OLD BABYLONIAN PERIOD

(2003–1595 BC)

THE ROYAL INSCRIPTIONS OF MESOPOTAMIA

Volumes Published

ASSYRIAN PERIODS

1 Assyrian Rulers of the Third and Second Millennia BC (TO 1115 BC)
A. KIRK GRAYSON

EARLY PERIODS

4 Old Babylonian Period (2003–1595 BC)
DOUGLAS FRAYNE

SUPPLEMENTS

1 Royal Inscriptions on Clay Cones from Ashur now in Istanbul
V. DONBAZ and A. KIRK GRAYSON

THE ROYAL INSCRIPTIONS OF MESOPOTAMIA

EARLY PERIODS / VOLUME 4

Old Babylonian Period

(2003–1595 BC)

DOUGLAS FRAYNE

UNIVERSITY OF TORONTO PRESS

Toronto Buffalo London

Toronto Buffalo London
Printed in Canada
Reprinted in 2018
ISBN 0-8020-5873-6
ISBN 978-1-4875-7230-3 (paper)

Printed on acid-free paper

Canadian Cataloguing in Publication Data

Frayne, Douglas.
Old Babylonian period (2003–1595 BC)

(The Royal inscriptions of Mesopotamia.
Early periods; v. 4)
Includes bibliographical references.
ISBN 0-8020-5873-6

1. Assyria – Kings and rulers. 2. Assyria – History – Sources. 3. Cuneiform inscriptions, Sumerian. 4. Cuneiform inscriptions, Akkadian. 5. Sumerian language – Texts. 6. Akkadian language – Texts. I. Title. II. Series.

PJ3815.F73 1990 953 C90-094508-7

The research and publication of this volume
have been supported by
the Social Sciences and Humanities Research Council of Canada
and the University of Toronto.

To

my parents, in appreciation of their support
and encouragement through the years.

Contents

Foreword

The ancient kings of Mesopotamia ruled one of the two great literate civilizations that set the course of the earliest history of the ancient Near East. Their temples and tombs do not waken vivid images in the minds of the modern reader or television viewer, as do those of the other great centre of early Near Eastern civilization, Egypt. But their cities, some with such familiar names as Babylon, Nineveh, and Ur, have been excavated over the past century and a half, according to the standards of the time, and have yielded an abundance of records of the boasted accomplishments of these kings. These are the Royal Inscriptions of Mesopotamia, mostly telling of building projects and battles, all done ad maiorem gloriam deorum.

The inscriptions, in a cuneiform script, are found on objects of various kinds including tablets, prisms, and vases of clay or steles, doorpost sockets, and sculpted wall panels of stone. Inscribed bricks are very common. A tiny cylinder seal, often known only from its impression on a clay tablet, or an engraved gem may give the name and titles of a king. The languages are Sumerian and Akkadian, the latter usually in its Babylonian dialect but with varying admixtures of the Assyrian dialect in documents from the north, in the region around modern Mosul.

The objects on which the inscriptions are found are now for the most part scattered around the world in various museums, although inscriptions cut on the face of rocks or on stone building blocks are often still in situ. The principal museums with collections of these kinds of antiquities are in Baghdad, Istanbul, Berlin (East), Paris, London, Philadelphia, and Chicago. The dispersal of the inscribed objects around the world makes their systematic study difficult, and the difficulty is compounded by the practical inaccessibility of many of the journals and monographs in which studies of the inscriptions have been published over the past century and more.

The purpose of the Royal Inscriptions of Mesopotamia Project is to make these texts available to layman and specialist alike by publishing standard editions, with English translations, in a series of volumes. To carry out this purpose an international editorial board has been formed and a staff of researchers and support staff assembled. This process began in the late 1970s with funding from the University of Toronto. In 1981 the Project was awarded full funding by the Negotiated Grants Section of the Social Sciences and Humanities Research Council of Canada.

The unique features of these editions are:

1. Complete corpora of inscriptions are edited, not just selections.
2. Every inscription is collated against the original when humanly possible.
3. To ensure accuracy the camera-ready copy is prepared by Project staff.

Toronto
March 1990

R.F.G. SWEET
Editor-in-Chief

Preface

This volume, the result of several years' work, was possible only with the assistance of numerous people, whom I would like to thank here.

First and foremost, I must express my deep gratitude to A.K. Grayson, whose vision in conceiving the Royal Inscriptions of Mesopotamia Project and persistence in bringing it into being made this volume possible in the first place. Professor Grayson, in his preface to RIMA 1, has noted the key figures of the Social Science and Humanities Research Council of Canada and the University of Toronto who took the concept of the RIM Project and marshalled the necessary resources to make it possible.

Two scholars advised me in the early stages of the preparation of the volume, the late E. Sollberger and D. Edzard. Their useful comments with respect to the system of transliteration and format of the volume are gratefully acknowledged. Once a preliminary manuscript was prepared, it was sent to three readers: M. Civil, D. Edzard, and W. Lambert, all of whom made numerous comments which greatly improved the volume. Their time and care in reading the manuscript are greatly appreciated.

Collation of the texts in various museums and collections was facilitated by the co-operation of many people: J.A. Brinkman at the Oriental Institute, Chicago, W. Hallo at Yale, A. Sjöberg at the University Museum, Philadelphia, C. Walker at the British Museum, R. Moorey at the Ashmolean Museum, B. André at the Louvre, L. Jakob-Rost as well as E. Klengel-Brandt and J. Marzahn at the Vorderasiatisches Museum, Berlin, V. Donbaz at the Archaeological Museums, Istanbul, and B. Ismail-Khalil as well as F. Rashid and R. Rashid-Jassim at the Iraq Museum, Baghdad. I am particularly indebted to the State Organization of Antiquities and Heritage of the Republic of Iraq and its president M. Damerji for permission to collate texts in the Iraq Museum. I would also like to thank M. Böhmer of the Deutsche Archäologisches Institut, Abteilung Baghdad, for permission to examine the records and photographs of the Uruk expedition, B. Hrouda of the Universität München for information on findspots and excavation numbers for the Isin expedition, D. Arnaud for information on the inscriptions from the Larsa expedition, R. Whiting for helpful comments about the Ešnunna material, and D. Charpin for help with the Mari materials.

People who kindly collated texts for me are too numerous to list here; while they are noted under the particular texts in question, their collective help is gratefully acknowledged here. Similarly, people who contributed new texts for this volume are noted under the individual texts. Their contributions have no doubt greatly added to the value of the volume and their assistance is greatly appreciated.

I must offer a word of special thanks to the RIM Headquarters staff: K. Glaser, Project Manager; H. Grau, Project Secretary; R. Westerby, Assistant Systems Manager; D. Kriger and D. Gorzo, Editorial Assistants. By their careful entry of the text data and constant checking of the computer files they were able to correct numerous slips in style and consistency, for which I am grateful. R. Westerby also prepared the indexes. G. Frame and R. Sweet made several collations for me and offered many constructive suggestions for various texts. L. Ourom of the University of Toronto Press is to be thanked for her careful reading of the manuscript and her professional advice on the style and format of the volume, which proved to be indispensable. Of course, any errors or omissions in the volume are solely the responsibility of the author.

Toronto
February 1990

D.R.F.

Editorial Notes

A detailed presentation of the principles, policies, and procedures of the Project will be found in the Editorial Manual (Toronto, 1983). However, the following summary should prove sufficient for the immediate needs of most readers of the present volume. The corpus of inscriptions has been divided into three sub-series: Assyrian Periods, Babylonian Periods, and Early Periods. The following description applies to all three. The purpose of the publication is to present complete groups of texts in reliable editions. It is not intended to provide analytical or synthetic studies, but rather to lay the foundation for such studies. Thus the heart of each volume is the edition of the texts; extensive discussions of the contents of the text are excluded. If such studies are developed by individuals in the course of editing the texts, it is intended that they be published elsewhere. Hand-copies and photographs are not included; if such are thought necessary by an editor, they will be published, at his discretion, outside the main series. To a certain extent the series the Royal Inscriptions of Mesopotamia: Supplements may be able to accommodate such publications.

The term 'exemplar' is used in these editions to refer to a single inscription found on one object. The term 'text' refers to an inscription which existed in antiquity and which may be represented in a number of exemplars which are more or less duplicates. In these editions exemplars of one text are edited together as a 'master text,' with a single transliteration and translation. Variants and other details about the exemplars are provided in the apparatus criticus. Further information about this is given below. When there is difficulty in deciding on the grouping of inscriptions under specific texts, more information is given in the editions. The editorial principle is that, regardless of how inscriptions are arranged and published, the reader must be provided with full information on what each exemplar contains.

The Project employs the resources of modern computer technology. A text is entered on the computer at the earliest stage when the preliminary edition is prepared. Thereafter a series of editing and proofing stages occur until the material is transferred directly onto the photocompositor to produce camera-ready copy for publication. The fact that the material is entered on the computer only once, and is regularly corrected and improved thereafter, drastically reduces the possibility of typographical errors. During the editing process the computer is used for a variety of other purposes, such as preparing concordances of words to assist in the identification of fragments.

The system of numbering the texts throughout the series requires some explanation. The first letter stands for the general period: A = Assyrian Periods, B = Babylonian Periods, and E = Early Periods. The number following this stands for the dynasty. In Assyrian Periods this is always 0 (zero) since the question of dynasty number is inapplicable. Details regarding the dynasty numbers for the other two sub-series will be found in the relevant volumes. In the third position appears the ruler number; once again, the details for each period will be found in the relevant sub-series. In the fourth position is the text number. Texts are arranged and numbered according to principles stated in each volume. In the fifth position is the exemplar number, where applicable. Thus A.0.77.1.13 is to be interpreted as follows: A = Assyrian Periods; 0 = Dynasty Inapplicable; 77 = Shalmaneser I; 1 = Text 1; 13 = Exemplar 13.

Texts which cannot be assigned definitely to a particular ruler are given text numbers beginning at 1001 (thus clearly distinguishing them from identified texts) and placed under a ruler according to the following principles. If at all possible, such a text is placed under the most probable ruler. In cases where a text can only be placed in a general period of several rulers, it is assigned to the ruler who is numerically in the middle. Fragments which cannot be identified at all are placed at the end of the book and given a ruler number of zero. Some private inscriptions which give information relevant for establishing royal names and titles — e.g. 'servant seals' — are included and have been given numbers beginning at 2001.

Each text edition is normally supplied with a brief introduction containing general information. This is followed, if there is more than one exemplar, by a catalogue containing basic information about all exemplars. This includes museum and excavation numbers, provenance, dimensions of the object (in the case of broken objects the symbol + is added), lines preserved, and indication of whether or not the inscription has been collated (c = collated with the original, p = collated with a photo, and n = not collated; a column with this information has cpn at its head). The next section is normally a commentary containing further technical information and notes. The bibliography then follows. Items are arranged chronologically, earliest to latest, with notes in parentheses after each item. These notes indicate the exemplars with which the item is concerned and the nature of the publication, using the following key words: provenance, photo, copy, edition, translation, and study. Some standard reference works are not normally cited, although they are fundamental in the collecting and editing of these texts, viz. the bibliographies by R. Caplice et al., entitled Keilschriftbibliographie and published in Orientalia; the annotated bibliography by Borger, HKL 1–3; the dictionaries AHw and CAD; and the study of epithets by Seux, ERAS.

In the editions proper, each page gives all the information the vast majority of readers will need in order to understand the text transliterated on that page. In the left-hand column is the transliteration, in the right-hand column the English translation, and at the bottom of the page an apparatus criticus of the variants found in the different exemplars of the text. The distinction between major and minor textual variants found in RIMA 1 is not observed in this volume; all variants are simply listed in one apparatus criticus. In the apparatus criticus, the text line numbers are in bold-face, followed after a period by the exemplar number(s) in normal typeface.

Lines are numbered in succession, and no indication of reverse or column numbers is normally given except 1) in a summary form in a commentary, 2) if a text is broken, or 3) in the case of multi-column inscriptions, if there are several hundreds of lines. If a text is divided into sections by horizontal lines, such lines are drawn across the transliterations and translations.

In the transliterations, lower-case Roman is used for Sumerian and lower-case italics for Akkadian. Logograms appear in small capitals. Italics in the translation indicate either an uncertain translation or a word in the original language. The system of sign values in Borger, Zeichenliste, is followed. Akkadian is usually left in transliteration with logograms uninterpreted. When, however, it is transcribed and logograms are interpreted, the system of AHw is followed. This happens, for example, in restorations. Further technical details about the system of transliteration are given in the Editorial Manual.

Toronto
March 1990

R.F.G. SWEET
Editor-in-Chief

Bibliographical Abbreviations

AAAS	Les annales archéologiques arabes syriennes. Damascus, 1951–
AASOR	The Annual of the American Schools of Oriental Research. New Haven, 1919–
AcOr	Acta Orientalia. Copenhagen, 1922–
Adams, Baghdad	R.McC. Adams, The Land behind Baghdad: A History of Settlement on the Diyala Plains. Chicago and London, 1965
Adams, Countryside	R.McC. Adams, The Uruk Countryside: The Natural Setting of Urban Societies. Chicago and London, 1972
AfK	Archiv für Keilschriftforschung, vols. 1–2. Berlin, 1923–25
AfO	Archiv für Orientforschung, vol. 3– (vol. 1–2 = AfK). Berlin, Graz, and Horn, 1926–
AfO Beih.	Archiv für Orientforschung, Beiheft. Berlin, Graz, and Horn, 1933–
AION	Annali dell'Istituto Orientale di Napoli. Naples, 1929–
AIPHOS	Brussels, Université libre de Belgique, Annuaire de l'Institut de Philologie et d'Histoire Orientales et Slaves. Brussels, 1932–
AJ	The Antiquaries Journal, Being the Journal of the Society of Antiquaries of London. London, 1921–
AJSL	American Journal of Semitic Languages and Literatures. Chicago, 1884–1941
AMI	Archäologische Mitteilungen aus Iran, vols. 1–9. Berlin, 1929–38
Amiet, MDP 43	P. Amiet, Glyptique susienne des origines à l'époque de Perses achéménides. Cachets, sceaux-cylindres et empreintes antiques découverts à Suse de 1913 à 1967, 2 vols. Paris, 1972
Andrae, AIT	W. Andrae, Die archaischen Ischtar-Tempel in Assur (= WVDOG 39). Leipzig, 1922
André-Leicknam, Naissance de l'écriture	B. André-Leicknam, Naissance de l'écriture cunéiformes et hiéroglyphes, 4e édition. Paris, 1982
ANET^3	J.B. Pritchard (ed.), Ancient Near Eastern Texts Relating to the Old Testament, 3rd edition. Princeton, 1969
AnSt	Anatolian Studies, Journal of the British Institute of Archaeology at Ankara. London, 1951–
AOAT	Alter Orient und Altes Testament. Neukirchen-Vluyn, 1968–
AoF	Altorientalische Forschungen. Berlin, 1974–
AOS	American Oriental Studies. New Haven, 1935–
Arch.	Archaeologia, vols. 1–100. London, 1888–1966
ARM	Archives royales de Mari. Paris, 1946–
ARMT	Archives royales de Mari, textes transcrits et traduits. Paris, 1950–
ArOr	Archiv Orientální. Prague, 1930–
ARRIM	Annual Review of the Royal Inscriptions of Mesopotamia Project. Toronto, 1983–
AS	Assyriological Studies. Chicago, 1931–
ATAT^2	H. Gressmann (ed.), Altorientalische Texte zum Alten Testament, 2. Auflage. Berlin and Leipzig, 1926
BA	Beiträge der Assyriologie und semitischen Sprachwissenschaft, vols. 1–10. Leipzig, 1890–1927
Babyloniaca	Babyloniaca, études de philologie assyro-babylonienne. Paris, 1907–37
Bagh. Mitt.	Baghdader Mitteilungen. Berlin, 1960–
Balkan, Kassit. Stud.	K. Balkan, Kassitenstudien 1. Die Sprache der Kassiten (= AOS 37). New Haven, 1954
Bardet, et al., ARMT 23	G. Bardet, F. Joannès, B. Lafont, D. Soubetran, and P. Villard, Archives administratives de Mari I. Paris, 1984
Barton, RISA	G.A. Barton, The Royal Inscriptions of Sumer and Akkad (= Library of Ancient Semitic Inscriptions 1). New Haven, 1929
BASOR	Bulletin of the American Schools of Oriental Research. New Haven, 1919–
Batto, Women at Mari	B.F. Batto, Studies on Women at Mari. Baltimore and London, 1974
BE	Babylonian Expedition of the University of Pennsylvania, Series A: Cuneiform Texts, vols. 1–14. Philadelphia, 1893–1914
Beer-Sheva	Beer-Sheva. Journal of the Department of Biblical and Oriental Studies. Beer-Sheva, 1985–
Behrens, Enlil und Ninlil	H. Behrens, Enlil und Ninlil: Ein sumerischer Mythos aus Nippur (= Studia Pohl: Maior 8). Rome, 1978

Belleten	Türk Tarih Kurumu, Belleten. Ankara, 1937–
BE Res	Babylonian Expedition of the University of Pennsylvania, Series D: Researches and Treatises, vols. 1, 3–5. Philadelphia, 1904–10
Bezold, Cat.	C. Bezold, Catalogue of the Cuneiform Tablets in the Kouyunjik Collection of the British Museum, 5 vols. London, 1889–99
Bezold, Literatur	C. Bezold, Babylonisch-Assyriche Literatur. Leipzig, 1886
BibMes	Bibliotheca Mesopotamica. Malibu, 1975–
BIN	Babylonian Inscriptions in the Collection of J.B. Nies. New Haven, 1917–
BiOr	Bibliotheca Orientalis. Leiden, 1943–
Birot, ARMT 9	M. Birot, Textes administratifs de la salle 5 du palais, transcrits, traduits et commentés. Paris, 1960
Birot, et al., ARMT 16/1	M. Birot, J.-R. Kupper, and O. Rouault, Répertoire Analytique (2e volume) tomes I–XIV, XVIII, et textes divers hors-collection, première partie: Noms propres. Paris, 1979
BM Guide	British Museum. A Guide to the Babylonian and Assyrian Antiquities, 3rd edition. London, 1922
BMQ	British Museum Quarterly, vols. 1–37. London, 1926–73
Böhl, Chrestomathy	F.M.T. Böhl, Akkadian Chrestomathy, vol. 1: Selected Cuneiform Texts. Leiden, 1947
Böhl, Leiden Coll.	F.M.T. Böhl, Medeelingen uit de Leidische Verzameling van spijkerschrift-Inscripties, 3 vols. Amsterdam, 1933
BOR	Babylonian and Oriental Record, vols. 1–9. London, 1886–1909
Borger, BAL[1]	R. Borger, Babylonisch-Assyrische Lesestücke, 3 vols. Rome, 1963
Borger, BAL[2]	R. Borger, Babylonisch-Assyrische Lesestücke (= AnOr 54), 2 vols. Rome, 1979
Borger, EAK 1	R. Borger, Einleitung in die assyrischen Königsinschriften, Erster Teil: Das zweite Jahrtausend v. Chr. (= Handbuch der Orientalistik Ergänzungsband v/1/1). Leiden, 1961
Borger, HKL	R. Borger, Handbuch der Keilschriftliteratur, 3 vols. Berlin, 1967–75
Borger, Zeichenliste	R. Borger, Assyrisch-babylonische Zeichenliste, 2. Auflage (= AOAT 33/33A). Neukirchen-Vluyn, 1981
Bothmer, Ancient Art	D. von Bothmer, Ancient Art from New York Private Collections. Catalogue of an Exhibition Held at the Metropolitan Museum of Art December 17, 1959 - February 28, 1960. New York, 1961
Bottéro, ARM 7	J. Bottéro, Textes administratifs de la salle 110 (= TCL 28). Paris, 1956
Bottéro, ARMT 7	J. Bottéro, Textes économiques et administratifs. Paris, 1957
Boyer, ARM 8	G. Boyer, Textes juridiques et administratifs (= TCL 29). Paris, 1957
Boyer, ARMT 8	G. Boyer, Textes juridiques, transcrits, traduits et commentés. Paris, 1958
Boyer, Contribution	G. Boyer, Contribution à l'histoire juridique de la 1re dynastie babylonienne. Paris, 1928
BRM	Babylonian Records in the Library of J. Pierpont Morgan, 4 vols. New Haven, New York, 1912–23
Buchanan and Gurney, Ashmolean 1	B. Buchanan and O.R. Gurney, Catalogue of Ancient Near Eastern Seals in the Ashmolean Museum, vol. I: Cylinder Seals. Oxford, 1966
Buchanan and Hallo, Early Near Eastern Seals	B. Buchanan and W.W. Hallo, Early Near Eastern Seals in the Yale Babylonian Collection. New Haven and London, 1981
Burke, ARMT 11	M.L. Burke, Textes administratifs de la salle 111 du palais, transcruits, traduits et commentés. Paris, 1963
CAD	The Assyrian Dictionary of the Oriental Institute of the University of Chicago. Chicago, 1956–
Cameron, Iran	G.G. Cameron, History of Early Iran. Chicago, 1936
Chabouillet, Catalogue	Chabouillet, Catalogue. 1848
Charpin, Archives Épistolaires	D. Charpin, et al., Archives Épistolaires de Mari 1/2 (= ARM 26). Paris, 1988
Charpin, Le clergé d'Ur	D. Charpin, Le clergé d'Ur au siècle d'Hammurabi (XIXe–XVIIIe siècles av. J.-C.) (= Hautes études orientales 22). Geneva and Paris, 1986
Charpin and Durand, Documents Strasbourg	Charpin and Durand, Documents Cunéiformes de Strasbourg (= Recherche sur les grandes civilisations, Cahier n° 4). Paris, 1981
Chiera, PBS 8/2	E. Chiera, Old Babylonian Contracts. Philadelphia, 1922
Chiera, SRT	E. Chiera, Sumerian Religious Texts (= Crozier Theological Seminary Babylonian Publications 1). Upland, 1924
Clay, BRM 4	A. Clay, Epics, Hymns, Omens and Other Texts. New Haven, 1923
Clay, YOS 1	A. Clay, Miscellaneous Inscriptions in the Yale Babylonian Collection. New Haven, 1915
de Clercq, Collection	H.F.X. de Clercq and J. Ménant, Collection de Clercq, catalogue méthodique et raisonné, antiquités assyriennes, cylindres orientaux, cachets, briques, bronzes, bas-reliefs etc., 2 vols. Paris, 1888/1903
Collon, AOAT 27	D. Collon, The Seal Impressions from Tell Atchana/Alalakh. Neukirchen-Vluyn, 1975
Collon, The Alalakh Cylinder Seals	D. Collon, The Alalakh Cylinder Seals: A New Catalogue of the Actual Seals Excavated by Sir Leonard Woolley at Tell Atchana, and from Neighbouring Sites on the Syrian-Turkish Border (= British Archaeological Reports, International Series 132). Oxford, 1982

Collon, Cylinder Seals 2	D. Collon, Catalogue of the Western Asiatic Seals in the British Museum. Cylinder Seals II: Akkadian, Post Akkadian, Ur III Periods. London, 1982
Collon, Cylinder Seals 3	D. Collon, Catalogue of the Western Asiatic Seals in the British Museum. Cylinder Seals III: Isin-Larsa and Old Babylonian Periods. London, 1986
Collon, First Impressions	D. Collon, First Impressions: Cylinder Seals in the Ancient Near East. London, 1987
Contenau, Manuel	G. Contenau, Manuel d'archéologie orientale, 4 vols. Paris, 1927–47
CRAIB	Comptes-rendus des séances de l'académie des inscriptions et belles-lettres. Paris, 1857–
Crawford, BIN 9	V.E. Crawford, Sumerian Economic Texts from the First Dynasty of Isin. New Haven, 1954
Cros, Tello	G. Cos, Nouvelles fouilles de Tello, Mission française de Chaldée. Paris, 1910
CRRA	Compte Rendu de la Rencontre Assyriologique Internationale. [various locations], 1950–
CRRA 15	J.-R. Kupper (ed.), La civilisation de Mari (= Les Congrès et colloques de l'Université de Liège 42, = Bibliothèque de la Faculté de Philosophie et Lettres de l'Université de Liège 172). Paris, 1967
CT	Cuneiform Texts from Babylonian Tablets in the British Museum. London, 1896–
Cullimore, Oriental Cylinders	Cullimore, Oriental Cylinders. Impressions of Ancient Oriental Cylinders, or Rolling Seals of the Babylonians, Assyrians, and Medo-Persians. London, 1842–43
Dalley, OBTR	S. Dalley, C.F.B. Walker, and J.D. Hawkins, The Old Babylonian Tablets from Tell al Rimah. London, 1976
Delaporte, Bibliothèque Nationale	L. Delaporte, Catalogue des cylindres orientaux et des cachets assyro-babyloniens, perses et syro-cappadociens de la Bibliothèque Nationale. Paris, 1910
Delaporte, Louvre 2	L. Delaporte, Musée du Louvre. Catalogue des cylindres, cachets et pierres gravées de style oriental, tome II: Acquisitions. Paris, 1923
Delitzsch, AL[5]	F. Delitzsch, Assyrische Lesestücke mit den Elementen der Grammatik und vollständigem Glossar (= Assyriologische Bibliothek 16), 5. Auflage. Leipzig, 1912
Delougaz, Pottery	P. Delougaz, Pottery from the Diyala Region (= OIP 63). Chicago, 1952
van Dijk, TIM 2	J. van Dijk, Cuneiform Texts: Old Babylonian Letters and Related Material. Wiesbaden, 1965
van Dijk, TIM 4	J. van Dijk, Cuneiform Texts: Old Babylonian Contracts and Juridical Texts. Wiesbaden, 1967
van Dijk, TIM 5	J. van Dijk, Cuneiform Texts: Old Babylonian Contracts and Related Material. Wiesbaden, 1968
van Dijk, TIM 9	J. van Dijk, Cuneiform Texts: Texts of Varying Content. Leiden, 1976
van Dijk, TLB 2	J. van Dijk, Textes divers. Leiden, 1957
van Dijk, VAS 17	J. van Dijk, Nicht-kanonische Beschwörungen uns sonstige literarische Texte. Berlin, 1971
Dougherty, AASOR 7	R.P. Dougherty, Searching for Ancient Remains in Lower ʿIrâq. New Haven, 1927
Durand, ARM 21	J.-M. Durand, Textes administratifs des salles 134 et 160 du palais de Mari. Paris, 1982
Durand, ARMT 21	J.-M. Durand, Textes administratifs des salles 134 et 160 du palais de Mari, transcrits, traduits et commentés. Paris, 1983
Durand, Doc. Cun. 1	J.-M. Durand, Documents Cunéiformes de la IVe Section de l'Ecole pratique des Hautes Etudes, tome I: Catalogue et copies cunéiformes. Paris, 1982
Dussaud Festschrift	Mélanges syriens offerts à M.R. Dussaud par ses amis et élèves. Paris, 1939
Halil Edhem Memorial Volume	Halil Edhem Hâtıra Kitabı Cilt 1 (= TTKY 7/5). Ankara, 1947
Edzard, Zwischenzeit	D.O. Edzard, Die 'Zweite Zwischenzeit' Babyloniens. Wiesbaden, 1957
Eisen, Moore	G. Eisen, Ancient Oriental Cylinder and Other Seals, with a Description of the Collection of Mrs. W.H. Moore (= OIP 47). Chicago, 1940
Ellis, Foundation Deposits	R.S. Ellis, Foundation Deposits in Ancient Mesopotamia (= YNER 2). New Haven and London, 1968
Faust, YOS 8	D. Faust, Contracts from Larsa Dated in the Reign of Rim-Sin. New Haven, 1941
Feigin, YOS 12	S.I. Feigin, Legal and Administrative Texts of the Reign of Samsu-iluna. New Haven and London, 1979
Figulla, Cat.	H.H. Figulla, Catalogue of the Babylonian Tablets in the British Museum, vol. 1. London, 1961
Figulla, VAS 13	H.H. Figulla, Altbabylonische Verträge. Leipzig, 1914
Figulla and Martin, UET 5	H.H. Figulla and Martin, Letters and Documents of the Old Babylonian Period. London, 1953
Finkelstein, CT 48	J.J. Finkelstein, Old Babylonian Legal Documents. London, 1968
Essays Finkelstein	M. de Jong Ellis (ed.), Essays on the Ancient Near East in Memory of J.J. Finkelstein. Hamden, 1977
Finkelstein, YOS 13	J.J. Finkelstein, Late Old Babylonian Documents and Letters. New Haven and London, 1972
Frankena, Catalogue sommaire	A.N. Zadoks-Josephus Jitta and R. Frankena, Catalogue sommaire des cylindres orientaux au Cabinet Royal des Médailles à la Haye. La Haye, 1952
Frankfort, Art and Architecture	H. Frankfort, The Art and Architecture of the Ancient Orient. Harmondsworth, 1954
Frankfort, Cylinder Seals	H. Frankfort, Cylinder Seals: A Documentary Essay on the Art and Religion of the Ancient Near East. London, 1939
Freedman, St. Louis	R.D. Freedman, The Cuneiform Tablets in St. Louis. Columbia University PhD Dissertation, 1975
Gadd, Early Dynasties	C.J. Gadd, The Early Dynasties of Sumer and Akkad. London, 1921

Gadd, Reading-book	C.J. Gadd, A Sumerian Reading-book. Oxford, 1924
Gadd, UET 1	C.J. Gadd, L. Legrain, and S. Smith, Royal Inscriptions. London, 1928
Gelb, Hurrians	I.J. Gelb, Hurrians and Subarians (= Studies in Ancient Oriental Civilization 22). Chicago, 1944
Gelb, Lingua degli Amoriti	I.J. Gelb, La Lingua degli Amoriti, Rendiconti della Classe di Scienza morali, storiche e filologiche della Accademia Nazionale dei Lincei 8/13/3-4 (1958) pp. 143-64
Gelb, MAD 2^2	I.J. Gelb, Old Akkadian Writing and Grammar, 2nd edition. Chicago, 1961
Gelb, MAD 3	I.J. Gelb, Glossary of Old Akkadian. Chicago, 1957
de Genouillac, Kich	H. de Genouillac, Premières recherches archéologique à Kich (Fouilles françaises d'El-ᵓAkhymer, mission d'Henri de Genouillac, 1911-12), 2 vols. Paris, 1924/25
Gibson and Biggs, Seals	M. Gibson and R.D. Biggs, Seals and Sealing in the Ancient Near East (= BibMes 6). Malibu, 1977
Gordon, Smith College	C.H. Gordon, Smith College Tablets, 110 Cuneiform Tablets Selected from the College Collection (= Smith College Studies in History 38). Northhampton (Mass.), 1952
Grant, Business Doc.	E. Grant, Babylonian Business Documents of the Classical Period. Philadelphia, 1919
Grayson, ARI	A.K. Grayson, Assyrian Royal Inscriptions, 2 vols. Wiesbaden, 1972/76
Grayson, RIMA 1	A.K. Grayson, Assyrian Rulers of the Third and Second Millennia BC (to 1115 BC). Toronto, 1987
Greengus, Ishchali Documents	S. Greengus, Studies in Ishchali Documents (= BibMes 19). Malibu, 1986
Greengus, OBTI	S. Greengus, Old Babylonian Tablets from Ishchali and Vicinity (= Uitgaven van het Nederlands Historisch-Archaeologisch Instituut te Istanbul 44). Leiden, 1979
Grégoire, MVN 10	J.-P. Grégoire, Inscriptions et archives administratives cunéiformes (1e partie). Rome, 1981
Grice, YOS 5	E. Grice, Records from Ur and Larsa Dated in the Larsa Dynasty. New Haven, 1919
Groneberg, Rép. Géogr. 3	B. Groneberg, Die Orts- und Gewässernamen der altbabylonischen Zeit. Wiesbaden, 1980
Hall, Sculpture	H.R. Hall, Babylonian and Assyrian Sculpture in the British Museum. Paris and Brussels, 1928
Hallo, Royal Titles	W.W. Hallo, Early Mesopotamian Royal Titles, a Philologic and Historical Analysis (= AOS 43). New Haven, 1957
Handcock, Mesopotamian Archaeology	S.P. Handcock, Mesopotamian Archaeology: An Introduction to the Archaeology of Babylonia and Assyria. London, 1912
Heidelberger Studien	Heidelberger Studien zum Alten Orient, A. Falkenstein zum 17. September 1966. Wiesbaden, 1967
Heltzer, Suteans	M. Heltzer, The Suteans (= Istituto Universitario Orientale, Seminario di Studi Asiatici, Series Minor 13). Naples, 1981
Heuzey, Catalogue Louvre	L. Heuzey, Catalogue des antiquités chaldéennes, sculpture et gravure à la pointe. Paris, 1902
Heuzey, Origines	L. Heuzey, Les origines orientales de l'art. Paris, 1891-1915
Heuzey, Palais Chaldéen	L. Heuzey, Un palais chaldéen d'après les découvertes de M. de Sarzec. Paris, 1888
Hilprecht, Assyriaca	H.V. Hilprecht, Assyriaca: Eine Nachlese auf dem Gebiete der Assyriologie (= Publications of the University of Pennsylvania, Series in Philology, Literature and Archaeology 3/1). Boston, 1984
Hilprecht, BE 1	H.V. Hilprecht, Old Babylonian Inscriptions Chiefly from Nippur, 2 vols. Philadelphia, 1893/96
Hilprecht, Deluge Story	H.V. Hilprecht, The Earliest Version of the Babylonian Deluge Story and the Temple Library of Nippur (= BE Res 5/1). Philadelphia, 1910
Hilprecht, Explorations	H.V. Hilprecht, Explorations in Bible Lands during the 19th Century. Philadelphia, 1903
Holma, ZATH	H. Holma, Zehn Altbabylonische Tontafeln in Helsingfors (= Acta Societatis Scientiarum Fennicae 45/3). Helsingfors, 1914
Hommel, Semiten	F. Hommel, Die semitischen Volker und Sprachen. Leipzig, 1883
Hrouda, Isin 1	B. Hrouda (ed.), Isin-Išān Baḥrīyāt I. Die Ergebnisse der Ausgrabungen 1973-1974 (= Bayerische Akademie der Wissenschaften philosophisch-historische Klasse NF 79). Munich, 1977
Hrouda, Isin 2	B. Hrouda (ed.), Isin-Išān Baḥrīyāt II. Die Ergebnisse der Ausgrabungen 1975-1978 (= Bayerische Akademie der Wissenschaften philosophisch-historische Klasse NF 87). Munich, 1981
Hrouda, Isin 3	B. Hrouda (ed.), Isin-Išān Baḥrīyāt III. Die Ergebnisse der Ausgrabungen 1983-1984 (= Bayerische Akademie der Wissenschaften philosophisch-historische Klasse NF 94). Munich, 1987
Hrouda, Edzard, and Trümpelmann, Iranische Denkmäler 2/7	B. Hrouda, D.O. Edzard, and L. Trümpelmann, Iranische Felsreliefs C: Sarpol - I Zohāb, Die Felsreliefs I-IV. Berlin, 1976
HUCA	Hebrew Union College Annual. Cincinnati, 1924-
Hunger, Kolophone	H. Hunger, Babylonische und assyrische Kolophone (= AOAT 2). Neukirchen-Vluyn, 1968
Huot, Larsa et 'Oueili 1978-1981	J.-L. Huot (ed.), Larsa (8eme et 9eme campagnes, 1978 et 1981) et 'Oueilli (2eme et 3eme campagnes, 1978 et 1981): Rapport Préliminaire (= Éditions Recherche sur les Civilisations, 'Mémoire' n° 26). Paris, 1983

Huot, Larsa et 'Oueili 1983	J.-L. Huot (ed.), Larsa (10e campagne, 1983) et 'Oueilli (4e campagne, 1983): Rapport Préliminaire (= Éditions Recherche sur les Civilisations, 'Mémoire' n° 73). Paris, 1987
ILN	The Illustrated London News. London, 1842–
Iraq Museum Guide	A Guide to the ʿIraq Museum Collections. Baghdad, 1942
JA	Journal asiatique. Paris, 1822–
Jacobsen, Cylinder Seals	H. Frankfort and T. Jacobsen, Stratified Cylinder Seals from the Diyala Region (= OIP 72). Chicago, 1955
Jacobsen, Gimilsin Temple	T. Jacobsen, The Gimilsin Temple and the Palace of the Rulers at Tell Asmar (= OIP 43). Chicago, 1940
Jacobsen, OIC 13	T. Jacobsen, H. Frankfort, and C. Preusser, Tell Asmar and Khafaje, the First Season's Work in Eshnunna. Chicago, 1932
Jacobsen, SKL	T. Jacobsen, The Sumerian King List (= AS 11). Chicago, 1939
JANES	Journal of the Ancient Near Eastern Society of Columbia University. New York, 1968–
JAOS	Journal of the American Oriental Society. New Haven, 1893–
Jastrow, Bildermappe	M. Jastrow, Bildermappe mit 273 Abbildungen samt Erklärungen zur Religion Babyloniens und Assyriens. Giessen, 1912
JCS	Journal of Cuneiform Studies. New Haven and Cambridge, Mass., 1947–
Jensen, KB 3/1	P. Jensen, et al., Historische Texte altbabylonischer Herrscher. Berlin, 1892
Jensen, KB 6/1	P. Jensen, Assyrisch-babylonische Mythen und Epen. Berlin, 1900
JEOL	Jaarbericht van het Vooraziatisch-Egyptisch Genootschap 'Ex Oriente Lux'. Leiden, 1933–
JHS	Journal of Hellenic Studies. London, 1880–
JKF	Jahrbuch für kleinasiatische Forschung, 2 vols. Heidelberg, 1950/53
JM(E)OS	Journal of the Manchester (Egyptian and) Oriental Society. Manchester
JNES	Journal of Near Eastern Studies. Chicago, 1942–
Johns, Ur-Engur	C.H.W. Johns, Ur-Engur: A Bronze of the Fourth Millennium in the Library of J. Pierpont Morgan. New York, 1908
Jones and Snyder, Econ. Texts	T.B. Jones and J. Snyder, Sumerian Economic Texts from the Third Ur Dynasty, a Catalogue and Discussion of Documents from Various Collections. Minneapolis, 1961
Jordan, Uruk-Warka	J. Jordan, Uruk-Warka nach den Ausgrabungen durch die Deutsche Orient-Gesellschaft (= WVDOG 51). Leipzig, 1928
JRAS	Journal of the Royal Asiatic Society. London, 1834–
JRGS	Journal of the Royal Geographical Society. London, 1830–
JSOR	Journal of the Society of Oriental Research, vols. 1–16. Chicago and Toronto, 1917–32
JSS	Journal of Semitic Studies. Manchester, 1956–
Kärki, KDDU	I. Kärki, Die Königsinschriften der dritten Dynastie von Ur, (= Studia Orientalia 58). Helsinki, 1986
Kärki, SAKAZ 1	I. Kärki, Die sumerischen und akkadischen Königsinschriften der altbabylonischen Zeit, I: Isin, Larsa, Uruk (= Studia Orientalia 49). Helsinki, 1980
Kärki, SAKAZ 2	I. Kärki, Die sumerischen und akkadischen Königsinschriften der altbabylonischen Zeit, II: Babylon (= Studia Orientalia 55/1). Helsinki, 1983
Kärki, SKFZ	I. Kärki, Die sumerischen Königsinschriften der frühaltbabylonischen Zeit, in Umschrift und Übersetzung. Helsinki, 1968
KB	Keilinschriftliche Bibliothek, Sammlung von assyrischen und babylonischen Texten in Umschrift und Übersetzung, vols. 1–6. Berlin, 1889–1915
Keiser, BIN 2	C. Keiser and J.B. Nies, Historical Religious and Economic Texts and Antiquities. New Haven, 1920
Keiser, BRM 3	C. Keiser, Cuneiform Bullae of the Third Millennium B.C. New York, 1914
al Khalesi, Mari Palace	Y.M. al Khalesi, The Court of the Palms: A Functional Interpretation of the Mari Palace (= BibMes 8). Malibu, 1978
Kienast, Kisurra	B. Kienast, Die altbabylonischen Briefe und Urkunden aus Kisurra (= Freiburger Altorientalische Studien 2), 2 vols. Wiesbaden, 1978
King, Early History	L.W. King, A History of Sumer and Akkad: An Account of the Early Races of Babylonia from Prehistoric Times to the Foundation of the Babylonian Monarchy. London, 1910
King, First Steps	L.W. King, First Steps in Assyrian: A Book for Beginners. London, 1898
King, History	L.W. King, A History of Babylon from the Foundation of the Monarchy to the Persian Conquest. London, 1915
King, LIH	L.W. King, The Letters and Inscriptions of Hammurabi, King of Babylon, about 2000 B.C. to Which Are Added a Series of Letters of Other Kings of the First Dynasty of Babylon, 3 vols. (= Luzac's Semitic Text and Translation Series vols. 2-3 and 8). London, 1898–1900
King and Hall, EWA	L. King and H.R. Hall, Egypt and Western Asia in the Light of Recent Discoveries. London, 1907
Klein, Three Šulgi Hymns	J. Klein, Three Šulgi Hymns: Sumerian Royal Hymns Glorifying King Šulgi of Ur. Ramat-Gan, 1981

Knopf, USCS 2	C.S. Knopf, An Ancient Inscribed Cone of Sin-gashid, King of Erech (=University of Southern California Studies 2). Los Angeles, 1930
25. Kongress	Trudy Dvatcat' pjatogo Mezdunarodnogo Kongressa Vostokovedov, Moskva 9-16 avgusta 1960, 2 vols. (=25e Congrès international des Orientalistes, compte rendu). Moscow, 1962
Kramer, ISET 2	S.N. Kramer, Istanbul Arkeoloji Müzelerinde Bulunan: Sumer Edebî Tablet ve Parçaları 2 (=TTKY 6/13a). Ankara, 1976
Kramer, Çıg, and Kızılyay, ISET 1	S.N. Kramer, M. Çıg, and H. Kızılyay, Istanbul Arkeoloji Müzelerinde Bulunan: Sumer Edebî Tablet ve Parçaları 1 (=TTKY 6/13). Ankara, 1969
Kramer Anniversary	B. Eichler (ed.), Kramer Anniversary Volume: Cuneiform Studies in Honor of Samuel Noah Kramer (=AOAT 25). Neukirchen-Vluyn, 1976
Kraus, Edikt	F.R. Kraus, Ein Edikt des Königs Ammi-ṣaduqa von Babylon (=Studia et Documenta ad Iura Orientis Antiqui Pertinentia 5). Leiden, 1958
Kraus, Königl. Verfüg.	F.R. Kraus, Königliche Verfügungen in Altbabylonischer Zeit (=Studia et Documenta ad Iura Orientis Antiqui Pertinentia 11). Leiden, 1984
Kraus, Könige	F.R. Kraus, Könige, die in Zelten wohnten. Betrachtungen über den Kern der assyrischen Königsliste (=Mededelingen der Koninklijke Nederlandse, Nieuwe reeks 28/2). Amsterdam, 1965
Kraus Festschrift	G. van Driel, Th.J.H. Krispijn, M. Stol, and K.R. Veenhof (eds.), Zikir Šumim. Assyriological Studies Presented to F.R. Kraus on the Occasion of His Seventieth Birthday. Leiden, 1982
Kupper, Amurru	J.-R. Kupper, L'iconographie du dieu Amurru dans la glyptique de la 1re dynastie babylonienne. Brussels, 1961
Kupper, ARMT 22	J.-R. Kupper, Documents administratifs de la salle 135 du palais de Mari, transcrits et traduits, 2 vols. Paris, 1983
Kupper, Nomades	J.-R. Kupper, Les nomades en Mésopotamie au temps des rois de Mari. Paris, 1957
Kutscher, Brockmon Tablets	R. Kutscher, The Brockmon Tablets of the University of Haifa: Royal Inscriptions (=Shay Series of the Zinman Institute of Archaeology). Haifa, 1989
LAK	A. Deimel, Liste der archaischen Keilschriftzeichen von Fara (=WVDOG 40). Leipzig, 1922
Landsberger, Date Palm	B. Landsberger, The Date Palm and Its By-products According to the Cuneiform Sources (=AfO Beih. 17). Graz, 1967
Landsberger, MSL 2	B. Landsberger, Die Serie Ur-e-a = *nâqu*. Rome, 1951
Landsberger Festschrift	H.G. Güterbock and T. Jacobsen (eds.), Studies in Honor of B. Landsberger on His Seventy-fifth Birthday, April 21, 1965 (=AS 16). Chicago, London, and Toronto, 1965
Langdon, Kish	S. Langdon and L. Watelin, Excavations at Kish, the Hebert Weld and Field Museum of Natural History Expedition to Mesopotamia, 4 vols. Paris, 1924-34
Langdon, OECT 1	S. Langdon, The H. Weld-Blundell Collection in the Ashmolean Museum, vol. 1: Sumerian and Semitic Religious and Historical Texts. Oxford, 1923
Layard, Discoveries	A.H. Layard, Discoveries among the Ruins of Nineveh and Babylon, with Travels in Armenia, Kurdistan and the Desert. London, 1853
Leemans, SLB 1/1	W.F. Leemans, Ishtar of Lagaba and Her Dress. Leiden, 1952
Leemans, SLB 1/2	W.F. Leemans, Legal and Economic Records from the Kingdom of Larsa. Leiden, 1954
Legrain, PBS 13	L. Legrain, Historical Fragments. Philadelphia, 1922
Legrain, PBS 14	L. Legrain, The Culture of the Babylonians from Their Seals in the Collections of the Museum. Philadelphia, 1925
Legrain, PBS 15	L. Legrain, Royal Inscriptions and Fragments from Nippur and Babylon. Philadelphia, 1926
Legrain, UE 10	L. Legrain, Seal Cylinders. London and Philadelphia, 1951
Lenormant, Choix	F. Lenormant, Choix de textes cunéiformes inédits ou incomplètement publiés. Paris, 1873-75
Lenormant, Études accadiennes	F. Lenormant, Études accadiennes, 3 vols. (=Lettres assyriologiques, seconde série). Paris, 1873
Levine and Young, Mountains and Lowlands	L.D. Levine and T.C. Young, Mountains and Lowlands: Essays in the Archaeology of Greater Mesopotamia (=BibMes 7). Malibu, 1977
Levy and Artzi, ʿAtiqot 4	S. Levy and P. Artzi, Sumerian and Akkadian Documents from Public and Private Collections in Israel. Jerusalem, 1965
Limet, Sceaux cassites	H. Limet, Les légendes des sceaux cassites. Brussels, 1971
Loftus, Travels	W.K. Loftus, Travels and Researches in Chaldea and Susiana with an Account of Excavations at Warka, the 'Erech' of Nimroud, Shush, 'Shushian the Palace' of Esther, in 1849-52. New York, 1857
de Longpérier, Notice³	A. de Longpérier, Notice des antiquités assyriennes, babyloniennes, perses, hébraïques, exposées dans les galeries du Musée du Louvre, 3e édition. Paris, 1854
de Longpérier, Musée Napoléon III	A. de Longpérier, Musée Napoléon III: Choix de monuments antiques pour servir à l'histoire de l'art en Orient et en Occident, 4 vols. Paris, 1868-74
Luckenbill, Adab	D.D. Luckenbill, Inscriptions from Adab (=OIP 14). Chicago, 1930
MAD	Materials for the Assyrian Dictionary. Chicago, 1952-
MAIB	Mémoires de l'institut national de France, académie des inscriptions et belles-lettres. Paris, 1899-

MAIS	Missione Archeologica Italiana in Siria. Rome, 1965–
MAM	Mission Archéologique de Mari. Paris, 1956–
MAOG	Mitteilungen der Altorientalischen Gesellschaft. Leipzig, 1925–43
MAOV	Mitteilungen des Akademisch-Orientalistischen Vereins zu Berlin. Berlin, 1887–
MARI	Mari, Annales de Recherches Interdisciplinaires. Paris, 1982–
Matthews, First Dynasty of Babylon	L.P. Matthews, The First Dynasty of Babylon: History and Texts. Birmingham University PhD Dissertation, 1970
McCown, Nippur 1	D.E. McCown, R.C. Haines, and D. Hansen, Nippur I: Temple of Enlil, Scribal Quarter, and Soundings (= OIP 78). Chicago, 1967
MCS	Manchester Cuneiform Studies, vols. 1–9. Manchester, 1951–64
MDOG	Mitteilungen der Deutschen Orient-Gesellschaft. Berlin, 1898–
MDP	Mémoires de la Délégation en Perse. Paris, 1900–
Meissner, Warenpreise	B. Meissner, Warenpreise in Babylonien (= Abhandlungen der Preussischen Akademie der Wissenschaften, philosophisch-historische Klasse 1936/1). Berlin, 1936
Mélanges Birot	J.-M. Durand and J.-R. Kupper (eds.), Miscellanea babyloniaca. Mélanges offerts à Maurice Birot. Paris, 1985
Ménant, Catalogue la Haye	J. Ménant, Catalogue des cylindres orientaux du Cabinet Royal des Médailles de la Haye. La Haye, 1878
Ménant, Glyptique	M.J. Menant, Les pierres gravées de la Haute-Asie, recherches sur la glyptique orientale, 2 vols. Paris, 1883/86
Ménant, Inscriptions de Hammourabi	J. Ménant, Inscriptions de Hammourabi, roi e Babylone (XVIe siècle avant J.-C.). Paris, 1863
Ménant, Manuel	J. Ménant, Manuel de la langue assyrienne. Paris, 1880
Mesopotamia	Meopotamia: Rivista di Archeoligia. Turin, 1966–
E. Meyer, Sumerier und Semiten	E. Meyer, Sumerier und Semiten in Babylonien. Berlin, 1906
G.R. Meyer, Altorientalische Denkmäler	G.R. Meyer, Altorientalische Denkmäler im Vorderasiatischen Museum zu Berlin. Leipzig, 1965
de Meyer (ed.), Tell ed-Dēr 3	L. de Meyer (ed.), Tell ed-Dēr: Soundings at Abū Ḥabbah (Sippar). Louvain, 1980
van de Mieroop, BIN 10	M. van de Mieroop, Sumerian Administrative Documents from the Reigns of Išbi-Erra and Šū-ilišu. New Haven and London, 1987
MJ	Museum Journal of the University Museum, University of Pennsylvania, vols. 1–24. Philadelphia, 1910–35
Moorey, Kish	P.R.S. Moorey, Kish Excavations 1923–33 with a Microfiche Catalogue of the Objects in Oxford Excavated by the Oxford-Field Museum, Chicago Expedition to Kish in Iraq. Oxford, 1978
Moorey, et al., Ancient Bronzes	P.R.S. Moorey, E.C. Bunker, E. Porada, and G. Markoe, Ancient Bronzes, Ceramics, and Seals. Los Angeles, 1981
Moortgat, VAR	A. Moortgat, Vorderasiatische Rollsiegel: Ein Beitrag zur Geschichte der Steinschneidekunst. Berlin, 1940
de Morgan, MSP 4/1	J. de Morgan, Mission scientifique en Perse 4/1. Paris, 1896
MP	Monuments et mémoires publiés par l'académie des inscriptions et belles-lettres. Paris
MSL	Materials for the Sumerian Lexicon. Rome, 1937–
Muscarella (ed.), Ladders to Heaven	O.W. Muscarella (ed.), Ladders to Heaven: Art Treasures from Lands of the Bible. Toronto, 1981
Muséon	Le Muséon, revue d'études orientales. Louvain, 1888–
MVN	Materiali per il vocabolario neosumerico. Rome, 1974–
NABU	Nouvelles assyriologiques brêves et utilitaires. Paris, 1987–
Nakahara, Sumerian Tablets Kyoto	Y. Nakahara, The Sumerian Tablets in the Imperial University of Kyoto (= Memoirs of the Research Department of the Toyo-Bunko 3). Tokyo, 1928
Oberhuber, Florenz	K. Oberhuber, Sumerische und akkadische Keilschriftdenkmäler des Archäologischen Museums zu Florenz, 2 vols (= Innsbrucker Beiträge zur Kulturwissenschaft 7–8). Innsbruck, 1958/60
Oberhuber Festschrift	W. Meid and H. Trenkwalder (eds.), Im Bannkreis des Alten Orients: Studien zur Sprach- und Kulturgeschichte des Alten Orients und seines Ausstrahlungsraumes. Karl Oberhuber zum 70. Geburtstag gewidmet (= Innsbrucker Beiträge zur Kulturwissenschaft 24). Innsbruck, 1986
OECT	Oxford Editions of Cuneiform Texts. Oxford, London, and Paris, 1923–
OIC	Oriental Institute Communications. Chicago, 1922–
OIP	Oriental Institute Publications. Chicago, 1924–
OLZ	Orientalistische Literaturzeitung. Berlin and Leipzig, 1898–
M. von Oppenheim Festschrift	Aus fünf Jahrtausenden morgenländischer Kultur, Festschift M. von Oppenheim zum 70. Geburtstag gewidmet von Freunden und Mitarbeitern (= AfO Beih. 1). Berlin, 1933
Oppert, EM 1	J. Oppert, Expédition scientifique en Mésopotamie ... Tome 1: Relation du voyage et résultats de l'expédition. Paris, 1863

OrAnt	Oriens Antiquus, Rivista del Centro per le Antichità e la Storia dell'Arte del Vicino Oriente. Rome, 1962–
Orthmann (ed.), Der alte Orient	W. Orthmann (ed.), Der alte Orient (= Propyläen Kunstgeschichte vol. 14). Berlin, 1975
van der Osten, Brett	H. van der Osten, Ancient Oriental Seals in the Collection of Mrs. A. Baldwin Brett (= OIP 37). Chicago, 1936
van der Osten, Newell	H. van der Osten, Ancient Oriental Seals in the Collection of Mr. Edward Newell (= OIP 22). Chicago, 1934
Owen, MVN 3	D. Owen, The John Frederick Lewis Collection. Rome, 1975
Parrot, Documents	A. Parrot, Le palais, documents et monuments (= MAM 2/3). Paris, 1959
Parrot, Glyptique mésopotamienne	A. Parrot, Glyptique mésopotamienne: Fouilles de Lagash (Tello) et de Larsa (Senkereh) (1931–1933). Paris, 1954
PBS	Publications of the Babylonian Section, University Museum, University of Pennsylvania, 15 vols. Philadelphia, 1911–26
Perrot and Chipiez, Chaldée et Assyrie	G. Perrot and C. Chipiez, Histoire de l'art dans l'antiquité, tome 2: Chaldée et Assyrie. Paris, 1884
Peters, Nippur	J.P. Peters, Nippur, or Explorations and Adventures on the Euphrates. The Narrative of the University of Pennsylvania Expedition to Babylonia in the Years 1888–1890, 2 vols. New York and London, 1897
Pinches, CT 45	T.G. Pinches, Old-Babylonian Business Documents. London, 1964
Pinches, Old Testament	T.G. Pinches, The Old Testament in the Light of the Historical Records and Legends of Assyria and Babylonia. London, 1902
Poebel, AS 3	A. Poebel, Das appositionell bestimmte Pronomen der 1. Pers. Sing. in den westsemitischen Inschriften und im Alten Testament. Chicago, 1932
Poebel, Grammatik	A. Poebel, Grundzüge der sumerischen Grammatik (= Rostocker orientalistische Studien 1). Rostock, 1923
Poebel, PBS 4/1	A. Poebel, Historical Texts. Philadelphia, 1914
Poebel, PBS 5	A. Poebel, Historical and Grammatical Texts. Philadelphia, 1914
Porada, Corpus	E. Porada, Corpus of Ancient Near Eastern Seals in North American Collections, 1: The Collection of the Pierpont Morgan Library (= Bollingen Series 14). Washington, 1948
Potts (ed.), Dilmun	D.T. Potts (ed.), Dilmun: New Studies in the Archaeology and Early History of Bahrain (= Berliner Beiträge zum Vorderen Orient 2). Berlin, 1983
Price, Rim-Sin	I.M. Price, Some Literary Remains of Rim-Sin (Arioch), King of Larsa, about 2285 B.C. (= Decennial Publications vol. 5 pp. 167–91). Chicago, 1904
Pritchard, ANEP^2	J.B. Pritchard, The Ancient Near East in Pictures Relating to the Old Testament, 2nd edition. Princeton, 1969
PSBA	Proceedings of the Society of Biblical Archaeology, vols. 1–40. London, 1878–1918
1 R	H.C. Rawlinson and E. Norris, The Cuneiform Inscriptions of Western Asia, vol. 1: A Selection from the Historical Inscriptions of Chaldaea, Assyria, and Babylonia. London, 1861
4 R^2	H.C. Rawlinson and T.G. Pinches, The Cuneiform Inscriptions of Western Asia, vol. 4: A Selection from the Miscellaneous Inscriptions of Assyria, 2nd edition. London, 1891
RA	Revue d'assyriologie et d'archéologie orientale. Paris, 1886–
Radau, EBH	H. Radau, Early Babylonian History down to the End of the Fourth Dynasty of Ur. New York and London, 1900
Ranke, BE 6/1	H. Ranke, Babylonian Legal and Business Documents from the Time of the First Dynasty of Babylon, Chiefly from Sippar. Philadelphia, 1906
REC	Thureau-Dangin, Recherches sur l'origine de l'écriture cunéiformes, 1re partie: Les formes archaïques et leurs équivalents modernes. Paris, 1898
Rép. Géogr.	W. Röllig (ed.), Beihefte zum Tübinger Atlas des vorderen Orients, Reihe B, Nr. 7: Répertoire géographique des texts cunéiformes. Wiesbaden, 1974–
RHA	Revue Hittite et Asianique. Paris, 1930–
RHR	Revue de l'histoire des religions. Annales du Musée Guimet. Paris, 1880–
RIMA	The Royal Inscriptions of Mesopotamia, Assyrian Periods
RIME	The Royal Inscriptions of Mesopotamia, Early Periods
RLA	Reallexikon der Assyriologie. Berlin, 1932–
RLV	Reallexikon der Vorgeschichte, vols. 1–15. Berlin, 1924–32
Römer, Königshymnen	W.H.Ph. Römer, Sumerische Königshymnen der Isin-Zeit. Leiden, 1965
Rouault, TFR 1	O. Rouault, Terqa Final Reports No. 1: L'Archive de Puzurum (= BibMes 16). Malibu, 1984
Rouault, TPR 7	O. Rouault, Terqa Preliminary Reports No. 7: Les Documents épigraphiques de la troisième saison (= Syro-Mesopotamian Studies 2/7). Malibu, 1979
RP NS	Records of the Past, Being English Translations of the Ancient Monuments of Egypt and Western Asia, New Series, 6 vols. London, 1888–
RP OS	Records of the Past, Being English Translations of the Assyrian and Egyptian Monuments, Old Series, 12 vols. London, 1873–81
RSO	Rivista degli studi orientali. Rome, 1907–

RT	Receuil de travaux relatifs à la philologie et à l'archéologie égyptiennes et assyriennes, vols. 1–40. Paris, 1870–1923
Sachs Memorial	E. Leichty, M. deJ. Ellis, and P. Gerardi (eds.), A Scientific Humanist: Studies in Memory of Abraham Sachs (=Occasional Publications of the Samuel Noah Kramer Fund 9). Philadelphia, 1988
Salonen, Hausgeräte 2	A. Salonen, Die Hausgeräte der alten Mesopotamier nach sumerisch-akkadischen Quellen, Teil II: Gefässe. Helsinki, 1966
de Sarzec, Découvertes	E. de Sarzec, Découvertes en Chaldée par Ernest de Sarzec, ouvrage acompagné de planches, publié par les soins de Léon Heuzey, avec le concours de Arthur Amiaud et François Thureau-Dangin pour la partie épigraphique, 2 vols. Paris, 1884/1912
Scheil, MDP 2	V. Scheil, Textes élamites-sémitiques, 1e série. Paris, 1900
Scheil, MDP 14	V. Scheil, Textes élamites-sémitiques, 5e série. Paris, 1913
Scheil, Sippar	V. Scheil, Une saison de fouilles à Sippar (=Mémoires publiés par les membres de l'Institut Français d'Archéologie Orientale du Caire 1/1). Cairo, 1902
Schorr, Urkunden	M. Schorr, Urkunden des altbabylonischen Zivil- und Prozessrechts (=VAB 5). Leipzig, 1913
Schott, Eanna	A. Schott, Nebst den inschriftlichen Quellen zur Geschichte Eannas (=UVB 1). Berlin, 1930
Schroeder, KAH 2	O. Schroeder, Keilschrifttexte aus Assur historischen Inhalts, Zweites Heft (=WVDOG 37). Leipzig, 1922
Schroeder, VAS 16	O. Schroeder, Altbabylonische Briefe. Leipzig, 1917
Seux, ERAS	J.-M. Seux, Épithètes royales akkadiennes et sumériennes. Paris, 1967
Shileiko, VN	V.K. Shileiko, Votivnie nadpisi šumerijskich pravitelej. Petrograd, 1915
Sigrist, Sattukku	R.M. Sigrist, Les *sattukku* dans l'Ešumeša durant la période d'Isin et Larsa (=BibMes 11). Malibu, 1984
Simmons, YOS 14	S.D. Simmons, Early Old Babylonian Documents. New Haven and London, 1978
SLB	Studia ad tabulas cuneiformes collectas a F.M.Th. d Liagre Böhl pertinentia. Leiden, 1952–
Snell, MVN 9	D. Snell, The E.A. Hoffman Collection and other American Collections. Rome, 1979
von Soden, AHw	W. von Soden, Akkadisches Handwörterbuch, 3 vols. Wiesbaden, 1965–81
Sollberger, UET 8	E. Sollberger, Royal Inscriptions Part 2. London, 1965
Sollberger and Kupper, IRSA	E. Sollberger and J.R. Kupper, Inscriptions royales sumériennes et akkadiennes. Paris, 1971
SPAW	Sitzungsberichte der Preussischen Akademie der Wissenschaften, philosophisch-historische Klasse. Berlin, 1922–38, 1948–49
Speleers, Recueil	L. Speleers, Recueil des inscriptions de l'Asie antérieure des Musées Royaux du Cinquantenaire à Bruxelles. Textes sumeriens, babyloniens et assyriens. Brussels, 1925
Stephens, YOS 9	F.J. Stephens, Votive and Historical Texts from Babylonia and Assyria. New Haven, 1937
Stol, AbB 9	M. Stol, Letters from Yale (=Altbabylonische Briefe in Umschrift und Übersetzung 9). Leiden, 1981
Strommenger and Hirmer, Mesopotamien	E. Strommenger and M. Hirmer, Fünf Jahrtausende Mesopotamien: Die Kunst von den Anfängen um 5000 v. Chr. bis zu Alexander dem Grossen. Munich, 1962
Studi Levi della Vida	Studi orientalistici in onore di Giorgio Levi della Vida. Rome, 1956
Studia Mariana	A. Parrott (ed.), Studia Mariana (=Documenta et Monumenta Orientalis Antiqui 4). Leiden, 1950
Studies Albright	H. Goedicke (ed.), Near Eastern Studies in Honor of W.F. Albright. Baltimore and London, 1971
Szlechter, Geneva	E. Szlechter, Tablettes juridiques de la 1re dynastie de Babylone conservées au Musée d'Art et d'Histoire de Genève, 2 parts (=Publications de l'Institut de Droit Romain de l'Université de Paris 16). Paris, 1958
Szlechter, Manchester	E. Szlechter, Tablettes juridiques et administratives de la IIIe dynastie d'Ur et de la 1re dynastie de Babylone conservées au Musée de l'Université de Manchester et, à Cambridge, au Musée Fitzwilliam, à l'Institut d'Études Orientales et à l'Institut d'Égyptologie, 2 parts (=Publications de l'Institut de Droit Romain de l'Université de Paris 21). Paris, 1963
Talon, ARMT 24	P. Talon, Textes administratifs des salles 'Y et Z' du palais de Mari. Paris, 1985
TCL	Textes cunéiformes du Musée du Louvre, Département des Antiquités Orientales. Paris, 1910–
Teissier, Marcopoli	B. Teissier, Ancient Near Eastern Cylinder Seals from the Marcopoli Collection. Berkeley, Los Angeles, and London, 1984
Thureau-Dangin, ISA	F. Thureau-Dangin, Les inscriptions de Sumer et d'Akkad, transcription et traduction. Paris, 1905
Thureau-Dangin, SAK	F. Thureau-Dangin, Die sumerischen und akkadischen Königsinscriften (=VAB 1). Leipzig, 1907
Thureau-Dangin, TCL 1	F. Thureau-Dangin, Lettres et contrats de l'époque de la première dynastie babylonienne. Paris, 1910
TSBA	Transactions of the Society of Biblical Archaeology. London, 1872–93
TTKY	Türk Tarih Kurumu Yayınlarından. Ankara
TUAT	O. Kaiser (ed.), Texte aus der Umwelt des Alten Testaments. Gütersloh, 1982–
UCP	University of California Publications in Semitic Philology, vols. 1–24. Berkeley, 1907–63

UE	Ur Excavations. Oxford, London, and Philadelphia, 1926–
UET	Ur Excavations, Texts. London, 1928–
UF	Ugarit-Forschungen, Internationales Jahrbuch für die Altertumskunde Syrien-Palästinas. Neukirchen-Vluyn, 1969–
Unger, Babylon	E. Unger, Babylon, die heilige Stadt nach der Beschreibung der Babylonier. Berlin and Leipzig, 1931
Unger, Katalog 3	E. Unger, Kaiserlich Osmanische Museen, Katalog der babylonischen und assyrischen Sammlung 3: Geräte. Constantinople, 1918
Unger, Siegelbildforschung	E. Unger, Der Beginn der altmesopotamischen Siegelbildforschung: Eine Leistung der Österreichischen Orientalistik (= Sitzungsberichte der Österreichenische Akademie der Wissenschaften, philosophisch-historische Klasse 250/2). Vienna, 1966
Unger, SuAK	E. Unger, Sumerische und akkadische Kunst. Breslau, 1926
Ungnad, HG	A. Ungnad and J. Kohler, Hammurabi's Gesetz, 6 vols. Leipzig, 1909–23
Ungnad, VAS 9	A. Ungnad, Altbabylonische Privaturkunden, part 3. Leipzig, 1909
UVB	Vorläufiger Bericht über die von (dem Deutschen Archäologischen Institut und der Deutschen Orient-Gesellschaft aus Mitteln) der Deutschen Forschungsgemeinschaft unternommenen Ausgrabungen in Uruk-Warka. Berlin, 1930–
VAB	Vorderasiatische Bibliothek. Leipzig, 1907–16
Van Buren, Found.	D. Van Buren, Foundation Figurines and Offerings. Berlin, 1931
VAS	Vorderasiatische Schriftdenkmäler der Königlichen Museen zu Berlin. Leipzig and Berlin, 1907–
Virolleaud, Danel	C. Virolleaud, La légende phénicienne de Danel (= Mission Ras-Shamra 1). Paris, 1936
Walker, CBI	C.B.F. Walker, Cuneiform Brick Inscriptions in the British Museum, the Ashmolean Museum, Oxford, the City of Birmingham Museums and Art Gallery, the City of Bristol Museum and Art Gallery. London, 1981
M. Walker, The Tigris Frontier	M. Walker, The Tigris Frontier from Sargon to Hammurabi: A Philologic and Historical Synthesis. Yale University PhD Dissertation, 1985
Walters, Water	S.D. Walters, Water for Larsa: An Old Babylonian Archive Dealing with Irrigation (= YNER 4). New Haven and London, 1970
Ward, Morgan	W.H. Ward, Cylinders and Other Ancient Oriental Seals in the Library of J. Pierpont Morgan. New Haven, 1920
Ward, Seals	W.H. Ward, The Seal Cylinders of Western Asia. Washington, 1910
Waterman, Bus. Doc.	L. Waterman, Business Documents of the Hammurapi Period from the British Museum. London, 1916
Weissbach, Miscellen	F.H. Weissbach, Babylonische Miscellen (= WVDOG 4). Leipzig, 1903
Willams-Forte, Ancient Near Eastern Seals	E. Williams-Forte, Ancient Near Eastern Seals: A Selection of Stamp and Cylinder Seals from the Collection of Mrs. William H. Moore. New York, 1976
Winckler, AOF	H. Winckler, Altorientalische Forschungen, 3 vols. Leipzig, 1893–1905
Winckler, KB 3/1	H. Winckler, et al., Historische Texte altbabylonischer Herrscher. Berlin, 1892
Winckler, Untersuchungen	H. Winckler, Untersuchungen zur altorientalischen Geschichte. Leipzig, 1889
Winckler and Böhden, ABK	H. Winckler and E. Böhden, Altbabylonische Keilschrifttexte zum Gebrauch bei Vorlesungen. Leipzig, 1892
Wiseman, Alalakh	D.J. Wiseman, The Alalakh Tablets. London, 1953
Wiseman, Illustrations	D.J. Wiseman, Illustrations from Biblical Archaeology. London, 1958
Witzel, KSt 7	M. Witzel, Perlen sumerischer Poesie 3: Die Grosse Ischmedagan-Liturgie (= Keilinschriftliche Studien 7). Jerusalem, 1930
WO	Die Welt des Orients. Wuppertal, Stuttgart, and Göttingen, 1947–
Woolley, Alalakh	C.L. Woolley, Alalakh: An Account of the Excavations at Tell Atchana in the Hatay, 1937–1949 (= Reports of the Research Committee of the Society of Antiquaries of London 18). London, 1955
Woolley, UE 5	C.L. Woolley, The Ziggurat and Its Surroundings. London and Philadelphia, 1939
Woolley, UE 6	C.L. Woolley, The Buildings of the Third Dynasty. London and Philadelphia, 1974
Woolley, UE 8	C.L. Woolley, The Kassite Period and the Period of the Assyrian Kings. London, 1965
Woolley and Mallowan, UE 7	L.W. Woolley and M. Mallowan, The Old Babylonian Period. London and Philadelphia, 1976
WVDOG	Wissenschaftliche Veröffentlichungen der Deutschen Orient-Gesellschaft. Leipzig and Berlin, 1901–
WZJ	Wissenschaftliche Zeitschrift der Friedrich Schiller Universität Jena. Jena, 1951–
WZKM	Wiener Zeitschrift für die Kunde des Morgenlandes. Vienna, 1887–
YNER	Yale Near Eastern Researches. New Haven and London, 1967–
YOS	Yale Oriental Series, Babylonian Texts. New Haven, 1915–
Young (ed.), Mari at 50	G.W. Young (ed.), Mari at 50. Winona Lake, 1988
ZA	Zeitschrift für Assyriologie und Verwandte Gebiete. Berlin, 1886–
ZDMG	Zeitschrift der Deutschen Morgenländischen Gesellschaft. Leipzig and Wiesbaden, 1879–

Other Abbreviations

c	collated
c.	circa
cm	centimetre(s)
col(s).	column(s)
dia.	diameter
DN	divine name
dupl.	duplicate
ed(s).	editor(s)
ex(s).	exemplar(s)
fig.	figure(s)
frgm(s).	fragment(s)
masc.	masculine
MB	Middle Babylonian
MN	month name
n	not collated
n(n).	note(s)
NB	Neo-Babylonian
no(s).	number(s)
NS	New Series
OB	Old Babylonian
obv.	obverse
OS	Old Series
p	collated from photo
p(p).	page(s)
pl(s).	plate(s)
PN	personal name
rev.	reverse
RN	royal name
var(s).	variant(s)
vol(s).	volume(s)

+	1) Between object numbers indicates physical join
	2) After dimensions indicates part of object missing
(+)	Indicates fragments from same object but no physical join

Object Signatures

When the same signature is used for more than one group, the first group in this list is meant unless otherwise indicated. For example, 'A' always means the Chicago collection unless stated otherwise.

A	1) Asiatic collection of the Oriental Institute, Chicago
	2) Mari collection of the Musée du Louvre, Paris
	3) Wellcome collection
Ac	Acem höyük
AH	Abu Habba collection of the British Museum, London
AO	Collection of Antiquités Orientales of the Musée du Louvre, Paris
As	Excavation numbers of the Chicago excavations at Tell Asmar, Iraq
Ash	Collection of the Ashmolean Museum, Oxford
Bab	Excavation numbers of the German excavations at Babylon
BCM	Birmingham City Museum
BE	1) Signature of objects in the Babylon collection of the Vorderasiatische Museum, Berlin
	2) Prefix of excavation numbers from the German excavations at Babylon
BM	British Museum, London
Bu	Budge collection in the British Museum, London
CBS	Babylonian Section of the University Museum, Philadelphia
EAH	E.A. Hoffman collection of the General Theological Seminary, New York
EŞ	Eski Şark Eserleri Müzesi of the Arkeoloji Müzeleri, Istanbul
FLP	John Frederick Lewis collection of the Free Library of Philadelphia
FM	Fitzwilliam Museum
FMNH	Signature of objects in the collections of the Field Museum for Natural History, Chicago
HMR	Excavation numbers of the Oxford-Field Museum expedition to Kiš
HS	Hilprecht collection of Babylonian Antiquities of Fr. Schiller University, Jena
IA	Australian Institute of Archaeology, Melbourne
IAC	Claremont College, California
IB	Excavation numbers of the Munich expedition to Isin-Išān Baḥrīyāt
IES	Institute of Egyptian Studies, Cambridge
IM	Iraq Museum, Baghdad
K	Kuyunjik collection of the British Museum, London
Kh	Prefix of field numbers from the American excavation at Khafajah
Ki	L.W. King collection of the British Museum, London
L	1) Signature of objects in the collection of the University Museum, Philadelphia
	2) Prefix of excavation numbers of the American excavations at Tell Leilan, Syria
	3) Larsa excavations
LB	Tablets in the Liagre Böhl collection
LBAF	Lands of the Bible Archaeology Foundation
M	1) Signature of objects in the Mari collection of the Musée du Louvre, Paris
	2) Prefix of excavation numbers from the French excavations at Mari, Syria
MAH	Musée d'Art et d'Histoire, Geneva
ME	Prefix of excavation numbers from the French excavations at Mari, Syria
MFAB	Museum of Fine Arts, Boston
MLC	J. Pierpont Morgan collection of the Yale University Library, New Haven
MM	1) Signature of objects in the collection of the Museo Monserrat
	2) Medelhavsmuseet, Stockholm
MMA	Metropolitan Museum of Art, New York
MN(B)	Musées Nationaux of the Musée du Louvre, Paris
MWA	Mission Museum of Wert, West Germany

N	1) Nippur collection of the University Museum, Philadelphia
	2) Nabû Temple collection of the British Museum, London
N III	Musée Napoleon III of the Musée du Louvre, Paris
N-T	Excavation numbers of inscribed objects from the American excavations at Nippur
NBC	James B. Nies collection of the Yale University Library, New Haven
NCBS	James B. Nies collection of the Yale University Library, New Haven
OI	Oriental Institute, Chicago
O-M	University of Illinois, Urbana
P	Photo numbers of the Oriental Institute in Chicago
PS	Piepkorn collection
RFH	R.F. Harper collection
ROM	Royal Ontario Museum, Toronto
S	Mari collection of the Musée du Louvre, Paris
Sb	Susa collection of the Musée du Louvre, Paris
S-G	Collection of F. Seidl-Geuthner, Paris
SH	Prefix of excavation numbers from the Danish excavation at Tell Šamšārah
TR	Prefix of excavation numbers from the British excavations at Tell al Rimah, Iraq
U	Prefix of excavation numbers from the British-American excavations at Ur, Iraq
UCLMA	Lowie Museum of Anthropology, University of California, Berkeley
UIOM	University of Illinois Oriental Museum, Urbana
UM	University Museum, Philadelphia
UMM	University Museum, Manchester
VA	Vorderasiatische Museum, Berlin
VA Bab	Babylon collection of the Vorderasiatische Museum, Berlin
VAT	Tablets in the collection of the Vorderasiatische Museum, Berlin
W	Excavation numbers of the German excavations at Uruk/Warka
WAG	Walters Art Gallery, Baltimore
YBC	Babylonian collection of the Yale University Library, New Haven

Comparative Chart of the Major Dynasties

ISIN	LARSA	URUK	EŠNUNNA
IŠBI-ERRA* (2073)			
			Nūr-aḫum*
	Iemṣium (2060)		
			Kirikiri*
			Bilalama*
ŠŪ-ILĪŠU* (2040)			
	Sāmium (2032)		
IDDIN-DAGĀN* (2030)			
			Išar-rāmāšu*
			Uṣur-awassu*
IŠME-DAGĀN* (2009)			
	Zabāia* (1997)		Azūzum*
LIPIT-EŠTAR* (1990)	GUNGUNUM* (1988)		
			Ur-Ninmar*
UR-NINURTA* (1979)			
	Abī-sarē* (1961)		Ur-Ningišzida*
BŪR-SÎN* (1951)	SŪMŪ-EL* (1950)	(Ikūn-pî-Eštar*)	Ipiq-Adad I*
		(Alila-ḫadûm)	Šarrīia*
LIPIT-ENLIL (1929)		(Sūmû-kanasa)	Warassa*
ERRA-IMITTĪ* (1929)	NŪR-ADAD* (1921)		Bēlakum*
ENLIL-BĀNI* (1916)			Ibāl-pî-El I*
			Ipiq-Adad II*
	SÎN-IDDINAM* (1905)	Sîn-kāšid*	
	SÎN-IRĪBAM* (1898)		
	SÎN-IQĪŠAM* (1896)		
ZAMBĪIA* (1892)	ṢILLĪ-ADAD* (1891)		
ITER-PĪŠA (1889)	WARAD-SÎN* (1890)	Sîn-irībam	
UR-DUKUGA* (1886)		Sîn-gāmil*	
SÎN-MĀGIR* (1883)	RIM-SÎN I* (1878)	Ilum-gāmil*	
DAMIQ-ILĪŠU* (1872)		Etēia	
		Anam*	Narām-Sîn*
		IR-ne-ne* (1871)	
		(1859)	Ibni-Erra
(1850)			Iqīš-Tišpak*
			Dannum-tāḫaz*
			Dāduša*
			Ibāl-pî-El II* (1789)
			(Elamite interregnum)
			Ṣillī-Sîn*
	(1819)		
	Rīm-Sîn II*		Iluni*
		Rīm-Anum*	
		Nabi-ilīšu*	
			Aḫūšina

BABYLON	MARI	MANANĀ	MARAD/ KAZALLU	OTHER
				Iddi(n)-Sîn* (Simurrum)
				Zabazuna* (Simurrum)
				Ilum/Anum-muttabbil* (Dēr)
				(destruction of Nippur and Ešnunna)
				Itūr-Šamaš* (Kisurra)
		Ḫalium		Iawiʾum* (Kiš)
Sūmû-abum* (1950)		Abdi-Eraḫ* (1950)	Ibni-šadûm	
		Mananā	Sūmû-ditān	Šamḫum* (Diyala)
			Iamsi-El	
Sūmû-la-Il* (1936)			Alum-pīʾū	
		Nāqimum		
		Aḫī-maraṣ	Sūmû-numḫim	
		Sūmû-iamutbala*		
		Manium*		Itūr-šarrum* (Diniktum)
Sābium (1900)				
Apil-Sîn (1886)				
Sîn-muballiṭ (1868)				
	Iaḫdun-Līm*			
	Sūmû-Iamam			
	Šamšī-Adad			
ḪAMMU-RĀPI* (1848)	Iasmaḫ-Addu*	**IAMḪAD**		
				Bunu-Eštar* (Qabarā)
		Iarīm-Līm I*		
	Zimrī-Līm* (1831)			
				Sîn-gāmil* (Diniktum)
		Ḫammu-rāpi I*		Iašūb-Iaḫad (Dēr)
SAMSU-ILUNA* (1805–1768)	**ḪANA**			
		Abba-Il*		
	Iapaḫ-sūmû-abu			
	Iṣi-sūmû-abu			
	Iadiḫ-abu			
	Kaštiliašu*			
Abī-ešuḫ* (1767–1740)				
	Šunuḫrû-Ammu			

Accession years are listed according to the long chronology (Ammī-ṣaduqa 1 = 1702 BC) favoured by P. Huber, Astronomical Dating of Babylon I and Ur III p. 42. Rulers whose inscriptions appear in the present volume are indicated by an asterisk. Rulers who were recognized at Nippur appear in capital letters. Rulers whose dynastic affiliations are obscure appear in parentheses.

OLD BABYLONIAN PERIOD

(2003–1595 BC)

INTRODUCTION

The time period covered by the inscriptions edited in this volume extends from the accession of Išbi-Erra, first king of the First Dynasty of Isin, to the death of Samsu-ditāna, last king of the First Dynasty of Babylon, in all a period of about 422 years.

At the beginning of this period Isin (E4.1) controlled a major part of the domains which had once been part of the Ur III empire including the dynastic capital Isin, the religious capital Nippur, and the former Ur III capital, Ur. Inscriptions of the first four Isin rulers are known from those cities. However, by the time of year 10 of Gungunum of Larsa, Larsa (E4.2) had gained control over the old capital Ur, in whose hands it was to remain until the fall of the Larsa dynasty. Because of the extensive excavations carried out by Sir Leonard Woolley at Ur, we find at Ur, beginning with Gungunum, an ever increasing number of royal inscriptions of the Larsa kings. These reach a climax with the reigns of Warad-Sîn and Rīm-Sîn I. Because Larsa itself has been much less extensively examined, the number of inscriptions of the Larsa kings from that site is at present rather meagre. Inscriptions of the Isin kings continue in comparatively small numbers during this period down to the reign of Damiq-ilīšu, the last king of the dynasty, mainly from the cities of Isin and Nippur.

Probably some time during the reign of Nūr-Adad of Larsa, an Amorite leader Sîn-kāšid installed himself as ruler at Uruk and established a short-lived dynasty. This lasted until year 20 of Rīm-Sîn I when the city was defeated by Larsa. The inscriptions of Sîn-kāšid and his successors are edited in section E4.4.

Meanwhile, in the north, another independent Amorite dynasty was established at Babylon. Its earliest rulers, known from king lists and date lists, are otherwise attested only from seal impressions of servants of the king. However, beginning with its sixth ruler Ḫammu-rāpi, we have genuine royal inscriptions inscribed on bricks, cones, and steles. Royal inscriptions of Ḫammu-rāpi's son, Samsu-iluna, are also fairly numerous, but few inscriptions are attested for the last four kings of the dynasty. The inscriptions of the Babylon dynasty are edited in section E4.3.

At Ešnunna a long series of governors of the city is attested, mainly from brick inscriptions. They span the time period from Išbi-Erra down to the reign of Ḫammu-rāpi of Babylon, who defeated the city. The Ešnunna inscriptions are edited in section E4.5.

At Mari a series of military governors is attested from the time of Išbi-Erra on, these known for the most part from seal impressions. Unfortunately, a complete roster of these governors is not at present known. An independent dynasty of rulers styling themselves 'king' (*šarrum*) emerges with the accession of Iaḫdun-Līm. This dynasty in turn was deposed by Šamšī-Adad, who installed his son Iasmaḫ-Addu as ruler in Mari. The line of Iaḫdun-Līm was restored when his son, Zimrī-Līm, deposed Iasmaḫ-Addu and ruled in Mari for about 15 years. The dynasty was brought to an end by Ḫammu-rāpi of Babylon. The Mari inscriptions are edited in section E4.6.

In addition to these six major dynasties, a number of small states with independent rulers are known for the Isin-Larsa/Old Babylonian period. Their inscriptions are edited in sections E4.7–36. These are edited in roughly geographical order from south-east to north-west in this volume. A number of rulers attested from servant seals who are otherwise unattested have texts in section E4.0.

Within a given dynasty the texts are edited in chronological order by ruler as best can be determined by king lists and other historical documents. For each ruler an attempt has been made to arrange the texts in chronological order within the reign. Such a scheme has been determined to a large degree by correlations with year names of the king. During the period treated in this volume, a system of dating was used by which each year was given a name. For many rulers the order of these year names is known. Many of the events commemorated in the year names also figure in the royal inscriptions. In addition, several of the events described in year names figure in temporal clauses which appear in the royal inscriptions. The chronological arrangement of the texts allows one in many cases to see the development of the titulary of the king. This in turn often helps to place inscriptions in their correct chronological setting even if the inscription does not correlate to a year name. A chronological arrangement also permits the grouping of texts dealing with one event which are inscribed on different objects. In this respect this volume differs from the previous bibliography of Hallo and the edition of Kärki which grouped the texts typologically.

The usefulness of this approach is best illustrated by an example. The name of year 10 of Warad-Sîn deals with the construction of the wall of Ur. This event is described in a brick inscription of 22 lines (E4.2.13.18), on foundation tablets of 27 lines (E4.2.13.19), on a cone inscription of 56 lines (E4.2.13.20), and on a barrel inscription of 116 lines (E4.2.13.21). The phraseology of the four texts is very similar – each succeeding version is slightly different and gives more detail. The grouping of the four texts together allows for easy comparison, while a typological arrangement separates the texts.

For any one given inscription the exemplars are listed, as a general rule, according to the excavation number of the piece if this is known. This means that in many cases the master text which serves as a basis for the transliteration is not the first text listed in the catalogue. For cone inscriptions the catalogue indicates if these are inscribed on the head or shaft. Although the head and shaft may be preserved in one object, these are given separate exemplar numbers for ease of citation. For cone shafts the dimensions refer to the length of the piece; for cone heads the dimensions refer to the diameter.

Concerning the transliteration of texts the following may be noted. An attempt has been made to differentiate between the signs ÌR and IR_{11} (ÌR × KUR) in servant seals, but because in many cases the seal was not available for collation or the sign was too small for the inscribed KUR to be seen, there is some uncertainty in this respect. Similarly, an attempt has been made to distinguish between uri_5 (ŠEŠ.AB) and úri (ŠEŠ.UNUG), but in many cases uncertainty remains. The logogram for the moon god is rendered ^{d}EN.ZU in this volume. The logogram for the wind god ^{d}IŠKUR is always rendered Adad in Akkadian and Addu in Amorite names.

Concerning the bibliographies it may be noted that in a number of cases we were not able to locate copies of some old volumes which were referred to by other sources. In these cases the particular bibliographical reference is cited without a description of what it contained since we were not able to consult it.

With respect to the numbering of the texts we note that the main series refers to royal inscriptions of the kings, the 1000 series to royal inscriptions the attribution of which is not entirely certain, and the 2000 series to servant seals and votive inscriptions. If a seal or a votive inscription belongs to the king or any member of his family, it is treated in the main series.

ISIN

E4.1

After assuming independence from the Ur III king Ibbi-Sîn under the energetic governor Išbi-Erra, Isin remained an independent city-state for about 225 years until its defeat at the hands of Rīm-Sîn of Larsa. Originally controlling most of the cities of the Sumerian south such as Uruk and Ur, as well as territory as far north as Apiak, Isin's domains greatly diminished during this period. This was due to the rise of small independent states such as Uruk and Kisurra, as well as the expansionist policies of its arch-rival Larsa. After the reign of Lipit-Eštar almost all our inscriptions dealing with the Isin kings come from either Isin or Nippur.

Fifteen kings are known for this dynasty, and most have left us royal inscriptions.

Išbi-Erra

E4.1.1

According to the Sumerian King List, Išbi-Erra had a relatively long reign of 33 years. However, surprisingly few royal inscriptions are extant for this king.

1

Apart from seal impressions of servants of the king, only one royal inscription is known for Išbi-Erra. This is a text dealing with the construction of a great lyre for the god Enlil known from a contemporary copy on a tablet.

COMMENTARY

The text is IM 58336, excavation number 3N–T20, from Nippur, TB iv 2b, locus unknown. It appears in OI photo no. 3/101 and P47149/50. The text is inscribed on a clay tablet 9.2×5.5 cm and was collated from the excavation photo.

A certain confusion has existed in the literature about this inscription. Its existence was first signalled by T. Jacobsen in JCS 7 (1953) p. 44 (where the king's title is incorrectly given as lugal-kalam-ma-na). The Jacobsen piece was referred to by W. Hallo, Royal Titles p. 19. A photo of the tablet entered the Oriental Institute archives as no. 3/101, and a transliteration of this photo entered I. Gelb's files. This transliteration is referred to by Hallo, Royal Titles p. 19 n. 6. Hallo thought that the transliteration in Gelb's files was a separate text from that referred to by Jacobsen, but a comparison of Gelb's transliteration and photos P47149/50 indicates that it is the same text.

Although Hallo thought the tablet to be a late copy of an Išbi-Erra text, the provenance and palaeography of the tablet indicate that it is a contemporary copy.

BIBLIOGRAPHY

1953 Jacobsen, JCS 7 p. 44 (study)
1957 Hallo, Royal Titles pp. 19–20 and n. 6 (study)
1961 Hallo, BiOr 18 p. 5 Išbi-Irra 2 (study)
1968 Kärki, SKFZ p. 1 Išbierra 2 (study)
1980 Kärki, SAKAZ 1 p. 2 Išbierra 2 (study)
1982 Frayne, AfO Beih. 19 p. 27 and nn. 34–35 (study)
1987 Civil, NABU pp. 14–15 no. 28 (copy, edition)

TEXT

1) [d]en-líl
2) lugal-kur-kur-ra
3) lugal-a-ni-ir
4) [d]*iš-bi-èr-r*[*a*]
5) lugal-kala-ga

1–3) For the god Enlil, lord of the foreign lands, his lord,

4–6) Išbi-Err[a], mighty king, lord of ⟨his⟩ land,

6) lugal-⸢ma⸣-da-⟨na⟩-ke$_4$
7) balag-⸢maḫ⸣
8) šà tu-x-da
9) mu-na-an-dím
10) nam-ti-la-[ni-šè]
11) a mu-na-ru
12) balag-ba
13) ᵈ*iš-bi-èr-ra*
14) ᵈen-líl-da ⸢nir⸣-gál
15) mu-bi-⸢im⸣

7–9) fashioned a great lyre for him, which ... the heart.

10–11) He dedicated it [for his own] life.

12–15) The name of this lyre is 'Išbi-Erra trusts in the god Enlil'.

2001

A rather large corpus of administrative texts from ancient Isin dating to the time of Išbi-Erra and Šū-ilīšu have been studied by V. Crawford and M. van de Mieroop. On these tablets are seal impressions of various officials. These are edited in order according to the date of the tablet on which they appear.

Ur-Šubula, possibly the *šà-tam* official of the same name, appears in a seal impression dating to year B. Year B dates to the very early period of Išbi-Erra's reign (see M. van de Mieroop, BIN 10 p. 2). Išbi-Erra's name is written here without the prefixed DINGIR sign.

COMMENTARY

The seal impression is found on YBC 9759, from Isin. It measures 0.9×2.1 cm and was collated.

BIBLIOGRAPHY

1954 Crawford, BIN 9 pl. XCIII P (copy)
1961 Hallo, BiOr 18 p. 5 Išbi-Irra 1: vi (study)
1968 Kärki, SKFZ p. 1 Išbierra 1 (edition)
1980 Kärki, SAKAZ 1 p. 1 Išbierra 1 (edition)

TEXT

1) ur-ᵈ⸢šu⸣-bu-⸢la⸣
2) dumu-*ša*-[...]-*a*
3) ìr-*iš-bi-èr-ra*

1) Ur-Šubula,
2) son of Ša[...]a,
3) servant of Išbi-Erra.

2002

A tablet dating to year x+5 of Išbi-Erra has the seal impression in Akkadian of a servant of Išbi-Erra.

COMMENTARY

Several impressions of this seal are found on NBC 8437. They were all collated to produce a conflated transliteration. The reading given here differs from the copy of Crawford in BIN 9. The seal impression measures 1.9×2.2 cm.

Lu-Ninšubur often occurs in the BIN 9 texts receiving bags for drinking purposes so the occupation 'brewer' (LÚ.KAŠ) found in line 6 is not unexpected.

BIBLIOGRAPHY

1954 Crawford, BIN 9 pl. XCIII F (copy)
1961 Hallo, BiOr 18 p. 5 Išbi-Irra 1: iv (study)
1968 Kärki, SKFZ p. 1 Išbierra 1 (edition)
1980 Kärki, SAKAZ 1 p. 2 Išbierra 1 (edition)

TEXT

1) *iš-bi-èr-ra*
2) *da-núm*
3) *be-al ma-ti-šu*
4) LÚ-dNIN-ŠUBUR
5) DUMU UR-d[...]
6) LÚ.KAŠ [x]
7) ÌR.ZU

1) Išbi-Erra,
2) the mighty,
3) lord of his land,
4) Lu-Ninšubur,
5) son of Ur-[...],
6) the brewer [...],
7) your servant.

2003

A group of tablets purchased by the Ashmolean Field Museum Kish expedition belong to the same group as the BIN 9 tablets. One dating to year x+7 has the seal of a cupbearer. Unfortunately, his name is not complete.

COMMENTARY

The seal impression is on Ash 1932,259.

BIBLIOGRAPHY

1987 van de Mieroop, BIN 10 pl. LXXIV seal j (copy)

TEXT

1) d*iš-bi-èr-ra*
2) lugal-kala-ga
3) lugal-ma-da-na
4) ki-ág-den-líl
5) ù dni[n]-in-si-[na]
6) d*en-⸢líl⸣*-[x]-*um*(?)-*iš-bi-èr-ra*
7) sagi
8) ir_{11}-zu

1) Išbi-Erra,
2) mighty king,
3) lord of his land,
4) beloved of the god Enlil
5) and the goddess Ni[n]isi[na],
6) Enlil-[...]um-Išbi-Erra,
7) cupbearer,
8) your servant.

2004

An impression of a servant seal in Akkadian is found on a tablet dating to year x+9 of Išbi-Erra.

COMMENTARY

The impression is on NBC 6517, and was collated by W. Hallo. The reading of line 3 differs from that indicated by the copy in BIN 10.

BIBLIOGRAPHY

1987 van de Mieroop, BIN 10 pl. LXXIV seal a (copy)

TEXT

1) *iš-bi-èr-ra*	1) Išbi-Erra,
2) *da-núm*	2) the mighty,
3) *be-al ma-ti-šu*	3) lord of his land,
4) [...]	4) [...]
5) DUB.[SAR]	5) scr[ibe]
6) DUMU x [...]	6) son of ... [...]
7) [ÌR].ZU	7) your [servant].

2005

Šū-Erra, servant of Išbi-Erra, is attested in an impression dating to year x+9.

COMMENTARY

The seal impression is found on NBC 7194, from Isin. The name *šu-[èr-ra]* is restored from line 6 of the tablet which has this seal (BIN 9 no. 125).

BIBLIOGRAPHY

1954 Crawford, BIN 9 pl. XCIII S (copy)
1961 Hallo, BiOr 18 p. 5 Išbi-Irra 1: v (study)
1968 Kärki, SKFZ p. 1 Išbierra 1 (edition)
1971 Sollberger and Kupper, IRSA IVA1b (translation)
1980 Kärki, SAKAZ 1 p. 1 Išbierra 1 (edition)

TEXT

1) ^d^*iš-bi-èr-ra*
2) lugal-kala-ga
3) lugal-an-ub-da-límmu-ba
4) *šu*-[*èr-ra*]
5) GÌR.[NÍTA]
6) dumu-*tu-r*[*a-am*]-*ì*-[*lí*]
7) ìr-[zu]

1) Išbi-Erra,
2) mighty king,
3) king of the four quarters,
4) Šū-[Erra],
5) military [governor],
6) son of Tūr[am]-i[lī],
7) [your] servant.

2006

The impression of a seal of a servant of Išbi-Erra is found on a tablet dating to year x + 9.

COMMENTARY

The impression is on NBC 5617. The tablet indicates that it was sealed by the *šatam* officials. *A-lí-šu-nu* appears as a *šatam* official in BIN 10 no. 118 line 7. This accounts for the restoration of the name in this seal impression.

BIBLIOGRAPHY

1987 van de Mieroop, BIN 10 pl. LXXIV seal b (copy)

TEXT

1) ^d^[*iš-bi-èr*]-*ra*
2) lugal-kala-ga
3) lugal-an-ub-da-límmu-ba
4) [ki-á]g-^d^en-[l]íl
5) [ù ^d^nin-in-si-na]
6) *a-lí*-[*šu-nu*]
7) dub-[sar]
8) dumu-[...]-ke_4
9) [ìr-zu]

1) [Išbi-Er]ra,
2) mighty king,
3) king of the four quarters,
4) [bel]oved of the god En[l]il,
5) [and the goddess Ninisina],
6) Alī[šunu],
7) scr[ibe],
8) son of [...],
9) [your servant].

2007

Išbi-Erra-mālik, the *rá-gaba* official, is attested from two separate seal impressions. One is found on a tablet dated to year x + 14b.

COMMENTARY

The tablet is NBC 7104, from Isin. Dimensions of the seal are undeterminable.

The translation 'lord' for lugal in the expression lugal-ma-da-na is based on the Akkadian equivalent *be-al ma-ti-šu* found in E4.1.1.2002 and 2004.

BIBLIOGRAPHY

1954 Crawford, BIN 9 pl. XCIII Q (copy)
1961 Hallo, BiOr 18 p. 5 Išbi-Irra 1: iii (study)
1968 Kärki, SKFZ p. 1 Išbierra 1 (edition)
1971 Sollberger and Kupper, IRSA IVA1a n. 1 (study)
1980 Kärki, SAKAZ 1 p. 1 Išbierra 1 (edition)

TEXT

1) ^{d}*iš-bi-èr-ra*	1) Išbi-Erra,
2) lugal-kala-g[a]	2) might[y] king,
3) lugal-ma-da-[na]	3) lord of [his] land,
4) ^{d}*iš-bi-èr-r*[*a-ma-lik*]	4) Išbi-Err[a-mālik],
5) [ìr-zu]	5) [your servant].

2008

The impression of a seal of a servant of Išbi-Erra is found on a tablet (NBC 7568) dating to year x + 16.

BIBLIOGRAPHY

1987 van de Mieroop, BIN 10 pl. LXXIV seal e (copy)

TEXT

1) ^{d}*iš-bi-*[*è*]*r-ra*	1) Išbi-[E]rra,
2) lugal-kala-ga	2) mighty king,
3) lugal-ma-da-na	3) king of his land,
4) ur-al-l[a]	4) Ur-All[a],
5) dumu-*ku*-[...]	5) son of Ku-[...],
6) ìr-[zu]	6) [your] servant.

2009

A second seal of Išbi-Erra-mālik is found on three tablets dating to years x + 17b–19.

COMMENTARY

The impressions are on NBC 7087, 7387, and 6421, from Isin. The seal impression measures 3.1 × 1.5 cm and the inscription was collated.

BIBLIOGRAPHY

1954 Crawford, BIN 9 pl. XCIII D (exs. 1-3, composite copy)
1961 Hallo, BiOr 18 p. 5 Išbi-Irra 1: ii (study)
1968 Kärki, SKFZ p. 1 Išbierra 1 (edition)
1971 Sollberger and Kupper, IRSA IVA1a (translation)
1980 Kärki, SAKAZ 1 p. 1 Išbierra 1 (edition)

TEXT

1) ^{d}*iš-bi-èr-ra*	1) Išbi-Erra,
2) dingir-kalam-ma-na	2) god of his nation,
3) lugal-kala-ga	3) mighty king,
4) lugal-ma-da-na	4) lord of his land,
5) ^{d}*iš-bi-èr-ra-ma-lik*	5) Išbi-Erra-mālik,
6) [ìr-zu]	6) [your servant].

2010

KALbaba, the bowmaker, is attested in a seal impression on a tablet dating to year x + 17b.

COMMENTARY

The seal impression is found on NBC 7153, from Isin, and measures 1.4 × 2.7 cm. The reading of the personal name is uncertain.

BIBLIOGRAPHY

1954 Crawford, BIN 9 pl. XCIII I (copy)
1961 Hallo, BiOr 18 p. 5 Išbi-Irra 1: i (study)
1968 Kärki, SKFZ p. 1 Išbierra 1 (edition)
1980 Kärki, SAKAZ 1 p. 1 Išbierra 1 (edition)

TEXT

1) KAL-ba-ba	1) KALbaba,
2) GIŠ.ban-d[í]m	2) bowma[k]er,
3) ir_{11}-^{d}*iš-bi-[èr-ra]*	3) servant of Išbi-[Erra].

2011

A second Ashmolean tablet, this dating to year x + 18b, has the seal impression of Libūr-bēlī.

COMMENTARY

The seal impression is on Ash 1932,251, measuring 1.2 × 2.6 cm.

The name in line 4 is restored from the tablet. The omission of the DINGIR sign in the writing of Išbi-Erra's name at this late date in the reign is curious.

BIBLIOGRAPHY

1987 van de Mieroop, BIN 10 pl. LXXIV seal h (copy)

TEXT

1) *iš-bi-èr-ra*	1) Išbi-Erra,
2) lugal-kala-ga	2) mighty king,
3) lugal-ma-da-na	3) lord of his land,
4) *li-*[*bur-be*]*-lí*	4) Li[būr-bē]lī,
5) rá-rá	5) (oil) presser,
6) ìr-[zu]	6) [your] servant.

2012

A number of tablets dating to the period of the early Isin kings were excavated from house levels in TB at Nippur. Seal impressions of two servants of Išbi-Erra figure on these tablets. The first of these belongs to Abūni, the chief steward.

COMMENTARY

The seal impression is found on three tablets: A 30013a–b, A 30006, and A 30004, excavation nos. 2N–T578, 2N–T569, and 2N–T567, respectively. All the tablets were at Nippur, locus 153, level III 1, TB.

BIBLIOGRAPHY

1986 van de Mieroop, JANES 18 p. 43 no. 5 seal (copy)

TEXT

1) ᵈ*iš-bi-èr-ra*	1) Išbi-Erra,
2) lugal-kala-ga	2) mighty king,
3) lugal-ma-da-na	3) lord of his land,
4) *a-bu-ni*	4) Abūni,
5) agrig	5) chief steward,
6) dumu-*nu-úr-ì-lí*	6) son of Nūr-ilī,
7) ìr-zu	7) your servant.

2013

Another seal impression from Nippur belongs to a scribe whose name is not fully preserved.

COMMENTARY

The seal impression is on A 30014, excavation no. 2N-T579. It is on a tablet found at Nippur, locus 153, level III 1, TB.

BIBLIOGRAPHY

1986 van de Mieroop, JANES 18 p. 48 no. 19 seal (copy)

TEXT

1) ᵈ*iš*-[*b*]*i-èr*-[*ra*]	1) Iš[b]i-Er[ra],
2) lugal-ma-da-[na]	2) lord of [his] land,
3) lú-ᵈni[n-...]	3) Lu-Ni[n...],
4) dub-sar [ìr-zu]	4) scribe, [your servant].

Šū-ilīšu

E4.1.2

According to the Sumerian King List Šū-ilīšu reigned 10 years. Three monumental texts are extant for this king.

1

Šū-ilīšu, successor of Išbi-Erra, continued the restoration work at Ur that had begun late in the reign of his father. The name of what is probably his second year reads: 'The year he confirmed Ur in its residence' (mu uri₅.KI ki-tuš-ba bí-in-ge-en). As part of the restoration work the Dublamaḫ was rebuilt. Two pivot stones originally placed by Šū-ilīšu in the Dublamaḫ deal with this construction.

CATALOGUE

Ex.	Museum number	Excavation number	Photo number	Provenance	Dimensions (cm)	Lines preserved	cpn
1	CBS 15324	U 420	U 19, 32, 68	Ur, against the western door jamb in Enunmaḫ 13 (=TTB 7), reused in the Persian period	50×22	1-31	p
2	IM 373	U 421	U 18, 67	In the NW doorway of Enunmaḫ 19	50×28	1-31	p

COMMENTARY

The master text is ex. 2. The inscription was collated from excavation photos.

The pivot stones were reused much later for doors in the neighbouring Enunmaḫ where they were excavated by Woolley. The emphasis in the inscription on the doors of the Dublamaḫ is undoubtedly so because the texts were carved on pivot stones.

BIBLIOGRAPHY

1928 Gadd, UET 1 no. 100 (exs. 1-2, edition) and pl. N (ex. 2, photo)
1929 Barton, RISA pp. 304-305 Gimil-ili-shu 1 (edition)
1961 Hallo, BiOr 18 p. 5 Šu-ilišu 1 (study)
1965 Woolley, UE 8 p. 101 (exs. 1-2, provenance)
1968 Kärki, SKFZ pp. 1-2 Šuilīšu 1 (edition)
1971 Sollberger and Kupper, IRSA IVA2a (translation)
1974 Woolley, UE 6 pp. 51 and 90 (ex. 1, provenance)
1980 Kärki, SAKAZ 1 pp. 2-3 Šuilīšu 1 (edition)
1985 Lambert, Orientalia NS 54 p. 192 (study)

TEXT

1) ^{d}nanna
2) sag-íl-maḫ-
3) ^{d}a-nun-na-ke$_4$-ne
4) lugal-a-ni-ir
5) ^{d}*šu-ì-lí-šu*
6) nita-kala-ga
7) lugal-uri$_5$.KI-ma-ke$_4$
8) u$_4$ ^{d}nanna
9) an-ša-an.KI-ta
10) uri$_5$.KI-šè
11) mu-un-túm-ma-a
12) dub-lá-maḫ
13) ki-di-ku$_5$-da-ni
14) mu-na-dù
15) GIŠ.ig zà-mí ma-gùn-a
16) mu-na-an-gub
17) nam-ti-la-ni-šè
18) a mu-na-ru
19) lú á-nì-ḫul-dím-ma
20) íb-ši-ág-ge$_{26}$-a
21) é-nì-GA-ra
22) i-ni-ib-ku$_4$-ku$_4$-a
23) áš-bal-a-ba-ke$_4$-eš
24) lú-kúr
25) šu ba-an-zi-zi-a
26) lú-ba
27) ^{d}nanna
28) lugal-mu
29) ^{d}nin-gal
30) nin-mu
31) nam ḫa-ba-an-da-ku$_5$-ru-ne

1–4) For the god Nanna, supreme proud one of the Anuna gods, his lord,

5–7) Šū-ilīšu, mighty man, king of Ur,

8–11) when he brought (back the statue of) the god Nanna from Anšan to Ur,

12–16) built the Dublamaḫ, his place of judgement. He set up for him a door ... *brightly coloured*,

17–18) (and) dedicated it for his own life.

19–25) (As for) the man who gives orders to do evil against it, has it brought into a storehouse (or) on account of this curse incites another to do so,

26–31) may the god Nanna, my lord, (and) the goddess Ningal, my lady, curse that man.

2

The name of what is probably the third year of Šū-ilīšu (see C. Wilcke, Orientalia NS 54 p. 308) commemorates the construction of a standard for the god Nanna of Ur. This work is described in a school copy excavated by Woolley at Ur.

COMMENTARY

The inscription is found on IM 85680, a tablet 7×11×3.5 cm. It was collated.

Since the provenance and excavation no. of this tablet were not known it was assigned an arbitrary excavation no. U r by Sollberger. It may have come from the house at no. 7 Quiet Street where copies of a number of royal inscriptions were found.

Col. ii 1–6 are restored following a suggestion of C. Wilcke in Orientalia NS 54 p. 306.

BIBLIOGRAPHY

1965 Sollberger, UET 8 no. 62 (copy, study)
1966 Falkenstein, BiOr 23 p. 166 (study)
1971 Sollberger and Kupper, IRSA IVA2b (translation)
1980 Kärki, SAKAZ 1 pp. 3–5 Šuilīšu 2 (edition)
1985 Wilcke, Orientalia NS 54 p. 306 (study)

TEXT

Col. i
1) ^{d}nanna
2) nir-gál-an-ki-a
3) dumu-NUN-zi-
4) ^{d}en-líl-lá
5) en aša-ni an-ki-šè
6) dingir-re-ne-er zà-díb-ba
7) lugal-a-ni-ir

i 1–7) For the god Nanna, trusted one of heaven and earth, true princely son of the god Enlil, the lord alone, surpasses as far as heaven and earth, surpasses the gods, his lord,

8) ^{d}*šu-ì-lí-šu*
9) dingir-kalam-ma-na
10) lugal-kala-ga
11) lugal-uri$_{5}$.KI-ma
12) ki-ág-an
13) ^{d}en-líl
14) ù ^{d}nanna-ke$_{4}$

i 8–14) Šū-ilīšu, god of his nation, mighty king, king of Ur, beloved of the gods An, Enlil, and Nanna,

15) ^{d}šu-nir-gal
16) giš buru$_{14}$-a tum$_{4}$-ma
17) u$_{6}$-di-dè ḫé-du$_{7}$
18) kù-GI
19) kù za-gìn-na gùn-⌜a⌝
20) mí-ul-lá sig$_{7}$-[ga]
21) alam kù-[babbar]
22) x x ⌜gi⌝ x [x x]
Lacuna

i 15–22) a great divine standard, a tree fit for a (rich) harvest, evoking wonder, coloured with gold, silver, and shining lapis lazuli, ..., a sil[ver] image ...
Lacuna

Col. ii
1) [u$_{4}$ ...]
2) m[u-...]
3) u[ri$_{5}$.KI(?) ...]
4) x-[...]
5) zà-a[n-ša-an.KI-na-šè] ság-d[u$_{11}$-ga]
6) ki-tuš-ba gi-n[a-a]
7) mu-na-dím

ii 1–7) he fashioned for him [when] he establish[ed in] U[r the people] scattered as far as A[nšan], in their abode,

8) nam-ti-la-ni-šè
9) a mu-na-[r]u

ii 8–9) He dedicated it for his own life.

10) l[ú á-nì-ḫul-dím-ma]
11) [... íb-ši-ág-ge$_{26}$-a]
12) m[u-sar-ra-ba]
13) šu [bí-íb-ùr-a]
14) m[u-ni bí-íb-sar-re-a]
15) x [...]
16) x [...]
Lacuna

ii 10–16) (As for) the m[an who gives orders to do evil against it] ... era[ses its] i[nscription and writes his] n[ame on it ...]
Lacuna

Col. iii
1′) PA N[I ...]-da-a[b ...]
2′) GIŠ.gu-[za-na]
3′) suḫuš-bi na-a[n-na-ge-en]

iii 1′–15′) ... may the foundation of [his] thr[one] not be [secure] for him, may he [sit] in the dust. May the walls of his shrine [resound] with

4′) sahar-ra ha-ab-d[a-tuš]
5′) bára-ga-na SIG4.Z[I-bi] a-nir ha-ab-d[a-gi4-gi4]
6′) tùr-ra-ni hé-[...]
7′) amaš(*)-a-ni hé-x-[...]
8′) [d]en-ki-ke4
9′) hé-gál-an-ki-ka
10′) KA a-ba-an-da-an-gi4
11′) i7-mah a-KU6.eštub DU-a-na
12′) sahar ha-an-⌜da-si⌝-[si]
13′) ma-x-[...]
14′) AN [...]
15′) x [...]
Lacuna

laments. May his cattle pens [...] (and) his sheepfolds [...]. May the god Enki, after stopping the abundance of heaven and earth, silt up the great canal which (used to) bring the early flood.
Lacuna

Col. iv
1′) x x x [x x x]
2′) u4-da-rí-šè x
3′) [d]šu-nir-ba
4′) [d]nun-bi bar-an-ki
5′) mu-bi
(blank)
x (erasure)
Upper Edge: u4 (erasure)

iv 1′-2′) ... forever.

iv 3′-5′) The name of this divine standard is 'Its divine prince is light of heaven and earth'.

3

The name of year 7 of Šū-ilīšu commemorates the construction of the wall of Isin. This deed is described in a cone inscription recently excavated by the Munich expedition to Isin.

CATALOGUE

Ex.	Museum number	Excavation number	Provenance	Object	Dimensions (cm)	Lines preserved	cpn
1	IM 95454	IB 1387	Isin, 908.65N, 299.35 E, +6.53, from a robber's pit	Clay cone head	10.7 dia.	1–13	c
2	IM 95454	IB 1387	As ex. 1	Clay cone shaft	8.5	1–13	c

COMMENTARY

Although not found in situ, the provenance of the cone in the extreme north-east corner of the tell suggests that the city wall built by Šū-ilīšu may have once stood in this area.

iii 7′ AMAŠ.ME.

BIBLIOGRAPHY

1985 Wilcke, Orientalia NS 54 pp. 304–308 (edition) and pl. I (photo)
1987 Wilcke in Hrouda, et al., Isin 3 p. 113 (edition)

TEXT

1) ^{d}*šu-ì-lí-šu*
2) lugal-kala-ga
3) lugal-ki-en-gi-ki-uri-ke$_4$
4) nam-gal-ki-ág-
5) ^{d}nin-in-si-na-ta
6) ì-si-in.KI-da
7) ma-da-sig-nim ság-du$_{11}$-ga
8) ki-tuš-ba gi-né-dè
9) bàd-gal me-lám-ba gù lú nu-gá-gá
10) mu-dù
11) bàd-ba
12) ^{d}*šu-ì-lí-š*[*u*]*-ri-im-eš*$_4$-[*tár*]
13) mu-bi-i[m]

1–3) Šū-ilīšu, mighty king, king of the land of Sumer and Akkad,

4–5) on account of the great love of/for the goddess Ninisina,
6–8) in order to settle in their residence around Isin the scattered (people) of the upper and lower lands
9–10) he built the great wall in whose aura no one makes a noise.
11–13) The name of this wall is 'Šū-ilīš[u] is the beloved of (the goddess) Eš[tar]'.

4

The impression of a royal seal of Šū-ilīšu was excavated in the Bilalama palace at Ešnunna.

COMMENTARY

The impression is on As. 30:T.734, a clay sealing 4.5×3.5 cm. T. Jacobsen, Gimilsin Temple p. 149, indicates that the sealing was found in O 30:18; R. Whiting indicates that the field catalogue lists its provenance as O 30:4 (above O 30:18), the 'burned level' in the Bilalama palace. It was collated by Whiting.

Although Jacobsen suggested that the seal impression was to be read in Akkadian, collation reveals that it was inscribed in Sumerian. Unless the inscription has a third col., now broken away, which seems unlikely, the impression must be that of a royal seal of Šū-ilīšu himself. Hallo, followed by Kärki, thought that this impression might refer to Damiq-ilīšu of Isin. However, the spacing of the writing on the impression, the stratigraphy, and the titulary all argue in favour of Jacobsen's original attribution to Šū-ilīšu.

BIBLIOGRAPHY

1940 Jacobsen, Gimilsin Temple p. 149 no. 25 (edition)
1957 Hallo, Royal Titles p. 139 n. 3 (study)
1980 Kärki, SAKAZ 1 p. 39 Damiqilīšu 3 (edition)
1987 Whiting, AfO 34 pp. 30–34 (copy, edition)

TEXT

1) [^{d}*šu*]*-ì-lí-*⌜*šu*⌝
2) lugal-kala-ga
3) [lugal-u]ri$_5$.[KI-m]a
4) ki-[ág]-^{d}e[n-líl]
5) ù ^{d}n[in]-in-si-na

1) [Šū]-ilīšu,
2) mighty king,
3) [king of U]r,
4) belo[ved] of the god E[nlil]
5) and the goddess N[in]isina.

2001

A tablet excavated from a house in the TB area of Nippur bears the seal impressions of two scribes, servants of Šū-ilīšu. The tablet itself, dated to the last year of Šū-ilīšu, was used by Steele to determine the sequence of most of the king's year names.

COMMENTARY

The seal impression is on UM 55-21-125; excavation no. 2N-T668. It was found at Nippur, locus 201/213, level IV 1, TB. The seal impression measures 1.3×2.8 cm and the inscription was collated.

BIBLIOGRAPHY

1951 Steele, BASOR 122 p. 47 (copy)

TEXT

1) ᵈ*šu-ì-lí-šu*	1) Šū-ilīšu,
2) lugal-kala-ga	2) mighty king,
3) lugal-ma-da-na	3) lord of his land,
4) ⸢er$_{11}$-ra⸣-x-x-ni	4) Erra-...ni,
5) dub-sar	5) scribe,
6) dumu-lú-bala-sa$_{6}$-ga	6) son of Lu-bala-saga.

2002

The name of a second servant of Šū-ilīšu is known from the Nippur tablet edited by Steele.

COMMENTARY

The impression is found on the same tablet as E4.1.2.2001. It measures 1.1×2.7 cm and the inscription was collated.

BIBLIOGRAPHY

1951 Steele, BASOR 122 p. 47 (copy)

TEXT

1) ^{d}*šu-ì-lí-šu*	1) Šū-ilīšu,
2) nita-kala-ga	2) mighty man,
3) [lugal-ma-d]a-[na]	3) [lord of his l]an[d],
4) ^{d}šara-mu-túm	4) Šara-mutum,
5) dub-sar	5) scribe,
6) dumu ur-^{d}šul-pa-⌈è⌉	6) son of Ur-Šulpae.

2003

The impression of the seal of a servant of Šū-ilīšu is found on a clay sealing excavated at Nippur.

COMMENTARY

The impression is found on 2D 812, found at locus TB 222 IV 2 at Nippur. It was not collated.

BIBLIOGRAPHY

1967 McCown, Nippur 1 pl. 119 no. 1 (transliteration)

TEXT

1) lú-[...]	1) Lu-[...],
2) dumu ... [...]	2) son of ...[...],
3) ìr-^{d}*šu-ì-*[*lí-šu*]	3) servant of Šū-i[līšu].

Iddin-Dagān

E4.1.3

According to the Sumerian King List, Iddin-Dagān reigned 21 years. One contemporary monumental text is extant for the king; two are known from later copies.

1

A fragment of a stone statue, now in Stockholm, dedicated to Ninisina by Iddin-Dagān is the only extant contemporary monumental text of this king.

COMMENTARY

The statue is MM [Medelhavsmuseet] 1974:26 and measures 16 cm high. The inscription was collated from the published photo. The provenance of this purchased piece is unknown; it probably came from Isin.

BIBLIOGRAPHY

1977 Haldar, Medelhavsmuseet Bulletin 12 pp. 3–6 (photo, edition)

TEXT

1) [^{d}nin-in-si]-na 2) nin-a-ni-ir	1–2) To the goddess [Ninisi]na, his lady,
3) ^{d}*i-din-*^{d}*da-gan* 4) lugal-kala-ga 5) lugal-ì-si-in.KI-na 6) lugal-ki-en-gi-ki-uri-ke$_4$	3–6) Iddin-Dagān, mighty king, king of Isin, king of the land of Sumer and Akkad,
7) nam-ti-la-ni-šè 8) a mu-na-ru	7–8) dedicated (this statue) to her for his own life.
9) lú á-nì-ḫul-[dím-ma]	9) (As for) the man [who gives] orders [to do] evil [against it ...]
Lacuna	Lacuna
1′) ^{d}nin-in-si-na 2′) nin-mu 3′) ^{d}da-mu 4′) lugal-mu 5′) nam ḫa-ba-an-da-ku$_5$-ru-ne	1′–5′) may the goddess Ninisina, my lady, (and) the god Damu, my lord, curse [that man].

2

Two clay tablets found in a hoard in a house at Ur by Woolley contain later copies of a royal inscription of Iddin-Dagān.

CATALOGUE

Ex.	Museum number	Excavation number	Provenance	Dimensions (cm)	Lines preserved	cpn
1	IM 85467	U 7728	Ur, from a hoard in no. 7 Quiet Street, in the burnt level over upper floor of rooms 5–6	10.5×6×2.7	1–41	c
2	IM 85466	U 7757	As ex. 1	7.8×7.0×2.5	1–11, 19–24, 39–41	c

COMMENTARY

The master text is ex. 1. The line count differs from the previous edition in counting the old line 7 as lines 7 and 8.

The inscription deals with the construction of some object for the god Nanna (of Ur) by the king. Unfortunately, the text omits the name of the object in question. A year name of Iddin-Dagān does deal with his fashioning of a throne (and dais) for Nanna's Dublamaḫ, but no firm connection between this royal inscription and that year name can be demonstrated at present.

The two tablets with this inscription came from the house at no. 7 Quiet Street which contained a number of copies of royal inscriptions, and literary and mathematical texts. Woolley and Mallowan have suggested that it may have been a school.

BIBLIOGRAPHY

1928 Gadd, UET 1 no. 293 (ex. 2, copy, edition) and no. 294 (ex. 1, copy, edition)
1961 Hallo, BiOr 18 p. 5 Iddin-Dagan 2 (study)
1964–66 Landsberger, WO 3 p. 73 n. 97e (study)
1968 Kärki, SKFZ pp. 2–3 Iddindagān 2 (edition)
1971 Sollberger and Kupper, IRSA IVA3a (translation)
1976 Woolley and Mallowan, UE 7 pp. 112–13 n. 11 and 228–29 (exs. 1–2, provenance)
1980 Kärki, SAKAZ 1 pp. 5–7 Iddindagān 2 (edition)
1986 Charpin, Le clergé d'Ur p. 35 (provenance)

TEXT

1) ^{d}nanna
2) sag-gal-dingir-dingir-a-nun-ke$_{4}$-ne
3) nir-gál-é-kur-ra
4) me-ni an-ki-da gú-lá-a
5) u$_{18}$-ru ság nu-di
6) en aša-ni dingir pa-è-a
7) dumu-sag-^{d}en-líl-lá
8) me-ul-lí-a ki-bé gi$_{4}$-gi$_{4}$
9) giš-ḫur-úri.K[I]-ma
10) si-sá-sá-x-[d]a
11) ⸢dumu⸣-NUN-e é-kur-ta
12) me-maḫ íb-ta-an-è
13) ⸢^{d}⸣[*i-d*]*in-*^{d}*da-gan*
14) géštu-sum-ma-^{d}en-ki-ka-ra
15) mas-sú inim-pà-dè

1–7) The god Nanna, foremost one of the Anuna gods, trusted one of the Ekur, whose *me*s embrace heaven and earth (and) are those which no storm can disperse, the lord who alone is a god, who shines forth, first-born son of the god Enlil,

8–12) in order to restore the ancient *me*s (and) to put in order the ground plan of Ur, the princely son (Nanna) brought forth the best *me*s from the Ekur.

13–18) To [Id]din-Dagān, the one given wisdom by the god Enki, to the leader who finds the (right) words, to the one who has knowledge of

16) nì-nam gal-zu-ra
17) sipa-zi ki-ág-gá-ni-ir
18) šu-né im-ma-an-sum
19) ^{d}*i-din-*^{d}*da-gan*
20) lugal-kala-ga lugal-úri.KI-ma
21) lugal-ki-en-gi-ki-uri
22) ki-ág-^{d}nanna ù ^{d}nin-gal-ke$_{4}$
23) mu-na-dím nam-ti-la-ni-šè
24) a mu-na-ru
25) lú-á-nì-ḫul-dím-[ma]
26) [í]b-ši-ág-ge$_{26}$-a nì-d[ím-ma-mu]
27) íb-zi-re-[a]
28) mu-sar-ra-ba šu bí-í[b-ùr-a]
29) mu-ni bí-íb-sar-[re-a]
30) áš-bal-a-ba-ke$_{4}$-eš lú-⌜kúr⌝
31) šu ba-an-zi-zi-a
32) lú-bi lugal ḫé-a
33) en ḫé-a ù lú-ulu$_{4}$-sag-zi-gál
34) mu-ni sa$_{4}$-a ḫé-a
35) lú-bé mu na-an-tuk-tuk
36) numun na-mi-i-i
37) lú-ba ^{d}nanna lugal-mu
38) ^{d}nin-gal nin-mu
39) nam ḫa-ba-an-da-kuru$_{5}$-ne
40) ^{d}utu ^{d}inanna maškim nu-kuru$_{5}$-bi ḫé-a
41) u$_{4}$-da-ri-šè

everything, to his beloved reliable shepherd, (Nanna) handed them over.

19–22) (Therefore) Iddin-Dagān, mighty king, king of Ur, king of the land of Sumer and Akkad, beloved of the god Nanna and the goddess Ningal, fashioned (this object) for him. 23–24) He dedicated it to him for his own life.

25–31) (As for) the man who gives orders to do evi[l] against it, has [my] handi[work] destroyed, (or) [erases] its inscription (and) write[s] his name on it, (or) on account of this curse incites another to do so,

32–41) whether he be a king, an *en* priest, or an ordinary human being, may that man not get a name or beget any descendants. May the god Nanna, my lord, (and) the goddess Ningal, my lady, curse him, (and) may the god Utu and the goddess Inanna forever be its (the curse's) evil spirit who cannot be countermanded.

3

An inscription of the Isin king Enlil-bāni deals with the transfer from Isin to Nippur of two statues that had been fashioned by Iddin-Dagān (see E4.1.10.11). The inscription presumably gives the text that may have been carved on the statues by Iddin-Dagān.

COMMENTARY

The inscription is lines 26–37 of the tablet UM L-29-578, from Nippur. It measures 8.5×5.2×2.2 cm and was collated.

In line 37 the suffix -gá instead of the -mu found in line 36 is unexpected.

BIBLIOGRAPHY

1973 Loding, AfO 24 pp. 47–50 (photo, edition)
1980 Kärki, SAKAZ 1 p. 7 Iddindagān 3 (edition)

28.1 Copy omits šu, which is clear on the tablet.

TEXT

26) ^{d}nin-líl nin-dingir-re-e-ne-ra
27) ^{d}*i-din-*^{d}*da-gan* lugal-kala-ga
28) URUDU.alam-EZEN-X-ma mu-na-dím
29) igi-ni-šè in-de$_{6}$
30) nam-ti-la-ni-šè a mu-na-ru
31) lú á-nì-ḫul-dím-ma íb-ši-ág-[ge$_{26}$-a]
32) nì-dím-ma-mu íb-x-bé-⟨a⟩
33) mu-sar-ra-ba mu-ni bí-⟨íb-sar-re-a⟩
34) áš-bala-ba-a-ke$_{4}$-eš
35) ⟨lú-kúr šu ba-an-zi-zi-a⟩
36) lú-ba ^{d}en-líl lugal-mu ^{d}nin-líl nin-mu
37) ^{d}da-gan dingir-gá nam ḫa-ba-an-da-ku$_{5}$-ru-ne

26–28) For the goddess Ninlil, queen of the gods, Iddin-Dagān, mighty king, fashioned a ... copper *festival* statue for her.
29) He brought it in before her.
30) He dedicated it to her for his own life.
31–35) (As for) the man who giv[es] orders to do evil against it (and) has my handiwork *destroyed* (and) ⟨writes⟩ his name on its inscription, (or) because of this curse ⟨incites another to do so⟩,

36–37) May the god Enlil, my lord, the goddess Ninlil, my lady, (and) the god Dagān, my (personal) god, curse that man.

2001

A tablet found in the Enunmaḫ at Ur dated to the fourteenth year of Gungunum of Larsa bears the seal impression of a servant of Iddin-Dagān. The impression demonstrates how long a seal could remain in use, since it must have been at least 35 years old when used on this tablet.

COMMENTARY

The seal impression is on a clay tablet, museum no. unknown, excavation no. U 2682. It was found at Ur under the wall of Kudur-mabuk dividing Enunmaḫ room 32 from Emurianabak (formerly TTB 34).

BIBLIOGRAPHY

1928 Gadd, UET 1 no. 229 (copy, study)
1957 Hallo, Royal Titles pp. 16–17 (study)
1968 Kärki, SKFZ p. 2 Iddindagān 1 (edition)
1976 Woolley and Mallowan, UE 7 pp. 218–19 (provenance)
1980 Kärki, SAKAZ 1 p. 5 Iddindagān 1 (edition)

TEXT

1) ^{d}*i-din-*^{d}*da-gan*
2) nita-kala-ga
3) (blank)
4) [...]
5) dumu [...]
6) dub-[sar]
7) ir$_{11}$-[zu]

1) Iddin-Dagān,
2) mighty man,
3) (blank)
4) [...]
5) son of [...],
6) scr[ibe],
7) [your] servant.

Išme-Dagān

E4.1.4

According to the Sumerian King List, Išme-Dagān ruled 20 years. There is an increase in the number of extant royal inscriptions for this ruler compared with the earlier Isin kings, but the number is still not large. Recent research on Išme-Dagān's year names allows a chronological arrangement of a number of the king's inscriptions.

1

Išme-Dagān's standard inscription occurs in two slightly variant forms. One is an 11-line stamped brick known at present from Ur and Isin.

CATALOGUE

Ex.	Museum number	Excavation number	Registration number	Provenance	Dimensions (cm)	Lines preserved	cpn
1	BM 90170	From Taylor's excavations at Ur, no excavation numbers	1979-12-20,86	Ur, from the interior facing of the walls of the temple on the southern mound of Mugheir	31.0×27.0×8.0	1-11	c
2	BM 90171	As ex. 1	1979-12-20,87	As ex. 1	29.5×29.5×6.0	1-11	c
3	BM 90172	As ex. 1	1979-12-20,88	As ex. 1	29.0×29.5×6.0	1-11	c
4	BM 90173	As ex. 1	1979-12-20,89	As ex. 1	30.5×25.5	1-11	c
5	BM 90174	As ex. 1	1979-12-20,90	As ex. 1	32.0×31.5×8.1	3-6, 9-11	c
6	BM 90175	As ex. 1	1979-12-20,91	As ex. 1	15.5×15.0×8.0	1-6	c
7	BM 90176	As ex. 1	1979-12-20,92	As ex. 1	30.0×29.0×6.0	1-11	c
8	BM 90177	As ex. 1	1979-12-20,93	As ex. 1	24.0×14.5×6.5	1-11	c
9	BM 90178	As ex. 1	1979-12-20,94	As ex. 1	30.0×29.0×6.0	1-11	c
10	BM 90179	As ex. 1	1979-12-20,95	As ex. 1	26.5×21.0×7.0	1-10	c
11	BM 90180	As ex. 1	1979-12-20,96	As ex. 1	30.5×28.0×7.5	1-11	c
12	BM 90181	As ex. 1	1979-12-20,97	As ex. 1	32.0×15.5×8.0	1-11	c
13	BM 90182	As ex. 1	1979-12-20,98	As ex. 1.	26.5×30.5×7.0	1-11	c
14	BM 90183	As ex. 1	1979-12-20,99	As ex. 1	25.5×30.0×7.0	1-11	c
15	BM 90377+90762	As ex. 1	1979-12-20,221	As ex. 1	26.5×22.5×6.5	1-11	c
16	VA 2103	By German expedition of 1886/87	–	Ur, in a building east of the great temple	30.0×30.0×6.4	1-11	c
17	CBS 16467	U 2566	–	Ur, from 'PAT'	15.0×30.0×6.0	–	n
18	CBS 16468	U 2566	–	As ex. 17	33.0×21.0×8.0	1-11	c
19	CBS 16539	U 2566	–	As ex. 17	31.0×31.0×7.0	–	n
20	IM 892A	U 2566	–	As ex. 17	32.0×29.0×6.0	–	n
21	IM 892B	U 2566	–	As ex. 17	26.0×14.0×7.0	–	n
22	CBS 16544	U 2817	–	Ur, from 'S.F.'	15.0×13.5×4.5	1-5	n
23	CBS 8639	–	–	Ur, –	17.5×6.5	–	n
24	UM 84-26-46	–	–	–	33.0×18.0×7.5	–	n

Ex.	Museum number	Excavation number	Registration number	Provenance	Dimensions (cm)	Lines preserved	cpn
25	Australian Institute of Archaeology IA7.16	–	–	Ur(?)	–	6–11	p
26	–	Isin-Munich expedition	–	Isin, from the surface of the mound	–	–	n
27	–	As ex. 26	–	Isin, from the SE cutting	–	–	n
28	Ash 1924,629	Isin-Oxford Field Museum expedition	–	Isin, provenance not indicated		1–11	c

COMMENTARY

Exs. 1–15 were excavated by Taylor at Ur. Ex. 16 is from the German expedition of 1886/7 to Ur. Exs. 17–24 were excavated by Woolley at Ur. Exs. 26–27 were found at Isin by the Munich expedition and ex. 28 from the same site was found by Langdon.

BIBLIOGRAPHY

1861 1 R pl. 2 no. v 1 (exs. 1–15, composite copy)
1872 G. Smith, TSBA 1 p. 38 (translation)
1874 Lenormant, Études accadiennes 2 p. 332
1875 Ménant, Annales des rois d'Assyrie (Paris) p. 17
1875 Ménant, Babylone et la Chaldée (Paris) p. 78 (translation)
1883 Hommel, Semiten I p. 231 (translation)
1892 Winckler, KB 3/1 pp. 86–87 Išmí-Dagan (edition)
1899 Bezold, Cat. 5 p. 2233 (exs. 1–15, study)
1905 Thureau-Dangin, ISA pp. 292–93 Išme-dagan (edition, see n. 14)
1905 King, CT 21 pl. 21 (ex. 4, copy)
1907 Messerschmidt, VAS 1 no. 29 (ex. 16, copy)
1907 Thureau-Dangin, SAK pp. 206–207 Išme-dagan n. a (edition)
1910 King, Early History pl. xxxii facing p. 310 (ex. 9, photo)
1922 BM Guide p. 61 (study)
1924 Langdon, Kish 1 p. 111 B (ex. 28, edition)
1926 Bezold, Ninive und Babylon (Leipzig) fig. 32 (photo)
1928 Gadd, UET 1 p. xxiv (exs. 17–22, study)
1929 Barton, RISA pp. 304–305 Ishmi-Dagan 1 (edition)
1961 Hallo, BiOr 18 p. 5 Išme-Dagan 1 (study)
1968 Kärki, SKFZ pp. 3–4 Išmedagān 1 (study)
1975 von Soden, ZA 64 p. 38 (ex. 26, study)
1976 Woolley and Mallowan, UE 7 p. 219 (exs. 17–22, provenance, study)
1977 Edzard and Wilcke in Hrouda, Isin 1 p. 87 (ex. 26, study)
1980 Kärki, SAKAZ 1 pp. 7–8 Išmedagān 1 (edition)
1981 Walker, CBI no. 28 (exs. 1–5, 28, study)
1981 Walker in Hrouda, Isin 2 p. 94 (ex. 27, study)
1981 Grégoire, MVN 10 no. 25 (ex. 28, copy, study)

TEXT

1) ^{d}*iš-me-*^{d}*da-gan*	1) Išme-Dagān,
2) ú-a-nibru.KI	2) provider of Nippur,
3) sag-ús-	3–4) constant (attendant) of Ur,
4) uri$_5$.KI-ma	
5) u$_4$-da gub	5–6) who is daily at the service of Eridu,
6) eridu.KI-ga	
7) en-unu.KI-ga	7) *en* priest of Uruk,
8) lugal-ì-si-in.KI-na	8) king of Isin,
9) lugal-ki-en-gi-ki-uri	9) king of the land of Sumer and Akkad,
10) dam-ki-ág-	10–11) beloved spouse of the goddess Inanna.
11) ^{d}inanna	

2

The standard inscription of Išme-Dagān also occurs in a 12-line inscribed brick version.

CATALOGUE

Ex.	Museum number	Excavation number	Registration number	Provenance	Dimensions (cm)	Lines preserved	cpn
1	BM 90200	From Taylor's excavations, no excavation numbers	1979-12-20,116	Ur, from the interior facing walls of the temple on the southern mound of Mugheir	33.0×32.0×8.5	1-12	c
2	BM 90201	As ex. 1	1979-12-20,117	As ex. 1	32.0×31.0×8.0	1-12	c
3	BM 90202	As ex. 1	1979-12-20,118	As ex. 1	32.0×30.5×8.0	1-8, 10-12	c
4	BM 90203	As ex. 1	1979-12-20,119	As ex. 1	31.5×15.0×8.5	1-12	c
5	BM 90204	As ex. 1	1979-12-20,120	As ex. 1	33.5×31.0×7.5	1-12	c
6	BM 90205	As ex. 1	1979-12-20,121	As ex. 1	33.0×33.0×8.0	1-12	c
7	BM 90206	As ex. 1	1979-12-20,122	As ex. 1	33.0×31.5×8.0	1-12	c
8	BM 90207	As ex. 1	1979-12-20,123	As ex. 1	32.0×21.0×8.5	1-12	c
9	BM 90210	As ex. 1	1979-12-20,317	As ex. 1	33.0×32.5×8.0	5-12	c
10	BM 90720	As ex. 1	1979-12-20,323	As ex. 1	–	4-12	c
11	BM 90761	As ex. 1	1979-12-20,339	As ex. 1	26.0×15.0×8.0	1-12	c
12	IM 2559A	U 92	–	–	–	–	n
13	IM 2559B	U 92	–	–	–	–	n
14	CBS 15347	U 195	–	–	32.0×33.0×8.0	–	n
15	CBS 16540	U 2566b	–	From 'PAT'	32.0×34.0×8.0	–	n
16	CBS 16541	–	–	–	32.0×32.0×8.0	–	n
17	YBC 2434	–	–	–	18.4×7.6×8.0	1-10	c

COMMENTARY

Exs. 1-11 were excavated by Taylor at Ur. Exs. 12-16 were excavated by Woolley at Ur. The provenance of ex. 17 is not known.

BIBLIOGRAPHY

1861 1 R pl. 2 no. v 2 (exs. 1-11, composite copy)
1872 G. Smith, TSBA 1 p. 38 (translation)
1874 Lenormant, Études accadiennes 2 p. 332
1875 Ménant, Annales des rois d'Assyrie (Paris) p. 17
1875 Ménant, Babylone et la Chaldée (Paris) p. 78 (translation)
1883 Hommel, Semiten I p. 231 (translation)
1892 Winckler, KB 3/1 pp. 86-87 Išmí-Dagan (edition)
1899 Bezold, Cat. 5 p. 2233 (exs. 1-11, study)
1905 Thureau-Dangin, ISA pp. 292-93 Išme-dagan (edition)
1905 King, CT 21 pl. 20 (ex. 2, copy)
1907 Thureau-Dangin, SAK pp. 206-207 Išme-dagan (edition)
1922 BM Guide p. 61 (study)
1929 Barton, RISA pp. 304-305 Ishmi-Dagan 2 (edition)
1928 Gadd, UET 1 p. xxiv (exs. 12-15, study)
1961 Hallo, BiOr 18 p. 5 Išme-Dagan 2 (study)
1968 Kärki, SKFZ p. 4 Išmedagān 2 (edition)
1980 Kärki, SAKAZ 1 p. 8 Išmedagān 2 (edition)
1981 Walker, CBI no. 29 (exs. 1-11, study)

TEXT

1) ^{d}*iš-me-*^{d}*da-gan*
2) ú-a-nibru.KI
3) sag-ús-
4) uri$_5$.KI-ma
5) u$_4$-da gub
6) eridu.KI-ga
7) en-unu.KI-ga
8) lugal-kala-ga
9) lugal-ì-si-in.KI-na
10) lugal-ki-en-gi-ki-uri
11) dam-ki-ág-
12) ^{d}inanna-ka

1) Išme-Dagān,
2) provider of Nippur,
3-4) constant (attendant) of Ur,
5-6) who is daily at the service of Eridu,
7) *en* priest of Uruk,
8) mighty king,
9) king of Isin,
10) king of the land of Sumer and Akkad,
11-12) beloved spouse of the goddess Inanna.

3

Early in the reign of Išme-Dagān the king named one of his years after the installation of his daughter as *en* priestess of the god Nanna in Ur under the name En-ana-tuma (see S. Simmons, YOS 14 no. 314). The standard inscription of this personage appears in two slightly variant forms. These were treated together as Išme-Dagān 4 by Hallo and Kärki, but are kept separate here. One is a six-line inscribed brick found by Woolley in the Gipar-ku, the residence of En-ana-tuma in Ur. A slightly variant version of this text is found on a clay cone from Ur, whose provenance is not known.

CATALOGUE

Ex.	Museum number	Excavation number	Registration number	Provenance	Object	Dimensions (cm)	Lines preserved	cpn
1	CBS 15340	U 52(?)	–	Ur, –	Stamped brick	30.0×18.0×6.0	–	n
2	BM 137352	U 6743	1935-1-13,12	From the Gipar-ku	Inscribed brick	31.0×18.0×7.0	1-6	c
3	CBS 16543a	U 6743	–	As ex. 3	Inscribed brick	31.0×19.0×7.0	1-6	c
4	IM 25579A	U 6743	–	As ex. 3	Inscribed brick	–	–	n
5	IM 25579B	U 6743	–	As ex. 3	Inscribed brick	–	–	n
6	IM 25579C	U 6743	–	As ex. 3	Inscribed brick	–	–	n
7	IM 45697	–	–	–	Inscribed brick	–	1-6	c
8	UM 84-26-13	–	–	–	Inscribed brick	22.0×12.0×5.5	–	n
9	IM 92813	U 754	–	–	Clay cone shaft	5.6	1-6	c
10	IM 92813	U 754	–	–	Clay cone head	6.5 dia.	1-6	c

COMMENTARY

Ex. 1 is a stamped brick; the rest are all inscribed. Ex. 7 is on display in the Iraq Museum.

BIBLIOGRAPHY

1928 Gadd, UET 1 no. 105 (partial copy, edition)
1961 Hallo, BiOr 18 p. 5 Išme-Dagan 4 (study)
1965 Sollberger, UET 8 p. 26 no. 13 (exs. 9–10, study)
1968 Kärki, SKFZ p. 5 Išmedagān 4 (edition)
1976 Woolley and Mallowan, UE 7 p. 255 (exs. 2–6, provenance)
1976 Basmachi, Treasures of the Iraq Museum (Baghdad) p. 206 no. 11 (ex. 7, study)
1980 Kärki, SAKAZ 1 p. 9 Išmedagān 4 (edition)
1981 Walker, CBI no. 31 (ex. 2, study)
1986 Charpin, Le clergé d'Ur p. 195 (study)

TEXT

1) en-an-na-túm-ma	1) En-ana-tuma,
2) zirru$_x$(EN.MÍ.ME.NUNUZ.ZI.^{d}NANNA)	2) *zirru* priestess,
3) en-^{d}nanna	3–4) *en* priestess of the god Nanna, in Ur,
4) šà-uri$_5$.KI-ma	
5) dumu-^{d}*iš-me*-^{d}*da-gan*	5) daughter of Išme-Dagān,
6) lugal-ki-en-gi-ki-uri	6) king of the land of Sumer and Akkad.

4

A variant of En-ana-tuma's standard inscription is found in a six-line stamped brick from Ur.

CATALOGUE

Ex.	Museum number	Excavation number	Registration number	Provenance	Dimensions (cm)	Lines preserved	cpn
1	BM 90163	From Taylor's excavations at Ur, no excavation numbers	1979-12-20,79	Ur, from the tomb mound near the western wall of Mugheir	30.0×18.0×6.0	Traces only	c
2	BM 90164	As ex. 1	1979-12-20,80	As ex. 1	31.0×18.0×7.0	Traces only	c
3	BM 90165	As ex. 1	1979-12-20,81	As ex. 1	31.0×19.0×7.0	1–6	c
4	BM 90166	As ex. 1	1979-12-20,82	As ex. 1	–	1–6	c
5	BM 90167	As ex. 1	1979-12-20,83	As ex. 1	–	1–6	c
6	BM 90168	As ex. 1	1979-12-20,84	As ex. 1	–	1–6	c
7	BM 90169	As ex. 1	1979-12-20,85	As ex. 1	–	Only traces visible	c
8	BM 90388	As ex. 1	1979-12-20,225	As ex. 1	22.0×12.0×5.5	–	n
9	BM 137355	Ur, Woolley's excavations	1935-1-13,15	Ur, TTB 12	–	1–6	c
10	BM 137388	As ex. 9	1979-12-18,23	–	–	1–6	c
11	BM 137389	As ex. 9	1979-12-18,24	–	–	1–6	c
12	BM 137390	As ex. 9	1979-12-18,25	–	–	1–6	c
13	CBS 16542	U 2569	–	From 'PAT'	28.0×28.0×8.5	1–6	c
14	IM 893A	U 2569	–	As ex. 13	–	–	n
15	IM 893B	U 2569	–	As ex. 13	–	–	n
16	CBS 16469	–	–	–	30.0×19.0×9.0	–	n
17	CBS 16543b	–	–	–	30.0×18.0×7.0	–	n
18	CBS 16543c	–	–	–	31.0×18.0×6.0	–	n
19	UM 84-26-14	–	–	–	30.0×20.0×8.5	–	n
20	Ash 1961,238	–	–	–	–	1–6	c

5.9 adds lugal-[kala-ga] lugal-ì-s[i-in.KI-na] before line 6.

COMMENTARY

Exs. 1-8 were found by Taylor at Ur. Exs. 13-19 were found by Woolley at Ur; exs. 9-12 were probably found by the same excavator. Ex. 17 is inscribed; the rest are stamped. The provenance of ex. 20 is not known — it presumably came from Ur. In the copy of this text in UET 1 no. 104 Gadd inadvertently omitted line 3. No ex. with this omission could be found.

BIBLIOGRAPHY

1861 1 R pl. 2 no. VI 2 (exs. 2-7, composite copy)
1872 G. Smith, TSBA 1 p. 38 (translation)
1875 Ménant, Babylone et la Chaldée (Paris) p. 79 (translation)
1892 Winckler, KB 3/1 pp. 86-87 Gungunu 2 (edition)
1899 Bezold, Cat. 5 p. 2233 (exs. 2-3, 5-7, study)
1905 King, CT 21 pl. 21 (ex. 4, copy; exs. 1-6, study)
1905 Thureau-Dangin, ISA pp. 294-95 Époque de Gungunu (edition)
1907 Thureau-Dangin, SAK pp. 206-207 Aus der Zeit Gungunus (edition)
1922 BM Guide p. 61 (study)
1928 Gadd, UET 1 no. 104 (exs. 13-19?, composite copy [omits line 3], edition)
1929 Barton, RISA pp. 310-11 Time of Gungunu 1 (edition)
1961 Hallo, BiOr 18 p. 5 Išme-Dagan 5 (study)
1968 Kärki, SKFZ p. 5 Išmedagān 5 (edition)
1976 Woolley and Mallowan, UE 7 p. 219 (exs. 13-19?, provenance)
1980 Kärki, SAKAZ 1 pp. 9-10 Išmedagān 5 (edition)
1981 Walker, CBI no. 32 (exs. 1-12, 18, study)
1986 Charpin, Le clergé d'Ur p. 195 (study)

TEXT

1) en-an-na-túm-ma	1) En-ana-tuma,
2) en ki-ág-^{d}nanna	2) *en* priestess beloved of the god Nanna,
3) en-^{d}nanna	3-4) *en* priestess of the god Nanna, in Ur,
4) šà-uri$_5$.KI-ma	
5) dumu-^{d}*iš-me*-^{d}*da-gan*	5) daughter of Išme-Dagān,
6) lugal-ki-en-gi-ki-uri	6) king of the land of Sumer and Akkad.

5

A number of cones recently excavated at Isin as well as earlier purchased exemplars deal with the construction of a wall in Isin by Išme-Dagān.

CATALOGUE

Ex.	Museum number	Excavation number	Provenance	Object	Dimensions (cm)	Lines preserved	cpn
1	–	IB 311	Isin, 70 S/40 W	Head	12 dia.	1-4, 10-16	c
2	–	IB 335	72.20 S/8.90 E 35 cm under the surface	Shaft	5.3	10-18	c
3	IM 77902	IB 774	117.40 W/49.10 N +11.30 in area of Gula temple	Shaft	20	1-18	c
4	IM 79902	IB 774	As ex. 3	Head	11 dia.	5-10, 15-18	c
5	IM 80860	IB 1084	North Cutting II	Shaft	7.5	1-17	c
6	–	IB 1607a	Debris on top of the temenos wall 146.60 N/81.90 W, +8.95	Shaft	12	1-18	c
7	–	IB 1607b	As ex. 6	Shaft	12	1-18	c
8	–	IB 1608	As ex. 6, wall 147.30 N/82.30 W, 25 cm below the surface	Shaft	11.2	1-18	c
9	–	IB 1609	As ex. 6, 147.80 N/83.20 W, 25 cm below the surface	Shaft	11.5	1-5, 8-18	c

Ex.	Museum number	Excavation number	Provenance	Object	Dimensions (cm)	Lines preserved	cpn
10	–	IB 1639	Between the bricks in the top layer of the wall, 144.90 N/81.50 W, +9.00	Shaft	11.5	1–18	c
11	–	IB 1640	As ex. 10, 145.00 N/82.75 W, +9.03	Shaft	9.3	1–18	c
12	–	IB 1641	As ex. 10, 145.60 N/82.80 W, +8.92	Shaft	11.3	1–18	c
13	IM 42714A	–	–	Shaft	12.5	1–18	c
14	IM 11008	–	–	Cone	–	–	n
15	NBC 6058	–	–	Shaft	12.2	1–18	c
16	HS 1966	–	–	Shaft	11.4	1–4, 6–18	c

COMMENTARY

Exs. 1–12 were recently excavated at Isin by the Munich expedition. Exs. 13–14 were confiscated or purchased by the Iraq Museum. Ex. 15 was purchased by the Yale collection; ex. 16 is in the Hilprecht Sammlung in Jena.

In 1985 the Munich expedition to Isin recovered parts of a temenos wall surrounding the Gula temple. This wall, lower in position on the mound than the Kassite temple levels, dates to an earlier period. Exs. 6–12, small headless cones, were found in debris on top of the wall or in situ between bricks of the temenos wall. This indicates that the wall, at least in one of its constructions, dates to the time of Išme-Dagān.

BIBLIOGRAPHY

1937 Stephens, YOS 9 no. 25 (ex. 15, copy)
1951 Kraus, JCS 3 pp. 28–29 (study)
1957 Edzard, Zwischenzeit p. 81 (study)
1958 Kraus, Edikt p. 197 (study)
1961 Hallo, BiOr 18 p. 5 Išme-Dagan 7 (study)
1968 Kärki, SKFZ p. 5 Išmedagān 7 (edition)
1969 Oelsner, WZJ 18 p. 54 no. 28 (ex. 16, study)
1971 Sollberger and Kupper, IRSA IVA4c (translation)
1977 Edzard and Wilcke in Hrouda, Isin 1 p. 87 (exs. 1–2, study)
1980 Kärki, SAKAZ 1 pp. 10–11 Išmedagān 7 (edition)
1981 Walker and Wilcke in Hrouda, Isin 2 p. 93 (exs. 3–5, study)
1984 Kraus, König. Verfüg. p. 17 (study)
1987 Wilcke in Hrouda, et al., Isin 3 pp. 113–14 (exs. 6–12, study)

TEXT

1) ^{d}*iš-me-*^{d}*da-gan*
2) nita-kala-ga
3) lugal-ì-si-in.KI-na
4) lugal-an-ub-da-límmu-ba-ke$_4$
5) u$_4$ nibru.KI
6) uru-ki-ág-
7) ^{d}en-líl-lá-⟨ka⟩
8) gú-bi
9) mu-un-du$_8$
10) éren-bi kaskal-ta
11) ba-ra-an-zi-ga-a
12) bàd-gal-
13) ì-si-in.KI-na
14) mu-un-dù
15) bàd-ba
16) ^{d}*iš-me-*^{d}*da-gan*
17) ^{d}en-líl-da á-an-gal
18) mu-bi-im

1–4) Išme-Dagān, mighty man, king of Isin, king of the four quarters,

5–11) when he cancelled the tribute of Nippur, the city beloved of the god Enlil, (and) relieved its men of military service,

12–14) he built the great wall of Isin.

15–18) The name of that wall is 'Išme-Dagān is a great ... beside the god Enlil.'

3.15 ì-si-in.⟨KI⟩-na. **11**.2, 5 omit -an-. **11**.15 ba-ra-«BI»-zi-ga-a. **11**.3 ba-ra-an-zi-ga-⟨a⟩. **13**.15 ì-si-in.⟨KI⟩-na. **15**.15 bàd-gal. **17**.8 ^{d}en-líl-lá-da. **17**.15 omits ^{d}en-líl-da.

6

A Sammeltafel in the Philadelphia collection published by Poebel contains copies of a number of royal inscriptions of Išme-Dagān. Unfortunately, the tablet is not fully preserved so one cannot determine at present exactly where one inscription ended and another started. All the preserved inscriptions allude to the cancelling of corvée duty for the men of Nippur. This indicates that the inscriptions probably date to an early phase of Išme-Dagān's reign. One of the inscriptions deals with the construction of a du$_8$-maḫ, possibly a cauldron, an object which also figures in E4.2.8.3.

COMMENTARY

The inscriptions are found on the clay tablet CBS 13996, excavated by the Hilprecht expedition, provenance unknown. Its dimensions are 7.6×5.8×3.2 cm, and it was collated.

BIBLIOGRAPHY

1914 Poebel, PBS 5 no. 66 (copy)
1951 Kraus, JCS 3 p. 29 (study)
1957 Edzard, Zwischenzeit pp. 81–82 (study)
1958 Kraus, Edikt pp. 197–98 (study)
1961 Hallo, BiOr 18 p. 6 Išme-Dagan 12 (study)
1968 Kärki, SKFZ pp. 7–9 Išmedagān 12 (edition)
1980 Kärki, SAKAZ 1 pp. 13–15 Išmedagān 12 (edition)
1984 Kraus, König. Verfüg. pp. 17–18 (study)

TEXT

Col. i
1) ⌈^{d}⌉en-líl
2) an-ki-šè lugal-àm
3) aša-ni dingir-ra-àm
4) ^{d}nu-nam-nir
5) kur-zà-til-la-šè
6) [...] x en-zi-bi-im
7) [... z]i-šè
8) [...]-⌈e⌉
Lacuna

i 1–8) For the god Enlil, who is lord as far as heaven and earth (extends), who alone is a god, the god Nunamnir, who to the limits of the foreign land ... is their reliable lord, ...
Lacuna

Col. ii
1) u$_4$ dumu-nibru.KI
2) kaskal-ta
3) ba-ra-an-zi
4) ⌈é⌉-^{d}en-líl
5) ^{d}nin-líl
6) ù ^{d}nin-urta-ke$_4$
7) ba-ra-an-g[ar]
8) ki-en-gi [ki-uri]
9) zà-u-[bi]
10) [m]u-[un-du$_8$]
11) [su-kalam-ma]
12) [mu-un-du$_{10}$-ga]
Lacuna

ii 1–12) when (Išme-Dagān) relieved the citizens of Nippur from military service, removed (obligations) from the temples of the gods Enlil, Ninlil, and Ninurta, [ca]nce[lled] the tithe of the land of Sumer (and) [Akkad, (and) made the nation content]
Lacuna

Col. iii
1) [...]
2) [...]
3) [...]
4) x [...]
5) x [...]
6) x [...]
Lacuna
(Col. iv missing)
Col. v
Lacuna
1′) [u$_4$ dumu-nibru.KI]
2′) kaska[l-ta ba-ra-an-zi]
3′) é-[^{d}]e[n-líl]
4′) ^{d}nin-[líl]
5′) ù ^{d}nin-u[rta]
6′) ba-ra-an-[gar]
7′) ^{d}*iš-me-*^{d}*da-ga*[*n*]
8′) dumu-^{d}da-ga[n-na-(ke$_4$)]
9′) gú-un-[bi]
10′) ba-an-[du$_8$]
11′) ki-en-gi ki-[uri]
12′) zà-u-bi mu-u[n-du$_8$]
13′) su-kalam-[ma]
14′) mu-un-du$_{10}$-g[a]
15′) u$_4$-ba du$_8$-ma[ḫ]
Col. vi
Lacuna
1′) x-gin$_7$
2′) x til-bi-šè
3′) m[u-m]u gá-gá-dè
4′) ⸢^{d}en⸣-ki-ke$_4$
5′) géštu-dagal
6′) nì-nam bùru-bùru-dè
7′) me un-e sum-mu-⟨dè⟩
8′) ^{d}a-nun-na
9′) en nam-tar-re-gin$_7$
10′) nì-nam-e sa-di
11′) nitadam-a-ni
12′) kur-gal ^{d}en-líl-lá
13′) al im-ma-an-ni-in-du$_{11}$
Col. vii
Lacuna
1′) [...]-⸢a⸣-ni
2′) [...]-me-en
3′) [^{d}*iš-me*]-⸢^{d}⸣*da-gan*
4′) [luga]l-kala-ga
5′) [lugal-ì-si-i]n.KI-na
6′) [lugal-ki-e]n-gi-[ki-uri]-me-en
7′) [... m]u-na-dím
8′) [nam-ti-(la)]-mu-šè
9′) [a m]u-na-ru
10′) [u$_4$-da-rí]-šè
11′) [u$_4$-da e]gir-bi-šè
12′) [an-k]i-šú-a

iii) No translation warranted.

iv) (missing)

Lacuna
v 1′–6′) [When (Išme-Dagān) relieved the citizens of Nippur from] military service, removed (obligations) from the temples of the gods E[nlil], Nin[lil], and Ninu[rta],

v 7′–14′) Išme-Dagā[n], son of the god Dagā[n, cancelled their] tribute, [cancelled] the tithe of the land of Sumer (and) [Akkad], made the nation content,

v 15′) At that time a grea[t] *cauldron*

Lacuna
vi 1′–7′) ... in order to establish *m*[*y na*]*me* to their (the lands') limits like a [...], ⟨in order⟩ that the god Enki whose broad wisdom is able to fathom everything, give the *me*'s to the people,

vi 8′–10′) the Anuna gods, as if lords who determine destinies, who achieve everything,

vi 11′–13′) (had the goddess Ninlil) ask her spouse, the great mountain Enlil ...

Lacuna
vii 1′–6′) ... his ... am I. I, [Išme]-Dagān, mighty [king, king of Isi]n, [king of the land of S]umer [and Akkad],

vii 7′) fashioned a ... for him/her.
vii 8′–9′) I [de]dicated it for my own [life].

vii 10′–13′) [Forev]er, [in days] to come, in all [of heaven and ear]th, till the distant [future] ...

13′) [u$_{4}$-s]ù-rá-šè
Left Edge
1) x-ZI x-da ul-x-[...]
2) lugal ^{d}en-líl-le ⌜é⌝-[kur-ta]
3) ⌜gù⌝-zi dé-⌜a⌝-[me-en]
Lacuna

left edge 1–3) ... [I am] the one truly called by king Enlil from the E[kur].
Lacuna

7

After regaining control over the city of Nippur, Išme-Dagān fashioned a number of cult objects for the chief gods of that city, Enlil, Ninlil, and Ninurta. One such act was the fashioning of the mace with fifty heads for the god Ninurta. While the mace itself has not been found, a number of bricks inscribed or stamped which may have formed the socle on which it once stood have been recovered.

CATALOGUE

Ex.	Museum number	Excavation number	Registration number	Provenance	Dimensions (cm)	Lines preserved	cpn
1	BM 90385	–	51-10-9,87	Nippur	13.0×13.0×5.5	6–12	c
2	BM 137446	–	51-10-9,26	–		3–6	c
3	CBS 8634	From the Hilprecht expedition		From a platform located to the south of the Ekur	31.5×27.0×7.0	–	n
4	CBS 8641	As ex. 3		–	16.0×12.0×6.0	7–12	n
5	CBS 8649	As ex. 3		–	32.0×28.0×7.0	1–12	p
6	CBS 8650	As ex. 3		–	31.0×23.0×6.0	1–12	n
7	EŞ 528	As ex. 3		–	31.0×27.4×6.3	1–12	p
8	EŞ 529	As ex. 3		–	31.0×28.0×6.7	1–12	p
9	EŞ 530	As ex. 3		–	32.0×27.0×5.5	1–12	p
10	EŞ 8948	As ex. 3		–	–	1–12	p
11	EŞ 8949	As ex. 3		–	30.5×27.0×6.4	1–12	p
12	Istanbul no number	As ex. 3		–	–	1–12	p
13	Istanbul no number	As ex. 3		–	–	1–12	p
14	Istanbul no number	As ex. 3		–	–	1–12	p
15	Istanbul no number	As ex. 3		–	–	–	n
16	IM –	5N-T692		Nippur, trench SB 13, below level II, fill of the Parthian platform of the Inanna temple	–	1–12	c
17	FLP 2625	–		–	–	1–12	c

COMMENTARY

Exs. 1–2, from Rawlinson's collections, were picked up from Nippur sometime before 1851. Exs. 2–15 all come from the Hilprecht expedition to Nippur. Some if not all of these come from a brick platform described by Peters (Nippur 2 p. 146). It was located to the south of the Ekur. Exs. 1–2 were purchased from Rawlinson.

BIBLIOGRAPHY

1897 Peters, Nippur 2 p. 146 (exs. 3–15, provenance)
1926 Legrain, PBS 15 no. 46 (ex. 6, copy, edition)
1929 Barton, RISA pp. 304–305 Ishmi-Dagan 2 (edition)
1961 Hallo, BiOr 18 p. 5 Išme-Dagan 3 (study)
1968 Kärki, SKFZ p. 4 Išmedagān 3 (edition)
1969 Pritchard, ANEP^{2} no. 253 (ex. 5, photo, study)
1971 Sollberger and Kupper, IRSA IVA4a (translation)
1976 Basmachi, Treasures of the Iraq Museum (Baghdad) p.

205 no. 9 (ex. 16, study)
1980 Kärki, SAKAZ 1 pp. 8–9 Išmedagān 3 (edition)
1981 Walker, CBI no. 30 (exs. 1–2, study)

TEXT

1) ^{d}*iš-me-^{d}da-gan*
2) lugal-ki-en-gi-ki-uri-ra
3) u$_4$ ^{d}en-líl-le
4) ^{d}nin-urta
5) ur-sag-kala-ga-ni
6) maškim-šè
7) mu-ni-in-tuk-a
8) šíta mi-tum sag-ninnu
9) mu-na-dím
10) sig$_4$-al-ùr-ra
11) GIŠ.tukul ki-ág-a-ni
12) mu-na-an-gub-ba-àm

1–7) When the god Enlil had Išme-Dagān, king of the land of Sumer and Akkad, take the god Ninurta, his mighty champion, as bailiff,

8–9) (Išme-Dagān) fashioned for him (Ninurta) the *šita*-weapon, the mace with fifty heads,
10–12) (and) set up his beloved weapon on a baked brick platform for him.

8

A tablet from Nippur now in Istanbul contains on its reverse a copy of a text which may have once been carved on a statue of Išme-Dagān. The inscription seems to deal with Išme-Dagān's setting up of a statue of himself as a 'runner', emulating the actions of his predecessor Šulgi.

COMMENTARY

The text is on a clay tablet, Ni 2432, excavated by the Hilprecht expedition, provenance not known. The tablet measures 14.8×7.4×3.1 cm. The inscription was collated by J. Klein. Klein has demonstrated that the Išme-Dagān text commences on line 3 of the rev. of the tablet. We have maintained the line count of Chiera's copy for our edition.

BIBLIOGRAPHY

1924 Chiera, SRT no. 13 (copy)
1930 Witzel, KSt 7 pp. 66–69 and 128–30 (edition)
1961 Sjöberg, ZA 54 p. 70 (study)
1965 Römer, Königshymnen pp. 18–20 (edition)
1966 Sjöberg, Orientalia NS 35 p. 291 (study)
1981 Klein, Three Šulgi Hymns p. 42 n. 81 (study)
1983 Frayne, JAOS 103 pp. 745–47 (study)
1986 Klein, Beer-Sheva 2 pp. 7–38 (edition)

3.14 ^{d}en-líl-lá.

TEXT

3) ^{d}en-líl du$_{11}$-ga u$_{18}$-ru di-zu sukud-dagal-là[m]
4) ⌜ka⌝-aš-bar è du$_{11}$-ni nu-kàm-me-da TÚG-X šu-ni-šè gar
5) ^{d}*iš-me-^{d}da-gan* guruš-kala sa-su-pirig šul-kala ní-gál-la
6) AŠ-(x)-ni maḫ en mu-du$_{10}$-sa$_{4}$-a-ni kur-šár-ra pà-d[a]
7) e-⌜ne-da⌝ [z]i-gál-la im-mi-in-l[u(?)-a(?)]
8) á-bàd un-dúr-ru-na-bi-šè sag(?)-gi$_{6}$ šu mu-na-[su]m(?)-ma
9) nisag(?)-kur-ra-da si ša-mu-na-ni-ib-sá-aš
10) é-gal-du$_{10}$-ga-na ki la-ba-na-tag-ge

3–4) O god Enlil, (whose) word is mighty, (whose) judgement is tall and broad, who issues verdicts, whose word cannot be overturned, who holds the ... in his hands, – 5–10) Išme-Dagān, the mighty young man with muscles and body of a lion, mighty youth who possesses fearsome splendour, who alone is supreme, the lord whose good name is called by the numerous foreign lands, thanks to whom the living ones mul[tiply], for the settled people of the strongholds, had the black-headed people who had been entrusted to him proceed to him with the first-fruit offerings of the foreign lands. He does not *put them* in his good palace.

11) u$_{4}$-ba ^{d}*iš-me-^{d}da-gan* šul ur-sag-gìr-du$_{10}$-gál-e-ne-ke$_{4}$
12) nibru.KI uru numun-un-šár-ra i-i ti-le ù-tu gál-la-šè
13) kas$_{4}$-di-ḫu-luḫ-e gi$_{6}$-an-bar$_{7}$-ba gub-bu mùš nu-túm-mu
14) u$_{4}$-šú-uš nì-nam tùm sá gal-e-eš na-an-gar

11–14) At that time, Išme-Dagān, the young man, champion of the runners, to Nippur, being the city where the seed of the numerous people sprang up, where the living were born, the fearsome runner who serves night and day without ceasing, who brings everything daily (that is needed), reached a great decision (to run there).

15) zi-ga-ni u$_{18}$-lu a-ma-ru ní-súr-ba DU-a
16) á-na bad-rá-a-ba gá-gá-gá da-na sù-ud-bi-šè mu-gír-gír-re
17) pirig-ḫuš-eden-na-gin$_{7}$ usu-nam-šul-ba DU-a
18) du$_{10}$ kaskal-la bad-bad-da-ni-a giš-lá mè-[šè gub-bu]
19) ANŠE.ZI.ZI ḫar-ra-an-na kun-sù-sù [...]
20) máš-dàra-gin$_{7}$ KAS$_{4}$.KAS$_{4}$-e x x ba [...]
21) du$_{10}$-ub šu bar-ra nu-kúš-ù-x [...]
22) dumu nì-túm-túm-^{d}en-líl-lá-ka
23) nì-šà-ḫúl-ḫúl-^{d}nin-líl-lá-ka
24) lugal-e èš-za-gìn-na-šè mùš la-ba-ra-túm-mu

15–24) (He) whose surge is a hurricane, a flood, a wind raging in its fury, who by moving his swinging arms *runs* miles into the distance, who like a fierce lion of the steppe proceeds with might and vigour, who strides along the road [approaching] battle and combat, who like a horse with its tail streaming behind on the highway, like a buck ... in running, who once started (running) is untiring, the son who brings (every)thing for the god Enlil, who causes joy for the goddess Ninlil's heart – the king does not stop until (he reaches) the shining shrine.

25) u$_{4}$-ba ^{d}*iš-me-^{d}da-gan* URUDU.alam mer-re-e KAS$_{4}$.KAS$_{4}$-e ḫu-luḫ-ḫa-na
26) é-ní-gùr bára-kal-kal-[l]a-na
27) mu-ni-in-gub še-er-zi-dè-eš bí-in-gùn
28) nun-gal zà-an-na en du$_{11}$-ga nu-kàm-me-da
29) sag-ki-zalag igi-zi íl-la-na-«šè»
30) ḫé-en-ši-ni-gál sipa-zi tu-da-ni-šè

25–30) At that time Išme-Dagān erected a statue (depicting himself) inspiring terror as he runs in the storm, in the temple which bears a fearsome splendour, on his very precious dais, and brilliantly decorated it with colours. May the great prince of the entire heaven, the lord whose utterance cannot be overturned, turn his shining face and trusty lifted eye toward the reliable shepherd whom he has engendered.

31) lugal á-nì-ḫul-dím-ma íb-ši-ág-e-a
32) mu-sar-ra-ba šu bí-íb-〈ùr〉-ra-a mu-ni bí-íb-sar-a
33) áš-bal-a-ba-ke$_{4}$-eš lú-kúr šu ba-an-zi-zi-i-a
34) lú-ba ^{d}en-líl lugal-mu ^{d}nin-líl nin-mu nam ḫa-ba-an-d[a-ku$_{5}$-ru-ne]

31–36) As for the king who gives orders to do evil against it (or) er[as]es its inscription (and) writes his name on it, (or) on account of this curse incites another to do so, may the god Enlil, my lord, and the goddess Ninlil, my lady, [curse] that man. May the gods Enki, Iškur, Ezinu, (and)

7 im-mi-in-l[u-a] (collated). **8** dúr-ru-na-bi-šè sag-gi$_{6}$ šu mu-na-[su]m-ma (collated). **9** nisag (collated). **15** a-ma-ru (collated). **20** máš-dàra-gin$_{7}$ (collated). **31** íb-ši-ág-e-a (collated). **33** áš-bal-a-ba-ke$_{4}$-eš (collated).

35) ^{d}en-ki ^{d}iškur ^{d}ezinu ^{d}šàkan en ḫé-gál-la-k[e$_{4}$-ne]
36) ḫé-gál an-ki-a a-ba-da-an-ge$_{4}$-eš ḫu[l]-bi ḫa-ba-[...]

Šakkan, the lords of abundance, having withheld the abundance of heaven and earth from him, [destroy] him cruelly.

9

Two archival texts dating to the time of Lipit-Eštar (see D. Loding, JCS 28 [1976] pp. 239–40 nos. 2 and 6) deal with rations for Ḫala-Ningal, the *en* priestess of Inanna in Ur. An inscription in Akkadian probably belonging to Išme-Dagān found on a clay tablet excavated at Isin deals, among other things, with the choosing of this priestess.

COMMENTARY

The tablet is IB 1537 found in the south sounding by the north enclosure wall — 138 N, 61.50 W, +8.10. It is a fragment of a very large tablet with the remains of five cols. on the obv. and seven cols. on the rev. The Išme-Dagān text(s) correspond(s) to cols. i′-v′ of the obv. and i′-iv′ of the rev.

BIBLIOGRAPHY

1987 Wilcke in Hrouda, et al., Isin 3 pp. 108–10 D2.3 (transliteration, study) and pl. 44 (photo)

TEXT

Obverse
Col. i′
Lacuna
1′) [... R]U X [X]
2′) [...]-GA-*am*
3′) [...-*l*]*a*(?)-*am*
4′) [...]-ZI-*am*
5′) [...] X NI-*si*(?)-*am*
6′) [...] KI(?)-*a-am*
7′) [...] X X X-*am*
8′) [...] X AN X X

Lacuna
i′ 1′–8′) No translation warranted.

9′) [^{d}*i*]*š-me*-^{d}⸢*da-gan*⸣
10′) [...] ⸢LUGAL(?)-*ru*(?)⸣
11′) [...] X AN.KI
12′) [*i-d*]*u-uk*

i′ 9′–12′) [I]šme-Dagān, the *kings*, ... [de]feated.

13′) [...] X IB
14′) [...] X DA X
15′) [...]-*na-ki*
16′) [...]-*šu*
17′) [...] X
18′) [...] X
Lacuna

i′ 13′–18′) No translation warranted.
Lacuna

Col. ii′
Lacuna
1′) *pa-al-ḫ*[*a-ti-ša*]

Lacuna
ii′ 1′–4′) ... He ... [her] fearsome [..., he]r

2′) *na-am-ri-r*[*a-š*]*a*
3′) *me*-«A»-*lám-ma-ša*

radiance, (and) her aura.

4′) É-*ra-am*
5′) *eš*$_4$-*tár*
6′) *ḫi-ra-at-sú*
7′) *ap-lu-ḫa-ta-šu*
8′) *ta* X RU *ra*(?) X *uš*(?)

ii′ 5′–8′) Eštar, his spouse ... his armour.

9′) X ⸢IB(?)⸣
10′) ⸢AN(?)⸣ NI-*šu*

ii′ 9′–10′) No translation warranted.

11′) ^{d}*nin-urta*(?)
12′) *a-pi*$_5$-*il*
13′) ^{d}*en-líl*
14′) *qar-dum*
15′) *mu-ta-ar-ri*
16′) [*a*]-*bu-ši-im*
17′) X NE X X
Lacuna

ii′ 11′–17′) The god Ninurta, valiant heir of Enlil, leader of ...
Lacuna

Col. iii′
Lacuna
1′) X X [...]
2′) X-BU-⸢*uḫ*(?)⸣
3′) X-*ri*-IS
4′) [X] X-LUM
5′) [^{d}E]N.[L]ÍL-*ti-šu-un*
6′) [X]-*ta-an*
7′) X X *ap-lu-sà*
8′) X NI GAR
9′) *ta-am*-«X»-*tá*
10′) X *me-e*
11′) ⸢*ša*(?)-*am-ša*(?)⸣-*ti-iš*
12′) Ú.UGU.LÚ.DIŠ.RA
13′) *ra-aš* ÚR(?) X X
14′) [*t*]*a-ar*-X X ⸢KI(?)⸣

Lacuna
iii′ 1′–14′) ..., their [E]n[l]il-ship ... her inheritance ... the sea (and) water ... to the *sun disc*, ... to the one who possesses ... she ...

15′) ^{d}EN.[X]
16′) *ù* ^{d}*n*[*in*-X]
Lacuna

iii′ 15′–16′) The god En[...] and goddess Ni[n...]
Lacuna

Col. iv′
Lacuna
1′) X [...]
2′) LU [...]
3′) *a-ba*-X [...]
4′) AN.X ^{d}*iš*-[X]
5′) X-*šu-nu-ma*(?)
6′) *i-na*
7′) KI.TA-*im*
8′) *uš-zi-i*[*z*]
9′) *ik*(?)-*ru*(?)-⸢*ub*⸣
10′) X-*na-ti-im*
11′) [X X] X [...]
Lacuna

Lacuna
iv′ 1′–11′) ... the gods ... and ... ... he set below and *dedicated* (it) ...
Lacuna

Col. v′
Lacuna
1′) AN [...]
2′) *i*-[...]
3′) X [...]

Lacuna
v′ 1′–4′) No translation warranted.
Lacuna

4′) x […]
Lacuna
Reverse
Col. i′
Lacuna
1′) x […]
2′) x […]
3′) x […]
Lacuna

Lacuna
rev. i′ 1′–3′) No translation warranted.
Lacuna

Col. ii′
Lacuna
1′) x […]
2′) *na*[*m-*…]
3′) *ta-a*[*l-*…]
4′) NA$_4$.ZA.G[ÌN]
5′) NA$_4$.GU[G]
6′) *uš-na-w*[*i-ir*]
7′) *tu-uš-z*[*i*(?)*-iz*]
8′) *ú-me-ni-*[x]
9′) *ma-su*(?)*-am š*[*a*]
10′) *ì-lí-iš* [x]
11′) ⸢*é-ra*(?)*-am*⸣ [x]
12′) *ma*(?)*-tu-uš-šu*
13′) *mas-su-am*
14′) *e-te-ep-še-im*
15′) *e-em-qi$_4$-im*
16′) *be-el uz-ni-im*
17′) ⸢MI.ŠU.IŠ⸣
Lacuna

Lacuna
rev. ii′ 1′–2′) …
rev. ii′ 3′) she …
rev. ii′ 4′–6′) He made (it) shi[ne] with lapis lazu[li] and carne[lian].
rev. ii′ 7′) She se[t (it) up].
rev. ii′ 8′) He ….
rev. ii′ 9′–17′) The leader whom to the gods he … In his *land*, the leader, ⟨to⟩ the capable, wise one, the lord of wisdom, … (the god Enki) …
Lacuna

Col. iii′
Lacuna
1′) x x (x)
2′) *eridu*.KI
3′) x x*-la-sí-im*
4′) *ù ši-ma-il-tum*
5′) AMA x*-ra-at*(?)
6′) *bí-in-ta-šu*
7′) EGE.ZI*-tum*
8′) *qá-ar-ni*
9′) É(?) *ur-ši-im*
10′) *iš-tu pa-ti-im*
11′) AN(?) x AB
12′) *na-ši-at*
13′) *ù ta-ra-am-pa-la-mi-ig-ri-ša*
14′) *an-nu-ni-tum*
15′) AMALU *ma-dì-iš*
16′) *te-ri-iš-ši-ma*
17′) K[I …] x
Lacuna

Lacuna
rev. iii′ 1′–3′) … (*in*) Eridu … to her
rev. iii′ 4′–12′) Now Šīma-iltum, the …, his daughter, the *egiṣītum* priestess bore the horns *of the bedroom* from the …
rev. iii′ 13′–17′) Now as for Tarām-pala-migrīša, Annunītum, urgently asked her to be an *amalūtum* priestess. …
Lacuna

Col. iv′
Lacuna
1′) x […]
2′) EZEN […]
3′) WA *ra* KI […]

Lacuna
rev. iv′ 1′–3′) …

4′) *ta-ki-i*[*l*$_5$]-⌜*tum*⌝
5′) *eš*$_4$*-tár*
6′) ⌜*te-ri-iš-šu-ma*⌝
7′) É.TILMUN-*ša*
8′) *ú-ru*
9′) *ḫa-la-*^{d}*nin-gal*
10′) IGI.ÍL-*ši-im*
11′) *in* [ŠEŠ].AB.KI
12′) x [x x] x x-*iš*
13′) *na-ši*
14′) NAM.MEN(?)-*nam*
15′) *wa-li-da*
16′) NAM.MEN-*ni*
17′) *na-ap-ḫa-ar-šu-nu*
18′) *mu-ša-ak-*⌜*li*⌝-x
19′) WA x [...]
Lacuna

rev. iv′ 4′–19′) Eštar asked him for Taki[l]tum and he brought (her) into her Etilmun. He chose Ḫala-Ningal for her and elevated (her) to *office* in [U]r. They both gave birth to a ... all their ....
Lacuna

10

A diorite stele fragment found at Nippur south of Enlil's ziqqurrat by the Hilprecht expedition contains part of a royal inscription of Išme-Dagān. Unfortunately, little of the text is preserved.

COMMENTARY

The text is on CBS 3243, a diorite slab 8.1 × 10.5 × 5.6 cm. It was not collated.

BIBLIOGRAPHY

1893 Hilprecht, BE 1/1 no. 17 (copy)
1929 Barton, RISA pp. 304–305 Ishmi-Dagan 3 (edition)
1968 Kärki, SKFZ p. 7 Išmedagān 11 (edition)
1980 Kärki, SAKAZ 1 p. 13 Išmedagān 11 (edition)

TEXT

Col. i
Lacuna
1′) [...] x
2′) [...]-ZU-ta
3′) [...]-ta
Lacuna
Col. ii
Lacuna
1′) [...]
2′) ⌜^{d}⌝*iš-me-*⌜^{d}⌝[*d*]*a-gan*-e
3′) kin [x x] x x m[a-...]
Lacuna
Col. iii
Lacuna

i–iii) No translation warranted.

1′) B[I ...]
2′) ki[n-...]
Lacuna

11

A cone of unknown provenance in the Yale collection deals with the construction of the wall of Dūrum, a city which the text tells us is where Išme-Dagān had once served as military governor.

CATALOGUE

Ex.	Museum number	Provenance	Object	Dimensions (cm)	Lines preserved	cpn
1	YBC 2290	Presumably ancient Dūrum	Clay cone shaft	13	1–15	c
2	YBC 2290	As ex. 1	Clay cone head	10 dia.	1–15	c

COMMENTARY

Although the BÀD.KI which figures in this text was once thought to refer to the city of Dēr, it seems more likely that if refers to the city of Dūrum, a small settlement not far from Uruk. In this city the Ur III prince Šū-Sîn served as military governor prior to his enthronement. The same seems to have been true for Išme-Dagān. Both exs. were purchased.

BIBLIOGRAPHY

1937 Stephens, YOS 9 nos. 22–23 (exs. 1–2, copy)
1957 Edzard, Zwischenzeit pp. 73–74 (study)
1961 Hallo, BiOr 18 p. 5 Išme-Dagan 6 (study)
1968 Kärki, SKFZ p. 5 Išmedagān 6 (edition)
1971 Sollberger and Kupper, IRSA IVA4b (translation)
1977 Michalowski, Mesopotamia 12 p. 90 n. 38 (study)
1980 Kärki, SAKAZ 1 p. 10 Išmedagān 6 (edition)

TEXT

1) ^{d}*iš-me-*^{d}*da-gan*
2) ú-a-nibru.KI
3) sag-ús-
4) uri$_5$.KI-ma
5) u$_4$-da gub-
6) eridu.KI-ga
7) en-unu.KI-ga
8) lugal-ì-si-in.⌜KI⌝-⟨na⟩
9) lugal-ki-en-gi-⌜ki⌝-uri
10) dam-ki-á[g]-
11) ^{d}inanna-ka-ke$_4$
12) bàd-gal-BÀD.KI
13) uru.KI-nam-GÌR.NÍTA
14) nam-dumu-na-ka-ni
15) mu-un-dù

1–11) Išme-Dagān, provider of Nippur, constant (attendant) of Ur, who is daily at the service of Eridu, *en* priest of Uruk, king of Isin, king of the land of Sumer and Akkad, belov[ed] spouse of the goddess Inanna,

12–15) built the great wall of Dūrum, city of the military governorship (and) his princeship.

12

A calcite vase found in the Gipar-ku at Ur by Woolley contains a dedication to the god Nanna by Išme-Dagān.

COMMENTARY

The object is CBS 16206, U 6358, found in the Gipar-ku room C.21. This was below the doorway leading between rooms 63 and 57 of the Gipar-ku of Kurigalzu. The height of the vase is 35.6 cm, the dia. 13 cm. The inscription was collated.

BIBLIOGRAPHY

1926 Woolley, AJ 6 p. 377 (provenance)
1928 Gadd, UET 1 no. 102 (copy, edition) and pl. N (photo)
1929 Barton, RISA pp. 370–71 Ishmi-Dagan 2 (edition)
1961 Hallo, BiOr 18 p. 6 Išme-Dagan 9 (study)
1965 Woolley, UE 8 p. 41 (provenance)
1968 Kärki, SKFZ pp. 6–7 Išmedagān 9 (edition)
1971 Sollberger and Kupper, IRSA IVA4d (translation)
1976 Woolley and Mallowan, UE 7 pp. 56 and 223 (provenance)
1980 Kärki, SAKAZ 1 p. 12 Išmedagān 9 (edition)

TEXT

1) ^{d}nanna
2) dumu-sag-
3) ^{d}en-líl-lá
4) lugal-a-ni-ir
5) ^{d}*iš-me-*^{d}*da-gan*
6) ú-a-nibru.KI
7) sag-ús-
8) uri$_5$.KI-ma
9) u$_4$-da-gub-
10) eridu.KI-ga
11) en-unu.KI-ga
12) [l]ugal-ì-si-in.KI-na
13) [l]ugal-ki-en-gi-ki-uri
14) [da]m-ki-á[g]-
15) [^{d}]inanna-ka-ke$_4$
16) [nam-t]i-la-ni-šè
17) [a mu-na]-ru

1–4) For the god Nanna, first-born son of the god Enlil, his lord,

5–15) Išme-Dagān, provider of Nippur, constant (attendant) of Ur, who is daily at the service of Eridu, *en* priest of Uruk, [k]ing of Isin, [k]ing of the land of Sumer and Akkad, belov[ed spo]use of the [goddess] Inanna,

16–17) [dedic]ated (this vase) [to him] for his own [l]ife.

13

A diorite statuette found in the Gipar-ku at Ur by Woolley was dedicated by En-ana-tuma, the *en* priestess, to Ningal.

COMMENTARY

The piece is a diorite statuette, U 6352 now CBS 16229, from the Gipar-ku, room C.22. It is 24.5 cm high and 11.5 cm wide. The inscription was collated from a photo.

The statuette was found in the second small room off the main courtyard of the Ningal temple section of the Gipar-ku. If this Ningal temple was similar to the temple of Bēlet-Apim at Šubat-Enlil described in a tablet published by D. Charpin in Iraq 45 (1983) pp. 57–59, then room C.22 should be the *kummu* or 'bedroom'. This accords well with the inscription on the statuette, which says that it was brought into the *agrun* = Akkadian *kummu*; see D. Charpin, Le clergé d'Ur, p. 213.

BIBLIOGRAPHY

1926 Woolley, AJ 6 p. 376 (provenance) and pl. liia (photo); Woolley, MJ 18

1928 Gadd, UET 1 no. 103 (copy, edition)

1929 Barton, RISA pp. 370–71 Ishmi-Dagan 3 (edition)

1935 Zervos, L'art de la Mésopotamie p. 114 (photo)

1954 Frankfort, Art and Architecture pp. 55–56 (study) and pl. 57 (photo)

1961 Hallo, BiOr 18 p. 5 Išme-Dagan 8 (study)

1968 Kärki, SKFZ p. 6 Išmedagān 8 (edition)

1971 Sollberger and Kupper, IRSA IVA4e (translation)

1976 Woolley and Mallowan, UE 7 pp. 57 and 223 (provenance), p. 169 (study), and pl. 55a (photo)

1980 Kärki, SAKAZ 1 p. 11 Išmedagān 8 (edition)

TEXT

1) ^{d}nin-gal
2) SAL + ŠÈ sag-íl
3) me-ni me-nu-sá
4) ad-gi$_4$-gi$_4$-gal-zu
5) nam-nin-a túm-ma
6) nin-a-ni-ir
7) en-an-na-túm-ma
8) en-ki-ág-^{d}nanna
9) en-^{d}nanna
10) šà-uri$_5$.KI-ma
11) dumu-^{d}*iš-me-^{d}da-gan*
12) lugal-ki-en-gi-ki-uri-ke$_4$
13) ⌜alam⌝-ba
14) agrun-na-šè
15) mu-na-de$_6$
16) nam-ti-la-ni-šè
17) a mu-na-ru

1–6) For the goddess Ningal, proud *lady*, whose *me*s no *me*s can rival, wise counsellor, the one suitable for ladyship, her lady,

7–12) En-ana-tuma, *en* priestess beloved of the god Nanna, *en* priestess of the god Nanna, in Ur, daughter of Išme-Dagān, king of the land of Sumer and Akkad,

13–15) brought this statue to her to the bedroom.

16–17) She dedicated it to her for her own life.

14

A seal impression found on two tablets belongs to a son of the *en* priestess En-ana-tuma.

CATALOGUE

Ex.	Museum number	Excavation number	Ur provenance	Dimensions (cm)	Lines preserved	cpn
1	YBC 4771	–	–	–	–	n
2	YBC 4854	–	–	–	1–3	n
3	YBC 4862	–	–	–	–	n
4	–	U 581	Enunmaḫ, room 22	0.5 × 0.25	1–3	n

BIBLIOGRAPHY

1919 Grice, YOS 5 no. 46a (copy)
1967 Renger, ZA 58 pp. 120–21 (study)
1974 Woolley, UE 6 pp. 53 and 91 (ex. 4, study)
1986 Charpin, Le clergé d'Ur p. 218 n. 5 (edition)

TEXT

1) a-ab-ba
2) dumu-en-an-[na]-⸢túm⸣-ma
3) en-^{d}nanna

1) A-ab-ba,
2) son of En-an[a]-tuma,
3) *en* priestess of the god Nanna.

15

A tablet in the Philadelphia collection appears to be a copy of various royal inscriptions of Išme-Dagān. The best preserved section deals with the setting up of the mace with fifty heads for the god Ninurta.

COMMENTARY

The tablet is N 1320 from Nippur, excavated by the Hilprecht expedition, provenance not known. The tablet measures 6×6.3×3.2 cm. It appears to be the lower third of a tablet. Previously unpublished, it is offered here through the courtesy of A. Sjöberg.

It is not certain whether this fragment is part of a collection of royal inscriptions or a royal hymn. Normally we do not find royal inscriptions with addresses in the second person. The text is narrative in style like that of a royal inscription and does contain the standard titulary of Išme-Dagān at the end. It may represent a composition similar to E4.1.6.2 edited below, which has a curse formula characteristic of a royal inscription, but has various discourses characteristic of royal hymns.

The first section of the composition deals with the fashioning of some object made of copper which stood in the great dining hall of the god. In light of the evidence of E4.2.8.3 this might be a du$_8$-maḫ, since this object, perhaps a cauldron, stood with the oven in the kitchen of the god Nanna at Ur. In view of the previous inscription of Išme-Dagān which mentions the fashioning of a du$_8$-maḫ this does not seem an unlikely restoration in our text.

The second section of the text, lines 7′–16′, deals with the construction of the mace with fifty heads for the god Ninurta. The composition seems to have an address to the god Ninurta. The last section, lines 17′–20′, which lists the titulary of the king, may have begun another inscription.

TEXT

Lacuna
1′) (traces)
2′) URUDU.[du$_8$-m]aḫ ní gal-le-eš [...]
3′) bára-kù-za bí-in-[...]
4′) un-e u$_6$-di-d[è ...]
5′) kin-gal únu-gal-z[a]
6′) u$_4$-ul-lí-a-šè sá-du$_{11}$-šè ma-ra-ni-[...]
7′) G[IŠ.mi-tu]m sag-ninnu ki-bala gul-gul-lu
8′) [...] bára-maḫ-zu-šè pà-[da]
9′) [ì-si]-in.KI uru.KI-nam-lug[al-la-ka]
10′) [^{d}*i*]*š-me-*^{d}*da-gan*-e kin [...]
11′) mu-ninnu ma-ra-⸢an⸣-x x
12′) nibru.KI uru-ul ki-⸢gar⸣-[ra]

1′–6′) ... a great copper [*cauldron*] grandly [*casting*] a fearful splendour, on your shining dais [*he set up*]. In order that the people marvel at it he [*put*] the masterpiece i[n] your great dining hall for you for regular offerings to the distant future.

7′–10′) The [mac]e with fifty heads, which destroys the rebellious land, ... chos[en] for your great dais, [*in* Is]in, the city of king[ship, I]šme-Dagān [finished] the work.

11′–16′) He [*called*] the fifty names for you. (*To*) Nippur, the ancient, established city, from Isin he

13′) ì-si-in.KI-ta ma-ra-⌜an⌝-[...]
14′) é-šu-me-ša$_4$ ki-tuš-maḫ ní-x [...]
15′) ká-igi-šu-galam ki-nam-tar-re-[dam]
16′) u$_6$-di-dè ma-ra-an-[...]
17′) ⌜^{d}*iš*⌝-*me*-^{d}*da-gan* ú-a-ni[bru.KI-a]
18′) sa[g]-ús-úri.K[I-ma]
19′) [u$_4$-da-D]U-eridu.[KI-ga]
20′) [en-unu.KI-ga] lugal-i-[si-in.KI-na]
Lacuna

[*brought*] it for you. In Ešumeša, the supreme residence which [casts] a fearsome splendour, at the gate in front of Šugalam, the place where fate is determined, he [*set it up*] for you as a wonder.
17′–20′) Išme-Dagān, provider of Ni[ppur], supporter of Ur [who is daily at the service of] Eridu, [*en* priest of Uruk], king of I[sin].
Lacuna

2001

A stone bowl found at Ur by Woolley was dedicated by a servant of the king for his master's life.

COMMENTARY

The fragment is CBS 14948, U 262, from the Enunmaḫ, '16–17' under pavement (Ur field cards), room 11 (UE 6). It is 14.5 cm in dia. and 4.2 cm high. The inscription was collated.

BIBLIOGRAPHY

1923 Woolley, AJ 3 p. 323 (provenance)
1928 Gadd, UET 1 no. 101 (copy, edition)
1929 Barton, RISA pp. 370–71 Ishmi-Dagan 1 (edition)
1961 Hallo, BiOr 18 p. 6 Išme-Dagan 10 (study)
1968 Kärki, SKFZ p. 7 Išmedagān 10 (edition)
1976 Woolley and Mallowan, UE 7 p. 215 (provenance)
1980 Kärki, SAKAZ 1 p. 12 Išmedagān 10 (edition)

TEXT

1) ^{d}[...]
2) lugal-a-[ni-ir]
3) nam-[ti]-
4) ^{d}*iš-me*-^{d}[*da-gan*]
5) lugal-k[ala-ga]
6) lugal u[ri$_5$.KI-ma-ka-šè]
7) mu-da-da-[x (x)]
8) dumu *šar-ru-um*-[x (x)]
9) ir$_{11}$-da-a-[ni]
10) a mu-na-[ru]

1–2) For the god ..., [his] lord,
3–6) for the li[fe] of Išme-[Dagān], m[ighty] king, king of U[r],
7–9) Mudada[...], son of Šarrum-[... his] servant,
10) dedi[cated] (this bowl) to him.

Lipit-Eštar

E4.1.5

According to the Sumerian King List, Lipit-Eštar ruled 11 years. A number of his year names are known, but their order has not yet been determined. Here, after the standard inscription, those inscriptions which deal with the city of Isin are edited first (E4.1.5.2–4) and then those which deal with Ur (E4.1.5.5–6).

1

The standard inscription of Lipit-Eštar is found on a 16-line stamped or inscribed brick inscription, known at present from Ur, Uruk, and Isin.

CATALOGUE

Ex.	Museum number	Excavation number	Provenance	Dimensions (cm)	Lines preserved	cpn
1	CBS 16536b	U 2880d	Ur, –	32.5×32.5×8.0	1–16	c
2	IM 1062	U 3191	Ur, loose on SW slope of western and highest hill	–	–	n
3	IM 25594A	U 3191	As ex. 2	–	–	n
4	IM 25594B	U 3191	As ex. 2	–	–	n
5	IM 25594C	U 3191	As ex. 2	–	–	n
6	IM 25594D	U 3191	As ex. 2	–	–	n
7	CBS 16546	U 3191	As ex. 2	31.0×31.0×7.0	–	n
8	–	U 6312	Ur, EH	–	–	n
9	BM 137351	U 6328	As ex. 8	31.0×31.0×7.0	1–16	c
10	CBS 16471	U 6328	As ex. 8	33.0×31.0×7.0	–	n
11	Berlin	W 3272	Uruk, Pd xv 4, in rubbish	–	2–10	n
12	–	IB 282A	Isin, surface find	–	–	n
13	–	IB 282B	As ex. 12	–	–	n
14	–	IB 282C	As ex. 12	–	–	n
15	–	Isin, not registered	Isin, west corner of the Gula temple	–	–	n

COMMENTARY

Exs. 1–10 were found by Woolley at Ur. Woolley (UE 7 p. 81) suggests that the bricks may have been made for the *gipar* of Ningubalag for which we have many cone inscriptions of Lipit-Eštar (see E4.1.5.6). Woolley suggests a location for this structure in the SM site. In addition to the bricks noted here, Woolley indicates one was reused in the pavement of no. 5 Quiet Street, and a number were found in the Gipar-ku of En-ana-tuma and the Eḫursag. Their excavation numbers could not be determined.

Exs. 12–15 are from Isin. Ex. 11, a brick fragment from Uruk, was noted by the epigrapher of the Uruk expedition as a duplicate of E4.1.5.6, the latter a cone dealing with the construction of a *gipar* at Ur. This was the only other Lipit-Eštar text available at the time for comparison. It is unlikely that the Uruk brick fragment is a duplicate of the cone inscription found at Ur. It is placed here as a duplicate of the standard inscription. However, since it is broken, it could be the beginning of a text unique to Uruk not otherwise attested.

Sollberger, UET 8/2 no. 15 listed two cone duplicates of this text, but collation of the cones reveals that they are duplicates of E4.1.5.5 instead. Hence, this standard inscription is found only on bricks, not bricks and cones as Kärki, SAKAZ 1 p. 15 indicates.

BIBLIOGRAPHY

1928 Gadd, UET 1 no. 110 (exs. 2–10, copy, edition)
1929 Barton, RISA p. 371 n. 6 (study)
1930 Schott, Eanna no. 5 (ex. 11, copy, edition)
1961 Hallo, BiOr 18 p. 6 Lipit-Ištar 1 (study)
1968 Kärki, SKFZ pp. 9–10 Lipiteštar 1 (edition)
1976 Woolley and Mallowan, UE 7 pp. 81, 220, and 222 (exs. 2–10, provenance)
1977 Edzard and Wilcke in Hrouda, Isin 1 p. 87 (exs. 12–14, study)
1980 Kärki, SAKAZ 1 pp. 15–16 Lipiteštar 1 (edition)
1981 Walker, CBI no. 33 (ex. 9, study)
1981 Walker in Hrouda, Isin 2 p. 94 (ex. 15, study)
1985 Behrens, JCS 37 p. 234 no. 24 (exs. 1, 7, 10, study)

TEXT

1) *^{d}li-pí-it-eš$_4$-tár*	1) Lipit-Eštar,
2) sipa-sun$_5$-na-	2–3) humble shepherd of Nippur,
3) nibru.KI	
4) engar-zi-	4–5) true farmer of Ur,
5) uri$_5$.KI-ma	
6) mùš nu-túm-mu-	6–7) unceasing (provider) for Eridu,
7) eridu.KI-ga	
8) en me-te-	8–9) *en* priest fit for Uruk,
9) unu.KI-ga	
10) lugal-ì-si-in.KI-na	10) king of Isin,
11) lugal-ki-en-gi-ki-uri	11) king of the land of Sumer and Akkad,
12) šà-ge DU-a-	12–13) favourite of the goddess Inanna,
13) ^{d}inanna	
14) lugal nì-si-sá	14–16) king who established justice in the land of Sumer and Akkad.
15) ki-en-gi ki-uri-a	
16) ì-ni-in-gar-ra	

2

The south-east area of the tell of Išān Bāḥriyāt (ancient Isin) contains a mound which the Munich expedition thought might cover the remains of the palace of Isin. Excavations carried out there revealed parts of a large building. The contents of the texts found there suggest that this building was the administrative centre for the city.

A cone recently published by G. Oller deals with the construction of a royal palace by Lipit-Eštar, presumably in Isin. This may possibly refer to the construction of the building recently excavated at Isin. The palace also figures in E4.1.5.3.

COMMENTARY

The piece is FLP 2636, a small headless cone, 9 cm long and 3.4 cm in dia. It is a purchased piece, probably from Isin.

BIBLIOGRAPHY

1987 Oller, ARRIM 5 p. 47 (copy, partial transliteration)

TEXT

1) [d]*li-pí-it-eš$_4$-tar*
2) sipa-sun$_5$-na-
3) nibru.KI
4) engar-zi-
5) [uri$_5$].KI-ma
6) [mùš-nu-t]úm-mu-
7) eridu.KI-ga
8) en me-te-
9) unu.KI-ga
10) lugal-ì-si-in.KI-na
11) lugal-ki-en-gi-ki-uri
12) šà-ge DU-a-
13) [d]inanna-me-en
14) u$_4$ nì-si-sá
15) ki-en-gi-ki-uri-a
16) i-ni-in-gar-[ra]
17) é-me-te-nam-lugal-[la]
18) é-ki-t[uš]-gu-la-mu
19) mu-dù

1–13) I, Lipit-Eštar, humble shepherd of Nippur, true farmer of [U]r, [unce]asing (provider) for Eridu, *en* priest suitable for Uruk, king of Isin, king of the land of Sumer and Akkad, favourite of the goddess Inanna,

14–16) when I establish(ed) justice in the land of Sumer and Akkad,

17–19) I built the Emetenamlugal[a] ('House — suitable for kingship'), my great resid[ence].

3

A large number of small headless cones found at Isin have an Akkadian text dealing with the construction by Lipit-Eštar of a pair of pot stands (*kannum*) at the gate of the palace.

CATALOGUE

Ex.	Museum number	Excavation number	Registration number	Provenance	Object	Dimensions (cm)	Lines preserved	cpn
1	–	IB 192		Isin, surface find	Cone	7.4×8.5×4.5	1–8, 22–32	n
2	–	IB 333		73.10 S, 8.10 E, +8.67	Cone	8.4	–	n
3	–	IB 336		75.50 S, 8.14 E, +8.21	Cone	4.8	–	n
4	–	IB 1016		N II, rubbish dump	Cone	–	26–29	n
5	IM 90017	IB 1289		262 E, 105 S, on surface	Shaft	10	5–10, 20–28	c
6	–	IB 1384		Surface near NO I	Cone shaft	–	–	n
7	BM 68463	–	Att 82-9-18,8461	–	Cone shaft	–	–	n
8	BM 114390	–	1920-3-15,1	–	Cone shaft	13.0	1–36	c
9	BM 114683	–	1920-10-9,1	–	Cone shaft	10.9	1–36	c
10	BM 115314	–	1921-7-12,1	–	Cone shaft	12.0	1–36	c
11	BM 117705	–	1925-5-9,527	–	Cone shaft	9.0	1–36	c

Ex.	Museum number	Excavation number	Registration number	Provenance	Object	Dimensions (cm)	Lines preserved	cpn
12	BM 117823	–	1925-10-15,3	–	Cone head	16.3	1-36	c
13	BM 117823	–	1925-10-15,3	–	Cone shaft	16.3	1-36	c
14	BM 138342	–	1980-12-14,1	–	Cone shaft	11.1	1-20, 22-36	c
15	YBC 2314	–		–	Shaft	15.4	1-36	c
16	YBC 2314	–		–	Head	11.9 dia.	1-36	c
17	YBC 2315	–		–	Shaft	11.6	2-36	c
18	YBC 2324	–		–	Shaft	10.5	1-36	c
19	EŞ 9261	–		–	Cone	–	–	n
20	IM 14041	–		–	Shaft	10.5	1-36	c
21	IM 14042	–		–	Shaft	11.7	1-27, 30-36	c
22	IM 14043	–		–	Cone	–	–	n
23	IM 14557	–		–	Cone	–	–	n
24	IM 49432	–		–	Cone	–	–	n
25	IM 51976A	–		–	Shaft	12.4	5-36	c
26	IM 51976B	–		–	Shaft	6.6	1-34	c
27	IM 51976C	–		–	Shaft	11	3-12,21-24	c
28	IM 52768A	–		–	Cone	–	–	n
29	IM 52768B	–		–	Cone	–	–	n
30	IM 55547	–		–	Shaft	10	1-26, 32-36	c
31	Kestner Museum 1926,1	–		–	Shaft	–	1-36	p
32	AO 8535	–		–	Shaft	11.2	1-36	c
33	AO 11252	–		–	Shaft	15.5	1-36	c
34	AO 11252	–		–	Head	11.5 dia.	1-36	c
35	UCLM 9-1778	–		–	Shaft	10.5	1-36	c
36	UCLM 9-1779	–		–	Shaft	11	1-36	c
37	Kelsey Museum, Ann Arbor	–		–	Cone	–	–	n
38	Australian Institute of Archaeology IA7 A Kirk	–		–	Shaft	–	1-7, 9-36	p
39	Tuffs University 2/5/8/2	–		–	Cone	–	1-21, 26-36	c
40	FLP, LI 2	–		–	Shaft	10.6	1-36	c
41	FLP, LI 3	–		–	Shaft	12	–	n
42	FLP, LI 4	–		–	Shaft	10.8	–	n
43	FLP, LI 5	–		–	Shaft	11.7	–	n
44	FLP, LI 6	–		–	Shaft	10.7	–	n
45	FLP, LI 7	–		–	Shaft	10.0	–	n
46	FLP, LI 8	–		–	Shaft	11.7	–	n
47	FLP, LI 9	–		–	Shaft	11.0	–	n
48	FLP, LI 10	–		–	Shaft	10	–	n
49	FLP, LI 11	–		–	Shaft	9.0	–	n
50	FLP, LI 12	–		–	Shaft	11.8	–	n
51	FLP, LI 13	–		–	Shaft	10.6	–	n
52	FLP, LI 14	–		–	Shaft	10.3	–	n
53	FLP, LI 15	–		–	Shaft	11.8	–	n
54	FLP, LI 16	–		–	Shaft	12.8	–	n
55	FLP, LI 17	–		–	Head	12.0 dia.	–	n
56	FLP, LI 17	–		–	Shaft	12.5	–	n
57	FLP, LI 18	–		–	Head	12.0 dia.	–	n
58	FLP, LI 18	–		–	Shaft	11.2	–	n

COMMENTARY

Exs. 1-5 were recently excavated by the Munich expedition to Isin. They come for the most part from the south-east sector of the tell where the palace probably lay.

Exs. 1 and 4 were entered in the scores from unpublished copies kindly provided by C. Wilcke. The remaining exs. were all purchased.

On the reading of the goddess's name in line 23 see S. Parpola, Death p. 177 n. 21b.

Ex. 19, according to Kraus, preserves 13 lines.

Exs. 25-27 were presented in 1947 to the Iraq Museum by S. Bishara. Ex. 28 was picked up in 1947 by F. Basmaji.

BIBLIOGRAPHY

1921 Gadd, Early Dynasties pp. 33–34 (ex. 9, edition) and pl. 3 (copy)
1922 Langdon, JRAS p. 431 (study)
1927 Dougherty, AASOR 7 p. 38 (study)
1937 Stephens, YOS 9 nos. 118–20 (exs. 4–5, study)
1947 Kraus, Halil Edhem Memorial Volume p. 113 (ex. 19, study)
1948 S. Lewy, Sumer 4 pp. 56–59 (exs. 25–27, composite copy, edition; exs. 28–29, study)
1952 Fish, MCS 2 p. 20 (ex. 31, study)
1957 Edzard, Sumer 13 p. 177 (exs. 20–30, study)
1960 Aynard, RA 54 p. 17 (exs. 33–34, study)
1961 Hallo, BiOr 18 p. 6 Lipit-Ištar 5 (study)
1971 Sollberger and Kupper, IRSA IVA5b (translation)
1975 Owen, MVN 3 p. 32 n. 19 (exs. 40–58, study)
1977 Edzard and Wilcke in Hrouda, Isin 1 p. 87 (exs. 1–3, study)
1978 Foxvog, RA 72 p. 42 (exs. 35–36, study)
1980 Kärki, SAKAZ 1 pp. 19–20 Lipiteštar 5 (edition)
1981 Walker in Hrouda, Isin 2 p. 93 (exs. 3–6, study)
1985 Wilcke, Orientalia NS 54 p. 309 (ex. 6, study)
1987 Wilcke in Hrouda, et al., Isin 3 p. 114 c (ex. 6, study)

TEXT

1) ^{d}*li-pí-it-eš$_4$-tár*	1–19) I, Lipit-Eštar, humble shepherd of Nippur, true farmer of Ur, unceasing (provider) for Eridu, *en* priest suitable for Uruk, king of Isin, king of the land of Sumer and Akkad, favourite of the goddess Eštar, fashioned
2) *re-i-um*	
3) *pa-li-iḫ*	
4) NIBRU.KI	
5) *i-ka-ru-um*	
6) *ki-nu-um*	
7) *ša* URI$_5$.KI-*im*	
8) *la mu-pa-ar-ki-um*	
9) *a-na* ERIDU.KI	
10) EN-*um*	
11) *sí-ma-at*	
12) UNUG.KI	
13) *šar ì-si-in*.KI	
14) *šar ma-at*	
15) *šu-me-ri-im*	
16) *ù a-kà-dì-im*	
17) *bí-bí-il*	
18) *li-i-ba eš$_4$-tár*	
19) *a-na-ku*	
20) *kà-ni-in*	20–23) a pair of pot stands, a gift (for) the hands of the gods Enlil and Ninlil,
21) *bí-bí-il*	
22) *i-dì* ^{d}*en-líl*	
23) *ù* ^{d}NIN.LÍL-*ti-im*	
24) *i-na ì-si-in*.KI	24–26) in Isin, the city of my kingship, at the palace gate.
25) *a-al šar-ru-ti-ia*	
26) *i-na ba-ab* É.GAL-*im*	
27) ^{d}*li-pí-it-eš$_4$-tár*	27–29) I, Lipit-Eštar, son of the god Enlil, (did this)
28) *ma-ru* ^{d}*en-líl*	
29) *a-na-ku*	
30) *i-nu-mi*	30–36) when I established justice in the land of Sumer and Akkad.
31) *ki-i-ta-am*	
32) *i-na ma-at*	
33) *šu-me-ri-im*	
34) *ù a-kà-dì-im*	
35) *aš-ku-nu-ni*	
36) *e-pu-uš*	

3.20 omits. **4**.20 omits. **6**.20 omits. **7**.8, 20 omit *-im*.
15.12 omits. **30**.15 *i-nu-ni*.

4

A large number of small headless cones were found at Isin dealing with the construction of the é-nì-si-sá 'House of Justice' by Lipit-Eštar. The construction of this edifice may have something to do with the king's promulgation of a lawcode, a deed alluded to in most of the king's inscriptions.

CATALOGUE

Ex.	Museum number	Excavation number	Provenance	Dimensions (cm)	Lines preserved	cpn
1	IM -	IB 322	Isin, 76.45 S, 13.30 E, 60 cm under the surface	9.5	–	n
2	IM 77067	IB 323	85.70 S, 13 E	10.5	–	n
3	IM 77068	IB 324	In dump of south cutting	12.2	–	n
4	IM 77069	IB 325	76.70 S, 12.66 E, +8.60 E	11.3	–	n
5	IM 77070	IB 334	77.75 S, 13.20 E, +8.84	10.1	–	n
6	IM -	IB 340	78.44 S, 14.40 E, +8.50	8.8	–	n
7	IM 77071	IB 341	77.84 S, 17.70 E, +8.52	11.4	–	n
8	IM 9372	–	–	–	–	n
9	IM 10008A	–	–	–	–	n
10	IM 10008B	–	–	–	–	n
11	IM 10008C	–	–	–	–	n
12	IM 10008D	–	–	–	–	n
13	IM 10583A	–	–	–	–	n
14	IM 10583B	–	–	–	–	n
15	IM 10749	–	–	–	–	n
16	IM 10754	–	–	–	–	n
17	IM 11007	–	–	–	–	n
18	IM 11055	–	–	–	–	n
19	IM 17736	–	–	–	–	n
20	IM 17737	–	–	–	–	n
21	IM 21027	–	–	–	–	n
22	IM 29033A	–	–	–	–	n
23	IM 29033B	–	–	–	–	n
24	IM 29033C	–	–	–	–	n
25	IM 29033D	–	–	–	–	n
26	IM 29033E	–	–	–	–	n
27	IM 29033F	–	–	–	–	n
28	IM 42714B	–	–	–	–	n
29	IM 42714C	–	–	–	–	n
30	IM 42714E	–	–	–	–	n
31	IM 42714F	–	–	–	–	n
32	IM 42714G	–	–	–	–	n
33	IM 42714H	–	–	–	–	n
34	IM 42714O	–	–	–	–	n
35	IM 45471	–	–	–	–	n
36	IM 46736	–	–	–	–	n
37	IM 51044	–	–	–	–	n
38	IM 51948	–	–	–	–	n
39	IM 51949	–	–	–	–	n
40	IM 55003/1	–	–	–	–	n
41	IM 55003/2	–	–	–	–	n
42	IM 55003/3	–	–	–	–	n
43	IM 55003/4	–	–	–	–	n
44	IM 55003/5	–	–	–	–	n
45	IM 55003/6	–	–	–	–	n
46	IM 55003/7	–	–	–	–	n
47	IM 55003/8	–	–	–	–	n
48	IM 55003/9	–	–	–	–	n
49	IM 55103	–	–	–	–	n
50	IM 55104	–	–	–	–	n
51	IM 59103	–	–	–	–	n

Ex.	Museum number	Excavation number	Provenance	Dimensions (cm)	Lines preserved	cpn
52	IM 59104	–	–	–	–	n
53	IM 59379	–	–	–	–	n
54	IM 59380	–	–	–	–	n
55	YBC 2190	–	–	11.4	1-21	c
56	YBC 2190	–	–	10.4	1-21	c
57	YBC 16657	–	–	10.5	1-21	c
58	New York – Public Library Eames Collection xx-1	–	–	11.5	1-21	n
59	LB 992	–	–	11.0	1-21	c
60	LB 993	–	–	–	1-21	c
61	Library of Centenary College Shreveport, Louisiana	–	–	–	–	n
62	Collection of J.R.Tournay			–	1-21	n
63	Allen Memorial Art Museum, Oberlin, Ohio, no. 42.135	–	–	12.0	1-21	n
64	University of Minnesota Library 15	–	–	11.1	1-21	n
65	Collection of J.B. Pabst	–	–	–	–	n
66	McGill Ethnological Collections 2.3	–	–	11.9	1-21	c
67	University of Cincinatti Classics Library Cone A	–	–	–	1-21	c
68	University of Cincinatti Classics Library Cone B	–	–	–	1-21	c
69	Bryn Mawr College no. 20	–	–	10.5	1-21	c
70	Australian Institute of Archaeology IA7.17	–	–	–	1-21	p
71	Australian Institute of Archaeology IA7.18	–	–	–	1-21	p
72	Hebrew Union College 78.39.3	–	–	–	–	c
73	Suffield Connecticut Historical Society	–	–	11.5	1-21	c
74	Drew University, New Jersey	–	–	12.0	1-21	c
75	Drew University, New Jersey	–	–	11.8	1-21	c
76	Drew University, New Jersey	–	–	12.0	1-21	c
77	New Brunswick Museum A44-313	–	–	11.2	1-21	c
78	Stovall Museum of the University of Oklahoma C 43-44.1	–	–	10.7	1-21	c
79	Private collection in France, no. 602	–	–	10.3	1-21	c
80	Idem. no. 603	–	–	10.5	1-21	c
81	Idem. no. 868	–	–	11.2	1-21	c
82	Idem. no. 869	–	–	11	1-21	c
83	Idem. no. 870	–	–	11.5	1-21	c
84	Idem. no. 885	–	–	9.2	1-21	c
85	Idem. no. 1100	–	–	8.4	1-3, 7-14, 20-21	c
86	Idem. no. 1101	–	–	8.8	1-21	c
87	Idem. no. 1102	–	–	–	1-4, 6-15	c
88	Idem. no. 1103	–	–	9.8	1-10, 12-20	c
89	Idem. no. 1104	–	–	13.2	5-7, 12-13, 21	c
90	Idem. no. 1105	–	–	12	7-11, 18-21	c
91	Idem. no. 1106	–	–	10	8-11, 16-21	c
92	Public Library of Cincinnati and Hamilton County	–	–	12.2	–	n

COMMENTARY

Exs. 1-7 were excavated by the Munich expedition to Isin, all in the area around 77S, 14E. This may give an indication of the general location of the é-nì-si-sá at Isin. The rest were confiscated or donated to the Iraq Museum or purchased by other collections.

In view of the large number of exemplars of this text an attempt was not made to collate all the exs. The vars. listed are a sampling of the possible vars.

The information on cones 79-91 is through the courtesy of J.-J. Glassner.

BIBLIOGRAPHY

1932 Stephens, JAOS 52 pp. 182–85 (ex. 55, copy, edition)
1937 Stephens, YOS 9 no. 26 (ex. 55, copy)
1950 Stephens, JAOS 70 pp. 179–81 (ex. 61, study)
1951–52 Lettinga, JEOL 12 p. 253 (exs. 59–60, edition)
1952 Tournay, RA 46 p. 110 (ex. 62, edition)
1957 Edzard, Sumer 13 p. 177 (exs. 8–54, study)
1958 Gordon, Allen Memorial Art Museum Bulletin (Oberlin) pp. 16–28 (ex. 63, edition)
1940 Schwarz, Bulletin of the New York Public Library 44 p. 807 no. 13 (ex. 58, study)
1961 Jones and Snyder, Econ. Texts no. 340 (ex. 64, study)
1961 Hallo, BiOr 18 p. 6 Lipit-Ištar 2 (study)
1968 Kärki, SKFZ p. 10 Lipiteštar 2 (edition)
1971 Sollberger and Kupper, IRSA ɪᴠA5c (translation)
1975 Sauren, Muséon 88 p. 185 (ex. 65, study)
1977 Edzard and Wilcke in Hrouda, Isin 1 p. 87 (exs. 1–7, study)
1979 M. Ellis, JCS 31 p. 32 no. 20 (ex. 69, study)
1980 Kärki, SAKAZ 1 pp. 16–17 Lipiteštar 2 (edition)
1983 Glassner, JCS 35 pp. 209–10 and 215 (exs. 79–91, copy, study)
1988 Obermark, JCS 40 p. 236 (ex. 92, study)

TEXT

1) *ᵈli-pí-it-eš₄-tár*
2) sipa-sun₅-na-
3) nibru.ᴋɪ
4) engar-zi-
5) uri₅.ᴋɪ-ma
6) mùš-nu-túm-mu-
7) eridu.ᴋɪ-ga
8) en me-te-
9) unu.ᴋɪ-ga
10) lugal-ì-si-in.ᴋɪ-na
11) lugal-ki-en-gi-ki-uri
12) šà-ge ᴅᴜ-a
13) ᵈinanna-me-en
14) u₄ nì-si-sá
15) ki-en-gi-ki-uri-a
16) i-ni-in-gar-ra-a
17) *nam-kà-ru-um*
18) ki-rib-ba-
19) dingir-re-e-ne-ka
20) é-nì-si-sá-a
21) mu-dù

1–13) I, Lipit-Eštar, humble shepherd of Nippur, true farmer of Ur, unceasing (provider) for Eridu, *en* priest fit for Uruk, king of Isin, king of the land of Sumer and Akkad, favourite of the goddess Inanna,

14–16) when I established justice in the land of Sumer and Akkad,

17–21) I built the 'House of Justice' by the irrigation canal, the pre-eminent place of the gods.

5

A year name of Lipit-Eštar commemorates restoration work that the king carried out at Ur; another records the digging of the Ninki canal (see R.M. Sigrist, RLA 7, p. 28). These two events may be alluded to in an inscription found on a large number of small headless clay cones found by Taylor and Woolley at Ur, mainly from the Royal Cemetery area. Sigrist suggests the restoration work may have been necessary after a campaign by Gungunum of Larsa against the city of Ur.

5.78 omits. **10**.58 ì-si-in.ᴋɪ-⟨na⟩. **10**.62 ì-si-in-na.ᴋɪ. **10**.82–83 ì-si-in.⟨ᴋɪ⟩-na. **11**.66, 78 ki-uri-a. **14**.56 nì-si-sá-a. **15**.56, 59–60, 62, 73, 79, 82–83 ki-uri-⟨a⟩. **16**.56, 83 -gar-ra-⟨a⟩. **16**.60, 78 i-ni-⟨in⟩-gar-. **20**.82–83 -si-sá-⟨a⟩.

CATALOGUE

Ex.	Museum number	Excavation number	Provenance	Dimensions (cm)	Lines preserved	cpn
1	BM 30066	–	Ur, no provenance	5.5	1–14	c
2	BM 30060	–	As ex. 1	5.2	6–11	c
3	IM 92835	U 7797	SW side of temenos Larsa houses	4.7	1–5, 11–15	c
4	IM 92769	U 7845a	Trial Trench E, 3 metres below surface	6.5	1–23	c
5	IM 92770	U 7845b	As ex. 4	8.0	1–23	c
6	IM 92785	U 7845c	As ex. 4	10.0	5–11, 17–22	c
7	IM 92838	U 10105e	Royal Cemetery, top filling	6	1–13, 17	c
8	IM 92767	U 10108a	As ex. 7	5.6	14–23	c
9	IM 92786	U 10108b	As ex. 7	9	14–23	c
10	IM 92784	U 11615a	Royal Cemetery area	7.3	1–14, 16–23	c
11	IM 92766	U 11615b	As ex. 10	7.2	1–13, 19	c
12	IM 92765	U 11615c	As ex. 10	4.5	14–23	c
13	IM 92775	U 11615d	As ex. 10	6	1–13, 17	c
14	IM 92774	U 13663	Royal Cemetery area – Larsa rubbish	6	1–16, 18–23	c
15	IM 22884	U 16034	Mausoleum site, filling under Temenos wall chamber	5.1	1–13, 15–19	c
16	IM 22887	U 16538	No. 4, Straight Street, below burnt brick pavement	4.8	10–12, 14–23	c
17	IM 22895	U 17229	AH site	5	1–13	c
18	IM 123118	U 17851	Royal Cemetery area under house ruin level	12.4	1–23	c
19	IM 92790	U 18808c	–	9	6–12, 17–22	c
20	IM 92791	U qb	–	9	6–13, 18–22	c
21	BM 138347	U -	–	9.5	1–16, 20–23	c

COMMENTARY

Exs. 1–2 are from Taylor's excavations at Ur, exs. 3–21 from Woolley's. Exs. 3 and 7 were assigned as duplicates of E4.1.5.1 by Sollberger (see UET 8 p. 27 no. 15) but collation reveals that they are duplicates of this text.

Ex. 2, published here for the first time through the courtesy of C.B.F. Walker, is fragmentary. The extant inscription could be either E4.1.5.5 or E4.1.5.6. The fact that it is a fragment of a small headless cone suggests that it is a duplicate of the former.

BIBLIOGRAPHY

1905 King, CT 21 pl. 19 (ex. 1, copy)
1907 Thureau-Dangin, SAK p. 204 n. g (ex. 1, edition [treated as part of E4.1.5.6])
1928 Gadd, UET 1 no. 295 (exs. 4–6, composite copy, edition)
1929 Barton, RISA pp. 306–307 Libit-Ishtar 1 (ex. 1, edition [treated as part of E4.1.5.6])
1957 Edzard, Sumer 13 pp. 177 and 182 (ex. 15–17, study)
1961 Hallo, BiOr 18 p. 6 Lipit-Ištar 3 (study)
1965 Sollberger, UET 8 p. 27 no. 15 (exs. 3, 7, study) and pp. 33–34 no. 37 (exs. 6, 8–14, 18–20, study)
1968 Kärki, SKFZ p. 11 Lipiteštar 3 (edition)
1971 Sollberger and Kupper, IRSA ɪᴠA5a (translation)
1980 Kärki, SAKAZ 1 pp. 17–18 Lipiteštar 3 (edition)

TEXT

1) ^{d}*li-pí-it-eš*$_4$*-tár*
2) sipa-sun$_5$-na-
3) nibru.ᴋɪ
4) engar-zi-
5) uri$_5$.ᴋɪ-ma
6) mùš-nu-túm-mu-

1–13) I, Lipit-Eštar, humble shepherd of Nippur, true farmer of Ur, unceasing (provider) for Eridu, *en* priest suitable for Uruk, king of Isin, king of the land of Sumer and Akkad, favourite of the goddess Inanna,

7) eridu.KI-ga	
8) en me-te-	
9) unu.KI-ga	
10) lugal-ì-si-in.KI	
11) lugal-ki-en-gi-ki-uri	
12) šà-ge DU-a-	
13) ^{d}inanna-me-en	
14) u$_{4}$ nì-si-sá	14–16) when I established justice in the land of Sumer and Akkad,
15) ki-en-gi ki-uri	
16) mu-ni-gar-ra-a	
17) du$_{11}$-du$_{11}$-ga-	17–21) by the decree of the gods Enlil and Nanna, I restored Ur.
18) ^{d}en-líl-	
19) ^{d}nanna-ta	
20) uri$_{5}$.KI	
21) ki-bé ḫé-bí-gi$_{4}$	
22) *ḫi-ri-tum*-bi	22–23) I dug its moat.
23) ḫu-mu-ba-al	

6

A large number of cones, for the most part excavated by Woolley at Ur, deal with the construction of a *gipar* for the residence of En-nin-sún-zi, the *en* priestess of Ningubalag, daughter of Lipit-Eštar. The oracular designation of the same person figures in a year name of Lipit-Eštar (see R.M. Sigrist, RLA 7 p. 28).

CATALOGUE

Ex.	Museum number	Excavation number	Registration number	Provenance	Object	Dimensions (cm)	Lines preserved	cpn
1	BM 30063	Taylor's excavations at Ur, no excavation numbers	56-9-3,1476	Ur, –	Shaft	6.8	1–15, 20–26	c
2	YBC 2179	–		–	Head	10.9 dia.	1–28	c
3	YBC 2179	–		–	Shaft	10.3	1–15	c
4	BM 114181	Hall's excavations at Ur	1919-10-11,271	Ur	Shaft	6.0	4–8, 16–28	c
5	–	U 4		Trial Trench A, SE end	Cone	–	–	n
6	–	U 74		As ex. 5	Cone	10, 5.5 dia.	–	n
7	BM 119043	U 3109	1927-10-3,38	Edublalmaḫ	Head	9.6 dia.	1–11, 16–20	c
8	BM 119051	U 3245	1927-10-3,46	W side of Edublalmaḫ	Head	4.3 dia.	1–2, 14–15	c
9	BM 119053	U 3251	1927-10-3,48	SW of Edublalmaḫ	Cone	9.5	1–11, 16–25	c
10	IM 1529	U 6129		Loose in soil of EH	Head	10.4 dia.	–	n
11	–	U 6308		Surface of EH	Shaft	–	–	n
12	–	U 6325		KPS	Cone	–	–	n
13	IM 92808	U 6330		EH, grave 49	Shaft	7.8	16–28	c
14	IM 92824	U 6340a		–	Shaft	6.8	1–7	c
15	IM 92810	U 6340b		–	Shaft	4.8	16–28	c
16	IM 1606	U 6964		Eḫursag	Shaft	9.8	1–28	c
17	IM 3566/A	U 7702		Loose in soil of EM site and TT D and E	Shaft	11.0	1–28	c
18	IM 3566/B	U 7702		As ex. 17	Head	7.0 dia.	3–12	c
19	IM 3566/B	U 7702		As ex. 17	Shaft	9	1–15	c
20	IM 3566/C	U 7702		As ex. 17	Shaft	5.5	10, 16–28	c
21	IM 3566/D	U 7702		As ex. 17	Shaft	7.8	1–13, 15–28	c
22	IM 3566/E	U 7702		As ex. 17	Shaft	5.5	1–9, 11–15	c

Ex.	Museum number	Excavation number	Registration number	Provenance	Object	Dimensions (cm)	Lines preserved	cpn
23	IM 3566/F	U 7702		As ex. 17	Shaft	5.5	1-6, 15,23	c
24	IM -	U 10105a		Royal Cemetery top filling	Cone	–	–	n
25	IM 92809	U 10105b		As ex. 24	Shaft	9	8-13, 20-27	c
26	IM 92811	U 10105c		As ex. 24	Head	10.8 dia.	1-28	c
27	IM 92811	U 10105c		As ex. 24	Shaft	6.4	3-9	c
28	IM -	U 10105d		As ex. 24	Cone	–	–	c
29	IM -	U 10137		Royal Cemetery	Cone shaft	6	16-28	c
30	IM 22867/A	U 11607a		Royal Cemetery and NE city wall	Head	11 dia.	1-11, 14-28	c
31	IM 22867/A	U 11607a		As ex. 30	Shaft	6.5	1-15	c
32	IM 22867/B	U 11607b		As ex. 30	Head	8.2	16-28	c
33	IM 22867/B	U 11607b		As ex. 30	Shaft	8	1-15	c
34	IM 22867/C	U 11607c		As ex. 30	Shaft	9.5	1-28	c
35	IM 22867/D	U 11607d		As ex. 30	Shaft	7.2	19-27	c
36	–	U 13605a		Royal Cemetery, 6.7 m down	Cone frgm.	–	–	n
37	–	U 13605b		As ex. 36	Cone	–	–	n
38	–	U 13605c		As ex. 36	Cone	–	–	n
39	–	U 13605d		As ex. 36	Cone	–	–	n
40	–	U 13605e		As ex. 36	Cone	–	–	n
41	IM 92823	U 13605f		As ex. 36	Cone	–	–	n
42	IM 92822	U 13605g		As ex. 36	Shaft	5	5-9, 11-15	c
43	IM 92821	U 13605h		As ex. 36	Shaft	6	2-12	c
44	IM 92820	U 13605i		As ex. 36	Shaft	10.4	1-28	c
45	IM 92820	U 13605i		As ex. 36	Head	11 dia.	–	n
46	IM 92817	U 13605j		As ex. 36	Head	11 dia.	1-28	c
47	IM 92817	U 13605j		As ex. 36	Shaft	8	1-15	c
48	IM 92818	U 13605k		By the mud brick wall of the inner fort	Head	10.5 dia.	1-13, 16-26	c
49	IM 92818	U 13605k		As ex. 48	Shaft	4.5	1-11	c
50	IM 92819	U 13605l		–	Head	5.8 dia.	1-4, 16-19	c
51	IM 92815	U 13605m		–	Shaft	6.8	7-11	c
52	IM 92816	U 13605		–	Shaft	9.7	1-3, 10-13, 15-28	c
53	IM 22873	U 16012		Mausoleum site, filling top level	Shaft	5.5	16-28	c
54	IM 22880	U 16018		Ur, –	Head	9 dia.	2, 4-12, 16-24	c
55	IM 22880	U 16018		Ur, –	Shaft	6	1-3, 13-15	c
56	IM 23087/1	–		Ur, –	Head	10.5 dia.	1-28	c
57	IM 23087/1	–		Ur, –	Shaft	10	1-21	c
58	IM 23087/2	U 16055		Ur, –	Shaft	7.8	1-28	c
59	IM 22906	U 16276		Ur, –	Shaft	8.2	1-5, 15-20, 27-28	c
60	IM 22886	U 16537		No. 4 Straight Street below burnt brick pavement	Head	–	24-28	c
61	IM 22891	U 16588		AH, House 17, level II = nos. 10, 12 Straight Street	–	–	–	n
62	IM 22903	U 17644		Warad-Sîn bastion under the foundation of the steps	Shaft	9.1	1-12, 15-28	c
63	IM 22904	U 17864		Royal Cemetery about 4.5 m down, loose in rubbish close to south corner of Durgi building	Shaft	8.2	1-28	c
64	IM 22905	U 17884		As ex. 63	Head	10.5 dia.	1-28	c
65	IM 22905	U 17884		As ex. 63	Shaft	14	1-28	c
66	IM 92848	U 18808a		Extension of Royal Cemetery level 1600-1700	Shaft	7.5	5-15, 20-28	c
67	IM 92847	U 18808b		As ex. 66	Shaft	8	1-10, 16-28	c
68	IM -	U 18808c		As ex. 66	Shaft	–	–	n
69	BM 119057	U ta	1927-10-3,52		Head	4.3 dia.	16-22	c
70	IM 92849	U ua		–	Head	6 dia.	8-9, 21-28	c
71	IM 92849	U ua		–	Shaft	7.5	2-11	c
72	IM 92850	U va		–	Shaft	8	1-28	c
73	IM 92837	U wa		–	Shaft	6.2	1-2, 11, 16-28	c
74	IM 92836	U xa		–	Shaft	5.2	16-28	c
75	IM 26911	U -		–	Cone	–	11-15, 24-28	c
76	IM 26912	U -		–	Cone	–	1-15	c
77	BCM 287 '35D	U -		–	Shaft	10.0	1-28	c

COMMENTARY

Woolley (UE 7 p. 81), who is followed by Charpin (Le clergé d'Ur pp. 222–23), suggested that the *gipar* of En-nin-sún-zi is to be identified with the ruined structure found in the SM site. The distinction between uri$_5$ and úri noted in the scores is not recorded in the critical apparatus. Exs. 2 and 3 were purchased.

BIBLIOGRAPHY

1861 1 R pl. 5 no. XVIII (ex. 1, copy)
1872 G. Smith, TSBA 1 pp. 37–38 (ex. 1, translation)
1874 Lenormant, Études accadiennes 2 pp. 330 and 338
1892 Winckler, KB 3/1 pp. 86–87 Libit-Ištar (ex. 1, edition)
1899 Bezold, Cat. 5 p. 2234 (ex. 1, study)
1905 Thureau-Dangin, ISA pp. 290–91 Lipit-ištar (ex. 1, edition)
1905 King, CT 21 pl. 18 (ex. 1, copy)
1907 Thureau-Dangin, SAK pp. 204–205 Lipit-ištar (ex. 1, edition)
1915 Clay, YOS 1 no. 27 (ex. 2, copy)
1928 Gadd, UET 1 no. 106 (exs. 4–15, composite copy, edition)
1929 Barton, RISA pp. 370–71 Libit-Ishtar 1 (edition)
1957 Edzard, Sumer 13 pp. 176 and 182 (exs. 10, 16–23, 30–35, 53–58, 60–65, 75–76, study)
1961 Hallo, BiOr 18 p. 6 Lipit-Ištar 4 (study)
1965 Sollberger, UET 8 pp. 26–27 no. 14 (exs. 17–29, 36–51, 66–69, study)
1968 Kärki, SKFZ pp. 11–12 Lipiteštar 4 (edition)
1976 Woolley and Mallowan, UE 7 p. 81 (provenance)
1979 George, Iraq 41 p. 122 no. 28 (ex. 77, study)
1980 Kärki, SAKAZ 1 pp. 18–19 Lipiteštar 4 (edition)
1986 Charpin, Le clergé d'Ur pp. 220–21 (provenance, edition)

TEXT

1) ^{d}*li-pí-it-eš*$_4$*-tár*
2) sipa-sun$_5$-na-
3) nibru.KI
4) engar-zi-
5) uri$_5$.KI-ma
6) mùš-nu-túm-mu-
7) eridu.KI-ga
8) en me-te-
9) unu.KI-ga
10) lugal-ì-si-in.KI-na
11) lugal-ki-en-gi-ki-uri
12) šà-ge DU-a-
13) ^{d}inanna-ke$_4$

1–13) Lipit-Eštar, humble shepherd of Nippur, true farmer of Ur, unceasing (provider) for Eridu, *en* priest suitable for Uruk, king of Isin, king of the land of Sumer and Akkad, favourite of the goddess Inanna,

14) é-gi$_6$-pàr
15) en-nin-sún-zi
16) en-^{d}nin-gubalag
17) uri$_5$.KI-ma
18) agrig-zi-
19) ^{d}nin-é-ì-gára-ka
20) KA-nam-šita$_x$(REC 316)-zi du$_7$
21) gá-bur-ra-ka
22) a-ra-zu-ni-šè gub-ba
23) dumu-ki-ág-gá-ni-ir

14–23) the *gipar* house for En-nin-sun-zi, the *en* priestess of the god Ningubalag in Ur, the true stewardess of the goddess Nineigara, the one suited for true words of supplication, who stands (making) prayers for him in the Gabura (temple), for his beloved daughter,

24) u$_4$ nì-si-sá
25) ki-en-gi-ki-uri-a
26) i-ni-in-gar-ra-a

24–26) when he established justice in the land of Sumer and Akkad,

27) šà-uri$_5$.KI-ma-ka
28) mu-na-dù

27–28) he built it for her in Ur.

20.2 Clay mistakenly omits šita$_x$.

7

An inscription found on two cones deals with the construction by Lamassatum, the mother of Lipit-Eštar, of a storehouse for the goddess Inanna of Mur(um).

CATALOGUE

Ex.	Museum number	Object	Dimensions (cm)	Lines preserved	cpn
1	Private Collection in France, no. 883	Head	10.5 dia.	1–16	c
2	Idem. no. 883	Shaft	15.5	1–16	c
3	Idem. no. 884	Head	11.5	7–11, 13–16	c
4	Idem. no. 884	Shaft	16.8	2–11, 13–16	c

COMMENTARY

The cones were collated by J.-J. Glassner.

The name Mur probably refers to the city of Mur(um) located on the Araḫtum canal north-west of Isin. It was the cult centre of the goddess Ningilin. Although the cones do not have a known provenance, the fact that the inscription says that the storehouse stood in Isin indicates that they came from that city.

BIBLIOGRAPHY

1983 Glassner, JCS 35 pp. 210 and 216 (exs. 1–2, composite copy, study)

TEXT

1) ^{d}inanna-
2) mu-ur$_5$.KI
3) ^{d}inanna-ka-ni(*)-ir
4) nam-ti-
5) ^{d}*li-pí-it-eš$_4$-tár*
6) sipa giš-tuk-
7) dingir-re-e-ne
8) lugal-ki-en-gi-ki-uri
9) dam-^{d}inanna-ka-šè
10) *la-ma-sà-tum*
11) ama-ni
12) ù nam-ti-la-ni-šè
13) é-mar-uru$_5$
14) é-šutum-ki-ág-gá-ni
15) šà-ì-si-in.KI-na-ka
16) mu-na-dù

1–3) For the goddess Inanna of Mur(um), her personal goddess,

4–9) for the life of Lipit-Eštar, the shepherd who heeds the gods, king of the land of Sumer and Akkad, spouse of the goddess Inanna,

10–12) and for her own life, Lamassatum, his (Lipit-Eštar's) mother,

13–16) built for her the Emaruru ('House of the flood'), her beloved storehouse in Isin.

3.1–2 ^{d}ḪU for ^{d}inanna. **3** Copy: -ir. **16**.3–4 mu-dù.

8

An eye-stone in the Yale collection deals with a dedication by Lipit-Eštar to the goddess Ninlil.

COMMENTARY

The text is on YBC 2374, purchased in Mosul, a highly polished eye-stone of chalcedony and agate, 2.8 × 2.4 × 0.9 cm. The inscription was collated.

In line 3, sag-du is a phonetic writing for Sumerian sag-dù, Akkadian *bān qaqqadīia*.

BIBLIOGRAPHY

1925 Barton, JAOS 45 pp. 154–55 (copy, edition)
1929 Barton, RISA pp. 306–307 Libit-Ishtar 3 (edition)
1937 Stephens, YOS 9 no. 68 (copy)
1961 Hallo, BiOr 18 p. 6 Lipit-Ištar 7 (study)
1968 Kärki, SKFZ pp. 12–13 Lipiteštar 7 (edition)
1971 Sollberger and Kupper, IRSA IVA5d (translation)
1980 Kärki, SAKAZ 1 pp. 21–22 Lipiteštar 7 (edition)

TEXT

1) ^{d}nin-líl
2) nin-dingir-re-e-ne
3) ^{d}inanna sag-du-gá
4) ama-tú-mu-ra
5) ^{d}*li-pí-it-eš$_4$-tár*
6) lugal-ki-en-gi-ki-uri-me-en
7) u$_4$ nì-si-sá
8) ki-en-gi-ki-uri-a
9) i-ni-in-gar-ra-a
10) nam-ti-mu-šè
11) a mu-na-ru

1–4) To the goddess Ninlil, queen of the gods, goddess who created me (and) mother who gave birth to me,

5–6) I, Lipit-Eštar, king of the land of Sumer and Akkad,
7–9) when I established justice in the land of Sumer and Akkad,

10–11) dedicated this (eye-stone) to her for my own life.

2001

A tablet excavated by Woolley at Ur has a seal impression of a certain Aa-duga, servant of Lipit-Eštar.

COMMENTARY

The present location of the tablet has not been determined; the excavation no. is U 6874. It comes from the Eḫursag, 'loose'. The seal impression is 2.6 × 2.3 cm, and was not collated.

BIBLIOGRAPHY

1928 Gadd, UET 1 no. 107 (copy, edition)
1929 Barton, RISA pp. 372–73 Libit-Ishtar 3 (edition)
1951 Legrain, UE 10 no. 440 (photo, translation, study)
1961 Hallo, BiOr 18 p. 6 Lipit-Ištar 8 (study)
1968 Kärki, SKFZ p. 13 Lipiteštar 8 (edition)
1971 Sollberger and Kupper, IRSA ɪᴠA5e (translation)
1976 Woolley and Mallowan, UE 7 p. 226 (provenance)
1980 Kärki, SAKAZ 1 p. 22 Lipiteštar 8 (edition)

TEXT

1) ^{d}*li-pí-it-eš$_4$-tár*
2) lugal-kala-ga
3) lugal-uri$_5$.ᴋɪ-ma
4) a-a-du$_{10}$-ga
5) gudu$_4$-abzu-^{d}nanna
6) ù šita$_x$(REC 316)-èš
7) dumu-du$_{11}$-ga-zi-da
8) ir$_{11}$-zu

1) Lipit-Eštar,
2) mighty king,
3) king of Ur,
4) Aa-duga,
5) *gudapsûm* priest of the god Nanna
6) and *šita-eš* priest,
7) son of Duga-zida,
8) your servant.

2002

A seal impression on a tablet excavated by Woolley at Ur mentions Iddin-Dagān-waqar, servant of Lipit-Eštar.

COMMENTARY

The tablet in the University Museum, Philadelphia was found among a group of tablets under the wall of Kudur-mabuk dividing Enunmaḫ room 32 from Emurianabak room 5. Its excavation no. is U 2583. The dimensions of the impression are 3.5×1.9 cm. The transliteration is from the copy of Legrain – the impression is now obliterated.

In line 3, parallels with the titulary of Išbi-Erra would suggest a reading lugal-ma-da-na 'lord of his land'. Unfortunately, the seal impression was not available for collation.

BIBLIOGRAPHY

1928 Gadd, UET 1 no. 108 (copy, edition)
1929 Barton, RISA pp. 372–73 Libit-Ishtar 3 (edition)
1957 Edzard, Zwischenzeit p. 95 n. 460 (study)
1961 Hallo, BiOr 18 p. 6 Lipit-Ištar 9 (study)
1968 Kärki, SKFZ p. 13 Lipiteštar 9 (edition)
1971 Sollberger and Kupper, IRSA ɪᴠA5f (translation)
1976 Woolley and Mallowan, UE 7 pp. 218–19 (provenance)
1976 Loding, JCS 28 pp. 234 and 242 no. 6 (copy, study)
1980 Kärki, SAKAZ 1 p. 22 Lipiteštar 9 (edition)
1986 Charpin, Le clergé d'Ur p. 241 n. 6 (study)

TEXT

1) ^{d}*li-pí-it-eš$_4$-tár*
2) lugal-kala-ga
3) lugal-ma-da
4) ^{d}*i-din-*^{d}*da-gan-wa-qar*
5) ab-a-ab-da
6) dumu-^{d}nanna-ì-sa$_6$
7) ir$_{11}$-zu

1) Lipit-Eštar,
2) mighty king,
3) king of the land,
4) Iddin-Dagān-waqar,
5) *ababdûm* official,
6) son of Nanna-isa,
7) your servant.

2003

A tablet excavated by Woolley at Ur has the seal impression of a servant of Lipit-Eštar whose name is not fully preserved.

COMMENTARY

The location of the tablet is not known; the excavation no. is U 6720. The tablet is from the Gipar-ku; dimensions of the impression are 3.1 × 1.5 cm. The inscription was not collated.

BIBLIOGRAPHY

1928 Gadd, UET 1 no. 109 (copy, edition)
1929 Barton, RISA pp. 372–73 Libit-Ishtar 4 (edition)
1961 Hallo, BiOr 18 p. 6 Lipit-Ištar 10 (study)
1968 Kärki, SKFZ p. 13 Lipiteštar 10 (edition)
1976 Woolley and Mallowan, UE 7 p. 255 (provenance)
1980 Kärki, SAKAZ 1 p. 23 Lipiteštar 10 (edition)

TEXT

1) [d]*li-pí-it-eš$_4$-tár*
2) lugal-kala-ga
3) lugal-uri$_5$.KI-ma
4) ur-[...]
5) dub-sar
6) dumu-lú-[d]inanna
7) ir$_{11}$-zu

1) Lipit-Eštar,
2) mighty king,
3) king of Ur,
4) Ur-[...],
5) scribe,
6) son of Lu-Inanna,
7) your servant.

2004

A tablet excavated at Ur bears a partially preserved seal impression probably belonging to a servant of Lipit-Eštar.

COMMENTARY

The impression, published as UET 5 no. 778, may be in the Iraq Museum. It was not located and hence not collated.

BIBLIOGRAPHY

1953 Figulla and Martin, UET 5 no. 778 (copy)

TEXT

1) ^{d}*li-pí-it-eš$_4$-tár*	1) Lipit-Eštar,
2) lugal-kala-ga	2) mighty king,
Lacuna	Lacuna

Ur-Ninurta

E4.1.6

According to the Sumerian King List, Ur-Ninurta ruled 28 years. Two inscriptions are extant for the king.

1

The standard inscription of Ur-Ninurta is found in a 13-line brick which is generally inscribed, occasionally stamped. It is at present known from Nippur, Isin, Uruk, and Išān Ḥāfudh.

CATALOGUE

Ex.	Museum number	Excavation number	Registration number	Provenance	Dimensions (cm)	Lines preserved	cpn
1	BM 90378	From Rawlinson's collections	51-10-9,77	Nippur	–	7-13	c
2	BM 90726	As ex. 1	51-10-9,85	Nippur	21.5×16.0×7.0	10-13	c
3	BM 90727+90728	As ex. 1	51-10-9,90+88	Nippur	17.0×14.5×6.0	6-11	c
4	BM 90729	As ex. 1	51-10-9,83	Nippur	20.0×14.0×6.5	1-3	c
5	BM 90730	As ex. 1	51-10-9,91	Nippur	18.0×15.5×6.0	1-7	c
6	BM 90814	As ex. 1	51-10-9,76	Nippur	22.5×22.5	5-13	c
7	EŞ 1060	From Hilprecht expedition		Nippur	20.5×9.3	–	n
8	EŞ 1061	As ex. 7		Nippur	22.0×9.8	1-13	p
9	EŞ 1063	As ex. 7		Nippur, from c. 10 m below surface underneath SE buttress of ziqqurrat from a pavement of Ur-Ninurta	31.0×15.0×7.0	1-13	p
10	EŞ 8952	As ex. 7		Nippur	32.5×26.7×6.6	2-13	p
11	EŞ 8953	As ex. 7		Nippur	31.0×31.0×7.0		p
12	EŞ 8955	As ex. 7		Nippur	19.4×11.5×6.5	8-13	p
13	EŞ 8956	As ex. 7		Nippur	31.0×15.0×7.0	1-13	p
14	EŞ 8957	As ex. 7		Nippur	31.0×16.0×7.0	1-13	p
15	EŞ 8959	As ex. 7		Nippur	33.0×15.0×7.3	1-13	p
16	EŞ 8960	As ex. 7		Nippur	30.4×15.0×7.8	1-13	p
17	Istanbul no number	As ex. 7		Nippur	32.0×32.0×8.0	1-13	p
18	Istanbul no number	As ex. 7		Nippur	15.5×10.5×7.0	11-13	p
19	Istanbul no number, on display	As ex. 7		Nippur	–	1-13	p
20	Istanbul no number	As ex. 7		Nippur	–	–	n
21	Istanbul no number	As ex. 7		Nippur	–	–	n
22	Istanbul no number	As ex. 7		Nippur	–	–	n
23	Istanbul no number	As ex. 7		Nippur	–	–	n
24	CBS 8651	As ex. 7		Nippur	15.5×14.0×6.5		n
25	CBS 8652	As ex. 7		Nippur	17.5×15.0×6.5	–	n
26	UM 84-26-45	As ex. 7		Nippur	32.0×22.0×8.0	–	n
27	CBS 9021	As ex. 7		Found out of place in a later structure on the SE side of the ziqqurrat	32.0×33.0×8.0	1-13	n
28	UM 84-26-39	As ex. 7		Nippur	15.5×11.0×7.5	1-3	n
29	UM 84-26-40	As ex. 7		Nippur	17.0×8.0×6.5	8-13	n

Ex.	Museum number	Excavation number	Registration number	Provenance	Dimensions (cm)	Lines preserved	cpn
30	UM 84-26-41	As ex. 7		Nippur	34.0×34.0×6.5	1-13	n
31	UM 84-26-45	As ex. 7		Nippur	32.0×22.0×7.5	–	n
32	IM 56105	2N-T46		Nippur, EN surface	10.4×22.5	1-13	n
33	IM -	5N-T691		Nippur, ziqqurrat east stairs from fill	–	1-13	n
34	IM 61771	6N-T1140		Nippur, ZB 4	–	1-13	n
35	A 31072	6N-T1141		Nippur, ZB 4	32.0×31.2×6.7	1-13	c
36	–	–	–	Nippur, in room 13a of Enlil temple from a square base	–	–	n
37	–	–	–	From street 22 beside Enlil temple, revetment over drain	–	–	n
38	IM 25595	–	–	–	–	–	n
39	IM 26135	–	–	–	–	–	n
40	IM 78634	IB 937		Isin, from fill in the Gula temple 85 N, 122 W	33.0×33.0×8.0	–	n
41	Ash 1924,626			From Isin or Nippur, Oxford-Field Museum expedition	32.0×32.0×7.0	1-13	c
42	–	W 3365		Uruk, Qb/c xvi 1, in rubble	7 thick	1-9	n
43	–	–	–	Išān Ḥāfudh	–	1-13	n
44	VA 3039	–	–	–	31.5×15.5	1-13	n
45	VA 3130	–	–	–	32.0×13.0	1-13	c
46	Australian Institute of Archaeology IA7.1000	–	–	–	–	1-11	p
47	Royal Albert Memorial Museum, Exeter 366+399, 1974	–	–	–	–	1-6	c

COMMENTARY

Exs. 1-6, from Rawlinson's collections, presumably came from Nippur, provenance unknown. Exs. 7-31 all came from the Hilprecht expedition to Nippur. Peters (Nippur 2 pp. 125 and 157) describes the finding of a courtyard of the Ekur temple at Nippur paved with bricks of Ur-Ninurta. Ex. 9 (EŞ 1063) is known to have come from this pavement and several of the other bricks listed here probably come from the same pavement. Some of them, however, such as ex. 27, are known to have come from other locations at Nippur. Exs. 32-37 come from the more recent American expedition to Nippur, ex. 40 from Isin, ex. 41 from Isin or Nippur. The existence of ex. 42, from Uruk, suggests that Ur-Ninurta may have controlled that city for awhile. Ex. 43 is from Išān Ḥāfudh, a small site south-east of Tell Drehem.

BIBLIOGRAPHY

1861 1 R pl. 5 no. xxiv (ex. 6, copy)
1872 G. Smith, TSBA 1 p. 37 (exs. 1-6, translation)
1874 Lenormant, Études accadiennes 2 p. 328
1875 Lenormant, Choix no. 65 (ex. 6, copy)
1891 4 R² pl. 35 no. 5 (ex. 6, copy [restored from exs. 1-5])
1892 Winckler, KB 3/1 pp. 84-85 Gamil-Ninib (edition)
1893 Hilprecht, BE 1/1 no. 18 (ex. 27, provenance, copy, study)
1896 Hilprecht, BE 1/2 no. 65 (ex. 9, provenance, copy, study)
1897 Peters, Nippur 2 pp. 125 and 157 (provenance, study), pl. i beside p. 374 (photo), and p. 375 (provenance, study)
1900 Radau, EBH p. 230 (edition)
1903 Hilprecht, Explorations p. 378 (provenance, translation)
1905 Thureau-Dangin, ISA pp. 290-91 Ur-nin-ib (edition)
1907 Thureau-Dangin, SAK pp. 204-205 Ur-nin-ib (edition)
1922 BM Guide p. 61 no. 119 (ex. 6, study)
1926 Dougherty, BASOR 23 p. 24 (ex. 43, photo)
1927 Dougherty, AASOR 7 p. 83 no. 26 (ex. 43, photo)
1929 Barton, RISA pp. 306-307 Ur-Ninurta 1 (edition)
1930 Schott, Eanna no. 6 (ex. 42, copy, edition)
1961 Hallo, BiOr 18 p. 6 Ur-Ninurta 1 (study)
1967 McCown, Nippur 1 p. 8 (ex. 35, provenance), p. 11 (ex. 36, provenance), and p. 20 (ex. 32, provenance)
1968 Kärki, SKFZ pp. 13-14 Urninurta 1 (edition)
1971 Sollberger and Kupper, IRSA ivA6a (translation)
1980 Kärki, SAKAZ 1 pp. 23 Urninurta 1 (edition)

1981 Grégoire, MVN 10 no. 26 (ex. 41, copy, translation, study)
1981 Walker, CBI no. 34 (exs. 1–6, 41, study)
1981 Walker in Hrouda, Isin 2 p. 94 (ex. 39, study)
1985 Behrens, JCS 37 pp. 234–35 no. 25 (exs. 24–31, study)

TEXT

1) ^{d}ur-^{d}nin-urta
2) sipa nì-nam-íl-
3) nibru.KI
4) na-gada-
5) uri_5.KI-ma
6) išib-šu-sikil-
7) eridu.KI-ga
8) en-še-ga-
9) unu.KI-ga
10) lugal-ì-si-in.KI-na
11) lugal-ki-en-gi-ki-uri
12) dam-igi-íl-la-
13) ^{d}inanna

1) Ur-Ninurta,
2–3) shepherd who offers everything for Nippur,
4–5) herdsman of Ur,
6–7) *išippum* priest with clean hands for Eridu,
8–9) favourite *en* priest of Uruk,
10) king of Isin,
11) king of the land of Sumer and Akkad,
12–13) spouse chosen by the goddess Inanna.

2

A copy of an inscription of Ur-Ninurta on a tablet excavated at Nippur deals with the setting up, in the courtyard of Ninlil's Gagiššua temple, of an image of the king holding an offering of a votive goat (máš-kadra).

COMMENTARY

The tablet is CBS 12694, found at Nippur by the Hilprecht expedition in the third season out of place in a later structure on the south-east side of the ziqqurrat. The tablet measures 30.5×20×6.5 cm and the inscription was collated.

The tablet is a Sammeltafel with at least two inscriptions. The first deals with Šū-Sîn's fashioning of a goat figurine, booty from Anšan, and will be edited in RIME 3. The second text deals with the fashioning of the king's image holding a goat. That there was a statue of the king in Nippur of this type is confirmed by later *sattukku* offering lists from Nippur which record offerings for the alam-máš-gaba 'image of the goat (held at) the breast' (see Sigrist, Sattukku p. 149).

Col. vi 8′–9′ are restored from line 302 of the hymn Enlil Diriše (ms. Eichler) which is identical to them. The verb tur-tur in col. vi 9′ means 'to clasp, hold tightly' (Civil).

BIBLIOGRAPHY

1914 Poebel, PBS 5 no. 68 (copy)
1914 Poebel, PBS 4/1 pp. 137–38 (study)
1928 de Genouillac, RA 25 p. 143 (study)
1936 Cameron, Iran p. 65 n. 63 (study)
1949 Falkenstein, ZA 49 p. 81 and n. 3 (study)
1961 Hallo, BiOr 18 p. 6 Ur-Ninurta 2 (study)
1968 Kärki, SKFZ pp. 14–16 Urninurta 2 (edition)
1980 Kärki, SAKAZ 1 pp. 24–26 Urninurta 2 (edition)

TEXT

Col. i

16′) ^{d}nin-líl nin-maḫ-
17′) ⌜^{d}a⌝-nun-ke$_{4}$-ne pa-è
18′) [...] an-[k]i-a
19′) [...] x x gin$_{7}$
20′) [...] x
Lacuna

i 16′–20′) (For) the goddess Ninlil, supreme lady of the Anuna gods, radiant one, ... of heaven and [ea]rth, like ...,

Col. ii

1′) [...] x [...]
2′) [x] KI x [...]
3′) bára-bára-bi [...]
4′) nam-lugal-šè [...]
5′) men gidri sum-m[a-àm]

ii 1′–5′) ... their chapels/daises [...] for kingship [...] granted the crown and the sceptre

6′) ama-gal-^{d}a-nun-[ke$_{4}$-ne]
7′) nin-ki-ùr-ra [...]
8′) é-kur èš-maḫ-[a]
9′) me-bi bar-tam-e-⌜dè⌝
10′) èš-nibru.KI du[r-an-ki-ka]
11′) šu-luḫ-bi sikil-⌜e⌝-[dè]
12′) garza šu-ta š[ub-ba-bé]
13′) dalla-maḫ-⌜è⌝-[dè]
14′) nibru.KI máš-sa[g-kalam-ma]
15′) ki-bé gi$_{4}$-gi$_{4}$-[dè]

ii 6′–15′) for the great mother of the Anuna gods, the lady of the Kiur [...], in order to choose the *me*s of the Ekur, the supreme shrine, [in order] to purify the cleansing rites of shrine Nippur, the bon[d of heaven and earth, in order] to make the neg[lected] rites appear magnificently, [in order] to restore Nippur, the lea[d] goat [of the nation],

16′) ur-^{d}nin-urta-k[e$_{4}$]
17′) é-kur-šè gub-ba-[àm]
18′) ^{d}en-líl lugal-kur-kur-[ra-ke$_{4}$]
19′) un-dagal-šár-ra-d[a]
20′) igi mi-ni-in-í[l]
21′) zi-dè-⌜eš bí⌝-[in-pà]
Lacuna

ii 16′–21′) it was Ur-Ninurta, who devoted himself to the Ekur, upon whom the god Enlil, king of the foreign lands, look[ed] am[ong] the broad, numerous people and truly [chose].

Col. iii–v (not preserved)

iii–v) (not preserved)

Col. vi

1′) x x x x [...]
2′) an ^{d}en-líl ^{d}nin-líl x
3′) [nì]-ḫul im-ta-bu-úr

vi 1′–3′) (I, Ur-Ninurta)..., (for) the gods An, Enlil, (and) Ninlil removed evil from ...

4′) [é]-kur-za-gìn uru x ki x x
5′) [x] mu-ne-su$_{8}$

vi 4′–5′) and set up for them a ... (*in*) the shining [E]kur, (*in*) the ... city

6′) [URUDU].alam me-dím-bi
7′) mùš-me-gá sì-ga
8′) máš-ka[dr]a-ka
9′) im-tur-tur-re
10′) nam-šita$_{x}$(REC 316)-mu-šè gub-ba
11′) kisal-maḫ-gá-giš-šú-a-k[a]
12′) me-te-bi mu-na-dím

vi 6′–12′) I fashioned (for Ninlil) a [copper] image, whose form was endowed with my face, clasping a votive kid, standing to make supplications for me, an ornament of the main courtyard of the Gagiššua (temple).

13′) nam-ti-la-mu-šè
14′) a mu-na-ru

vi 13′–14′) I dedicated it to her for my own life.

15′) lú á-nì-ḫul-dím-m[a]
16′) ⌜íb⌝-[š]i-ág-ge$_{26}$-a
17′) [nì-dím]-m[a-m]u
18′) [íb-zi-re-a]
Lacuna

vi 15′–18′) (As for) the man who gives orders to do evil against it, who [destroys m]y [handi]work

Edge
1) [x] x-maḫ ^{d}en-líl-lá-ke_4
2) x x x mu-pà-da-né
3) [é-k]ur-ta KA [ḫ]é-mi-íb-gi_4-gi_4
4) [^{d}n]in-urta ur-sag-kala-ga-^{d}en-líl-lá
5) maškim ⟨nu⟩-ku_5-ru-bi ḫ[é-a]
6) u_4-da-rí-[šè]

edge 1–6) ... the supreme ... of the god Enlil, may the ... which proclaims his name be revoked from the [Ek]ur. M[ay the god N]inurta, the mighty champion of the god Enlil, forever b[e] its (the curse's) evil spirit who cannot be countermanded.

Būr-Sîn

E4.1.7

According to the Sumerian King List Būr-Sîn reigned 21 years.

1

The standard inscription of Būr-Sîn occurs in 10-line inscribed or stamped bricks known from Nippur and Isin.

CATALOGUE

Ex.	Museum number	Excavation number	Provenance	Dimensions (cm)	Lines preserved	cpn
1	CBS 8642	Hilprecht expedition	Nippur, found out of place in a later structure on the SE side of the ziqqurrat	30.0 × 18.0 × 6.0	1–10	n
2	EŞ 1062	As ex. 1	Nippur, –	–	1–10	p
3	IM -	5N-T694	Nippur, fill below SB level II, fill of the Parthian platform of the Inanna temple	–	–	n
4	MMA 59.41.84	6N-T1139	Nippur, ZB 4 (from a courtyard of the ziqqurrat, room 4)	28.5 × 17.0 × 7.0	1–6	c
5	–	Joint Chicago-Pennsylvania expedition	Nippur, on the SE side of street 22 from a brick revetment	–	–	n
6	IM 25596	–	(?)	–	–	n
7	IM 76546	–	Isin, surface find in rubble	32/33 × 36.5 × 8.0	–	n
8	–	–	Isin, 11 examples from the fill of the Gula temple, none registered	–	–	n

COMMENTARY

Exs. 1–2 are from the Hilprecht expedition to Nippur, exs. 3–5 from the Joint Chicago-Pennsylvania expedition to that city. Exs. 7–8 were found by the Munich expedition to Isin.

BIBLIOGRAPHY

1893 Hilprecht, BE 1/1 no. 19 (ex. 1, provenance, copy, study)
1905 Thureau-Dangin, ISA pp. 290–91 Pûr-sin a (edition)
1907 Thureau-Dangin, SAK pp. 204–205 Pûr-sin a (edition)
1900 Radau, EBH p. 231 (translation)
1929 Barton, RISA pp. 308–309 Bur-Sin 1 (edition)
1961 Hallo, BiOr 18 p. 6 Bur-Sin 1 (study)
1967 McCown, Nippur 1 p. 8 (ex. 5, provenance)
1968 Kärki, SKFZ p. 16 Būrsîn 1 (edition)
1971 Sollberger and Kupper, IRSA IVA7a (translation)
1977 Edzard and Wilcke in Hrouda, Isin 1 p. 87 (ex. 7, study)
1980 Kärki, SAKAZ 1 p. 26 Būrsîn 1 (edition)
1981 Walker in Hrouda, Isin 2 p. 94 (ex. 8, study)
1985 Behrens, JCS 37 p. 235 no. 26 (ex. 1, study)

TEXT

1) ^{d}*bur*-^{d}EN.ZU
2) sipa šà-nibru.KI du_{10}-du_{10}
3) engar-kala-ga-
4) úri.KI-ma
5) giš-ḫur-eridu.KI-ga ki-bé gi_4
6) en-me-a-túm-ma-
7) unu.KI-ga
8) lugal-ì-si-in.KI-na
9) lugal-ki-en-gi-ki-uri
10) dam me-te-úr-kù-^{d}inanna

1) Būr-Sîn,
2) shepherd who makes Nippur content,
3–4) mighty farmer of Ur,

5) who restores the designs of Eridu,
6–7) *en* priest fit for the *me*s, for Uruk,

8) king of Isin,
9) king of the land of Sumer and Akkad,
10) spouse suitable for the shining knee of the goddess Inanna.

2

This inscription is found on a statuette fragment dedicated to the goddess Inanna by Būr-Sîn.

COMMENTARY

The fragment is of red-brown agate and was in the private possession of Frau G. Strauss, present location unknown. It measures 2×3.5×2 cm, and the inscription was not collated.

BIBLIOGRAPHY

1927 Weidner, AfO 4 pp. 133–34 (photo, copy, edition)
1961 Hallo, BiOr 18 p. 6 Bur-Sin 2 (study)
1968 Kärki, SKFZ pp. 16–17 Būrsîn 2 (edition)
1971 Sollberger and Kupper, IRSA IVA7b (translation)
1980 Kärki, SAKAZ 1 pp. 26–27 Būrsîn 2 (edition)

TEXT

1) ^{d}inanna
2) nin-a-ni-ir
3) ^{d}*bur*-^{d}EN.ZU
4) lugal-kala-ga
5) lugal-ki-en-gi-ki-uri
6) mu-na-dí[m]
7) nam-ti-la-ni-šè
8) a mu-na-[ru]

1–2) For the goddess Inanna, his lady,

3–5) Būr-Sîn, mighty king, king of the land of Sumer and Akkad,

6) fashion[ed] (this statuette) for her.
7–8) He dedic[ated] it to her for his own life.

3

A small plate was dedicated by Nanāia-ibsa, the *lukur* priestess, for the life of Būr-Sîn.

COMMENTARY

The piece is the Lagre Böhl collection LB 2120, provenance unknown. It is an agate plate 3.3 × 7.6 × 0.4 cm. The inscription was collated.

BIBLIOGRAPHY

1957 van Dijk, TLB 2 no. 17 (copy)
1961 Hallo, BiOr 18 p. 6 Bur-Sin 3 (study)
1968 Kärki, SKFZ p. 17 Būrsîn 3 (edition)
1971 Sollberger and Kupper, IRSA ɪᴠA7c (translation)
1980 Kärki, SAKAZ 1 p. 27 Būrsîn 3 (edition)

TEXT

1)	^{d}na-na-a	1–2) For the goddess Nanāia, her lady,
2)	nin-a-ni-ir	
3)	nam-ti	3–7) for the life of Būr-Sîn, king of the land of Sumer and Akkad, beloved of the goddesses In[anna] and Nanāia,
4)	^{d}*bur*-^{d}EN.ZU	
5)	lugal-ki-en-gi-ki-uri	
6)	ki-ág-^{d}in[anna]	
7)	ù ^{d}na-na-a-⸢šè⸣	
8)	^{d}na-na-a-íb-sá	8–10) and for her own life, Nanāia-ibsa, his beloved travelling escort,
9)	lukur-ki-ág-kaskal-la-ka-né	
10)	ù nam-ti-la-ni-šè	
11)	a mu-na-ru	11) dedicated (this plate) to her.
12)	lú a-gú-bi	12–17) (As for) the man who takes away this *agu* (plate) from the body of the goddess Nanāia and either uses it for offerings or destroys it,
13)	su-^{d}na-na-a-ta	
14)	íb-ta-ab-zi-zi-a	
15)	šà-ge-kára-šè	
16)	ù in-gá-gá-a	
17)	ù íb-zi-re-⸢a⸣	
18)	^{d}na-na-a	18–20) may the goddess Nanāia, my lady, inflict him with a terrible curse.
19)	nin-mu	
20)	áš-gig-ga ḫé-⸢en⸣-dab	

2001

This inscription is a dedication of a dog figurine by Enlil-ennam to the goddess Ninisina for the life of Būr-Sîn.

COMMENTARY

The inscription is on the back of a stone dog figurine, provenance alleged to be Hamadan. The height is about 17 cm. It was shown to the British Museum and subsequently sold by Sotheby's in 1983. The transliteration is given through the courtesy of E. Sollberger.

For line 3 cf. E4.2.13.22 line 3: zi-gál kalam-dím-dím-me, also an epithet of Ninisina.

TEXT

1) ^{d}nin-in-si.KI-na
2) nin-a-ni-ir
3) nin-lú-ku$_5$-da(?)-dím-dí[m]
4) nam-ti-
5) ^{d}*bur*-^{d}EN.ZU
6) lugal-kala-ga
7) lugal-ì-si-in.KI-na
8) ^{d}*en-líl-en-nam*
9) dumu-*zi-bu-ú-ni*
10) a mu-na-ru

1–3) For the goddess Ninisina, his lady, lady who creates ...,

4–7) for the life of Būr-Sîn, mighty king, king of Isin,

8–10) Enlil-ennam, son of Zibūni dedicated (this dog) to her.

2002

A tablet excavated at Nippur has the seal of a servant of Būr-Sîn.

COMMENTARY

The tablet is NBC 11285 (incorrectly published as NBC 11205), excavation no. 5N–T418, from Sounding B at Nippur, locus 13 (east) and locus 14, that is, fill below the original Parthian version of the Inanna temple at the north-west end of the platform. The impression measures 2.5 × 1.2 cm and was collated. The tablet itself dates to the fifth year of Būr-Sîn.

BIBLIOGRAPHY

1977 Sigrist, RA 71 p. 124 (copy, transliteration)

TEXT

1) ^{d}*bur*-^{d}EN.ZU
2) lugal-kala-ga
3) lugal-ki-en-gi-ki-uri
4) ab-ba-mu
5) dub-sar
6) dumu-lú-^{d}utu
7) ìr-zu

1) Būr-Sîn,
2) mighty king,
3) king of the land of Sumer and Akkad,
4) Abbamu,
5) scribe,
6) son of Lu-Utu,
7) your servant.

2003

A cylinder seal found in a grave at Ur belonged to a servant of Būr-Sîn.

COMMENTARY

The seal is in the Iraq Museum, excavation no. U 16804, from Ur, AH grave 202. The seal is of steatite, and measures 2.2 × 1.1 cm. The inscription was collated from the published photo of the impression.

BIBLIOGRAPHY

1951 Legrain, UE 10 no. 540 (photo, transliteration)
1968 Kärki, SKFZ p. 18 Būrsîn 6 (edition)
1975 Boehmer in Orthmann (ed.), Der alte Orient no. 267b (photo, study)
1980 Kärki, SAKAZ 1 p. 28 Būrsîn 6 (edition)

TEXT

1) ÌR-^{d}UTU
2) dumu *zi-ia-tum*
3) ìr-*bur*-^{d}EN.ZU

1) Warad-Šamaš,
2) son of Ziiatum,
3) servant of Būr-Sîn.

2004

A clay bulla bears seal impressions of a servant of Būr-Sîn.

COMMENTARY

The piece is supposed to be in the British Museum, but the number given by Legrain in UE 10 is incorrect and the piece has not been located. The excavation no. of the piece is U 16561B, provenance not known. The seal impressions were collated from the published photo.

BIBLIOGRAPHY

1951 Legrain, UE 10 no. 445 (photo, transliteration)
1968 Kärki, SKFZ p. 18 Būrsîn 7 (edition)
1976 Woolley and Mallowan, UE 7 p. 241 (study)
1980 Kärki, SAKAZ 1 p. 28 Būrsîn 7 (edition)

TEXT

1) [ur]-^{d}nin-[...]
2) [dub-sar]
3) dumu-^{d}*da-mu*-GAL
4) ir_{11}-^{d}*bur*-^{d}EN.ZU

1) [Ur]-Nin[...],
2) [scribe],
3) son of Damu-rabi,
4) servant of Būr-Sîn.

2005

A cylinder seal in Berlin belonged to a servant of Būr-Sîn.

COMMENTARY

The seal is VA 2720, purchased in London, provenance unknown. It is reddy-brown jasper and measures 2.8 × 1.7 cm. The impression was collated.

BIBLIOGRAPHY

1894 Lehmann(-Haupt), BA 2 pp. 589–621 (copy, edition)
1905 Thureau-Dangin, ISA pp. 290–91 Pûr-sin b (edition)
1907 Thureau-Dangin, SAK pp. 204–205 Pûr-sin b (edition)
1910 Ward, Seals no. 33 (copy)
1915 Prinz, Altorientalische Symbolik (Berlin) pp. 57–58 (edition) and pl. XII no. 13 (photo)
1926 Unger, RLV 4/2 pl. 158 p. 368 (photo)
1926 Unger, SuAK p. 104 fig. 55 (photo)
1929 Barton, RISA pp. 308–309 Bur-Sin 2 (edition)
1940 Moortgat, VAR no. 255 (photo, edition)
1961 Hallo, BiOr 18 p. 6 Bur-Sin 5 (study)
1968 Kärki, SKFZ pp. 17–18 Būrsîn 5 (edition)
1971 Sollberger and Kupper, IRSA IVA7d (translation)
1980 Kärki, SAKAZ 1 pp. 27–28 Būrsîn 5 (edition)

TEXT

1) ^{d}*bur*-^{d}EN.ZU	1) Būr-Sîn,
2) lugal-kala-ga	2) mighty king,
3) lugal-ki-en-gi-ki-uri	3) king of the land of Sumer and Akkad,
4) lú-^{d}en-líl-lá	4) Lu-Enlila,
5) dub-sar	5) scribe,
6) dumu-lugal-ezen	6) son of Lugal-ezen,
7) ìr-zu	7) your servant.

2006

A cylinder seal with an Ur excavation number belonged to a servant of Būr-Sîn.

COMMENTARY

The seal is in the Iraq Museum. It was given the excavation no. U 17217C, but records indicate that it was acquired by Woolley, not excavated at Ur. It has a U photo no. 1905. It is a haematite cylinder 1.9 × 0.8 cm and the impression was collated from the published photo. The reading of the name in line 2 is unclear in the photo.

BIBLIOGRAPHY

1951 Legrain, UE 10 no. 528 (photo, transliteration)
1961 Hallo, BiOr 18 p. 6 Bur-Sin 4 (study)
1968 Kärki, SKFZ p. 17 Būrsîn 4 (edition)
1975 Boehmer in Orthmann (ed.), Der alte Orient no. 267c (photo, study)
1980 Kärki, SAKAZ 1 p. 27 Būrsîn 4 (edition)

TEXT

1) DINGIR-*a-ḫu-ú* [(x)]	1) Ilum-aḫû,
2) ⌜ìr-*bur*-^{d}EN⌝.[ZU]	2) servant of Būr-[Sî]n.

Lipit-Enlil

E4.1.8

According to the Sumerian King List, Lipit-Enlil, son of Būr-Sîn, reigned five years. At present, no inscriptions are known for this king.

Erra-imittī

E4.1.9

According to the Sumerian King List, Erra-imittī reigned eight years.

2001

A cylinder seal bears the inscription of Iliška-uṭul, servant of Erra-imittī.

COMMENTARY

The seal is BM 130695 (1904-10-15,22) from the O. Raphael Bequest, provenance unknown. However, since both Iliška-uṭul and Sîn-ennam occur together, although not given as son and father, on a tablet from Kisurra (see B. Kienast, Kisurra no. 75a), the cylinder perhaps comes from that city. Erra-imittī probably controlled Kisurra for a while as is evidenced by a year name commemorating the defeat of the city (see Chiera, PBS 8/2 no. 103).

The seal is of haematite, 2.55 × 1.4 cm.

BIBLIOGRAPHY

1986 Collon, Cylinder Seals 3 no. 395 (photo, edition)

TEXT

1) *ì-lí-iš-ka-ú-ṭùl*	1) Iliška-uṭul,
2) dub-sar	2) scribe,
3) dumu [d]EN.ZU-*en-nam*	3) son of Sîn-ennam,
4) ìr [d]*èr-ra-i-mi-ti*	4) servant of Erra-imittī.

Enlil-bāni

E4.1.10

According to the Sumerian King List, Enlil-bāni ruled 24 years. A number of inscriptions are extant for this king.

1

The standard inscription of Enlil-bāni is found in a 13-line text on bricks at Isin.

CATALOGUE

Ex.	Museum number	Excavation number	Provenance	Dimensions (cm)	Lines preserved	cpn
1	Ash 1924,630	–	Isin	20.0×14.0×6.0	1–13	c
2	–	–	Isin	–	1–13	p
3	IM 52767	–	Isin	33.0×29.0×7.0	–	n
4	–	IB 594	Isin, surface find, many others found on surface	–	–	n
5	–	–	Isin, in situ at the edge of the Kurigalzu pavement in courtyard B of the Gula temple	33.0×33.0	–	n
6	–	–	As ex. 5	33.0×33.5	–	n
7	–	–	Isin, reused in a pavement in North Cutting II	–	–	n
8	–	–	Isin, from a pavement in the West Cutting	–	–	n
9	–	–	Isin, reused as a door socket in an Old Babylonian house in North Cutting II 344.75 N, 44.90 E, +7.99	–	–	n

COMMENTARY

Exs. 1–3 were picked up from the surface by S. Langdon, Dougherty, and F. Basmaji, respectively.

BIBLIOGRAPHY

1924 Langdon, Kish 1 pp. 110–11 (ex. 1, edition)

1927 Dougherty, AASOR 7 p. 38 (ex. 2, study) and p. 87 fig. 39 (ex. 2, photo)

1961 Hallo, BiOr 18 p. 7 Enlil-bani 1 (study)

1968 Kärki, SKFZ p. 18 Enlilbāni 1 (edition)

1975 von Soden, ZA 64 p. 38 (ex. 4, study)

1977 Edzard and Wilcke in Hrouda, Isin 1 p. 87 (ex. 4, study)

1980 Kärki, SAKAZ 1 pp. 28–29 Enlilbāni 1 (edition)

1981 Grégoire, MVN 10 no. 27 (ex. 1, copy, translation, study)

1981 Walker, CBI no. 35 (ex. 1, study)

1981 Walker in Hrouda, Isin 2 p. 94 (exs. 5–8, study)

TEXT

1) ^{d}*en-líl-ba-ni*
2) sipa nì-nam-šár-ra-
3) nibru.KI
4) engar še-maḫ-
5) uri$_5$.KI-ma
6) me-eridu.KI-ga
7) kù-kù-ge
8) en še-ga-
9) unu.KI-ga
10) lugal-ì-si-in.KI-na
11) lugal-ki-en-gi-ki-uri
12) dam-šà-ge-pà-da-
13) ^{d}inanna

1) Enlil-bāni,
2–3) shepherd who makes everything abundant for Nippur,
4–5) farmer (who grows) tall grain for Ur,
6–7) who purifies the *me*s of Eridu,
8–9) favourite *en* priest of Uruk,
10) king of Isin,
11) king of the land of Sumer and Akkad,
12–13) spouse chosen by the heart of the goddess Inanna.

2

A number of cones from Isin deal with Enlil-bāni's construction of the wall of Isin. The same text is also found on bricks from that site as well as from a copy on a tablet of unknown provenance.

CATALOGUE

Ex.	Museum number	Excavation number	Provenance	Object	Dimensions (cm)	Lines preserved	cpn
1	IM 77922	IB 688	Isin, 100 m north on the way to the canal	Shaft	10.0	1–17	c
2	IM 79910	IB 855	Isin, 50 m south of the house	Head	12.0 dia.	1–16	c
3	IM 85999	IB 1217	Isin, 118.80 S/246.20 E, +7.7	Shaft	9.4	–	n
4	Manchester		Isin(?)	Head		1–17	p
5	Manchester		Isin(?)	Shaft		1–17	p
6	CBS 16200		Nippur, from the 4th season, found in a box in room 44	Shaft	6.5	1–17	c
7	IM 42726		Isin(?)	Shaft	8.0	1–17	c
8	–		Isin(?)	Cone	–	–	n
9	–		Isin, surface find	Bricks	–	–	n
10	IM 11087,9		(?)	Tablet	6.0×7.0×3.0	1–17	n

COMMENTARY

Exs. 1–3 come from the Munich expedition to Isin. Exs. 4–5 and 7–9, although not scientifically excavated, presumably come from Isin. Ex. 6 was excavated by the Hilprecht expedition to Nippur. Nothing is known about the present location of ex. 8; it could be the same as that of exs. 4–5. The provenance of ex. 10 is not known.

BIBLIOGRAPHY

1911 Hogg, JM(E)OS 1 pp. 1-20 and pls. I-V (exs. 4-5, photo, copy, edition)
1911 Scheil, RT 33 p. 212 (ex. 8, partial translation)
1926 Legrain, PBS 15 no. 84 (ex. 6, copy)
1929 Barton, RISA pp. 390-91 Enlil-bani 1 (edition)
1957 Edzard, Sumer 13 pp. 177 and 183 (ex. 7, study)
1961 Hallo, BiOr 18 p. 7 Enlil-bani 2 (study)
1968 Kärki, SKFZ pp. 18-19 Enlilbāni 2 (edition)
1971 Sollberger and Kupper, IRSA IVA10a (translation)
1976 van Dijk, TIM 9 no. 37 (ex. 10, copy)
1977 Edzard and Wilcke in Hrouda, Isin 1 p. 87 (ex. 1, study) and p. 88 (ex. 9, study)
1980 Kärki, SAKAZ 1 pp. 29-30 Enlilbāni 2 (edition)
1981 Walker in Hrouda, Isin 2 p. 93 (exs. 2-3, study)

TEXT

1) ^{d}*en-lı̄l-ba-ni*
2) sipa nì-nam-šár-ra-
3) nibru.KI
4) lugal-kala-ga
5) lugal-ì-si-in.KI-na
6) lugal-ki-en-gi-ki-uri
7) dam-šà-ge-pà-da-
8) ^{d}inanna
9) ki-ág-^{d}en-líl
10) ù ^{d}nin-in-si-na-ka-ke$_4$
11) bàd-gal
12) ì-si-in.KI-na
13) mu-dù
14) bàd-ba
15) ^{d}*en-lı̄l-ba-ni*
16) SUḪUŠ-*ki-in*
17) mu-bi-im

1-10) Enlil-bāni, shepherd who makes everything abundant for Nippur, mighty king, king of Isin, king of the land of Sumer and Akkad, spouse chosen by the heart of the goddess Inanna, beloved of the god Enlil and the goddess Ninisina,

11-13) built the great wall of Isin.

14-17) The name of that wall is Enlil-bāni-išdam-kīn ('Enlil-bāni is firm as to foundation').

3

A slightly variant version of the text dealing with the construction of the wall of Isin is known from two cones.

CATALOGUE

Ex.	Museum number	Provenance	Object	Dimensions (cm)	Lines preserved	cpn
1	IM 10789	Isin(?)	Cone	–	–	n
2	UCLM 9-1791	Isin(?)	Shaft	–	1-13	c
3	UCLM 9-1791	Isin(?)	Head	11.0 dia.	1-13	c

BIBLIOGRAPHY

1957 Edzard, Sumer 13 pp. 177 and 183 (ex. 1, study)
1961 Hallo, BiOr 18 p. 7 Enlil-bani 2 (study [combined with E4.1.10.2])
1968 Kärki, SKFZ pp. 18-19 Enlilbāni 2 (edition [combined with E4.1.10.2])
1971 Sollberger and Kupper, IRSA IVA10a (translation [combined with E4.1.10.2])
1978 Foxvog, RA 72 p. 42 (exs. 2-3, transliteration, study)

TEXT

1) ^{d}*en-líl-ba-ni*
2) sipa nì-nam-šár-ra-
3) nibru.KI
4) lugal-kala-ga
5) lugal-ì-si-in.KI-na
6) lugal-ki-en-gi-ki-uri
7) dam-šà-ge-pà-da
8) ^{d}inanna
9) ki-ág-^{d}en-líl
10) ù ^{d}nin-in-si-na-ka-ke$_4$

1–10) Enlil-bāni, shepherd who makes everything abundant for Nippur, mighty king, king of Isin, king of the land of Sumer and Akkad, spouse chosen by the heart of Inanna, beloved of the god Enlil and the goddess Ninisina,

11) bàd-ì-si-in.KI-na
12) ba-sumun-na
13) gibil-bi-šè
14) in-dù

11–14) built anew the wall of Isin which had become dilapidated.

4

A text on two cones, one in the Israel Museum and one in a private collection, commemorates Enlil-bāni's construction of the é-ur-gi$_7$-ra, 'Dog House'.

CATALOGUE

Ex.	Museum number	Provenance	Object	Dimensions (cm)	Lines preserved	cpn
1	Israel Museum 74.49.249	Isin(?)	Shaft	14.5	1–17	n
2	Israel Museum 74.49.249	Isin(?)	Head	broken	4–8, 12–15	n
3	In possession of V. Glätzer, Wiesbaden	Isin(?)	Head	11.8 dia.	2–10, 12–17	c
4	As ex. 3	Isin(?)	Shaft	13.5	1–17	c

COMMENTARY

Although the provenance of the cone is not known, it probably came from Isin because of the dedication to Ninisina, chief goddess of Isin. The connection of Ninisina with dogs is well attested, as the previous editor of the text points out.

BIBLIOGRAPHY

1974 Shaffer, JCS 26 pp. 251–55 (exs. 1–2, copy, edition)
1980 Kärki, SAKAZ 1 p. 33 Enlilbāni 8 (exs. 1–2, edition)
1988 Livingstone, JCS 40 pp. 54–60 (exs. 3–4, copy, edition)

TEXT

1) ^{d}nin-in-si-na
2) nin-a-ni-ir

1–2) For the goddess Ninisina, his lady,

3) ^{d}*en-líl-ba-ni*
4) sipa nì-nam-šár-ra-

3–15) Enlil-bāni, shepherd who makes everything abundant for Nippur, farmer (who grows) tall

5) nibru.KI
6) engar še-maḫ-
7) uri$_5$.KI-ma
8) me-eridu.KI-ga kù-kù-ge
9) en ki-ág-
10) unu.KI-ga
11) lugal-kala-ga
12) lugal-ì-si-in.KI-na
13) lugal-ki-en-gi-ki-uri
14) dam šà-ge-pà-da-
15) ^{d}inanna-ke$_4$
16) é-ur-gi$_7$-ra
17) mu-na-dù

grain for Ur, who purifies the *me*s of Eridu, *en* priest beloved of Uruk, mighty king, king of Isin, king of the land of Sumer and Akkad, spouse chosen by the heart of the goddess Inanna,

16–17) built for her the Eurgira, ('Dog House').

5

An inscription known from two cones of unknown provenance deals with the construction of the temple of Ninibgal by Enlil-bāni.

CATALOGUE

Ex.	Museum number	Provenance	Object	Dimensions (cm)	Lines preserved	cpn
1	NBC 8955	Isin(?)	Shaft	14.0	1-20	c
2	NBC 8955	As ex. 1	Head	9.5 dia.	1-20	c
3	A 7461	As ex. 1	Head	9.0 dia.	1-20	c
4	A 7461	As ex. 1	Shaft	15.0	1-20, omits 9-10	c

COMMENTARY

Stephens suggested that the Yale cone might come from Umma, because of the mention of the goddess Ninibgal in Ur III texts from that city. However, this provenance is very unlikely, because it is doubtful whether Enlil-bāni ever controlled Umma. Since the duplicate cone in Chicago belongs to a group that seems to come from Isin, this city is a more likely provenance.

Exs. 3–4 are edited here for the first time. Exs. 1–2 were purchased in 1947, while exs. 3–4 were purchased in 1931, from E.S. David.

BIBLIOGRAPHY

1947 Stephens, JCS 1 pp. 267–73 (exs. 1–2, copy, edition)
1961 Hallo, BiOr 18 p. 7 Enlil-bani 3: ii (exs. 3–4, study)
1968 Kärki, SKFZ p. 19 Enlilbāni 3 (edition)
1971 Sollberger and Kupper, IRSA IVA10c (translation)
1980 Kärki, SAKAZ 1 p. 30 Enlilbāni 3 (edition)

5.3 EN.KI.LÍL.

TEXT

1) ^{d}nin-ib-gal
2) nin-šà-lá-sù
3) ga-ti-e ki-ág
4) šùd a-ra-zu-e giš-tuk
5) ama-zalag-a-ni-ir
6) ^{d}*en-líl-ba-ni*
7) sipa nì-nam-šár-ra-
8) nibru.KI
9) engar še-maḫ-
10) úri.KI-ma
11) me-eridu.KI-ga kù-kù-ge
12) en ki-ág-
13) unu.KI-ga
14) lugal-kala-ga
15) lugal-ì-si-in.KI-na
16) lugal-ki-en-gi-ki-uri
17) dam šà-ge-pà-da-
18) ^{d}inanna-ke$_4$
19) é-ki-ág-gá-ni
20) mu-na-dù

1–5) For the goddess Ninibgal, lady with patient mercy, who loves ex-votos, who heeds prayers and entreaties, his shining mother,

6–18) Enlil-bāni, shepherd who makes everything abundant for Nippur, farmer (who grows) tall grain for Ur, who purifies the *me*s of Eridu, *en* priest beloved of Uruk, mighty king, king of Isin, king of the land of Sumer and Akkad, spouse chosen by the heart of the goddess Inanna,

19–20) built her beloved temple for her.

6

A cone in Chicago, probably from Isin, deals with Enlil-bāni's construction of the temple of Nintinuga.

CATALOGUE

Ex.	Museum number	Provenance	Object	Dimensions (cm)	Lines preserved	cpn
1	A 7555	Isin(?)	Head	10.2 dia.	1–12	c
2	A 7555	As ex. 1	Shaft	–	1–12	c

COMMENTARY

The translation of line 2 assumes that this line is an etymology of the name in line 1. Cf. Reiner, Šurpu 7 73f.: ^{d}nin-tin-ug$_5$-ga = *bēltu muballiṭat mīti*. Exs. 1 and 2 were purchased from E.S. David.

BIBLIOGRAPHY

1959 Hallo, JNES 18 p. 54 (exs. 1–2, study), p. 60 (exs. 1–2, edition), pp. 62–63 (exs. 1–2, copy), and pp. 67–68 (exs. 1–2, photo)
1961 Hallo, BiOr 18 p. 7 Enlil-bani 4 (study)
1968 Kärki, SKFZ pp. 19–20 Enlilbāni 4 (edition)
1971 Sollberger and Kupper, IRSA IVA10b (translation)
1980 Kärki, SAKAZ 1 pp. 30–31 Enlilbāni 4 (edition)

9.4 omits. **10**.1 uri$_5$.KI-ma. **10**.4 omits. **13**.1 AB×ḪA.KI-ga. **19**.1–2 é-ki-ág-gá-IR.

TEXT

1) ^{d}nin-tin-ug$_5$-ga
2) nin ti-la ug$_5$-ga
3) nin-a-ni-ir
4) ^{d}*en-líl-ba-ni*
5) lugal-kala-ga
6) lugal-ì-si-in.KI-na
7) lugal-ki-en-gi-ki-uri
8) ki-ág-^{d}en-líl
9) ù ^{d}nin-in-si-na-ka-ke$_4$
10) é-ní-dúb-bu
11) é-ki-ág-gá-ni
12) mu-na-dù

1–3) For the goddess Nintinuga, lady who revives the dead, his lady,

4–9) Enlil-bāni, mighty king, king of Isin, king of the land of Sumer and Akkad, beloved of the god Enlil and the goddess Ninisina,

10–12) built for her the Enidubu ('House of relaxation'), her beloved temple.

7

An inscription known from two cones deals with Enlil-bāni's construction of the temple of the goddess Sud, tutelary deity of Šuruppak.

CATALOGUE

Ex.	Museum number	Excavation number	Provenance	Object	Dimensions (cm)	Lines preserved	cpn
1	UCLM 9-1783	–	Said to come from Khum near Fara	Head	10.5 dia.	1–8	c
2	IM 79940	IB 932	Isin, found in the fill of the street in North Cutting II, 338.28 N, 37.40 E, +7.97	Head	12.6 dia.	1–8	n
3	IM 79940	IB 932	As ex. 2	Shaft	–	–	n

COMMENTARY

Ex. 1 was collated by D. Foxvog. Ex. 2 was entered from a copy of C. Wilcke. No source was available for ex. 3.

BIBLIOGRAPHY

1978 Foxvog, RA 72 p. 42 (ex. 1, transliteration, study)
1980 Kärki, SAKAZ 1 pp. 33–34 Enlilbāni 9 (edition)
1981 Walker in Hrouda, Isin 2 pp. 93–94 (exs. 2–3, edition)

TEXT

1) ^{d}sùd
2) nin-a-ni-ir
3) ^{d}*en-líl-ba-ni*
4) lugal-kala-ga
5) lugal-ì-si-in-na.KI-na-ke$_4$

1–2) For the goddess Sud, his lady,

3–5) Enlil-bāni, mighty king, king of Isin,

6) é-dim-gal-an-na
7) é-ki-ág-gá-ni
8) mu-na-dù

6–8) built for her the Edimgalana ('House — great mast of heaven'), her beloved temple.

8

The reverse of a tablet from Nippur has a copy of an inscription of Enlil-bāni dealing with the god Enlil. Unfortunately, only the beginning of the text is preserved.

COMMENTARY

The tablet is UM 29-16-42, provenance Nippur. It measures 9×11.9×3.8 cm and the inscription was collated.

BIBLIOGRAPHY

1972 Sjöberg, JCS 24 pp. 72–73 (photo, edition)
1980 Kärki, SAKAZ 1 pp. 31–32 Enlilbāni 6 (edition)

TEXT

1) [d]en-líl lugal-kur-kur-[ra]
2) lugal-a-ni-[ir]
3) [d]*en-líl-ba-*[*ni*]
4) lugal-kala-ga lugal-ì-si-i[n.KI-na]
5) lugal-ki-en-[gi-ki-uri]
6) ki-ág-[[d]en-líl]
7) ù [d][nin-in-si-na-ka-ke₄]
8) nì-[...]
Lacuna

1) [For] the god Enlil, lord of all the foreign lands,
2) his lord,
3) Enlil-bā[ni],
4) mighty king, king of Isi[n],
5) king of the land of Su[mer and Akkad],
6–7) beloved of [the god Enlil] and [the goddess Ninisina]
8) ...
Lacuna

9

A clay impression mentions the construction by Enlil-bāni of a palace, a deed confirmed by E4.1.10.10.

COMMENTARY

The piece (IM 25874) was obtained at ʿAfak but probably originally came from Isin or Nippur. It measures 10.5×3.5 cm and was collated by Edzard.

E4.1.10.7 line 8.2 [m]u-⌜un⌝-na-dù.

BIBLIOGRAPHY

1959 Edzard, Sumer 15 pp. 27–28 (edition) and pl. 4 (copy)
1980 Kärki, SAKAZ 1 p. 31 Enlilbāni 5 (edition)

TEXT

1) ⌈^{d}⌉*en-líl-ba-ni*
2) si[pa n]ì-nam-šár-ra-
3) nibru.KI
4) engar še-⟨maḫ⟩-«KI»-
5) ⌈úri⌉.KI-ma
6) ⌈en⌉ me-te-unu.KI-[g]a
7) ⌈eridu⌉.KI-⌈ga⌉
8) dam šà-ge-pà-da-
9) ⌈^{d}⌉inanna-me-en
10) u$_4$ nì-si-sá
11) ki-en-gi-ki-uri
12) i-ni-in-gar-ra
13) é-gal x-bi
14) lugal-e-x
15) [m]u-d[ù]

1–9) I, Enlil-bāni, shep[herd] who makes [ev]erything abundant for Nippur, farmer (who grows) tall grain for Ur, *en* priest suitable for Uruk (and) Uruk, spouse chosen by the heart of Inanna,

10–12) when I established justice in the land of Sumer and Akkad,

13–15) I [b]uil[t] the ... palace.

10

Bricks with a two-line 'palace inscription' were found on the surface of the mound at Isin.

CATALOGUE

Ex.	Museum number	Excavation number	Provenance	Dimensions (cm)	Lines preserved	cpn
1	–	–	Isin, from the surface of the mound	–	1–2	c
2	–	IB 953	Isin, from the surface of the mound north of the North Cutting	24.0×20.5×8.0	1–2	c

BIBLIOGRAPHY

1977 Edzard and Wilcke in Hrouda, Isin 1 p. 88 (ex. 1, study)
1978 Walker, Sumer 34 pp. 100 and 103 (ex. 2, copy, edition)
1981 Walker in Hrouda, Isin 2 p. 94 (ex. 2, edition)

TEXT

1) é-gal
2) ^{d}*en-líl-ba-ni*

1–2) Palace of Enlil-bāni.

11

A tablet in Philadelphia has an inscription dealing with Enlil-bāni's introduction into Nippur of two statues for the goddess Ninlil which Iddin-Dagān had fashioned 117 years earlier, but had not been able to bring into the city.

COMMENTARY

The tablet is UM L-29-578, of unknown provenance, 8.8×5.2×2.2 cm. The inscription was collated. Lines 26–37 of this tablet are edited under E4.1.3.3.

BIBLIOGRAPHY

1973 Loding, AfO 24 pp. 47–50 (photo, edition)
1980 Kärki, SAKAZ 1 pp. 32–33 Enlilbāni 7 (edition)

TEXT

1) ^{d}nin-líl 2) nin-dingir-re-e-ne-ra	1–2) For the goddess Ninlil, queen of the gods,
3) ^{d}*i-din-*^{d}*da-gan* lugal-e 4) URUDU-urudu-alam-gal-gal-min-a-bi mu-na-dím 5) nibru.KI-šè nu-un-de$_6$	3–5) Iddin-Dagān, the king, fashioned two great copper statues (but) did not bring them into Nippur.
6) šu-^{d}*i-din-*^{d}*da-gan*-ta 7) en-na-^{d}en-líl-*ba-ni* lugal-e 8) mu-117-kam 9) šà-ì-si-in-na-ka ì-su$_8$-ge-eš-àm	6–9) From Iddin-Dagān until Enlil-bāni, the king, for 117 years they stood in Isin.
10) ^{d}nin-líl-le šà-ḫúl-la-ni-ta 11) al in-dù in-du$_{11}$-ma	10–11) The goddess Ninlil with joy conceived a wish and commanded.
12) ^{d}*en-líl-ba-ni* lugal-kala-ga 13) lugal-ì-si-in-na lugal-ki-en-gi-ki-uri 14) [k]i-ág ^{d}en-líl ù ^{d}nin-líl 15) [URU]DU-alam-gal-gal-min-a-bi 16) šà-ì-si-in-na-ta 17) nibru.KI-šè in-túm	12–17) Enlil-bāni, mighty king, king of Isin, king of the land of Sumer and Akkad, [be]loved of the god Enlil and the goddess Ninlil, brought the two great [cop]per statues from Isin to Nippur.
18) kisal-maḫ-é-gá-giš-šú-a-ka 19) ^{d}nin-líl nin-a-ni-ir mu-na-gub	18–19) He set them up for the goddess Ninlil, his lady, in the great courtyard of the Gagiššua temple.
20) mu-bi-šè ^{d}nin-líl-le 21) nam-ti-^{d}en-líl-*ba-ni* 22) ki-^{d}en-líl-lá-ta u$_4$-bi ba-ni-in-sù	20–22) On account of this the goddess Ninlil had the god Enlil lengthen the life-span of Enlil-bāni.
23) lú mu-sar-ra-ba šu bí-⟨ib-ùr-ra⟩	23) (As for) the man who e⟨rases⟩ this inscription,
24) ^{d}en-líl lugal-mu ù ^{d}nin-líl nin-mu 25) nam ḫa-ba-an-da-ku$_5$-ru-ne	24–25) may the god Enlil, my lord, and the goddess Ninlil, my lady, curse him.

1001

An inscription found on a clay tablet excavated at Nippur deals with various social measures enacted by a king of Isin whose name is only partially written, but which should be probably read as Enlil-bāni. According to Kraus, König. Verfüg. p. 28 n. 60, this composition should be classed as a royal inscription, not a royal hymn.

COMMENTARY

The tablet is CBS 13909. It was collated by H. Behrens.

BIBLIOGRAPHY

1914 Poebel, PBS 5 no. 74 (copy)
1951 Kraus, JCS 3 pp. 30–32 and 35–36 (partial edition)
1957 Edzard, Zwischenzeit pp. 83–84 (study)
1958 Kraus, Edikt p. 201 (study)
1965 Römer, SKIZ pp. 38–39 (partial edition)
1984 Kraus, König. Verfüg. pp. 28–30 (partial edition)

TEXT

Col. i
1) [...]
2) [...] x
3) [...] x-me-en
4) ⸢èš⸣-nibru.KI
5) du[r]-an-ki-a-šè
6) gù zi-dè-eš ma-an-dé
7) sag-ki-zalag-ga-ni
8) mu-ši-in-bar
9) nam-du$_{10}$ mu-un-tar

i 1–9) [...] am I. (Enlil) truly called me to shrine Nippur, bond of heaven and earth. He looked at me with his shining face. He determined a good destiny (for me saying):

10) ^{d}en-⟨líl-ba-ni⟩
11) šu-du$_{11}$-ga-mu-me-en
12) ⸢á⸣-nun
13) ḫu-mu-ta-gál
14) ^{d}[a]-nun-na
15) ⸢kù⸣-an-šè
16) [x] ḫé-ni-túm(?)-ma(?)
17) [x] x x x x
18) [...]
19) [...]

i 10–19) 'You are En⟨lil-bāni⟩, my creation. May supreme power be with you. The [...] which the [A]nuna gods brought to shining An, [...] ... [...]'

Col. ii
1) [...] x
2) x x
3) nam-⸢ḫe⸣
4) ḫu-mi-diri-ge
5) kalam-ma
6) x x x ul
7) ma-⸢ra(?)⸣-gál
8) an(?)-ub-⟨da⟩-límmu-ba

ii 1–24) [...] ... 'May you make abundance plentiful. I have put ... in the land for you. In the four quarters (of the world) may you have no rival. You please the black-headed people, you are their sun god. I have given to you year(s) of life, a reign with a long life-span. [May you carry] (your) head (literally: 'neck') hi[gh] (in) shrine Nippur. [...] ...'

9) gaba-ri
10) na-an-tuk-tuk-un
11) un-sag-gi$_6$-ge
12) ba-du$_{10}$-ge-me-en
13) ^{d}utu-bi
14) ḫé-me-en
15) mu-nam-ti-la
16) bala u$_4$-bi
17) sù-sù-rá
18) sag-e-eš
19) mu-rig$_7$
20) èš-nibru.KI
21) gú an-[šè ...]
22) [ḫé-em-mi-zi]
23) [...]
24) [...] x

Col. iii
1) ⌜ab⌝-sín-bi
2) mu-e-dagal
3) x x AN
4) ⌜ebur(?)⌝-luḫ
5) x-za-kù-ga-bi-šè
6) u$_4$-šú-uš
7) ḫa-ba-gub-bé-en
8) giš-tag-bi
9) níg mu-ši-bar-ra
10) ma-túm
11) sig$_4$-é-kur-ra-ke$_4$
12) ḫé-em-da-ḫúl
13) utu-è-ta
14) u$_4$-šú-uš
15) nam-sipa-bi
16) ma-ra-sum
17) nam-lugal-zu
18) pa-è bí-ak
19) u$_4$-bi
20) ma-ra-sù-ud
21) x x ma
22) [...]-šè
23) [...]
24) mu-ra-ge-en

iii 1–24) 'I have made their furrows broad for you. May you stand daily at their shining bright ... harvest. You have brought to me their offerings, a thing that I have seen. Brickwork Ekur rejoiced over them. From east to west I gave to you their shepherdship. I made magnificent your kingship. I prolonged their days for you, I established ... for you ... [...]'

Col. iv
1) aga-me-dè(?)
2) u$_6$-di-dè
3) ḫé-du$_7$
4) sag-za ba-kešd-re$_6$
5) zà-kur-ra-šè
6) mi-ni-maḫ-en
7) téš-bi-éš
8) mu-sè-ke-en
9) ki-bala-a
10) uru.KI du$_{11}$-ga-zu-ta
11) la-ba-x
12) bàd mu-gul
13) gìr-⌜zu-ta⌝

iv 1–23) 'You wear on your head the ... crown which evokes wonder. You are exalted to the farthest reach of the foreign land. You make (the land) peaceful. In the rebellious land you destroy the wall of the city that does not ... at your command. You put them in fetters at your feet. I have entrusted to you, forever, the *enkara* weapon, the staff (and) sceptre of righteousness which guides the black-headed people. [...] ... are you.'

14) giš ḫé-ši-šú-e
15) enkara ⌜šibir⌝
16) gidru nì-⌜gi⌝-na
17) un 〈sag〉-gi$_6$-〈ga〉
18) laḫ$_5$-laḫ$_5$-e
19) u$_4$-da-rí-šè
20) šu-zi
21) mu-x-⌜un⌝-gar
22) [...] x
23) [...] x me-en

Col. v
1) inim-x-x-zu
2) na-me
3) nu-kúr-ru-dam
4) nam-tar-ra-mu
5) du-rí-šè
6) ḫa-mu-x-gar
7) ^{d}en-〈líl〉-le(?)
8) sig$_4$-é-kur-ra-ta
9) nam-mu
10) mi-ni-in-tar-ra
11) ni[bru].KI
12) nì-si-sá
13) mu-ni-in-gar
14) nì-gi-[na]
15) pa bí-è
16) udu-gin$_7$ ka ú [k]ú
17) ba-ni-in-k[in]
18) ú-si[g$_7$-g]a bí-kú
19) GIŠ.šudul-dugud-da
20) gú-bi im-ta-zi
21) dúr(?)-gi-na bí-tuš
22) nibru.KI-a
23) nì-gi-na
24) mi-ni-in-gar-ra

v 1-24) Nobody can alter your ... word. You have established my destiny forever. O god Enlil (this) is my destiny which you established at brickwork Ekur: I established justice in Nippur. I made righte[ousness] appear. As (for) sheep I sought out food to eat (and) fed (them) with green plants. I lifted the heavy yoke from their necks. I settled (them) in a secure abode. The righteousness which I established in Nippur

Col. vi
1) šà-bi mu-du$_{10}$-ga
2) ì-si-in.KI
3) uru.KI an-né
4) ^{d}en-〈líl〉-le
5) ^{d}nin-in-si-na-ra
6) sag-e-eš
7) mu-un-ni-in-rig$_7$-eš
8) nì-gi
9) nì-si-sá
10) mu-ni-in-gar
11) šà-kalam-ma mu-du$_{10}$
12) še nì-ku$_5$-ra
13) igi-5-gál ì-me-a
14) igi-10-gál-la
15) ḫé-mi-ku$_4$
16) MAŠ.EN.KAK
17) itu-da
18) u$_4$-4-àm
19) ḫé-gub

vi 1-23) made (the inhabitants of Nippur) happy. I established righteousness and justice in Isin, the city which the gods An and Enlil gave to the goddess Ninisina. I made the land content. I reduced to one-tenth the grain tax that formerly was one-fifth. I made the commoner serve (only) four days a month. The cattle of the palace which (formerly) grazed in the ... field,

20) máš-anše
21) é-gal-la-ke_4
22) a-šà x x x a
23) x x

Col. vii
1) i-[d]utu
2) bí-in-eš-a
3) máš-anše
4) é-gal-la
5) ab-sín-ta
6) ḫé-em-ta-è
7) i-[d]utu sì-ga
8) nì-gig-ga
9) ḫé-ni-ku_4
10) di-ku_5 nì-gi-e
11) ki-ág-me-en
12) nì-érim
13) nì-á-zi
14) ú-gu ḫé-ni-dé
15) lú-si-sá
16) x-ge
17) ḫé-mi-gi_4

vii 1–17) (and about which) ... made a complaint — I removed (those) cattle of the palace from the (field) furrows. I made anybody with a complaint a taboo thing. I am a judge who loves righteousness. I destroyed evil and violence. I restored ... the just man ...

Zambīia

E4.1.11

According to the Sumerian King List, Zambīia ruled three years. One inscription is known for this king.

1

A number of cones found at Isin, none in situ, deal with Zambīia's construction of the wall of Isin.

CATALOGUE

Ex.	Museum number	Excavation number	Provenance	Object	Dimensions (cm)	Lines preserved	cpn
1	A 7557	–	Isin(?)	Head	10.2 dia.	1–22	c
2	A 7557	–	As ex. 1	Shaft	–	1–22	c
3	IM 77073	IB 380	Isin, N IIs, Room 1, 326.25 N, 33.05 E, 170 cm under the surface	Shaft	12.5	1–22	c
4	IM 77073	IB 380	As ex. 3	Head	11.0 dia.	1–6, 9–22	c
5	IM -	IB 1153	Isin, Gula temple 91.20 N, 98.50 W, in upper rubble of court filling	Head	10.2 dia.	8–11, 19–22	c
6	IM -	IB 1153	As ex. 5	Shaft	5.5	7–13, 15–16	c

COMMENTARY

Exs. 1 and 2 were purchased in 1932 from E.S. David.

BIBLIOGRAPHY

1959 Hallo, JNES 18 p. 55 (exs. 1–2, study), pp. 60–61 (exs. 1–2, edition), pp. 65–66 (exs. 1–2, copy), and pp. 71–72 (exs. 1–2, photo)

1961 Hallo, BiOr 18 p. 7 Zambia 1 (study)

1968 Kärki, SKFZ p. 7 Zambīja 1 (edition)

1971 Sollberger and Kupper, IRSA IVA11a (translation)

1975 von Soden, ZA 64 p. 39 (exs. 3–4, study)

1977 Edzard and Wilcke in Hrouda, Isin 1 p. 87 (exs. 3–4, study)

1980 Kärki, SAKAZ 1 p. 34 Zambīja 1 (edition)

1981 Walker in Hrouda, Isin 2 p. 94 (exs. 5–6, study)

1985 Wilcke, Orientalia NS 54 pp. 311–12 (edition of lines 1–10)

1987 Wilcke in Hrouda, et al., Isin 3 p. 114 d (ex. 7, study)

TEXT

1) ^{d}*za-am-bi-ia*
2) sipa ní-tuk-
3) nibru.KI
4) engar gu-maḫ túm
5) še-maḫ túm
6) èš-dur-an-ki-šè
7) ú-a-zi
8) kisal-é-gal-maḫ-a
9) nì-nam-ḫe si-si
10) lugal-ì-si-in.KI-na
11) lugal-ki-en-gi-ki-uri
12) dam-igi-íl-la-
13) ^{d}inanna
14) ki-ág-^{d}en-líl
15) ù ^{d}nin-in-si-na-ka-ke$_4$
16) bàd-gal
17) ì-si-in.KI-na
18) mu-dù
19) bàd-ba
20) ^{d}*za-am-bi-ia*
21) *na-ra-am eš$_4$-tár*
22) mu-bi-im

1–15) Zambīia, shepherd who reverences Nippur, farmer who brings tall flax and grain for shrine Duranki, true provider, who fills the courtyard of the Egalmaḫ with abundant things, king of Isin, king of the land of Sumer and Akkad, spouse chosen by the goddess Inanna, beloved of the god Enlil and the goddess Ninisina,

16–18) built the great wall of Isin.

19–22) The name of that wall is 'Zambīia is the beloved of the goddess Eštar'.

18.3 mu-NI.

Ītir-pîša

E4.1.12

According to the Sumerian King List, Ītir-pîša ruled four years. Four year names are known for this king, but no royal inscriptions.

Ur-dukuga

E4.1.13

According to the Sumerian King List, Ur-dukuga reigned four years. A few inscriptions are known for this king.

1

A year name of Ur-dukuga (see J. van Dijk, TIM 4 no. 12) deals with the construction of the temple of Dagān. This same event is recorded in a number of cones from Isin.

CATALOGUE

Ex.	Museum number	Object	Dimensions (cm)	Lines preserved	cpn
1	LB 990	Head	14.8 dia.	1–24	c
2	NBC 6110	Head	13.8 dia.	13–24	c
3	NBC 6110	Shaft	17	1–8	c
4	NBC 6112	Head	13.2 dia.	1–12, 14–24	c
5	NBC 6112	Shaft	22.5	1–3, 11–24	c
6	NBC 6111	Head	10.1 × 12.4	1–12, 14–24	c

BIBLIOGRAPHY

1933 Böhl, Leiden Coll. 1 p. 24 (ex. 1, edition)
1937 Stephens, YOS 9 nos. 27–30 (exs. 2–5, copy, study) and no. 121 (ex. 6, study)
1957 van Dijk, TLB 2 no. 13 (ex. 1, copy)
1961 Hallo, BiOr 18 p. 7 Ur-dukuga 1 (study)
1968 Kärki, SKFZ pp. 20–21 Urdukuga 1 (edition)
1971 Sollberger and Kupper, IRSA ɪvA3a (translation)
1980 Kärki, SAKAZ 1 pp. 34–35 Urdukuga 1 (edition)

TEXT

1) ^{d}*da-gan*
2) en-gal-kur-kur-ra
3) dingir-sag-du-ga-ni-ir
4) ^{d}ur-du$_{6}$-kù-ga
5) sipa nì-nam-tùm-
6) nibru.ᴋɪ
7) engar-maḫ-
8) an-^{d}en-líl-lá
9) ú-a-é-kur-ra
10) ḫé-gál-du$_{8}$-du$_{8}$-

1–3) For the god Dagān, great lord of the foreign lands, the god who created him,

4–20) Ur-dukuga, shepherd who brings everything for Nippur, supreme farmer of the gods An and Enlil, provider of Ekur, who provides abundance for Ešumeša (and) Egalmaḫ, who returned to the gods the regular offerings which had been expropriated from the sanctuaries, mighty king, king of Isin, king of the land of Sumer and

11) é-šu-me-ša$_4$ 12) é-gal-maḫ-a 13) sá-du$_{11}$ èš-ta ba-ba-a 14) dingir-re-e-ne-er 15) in-ne-éb-gur-ra 16) lugal-kala-ga 17) lugal-ì-si-in.KI-na 18) lugal-ki-en-gi-ki-uri 19) dam igi-zi-bar-ra- 20) ^{d}inanna-ke$_4$	Akkad, spouse steadfastly looked upon by the goddess Inanna,
21) é-tuš-ki-gar-ra 22) ì-si-in.KI-na 23) ki-tuš-kù-ki-ág-gá-ni 24) mu-na-dù	21–24) built for him the Etuškigara ('House — the well founded residence') in Isin, his shining, beloved residence.

2

A brick found at Isin deals with king Ur-dukuga. Since only the beginning of the inscription giving the titles of the king is preserved, we cannot determine which royal deed is commemorated by this inscription.

COMMENTARY

The brick has not yet been assigned an IM no.; the excavation no. is IB 1337. It was found at Isin on the surface, 200 N, 80 W. It is a stamped brick, 32.0 × 15.5 × 8.5 cm. The stamp measures 8.5 × 7.3 cm. Perhaps about one-half of the brick is preserved.

BIBLIOGRAPHY

1981 Walker in Hrouda, Isin 2 p. 94 (study)

TEXT

1) ⸢ur-dù⸣-k[ù-ga]	1) Ur-duk[uga],
2) ⸢sipa nì-nam-tùm⸣- 3) ⸢nibru.KI⸣	2–3) shepherd who brings everything for Nippur,
4) ⸢engar-maḫ⸣- 5) ⸢an ^{d}en-líl-lá⸣	4–5) supreme farmer of the gods An and Enlil,
6) ⸢ú-a-é-kur-ra⸣	6) provider of the Ekur,
Lacuna	Lacuna

3

A fragmentary cone shaft excavated at Isin deals with the construction of the temple of the god Lulal by Ur-dukuga.

COMMENTARY

The cone shaft is IM 95461, excavation no. IB 1411, found at Isin 923/926 N, 298/302 E, 60 cm under the surface. It measures 10 cm long and 4 cm in dia. Perhaps about one-third of the text is preserved. The inscription was collated.

The name in line 2 is restored from IB 1392; see C. Wilcke in Hrouda, et al., Isin 3 p. 118. A text cited by C. Wilcke (Isin 3 p. 95, A vi 14) indicates that Dul-eden was probably the cult city of the god Lulal. Dul-eden lay north-east of Nippur on the Iturungal canal.

BIBLIOGRAPHY

1985 Wilcke, Orientalia NS 54 pp. 312–13 (edition)
1987 Wilcke in Hrouda, et al., Isin 3 p. 114 (edition)

TEXT

1) [^{d}l]ú-làl
2) [du$_6$-ed]en(?)-na
3) [lugal-a-n]i-ir
4) [ur-du$_6$-kù]-ga
5) [sipa nì-nam-t]ùm-
6) [nibru.KI]
Lacuna
1′) [dam-igi-zi-bar-ra]
2′) [^{d}inanna]-ke$_4$
3′) [é-ki-á]g-gá-ni
4′) [mu-na]-dù

1) For [the god L]ulal,
2) [of (the city) *Dul-ed*]*ena*
3) [hi]s [lord],
4) [Ur-duku]ga,
5–6) [shepherd who br]ings [everything for Nippur],
Lacuna
1′–2′) [spouse steadfastly looked upon by the goddess Inann]a,
3′–4′) built his [bel]oved [temple for him].

Sîn-māgir

E4.1.14

According to the Isin King List, Sîn-māgir reigned 11 years. Six inscriptions are known for this king.

1

A year formula of Sîn-māgir deals with the construction of the wall named Dūr-Sîn-māgir. This is probably the same structure whose construction was commemorated in a cone inscription known from Isin and Babylon. The inscription indicates that this was the name of the wall of Dunnum, a city north-east of Nippur.

CATALOGUE

Ex.	Museum number	Excavation number	Photo number	Provenance	Object	Dimensions (cm)	Lines preserved	cpn
1	IM –	IB 1610	–	Isin, 850.95 N, 286.40 E, +4.92	Shaft	9.5	1–23	c
2	VA Bab 628	BE 14864	Bab. 1159	Babylon, in rubble in the courtyard of the é-ḫur-sag-ti-la temple, temple of Ninurta in the south end of the city	Head	10.5 dia.	1–3, 13–16, 20–23	c
3	VA Bab 609	BE 14850+	Bab. 1159	As ex. 2	Shaft frgm.	6.3	6–11, 13–22	c

COMMENTARY

Ex. 1 from Isin is complete. Exs. 2–3, which are fragmentary, are probably pieces of one and the same cone. Although incomplete, they totally agree, where preserved, with ex. 1 and are assumed to be duplicates of it.

Although Unger, followed by Hallo, indicated that exs. 2–3 probably came from the so-called Schlossmuseum of Nebuchadnezzar II at Babylon, the actual provenance indicated by Koldewey is from the area of the Ninurta temple in the south end of the city. For the reading of the Ninurta temple name see A. Cavigneaux, NABU 2, p. 13.

Rīm-Sîn, who captured the city of Dunnum the year before his defeat of Isin itself, calls Dunnum the chief city of the state of Isin. The pieces found at Babylon may have been taken first by Rīm-Sîn from Dunnum to Larsa as booty and thence to Babylon by Ḫammu-rāpi when the latter king defeated Larsa.

BIBLIOGRAPHY

1903 Weissbach, Miscellen no. 1 (exs. 2-3, copy, partial edition, study)
1905 Thureau-Dangin, ISA pp. 292–93 Sin-mâgir (edition)
1907 Thureau-Dangin, SAK pp. 204–205 Sin-mâgir (edition)
1911 Koldewey, Tempel p. 30 (provenance) and pp. 70–71 no. 6 (edition)
1929 Barton, RISA pp. 308–309 Sin-magir 1 (edition)
1931 Unger, Babylon p. 224 no. 6 (study)
1959 Hallo, JNES 18 p. 58 (study)
1961 Hallo, BiOr 18 p. 7 Sin-magir 1 (study)
1968 Kärki, SKFZ p. 21 Sînmāgir 1 (edition)
1980 Kärki, SAKAZ 1 pp. 35–36 Sînmāgir 1 (edition)
1987 Wilcke in Hrouda, et al., Isin 3 pp. 114–16 (edition, study)

TEXT

1) ^{d}EN.ZU-*ma-gir*
2) sipa ú-a-
3) é-an-^{d}en-líl-lá
4) nì-nam-du$_8$-du$_8$-
5) é-gal-maḫ-a
6) engar-sá-du$_{11}$-sum-sum-mu-
7) dingir-un-dù-a-bi-šè
8) šà-ḫúl-ḫúl-éren-a-na
9) mu-pà-da-^{d}nanna
10) še-ga-^{d}nin-in-si-na
11) nam-lugal an-da-ak-da-ni-šè
12) uru-na mu-un-suḫ-a
13) lugal-kala-ga
14) lugal-ì-si-in.KI-na
15) lugal-ki-en-gi-ki-uri
16) dam-šà-ki-ág-^{d}inanna
17) ki-ná-gi-rin-na túm-ma
18) bàd-gal-*du-nu-um*.KI-ma
19) mu-dù
20) bàd-ba
21) ^{d}EN.ZU-*ma-gir*
22) suḫuš-ma-da-na-ge-en-ge-en
23) mu-bi-im

1–17) Sîn-māgir, shepherd, provider for the temples of the gods An and Enlil, who makes everything abound for the Egalmaḫ, farmer who gives regular offerings for the gods of all the people, who makes his men rejoice, called by name by the god Nanna, favourite of the goddess Ninisina, who was chosen in his city for the exercise of kingship, mighty king, king of Isin, king of the land of Sumer and Akkad, spouse beloved of the heart of the goddess Inanna, suitable for the flowery bed,

18–19) built the great wall of Dunnum.

20–23) The name of that wall is 'Sîn-māgir makes the foundation of his land firm'.

2

A cone in Chicago deals with the construction by Nuṭuptum, the *lukur* priestess, of a storehouse for the goddess Aktuppītum of Kiritab for her own life and for the life of Sîn-māgir.

CATALOGUE

Ex.	Museum number	Excavation number	Provenance	Object	Dimensions (cm)	Lines preserved	cpn
1	A 17650	–	(?)	Head	–	1–14	c
2	A 17650	–	(?)	Shaft	–	1–9	c

COMMENTARY

Although Poebel wanted to read the place-name in line 2 as Aktab, other sources (see B. Landsberger, JCS 13 p. 129 line 199) indicate the name is to be read Kiritab or Giritab.

BIBLIOGRAPHY

1937 Poebel, JAOS 57 pp. 359–67 (exs. 1–2, copy, edition)
1961 Hallo, BiOr 18 p. 7 Sin-magir 2 (study)
1961 Gelb, MAD 2^2 p. 210 (study)
1968 Kärki, SKFZ p. 22 Sînmāgir 2 (edition)
1971 Sollberger and Kupper, IRSA IVA14a (translation)
1980 Kärki, SAKAZ 1 p. 36 Sînmāgir 2 (edition)

TEXT

1) ^{d}*ak-tup-pí-tum*
2) kiri$_8$-tab
3) nin-a-ni-ir
4) nam-t[i]-
5) ^{d}EN.ZU-*ma-gir*
6) lugal-kala-ga
7) lugal-ì-si-in.KI-na
8) lugal-ki-en-⸢gi⸣-ki-uri-k[e$_4$]
9) *nu-ṭù-up-tum*
10) lukur-ki-ág-[kaskal-l]a-ka-ni
11) [ama-ibi]la-na-ke$_4$
12) é-šútum-ki-ág-gá-ni
13) ù nam-ti-la-ni-šè
14) mu-na-dù

1–3) For the goddess Aktuppītum of Kiritab, her lady,

4–8) for the li[fe] of Sîn-māgir, mighty king, king of Isin, king of the land of Sumer and Akkad,

9–11) Nuṭuptum, his beloved [travelli]ng escort, [mother] of his [first] born,

12–14) and for her own life, built her beloved storehouse for her.

3

Three bricks from Isin bear the 'palace inscription' of Sîn-māgir.

CATALOGUE

Ex.	Museum number	Excavation number	Provenance	Dimensions (cm)	Lines preserved	cpn
1	IM 78635	IB 938	Isin, from the fill of the Gula temple, 63 N, 118 W	33.5×33.0×8.0	1–2	c
2	IM –	IB 939	Isin, As ex. 1	28.0×20.0×8.5	1–2	c
3	IM –	IB 422	Isin, from the surface near the North Cutting	Stamp 8.4×4.4	1–2	c

BIBLIOGRAPHY

1977 Edzard and Wilcke in Hrouda, Isin 1 p. 90 (ex. 3, study)
1978 Walker, Sumer 34 pp. 100 and 103 (exs. 1–3, composite copy, edition)
1981 Walker in Hrouda, Isin 2 p. 95 (exs. 1–3, edition)

TEXT

1) é-gal
2) ^{d}EN.ZU-*ma-gir*

1–2) Palace of Sîn-māgir.

2001

A seal bears the inscription of Iddin-Damu, servant of Sîn-māgir.

COMMENTARY

The present location of the seal is unknown. It belonged to the collection of Mr L. Naville. The provenance of the seal is not known. It was collated from the published photo.

BIBLIOGRAPHY

1925 Boissier, RA 23 p. 18 no. 7 (photo) and pp. 19–20 no. 7 (transliteration, study)
1953 Weidner, JKF 2 p. 127 (transliteration, study)
1961 Hallo, BiOr 18 p. 7 Sin-magir 3 (study)
1968 Kärki, SKFZ p. 22 Sînmāgir 3 (edition)
1971 Sollberger and Kupper, IRSA IVA4b (translation)
1980 Kärki, SAKAZ 1 p. 37 Sînmāgir 3 (edition)

TEXT

1) *i-din-*^{d}*da-mu*
2) šitim-gal
3) dumu-ia-a
4) ìr-^{d}en-ki
5) ù ^{d}EN.ZU-*ma-gir*

1) Iddin-Damu,
2) chief builder,
3) son of Iaia,
4–5) servant of Enki and Sîn-māgir.

2002

A cylinder seal originally from the Duke of Luynes collection bears the inscription of a servant of Sîn-māgir.

COMMENTARY

The seal is Bibliothèque Nationale no. 225, provenance unknown. It is a haematite seal, 2.5 × 1.5 cm, and was collated from the published photo.

BIBLIOGRAPHY

1883 Ménant, Glyptique 1 p. 161 fig. 99 (copy)
1910 Delaporte, Revue archéologique series 4 vol. 15 p. 31 fig. 4
1910 Delaporte, Bibliothèque Nationale no. 225 (photo, copy, edition)
1926 Unger, RLV 4/2 pl. 159c (photo)
1926 Unger, SuAK p. 105 fig. 56 (photo) and p. 57 (study)
1961 Hallo, BiOr 18 p. 7 Sin-magir 4 (study)

1968 Kärki, SKFZ p. 22 Sînmāgir 4 (edition)
1971 Sollberger and Kupper, IRSA IVA4c (translation)
1980 Kärki, SAKAZ 1 p. 37 Sînmāgir 4 (edition)

TEXT

1) *im-gur*-^{d}EN.ZU	1) Imgur-Sîn,
2) šabra	2) administrator,
3) dumu-^{d}EN.ZU-*i-din-na-am*	3) son of Sîn-iddinam,
4) ìr-^{d}EN.ZU-*ma-gir*	4) servant of Sîn-māgir.

2003

A seal impression on a tablet in the Yale collections bears the name of a servant of Sîn-māgir.

COMMENTARY

The impression is on NBC 6451, a clay tablet which was purchased. The provenance is probably Isin. The impression was not collated. The tablet is dated by a year formula of Sîn-māgir.

BIBLIOGRAPHY

1978 Simmons, YOS 14 pl. CXXIII seal no. 139 (copy)

TEXT

1) *a-na*-^{d}*da-mu-ták-la-ku*	1) Ana-Damu-taklāku,
2) (blank)	2) (blank)
3) dumu-*a-da-ta*	3) son of Adata,
4) ìr-^{d}EN.ZU-*ma-gir*	4) servant of Sîn-māgir.

Damiq-ilīšu

E4.1.15

According to a king list in Philadelphia (BE 20 no. 47), Damiq-ilīšu, the last king of the Isin dynasty, reigned 23 years. Four inscriptions are known for this king.

1

A year formula of Damiq-ilīšu records the construction of the wall of Isin. The same deed is commemorated in a cone inscription of the king.

CATALOGUE

Ex.	Museum number	Excavation number	Provenance	Object	Dimensions (cm)	Lines preserved	cpn
1	HS 2008	None, from the Hilprecht expedition, 3rd campaign	Nippur	Head	12.2 dia.	1–23	c
2	HS 2008	As ex. 1	As ex. 1	Shaft	7.3	1–23	c
3	CBS 9999	Hilprecht expedition	Nippur	Head	11.9	1–23	c
4	CBS 9999	As ex. 3	Nippur	Shaft	11.9	1–5, 16–23	c
5	IM –	IB 1090	Isin, from N IIn, room 345 N/45 E, in rubble	Shaft	2.7	11–15	c

COMMENTARY

Exs. 1–4 although dealing with a construction in Isin were excavated at Nippur by the Hilprecht expedition. Ex. 1 was published in photo by Legrain in PBS 15 pl. VIII mistakenly under the museum no. CBS 9999. This museum no. actually refers to our exs. 3–4. Ex. 5, from Isin, contains only lines 11–15, and is so fragmentary that it could belong to either E4.1.15.1, 2, or 3. It is arbitrarily assigned here to E4.1.15.1. Ex. 2 was collated through the courtesy of Dr J. Oelsner.

BIBLIOGRAPHY

1903 Hilprecht, Explorations pp. 417–18 (exs. 1–4, provenance)

1906 Hilprecht, BE 20/1 p. 50 (study)

1914 Poebel, PBS 5 no. 73 (exs. 3–4, photo, copy)

1926 Legrain, PBS 15 no. 85 (ex. 1, photo, edition)

1929 Barton, RISA pp. 390–91 Damiq-ilishu 1 (edition)

1961 Hallo, BiOr 18 p. 7 Damiq-ilišu 1 (study)

1968 Kärki, SKFZ pp. 22–23 Damiqilīšu 1 (edition)

1969 Oelsner, WZJ 18 p. 54 no. 29 (exs. 1–2, study)

1971 Sollberger and Kupper, IRSA IVA5a (translation)

1980 Kärki, SAKAZ 1 pp. 37–38 Damiqilīšu 1 (edition)

1981 Walker in Hrouda, Isin 2 p. 94 (ex. 5, study)

1982 Lieberman, RA 76 p. 106 n. 41 (study)

TEXT

1) ^{d}*da-mi-iq-ì-lí-šu*
2) sag-ús-
3) nibru.KI
4) sipa še-ga-an-na
5) ^{d}en-líl-da giš-tuk
6) nun šà-ki-ág-
7) ^{d}nin-in-si-na
8) engar nì-túm-túm
9) guru$_{7}$ gú-gur-gur-re
10) ú-a-zi-
11) èš é-gal-maḫ-a
12) lugal-kala-ga
13) lugal-ì-si-in.KI-na
14) lugal-ki-en-gi-ki-uri
15) me-te-nam-en-na
16) ^{d}inanna-ra túm-ma

1–16) Damiq-ilīšu, constant (attendant) of Nippur, shepherd, favourite of the god An, who heeds the god Enlil, prince beloved of the heart of the goddess Ninisina, farmer who piles up the produce (of the land) in granaries, true provider of the shrine Egalmaḫ, mighty king, king of Isin, king of the land of Sumer and Akkad, suitable for the office of *en* priest befitting the goddess Inanna,

17) bàd-gal-
18) ì-si-in.KI-na
19) mu-dù

17–19) built the great wall of Isin.

20) bàd-ba
21) ^{d}*da-mi-iq-ì-lí-šu-*
22) *mi-gir-*^{d}*nin-urta*
23) mu-bi-im

20–23) The name of the wall is 'Damiq-ilīšu is the favourite of the god Ninurta'.

2

An inscription known from two cones, one excavated at Isin, deals with Damiq-ilīšu's construction of a storehouse for the god Mardu.

CATALOGUE

Ex.	Museum number	Excavation number	Provenance	Object	Dimensions (cm)	Lines preserved	cpn
1	A 7556	–	Isin(?)	Head	11.5 dia.	1–21	c
2	A 7556	–	Isin(?)	Shaft	7.0	13–21	c
3	IM –	IB 1291	Isin, SE room 4 101.05 SA 237.55 E, +6.22	Cone		19–21	n

COMMENTARY

Ex. 3 was entered from a copy of C. Wilcke. Exs. 1 and 2 were purchased.

BIBLIOGRAPHY

1959 Hallo, JNES 18 p. 56 (study), p. 60 (edition), p. 64 (ex. 1, copy), and pp. 69–70 (exs. 1–2, photo)
1961 Hallo, BiOr 18 p. 7 Damiq-ilišu 2 (study)
1968 Kärki, SKFZ p. 23 Damiqilīšu 2 (edition)
1971 Sollberger and Kupper, IRSA IVA15b (translation)
1980 Kärki, SAKAZ 1 pp. 38–39 Damiqilīšu 2 (edition)
1981 Walker in Hrouda, Isin 2 p. 94 (ex. 3, study)

TEXT

1) ^{d}mar-dú
2) dumu-an-na
3) me-ni kù-kù-ga
4) dingir-ra-a-ni-ir

1–4) For the god Mardu, son of the god An, whose *me*s shine, his god,

5) ^{d}*da-mi-iq-ì-lí-šu*
6) sipa še-ga-an-na
7) ^{d}en-líl-da giš-tuk
8) nun šà-ki-ág-
9) ^{d}nin-in-si-na
10) engar nì-túm-túm
11) guru$_7$ gú-gur-gur-re
12) ú-a-zi-
13) èš é-gal-maḫ
14) lugal-kala-ga
15) lugal-ì-si-in.KI-na
16) lugal-ki-en-gi-ki-uri
17) me-te-nam-en-na
18) ^{d}inanna-ra túm-ma

5–18) Damiq-ilīšu, shepherd, favourite of the god An, who heeds the god Enlil, prince beloved of the heart of the goddess Ninisina, farmer who piles up the produce (of the land) in heaps, true provider of the shrine Egalmaḫ, mighty king, king of Isin, king of the land of Sumer and Akkad, suitable for the office of *en* priest befitting the goddess Inanna,

19) é-me-sikil
20) é-šútum-ki-ág-gá-ni
21) mu-na-dù

19–21) built for him the Emesikil ('House with pure *me*s'), his beloved storehouse.

3

A cone excavated at Isin deals with Damiq-ilīšu's construction of the temple é-ki-tuš-bi-du$_{10}$ for some god whose name is broken away. It may possibly have been Nergal of Uṣarpara(n).

COMMENTARY

The cone has not yet been assigned an IM no. but it has the excavation no. IB 1481. It was found at Isin, 855.45 N, 291.45 E, 6.5 cm down. The cone head measures 12.3 cm in dia.; the shaft is broken away.

BIBLIOGRAPHY

1987 Wilcke in Hrouda, et al., Isin 3 pp. 116–17 g (edition)

TEXT

1) [^{d}nè-eri$_{11}$-gal]
2) ú-ṣa-a[r-pa-ra-(an).KI]
3) [l]ugal-a-ni-i[r]

1–3) [For the god Nergal] of Uṣa[rpara], his lord,

4) ^{d}*da-mi-iq-ì-lí-šu*
5) sipa š[e]-ga-an-na
6) ^{d}en-líl-da giš-tuk
7) nun šà-ki-[á]g-
8) ^{d}nin-in-si-na

4–17) Damiq-ilīšu, shepherd, favourite of the god An, who heeds the god Enlil, prince beloved of the heart of the goddess Ninisina, farmer who piles up the produce (of the land) in granaries, true provider [of shrine Egalma]ḫ, [migh]ty

9) engar nì-túm-túm
10) guru$_{7}$ gú-gur-gur-re
11) ú-a-zi-
12) [èš é-gal-ma]ḫ
13) [lugal-kal]a-ga
14) lu[g]al-ì-si-in.KI
15) lugal-ki-en-gi-ki-uri
16) me-te-nam-en-na
17) ^{d}inanna-ra túm-ma
18) é-ki-tuš-bi-du$_{10}$
19) é-ki-ág-gá-ni
20) mu-na-dù

[king], king of Isin, king of the land of Sumer and Akkad, suitable for the office of *en* priest befitting the goddess Inanna,

18–20) built for him the Ekitušbidu ('House – its residence is good'), his beloved house.

4

A brick fragment bears the 'palace inscription' of Damiq-ilīšu.

COMMENTARY

The brick was picked up from the surface of Tulūl al-Humr, an Islamic tell south of Isin.

BIBLIOGRAPHY

1987–88 Krebernik, Sumer 45 pp. 32 and 37 (study)

TEXT

1) [É].GAL [*da*]-*mi-iq-ì-lí-šu*

1) [Pal]ace of [Da]miq-ilīšu.

2001

This inscription contains a dedication to the god Nergal of Apiak for the life of Damiq-ilīšu.

COMMENTARY

The inscription is found on a black stone figure of a recumbent lion shown to the British Museum and subsequently sold at Sotheby's July 12–13, 1976. The transliteration offered here of this previously unpublished text is through the courtesy of C.B.F. Walker.

The name in line 10 is read *pí-iq-qum* to agree with that found in E4.4.7.2001.

TEXT

1) ^{d}nè-eri$_{11}$-gal 2) a-pi$_{5}$-ak.KI 3) nir-alim pirig nè-tuku 4) dingir-ra-a-ni-ir	1–4) To the god Nergal of Apiak, distinguished prince, lion possessing might, his god,
5) nam-ti- 6) ^{d}*da-mi-iq-ì-lí-šu* 7) lugal-ki-en-gi-ki-uri-ka-šè	5–7) for the life of Damiq-ilīšu, king of the land of Sumer and Akkad,
8) ÌR-^{d}nanna 9) dub-sar-lugal 10) dumu-*pí-iq-qum*-ke$_{4}$ 11) ìr-da-ni	8–11) Warad-Nanna, royal scribe, son of Pīqqum, his servant,
12) a mu-na-ru	12) dedicated (this lion) to him.

LARSA

E4.2

The city of Larsa appears to have gained its independence at a relatively early date after the fall of Ur. Unfortunately, the history of Larsa at this early period is very obscure.

An important source for the history of Larsa is the Larsa King List, YBC 2142, published as YOS 1 no. 32. This list gives a total of 16 rulers of the city down to the time of Samsu-iluna. The city itself was independent until its defeat in year 30 of Ḫammu-rāpi.

Naplānum

E4.2.1

The first ruler in the Larsa King List is Naplānum, who is given a reign of 21 years. If we take into account later synchronisms between Isin and Larsa rulers and count backwards through the Larsa King List, Naplānum would appear to date to the beginning of the reign of Ibbi-Sîn. We have no inscriptions for this ruler.

Iemṣium

E4.2.2

Naplānum is followed in the Larsa King List by Iemṣium with a reign of 28 years. No inscriptions of Iemṣium have appeared.

Sāmium

E4.2.3

Iemṣium is followed in the Larsa King List by Sāmium, with a reign of 35 years. He is known to have been the father of Zabāia who succeeded him as ruler of Larsa.

Zabāia

E4.2.4

Sāmium was followed by his son Zabāia as ruler of Larsa. The Larsa King List gives him a reign of 9 years. For the first time we have inscriptions of a ruler who figures in the Larsa King List. In addition to these inscriptions, the king is mentioned in a letter published by Arnaud, RA 71 (1977) pp. 3–4.

1

On the surface of the tell at Larsa were found examples of a five-line stamped brick of Zabāia in Akkadian dealing with the construction of the Ebabbar temple.

CATALOGUE

Ex.	Museum number	Excavation number	Provenance	Dimensions (cm)	Lines preserved	cpn
1	–	L 67–	From the surface of the tell	Stamp 10.7×7.4	1-5	n
2	–	L 7091	From the surface of the tell, 'quartier ancien' between the ziqqurrat, sounding J. VIII and the palace of Nūr-Adad	–	–	n
3	–	L 7096	As ex. 2	–	–	n
4	–	L 70–	As ex. 2	Stamp 10.7×7.4	1-5	n
5	–	L 70–	As ex. 2	Stamp 10.7×7.4	1-5	n

COMMENTARY

None of these bricks has been collated. The text is that given by M. Birot for ex. 1. While the stamped area of exs. 4–5 is complete, the inscription there is illegible.

BIBLIOGRAPHY

1968 Birot, Syria 45 p. 243 no. 1 (ex. 1, copy, edition)
1971 Arnaud, Syria 48 p. 292 (exs. 2–5, study)
1971 Sollberger and Kupper, IRSA IVB4a (translation)
1980 Kärki, SAKAZ 1 p. 39 Zabāja 1 (edition)

TEXT

1) *za-ba-a-a*	1) Zabāia,
2) *ra-bí-an* MAR.DÚ	2) Amorite chief,
3) DUMU *sa-mi-um*	3) son of Sāmium,
4) É.BABBAR.RA	4–5) built the Ebabbar.
5) *i-pu-uš*	

2

A fragment of a cone excavated at Tell Abū Duwari, ancient Maškan-šāpir, gives the beginning of a royal inscription in Sumerian belonging to Zabāia.

COMMENTARY

The cone has the excavation no. AbD 88-286, and is edited here through the courtesy of P. Steinkeller.

TEXT

1) *za-ba-a-*[*a*]	1) Zabā[ia],
2) nita-kala-g[a]	2) mighty man,
3) *ra-b*[*í-an*-mar-dú]	3) [Amorite] chi[ef],
4) [dumu *sa-mi-um*]	4) [son of Sāmium].
Lacuna	Lacuna

3

A tablet recently excavated at Sippar contains a late copy of a dedicatory text of Zabāia that was once inscribed on a bronze tablet. The text has not yet been published.

BIBLIOGRAPHY

1987 Anon., Iraq 49 p. 249 (study)

2001

A seal of a servant of Zabāia is in Cincinnati.

COMMENTARY

The seal is in the possession of D. Weisberg, who will publish it, and through whose courtesy it is edited here.

TEXT

1) *i-ku-mi-š*[*ar*]	1) Ikū(n)-Mīš[ar],
2) ÌR *za-ba-a-a*	2) servant of Zabāia.

Gungunum

E4.2.5

Zabāia was succeeded by Gungunum as king of Larsa. He reigned 27 years. All of Gungunum's year names are known, a fact which sheds a good deal of light on the history of this period. A number of inscriptions are extant for this ruler.

A marked expansion of the realms of Larsa occurred during the reign of Gungunum. By year 10 of Gungunum the Larsa ruler had gained control over the city of Ur. He then assumed the title 'king of Ur' found in E4.2.5.1–2. A variety of evidence suggests that later in the reign Gungunum may have controlled Nippur for a short time. The name of year 19 mentions Gungunum acting at the command of Enlil and Nanna, city gods of Nippur and Ur. A hymn of Gungunum (see A. Sjöberg, ZA 63 [1973] pp. 24–31 no. 4) was transmitted in the schools of Nippur. The name of year 22 deals with the digging of the Išartum canal, a canal which probably flowed near Nippur. At this time Gungunum probably assumed the title 'king of Sumer and Akkad', a title which may reflect his recognition by the authorities at Nippur. The title is found in E4.2.5.3–4.

1

By year 10 of Gungunum Larsa gained control over Ur, which had previously been under the domination of Isin. En-ana-tuma, the daughter of Išme-Dagān of Isin, who had been installed as *en* priestess of Nanna by her father, continued in that role during the domination of the city by Larsa. We have two building inscriptions which she had inscribed on behalf of her new lord Gungunum. The first is a cone inscription dealing with the construction of a storehouse for the god Dagān. In this inscription Gungunum appears as 'king of Ur'.

CATALOGUE

Ex.	Museum number	Excavation number	Provenance	Object	Dimensions (cm)	Lines preserved	cpn
1	CBS 17224	U 8835	From the Royal Cemetery Trial Trench G, rubbish, near top	Head	–	1-9, 12	c
2	CBS 17224	U 8835	As ex. 1	Shaft	–	5-9, 13-17	c
3	IM 92961	U 13602	Larsa rubbish filling over the Royal Cemetery area	Head	7.3 dia.	1-9, 11-16	c
4	IM 92961	U 13602	As ex. 3	Shaft	6.7	1-9	c
5	IM 92960	U 15035	From the Royal Cemetery near the surface	Shaft	8.8	4-17	c

COMMENTARY

The text is a conflated one; lines 1–3 come from ex. 1, lines 4–17 from ex. 5.

BIBLIOGRAPHY

1928 Gadd, UET 1 no. 297 (ex. 1, composite copy, edition)
1957 Edzard, Zwischenzeit p. 101 (study)
1961 Hallo, BiOr 18 p. 7 Gungunum 2 (study)
1965 Sollberger, UET 8 no. 64 (exs. 3-5, composite copy; exs. 1-5, study)
1968 Kärki, SKFZ p. 24 Gungunum 2 (edition)
1971 Sollberger and Kupper, IRSA ɪᴠB5b (translation)
1980 Kärki, SAKAZ 1 p. 40 Gungunum 2 (edition)

TEXT

1) ^{d}*da-gan*
2) en-dingir-gal-gal-e-ne
3) dingir-ra-a-ni-ir
4) nam-ti-
5) *gu-un-gu-nu-um*
6) nita-kala-ga
7) lugal-uri₅.ᴋɪ-ma-ka-šè
8) en-an-na-túm-ma
9) en-ki-ág-^{d}nanna
10) [š]à-uri₅.ᴋɪ-ma
11) dumu-^{d}*iš-me*-^{d}*da-gan*
12) lugal-ki-en-gi-ki-uri-ke₄
13) é-èš-me-dagal-l[a]
14) é-šútum-kù-ga-ni
15) mu-na-dù
16) ù nam-ti-la-ni-šè
17) a mu-na-ru

1–3) For the god Dagān, lord of the great gods, her god,

4–7) for the life of Gungunum, mighty man, king of Ur,

8–12) En-ana-tuma, *en* priestess beloved of the god Nanna [i]n Ur, daughter of Išme-Dagān, king of the land of Sumer and Akkad,

13–15) built the Eešmedagala ('House — shrine of the broad *me*s'), his shining storehouse,

16–17) and dedicated it to him for her own life.

2

A cone inscription found at Ur deals with En-ana-tuma's construction of a temple for the sun god Utu for her lord Gungunum. In this inscription Gungunum appears as 'king of Ur'.

CATALOGUE

Ex.	Museum number	Excavation number	Provenance	Object	Dimensions (cm)	Lines preserved	cpn
1	BM 30062	From Taylor's excavations at Ur, no excavation number	In the interior facing of the walls of the temple on the southern mound	Shaft	14.5	1–22	c
2	IM 90933	U 6740	From the 'court of En-ana-tumma' in the Gipar-ku	Shaft frgm.	6.0	5–11	c
3	IM 3570	U 7767	From the SM site	Shaft	5.8	12, 15–22	c
4	IM 22883	U 16032	From the Mausoleum site, filling under the Temenos wall chamber	Shaft	7.3	12–22	c
5	IM 90930	U 18768 + 18785	From the extension of the Royal Cemetery area	Shaft	12.3	1–22	c
6	IM -	U 18878	From the extension of the Royal Cemetery 'about level 1450 in rubbish near the drain'	Head	–	–	n
7	IM -	U 18878	As ex. 6	Shaft	–	–	n
8	IM 90934	U 18894	From the extension of the Royal Cemetery 'in Larsa rubbish pit at level 1250'	Shaft	10.4	2–22	c

COMMENTARY

The master text is ex. 1. Ex. 1 comes from Taylor's excavations at Ur. Exs. 2–8 come from Woolley's excavations in that city.

BIBLIOGRAPHY

1861 1 R pl. 2 no. VI 1 (ex. 1, copy)
1872 G. Smith, TSBA 1 p. 38 (translation)
1874 Lenormant, Études accadiennes 2 p. 334
1875 Ménant, Babylone et la Chaldée p. 79 (translation)
1892 Winckler, KB 3/1 pp. 86–87 Gungunu 1 (edition)
1899 Bezold, Cat. 5 p. 2232 (ex. 1, study)
1900 Radau, EBH p. 25 (partial edition)
1905 Thureau-Dangin, ISA pp. 294–95 Gungunu b (edition)
1905 King, CT 21 pls. 22–23 (ex. 1, copy)
1907 Thureau-Dangin, SAK pp. 206–207 Gungunu b (edition)
1910 King, Early History pl. XXXIII facing p. 314 (ex. 1, photo)
1928 Gadd, UET 1 p. xxiv (ex. 2, study)
1929 Barton, RISA pp. 310–11 Gungunu 2 (edition)
1957 Edzard, Sumer 13 p. 175 (exs. 3–4, study)
1961 Hallo, BiOr 18 p. 7 Gungunum 3 (study)
1965 Sollberger, UET 8 p. 36 no. 48 (exs. 2, 5–8, study)
1968 Kärki, SKFZ pp. 24–25 Gungunum 3 (edition)
1980 Kärki, SAKAZ 1 p. 41 Gungunum 3 (edition)

TEXT

1) ^{d}utu
2) ù-tu-da-
3) ^{d}nanna
4) dumu.NE-
5) é-kiš.KI-nu-gál
6) ^{d}nin-gal-e tu-da
7) lugal-a-ni-ir

1–7) For the god Utu, offspring of the god Nanna, ... son of the Ekišnugal, whom the goddess Ningal bore, his lord,

8) nam-ti-
9) *gu-un-gu-nu-um*
10) nita-kala-ga
11) lugal-uri$_5$.KI-ma-ka-šè

8–11) for the life of Gungunum, mighty man, king of Ur,

12) en-an-na-túm-ma
13) zirru$_x$(EN.MUNUS.NUNUZ.ZI.^{d}NANNA)
14) en-^{d}nanna
15) šà-uri$_5$.KI-ma

12–17) En-ana-tuma, *zirru* priestess, *en* priestess of the god Nanna in Ur, daughter of Išme-Dagān, king of the land of Sumer and Akkad,

16)	dumu-^{d}*iš-me-*^{d}*da-gan*	
17)	lugal-ki-en-gi-ki-uri	
18)	é-ḫi-li-a-ni in-dù	18–20) built his Eḫili ('Charming house'), built his shining storehouse for him.
19)	é-šútum-kù-ga-ni	
20)	mu-na-dù	
21)	nam-ti-la-ni-šè	21–22) She dedicated it to him for her own life.
22)	a mu-na-ru	

3

The name of year 21 of Gungunum commemorates the construction of the wall of Larsa. This deed is also recorded in a 10-line stamped brick inscription found at Larsa and Umm al-Wawīya, the latter a small site between Larsa and Uruk. In this text Gungunum appears as 'king of Sumer and Akkad'.

CATALOGUE

Ex.	Museum number	Excavation number	Provenance	Dimensions (cm)	Lines preserved	cpn
1	AO 3764	–	Larsa	7.7×9.2×1.0	1–10	c
2	–	–	Larsa, picked up from the surface by tourists	–	1–10	n
3	–	L 7081	Larsa, surface find in the 'quartier ancien' between the ziqqurrat, sounding J. VIII and Nūr-Adad's palace	5.1×8.4	1–10	n
4	–	L 70–	Larsa	–	–	n
5	–	L 70–	Larsa, reused in the oval altar in the interior courtyard of the Ebabbar	–	–	n
6	–	L 69–	Larsa, from G. IX in the west	–	–	n
7	–	L 74–	Larsa	–	–	n
8	–	WS 439	Umm al-Wawīya	–	1–10	p
9	–	WS 439	As ex. 8	–	7–10	p
10	–	WS 439	As ex. 8	–	1–5	p
11	–	WS 439	As ex. 8	–	1–10	p
12	–	WS 439	As ex. 8	–	1–10	p
13	–	WS 439	As ex. 8	–	7–10	p
14	–	WS 439	As ex. 8	–	1–10	p

COMMENTARY

The master text is ex. 1. Exs. 2–3 are entered in the score from the published copy. Exs. 8–14 were collated from photos kindly provided by R. Adams and H. Nissen. Among the seven exs. collated from the photos are IM 70638, 70639, 70640, 70641, and 70642.

BIBLIOGRAPHY

1905 Thureau-Dangin, ISA pp. 292–95 Gungunu a (ex. 1, edition)
1907 Thureau-Dangin, SAK pp. 206–207 Gungunu a (ex. 1, edition)
1929 Barton, RISA pp. 310–11 Gungunu 1 (edition)
1958 Roux, RA 52 pp. 233–35 (ex. 2, copy, edition)
1961 Hallo, BiOr 18 p. 7 Gungunum 1 (study)
1968 Kärki, SKFZ p. 24 Gungunum 1 (edition)
1971 Sollberger and Kupper, IRSA IVB5a (translation)
1971 Arnaud, Syria 48 p. 292 (exs. 3–6, study)
1972 Arnaud, RA 66 p. 34 no. 1 (ex. 3, copy, edition)
1972 Adams, Countryside p. 217 (exs. 8–12, study)
1978 Arnaud, Sumer 34 pp. 165 and 175 n. 4 (ex. 7, study)
1980 Kärki, SAKAZ 1 pp. 39–40 Gungunum 1 (edition)

TEXT

1) *gu-un-gu-nu-um*
2) lugal-larsa.KI-ma
3) lugal-ki-en-gi-ki-uri
4) ibila-kala-ga-
5) *sa-mi-um*
6) bàd-gal-larsa.KI-ma
7) ᵈutu ki-bal-e sá-di
8) mu-bi-im
9) šà-mu-aš-ka sig₄-bi
10) ù bàd-bi mu-dù

1–5) Gungunum, king of Larsa, king of the land of Sumer and Akkad, mighty heir of Sāmium,

6–10) in the course of one year made the bricks and built the great wall of Larsa named Utu-kibale-sadi ('the god Utu overtakes the rebellious land').

4

V. Scheil reports finding a tablet with a votive inscription of Gungunum, but since the location of the tablet cannot be determined, nothing is known about the text more than the fact that it contained the name of the king and his titles.

BIBLIOGRAPHY

1902 Scheil, RT 24 p. 25 (study)

TEXT

1) *gu-un-gu-nu-um*
2) lugal-larsa.KI-ma
3) lugal-ki-en-gi-ki-uri

1) Gungunum,
2) king of Larsa,
3) king of the land of Sumer and Akkad ...

2001

A number of tablets in the Yale collections bear seal impressions of servants of Gungunum. The first of these is the impression of Sîn-iddinam.

COMMENTARY

The impression is found on MLC 1598 and YBC 10314 published as YOS 14 nos. 180 and 186 respectively. These date to the first and second years of Abī-sarē. They were not collated.

BIBLIOGRAPHY

1978 Simmons, YOS 14 pl. CXX seal no. 79 (exs. 1–2, composite copy)

TEXT

1) [^{d}]EN.ZU-*i-din-na-*[*am*]	1) Sîn-iddina[m],
2) DUMU *i-la-ti-ia*	2) son of Illatīia,
3) ÌR *gu-un-gu-nu-um*	3) servant of Gungunum.

2002

The name of a servant of Gungunum whose name is not preserved in his seal impression is found on a tablet in the Yale collections.

COMMENTARY

The impression is on YBC 10242 = YOS 14 no. 185. The tablet dates to year 26 of Gungunum. The inscription was not collated.

BIBLIOGRAPHY

1978 Simmons, YOS 14 pl. CXX seal no. 82 (copy)

TEXT

1) [...]	1) [...],
2) DUMU ^{d}*en-líl-ri-m*[*e-ni*]	2) son of Enlil-rēm[ēni],
3) IR_{11} *gu-un-g*[*u-nu-um*]	3) servant of Gung[unum].

2003

The impression of Nanna-ursag-kalama, servant of Gungunum, is found on a large number of tablets in the Yale collections.

COMMENTARY

The impression is on YOS 14 nos. 194, 197, 199, 201–203, 206, 210–211, and 213. The tablets date to years 5–7 and 10 of Abī-sarē and year 1 of Sūmû-El. The impressions were not collated.

BIBLIOGRAPHY

1978 Simmons, YOS 14 pl. cxxi seal no. 87 (copy)

TEXT

1) ^{d}nanna-ur-sag-kalam-ma	1) Nanna-ursag-kalama,
2) DUB.SAR DUMU *iṣ-ru*	2) scribe, son of Iṣru,
3) ÌR *gu-un-gu-[nu-um]*	3) servant of Gungu[num].

Abī-sarē

E4.2.6

Gungunum was succeeded by Abī-sarē as king of Larsa. He ruled 11 years. All his year names are known as well as a number of his royal inscriptions.

1

The name of the third year of Abī-sarē deals with the introduction of a silver statue into the temple of Nanna. This same deed is commemorated in a royal inscription of the king known from a later school copy on a clay tablet excavated at Ur.

COMMENTARY

The tablet is now in the Iraq Museum, museum no. as yet undetermined. It was not collated.

According to E. Sollberger, the excavation no. on the piece is U 7792, which is also found on a lexical tablet published as UET 7 no. 92. Sollberger, therefore, assigned the arbitrary designation U s for the Abī-sarē inscription. The reading 7792 might be a mistake for 7752, which the Ur catalogue indicates is a large tablet fragment. Both U 7752 and 7792 were found in the upper part of the ruins of no. 7 Quiet Street. A large number of copies of royal inscriptions came from that site.

Col. vi 12–16 are restored from an Ur-Nammu cone inscription (see I. Kärki, KDDU p. 17 Urnammu 28 lines 29–32). In vi 13 [GI.K]A is probably to be connected with Akkadian *šakka(n)num*, a kind of reed, but see AHw p. 1140.

BIBLIOGRAPHY

1965 Sollberger, UET 8 no. 65 (copy, study)
1966 Falkenstein, BiOr 23 pp. 166–67 (study)
1967 Pettinato, Orientalia NS 36 pp. 454–55 (study)
1971 Sollberger and Kupper, IRSA IVA6a (translation)
1977 Durand, RA 71 pp. 23–25 (study)
1980 Kärki, SAKAZ 1 pp. 42–46 Abīsarē 4 (edition)

TEXT

Col. i
Lacuna
1′) [é-ku]r-[r]a ḫé-du$_7$
2′) [dumu]-zil an-gal-e
3′) nir sum-ma
4′) me nì-nam-ma
5′) šu-ni-šè gál-la

Lacuna
i 1′–12′) [(For the god Nanna) ...] the one befitting *the* [*Eku*]*r*, princely [son] given authority by great An, into whose hands all the *me*s have been entrusted, shining god who resides in pure heaven, true supreme authority of the nation,

6′) dingir-kù an-sikil-la
7′) du$_{10}$-gar-ra
8′) nir-zi-maḫ-kalam-ma
9′) é ki-tuš-maḫ
10′) ki-kù-ga
11′) bára ri-a
12′) giri$_{17}$-zal-la dúr-gar

who set up a dais in the house, 'lofty residence', a shining place, who sits in splendour,

13′) gal-di gal-zu-maḫ
14′) eš-bar-e sa-di
15′) giri$_{17}$-zal-a-a-ugu-na
16′) ki-ág giškim-ti-
17′) é-kur-ra
18′) ^{d}nin-líl-le
19′) tu-da
20′) ^{d}nanna
21′) lugal-ki-ág-mu-ra

i 13′–21′) noble one, supreme in wisdom, who reaches (the right) decision, splendour of the father who engendered him, beloved, trust of the Ekur, born of the goddess Ninlil, for the god Nanna, my beloved lord,

22′) ⌜*a*⌝-*bí-sa-re-e*
23′) [sipa] giš-tuk
24′) [ki-á]g-^{d}EN.ZU-na
25′) [nit]a-kala-ga
26′) [lu]gal-uri$_5$.KI-ma
27′) *ra-bí-a-nu-um* mar-dú-me-en

i 22′–27′) I, Abī-sarē, heedful [shepherd, belo]ved of the god Sîn, mighty [ma]n, [ki]ng of Ur, Amorite chief,

28′) u$_4$-ul-lí-a-ta
29′) alam kù-babbar
30′) NA$_4$.NÌ.GUL.DA-ta ak-a
31′) nu-ub-ta-gál-la-àm

i 28′–31′) from the past no statue fashioned of silver and *carnelian* having existed,

Col. ii
Lacuna

Lacuna

1′) [géšt]u-m[aḫ]
2′) nì-nam-ma diri-ga
3′) gá-ra ḫa-ma-an-sum

ii 1′–3′) [... the god *Enki* ...] gave to me su[preme intellig]ence, surpassing everything

4′) alam kù-babbar
5′) NA$_4$.NÌ.GUL.DA-ta ak-a
6′) kin-gal-eš
7′) nam-kù-zu ak
8′) me-dím-bi
9′) me-dím-ma diri-ga
10′) nì ár-eš dib-b[a]
11′) gi$_{16}$-sa a[k]
12′) alam k[ù-babbar]
13′) nì-da-[rí]
14′) é-^{d}nann[a-ta]
15′) nu-kúr-[ru-da]
16′) é-^{d}nan[na-ka]
17′) a-ra im-[x x]

ii 4′–17′) (and) a statue fashioned of silver and *carnelian*, expertly formed as a masterpiece, bigger than life size, a thing surpassing praise, fashioned with jewels, a s[ilver statue], an etern[al] thing that [should not be] removed [from] the temple of the god Nann[a] but in the temple of the god Nan[na] ...,

18′) gá-[e]
19′) *a-bí-sa-*[*re-e*]
20′) lú sa-ra [...]
21′) sa-ra mu-[x x]
22′) alam-[mu]
23′) u$_4$-šú-[uš-e]
24′) sa$_6$-ga-[mu]
25′) géštu-^{d}[nanna-šè]
26′) ru-gú-[dè]
27′) mu-na-[gub]

ii 18′–27′) I, Abī-sa[rē], the one who ..., ..., [set it up] for him [in order that my] statue dai[ly] bring [my] favour to the attention of the god [Nanna].

28′) nam-t[i-mu-šè]
29′) a m[u-na-ru]

ii 28′–29′) I de[dicated it for my own l]ife.

30′) ala[m-ba]
31′) *a-b*[*í-sa-re-e*]

ii 30′–31′) [The name of that] stat[ue] is ‘Ab[ī-sarē …’].

Col. iii
1′) x […]
2′) x […]
3′) e x […]
4′) x […]
5′) ḫa-[…]
6′) KA[A …]
7′) ḫ[a …]
8′) x […]
9′) […]
Lacuna

iii) No translation warranted.

Col. iv
Lacuna
1′) x [..]
2′) x […]
3′) ki […]
4′) x […]
Lacuna

iv) No translation warranted.

Col. v
1) x […]
2) NE […]
3) nu-u[n-…]
4) lugal-[bi]
5) sag-k[i(?)-zalag-(ga)]
6) ^{d}nann[a]
7) an-ta ḫ[é-gi$_{4}$]
8) ^{d}nin-[gal]
9) ḫé-en-d[a-ḫúl]
10) é-kiš-nu-gá[l-la]
11) gú an-[šè]
12) ḫé-ni-in-[zi-zi]
13) ^{d}[alad]
14) x [(x)] x-gi$_{4}$-[x x]
15) KA ḫé-n[i-i]b-sa$_{6}$-[sa$_{6}$]
16) nì-gi-n[a]
17) i-^{d}utu-b[i]
18) u$_{4}$-šú-u[š-e]
19) ^{d}lamma-ra-ni ḫé-[še-še]
20) u$_{4}$-da-rí-š[è]

v 1–20) [*As for the king who preserves my work*] … may [that] king appear before the shining face of the god Nanna. May the goddess Nin[gal rejoice] over him. May he lift high his head in the Ekišnugal. May [a guardian spirit] …, pray (for him). May his protective genius [be favourable] dail[y] to (appeals for) justice and causes of complaint, forever.

21) lú á-nì-ḫul-dím-m[a]
22) íb-⟨ši-ág⟩-ge$_{26}$-a
23) nì-dím-ma-m[u]
24) íb-zi-re-a
25) mu-sar-ra-mu
26) šu bí-úb-ùr-a
27) mu-ni
28) bí-íb-sar-re-a
29) ki-gub-ba-bi
30) íb-ši-ib-kúr-a
31) é-nì-GA-ra
32) i-ni-ib-ku$_{4}$-ku$_{4}$-a

v 21–34) (As for) the one who gi[v]es orders to do evil ag[ainst it], who destroys m[y] handiwork, who erases my inscription (and) inscribes his [own] name, changes the place where it stands, has it brought into a storehouse [or] because of this [curs]e [incites another to do so …]

33) [áš-bal]a-ba-ke$_4$-eš
34) [lú-kúr šu ba-an-zi-zi-a]
35) [lú-ba ^{d}nanna]
Col. vi
1) lugal-mu
2) ^{d}nin-gal
3) nin-mu
4) nam ḫa-ba-an-da-kuru$_5$-ne
5) uru.KI-bi
6) du$_6$-du$_6$-ra
7) ḫé-en-šid
8) i$_7$-da-bé
9) a nam-tùm
10) a-šà-ga-né
11) še nam-tùm
12) [uru].KI-ni
13) [GI.K]A-ta
14) ḫ[é-ta-dag]-⌜dag-ge⌝
15) nam-ti
16) nì-gig-ga-ni ḫé-a
17) GIŠ.ÍSIMU.SAR-né
18) GIŠ.ÍSIMU.SAR
19) na-an-tuk-tuk
20) ^{d}nin-gír-su
21) lugal-GIŠ.tukul-ke$_4$
22) GIŠ.tukul-ni
23) ḫé-eb-ta-ḫaš-e
24) ^{d}nin-gubalag
25) dumu-sag-
26) ^{d}nanna-ke$_4$
27) maškim-
28) nu-kúr-ra-bi ḫé-a
29) u$_4$-da-rí-šè

35) [that man may the god Nanna ...]

vi 1–29) my lord, (and) the goddess Ningal, my lady, curse him. May his city be counted among the ruins. May its (city) canal not bring water (and) may his field not bring forth grain. May his [city] and [reed h]ut be torn down. May life be his misfortune. May his offspring beget no offspring. May the god Ningirsu, the lord of the weapon, smash (him) with his weapon. May the god Ningubalag, first-born son of the god Nanna, forever be its (the curse's) evil spirit who cannot be countermanded.

2

A stamped brick inscription in Akkadian found on the surface of the tell at Larsa deals with Abī-sarē's strengthening of the wall of Larsa and the construction of a palace. Surprisingly, neither event is commemorated in a year name of the king.

CATALOGUE

Ex.	Museum number	Excavation number	Provenance	Dimensions (cm)	Lines preserved	cpn
1	–	L 67–	From the surface of the tell	11.0×7.5	1–11	n
2	–	L 7098	As ex. 1	10.8×7.2	1–11	c

COMMENTARY

The text is a conflation of the evidence of exs. 1 and 2.

Ex. 2 was collated from a latex cast through the courtesy of D. Arnaud. The emendation in line 10 was suggested by Arnaud.

BIBLIOGRAPHY

1968 Birot, Syria 45 pp. 243–44 no. 2 (ex. 1, copy, edition)
1971 Arnaud, Syria 48 p. 293 (ex. 2, study)
1977 Durand, RA 71 p. 21 n. 2 (ex. 1, edition)
1980 Kärki, SAKAZ 1 pp. 46–47 Abīsarē 5 (edition)

TEXT

1) *a-bí-sa-re-e*
2) *da-an-nu-u*[*m*]
3) LUGAL *l*[*ars*]*a*.KI
4) *e-li* [*š*]*a* [...]
5) *e-li* [*š*]*a* [...]
6) *i-n*[*a* MU].1.[KA]M.M[A]
7) BÀD ^{d}[utu-ki-ba]l-e sá-[di]
8) BÀD.GAL [*lar*]*sa*.KI
9) *ú-d*[*a-a*]*n-ni-in*
10) É.GAL ⟨*da*⟩*-ad-me-e-šu*
11) *i-pu-uš*

1–3) Abī-sarē, the might[y], king of L[ars]a,

4–9) i[n] the course of one [year] str[eng]thened the great wall of [Lar]sa, the wall [Utu-kiba]le-s[adi] ('the god Utu conquers the rebellious land') more than ..., more than ...,

10–11) (and) built the palace of his ⟨se⟩ttlement.

2001

A mace head in the British Museum has a dedicatory inscription to the god Nergal by Ir-Utu, the engraver, for the life of Abī-sarē.

COMMENTARY

The mace head is BM 104838 (1912-7-6,102). Arnaud suggests that this mace head may have come from the temple of Nergal in Larsa, in sector O. XIV, through clandestine excavations. If this is true, then it would have had the same general provenance as the following inscription.

The mace head measures 6.2 cm high with a dia. of 5.2 cm. The inscription was collated.

In line 8, it is not certain whether the name is to be read in Sumerian — Ir-Utu, or in Akkadian — Warad-Šamaš.

BIBLIOGRAPHY

1912 King, CT 33 pl. 50 (copy)
1929 Barton, RISA pp. 310–11 Abisare 1 (edition)
1961 Hallo, BiOr 18 p. 7 Abisare 1 (study)
1968 Kärki, SKFZ p. 25 Abīsarē 1 (edition)
1971 Sollberger and Kupper, IRSA IVB6b (translation)
1980 Kärki, SAKAZ 1 pp. 41–42 Abīsarē 1 (edition)
1983 Arnaud, RLA 6/7–8 p. 497 §3.1.5 (study)

TEXT

1) ^{d}nergal
2) lugal-a-ni-ir
3) nam-ti-
4) *a-bí-sa-re-e*
5) nita-kala-ga
6) lugal-úri.KI-ma
7) lugal-larsa.KI-ma
8) ìr-^{d}utu
9) bur-gul
10) dumu-lú-^{d}en-ki-ka
11) nam-ti-la-ni-šè
12) a mu-na-ru

1–2) To the god Nergal, his lord,

3–7) for the life of Abī-sarē, mighty man, king of Ur, king of Larsa,

8–12) (and) for his own life Ir-Utu, the engraver, son of Lu-Enkika, dedicated (this seal).

2002

A cylinder seal excavated at Larsa bears a dedicatory inscription to Nergal by Puzur-Ninkarrak, the engraver, for the life of Abī-sarē.

COMMENTARY

The seal is IM 15218, excavation no. L [33]57A, from Larsa, sector O. XIV. Arnaud suggests this may be from the temple of Nergal at Larsa. The seal is of grey-blue steatite, measuring 4.2×2.7 cm. The inscription was collated from the published photo.

BIBLIOGRAPHY

1933 Parrot, RA 30 p. 179 (study)
1951 Porada and Basmachi, Sumer 7 pp. 66–68 (photo, copy, edition)
1954 Parrot, Glyptique mésopotamienne no. 260 (study); M. Lambert, no. 260 (photo, copy, edition)
1957–58 Nagel, AfO 18 p. 320 no. 6 (study) and p. 323 fig. 1 (photo)
1961 Hallo, BiOr 18 p. 7 Abisare 2 (study)
1968 Kärki, SKFZ pp. 25–26 Abīsarē 2 (edition)
1969 Pritchard, ANEP^2 no. 699 (photo, study)
1971 Sollberger and Kupper, IRSA IVB6c (translation)
1971 Limet, Sceaux cassites p. 114 no. 12.0 (edition)
1980 Kärki, SAKAZ 1 p. 42 Abīsarē 2 (edition)
1983 Arnaud, RLA 6/7–8 p. 497 §3.1.5 (study)

TEXT

1) ^{d}ner[gal]
2) lugal-a-ni-i[r]
3) nam-ti-
4) *a-bí-sa-re-e*
5) *puzur$_4$-^{d}nin-kar-ra-ak*
6) bur-gul
7) dumu-*ka-na-ti*
8) nam-ti-la-ni-šè
9) a mu-na-ru

1–2) Fo[r] the god Ner[gal], his lord,

3–4) for the life of Abī-sarē,

5–9) (and) for his own life, Puzur-Ninkarrak, the engraver, son of Kanati, dedicated (this seal).

2003

A number of clay tags from Larsa in the Yale collections bear the seal impressions of officials of Abī-sarē. The first of these is that of Ešūb-El.

COMMENTARY

The text is found on NBC 5422, a purchased tablet from Larsa. The seal impression measures 2.2×1.2 cm and was collated. The impression is also found on BIN 7 nos. 114, 117, 119–120, 122, 124–125, and 129, and YOS 14 no. 220.

BIBLIOGRAPHY

1943 Alexander, BIN 7 no. 115 (copy)
1951 Kraus, JCS 3 p. 47 (provenance)
1961 Hallo, BiOr 18 p. 7 Abisare 3 (study)
1968 Kärki, SKFZ p. 26 Abīsarē 3 (edition)
1971 Sollberger and Kupper, IRSA IVB6d (translation)
1978 Simmons, YOS 14 pl. CXXI seal no. 101 (copy)
1980 Kärki, SAKAZ 1 p. 42 Abīsarē 3 (edition)

TEXT

1) *e-šu-ub-èl*	1) Ešūb-El,
2) IR₁₁ *a-bi-sa-re-e*	2) servant of Abī-sarē,
3) DUMU *kà-ni-na-nu-um*	3) son of Kaninānum.

2004

The seal of Dannīia appears on a tablet at Yale.

COMMENTARY

The tablet is YBC 10297 = YOS 14 no. 207. The impression was not collated.

We note the appellation *rabiān* MARDU 'Amorite chief' for Abī-sarē in this seal inscription. This agrees with his title in E4.2.6.1 i 27′.

BIBLIOGRAPHY

1978 Simmons, YOS 14 pl. CXXI seal no. 93 (copy)

TEXT

1)	*dan-ni-i*[*a*]	1) Dannīi[a],
2)	UGULA ŠU.I	2) overseer of the barbers,
3)	ÌR *a-bí-sa-re-e*	3) servant of Abī-sarē,
4)	RA.BÍ.AN MAR.DÚ	4) Amorite chief.

2005

The seal impression of Warad-[...], servant of Abī-sarē, *sanga* priest of the goddess Ningal, is on a number of tablets in the Yale collections.

COMMENTARY

The impression is found on YOS 14 nos. 190, 208, and 210–211. It was not collated.

Simmons, YOS 14 p. 83, read the seal owner's name as Warad-^{d}[...]; on p. 66 he restores the name as Warad-[Išum], but without giving a reason for this restoration. We have left the name unrestored.

BIBLIOGRAPHY

1978 Simmons, YOS 14 pl. CXXI seal no. 88 (copy)

TEXT

1)	IR_{11}-^{d}[...]	1) Warad-[...],
2)	DUB.[SAR]	2) scr[ibe],
3)	DUMU lú-^{d}nin-šubur	3) son of Lu-Ninšubur,
4)	SANGA ^{d}nin-gal	4) *sanga* priest of the goddess Ningal,
5)	ÌR *a-bí-sa-re-e*	5) servant of Abī-sarē.

2006

The seal impression of Lugal-šuba, servant of Abī-sarē, is found on a number of tablets in the Yale collections.

COMMENTARY

The impression is on YBC 10279, 10318, 10254, and 10268 = YOS 14 nos. 182, 189, 193, and 198 respectively. It was not collated.

BIBLIOGRAPHY

1978 Simmons, YOS 14 pl. CXX seal no. 80 (copy)

TEXT

1) lugal-šuba
2) DUB.SAR
3) DUMU ur-du$_6$-kù-ga
4) ÌR *a-bí-sa-re-e*

1) Lugal-šuba,
2) scribe,
3) son of Urdukuga,
4) servant of Abī-sarē.

2007

The seal impression of Warad-Sîn, servant of Abī-sarē, is on a large number of tablets in the Yale collections.

COMMENTARY

The impression is found on YOS 14 nos. 219, 230–234, 237–240, 242, 245–247, 250, 264, 270, 277, 279–280, and 284. See the text volume for the relevant museum nos. It was not collated.

BIBLIOGRAPHY

1978 Simmons, YOS 14 pl. CXXI seal no. 104 (copy)

TEXT

1) IR$_{11}$-^{d}EN.ZU
2) DUB.SAR-sar
3) IR$_{11}$ *a-bí-sa-re-e*
4) DUMU *zi-na-at-i-lu-ma*

1) Warad-Sîn,
2) scribe,
3) servant of Abī-sarē,
4) son of Zinat-iluma.

Sūmû-El

E4.2.7

Abī-sarē was succeeded by Sūmû-El, who reigned 29 years.

1

A cone inscription from Ur deals with Sūmû-El's construction of a storehouse for the goddess Inanna.

CATALOGUE

Ex.	Museum number	Excavation number	Provenance	Object	Dimensions (cm)	Lines preserved	cpn
1	BM 119028	U 2634	NW terrace of ziqqurrat	Head	4.5 dia.	1-6	c
2	BM 119030	U 2778a	As ex. 1	Shaft	8.7	1-10	c
3	IM 942	U 2778b	As ex. 1	Shaft	–	1-10	c
4	IM 942	U 2778b	As ex. 1	Head	–	3-6, 8-10	c
5	IM 3573A	U 7772a	From Trial Trench D	Head	7.5 dia.	1-10	c
6	IM 3573A	U 7772a	As ex. 5	Shaft	4.3	1-6, 8-10	c
7	IM 3573B	U 7772b	As ex. 5	Shaft	9.2	1-10	c
8	IM 90990	U 7772c	As ex. 5	Head	8.2 dia.	1-10	c
9	IM 90990	U 7772c	As ex. 5	Shaft	9.1	1-10	c
10	IM 3573D	U 7772d	As ex. 5	Shaft	10.0	1-10	c
11	IM 3573D	U 7772d	As ex. 5	Head	4.7 dia.	5-7	c
12	IM 3573E	U 7772e	As ex. 5	Shaft	7.0	1-5	c
13	IM 3573F	U 7772f	As ex. 5	Head	8.2 dia.	1-10	c
14	IM 3573F	U 7772f	As ex. 5	Shaft	6.5	1-4	c
15	IM 3573G	U 7772g	As ex. 5	Shaft	11.5	1-5, 7-10	c
16	IM 3573H	U 7772h	As ex. 5	Shaft	8.5	4-10	c
17	IM 3573H	U 7772h	As ex. 5	Head	4.0	3-6, 10	c
18	IM 3573I	U 7772i	As ex. 5	Shaft	8.0	1-2, 4-10	c
19	BM 120523	U 7776a	From the Royal Cemetery area	Head	7.7 dia.	1-10	c
20	BM 120523	U 7776a	As ex. 19	Shaft	6.5	1-10	c
21	CBS 17226	U 7776b	As ex. 19	Head	8.0 dia.	1-10	c
22	CBS 17226	U 7776b	As ex. 19	Shaft	6.7	7-10	c
23	IM 90988	U 7776c	As ex. 19	Shaft	–	1-10	c
24	IM 92751	U 10103a	From the Royal Cemetery area, top filling	Head	7.2 dia.	5-10	c
25	IM 92751	U 10103a	As ex. 24	Shaft	7.7	1-10	c
26	IM 92756	U 10103b	As ex. 24	Head	8.0 dia.	1-10	c
27	IM 92755	U 10103c	As ex. 24	Head	7.7 dia.	1-10	c
28	IM 92755	U 10103c	As ex. 24	Shaft	6.8	1-8	c
29	IM 92753	U 10103d	As ex. 24	Head	6.0 dia.	3-7	c
30	IM 92753	U 10103d	As ex. 24	Shaft	6.5	1-10	c
31	IM 92747	U 10103e	As ex. 24	Head	8.0 dia.	1-10	c
32	IM 92747	U 10103e	As ex. 24	Shaft	9.0	1-10	c
33	IM 90986	U 10103f	As ex. 24	Shaft	8.5	1-10	c
34	–	U 10103g	As ex. 24	Cone	–	–	n
35	IM 90970	U 10103h	As ex. 24	Head	6.6 dia.	1-8	c
36	IM 90970	U 10103h	As ex. 24	Shaft	7.7	1-10	c
37	IM 90977	U 10103i	As ex. 24	Cone	–	–	n

Ex.	Museum number	Excavation number	Provenance	Object	Dimensions (cm)	Lines preserved	cpn
38	IM 92801	U 10103j	As ex. 24	Shaft	10.5	1–10	c
39	IM 92801	U 10103j	As ex. 24	Head	6.7 dia.	1–7	c
40	IM 92802	U 10103k	As ex. 24	Cone	7.0 dia.	1–10	c
41	IM 92802	U 10103k	As ex. 24	Shaft	6.0	1–10	c
42	IM 90984	U 10103l	As ex. 24	Shaft	9.6	1–10	c
43	IM 90981	U 10103m	As ex. 24	Shaft	7.2	1–10	c
44	IM 90982	U 10103n	As ex. 24	Shaft	8.4	1–10	c
45	IM 90982	U 10103n	As ex. 24	Head	5.0 dia.	6–8	c
46	IM 90980	U 10103o	As ex. 24	Shaft	13.0	6–8	c
47	IM 90979	U 10103p	As ex. 24	Shaft	10.6	1–10	c
48	IM 92747	U 10103q	As ex. 24	Shaft	9.8	1–10	c
49	IM 10865	U 10103r	As ex. 24	Head	9.0 dia.		c
50	IM 10865	U 10103r	As ex. 24	Shaft	6.7		c
51	IM 92754	U 11608a	From the Royal Cemetery area	Head	7.0 dia.	1–10	c
52	IM 92754	U 11608a	As ex. 51	Shaft	10.8	1–10	c
53	IM 90974	U 11608b	As ex. 51	Shaft	9.8	1–10	c
54	IM 90975	U 11608c	As ex. 51	Head	7.0 dia.	1–10	c
55	IM 90975	U 11608c	As ex. 51	Shaft	5.5	1–10	c
56	IM 90973	U 15025	From the Royal Cemetery area, near the surface	Head	7.2 dia.	1–7	c
57	IM 22869	U 16017	From the Mausoleum site, filling	Head	7.6 dia.	1–10	c
58	IM 22869	U 16017	As ex. 57	Shaft	5.5	1–10	c
59	IM 22896	U 17230	From AH site	Head	8.2 dia.	1–10	c
60	IM 22896	U 17230	As ex. 59	Shaft	7.8	1–6	c
61	IM 22899	U 17233	As ex. 59	Head	8.3 dia.	1–10	c
62	IM 22899	U 17233	As ex. 59	Shaft	6.5	1–10	c
63	IM 90972	U 18784a	From the extension of the Royal Cemetery on level 17.00	Head	8.5 dia.	1–10	c
64	IM 90972	U 18784a	As ex. 63	Shaft	6.0	1–10	c
65	IM 90976	U 18784b	As ex. 63	Head	8.0 dia.	1–10	c
66	IM 90976	U 18784b	As ex. 63	Shaft	8.0	1–10	c
67	IM 92752	U xa	–	Many small pieces of cone	–	–	n
68	AO 20016	–	–	Shaft	6.5	1–10	c

COMMENTARY

The master text is ex. 2.

BIBLIOGRAPHY

1928 Gadd, UET 1 no. 114 (exs. 1–2, composite copy, edition)
1929 Barton, RISA pp. 374–75 Sumu-ilu 1 (edition)
1957 Edzard, Sumer 13 pp. 177 and 183 (exs. 3–18, 57–62, study)
1960 Aynard, RA 54 p. 17 (ex. 68, study)
1961 Hallo, BiOr 18 p. 8 Sumu-il 1 (study)
1965 Sollberger, UET 8 pp. 27–28 no. 17 (exs. 5–67, study)
1968 Kärki, SKFZ pp. 26–27 Sumuel 1 (edition)
1971 Sollberger and Kupper, IRSA ɪvB7a (translation)
1980 Kärki, SAKAZ 1 p. 47 Sumuel 1 (edition)

TEXT

1) ᵈinanna
2) nin-a-ni-ir
3) ᵈ*su-mu-èl*
4) nita-kala-ga
5) lugal-uri$_5$.ᴋɪ-ma
6) lugal-ki-en-gi-ki-uri

1–6) For the goddess Inanna, his lady, Sūmû-El, mighty man, king of Ur, king of the land of Sumer and Akkad,

6.7, 10–11 ⟨ki⟩-uri; ex. 6 broken at this point.

7) é-šútum-kù
8) é-ki-ág-a-ni
9) šà-uri$_5$.KI-ma
10) mu-na-dù

7–10) built her shining storehouse, her beloved house, in Ur.

2

A cone inscription from Ur deals with Sūmû-El's construction of a temple for the goddess Nanāia.

CATALOGUE

Ex.	Museum number	Excavation number	Provenance	Object	Dimensions (cm)	Lines preserved	cpn
1	BM 118728	U 6955	Loose in the surface	Shaft	8.3	1–10	c
2	BM 120524	U 7777a	From the Royal Cemetery area	Head	8.1 dia.	1–10	c
3	BM 120524	U 7777a	As ex. 2	Shaft	8.1 dia.	1–10	c
4	BM 120525	U 7777b	As ex. 2	Shaft	6.2	1–10	c
5	IM 92750	U 10103q	As ex. 2	Head	7.3 dia.	3–10	c
6	IM 92854	U 10104	From the Royal Cemetery area, top filling	Shaft	8.0	1–10	c
7	IM 92857	U 11609a	As ex. 2	Head	8.2 dia.	1–10	c
8	IM 92857	U 11609a	As ex. 2	Shaft	6.3	1–10	c
9	IM 92856	U 11609b	As ex. 2	Head	6.5 dia.	1–10	c
10	IM 92851	U 12567	From the great Nanna courtyard in filling of Sîn-iddinam's base	Head	6.5 dia.	1–10	c
11	IM 92851	U 12567	As ex. 10	Shaft	6.0	1–10	c
12	IM 92852	U 15684	No provenance	Shaft	9.7	1–8	c
13	IM 22874	U 16007	From the Mausoleum site, filling	Head	7.2 dia.	1–10	c
14	IM 22874	U 16007	As ex. 13	Shaft	7.0	1–10	c
15	IM 22894	U 17228	From the AH site	Shaft	8.8	1–10	c
16	UM 32-40-401	U -	–	Head	7.1 dia.	1-6, 8–10	c
17	UM 32-40-401	U -	–	Shaft	6.2	1, 4–10	c

COMMENTARY

The master text is ex. 1.

The cones bearing E4.2.7.1–2 of Sūmû-El both came from the Royal Cemetery area at Ur. In view of the close connections between the goddesses Inanna and Nanāia, it is not unlikely that the two temples may have stood beside each other, and were built about the same time by Sūmû-El.

The nin ḫi-li-a-na in line 2 of the copy in UET 1 no. 115 is a mistake. Ex. 1 actually reads nin ḫi-li-a ⸢šu⸣-d[u$_7$].

8.19, 21 é-ki-ág-gá-a-ni; exs. 20, 22 broken at this point.
10.19–22, 30, 43, 55 mu-un-na-dù; exs. 29, 54 broken here.

BIBLIOGRAPHY

1928 Gadd, UET 1 no. 115 (ex. 1, edition; ex. 2, composite copy, vars.)
1929 Barton, RISA pp. 374–75 Sumu-ilu 2 (edition)
1957 Edzard, Sumer 13 pp. 177 and 183 (exs. 13–15, study)
1961 Hallo, BiOr 18 p. 8 Sumu-il 2 (study)
1965 Sollberger, UET 8 p. 28 no. 18 (exs. 2–12, study)
1968 Kärki, SKFZ p. 26 Sumuel 2 (edition)
1971 Sollberger and Kupper, IRSA ɪvB7b (translation)
1980 Kärki, SAKAZ 1 pp. 47–48 Sumuel 2 (edition)

TEXT

1) ᵈna-na-a-a 2) nin ḫi-li-a šu-du₇	1–2) For the the goddess Nanāia, the lady with perfect voluptuousness,
3) ᵈ*su-mu-èl* 4) nita-kala-ga 5) lugal-uri₅.ᴋɪ-ma 6) lugal-ki-en-gi-ki-uri	3–6) Sūmû-El, mighty man, king of Ur, king of the land of Sumer and Akkad,
7) é-iti-da-ka-ni 8) é-šà-ḫúl-a-ni 9) šà-uri₅.ᴋɪ-ma 10) mu-un-na-dù	7–10) built for her her Eitida ('House of the month'), her house which makes her rejoice, in Ur.

2001

A dog figurine excavated at Telloh was dedicated by Abba-duga to Ninisina, for the life of Sūmû-El.

COMMENTARY

The piece is AO 4349, excavated by Cros at Telloh, from the necropolis of Tell H, trench ᴠɪ. It is a dog figurine of steatite, 8.5 cm high, length of the base 11.6 cm. The inscription was collated.

BIBLIOGRAPHY

1907 Thureau-Dangin, RA 6 pp. 69–71 (copy, edition)
1907 Thureau-Dangin, SAK pp. 208–209 Sumu-ilu (edition)
1910 Cros, Tello pp. 134–35 (provenance, study) and p. 121 Plan E letter a (provenance); Thureau-Dangin, pp. 157–59 (copy, edition); Heuzy, pp. 160–66 (study)
1929 Barton, RISA pp. 312–13 Sumu-ilu 4 (edition)
1935 Rutten, Encyclopédie photographique de l'art 1 p. 254 (photo)
1954 Parrot, Syria 31 p. 7 fig. 4 (photo)
1961 Hallo, BiOr 18 p. 8 Sumu-il 4 (study)
1968 Kärki, SKFZ p. 27 Sumuel 4 (edition)
1971 Sollberger and Kupper, IRSA ɪvB7c (translation)
1977 Durand, RA 71 pp. 32–34 II (edition, study)
1980 Kärki, SAKAZ 1 pp. 48–49 Sumuel 4 (edition)
1988 Civil, NABU p. 31 no. 46 (study)

2.13 ḫi-li-⟨a⟩. **8**.1 Copy: é-ki-ág-a-ni; collation: ⌜é-šà-ḫúl⌝-a-ni. **10**.2–3, 7 mu-na-dù. **10**.5–6, 8, 10, 12, 15–17 These are broken so we cannot determine whether mu-un-na-dù or mu-na-dù occurs.

TEXT

1) ^{d}nin-ì-si-in.KI-na
2) nin KA×GÁNA-*tenû*-NE-du$_{10}$ a-zu-gizzal$_{x}$(GIŠ.TÚG.PI.NI)
3) nin-a-ni
4) nam-ti-
5) *su-mu-èl*
6) lugal-uri$_{5}$.KI-ma
7) ab-ba-du$_{10}$-ga lú-maḫ
8) dumu-uru-KA-gi-na
9) [g]ala-maḫ-gír-su.KI-kam
10) [u]r-zi ki-gál-la «ú»
11) ú-nam-ti-la
12) mu-bi-im
13) mu-nam-ár-e-ta
14) a mu-na-ru

1–3) For the goddess Ninisina, lady, good ..., wise physician, his lady,

4–6) for the life of Sūmû-El, king of Ur,

7–9) Abba-duga, the *lumaḫ* priest, son of Uru-KA-gina, chief cantor of Girsu,

10–14) dedicated to her *with* praise (this figurine) named 'Faithful dog, a stand for a pot of life-giving medication'.

2002

A vase fragment excavated at Ur was dedicated to the goddess Ningal on behalf of the life of Sūmû-El.

COMMENTARY

The piece is CBS 16207, excavation no. U 6362, from the Gipar-ku at Ur in front of the sanctuary, room A. 30. It is a calcite vase fragment measuring 13×8×9.5 cm and the inscription was collated.

BIBLIOGRAPHY

1928 Gadd, UET 1 no. 116 (copy, edition)
1929 Barton, RISA pp. 374–75 Sumu-ilu 3 (edition)
1961 Hallo, BiOr 18 p. 8 Sumu-il 3 (study)
1968 Kärki, SKFZ pp. 26–27 Sumuel 3 (edition)
1976 Woolley and Mallowan, UE 7 pp. 50 and 223 (provenance)
1980 Kärki, SAKAZ 1 p. 48 Sumuel 3 (edition)

TEXT

1) ^{d}nin-gal
2) [n]in-a-ni-ir
3) [n]am-ti-
4) [^{d}*su*]-*mu-èl*
5) [nita-kala]-ga
6) [lugal-uri$_{5}$.KI]-⸢ma⸣
Lacuna

1–2) For the goddess Ningal, his [l]ady,

3–6) for the [l]ife of [Sū]mû-El, [mig]hty [man], [king of U]r, [PN ... dedicated (this vase)].
Lacuna

2003

A seal impression of Lu-Ninšubur, servant of Sūmû-El, is on a large number of tablets in the Yale collections. The impression gives the titulary of the king as well as a phonetic rendering of his name.

COMMENTARY

The seal impression is found on YOS 14 nos. 236, 238, 245–246, 265, 268–271, 273, 275–276, 278, and 284. It was not collated.

BIBLIOGRAPHY

1978 Simmons, YOS 14 pl. cxxi seal no. 106 (copy)

TEXT

1) [*su*]-*mu*-⌜*i-la*⌝	1) [Sū]mû-Ila,
2) lugal-kala-ga	2) mighty king,
3) lugal-uri$_5$.KI-ma	3) king of Ur,
4) lugal-ki-en-gi-ki-uri-ke$_4$	4) king of the land of Sumer and Akkad,
5) lú-nin-šubur	5) Lu-Ninšubur,
6) dub-sar	6) scribe,
7) dumu-*ku-da-nu-um*	7) son of Kudānum,
8) ir$_{11}$-zu	8) your servant.

2004

A seal impression on a number of tablets from Larsa in the Yale collections bears the name of Iemṣium, the captain of the elite soldiers, servant of Sūmû-El.

COMMENTARY

The seal impression is taken from the tablet NBC 5433 = BIN 7 no. 116. The impression measures 1.1 × 1.9 cm and was collated. The same seal impression occurs on BIN 7 nos. 118, 121, 123, 128–129, 131, 132(?), 133, 134(?), and 135.

BIBLIOGRAPHY

1943 Alexander, BIN 7 no. 116 (copy)
1953 Weidner, JKF 2 p. 140 n. 4 (transliteration, study)
1961 Hallo, BiOr 18 p. 8 Sumu-il 5 (study)
1968 Kärki, SKFZ p. 27 Sumuel 5 (edition)
1970 Walters, Water p. 149 (discussion of Emṣium)
1971 Sollberger and Kupper, IRSA ivB7d (translation)
1980 Kärki, SAKAZ 1 p. 49 Sumuel 5 (edition)

TEXT

1)	*e-em-ṣi-um*	1) Iemṣium,
2)	UGULA AGA.ÚS.SAG.GÁ	2) captain of the elite soldiers,
3)	IR$_{11}$ *su-mu-èl*	3) servant of Sūmû-El,
4)	DUMU *ká-ni-na-nu-um*	4) son of Kaninānum.

2005

The seal impression of Ḫusanum, servant of Sūmû-El, is found on a tablet in the Yale collections.

COMMENTARY

The impression is on YBC 12111 = YOS 14 no. 214. It was not collated.

BIBLIOGRAPHY

1978 Simmons, YOS 14 pl. CXXI seal no. 98 (copy)

TEXT

1)	*ḫu-sa-mu-um*	1) Ḫusamum,
2)	[DU]MU *šu-te-da-um*	2) [s]on of Šuteda᾿um,
3)	[Ì]R *su-mu-èl*	3) [se]rvant of Sūmû-El.

2006

A seal impression in the Yale collections bears the name of Nūr-Sîn, servant of Sūmû-El.

COMMENTARY

The tablet is YBC 13113, provenance unknown, probably Larsa, a clay strip with a seal impression 2.7 cm high. It was not collated.

This might be the seal impression of the Nūr-Sîn who appears as the head of the Irrigation Bureau at Larsa during the reigns of Abī-sarē and Sūmû-El.

BIBLIOGRAPHY

1970 Walters, Water pp. 144–45 (discussion of Nūr-Sîn)
1981 Buchanan, Early Near Eastern Seals p. 279 figs. 753a–b (photo); Hallo, p. 455 no. 753 (edition)

TEXT

1) *nu-úr-*[d]EN.ZU
2) DUMU *at-ta-ma-nu-um*
3) ÌR *su-mu-èl*

1) Nūr-Sîn,
2) son of Attā-mannum,
3) servant of Sūmû-El.

2007

A seal impression found on a number of clay tablets excavated at Ur bears the name of Ku-Lugalbanda, the *šita-eš* priest of Ningal, servant of Sūmû-El.

CATALOGUE

Ex.	Museum number	Excavation number	Publication number	Provenance	Dimensions (cm)	Lines preserved	cpn
1	IM 67700	U 6389	UET 1, no. 240	Ur, from the Gipar-ku, room C. 26	–	1–4	n
2	UM 52-30-247	U –	UET 5, no. 766	Ur, provenance not known	1.1×2.0	2–4	c
3	UM 52-30-248	U –	UET 5, no. 767	As ex. 2	–	2–4	c
4	BM –	U –	UET 5, no. 784	As ex. 2	–	2–4	n

COMMENTARY

According to UET 5 p. 79, ex. 4 should be in the British Museum. Unfortunately, its BM no. could not be determined or the tablet located.

The finding of ex. 1 in the Gipar-ku at Ur accords well with the fact that this seal belongs to a priest of Ningal, whose temple formed part of that building.

BIBLIOGRAPHY

1928 Gadd, UET 1 no. 240 (composite copy, edition)
1953 Figulla and Martin, UET 5 nos. 766–67 and 784 (exs. 2–4, copy)
1961 Hallo, BiOr 18 p. 8 Sumu-il 6 (study)
1968 Kärki, SKFZ p. 27 Sumuel 6 (edition)
1969 Renger, ZA 59 p. 130 n. 669 (study)
1980 Kärki, SAKAZ 1 p. 49 Sumuel 6 (edition)
1986 Charpin, Le clergé d'Ur p. 214 (edition)

TEXT

1) kù-[d]lugal-bàn-da
2) $šita_x$(REC 316)-èš [d]nin-gal
3) DUMU na-sá
4) ÌR *su-mu-èl*

1) Ku-Lugalbanda,
2) *šita-eš* priest of the goddess Ningal,
3) son of Nasa,
4) servant of Sūmû-El.

Nūr-Adad

E4.2.8

The Larsa King List indicates a reign of 16 years for Nūr-Adad. A number of royal inscriptions are extant for this ruler.

1

The 'standard inscription' of Nūr-Adad is found in an 18-line stamped brick inscription from Larsa.

CATALOGUE

Ex.	Excavation number	Provenance	Dimensions (cm)	Lines preserved	cpn
1	L 67-	From the surface of the tell	–	1–13	n
2	L 7082	Door-sill between rooms 25 and 8, palace of Nūr-Adad	–	1–18	n
3	L 7092	Door-sill in between rooms 25 and 5, palace of Nūr-Adad	–	–	n
4	L 74101	–	–	–	n
5	L 74817	–	–	–	n

COMMENTARY

The master text is ex. 2.

None of these bricks were collated. Exs. 1–2 are entered in the score from the published copies. Exs. 2–3 were found in situ as door-sills in the 'Palace of Nūr-Adad' excavated by Parrot at Larsa in 1933. This enabled the excavator to attribute the building to Nūr-Adad. Unfortunately, the inscription was not published at that time. Parrot only indicated that is was a shortened form of UET 1 no. 111; it actually contains lines 5–32 of that text. The bricks were left in situ to be re-excavated in 1970.

The other exemplars of this inscription were found at other points on the mound at Larsa.

BIBLIOGRAPHY

1933 Parrot, RA 30 pp. 177 and 182 (exs. 2–3, provenance, study)

1968 Birot, Syria 45 pp. 244–45 no. 3 (ex. 1, copy, edition)

1970 Margueron, Syria 47 p. 269 fig. 6 (door-sill between rooms 25-5 and 25-8, exs. 2–3, provenance) and p. 271 (exs. 2–3, study)

1971 Arnaud, Syria 48 p. 289 (exs. 2–3, provenance, study)

1972 Arnaud, RA 66 p. 34 no. 2 (ex. 2, copy, edition) and n. 4 (ex. 3, study)

1976 Arnaud, Syria 53 p. 48 I–3 (exs. 4–5, study)

1978 Arnaud, Sumer 34 p. 165 I–3 (exs. 4–5, study)

1980 Kärki, SAKAZ 1 p. 56 Nūradad 7 (edition)

TEXT

1) *nu-úr*-^{d}IŠKUR
2) nita-kala-ga
3) ú-a-úri.KI-ma
4) lugal-larsa.KI-ma
5) sag-èn-tar-
6) èš é-babbar-ra
7) šul ^{d}utu
8) šà-kù-ga-ni-⌜a⌝
9) zi-dè-[eš]
10) bí-in-p[à-da]
11) kur-gú-gar-gar-^{d}utu-ke$_4$
12) mu-du$_{10}$-sa$_4$-⌜a⌝-
13) ^{d}iškur-ra-ke$_4$
14) lú GIŠ.gu-za-
15) larsa.KI-ma
16) suḫuš-bi mu-un-gi-né
17) un ság-du$_{11}$-ga-bi
18) ki-bé bí-in-gi$_4$-a

1) Nūr-Adad,
2) mighty man,
3) provider of Ur,
4) king of Larsa,
5-6) who cares for shrine Ebabbar,

7-10) whom the god, youth Utu has tru[ly] cho[sen] in his heart,

11) subduer of the foreign lands for the god Utu,
12-13) called by a good name by the god Iškur,

14-16) the one who has made the foundation of the throne of Larsa secure,

17-18) (and) regathered its scattered people.

2

A number of cones were found in the Enunmaḫ at Ur dealing with the construction of that building by Nūr-Adad.

CATALOGUE

Ex.	Museum number	Excavation number	Provenance	Object	Dimensions (cm)	Lines preserved	cpn
1	BM 30070	From Taylor's excavations at Ur, no excavation number	In the foundation of buildings south of the great mound at Mugheir	Shaft	10.0	1-12	c
2	–	U 327	From Enunmaḫ, room 15 against the NW wall, five courses below the top of the mud brick wall	Head	–	–	n
3	IM 92787	U 330	From the Enunmaḫ area ['room'] 24	Head	7.0 dia.	1-12	c
4	IM 92787	U 330	As ex. 3	Shaft	7.5	1-12	c
5	–	U 335	From the Enunmaḫ, room 22	Cone	–	–	n
6	–	U 876	From the Enunmaḫ, room 31	Head	5.5 dia.	1-5	n
7	IM 90966	U gd	Provenance not known	Head	7.2 dia.	2-12	c

COMMENTARY

The master text is ex. 1.

Ex. 1 from Taylor's excavations is said to have come from the same building as the brick published here as E4.2.13.9. The brick inscription deals with the construction of the Ga-nun-maḫ, so we can be fairly confident that the Taylor piece came from the same building.

BIBLIOGRAPHY

1861 1 R pl. 2 no. IV (ex. 1, copy)
1872 G. Smith, TSBA 1 p. 45 (translation)
1874 Lenormant, Études accadiennes 2 p. 341
1875 Ménant, Babylone et la Chaldée p. 89 (translation)
1892 Winckler, KB 3/1 pp. 90–91 Nur-Ramman (edition)
1899 Bezold, Cat. 5 p. 2233 (ex. 1, study)
1905 Thureau-Dangin, ISA pp. 296–97 Nûr-immer (edition)
1905 King, CT 21 pl. 29 (ex. 1, copy)
1907 Thureau-Dangin, SAK pp. 208–209 Nûr-immer (edition)
1910 King, Early History pl. XXXIII facing 314 (ex. 1, photo)
1929 Barton, RISA pp. 312–13 Nur-Adad 1 (edition)
1961 Hallo, BiOr 18 p. 8 Nur-Adad 2 (study)
1965 Sollberger, UET 8 p. 36 no. 49 (exs. 3–4, 7, study)
1968 Kärki, SKFZ p. 28 Nūradad 2 (edition)
1974 Woolley, UE 6 pp. 52–53 (exs. 2–6, provenance)
1980 Kärki, SAKAZ 1 pp. 50–51 Nūradad 2 (edition)

TEXT

1) [d]nanna
2) lugal-a-ni-ir
3) [d]*nu-úr*-[d]IŠKUR
4) nita-kala-ga
5) engar-uri₅.KI-ma
6) lugal-larsa.KI-ma
7) gá-nun-maḫ
8) é-me-te-ì-nun-ga-àra
9) [d]nanna
10) [d]nin-gal-ra
11) šà-uri₅.KI-ma
12) mu-na-dù

1–6) For the god Nanna, his lord, Nūr-Adad, mighty man, farmer of Ur, king of Larsa,

7–12) built the Ganunmaḫ, a proper house for butter and cheese, for the god Nanna (and) the goddess Ningal, in Ur.

3

A lengthy inscription of Nūr-Adad dealing with the construction for the god Nanna of an oven and a du₈-maḫ, the latter object possibly a cauldron, is known from three copper cylinders and several cones excavated at Ur.

CATALOGUE

Ex.	Museum number	Excavation number	Provenance	Object	Dimensions (cm)	Lines preserved	cpn
1	BM 119045	U 2676	From the great court of Nanna	Cone head	9.3	1–2, 17–24	c
2	BM 119036	U 2755	From the great Nanna courtyard 'over the ruins head of the east corner of Larsa range'	Cone head	–	1–10	c
3	IM 92953	U 2755a	As ex. 2	Cone head	2.1 dia.	1–8, 18	c
4	IM 1090	U 3267	From 'HD 21', i.e. near the great Nanna courtyard	Cone shaft	10.1	35–49	c
5	IM –	U 6310	Found loose on the surface in the Dim-tab-ba range	–	–	–	n
6	IM 92954	U 6973	From the Ehursag area	Cone head	Head 7.2×5.5	9–12, 20, 22–27	c
7	IM 92954	U 6973	As ex. 6	Cone shaft	8.1	30–37, 39–47	c
8	IM 92944	U 10635	No provenance indicated	Cone shaft	9.7	38–39, 41–51	c
9	IM 92942	U 12568	From the Royal Cemetery area	Cone head	6.2 dia.	1–8, 18–24	c

10.3 [d]nin-gal-⌜a(?)⌝.

Ex.	Museum number	Excavation number	Provenance	Object	Dimensions (cm)	Lines preserved	cpn
10	UM 32-40-437	U 17626a	From a brick box under the foundations of the Larsa sanctuary in the range facing the NW court of the ziqqurrat, room 6 west corner	Copper cylinder		1-56	c
11	IM 14320	U 17626b	As ex. 10	Copper cylinder	27 long, 6.6 dia.	1-45, 47-54	c
12	IM 14321	U 17627b	From a brick box under the SW corner of room 3 beside the ziqqurrat	Copper cylinder	27 long, 6.5 dia.	1-56	c
13	UM 32-40-429	U 17822	–	Cone head	–	1-5, 17-22	c
14	UM 32-40-429	U 17822	–	Cone shaft	–	49-56	c
15	BM 123121	U 17823	Loose in upper rubbish in 'LH' (Larsa houses?)	Cone shaft	7.6	40-44	c
16	IM -	U 18176	Found in XNCF, i.e. the building range on the NW wall of the temenos against the SW wall of the terrace tower, level VI	Cone head and shaft	Dia. of head: 12.0	–	n
17	IM 92947	U v	No provenance	Cone shaft	6.5	31-38	c
18	IM 92946	U w	No provenance	Cone shaft	10.2	35-49	c
19	BM 117145	U x	No provenance	Cone head	5.9×4.8	1-6, 17-19	c
20	BCM 61'76	U –	No provenance	Cone shaft	6.2	40-41, 43-49	c

COMMENTARY

The master text is ex. 10.

The copper cylinders were foundation deposits excavated from brick boxes in the foundations of the corners of rooms 6 (exs. 10–11) and 3 (ex. 12) in the north-east block of rooms beside the ziqqurrat (see UE 5 pl. 68). This block of rooms probably served as a kitchen area to provide food for the cult of Nanna. Their use is paralleled by a similar room with an oven found beside the Enlil temple in Nippur.

The cones with this inscription have a variety of provenances, mainly from the great Nanna courtyard. As in the case of the following cone inscription (E4.2.8.4), the inscription began on the head of the cone in two cols., roughly lines 1-16 and 17-29, and continued in one col. on the shaft, lines 30-56. Thus exs. 6–7 and 13–14 represent in fact only one text. They are listed separately here for ease of citation.

Exs. 2 and 4-6 were edited separately by Gadd in UET 1, but it was later realized first by Woolley (see UE 5 p. 38 n. 2) and then Hallo (see BiOr 18 [1968] p. 8 Nūr-Adad 3) that they were parts of the same text.

For the reading and translation of line 11 see J. Krecher, ZA 60 (1970) p. 198.

BIBLIOGRAPHY

1928 Gadd, UET 1 nos. 113 and 124 (exs. 2, 4–6, composite copy, edition)

1929 Barton, RISA pp. 372–73 Nur-Adad 2 (ex. 2, edition)

1932–33 Gadd, BMQ 7 pp. 43–44 (exs. 10–12, study)

1939 Woolley, UE 5 pp. 38 and 47 (exs. 10–12, provenance), p. 38 n. 2 (exs. 2–7, study), pl. 18a (exs. 10–11, photo of provenance), and pl. 18b (exs. 10–11, photo)

1957 Edzard, Sumer 13 pp. 177 and 183 (ex. 4, study)

1961 Hallo, BiOr 18 p. 8 Nur-Adad 3 (study)

1965 Sollberger, UET 8 no. 67 (exs. 10–12, 16, composite copy; exs. 2–19, study)

1968 Kärki, SKFZ pp. 28–29 Nūradad 3 (edition)

1971 Sollberger and Kupper, IRSA IVB8b (translation)

1979 George, Iraq 41 p. 122 no. 29 (ex. 20, study)

1980 Kärki, SAKAZ 1 pp. 51–52 Nūradad 3 (edition)

TEXT

1) ᵈnanna
2) men-an-ki
3) mùš-ḫi-li-sù
4) dumu-sag-
5) ᵈen-líl-lá
6) lugal-a-ni-ir

1–6) For the god Nanna, crown of heaven and earth, whose face is adorned with charming rays, the god Enlil's first-born son, his lord,

7) *nu-úr*-^{d}IŠKUR
8) nita-kala-ga
9) ú-a-uri$_5$.KI-ma
10) lugal-larsa.KI-ma
11) nisag-sar-re-
12) é-kiš-nu-gál-la
13) sag-èn-tar-
14) èš é-bábbar-ra
15) šul ^{d}utu
16) šà-kù-ga-ni-a
17) zi-dè-eš bí-in-pà-da
18) gidri-sum-ma-
19) ^{d}nanna-ke$_4$
20) kur-gú-gar-gar-
21) ^{d}utu-ke$_4$
22) mu-du$_{10}$-sa$_4$-a-
23) ^{d}iškur-ra-ke$_4$
24) šul ní-tuk
25) ù-ma-né sá-di

7–25) Nūr-Adad, mighty man, provider of Ur, king of Larsa, who makes first fruit offerings reach the Ekišnugal, who looks after the shrine Ebabbar, whom the youth, god Utu has truly chosen in his heart, given the sceptre by the god Nanna, subduer of the foreign lands for the god Utu, called by a good name by the god Iškur, reverent youth who achieves his victory,

26) u$_4$ šà-uri$_5$.KI-ma
27) bí-in-du$_{10}$-ga-a
28) nì-érim
29) i-^{d}utu
30) íb-ta-an-zi-ga
31) un-ság-du$_{11}$-ga-bi
32) ki-bé bí-in-gi$_4$-a
33) ^{d}nanna
34) lugal-a-ni-ir
35) ki-sur-ra-ka-ni
36) mu-na-an-sum-ma-a

26–36) when he had made Ur content, had removed evil (and the cause for any) complaint from it, had regathered its scattered people (and) had given to the god Nanna, his lord, his (proper) boundary,

37) u$_4$-bi-a
38) gir$_4$-maḫ
39) ú-sù-sù-^{d}EN.ZU-na-ka
40) ninda íl-e
41) kìlib-dingir-re-e-ne-er

37–41) at that time, a great oven for the meals of the god Suen which provides bread for all the gods

42) du$_8$-maḫ-
43) únu-gal-ba
44) mí zi-dè-eš du$_{11}$-ga
45) kin-sig kin-nim-ma
46) gù-nun-bi di-dam

42–46) (and) a great *cauldron* cared for in the (dining) hall, roaring loudly at the morning and evening meals,

47) nam-ti-la-ni-šè
48) mu-na-dù

47–48) he made for him (the god Nanna) and for his own life.

49) šu-luḫ-u$_4$-ul-lí-a-ka-ni
50) ki-bé mu-na-gi$_4$

49–50) he restored the traditional cleansing rites.

51) *nu-úr*-^{d}IŠKUR
52) sipa-nì-ge-na-ra
53) nam-ti-u$_4$-sù-rá
54) bala-nam-ḫé
55) é-kiš-nu-gál-ta
56) ḫu-mu-na-ra-è-e

51–56) May a long life-span (and) a reign of abundance come forth from the Ekišnugal for Nūr-Adad, shepherd of righteousness.

44.4 zi-⟨dè⟩-eš. **49**.8, 14 u$_4$-ul-⟨lí⟩-a-ka-ni.

4

A number of cones excavated in the Gipar-ku at Ur deal with the construction of a 'dressing-room' for the goddess Ningal by Nūr-Adad.

CATALOGUE

Ex.	Museum number	Excavation number	Provenance	Object	Dimensions (cm)	Lines preserved	cpn
1	BM 119037	U 2769	From 'Room 15th' in the great Nanna courtyard	Cone head	6.6 dia.	10–12, 31–32	c
2	CBS 16230	U 6359	From Gipar-ku, room C. 32	Head	11.0 dia.	1–25	c
3	CBS 16232	U 6359	As ex. 2	Shaft	17.0	30–40	c
4	IM 1527	U 6359	As ex. 2	Cone	–	–	n
5	IM 22865	U 6359	As ex. 2	Head and shaft	12.0 dia. Shaft 18.5 long	1–16, 26–40	c
6	IM 92855	U 6359b	As ex. 2	Cone head – six pieces glued together	12.0 dia.	1–28	c
7	IM 92839	U 6359c	As ex. 2	Shaft with a little bit of the head remaining	Shaft 9.5 long, Head 7 dia.	5–11, 25–30	c
8	IM 92828	U 6359d	As ex. 2	Head and shaft	Head 5.8 dia. Shaft 6.8 long	22–25, 32–36	c
9	IM 92827	U 6359e	As ex. 2	Head	8.6 dia.	1–14	c
10	IM 92841	U 6359f	As ex. 2	Head	9.8 dia.	1–13	c
11	IM 92831	U 6359g	As ex. 2	Head	4.7 dia.	1–5	c
12	IM 92832	U 6359h	As ex. 2	Head	8.5 dia.	1–7	c
13	IM 92829	U 6359i	As ex. 2	Head	6.4 dia.	19–26	c
14	IM 92830	U 6359j	As ex. 2	Head	5.0 dia.	7–21	c
15	IM 92840	U 6359k	As ex. 2	Shaft	8.8	28–32	c
16	IM –	U 6359l	As ex. 2	Shaft	–	–	n

COMMENTARY

The text is a conflated one: lines 1–28 come from ex. 6, line 29 from ex. 5, and lines 30–40 from ex. 3.

Most of these cones bear the excavation number U 6359.

Like the preceding text the inscription on these cones begins on the head in two cols., lines 1–14 and lines 15–28, and concludes, lines 29–40, on the shaft.

U 2676 = BM 119045 was listed by Gadd and Sollberger as a duplicate of this text, but it is actually a duplicate of E4.2.8.3.

BIBLIOGRAPHY

1928 Gadd, UET 1 no. 111 (composite copy, edition)
1929 Barton, RISA pp. 372–73 Nur-Adad 1 (edition)
1957 Edzard, Sumer 13 p. 177 (exs. 4–5, study)
1957 Edzard, Zwischenzeit pp. 114 and 117 (study)
1961 Hallo, BiOr 18 p. 8 Nur-Adad 4 (study)
1965 Sollberger, UET 8 p. 27 no. 16 (exs. 1–16, study)
1968 Kärki, SKFZ pp. 29–30 Nūradad 4 (edition)
1971 Sollberger and Kupper, IRSA ɪvB8c (translation)
1976 Woolley and Mallowan, UE 7 p. 223 (exs. 2–16, provenance)
1980 Kärki, SAKAZ 1 pp. 52–53 Nūradad 4 (edition)
1986 Charpin, Le clergé d'Ur p. 196 (edition)

TEXT

1) ^{d}nin-gal
2) nìta-dam-kù-
3) ^{d}aš-im$_{5}$-bábbar-ra
4) nin-ki-ág-a-ni-ir

1–4) For the goddess Ningal, shining spouse of the god Ašimbabbar, his beloved lady,

5) *nu-úr-*^{d}IŠKUR
6) nita-kala-ga
7) ú-a-uri$_{5}$.KI-ma
8) lugal-larsa.KI-ma
9) sag-èn-tar-
10) èš é-bábbar-ra
11) šul ^{d}utu
12) šà-kù-ga-ni-a
13) zi-dè-eš
14) bí-in-pà-da
15) gidri-sum-ma-
16) ^{d}nanna-ke$_{4}$
17) kur-gú-gar-gar-
18) ^{d}utu-ke$_{4}$
19) mu-du$_{10}$-sa$_{4}$-a-
20) ^{d}iškur-ra-ke$_{4}$
21) šul ní-tuk
22) ù-ma-né sá-di

5–22) Nūr-Adad, mighty man, provider of Ur, king of Larsa, who looks after shrine Ebabbara, whom the youth god Utu has truly chosen in his heart, given the sceptre by the god Nanna, subduer of the foreign lands for the god Utu, called by a good name by the god Iškur, reverent youth, who achieves his victory,

23) u$_{4}$ šà-uri$_{5}$.ki-ma
24) bí-in-du$_{10}$-ga-a
25) nì-érim i-^{d}utu
26) íb-ta-an-zi-ga
27) GIŠ.gu-za-
28) larsa.KI-ma
29) suḫuš-bi
30) mu-un-ge$_{4}$-né
31) un-ság-du$_{11}$-ga-bi
32) ki-bé bí-in-gi$_{4}$-a

23–32) when he had made Ur content, had removed evil (and the cause for any) complaint from it, had made firm the foundation of the throne of Larsa, (and) had regathered its scattered people,

33) agrun-kù
34) é-nam-mu$_{4}$-ka-ni
35) á-ná-da-
36) šul ^{d}EN.ZU-na-ka
37) nam-ti-la-ni-šè
38) mu-na-dù

33–36) he built for his own life the Agrun-kù ('shining (bed)room'), her dressing-room, the *sleeping-wing* of the god, youth Suen.

39) agrun nì-ul-e
40) ki-bé mu-na-gi$_{4}$

39–40) He restored the Agrun as an everlasting thing.

5

A year name found in an archive dating to the time of Nūr-Adad deals with the construction of the temple of Enki in Eridu (see D. Arnaud, Mélanges Birot p. 38 n. 11). Stamped bricks found on the

3.6, 9 ^{d}aš-ím. **14** According to Sollberger (UET 8 p. 27 no. 16), U 6359c has bí-in-pà-dè. **26**.6 omits -an-.

ziqqurrat at Eridu by Thompson and Safar record the construction of Enki's temple in that city by Nūr-Adad. The same construction is commemorated in a cone inscription, E4.2.8.6.

CATALOGUE

Ex.	Museum number	Excavation number	Provenance	Dimensions (cm)	Lines preserved	cpn
1	BM 114342	From Thompson's excavations, no excavation number	Eridu, probably from the ziqqurrat	29.0×18.5×8.5	1–15	c
2	BM 137405	–	Eridu(?)	29.0×18.5×8.5	1–15	c
3	BM 137406	–	Eridu(?)	24.5×18.5×8.5	1–15	c
4	IM 52366	Eridu 77	Eridu, among debris almost at the middle of the NE side of the ziqqurrat	25.0×17.5×6.0	1–15	n
5	CBS 16545	U –	Ur, provenance not known	28.0×18.0×8.0	–	n
6	CBS 16472	U –	Ur, provenance not known	29.0×18.0×7.5	–	n

COMMENTARY

The master text is ex. 1.

Ex. 1 comes from Thompson's excavations. The origin of exs. 2–3 is not known, but they presumably came from Eridu, possibly from Thompson's excavations as well. Ex. 4 was found by the Iraqi expedition to Eridu. Exs. 5–6, unexpectedly, came from Ur.

BIBLIOGRAPHY

1920 Thompson, Arch. 70 p. 115 fig. 6 (ex. 1, copy) and pp. 116–17 (ex. 1, edition)
1921 Gadd, CT 36 pl. 6 (ex. 1, copy)
1924 Gadd, Reading-book pp. 44–45 (ex. 1, copy, edition)
1928 Gadd, UET 1 p. xxiv (exs. 5–6, study)
1929 Barton, RISA pp. 312–13 Nur-Adad 2 (edition)
1947 Safar, Sumer 3 (Arabic section) fig. 1d facing p. 235 (ex. 4, copy)
1961 Hallo, BiOr 18 p. 8 Nur-Adad 1 (study)
1968 Kärki, SKFZ pp. 27–28 Nūradad 1 (edition)
1971 Sollberger and Kupper, IRSA ɪvB8a (translation)
1980 Kärki, SAKAZ 1 p. 50 Nūradad 1 (edition)
1981 Walker, CBI no. 36 (exs. 1–3, study)
1982 Safar, et al., Eridu (Baghdad) p. 65 (ex. 4, provenance) and p. 229 fig. 108 no. 4 (ex. 4, copy)
1985 Behrens, JCS 37 p. 235 no. 27 (exs. 5–6, study)

TEXT

1) *nu-úr*-^{d}IŠKUR
2) nita-kala-ga
3) engar-zi-uri$_5$.KI-ma
4) lugal-larsa.KI-ma
5) me-èš é-babbar-ra
6) kù-kù-ge
7) eridu.KI u$_4$-ul-lí-a-ta
8) šu mu-un-ḫul-a-ba
9) bala-nì-si-sá-mu-uš
10) dù-dè al bí-du$_{11}$
11) ^{d}en-ki-ke$_4$
12) ki-tuš-kù-ki-ág-gá-ni
13) mu-na-dù
14) giš-ḫur-ul-lí-a-ka-ni
15) ki-bé mu-na-gi$_4$

1–6) (I), Nūr-Adad, mighty man, true farmer of Ur, king of Larsa, who purifies the *me*s of shrine Ebabbar,

7–10) desired to (re)build Eridu, which had been ruined from the remote past, for my reign of justice.

11–13) I built for the god Enki his beloved, shining residence

14–15) (and) restored for him his ancient rites.

6

A previously unpublished cone in Chicago deals, in a longer form than the brick inscription, with the construction of Enki's Abzu temple in Eridu.

CATALOGUE

Ex.	Museum number	Excavation number	Provenance	Object	Dimensions (cm)	Lines preserved	cpn
1	A 21183	–	Eridu	Head	9.5 dia.	4–14, 19–28	c
2	A 21183	–	Eridu	Shaft	8.8	1–28	c

COMMENTARY

The cone was found at Abū Šaḫrain, ancient Eridu, by P. Delougaz and T. Jacobsen during a survey of sites.

The text is published through the courtesy of the trustees of the Oriental Institute.

TEXT

1) ⸢^{d}en⸣-[ki]
2) ⸢lugal-eridu⸣.[KI-ga]
3) ⸢lugal⸣-[a-ni-ir]
4) *nu-úr*-⸢^{d}⸣[IŠKUR]
5) nita-kala-ga
6) ú-a-úri.KI-⸢ma⸣
7) ⸢lugal-larsa⸣.KI-⸢ma⸣
8) kur-gú-gar-gar-^{d}utu-ke$_{4}$
9) u$_{4}$ úri.KI
10) larsa.KI-bi
11) ki-bé ⸢bí-in⸣-gi$_{4}$-a
12) un-ság-du$_{11}$-⸢ga-bi⸣
13) ki-tuš-bé mu-⸢gi-na⸣
14) un-dab$_{5}$-dab$_{5}$-a-bi
15) uš zi-dè-[eš ...]
16) eridu.KI [...]
17) u$_{4}$-ba ḫul-[gál]
18) ^{d}en-[ki ...]
19) šà-ba nu-un-[...]
20) en ^{d}nu-dím-⸢mud⸣
21) mu-ši-in-še
22) da é-u$_{4}$-ul-x-a-ni
23) abzu é-me-kù-kù-ga-a-ni
24) gibil-bi-àm mu-na-dù
25) GIŠ.gu-za GIŠ.šu-nir
26) gi$_{16}$-sa libir-a-ni
27) šà-bi-šè
28) mu-ni-ku$_{4}$

1–3) [For] the god En[ki], lord of Eridu, [his] lord,

4–8) Nūr-[Adad], mighty man, provider of Ur, king of Larsa, subduer of the foreign lands for the god Utu,

9–16) when he had restored Ur and Larsa, had resettled their scattered people in their residence, their *captive people* ... the foundation tru[ly ...], Eridu [...],

17–19) at that time (he did not let) any evil-doer (against) the god Enki [enter] it.

20–21) Divine lord Nudimmud was pleased at this.

22–24) Beside his ancient temple (Nūr-Adad) built anew for him (Enki) his Abzu, the Emekukuga ('House which purifies the *me*s').

25–28) Into it he brought his throne, standard, (and) ancient treasures.

7

A cone inscription from Larsa deals with the construction of the wall of Larsa by a king of Larsa whose name is not fully preserved in the extant text. The piece should be attributed to Nūr-Adad.

CATALOGUE

Ex.	Museum number	Excavation number	Provenance	Object	Dimensions (cm)	Lines preserved	cpn
1	BM 132226 (1957-10-15,1)	–	Larsa(?)	Clay cone shaft	18 long, 13 dia.	1′–85′ (cols. i–ii)	c
2	AO 25108	L [33]4	Larsa, from the surface	Cone shaft frgm.	6.7	57′–73′, 75′–82′, 84′–85′	n
3	AO 25109	L [33]25	Larsa, MXIII, palace	Cone shaft frgm.	5.6	81′–85′	n
4	AO 25111	L [33]298	Larsa, MV	Cone shaft frgm.	7.8	63′–70′	n

COMMENTARY

The master text is ex. 1.

Although the provenance of ex. 1, a purchased piece, was not previously known, the fact that the three other duplicates come from Larsa makes it virtually certain that the BM cone comes from that site as well.

According to E. Sollberger, col. i of ex. 1 is totally missing. However, collation of ex. 1 reveals no need to posit a missing col.

The inscription was attributed to Nūr-Adad by E. Sollberger, the editor of ex. 1, based on a restoration of the king's name in ii 17. D. Arnaud, however, attributed exs. 2–4 to Sîn-iddinam because the restoration of the in-dub of Utu mentioned at the end of the inscription is a deed which figures in other inscriptions of Sîn-iddinam.

In this connection we note the evidence of an archive of texts from Larsa edited by D. Arnaud (Birot Festschrift pp. 35–38) that tells us that the year name mu-ús-sa é-^{d}en-ki 'the year following the temple of Enki' was a provisional name equivalent to mu bàd-gal-larsa.KI ba-dù 'the year the great wall of Larsa was built'. We noted in E4.2.8.5 that a year name dealing with the temple of Enki should be attributed to Nūr-Adad. The evidence of the archive studied by Arnaud indicates that a year name dealing with the construction of the great wall of Larsa should be attributed to Nūr-Adad as well.

Such a supposition is supported by the evidence of NBC 9267 (Buchanan and Hallo, Early Near Eastern Seals no. 758), a tag which is dated mu bàd-gal-larsa.KI ba-dù 'the year the great wall of Larsa was built' and which bears a seal impression of a servant of Nūr-Adad (see E4.2.8.2013).

A comparison of the royal titulary of E4.2.8.1 and E4.2.8.7 confirms that this text belongs to Nūr-Adad.

BIBLIOGRAPHY

1977 Arnaud, RA 71 p. 5 (exs. 2–4, copy) and p. 6 (exs. 2–3, study)
1982 Sollberger, Kraus Festschrift pp. 342–46 (ex. 1, edition)

TEXT

Col. i
1) [u_4 ^{d}utu lar]sa.KI-ma
2) [nam-bi mu-un-tar]-ra-a
3) [GIŠ.gu-za-ba suḫuš]-bi
4) [sù-rá-šè] gí-né-dè
5) [bala]-sa_6-ga-bi
6) [mù]š nu-túm-mu-dè

i 1–16) [When the god Utu had decre]ed [the fate] of [Lar]sa; (and) the god, [youth] Utu had [tru]ly spoken his [command] which can[not] be altered to make firm [forever the foundation of] its [throne], to make [unc]easing its good [reign], to make [man]ifest its kings[hip], to [re]settle its

7) [na]m-lugal-bi
8) [pa]-è ak-dè
9) [un s]ág-du$_{11}$-ga-bi
10) [ki-b]a gá-gá-dè
11) [...] x ki-tuš-du$_{10}$-ga
12) [dù]-ù-dè
13) [šul] ^{d}utu
14) [inim nu]-kúr-ru-da-ni
15) [zi-d]è-eš
16) [bí-i]n-du$_{11}$-ga

[sc]attered [people], to [build ...] a pleasant residence,

17) [*nu-úr*]-^{d}IŠKUR
18) [sipa nì-g]i-na-me-en
19) [šà-sù-r]a-na
20) [zi-d]è-eš
21) [mu-un]-pà-dè-en

i 17–21) It was I, [Nūr]-Adad, [shepherd of right]eousness whom he [tru]ly chose in his [*unfathomable* heart].

22) [...]-na-mu-šè
23) [na]m-du$_{10}$ mu-un-tar
24) [uru].KI ba-tu-dè-en-na-gá
25) nam-sipa-bi ma-an-sum
26) nam-ú-a èš-e [ú]ri.KI-ma
27) [nam-sa]g-⸢èn-tar⸣ [èš é-babbar]-⸢ra⸣

i 22–27) On account of my [...] he decreed a good. He gave to me the shepherdship of the [city] in which I was born. The providing for the shrine [U]r, the [c]are of the [shrine Ebabbar] ...

28) [...]
29) [...]
30) [...]
31) [...]
32) [...]
33) [...]-x
34) [...]-x
35) [...]-x-[M]U
36) [...]-DU.DU
37) [...]-na
38) [...]-⸢ma⸣-a
39) [...]-x kù
40) [...]-ta
41) [...]-DU-a
42) [...]-al
43) [...]-⸢an⸣-DU
44) [...]-x-na
45) [...-g]ar-gar

i 28–45) No translation warranted.

Col. ii
46) gur$_7$-du$_6$ gur$_7$-maš
47) ^{d}utu-ra gú-bi mi-ni-gur-gur
48) tùr amaš mi-ni-dagal
49) ì gára mi-ni-šár-šár
50) un-mu ú-šár-ra
51) mi-ni-kú
52) a-ḫé-gál-la mi-ni-nag
53) šà-bi-a sa-gaz lú-ḫul-gál
54) lú-nì-erím mu-ḫa-lam
55) si-ga nu-mu-un-su lú-ki-gul-la
56) su-bi mi-ni-du$_{10}$

ii 46–56) I heaped up mounds and stacks (of barley) for the god Utu. I enlarged the cattle pens and sheepfolds. I made oil and butter abundant. I had my people eat food of all kinds, (and) drink abundant water. I destroyed the brigand, the wicked, and the evil-doer in their midst. I made the weak, widow, and orphan content.

57) u$_4$-bala-sa$_6$-ga-mu
58) 2 še gur-ta 2 (bán) ì-ta
59) 10 ma-na síg-ta
60) 10 gur zú-lum-ta-àm

ii 57–63) During my good reign, according to the market value which was in my land, thus one shekel of silver purchased 2 *gur* of barley, 2 *ban* of oil, 10 minas of wool, 10 *gur* of dates.

61) ganba-šà-ma-da-gá-ka
62) kù 1-gín-e
63) ur$_5$-gin$_7$ ba-ra-sa$_{10}$
64) u$_4$-bi-a bàd-gal-larsa.KI-ma
65) ḫur-sag-gin$_7$ ki-sikil-la mu-dù
66) á lú-1-e
67) 3 (bán) še-ta 2 sìla ninda-ta
68) 2 sìla kaš-ta
69) 2 gín ì-ta-àm
70) u$_4$-1-e ur$_5$-gin$_7$ šu ba-an-ti

ii 64–70) At that time I built the great wall of Larsa like a mountain in a pure place. The wages of each worker were 3 *ban* of barley, 2 *sila* of bread, 2 *sila* of beer, 2 shekels of oil; thus they received this in one day.

71) u$_4$-da-rí-šè mu-mu gá-gá-dè
72) bàd-gal-bi
73) temen-kù mi-ni-si
74) ^{d}utu ù-ma-ni
75) sá bí-in-du$_{11}$
76) mu-šè im-mi-sa$_4$
77) di-nì-gi-na-^{d}utu-ta
78) uru.KI x-šè ga-ba-al
79) mu-un-dù-a
80) bàd-bi du$_6$-du$_6$-ra mi-ni-šid
81) gú-nu-gar-ra-bi
82) gìr-^{d}utu lugal-gá-šè mi-ni-gam
83) in-dub-^{d}utu
84) lugal-gá-ke$_4$
85) ki-bé im-mi-gi$_4$

71–85) In order to establish my name forever, I determined the holy perimeter of this great wall (and) named it Utu-umani-sa-bindu ('The god Utu has achieved his triumph'). By the true judgement of the god Utu, I counted among the ruins the wall of the city ... with which I had joined battle. I made its (inhabitants) who did not submit bow down at the feet of the god Utu, my lord. I restored there the boundary of the god Utu, my lord.

2001–13

Impressions of seals of a number of different servants of Nūr-Adad are found on tablets in the Yale and University of Illinois Oriental Museum. These are edited here as inscriptions E4.2.8.2001–2013.

2001

The impression of Apil-kūbi is found on tablets from Larsa.

CATALOGUE

Ex.	Museum number	cpn
1	UIOM 2009	n
2	YBC 3268	n
3	YBC 4970	n

69.2 [...-t]a-⟨àm⟩.

BIBLIOGRAPHY

1914 Keiser, BRM 3 no. 17b (ex. 4, copy)
1950 Goetze, JCS 4 p. 114 (exs. 1–4, edition)
1961 Hallo, BiOr 18 p. 8 Nur-Adad 6: ii (study)
1968 Kärki, SKFZ pp. 30–31 Nūradad 6 (conflated edition)
1980 Kärki, SAKAZ 1 p. 54 Nūradad 6 (edition)

TEXT

1) *a-pil-ku-bi*
2) DUMU [d]EN.ZU-*na-da*
3) ÌR *nu-úr*-[d]IŠKUR

1) Apil-kūbi,
2) son of Sîn-nādā,
3) servant of Nūr-Adad.

2002

The impression of the seal of Zikir-ilīšu is found on two tablets.

CATALOGUE

Ex.	Museum number	cpn
1	YBC 3320	c
2	NBC 7646	n

BIBLIOGRAPHY

1919 Grice, YOS 5 no. 155a (ex. 1, copy)
1961 Hallo, BiOr 18 p. 8 Nur-Adad 6: xi (study)
1968 Kärki, SKFZ pp. 30–31 Nūradad 6 (conflated edition)
1978 Simmons, YOS 14 pl. CXXII seal no. 126 (ex. 2, copy)

TEXT

1) *zi-ki-ir-ì-lí-šu*
2) DUMU *ip-qú-ìl-a-ba*
3) ÌR *nu-úr*-[d]IŠKUR

1) Zikir-ilīšu,
2) son of Ipqu-Ilaba,
3) servant of Nūr-Adad.

2003

The impression of the seal of Sîn-bēl-ilī is found on three tablets.

CATALOGUE

Ex.	Museum number	cpn
1	YBC 5678	c
2	YBC 5732	n
3	YBC 6146	n

BIBLIOGRAPHY

1941 Faust, YOS 8 no. 39 seal b (ex. 1, copy)
1961 Hallo, BiOr 18 p. 8 Nur-Adad 6: viii (ex. 1, study)
1968 Kärki, SKFZ pp. 30–31 Nūradad 6 (ex. 1, edition)
1980 Kärki, SAKAZ 1 p. 54 Nūradad 6 (ex. 1, edition)
1987 van de Mieroop, AfO 34 pp. 27–28 (exs. 2–3, transliteration)

TEXT

1) ᵈEN.ZU-[*be-el*]-*ì-lí*	1) Sîn-[bēl]-ilī,
2) UGULA URU	2) overseer of the city,
3) DUMU *ḫa-li-lum*	3) son of Ḫalīlum,
4) IR₁₁ *nu-úr*-ᵈIŠKUR	4) servant of Nūr-Adad.

2004

The impression of the seal of Nawirum is found on YBC 5702.

BIBLIOGRAPHY

1919 Grant, Business Doc. no. 28 (copy)
1941 Faust, YOS 8 no. 56a (copy)
1961 Hallo, BiOr 18 p. 8 Nur-Adad 6: vi (study)
1968 Kärki, SKFZ pp. 30–31 Nūradad 6 (conflated edition)
1980 Kärki, SAKAZ 1 p. 54 Nūradad 6 (edition)

TEXT

1) ⸢*na-wi-ru*⸣-*um*	1) Nawirum,
2) MÁ.LAḪ₅	2) boatman,
3) DUMU *ku-lu-ú-a*	3) son of Kulūa,
4) ÌR *nu-úr*-ᵈIŠKUR	4) servant of Nūr-Adad.

2005

The impression of the seal of the diviner Nanna-mansum is found on tablets from Larsa.

CATALOGUE

Ex.	Museum number	cpn
1	UIOM 2009	n
2	UIOM 2010	n
3	UIOM 2011	n
4	UIOM 2012	n
5	UIOM 2013	n
6	UIOM 2014	n
7	UIOM 2015	n
8	UIOM 2016	n
9	YBC 3268	p

Ex.	Museum number	cpn
10	YBC 4970	p
11	YBC 5205	p

BIBLIOGRAPHY

1950 Goetze, JCS 4 p. 113 (exs. 1–12, edition)
1950 Porada, JCS 4 p. 160 fig. 14 (composite copy)
1961 Hallo, BiOr 18 p. 8 Nur-Adad 6: v (study)
1968 Kärki, SKFZ pp. 30–31 Nūradad 6 (conflated edition)
1971 Sollberger and Kupper, IRSA IVB8d (translation)
1980 Kärki, SAKAZ 1 p. 55 Nūradad 6 (edition)
1981 Buchanan, Early Near Eastern Seals p. 282 no. 760 (exs. 9–11, study) and p. 283 nos. 760a–c (exs. 9–11, photo); Hallo, p. 456 no. 760 (exs. 9–11, edition)

TEXT

1) ᵈnanna-ma-an-sum
2) MÁŠ.ŠU.GÍD.GÍD
3) ÌR ᵈnanna
4) [ù] *nu-úr-*ᵈIŠKUR

1) Nanna-mansum,
2) diviner,
3) servant of the god Nanna,
4) [and] Nūr-Adad.

2006

The impression of the seal of Lu-Dumuzida is found on a number of tablets.

CATALOGUE

Ex.	Museum number	cpn
1	UIOM 2018	n
2	UIOM 2026	n
3	UIOM 2027	n
4	UIOM 2028	n
5	UIOM 2033	n
6	YBC 4969	n
7	YBC 10249	n

BIBLIOGRAPHY

1950 Goetze, JCS 4 pp. 113–14 (exs. 1–7, edition)
1961 Hallo, BiOr 18 p. 8 Nur-Adad 6: iv (study)
1968 Kärki, SKFZ pp. 30–31 Nūradad 6 (conflated edition)
1980 Kärki, SAKAZ 1 p. 55 Nūradad 6 (edition)

TEXT

1) lú-ᵈdumu-zi-da
2) DUB.SAR
3) DUMU *i-ku-un-pi₄-*ᵈEN.ZU
4) ÌR *nu-úr-*ᵈIŠKUR

1) Lu-Dumuzida,
2) scribe,
3) son of Ikūn-pî-Sîn,
4) servant of Nūr-Adad.

2007

The impression of the seal of Adad-illassu is found on a number of tablets.

CATALOGUE

Ex.	Museum number	cpn
1	UIOM 2009	n
2	UIOM 2014	n
3	UIOM 2019	n
4	UIOM 2020	n
5	UIOM 2022	n
6	UIOM 2023	n
7	UIOM 2024	n
8	UIOM 2025	n
9	YBC 3268	n

BIBLIOGRAPHY

1950 Goetze, JCS 4 p. 114 (exs. 1–9, edition)
1961 Hallo, BiOr 18 p. 8 Nur-Adad 6: i (study)
1968 Kärki, SKFZ pp. 30–31 Nūradad 6 (conflated edition)
1980 Kärki, SAKAZ 1 p. 55 Nūradad 6 (edition)

TEXT

1) dIŠKUR-*illat*-[*su*]
2) DUMU *i-ku-pi*$_4$-dIŠKUR
3) ÌR d*nu-úr*-dIŠKUR

1) Adad-illas[su],
2) son of Ikū(n)-pî-Adad,
3) servant of Nūr-Adad.

2008

The impression of the seal of Sîn-iqīšam is found on a number of tablets.

CATALOGUE

Ex.	Museum number	cpn
1	UIOM 2010	n
2	YBC 4970	n
3	YBC 4974	n

BIBLIOGRAPHY

1950 Goetze, JCS 4 p. 115 (exs. 1–3, edition)
1961 Hallo, BiOr 18 p. 8 Nur-Adad 6: ix (study)
1968 Kärki, SKFZ pp. 30–31 Nūradad 6 (conflated edition)
1980 Kärki, SAKAZ 1 p. 55 Nūradad 6 (edition)

TEXT

1) ᵈEN.ZU-*i-qí-ša-am*
2) DUMU *nu-úr-*ᵈUTU
3) ÌR *nu-úr-*ᵈIŠKUR

1) Sîn-iqīšam,
2) son of Nūr-Šamaš,
3) servant of Nūr-Adad.

2009

The impression of the seal of Damu-mūde is found on a number of tablets.

CATALOGUE

Ex.	Museum number	cpn
1	UIOM 2013	n
2	UIOM 2015	n
3	UIOM 2016	n
4	UIOM 2019	n
5	UIOM 2020	n
6	UIOM 2021	n
7	UIOM 2025	n
8	UIOM 2030	n
9	YBC 4971	n

BIBLIOGRAPHY

1950 Goetze, JCS 4 p. 115 (exs. 1–9, edition)
1950 Porada, JCS 4 p. 159 fig. 3 (ex. 8, copy)
1961 Hallo, BiOr 18 p. 8 Nur-Adad 6: iii (study)
1968 Kärki, SKFZ pp. 30–31 Nūradad 6 (conflated edition)
1980 Kärki, SAKAZ 1 p. 55 Nūradad 6 (edition)

TEXT

1) ᵈ*da-mu-*GAL.ZU
2) DUMU *i-la-ni*
3) ÌR *nu-úr-*ᵈIŠKUR

1) Damu-mūde,
2) son of Ilani,
3) servant of Nūr-Adad.

2010

The impression of the seal of Nidnuša is found on two tablets.

CATALOGUE

Ex.	Museum number	cpn
1	UIOM 2010	n
2	YBC 4974	n

BIBLIOGRAPHY

1950 Goetze, JCS 4 p. 115 (exs. 1–2, edition)
1950 Porada, JCS 4 p. 159 fig. 6 (exs. 1–2, composite copy)
1961 Hallo, BiOr 18 p. 8 Nur-Adad 6: vii (study)
1968 Kärki, SKFZ pp. 30–31 Nūradad 6 (conflated edition)
1980 Kärki, SAKAZ 1 p. 55 Nūradad 6 (edition)

TEXT

1) *ni-id-nu-ša*	1) Nidnuša,
2) DUMU *a-[bi]-i-din-na-am*	2) son of A[bī]-iddinam,
3) ÌR *nu-úr*-^{d}IŠKUR	3) servant of Nūr-Adad.

2011

The impression of the seal of Sîn-[išme]ani is found on two tablets.

CATALOGUE

Ex.	Museum number	cpn
1	UIOM 2019	n
2	UIOM 2021	n

BIBLIOGRAPHY

1950 Goetze, JCS 4 p. 116 (exs. 1–2, edition)
1961 Hallo, BiOr 18 p. 8 Nur-Adad 6: x (study)
1968 Kärki, SKFZ pp. 30–31 Nūradad 6 (conflated edition)
1980 Kärki, SAKAZ 1 p. 55 Nūradad 6 (edition)

TEXT

1) ^{d}EN.ZU-[*iš-me*]-*a-ni*	1) Sîn-[išme]ani,
2) DUMU ÌR-[...]	2) son of Warad-[...],
3) ÌR *nu-úr*-[^{d}IŠKUR]	3) servant of Nūr-[Adad].

2012

The impression of a seal of a servant of Nūr-Adad whose name is not preserved is found on UIOM 2018. It was not collated.

BIBLIOGRAPHY

1950 Goetze, JCS 4 p. 117 (edition)
1968 Kärki, SKFZ pp. 30–31 Nūradad 6 (conflated edition)
1980 Kärki, SAKAZ 1 p. 56 Nūradad 6 (edition)

TEXT

1) [...]
2) DUMU ^{d}*na-bi-u*[*m-*...]
3) ÌR *nu-úr-*^{d}IŠKUR

1) [...],
2) son of Nabiu[m-...],
3) servant of Nūr-Adad.

2013

The impression of a seal of a servant of Nūr-Adad is found on a clay tag in the Yale Collections.

COMMENTARY

The impression is on NBC 9267. It was collated by G. Beckman. The year name on this tablet 'the year the great wall of Larsa was built' should be attributed to Nūr-Adad, not Sîn-iqīšam, as Hallo previously suggested.

BIBLIOGRAPHY

1981 Buchanan and Hallo, Early Near Eastern Seals no. 758 (study)
1988 Beckman, NABU pp. 8–9 no. 13 (transliteration, copy)

TEXT

1) ur-^{d}nin-x-x-x
2) DUMU x-*ì-lí-šu*
3) ÌR *nu-úr-*^{d}IŠKUR

1) Ur-Nin-...,
2) son of ...-ilīšu,
3) servant of Nūr-Adad.

Sîn-iddinam

E4.2.9

Nūr-Adad was succeeded by his son Sîn-iddinam, who reigned seven years. Despite a short reign, a large number of inscriptions are extant for this ruler.

1

A tablet in Berlin contains a copy of a lengthy text of Sîn-iddinam. The text is a collection of three inscriptions. The first deals with the construction by Sîn-iddinam of a statue of his father Nūr-Adad. This appears to be a copy of a genuine royal inscription which may have once been inscribed on the statue itself. We edit it here as the first inscription of Sîn-iddinam.

The second and third inscriptions, which are copies of letters addressed to the statue, recount the events of Nūr-Adad's reign. They belong to the genre of literary letters and are not edited here.

COMMENTARY

The text is on VAT 8515, a clay tablet 17.8×9 cm which was purchased. It probably originates from Larsa. The tablet was collated. The text follows the edition of van Dijk, which was partially based on old photos of the tablet which show it in a better state of preservation than that found at present.

BIBLIOGRAPHY

1965 van Dijk, JCS 19 pp. 1–25 (copy, edition)
1971 van Dijk, VAS 17 no. 41 (copy)
1976 Hallo, Kramer Anniversary p. 211 (study)
1980 Kärki, SAKAZ 1 pp. 68–76 Sîniddinam 13 (edition)
1980 Michalowski, RLA 6/1–2 p. 56 §5.2 (study)
1984 Römer, TUAT 1/4 pp. 320–25 (translation)

TEXT

Lacuna (5 lines)
6) x [...]-x-ga
7) en p[irig-gal ka-aš-b]ar-an-ki
8) a[m a]n-š[è iz]i-g[ar-gi]n$_7$ gá-gá
9) šu[l-zi ...] an-dagal-la
10) d[i-k]u$_5$ [...]-ra
11) ti-la u[g$_5$-ga èn-tar]-bi-im
12) me-bé aš-a-n[i šu-du$_7$-du$_7$]

Lacuna (5 lines)
6–18) [For the god Utu] ... lord, [great] l[ion, jud]ge of heaven and earth, wild bu[ll] who goes along in [hea]ven [li]ke a [t]or[ch, true] you[th] ... in broad heaven, j[ud]ge ... [who cares for] the living and the de[ad], who alone [perfectly executes] their *me*s, prince [youth Utu], ... [grandly su]itable for the shining crown, with

13) nun [šul ^{d}utu]
14) a[n-...] x x x [...-m]aḫ
15) men-kù-ga [gal-bi t]úm-ma
16) árḫuš-sù ga-ti-e ki-ág
17) a-ra-zu-e giš-tuk
18) lugal-a-ni-ir

patient mercy, who loves ex-votos, who heeds entreaties, his lord,

19) ^{d}EN.ZU-*i-din-nam* nita-kala-ga
20) ú-a-uri$_{5}$.KI-ma
21) sipa-zi-lársa.KI-ma
22) giš-ḫur-eridu.KI-ga
23) ki-bé bí-in-gi$_{4}$-a
24) me-šu-du$_{7}$-du$_{7}$-lagaš.KI
25) gír-su.KI-ke$_{4}$
26) ibila-kala-ga šà-a-a-na du$_{10}$-du$_{10}$
27) dumu-sag-^{d}iškur-ke$_{4}$

19–27) Sîn-iddinam, mighty man, provider of Ur, true shepherd of Larsa, who restored the rites of Eridu, who perfectly executes the *me*s of Lagaš and Girsu, mighty heir who pleases his father very much, first-born son of the god Iškur,

28) alam-gub-kù-babbar-a-a-ugu-na
29) *nu-úr*-^{d}IŠKUR
30) lugal-lársa.KI-ma-ke$_{4}$
31) [me-d]ím-sa$_{6}$-
32) i[m-s]ar-ra sì-ga
33) mu-na-dím

28–33) fashioned for him (Utu) a silver standing statue of the father who engendered him, Nūr-Adad, king of Larsa, endowed with beautiful i[nsc]ribed [li]mbs.

34) nam-ti-la-ni-šè
35) a mu-na-ru

34–35) He dedicated it to him for his own life.

36) k[isa]l-maḫ èš é-babbar-ra
37) ki-u$_{6}$-di-kalam-ma-ka
38) é-maḫ sískur-ra
39) ḫé-du$_{7}$-na
40) bí-in-gub

36–40) He set it up in the main cour[tya]rd of shrine Ebabbar, the place of wonder of the nation, in his lofty temple, suitable for the *siskur* offerings.

2

The name of the second year of Sîn-iddinam commemorates the digging of the Tigris. This deed is described in an inscription found on three barrel cylinders and a cone fragment.

CATALOGUE

Ex.	Museum number	Excavation number	Photo number	Provenance	Object	Dimensions (cm)	Lines preserved	cpn
1	–	–	OI photo 11033	Was in the possession of E.S. David, said to come from Bismayah	Hollow clay barrel	15.0 long, 5.0 dia.	1–70	p
2	Ash 1924,263	–	–	Purchased in Baghdad in 1923, provenance unknown	Hollow clay barrel	13.8 long, 9.8 dia.	1–70	c
3	AO 25109	L [33]7	–	Larsa	Frgm. of cone	6.4 long	1–7, 29–35	c
4	A 7467	–	–	Purchased from E.S. David, June 1931 (purportedly from Tell al-Buzekh)	Hollow clay barrel	13.5 long, 10.4 dia.	9–70	c

COMMENTARY

The master text is ex. 1. This ex., whose present whereabouts is unknown, was partially collated from OI photo 11033, which shows lines 24–35 and lines 59–70. Ex. 4 was collated by R. Biggs.

BIBLIOGRAPHY

1923 Langdon, OECT 2 pp. 27–30 (ex. 1, edition) and pl. VII (ex. 1, copy)
1929 Barton, RISA pp. 316–17 Sin-iddinam 5 (edition)
1936 Meissner, Warenpreise p. 38 (study)
1961 Hallo, BiOr 18 p. 8 Sin-iddinam 6 (study)
1968 Kärki, SKFZ pp. 33–35 Sîniddinam 6 (edition)
1971 Sollberger and Kupper, IRSA IVB9c (translation)
1977 Arnaud, RA 71 p. 5 (ex. 3, copy) and p. 6 (ex. 3, study)
1977 Gurney, Essays Finkelstein p. 93 (ex. 2, study)
1980 Kärki, SAKAZ 1 pp. 60–63 Sîniddinam 6 (edition)

TEXT

Text	Translation
1) ^{d}EN.ZU-*i-din-na-am*	1–9) I, Sîn-iddinam, mighty man, provider of Ur, king of Larsa, king of the land of Sumer and Akkad, king who built the Ebabbar, temple of the god Utu, who restored the rites of the temples of the gods,
2) nita-kala-ga	
3) ú-a-úri.KI-ma	
4) lugal-larsa.KI-ma	
5) lugal-ki-en-gi-ki-uri	
6) lugal é-babbar é-^{d}utu-ke$_4$	
7) mu-un-dù-a	
8) giš-ḫur-é-dingir-re-e-ne	
9) ki-bi-šè bí-gi$_4$-a-me-en	
10) u$_4$ an-né ^{d}en-líl ^{d}nanna ^{d}utu-bi	10–13) when the gods An, Enlil, Nanna, and Utu granted to me a good reign of justice, whose days are long,
11) bala-du$_{10}$-nì-si-sá	
12) u$_4$-bi sù-sù-ud-rá	
13) gá-ra sa$_{12}$-e-eš-e ma-ni-in-rig$_7$-eš-a	
14) géštu-dagal-la-mu	14–16) by means of my broad wisdom, supremely established, which excels,
15) maḫ-bi-šè gar	
16) sag-bi-šè è-a-ta	
17) uru.KI ma-da-mu-šè	17–22) in order to establish good water for my city (and) land (and) to make magnificent my ways, praise (and) valour for the future,
18) a-du$_{10}$ gá-gá-dè	
19) a-rá zà-mí	
20) nam-ur-sag-gá-mu	
21) u$_4$-da eger-bi-šè	
22) pa-è-maḫ-ak-dè	
23) an-ra ^{d}en-líl-ra	23–24) I prayed ardently to the gods An and Enlil.
24) KA in-sa$_6$-sa$_6$	
25) a-ra-zu-ge-na-mu-šè	25–26) They having agreed to my firm entreaty
26) ḫu-mu-ši-in-še-ge-eš-a	
27) I$_7$.idigna ba-al-la-a-da	27–32) commissioned (me), by their unalterable, to dig the Tigris, to restore (its banks, and) to establish my name for a long life-span.
28) ki-bi-šè gi$_4$-a-da	
29) u$_4$-ti-la-sù-ud-rá-šè	
30) mu-mu gá-gá-dè	
31) inim-nu-kúr-ru-bi-a	
32) á-bi ḫu-mu-da-an-ág-eš	
33) u$_4$-ba du$_{11}$-ga-du$_{11}$-ga-	33–38) At that time, by the decree of the gods An and Inanna, by the favour of the gods Enlil and Ninlil, by the god Iškur, my personal god, ... my
34) an ^{d}inanna-ta	
35) še-ga-^{d}en-líl ^{d}nin-líl-lá-ta	

9.2 bí-⌜in⌝-gi$_4$-a-me-en. **9**.4 ⌜bí⌝-g[i$_4$]-a-me-[en]. **15**.2, 4 ki-bi-šè. **24**.2, 4 KA in-ne-sa$_6$-sa$_6$. **27**.3 ba-al-la-da.

36) ^{d}iškur dingir-mu x [...]
37) á-[da]ḫ-gá-ta [x]
38) usu-maḫ-^{d}nanna ^{d}[utu]-ta
39) I$_{7}$.idigna
40) i$_{7}$-ḫé-gál-la-^{d}utu-ke$_{4}$
41) ù-ma-mu-ta
42) gal-bi ḫé-em-mi-ba-al
43) ki-sur-ra-in-dub-pà-mu-šè
44) ka-bi um-mi-tum$_{4}$
45) a-gam-ma-bi-šè
46) si-gal ḫé-em-mi-sá
47) a-da-rí
48) ḫé-gál mùš nu-túm-mu
49) larsa.KI kalam-ma-mu-šè
50) ḫé-em-mi-gar
51) u$_{4}$ I$_{7}$.idigna i$_{7}$-gu-la
52) mu-ba-al-la-a
53) á lú-1-e
54) še 1 gur-ta
55) ninda 2 sìla-ta
56) kaš 4 sìla-ta
57) ì 2 gín-ta-àm
58) u$_{4}$-aš-a
59) ur$_{5}$-gin$_{7}$ šu ḫa-ba-an-ti
60) lú á-lá
61) lú á-daḫ
62) ba-ra-bí-tuk
63) usu-ma-da-mu-ta
64) kin-bi ḫé-em-mi-til
65) KA ka-aš-bar
66) dingir-gal-e-ne-ta
67) I$_{7}$.idigna i$_{7}$-dagal-la
68) ki-bi-šè ḫé-em-mi-gi$_{4}$
69) u$_{4}$-ul-du-rí-šè
70) mu-mu ḫé-em-mi-gub

h[el]per, (and) by the supreme might of the gods Nanna and [Utu],

39–42) by means of my triumph I grandly dug there the Tigris, the river of abundance of the god Utu.

43–50) I connected its intake to the border, the boundary of my choice, and directed its great (course) straight into a swamp (thereby) providing perpetual water, unceasing abundance for Larsa, my land.

51–53) When I dug the Tigris, the great river, the wages of each worker were:

54–59) 1 *gur* of barley, 2 *sila* of bread, 4 *sila* of beer, 2 shekels of oil, in one day so they received this.

60–62) I let nobody take less or more.

63–64) By the might of my land I finished that work there.

65–70) By the decree (and) decision of the great gods, I restored (the banks) of the Tigris, the broad river, (and) set up my name for the distant future.

3

The name of the third year of Sîn-iddinam commemorates the laying of the foundation of the Ebabbar temple in Larsa. A number of inscriptions of Sîn-iddinam (E4.2.9.3–6) deal with this temple's construction. One of these is a 15-line stamped brick inscription found at Larsa.

36.2 Nothing after -mu. **37**.2 á-daḫ-mu-ta. **38**.2 ^{d}nanna dingir-kù-ta. **40**.1 i$_{7}$-⟨ḫé⟩-gál-la. **40**.2 i$_{7}$-ḫe-gál-la. **43**.4 in-dub-pà-mu(over erasure)-šè. **60**.1 Copy: DA-lá; text: á-lá. **61**.1 Copy: DA-daḫ; text: á-daḫ.

CATALOGUE

Ex.	Museum number	Excavation number	Larsa provenance	Dimensions (cm)	Lines preserved	cpn
1	BM 90721 (51-1-1,286)	–	–	34.0×16.0×9.0	1–15	c
2	–	L 67-	From the surface of the tell	16.7×6.0 (stamp?)	1–15	n
3	–	L 6911	From the surface of the tell between the ziqqurrat sounding, J. VIII, and the palace of Nūr-Adad	–	–	n
4	–	L 69-	As ex. 3	–	–	n
5	–	L 7039	As ex. 3	–	1–15	n
6	–	L 7099	As ex. 3	–	–	n
7	–	L 70101	As ex. 3	–	–	n
8	–	L 70-	As ex. 3	–	–	n

COMMENTARY

The master text is ex. 1. Exs. 2 and 5 were not collated but entered in the score from the published copy. Ex. 1 is from Loftus's excavations at Larsa.

BIBLIOGRAPHY

1968 Birot, Syria 45 pp. 245–46 no. 4 (ex. 2, copy, edition)
1971 Arnaud, Syria 48 p. 292 (exs. 3–8, study)
1972 Arnaud, RA 66 p. 35 no. 3 (ex. 5, copy, edition)
1976 Arnaud, Syria 53 p. 48 I-4 (exs. 3–8, study)
1980 Kärki, SAKAZ 1 p. 79 Sîniddinam 15 (edition)
1981 Walker, CBI no. 41 (ex. 1, study)
1982 Hibbert, OrAnt 21 p. 257 (ex. 1, study)

TEXT

1) ^{d}utu
2) lugal-a-ni-ir
3) ^{d}EN.ZU-*i-din-na-am*
4) nita-kala-ga
5) ú-a-uri$_5$.KI-ma
6) lugal-larsa.KI-ma
7) lugal-ki-en-gi-ki-uri-ke$_4$
8) é-babbar
9) é-ki-ág-gá-ni
10) nam-ti-la-ni-šè
11) mu-na-ni-in-dù
12) me giš-ḫur-
13) nam-en-na-ka-ni
14) u$_4$-ul-lí-a-aš
15) pa-gal mu-na-an-è

1–2) For the god Utu, his lord,

3–7) Sîn-iddinam, mighty man, provider of Ur, king of Larsa, king of the land of Sumer and Akkad,

8–11) built for him Ebabbar, his beloved temple, for his own life.

12–15) He made the *me*s and rites of his office of *en* priest magnificent for him to the distant future.

4

A 30-line inscription known from a brick stamp fragment and a brick fragment excavated at Larsa also deals with the construction of the Ebabbar temple by Sîn-iddinam.

CATALOGUE

Ex.	Museum number	Excavation number	Provenance	Dimensions (cm)	Lines preserved	cpn
1	AO 27586	L [33]307	Larsa, excavations of Parrot, sector M	9.2×6.7×4.2	18–30	p
2	–	L 7095	From the surface between the ziqqurrat, sounding J, and the palace of Nūr-Adad	8.0×18.2	1–25 (mostly illegible)	p

COMMENTARY

The text is a conflation of exs. 1 and 2. Lines 1–5 come from ex. 1 and lines 18–30 from ex. 2.

A photograph of ex. 2, previously unpublished, was kindly provided by D. Arnaud. It reveals a stamped inscription, extremely faint and almost totally illegible. However, collation of the photo and comparison with ex. 1 reveals that it is a duplicate of ex. 1. The traces of lines 6–17 in ex. 2 are too faint to provide a text.

Lines 18–22 may be compared with lines 22–26 of E4.2.9.2.

BIBLIOGRAPHY

1971 Arnaud, Syria 48 p. 293 (ex. 2, study)
1972 Arnaud, RA 66 pp. 35–36 no. 4 (ex. 1, copy, edition)
1980 Kärki, SAKAZ 1 p. 79 Sîniddinam 16 (ex. 1, edition)
1982 André-Leicknam, Naissance de l'écriture p. 327 no. 271 (ex. 1, photo, study)

TEXT

1) ⌜^{d}EN.ZU-*i-din-na-am*⌝
2) ⌜nita-kala-ga⌝
3) ⌜ú-a-úri.KI-ma⌝
4) ⌜lugal-larsa.KI-ma⌝
5) ⌜lugal-ki-en-gi-ki-uri-ke$_4$⌝
Lacuna (12 lines)
18) [x] x-dè
19) ^{d}utu lugal-mu
20) KA in-na-sa$_6$-sa$_6$
21) a-ra-zu-šà-ge-DU-a-gá
22) ḫu-mu-ši-in-še
23) u$_4$-bi-a še-ga-^{d}utu
24) lugal-gá-ta
25) é-babbar ⌜é⌝-ki-ág-gá-ni
26) ḫu-mu-na-dù
27) ḫur-sag-íl-la-gin$_7$
28) sag ḫu-mu-na-ni-íl
29) ki-tuš-šà-du$_{10}$-ga-na
30) ^{d}utu ḫé-em-mi-tuš

1–5) Sîn-iddinam, mighty man, provider of Ur, king of Larsa, king of the land of Sumer and Akkad,

Lacuna (12 lines)

18–20) in order to ... I prayed ardently to the god Utu, my lord.

21–22) He was favourable to the entreaties of my wishes.

23–24) At that time, by the favour of the god Utu, my lord,

25–26) I built for him Ebabbar, his beloved temple.

27–30) I raised (its) head for him there like a mountain raised high (and) installed the god Utu in his residence which pleases him.

5

A foundation inscription known from a limestone tablet and limestone cylinder fragment deals with the construction of the Ebabbar temple by Sîn-iddinam.

CATALOGUE

Ex.	Museum number	Provenance	Object	Dimensions (cm)	Lines preserved	cpn
1	WAG 41.222	Larsa(?)	Limestone foundation tablet	–	1–25	c
2	Crozer Theological Seminary 2	Larsa(?)	Limestone cylinder frgm. (top)	6.1 dia., 3.9 high	1–6, 7–12	n

COMMENTARY

Ex. 1 was in the possession of E.S. David and was offered for sale to the Oriental Institute, whose photos 12091–12092 show this object. The piece was subsequently purchased by the Walters Art Gallery. It was collated from the published photo.

The inscription probably dates to the very end of Sîn-iddinam's reign. The epithet sipa nì-nam-du_8-du_8-nibru.KI 'shepherd who makes everything abundant for Nippur' is found only in this text and E4.2.9.12. Texts from Nippur using a Sîn-iddinam year name date to the last year of the king (see R.M. Sigrist, Sattukku p. 100).

BIBLIOGRAPHY

1961 Hallo, BiOr 18 p. 8 Sin-iddinam 5 (ex. 1, study)
1968 Kärki, SKFZ p. 33 Sîniddinam 5 (study)
1969 Hallo, JCS 21 pp. 97–99 (ex. 1, photo, edition)
1973 Hallo, JANES 5 pp. 169–72 (ex. 2, copy, transliteration, study)
1980 Kärki, SAKAZ 1 p. 60 Sîniddinam 5 (edition)

TEXT

1) ^{d}utu
2) en di-ku_5-an-ki
3) gal-zu-eš-bar
4) nì-gi-e bar-tam-e
5) lugal-é-babbar-ra
6) lugal-a-ni-ir
7) ^{d}EN.ZU-*i-din-na-am*
8) sipa nì-nam-du_8-du_8-
9) nibru.KI
10) ú-a-uri_5.KI-ma
11) lugal-larsa.KI-ma
12) lugal-ki-en-gi-ki-uri-ke_4
13) é-babbar
14) é-ki-ág-gá-ni
15) nam-ti-la-ni-šè
16) mu-na-dù
17) diri-u_4-ul-lí-a-aš
18) ki-tuš-bi mu-na-an-dagal
19) nì-ak-bi-šè
20) ^{d}utu
21) ḫé-en-da-ḫúl
22) ti nì-du_{10}
23) u_4-bi íb-gu-ul-la
24) nì-ba-aš
25) ḫé-en-na-ba-e

1–6) For the god Utu, lord, judge of heaven and earth, wise in decisions, who chooses righteousness, lord of Ebabbar, his lord,

7–12) Sîn-iddinam, shepherd who makes everything abundant for Nippur, provider of Ur, king of Larsa, king of the land of Sumer and Akkad,

13–16) built for him Ebabbar, his beloved temple, for his own life.

17–18) He enlarged his residence from what it had been in the past.

19–21) May the god Utu rejoice with him at this deed,

22–25) (and) may he present to him as a gift, life, a splendid thing, whose days are increasingly numerous.

6

Near the door-sill of room 15, a small room off courtyard 1 of the Ebabbar temple in Larsa, a fragment of a foundation plaque with an inscription of Sîn-iddinam was excavated. The extant portion of this inscription duplicates the end of a text pieced together by E. Sollberger from several cones excavated at Ur. The Larsa text as a whole was probably a duplicate of the Ur cones. The text deals with Sîn-iddinam's construction of the Ebabbar temple.

CATALOGUE

Ex.	Museum number	Excavation number	Provenance	Object	Dimensions (cm)	Lines preserved	cpn
1	–	L 78300	Larsa, from room 15 facing courtyard 1 of the Ebabbar temple, 20 cm in front of door-sill leading to courtyard	Left bottom corner of limestone plaque	6.6×7.1×1.7	61–62, 68–78	n
2	BM 119044 (1927-10-3,39)	U 2637	Ur, from 'PDW', the great Nanna courtyard, west	Cone shaft	8.0	1–3, 27–37	c
3	IM 92945	U 13085	Ur, from NE of the city wall, central section	Cone shaft	6.8×6.2	24–40	c
4	IM –	U 13601	Ur, from 'Larsa rubbish filling'	Cone head	9.0 dia.	25–33, 51–65	c
5	IM 92941	U 13601	As ex. 4	Cone shaft	–	20–24, 27–34	c
6	IM 92951	U 13682	Ur, from 'Larsa rubbish', Royal Cemetery area	Cone shaft	10.5	4–24	c
7	IM 92946	U 15071	Ur, from the 'town wall'	Cone shaft	6.5×6.5	25–33, 58–60	c
8	BM 122939 (1931-10-10,7)	U 16047	Ur, from the 'upper filling' above the mausolea of Šulgi and Amar-Sîn	Cone shaft	9.7	14–33	c
9	BM 122939 (1931-10-10,7)	U 16047	As ex. 8	Cone head	7.0 dia.	29–32	c
10	BM 123120 (1932-10-8,4)	U ba	Ur, no provenance	Cone shaft	6.2×5.9	1–2, 26–33, 35, 37–39, 41–44, 62–72, 74, 76	c
11	IM 26913	U ca	Ur, no provenance	Cone shaft	–	22–38, 67–68, 70–74, 76–78	c
12	McGill Ethnological Collections, no. 16	U 187	Ur, Trial Trench B in brick rubbish near the wall face at the south end, about 030 above point of last brick-wall period	Cone shaft	11.1	55, 57–70	c

COMMENTARY

The text is a conflated one following that established by Sollberger in the copy in UET 8 no. 72 for lines 1–68 and ex. 1 for lines 69–78.

No common reading can be established for line 70 of the text.

A comparison of the Larsa plaque fragment with the Ur cones shows that the former was probably originally inscribed on both sides. Only the bottoms of the last two cols. of the rev. remain today. The stone plaque would have originally contained about 15 lines per col. About five lines are missing at the top of last col. in the extant fragment.

The cones from Ur were inscribed either on the head or shaft. The inscription was arranged in three cols. of about 25 lines each on the heads of the cones, and the same arrangement seems likely for the shafts. The discovery of the duplicate from Larsa helps explain why a text dealing solely with the construction of the

Ebabbar temple was found at Ur.

The restoration of lines 72–75 follows a partial parallel found in E4.2.13.21 lines 103–104.

BIBLIOGRAPHY

1928 Gadd, UET 1 no. 132 (ex. 2, copy, edition)
1957 Edzard, Sumer 13 p. 178 (ex. 11, study) and pl. 3a facing p. 185 (ex. 11, copy)
1965 Sollberger, UET 8 no. 72 (exs. 2–11, composite copy, study)
1971 Sollberger and Kupper, IRSA IVB9b (translation)
1976 Woolley and Mallowan, UE 7 p. 219 (ex. 2, provenance)
1980 Kärki, SAKAZ 1 pp. 76–79 Sîniddinam 14 (edition)
1981 Arnaud, Syria 58 pp. 43–44 no. 1 (ex. 1, study) and p. 83 (ex. 1, copy)
1983 Arnaud in Huot, Larsa et 'Oueili 1978–1981 p. 230 (ex. 1, study) and p. 252 no. 2 (ex. 1, copy)

TEXT

1) u$_4$ ^{d}utu èš é-babbar-ra
2) [n]am-bi mu-un-tar-ra-a

1–2) When the god Utu determined the destiny of shrine Ebabbar

3) [m]e giš-ḫur š[u-du$_7$-du$_7$-dè]
4) [...] x x x [...]
5) [ki]-tuš-bi daga[l-e-dè]
6) [ga]l-le-eš K[A ...]
7) x-aš mu-u[n-du$_{11}$-ga]

3–7) (and) [spoke of] p[erfectly executing] the *me*s and rites, ..., of enlar[ging] its [res]idence, [gra]ndly ...

8) ⸢u$_4$⸣-ba ^{d}EN.ZU-*i-d*[*in-na-am*]
9) nita-kala-[ga]
10) ú-a-uri$_5$.KI-[ma]
11) lugal-larsa.KI-[ma]
12) lugal-ki-en-⸢gi⸣-ki-uri-m[e-en]
13) šul ^{d}utu kur kìlib-ba-ni-[ta]
14) igi-zi mu-ši-i[n-bar]

8–14) at that time [it was] at me, Sîn-iddi[nam], mighty man, provider of Ur, king of Larsa, king of the land of Sumer and Akkad, whom the youth, god Utu, [from] among all his lands, truly loo[ked].

15) nam-sipa-larsa.KI-m[a-šè]
16) ḫu-mu-un-íl-[le-en]
17) éren-ma-da-lu-a-[bi]
18) inim-mu-šè ḫé-em-mi-i[n-tuš]
19) á-ág-gá-gal-gal-l[a-bi]
20) šu-mu-šè ḫé-em-mi-i[n-si]

15–20) He elevated [me to] the shepherdship of Larsa, made the troops of the numerous lands [dwell] at my command, and [entrusted] me with their great orders.

21) ki-tuš-šà-du$_{10}$-ga-na
22) šu-dagal di-d[è]
23) nam-ní-tuk-mu-šè
24) ⸢á⸣-bi ḫu-⸢mu⸣-da-an-ág

21–24) He commissioned me, on account of my reverence, t[o] enlarge his residence that pleases him.

25) ⸢u$_4$⸣-bi-a ^{d}utu lugal-mu-úr
26) KA-sa$_6$-sa$_6$-ge-mu-ta
27) uru.KI-gá i-^{d}utu
28) ḫé-éb-ta-zi

25–28) At that time, for the god Utu, my lord, with my ardent prayer, I removed (cause for) complaint from my city.

29) ugnim-larsa.KI-ma
30) aš-bi um-mi-tuš
31) á šà-gal ì-šeš$_4$
32) šà-du$_{10}$-ga-bi-dè
33) lú-kin-ak-bi-šè
34) ḫa-ba-sum-sum

29–34) I assembled the host of Larsa and gave to them, as its (Ebabbar's) workers, wages — food, annointing oil — (enough) to please them.

35) šà-mu-aš-ka
36) sig$_4$-al-ur$_5$-ra-bi
37) ḫé-bí-du$_8$

35–37) I baked its (Ebabbar's) baked brick in the course of one year

---

33.11 Copy: [lú-kin-ak]-bi-⟨šè⟩; text: [lú-kin-ak]-bi-šè.

38) é-babbar-ra [é-ki-ág]-gá-ni
39) [ḫ]ur-sag-gin$_7$ ki-siki[l-la]
40) [gi-gun$_4$-n]a-maḫ-bi
41) [ḫu-mu-n]a-dù
42) [u$_4$ èš é-babbar]-ra
43) [ḫu-mu-dù]-a
44) x [...]
Lacuna
49) [á lú-1-e]
50) [x še-gur-ta]
51) zú-lum 2 sìla-ta
52) ga-àra 2 sìla-ta
53) duḫ-še-giš-ì 2 sìla-ta
54) ì 2 gín-ta-àm
55) amaš nì-kú-e šub-ba
56) u$_4$-aš-a
57) ur-gin$_7$ šu ḫa-ba-ra-an-ti
58) u$_4$-[b]ala-sa$_6$-ga-gá
59) ^{d}utu lugal-mu
60) gá-ar ma-an-sum-ma-a
61) še 4 gur-ta
62) zú-lum 12 gur-ta
63) síg 15 ma-na-ta
64) ì-giš 3 bán-ta
65) ì-šaḫ 5 bán-ta-àm
66) ganba šà-uri$_5$.KI
67) larsa.KI ù ma-da-g[á-ka]
68) kù 1 gín-e
69) ur$_5$-gin$_7$ ḫa-ba-ra-[sa$_{10}$]
70) ^{d}EN.ZU-*i-din-n[a-am]* nun-gal x [...]
71) sig-tùm-tùm x [x x]
72) u$_4$-ba sag-k[i-zalag]
73) šà-ḫúl-uru.KI-gá-[ka]
74) èš é-babbar-r[a]
75) kin-bi ḫu-mu-ni-ti[l]
76) šà-^{d}utu
77) ù ^{d}šè-ri$_5$-da-ke$_4$
78) ḫu-mu-du$_{10}$

38–41) (and) I built for him (Utu) the lofty [*gigun*]*na* of Ebabbar, his [belove]d [temple], like a [m]ountain in a pur[e] place.

42–43) [When I built shrine Ebabba]r ...
Lacuna

49–55) [the wages of each (worker) were: x *gur* of grain] 2 *sila* of dates, 2 *sila* of cheese, 2 *sila* of sesame bran, 2 shekels of oil, not including food from the sheepfolds.

56–57) In one day so they received this.

58–69) In the days of my gracious [r]eign, which the god Utu, my lord gave to me, 4 *gur* of barley, 12 *gur* of dates, 15 minas of wool, 3 *ban* of vegetable oil, 5 *ban* of lard, according to the market value in Ur, Larsa and m[y] land, so much [was sold] per one shekel of silver.

70–71) I, Sîn-iddin[am], great prince, ... who carries off the Lower Land ...,
72–78) at that time, with [shining] fa[ce amidst] rejoicing [in] my city, I finishe[d] the construction work of shrine Ebabbar. I made the gods Utu and Šeridda content.

7

A cone from Larsa deals with some deed performed by Sîn-iddinam on behalf of the sun god Utu. Only the beginning of the text is preserved.

60.12 ma-an-[sum]-ma-⟨a⟩. **70**.1 nun-gal [...]. **70**.10 nun ⌜ní-tuk⌝ [...]. **70**.11 ú-a x [...].

COMMENTARY

The cone is BM 30215 (51-1-1,256) excavated by Loftus at Larsa, no excavation no. or provenance known. The cone is 4.9 cm long and 6 cm in dia., and the inscription was collated.

BIBLIOGRAPHY

1861 1 R pl. 3 no. IX (copy)
1872 G. Smith, TSBA 1 p. 44 (translation)
1875 Ménant, Babylone et la Chaldée p. 88 (translation)
1899 Bezold, Cat. 5 p. 2233 (study)
1905 Thureau-Dangin, ISA pp. 298–99 Sin-idinnam c (edition)
1905 King, CT 21 pl. 30 (copy)
1907 Thureau-Dangin, SAK pp. 210–11 Sin-idinnam c (edition)
1929 Barton, RISA pp. 314–15 Sin-iddinam 3 (edition)
1961 Hallo, BiOr 18 p. 8 Sin-iddinam 9 (study)
1968 Kärki, SKFZ pp. 36–37 Sîniddinam 9 (edition)
1980 Kärki, SAKAZ 1 pp. 65–66 Sîniddinam 9 (edition)

TEXT

1) ᵈ[utu]
2) en piri[g-gal]
3) GIŠ(*).si-gar-an-na-[ke₄ gál-tak₄]
4) di-ku₅-sig-IGI.NI[M-ma]
5) lugal-é-[babbar-ra]
6) lugal-a-n[i-ir]
7) ᵈEN.ZU-*i-[din-na-am]*
8) nita-kala-[ga]
9) [d]umu ga-eš.K[I-e ù-tu-da]
10) ú-a-ur[i₅KI]-m[a]
11) lugal-lars[a.KI-ma]
12) lugal-ki-e[n-gi] ki-u[ri]
Lacuna

1–6) [For the] god [Utu], lord, [great] lio[n], [who opens] the bolt of heaven, judge of the Upper and Lowe[r] (lands), lord of E[babbar], his lord,

7–12) Sîn-i[ddinam], mighty man, [s]on [born] in Gaʾeš, provider of U[r], king of Lars[a], king of the land of S[umer] and Ak[kad]
Lacuna

8

A brick fragment excavated at Larsa commemorates some deed of Sîn-iddinam. The broken nature of the brick prevents us from determining the purport of the text as a whole.

COMMENTARY

The brick fragment is IM 73345, excavation no. L [33]82 from Parrot's excavations in the so-called palace of Sîn-iddinam, sector E.F.IX. It is the lower left corner of a two(?)-col. brick 7.3 × 8.5 × 3.2 cm. The transliteration of this previously unpublished piece is offered through the courtesy of D. Arnaud. The inscription parallels some lines of UET 8 no. 68 but is not a duplicate of the Ur text.

3 Copy: GIGIR.

BIBLIOGRAPHY

1981 Arnaud, Syria 58 p. 43 n. 1 (study)
1983 Arnaud in Huot, Larsa et 'Oueili 1978–1981 p. 230 n. 14 (study)

TEXT

Lacuna	Lacuna
1′) [è]š é-bab[bar-ra]	1′) [who looks after s]hrine Ebab[bar],
2′) suḫuš-ma-da	2′–4′) who makes fi[rm] the foundation of the land for the god Utu,
3′) ge-en-ge-[en]	
4′) ^{d}utu-[ke$_4$]	
5′) bàd-gal-úr[i.KI-ma]	5′–6′) built for him the great wall of U[r],
6′) mu-na-dù	
7′) ḫur-sag-[gin$_7$]	7′–9′) [built] it in a [pure] place [like] a mountain.
8′) ki-[sikil-la]	
9′) mu-u[n-dù]	
10′) [... ú]ri.KI	10′–11′) [... U]r [...]
11′) [...-k]e$_4$	Lacuna
Lacuna	

9

An inscription found on cones excavated at Ur deals with two themes: that Sîn-iddinam has built the Ebabbar temple for the god Utu and the wish that the king be an everlasting provider of offerings in both the Ebabbar and Ekišnugal temples. The juxtaposition of the names of the two shrines in one text is noteworthy.

CATALOGUE

Ex.	Museum number	Excavation number	Ur provenance	Object	Dimensions (cm)	Lines preserved	cpn
1	BM 91152 (59-10-14,82)	–	–	Cone head	12.2 dia.	3–10, 13–20	c
2	BM 91152 (59-10-14,82)	–	–	Cone shaft	10	1–25	c
3	IM 972	U 2900	From south corner of the ziqqurrat terrace	Cone shaft	11.2	1–25	c
4	IM 972	U 2900	As ex. 3	Small cone head frgm.	7 dia.	6–7	c
5	BM 120522 (1928-10-9,5)	U 7798	From Enunmaḫ, under Nebuchadnezzar pavement	Cone	–	–	n
6	IM 92853	U 10136	From the Royal Cemetery area	Cone shaft	11.0	1–25	c
7	IM 22885	U 16536	From AH, extreme NE end, D.20 below Neo-Babylonian floor	Cone head	9.0 dia.	1–25	c
8	IM 22885	U 16536	As ex. 7	Cone shaft	11.0	2–10, 13–24	c

COMMENTARY

The master text is ex. 2.

Bezold, Literatur p. 51, described ex. 1 as coming from Larsa, probably because of the dedication to the sun god. The registration no. of the cone indicates that it was excavated by Taylor at Ur. Thus all the cones come from Ur and Kärki, SAKAZ 1 p. 64 'Sîniddinam 8 Tonnagel; Larsa, Ur' should be modified accordingly.

BIBLIOGRAPHY

1872 G. Smith, TSBA 1 pp. 44–45 (translation)
1873 Lenormant, Choix no. 6 (ex. 2, copy)
1886 Bezold, Literatur p. 51 (study)
1891 4 R^2 pl. 36 no. 2 (ex. 2, copy)
1899 Bezold, Cat. 5 p. 2241 (study)
1905 Thureau-Dangin, ISA pp. 298–99 Sin-idinnam b (edition)
1907 Thureau-Dangin, SAK pp. 208–11 Sin-idinnam b (edition)
1910 King, Early History pl. XXIII facing p. 258 (ex. 2, photo)
1928 Gadd, UET 1 no. 118 (exs. 3–5, composite copy, edition)
1929 Barton, RISA pp. 314–15 Sin-iddinam 2 (ex. 2, edition) and p. 374 Sin-iddinam 2 (exs. 3–5, edition)
1957 Edzard, Sumer 13 p. 177 (exs. 3–4, 7–8, study)
1961 Hallo, BiOr 18 p. 8 Sin-iddinam 8 (study)
1965 Sollberger, UET 8 p. 28 no. 19 (ex. 6, study)
1968 Kärki, SKFZ pp. 36–37 Sîniddinam 8 (edition)
1980 Kärki, SAKAZ 1 pp. 64–65 Sîniddinam 8 (edition)

TEXT

1) ^{d}utu
2) en-nì-ge
3) sag-kal-an-ki
4) diri-^{d}a-nun-ke$_4$-ne
5) lugal-a-ni-ir
6) ^{d}EN.ZU-*i-din-na-am*
7) nita-kala-ga
8) ú-a-uri$_5$.KI-ma
9) lugal-larsa.KI-ma
10) lugal-ki-en-gi-ki-uri-ke$_4$
11) é-babbar ki-tuš-kù-ki-ág-gá-ni
12) nam-ti-la-ni-šè
13) mu-na-ni-in-dù
14) me giš-ḫur
15) a-rá-maḫ-ka-né
16) sù-ud-rá-šè
17) pa-gal mu-na-an-è
18) du$_{11}$-ga-du$_{11}$-ga-
19) ^{d}nanna ^{d}utu-bi-ta
20) é-babbar
21) é-kiš-nu-gál-la-ka
22) ^{d}EN.ZU-*i-din-na-am*
23) ní-tuk-^{d}a-nun-ke$_4$-ne
24) nidba šu-du$_7$-du$_7$ ḫé-a
25) u$_4$-da-rí-šè

1–5) For the god Utu, lord of righteousness, foremost one of heaven and earth, the one greater than the Anuna gods, his lord,

6–10) Sîn-iddinam, mighty man, provider of Ur, king of Larsa, king of the land of Sumer and Akkad,

11–13) built for him for his own life the Ebabbar, his beloved shining residence.

14–17) He made magnificent for him to the distant future the *me*s and rites of his supreme ways.

18–25) By the decree of the gods Nanna and Utu may Sîn-iddinam, the one who reveres the Anuna gods, be one who makes perfect offerings in Ebabbar and Ekišnugal forever.

3.6 -an-ki-a. **10**.3 Last sign of line copied by Gadd as uri is indistinct on original. Duplicates suggest it should be -ke$_4$. **11**.6 -ki-ág-gá-a-ni. **12**.2 nam-ti-la-a-n[i-šè]. **12**.7 nam-ti-la-a-ni-šè. **15** Despite comments of Kärki, all texts have simply a-rá-. **15**.5–6 a-rá-maḫ-a-ka-né. **17**.8 ⌜mu-un⌝-n[a-...].

19.3 Copy: ^{d}nanna ^{d}utu-bi; text: ^{d}nanna ^{d}utu-t[a].
21.3 Copy: é-kiš-nu-gál-bi; text: é-kiš-nu-gál-l[a-x].
21.5 Gadd lists U 7798 as having é-kiš-nu-gál-la; although not collated we would expect é-kiš-nu-gál-la-ka. **23**.3 Copy: an-nun-ge-ne; text: ^{d}a-nun-ke$_4$-ne.

10

A number of bricks found at Ur deal with Sîn-iddinam's construction of the Ga-nun-maḫ.

CATALOGUE

Ex.	Museum number	Registration number	Excavation number	Provenance	Dimensions (cm)	Lines preserved	cpn
1	BM 114271	1919-10-11,4702	–	Ur, no provenance	9.0×8.5×7.0	11-18	c
2	BM 119276	1927-10-3,271	U 3115	Ur, loose NW of the ziqqurrat and behind the Edublamaḫ	28.0×18.5×9.0	2-17	c
3	BM 137347	1935-1-13,7	U 3115	As ex. 2	27.0×17.5×8.5	1-4, 8-18	c
4	IM 1032	–	U 3115	As ex. 2	25.0×18.0	–	n
5	CBS 16474	–	U 3315b	As ex. 2	28.0×12.5×8.0	1-18	c
6	BM 120521	1928-10-9,4	U 7715	From Diqdiqqah	18.0×17.0×9.0	1-18	c
7	BM 137407	1979-12-18,42	–	Ur(?), no provenance	27.5×18.0×9.0	1-2, 4-18	c

COMMENTARY

The master text is ex. 6. Ex. 1 was found by Hall at Ur, exs. 2-6 by Woolley.

BIBLIOGRAPHY

1928 Gadd, UET 1 no. 117 (exs. 2-4, 6, composite copy, edition)
1929 Barton, RISA pp. 374-75 Sin-iddinam 1 (edition)
1961 Hallo, BiOr 18 p. 8 Sin-iddinam 2 (study)
1968 Kärki, SKFZ pp. 31-32 Sîniddinam 2 (edition)
1971 Sollberger and Kupper, IRSA IVB9a (translation)
1980 Kärki, SAKAZ 1 pp. 57-58 Sîniddinam 2 (edition)
1981 Walker, CBI no. 38 (exs. 1-3, 6-7, study)
1976 Woolley and Mallowan, UE 7 p. 220 (exs. 5-6, provenance)

TEXT

1) ^{d}EN.ZU-*i-din-na-am*
2) nita-kala-ga
3) ú-a-úri.KI-ma
4) lugal-larsa.KI-ma
5) lugal giš-ḫur-úri.KI
6) eridu.KI-ga
7) ki-bé bí-in-gi$_4$-a

1-7) Sîn-iddinam, mighty man, provider of Ur, king of Larsa, king who restored the rites of Ur and Eridu,

8) gá-nun-maḫ
9) u$_4$-ul-lí-a-ta
10) lugal-IGI.DU-na-ne
11) ki-bé li-bí-gi$_4$

8-11) from past days no royal ancestor of his had restored the Ganunmaḫ.

12) du$_{11}$-ga-^{d}nanna
13) lugal-gá-ta
14) èš-gal-maḫ nì-GA-ra-kam

12-18) By the decree of the god Nanna, my lord, I built for him the Eešgalmaḫ ('Supreme great shrine') of the storehouse, which none among the

9.6 u$_4$-ul-a-lí-ta. **11** Copy: šà-bé; all exs.: ki-bé. **13**.2-3, 5 lugal-maḫ-ta.

15) un-šár-e nu-sá
16) nam-ti-ad-da-gá
17) ù nam-ti-mu-uš
18) mu-na-dù

numerous people can rival, for the life of my father and for my own life.

11

An inscription found stamped on bricks excavated by Taylor at Ur deals with the construction by Sîn-iddinam for the god Nanna of the temple Enamnuna.

CATALOGUE

Ex.	Museum number	Registration number	Excavation number	Provenance	Dimensions (cm)	Lines preserved	cpn
1	BM 90031	59-10-14,31	–	Ur, from the extreme northern mounds at Mugheir	31.5×15.0	1-30	c
2	BM 90251	59-10-14,40	–	As ex. 1	35.5×17.0×7.5	1-14	c
3	BM 90356	59-10-14,38	–	As ex. 1	30.0×22.0×8.0	1-30	c
4	BM 90357	59-10-14,32	–	As ex. 1	20.0×18.0×8.0	1-13, 16-17	c
5	BM 90358+ BM 90393	59-10-14,36+ 59-10-14,30	–	As ex. 1	29.5×18.0×9.0	1-18, 20-30	c
6	BM 90381+ BM 90389	59-10-14,28+ 59-10-14,35	–	As ex. 1	34.0×30.0×8.0	1-15, 17-30	c
7	BM 90383	59-10-14,39	–	As ex. 1	21.0×11.0×8.0	5-14, 17-23	c
8	BM 90387	59-10-14,15	–	As ex. 1	14.5×11.0×7.0	11-30	c
9	BM 90395	59-10-14,37	–	As ex. 1	19.0×12.0×8.5	face: 15-30	c
10	BM 90395	59-10-14,37	–	As ex. 1	19.0×12.0×8.5	edge: 9-20	c
11	BM 90690	59-10-14,29+34	–	As ex. 1	18.0×16.0×6.0	17-30	n
12	BM 90704+ BM 90718	59-10-14,33 59-10-14,33	–	Ur, from the extreme northern mounds	33.5×16.5×9.5	1-15, 17-30	c
13	IM 108	–	U 254	Ur, –	18.0×10.0	–	n
14	CBS 16473	–	U 3315a	Ur, no provenance	32.5×33.0×8.0	–	n

COMMENTARY

The master text is ex. 1.

Exs. 1-12 come from Taylor's excavations at Ur, exs. 13-14 from Woolley's.

The number U 254 for ex. 13 = IM 108 is from records in Baghdad. It does not agree with the Ur registry which indicates that U 254 is a vase fragment.

For the meaning 'to agree to' for -gin in line 23, cf. CT 11 pl. 31 iv 24: $^{\text{gi-in}}$gin = *ma-ga-rum*.

BIBLIOGRAPHY

1861 1 R pl. 5 no. xx (exs. 1-12, composite copy)
1872 G. Smith, TSBA 1 p. 44 (translation)
1874 Lenormant, Études accadiennes 2 pp. 373-74
1875 Ménant, Babylone et la Chaldée pp. 88-89 (translation)
1892 Winckler, KB 3/1 pp. 92-93 Sin-iddina 2 (edition)
1899 Bezold, Cat. 5 p. 2233 (study)
1905 Thureau-Dangin, ISA pp. 298-301 Sin-idinnam d (edition)
1907 Thureau-Dangin, SAK pp. 210-11 Sin-idinnam d (edition)
1915 King, History pl. VII facing p. 90 (ex. 2, photo)
1922 BM Guide p. 61 no. 120 (exs. 1-2, study)

16 Gadd, UET 1 p. 28, suggests var. ad-da-mu; collation reveals ad-da-⸢gá⸣. **17** Copy: nam-ti-mu-šè; all exs.: nam-ti-mu-uš.

1961 Hallo, BiOr 18 p. 8 Sin-iddinam 3 (study)
1968 Kärki, SKFZ pp. 32–33 Sîniddinam 3 (edition)
1980 Kärki, SAKAZ 1 pp. 58–59 Sîniddinam 3 (edition)
1981 Walker, CBI no. 39 (exs. 1–12, study)

TEXT

1) ^{d}EN.ZU-*i-din-na-am*
2) nita-kala-ga
3) ú-a-úri.KI-ma
4) lugal-larsa.KI-ma
5) lugal-ki-en-gi-ki-uri
6) lú in-dub-libir
7) ki-bé bí-in-gi$_4$-a

1–7) Sîn-iddinam, mighty man, provider of Ur, king of Larsa, king of the land of Sumer and Akkad, the one who restored the old boundary –

8) u$_4$ GIŠ.gu-za-larsa.KI-ma
9) suḫuš mu-un-ge-na-a
10) GIŠ.tukul-ta gú-érim-bé
11) gàr bí-in-dar-ra-a

8–11) when he had made firm the foundation of the throne of Larsa, had defeated all (his) enemies with weapons,

12) I$_7$.idigna
13) i$_7$-šà-du$_{10}$-ga-na
14) usu-ma-da-ni-ta
15) im-mi-in-ba-al-la-a
16) a-da-rí
17) ḫé-gál nì-nu-til-e
18) uru.KI ma-da-ni-šè
19) im-mi-in-gar-ra-a

12–19) had dug there, by the might of his land, the Tigris, the river which is pleasing to him, (and) had provided perpetual water, abundance without end for his city and land,

20) šùd-dè nam-šita$_x$(REC 316) a-ra-zu-ni
21) ^{d}nanna
22) dumu-sag-^{d}en-líl-lá-ke$_4$
23) in-dè-gen-na-aš

20–23) because the god Nanna, first-born son of the god Enlil, agreed to his prayers, supplications, and entreaties,

24) géštu-dagal
25) KA-ša$_6$-ša$_6$-ge-ni-ta
26) ki-úri.KI-ma-ka
27) mu-maḫ-a-ni bí-in-gub

24–27) by his broad wisdom (and) prayers he set up his supreme name in the land of Ur.

28) é-nam-nun-na-ka-ni
29) ^{d}nanna-ar
30) mu-na-an-dù

28–30) He built for the god Nanna his Enamnuna ('House of princeship').

12

A stamped brick inscription from Ur refers to the setting up of a great statue of the god Nanna by Sîn-iddinam.

CATALOGUE

Ex.	Museum number	Excavation number	Provenance	Dimensions (cm)	Lines preserved	cpn
1	–	U 2725	Ur, from the east corner of the great Nanna court	? × 17.0 × 5.0	1–8	n
2	CBS 16548	U 6324	Ur, from KPS (a southern extension of Gipar-ku site of Larsa and later dates)	17.0 × 16.0 × 6.0	–	n
3	–	U 11662	Ur, from room 2 of the great Nanna courtyard	–	1–6	n

Ex.	Museum number	Excavation number	Provenance	Dimensions (cm)	Lines preserved	cpn
4	UM 31-16-358	U 13108	Ur, from 'courtyard of house at NW end of the NE city wall', central section	32.0×32.0×6.5	1–18	n
5	BM 137385 (1979-12-18,20)	–	Ur(?)	13.5×10.5×5.0	7–15	c
6	BM 137415 (1979-12-18,50)	–	Ur(?)	25.5×18.0×6.0	1–14	c

COMMENTARY

The master text is ex. 4 entered from H. Behren's transliteration.

This inscription probably dates to the very end of Sîn-iddinam's reign because of the epithet sipa nì-nam-du$_8$-du$_8$-nibru.KI (see commentary to E4.2.9.5).

Concerning the provenance of these bricks, it is likely that they formed the socle on which the statue of Sîn-iddinam once stood. A number of Isin-Larsa inscriptions from Ur refer to the setting up of statues in the kisal-maḫ 'main courtyard', which has been identified with the great Nanna courtyard east of the ziqqurrat. Exs. 1 and 3 are said to have come from this courtyard. The 'Sîn-iddinam base', a brick platform in the great Nanna courtyard, may have served as a base for this statue (see Figulla and Martin, UE 5 p. 83). A brick, U 12570, is said to have come from this base, but the brick with this number bears the inscription dealing with the construction of the wall of Ur. Curiously, another brick, U 13108, bearing the inscription dealing with this statue, is said to have come from a courtyard of a house near the city wall. In view of these coincidences we might conjecture that the two bricks were accidentally interchanged when being registered, and that the one dealing with the statue came from the 'Sîn-iddinam base' and the one dealing with the city wall from the courtyard of the house near the city wall. The bricks in question bear consecutive museum numbers. However, this is only a conjecture, which cannot be proved from the records at hand.

Ex. 2, U 6324, was said by Woolley and Mallowan, UE 7 p. 222, to be a duplicate of UET 1 no. 119 = E4.2.9.13. Collation by Behrens reveals that it is a duplicate of this text.

BIBLIOGRAPHY

1928 Gadd, UET 1 no. 120 (ex. 1, copy, edition)
1929 Barton, RISA pp. 376–77 Sin-iddinam 4 (edition)
1961 Hallo, BiOr 18 p. 8 Sin-iddinam 4 (edition)
1965 Sollberger, UET 8 no. 69 (ex. 3, copy; ex. 3–4, study)
1968 Kärki, SKFZ p. 33 Sîniddinam 4 (edition)
1980 Kärki, SAKAZ 1 pp. 59–60 Sîniddinam 4 (incomplete edition)
1981 Walker, CBI no. 40 (exs. 5–6, study)
1985 Behrens, JCS 37 pp. 235–36 no. 31 (ex. 4, transliteration; exs. 2, 4, study)

TEXT

1) ^{d}nanna
2) dumu-sag-^{d}en-líl-lá
3) lugal-a-ni-ir
4) ^{d}EN.ZU-*i-din-na-am*
5) sipa nì-nam-du$_8$-du$_8$-
6) nibru.KI
7) ú-a-úri.KI-ma
8) lugal-larsa.KI-ma
9) lugal-ki-en-gi-ki-uri-ke$_4$
10) URUDU.alam-gu-la
11) nam-ti-la-ni-šè
12) mu-na-dím
13) é-^{d}nanna
14) ki-u$_6$-di-⌜kalam-ma⌝-k[a]
15) bí-in-⌜ku$_4$⌝

1–3) For the god Nanna, first-born son of the god Enlil, his lord,

4–9) Sîn-iddinam, shepherd who makes everything abundant for Nippur, provider of Ur, king of Larsa, king of the land of Sumer and Akkad,

10–12) fashioned for him, for his own life, a great copper statue.

13–15) He brought it into the temple of the god Nanna, in[to] the place of wonder of the nation.

16) ⸢bala⸣-nam-lugal-la-ka-ni
17) sù-rá u$_4$-ul-lí-a-⸢aš⸣
18) [pa-gal mi-ni]-in-è

16–18) He made resplendent to remote places (and) to the distant future his reign of kingship.

13

A number of stamped bricks found at Ur deal with Sîn-iddinam's construction of the wall of Ur.

CATALOGUE

Ex.	Museum number	Excavation number	Provenance	Dimensions (cm)	Lines preserved	cpn
1	BM 30217 (59-10-14,94)	Taylor's excavations	Ur, no provenance	7.0×6.0×3.0	3–11	c
2	BM 137383 (1979-12-18,18)	–	Ur(?), no provenance	16.0×11.0×4.0	8–26	c
3	–	U 6324(?) (see commentary)	Ur, from KPS (southern extension of the Gipar-ku site)	32.0×32.0×8.0	1–15	n
4	UM 31-16-359	U 12570	Ur, from the 11th course of the great base or pedestal of Sîn-iddinam in the great Nanna courtyard	35.0×35×8.0	1–30	c
5	–	U 15066A	Ur, from the NE city wall, central section	–	–	n
6	–	U 15066B	From Diqdiqqah 'near the railway'	–	–	n
7	–	U 15066C	Ur, from just inside the city wall behind the Ningišzida temple in the SW part of the city	–	–	n
8	–	U 15066D	As ex. 7	–	–	n

COMMENTARY

The text is a composite of exs. 1–3 and the copy published as UET 8 no. 68.

Ex. 3 was published in copy by Gadd as UET 1 no. 119. According to Gadd this is U 6324. UE 7 p. 222 states that U 6324 = CBS 16548. However, Behrens (JCS 37 p. 235, no. 31) indicates that CBS 16548 is a duplicate of E4.2.9.12. There is obviously some confusion here. Ex. 3 is simply entered in the score from the copy of Gadd in UET 1 no. 119.

Exs. 5–8, as yet unlocated, were used by Winckworth to make a composite copy published in UET 8 no. 68. This copy provides us with the end of the inscription. What was actually preserved on the individual bricks cannot be determined at present.

It is interesting to note that exs. 5 and 7–8 of this text dealing with the construction of the city wall were all found in or near the city wall.

BIBLIOGRAPHY

1928 Gadd, UET 1 no. 119 (ex. 3, copy, edition)
1929 Barton, RISA pp. 374–75 Sin-iddinam 3 (ex. 3, edition)
1961 Hallo, BiOr 18 p. 8 Sin-iddinam 1 (study)
1965 Sollberger, UET 8 no. 68 (exs. 4–8, composite copy, study)
1968 Kärki, SKFZ p. 31 Sîniddinam 1 (edition)
1980 Kärki, SAKAZ 1 pp. 56–57 Sîniddinam 1 (edition)
1981 Walker, CBI no. 37 (exs. 1–2, study)

TEXT

1) ^{d}EN.ZU-*i-din-n*[*a-am*]
2) nita-kala-g[a]
3) ú-a-úri.KI-ma
4) lugal-larsa.KI-ma
5) sag-èn-tar-
6) èš é-babbar-ra
7) suḫuš-ma-da-
8) ge-en-ge-en-
9) ^{d}utu-ke$_4$
10) si-sá-ni-šè
11) inim-nì-ge-na-ni-šè
12) ^{d}nanna a-ra-zu-ni
13) in-dè-gen
14) ḫul-du-ni
15) šu-ni-šè im-mi-in-si
16) ki-bal-ni
17) gìr-ni-šè im-mi-in-gúr
18) GIŠ.gu-za-larsa.KI-ma
19) suḫuš-bi mu-na-an-ge-en
20) bala-si-sá
21) šu mu-na-ni-in-du$_7$
22) ki-bal-a-na
23) sag giš mi-ni-in-ra-ta
24) GIŠ.tukul-lú-érim-ma-na
25) íb-ta-an-ḫaš-a-ta
26) u$_4$-bi-a du$_{11}$-ga-du$_{11}$-ga-
27) ^{d}nanna ^{d}nin-gal-ta
28) bàd-gal-úri.KI-ma
29) ḫur-sag-gin$_7$
30) ki-sikil-la mu-un-dù

1–9) Sîn-iddin[am], mighty man, provider of Ur, king of Larsa, who looks after the shrine Ebabbar, who makes firm the foundation of the land for the god Utu,

10–17) on account of his order and his steadfast words the god Nanna agreed to his entreaty to deliver his enemies into his hands (and) make the land that rebelled against him bow down at his feet.

18–21) He made firm the foundation of the throne of Larsa for him (and) perfectly carried out a reign of order.

22–25) After he smote with weapons the land that rebelled against him (and) smashed the weapon of his enemy,

26–30) at that time, by the decree of the god Nanna and the goddess Ningal, he built the great wall of Ur like a mountain in a pure place.

14

A cone in Berlin deals with the construction of the wall of Bad-tibira by Sîn-iddinam.

COMMENTARY

The cone is VA 3611, formerly in the private collection of F. Delitzsch. It presumably originally came from ancient Bad-tibira, modern Tell al-Medāʾin. The cone is headless and measures 16.5 cm long, 6.5 cm in dia. The text is written around the shaft in two cols. Col. i has lines 1–20, col. ii lines 21–38. It was collated.

BIBLIOGRAPHY

1890 Delitzsch, BA 1 pp. 301–11 (photo, copy, edition)
1892 Winckler, KB 3/1 pp. 90–93 Sin-iddina 1 (edition)
1905 Thureau-Dangin, ISA pp. 296–97 Sin-idinnam a (edition)
1907 Thureau-Dangin, SAK pp. 208–209 Sin-idinnam a (edition)
1929 Barton, RISA pp. 312–13 Sin-iddinam 1 (edition)
1961 Hallo, BiOr 18 p. 8 Sin-iddinam 7 (study)
1968 Kärki, SKFZ pp. 35–36 Sîniddinam 7 (edition)
1980 Kärki, SAKAZ 1 pp. 63–64 Sîniddinam 7 (edition)

TEXT

1) ^{d}EN.ZU-*i-din-na-am*
2) nita-kala-ga
3) ú-a-uri$_5$.KI-ma
4) lugal-larsa.KI-ma
5) lugal-ki-en-gi-ki-uri-ke$_4$
6) lú é-babbar
7) é-^{d}utu-ke$_4$
8) mu-un-dù-a
9) me giš-ḫur-
10) ^{d}a-nun-na-ke$_4$-ne
11) ki-bi-šè bí-in-gi$_4$-a
12) lú I$_7$.idigna
13) i$_7$-dagal-la
14) mu-un-ba-al-la-a
15) a-du$_{10}$ ḫé-gál
16) nì nu-til-le-da
17) uru.KI ma-da-ni-šè
18) im-mi-in-gar-ra-a
19) dumu-*nu-úr*-^{d}IŠKUR
20) lugal-larsa.KI-ma-ke$_4$
21) ma-da-na
22) ki-tuš-ne-ḫa tuš-ù-dè
23) éren-dagal-la-na
24) ù-du$_{10}$ ku-ku-dè
25) u$_4$-ul-lí-a-aš
26) ár-nam-lugal-la-ka-ni
27) un-e ak-ak-dè
28) bàd-gal-
29) bàd-tibira.KI
30) ù-ma-ni-ta
31) gal-bi im-mi-in-dù
32) ^{d}EN.ZU-*i-din-na-am*
33) sipa-nì-ge-na-ke$_4$
34) šà-^{d}utu ⸢ù⸣ ^{d}dumu-zi-bi
35) mu-un-du$_{10}$
36) u$_4$-bala-a-na
37) nì nu-kúr-ru ḫé-a
38) u$_4$-da-rí-šè

1–20) Sîn-iddinam, mighty man, provider of Ur, king of Larsa, king of the land of Sumer and Akkad, the one who built Ebabbar, the temple of the god Utu, who restored the *me*s and rites of the Anuna gods, the one who dug the Tigris, the broad river, who supplied good water, abundance without end for his city (and) land, son of Nūr-Adad, king of Larsa —

21–27) in order to settle his land in quiet abodes, in order that his many men sleep soundly, in order that the people praise his kingship in the future,

28–31) by means of his triumph he built in a grand fashion the great wall of Bad-tibira.

32–35) Sîn-iddinam, the shepherd of righteousness, made both the gods Utu and Dumuzi content.

36–38) May the days of his reign be an unalterable thing, forever.

15

A copy of a royal inscription of Sîn-iddinam deals with the construction of a throne for the god Iškur.

COMMENTARY

The text is inscribed on YBC 4624, a late tablet copy written in 4 cols. (2 on obv., 2 on rev.). The tablet measures 14.4×9.2×2.5 cm. The provenance of the tablet is unknown but may have been Larsa. For the animal which appears in line 79 see F. Pomponio, AION 40 (1980) pp. 549–53. The description of the divine throne in lines 72–82 may be compared with that found in E4.2.13.13.

BIBLIOGRAPHY

1969 Hallo, JCS 21 p. 96 Sin-iddinam 12 (study)
1988 Michalowski, Sachs Memorial pp. 265–75 (photo, edition)

TEXT

1) ^{d}iškur en ud-ḫu[š ...] ud-gal-a[n-ki]	1) For the god Iškur, lord, an[gry] storm, [...] great storm of heav[en and earth],
2) nam-maḫ-a-ni-šè nir-gál	2) who trusts in his supremacy,
3) sag-kal KA-mud-gál dumu-an-na	3) foremost one, ..., son of An,
4) sag gìr-ra gú-è-a	4) whose head is clothed in magnificence,
5) en sag-ḫuš ud-gal-la x-bi-a gaba-⸢šu⸣-gar nu-tuk	5) lord, raging *leader*, great storm, in whose ... has no rival,
6) dungu sír-re	6) who masses the clouds,
7) mir-a kas$_{4}$-kas$_{4}$-x-da-ni	7) at his rushing in the storm wind
8) ki mu-un-da-tuk$_{4}$-e	8) he causes the earth to tremble.
9) an-dagal-la im-maḫ gù ru-ru-gú	9) In broad heaven he is a mighty wind which roars,
10) [za-pa]-ág-bi ḫé-gál-àm	10) whose [rum]ble is abundance.
11) KA×[ŠID]-gi$_{4}$-ni-šè kalam ḫur-sag-gal-gal	11–12) At his roar the land and the great mountains are afraid.
12) ní-bi ba-an-da-ab-gi$_{4}$	
13) ur-sag-gal šibir-ta šu(?)-dab$_{5}$-e	13) Great champion, who holds the sceptre in the hand
14) nam-nir-ra zà-kéš	14) (and) is clothed in authority.
15) a-aba ur$_{5}$-ša$_{4}$-ni	15) At his thundering (over) the sea
16) me-⟨lám⟩ kalam-ma dul-la-šè	16) (and) covering the land with ra⟨diance⟩,
17) na$_{4}$-gal-gal BÀD šeg$_{x}$(IM.A) gil	17) great (hail)stones ... rain ... are difficult to see through,
18) x-x-ba mu-un-na-gub-bé-eš	18) In their ... they set up for him ...
19) [...]	19–21) [...] ... like a reed.
20) [...]	
21) ⸢gi-gin$_{7}$⸣ x x [x]	
22) ní-bi gál-la-ni-šè	22–23) On their own accord, at his presence *they* lift ... to him.
23) x di mu-un-na-íl	
24) un-šár-ra-ba igi-bi im-ši-gál	24) He spies the numerous people.
25) en nam-ḫé giri$_{17}$-zal lu-lu-lu	25) Lord of abundance, who makes splendour plentiful,

26) zi-kalam-ma sum-mu	26) who gives sustenance to the nation,
27) nun šà-gur-ru šu-nigin$_{4}$-bi du$_{10}$	27) merciful prince whose compassion is good,
28) an-dùl-larsa.KI-ma	28) shade of Larsa,
29) á-daḫ-^{d}EN.ZU-*i-din-na-am* ki-mè-ka	29) helper of Sîn-iddinam in the field of battle,
30) šen-šen-na érin zag-ga-na gub-bu	30) who stands in combat with the troops at his side,
31) en-gal kù-gál-an ^{d}en-líl-ka	31) great lord, canal inspector of the gods An and Enlil,
32) nam-ma-ni zà nu-di	32) whose destiny cannot be rivalled,
33) lugal-a-ni-ir	33) for his lord,
34) ^{d}EN.ZU-*i-din-na-am* nita-kala-ga	34) Sîn-iddinam, mighty man,
35) nun-sun$_{5}$-na ní-tuk-^{d}en-líl-lá	35) humble prince, who reverences the god Enlil
36) ḫé-àm-é-kur-ra-kam	36) – he is the 'yea' of the Ekur –
37) šul mu-du$_{10}$-sa$_{4}$-^{d}nanna-ke$_{4}$	37) youth called by a good name by the god Nanna,
38) ú-a-⌜uri$_{5}$⌝.KI-ma	38) provider of Ur,
39) lugal-larsa.KI-ma	39) king of Larsa,
40) lugal-ki-en-gi-ki-uri-ke$_{4}$	40) king of the land of Sumer and Akkad
41) géštu-dagal igi-gál-diri sum-ma	41–42) given broad wisdom and surpassing intelligence by the god Nudimmud,
42) ^{d}nu-dím-mud-ke$_{4}$	
43) bala-du$_{10}$ ti-u$_{4}$-sù-rá ḫé-gál nì-nu-til-e	43–45) granted a good reign, a long life-span, and abundance without end by the god Iškur, his personal deity,
44) ^{d}iškur dingir-ra-ni	
45) sa$_{12}$-e-eš-e rig$_{7}$-ga	
46) giš-ḫur-eridu.KI-ga si-sá-sá	46) who puts in order the rites of Eridu,
47) nidba-	47–48) who perfects the offerings of the gods,
48) dingir-re-e-ne šu-du$_{7}$-du$_{7}$	
49) gal-an-zu me-libir(?)	49–50) wise one, who [r]estored the *old mes*,
50) [k]i-bé bí-in-gi$_{4}$-a	
51) [...] x un-šár-ra-né	51–53) the one whom his numerous people [tru]ly [ch]ose –
52) [zi-d]è-eš	
53) [mu-u]n-pà-da	
54) [GIŠ.gu-z]a-maḫ	54) a lofty [thron]e,
55) [...] me-dím-ta diri	55) [...] with surpassing form,
56) [dingir]-ra-ni-ir sì-ga	56) placed for his [personal deity],
57) [...] kù-luḫ-ḫa	57–58) [grand]ly made with [...] refined silver,
58) [gal-l]e-eš ak	
59) [...] ka an-sig$_{7}$-ga	59) [...] of the green heaven,
60) [...]	60–63) [...],
61) [...]	
62) [...]	
63) [...]	
64) me-te-nam-u$_{11}$-ru-ka-ni	64) befitting his greatness,
65) du$_{10}$-gál-le bí-du$_{7}$-a	65) suitable for *sitting on* –
66) šà-la-la gál-la-na	66) amidst jubilation
67) kin-bi im-mi-in-til	67) he finished the work there.
68) u$_{4}$-bi-a ^{d}iškur dingir-ra-ni	68) At that time, the god Iškur, his (personal) deity,
69) GIŠ.gu-za-ka-silim-ma-ka-na	69–70) grandly sat down there on his throne of glory.
70) gal-bi dúr mi-ni-in-gar	
71) u$_{4}$-a u$_{4}$-ul-lí-a-aš	71) Then, for the future
72) me-dím-bi im-mi-in-diri	72) (Sîn-iddinam) made its form surpassing.
73) giš-ḫur me-maḫ-bi	73–74) He sought out a place for its rites and supreme *me*s.
74) ki-bi mi-ni-in-kin-kin	
75) 2-am-gal ki-aš-te	75–78) He set below, on the right and left, two

76) érim-lugal-la du$_7$-d[è]
77) zi-da gáb-bu-[bi]
78) sig-ta im-mi-in-[gar]
79) ÉREN + PIRIG x x x [x x]
80) ḫé-gál-⌜la⌝ ^{d}a-n[un-na]
81) me-šè an-úr [x x x]
82) mu-u[n]-na-da-su$_8$-s[u$_8$-ge-eš]
83) alam-bi mi-ni-i[n-dím]
84) du$_{10}$-ub-ba im-mi-in-[gub]
85) [...] im-mi-[in-...]
86) [...]
87) [...]
88) [...]

great wild bulls at the throne butt[ing] at the enemies of the king,

79) A ... beast ...,
80–82) the A[nuna gods] set u[p] abundance [from] the horizon ... beside him.

83) He [fashioned] its (cult) statue
84) and [set it] on its (the throne's) lap.
85–88) He ... there. [...]

16

The name of the seventh year of Sîn-iddinam commemorates the construction of the wall of Maškan-šāpir. This deed is recorded in an inscription known from several barrel cylinder fragments from a pit beside an ancient wall that was excavated by E. Stone at Tell Abū Duwari, ancient Maškan-šāpir. The text will be published by P. Steinkeller. It was mentioned by E. Stone and P. Steinkeller in The Location of Maškan-šāpir, a paper delivered to the annual meeting of the American Oriental Society, New Orleans, 13 March 1989.

2001

The seal of Sîn-imittī, servant of Sîn-iddinam, is found on a number of tablets.

CATALOGUE

Ex.	Museum number	cpn
1	MLC 2517	n
2	UIOM 2011	n
3	UIOM 2013	n
4	UIOM 2020	n
5	UIOM 2022	n
6	UIOM 2023	n
7	UIOM 2024	n
8	UIOM 2027	n
9	UIOM 2028	n
10	UIOM 2030	n
11	UIOM 2032	n
12	YBC 4970	n
13	YBC 4973	n
14	YBC 4974	n
15	YBC 5606	n
16	YBC 10249(?)	n

BIBLIOGRAPHY

1914 Keiser, BRM 3 no. 17a (ex. 1, copy)
1950 Goetze, JCS 4 p. 115 (exs. 1–16, edition)
1968 Kärki, SKFZ pp. 37–38 Sîniddinam 10 (conflated edition)
1980 Kärki, SAKAZ 1 p. 66 Sîniddinam 10 (edition)

TEXT

1) dEN.ZU-*i-mi-ti*
2) DUMU DINGIR-*i-din*
3) ÌR dEN.ZU-*i-din-na-am*

1) Sîn-imittī,
2) son of Ilum-iddin,
3) servant of Sîn-iddinam.

2002

The impression of the seal of Warad-Nanna is found on a number of tablets from Larsa.

CATALOGUE

Ex.	Museum number	cpn
1	MLC 2517	n
2	UIOM 2010	n
3	UIOM 2013	n
4	UIOM 2015	n
5	UIOM 2034	n
6	YBC 4972	n
7	YBC 4974	n
8	YBC 5205	n
9	YBC 8728	n

BIBLIOGRAPHY

1914 Keiser, BRM 3 no. 17c (ex. 1, copy)
1950 Goetze, JCS 4 p. 115 (exs. 1–9, edition)
1950 Porada, JCS 4 p. 159 fig. 2 (exs. 3, 5, composite copy)
1968 Kärki, SKFZ pp. 37–38 Sîniddinam 10 (conflated edition)
1980 Kärki, SAKAZ 1 p. 66 Sîniddinam 10 (edition)

TEXT

1) ÌR-d*nanna*
2) DUMU dEN.ZU-*i-qí-ša-am*
3) ÌR dEN.ZU-*i-din-nam*

1) Warad-Nanna,
2) son of Sîn-iqīšam,
3) servant of Sîn-iddinam.

2003

The impression of the seal of Ali-waqrum is found on a large number of tablets from Larsa.

CATALOGUE

Ex.	Museum number	cpn
1	MLC 2517	n
2	UIOM 2009	n
3	UIOM 2010	n
4	UIOM 2012	n
5	UIOM 2013	n
6	UIOM 2014	n
7	UIOM 2016	n
8	UIOM 2017	n
9	UIOM 2018(?)	n
10	UIOM 2019	n
11	UIOM 2020	n
12	UIOM 2021	n
13	UIOM 2022	n
14	UIOM 2023	n
15	UIOM 2024	n
16	UIOM 2025	n
17	UIOM 2027	n
18	UIOM 2028	n
19	UIOM 2030	n
20	UIOM 2031	n
21	UIOM 2032	n
22	UIOM 2033	n
23	YBC 3268	n
24	YBC 4456	n
25	YBC 4970	n
26	YBC 4971	n
27	YBC 4972	n
28	YBC 5606	n
29	YBC 8728	n
30	YBC 10249	n
31	YBC 10572	n
32	RFH Coll. no. 13	n

BIBLIOGRAPHY

1914 Keiser, BRM 3 no. 17d (ex. 1, copy)
1916–17 Meek, AJSL 33 p. 229 no. 13 (ex. 32, copy)
1950 Goetze, JCS 4 p. 113 (exs. 1–32, edition)
1968 Kärki, SKFZ pp. 37–38 Sîniddinam 10 (conflated edition)
1980 Kärki, SAKAZ 1 p. 66 Sîniddinam 10 (edition)

TEXT

1) *a-lí-wa-aq-ru-um*
2) DUMU ^d^*qud-ma*-SIPA
3) DUB.SAR
4) ÌR ^d^EN.ZU-*i-din-na-am*

1) Ali-waqrum,
2) son of Qudma-rēʾi,
3) scribe,
4) servant of Sîn-iddinam.

2004

A tablet envelope in Berlin bears the seal impression of a servant of Sîn-iddinam.

COMMENTARY

The impression is on VAT 7721. It was not collated.

BIBLIOGRAPHY

1914 Figulla, VAS 13 no. 56a seal B 2 (copy)
1968 Kärki, SKFZ pp. 37–38 Sîniddinam 10 (conflated edition)
1980 Kärki, SAKAZ 1 p. 66 Sîniddinam 10 (edition)

TEXT

1) *akšak*.KI-*i-din-*[*na*]-*am*
2) DUMU ^{d}*en-líl-ma-lik*
3) [ÌR] ^{d}EN.ZU-*i-din-n*[*am*]

1) Akšak-iddinam,
2) son of Enlil-mālik,
3) [servant] of Sîn-iddin[am].

2005

The impression of a seal of Nanna-mansum is found on a number of tablets.

CATALOGUE

Ex.	Museum number	n
1	UIOM 2010	n
2	YBC 4970	n
3	YBC 4974	n
4	YBC 10572	n

BIBLIOGRAPHY

1950 Goetze, JCS 4 p. 114 (exs. 1–4, edition)
1968 Kärki, SKFZ pp. 37–38 Sîniddinam 10 (conflated edition)
1980 Kärki, SAKAZ 1 p. 67 Sîniddinam 10 (edition)

TEXT

1) ^{d}NANNA-MA-AN-SUM
2) DUMU *ia-šu-ḫu-um*
3) ÌR ^{d}EN.ZU-*i-din-na-am*

1) Nanna-mansum,
2) son of Iašuḫum,
3) servant of Sîn-iddinam.

2006

The impresssion of the seal of Šamaš-gāmil is found on a number of tablets.

CATALOGUE

Ex.	Museum number	cpn
1	UIOM 2009	n
2	UIOM 2011	n
3	YBC 4970	n

BIBLIOGRAPHY

1950 Goetze, JCS 4 p. 114 (exs. 1–3, edition)
1968 Kärki, SKFZ pp. 37–38 Sîniddinam 10 (conflated edition)
1980 Kärki, SAKAZ 1 p. 67 Sîniddinam 10 (edition)

TEXT

1) dUTU-*ga-mi-il*
2) DUMU *a-na*-dEN.ZU-*ták-la-ku*
3) ÌR dEN.ZU-*i-din-na-am*

1) Šamaš-gāmil,
2) son of Ana-Sîn-taklāku,
3) servant of Sîn-iddinam.

2007

The impression of the seal of Nawram-šarūr is found on a number of tablets.

CATALOGUE

Ex.	Museum number	cpn
1	UIOM 2012	n
2	UIOM 2019	n
3	UIOM 2020	n
4	UIOM 2021	n
5	YBC 10572	n

BIBLIOGRAPHY

1950 Goetze, JCS 4 p. 115 (exs. 1–5, edition)
1968 Kärki, SKFZ pp. 37–38 Sîniddinam 10 (conflated edition)
1980 Kärki, SAKAZ 1 p. 67 Sîniddinam 10 (edition)

TEXT

1) *na-aw-ra-am-ša-ru-ur*	1) Nawram-šarūr,
2) ÌR ^{d}EN.ZU-*i-din-na-am*	2) servant of Sîn-iddinam.

2008

The impression of a seal of a servant of Sîn-iddinam whose name is not preserved is found on a tablet at Yale.

COMMENTARY

The tablet is YBC 4974. The impression was not collated.

BIBLIOGRAPHY

1950 Goetze, JCS 4 p. 115 (edition)
1968 Kärki, SKFZ pp. 37–38 Sîniddinam 10 (conflated edition)
1980 Kärki, SAKAZ 1 p. 67 Sîniddinam 10 (edition)

TEXT

1) [...]	1) [...],
2) DUMU *ì-[lí-pu-uṭ]-ra-am*	2) son of I[lī-puṭ]ram,
3) ÌR ^{d}EN.ZU-*i-din-na-am*	3) servant of Sîn-iddinam.

2009

The impression of the seal of Ilī-puṭram is found on a number of tablets.

CATALOGUE

Ex.	Museum number	cpn
1	UIOM 2015	n
2	UIOM 2022	n
3	UIOM 2024	n
4	UIOM 2025	n
5	YBC 3268	n
6	YBC 5205	n

BIBLIOGRAPHY

1950 Goetze, JCS 4 p. 116 (exs. 1–6, edition)
1968 Kärki, SKFZ pp. 37–38 Sîniddinam 10 (conflated edition)
1980 Kärki, SAKAZ 1 p. 67 Sîniddinam 10 (edition)

TEXT

1) *ì-lí-pu-uṭ-ra-am*
2) ÌR [d]EN.ZU-*i-din-na-am*

1) Ilī-puṭram,
2) servant of Sîn-iddinam.

2010

The impression of the seal of Sîn-muballiṭ is found on a large number of tablets.

CATALOGUE

Ex.	Museum number	cpn
1	UIOM 2015	n
2	UIOM 2016	n
3	UIOM 2030	n
4	UIOM 2031	n
5	UIOM 2033	n
6	YBC 4456	n
7	YBC 4971	n
8	YBC 4972	n
9	YBC 4973	n
10	YBC 5205	n
11	YBC 5606	n
12	YBC 8728	n
13	YBC 3320	n
14	RFH Coll. no. 13	n

BIBLIOGRAPHY

1950 Goetze, JCS 4 p. 114 (exs. 1–14, edition)
1968 Kärki, SKFZ pp. 37–38 Sîniddinam 10 (conflated edition)
1980 Kärki, SAKAZ 1 p. 67 Sîniddinam 10 (edition)

TEXT

1) [d]EN.ZU-*mu-ba-lí-iṭ*
2) DUMU lú-ga-a-a
3) ÌR [d]EN.ZU-*i-din-na-am*

1) Sîn-muballiṭ,
2) son of Lu-gaia,
3) servant of Sîn-iddinam.

2011

The seal of a servant of Sîn-iddinam whose name is only partially preserved is found on a tablet at Yale.

COMMENTARY

The impression is on YBC 5205. It was not collated.

BIBLIOGRAPHY

1950 Goetze, JCS 4 p. 116 (edition)
1968 Kärki, SKFZ pp. 37–38 Sîniddinam 10 (conflated edition)
1980 Kärki, SAKAZ 1 p. 67 Sîniddinam 10 (edition)

TEXT

1) x x x x	1) ...,
2) DUMU lú-^{d}ba-ba$_{6}$	2) son of Lu-Baba,
3) ÌR ^{d}EN.ZU-*i-din-na-am*	3) servant of Sîn-iddinam.

2012

The impression of the seal of Išḫi-ilīšu is found on a tablet in Urbana, Illinois.

COMMENTARY

The impression is on UIOM 2027. It was not collated.

BIBLIOGRAPHY

1950 Goetze, JCS 4 p. 117 (edition)
1968 Kärki, SKFZ pp. 37–38 Sîniddinam 10 (conflated edition)
1980 Kärki, SAKAZ 1 p. 68 Sîniddinam 10 (edition)

TEXT

1) *iš-[ḫi]-ì-lí-šu*	1) Iš[ḫi]-ilīšu,
2) DUMU [x x]-*a*-[x]	2) son of [...]a[...],
3) ÌR ^{d}EN.ZU-*i-din-na-am*	3) servant of Sîn-iddinam.

2013

The impression of a seal of Sîn-ḫāzir is found on three tablets.

CATALOGUE

Ex.	Museum number	cpn
1	UIOM 2021(?)	n
2	UIOM 2032	n
3	YBC 4973(?)	n

BIBLIOGRAPHY

1950 Goetze, JCS 4 p. 117 (exs. 1–3, edition)
1968 Kärki, SKFZ pp. 37–38 Sîniddinam 10 (conflated edition)
1980 Kärki, SAKAZ 1 p. 68 Sîniddinam 10 (edition)

TEXT

1) ᵈEN.ZU-[*ḫa*]-*zi-ir*	1) Sîn-[ḫā]zir,
2) DUMU [*i-ku-un*]-*pi₄-ša*	2) son of [Ikūn]-pîša,
3) ÌR ᵈ[EN.ZU-*i-din-na-am*]	3) servant of [Sîn-iddinam].

2014

The impression of the seal of Šamaš-nāṣir is found on a tablet envelope at Yale.

COMMENTARY

The impression is on YBC 5472. It was collated from the published photo.

BIBLIOGRAPHY

1981 Buchanan, Early Near Eastern Seals p. 282 no. 761 (photo, study); Hallo, p. 451 no. 761 (edition)

TEXT

1) ᵈUTU-*na-ṣi-*[*ir*]	1) Šamaš-nāṣi[r],
2) DUMU *šu-mi-a-ḫi-*⌜*ia*⌝	2) son of Šumi-aḫīia,
3) ÌR ᵈEN.ZU-*i-d*[*in-na-am*]	3) servant of Sîn-idd[inam].

Sîn-irībam

E4.2.10

Sîn-iddinam was succeeded by Sîn-irībam, who reigned only two years. No monumental texts of this king survive, only a weight stone and two servant seal impressions.

1

A fragmentary weight stone in the Yale collections is inscribed with the name of Sîn-irībam.

COMMENTARY

The stone is YBC 2163, a purchased piece, provenance unknown. It is a fragment of diorite, 14.3 × 12 × 5.5 cm. The inscription was collated.

BIBLIOGRAPHY

1915 Clay, YOS 1 no. 30 (copy, study)
1929 Barton, RISA pp. 316–17 Siniribam 1 (edition)
1961 Hallo, BiOr 18 p. 8 Sin-eribam 1 (study)
1968 Kärki, SKFZ p. 38 Sînirībam 1 (study)
1971 Sollberger and Kupper, IRSA IVB10a (translation)
1980 Kärki, SAKAZ 1 p. 80 Sînirībam 1 (edition)

TEXT

1) na$_4$-aš-gú	1) Stone (weight): one talent,
2) é-gal-^{d}EN.ZU-*i-ri-ba-am*	2) palace of Sîn-irībam.

2001

A seal now in the Oriental Institute, Chicago, bears the name of a servant of Sîn-irībam.

COMMENTARY

The seal is A 3709, formerly in the Haskell Oriental Museum, a purchased piece, provenance unknown. It is an agate cylinder seal 2.5 × 1.4 cm and the impression was collated.

The Amorite name in line 1 is restored from Gelb, AS 21 p. 112.

BIBLIOGRAPHY

1927–28 Williams, AJSL 44 pp. 242–43 (edition) and pl. following p. 252 no. 32 (photo)
1961 Hallo, BiOr 18 p. 9 Sin-eribam 2 (study)
1968 Kärki, SKFZ p. 38 Sînirībam 2 (edition)
1980 Kärki, SAKAZ 1 p. 80 Sînirībam 2 (edition)

TEXT

1) *i-ṣi-qá-*[*ṭar*]
2) DUMU *ka-mi-zu-um*
3) ÌR ^{d}EN.ZU-*i-ri-ba-am*

1) Iṣi-qa[ṭar],
2) son of Kamizum,
3) servant of Sîn-irībam.

2002

A seal impression on a tablet in the Yale collections bears the name of a servant of Sîn-irībam.

COMMENTARY

The tablet is YBC 3320, a purchased tablet originally from Larsa. The seal impression was not collated.

BIBLIOGRAPHY

1919 Grice, YOS 5 no. 155b (copy)
1961 Hallo, BiOr 18 p. 9 Sin-eribam 3 (study)
1968 Kärki, SKFZ p. 38 Sînirībam 3 (edition)
1980 Kärki, SAKAZ 1 p. 80 Sînirībam 3 (edition)

TEXT

1) ^{d}EN-ZU-⸢*i*⸣-*mi-ti*
2) DUMU ^{d}[...]-*i-din*
3) ÌR ^{d}EN.ZU-*i-ri-ba-am*

1) Sîn-imittī,
2) son of [...]-iddin,
3) servant of Sîn-irībam.

Sîn-iqīšam

E4.2.11

Sîn-irībam was succeeded by his son Sîn-iqīšam as king of Larsa. He ruled five years. A handful of inscriptions are extant for this king.

1

The name of the fourth year of Sîn-iqīšam commemorates the introduction of fourteen statues into Nippur as well as the entry of three thrones and statues of the gods Utu and Šerida into Larsa. The first of these deeds is described in a royal inscription known from a copy on a clay tablet from Nippur published by M. Green. Although the king's name on the tablet is not fully preserved, the attribution of the inscription to Sîn-iqīšam seems reasonably certain.

COMMENTARY

The inscription is found on CBS 7861 + 7865, a clay tablet 10 × 12.4 × 1.7 cm. It was excavated by the Hilprecht expedition to Nippur, provenance not known.

The epithet in ii 14–15, 'The one who built the great wall of Larsa', accords well with the fact that the name of year three of Sîn-iqīšam, the year name which precedes that named for the fashioning of the fourteen statues, records the building of the wall of Larsa. A parallel to i 5 is found in E4.2.13.21, line 38.

BIBLIOGRAPHY

1988 Green and Frayne, ARRIM 6 pp. 25–32 (copy, edition)

TEXT

Obverse
Col. i

1) [^{d}]⸢en-líl⸣
2) en-u$_{18}$-ru
3) aš-a-ni maḫ
4) zà-dib an-ki-a
5) sipa-gin$_{7}$ edin
6) [k]ìlib zi-gál túm-túm-mu
7) nì-a-na
8) mu-sa$_{4}$-a
9) èn tar-ra

i 1–9) For the [god] Enlil, mighty lord, who is uniquely supreme, who surpasses (those) in heaven and earth, who like a shepherd cares for [a]ll living creatures (of) the steppe, who looks after anything whatsoever,

10) x x-na-ús(?)
11) [x] x ⸢ni⸣
12) [...]
13) [...]
14) [...]
15) [...]
16) [... n]i
17) [...] x DI
18) [...] ⸢ni⸣
19) [...] x
20) [...] x
Lacuna

i 10–20) No translation warranted.

Col. ii
1) [...]
2) [...]
3) en x [...]

ii 1–3) [...] ... [...]

4) un-šár x [x (x)]
5) me kìlib-ba zà-k[éš]
6) lugal-mu-r[a]

ii 4–6) the numerous people ..., clothed in all the *me*s, for my lord,

7) ^{d}EN.⟨ZU-*i-qí-ša-am*⟩
8) nita-kala-ga
9) sipa šà-du$_{10}$-du$_{10}$ nibru.KI-k[e$_4$]
10) ú-a-ú[ri.K]I-ma
11) lugal-[larsa.KI]-⸢ma⸣
12) lug[al-ki-e]n-[gi]
13) [k]i-ur[i]-me-⸢en⸣

ii 7–13) I, S⟨în-iqīšam⟩, mighty man, shepherd who makes Nippur content, provider of U[r], king of [Lars]a, ki[ng of the land of S]um[er] (and) Akka[d].

---

14) lú bàd-gal-
15) larsa.KI-ma mu-dù-a
16) larsa.KI uru-ul x an-k[i]
17) mu-maḫ bí-in-tuk-me-e[n]
18) sipa ní-tuk
19) [^{d}]e[n]-líl ^{d}nin-l[íl]
20) [...]
Lacuna

ii 14–20) who built the great wall of Larsa, I, who caused Larsa, the ancient city ... of heaven (and) [earth], to have a supreme name, reverent shepherd, who reverences the gods E[n]lil and Ninl[il] ...
Lacuna

Col. iii
1) nam-šita$_x$(REC 316)-aš gub-ba-me-e[n]
2) ⸢alam-zabar⸣ 7-ta x
3) [...]
4) [...]
5) [...]
6) [...]
7) [...] x
8) [...] x

iii 1–8) I, who stand for supplication, seven bronze statues [...]

9) [... zab]ar-x-ra
10) š[u ...] x-du$_7$
11) [...] x
12) [...] x

iii 9–12) had them perfectly [made] of [b]ronze [...]

13) ⸢èš⸣ [é]-kur-ra-ka
14) sag-g[á] tuk-tu[k-d]è
15) inim-du$_{10}$ zà-mí nam-lugal-gá
16) x ki gá-gá-dè
17) [alam]-⸢né⸣-[né]
18) dumu-⸢né-né⸣
19) ìr lú x-x-[x]

iii 13–20) in order to make shrine Ekur have a ..., in order to establish sweet words of the praise of my kingship, *I* fashioned [the statue of so-and]-so, son of so-and-so, the servant of ...

20) bí-in-dím
21) [m]u-du-rí gi$_4$-dè
22) [...]
23) [...]
24) [...]
25) [...]
26) [...-b]i
27) [...]
28) [... lug]al
29) [...]-a(?)
Lacuna

iii 21) To return eternal fame
iii 22–29) No translation warranted.

Col. iv
1) [x] + 6 sìla ninda-ta
2) [x s]ìla kaš-ta
3) [x sìl]a kùrun-ta
4) [x sìla] ninda-duḫ-ta
5) [sá(?)]-du$_{11}$-⟨šè⟩
6) [alam-n]é-né
7) ìr-gá-ka
8) u$_4$-aš-a ur$_5$-gin$_7$ ḫu-mu-ni-gar

iv 1–8) For one day so I established [x] + 6 *sila* of bread, [x *s*]*ila* of beer, [x *sil*]*a* of wine, [x *sila*] of bran bread, ⟨as⟩ regular offerings [for the statue of so-and]-so, my servant.

9) u$_4$-me-da u$_4$-da egir-bi-šè
10) lú alam-né-né
11) dumu-né-né
12) ìr-gá
13) nì-mu-sa$_4$-a
14) an-zil i-ni-in-gar-ra
15) nu-ub-zi-re-a
16) mu-ni li-bí-íb-ḫa-lam-e-a
17) ki-gub-ba-bi
18) [n]u-ub-da-ab-kúr-ru-a
19) é-nì-GA-ra
20) nu-b[í]-íb-[ku$_4$-ku$_4$-a]

iv 9–20) (As for) the one who forever and ever does not destroy the statue of so-and-so, son of so-and-so, my servant, a thing given a name, and ..., does not deface his (the original owner's) name, does [n]ot alter the place where it stands, does not [bring it] into a storehouse,

21) [...]
22) [...]

iv 21–22) [...]

23) [ka]š ninda ⌜u$_6$⌝-[di-dè]
24) im-mi-ib(?)-gub(?)-b[a(?)-a]
25) alam-né-né
26) ìr-gá
27) nu-ub-ta-ku$_5$-ru-a

iv 23–27) does not cut off the [be]er and bread (offerings) wondr[ously] established there (for) the statue of so-and-so, my servant,

28) lú-bi bala-a-ni
29) du-rí ḫé-im
30) GIŠ.tukul-bi ki-mè-ka
31) [gaba-r]i na-an-tuk-tuk
32) [...] x-bi
33) [ḫé-im]-⌜ta⌝-sìg
Lacuna

iv 28–33) that man — may his reign exist forever. In the field of battle may his weapon find no [riv]al. [May] he smite [...] with ... its ...
Lacuna

Col. v
1) u$_4$ ⌜^{d}en⌝-[líl]
2) enkar GIŠ.[...]
3) nam-sipa-kalam-ma-šè x [x]
4) íb-ši-gá-gá-a

v 1–4) When *the god En*[*lil*] places, [*for a future ruler*], the staff (and) [sceptre] for the shepherdship of the nation

5) tukum-bi
6) alam-a-ni ḫé-a
7) alam-ìr-da-ni ḫé-a
8) é-kur

v 5–10) if (that ruler) brings either his own statue or the statue of his servant into Ekur, the temple of Enlil,

9) é-^{d}en-líl-lá-šè
10) i-ni-in-ku$_4$-ku$_4$
11) alam-ìr-gá
12) ki-gub-ba-bi
13) nam-ba-da-ab-kúr-re

v 11–13) may he not alter the place where the statue of my servant stands,

14) alam-a-ni
15) igi-alam-ìr-da-ni
16) ki-ba nam-ba-ab-gub-bé

v 14–16) may he not set up his own statue in that place in front of the statue of his servant,

17) ki-bi-šè na-ab-gub-bé
18) bar-bi-šè ḫé-bí-íb-gub-bé

v 17–18) may he not set it up in that place, (but rather) set it up outside.

19) lú-á-nì-ḫul-dím-ma
20) íb-ši-ág-ge$_{26}$-e
21) alam-zabar-
22) né-né
23) dumu-né-né
24) ìr-gá
25) nì-mu-sa$_4$-a
26) [an]-zil i-ni-in-gar-ra
27) [íb-zi-re-a]
28) [mu]-ni
29) [bí-íb-ḫa-lam-e]-a
30) ki-g[ub-ba-b]i
31) íb-da-ab-⸢kúr-ru-a⸣
32) alam-a-ni
33) igi-alam-
34) né-né
35) ìr-gá-ka
36) bí-íb-gub-bu-a
37) é-nì-GA-ra
38) alam-[né-né]
39) ì[r-gá]
40) [bí-íb-ku$_4$-ku$_4$-a]
Lacuna

v 19–40) (As for) the man who gives orders to do evil against it, [destroys] the bronze statue of so-and-so, son of so-and-so, my servant, a thing given a name, and ... who [defaces] his (the original owner's) [name], (or) moves the place [where it stands], sets up his own statue in front of the statue of so-and-so, my servant, (or) [brings] the statue of [so-and-so, my] se[rvant], into a storehouse,
Lacuna

Col. vi
1) [...]
2) [...]
3) x [...]
4) x [...]
5) íb-t[a-...]

vi 1–5) [...] ...

6) mu-s[ar-ra-ba]
7) šu b[í-íb-ùr-ru-a]
8) mu-n[i bí-íb-sar-re-a]
9) áš-b[al-a-ba-ke$_4$-eš lú-kúr]
10) š[u ba-an-zi-zi-a]

vi 6–10) (or) er[ases its] in[scription], (and) [writes] his own name [on it, or on account of this] cur[se] in[cites another to do so],

11) [...]
12) [...]
13) [...]
14) [...]
15) x [...]

vi 11–15) [...]

16) lú-[bi lugal ḫé-a en ḫé-a]
17) ù l[ú-ùlu sag-zi-gál]
18) mu-s[a$_4$-a ḫé-a]
19) lú-[ba]
20) m[u na-an-tuk-tuk]
21) ^{d}[...]

vi 16–23) [Whether he be a king, an *en* priest], or an or[dinary human being] — may [that] man [not get] any of[fspring]. May the god [Enlil] and the goddess [Ninlil] cu[rse him].

22) ^{d}[...]
23) n[am ḫa-ba-an-da-ku$_{5}$-ru-ne]
24) k[i(?) ...]
25) [...]
26) x [...]
27) ḫu-m[u-...]

vi 24–27) No translation warranted.

28) ^{d}en-[ki ...]
29) nun x [...]
30) I$_{7}$.x [...]

vi 28–30) May the god En[ki ...] prince [...] the canal [...]

31) ⸢a⸣ x [...]
32) ⸢ù(?)⸣ [...]
33) x [...]

vi 31–33) No translation warranted.

Lacuna

Reverse

Col. i

Lacuna

1′) x [...] in-n[a-...]
2′) ki-ḫub x [...] l[ú ...]
3′) lú-érim-n[i ...]
4′) ka-a ki [...] DU [...]
5′) gìri šu [...]

Lacuna

rev. i 1′–5′) ... the place of defeat ... his enemy ... mouth ... foot ...

6′) [...]
7′) [...]
8′) [...]
9′) [...]
10′) [...]
11′) šà-[...]
12′) gam [...] x [...]
13′) igi-lá m[u-...]
14′) ḫé-e[n-...]
15′) a kal [...]
16′) nam-TAR x [...]
17′) x [...]
18′) x [...]

rev. i 6′–18′) No translation warranted.

Lacuna

Col. ii

Lacuna

1′) x [...]

Lacuna

rev. ii 1′) ...

2′) un-un-bi
3′) ⸢GIŠ.tukul⸣ ḫé-en-da-šub-bé
4′) uru-ni é-ri-a
5′) ⸢ár(?)-ár(?)⸣ ḫé-im
6′) kalam-ma-ni ḫé-en-šub
7′) du$_{6}$-du$_{6}$-ra ḫé-en-šid

rev. ii 2′–7′) May it fell its people with weapons. May his city become a waste ... May his land tumble down (and) be counted among the rubble heaps.

8′) lú ^{d}suen-a
9′) ^{d}nanna-gin$_{7}$
10′) lú mu-ši-da-b[é]
11′) sag ḫé-x [...]
12′) šu-maḫ-ni ḫé-x-x
13′) sù-da ḫa-ra-ab-dab$_{5}$

rev. ii 8′–13′) ...

14′) nì-tuk nì-sa$_{6}$-ga
15′) a-ba-da-an-tak$_{4}$
16′) uru ki nu-zu-na
17′) šu ḫé-en-dag-ge$_{4}$
18′) ⸢ḫé-gál sì-sì-ga⸣

rev. ii 14′–19′) May the wealthy man, having lost his fine possessions, wander through his city that is unfamiliar to him. May ... seize the one who was (once) endowed with abundance.

19′) x ⸢šu ḫé-en-da-an-dab$_{5}$⸣
20′) mìn-kam-ma-šè tukum-bi
21′) ⸢u$_{4}$-da⸣ lú
22′) [...] x
Lacuna

rev. ii 20′–22′) For a second time, if when [that] man [...]
Lacuna

Col. iii
Lacuna
1′) [x] ⸢na⸣ x x
2′) x ⸢ak-a-gin$_{7}$⸣
3′) ^{d}utu-ra ḫé-en-ta-gi$_{4}$-gi$_{4}$
4′) kar x x x x
5′) lú kas$_{4}$(?)-a-aš ḫa-ba-an-ku$_{4}$-ku$_{4}$
6′) [x] ⸢é⸣-gal-la-ke$_{4}$
7′) a-gin$_{7}$ ki-⟨a⟩-še-er-ra ḫé-em-búr-e
8′) nì-gig é-gal-šè
9′) ḫé-ni-in-ku$_{4}$-ku$_{4}$
10′) uru-ni ⸢ur-gi$_{7}$-gin$_{7}$⸣
11′) šu ḫé-en-da-ab-zi
12′) mu-ni ḫé-en-nigin
13′) mu-pà-da-ni
14′) kalam-ma na-an-gá-gá

Lacuna
rev. iii 1′–14′) ..., like the one who does ..., may he *answer* to the god Utu. ... Thus, may the ... of his palace turn into a treacherous place and may he be turned into a taboo (person) at the palace. May his city drive him out like a dog. May his name be cut off. May he have no one proclaiming his name in the nation.

15′) [x]-⸢ta⸣ x x x
16′) [x] ⸢ab-ta⸣-x-x
17′) [x x] ⸢an⸣ x x [x]
18′) x [...]-⸢bi⸣
19′) [...]-e
Lacuna

rev. iii 15′–19′) No translation warranted.

Col. iv
Lacuna
1′) [...] ⸢ìr-gá⸣
2′) mu-dím-ma-šè
3′) *za-ri-ku*
4′) lú-más-su
5′) nì-na-me na-ab-bé
6′) ìr-gá šu-zi ba-ni-in-gar
7′) alam-a-ni mu-dím

Lacuna
rev. iv 1′–7′) to [the statue] of my servant which he fashioned, Zariku, the leader, said nothing to him. My servant truly *handed it over* to him. I fashioned a statue in his likeness.

8′) u$_{4}$-ul-lí-a-šè
9′) ⸢egir⸣ u$_{4}$-da-šè
10′) ìr lugal-a-ni-ir
11′) [š]u-zi bí-in-gar-ra
12′) alam-a-ni [b]í-in-dím-⟨ma⟩
Lacuna

rev. iv 8′–12′) For the future, for time to come, what a servant has truly *handed over* to his lord, a statue *which* he fashioned in his likeness
Lacuna

Col. v
Lacuna
1′) x ⸢me⸣ x x
2′) x AB ni-du$_{8}$-šè
3′) é-a ku$_{4}$-ra
4′) ⸢é⸣-a ti-la ḫé-a

Lacuna
rev. v 1′–4′) ... ... to the *doorman*, having entered the temple, may it be a living (thing) in the temple.

5′) lú-inim-gar
6′) alam-né-né ìr-gá
7′) bí-íb-ḫul-a

rev. v 5′–7′) (As for) a man of (bad) reputation who damages the statue of so-and-so, my servant,

8′) mùš-me alam-a-ni
9′) nì-sa$_{6}$-⟨ga⟩-bi-a
10′) šu-x-x-bu-da
11′) bí-íb-sì-ga

rev. v 8′–11′) who lays a ... hand on the face of his statue and its beautiful (adornments),

12′) kaš ninda u_6 di-dè
13′) ⌜im-mi⌝-[ib-gub-ba-a]
14′) [alam-né-né]
15′) [ìr-gá]
16′) [íb-ta-ku_5-ru-a]
Lacuna
Col. vi
Lacuna
1′) […]-⌜a⌝
2′) […]-ta
3′) […] x
4′) […] x
5′) […] x
6′) […]-NE
7′) […] x
8′) […] x
Lacuna

rev. v 12′–16′) [who cuts off] the beer and bread (offerings) wondrously [established there (for) the statue of so-and-so, my servant]
Lacuna

Lacuna
rev. vi 1′–8′) No translation warranted.

2

A cone fragment excavated at Ur deals with the construction of the temple of Ningišzida by Sîn-iqīšam.

COMMENTARY

The fragment is IM 92950, excavation no. U 10100, from the Royal Cemetery area, 'top filling'. It is a fragment of a cone shaft 11 cm long, 4.2 cm dia., and was collated.

The provenance of this cone suggests that it may have come from a double temple of Ningišzida and Ningubalag which may once have stood in the SM area at Ur; see D. Charpin, Le Clergé d'Ur, p. 223.

BIBLIOGRAPHY

1965 Sollberger, UET 8 no. 73 (copy, study)
1976 Woolley and Mallowan, UE 7 p. 232 (provenance)
1971 Sollberger and Kupper, IRSA IVB11a (translation)
1980 Kärki, SAKAZ 1 pp. 80–81 Sîniqīšam 1 (edition)

TEXT

1) ^{d}nin-giš-zi-da
2) GÌR.NÍTA-uri_5.KI-ma
3) ^{d}EN.ZU-*i-qí-ša-am*
4) nita-kala-ga
5) dumu-^{d}EN-ZU-*i-ri-ba-am*
6) ú-a-uri_5.KI-ma
7) lugal-lársa.KI-ma
8) [é]-nì-ge-na
9) [é]-ki-tuš-
10) [ki]-ága-ni
11) [mu]-na-dù

1–2) For the god Ningišzida, 'governor' of Ur,

3–7) Sîn-iqīšam, mighty man, son of Sîn-irībam, provider of Ur, king of Larsa,

8–11) built for him the [E]-nigena ('[House] of justice'), his [be]loved [re]sidence.

3

A cone fragment excavated at Ur deals with the construction of a temple for some god, by a king of Larsa whose name is not fully preserved. It may be Sîn-iqīšam.

COMMENTARY

The cone is IM 92922, excavation no. U 11692, from the Royal Cemetery area, rubbish under the Temenos wall. It is a fragment of a head of a clay cone and the inscription was not collated.

The divine beneficiary of this inscription should probably be restored as Nanna, as Sollberger suggests. The king's name, which is broken away, begins with a divine name. The king's father's name, which is also broken away, also begins with a divine name. In the entire Larsa dynasty only two possibilities would fit this pattern. Either the king was Sîn-irībam or Sîn-iqīšam. The titulary of the king in this inscription agrees perfectly with that found for Sîn-iqīšam in the following inscription. Unfortunately, we have no comparable text of Sîn-irībam giving the king's titulary to make a comparison. The fragment has been arbitrarily edited here as an inscription of Sîn-iqīšam, bearing in mind that it could equally well belong to Sîn-irībam.

The mention of a bed(?) in line 12 suggests that this text might have dealt with the construction of Nanna's bedroom.

BIBLIOGRAPHY

1965 Sollberger, UET 8 p. 20 no. 89 (study) and pl. XXII no. 88 [sic!] (copy)

TEXT

1) ⸢^{d}⸣[nanna]
2) dum[u-sag]-
3) ⸢^{d}⸣[en-líl-lá]
4) lug[al-a-ni-ir]
5) ^{d}E[N.ZU-*i-qí-ša-am*]
6) nita-[kala-ga]
7) dumu-⸢^{d}⸣[EN.ZU-*i-ri-ba-am*]
8) ú-a-u[ri$_{5}$.KI-ma]
9) lugal-l[arsa.KI-ma]
10) lugal-ki-[en-gi-ki-uri]
11) é-[...]
12) x-n[á-...]
Lacuna

1–4) For the god [Nanna, most important] so[n] of the god [Enlil, his] lo[rd],

5–10) S[în-iqīšam, mighty] man, son of [Sîn-irībam], provider of U[r], king of L[arsa], king of the land [of Sumer and Akkad],

11–12) the temple [...], ... *bed* ... [he built].
Lacuna

2001

A fragment of a calcite bowl excavated at Ur contains a dedication for the life of Sîn-iqīšam.

COMMENTARY

The present location of the piece is not known. It bears the excavation no. U 16529 and was found in wagon dirt at the main Isin-Larsa and later residential quarter. A duplicate no. U 16529 is the tablet UM 52-30-66 in Philadelphia, published as UET 5 no. 51. Our piece is a fragment of a white calcite bowl.

BIBLIOGRAPHY

1965 Sollberger, UET 8 no. 74 (copy, study)
1980 Kärki, SAKAZ 1 p. 81 Sîniqīšam 2 (edition)

TEXT

1) ^{d}[...]	1) For the god [...],
2) dingir-ra-[ni-ir]	2) [his] god,
3) nam-[ti]-	3) for the li[fe]
4) ^{d}EN.ZU-*i-qí-š*[*a-am*]	4) of Sîn-iqīš[am],
5) *za-a-a-*[x]	5) Zaia-[...]
Lacuna	Lacuna

2002

The impression of what is probably a seal of a servant of Sîn-iqīšam is found on a tablet at Yale.

COMMENTARY

The impression is on YBC 10294 dated to year 3 of Sîn-iqīšam. It was not collated.

BIBLIOGRAPHY

1978 Simmons, YOS 14 pl. CXXII Seal no. 127 (copy)

TEXT

1) *ig-mi-il-*x [x x]	1) Igmil-...[...],
2) DUMU *na-ši-*x [x x]	2) son of Naši-...[...],
3) IR$_{11}$ ^{d}EN.Z[U-*i-qí-ša-am*]	3) servant of Sî[n-iqīšam].

Ṣillī-Adad

E4.2.12

Sîn-iqīšam was succeeded by Ṣillī-Adad, who may not have reigned even one full year. Only two inscriptions are extant for this ruler.

1

A number of bricks excavated at Ur, some from the south-west or north-west corners of the ziqqurrat terrace, deal with the strengthening and restoration of the base (úr) of the temenos by Ṣillī-Adad. The same inscription is found on a number of cones excavated at Ur.

CATALOGUE

Ex.	Museum number	Registration number	Excavation number	Ur Provenance	Object	Dimensions (cm)	Lines preserved	cpn
1	BM 119272	1927-10-3,267	U 2669	From the NW or SW corner of the ziqqurrat terrace	Stamped brick	30.0×20.5×8.5	1-13	c
2	IM 913	–	U 2669	As ex. 1	Stamped brick	22.0×24.0×7.5	–	n
3	CBS 16475	–	U 2833a	From SF	Stamped brick	30.0×28.0×7.5	–	n
4	CBS 16547	–	U 2883b	As ex. 3	Stamped brick	30.0×32.0×7.0	–	n
5	–	–	U 6323	From KPS	Stamped brick	–	–	n
6	BM 137356	1935-1-13,16	–	Trial Trench B, ES	Stamped brick	19.0×16.0×7.0	1-7	c
7	BM 137393	1979-12-18,28	–	–	Stamped brick	20.0×18.0×7.5	1-7	c
8	BM 137394	1979-12-18,29	–	–	Stamped brick	23.5×20.0×7.0	4-13	c
9	BM 137395	1979-12-18,30	–	–	Stamped brick	31.0×19.0×6.5	1-8	c
10	BM 137396	1979-12-18,31	–	–	Stamped brick	23.0×22.5×7.5	3-13	c
11	BM 137397	1979-12-18,32	–	–	Stamped brick	31.0×27.0×7.0	1-13	c
12	CBS 15614	–	U 1355	Debris of great court NE of ziqqurrat	Cone shaft	7.3	1-9	c
13	IM 92872	–	U 15023a	From the Royal Cemetery area, 'near surface'	Cone head	–	9-13	c
14	IM 92863	–	U 15023b	As ex. 13	Cone shaft	–	1-13	c

COMMENTARY

Exs. 1-11 are bricks, exs. 12-14 cones. Exs. 6-11 have no registration numbers indicating when they actually entered the museum; the registration numbers they bear are recent ones. Exs. 7-11 are probably from Woolley's excavations.

BIBLIOGRAPHY

1928 Gadd, UET 1 no. 121 (exs. 1–5, composite copy, edition)
1929 Barton, RISA pp. 376–77 Ṣilli-Adad 1 (edition)
1961 Hallo, BiOr 18 p. 9 Ṣilli-Adad 1 (study)
1965 Sollberger, UET 8 pp. 28–29 no. 20 (exs. 13–14, study)
1968 Kärki, SKFZ p. 38 Ṣillīadad 1 (edition)
1971 Sollberger and Kupper, IRSA IVB12a (translation)
1980 Kärki, SAKAZ 1 pp. 81–82 Ṣillīadad 1 (edition)
1981 Walker, CBI no. 42 (exs. 1, 6–11, study)

TEXT

1) ^{d}nanna 2) lugal-a-ni-ir	1–2) For the god Nanna, his lord,
3) *ṣi-li*-^{d}IŠKUR 4) ú-a-nibru.KI 5) énsi- 6) úri.KI 7) larsa.KI 8) lagaš.KI 9) ù ma-da- 10) *ku-ta-al-la*.KI-a-ke_4	3–10) Ṣillī-Adad, provider of Nippur, governor of Ur, Larsa, Lagaš, and the land of Kutalla,
11) úr-é-temen-ní-gùru 12) bí-in-gur	11–12) reinforced the base of Etemenniguru ('House — foundation which bears a fearful splendour')
13) ki-bé bí-in-gi_4	13) (and) restored it.

2

A cone excavated at Ur deals with the strengthening and restoration of the terrace of Ningal's é-i_7-lú-ru-gú-kalam-ma temple by a Larsa king, probably Ṣillī-Adad.

COMMENTARY

The cone is IM 92977, excavation no. U 18762, from the extension of the Royal Cemetery area about 3 m below the modern surface. It is a fragment of a head of a clay cone 10.5×6 cm and the inscription was collated.

The first preserved line of the cone is broken but reads: *ku*-⌈*ta*⌉-[*al-la*.KI]-⌈a⌉-ke_4. This phrase could be part of the titulary of either Ṣillī-Adad or Warad-Sîn. Sollberger, followed by Kärki, attributed it to Warad-Sîn. An inscription slightly different from this one dealing with repair work by Warad-Sîn on the terrace of the é-i_7-lú-ru-gú-kalam-ma temple (E4.2.13.1) dates to the first year of Warad-Sîn's reign. It seems unlikely that Warad-Sîn would have commissioned two separate cone inscriptions inscribed in one year to commemorate work on the same temple. This fact, coupled with the similarity of the present text to E4.2.12.1, suggests that this fragment should be assigned to Ṣillī-Adad. If this be correct, then it would indicate that work on the terrace of Ningal's temple was begun during the one-year reign of Ṣillī-Adad and continued, as commemorated in a slightly different inscription, in the first year of Warad-Sîn.

The cone inscription is restored on the basis of E4.2.12.1.

4.12 [...-ni]bru.KI-a. **10**.14 [*k*]*u-ta-al-la*.KI-⟨a⟩-ke_4. **12** Copy of Gadd has bí-in-du_{11}; all exs. where collated have bí-in-gur. **13**.14 ki-bé bí-in-gi_4-a.

BIBLIOGRAPHY

1965 Sollberger, UET 8 no. 78 (copy, study)
1980 Kärki, SAKAZ 1 p. 134 Waradsîn 34 (edition)

TEXT

1) [^{d}nin-gal]	1–2) [For the goddess Ningal, his lady],
2) [nin-a-ni-ir]	
3) [*ṣi-lí*-^{d}IŠKUR]	3–10) [Ṣillī-Adad, provider of Nippur, governor of Ur, Larsa, Lagaš, and the land of] Kuta[lla],
4) [ú-a-nibru.KI]	
5) [énsi]-	
6) [úri.KI]	
7) [larsa.KI]	
8) [lagaš.KI]	
9) [ù ma-da]-	
10) *ku*-⸢*ta*⸣-[*al-la*.KI]-⸢a⸣-ke$_4$	
11) úr-é-i$_7$-⸢lú-ru⸣-[g]ú-kalam-ma	11–12) reinforced the base of Eiluru[g]ukalama ('House – ordeal river of the nation')
12) bí-in-gur	
13) ki-bé bí-in-gi$_4$-a	13) (and) restored it.

Warad-Sîn

E4.2.13

Kudur-mabuk, the Amorite chief, installed his son, Warad-Sîn, as king of Larsa following the expulsion of Ṣillī-Adad. Although a date list published by M. Stol (Studies in Old Babylonian History pp. 2–3) indicates that Warad-Sîn ruled 13 years, new evidence discussed by M. Sigrist (RA 79 [1985] p. 168) indicates that the king reigned only 12 years.

Although he did not have a particularly long reign, there are more royal inscriptions extant for Warad-Sîn than any other king of the Larsa dynasty. Many of these inscriptions describe deeds which were also commemorated in year names of the king. The inscriptions are edited here in the order determined by these correlations with the king's year names. The numbering of the year names follows the scheme proposed by Sigrist.

Correlations with the names of Warad-Sîn's years can also be found in the titulary found in three inscriptions, E4.2.13.14, 17, and 27. The latest and most complete form is found in E4.2.13.27, where the following epithets may be correlated with the names of years 7–10:

Line 14: šul á-ág-gá kin-kin 'youth who seeks out the (proper) omens' probably refers to the oracular designation and subsequent installation of the *en* priestess, the latter event providing the name of year 7 of Warad-Sîn.

Lines 16–17: é-dingir-re-e-ne šu-gibil bí-in-ak 'who renewed the temples of the gods' may allude to the construction work on the temple of the god Nanna which figures in the name of year 8 of the king.

Lines 18–20: URUDU.alam-gal-gal-mu-pà-da-nam-lugal-la-ka-na gal-bi bí-in-su_8-ga 'who grandly set up statues which call his royal name' may allude to the introduction of the statue of Kudur-mabuk into the temple of the god Utu in Larsa which figures in the name of year 9.

Lines 21–22: uru-šub-šub-ba-bi bàd-bi ḫu-mu-dù-a 'who built the walls of the fallen down cities' probably alludes to the construction of the wall of Ur commemorated in the name of year 10.

E4.2.13.14 and 17 only have part of this titulary, a fact which may help to date these inscriptions.

Another indication for the relative dating of Warad-Sîn's inscriptions is the title used for Kudur-mabuk. He appears as ad-da-kur-mar-dú 'father of the Amorite land' in inscriptions correlating to the names of years 1–6, and ad-da-*e-mu-ut-ba-la* 'father of Emutbala' in inscriptions correlating to the names of years 7–12. The second title was probably adopted concurrent with the recognition of his son, Warad-Sîn, by the Nippur authorities, an event commemorated, as it was by his predecessor, Sîn-iqīšam, by the introduction of 14 statues into Nippur, as recorded in a variant to the name of year 6 of

Warad-Sîn (see E4.2.13.13). The names of Warad-Sîn years 7, 9, 10, and 11 are attested on archival texts from Nippur (see R.M. Sigrist, Ninurta à Nippur, p. 70).

1

A number of cones found at Ur, at least one of which came from the Gipar-ku, deal with repair work by Warad-Sîn on Ningal's é-i$_7$-lú-ru-gú-kalam-ma temple. This was probably a continuation of work begun by Ṣillī-Adad (see commentary to E4.2.12.2). The titulary of the king used here indicates that the text dates to year 1 of Warad-Sîn.

CATALOGUE

Ex.	Museum number	Excavation number	Ur provenance	Object	Dimensions (cm)	Lines preserved	cpn
1	BM 30069 (56-9-3,1483)	Loftus's excavations	–	Shaft	6.5 dia.	1–10, 14–21	c
2	CBS 16233	U 6338	From the Gipar-ku room C. 10	Head	13.2 dia.	1–4, 12–20	c
3	CBS 16233	U 6338	–	Shaft	13.0	1–21	c
4	IM 1528	U 6338	–	Cone	–	–	n
5	IM 92870	U cb	–	Head	11.3 dia.	1–5, 12–16	c
6	IM 92868	U db	–	Shaft	11.5	1–21	c
7	IM 92866	U eb	–	Shaft	6.0	1–6	c

COMMENTARY

The master text is ex. 3.

Ex. 1, edited here for the first time through the courtesy of C.B.F. Walker, was found by Loftus at Ur. The remainder are from Woolley's excavations.

In room C. 10 of the Gipar-ku at Ur Woolley excavated a sloped mud brick revetment against which ex. 2 was found. The cone inscription indicates that this mud brick repair work (*takšīrum*) was done by the hand of Warad-Sîn. It also tells us that é-i$_7$-lú-ru-gú-kalam-ma 'House of the ordeal river of the nation' was the name of section C of the Gipar, the residence of the goddess Ningal, within the Gipar complex.

BIBLIOGRAPHY

1928 Gadd, UET 1 no. 126 (exs. 2–3, composite copy, edition)
1929 Barton, RISA pp. 378–79 Warad-Sin 4 (edition)
1934 Meissner, SPAW p. 917 n. 2 (study)
1957 Edzard, Sumer 13 p. 177 (ex. 4, study)
1961 Hallo, BiOr 18 p. 9 Warad-Sin 14 (study)
1965 Sollberger, UET 8 p. 29 no. 24 (exs. 5–7, study)
1968 Kärki, SKFZ p. 52 Waradsîn 14 (edition)
1975 Weadcock, Iraq 37 p. 109 n. 62 (study)
1976 Woolley and Mallowan, UE 7 p. 55 (ex. 2, provenance, study)
1980 Kärki, SAKAZ 1 pp. 101–102 Waradsîn 14 (edition)
1986 Charpin, Le clergé d'Ur pp. 198–99 (edition)

TEXT

1) ^{d}nin-gal
2) nin maḫ-di
3) me-kìlib-ba sag-íl
4) nin-a-ni-ir

1–4) For the goddess Ningal, highest lady, who is exalted with all the *me*s, his lady,

5) IR$_{11}$-^{d}EN.ZU
6) ú-a-nibru.KI

5–10) Warad-Sîn, provider of Nippur, governor of Ur, Larsa, Lagaš, and the land of Kutalla,

7) énsi-uri$_5$.KI	
8) larsa.KI	
9) lagaš.KI	
10) ù ma-da-*ku-ta-al-la*.KI-ke$_4$	
11) u$_4$ ^{d}nin-gal	11–13) when the goddess Ningal went to bless him,
12) šùd-da-a-ni	
13) in-dè-DU-a	
14) é-i$_7$-lú-ru-gú-kalam-ma	14–18) he did not alter the perimeter of the Eilurugukalama ('House — ordeal river of the nation'), her beloved temple — it had been built in the past and its foundation and wall had become dilapidated.
15) é-ki-ág-gá-ni	
16) u$_4$-ul ba-dù-a-ta	
17) uru$_4$ é-gar$_8$-bi ba-sun	
18) temen-bi nu-mu-un-kúr	
19) úr-libir-a-bé	19–20) On its old base he did repair work.
20) *ták-ší-ru-um* bí-in-ak	
21) ki-bé mu-na-gi$_4$	21) He restored it for her.

2

A cone shaft fragment excavated at Ur deals with the construction of the temple of Ninisina in Ur by a king whose name should be restored as Warad-Sîn. The titulary of the king used in this text indicates that the inscription dates to year 1 of Warad-Sîn.

COMMENTARY

The piece is IM 92963, excavation no. U 12972, from the central section of the north-east city wall at Ur. It is a frgm. of a cone shaft 8.5 cm long, 6 cm in dia. The inscription was collated.

This inscription was not given a definite attribution by Sollberger, who suggested that it might belong to Būr-Sîn of Isin. The fragmentary titulary of the king indicates that it could belong to either Ṣillī-Adad or Warad-Sîn. The fact that the king's name in line 5 ends [...]-Sîn clinches the case for the latter king. It was edited as an inscription of Warad-Sîn by Kärki.

Lines 13–15 are restored from E4.2.13.1 lines 11–13. The fact that only these two inscriptions (E4.2.13.1–2) have the titulary referring to Warad-Sîn as *ensi* of Ur makes such a restoration likely.

Line 13 ends in KI as copied. It is emended here to read -na.

The restoration of line 16 is based on the guess that Ninisina's temple in Ur may have had the same name as her temple in Isin. Such a hypothesis is supported by the occurrence of this same name for the temple of Ninisina in Uruk (see E4.4.1.11).

Lines 17–18, as in Sollberger's copy, are separated by a ruling. The restoration proposed by Kärki, followed here, treats lines 17–18 as one line, with the second half indented. In this case the ruling may have been drawn first by the scribe and filled in as dictated by the needs of the inscription.

In line 26 the form of the phrase [nam]-e-eš ḫé-en-na-tar-re is probably influenced by the verb sag-e-eš ... rig$_7$ often found at the end of these inscriptions.

BIBLIOGRAPHY

1965 Sollberger, UET 8 no. 63 (copy, study)
1980 Kärki, SAKAZ 1 p. 132 Waradsîn 30 (edition)

19.2 úr-libir-⟨a⟩-bé. **20**.2 Copy has *ká-si-ru-um*; collation reveals *ták-ší-ru-um*.

TEXT

1) [^{d}nin-i]n-si-na
2) [dumu-sa]g-an-na
3) [é-gi$_4$]-⸢a⸣-é-kur-ra
4) [nin-a]-ni-ir
5) [IR$_{11}$-^{d}]EN.ZU
6) [ú-a-nib]ru.KI
7) [én]si
8) [úri].KI
9) [larsa].KI
10) [lagaš].KI
11) [ù-ma]-da-
12) [*ku-ta-al-la*.KI-(a)]-ke$_4$
13) [u$_4$ ^{d}nin-in-si]-na(*)
14) [šùd-da-a]-ni
15) [in-dè-DU]-a
16) [é-gal]-maḫ
17) [ki-tuš-kù-ki]-ág-[g]á-ni
18) [šà-úri.K]I-ma-ka
19) [nam-ti-l]a-ni-šè
20) [mu-na-ni]-in-dù
21) [nì-ak]-bi-šè
22) [^{d}ni]n-in-si-na
23) [ḫé-e]n-da-UD
24) [nam-ti u$_4$]-maḫ-bi
25) [nam-luga]l-šà-ḫúl-la
26) [nam]-e-eš ḫé-en-na-tar-re

1–4) For [the goddess Nini]sina, [first-bor]n [daughter] of the god An, [daughter-in-l]aw of the Ekur, his [lady],

5–12) [Warad]-Sîn, [provider of Nip]pur, [gove]rnor of [Ur, Larsa, Lagaš, and the la]nd of [Kutalla],

13–15) [when the goddess Ninisi]na [went to bless] him,

16–20) he built [for her] for his own [lif]e the [Egal]maḫ, her [bel]oved [residence in Ur].

21–26) [May the goddess Ni]nisina shine at this [deed] (and determine) for him as [(his) destiny]: a very great [life-span (and) a kingshi]p of joy.

3

The name of the second year of Warad-Sîn commemorates the destruction of the wall of Kazallu and the smiting of the army of Mutiabal in Larsa. These same events are alluded to in two inscriptions of Warad-Sîn. The first is a cone inscription from Uruk dealing with Kudur-mabuk's construction of the temple of Nergal, presumably in Uruk, for his own life and the life of Warad-Sîn. The construction work probably dates to a period early in the reign of Warad-Sîn.

CATALOGUE

Ex.	Museum number	Excavation number	Provenance	Object	Dimensions (cm)	Lines preserved	cpn
1	AO 6209	–	Uruk(?), no provenance	Head	11.7 dia.	1–39	c
2	AO 6209	–	As ex. 1	Shaft	4.8	1–19	c
3	IM 49816	W 18524	Uruk, Od XIV 4	Head	10.3	25–39	p
4	IM 49816	W 18524	As ex. 3	Shaft	5.6	9–11, 13–18	p

13 Text: KI.

COMMENTARY

The master text is ex. 1.

Exs. 1–2 were acquired by the Louvre; the provenance of the cone at the time of purchase was unknown. Exs. 3–4 were excavated at Uruk. This provides a provenance for the inscription. Exs. 3–4 were collated from the Warka excavation photos through the courtesy of R. Boehmer.

For the translation 'eldest son' for dumu-pa$_4$-šeš in line 4, see A. Sjöberg, Heidelberger Studien p. 217.

ḫaš...gur of line 5 is elsewhere attested with the meaning 'to turn back' (Civil).

BIBLIOGRAPHY

1912 Thureau-Dangin, RA 9 pp. 121–24 (exs. 1–2, copy, edition)
1929 Barton, RISA pp. 324–25 Warad-Sin 9 (edition)
1957 Edzard, Sumer 13 pp. 177 and 183 (exs. 3–4, study)
1961 Hallo, BiOr 18 p. 9 Warad-Sin 13 (study)
1960 Aynard, RA 54 p. 17 (study)
1968 Kärki, SKFZ pp. 50–52 Waradsîn 13 (edition)
1971 Sollberger and Kupper, IRSA IVB13i (translation)
1980 Kärki, SAKAZ 1 pp. 100–101 Waradsîn 13 (edition)

TEXT

1) ^{d}nergal en-gal
2) usu-ir$_9$-ra
3) ní me-lám gùr-ru
4) šul-kala-ga dumu-pa$_4$-šeš-kur-gal-la
5) ḫáš-ba gur-ru-bi du$_{10}$
6) lugal-a-ni-ir

1–6) For the god Nergal, great lord, (with) powerful might, who bears a fearsome splendour and an aura, mighty youth, eldest son of the great mountain (Enlil), whose *withdrawal* is good, his lord,

7) *ku-du-ur-ma-bu-uk*
8) ad-da-kur-mar-dú
9) dumu-*si-im-ti-ši-il-ḫa-ak*
10) lú šu-gar-é-babbar-ra-ke$_4$
11) bí-in-gi$_4$-a
12) ugnim-ka-zal-lu.KI
13) ù *mu-ti-a-ba-al-la*-ke$_4$
14) šà-larsa.KI šà-*e-mu-ut-ba-la*-ke$_4$
15) sag giš bí-in-ra-a

7–15) Kudur-mabuk, father of the Amorite land, son of Simti-šilḫak, the one who repaid a favour for the Ebabbar, who smote the army of Kazallu and Muti-abal in Larsa (and) Emutbala,

16) du$_{11}$-du$_{11}$-ga-^{d}nanna ^{d}utu-ta
17) ka-zal-lu i-ni-in-dab$_5$-ba
18) bàd-bi i-ni-in-sì-ga
19) ka-si-il-la-aš i-ni-in-gar-ra-a

16–19) who by decree of the gods Nanna and Utu seized Kazallu, tore down its wall, (and) made it submit,

20) u$_4$-bi-a ^{d}nergal
21) lugal-a-ni-ir
22) nam-⟨ga⟩-me-èš-a-ni-ta

20–22) at that time, for the god Nergal, his lord, having (established) a colleagueship (with him),

23) é-me-te-ir$_9$-ra
24) ki-tuš-nam-ur-sag-gá-ka-ni
25) i-ŠI ní šu-si-a
26) nam-ti-la-ni-šè
27) ù nam-ti-IR$_{11}$-^{d}EN.ZU dumu-ni
28) lugal-larsa.KI-ma-šè
29) mu-na-ni-in-dù

23–29) he built for him Emetegira ('House — suitable for the mighty one') his residence of valour, filled with a radiance and a fearsome splendour, for his own life and for the life of Warad-Sîn, his son, king of Larsa.

30) mu nam-maḫ-bi-gin$_7$
31) sag-bi ḫu-mu-ni-in-íl

30–31) He raised its head commensurate with its name and greatness.

22.1 Restore nam-⟨ga⟩-me-èš-a-ni-ta.

32) ^{d}nergal lugal-mu
33) za-e-me-en ba-e-a-ak
34) gá-e a-na-mu-me-en
35) nì-ak-bi-šè ^{d}nergal
36) dingir-ra-na ḫé-en-ši-ḫúl
37) nam-ti u$_{4}$-maḫ-bi
38) bala-da-rí sa$_{12}$-e-eš
39) ḫé-en-na-rig$_{7}$-ge

32–34) 'Nergal, my lord, it is you who has done it, (as for) myself, what am I?'

35–36) May the god Nergal, his lord, rejoice at this deed,
37–39) (and) may he grant a very great life-span (and) an eternal reign.

4

A cone shaft fragment probably from Woolley's excavations at Ur alludes to the events of the name of year 2 of Warad-Sîn and seems to deal with the construction(?) of the Gabura temple in Ur.

COMMENTARY

The frgm. is IM 22900, Ur excavation number as yet undetermined. It is a cone shaft, dimensions not known. The inscription was collated by D. Edzard.

Charpin (Le clergé d'Ur p. 223) suggests that the Gabura temple of Ningubalag is to be identified with the ruined building in the EM site.

BIBLIOGRAPHY

1957 Edzard, Sumer 13 p. 178 (study) and pl. 3 after p. 188 (copy)
1961 Hallo, BiOr 18 p. 9 Warad-Sin 16 (study)
1968 Kärki, SKFZ p. 53 Waradsîn 16 (edition)
1980 Kärki, SAKAZ 1 p. 103 Waradsîn 16 (edition)

TEXT

Lacuna
1′) [...] si [...]
2′) [Ì]R$_{11}$-^{d}EN.ZU l[ugal]-
3′) lars[a.KI-ma]
4′) [u]gnim [k]a-zal-⌜lu.KI⌝
5′) [ù *m*]*u-ti-a-ba-a*[*l*]-*la*-⌜ke$_{4}$⌝
6′) [šà]-larsa.KI
7′) šà-*e-mu-ut-ba*-⌜*la*⌝-ka
8′) [s]ag giš BI bí-in-r[a-a]
9′) [é-g]á-bur-ra
10′) [...] x NI dù-a [...]
Lacuna

Lacuna
1′) [For the god Ningubalag] ...
2′–3′) [Wa]rad-Sîn, k[ing] of Lars[a],

4′–8′) the one who smote the [ar]my of [K]azallu [and M]uti-abal [in] Larsa (and) Emutbala,

9′–10′) [built for him Eg]abura, built ...
Lacuna

38.1 bala-da-rí «ki». **38**.3 [ba]la-du-rí. **39**.3 ḫé-en-na-rig$_{8}$ (PA.ḪÚB)-ge.

5

Early in the reign of Warad-Sîn Kudur-mabuk had the é-èš-ki-te shrine of the god Nanna constructed in Ur. This work is commemorated in brick and cone inscriptions. A third text known from a school copy deals with the erection of a statue, probably in the courtyard of the same temple.

Here the brick inscription dealing with the é-èš-ki-te shrine is edited first.

COMMENTARY

The inscription is found on BM 137384 (1979-12-18, 19), no excavation no. known, provenance unrecorded, although undoubtedly from Ur. It probably came from Woolley's excavations. It was collated by C.B.F. Walker. The brick is stamped and measures 34.5 × 29.5 × 8.5 cm.

The titulary of Kudur-mabuk found in this text exactly parallels that found in E4.2.13.3 with the omission of the reference to the defeat of the army of Kazallu and Mutiabal. This argues for a date for this inscription early in the reign. The epithet ad-da-kur-mar-dú 'father of the Amorite land' indicates that it pre-dates year 7, when the title ad-da-*e-mu-ut-ba-la* 'father of Emutbala' replaced it.

BIBLIOGRAPHY

1981 Walker, CBI no. 46 (transliteration, study)

TEXT

1) ⸢^{d}nanna⸣	1–4) [For] the god Nanna, lord of offerings, who lights up [heaven] (and) earth, first-born son of the god E[nli]l, [his] lord,
2) ⸢en⸣-sískur [an]-⸢ki zalag⸣	
3) dumu-sag-^{d}e[n-lí]l-⸢lá⸣	
4) ⸢lugal⸣-[a-ni-ir]	
5) *ku-du-*⸢*ur*⸣*-m*[*a-bu*]-⸢*uk*⸣	5–9) Kudur-m[ab]uk, father of the [Amo]rite land, son of Simti-šilḫak, the one who repaid a favour for the Ebabbar,
6) ad-da-kur-[mar]-⸢dú⸣	
7) ⸢dumu⸣-*si-im-ti-ši-*⸢*il*⸣*-ḫa-*⸢*ak*⸣	
8) lú-⸢šu-gar⸣-é-babbar-⸢ra-ke$_4$⸣	
9) ⸢bí-in⸣-gi$_4$-a	
10) [nam]-ti-⸢la⸣-ni-⸢šè⸣	10–13) for his own [li]fe [and] for the life of Warad-Sîn, his son, king of Larsa,
11) [ù] ⸢nam⸣-ti-	
12) ⸢IR$_{11}$⸣-^{d}EN.ZU ⸢dumu-ni⸣	
13) ⸢lugal⸣-larsa.KI-ma-⟨šè⟩	
14) [é]-èš-ki-te	14–16) built the [E]eškite, his [re]sidence of rejoicing.
15) [ki]-⸢tuš-šà-ḫúl-la-ka⸣-ni	
16) ⸢mu⸣-na-dù	
17) ⸢ḫur-sag⸣-gin$_7$ ⸢bí-in-sukud⸣	17–18) He made it high as a mountain (and) made (its) head touch heaven.
18) ⸢sag⸣ an-⸢e ši⸣-bí-⸢in-ús⸣	
19) ⸢nì⸣-ak-bi-⸢šè⸣	19–22) On account of this deed the gods Nanna and Ningal rejoiced.
20) ^{d}⸢nanna⸣	
21) ⸢^{d}nin-gal⸣-bi	
22) [ḫé]-⸢en-ši-ḫúl-le-eš⸣	
23) [nam-ta]r-⸢nam-ti-la⸣	23–26) [May] they grant to him a [dest]iny of life, a long reign, (and) a firm foundation.
24) ⸢bala-sù-rá suḫuš-ge⸣-na	
25) ⸢sag-e-eš⸣	
26) [ḫé]-en-na-rig$_7$-ge-ne	

6

The construction of Nanna's é-èš-ki-te temple is also recorded in a cone inscription excavated by Woolley at Ur.

CATALOGUE

Ex.	Museum number	Registration number	Excavation number	Photo number	Ur provenance	Object	Dimensions (cm)	Lines preserved	cpn
1	BM 119022	1927-10-3,17	U 2801	U 388	From Edublalmaḫ, room 7	Shaft	8.3	1–29	c
2	BM 119022	1927-10-3,17	U 2801	U 388	As ex. 1	Head	15.7 dia.	4–8, 19–25	c

COMMENTARY

The master text is ex. 1.

The end of line 2 reads: an-na zalag 'who shines in heaven' in contrast to the phrase an-ki zalag 'who lights up heaven and earth' found in the corresponding lines of the two parallel inscriptions.

BIBLIOGRAPHY

1928 Gadd, UET 1 no. 122 (ex. 1, copy, edition)
1929 Barton, RISA pp. 376–77 Warad-Sin 1 (edition)
1961 Hallo, BiOr 18 p. 9 Warad-Sin 9 (study)
1965 Sollberger, UET 8 p. 29 no. 21 (exs. 1–2, study)
1968 Kärki, SKFZ pp. 45–46 Waradsîn 9 (edition)
1980 Kärki, SAKAZ 1 pp. 93–94 Waradsîn 9 (edition)
1981 Walker, CBI no. 46 (ex. 1–2, study)

TEXT

1) ^{d}nanna
2) en-sískur an-na zalag
3) dumu-sag-^{d}en-líl-lá
4) lugal-a-ni-ir

1–4) For the god Nanna, lord of offerings, who shines in heaven, first-born son of Enlil, his lord,

5) *ku-du-ur-ma-bu-uk*
6) ad-da-kur-mar-dú
7) dumu-*si-im-ti-ši-il-ḫa-ak*
8) lú-šu-gar-é-babbar-ra-ke$_{4}$
9) bí-in-gi$_{4}$-a
10) abul-larsa.KI-ke$_{4}$ bàd-da
11) gál bí-in-tak$_{4}$-a
12) un-šár-ra-bi-šè
13) u$_{4}$ íb-ta-an-è-a
14) úri.KI larsa.KI-bi
15) ⸢ki-tuš-ne⸣-ḫa bí-in-tuš-a

5–15) Kudur-mabuk, father of the Amorite land, son of Simti-šilḫak, the one who repaid a favour for the Ebabbar, who opened the gate of Larsa in the wall (and) caused the daylight to come forth for all the people, who settled Ur and Larsa in peaceful abodes,

16) [nam-ti]-la-ni-šè
17) [ù nam-t]i-IR$_{11}$-^{d}EN.ZU dumu-ni
18) [lugal-lars]a.KI-ma-šè

16–18) for his own [life and] for the [li]fe of Warad-Sîn, his son, [king of Lars]a,

19) ⸢é⸣-[è]š-ki-te
20) ki-tuš-šà-ḫúl-la-ka-ni
21) ḫur-sag-gin$_{7}$ bí-in-sukud

19–21) made high as a mountain the E[e]škite, his residence of rejoicing.

22) sag an-e ši-⸢bí⸣-in-ús

22–24) He made (its) head touch heaven and set it

23) u_6-di-kalam-ma-ka
24) [u_4-da-rí-šè] bí-in-gub
25) [nì-ak]-bi-šè
26) [^{d}]nanna ^{d}nin-gal-bi
27) ḫé-en-ši-ḫúl ⸢nam-tar⸣-nam-ti-la
28) bala-⸢du_{10} suḫuš⸣-gi-na
29) sa_{12}-e-⟨eš⟩ ḫé-en-rig_7

up there to the wonder of the nation, [forever].

25–29) On account of this [deed] may the gods Nanna and Ningal rejoice and grant (to him) a destiny of life, a good reign, (and) a firm foundation.

7

An inscription of Kudur-mabuk known from a school copy on a tablet deals with the erection of a statue for the god Nanna in the courtyard of some temple. The inscription bears striking parallels to the two previous inscriptions dealing with Nanna's é-èš-ki-te temple. In view of these parallels, the courtyard mentioned in the text was probably that of the é-èš-ki-te temple.

COMMENTARY

The inscription is found on IM 85468, excavation no. U 7733, from no. 7 Quiet Street, rooms 5–6. It is a copy on a clay tablet measuring 9.5×8×2.7 cm and was collated.

The provenance of this tablet has been identified by the excavator as the site of a school. A large number of copies of royal inscriptions was found there.

In iii 3–4 the translation given assumes that the Sumerian there represents what should appear in Sumerian as mu-nam-lugal-la-ka-ni pà-da. The word order in the extant text probably represents a translation from an original Akkadian expression.

In iii 5, kalam-maḫ is probably a mistake for kalam-ma-ka; cf. E4.2.13.14 line 21′: šà-kalam-ma-ka.

In iv 2′ the expression ru-gál does not appear to make any sense. This might be a mistake for ru-gú, the whole phrase lú-ru-gú meaning 'confronting a man'.

The bottom edge of the rev. of the tablet is preserved, and it is clear that the curse is not complete.

BIBLIOGRAPHY

1928 Gadd, UET 1 no. 299 (copy, edition)
1961 Hallo, BiOr 18 p. 10 Warad-Sin 26 (study)
1965 Sollberger, UET 8 p. 34 no. 38 (study)
1968 Kärki, SKFZ pp. 65–66 Waradsîn 26 (edition)
1976 Woolley and Mallowan, UE 7 p. 228 (provenance)
1980 Kärki, SAKAZ 1 pp. 118–19 Waradsîn 26 (edition)

TEXT

Col. i
1) ^{d}nanna
2) en-sískur
3) an-ki zalag
4) dumu-sag-
5) ^{d}en-líl-lá
6) lugal-a-ni-⸢ir⸣

i 1–6) For the god Nanna, lord of offerings, who lights up heaven (and) earth, first-born son of the god Enlil, his lord,

7) *ku-du-*[*ur*]-⸢*ma*⸣-[*bu*]-*uk*
8) ad-⸢da⸣-kur-mar-dú

i 7–11) Kudu[r]-ma[b]uk, father of the Amorite land, son of Simti-šilḫak, the one who [repaid] a

29.1 Restore sag-e-⟨eš⟩.

9) dumu-*si-im-ti-ši-il-ḫa-ak*
10) lú-šu-gar-⌜é⌝-babbar-r[a-ke$_4$]
11) [bí-in-gi$_4$-a]
Lacuna

favour for the Ebabbar,
Lacuna

Col. ii
1) ù-ma-ni-ta
2) úgu-BI.BI-gub-bu-a
3) mu-na-dím

ii 1-3) ... he fashioned for him a ... according to his victory.

4) [n]am-ti-la-ni-šè
5) ù nam-ti-
6) IR$_{11}$-^{d}EN.ZU dumu-ni
7) lugal-larsa.KI-ma-šè
8) a mu-na-ru

ii 4-8) He dedicated it to him for his own [l]ife and for the life of Warad-Sîn, his son, king of Larsa.

9) ⌜kisal-maḫ⌝ [x x]
Lacuna

ii 9) [He set it up] in the main courtyard of [*Eeškite*] ...
Lacuna

Col. iii
1) šà-íb-ba-bi-a
2) igi-suḫ ù-mu-ni-in-ak-eš
3) mu-pà-da
4) nam-lugal-la-ka-ni
5) kalam-maḫ (sic)
6) nam-mu-ni-íb-gá-gá-ne
Lacuna

iii 1-6) [May the gods ...] look at him with an evil eye in their anger, and cause *no one proclaiming his royal name* to exist in the land.
Lacuna

Col. iv
Lacuna
1′) ⌜URUDU⌝.a[lam]
2′) lú-ru-gál x [x]
3′) mu-na-⌜dím⌝

Lacuna
iv 1′-3′) He fashioned for him a copper st[atue], (depicting him) ... a man.

4′) nam-ti-la-ni-šè
5′) ù nam-ti-
6′) IR$_{11}$-^{d}EN.ZU dumu-ni
7′) lugal-larsa.KI-ma-šè
8′) a mu-na-ru

iv 4′-8′) He dedicated it to him for his own life and for the life of Warad-Sîn, his son, king of Larsa.

9′) lú mu-sar-ra-ba
10′) šu bí-íb-ùr-a
11′) mu-ni bí-íb-sar-re-a

iv 9′-11′) (As for) the one who erases this inscription (and) writes his own inscription ...

8

The name of year 4 of Warad-Sîn commemorates the construction of the main courtyard of the Ebabbar temple in Larsa. This is the only building activity of Warad-Sîn in Larsa commemorated in the king's year names. A fragment of a barrel inscription of Warad-Sîn was found in a room off courtyard 1 of the Ebabbar complex in Larsa. Although the piece is too fragmentary to determine what royal act it commemorated, it probably recorded some construction work in Larsa.

COMMENTARY

The barrel fragment is IM 85794, excavation no. L 78250, from the west corner of room 15 of the courtyard of the Ebabbar temple. It measures 10.4 cm long with a maximum dia. of 7 cm. The inscription was collated by J. Black.

The inscription is restored based on parallels with E4.2.13.21 lines 38–43 and E4.2.14.15 lines 30–31.

Line 9′ finds a parallel in E4.2.13.10 line 42.

BIBLIOGRAPHY

1981 Arnaud, Syria 58 p. 44 no. 2 (study) and p. 83 (copy)

1983 Arnaud in Huot, Larsa et 'Oueili 1978–1981 p. 230 II-2 (study) and p. 253 no. 1 (copy)

TEXT

Lacuna

1′) [...-d]è

2′) [...]-⸢dè⸣

3′) [šà-mu ḫé-bí-in]-túm

4′) [nam-bi-šè ÌR$_{11}$]-⸢^{d}⸣EN.ZU

5′) [x] ⸢é⸣-babbar-da ní-tuk-me-en

6′) [^{d}utu š]u-mu mu-un-dab$_5$-ba

7′) [...] x galga-x-ga-ni-šè

8′) [mu-un-ga]r-re-en

9′) [...]-x ḫa-ma-ḫúl-⸢e⸣

10′) [...]-gá(?)

11′) [... u$_4$-ul-l]í-a-aš

12′) [...]-x-dagal

13′) [...]-du$_{11}$

14′) [...]-ke$_4$

15′) [...]-re

16′) [...] ⸢ki(?)⸣

Lacuna

Lacuna

1′–3′) ... in order to ..., in order to ..., [*verily my heart* was mov]ed.

4′–8′) [On account of this] it was me, [Warad]-Sîn, ... who reverences the Ebabbar, whom [the god Utu], having taken my [h]and, [appo]inted for his ... counselor.

9′–16′) May he rejoice at me. He commanded [me] ... (to) enlarge ... for the [futu]re ...

Lacuna

9

The name of year 5 of Warad-Sîn commemorates two events. The first is the construction of the Ganunmaḫ for the god Nanna at Ur. This deed is commemorated by an inscription recorded on a large number of stamped bricks excavated at Ur by Loftus, Taylor, Hall, and Woolley.

CATALOGUE

Ex.	Museum number	Registration number	Excavation number	Ur provenance	Dimensions (cm)	Lines preserved	cpn
1	BM 90032	1979-12-20,28	–	–	22.0×24.0		
2	BM 90047	1979-12-20,38	–	–	19.0×17.5×8.0	1–10	c
3	BM 90054	1979-12-20,44	–	–	33.5×22.5×8.0	1–15	c
4	BM 90093	1979-12-20,181	–	–	18.0×17.0×8.0	12–15	c
5	BM 90321	1979-12-20,189	–	–	15.0×14.0×7.5	1–6	c

Ex.	Museum number	Registration number	Excavation number	Ur provenance	Dimensions (cm)	Lines preserved	cpn
6	BM 90322	1979-12-20,190	–	–	16.0×11.5×7.5	1-5	c
7	BM 90323	1979-12-20,191	–	–	25.0×20.5×8.0	2-15	c
8	BM 90324	1979-12-20,192	–	–	26.0×25.5×8.0	1-11	c
9	BM 90325	1979-12-20,193	–	–	18.5×19.5×7.5	1-6	c
10	BM 90326	1979-12-20,194	–	–	18.0×16.0×7.5	1-10	c
11	BM 90327	1979-12-20,195	–	–	24.0×16.5×9.0	1-4 (traces), 5-15	c
12	BM 90328	51-1-1,343	–	–	19.0×16.5×8.0	7-15	c
13	BM 90329	51-1-1,341	–	–	23.0×21.0×7.5	1-14	c
14	BM 90331	1979-12-20,196	–	–	21.0×13.0×8.0	1-15	c
15	BM 90332	1979-12-20,197	–	–	30.5×23.0×7.5	1-15	c
16	BM 90333	1979-12-20,198	–	–	19.5×13.0×9.0	2-15	c
17	BM 90334	1979-12-20,199	–	–	17.0×16.0×8.0	4-12	c
18	BM 90335	1979-12-20,200	–	–	23.0×18.5×8.0	1-6	c
19	BM 90343	1979-12-20,206	–	–	22.5×12.5×8.0	1-13	c
20	BM 90351	1979-12-20,209	–	–	19.0×18.0×8.0	7-15	c
21	BM 90394	1979-12-20,228	–	–	16.0×14.5×8.0	13-15	c
22	BM 90723	1979-12-20,325	–	–	18.0×11.0×7.5	9-15	c
23	BM 114276	1919-10-11,4707	–	–	19.0×13.0×6.5	5-15	c
24	CBS 15349	–	U 85	–	33.0×17.0×8.0	–	n
25	IM 109	–	U 255	–	33.0×33.0	–	n
26	BM 137343	1935-1-13,3	U 973	From Trial Trench B, 34, i.e. under wall of Kudur-mabuk dividing Enunmaḫ room 32 from Emurianabak room 5	14.5×10.0×8.5	10-15	c
27	CBS 16550	–	U 2882a	From the arched wall in room 34 of Enunmaḫ	33.5×16.0×8.0	–	n
28	CBS 16476	–	U 2882a	As ex. 27	31.0×31.0×7.5	–	n
29	UM 33-35-179	–	–	–	33.0×33.0×7.5	–	n

COMMENTARY

The master text is ex. 3.

Exs. 12-13 come from Loftus's excavations at Ur. The remainder, exs. 1-22, probably come from the excavations of either Loftus or Taylor. Taylor describes excavating a building at Ur that can be identified on the basis of later excavations with the Ganunmaḫ and describes finding a number of inscribed bricks in this structure. Ex. 23 comes from Hall's excavations and exs. 24-29 from Woolley's.

BIBLIOGRAPHY

1855 Taylor, JRAS p. 265 (provenance)
1861 1 R pl. 2 no. III (exs. 1-22, composite copy)
1872 G. Smith, TSBA 1 p. 43 (translation)
1874 Lenormant, Études accadiennes 2 pp. 346-47
1875 Ménant, Babylone et la Chaldée p. 86 (translation)
1892 Winckler, KB 3/1 pp. 92-93 Kudur-mabuk and Rim-Sin 1 (edition)
1899 Bezold, Cat. 5 p. 2233 (study)
1904 Price, Rim-Sin pp. 6-7 no. I (edition)
1905 Thureau-Dangin, ISA pp. 300-301 Arad-sin a (edition)
1905 King, CT 21 pl. 33 (ex. 1, copy)
1907 Thureau-Dangin, SAK pp. 210-11 Arad-sin a (edition)
1907 King and Hall, EWA pl. facing p. 241 (ex. 3, photo)
1922 BM Guide p. 61 nos. 121-24 (exs. 1-4, study)
1928 Gadd, UET 1 p. xxiv (exs. 27-28, study)
1929 Barton, RISA pp. 318-19 Warad-Sin 1 (edition)
1961 Hallo, BiOr 18 p. 9 Warad-Sin 3 (edition)
1968 Kärki, SKFZ p. 40 Waradsîn 3 (study)
1971 Sollberger and Kupper, IRSA IVB13g (translation)
1980 Kärki, SAKAZ 1 p. 86 Waradsîn 3 (edition)
1981 Walker, CBI no. 45 (exs. 1-23, 26, study)

TEXT

1) ^{d}nanna
2) lugal-a-ni-ir
3) *ku-du-ur-ma-bu-uk*
4) ad-da-kur-mar-dú
5) dumu-*si-im-ti-ši-il-ḫa-ak*

1-2) For the god Nanna, his lord,

3-5) Kudur-mabuk, father of the Amorite land, son of Simti-šilḫak,

6) u$_4$ ^{d}nanna
7) a-ra-zu-ni
8) mu-ši-gin-na-a
9) gá-nun-maḫ-
10) ^{d}nanna-kam
11) nam-ti-la-ni-šè
12) ù nam-ti-
13) IR$_{11}$-^{d}EN.ZU dumu-ni
14) lugal-larsa.KI-ma-šè
15) mu-na-ni-in-dù

6–8) when the god Nanna agreed to his entreaty,

9–15) he built for him there the Ganunmaḫ of the god Nanna, for his own life and for the life of Warad-Sîn, his son, king of Larsa.

10

The construction of the Ganunmaḫ is also recorded in an inscription found on a large number of cones excavated by Woolley at Ur.

CATALOGUE

Ex.	Museum number	Excavation number	Ur provenance	Object	Dimensions (cm)	Lines preserved	cpn
1	–	U 188	From Enunmaḫ, room 7, with broken vases	Cone		–	n
2	McGill Ethnological Collections no. 7	U 212	Enunmaḫ, room 19	Head	10 dia.	1–7, 26–29	c
3	BCM 287 '35A	U 217	Enunmaḫ, room 19, NE corner below rammed mud floor of first brick building (=TTB 19)	Shaft	17.0	1–50	c
4	McGill Ethnological Collections no. 5	U 325	Enunmaḫ '3A' (=34?) =Emurianabak, room 5	Head	11.0 dia.	6–20, 26–48	c
5	–	U 333	Emurianabak, room 2 (=TTB 27)	Head	8.5 dia.	–	n
6	BCM 287 '35C	U 750	Found in well no. 1	Shaft	8.5	7–29	c
7	IM 92760	U 861	Enunmaḫ '34' =Emurianabak room 5/SW wall of Enunmaḫ	Head	16.5 dia.	1–50	c
8	–	U 862	Against SW wall of Enunmaḫ, TTB 34	–	–	–	n
9	Ash 1935,775	U 863	TTB 34	Shaft	12.0	1–50	c
10	BCM 287 '35G	U 864	As ex. 8	Head	9.6	17–25, 54–50	c
11	–	U 865	As ex. 8	Cone	–	–	n
12	McGill Ethnological Collections no. 8	U 866A+866B	As ex. 8	Head	8.5 dia.	1–14, 26–31	c
13	McGill Ethnological Collections no. 9	U 867	As ex. 9	Head	11.8	2–16	c
14	–	U 868	As ex. 9	Shaft	8.0	–	n
15	–	U 869	As ex. 9	Shaft	3.0	–	n
16	–	U 870	As ex. 9	Cone	2.0	–	n
17	–	U 919	Against SW wall of Enunmaḫ	Cone	–	–	n
18	–	U 920	As ex. 17	Cone	–	–	n
19	BM 117140 (1924-9-20,389)	U 1197	From outside the works	Head (5 frgms. joined)	–	1–50	c

Ex.	Museum number	Excavation number	Ur provenance	Object	Dimensions (cm)	Lines preserved	cpn
20	Philadelphia no number	U 2611	From opposite SE angle of Great Court of Nanna, below pavement	Head	15.3 dia.	1–22, 26–39	c
21	Philadelphia no number	U 2611	As ex. 20	Shaft	8.1	1, 3–5, 8–17	c
22	BM 119031 (1927-10-3,26)	U 2614	Opposite SE corner of Great Court of Nanna	Head	8.3 dia. 50	16–25, 40–46, 48,	c
23	BM 119031 (1927-10-3,26)	U 2614	As ex. 22	Shaft	5.7	26–33	c
24	BM 119052 (1927-10-3,48)	U 2679	From Great Court of Nanna	Head	11.4 dia.	1–4, 26–45	c
25	IM 946	U 2794	From Edublalmaḫ	Shaft	13.5	1–50	c
26	IM 92861	U 6329	From 'trench behind Hall's excavations'	Head	6.2 dia.	26–33	c
27	IM 2794	U –	–	Cone	–	–	n
28	IM 3571A	U 7768	From SM site, Trial Trench D	Shaft	11.0	16–32, 38–45	c
29	IM 3571B	U 7768	As ex. 28	Head	8.0×6.2	35–46	c
30	IM 3579	U 7817	From Enunmaḫ, loose in soil, widely separated	Head	12.5 dia.	1–15, 17–20, 26–41	c
31	IM 4072	U 8838	From Trial Trench G	Shaft	13.0	1–18, 33–34, 36–37, 39–42, 44–45, 47–50	c
32	IM 22881	U 16027	Under the Temenos wall chamber	Head	13 dia.	4–25, 27–50	c
33	IM 22881	U 16027	As ex. 32	Shaft	8.0	1–22, 25–50	c
34	IM 16493	U 18227	XNCF 1932, Room 1932/8	Head	15.3 dia.	1–50	c
35	IM 26914	U –	–	Shaft	12.8	6–50	c
36	–	U ya	–	Head	–	–	n
37	–	U ya	–	Shaft	–	–	n
38	IM 92860	U za	–	Head	11.7 dia.	18–25, 39–50	c
39	IM 92860	U za	–	Shaft	4.3	26–31	c
40	IM 92862	U ab	–	Shaft	12.0	6–20	c
41	–	U bb	–	Shaft (2 frgms. joined)	–	–	n
42	McGill Ethnological Collections no. 10	U –	–	Head	10.7 dia.	4–23	c
43	BM 138211 (1935-1-13,360)	U –	–	Head	–	1–50	c
44	BM 138211 (1935-1-13,360)	U –	–	Shaft	–	1–50	c
45	UM 32-40-433	U –	–	Head	16 dia.	19–25, 27–50	c

COMMENTARY

The master text is ex. 7.

BIBLIOGRAPHY

1928 Gadd, UET 1 no. 123 (exs. 1–5, 7, 20–26, composite copy, edition)
1929 Barton, RISA pp. 376–77 Warad-Sin 1 (edition)
1957 Edzard, Sumer 13 p. 177 (exs. 25, 27–35, study)
1961 Hallo, BiOr 18 p. 9 Warad-Sin 11 (study)
1965 Sollberger, UET 8 p. 29 no. 22 (exs. 36–41, study)
1968 Kärki, SKFZ pp. 48–49 Waradsîn 11 (edition)
1974 Woolley, UE 6 p. 93 (exs. 7–16, provenance)
1979 George, Iraq 41 p. 122 nos. 34–36 (exs. 3, 6, 10, study)
1980 Kärki, SAKAZ 1 pp. 97–98 Waradsîn 11 (edition)

TEXT

1) ᵈnanna
2) en an-kù-ge dalla-è
3) dumu-sag-ᵈen-líl-lá
4) lugal-a-ni-ir

1–4) For the god Nanna, lord who beams forth brightly in shining heaven, first-born son of the god Enlil, his lord,

5) *ku-du-ur-ma-bu-uk*
6) ad-da-kur-mar-dú
7) dumu-*si-im-ti-ši-il-ḫa-ak*
8) igi-du$_8$-^{d}en-líl-lá
9) ^{d}nin-líl-da še-ga-àm
10) é-babbar-da ní-tuk
11) ú-a-é-kur-ra
12) sag-ús-é-kiš-nu-gál
13) lú šà-nibru.KI du$_{10}$-du$_{10}$-me-en
14) u$_4$ ^{d}nanna a-ra-zu-mu
15) mu-ši-in-še-ga-àm
16) ḫul-gál-e-ne sag-é-babbar-ra
17) bí-in-sal-eš-a
18) šu-mu-šè bí-in-si-a
19) maš-gán-ŠABRA.KI
20) kar-ra-^{d}utu.KI-ke$_4$
21) larsa.KI-šè ḫé-em-mi-gi$_4$
22) ^{d}nanna lugal-mu
23) za-e-me-en ba-e-ak
24) gá-e a-na-mu-me-en
25) nam-bi-šè
26) ^{d}nanna lugal-mu
27) KA-sa$_6$-sa$_6$-ge-da-gá
28) gá-nun-maḫ
29) é-kù-babbar-kù-GI
30) ùru-èrim-dugud
31) ^{d}EN.ZU-na-ka
32) u$_4$-ul-lí-a-ta
33) ba-dù-a-ba ba-sun
34) nam-ti-mu-šè
35) ù nam-ti-
36) ìr-^{d}EN.ZU dumu-mu
37) lugal-larsa.KI-ma-šè
38) mu-na-dù
39) ki-bi-šè ḫé-em-mi-gi$_4$
40) nì-ak-mu-šè
41) ^{d}nanna lugal-mu
42) ḫa-ma-ḫúl-e
43) nam-tar-nam-ti-la
44) bala-du$_{10}$-ga
45) GIŠ.gu-za suḫuš-gi-na
46) sa$_{12}$-e-eš
47) ḫa-ma-ab-rig$_7$-ge
48) sipa-ki-ág-
49) ^{d}nanna ḫé-me-en
50) u$_4$-mu ḫé-sù-sù-ud

5–13) I, Kudur-mabuk, father of the Amorite land, son of Simti-šilḫak, the one who is attentive to the god Enlil, who finds favour with the goddess Ninlil, who reverences the Ebabbar, provider of the Ekur, constant (attendant) for the Ekišnugal, the one who makes Nippur content,

14–15) when the god Nanna agreed to my entreaty

16–18) (and) delivered into my hands the enemies who had thrown down the top of the Ebabbar temple,
19–21) he (the god Nanna) returned to Larsa Maškan-šāpir and Kār-Šamaš.

22–24) 'Nanna, my lord, it is you who has done it, (as for) myself, what am I?'

25–27) In respect of this, to the god Nanna, my lord, as I prayed fervently

28–38) I built the Ganunmaḫ, the house of silver and gold, the god Suen's storehouse with heavy treasure — it had been built in the past (and) had become dilapidated — for my own life and for the life of Warad-Sîn, my son, king of Larsa.

39) I restored it.
40–42) May the god Nanna, my lord, rejoice at my deed

43–47) (and) grant to me a destiny of life, a good reign, (and) a throne with a secure foundation.

48–49) May I be the shepherd, beloved of the god Nanna.
50) May my days be long.

6.25 ad-⟨da⟩-kur-mar-dú. **13**.25 omits du$_{10}$-du$_{10}$. **15**.6, 19–20 mu-ši-in-še-ga-a. **17**.20 bí-in-sal-eš-⟨a⟩. **37**.3 [lug]al-larsa.KI-ma-⟨šè⟩. **39**.38 ki-bé-⟨šè⟩. **42**.3 ḫa-ma-ḫúl-le. **42**.43 ḫa-ma-ḫúl-l[e].

11

The second part of the name of year 5 of Warad-Sîn deals with the construction of the temple of the goddess Inanna in Zabala. This deed is commemorated in an inscription found on a stone foundation cylinder and tablets.

CATALOGUE

Ex.	Museum number	Photo number	Provenance	Object	Dimensions (cm)	Lines preserved	cpn
1	BM 91085 (82-7-4,1)	–	Said to be from Babylonia, presumably originally from Zabala	Stone foundation cylinder	14.1 high, 4.8 dia.	1–18	c
2	–	–	Presumably originally from Zabala	Stone tablet(?)	–	1–18	n
3	–	OI 12488/12487	As ex. 2	Stone tablet	–	1–18	p

COMMENTARY

The master text is ex. 1.

Ex. 1, a foundation cylinder, was purchased from Spartoli and ex. 2 was in the private collection of S. Mercer; their present whereabouts are unknown. Mercer does not indicate the type of object on which the inscription was incised. Since the rest of the objects published by him (see bibliography) are stone tablets, we may guess that it was a stone tablet as well. Ex. 2 is entered in the score from the copy of Mercer. Ex. 3, a stone tablet, was in the collection of E.S. David. It was offered for sale to the Oriental Institute, which did not purchase it, but did take photos OI 12488/12487 of it, which were examined. It is possible that exs. 2–3 are the same object.

In line 3 of ex. 2 the copyist has indicated the first sign as ìr. In view of the ir_{11} appearing in the other two exemplars of this text, this may be a mistake.

BIBLIOGRAPHY

1887 Winckler, MAOV 1 p. 16 no. 2 (ex. 1, copy)
1892 Winckler, KB 3/1 pp. 94–97 Kudur-mabuk and Rim-Sin 4 (edition)
1899 Ball, Light from the East (London) p. 67 (ex. 1, photo)
1904 Price, Rim-Sin p. 16 no. x (edition)
1905 Thureau-Dangin, ISA pp. 304–305 Arad-sin e (edition)
1907 Thureau-Dangin, SAK pp. 214–15 Arad-sin e (edition)
1915 King, History pl. xii facing p. 152 (ex. 1, photo)
1928 Mercer, JSOR 12 pp. 147–48 and 150 no. 36 (ex. 2, copy, edition)
1929 Barton, RISA pp. 322–23 Warad-Sin 6 (edition)
1961 Hallo, BiOr 18 p. 9 Warad-Sin 5 (study)
1964 Bergmann, ZA 56 p. 7 (study)
1968 Kärki, SKFZ p. 41 Waradsîn 5 (edition)
1971 Sollberger and Kupper, IRSA ivB13d (translation)
1980 Kärki, SAKAZ 1 pp. 87–88 Waradsîn 5 (edition)

TEXT

1) ^{d}inanna-zabala.KI 2) nin-mu-ra	1–2) For the goddess Inanna of Zabala, my lady,
3) IR_{11}-^{d}EN.ZU 4) lugal-larsa.KI-ma	3–4) (I), Warad-Sîn, king of Larsa,
5) nam-ti-mu-šè 6) ù nam-ti- 7) *ku-du-ur-ma-bu-uk* 8) a-a-ugu-gá-ka	5–8) for my life and the life of Kudur-mabuk, the father who engendered me,
9) gi-gun_4-na-kù 10) ki-tuš-nam-ur-sag-gá-ka-ni	9–11) built for her the shining *gigunû*, her residence of valour.

11) mu-na-dù
12) kur-sukud-rá-gin$_7$
13) sag-bi ḫu-mu-ni-in-íl
14) nì-ak-mu-šè
15) ḫa-mu-ḫúl-e
16) nam-ti-u$_4$-su$_{13}$-rá
17) nì-ba-aš
18) ḫa-ma-an-ba-e

12–13) I raised its head there like a lofty mountain.
14–18) May she rejoice at my deed (and) grant to me as a gift a long life-span.

12

The construction of the temple of Inanna in Zabala by Warad-Sîn is also commemorated in an inscription found on two bronze canephores.

CATALOGUE

Ex.	Museum number	Registration number	Provenance	Dimensions (cm)	Lines preserved	cpn
1	BM 91144	1890-5-10,1	Said to come from Tello, presumably originally from Zabala	27.7 high, 5.3 wide at arms, 4 wide at waist	1–29	c
2	MFAB 37.1151	–	Zabala(?)	26 high	1–29	c

COMMENTARY

The master text is ex. 1, which was purchased from J. Shemtob. Ex. 2 was purchased from a New York dealer in 1937 by the Otis Norcross fund.

BIBLIOGRAPHY

1891 Evetts, PSBA 13 pp. 156–59 (ex. 1, photo, copy, edition)
1904 Price, Rim-Sin pp. 11–12 no. VI (edition)
1905 Thureau-Dangin, ISA pp. 306–307 Arad-sin f (edition)
1905 King, CT 21 pls. 31–32 (ex. 1, copy)
1907 Thureau-Dangin, SAK pp. 214–15 Arad-sin f (edition)
1922 BM Guide p. 87 no. 89 (ex. 1, photo, study)
1929 Barton, RISA pp. 322–23 Warad-Sin 7 (edition)
1961 Hallo, BiOr 18 p. 9 Warad-Sin 6 (study)
1962 Terrace, The Art of the Ancient Near East in Boston no. 11 (ex. 2, photo, study)
1968 Kärki, SKFZ pp. 41–42 Waradsîn 6 (edition)
1980 Kärki, SAKAZ 1 pp. 88–89 Waradsîn 6 (edition)

TEXT

1) ^{d}inanna-zabala.KI
2) dumu-munus-^{d}EN.ZU-na
3) nin-mu-ra
4) IR$_{11}$-^{d}EN.ZU
5) lugal-larsa.KI-me-en
6) nam-ti-mu-šè
7) ù nam-ti-
8) *ku-du-ur-ma-bu-uk*

1–3) For the goddess Inanna of Zabala, daughter of the god Suen, my lady,
4–5) I, Warad-Sîn, king of Larsa,
6–9) for my life and for the life of Kudur-mabuk, the father who engendered me –

16.3 -sù-rá.

9) a-a-ugu-gá-šè
10) gi-gun$_4$ ki-kù
11) é-sag-í[l]
12) ki-tuš-nam-ur-sag-gá-ka-ni
13) ⌜lugal⌝ ŠU.IGI.DU-gá-ke$_4$
14) dù-ù-dè
15) nu-un-še-ga
16) gá-ra sag-ki-UD.UD-ga-ni-ta
17) gibil-gibil-bi
18) ma-an-du$_{11}$-ga
19) gi-gun$_4$ ki-kù mu-dù
20) kur-sukud-rá-gin$_7$
21) su-lim-ma ši-bí-in-íl
22) u$_6$-di-kalam-ma-ka
23) ḫé-bí-gub
24) KA-sa$_6$-sa$_6$-ge-da-gá
25) igi-zi ḫé-en$_6$-ši-bar
26) bala gù-téš-sì-ke
27) mu-šà-du$_{10}$-du$_{10}$-ga
28) sa$_{12}$-e-eš
29) ḫu-mu-ni-rig$_7$

10–15) (the goddess Inanna), having favoured none of my royal ancestors to build her *gigunû*, a shining place, a house with a rais[ed] head, her residence of valour,

16–18) (but) with a shining face having commanded its renovation to me

19) I built (her) *gigunû*, a shining place.
20–21) Like a lofty mountain I made it rise up in awe-inspiring radiance.
22–23) I erected it there to the wonder of the nation.
24–25) As I fervently pray (to her) may she look steadfastly at me
26–29) (and) grant me a peaceful reign and year(s) of happiness.

13

The name of year 6 of Warad-Sîn commemorates the introduction of thrones and daises into the temples of the gods Nanna, Ningal, and Utu. An inscription dealing with Kudur-mabuk's construction of the throne of the god Nanna of Ur for his son Warad-Sîn, known from two school copies on tablets excavated at Ur, is to be correlated to this year name. The mention in lines 7–9 of the same text of the god Nanna's receiving the 'true decision' from the god Enlil in Nippur probably alludes to Warad-Sîn's gaining control over the city of Nippur at this time, a deed commemorated in a variant of the year 6, recording the introduction of fourteen statues into Nippur (see M. Stol, Studies in Old Babylonian History, p. 15).

CATALOGUE

Ex.	Museum number	Excavation number	Ur provenance	Dimensions (cm)	Lines preserved	cpn
1	IM 85469	U 7743	From no. 7, Quiet Street in 'burnt level over the upper floor of rooms 5–6'	13.4 × 8.5 × 2.5	1–20, 22–114	c
2	IM 85470	U 16835	From the 'Isin-Larsa' school house = no. 1 Broad Street	8.0 × 4.7	1–47	c

COMMENTARY

The master text is ex. 1, which is followed except in lines 21 and 46–47, where ex. 2 has the more complete version. The translation follows ex. 1 except where noted.

The description of the throne of Nanna in lines 59–82 may be compared with depictions of thrones found in the art of ancient Mesopotamia.

Lines 68–71 refer to a pair of *lamassu* figures

standing at the side of the throne to protect it. Lines 76–77 probably refer to a calf head mounted at the back of the throne pointing to the rear. Lines 78–79 probably refer to four bull heads mounted at the four corners of the seat of the throne.

In line 12, ex. 2 has a phonetic writing šu-de for šùd. Ex. 1 has a prefixed phonetic complement šu.

In line 29 the translation 'snare' follows ex. 2 GIŠ.búr.

In line 30 the translation follows ex. 2.

In line 32 we understand the phrase ki-tuš-NUN to be in the locative — read ki-tuš-nuna.

In line 41, the translation follows ex. 2, which has un 'nation' instead of UD in ex. 1.

In line 71 Sollberger reads ḫé-bí-gin-n[é]. The regular meaning of gin, *ḫamṭu* of DU 'to go', does not seem to fit this passage. We have read the verb ḫé-bí-gub-x 'I set up there.'

Line 72 has a phonetic writing for šùd.

In line 77 the locative infix is rendered -bi(PI).

For nir-nir in line 81 cf. Ur$_5$-ra = *ḫubullu* V 308: giš.nir.ra = *iṣ ni-ri*, 'yoke, cross-piece'.

In line 80 giš-gána$^{a\text{-}núm}$ corresponds to Akkadian *kiškanûm*, a kind of wood used to make chairs.

In line 90 the sign at the end of the line is unclear.

BIBLIOGRAPHY

1928 Gadd, UET 1 no. 300 (ex. 1, copy, edition)
1961 Hallo, BiOr 18 p. 10 Warad-Sin 28 (study)
1965 Sollberger, UET 8 p. 34 no. 39 (ex. 2, study)
1968 Kärki, SKFZ pp. 67–71 Waradsîn 28 (edition)
1980 Kärki, SAKAZ 1 pp. 122–26 Waradsîn 28 (edition)

TEXT

1) ^{d}nanna en-gal
2) u$_4$ an-kù-ge si
3) men-nun-na sag-íl
4) dingir-zi u$_4$ ge$_6$-bi ḫé-ḫé
5) iti ge-en-ge-en
6) mu silim-ma
7) šà-é-kur-ra-ke$_4$ sun$_5$-na
8) eš-bar-zi šu-ti
9) ki-a-a-ugu-na-ke$_4$
10) dumu-ki-ág-^{d}nin-líl-lá
11) ^{d}aš-ím-babbar-re
12) ^{šu}šùd a-ra-zu giš-tuk
13) lugal-a-ni-ir
14) ^{m}*ku-du-ur-ma-bu-uk*
15) ad-da-kur-mar-dú
16) dumu-*si-im-ti-ši-il-ḫa-ak*
17) lú šu-gar-é-bábbar-ra-ke$_4$
18) bí-in-gi$_4$-a
19) ^{d}utu lugal-a-ni-ir
20) šu bí-in-tag-ga-àm
21) un-bir-re-a
22) gú-bi kár-kár-ra
23) [é]ren-sùḫ-sùḫ-a-bi
24) si bí-in-si-sá
25) gù-ma-da-na
26) téš-bi íb-ta-sì-ga
27) sag-du ḫul-du-bi

1–6) For the god Nanna, great lord, light which fills shining heaven, who holds the princely crown aloft, reliable god, who *alternates* days and nights, who establishes the months, who completes the year.

7–9) In the Ekur he humbly receives the true decisions from the father who engendered him (Enlil) —

10) son beloved of the goddess Ninlil,

11–13) (for) the god Ašimbabbar, who listens to prayers and entreaties, his lord,

14–35) (I), Kudur-mabuk, father of the Amorite land, son of Simti-šilḫak, the one who repaid a favour for the Ebabbar temple (and) adorned it for the god Utu, his lord, who gathered the scattered people (and) put in order their disorganized troops, who made his land peaceful, who smote the head of its foes, snare of his land, who smashed all the enemies, who made the youth, god Utu, supreme judge of heaven and earth, reside contently (*in*) his princely residence, in Larsa, the *place* of regular offerings.

2.2 an-kù-ge$_4$. **3**.1–2 Both exs. have men- not men$_4$-. **3**.1 KA-íl for sag-íl. **3**.2 -nun-e. **4**.2 ḫe-ḫe. **7**.2 šà-é-kur-ra-⟨ke$_4$⟩ sun$_5$-né. **9**.2 ki-a-a-ugu-⟨na⟩-ke$_4$. **11**.2 ^{d}aš-ím-babbar-⟨re⟩. **12**.2 šu-de a-ra-zu-e. **14**.2 ⟨^{m}⟩*ku-du-ur-ma-bu-úk*. **17**.2 é-babbar-ra-ke$_4$. **22**.2 gar-gar-ra. **23**.2 [é]ren-sùḫ-sùḫ-ga-bi. **24**.2 si bí-in-si-sá-e. **26**.2 íb-ta-an-sì-ga-àm.

28) tibir$_x$(TAG×NE)-ra bí-ra
29) giš-bur-ma-da-na
30) gú-érim-gál-la-àm
31) bí-in-ḫaš-àm
32) ki-tuš-NUN šul ^{d}utu
33) di-ku$_5$-maḫ-an-ki
34) larsa.KI-ma nì-sá-du$_{11}$-gin-na-ka
35) su-du$_{10}$ bí-in-tuš-àm
36) ^{m}*ku-du-ur-ma-bu-uk* sipa-sun$_5$-na
37) èš é-bábbar-ra-šè
38) nam-šita$_x$(REC 316)-a-aš gub-ba-me-en

36–38) I, Kudur-mabuk, humble shepherd, who stands in supplication for the shrine Ebabbar,

39) u$_4$ an-né ^{d}en-líl-le
40) ^{d}en-ki ^{d}nin-maḫ-bi
41) GIŠ.gidru-zi un$_5$ laḫ$_4$-laḫ$_4$ ḫé-du$_7$
42) bala-me-da-rí
43) me-bi nu-kúr-ru-dè
44) du$_{11}$-ga-maḫ-^{d}nanna ^{d}utu-ta
45) nam-si-sá-a-mu-šè
46) ma-ni-in-sum-mu-uš(*)-àm

39–46) when the gods An, Enlil, Enki, and Ninmaḫ had given to me, on account of my order by the supreme decree of the gods Nanna and Utu, the true sceptre suitable to lead the people (and) a reign with eternal *me*s, whose *me*s cannot be altered,

47) nam-bi-šè KA-sa$_6$-sa$_6$-ge-en-mu-dè

47) on account of this, as I made an ardent prayer ...

48) x ⸢NI⸣ [...]
49) [...]
50) x x [...]
51) igi-a x [...]
52) mul-k[ù ...]
53) su-lim [...]
54) GIŠ.g[u-za ...]
55) ba-x [...]
56) šà-[...]
57) ⸢ra⸣ [...]
58) x [...]

48–58) ..., shining star(s) ... awe-inspiring radiance ... a th[rone] ...

59) GIŠ.gu-⸢za-a⸣-b[i ...]
60) kù-GI-ḫ[u]š-a [gar-ra]

59–60) that throne [was inlaid] with red gold,

61) u$_4$-ti-le-m[u ...]
62) kin-gá re-eš x [...]
63) alam-^{d}nanna me-d[ím-bi]
64) zi-da ak-da-x [...]
65) x [...]
66) x x x x [...]
67) gal-le-eš x [...]

61–67) [...] the days which I live ... a work ... [...] a statue of the god Nanna [whose] fo[rm] was fashioned correctly ..., [...], ... grandly I ...

68) 2-^{d}lamma di na[m-...]
69) i$_5$-gar-sa$_6$-sa$_6$-g[e-a-mu-šè]
70) u$_4$-šú-uš gál-la nu-UŠ x [...]
71) zà-zà-bé ḫé-bí-gub-x

68–71) A pair of protective genii ... [giving] good omens [...], being there daily ... [...] I *set up* on either side of it.

72) alam šu-de-a-mu-šè
73) šu-íl-lá-gibil-lá
74) a-rá-zu-gin$_7$ ma-ab-lá te-GIŠ.gu-za-a-ba
75) ḫé-bí-ge-en-ge-en

72–75) I *fixed* (them) there at the perimeter of that throne (area with their hands) stretched out towards the statue of me praying, as if (making) new *šu-ila* prayers and entreaties.

76) amar-an-na kìlib-ba kin-galam-ma-ka

76–77) I sought out well-chosen *me*s for the calf

28.2 tibir$_x$(TAG×ŠE) ⸢bí⸣-ra-a. **29**.2 GIŠ.búr-ma-da-⟨na⟩. **30**.1 gú-BI.RU-gál-la-àm. **30**.2 gú-érim-gál-x-la. **33**.2 di-ku$_5$-maḫ-^{d}utu. **34**.2 lársa.KI-ma. **36**.2 ⟨^{m}⟩*ku-du-⸢ur⸣-ma-bu-úk*. **37**.2 é-babbar-ra-šè. **38**.2 na[m]-šita$_x$(REC 316)-aš. **41**.2 GIŠ.gidru-zi un laḫ$_5$-laḫ$_5$-e-dè. **45**.2 ⸢nam-si⸣-sá-⟨a⟩-mu-šè. **46**.2 -sum-mu-ba-àm.

77) me zà-zà-bé ḫé-bì-kin-kin
78) gu$_4$-áb-ba límmu-bi
79) ḫé-bì-ge-en-ge-en
80) dúr(*)-gal-bi giš-gána(*)$^{a-núm}$-ta
81) nir-nir-ra pirig máš šub-àm
82) kù-luḫ-ḫa gar-ra
83) zi-nam-ti-la-⌜mu⌝-šè
84) ù nam-ti-IR$_{11}$-⌜^{d}⌝[EN.ZU]
85) dumu-mu mu-ú-numun-x-[...]
86) mu-da-rí dumu-x [...]
87) ú-⟨a⟩-uri$_5$.KI-ma é-[babbar-du ní-tuk]
88) [lugal]-larsa.KI-ma a mu-[na-r]u
89) ⌜u$_4$⌝-a u$_4$-da eger-[bi-š]è
90) [lú] GIŠ.gu-za-[ba á-nì-ḫul-dí]m-ma
91) [i]b-ši-⟨ág⟩-gá-àm
92) [nì]-dím-ma-mu íb-zi-re-a
93) [é]-nì-GA(*)-ra i-ni-in-ku$_4$-ku$_4$-a
94) [x-t]i-si-sá-ka íb-zi-re-ba
95) [GIŠ].gu-za-a-bi-šè
96) [í]b-ta-kúr-ru-ú-a
97) nisag$_x$(LAK 159)-á-ki-te x-[... l]a
98) ki-nag-abzu-a-šè
99) u$_4$-tu-ud-bi-da è-a
100) u$_4$ NA$_4$.X GIŠ.gu-za-a-ba
101) ù-mu-dím
102) ^{d}nanna lugal-la-ni
103) èn-bi-eš gá-gá-àm
104) a-ba-an(*)-ge
105) á-nì-ḫul-da-ni-ta
106) íb-ta-kúr-ru-a
107) dingir-kúr-ra ù lugal-e
108) gaba-ri-ni-ta
109) nì-ba ba-ab-sum-mu-a
110) mu-sar-ra-a-ba
111) šu bí-íb-⟨ùr⟩-ra-ge
112) mu-ni íb-sar-re-dè
113) ⌜áš⌝-bal-lá-ba-ke$_4$-⟨eš⟩
114) [l]ú-kúr šu ba-an-zi-zi

of heaven, that was in its entirety a masterpiece.
78–79) I fixed there four breed bulls.

80–82) Its great *seat* was of *kiškanûm* wood. Its crosspieces, (depicting) a lion seizing a kid, were inlaid with refined silver.
83–88) I dedicated it to him for my life and for the life of Warad-[Sîn], my son, offspring of ..., eternal name, son of ..., provider of Ur, [who reverences] the E[babbar, king] of Larsa.

89–96) (As for) [the one] who in the future [gives or]ders [to do ev]il against that throne, has my [ha]ndiwork destroyed, has it brought into a store[house], (or) having ... destroyed its well-ordered ..., having removed for that throne ...,

97–99) first fruit offerings of the *Akitu* (festival) to the drink offering place of the apsû coming forth from its day of birth ...
100–104) after having affixed ... stones on that throne, (and) having returned it (to) the god Nanna, his lord, ...,

105–114) removes it on account of his malevolence, (and) gives it as a gift to another deity or a king who is his peer, (or) [era]ses its inscription, (or) ⟨because⟩ of this curse incites [an]other to write his inscription on it ...

14

This inscription, a copy on a clay tablet, has a titulary similar in many aspects to that found in E4.2.13.17 and 27 (see discussion in introduction to Warad-Sîn). However, it has none of the epithets alluding to the year names of years 7–12, and thus probably pre-dates year 7. It deals with the fashioning by Warad-Sîn of seven 'river statues' for the god Nanna in order to provide beer and wine for festival offerings.

80.1 éš-gal-bi. **80.1** kár. **93.1** [é]-ní-U.GA-ra. **104.1** a-ba-BE-ge.

COMMENTARY

The inscription is found on a clay tablet, IM 85471, U 7732, a school copy from no. 7 Quiet Street, rooms 5–6. Part of the top of col. ii is missing; the tablet measures 12×8 cm. The inscription was collated.

The description in the inscription of seven statues holding copper vessels with holes in them recalls the façade of the Karaindaš temple in Uruk, which consists of various figures holding flowing vases.

Lines 10–17 of this inscription are identical to col. i lines 6′–13′ of E4.2.13.17 and lines 6–13 of E4.2.13.27.

The more complete readings of lines 1–7 are a result of collation.

For the URUDU.nì-dúr-bùr = Akkadian *namzītum*, found in lines 22 and 11′, see A. Salonen, Hausgeräte 2 p. 189. It appears to be a vat with holes in its bottom that was used to make beer. See also R. Ellis in Levine and Young (eds.), Mountains and Lowlands pp. 29–34 and M.-H. Gates, BASOR 270 (1988) pp. 66–68.

BIBLIOGRAPHY

1928 Gadd, UET 1 no. 301 (copy, edition)
1961 Hallo, BiOr 18 p. 10 Warad-Sin 27 (study)
1968 Kärki, SKFZ pp. 66–67 Waradsîn 27 (edition)
1976 Woolley and Mallowan, UE 7 p. 228 (provenance)
1980 Kärki, SAKAZ 1 pp. 120–21 Waradsîn 27 (edition)
1983 Kärki, SAKAZ 2 p. 48 (study)

TEXT

1) [^{d}]nann[a]
2) [an-kù-t]a pa è-⌜a⌝
3) me[n]-x x-⌜šè⌝ túm-ma
4) šul ḫi-li
5) ⌜zi⌝-šà(*)-gál tu
6) mu-ni a-re-eš kal
7) ⌜DUMU⌝.NÍTA šà-zi-ta è-a
8) ki-ág-é-kur-ra
9) lugal-a-ni-ir
10) ⌜IR$_{11}$⌝-^{d}EN.ZU
11) nun še-ga-nibru.KI
12) ú-a-uri$_5$.KI-ma
13) sag-èn-tar-gìr-su.KI-
14) ki-lagaš.KI-[a]
15) é-babbar-d[a ní-te-g]e$_{26}$
16) l[ugal-l]arsa.⌜KI⌝-ma
17) lugal-ki-en-gi-ki-uri-ke$_4$
18) u$_4$ ^{d}nanna lugal-a-né
19) šùd a-ra-zu-ni
20) in-ši-in-še-ga
21) 7 URUDU.alam-i$_7$-da
22) URUDU.nì-dúr-bùr-ḫé-gál-la
23) šu-bi-a
24) mu-un-né-gál
25) u$_4$-ezen-sískur-ra-ka
26) kaš geštin ulušin

Lacuna (c. 9 lines)

1′) l[ú á-nì-ḫul-dím-ma]
2′) í[b-ši-ág-ge$_{26}$-a]
3′) n[ì-dím-ma-mu]
4′) [íb-zi-re-a]

1–9) For the [god] Nann[a], who beams forth [fr]om [shining heaven], the one suitable for the ... crown, charming youth, who gives birth to the living, whose name is precious enough to praise, first-born son come forth from the true womb, beloved of the Ekur, his lord,

10–17) Warad-Sîn, prince, favourite of Nippur, provider of Ur, who looks after Girsu (and) the land of Lagaš, who [reverences] the Ebabbar, ki[ng of L]arsa, king of the land of Sumer and Akkad,

18–20) when the god Nanna, his lord, was favourable to his prayers and entreaties,

21–24) he placed seven copper river statues with copper vats of abundance in their hands.

25–26) On the day of the offering festival, beer, wine, and emmer beer ...

Lacuna (c. 9 lines)

1′–11′) (As for) the on[e] who g[ives orders to do evil against it, has my] ha[ndiwork destroyed, brings it into a storehouse] (or) because of this curse incites another to do so, neglects to bring

---

5 Tablet has: nun(?).

5′) [é-nì-GA-ra]
6′) i-ni-í[b-ku$_4$-ku$_4$-a]
7′) áš-bal-a-ba-ke$_4$-eš
8′) lú-kúr
9′) šu ba-an-zi-zi-a
10′) u$_4$-ezen-sískur-ra-ka
11′) URUDU.nì-dúr-bùr-bi è-dè íb-TAG$_4$.TAG$_4$-a
12′) lú-ba
13′) ^{d}en-líl
14′) ^{d}EN.ZU
15′) ^{d}en-ki
16′) ^{d}nin-maḫ-bi
17′) kìlib-dingir-gal-gal-e-ne
18′) ki-nam-tar-re-da
19′) inim-ma-ni un-kíd-da
20′) e-ne ù numun-a-ni
21′) šà-kalam-ma-ka
22′) nam-mu-ni-íb-gá-gá-e-ne
23′) eš

out the copper vats on the day of the offering festival,

12′–23′) may the gods Enlil, Sîn, Enki, Ninmaḫ, and all the great gods, slander that man in the place where destinies are determined, and cause him and his seed not to remain in the nation.

15

The name of year 7 of Warad-Sîn commemorates the installation of the *en* priestess of Nanna, En-ane-du. Fragments of a large stone tablet, smashed in antiquity, were excavated by Woolley at Ur. The inscription on the tablet appears to deal with events involved with the installation of En-ane-du.

COMMENTARY

The fragments bear the museum no. CBS 16205. They were found in room C. 7, the great courtyard in the Ningal temple section of the Gipar-ku at Ur. The various excavated stone bits were assembled and mounted in a plaster reconstruction now in Philadelphia. Unfortunately, because of the broken nature of the text, the placement of a number of pieces is uncertain. Although described by Woolley as fragments of a stele, the configuration of the reconstruction in Philadelphia resembles more that of a stone tablet than a stele, since the text is read by turning over the stone in the manner of a tablet. Since the text mentions at the end the setting up of a statue, possibly one of the *en* priestess herself, this tablet may be the one which accompanied the statue set up in the Gipar-ku.

In the copy of the text found in UET 1 no. 137 Gadd attempted an arrangement of most of the pieces. Unfortunately, Gadd's copy does not indicate what pieces are found on the obv., rev., or edges of the tablet, a fact which led to an erroneous order of the fragments in Kärki's edition. The edition offered here is based on a collation of the reconstruction now in Philadelphia. Unfortunately, some of the pieces copied by Gadd were not incorporated into that reconstruction, and their present whereabouts are not known.

The reconstruction of the text offered here differs from the published copy and Philadelphia reconstruction by the join of the fragment which appears in the copy as rev. ii 30, [...]-du$_7$, to rev. i 36, en-an-e-[...], giving en-an-e-du$_7$. This necessitates a shift of what appears as cols. iii–v in the copy to cols. ii–iv, and changes their placement with respect to the fragments copied at the bottom of UET 1 pl. XXVIII. It results in a reconstruction of a tablet containing five cols. per side instead of six.

Rather than attempting to render a connected text reflecting the copy in UET 1 no. 137, we have given each separate fragment a number and edited them in order of their probable position in the original monument.

While the broken nature of the text prevents us from gaining a complete understanding of it, its general content is clear. The inscription as a whole bears striking similarities to a cylinder of Nabonidus describing the installation of his daughter as *en* priestess of the god Nanna. In the En-ane-du text it appears that the priestess was chosen by the god Nanna. The text goes on to describe various rebuildings of some structure, almost certainly the gipar, by various *en* priestesses who preceded En-ane-du. The text then records the construction of that structure for En-ane-du herself, undoubtedly in preparation for her installation in it.

Col. iii of our text refers to various fields which formerly were barren. Undoubtedly, with the installation of the new *en* priestess fertility was returned to the land.

The obv. of col. v continues with a description of a statue and recounts the regular offerings established for it. A letter of Kudur-mabuk found at Ur refers to the fashioning of a statue of an *en* priestess. This, as Renger (ZA 58 [1967] p. 120 n. 51) suggests, may have been made to accompany the installation of Enanedu. The rev. of col. v relates curses against the one who might be tempted to remove the jewels from the statue or otherwise deface it.

Frgm. 1 line 3 is restored from E4.2.13.14 line 6.

BIBLIOGRAPHY

1928 Gadd, UET 1 no. 137 (copy, edition)
1931 Landsberger, OLZ 34 129 and 135–36 (study)
1951 Gadd, Iraq 13 p. 29 (study)
1957 Hallo, Royal Titles p. 110 (study)
1961 Hallo, BiOr 18 p. 10 Warad-Sin 19 (study)
1968 Kärki, SKFZ pp. 56–63 Waradsîn 19 (edition)
1976 Woolley and Mallowan, UE 7 p. 223 (provenance)
1980 Kärki, SAKAZ 1 pp. 106–17 Waradsîn 19 (edition)
1986 Charpin, Le clergé d'Ur pp. 218–19 (study)

TEXT

Frgm. 1 (On edge)
1) [u$_4$ ^{d}nan]na
2) [...-m]aḫ
3) [mu-ni a-re-eš] kal

Frgm. 1) [When the god Nan]na, [su]preme [..., whose word is] worthy [of praise] ...

Col. i Obverse
Lacuna (of about 30 lines)
Frgm. 2
1′) [x x x x] x x x [x]
2′) [x] x x [...] galam-ma-mu [x]
Lower edge col. i
3′) [ma]-a[n]-sum-mu-[uš]
4′) [...]
5′) [...]
6′) [...]
7′) [... s]i-šè
8′) [...].KI
9′) [...]
10′) [...]
11′) [...]
12′) [...]

Frgm. 2) ... they gave [to me] my artful ..., ...

Col. i Reverse
Lacuna (c. 10 lines)
Frgm. 3
1′) [...] x
2′) [...] x
3′) [...]-na
4′) [šà-g]e-pà-da
5′) [^{d}]nanna-ke$_4$
6′) [...] agrun-kù
7′) [...]-ba-ni

Frgm. 3) ..., chosen by the [heart] of the god Nanna, [...] the shining room, his/her [...], I, who am pleasing to [the goddess Ninga]l, who [perfectly executes the *me*s and ri]tes for [Ekišn]ugal, ...

8′) [^{d}nin-ga]l-da še-ga
9′) [me gi]š-ḫur
10′) [é-kiš-n]u-gál-šè
11′) [šu-du$_7$-du$_7$]-me-en
12′) [...] x si-ga
13′) [...]-šè
14′) [...] x
Lacuna
Frgm. 4
1′) [iti]-⸢1-a-kam⸣ ḫ[u-mu-gar]
2′) en-an-e-du$_7$
3′) z[i]-nam-ti-la en-n[a]
4′) u$_4$-[s]ù-rá-šè x [...]
5′) ugu-nì-[ba]
6′) diri-u$_4$-[bi-ta-šè]
7′) ^{d}[...]
8′) KA-sa$_6$-s[a$_6$-ge-da-gá]
9′) é-kiš-[nu-gál-šè]

Frgm. 4) ... I e[stablished as regular offerings] for each [mon]th. I, En-ane-du, (for my) life ... as far as the distant future, more than ..., surpassing what [came before], the god ..., [as I made a] pra[yer] (for) Ekiš[nugal] ...,

Col. ii (On edge)
Frgm. 5
1) IM [...]
2) é-bi [...]
3) ḫu-mu-[...]
4) [...]
5) ⸢é⸣-ki-[ág]-
6) [...]
7) ⸢é⸣ èš [...]
8) [...]-bi [...]
Lacuna

Frgm. 5) ... that house ..., ..., house bel[oved of ...], house, shrine ..., its [...]

Frgm. 6 Col. ii (Obverse)
1′) [en]-an-na-[túm-ma]
2′) [dumu-^{d}]*iš-me*-⸢^{d}⸣[*da-gan*]
3′) [...] x [...]

Frgm. 6) [En]-ana-[tuma, daughter of] Išme-[Dagān] ..., (restored it).

Frgm. 7 (Lower edge col. ii)
Lacuna (4 lines)
1′) en-[...]
2′) en-gal x [...]
3′) ki-bi-šè x [...]
4′) é ḫé-x-[...]
Lacuna (2 lines)

Frgm. 7) En-[...], great *en* priestess [...], res[tored it]. The house ...

Col. ii (Reverse)
Frgm. 8
1) ^{d}*su-mu-èl*
2) ad-da-en-šà-ki-ág-^{d}nanna
3) ⸢é-babbar-ra bí⸣-[...]
4) [é]-babbar-ra-⸢šè⸣ [...]
Lacuna

Frgm. 8) Sūmû-El, father of En-šakiag-nanna, [...] in Ebabbar. For [E]babbar [...]

Frgm. 9
1′) rig$_7$-[ge-a]
2′) nun-nì-ge-[na]
3′) šà-še-ga-^{d}[...]
4′) dumu-*ku-du-u*[*r-ma-bu-uk*]
5′) ad-da-*e*-[*mu-ut-ba-la*]
6′) šeš-^{d}IR$_{11}$-[^{d}EN.ZU]

Frgm. 9) [...] grant[ed ...], the prince of justice, who pleases the heart of the god/goddess [...], son of Kudu[r-mabuk] father of E[mutbal]a, brother of Warad-[Sîn], king of Lar[sa], beside ..., the house ..., the work ..., everythi[ng ...] When [...], the wo[rd ...], the cr[own] ...

7′) lugal-lar[sa.KI-ma]
8′) da-[...]
9′) é-[...]
10′) kin [...]
11′) nì-na[m ...]
12′) u$_4$ [...]
13′) K[A ...]
14′) me[n ...]
15′) x [...]
Lacuna
Frgm. 10
1′) [šu]-luḫ x x
2′) [si-s]á-sá-e-dè
3′) [á gá-a-a]r mu-un-ág-en
4′) [...] TUR.TUR
5′) [kì]ri-šu-gál-la-mu
6′) [mu-ši]-i[n]-še-ga-a
7′) [...]-bi [...]
8′) [...]
Lacuna

Frgm. 10) ... ordered [m]e to put in ord[er] the [lus]tration rites, ..., the *small* ..., which was favourable to my [p]rayer, ...

Col. iii (Obverse)
Lacuna
Frgm. 11
1′) [*ku-d*]*u-ur-ma-*[*bu-uk*]
2′) [a]d-da-m[u]
3′) [(x)] IR$_{11}$-^{d}EN.ZU
4′) [šeš-ta]m-ma-mu
5′) [x x] ma-ar-ta-aš
6′) [ki]-tuš-mu
7′) x-ba-bi ḫé-bí-gar
8′) [m]u-mu gi$_{16}$-sa-aš
9′) [k]a-ka ḫé-em-mi-gál
10′) [nì-ak]-ak-da-mu-uš
11′) [^{d}nann]a lugal-mu
12′) [^{d}nin-gal n]in-mu
13′) [ḫa-ma-ši-ḫúl-e]š-àm
14′) [...]-na
Lacuna

Frgm. 11) [Kud]ur-ma[buk], m[y] f[ather], Warad-Sîn, my [tw]in [brother], ... I established my [res]idence there ... I established my [fame] forever there as treasure in the [mo]uths (of the people). May it be [the god Nann]a, my lord, and [the goddess Ningal], my [l]ady, who [rejoice at me] for my (good) [de]eds.

Col. iii (Reverse)
Lacuna
Frgm. 12
1′) [...]
2′) x [...]
3′) an-[ta-s]ur-ra.KI
4′) mu [ḫ]é-em-mi-s[a$_4$]
5′) a-š[à] a-gar-sun-na
6′) u$_4$-[ul-l]a-ta šub-ba
7′) m[áš-z]i ba-ra-gál-la
8′) [en-a]n-e-du$_7$
9′) [...] x [...] x
10′) [n]am-kù-babb[ar ...]
11′) [...] ⸢gal⸣ [...]
12′) [...]
Lacuna

Frgm. 12) '... An[tas]ura' I named it. (As for) the fiel[d] of the old tract which l[on]g ago had fallen (into disarray) and did not yield a [relia]ble in[come], (I), [En-a]ne-du, ..., the brightness, ...

Frgm. 13 (Top edge, end of col. iii)
Lacuna
1′) ḫé-e[m-mi-...]
2′) gána-A[N ...] x x [...]
3′) [...] x-ma KI
4′) [...] a-ru-a
5′) ^{d}nin-gal-ke$_{4}$
6′) a-šà a-gàr-dag[al-la]
7′) a nu-mu-un-d[é-a]
8′) ⌜máš-zi⌝ x x x [...]
9′) [ḫ]é-[...]
10′) [...]

Frgm. 13) ... I ...-ed there. The field ..., ... votive gift of the goddess Ningal, the field of the bi[g] tract, which had not been irriga[ted] and which [did not *yield*] a reliable income, I ...

Col. iv (Obverse)
Frgm. 14
Lacuna
1′) [...]
2′) [...]-šè
3′) x [...]-mu
4′) su-^{d}[nanna]-lugal-gá
5′) ù ^{d}nin-g[al n]in-gá
6′) ì-li-gin$_{7}$ ḫ[a-ba]-du$_{10}$
7′) mu-sù-rá
8′) nam-ti-šà-⌜du$_{10}$⌝-ga
9′) nì-ba-aš ḫa-ma-ba-e-ne
10′) uri$_{5}$.KI-ma
11′) uru-nam-en-na-mu
12′) nì-sa$_{6}$-ga-mu ḫa-ba-[...]
13′) u$_{4}$ ^{d}nin-gal nin-m[u]
14′) mu-sa$_{6}$-ga-[mu]
15′) [g]ù-zi bí-in-[dé-a]
16′) [...] DA x [...]
Lacuna

Frgm. 14) ... May my ... be pleasing to the god [Nanna], my lord, and the goddess Ning[al], my [l]ady, like finest oil. May they present to me as a gift long year(s) and a life of happiness. In Ur, the city *of* my *en*-ship, may they [...] my good deeds. When the goddess Ningal, m[y] lady, truly cal[led my] good name, ...

Col. iv (Obverse)
Frgm. 15
Lacuna
1′) [...]-uš
2′) [...]-ga
3′) [...]-⌜e⌝-ne
4′) [...]-kù
5′) [...] x E BU
6′) [... g]al-ka
7′) [... ka]la-ga
8′) [...] NE túm-mu
9′) [...] nin-gá
10′) [... d]è-eš
11′) [...]-ta
12′) [...]-a
13′) [...]-gar
14′) [... s]i
15′) [...] x
16′) [...]-dù
17′) [...].KI
18′) [...]-sa$_{4}$
19′) [...]-na
20′) [...] x

Frgm. 15) No translation warranted.

Lacuna
Col. iv (Reverse)
Frgm. 16
Lacuna
1′) [n]a$_4$.nír-k[ù]
2′) [aš]-me kù-GI-ḫuš
3′) ki-lá-bi maš ma-na
4′) zi-pa-ág-gá-na
5′) u$_4$-gin$_7$ kár-kár-ka
6′) me-te nam-dingir-bi-šè túm-ma
7′) ù-mu-dím
8′) nam-ti-mu-šè
9′) [ḫu]-mu-ba
10′) [x x] é-NIM-ma
11′) [...] x-i-lim-ḫú[š]
12′) [...] x [...]
13′) gal-bi ḫé-[...]
Lacuna

Frgm. 16) I fashioned ... a ... of shin[ing] *ḫulālu* stones, a [sun] disc of red gold, with a weight of half a mina, shining like the sun on her throat, a thing suitable for her divinity, and presented it for my life ... the ENIMA ... (with) a fur[ious] radiance ... grandly I ...

Frgm. 17 Col. iv (Top edge, end of column)
Lacuna
1′) [...]-ge-a
2′) [sag-e-eš r]ig$_7$-ge-a
3′) [... gur] še-ta
4′) s[á]-du$_{11}$-šè gi-na
5′) iti-1-a-kam
6′) ḫu-mu-gar
7′) GIŠ.gu-[za]-⌜du$_{10}$⌝-ba kù-GI
8′) [...] 3-ta gar-ra
9′) [giš]-nú-^{d}nin-[gal]

Frgm. 17) ... [gra]nted, [so many] *gur* grain, as regular of[fe]rings each month I established. The thro[ne], its knee inlaid with gold of three ..., ..., the [b]ed of the goddess Nin[gal(?)] ...

Col. v (Obverse)
Frgm. 18
Lacuna
1′) ki-tuš-nam-[en-na-gá]
2′) gal-bi ḫé-[...]
3′) alam me-[dím-bi ...] x
4′) mùš-me-bi k[ù-babbar k]ù-GI
5′) kin nam-[...]-gar-ra
6′) ù-[mu]-dím
7′) šà-ba DU[G ...-N]E
8′) 1 di[da](KAS.Ú.[SA])
9′) 5 sìla zì-[dub-dub]
10′) 2 sìla x [...]
11′) 2 sìla ninda-⌜ì⌝-[dé-a]
12′) 1 uzu [...]
13′) 1 [...]
14′) [...]
15′) ⌜^{d}⌝ [...]
16′) na[m-...]
17′) 5 sìla [...]
18′) sá-d[u$_{11}$-šè gi-na]
19′) ḫé-[em-mi-gar]
20′) ⌜1 sìla⌝ [...]
Lacuna
Frgm. 19 (Bottom edge col. v)
Lacuna (about 8 lines missing)

Frgm. 18) ... [*in*] the residence of [my *en*-ship, I grandly [*set it up*], I fas[hio]ned a statue with ... fo[rm], whose face was inlaid with [... si]lver and [g]old, a ... work, [and I established] there [as] re[gular offerings] ..., one jug of mixed [beer], five *sila* of [offering] flour, two *sila* of ..., two *sila* of bread [*mixed with*] oil, one portion meat, ..., one ..., ..., the god ..., ..., five *sila* of ..., 1 *sila* of ...

1′) [...] bar [...]
2′) [i]ti-1-kam ḫé-em-m[i-gar]
3′) é-gá-gú-x [...]
Lacuna

Frgm. 19) ... I es[tablished] for each [m]onth. The house ...

Col. v (Reverse)
Frgm. 20
Lacuna
1′) [...] x [...]
2′) [šà]-⌜íb-ba⌝-[x x]
3′) [x di$_4$]-di$_4$-lá-bi
4′) [igi-suḫ] a-ba-ni-in-ak
5′) [š]à-ga-ni
6′) [nì]-érim
7′) [... t]a-an-túm
8′) [...^{d}]nin-gal nin-mu
9′) [...] x kù
10′) [...-í]b-zi-g[e]
11′) [...]-gál
Lacuna

Frgm. 20) ... (as for the one who) [an]grily [looks] at its [sm]all [...] with [an evil eye], and his [he]art is moved (to) [male]volence ... the goddess Ningal, my lady, the shining ..., takes away ...

Frgm. 21
Lacuna
1′) [...]
2′) ⌜^{d}⌝ [...]
3′) nin-ga[l-...]
4′) [...]
5′) dumu [...]
6′) KA [...]
7′) x [...]
Lacuna(?)

Frgm. 21) ..., the goddess ..., gr[eat] lady ..., ..., the son ..., ...

Frgm. 22 (very bottom of Reverse col. v)
1′) [^{d}nanna lugal]-mu
2′) [^{d}nin-gal nin]-mu
3′) [kilib-dingir-gal-gal-e]-ne-ne
4′) [áš-g]ig-[ga]
5′) [ḫé-n]i-in-bal-e-[ne]
6′) [e-ne] ù numun-a-ni
7′) [šà-kalam-ma]-ka
Frgm. 23
(Left edge, follows immediately on line 7′)
1′) [nam-mu-ni-í]b-gá-gá-ne
2′) [...]-⌜ta⌝

Frgm. 22–23) ... May [the god Nanna], my [lord], and [the goddess Ningal], my [lady, and all the great god]s inflict on him a [t]errible [curse] (and) may [he] and his offspring [not] remain [in the nation].

Frgm. 24 (Left edge)
1′) [...]-kešda
2′) [...] x kal aš-ša
3′) [...]-ba sag-íl
4′) [š]à-du$_{10}$-du$_{10}$-a-a-ugu-na
5′) [...] x ⌜ḫúl-dím-ma-ni⌝
Lacuna

Frgm. 24) ..., ... worthy ..., proudly ..., who [p]leases the father who engendered her/him ... his evil [deed] ...,

Frgm. 25 (Left edge)
1′) [...]-^{d}nanna
2′) en-IGI-DU-mu [...]

Frgm. 25) ... of the god Nanna, the *en* priestesses who preceded me ...

Frgm. 26
Lacuna
1′) [...]-a
2′) [... R]I-a

Frgm. 26–28) No translation warranted.

3′) [...]-eš
4′) [...]-mu
5′) [...]-a
Frgm. 27
Lacuna
1′) [...]-⌜gar⌝
2′) [...]-šè
3′) [...] x
Frgm. 28
Lacuna
1′) [...] x
2′) [...]-ba
3′) [...]-a
4′) [...]-x-sì-ga
5′) [...]-gál
6′) [...]-a

16

The name of year 8 of Warad-Sîn records the construction of the courtyard of the temple of the god Nanna in Ur. A cone inscription known from numerous exemplars found at various points in the Great Nanna Courtyard, the Ziqqurrat Terrace, as well as beside the ziqqurrat staircase at Ur, deals with Warad-Sîn's construction of the *temenos* é-temen-ní-gùru for the god Nanna.

CATALOGUE

Ex.	Museum number	Registration number	Excavation number	Ur provenance	Object	Dimensions (cm)	Lines preserved	cpn
1	BM 30050	59-10-14,81	–	–	Head	–	1-18, 26-41	c
2	BM 30050	59-10-14,81	–	–	Shaft	8.5	1-31	c
3	BM 91149	59-10-14,83	–	–	Head	11.4 dia.	1-6, 9, 26-38	c
4	BM 91149	59-10-14,83	–	–	Shaft	6.0	2-8, 29-31	c
5	BM 138209	1935-1-13,628	U 19	Surface find	Head	15.5 dia.	8-11, 13-50	c
6	BM 138209	1935-1-13,628	U 19	As ex. 5	Shaft	–	1-26, 41-44	c
7	BM 138210	1935-1-13,630	U 700	From well no. 1	Cone	16.0 dia.	–	n
8	BCM 287'35F	–	U 751	As ex. 7	Head	12.0 dia.	18-26, 40-50	c
9	BCM 287'35H	–	U 753	As ex. 7	Head	12.0 dia.	23-25, 47-50	c
10	–	–	U 778	As ex. 7	Cone frgms.	–	–	n
11	IM 612	–	U 1200	Found in situ in inner Temenos wall, north of ziqqurrat	Head	14.0 dia.	1-50	c
12	IM 612	–	U 1200	As ex. 11	Shaft	12.5	1-37, 39-50	c
13	BM 117144	1924-9-20,393	U 1351	From Great Nanna Courtyard, NE of ziqqurrat	Head	7.3 dia.	1-6	c
14	IM 740	–	U 1515	From wall NE of ziqqurrat near U 1200	Cone	–	–	n
15	–	–	U 2565	WPD = west Great Nanna Courtyard	Cone	5.0×4.5	ends of col. i, 30-39, 48-50	n
16	BM 119039	1927-10-3,34	U 2612	Opposite SE corner of Great Nanna Courtyard	Shaft	6.0	17, 30-50	c
17	BM 119032	1927-10-3,27	U 2613	As ex. 16	Shaft	7.3	16-21, 24, 45-49	c
18	BM 119038	1927-10-3,33	U 2617B	As ex. 16	Head	10.0 dia.	24-25, 49-50	c
19	Philadelphia, no number	–	U 2622	As ex. 16	Head	13.7 dia.	1-50	c
20	–	–	U 2651	PDW = Great Nanna Courtyard W, rooms 29-30	Cone	–	36-50	n
21	–	–	U 2659	Provenance not known	Head	11.0 dia.	15-25, 35-50	n

Ex.	Museum number	Registration number	Excavation number	Ur provenance	Object	Dimensions (cm)	Lines preserved	cpn
22	BM 119016	1927-10-3,11	U 2759A	From side of staircase, west angle of Great Temple Extension	Shaft	19.0	1-50	c
23	BM 119016	1927-10-3,11	U 2759A	As ex. 22	Head	14.0 dia.	1-50	c
24	–	–	U 2759B	As ex. 22	Cone	–	–	n
25	–	–	U 2759C	As ex. 22	Cone	–	–	n
26	–	–	U 2759D	As ex. 22	Cone	–	–	n
27	Philadelphia, no number	–	U 2759E	As ex. 22	Shaft	17.0	1-50	c
28	Philadelphia, no number	–	U 2759E	As ex. 22	Head	15.0 dia.	1-50, much of head covered with dirt	c
29	BM 119015	1927-10-3,10	U 2759F	As ex. 22	Head	13.6 dia.	1-50	c
30	BM 119015	1927-10-3,10	U 2759F	As ex. 22	Shaft	18.0	1-13, 15-23, 26-50	c
31	–	–	U 2759G	As ex. 22	Cone	–	–	n
32	IM 935H	–	U 2759H	As ex. 22	Head	15.0 dia.	1-50	c
33	IM 935H	–	U 2759H	As ex. 22	Shaft	19.0	1-50	c
34	IM 935I	–	U 2759I	As ex. 22	Head	15.0 dia.	1-50	c
35	IM 935I	–	U 2759I	As ex. 22	Shaft	16.0	1-50	c
36	IM 935J	–	U 2759J	As ex. 22	Head	15.5 dia.	1-50	c
37	IM 935J	–	U 2759J	As ex. 22	Shaft	17.5	1-50	c
38	IM 935K	–	U 2759K	As ex. 22	Head	14.2 dia.	6-50	c
39	IM 1079	–	U 3247	From SW of Edublalmaḫ	Shaft	7.3	30-50	c
40	IM 1115	–	U 3338	HDB	Shaft	6.7	27-50	c
41	IM 3581	–	U 7829	North corner of Great Courtyard of Nanna	Head	14.3 dia.	1-23, 26-49	c
42	IM 3581	–	U 7829	As ex. 41	Shaft	10.5	1-6, 19-25	c
43	IM 92859	–	U 12970	From NE city wall, central section	Shaft	8.2	1-10, 12-13, 28-33	c
44	IM 92859	–	U 12970	As ex. 43	Head	8.5 dia.	26-40	c
45	–	–	U 12971	No provenance given	3 cone frgms.	–	–	n
46	–	–	U 16015	BC (Mausolea of Shulgi and Bur-Sin), filling under Temenos	Cone	–	–	n
47	IM 22882	–	U 16028	From Mausoleum site, filling under Temenos wall chamber	Shaft	11.5	1-23, 25-39, 41, 46-48, 50	c
48	UM 31-43-248	–	U 16582	A.H.	Shaft	9.8	1-2, 17-38, 40-50	c
49	UM 31-43-248	–	U 16582	A.H.	Head	8.5 dia.	2-11, 13-23, 28-37	c
50	IM 22902	–	U 17628	From 'behind the half-columned façade of Warad-Sîn and just in front of the mud-brick Isin façade', NW face of ziqqurrat terrace	Shaft	13.0	1-34, 41-50	c
51	UM 32-40-429	–	U 17654B	From the 'outer face of the pillared mud brick wall of Warad-Sîn's fort on the NW side of the ziqqurrat terrace'	Head	14.0 dia.	1-50	c
52	UM 32-40-429	–	U 17654B	As ex. 51	Shaft	19.0	1-50	c
53	IM 20871	–	U 17654A	As ex. 51	Head	15.4 dia.	1-50	c
54	IM 20871	–	U 17654A	As ex. 51	Shaft	15.5	1-50	c
55	BM 123117	1932-10-8,1	U 18107	From building range on NW wall of Temenos 150 below foundations of inner wall of SE range, 600 ft. from east corner of courtyard	Head	12.4 dia.	1-25, 27-50	c
56	BM 123117	1932-10-8,1	U 18107	As ex. 55	Shaft	11.3	1-25, 34-45	c
57	IM 92763	–	U 18828	Loose in soil about level 1500 in extension of Royal Cemetery	Head	12.0 dia.	1-47	c
58	IM 48411	–	U 18336	XNCF 1933, against buttressed NE wall of Kurigalzu's addition to Warad-Sîn fort	Head	–	1-19, 26-44	c
59	IM 48411	–	U 18336	As ex. 58	Shaft	–	17-22	c
60	IM 92762	–	U 19488	No provenance given	Head	13.0 dia.	1-11, 13, 27-44	c
61	IM 92762	–	U 19488	As ex. 60	Shaft	8.0	1-7	c
62	BM 119033	1927-10-3,28	U fb	–	Shaft	6.5	37-50	c
63	BM 119034	1927-10-3,29	U gb	–	Head	13.1 dia.	6-25	c
64	BM 119035	1927-10-3,30	U hb	–	Head	7.2	2-16	c
65	BM 119035	1927-10-3,30	U hb	–	Shaft	4.5	22-23, 34-38, 40-42	c
66	BM 119046	1927-10-3,41	U ib	–	Head	10.3 dia.	16, 18-25, 34-50	c
67	BM 119050	1927-10-3,45	U jb	–	Shaft	–	1-13, 30-40	c
68	BM 119058	1927-10-3,53	U kb	–	Head	6.1 × 3.6	44-50	c

Ex.	Museum number	Registration number	Excavation number	Ur provenance	Object	Dimensions (cm)	Lines preserved	cpn
69	IM 92776	–	U lb	–	Shaft	13.5	1–50	c
70	IM 92777	–	U mb	–	Head	8.2 dia.	26–46	c
71	BCM 59'76	–	–	–	Head	5.0 dia.	46–50	c
72	McGill Ethnological Collections no. 4	–	–	–	Shaft	16.0	1–50	c
73	McGill Ethnological Collections no. 6	–	–	–	Head	14.0	1–12, 16–20, 23–50	c
74	UM 32-40-434	–	–	–	Head	6.1 dia.	40–50	c
75	UM 32-40-430	–	–	–	Shaft	12.2	1–7, 24–26	c
76	IM 23090/29	–	–	–	Shaft	7.0	43–50	c
77	IM no number	–	–	–	Shaft	6.5	8–19, 37–48	c
78	BM 117143	1924-9-20,392	U 1697	Debris from NW face of ziqqurrat	Cone	4.1 dia.	8–12	c
79	IM 20870	–	U 16016	From mausoleum site, filling	Shaft	8.4	1–11, 19–26, 45–50	c

COMMENTARY

The edition is a conflated one. The line count follows ex. 2 for lines 1–25, ex. 1 for lines 26–41, and ex. 21 for lines 42–50.

Exs. 1–4 come from Taylor's excavations at Ur; the rest were excavated by Woolley. The vars. for ex. 7, which was not collated, are those indicated by E. Sollberger in UET 8 p. 31. In line 48 the distinction between su$_{13}$ and sù is not made.

BIBLIOGRAPHY

1872 G. Smith, TSBA 1 p. 43 no. 23 (exs. 1–2, translation)
1875 Lenormant, Choix no. 67 (ex. 1, copy)
1875 Ménant, Babylone et la Chaldée p. 87 (translation)
1891 4 R² pl. 35 no. 6 (exs. 1–2, composite copy; exs. 3–4, vars.)
1892 Winckler, KB 3/1 pp. 96–99 Kudur-maduk and Rim-Sin 6 (edition)
1904 Price, Rim-Sin pp. 10–11 no. v (edition)
1905 Thureau-Dangin, ISA pp. 302–303 Arad-sin c (edition)
1907 Thureau-Dangin, SAK pp. 212–13 Arad-sin c (edition)
1928 Gadd, UET 1 no. 131 (exs. 5–8, 10, 19–21, 40, conflated edition; ex. 21, copy)
1929 Barton, RISA pp. 318–19 Warad-Sin 3 (exs. 1–2, edition) and Warad-Sin 9 (edition)
1957 Edzard, Sumer 13 pp. 177 and 183 (exs. 11–12, 14, 32–38, 40–41, 46–47, 50, 53–54, 58, study)
1961 Hallo, BiOr 18 p. 9 Warad-Sin 10 (study)
1965 Sollberger, UET 8 p. 30 no. 27 (exs. 13, 16–18, 22–23, 29–30, 43–45, 55–57, 60–70, study)
1968 Kärki, SKFZ pp. 46–48 Waradsîn 10 (edition)
1980 Kärki, SAKAZ 1 pp. 94–96 Waradsîn 10 (edition)

TEXT

1) ^{d}nanna
2) en dumu-nun
3) an-kù-ge dalla-è
4) nam-šita$_{x}$(REC 316) a-ra-zu-e giš-tuk
5) lugal-mu-ra

1–5) For the god Nanna, lord, princely son, who shines forth brightly in shining heaven, who listens to supplications and entreaties, my lord,

6) IR$_{11}$-^{d}EN.ZU
7) ú-a-é-kur-ra
8) sipa sag-èn-tar-
9) é-kiš-nu-gál
10) lú ní-tuk-
11) èš é-babbar-ra
12) me giš-ḫur-
13) eridu.KI-ga šu-du$_{7}$-du$_{7}$
14) lú nidba-gu-ul-gu-ul-
15) é-ninnu-me-en

6–24) I, Warad-Sîn, provider of the Ekur, shepherd who looks after the Ekišnugal, the one who reverences the shrine Ebabbar, who perfectly executes the *me*s and rites of Eridu, the one who abundantly makes offerings for the Eninnu, who restores Lagaš and Girsu, I, who renovated the cities of the gods of their lands (and) put the gods Nanna and Utu in a good, peaceful residence, reverent prince who stands for his life at the house of his lord,

---

4.12 a-⟨ra⟩-zu-e. **5**.19, 32–33, 46, 49, 57, 60, 72–73, 75, 79 lugal-mu-úr. **5**.61 broken at this point. **11**.41 èš é-bábbar(UD.UD)-ra.

16) lagaš.KI gír-su.KI
17) ki-bé gi$_{4}$-gi$_{4}$-me-en
18) uru.KI-dingir-ma-da-bé-ne
19) šu-gibil bí-in-ak-a
20) ^{d}nanna ^{d}utu-bi
21) ki-tuš-ḫun-gá-du$_{10}$ mu-un-ne-gál-la
22) nun ní-te-ge$_{26}$
23) é-lugal-la-na-šè
24) zi-ti-le-ni-šè gub-ba-me-en

25) u$_{4}$ ^{d}aš-ím-babbar
26) giskim-sa$_{6}$-ga-né
27) igi ma-ni-in-du$_{8}$-a
28) igi-nam-ti-la-ka-ni
29) mu-ši-in-bar-ra-a
30) é-a-ni dù-ù-dè
31) ki-bé gi$_{4}$-gi$_{4}$-dè
32) gá-a-ar ma-an-du$_{11}$-ga

25–32) when the god Ašimbabbar let me see his favourable omen, looked at me with his eye of life, (and) ordered me to build his temple, to restore it,

33) nam-ti-mu-šè
34) ù nam-ti-
35) *ku-du-ur-ma-bu-uk*
36) a-a-ugu-gá-ke$_{4}$

33–36) for my own life and for the life of Kudurmabuk, the father who engendered me,

37) é-šà-ḫúl-la-ka-ni
38) é-temen-ní-gùr-ru
39) mu-na-dù
40) me-te-u$_{6}$-di-kalam-ma-ka
41) u$_{4}$-da-rí-šè bí-in-gub

37–41) I built for him his house of rejoicing, the Etemeniguru ('House — foundation which bears a fearsome splendour'). I set it up forever, suitable for the wonder of the nation.

42) ^{d}nanna lugal-mu
43) za-e-me-en ba-e-a-ak
44) gá-e a-na-mu-me-en

42–44) 'O god Nanna, my lord, it is you who has done it; (as for) myself, what am I?'

45) nì-ak-ak-da-gá
46) ^{d}nanna en-an-ki
47) ḫu-mu-ḫúl-le-en
48) nam-tar-nam-ti-la bala-sù-rá
49) GIŠ.gu-za-suḫuš-gi-na
50) sa$_{12}$-e-eš ḫa-ma-ab-rig$_{7}$-ge

45–50) May the god Nanna, the lord of heaven (and) earth, rejoice at my deeds (and) grant me a fate of life, a long reign, and a throne with a secure foundation.

17

This inscription has a titulary of the king similar to that found in E4.2.13.14, with the addition of epithets alluding to the events commemorated in the names of years 7–8 of Warad-Sîn (see introduction to Warad-Sîn). Since the inscription has no epithets alluding to the name of year 10 or later years, this inscription was probably composed around year 9.

16.7 gír-su.⟨KI⟩. **19**.19 bí-in-ak-⟨a⟩. **21**.7, 72 ki-tuš-ḫun-gá-KU. **21**.7 mu-⟨un⟩-ne-gál-la (shaft only). **21**.69 mu-un-ne-⟨gál-la⟩. **26**.7–8, 72–73, 79 giskim-sa$_{6}$-ga-a-né. **26**.11, 69 giskim-sa$_{6}$-KA(?)-né. **27**.27–28 igi ma-ni-in-ak-a. **29**.3, 11–12, 22–23, 27–30, 34–37, 41, 44, 50–54, 57–58, 69–70 mu-ši-in-bar. **30**.69 dù-ù-TU. **31**.72 ki-⟨bé⟩ gi$_{4}$-gi$_{4}$-dè. **37**.33, 62 é-šà-ḫúl-la-ka-a-ni. **37**.60 é-šà-ḫúl-la-ka-a-bi. **38**.11, 22–23, 27–30, 35–39, 41, 44, 51–54, 57, 66, 69–70, 77 é-temen-ní-gùru. **40**.27 kalam-ma-NE. **40**.28 kala̩m-ma-x. **42**.36 ^{d}aš-ím-babbar for ^{d}nanna. **42**.39 [l]ugal-gá. **43**.62 ba-⟨e⟩-a-ak. **44**.21 (From copy, not collated): gá-e-men$_{x}$(MIN). **46**.30, 68 en-an-na. **47**.5, 8, 19, 32–33, 40, 62, 72–73 ḫu-mu-ḫúl-le-en. **47**.22–23, 29–30, 69 ḫu-mu-ḫúl-ḫúl-le. **48**.33 ⌜bala⌝-DU-rá. **48**.39 bala-sù-da. **49**.27–28 suḫuš-ge-en. **50**.11 -rig$_{7}$-⟨ge⟩.

COMMENTARY

The inscription is found on IM 85686, a clay tablet, excavation no. U ja, provenance not known. It is the lower left corner of a thick tablet 8.8×6.5×2.4 cm. The inscription was collated.

The original number of cols. on this tablet is not definitely known. It probably contained three cols. per side.

The fragmentarily preserved subscript, if correctly read, indicates that this text was inscribed on a ⸢na-ru-a⸣, 'stone monument'.

In lines i 9′–12′ the epithets are restored from E4.2.13.27. The copyist of this tablet has apparently not respected the line division of the original monument, if this corresponded to what is found in E4.2.13.27.

Although the copy comes from Ur, it deals exclusively with the god Utu and his wife Šeridda, and probably commemorates some deed that took place in Larsa. In col. v, a fragmentary section seems to deal with offerings established by the king. The parallel of this section with iv 1–8 of E4.2.11.1 suggests that this passage refers to daily offerings that were established for some cult object. It might have been the statue of Kudur-mabuk whose construction provided the name of year 9 of Warad-Sîn.

Col. i line 3′ should not be restored ^{d}I[R$_{11}$-^{d}EN.ZU ...], as Kärki suggests, since it appears that the king's name was never written with the prefixed DINGIR sign. It appears without the DINGIR sign in i 9′.

At the end of i 12′ one would expect the restoration [šu-gibil bí-in-ak] but there does not seem to be enough room for it.

Col. v lines 5–9 are restored from the partial parallel found in E4.2.14.15 lines 57–58.

BIBLIOGRAPHY

1965 Sollberger, UET 8 no. 93 (copy, study)
1980 Kärki, SAKAZ 1 pp. 140–41 Waradsîn 39 (edition)

TEXT

Col. i
Lacuna
1′) ⸢^{d}⸣x [...]
2′) lú x [...]
3′) ^{d}x [...]
4′) lug[al-kala-ga ...]
5′) luga[l-larsa.KI-ma]
6′) luga[l-ki-en-gi-ki-uri]
7′) dumu-[*ku-du-ur-ma-bu-uk*]
8′) a[d-da-*e-mu-ut-ba-la*]
9′) IR$_{11}$-[^{d}EN.ZU nun]-
10′) še-g[a-nibru.KI šul]
11′) ⸢á⸣-[á]g-⟨gá⟩-⟨kin⸣-k[in x x x]
12′) [é]-dingir-re-e-n[e x x]
13′) giš-ḫur šu-du$_{7}$-[du$_{7}$]
14′) ní-tuk ù-nu-ku-kalam-m[a-me-en]
15′) u$_{4}$ ^{d}utu lugal-mu gù-z[i ma]-ni-in-d[é-a]

Lacuna
i 1′–14′) the god ..., the one who ..., the god ... [mighty] ki[ng ...], ki[ng of Larsa], ki[ng of the land of Sumer and Akkad], son of [Kudur-mabuk], f[ather of Emutbala], I, Warad-[Sîn, prince], fav[ourite of Nippur, youth] who seeks out the omens, who [renovated the temples of the gods], who properly executes the rites, reverent one who never sleeps (in order that he serve) the nation.

i 15′) When the god Utu, my lord spoke [to me] tru[ly] ...

Col. ii–iv (missing)
(ii–iv missing)

Col. v
1) z[ú-lum x-sìla-ta]
2) zì [x-sìla-ta]
3) ka[š x-sìla-ta]
4) m[u-ni-gar]
5) na[m-bi-šè]
6) ^{d}[utu]
7) bal[a-ḫé-gál-la]

v 1–4) He established there [so many *sila*] of da[tes, so many *sila*] of flour, [so many *sila*] of beer.

v 5–11) [On] acco[unt of this], may the god [Utu *grant* to me] a re[ign of abundance in] the shri[ne of Larsa].

8) è[š-larsa.KI-ma-ka]
9) ḫ[u-...]
10) ^{d}[...]
11) x [...]
Lacuna
Col. vi
1) á-gál-é-babbar
2) inim-ma-ni še-ga
3) igi-^{d}utu ù ^{d}šè-ri$_{5}$-da-bi
4) i$_{5}$-gar-bi ḫul-ḫul-dè
5) u$_{4}$-bi-šè
6) sag-bi ḫé-ḫa-za
7) ^{d}LÚ.ḪUŠ.GAL
8) kar igi(?) nu-túm-mu
9) sag šu-bal-e
10) a-ba-ni-in-tuk
11) maškim ḫul-gar nì-nu-kúr-ru-a ḫé-a
12) u$_{4}$-da-rí-šè
Subscript: ⸢na-ru-a IR$_{11}$⸣-[^{d}EN.ZU]

Lacuna

vi 1–6) (May the god ...), strength of the Ebabbar, whose word is favourable, in order to make (the evil-doer's) reputation bad before the gods Utu and Šeridda, firmly take hold of (the evil-doer) at that time.

vi 7–12) May the god LÚ.ḪUŠ.GAL, who does not ... the runaway, having taken hold of the person who altered (the inscription), forever be its (the curse's) evil spirit who cannot be countermanded.

Subscript: Monument of Warad-[Sîn].

18

The name of year 10 of Warad-Sîn commemorates the building of the wall of Ur. This deed is recorded on bricks, foundation tablets, cones, and foundation cylinders found at Ur (E4.2.13.18–21).

A 22-line inscription is found on stamped bricks from Ur.

CATALOGUE

Ex.	Museum number	Excavation number	Ur provenance	Dimensions (cm)	Lines preserved	cpn
1	BM 90033	59-10-14,14	From the eastern line of mounds	34.0×32.5	1–22	c
2	BM 90053	59-10-14,13	As ex. 1	33.0×34.0×18.5	1–22	c
3	BM 90055	59-10-14,11	As ex. 1	33.0×34.0	1–22	c
4	BM 90059	59-10-14,12+ 59-10-14,52	As ex. 1	20.0×33.5×9.0	1–9, 12–17	c
5	BM 90330	59-10-14,17	As ex. 1	16.5×15.0×8.0	8–11, 17–22	c
6	BM 90347	59-10-14,19+ 59-10-14,20	As ex. 1	26.0×15.5×8.5	4, 6–11, 14–22	c
7	BM 90350+ BM 90397	59-10-14,47+ 59-10-14,16	As ex. 1	30.5×21.0×9.0	6–11,18–22	c
8	BM 90391	59-10-14,21	As ex. 1	14.0×14.0×7.5	1–9	c
9	BM 90703	59-10-14,18	As ex. 1	24.0×18.0×8.5	18–22	c

COMMENTARY

The master text is ex. 1.

Exs. 1–9 were all excavated by Taylor. In a description of soundings made in the easternmost part of the tell Taylor writes, '... I came upon another brick wall, running at an oblique angle to the bastion I was digging along; this wall ran apparently into the ruins. The bastion or buttress was 5 yards 20 inches long, and 2 yards 23 inches broad. The bricks composing it [imbedded in bitumen] were 13 inches long, 12 broad, and 3 thick ... The bricks were inscribed on the sides only, but so ruined that I did not procure one perfect.' The size and state of preservation of the bricks described by Taylor matches our exs. 1–9. Presumably the 'bastion' mentioned by Taylor was the wall of Ur constructed with Warad-Sîn bricks. Curiously, Woolley does not report finding any of these bricks in his excavations.

In lines 5 and 10 the worn nature of some of the inscriptions makes it difficult to tell whether ŠEŠ.AB.KI or ŠEŠ.UNUG.KI occurs as a writing for the city name Ur. For the translation of line 16 see A. Sjöberg, AfO 20 (1963) p. 173.

BIBLIOGRAPHY

1855 Taylor, JRAS p. 275 (provenance)
1861 1 R pl. 5 no. XVI (exs. 1–9, composite copy)
1872 G. Smith, TSBA 1 p. 43 (translation)
1874 Lenormant, Études accadiennes 2 pp. 348–49
1875 Ménant, Babylone et la Chaldée p. 87 (translation)
1892 Winckler, KB 3/1 pp. 94–95 Kudur-mabuk and Rim-Sin 2 (edition)
1899 Bezold, Cat. 5 p. 2234 (study)
1904 Price, Rim-Sin pp. 8–9 no. III (edition)
1905 Thureau-Dangin, ISA pp. 300–301 Arad-sin b (edition)
1907 Thureau-Dangin, SAK pp. 212–13 Arad-sin b (edition)
1915 King, History pl. IX facing p. 104 (ex. 3, photo)
1922 BM Guide p. 61 nos. 125–28 (study)
1929 Barton, RISA pp. 318–19 Warad-Sin 2 (edition)
1961 Hallo, BiOr 18 p. 9 Warad-Sin 1 (study)
1968 Kärki, SKFZ p. 39 Waradsîn 1 (edition)
1980 Kärki, SAKAZ 1 pp. 84–85 Waradsîn 1 (edition)
1981 Walker, CBI no. 43 (exs. 1–9, study)

TEXT

1) IR$_{11}$-^{d}EN.ZU
2) nita-kala-ga
3) sipa-nì-ge
4) ^{d}en-líl-le gar-ra
5) ú-a-uri$_{5}$.KI-ma
6) lugal-larsa.KI-ma
7) lugal-ki-en-gi-ki-uri-ke$_{4}$
8) dumu-*ku-du-ur-ma-bu-uk*
9) ad-da-*e-mu-ut-ba-la*-me-en
10) úri.KI dagal-e-dè
11) mu-maḫ tuk-tuk-dè
12) sun$_{5}$-na-bi
13) ù-gul im-ma-an-gá-gá
14) ^{d}nanna lugal-mu
15) mu-ši-in-še
16) bàd-gal ḫur-sag-íl-la-gin$_{7}$ šu nu-tu-tu
17) ní-bi-šè è-a
18) mu-na-dù
19) uru-ni ḫé-em-mi-da$_{5}$
20) bàd-ba
21) ^{d}nanna suḫuš-ma-da ge-en-ge-en
22) mu-bi-im

1–9) I, Warad-Sîn, mighty man, shepherd of righteousness, appointed by the god Enlil, provider of Ur, king of Larsa, king of the land of Sumer and Akkad, son of Kudur-mabuk, father of Emutbala,

10–15) in order to enlarge Ur, in order that it acquire a lofty reputation, I implored him humbly, (and) the god Nanna, my lord, was favourable (to my prayer).

16–18) I built for him the great wall, which like a mountain raised high cannot be touched, which comes forth on its own accord.

19) I surrounded his city.

20–22) The name of that wall is Nanna-suḫuš-mada-gengen ('The god Nanna makes the foundation of the land firm').

19

Two foundation tablets excavated by Woolley deal with Warad-Sîn's construction of the wall of Ur.

CATALOGUE

Ex.	Museum number	Registration number	Excavation number	Ur provenance	Object	Dimensions (cm)	Lines preserved	cpn
1	BM 119011	–	U 3021	Reburied in the NB Ningal temple of Sîn-balaṭsu-iqbi, room 3	Copper foundation tablet	14.3×8.0	1–27	c
2	BM 119010	1927-10-3,5	U 3020	As ex. 1	Soapstone foundation tablet	14.2×7.8×2.0	1–27	c

COMMENTARY

The master text is ex. 1.

BIBLIOGRAPHY

1925 Woolley, AJ 5 pl. XXXVI 1 (exs. 1-2, photo)
1928 Gadd, UET 1 no. 129 (exs. 1-2, composite copy, edition)
1929 Barton, RISA pp. 380-81 Warad-Sin 7 (edition)
1939 Woolley, UE 5 p. 63 (exs. 1-2, provenance)
1961 Hallo, BiOr 18 p. 9 Warad-Sin 4 (study)
1965 Sollberger, UET 8 p. 30 no. 26 (study)
1968 Kärki, SKFZ pp. 40-41 Waradsîn 4 (edition)
1971 Sollberger and Kupper, IRSA IVB13b (translation)
1980 Kärki, SAKAZ 1 pp. 86-87 Waradsîn 4 (edition)

TEXT

1) IR$_{11}$-^{d}EN.ZU
2) nita-kala-ga
3) ú-a-úri.KI-ma
4) lugal-larsa.KI-ma
5) lugal-ki-en-gi-ki-uri
6) dumu-*ku-du-ur-ma-bu-uk*
7) ad-da-*e-mu-ut-ba-la*

1–7) (I), Warad-Sîn, mighty man, provider of Ur, king of Larsa, king of the land of Sumer and Akkad, son of Kudur-mabuk, father of Emutbala.

8) uri$_{5}$.KI dagal-e-dè
9) ki-sá-a-bi šu-peš$_{11}$-e-dè
10) mu-maḫ tuk-tuk-dè
11) ^{d}nanna lugal-mu
12) mu-ši-in-še

8–12) The god Nanna, my lord, was favourable to (my prayer) to enlarge Ur, to reinforce its supporting wall, to have it acquire a lofty reputation.

13) bàd-gal ḫur-sag-íl-la-gin$_{7}$
14) šu nu-tu-tu-dè
15) ní-bi-šè è-a
16) mu-na-dù

13–16) I built for him the great wall, which like a mountain raised high cannot be touched, which comes forth on its own accord.

17) bàd-ba
18) ^{d}nanna-suḫuš-ma-da-ge-en-ge-en
19) mu-bi-im

17–19) The name of that wall is Nanna-suḫuš-mada-gengen ('The god Nanna makes the foundation of the land firm').

20) nì-ak-ak-da-gá
21) ^{d}nanna lugal-mu
22) ḫu-mu-ḫúl-le-en
23) nam-tar-nam-ti-la
24) bala-sù-rá
25) GIŠ.gu-za-suḫuš-gi-na
26) sa$_{12}$-e-eš
27) ḫa-ma-ab-rig$_{7}$-ge

20–27) May you Nanna, my lord, rejoice at my deeds and grant me a fate of life, a long reign, (and) a throne with a secure foundation.

6.2 *-úk*.

20

An inscription dealing with the construction of the wall of Ur by Warad-Sîn is found on seven cone fragments excavated at Ur.

CATALOGUE

Ex.	Museum number	Registration number	Excavation number	Provenance	Object	Dimensions (cm)	Lines preserved	cpn
1	BM 30058	59-10-14,92	–	–	Shaft	4.0 dia.	34-49	c
2	BM 30059	59-10-14,123	–	–	Shaft	6.5 dia.	38-47	c
3	BM 30221	59-10-14,121	–	–	Head	3.5×4.2×2.7	26-31	c
4	McGill Ethnological Collections no. 21	–	U 334	From Enunmaḫ, room 18	Head	8.4×8.6	5-23, 41-47	c
5	BM 119047	1927-10-3,42	U 3112	Near Great Nanna Courtyard	Shaft	6.9	1-9	c
6	IM 92957	–	U 15053	From 'Larsa and other rubbish' Royal Cemetery area	Shaft	7.7	14-15, 26-45	c
7	IM 92975	–	U 15068	From 'wall Larsa pavement' between Neo-Babylonian graves 68 and 69 in the AH site	Shaft	10.0	33-40, 51-56	c

COMMENTARY

The text, which is a conflated one, is almost complete; only lines 24-25 and 50 are entirely absent from the sources at present available. The text is established as follows: lines 1-4, ex. 5; lines 5-23, ex. 4; lines 26-31, ex. 3; line 32, ex. 6; lines 33-40, ex. 7; lines 41-47, ex. 4; lines 48-49, ex. 1; and lines 51-56, ex. 7. Lines 22-32 can be restored in their entirety from E4.2.13.21 lines 66-75, as can line 50 from line 107 of the same text.

Exs. 1-3, from Taylor's excavations, are edited here for the first time through the courtesy of the trustees of the British Museum. Exs. 4-7 come from Woolley's excavations.

Although some portions of the text were previously published, the text is offered here in its entirety for the first time. Exs. 4, 5, and 6-7 were previously edited separately by Kärki as Waradsîn 18, 32, and 36 respectively.

As Sollberger points out, the provenance of ex. 7, from the 'wall Larsa pavement', is significant.

BIBLIOGRAPHY

1928 Gadd, UET 1 no. 134 (ex. 4, copy, edition)
1961 Hallo, BiOr 18 p. 10 Warad-Sin 18 (study)
1965 Sollberger, UET 8 no. 76 (ex. 5, copy) and no. 81 (exs. 6-7, composite copy)
1968 Kärki, SKFZ pp. 54-55 Waradsîn 18 (ex. 4, edition)
1980 Kärki, SAKAZ 1 pp. 105-106 Waradsîn 18 (ex. 4, edition), p. 133 Waradsîn 32 (ex. 5, edition), and pp. 136-37 Waradsîn 36 (exs. 6-7, edition)

TEXT

1) [I]R$_{11}$-^{d}EN.Z[U]
2) [n]ita-kala-g[a]
3) sipa nì-ge m[ú-mú]
4) ki-ág-^{d}e[n-líl]
5) ^{d}nanna ^{d}utu-bi
6) é-babbar-da ní-t[uk]
7) ú-a-é-kur-[ra]
8) lú šà-nibru.KI du$_{10}$-[du$_{10}$]
9) sag-ús-é-kiš-nu-gá[l]

1-13) I, [Wa]rad-Sîn, mighty [m]an, shepherd who makes righteousness inc[rease], beloved of the gods E[nlil], Nanna, and Utu, who re[verences] the Ebabbar, provider of Ekur, the one who makes Nippur content, supporter of Ekišnuga[l], king of Larsa, king of the land of Sumer and Akkad, son of Kudur-mabuk, father of Emutbala,

10) lugal-larsa.KI-ma 11) lugal-ki-en-gi-ki-uri 12) dumu-*ku-du-ur-ma-bu-uk* 13) ad-da-*e-mu-ut-ba-la*-me-en	
14) ^{d}nanna lugal-mu KA-sa$_6$-sa$_6$-ge-da-mu 15) úri.KI dagal-e-dè 16) ki-sá-a-bi šu-peš$_{11}$-e-dè 17) diri-nì-u$_4$-bi-da-ka 18) ki-gar-bi gu-ul-lu-dè 19) mu-maḫ tuk-tuk-dè 20) èn ù-bí-tar 21) [egi]r-a-ni bí-zukum 22) [sun$_5$-na-b]i ù-gul im-m[a-an-gá-gá]	14–22) I asked and enquired of the god Nanna (with) my ardent prayer about enlarging Ur, of reinforcing its supporting wall, about making its foundation greater than it had been previously, of having it acquire a lofty reputation, (and) imp[lored him humbly].
23) [^{d}nanna lugal-m]u mu-[ši-in-še]	23) [The god Nanna], [m]y [lord, was favourable (to my prayer)].
24) [nam-ti-mu-še ù nam-ti]-	24) [For my life and the life]
25) [*ku-du-ur-ma-bu-uk* a-a-tu-da-gá-ke$_4$]	25) [of Kudur-mabuk, the father who engendered me].
26) [uru kur-n]am-ti-l[a] 27) [ki-ḫé-gál]-la-k[a] 28) [ki-tuš nigin-gál-dingir-re]-e-ne-ke$_4$ 29) [nam-bi mu-u]n-tar-ra 30) [mu-ni-gin$_7$] diri-ga 31) [sag an]-e ús-sa 32) [á-bi šu-ta kin ki èn-tar ga]r-r[a] 33) an-dùl-dagal-la-ni kur-kur-ra ša-mu-un-me 34) un-sag-gi$_6$-ga úr-bé mu-un-lu-lu 35) nam-ti kar-kar-re-me-eš 36) [bà]d-gal-bi ḫu-mu-dù	26–36) [(Ur) — the city, mountain of l]if[e, place of abund]ance, [residence whose destiny all the gods] determined, [which like his name] is surpassing, [whose head] reaches [heaven, whose arm ... the place where a ... is pl]aced, whose broad shadow is spread over the foreign lands, at whose base the black-headed people multiply (and) are able *to save* their lives — I built its great [wa]ll.
37) ḫur-sag-sig$_7$-ga-gin$_7$ ki-sikil-la ḫé-bí-mú 38) mu nam-maḫ-bi-⟨gin$_7$⟩ sag-bi ḫu-mu-ni-in-íl 39) u$_6$-di-⌜kalam⌝-ma-šè pa gal-le-eš ḫé-bí-in-è	37–39) Like a verdant mountain I caused it to grow up there in a pure place. I lifted its head ⟨commensurate⟩ with its name (and) greatness. I caused it to shine forth splendidly to the wonder of the nation.
40) u$_4$ b[àd-ú]ri.KI-ma mu-dù-a 41) ⌜á⌝ lú-1-e 3 bán še-ta 42) ⌜2⌝ [sìla] ninda-ta 2 sìla kaš-ta 43) ⌜2⌝ gín ì-giš-ta 44) u$_4$-aš-a ur$_5$-gin$_7$ šu ḫa-ba-an-ti	40–44) When I built the w[all of U]r, the wages of each man were 3 *ban* of barley, 2 [*sila*] of bread, 2 *sila* of beer, 2 *shekels* of vegetable oil; in one day so each one received this.
45) šà-ma-da-gá-ka i-^{d}utu ḫé-éb-ta-zi	45) I removed (any cause for) complaint from my land.
46) sag-ki-zalag-šà-ḫúl-la-gá-ka 47) kin-bi asila^{lá} ul$_4$-le-eš ḫé-em-mi-til	46–47) With my shining face (and) happy heart, I joyfully, quickly finished [that] work.
48) [géštu-dagal nam-kù-zu-m]u-šè gal-bi ḫu-mu-dù	48) On account of m[y broad wisdom and intelligence] I built it in a grand fashion.
49) [bàd-bi ^{d}nanna suḫuš]-⌜ma-da⌝ [ge-en-ge-en] 50) [mu-šè ḫé-em-mi-sa$_4$]	49–50) [I named that wall Nanna-suḫuš]-mada-[gengen] (‘[The god Nanna makes the foundation of the] land firm’).
51) [nì-ak-mu-š]è 52) ⌜^{d}nanna lugal-mu ḫu-mu-ḫúl⌝-le-⌜en⌝ 53) u$_4$-šà-ḫúl-la bala-nam-ḫé-a 54) ti nì-du$_{10}$ mu-ḫé-gál-la-ka 55) GIŠ.gu-za suḫuš-gi-na 56) sa$_{12}$-e-eš ḫa-ma-ab-rig$_7$-ge	51–56) May you, god Nanna, my lord, rejoice at [my deed] and grant me days of rejoicing, a reign of abundance, life, a good thing, years of plenty, (and) a throne with a secure foundation.

21

The building of the wall of Ur is also recorded in a long barrel inscription known from two exemplars.

CATALOGUE

Ex.	Museum number	Excavation number	Provenance	Dimensions (cm)	Lines preserved	cpn
1	VA 5950	BE 46431	Babylon, from the Old Babylonian house in 22 K$_2$	24.5 long, 14.5 dia.	1–116	c
2	IM 92920	U 12974	Ur, from the NE city wall, central section	–	2–12	n

COMMENTARY

Ex. 1, from Babylon, may have been taken there as a piece of booty from Ur. Ex. 2 was previously unattributed. Its provenance, from the north-east city wall of Ur, is significant in view of the content of the inscription.

BIBLIOGRAPHY

1964 Falkenstein, Bagh. Mitt. 3 pp. 25–40 (ex. 1, edition)
1965 Sollberger, UET 8/1? no. 91 (ex. 2, copy)
1966 Falkenstein, BiOr 23 pp. 166 and 167b (ex. 1, study)
1971 Sollberger and Kupper, IRSA ɪᴠB13a (translation)
1980 Kärki, SAKAZ 1 pp. 126–32 Waradsîn 29 (edition)

TEXT

1) u$_4$ an ^{d}en-líl-bi
2) nun-da-rí a-a-dingir-re-e-ne
3) nam-tar-tar-re-me-eš

1–3) When the gods An and Enlil, eternal princes, fathers of the gods, who decide the fates,

4) ^{d}nanna dumu-zi-le
5) ki-ág-é-kur-ra-ra
6) u$_4$-šú-uš nam-sun$_5$-na
7) šu-kin-dab$_5$-bé-da-ni-šè
8) igi-bi-a al-gub-ba
9) ka-ba-bi-šè gizzal im-ši-⟨ak⟩
10) du$_{11}$-ga-bi-šè mu-un-gur-e
11) gù-ḫúl mu-ni-in-dé-eš

4–11) spoke joyously to the god Nanna, the handsome son, beloved of the Ekur, who daily humbly stands before them in reverence, who pays attention to what they say, who bows to their word –

12) ad-gi$_4$-an-ki-ka
13) umuš ka-aš-bar-re-^{d}a-nun-na
14) šu-na bí-in-gar-re-eš

12–14) they entrusted his hands with the counsel of heaven and earth, the advice and decisions of the Anuna gods.

15) úri.ᴋɪ ki-sur-ra dingir-re-ne gar-ra-na
16) bala-sa$_6$-ga sù-rá-šè ak-dè
17) bára-bi sukud-íli-dè
18) kìlib-da-ga-an-sag-zi-gál-la
19) gú-un íl-i-dè
20) gìri-né šu-né ri-e-dè
21) ini[m]-kù nì-nu-kúr-ru-da-ne-ne
22) gi-né-šè bí-in-ne-eš-àm

15–22) By their pure word, a thing which cannot be altered, they firmly commanded him in his Ur, the boundary established by the gods, to exercise a good reign for the future, to raise high its shrines, to have all living things bear tribute (and) lay it at his feet and hands.

23) u$_4$-bi-a ^{d}aš-ím-babbar-re
24) eš-bar-re gal-zu dumu-^{d}nin-líl-lá-ke$_4$
25) igi-an-^{d}en-líl-bi-ta
26) sag-íl-la ul-le-eš è-da-ni
27) ma-da inim-a-né te-en-te-ne
28) sag-gi$_6$ zi-dè-eš bí-in-è-a
29) un-šár-ra-bi-šè arḫuš bí-in-tuk-àm
30) uru-ni uri$_5$.KI-ma ama-sig^{ig}-kur-ra
31) sag-ki-zalag šà-ḫúl-la-ni-ta
32) mu-un-na-ši-bar-re-en
33) sag-n[i b]í-in-íl-la
34) mu-maḫ bí-in-tuk-àm
35) ḫur-sag a-ab-ba nam-ḫé-bi kú-dè
36) mè-šen kalam-ma ḫúb-sa-ra ak-ak-dè
37) sa$_{12}$-e-eš im-mi-in-rig$_7$

23–37) At that time, the god Ašimbabbar, wise in decisions, son of the goddess Ninlil, who proudly goes forth in beauty before the gods An and Enlil, whose word soothes the land, who steadily goes forth among the black-headed (people), showed mercy to all the people. He looked with shining face and joyous heart at his city, Ur, the *old woman* of the land. He raised hi[s] head, caused (Ur) to have a lofty reputation, granted to it to enjoy the abundance of the mountain and sea, (and) to charge in the battles and combat of the nation.

38) sipa-gin$_7$ ⌜zi⌝-gál túm-túm-e-dè
39) ma-da-bi-im šu-a gi$_4$-gi$_4$-dè
40) šà-bé a gá-gá-dè u$_4$-bi sù-sù-u$_5$-dè
41) inim sikil-bi bí-in-tùm

38–41) Their (An and Enlil's) word purely moved him to care for the living ones like a shepherd, to make their land safe, to establish water in their midst, to make their days long.

42) nam-bi-šè ìr-^{d}EN.ZU
43) gal-zu géštu-tuk-tuk nì-ge-na ki-ág-me-en
44) šà-ama-ugu-mu-ta kù-ge-eš gùn-a-me-en
45) nam-sipa kalam-ma-na mu-un-gar-re-en

42–45) For this purpose it was me, Warad-Sîn, the wise one possessing wisdom, who loves righteousness, who was purely *formed* in the womb of the mother who bore me, whom (the god Nanna) appointed (for) shepherdship of his nation,

46) nam-si-sá-gá gidru ma-an-sum
47) bala-ḫúl-la šu-zi ma-ni-in-gar
48) 〈*ni*〉-*šì*-lu-lu-a-ni KA-mu-šè ma-ni-in-dúr

46–48) he gave to me, (because of) my rectitude, the sceptre and entrusted to me a joyous reign. He made his numerous people dwell under my decree.

49) é-temen-ní-gùr-ru gibil-gibil-dè
50) ùr-èš-é-babbar gur-re-dè
51) uru.KI-dingir-ma-da-bé-e(*)-ne dù-ù-dè
52) DA.GABA-šub-ba-bi ŠUKU.KU.ŠUKU-dè
53) giš-ḫur-libir sukud-íli-dè
54) šu-luḫ-ḫa-lam-ma-bi ki-bé gi$_4$-gi$_4$-dè
55) ^{d}nanna en me-an-ki šu-du$_7$
56) nam-ní-tuk-mu-šè á-bi ḫu-mu-da-«KI»-ág

49–56) The god Nanna, lord who perfectly executes the *me*s of heaven and earth, on account of my reverence, ordered me to renovate Etemeniguru, to strengthen the base of shrine Ebabbar, to build the cities of the gods of the land, to ... their fallen ..., to raise high their ancient rites, to restore their forgotten lustration rites.

57) ad-gi$_4$-a-mu ki-bi-šè nì-sag-bi-šè è-a
58) èn-tar-galam-ma-mu nì ság-nu-di-dam

57–58) My counsel for that is a thing which excels, my skilful care is a thing which cannot be frustrated.

59) a-rá-nam-lugal-la-gá un-gá zu-zu-dè
60) nam-gal nam-maḫ-gá u$_4$-da-rí-šè gál-le-dè
61) uri$_5$.KI dagal-e-dè
62) ki-sá-a-bi šu-peš$_{11}$-e-dè
63) diri-nì-u$_4$-bi-ta-ka
64) ki-gar-bi gu-ul(*)-[lu]-dè
65) èn ù-bí-tar egir-[a-ni b]í-zukum
66) sun$_5$-na-bi ù-gúl m[u-na-n]i-in-gar

59–66) I asked and enquired (of the god Nanna) about making the people know the ways of my kingship, of making my greatness and supremacy exist forever, about enlarging Ur, and reinforcing its supporting wall, of making its foundation greater than it had been previously and I implored the god (Nanna) humbly.

67) ^{d}nanna lugal-〈mu〉 mu-ši-[i]n-še

67) The god Nanna, 〈my〉 lord, was favourable (to my prayer).

68) nam-ti-mu-šè ⌜ù⌝ nam-ti-
69) *ku-du-ur-ma-bu-uk* a-a-tu-⌜da⌝-gá-ke$_4$

68–69) For my life and for the life of Kudur-mabuk, the father who engendered me —

51.1 ma-da-bé-ke$_4$-ne. **64**.1 gu-lu-[x]-dè.

70) uru kur-nam-ti-l[a k]i-ḫé-gál-la-ka
71) ki-tuš nigin-gál-dingir-re-e-ne-ke$_4$
72) nam-bi mu-un-tar-r[e-š]a(?)
73) mu-ni-gin$_7$ diri-ga
74) sag an-e ús-sa
75) á-bi šu-ta kin ki èn-tar gar-ra
76) an-dùl-dagal-la-ni kur-kalam-ma dul
77) úr-du$_{10}$-ga-ni-ta un-sag-gi$_6$-ga
78) mu-un-lu-lu nam-ti kar-kar-re-meš
79) bàd-bi dù-ù-dè šu-gá im-mi-gar
80) muru$_4$-ba itu-5-àm ba-ra-ab-zal
81) sig$_4$-bi ḫu-mu-du$_8$
82) bàd-gal-bi ḫu-mu-til
83) bàd-si-bi ḫu-mu-íl
84) ḫur-sag-sig$_7$-ga-gin$_7$ ki-sikil-la ḫé-bí-mú
85) sukud-rá-bi ḫé-bí-diri su-ŠI ḫé-bí-du$_8$-du$_8$
86) mu nam-maḫ-bi-gin$_7$ sag-bi ḫu-mu-ni-in-íl
87) u$_6$-di-kalam-ma-šè
88) pa gal-le-eš ḫé-bí-in-è
89) uru$_4$-ba temen-nam-lugal-la-gá
90) ki ḫé-em-ma-ni-in-pà
91) abul-la-ba sag ḫé-bí-íl
92) e-ek-sur-ra-bi ḫu-mu-kala
93) sig$_4$-bi ḫu-mu-da
94) *ḫi-rí-tum*-bi ḫu-mu-ba-al
95) *ma-du-um*-bi ḫu-mu-dub

70–79) (The god Nanna) entrusted me to build the wall (of Ur) – the city, mountain of li[fe, p]lace of abundance, residence whose destiny all the gods decided, which like its name is surpassing, whose head reaches heaven, whose arm ... the place where enquiries are put, whose broad shadow covers the foreign land and nation, at whose fine base the black-headed people multiply and are able to *save* their lives – (The god Nanna) entrusted me the building of its wall.

80–95) In the course of that (year) five months had not passed (when) I baked its bricks. I finished that great wall (and) raised up its parapet. Like a verdant mountain I caused it to grow up in a pure place. I made its height surpassing, had it release its terrifying aura. I raised its head commensurate with its name and greatness. I caused it to shine forth splendidly to the wonder of the nation. I chose the place for my royal foundation inscription in its foundation, (and) raised the head of its gate there. I made its fosse strong, circled it with bricks, (and) dug its moat. I heaped up its ...

96) u$_4$ bàd-uri$_5$.KI-ma
97) mu-dù-a
98) á lú-1-e 3 bán [š]e-ta
99) 2 sìla ninda-ta 2 sìla kaš-ta 2 gín ì-giš-ta
100) u$_4$-aš-a ur$_5$-gin$_7$ šu ḫa-ba-an-ti

96–100) When I built the wall of Ur, the wages of each man were 3 *ban* of [b]arley, 2 *sila* of bread, 2 *sila* of beer, 2 shekels of vegetable oil – in one day so each one received this.

101) šà-ma-da-gá-ka
102) i-^{d}utu ḫé-éb-ta-zi

101–102) I removed (any cause for) complaint from my land.

103) sag-ki-zalag-šà-ḫúl-la-gá-ka
104) kin-bi asila^{lá}-a ul$_4$-le-«dè»-eš ḫé-em-mi-til

103–104) With my shining face and happy heart I joyfully, quickly finished the work.

105) géštu-dagal nam-kù-zu-mu-ta gal-bi 〈ḫe〉-em-mi-kin

105) With my broad wisdom and intelligence I performed the work in a grand fashion.

106) bàd-ba ^{d}nanna suḫuš-ma-da ge-en-ge-en
107) mu-šè ḫé-em-mi-sa$_4$

106–107) I called that wall Nanna-suḫuš-mada-gengen ('The god Nanna makes the foundation of the land firm').

108) nì-ak-mu-šè ^{d}nanna lugal-mu ḫu-mu-ḫúl-le-en

108) May you, Nanna, my lord, rejoice at my deed

109) u$_4$-šà-ḫúl-la bala-nam-〈ḫé〉-a
110) nam nu-kám-me mu-ḫé-gál-la-ka
111) giš-šub ti nì-du$_{10}$ ḫa-la-nam-lugal-la
112) sa$_{12}$-e-eš ḫa-ma-ab-rig$_7$-ge

109–112) and grant me day(s) of rejoicing, a reign of abundance, a destiny that cannot be overturned, year(s) of plenty, (and) as my lot – life – a good thing, the allotment of kingship.

113) nam-sipa-mu nibru.KI-a uri$_5$.KI larsa.KI-bi
114) sù-ud-šè nam-ba-kúr-ru

113–114) May my shepherdship never be altered in Nippur, Ur, and Larsa.

115) nun-ki-ág-^{d}nanna-^{d}nin-gal-bi ḫé-em

115) May I be the prince beloved of the gods Nanna and Ningal.

116) u$_4$-mu ḫé-sù-sù-ud

116) May my day(s) be long.

22

The remaining inscriptions of Warad-Sîn cannot be precisely dated because they do not correlate to specific year names of the king. E4.2.13.22–25 do, however, exhibit a titulary which resembles that found in E4.2.13.18, an inscription dealing with events commemorated in the name of year 11. These inscriptions probably date to the general time period around year 11.

The first of the undated texts is an inscription dealing with the construction of the temple of the goddess Ninisina. It is inscribed on stone foundation tablets.

CATALOGUE

Ex.	Museum number	Registration number	Dimensions (cm)	Lines preserved	cpn
1	BM 21890	96-4-4,1	13.0×8.5×1.8	1-41	c
2	BM 21891	96-4-4,2	14.5×8.7×2.1	1-41	c
3	BM 21892	96-4-4,3	14.0×7.7×2.5	1-41	c
4	BM 21893	96-4-4,4	12.6×7.3×2.6	1-41	c
5	AO 3003	–	13.3×8.8×3.0	1-41	c
6	Hermitage(?)	–	–	1-41	p
7	Collection of Mercer	–	–	1-20, 25-41	n
8	MFAB 41.814	–	14.5×7.9×4.4	1-41	p
9	OI Photo(?)	–	–	–	n
10	WAG 41.223	–	–	1-41	c
11	WAG 41.224	–	–	1-41	c
12	Private collection	–	–	–	n

COMMENTARY

The master text is ex. 2.

All the exemplars were purchased, none scientifically excavated. As a consequence, their provenance was not known. However, the phrase near the end of the text, 'in the shrine Larsa, the city where I was created', suggests that the temple was constructed in Larsa, as Renger (Heidelberger Studien p. 147) proposed.

This temple in Larsa might be the same one built by Gungunum as recorded in the name of his 24th year.

Ex. 6 was collated from the published photo. Ex. 7, previously in the private collection of S. Mercer, could not be located but was entered in the score from the copy of Mercer. Ex. 9 is supposed to be on a photo in Chicago that was mentioned by Hallo. This photo could not be located. It might be a photo of one of the pieces, exs. 10–11 that are now in the Walters Art Gallery. These were kindly collated by J. Cooper. No complete transliteration is available for ex. 12; the vars. indicated are those given by D. Arnaud.

BIBLIOGRAPHY

1896 King, CT 1 pls. 45–46 (ex. 2, copy; exs. 1–4, vars.)
1904 Price, Rim-Sin pp. 12–13 no. VII and pls. IX–X (ex. 5, copy, edition)
1905 Thureau-Dangin, ISA pp. 302–303 Arad-sin d (edition)
1907 Thureau-Dangin, SAK pp. 214–15 Arad-sin d (edition)
1915 Shileiko, VN pp. 20–21 no. x and pl. III no. 1 (ex. 6, photo, edition)
1928 Mercer, JSOR 12 pp. 148 and 150 no. 37 (ex. 7, copy, edition)
1929 Barton, RISA pp. 320–21 Warad-Sin 5 (edition)
1961 Hallo, BiOr 18 p. 9 Warad-Sin 7 (study, including ex. 9)
1968 Kärki, SKFZ pp. 42–44 Waradsîn 7 (edition)
1971 Gordon and Owen, JCS 23 p. 72 no. 5 (ex. 8, study) and p. 74 (ex. 8, photo)
1980 Kärki, SAKAZ 1 pp. 89–91 Waradsîn 7 (edition)
1981 Arnaud, Syria 58 p. 79 n. 1 (ex. 12, study)
1983 Arnaud in Huot, Larsa et 'Oueili 1978–1981 p. 250 n. 45 (ex. 12, study)

TEXT

1) ^{d}nin-in-si-na
2) nin-gal ama-kalam-ma
3) zi-gál kalam-dím-dím-me
4) dumu-sag-an-kù-ga
5) nin-a-ni-ir
6) IR$_{11}$-^{d}EN.ZU
7) nita-kala-ga
8) ú-a-uri$_5$.KI-ma
9) lugal-larsa.KI-ma
10) lugal-ki-en-gi-ki-uri
11) sipa-nì-ge giš-ḫur šu-du$_7$-du$_7$-me-en
12) é-ú-nam-ti-la
13) unu$_7$-kù-ga
14) ki-ní-dúb-bu-da-ni
15) é-a-ni nì u$_4$-ul-lí-a-ta
16) ba-dù-a-ba ba-sun
17) nam-ti-mu-šè
18) ù nam-ti-
19) *ku-du-ur-ma-bu-uk*
20) a-a-ugu-gá-ke$_4$
21) ḫu-mu-na-dù
22) ki-bé ḫé-em-mi-gi$_4$
23) ki-tuš-šà-du$_{10}$-ga-na
24) gal-le-eš ḫé-em-mi-tuš
25) mu-nam-lugal-la-gá
26) du-rí-šè ḫé-em-mi-gál
27) egir-u$_4$-da-aš
28) ár-mu ak-ak-dè
29) temen-ár-nam-nun-na-gá
30) uru$_4$-bé ki ḫé-bí-túm
31) é-gar$_8$-sikil-bi ḫé-bí-si
32) nì-ak-mu-šè
33) ^{d}nin-in-si-na
34) nin-mu ḫu-mu-ḫúl-le-en
35) nam-tar-nam-ti-la
36) bala-sù-ud mu-ḫé-gál-la
37) GIŠ.gu-za-suḫuš-gi-né
38) sa$_{12}$-e-eš ḫa-ma-ab-rig$_7$-ge
39) èš-larsa.KI-ma-ka
40) uru ba-dím-me-na-gá
41) u$_4$-mu ḫé-sù-sù-ud

1–5) For the goddess Ninisina, great lady, mother of the nation, the one possessing life, who creates the nation, first-born child of shining An, his lady,

6–11) I, Warad-Sîn, mighty man, provider of Ur, king of Larsa, king of the land of Sumer and Akkad, shepherd of righteousness who perfectly executes the rites,

12–21) built the Eunamtila ('House – plant of life'), her shining hall, her place of relaxation – her temple built in the past had become dilapidated – for my life and for the life of Kudur-mabuk, the father who engendered me,

22) I restored it.

23–24) I installed her grandly in her residence that pleases her.

25–26) I put there forever my royal name.

27–31) In order to make praise of me for the future I deposited a foundation inscription of my princely praise, in its foundation,

32–38) (and) filled it up with a clean brick wall. May you goddess Ninisina, my lady, rejoice at my deed, and grant me a fate of life, a long reign, year(s) of abundance, (and) a throne with a secure foundation.

39–41) In the shrine of Larsa, the city where I was created, may my life-span be long.

9.7, 10–11 lugal-larsa.⟨KI⟩-ma. **11**.10–12 šu-du$_7$-⟨du$_7$⟩-me-en. **22**.3 TA-em-mi-gi$_4$. **23**.8 ki-SI-. **33**.1 ^{d}nin-in-si$_4$-na.

23

An inscription known from two cones excavated at Ur deals with Warad-Sîn's construction of the temple of the god Nergal in that city.

CATALOGUE

Ex.	Museum number	Registration number	Excavation number	Provenance	Object	Dimensions (cm)	Lines preserved	cpn
1	BM 118727	1927-5-27,255	U 6966	Ur, from Eḫursag, loose	Head	14.7 dia.	1–18, 21–37	c
2	BM 118727	1927-5-27,255	U 6966	As ex. 1	Shaft	6.3	2–5, 10–22	c
3	UM 33-35-192	–	U 18228	Ur, XNNCF 1932, cemetery near Nebuchadnezzar's fortress Room 1932/10	Shaft	13.5	1–37	c

COMMENTARY

The master text is ex. 1.

Ex. 3 is edited here for the first time through the courtesy of A. Sjöberg.

The line count follows ex. 1.

There is a ruled line between lines 17 and 18 in the copy in UET 1 which is not found in the original. The reconstruction of line 17 given by Sollberger in UET 8 p. 29 is incorrect in including the DINGIR sign, which is actually at the beginning of Nergal's name.

BIBLIOGRAPHY

1928 Gadd, UET 1 no. 125 (ex. 1, copy, edition)
1929 Barton, RISA pp. 378–79 Warad-Sin 3 (edition)
1961 Hallo, BiOr 18 p. 9 Warad-Sin 12 (study)
1965 Sollberger, UET 8 p. 29 no. 23 (exs. 1–2, study)
1968 Kärki, SKFZ pp. 49–50 Waradsîn 12 (edition)
1980 Kärki, SAKAZ 1 pp. 98–99 Waradsîn 12 (edition)

TEXT

1) ^{d}nergal
2) en-ir$_9$-kur á-gál
3) dumu-sag-^{d}en-líl-lá
4) lugal-mu-úr
5) IR$_{11}$-^{d}EN.ZU
6) sag-èn-tar-é-babbar-ra
7) ú-a-uri$_5$.KI-ma
8) ^{d}en-líl-le gar-ra
9) ^{d}nanna ^{d}utu-bi ki-ág
10) lugal-larsa.KI-ma
11) lugal-ki-en-gi-ki-uri
12) dumu-*ku-du-ur-ma-bu-uk*
13) ad-da-*e-mu-ut-ba-la*
14) lú šu-gar é-babbar-ra-ke$_4$
15) bí-in-gi$_4$-a
16) sun$_5$-sun$_5$-na dingir-gal-gal-e-ne-er

1–4) For the god Nergal, powerful lord of the underworld, strong one, first-born son of the god Enlil, my lord,

5–17) I, Warad-Sîn, who looks after the Ebabbar, provider of Ur, appointed by the god Enlil, beloved of the gods Nanna and Utu, king of Larsa, king of the land of Sumer and Akkad, son of Kudur-mabuk, father of Emutbala, the one who repaid a favour for the Ebabbar, who stands humbly for the great gods for his own life,

8.3 [^{d}e]n-líl-⟨le⟩.

17) zi-ti-le-ni-šè gub-ba-me-en
18) ^{d}nergal
19) na[m-(x)] x-⸢ni-ta⸣
20) á-daḫ-GIŠ.tukul-la-gá
21) nam-ga-me-èš-ak-da-gá
22) é-libir-ra-ka-ni
23) é-kù-ga ki-tuš-šà-du$_{10}$-ga-na
24) nam-ti-mu-šè
25) ù nam-ti-
26) *ku-du-ur-ma-bu-uk*
27) a-a-ugu-gá-šè
28) mu-na-dù
29) ḫur-sag-sù-rá-gin$_{7}$
30) u$_{6}$-di-un-šár-ra-ba ḫé-bí-gub

18–30) (for) the god Nergal, on account of his ..., the helper of my weapon, as I established a colleagueship (with him), I (re)built for him his old temple, the Ekuga ('Shining house'), the residence which pleases him, for my life and for the life of Kudur-mabuk, the father who engendered me. I set it up there like a distant mountain to the wonder of the numerous people.

31) nì-ak-ak-da-gá
32) ^{d}nergal dingir-mu
33) ḫu-mu-ḫúl-le
34) nam-tar-nam-ti-la
35) bala-sù-rá
36) GIŠ.gu-za-gi-na
37) sa$_{12}$-e-eš ḫa-ma-ab-rig$_{7}$

31–37) May the god Nergal, my god, rejoice at my deeds (and) grant to me a fate of life, a long reign, (and) a throne with a secure foundation.

24–26

E4.2.13.24–26 are edited here together because of their similar structure. All begin with a divine dedication in the third person (...-a-ni-ir), but subsequently switch to first person in the middle of the inscription. They all contain a nominalized section probably indicating indirect discourse (see Thomsen, Sumerian Grammar pp. 241–42 §484).

24

This text, known from two cones excavated at Ur, deals with Warad-Sîn's construction of the temple of the god Zababa in that city.

CATALOGUE

Ex.	Museum number	Registration number	Excavation number	Ur provenance	Object	Dimensions (cm)	Lines preserved	cpn
1	BM 116424	1923-11-10,9	U 779	From well no. 1	Head	12.5 dia.	1–29	c
2	BM 116424	1923-11-10,9	U 779	As ex. 1	Shaft	6.8	1–29	c
3	IM 1531	–	U 6313	Loose in soil of EH	Head	7.6 dia.	14–29	c
4	IM 1531	–	U 6313	As ex. 3	Shaft	7.2	3, 25–28	c

20.2 ⸢á⸣ sign at beginning of line not entirely certain.
37.1 PA.ḪÚB.[DU]. **37.3** [...-r]ig$_{7}$-ga.

COMMENTARY

The master text is ex. 1.

Edzard, Sumer 13 p. 177, lists IM 1531 as being a duplicate of E4.2.13.16, but collation of the piece reveals that it is a duplicate of this inscription.

Lines 1–14 appear to be in the third person, lines 17–19 a nominalized clause indicating indirect discourse, and lines 19–29 are in first person. The phrase ki-šu-íl-la-gá (line 15) 'in my place of *šu-il-la* prayer' also occurs in E4.2.13.25.

BIBLIOGRAPHY

1928 Gadd, UET 1 no. 128 (exs. 1–4, composite copy, edition)
1929 Barton, RISA pp. 380–81 Warad-Sin 6 (edition)
1961 Hallo, BiOr 18 p. 9 Warad-Sin 15 (study)
1968 Kärki, SKFZ pp. 52–53 Waradsîn 15 (edition)
1980 Kärki, SAKAZ 1 pp. 102–103 Waradsîn 15 (edition)

TEXT

1) ^{d}za-ba$_4$-ba$_4$
2) en ur-sag-gal
3) dumu-maḫ-^{d}en-líl-lá
4) dingir-ir$_9$ igi-šen-šen-na du
5) á-daḫ-GIŠ.tukul-la-ka-ni-ir

1–5) For the god Zababa, lord, great champion, lofty son of the god Enlil, powerful god, who goes at the van of battle, the helper of his weapon,

6) IR$_{11}$-^{d}EN.ZU
7) ú-a-uri$_5$.KI-ma
8) lugal-larsa.KI-ma
9) lugal-ki-en-gi-ki-uri
10) dumu-*ku-du-ur-ma-bu-uk*
11) ad-da-*e-mu-ut-ba-la*
12) sipa-nì-si-sá
13) un-dagal-la-na
14) ú-sal bí-in-nú-a

6–14) Warad-Sîn, provider of Ur, king of Larsa, king of the land of Sumer and Akkad, son of Kudur-mabuk, father of Emutbala, shepherd of justice, who made his broad people lie down in rich pastures.

15) mu ki-šu-íl-la-gá
16) mu-un-ús-en
17) érim-gál-gá
18) šu-mu-uš bí-in-si-a

15–18) Since (the god Zababa) supported me in my place of prayer that he deliver my enemies into my hands,

19) ur$_5$-šè-àm
20) ^{d}za-ba$_4$-ba$_4$
21) en-giškim-sa$_6$-ga-gá
22) nam-ga-me-èš-ak-da-gá
23) é-a-ni
24) šà-uri$_5$.KI-ma
25) nam-ti-mu-šè
26) ḫu-mu-na-dù
27) é-ba
28) é-ki-tuš-šà-te-en-bi
29) mu-bi ḫé-em-mi-sa$_4$

19–29) on account of this, for the god Zababa, the lord of my favourable omen, as I established a colleagueship with him, I built for him his temple in Ur for my own life. I called that temple Ekitušatenbi ('House — residence that soothes the heart').

4.2 dingir-⌜ug⌝ [...].

25

A number of bricks excavated by Woolley at Diqdiqqah deal with the digging and restoration of a canal.

CATALOGUE

Ex.	Museum number	Registration number	Excavation number	Provenance	Dimensions (cm)	Lines preserved	cpn
1	CBS 15343	–	U 158	Diqdiqqah, from outskirts of site	15×16×6	6–14	n
2	IM 84	–	U 161	Diqdiqqah	17.8×25.4	–	n
3	BM 137391	1979-12-18,26	–	Not recorded, probably as ex. 1	25×17×7	1–14	c
4	BM 137392	1979-12-18,27	–	As ex. 3	17×17×7.5	1–14	c
5	BM 137453	1927-5-27,311	–	As ex. 3	25.5×16×7.5	1–14	c
6	CBS 15332	–	–	As ex. 3	25×16×7	1–14	p

COMMENTARY

The master text is ex. 6.

Jacobsen, Iraq 22 (1960) p. 184, suggested that these bricks might come from Diqdiqqah. This is confirmed by UE 7 p. 84. Many inscriptions dealing with the digging of canals came from this site.

Behren's comment (JCS 37 [1985] p. 236 no. 33) that -a is omitted in line 11 of ex. 6 is confusing because this line does not contain -a.

Lines 1-6 appear to be in the third person, lines 7-11 in the first person, and lines 13-14 contain nominalized verb forms.

BIBLIOGRAPHY

1925 Woolley, MJ 16 p. 303 (ex. 6, photo)
1928 Gadd, UET 1 no. 136 (composite copy, edition)
1929 Barton, RISA pp. 382-83 Warad-Sin 10 (edition)
1960 Jacobsen, Iraq 22 p. 184 d (study)
1961 Hallo, BiOr 18 p. 9 Warad-Sin 2 (study)
1968 Kärki, SKFZ pp. 39-40 Waradsîn 2 (edition)
1971 Sollberger and Kupper, IRSA IVB13c (translation)
1976 Woolley and Mallowan, UE 7 p. 84 and n. 10 (provenance)
1980 Kärki, SAKAZ 1 p. 85 Waradsîn 2 (edition)
1981 Walker, CBI no. 44 (exs. 3-5, study)
1985 Behrens, JCS 37 p. 236 no. 33 (exs. 1, 6, study)

TEXT

1) ^{d}nanna
2) lugal-a-ni-ir
3) IR$_{11}$-^{d}EN.ZU
4) ú-a-uri$_{5}$.KI-ma
5) é-babbar-da ní-tuk
6) lugal-larsa.KI-ma
7) u$_{4}$ ^{d}nanna
8) ^{d}nin-gal-bi
9) šà-ne mu-un-ne-ša$_{4}$-aš
10) ki-šu-íl-la-gá
11) mu-un-ús-en
12) i$_{7}$-^{d}nanna-ḫúl
13) mu-ba-al-la-a
14) ki-bé bí-in-gi$_{4}$-a

1-2) For the god Nanna, his lord,

3-6) Warad-Sîn, provider of Ur, who reverences the Ebabbar, king of Larsa,

7-14) when I implored the gods Nanna and Ningal, they supported me in my place of prayer that I dig the canal Nanna-ḫul ('The god Nanna rejoices') (and) that I restore (its banks).

26

A number of cones excavated by Woolley at Ur deal with Warad-Sîn's construction of Ningubalag's temple in that city.

CATALOGUE

Ex.	Museum number	Excavation number	Ur provenance	Object	Dimensions (cm)	Lines preserved	cpn
1	BM 117141 (1924-9-20,390)	U 1368	From debris of Great Nanna Courtyard	Shaft	4.1	15-25	c
2	IM 92871	U 6963	From Eḫursag area, loose	Head	9.0 dia.	4-11, 19-27	c
3	IM 92759	U 7781	From Larsa houses on SW side of Temenos	Shaft	8.0	1-11, 27-30	c
4	IM 92948	U 125969	From Royal Cemetery area	Shaft	9.0	12-26	c
5	IM 92949	U 13632	From 'Larsa rubbish filling' over Royal Cemetery area	Shaft	7.4	13-24	c
6	IM 92924	U 15069	From room 9 of Enki temple	Head	12.0 dia.	8-15, 21-26, 28-30	c
7	IM 92924	U 15069	As ex. 6	Shaft	6.5	11-26	c
8	BM 122940 (1931-10-10,8)	U 17225	From main Isin-Larsa residential quarter	Shaft	6.9	12-23	c
9	IM 92858	U ea	–	Shaft	–	13-23	n

COMMENTARY

The text is a conflated one, established in the following manner: lines 1–8, ex. 3; lines 9–11, ex. 2; lines 12–26, ex. 4; and lines 28–30, ex. 6.

Lines 1–8 are in the third person; lines 18–19 contain a nominalized clause to indicate indirect discourse. Lines 20–30 are in the first person.

This inscription probably commemorates reconstruction work of Warad-Sîn on the Gabura temple, if E4.2.13.4 edited above, which dates to an earlier period of the reign, also deals with work on this same temple. Charpin (Le clergé d'Ur p. 223) suggests that the Gabura of Ningubalaga may possibly be identified with the ruined building found in the EM site. Some cones with this inscription were found scattered in the area around this building.

The copy in UET 1 no. 130 ii 15 indicates nam where the other texts read nì-dab$_5$. Collation of the piece confirms a reading nì-dab$_5$ (line 24).

BIBLIOGRAPHY

1928 Gadd, UET 1 no. 130 (ex. 2, copy, edition) and no. 308 (ex. 3, copy, edition)

1929 Barton, RISA pp. 382–83 Warad-Sin 8 (edition)

1957 Edzard, Zwischenzeit p. 174 n. 955 (study)

1961 Hallo, BiOr 18 p. 9 Warad-Sin 17 (study)

1965 Sollberger, UET 8 no. 80 (exs. 1–9, composite copy, study)

1966 Falkenstein, BiOr 23 p. 167 (study)

1967 Pettinato, Orientalia NS 36 p. 457 (study)

1968 Kärki, SKFZ pp. 53–54 Waradsîn 17 (edition)

1971 Sollberger and Kupper, IRSA IVB13e (translation)

1980 Kärki, SAKAZ 1 pp. 103–104 Waradsîn 17 (edition)

TEXT

1) [^{d}nin]-gubalag
2) [igi]-gál-šen-šen-na
3) [...] TÚG
4) [x] x gal dar-dar-re
5) [x]-⌜^{d}⌝en-líl-lá
6) [^{d}]lamma-é-kiš-nu-gál
7) [šà-u]ri$_5$.KI-ma

1–8) For [the god Nin]gubalag, [w]ise in combat, ..., who *splits* the great ..., ... of the god Enlil, protective genius of the Ekišnugal [in U]r, his royal helper,

8) ⸢á⸣-daḫ-nam-lugal-la-ka-ni-ir
9) ⸢IR$_{11}$⸣-[^{d}]⸢EN⸣.ZU
10) [nita-kala]-ga
11) [ú]-⸢a-uri$_5$⸣.KI-ma
12) lugal-larsa.KI-ma
13) lugal-ki-⸢en⸣-gi-ki-uri
14) dumu-*ku-d[u]-ur-ma-bu-uk*
15) ad-da-⸢*e*⸣-*mu-ut-ba-la*-me-en

9–15) I, Warad-Sîn, [might]y [man, pro]vider of Ur, king of Larsa, king of the land of Sumer and Akkad, son of Kudur-mabuk, father of Emutbala,

16) u$_4$ ^{d}nin-gubalag lugal-mu
17) á-á[g]-gá-ni [i]n-DU-a
18) un-lú-kúr-ra-gá mu-un-gúr-en
19) lugal-gú-dù-a-gá inim-gá bí-in-tuš-a

16–19) when the god Ningubalag, my lord, had brought his commission – that I might make the people who were hostile to me bow down, that the kings inimical to me might dwell under my command.

20) nam-bi-šè
21) KA-sa$_6$-sa$_6$-ge-da-gá
22) é-gá-bur-ra
23) tùr-ì-gára kur-ḫé-gál-la
24) unu$_7$(TE.UNU)-kù-ga nì-dab$_5$-dingir-ra-na
25) a-kilib-ba ḫu-mu-dù
26) ki-bé ḫé-em-mi-gi$_4$

20–26) On account of this, as I said an ardent prayer, I built the Egabura, (providing) a cattle pen of butterfat, a mountain of abundance, his shining hall with provisions for deity and with all (kinds) of drinks. I restored it.

27) nam-⸢gal⸣-nam-⸢lugal-la-gá⸣
28) kalam-ma igi ḫé-bí-in-du$_8$
29) mu-maḫ-gá
30) du-rí-šè ḫé-em-mi-gar

27–30) I let the nation see the greatness of my kingship (and) established my exalted reputation forever.

27

An inscription found on several cones excavated at Ur deals with the construction of Inanna's temple in that city by Warad-Sîn.

CATALOGUE

Ex.	Museum number	Excavation number	Ur provenance	Object	Dimensions (cm)	Lines preserved	cpn
1	YBC 2174	–	–	Shaft	19.7	1–50	c
2	YBC 2174	–	–	Head	5.2 dia.	1–50	c
3	CBS 14181	–	Supposedly from Warka according to dealer	Head	–	1–50	c
4	CBS 14181	–	As ex. 3	Shaft	–	1–2, 8–25	c
5	NBC 6064	–	–	Shaft	8.9	7–11, 16, 26–50	c
6	Was in Walker Art Center Minneapolis as no. 16, present location unknown	–	–	Head	–	1–50	n
7	WAG 48.1801	–	–	Cone	–	1–50	c
8	Photo I.J. Gelb	–	–	Cone	–	–	n
9	BM 113914 (1919-10-11,4)	–	–	Head	8.0 dia.	19–25, 42–50	c
10	CBS 15616	U 166	–	Shaft	5.4	9–14, 26–31, 33–40, 42–50	c
11	BM 116420 (1923-11-10,5)	U 641	From well no. 1	Head	15.0 dia.	1–50	c
12	BM 116420 (1923-11-10,5)	U 641	As ex. 11	Shaft	10.0	1–10, 15–25	c
13	IM 92867	U 10653	From ziqqurrat courtyard	Shaft	8.0	1–10, 26–34	c

17.4 á-⟨ág⟩-gá-ni.

Ex.	Museum number	Excavation number	Ur provenance	Object	Dimensions (cm)	Lines preserved	cpn
14	IM 92864	U 15651	From city wall, central section 0 45	Shaft	–	2–14	c
15	IM 92864	U 15651	As ex. 14	Head	–	1-3, 26-29	c
16	IM 22892	U 16817	From no. 2 Paternoster row, lower filling	Shaft	16.0	1-50	c
17	IM 22893	U 17227	From AH site	Head	13.0 dia.	19-25, 40-50	c
18	IM 22897	U 17231	–	Shaft	13.5	5-23, 32-33, 37-38, 40-49	c
19	IM 22901	U 17252	–	Shaft	6.7	5-18, 47	c
20	IM 20871	U 17654A	–	Shaft	15.5	1-50	c
21	IM 92870	U 18895	From Larsa rubbish pit at level 1250	Shaft	11.0	1-18, 34, 36, 38-39, 41-46, 48-50	c

COMMENTARY

The master text is ex. 1.

Exs. 1-8 are purchased cones now in various collections. Ex. 9 was excavated by Hall at Ur, exs. 10-20 by Woolley at Ur. The Ur provenances are varied and do not indicate where the temple once lay.

Ex. 6 was in the Walker Art Center in Minneapolis, but this collection was sold and the cone's present whereabouts is not known. According to T. Jones (personal communication), the cone was complete.

Ex. 7, in the Walters Art Gallery, was kindly collated by J. Cooper. Ex. 8, a photo mentioned by Hallo (BiOr 18 p. 9 viii), could not be located. It may well be a photo of ex. 7.

IM 1079 was listed by Edzard (Sumer 13 p. 178) as an ex. of this text, but collation reveals that it is actually an ex. of E4.2.13.16.

Sollberger, UET 8 p. 30 no. 25, lists U 983 as a duplicate of this text, but this text, IM 92872, is actually a cone of Ṣillī-Adad (E4.2.12.1 ex. 13).

In line 36 the sign asila$_{x}$ is represented by EZEN with some sign such as LÁL, TAB, or ŠID inscribed in it. In many cases the inscribed sign is too small to be identified and it has not been indicated in this edition.

In line 36 of ex. 2 the scribe has a partial dittography of the preceding line.

In lines 46 and 50 the verb forms are strictly speaking *ḫamṭu* in form, but they are given a precative meaning based on the parallels found in other royal inscriptions.

The epithets of the king found in lines 16–22 probably allude to the events commemorated in the names of years 8–10 of Warad-Sîn. This indicates that this inscription dates to the time of year 10 or later. The epithets in lines 6–10 are similar to those found in E4.2.13.14 and 17.

BIBLIOGRAPHY

1915 Clay, YOS 1 no. 31 (ex. 1, copy; exs. 1-2, edition)
1922 Legrain, PBS 13 no. 18 (ex. 3, copy, edition)
1928 Gadd, UET 1 no. 127 (exs. 11-12, composite copy, edition)
1929 Barton, RISA pp. 320-21 Warad-Sin 4 (exs. 1-3, edition) and pp. 380-81 Warad-Sin 5 (exs. 11-12, edition)
1957 Edzard, Sumer 13 pp. 178 and 183 (exs. 16–19, study)
1961 Hallo, BiOr 18 p. 9 Warad-Sin 8 (study)
1961 Jones and Snyder, Econ. Texts no. 341 (ex. 6, study)
1965 Sollberger, UET 8 p. 30 no. 25 (exs. 13-14, 21, study)
1968 Kärki, SKFZ pp. 44-45 Waradsîn 8 (edition)
1980 Kärki, SAKAZ 1 pp. 91-93 Waradsîn 8 (edition)

TEXT

1) ^{d}inanna
2) nin ní-gal-gùr-ru
3) me-šár-ra tab-ba
4) dumu-gal-^{d}EN.ZU-na
5) nin-a-ni-ir

1–5) For the goddess Inanna, lady who bears a fearsome splendour, who holds the numerous *me*s, the god Suen's great daughter, his lady,

6) IR$_{11}$-^{d}EN.ZU

6–13) I, Warad-Sîn, prince, favourite of Nippur,

1.1 ^{d}MÚŠ.

7) nun še-ga-nibru.KI
8) ú-a-uri$_5$.KI-ma
9) sag-èn-tar-gír-su.KI
10) ki-lagaš.KI-a
11) é-babbar-da ní-te-ge$_{26}$
12) lugal-larsa.KI-ma
13) lugal-ki-en-gi-ki-uri

provider of Ur, who looks after Girsu (and) the district of Lagaš, who reverences the Ebabbar, king of Larsa, king of the land of Sumer and Akkad,

14) šul á-ág-gá kin-kin
15) giš-ḫur šu-du$_7$-du$_7$
16) é-dingir-re-e-ne
17) šu-gibil bí-in-ak
18) URUDU.alam-gal-gal
19) mu-pà-da-nam-lugal-la-ka-na
20) gal-bi bí-in-su$_8$-ga
21) uru-šub-šub-ba-bi
22) bàd-bi mu-dù-a
23) ma-da-dagal-la-na
24) é-ne-ḫa bí-in-tuš-a
25) ní-tuk šà-KA-gál
26) éren šu-a gi$_4$-gi$_4$-a-me-en

14–26) youth who seeks out the (appropriate) omens, who properly executes the rites, who renovated the temples of the gods, who grandly set up great statues that call his royal name, who built the walls of the fallen-down cities, who settled his broad land in peaceful abodes, reverent one ..., who keeps the troops safe,

27) géštu-dagal
28) kin-da-rí dím-me-dè
29) ^{d}en-ki-ke$_4$ ma-an-sum-ma
30) nam-bi-šè ^{d}inanna nin-gá
31) KA-sa$_6$-sa$_6$-ge-da-gá
32) é-tilmun-na
33) ki-tuš-ní-dúb-bu
34) šà-ḫúl-la-ka-ni
35) igi-du$_8$-ù-dè
36) šà-bé asila$_x$-si
37) diri-u$_4$-bi-da-ke$_4$
38) é-šu-sì-ga-bi
39) ù-mu-dagal
40) u$_4$-ul-šè
41) nam-ti-mu-šè ḫu-mu-dù

27–41) the god Enki gave to me the broad wisdom to create eternal works (and) on account of this, in order that the goddess Inanna, my lady, as I said an ardent prayer, might joyfully look upon Etilmun ('Solemn house'), her residence of relaxation (and) rejoicing whose interior resounds with joy, I enlarged its *ešusiga* more than it had been previously and built it for the future, for my own life.

42) sag-bi mu-ni-íl
43) ḫur-sag-gin$_7$ ḫu-mu-mú

42–43) I raised its head (and) caused it to grow up like a mountain.

44) nì-ak-ak-da-gá-ne-e-šè
45) ^{d}inanna nin-mu
46) ḫa-ma-ši-ḫúl
47) u$_4$-sù-rá mu-ḫé-gál-la
48) aš-te-suḫuš-gi-na
49) gidru un gúr-gúr
50) sa$_{12}$-e-eš ḫa-ma-ni-in-rig$_7$

44–50) May the goddess Inanna, my lady, rejoice at me for these my deeds (and) grant me long days, years of abundance, a throne with a secure foundation, (and) a sceptre before which the people bow down.

8.7, 11–12, 18, 21 uri$_5$.KI-ma. **14**.1 DA-ág-gá. **14**.18–19 á-ág-⟨gá⟩. **14**.3 á-ág-gá ur$_4$-ur$_4$. **18**.20 -gal-gal-la. **19**.18 [mu-p]à-da-⟨nam⟩-lugal-la-ka-na. **22**.1, 20 ḫu-mu-dù-a. **24**.3–4 dag-ne-ḫa. **25**.17 šà-KA×ÁB-gál. **26**.5–6, 10–11, 16, 20 gi$_4$-gi$_4$-⟨a⟩-me-en. **30**.5 ^{d}MÚŠ. **36**.7 asila$_x$(EZEN×TAB). **36**.16 asila$_x$(EZEN×ŠID). **41**.3, 20 nam-⟨ti⟩-mu-šè. **42**.20 ḫu-⟨mu⟩-ni-in-íl. **43**.5 ḫur-sag-gi. **44**.1, 3 nì-ak-ak-da-⟨gá⟩-ne-e-šè. **44**.2 nì-ak-ak-ge-da-gá. **44**.17 nì-ak-ak-da-gá-ne-⟨e⟩-šè. **45**.2, 11, 16 nin-gá. **45**.5 ^{d}MÚŠ. **48**.10 [su]ḫuš-gi-NI. **50**.3 sag-e-⟨eš⟩.

28

A fragment of a clay knob excavated at Ur deals with some deed of Warad-Sîn.

COMMENTARY

The fragment is IM 92976, excavation no. U 12973, from the north-east city wall, central section. It is a fragment of a hollow globular knob 7 cm long, 5 cm in dia. The inscription was collated.

Too little of the text remains to determine the purport of this inscription.

Line 5′ is restored by comparison with E4.2.13.1002 iii 11′. It is not certain if these ḫé/ḫu forms are precative or affirmative. The verbal root in E4.2.13.1002 appears to be *ḫamṭu*, which suggests an affirmative form. The meaning 'to place' for gál is normally found with a bí- or -ni in the verbal chain, which is not found, however, in E4.2.13.1002.

BIBLIOGRAPHY

1965 Sollberger, UET 8 no. 77 (copy, study)
1980 Kärki, SAKAZ 1 pp. 133–34 Waradsîn 33 (edition)

TEXT

1) I[R$_{11}$-^{d}EN.ZU]
Lacuna (15–20 lines)
1′) bala-nì-si-sá m[u-ḫé-gál-la]
2′) sag-eš ḫa-ma-ab-[rig$_7$-ge]
3′) mu-pà-da-mu nam-[...]
4′) é-kiš-nu-gál-la KA [...]
5′) igi-bi-a(*) ḫ[é-bí-gál]
Subscript: a x ḪAL

1) War[ad-Sîn],
Lacuna (15–20 lines)
1′–5′) may he [grant] me a reign of justice (and) ye[ars of abundance], m[ay] my invoked name not [...], may it/them be before it [...] in Ekišnugal.

Subscript: ...

29

A cylinder fragment in the British Museum contains an inscription of Warad-Sîn. Its contents are too fragmentarily preserved to determine which deed they commemorated.

COMMENTARY

The piece is BM 30216 (59-10-14,93) from Taylor's excavations at Ur. The text, collated by G. Frame, is published for the first time through the courtesy of the trustees of the British Museum.

5′ igi-bi-a(text: ZA).

TEXT

Col. i
1′) l[ugal]-⌜larsa⌝.K[I]-m[a]
2′) lugal-ki-en-gi-⟨ki⟩-uri-k[e$_{4}$(?)]
3′) ⌜dumu⌝-*ku-du-ur-ba-bu-uk*
4′) ad-da-*e-mu-ut*-⌜*ba*⌝-[*la*-m]e-en
5′) lú šu-gar é-babbar-ra-[k]e$_{4}$ bí-in-g[i$_{4}$-a]
6′) ù a x ⌜a(?)⌝
7′) ⌜lú-šà⌝-uru-na-⌜du$_{10}$-du$_{10}$-e⌝-[x]
8′) u$_{4}$ ^{d}nanna ^{d}nin-gal-bi mu-x-x-a
9′) x-x-bi bí-in-⌜sa$_{4}$⌝-a
10′) en aš-ím-babbar maḫ-a-mu x (x)
11′) ⌜bí-in⌝-diri x [...]
12′) ⌜sa$_{12}$⌝-e-eš mu-⌜ri-eš-rig$_{7}$⌝-[...]
13′) suḫuš GIŠ.gu-za x x x x
14′) ⌜nam-ti⌝ x x x x
15′) x x mu x x x
16′) [...] x x [(x)]
Col. ii
Lacuna
1′) [...]
2′) x [...]
3′) [x] x x [...]
4′) x ^{d}nan[na(?) ...]
5′) x x x [...]
6′) x x x [...]
7′) [x x] ⌜maḫ(?)⌝ [...]
8′) [x x x] x ḪA za x [...]
9′) ⌜gú⌝-un-dugud [...]
10′) ⌜mùš(?) nu-tùm(?)⌝ x [...]
11′) [x x] ⌜dù(?)⌝-a SAR ⌜a⌝ [...]
12′) x x x mu NE x [...]
13′) x x x ma ma-an-x-[...]
14′) ⌜u$_{4}$⌝ x x ^{d}nin-gal x [...]
15′) KA-sa$_{6}$-sa$_{6}$-ge-x [...]
16′) x x-galam/sukud-bi-šè x [...]
17′) [x] x [x] x x [...]
18′) [...] x [...]
Lacuna

i 1′) I, (Warad-Sîn,) k[ing] of Larsa,
i 2′) king of the land of Sumer and Akkad,
i 3′) son of Kudur-mabuk,
i 4′) father of Emutba[la],
i 5′) the one repaid a favour for Ebabbar,
i 6′) ...
i 7′) the one who made his city content –
i 8′) When the god Nanna and goddess Ningal
i 9′) called its ...
i 10′) Lord Ašimbabbar ...
i 11′) made ... surpassing,
i 12′) (*he*) gave to *you* ...
i 13′) a foundation, a throne ...
i 14′–16′) [for] the life of ...

Lacuna
ii 1′–8′) ...,

ii 9′–10′) heavy tribute ..., unceasing ...,

ii 11′–13′) ...,

ii 14′) *When* ... (*and*) the goddess Ningal
ii 15′) [heard my] prayers ...
ii 16′) towards their clever/lofty ...,
ii 17′–18′) ...
Lacuna

30

An inscription in the Louvre bears a dedication to the god Nanna by Warad-Sîn.

COMMENTARY

The inscription is found on AO 4504, an agate eye-stone, 3.4 cm in dia., 1.4 cm thick. It was collated from the published photo.

The title 'governor of Utu' for Warad-Sîn instead of the usual 'king of Larsa' is noteworthy and probably indicates an early date for this inscription.

BIBLIOGRAPHY

1910 Thureau-Dangin, RT 32 p. 44 (copy, edition)
1923 Delaporte, Louvre 2 p. 179 no. 817 (edition) and pl. 93 8a–b (photo)
1929 Barton, RISA pp. 324–25 Warad-Sin 8 (edition)
1961 Hallo, BiOr 18 p. 10 Warad-Sin 20 (study)
1968 Kärki, SKFZ pp. 63–64 Waradsîn 20 (edition)
1980 Kärki, SAKAZ 1 p. 117 Waradsîn 20 (edition)

TEXT

1) ^{d}nanna
2) lugal-a-ni-ir
3) IR$_{11}$-^{d}EN.ZU
4) énsi-
5) ^{d}utu
6) dumu-*ku-du-ur-ma-bu-uk*
7) ad-da-kur-mar-dú
8) a mu-na-ru

1–2) For the god Nanna, his lord,

3–7) Warad-Sîn, governor of the god Utu, son of Kudur-mabuk, father of the Amorite land,

8) dedicated (this eye-stone).

31

An impression of a royal seal of Warad-Sîn is on a tablet from Larsa.

COMMENTARY

The impression is found on YBC 6978 and measures 1.1×2.7 cm. It was collated. The tablet dates to year 5 of Warad-Sîn.

BIBLIOGRAPHY

1919 Grice, YOS 5 no. 165 (copy)
1956 Gelb, Studi Levi della Vida 1 p. 386 (study)
1961 Hallo, BiOr 18 p. 10 Warad-Sin 21 (study)
1968 Kärki, SKFZ pp. 64–65 Waradsîn 21 (edition)
1980 Kärki, SAKAZ 1 p. 117 Waradsîn 21 (edition)

TEXT

1) IR$_{11}$-^{d}EN.ZU
2) lugal-larsa.KI-ma
3) dumu-*ku-du-ur-ma-bu-uk*

1) Warad-Sîn,
2) king of Larsa,
3) son of Kudur-mabuk.

32

A seal impression of the *en* priestess Enanedu is found on a clay tablet envelope excavated at Ur.

COMMENTARY

The impression is on UM 52-30-126, excavation no. U 7836 psi. It was found in room 11, no. 7 Quiet Street, and was collated by D. Charpin. The tablet is dated to year 11 of Rīm-Sîn.

Although listed separately by Hallo (BiOr 18 p. 10 Warad-Sin 22 and 24), it seems reasonably certain that UET 1 no. 303 and UET 5 no. 272, which are said to have the same U no., refer to the same object. The copy in UET 5 has omitted the first line of the inscription since it is worn away. Therefore, we do not have two different line arrangments of the same text as Kärki, SAKAZ 1 p. 118, indicates, but rather two published copies of one impression.

Although the name of the priestess has to be largely restored in the seal impression, the restoration is secure because the envelope bears the notation kišib en-an-e-du$_7$ 'seal of Enanedu'.

The title 'brother of Warad-Sîn' for Enanedu is noteworthy and finds a parallel in E4.2.13.15, frgm. 9 line 6′.

BIBLIOGRAPHY

1928 Gadd, UET 1 no. 303 (copy, edition)
1953 Figulla and Martin, UET 5 no. 272 (copy)
1955 Leemans, BiOr 12 p. 112 (edition)
1961 Hallo, BiOr 18 p. 10 Warad-Sin 22 and 24 (study)
1968 Kärki, SKFZ p. 64 Waradsîn 22 and 24 (edition)
1980 Kärki, SAKAZ 1 pp. 117–18 Waradsîn 22 and 24 (edition)
1986 Charpin, Le clergé d'Ur pp. 60–61 (edition)

TEXT

1) [en-an-e-du$_7$]
2) ⌜en⌝-^{d}[nanna]
3) [u]ri$_5$.KI-[ma]
4) dumu-*ku-du-ur-ma-bu-[uk]*
5) [š]eš-IR$_{11}$-^{d}EN.[ZU]
6) lugal-larsa.KI-m[a]

1) [Enanedu],
2–3) *en* priestess of the god [Nanna of U]r,
4) son of Kudur-mabu[k],
5–6) [br]other of Warad-Sî[n], king of Larsa.

33

The impression of a seal of a certain Rīm-Sîn, son of Warad-Sîn, king of Larsa, is found on a tablet envelope excavated at Ur.

COMMENTARY

The tablet envelope is in London. The excavation no. is U 7833M, from room 11, no. 7 Quiet Street. The impression was collated by D. Charpin.

The text is established from two partially preserved impressions on the envelope.

The Rīm-Sîn in this impression is not Rīm-Sîn I of Larsa, since the king was a brother, not a son, of Warad-Sîn. Although Sollberger and Kupper, IRSA p. 211, suggest that this Rīm-Sîn might be Rīm-Sîn II, the fact that he already had a seal inscribed for himself during the reign of Warad-Sîn indicates that he would have been over 70 years old at the time of Rīm-Sîn II's revolt against Samsu-iluna. It seems unlikely, therefore, that the Rīm-Sîn of this impression is the later Rīm-Sîn II.

BIBLIOGRAPHY

1928 Gadd, UET 1 no. 302 (copy, edition)
1968 Kärki, SKFZ p. 64 Waradsîn 23 (edition)
1971 Sollberger and Kupper, IRSA IVB15a (translation)
1980 Kärki, SAKAZ 1 p. 118 Waradsîn 23 (edition)
1986 Charpin, Le clergé d'Ur p. 40 (edition)

TEXT

1) *ri-im*-[d]EN.[ZU]
2) dumu-IR11-dEN.[ZU]
3) lugal-lár[sa.KI]-m[a]

1) Rīm-Sî[n],
2) son of Warad-Sî[n],
3) king of Lar[sa].

1001

A fragmentary cone excavated by Woolley at Ur deals with the construction by a king of Larsa of a temple for a god whose name is broken away. The one partially preserved line of the titulary of the king, if restored correctly, indicates that this inscription belongs to Warad-Sîn and dates to his first year.

CATALOGUE

Ex.	Museum number	Excavation number	Ur provenance	Object	Dimensions (cm)	Lines preserved	cpn
1	IM 92923	U 15067	From outside north corner of Enki temple in street	Head	12.0 dia.	10, 13–18, 21–36	c
2	IM 92923	U 15067	As ex. 1	Shaft	–	10–16	c

COMMENTARY

The text is a conflated one combining the evidence of the cone head and shaft.

Based on parallels with other Warad-Sîn texts, it is certain that there are two lines missing at the beginning of col. ii on the head of the cone. This means that the second col. originally contained 18 lines. Assuming the same number of lines in col. i, the whole inscription would have contained 36 lines. Thus col. i contained lines 1–18 and col. ii lines 19–36.

The restoration of lines 16–21 is based on the parallel with E4.2.13.23 lines 23–28. This permits a relative placement of the shaft fragment within the inscription as a whole.

BIBLIOGRAPHY

1965 Sollberger, UET 8 no. 83 (copy, study)
1980 Kärki, SAKAZ 1 pp. 138–40 Waradsîn 38 (edition)

TEXT

1) [^{d}...]
2) [...]
3) [lugal-a-ni-ir]
4) [IR$_{11}$-^{d}EN.ZU]
5) [ú-a-nibru.KI]
6) [énsi-uri$_{5}$.KI]
7) [larsa.KI]
8) [lagaš.KI]
9) [ù ma-da]-
10) *ku*(?)-⸢*ta*(?)⸣-[*al-la*.KI-k]e$_{4}$
11) é-KUŠ.suḫub(ŠÚ.MUL)-⸢bi⸣ x [...]
12) giš a x x [...]
13) èš-ur[i$_{5}$.KI x] x
14) uru ki-[ág-x] x
15) kalam [...]-šè
16) ki-[tuš šà-du$_{10}$-ga]-na
17) n[am-ti-mu-šè]
18) ⸢ù⸣ [nam]-ti-
19) [*ku-du-ur-ma-bu-uk*]
20) [a-a-ugu-gá-ke$_{4}$]
21) [ḫu-mu]-⸢na⸣-dù
22) [diri-u$_{4}$-bi]-⸢ta⸣-x-k[a]
23) [é-šu]-⸢si⸣-ga-bi
24) [ḫé]-bí-gu-ul
25) [ḫ]ur-sag-gin$_{7}$ sag-bi ḫu-mu-ni-íl
26) u$_{6}$(*)-di-kalam-ma-šè
27) ḫé-bí-gub
28) ní-tuk-mu-šè
29) [K]A-sa$_{6}$-sa$_{6}$-ge-da-mu
30) á-ág-gá-lugal-gá
31) sá-di mu-un-zu-a-ar
32) sag-ki-zalag-ga-bi
33) igi-ḫúl ḫé-en-ši-bar
34) ti-u$_{4}$-sù-rá
35) bala-šà-ḫúl-la-da
36) sag-e-eš ḫa-ma-ab-rig$_{7}$-ge

1–3) [For the god ..., ..., his lord,]

4–10) [(I), Warad-Sîn, provider of Nippur, governor of Ur, Larsa, Lagaš, and the land of] Kuta[lla],

11–21) built the Ešuḫubbi [...] ('House – whose shoes [...]'), a tree ..., (*in*) shrine U[r ...], the city be[loved of ...], for [...] the nation, the res[idence which pleases] him, for [m]y [life, and the li]fe [of Kudur-mabuk, father who engendered me].

22–27) I made its [*e*]*šusiga* greater than it had been [previou]sly. I raised its head like a [m]ountain (and) set it up there to the wonder of the nation.

28–36) On account of my reverence (*and*) my fervent prayer may the god ... look (at me), the one who knows how to achieve the commissions of his lord, with a shining face (and) a joyous eye. May he grant to me a life of long days and a reign of joy.

1002

A fragment of a tablet excavated by Woolley at Ur has a copy of a text that deals with the fashioning of a lyre and bronze kettledrum by a king of Larsa whose name is not preserved. The inscription could belong to either Warad-Sîn or Rīm-Sîn I and is arbitrarily placed here.

26 u$_{6}$; tablet has: KA.

COMMENTARY

The tablet is at present in the Iraq Museum, but the IM no. has not been determined. It was given the arbitrary excavation no. U da, with provenance unknown. Only the lower right-hand corner of the tablet remains. The inscription, probably a school copy of a royal inscription, was not collated.

After ii 10′ there is a dividing line. However, following Kärki, we have taken lines 10′–11′ as one line.

BIBLIOGRAPHY

1965 Sollberger, UET 8 no. 79 (copy, study)
1980 Kärki, SAKAZ 1 pp. 134–35 Waradsîn 35 (edition)

TEXT

Col. i (missing)

(i missing)

Col. ii
Lacuna
1′) [...] x [x]
2′) [...] x x x [x]
3′) [...] TÚG KI x x
4′) [...] x ma-ni-in-gar
5′) [...]-dúr-ru-ke$_{4}$-ne-ka
6′) [... m]a-ni-in-íl
7′) [... m]u-un-tar
8′) [nam-b]i-šè(*)
9′) [^{d}...l]ugal-mu-úr
10′) [KA-s]a$_{6}$-sa$_{6}$-ge-da-gá

Lacuna
ii 1′–7′) ..., he established for me, ... he raised up for me in ... he determined.

ii 8′–10′) On account of this, [for the god ...,] my [l]ord, as I said an ardent [p]rayer

Col. iii
Lacuna
1′) [...] x x
2′) [...]-le nì-dím-m[a]
3′) [g]éštu sì(*)-ge-dè
4′) nam-ti-mu-šè
5′) ù nam-ti-
6′) *ku-d*[*u*]*-ur-ma-*⟨*bu*⟩*-uk*
7′) a-a-u[g]u-gá(*)-ke$_{4}$(*)
8′) balag [l]i-li-ìs-za[bar]
9′) mu-[n]a-dím
10′) du-rí-šè
11′) igi-bi-a ḫu-mu-gál

Lacuna
iii 1′–11′) ..., ... the handiwork, in order to establish wisdom, I fashioned for (the god ...), for my life and the life of Kudur-ma⟨bu⟩k, the father who engendered me, a lyre and a bronze [ke]ttledrum. I put them in front of it/them forever.

Col. iv
1) u$_{4}$-[me-da]
2) u$_{4}$-da-eg[ir-bi-šè]
3) lú(*) á-nì-[ḫul-dím-ma]
4) íb-ši-á[g-ge$_{26}$-a]
5) nì-dím-ma-m[u]
6) íb-zi-re-[a]
7) é-nì-GA-ra
8) i-n[i-ib]-ku$_{4}$-ku$_{4}$-a
9) x [...] x a

iv 1–11) (As for) the one who in the future g[ives] orders to do ev[il] against it, has m[y] handiwork destroyed, has it brought into a storehouse ...
Lacuna

---

ii 8′ šè (text: TÚG). **ii 10′** A dividing line occurs between ge and da. **iii 3′** Text: UB. **iii 7′** gá sign with additional horizontal. **iii 7′** Sign looks like a -ke$_{4}$ with -šè written on top of it. **iv 3** lú (text: GÁ × AŠ).

10) [...]-gi$_4$-a
11) [...] x [x]
Lacuna
Col. v
1) [(an) ^{d}]⸢en-líl⸣
2) [(^{d}EN.ZU) ^{d}e]n-ki
3) [^{d}ni]n-maḫ-bi
4) x bi-šè
5) [(x)] da ^{d}nanna
6) [inim-nu]-kúr-ru-bi-a
7) [áš-g]ig ù-mu-ni-i[n-ba]l-⟨eš⟩
8) [^{d}]nanna
9) [x] x x x
Lacuna
Col. vi (missing)

v 1–9) May [the gods (An)], Enlil, [(Sîn), E]nki, and [Ni]nmaḫ, ..., ... Nanna, with their [un]alterable [decree], inflict on him a terrible [curse] and may [the god] Nanna ...
Lacuna

(vi missing)

1003

This inscription, dealing with the goddess Ninmaḫ, may perhaps be attributed to Warad-Sîn.

COMMENTARY

The inscription is found on IM 85685, from Ur, excavation no. U 16836, from the Isin-Larsa 'school-house', no. 1 Broad Street. The text is a school copy on a clay tablet and was not collated.

The inscription stops after the dedication to Ninmaḫ, not giving the name or titles of the king responsible for the deed which would have been commemorated in the rest of the inscription. Ninmaḫ was the tutelary deity of Šarrakum/Keš. This inscription might possibly be connected with the restoration of Šarrakum to Larsa recorded in the name of the 11th year of Warad-Sîn.

In line 7 šar-ra is probably a phonetic variant for šár-ra.

BIBLIOGRAPHY

1965 Sollberger, UET 8 no. 94 (copy, study)

TEXT

1) [^{d}ni]n-maḫ
2) [é-g]i$_4$-a-uri$_5$.KI-ma
3) x du$_{11}$-ga-a-a-ni-ta
4) dalla-É.NUN.NA
5) me-te-unu$_7$-gal
6) giš-ḫur-bi sikil-la
7) nitadam$_x$(MUNUS.UŠ.DI.DAM)-kù nin-šar-ra zà-dib
8) sag-èn-tar-
9) x-dingir-dingir-re-e-ne
10) nidba-gal sum-ma
11) nam-nun-na diri-ga

1–15) For the [goddess Ni]nmaḫ, [bet]rothed of Ur, ... from her father, beaming one of the Enuna, suitable for the great hall, whose rites are pure, shining wife, who surpasses *all other* ladies, who looks after the ... of the great gods, who is given great offerings, surpassing in dominion, fit for the great *me*s, beloved of the handsome son (Nanna), who listens to prayers, his lady ...

12) me-gal-gal-la ⸢túm⸣-ma
13) ki-ág-dumu-zil-e
14) šud-dè géštu-tuk
15) nin-a-⸢ni⸣-ir

2001

A limestone fragment excavated at Ur has a dedicatory inscription by Alla-rāpi for the life of Warad-Sîn.

COMMENTARY

The fragment is UM 32-40-435, excavation no. U 17853, from Ur, the 'Ziqqurrat NW' 'under the Nebuchadnezzar Corner Fort'. It was found by the door jamb of room 1 in the third building. The piece was collated.

A space occurs before the first ú sign in line 7. The stone is worn at this point, so it is difficult to tell if a sign was originally there or not.

The sign at the end of line 8 is only partially preserved, but a reading ⸢šè⸣ seems reasonably certain. For a similar use of -šè compare E4.3.6.2002 line 12.

BIBLIOGRAPHY

1965 Sollberger, UET 8 no. 75 (copy, study)
1980 Kärki, SAKAZ 1 pp. 132–33 Waradsîn 31 (edition)

TEXT

1) ^{d}DINGIR.MAR.D[Ú]	1–2) To the god DINGIR-MARDU, his god,
2) dingir-a-ni-ir	
3) nam-ti-	3–5) for the life of Warad-Sîn, king of Larsa,
4) IR$_{11}$-^{d}EN.ZU	
5) lugal-larsa.KI-ma	
6) *al-la-ra-pi*	6–9) Alla-rāpi, [*son* of] Ukuʾa, [dedic]ated (this object) as his [ser]vant.
7) [x] *ú*-KU-*ú-a*	
8) [ìr]-da-a-ni-⸢šè⸣	
9) [a mu]-⸢na⸣-r[u]	

2002

The impression of the seal of the important figure Ur-Nanna, *gudapsûm* priest of the god Nanna, is found on a number of tablets in the Yale collections, presumably from Ur.

CATALOGUE

Ex.	Museum number	cpn
1	YBC 4854	n
2	YBC 4772	n
3	YBC 4771	n
4	YBC 4862	n
5	YBC 4769	n
6	YBC 4762	n

COMMENTARY

The tablets with this seal impression date to years 2 and 5 of Warad-Sîn. They are YOS 5 nos. 46 and 50–53 (year 2), and YOS 5 no. 47 (year 5). The impressions were not collated.

For the career of Ur-Nanna, see most recently Charpin, Le clergé d'Ur pp. 47–48.

BIBLIOGRAPHY

1919 Grice, YOS 5 no. 46b (copy)
1961 Hallo, BiOr 18 p. 10 Warad-Sin 25: iii (study)
1968 Kärki, SKFZ p. 64 Waradsîn 25 (conflated edition)
1980 Kärki, SAKAZ 1 p. 118 Waradsîn 25 (edition)
1986 Charpin, Le clergé d'Ur pp. 47–48 (edition)

TEXT

1) ur-^{d}nanna	1) Ur-Nanna,
2) GUDU$_{4}$.ABZU ^{d}nanna	2) *gudapsûm* priest of the god Nanna,
3) DUMU kù-^{d}nin-gal	3) son of Ku-Ningal,
4) ŠA$_{13}$.DUB.BA ^{d}nanna	4) archivist of the god Nanna,
5) IR$_{11}$ IR$_{11}$-^{d}EN.ZU	5) servant of Warad-Sîn.

2003

Impressions of a second seal of Ur-Nanna in which he appears as *šandabakkum* of the god Nanna are found on tablets dating to year 10 of Warad-Sîn and year 2 of Rīm-Sîn I.

COMMENTARY

The impressions are on YBC 5709 (ex. 1) and U 16830C (ex. 2).

BIBLIOGRAPHY

1919 Grice, YOS 5 no. 122 (ex. 1, copy)
1953 Figulla and Martin, UET 5 no. 476 seal 2 (ex. 2, copy)
1986 Charpin, Le clergé d'Ur p. 48 (edition)

TEXT

1) ur-^{d}nanna GUDU$_4$.ABZU	1) Ur-Nanna, *gudapsûm* priest,
2) ŠA$_{13}$.DUB.BA ^{d}nanna	2) archivist of the god Nanna,
3) DUMU [kù]-^{d}nin-gal	3) son of [Ku]-Ningal,
4) [IR$_{11}$ IR$_{11}$-^{d}EN.ZU]	4) [servant of Warad-Sîn].

2004

The impression of a seal of a servant of Warad-Sîn is found on a tablet in the Yale collections.

COMMENTARY

The impression is on YBC 5709, dating to year 10 of Warad-Sîn. It was not collated.

The seal owner's name could be read either Anum-pîšu or Ilum-pîšu.

BIBLIOGRAPHY

1919 Grice, YOS 5 no. 122b (copy)
1961 Hallo, BiOr 18 p. 10 Warad-Sin 25: i (study)
1968 Kärki, SKFZ pp. 64–65 Waradsîn 25 (conflated edition)
1980 Kärki, SAKAZ 1 p. 118 Waradsîn 25 (edition)
1986 Charpin, Le clergé d'Ur p. 50 seal b (transliteration)

TEXT

1) AN-*pi$_4$-šu*	1) Anum-pîšu,
2) DUMU ur-dub-šén-na	2) son of Ur-dubšena,
3) IR$_{11}$ IR$_{11}$-^{d}EN.ZU	3) servant of Warad-Sîn.

2005

The impression of a seal of Bala-munamḫe, an important figure at Larsa, is found on a tablet at Yale and three tablet fragments excavated at Ur. The Ur pieces are probably fragments of envelopes of letters sent from Bala-munamḫe at Larsa to Ur-Nanna at Ur.

CATALOGUE

Ex.	Museum number	Excavation number	Provenance	Lines preserved	cpn
1	YBC 5414	–	Larsa	1-3	n
2	BM no number	U 7833E	Ur, no. 7 Quiet Street	–	c
3	BM no number	U 7833F	As ex. 2	–	c
4	BM no number	U 7833G	As ex. 2	–	c

COMMENTARY

Exs. 2–4 were collated by D. Charpin.

BIBLIOGRAPHY

1941 Faust, YOS 8 no. 71 (ex. 1, copy)
1961 Hallo, BiOr 18 p. 10 Warad-Sin 25: ii (study)
1968 Kärki, SKFZ pp. 64–65 Waradsîn 25 (conflated edition)
1980 Kärki, SAKAZ 1 p. 118 Waradsîn 25 (edition)
1986 Charpin, Le clergé d'Ur p. 49 (exs. 2–4, composite copy, edition)

TEXT

1) bala-mu-nam-ḫé	1) Bala-munamḫe,
2) DUMU [d]EN.ZU-*nu-úr-ma-tim*	2) son of Sîn-nūr-mātim,
3) IR$_{11}$ IR$_{11}$-[d]EN.ZU	3) servant of Warad-Sîn.

Kudur-mabuk

E4.2.13a

A number of inscriptions edited in this volume under the heading Warad-Sîn are actually inscriptions of Kudur-mabuk in which he performs some deed for the gods on behalf of his son Warad-Sîn. In contrast to these are three texts edited here in which Kudur-mabuk appears alone without reference to his son. The precise date of these inscriptions is uncertain.

1

A tablet excavated at Nippur contains the copy of a caption found on a stele which depicted Kudur-mabuk smiting Ṣillī-Eštar, king of Maškan-šāpir. The text informs us that this stele was set up in the courtyard of Ninlil's Gagiššua temple in Nippur.

COMMENTARY

The inscription is found on Ni 2760, from the Hilprecht expedition to Nippur, provenance not known. It is a clay tablet 14.5×7.7×3.8 cm and the inscription was collated.

The capture of Maškan-šāpir by Kudur-mabuk is alluded to in lines 19–21 of E4.2.13.10, an inscription that may be correlated with the name of year 5 of Warad-Sîn. This indicates that Kudur-mabuk's capture of Maškan-šāpir pre-dated year 5 of Warad-Sîn.

BIBLIOGRAPHY

1959–60 Kramer, AfO 19 pl. III after p. 304 (copy)
1963 Edzard, AfO 20 pp. 159–61 (edition)
1967 Landsberger, Date Palm p. 28 (study)
1976 Kramer, ISET 2 pl. 126 (copy)
1980 Kärki, SAKAZ 1 pp. 83–84 Kudurmabuk 2 (edition)

TEXT

1) me-dím-⸢*ṣi*⸣-*lí-eš*$_4$*-tár*
2) lú-maš-kán-ŠABRA.KI
3) lú-érim-larsa.KI-ma
4) ḫul-gál-*e-mu-ut-ba-lum*.KI-šè
5) igi-^{d}nanna-^{d}utu-bi-ir
6) nì-ḫa-lam-ma-bi
7) bí-in-⸢dúb(?)⸣-ba
8) *ku-du-ur-ma-b*[*u*]*-úk*

1–7) Depiction of Ṣillī-Eštar, ruler of Maškan-šāpir, enemy of Larsa, evil-doer against Emutbala, who ... their (Larsa and Emutbala's) forgotten things before the gods Nanna and Utu,

8–19) (*and*) of Kudur-mab[u]k, king who returns

9) lugal lú mu-ni-in-sa$_6$-ga-ni
10) nam-maḫ bí-in-gi$_4$-a
11) du$_{11}$-ga-maḫ-^{d}en-líl ^{d}nin-urta
12) ^{d}nanna ^{d}utu-bi
13) šu-né [sá bí-in]-du$_{11}$-ga
14) g[ìr (x) b]í-in-gub-ba
15) ra[b LÚ]Ú × KÁRA-a-bi
16) kisal-maḫ-gá-giš-šú-a
17) é-^{d}nin-líl-lá-ka
18) du$_{10}$-bad-rá-a-ni-ta
19) sag(*)-ra gìr ús-sa
20) mu-sar-ra *ṣi-lí-eš$_4$-tár*

the best (favour) for the one who does a good favour for him, (who) by the supreme decree of the gods Enlil, Ninurta, Nanna, and Utu, having conquered (Ṣillī-Eštar) (and) having set (his) f[oot ...], a captive (in) a hand-stock, in the main courtyard of the Gagiššua (temple), the temple of the goddess Ninlil, striding with (his) foot placed on (Ṣillī-Eštar's) head.

20) Inscription (beside) Ṣillī-Eštar.

2

A cone inscription in Akkadian deals with Kudur-mabuk's construction of a baked brick house, shelter for a stele.

COMMENTARY

The inscription is found on AO 6445, a purchased piece, provenance unknown. It is a clay cone, 15.8 cm long, 15.5 cm in dia. Ex. 1 is the inscription on the head, ex. 2 the traces found on the shaft. It was collated.

The title *a-bu e-mu-ut-ba-la* 'father of Emutbala' indicates that this inscription dates to year 8 or later in the reign of Warad-Sîn, since this title was adopted at that time.

BIBLIOGRAPHY

1914 Thureau-Dangin, RA 11 pp. 91–96 (copy, edition)
1960 Aynard, RA 54 p. 17 (study)
1961 Hallo, BiOr 18 p. 9 Kudur-mabuk 1 (study)
1964–66 Landsberger, WO 3 p. 73 n. 97 (study)
1971 Sollberger and Kupper, IRSA IVB13j (translation)
1980 Kärki, SAKAZ 1 pp. 82–83 Kudurmabuk 1 (edition)

TEXT

1) *ku-du-ur-ma-bu-uk*
2) *a-bu e-mu-ut-ba-la*
3) DUMU *si-im-ti-ši-il-ḫa-ak*
4) *a-na larsa*.KI *ù e-mu-ut-ba-la*
5) *mi-im-ma ú-la ú-ga-le-el*
6) *ša e-li* ^{d}UTU *la ṭa-ba*
7) *ú-la e-pu-uš*

1–7) Kudur-mabuk, father of Emutbala, son of Simti-šilḫak: he did no wrong to Larsa and Emutbala, did not do anything that was not pleasing to the god Šamaš.

8) *i-na ú-zu-un* IGI.GÁL-*im*
9) *ša i-lum i-di-nu-šum*
10) *em-qì-iš iš-ti-i-ma*
11) *i-na aš-ri-im ša-qú-um-mi-im*
12) *a-šar še$_{20}$-pu-um pa-ar-sú-ú*
13) *bi-it a-gu-ur-ri-im*

8–20) With the wise understanding that the god gave to him, (he) searched wisely (and) in a quiet, inaccessible place built for eternity a house of baked bricks, a pure residence, a stand for a stele for daily regular offerings in it.

19 Text: SAG plus extra horizontal.

14) *šu-ub-tam el-le-tam*
15) *ma-an-za-az na-re-e-em*
16) *ša* u_4*-mi-ša-am*
17) *i-na li-ib-bi-šu*
18) *ni-qú ka-a-nu-ú*
19) *a-na da-ri-iš* u_4*-mi*
20) *i-pu-uš-ma*
21) *šum-šu kab-tam iš-ku-un*
22) *a-na ṣi-a-at ni-ši*
23) *na-*PI*-tam uš-zi-iz*

21–23) He established his name as important. He set up for future generations a ...

24) *a-na ma-ti-i-ma*
25) *a-na wa-ar-ki-a-at* u_4*-mi*
26) *ša bi-it a-gu-ur-ri-im šu-a-ti*
27) *i-nu-ma il-ta-bi-ru*
28) *la ú-da-an-na-nu-šu*
29) *a-sú-ur-ra-šu*
30) *la i-ka-aš-ša-ru*
31) GIŠ.IG*-sú i-na-sà-ḫu-ú*
32) *sí-ip-pi-šu i-na-ṣú-ú*
33) *pi-sà-an-na-šu i-na ma-qá-tim*
34) *a-na aš-ri-i-šu*
35) *la ú-te-er-ru*
36) *i-na i-da-at*
37) *le-mu-ut-tim*
38) *i-na-aq-qá-ru-ú-ma*
39) *uš-ši-i-šu ša-am-ša-am*
40) *ú-ka-al-la-mu*
41) *a-na ni-pi er-ṣe-e-tim*
42) *ú-ta-ar-ru-šu*

24–42) (As for) the one who in future, until distant days, when this baked brick house has become old, does not strengthen it or repair its foundation, who rips out its door leaves and tears out its door jambs, who does not put back its fallen-down *drain-pipe*, who with evil intent destroys (it) and exposes its foundation to the sun, who turns it into a field of wild growth,

43) *a-wi-lam šu-a-ti lu* LUGAL *lu* EN
44) ^{d}*nergal*
45) *i-lum ba-ni qá-aq-qá-di-ia*
46) *a-gi-iš i-na ú-zi-šu*
47) *li-ib-ba-šu li-is-sú-uḫ*
48) ^{d}UTU *be-el ša-me-e*
49) *ù er-ṣe-e-tim*
50) *er-re-tam ma-ru-uš-tam*
51) *li-ru-ur-šu*

43–51) that man, whether king or *en* priest, may the god Nergal, the god who created me, angrily remove his sense in his rage. May the god Šamaš, the lord of heaven and earth, inflict him with a terrible curse.

3

A stone pendant found at Tell ʿAšarah, ancient Terqa, bears part of a dedicatory inscription of Kudur-mabuk.

COMMENTARY

The piece, TQ4–T87 = TFR 1 no. 58, was found at Tell ʿAšarah, area C, in the street STCC which separates the temple of Ninkarrak (STCD) from the house of Puzurum (STCA). It is a fragment of a stone pendant or eye-stone, the preserved length of which is about 6.8 cm, preserved height 6 cm. The inscription was collated from the published photo. The text was identified by C. Wilcke as belonging to Kudur-mabuk.

The provenance of this piece, immediately adjacent to the temple of Ninkarak, raises the possibility that the stone might have been dedicated to the goddess Ninkarak.

BIBLIOGRAPHY

1984 Rouault, TFR 1 p. 61 (transliteration, study), p. 92 TFR1 58 (copy), and pl. I no. 4 (photo)

TEXT

1) [ᵈ...]	1) [For the god(dess) ...]
2) [lugal/nin-a-ni-ir]	2) [his lord/lady],
3) [*ku-du-ur-m*]*a*-⌜*bu*⌝-*uk*	3) [Kudur-m]abuk,
4) [dumu-*si-im-t*]*i-ši-il-ḫa-ak*	4) [son of Simt]i-šilḫak,
5) [nam-ti-l]a-ni-šè	5–6) [dedicated (this object)] for his [life].
6) [a mu-na-ru]	

2001

The impression of a seal of a servant of Kudur-mabuk was published by V. Scheil.

COMMENTARY

The former and present whereabouts of this seal impression are not known; the impression was not collated.

The divine name ᵈ*la-ḫu-ra-til* occurs in Šurpu II line 162 in connection with the god Inšušinak at Susa. It is probably a variant form of the god Ruḫuratir.

BIBLIOGRAPHY

1916 Scheil, RA 13 p. 10 (copy, transliteration)

TEXT

1) ᵈ*la-ḫu-ra-*[*til-*...]	1) Laḫura[til-...],
2) DUMU *a-bi-li-*[...]	2) son of Abili-[...],
3) ÌR *ku-du-ur-ma-bu-uk*	3) servant of Kudur-mabuk.

Rīm-Sîn I

E4.2.14

Warad-Sîn was succeeded by his brother Rīm-Sîn I, who reigned 60 years. During the first half of his reign there was a considerable expansion in the realms of Larsa, culminating with the taking of the city of Isin, a deed commemorated in the name of year 30 of the king.

The various royal inscriptions of Rīm-Sîn I may be divided chronologically into at least seven groups.

1. E4.2.14.1-5 date to a time period before year 8. All these inscriptions refer to Kudur-mabuk, father of Rīm-Sîn I, indicating that he was alive at this time. In these inscriptions Rīm-Sîn I appears as nun ní-tuk-nibru.KI 'prince who reverences Nippur', an epithet that reflects the king's control over Nippur at this time. The king's name is written without the prefixed DINGIR sign.

2. E4.2.14.6 deals with the construction of the temple of Enki, a deed commemorated in the name of year 8 of the king. In this inscription there is no mention of Kudur-mabuk, so we may assume that he had died by this time. Rīm-Sîn I still holds the title nun ní-tuk-nibru.KI 'prince who reverences Nippur', a reflection of the fact that Larsa still controlled Nippur. The king's name is written without the DINGIR sign. E4.2.14.7, which is broken, probably dates to this same general time period.

3. Inscriptions E4.2.14.8–10 date to the next period. The name of year 14 of Rīm-Sîn I commemorates a great victory over the coalition army of Uruk, Isin, Babylon, and others, and this deed is alluded to in these inscriptions. During the time period of years 11–19 Nippur was lost from Larsa to Damiq-ilīšu of Isin and in inscriptions 8–10 the earlier epithet 'who reverences Nippur' is replaced by another: sipa KA-sa$_6$-sa$_6$-ge-nibru.KI 'shepherd who fervently prays for Nippur'. The new epithet probably reflects Larsa's changed relationship with respect to Nippur.

4. The next group includes E4.2.14.11. Probably sometime during year 20, Rīm-Sîn I regained control over Nippur. This deed is reflected in the new epithet gu-ún-kár-nibru.KI 'who bears tribute for Nippur'. This epithet appears in inscription E4.2.14.11 and subsequent inscriptions. About this time the prefixed DINGIR sign was adopted to write the king's name, a writing which does not, however, occur in E4.2.14.11.

5. The next group includes E4.2.14.12–13. In these texts there is an allusion to the taking of the city of Uruk, a deed commemorated in the name of year 21. In these inscriptions the king's name is consistently written with the DINGIR sign.

6. The next group includes E4.2.14.14–15. After his great military triumphs, Rīm-Sîn I concentrated a great deal of energy on canal digging, and the names of years 22–24 and 26–27 deal with such work.

E4.2.14.15 certainly deals with the digging of a canal and probably dates to this time period. It may possibly be connected with the name of year 24 of the king. E4.2.14.14 must post-date year 21 and possibly refers to the digging of a canal.

7. The next group includes E4.2.14.18–20. The last notable event in the reign of Rīm-Sîn I was the taking of the city of Isin, which provided the name for the 30th year of the king. This deed is alluded to in E4.2.14.19, and in an indirect way in E4.2.14.18 and 20.

While a few of the inscriptions of Rīm-Sîn I which remain cannot be given a relative dating, the preceding summary gives a good idea of the development of the titulary during the king's reign. The relative lack of royal inscriptions from the last half of the reign is noteworthy.

1

An inscription known from a tablet and a cone excavated by Woolley at Ur deals with the construction of the temple of Iškur. The titulary of the king used in this text indicates a date early in the reign.

CATALOGUE

Ex.	Museum number	Excavation number	Ur provenance	Object	Dimensions (cm)	Lines preserved	cpn
1	IM 3	U 223	From Enunmaḫ, room 11, below mud floor (= TTB 19)	Steatite tablet	7.0 × 6.5	1–10, 23–30	n
2	IM 92921	U 18761	From extension of Royal Cemetery area about 3 metres below modern surface	Cone head	11.0 dia.	1–11, 17–26	c

COMMENTARY

The text offered here is a conflated one. The line count follows ex. 2 for lines 1–11 and 17–22, and ex. 1 for lines 23–30. Unfortunately the name of the temple built by Rīm-Sîn I is not preserved.

A gap of five lines is estimated in the middle of both exs.

In line 5 J. Krecher, ZA 60 (1970) p. 199, suggests that the dungu-TAR of our text may represent dungu-sila and be a Hörfehler for dungu-sír-ra, a well-attested phrase.

BIBLIOGRAPHY

1928 Gadd, UET 1 no. 145 (ex. 1, copy, edition)
1929 Barton, RISA pp. 388–89 Rim-Sin 7 (edition)
1961 Hallo, BiOr 18 p. 10 Rim-Sin 2 (study)
1965 Sollberger, UET 8 no. 87 (ex. 2, copy; exs. 1–2, study)
1966 Falkenstein, BiOr 23 p. 168 (study)
1968 Kärki, SKFZ pp. 71–72 Rīmsîn 2 (edition)
1970 Krecher, ZA 60 pp. 198–99 (study)
1980 Kärki, SAKAZ 1 pp. 142–43 Rīmsîn 2 (edition)

TEXT

1) ^{d}iškur
2) en ur-sag dumu-an-na
3) su-zi-maḫ ri-a

1–8) For the god Iškur, lord, champion, son of the god An, clothed in frightful radiance, who by means of his thunder gathers the *thick* clouds,

3.1 Copy of Gadd has TE-zi, collation reveals su-zi.

4) te-eš-du$_{11}$-ga-ni-ta
5) dungu-TAR ka-kéš-re
6) ubur-utaḫ-ḫe tag$_{4}$-lá
7) ki-šár-ra ma-dam ḫé-gál šár-re
8) lugal-a-ni-ir

who opens the teat of heaven, who makes produce and abundance plentiful everywhere, his lord,

9) [*r*]*i-im*-^{d}EN.ZU
10) [nun ní-tuk n]ibru.KI
11) [ú-a úri.K]I-m[a]
12) [lugal-larsa.KI-ma]
13) [lugal-ki-en-gi-ki-uri-ke$_{4}$]

9–13) [R]īm-Sîn, [prince who reverences N]ippur, [provider of U]r, [king of Larsa, king of the land of Sumer and Akkad],

14) [...]
15) [...]
16) [é-...]
17) ki-tuš-ní-dúb-bu
18) me-te nam-dingir-ra-né ì-túm-ma
19) nam-ti-la-ni-šè
20) ù nam-⸢ti⸣-
21) *ku-du-ur-ma-b*[*u-uk*]
22) a-a-ugu-n[a-šè]
23) u$_{4}$-ul-šè m[u-na]-dù

14–23) he built [for him] for the future, for his own life and (for) the life of Kudur-mabuk, the father who engendered him, [the temple ...], a residence of relaxation suitable for his divinity.

24) ur$_{5}$-šè-àm
25) ^{d}iškur lugal-a-ni
26) ù-mu-un-ši-ḫúl
27) u$_{4}$-bal-a-na-šè mu-bi su$_{13}$-rá
28) im-ḫé-gál-la
29) ab-sín zi-kalam-ma
30) sa$_{12}$-e-eš ḫé-en-na-rig$_{7}$

24–30) On account of this, may the god Iškur, his lord, rejoice at him and grant him for the days of his reign, whose years are long, abundant rain (and) furrows, the sustenance of the land.

2

The name of the fourth year of Rīm-Sîn I commemorates the building of a number of temples in Larsa. Among these is the temple of the goddess Inanna. The construction of this temple is recorded in an inscription of Rīm-Sîn I known from three bronze foundation canephores and three stone foundation tablets.

CATALOGUE

Ex.	Museum number	Provenance	Object	Dimensions (cm)	Lines preserved	cpn
1	AO 25580	Larsa(?), said to have been found at Afaj	Bronze canephore	26.2 long, 10.0 wide at the arms	1–28	c
2	VA 2922	Larsa(?)	Bronze canephore	24.5 long, 9.9 wide at the arms	1–28	c
3	BM 102462 (1907-6-8,1)	Larsa(?)	Bronze canephore	26.0 long, 10.0 wide at the arms	1–28	c
4	LBAF C. 12	Larsa(?)	Stone tablet	13.7 × 6.5 × 3.2	1–28	p
5	Musée de Picardie, Amiens	Larsa(?)	Stone tablet	–	1–28	n
6	YBC 13526	Larsa(?)	Stone tablet	10.8 × 6.9 × 2.8	2–27	c

23.1 -dù (text: NI).

COMMENTARY

The master text is ex. 2.

All the exs. were purchased, none scientifically excavated. Ex. 1 was said to come from Afaj on the Tigris. W. Hallo thought this was a reference to Ḫafāji, ancient Tutub, but this appears doubtful, because there is no reason to believe that Rīm-Sîn I ever controlled Tutub.

Emeurur is the name of the temple of Inanna in Larsa (see RLA 5 p. 78). We may be confident, therefore, that the exemplars come from that city.

Ex. 5 was not collated, but entered in the score from the copy by Arnaud. Ex. 6 is edited here for the first time through the courtesy of W. Hallo.

BIBLIOGRAPHY

1868 de Longpérier, Musée Napoléon III pl. 1 no. 1 (ex. 1, copy)
1872 G. Smith, Notes on the Early History of Assyria and Babylonia pp. 9–26 (ex. 1, copy, edition)
1875 Lenormant, Choix no. 70 (ex. 1, copy)
1883 Ménant, Glyptique 1 p. 171 §106 (ex. 1, copy, study)
1884 Perrot and Chipiez, Chaldée et Assyrie 2 p. 329 (copy, study)
1888 Hommel, Geschichte Babyloniens und Assyriens (Berlin) p. 358 (ex. 1, copy)
1891 Heuzey, Origines p. 103
1892 Winckler, KB 3/1 pp. 98–99 Nachtrag zu den Inschriften Kudurmabuk's und Rim-Sin's (ex. 1, edition)
1900 Koldewey, MDOG 5 p. 17 (exs. 1–2, study)
1902 Heuzey, Catalogue Louvre pp. 314–17 no. 164 (ex. 1, drawing, study)
1904 Price, Rim-Sin p. 7 no. II (edition)
1905 Thureau-Dangin, ISA pp. 312–13 Rîm-sin e (edition)
1907 Messerschmidt, VAS 1 no. 31 (ex. 2, copy)
1907 Thureau-Dangin, SAK pp. 218–21 Rîm-sin e (edition)
1912 Handcock, Mesopotamian Archaeology p. 247 §39 (ex. 1, copy)
1920 Johns, Ur-Engur pp. 16–17 pl. xi b (ex. 1, photo, study) and p. 19 pl. xv (ex. 2, photo, study)
1922 BM Guide p. 86 no. 82 (ex. 3, study)
1929 Barton, RISA pp. 330–31 Rim-Sin 6 (edition)
1931 Van Buren, Found. fig. pp. 30–32 (exs. 1–3, study), pl. XI §23 (ex. 2, photo), and pl. XIV §26 (ex. 3, photo)
1961 Hallo, BiOr 18 p. 10 Rim-Sin 4 (study)
1965 G.R. Meyer, Altorientalische Denkmäler pp. 55–56 (ex. 2, photo)
1968 Kärki, SKFZ pp. 72–73 Rīmsîn 4 (edition)
1975 Borger et al., Die Welt des Alten Orients (Göttingen) no. 133 (ex. 2, photo)
1980 Kärki, SAKAZ 1 pp. 145–46 Rīmsîn 4 (edition)
1981 Sweet in Muscarella (ed.), Ladders to Heaven no. 60 (ex. 4, photo, edition)
1981 Arnaud, Syria 58 p. 98 (ex. 5, copy) and p. 80 (exs. 1–3, 5, study)
1983 Arnaud in Huot, Larsa et 'Oueili 1978–1981 p. 250 v (exs. 1–3, 5, study), p. 289 no. 2, and p. 290 no. 1 (ex. 5, copy)

TEXT

1) ^{d}inanna nin-gú-sag
2) me-kilib-ba du$_{10}$-gál
3) á-ág-gá-kalam šu-dab$_{5}$-bé
4) dumu-gal-^{d}EN.ZU-na
5) nin-a-ne-ne-er

1–5) For the goddess Inanna, mistress of everything, who has gathered all the *me*s, who holds the commissions of the nation in (her) hand, great daughter of the god Sîn, their lady,

6) *ku-du-ur-ma-bu-uk*
7) ad-da-*e-mu-ut-ba-la*
8) dumu-*si-im-ti-ši-il-ḫa-ak*
9) ù *ri-im*-^{d}EN.ZU dumu-ni
10) nun ní-tuk-nibru.KI
11) ú-a-uri$_{5}$.KI-ma
12) lugal-larsa.KI-ma
13) lugal-ki-en-gi-ki-uri-ke$_{4}$

6–13) Kudur-mabuk, father of Emutbala, son of Simti-šilḫak, and Rīm-Sîn, his son, prince who reverences Nippur, provider of Ur, king of Larsa, king of the land of Sumer and Akkad,

14) é-me-ur$_{4}$-ur$_{4}$
15) ki-tuš-ki-ág-gá-ni

14–17) built for her, for their own lives, the Emeurur ('House which gathers the *me*s'), her

---

6.5–6 *-uk*. **10**.1 Copy of F. Lenormant: sipa ní-tuk; canephore: nun ní-túk. **11**.4 úri.KI-ma.

16) nam-ti-la-ne-ne-šè
17) mu-na-dù-uš
18) sag-bi mu-ni-in-íl-iš
19) ḫur-sag-gin$_7$ bí-in-mú-uš
20) nam-bi-šè
21) ^{d}inanna nin-an-ki-ke$_4$
22) ù-mu-ne-ḫúl
23) nam-ti u$_4$-maḫ-ba
24) mu-su$_{13}$-rá bala-gi-na
25) gù-kalam téš-a sì-ke
26) nam-lugal du-rí-šè ak-dè
27) mu-ru-ub-dingir-gal-gal-e-ne-ta
28) nam ḫé-en-ne-éb-tar-re

beloved residence.

18–19) They raised its head there (and) caused it to grow up like a mountain.
20–28) On account of this may the goddess Inanna, lady of heaven and earth, rejoice at them, and determine in the midst of the great gods a destiny for them — life with exalted days, long years, a firm reign that makes the nation peaceful, (and) the exercise of kingship forever.

3

An inscription known from one bronze foundation canephore and three stone foundation tablets deals with the construction of the temple of the goddess Nanāia by Kudur-mabuk and Rīm-Sîn I. The titulary of the king, phraseology, and literary structure of this inscription are strikingly similar to those of the preceding inscription. In view of the close connections between the goddesses Inanna and Nanāia, it is not unlikely that the temples commemorated in E4.2.14.2–3 may have been situated beside each other in Larsa, and may have been built about the same time by Rīm-Sîn I. Although all the exemplars of this inscription were purchased, so we do not know their provenance, it is probable that they came from Larsa.

CATALOGUE

Ex.	Museum number	Object	Dimensions (cm)	Lines preserved	cpn
1	VA 3025	Bronze canephore	26.0 long, 10.0 wide at arms	1–28	c
2	AO 4412	Stone tablet	12.4×7.4×2.7	1–28	c
3	Hermitage(?)	Stone tablet	–	1–28	p
4	LB 997	Stone tablet	12.4×7.2	1–28	c

COMMENTARY

The master text is ex. 1. Exs. 2–3 agree in all their vars. and appear to have an inferior version, with several mistakes.

24.1–2, 4, 6 mu-sù-rá.

BIBLIOGRAPHY

1900 Koldewey, MDOG 5 pp. 18–21 and figs. 4–5 (ex. 1, photo, study)
1905 Thureau-Dangin, ISA pp. 312–13 Rîm-sin f (edition)
1907 Messerschmidt, VAS 1 no. 30 (ex. 1, copy)
1907 Thureau-Dangin, SAK pp. 220–21 Rîm-sin f (edition)
1915 Shileiko, VN pp. 23–24 no. XI and pl. II no. 2 (ex. 3, photo, edition)
1929 Barton, RISA pp. 330–31 Rim-Sin 7 (edition)
1933 Böhl, Leiden Coll. 1 pp. 28–29 (ex. 4, translation)
1957 van Dijk, TLB 2 no. 18 (ex. 4, copy)
1961 Hallo, BiOr 18 p. 10 Rim-Sin 5 (study)
1968 Kärki, SKFZ pp. 73–74 Rīmsîn 5 (edition)
1971 Sollberger and Kupper, IRSA IVB14a (translation)
1980 Kärki, SAKAZ 1 pp. 146–47 Rīmsîn 5 (edition)

TEXT

1) ^{d}na-na-a
2) nin ḫi-li še-er-ka-an-di
3) nam-sa$_6$-ga-ni gal diri
4) dumu-zi-le-an-gal-la
5) nin-a-ne-ne-er
6) *ku-du-ur-ma-bu-uk*
7) ad-da-*e-mu-ut-ba-la*
8) dumu-*si-im-ti-ši-il-ḫa-ak*
9) ù *ri-im*-^{d}EN.ZU dumu-ni
10) nun ní-tuk-nibru.KI
11) ú-a-uri$_5$.KI-ma
12) lugal-larsa.KI-ma
13) lugal-ki-en-gi-ki-uri-ke$_4$
14) é-šà-ḫúl-la
15) ki-tuš-ki-ág-gá-ni
16) nam-ti-la-ne-ne-šè
17) mu-na-dù-uš
18) sag-bi mu-ni-in-íl-iš
19) ḫur-sag-gin$_7$ bí-in-mú-uš
20) ur$_5$-šè-àm
21) ^{d}na-na-a
22) nin-^{d}lamma-ke$_4$
23) ù-mu-ne-ḫúl
24) nam-lugal-šà-ḫúl-la
25) bala-nam-sa$_6$-ga
26) ^{d}lamma šu-a gi$_4$-gi$_4$
27) ki-an ^{d}inanna-ta
28) al ḫu-mu-un-ne-dè-bé

1–5) For the goddess Nanāia, lady adorned with voluptuousness, whose beauty is excessively great, comely daughter of great An, their lady,

6–13) Kudur-mabuk, father of Emutbala, son of Simti-šilḫak, and Rīm-Sîn his son, prince who reverences Nippur, provider of Ur, king of Larsa, king of the land of Sumer and Akkad,

14–17) built for her, for their own lives, the Ešaḫula ('House of rejoicing'), her beloved residence.

18–19) They raised its head there (and) caused it to grow up like a mountain.

20–28) On account of this, may the goddess Nanāia, lady of the protective genii, rejoice at them, and request for them from the god An and the goddess Inanna a kingship of joy, a gracious reign, (and) a protective genius which keeps (them) safe.

4

Two cone inscriptions excavated by Woolley at Ur date to the early part of the reign of Rīm-Sîn I when Kudur-mabuk was still alive. The titulary of the king found in these texts is identical to that in E4.2.14.1–3. The first of these inscriptions deals with the construction of the temple of the god Dumuzi in Ur.

2.2–3 še-er-SAG-an-di. **6**.4 *-uk*. **12**.2–3 lársa(UD.AB).KI-ma. **18**.2–3 KA-bi. **18**.2–3 im-mi-in-íl-i-iš. **19**.2–3 UḪ-sag. **20**.2–3 UḪ-šè-àm. **28**.2–3 ḫu-mu-un-ne-dè-éb-bé.

CATALOGUE

Ex.	Museum number	Registration number	Excavation number	Photo number	Ur provenance	Object	Dimensions (cm)	Lines preserved	cpn
1	BM 116422	1923-11-10,7	U 780	U 89	From well no. 1	Head	12.5 dia.	1-24	c
2	BM 116422	1923-11-10,7	U 780	U 89	As ex. 1	Shaft	12.5	1-24	c
3	McGill Ethnological Collections no. 14	–	U 327(?)	–	From the Enunmaḫ	Shaft	7.0	1-9, 21-24	c

COMMENTARY

The master text is ex.1.

The cone with exs. 1-2, like many other Rīm-Sîn I inscriptions from Ur, was found in well no. 1. Ex. 3 appears to bear a number 327, presumably U 327. According to the Ur registry this is an inscription of Nūr-Adad found in the Enunmaḫ. The discrepancy between the catalogue entry for U 327 and the number on ex. 3 cannot be resolved at present.

For the reading túm-túm in line 5, cf. E4.2.11.1 i 5-6: sipa-gin$_{7}$ edin [k]ilib zi-gál túm-túm-mu 'who like a shepherd cares for [a]ll the living creatures (of) the steppe' and cf. E4.2.13.21 line 38: sipa-gin$_{7}$ ⸢zi⸣-gál túm-túm-e-dè 'in order to care for the living like a shepherd'.

BIBLIOGRAPHY

1928 Gadd, UET 1 no. 142 (exs. 1-2, composite copy, edition)
1929 Barton, RISA pp. 386-87 Rim-Sin 5 (edition)
1961 Hallo, BiOr 18 p. 10 Rim-Sin 9 (study)
1965 Sollberger, UET 8 p. 32 no. 31 (study)
1968 Kärki, SKFZ pp. 78-79 Rīmsîn 9 (edition)
1974 Woolley, UE 6 p. 89 (ex. 3, provenance)
1980 Kärki, SAKAZ 1 p. 153 Rīmsîn 9 (edition)

TEXT

1) ^{d}dumu-zi
2) en-sískur
3) nita-dam-ki-ág-^{d}inanna
4) sipa-eden-dagal-la
5) túm-túm-e ḫé-du$_{7}$
6) lugal-a-ni-ir

1-6) For the god Dumuzi, lord of offerings, beloved husband of the goddess Inanna, shepherd of the broad steppe, fit to to care for (all the creatures), his lord,

7) *ri-im*-^{d}EN.ZU
8) ⸢nita⸣ ní-tuk-nibru.KI
9) ⸢ú⸣-a-uri$_{5}$.KI-ma
10) lugal-larsa.KI-ma
11) lugal-ki-en-gi-ki-uri-ke$_{4}$

7-11) Rīm-Sîn, prince who reverences Nippur, provider of Ur, king of Larsa, king of the land of Sumer and Akkad,

12) é-ì-gára-sù
13) ki-tuš-ki-ág-gá-ni
14) tuš-a-ni-šè túm-ma
15) nam-ti-la-ni-šè
16) ù nam-ti-
17) *ku-du-ur-ma-bu-uk*
18) a-a-ugu-na-šè
19) u$_{4}$-ul-šè mu-dù

12-19) built for the future the Eigarasu ('House filled with butterfat'), his beloved residence suitable for his habitation, for his own life and for the life of Kudur-mabuk, the father who engendered him.

20) ur$_{5}$-šè-àm
21) ^{d}dumu-zi lugal-a-ni
22) ù-mu-un-ši-ḫúl
23) tùr amaš-a
24) gu$_{4}$ udu ḫé-ni-in-šár-šár

20-24) On account of this may the god Dumuzi, his lord, rejoice at him and multiply cattle and sheep for him in the pens and folds.

5

Another cone inscription from Ur dating to the early part of Rīm-Sîn I's reign deals with the construction of the temple of the god Nergal in that city.

CATALOGUE

Ex.	Museum number	Excavation number	Ur provenance	Object	Dimensions (cm)	Lines preserved	cpn
1	BM 116423 (1923-11-10,8)	U 640	From well no. 1	Head	12.5 dia.	1–14, 16, 18–22, 24–28	c
2	BM 116423 (1923-11-10,8)	U 640	As ex. 1	Shaft	15.0	1–28	c
3	CBS 17227	U 7719	Ur, EM loose	Shaft	9.5	1–22	c
4	CBS 17227	U 7719	–	Head	12.3 dia.	1–14, 16–28	c
5	IM 22898	U 17232	From AH site	Shaft	9.0	1, 3–14	c
6	IM 92780	U nb	–	Shaft	7.0	15–28	c

COMMENTARY

The master text is ex.2.

BIBLIOGRAPHY

1928 Gadd, UET 1 no. 141 (exs. 1–2, copy, edition)
1929 Barton, RISA pp. 386–87 Rim-Sin 4 (edition)
1957 Edzard, Sumer 13 pp. 178 and 185 (ex. 5, study)
1961 Hallo, BiOr 18 p. 11 Rim-Sin 12 (study)
1965 Sollberger, UET 8 p. 31 no. 30 (study)
1968 Kärki, SKFZ pp. 82–83 Rīmsîn 12 (edition)
1980 Kärki, SAKAZ 1 pp. 157–58 Rīmsîn 12 (edition)

TEXT

1) ^{d}nergal en-maḫ
2) usu-gal tuk
3) ní me-lam šu-du$_7$
4) sag-kal kur-gú-érim šu-ḫul-di
5) ki-bal zar-re-eš du$_8$
6) dingir-ra-ni-ir

1–6) For the god Nergal, supreme lord, who possesses great might, the one with a perfect fearsome splendour and aura, foremost one, who destroys all the evil foreign lands (and) piles up the rebellious land in heaps, his god,

7) *ri-im-*^{d}EN.ZU
8) nun ní-tuk-nibru.KI
9) ú-a-uri$_5$.KI-ma
10) lugal-larsa.KI-ma
11) lugal-ki-en-gi-ki-uri-ke$_4$

7–11) Rīm-Sîn, prince who reverences Nippur, provider of Ur, king of Larsa, king of the land of Sumer and Akkad,

12) é-érim-ḫaš-ḫaš
13) ki-tuš-nam-ur-sag-gá-ka-ni
14) tuš-ù-dè ba-ab-du$_7$-a
15) nam-ti-la-ni-šè
16) ù nam-ti-
17) *ku-du-ur-ma-bu-uk*
18) a-a-ugu-na-šè
19) u$_4$-sù-rá-šè mu-dù

12–19) built for the future Eerimḫašḫaš ('House which smashes the enemy'), his residence of valour suitable for habitation, for his own life and for the life of Kudur-mabuk, the father who engendered him.

20) ur$_5$-šè-àm
21) ^{d}nergal
22) dingir-sag-du-ga-na
23) igi-zalag ù-mu-un-ši-in-bar
24) ki-mè-ka
25) á-zi-da-na
26) ḫé-en-da-ab-ri
27) kur nì-bal-a-na
28) šu-né sá ḫé-éb-bé

20–28) On account of this may the god Nergal, his divine creator, look at him with shining eyes, *and dwell* at his right side in the field of battle. May he conquer the foreign land that rebels against him.

6

The name of the eighth year of Rīm-Sîn I commemorates the construction of the temple of the god Enki in Ur. This structure was excavated by Woolley in the south-west sector of the city. From the west buttress of the temple came a foundation deposit with a bronze canephore and a stone tablet. The inscription on these describes the building of the temple of the god Enki. Cones excavated in and about the temple area also bore the same inscription. Another set of canephore and tablet with this inscription appeared on the market before Woolley's excavations and may have come from the eroded east buttress of the temple.

CATALOGUE

Ex.	Museum number	Excavation number	Ur provenance	Object	Dimensions (cm)	Lines preserved	cpn
1	UM 31-17-8	U 15065	From a foundation box in west buttress of Enki temple	Copper canephore	–	1–31	c
2	UM 31-17-7	U 15064	As ex. 1	Stone tablet	–	1–31	p
3	A 29804	–	Possibly from eroded-away east buttress of Enki temple	Copper canephore	31.8 long, 10.2 wide at arms	1–22, 24–31	c
4	A 29805	–	As ex. 3?	Stone tablet	14.4×8.4×2.1	1–31	c
5	UM 31-17-9	U 15063a	At foot of Enki temple wall, near city wall	Cone head	–	1–16, 19–30	c
6	UM 31-17-9	U 15063a	As ex. 5	Cone shaft	–	1–31	c
7	BM 122869 (1930-12-13,169)	U 15063b	As ex. 5	Cone head	13.0 dia.	1–31	c
8	IM 92952	U 15063c	From room 15 of Enki temple	Cone head	11.2 dia.	1–31	c

COMMENTARY

The master text is ex. 7.

Ex. 3 was purchased from C. Morley, New York. It gives a different temple name in line 25.

In line 10 we have not attempted to determine which sign is inscribed inside the EZEN sign as a writing for Sumerian asila. It normally is LÁL, A.LÁ, or A.LÁL.

In this text Kudur-mabuk is not mentioned, so we may assume that by year 8 of Rīm-Sîn he had died.

The é-šu-sì-ga that occurs in line 29 here, and in other Rīm-Sîn inscriptions, may be related to the [é-šu-sum-ma $^{\text{e-šu]-šum-ma}}$ = *bi-it šu-šum-ma* 'delivery house' of a lexical text (see AHw p. 1288).

BIBLIOGRAPHY

1930 Woolley, AJ 10 p. 323 (provenance) and pl. XXXVIII (exs. 1–2, photo)
1930 Woolley, MJ 21 pl. x (ex. 1–2, photo)
1931 Langdon, RA 28 p. 115 (study)
1961 Hallo, BiOr 18 p. 10 Rim-Sin 3 (study)
1965 Sollberger, UET 8 no. 84 (ex. 7, copy; exs. 1–8, study)
1968 R. Ellis, Foundation Deposits p. 70 (exs. 1–2, provenance; exs. 3–4, study)
1971 Sollberger and Kupper, IRSA IVB14b (translation)
1976 Woolley and Mallowan, UE 7 p. 64 (exs. 1–2, 5–8, provenance; exs. 3–4, study)
1980 Kärki, SAKAZ 1 pp. 143–44 Rīmsîn 3 (edition)

TEXT

1) ^{d}en-ki
2) en nam-gal tar-tar-re
3) á-kìlib-ba ág-e
4) gal-zu en sá-gar
5) dingir-gal-gal-e-ne-er
6) umuš galga sum-mu
7) nun-gal du$_{11}$-ga-ni nu-kàm-me-dam
8) inim-ma-ni u$_{18}$-ru
9) ḫé-gál šár-re
10) un-e asila$_x$ si-si
11) zi-gál-la-aš ḫa-la sum-mu
12) lugal-a-ni-ir

1–12) For the god Enki, lord who determines the great destinies, who gives all the commissions, wise one, lord, adviser for the great gods, who gives instruction and counsel, great prince, whose utterance cannot be overturned, whose word is mighty, who makes abundance plentiful, who fills the people with joy, who assigns lots to the living, for his lord,

13) *ri-im*-^{d}EN.ZU
14) nun ní-tuk-nibru.KI
15) ú-a-úri.KI-ma
16) sag-èn-tar-
17) gír-su.KI ki-lagaš.KI-a
18) me giš-ḫur-eridu.KI-ga šu-du$_7$-du$_7$
19) é-babbar-da ní-te-ge$_{26}$
20) lugal-larsa.KI-ma
21) lugal-ki-en-gi-ki-uri
22) lú é-dingir-re-e-ne šu-gibil bí-in-ak
23) giš-ḫur šu-luḫ-gal-bi šu im-mi-in-du$_7$-a
24) nam-šita$_x$(REC 316) a-ra-zu-e u$_4$-šú-uš-e gub-ba

13–24) Rīm-Sîn, prince who reverences Nippur, provider of Ur, who looks after Girsu (and) the district of Lagaš, who perfectly executes the *me*s and rites of Eridu, who is in awe of Ebabbar, king of Larsa, king of the land of Sumer and Akkad, who renovated the temples of the gods, who perfectly executed the rites and great lustration ceremonies, who stands daily in supplication and entreaty,

25) é-géštu-šu-du$_7$
26) ki-tuš-ki-ág-gá-ni
27) mu-na-dù
28) diri-u$_4$-bi-ta-šè
29) é-šu-sì-ga-bi mu-dagal
30) sag-bi im-mi-in-íl
31) ḫur-sag-gin$_7$ bí-in-mú

25–31) has built for him the Egeštušudu ('House of perfect wisdom'), his beloved residence. He enlarged its *ešusiga* from what it had been previously. He raised its head there (and) caused it to grow up there like a mountain.

5.5–6 dingir-gal-gal-e-ne-⟨er⟩. **5**.8 puts the -er at the end of the next line. **7**.7 SAG-ga-ni. **8**.7 As copied, badly made u$_{18}$ sign. **10**.8 un-⟨e⟩. **15**.7–8 úri.KI-ma. **18**.7 giš-TE. **18**.8 eridu.KI-«du$_{10}$»-ga. **21**.7 ki-en-gi$_4$. **22**.2, 4, 8 šu-gibil$_4$. **22**.5–7 bi$_5$-in-ak. **23**.7 giš-TE. **24**.2, 4, 7, 8 a-ra-zu di. **25**.3 é-⌜eš-bar(?)⌝-si-sá [(x)]. **26**.3 ki-tuš-ní-dúb-b[u] ki-ág-gá-ni. **26**.7 ki-TÚG. **29**.7 é-šu-sì-ga-⟨bi⟩. **31**.6, 8 bí-⟨in⟩-mú. **31**.8 TE-sag-gin$_7$.

7

An inscription on a cone shaft fragment, presumably excavated by Woolley at Ur, deals with the construction of a temple for a god whose name is not preserved. The titulary of the king found in this inscription most closely resembles that of the preceding inscription and probably dates to this general time period in the reign.

COMMENTARY

The cone shaft fragment is IM 22890, U no. as yet undetermined. It is 6.5 cm in dia. and the inscription was collated by D. Edzard.

BIBLIOGRAPHY

1957 Edzard, Sumer 13 pp. 178, 185, and pl. 3 (copy, edition)
1961 Hallo, BiOr 18 p. 11 Rim-Sin 17 (study)
1968 Kärki, SKFZ pp. 88–89 Rīmsîn 17 (edition)
1980 Kärki, SAKAZ 1 p. 165 Rīmsîn 17 (edition)

TEXT

Lacuna
1′) [sag-è]n-tar
2′) [gír]-su.KI
3′) [ki-l]agaš.KI-⌜a⌝
4′) me giš-ḫur-eridu.KI-ga šu-du$_7$-d[u$_7$]
5′) é-babbar-da ní-te-ge$_{26}$
6′) lugal-larsa.KI-m[a]
7′) lugal-ki-en-gi-ki-uri-ke$_4$
8′) é-ì-rá-rá
9′) ir-si-im-bi du$_{10}$-ga-à[m]
10′) [g]iš-ḫi-a-bi peš-peš
11′) [m]u-na-dù
12′) [...] x NI [...]
Lacuna

Lacuna
1′–7′) [(For the god/goddess ..., Rīm-Sîn, ...)], who [looks af]ter [Gir]su [(and) the district of L]agaš, who perfectly executes the *me*s and rites of Eridu, who is in awe of Ebabbar, king of Larsa, king of the land of Sumer and Akkad,

8′–12′) built for him/her the Eirara ('House of the perfumer'), whose fragrance is sweet, whose various (aromatic) woods are costly, ...
Lacuna

8

The name of year 14 of Rīm-Sîn I commemorates a great battle against the coalition army of Uruk, Isin, and others. In this battle, ÌR-ne-ne, king of Uruk, was defeated. This major event is alluded to in three separate inscriptions of Rīm-Sîn I, which must date to the time period of years 14–20 of the reign.

The first inscription, found on clay cones, deals with the construction of the temple of the goddess Ninšubur in Ur by Rīm-Sîn I.

CATALOGUE

Ex.	Museum number	Registration number	Excavation number	Ur provenance	Object	Dimensions (cm)	Lines preserved	cpn
1	BM 116421	1923-11-10,6	U 642	From well no. 1	Head	14.3 dia.	1-36	c
2	BM 116421	1923-11-10,6	U 642	As ex. 1	Shaft	17.5	1-36	c
3	IM 92778	–	U 702	As ex. 1	Head	14.0 dia.	1-14, 18-31	c
4	IM 92778	–	U 702	As ex. 1	Shaft	9.0	1-36	c

COMMENTARY

The master text is ex. 1.

This inscription deals with Ninšubur in her female aspect. In this text the king's name is written without the prefixed DINGIR sign.

BIBLIOGRAPHY

1923 Woolley, AJ 3 p. 318 and pl. XXXIV (exs. 1-2, provenance, photo)
1928 Gadd, UET 1 no. 138 (exs. 1-2, composite copy, edition)
1929 Barton, RISA pp. 382-85 Rim-Sin 1 (edition)
1957 Edzard, Zwischenzeit p. 155 (study)
1961 Hallo, BiOr 18 p. 11 Rim-Sin 15 (study)
1965 Sollberger, UET 8 p. 31 no. 28 (exs. 1-4, study)
1968 Kärki, SKFZ pp. 86-87 Rīmsîn 15 (edition)
1980 Kärki, SAKAZ 1 pp. 162-63 Rīmsîn 15 (edition)

TEXT

1) ^{d}nin-šubur
2) nin sukkal-zi-an-na
3) me-kù-ga šu-du$_7$
4) sag-íl igi-šè-du-dingir-re-e-ne
5) á-ág-gá sum-mu gal-zu
6) šà-kúš šà-du$_{10}$-du$_{10}$-^{d}inanna
7) nam-šita$_x$(REC 316)-e ki-ág
8) nin-a-ni-ir

1-8) For the goddess Ninšubur, lady, reliable messenger of the god An, who perfectly executes the shining *me*s, proud one who goes at the fore of the gods, who knows how to give commands, who advises and pleases the goddess Inanna, who loves (to receive) supplication, his lady,

9) *ri-im*-^{d}EN.ZU
10) nita-kala-ga
11) sipa KA-sa$_6$-sa$_6$-ge-nibru.KI
12) ú-a-uri$_5$.KI-ma
13) é-babbar-da ní-te-ge$_{26}$
14) me-eridu.KI-ga šu-du$_7$-du$_7$
15) sag-èn-tar-gír-su.KI-ki-lagaš.KI-a
16) lú é-dingir-re-e-ne šu-gibil bí-in-ak
17) lugal-larsa.KI-ma
18) lugal-ki-en-gi-ki-uri-ke$_4$

9-18) Rīm-Sîn, mighty man, shepherd who prays ardently for Nippur, provider of Ur, who is in awe of Ebabbar, who perfectly executes the *me*s of Eridu, who looks after Girsu (and) the district of Lagaš, who renovated the temples of the gods, king of Larsa, king of the land of Sumer and Akkad,

19) u$_4$ ugnim-unu.KI-ga
20) ì-si-in.KI
21) KÁ.DINGIR.RA.KI
22) *ra-pí-qum*.KI
23) *su-ti-um*.KI-bi
24) GIŠ.tukul in-sìg-ga
25) mè-ba
26) ÌR-ne-ne lugal-unu.KI-ga in-dab$_5$-ba
27) muš-gin$_7$ sag-gá-né

19-28) when he smote with weapons the army of Uruk, Isin, Babylon, Rapiqum, and Sutium, captured ÌR-ne-ne, king of Uruk, in that battle, (and) laid his foot on his head as if he were a snake,

---

16.2 bí-in-⟨ak⟩.

28) gìri-ni in-ús-sa
29) u$_4$-ba é-nin-bé-túm
30) ki-tuš-ki-ág-gá-ni
31) nam-ti-la-ni-šè
32) mu-na-dù
33) diri-u$_4$-bi-ta-šè
34) é-šu-sì-ga-bi mu-dagal
35) sag-bi im-mi-in-íl
36) gal-le-eš mu-na-an-gùn

29–36) at that time he built for her, for his own life, the Eninbetum ('House suitable for its lady'), her beloved residence. He enlarged *ešusiga* more than it had been previously. He raised its head there (and) grandly decorated it with colours for her.

9

A second inscription alluding to ÌR-ne-ne's defeat deals with the construction in Ur of the temple of the goddess Ninlil.

COMMENTARY

The piece is BM 116428, excavation no. U 783, found in well no. 1 at Ur. It is a fragment of a cone shaft, 13.2 cm long, 7.3 cm in dia. The inscription was collated.

After line 13 the cone head is worn away for a few lines. Kärki restored these lines omitting the titles 'king of Larsa, king of the land of Sumer and Akkad'. However, since these lines always appear when the king's titulary is given, we have provided them here, offering a slightly different restoration for these lines from that given previously by Kärki.

In line 8 only the end of Rīm-Sîn I's name is preserved, so we cannot determine whether the name was written with the prefixed DINGIR sign or not. If the text dates before year 20 we would not expect to find it.

Line 35 should perhaps end in a -ra based on the parallel found in E4.2.14.10 line 37. It is unclear why this verb has been nominalized.

In line 45 the meaning of the verb zà at the end of the line is uncertain. In all other comparable cases the verb dagal is found. This accounts for the translation given here.

BIBLIOGRAPHY

1928 Gadd, UET 1 no. 144 (copy, edition)
1929 Barton, RISA pp. 386–89 Rim-Sin 6 (edition)
1961 Hallo, BiOr 18 p. 10 Rim-Sin 9 (study)
1965 Sollberger, UET 8 p. 32 no. 32 (study)
1968 Kärki, SKFZ pp. 79–80 Rīmsîn 10 (edition)
1980 Kärki, SAKAZ 1 pp. 153–55 Rīmsîn 10 (edition)

TEXT

1) [^{d}nin]-líl
2) [...] me-lám-ma sag-íl
3) [... gal]-le-eš gar-ra
4) [...]-x-a
5) [...] tar-ra
6) [...]-ḫa
7) [nin-a-ni]-ir

1–7) For [the goddess Nin]lil, who raises (her) head in an aura, [... grand]ly established, ..., ..., ..., for [his lady],

8) [*ri-im*-^{d}E]N.ZU
9) [nita-ka]la-ga

8–14) [Rīm-S]în, [migh]ty [man, shepherd who ardently pray]s for Nippur, [provider of U]r,

4 Copy: [...]-a; text: [...]-x-a.

10) [sipa KA-sa$_6$-sa$_6$-g]e-nibru.KI
11) [ú-a-úri.KI]-ma
12) [me-giš-ḫur-eridu.KI-ga šu-du$_7$]-d[u$_7$]
13) [sag-èn-tar-gír-s]u.KI-
14) [ki-lagaš.KI-a-ke$_4$]
15) [lugal-larsa.KI-ma]
16) lugal-ki-en-gi-ki-uri-ke$_4$]
17) [u$_4$ ugnim-unu.KI-ga]
18) [ì-si-in.KI KÁ.DINGIR.RA.K]I
19) [ra-pí-qum].KI
20) [su-ti-um].KI-b[i]
21) [GIŠ.tukul in]-sìg-ga
22) [(mè-ba) ÌR-n]e-ne
23) [lugal-unu.KI-g]a in-dab$_5$(*)-ba
24) [(muš-gin$_7$) sag-gá]-na [gìri-n]i in-ús-sa
25) [uru-didli-ma]-da-[unu].KI-ga
26) [...] šà ^{d}[e]n-[l]íl-le
27) [mu-na-a]n-sum-ma-a
28) [GIŠ.tukul-ka]la-ga-^{d}nin-urta
29) á-zi-da-du-na-ta
30) giskim-sa$_6$-ga-^{d}nanna-t[a]
31) nam-nir-gál-^{d}ne[rgal]
32) ⌜dingir⌝-sa[g]-du-g[a-na-ta]
33) GIŠ.esi-da-b[i x x x]
34) nam-ra-ak ⌜ù⌝ [x x]
35) larsa.KI-«ma»-šè mu-un-[ku$_4$-(ra)]
36) ^{d}nin-líl nin-a-né
37) KA-sa$_6$-sa$_6$-ge-da-né
38) [š]ùd-da-a-né giš in-ni-in-tuk-àm
39) šu-íl-la-a-ni in-ši-in-še-ga-àm
40) u$_4$-ba é-nin-bi-šè-túm
41) ki-tuš-ki-ág-gá-ni
42) nam-ti-la-ni-šè
43) mu-na-dù
44) diri-u$_4$-bi-da-šè
45) é-šu-⌜si⌝-[ga]-bi mu-zà
46) sag-bi im-mi-in-íl
47) ḫur-sag-gin$_7$ mu-na-mú

[who perfectly exe]cutes [the *me*s and rites of Eridu, looks after Girs]u [(and) the district of Lagaš, king of Larsa, king of the land of Sumer and Akkad],

15–25) [when] he smote [with weapons the army of Uruk, Isin, Babylon, Rapiqum], and [Sutium], seized [ÌR-n]e-ne, [king of Uru]k, [(in that battle)], (and) put [h]is [foot] on his [head (as if he were a snake), the various cities of the la]nd of [Ur]uk,

26–31) (by) the ... which the god Enlil gave [to him], by means of the [m]ighty [weapon] of the god Ninurta which goes at his right side, b[y] the favourable omen of the god Nanna, (and) [by] the authority of the god Ne[rgal], the god who created [him],

32–34) the *ebony* wood ..., the booty and ... which he [brought into] Larsa ...

35–38) The goddess Ninlil, his lady, listened to his ardent prayers and [e]ntreaties and was favourable to his *šu-ila* prayer.

39–46) At that time he built for her, for his own life, the Eninbišetum ('House suitable for its lady'), her beloved residence. He made its *ešusiga greater* than it had been previously. He raised its head (and) made it grow up like a mountain for her.

10

A third text of Rīm-Sîn I alluding to the defeat of ÌR-ne-ne is found in a cone inscription that deals with the construction of the Ningišzida temple in Ur.

---

23 Text: in-TÚG-ba. **32** (in copy line 31): MÍ KA; text: ⌜dingir⌝ SA[G].

CATALOGUE

Ex.	Museum number	Excavation number	Ur provenance	Object	Dimensions (cm)	Lines preserved	cpn
1	CBS 15619	U 1454	From a mound called Umm Faisit, on other side of railway from Tell el Obeid	Head	13.0 dia.	1–6, 21–35	c
2	IM 92919	U 15070	From town wall (presumably in SW near Ningišzida temple?)	Head	15.5 dia.	1–10, 21–45	c
3	IM 92919	U 15070	As ex. 2	Shaft	16.0	1–45	c
4	IM 92956	U 15652	From Ningišzida temple, just east of city wall in SW section of city	Shaft	5.2	18–36, 38, 40	c
5	BM 122870 (1930-12-13,170)	U 15662	From Ningišzida temple	Shaft	–	1–45	c
6	IM 22875	U 16001a	From room 11 of Ningišzida temple in a trench dug for foundation of Kassite period temple	Cone	–	–	n
7	IM 22876	U 16001b	From room 11 of Ningišzida temple, about 4 m from ex. 6	Shaft	14.0	1–25, 27, 30, 36, 45	c
8	IM 22877	U 16001c	As ex. 7	Shaft	12.5	1–26, 28–34, 36–45	c
9	IM 92955	U fa	–	Shaft	6.6	4–6, 8–10	c

COMMENTARY

All the exs., as far as can be determined, came from the Ningišzida temple and its vicinity, in the south-west section of the city, with the exception of ex. 1 from Umm Faisit.

Ex. 1 is edited here for the first time through the courtesy of A. Sjöberg.

The edition is a conflated one using as a basis ex. 8 for lines 1–22 and ex. 2 for lines 23–45.

All exs. where preserved are consistent in rendering the king's name with the prefixed DINGIR sign.

For Ningišzida as chair-bearer of the underworld, see CT 16 pl. 13 col. ii line 44: zi ^{d}nin-giš-zi-da gu-za-lá-kur-ra-ke$_4$ ḫé-⟨pà⟩ 'Be adjured by Ningišzida, chair-bearer of the netherworld'. See also AfO 14 p. 146 line 124 = 4 R^2 no. 21 col. ii line 15: *ana* ^{d}nin-giš-zi-da GU.ZA.LÁ KI-*tim* DAGAL-*tim* 'to Ningišzida, chair-bearer of the broad underworld'.

BIBLIOGRAPHY

1965 Sollberger, UET 8 no. 85 (ex. 5, copy; exs. 2–9, study)
1971 Sollberger and Kupper, IRSA IVB14c (translation)
1976 Woolley and Mallowan, UE 7 p. 71 (exs. 4–8, provenance)
1980 Kärki, SAKAZ 1 pp. 171–72 Rīmsîn 26 (edition)

TEXT

1) ^{d}nin-giš-zi-da
2) ur-sag i-ši ní di sag-ki-bi súr ḫu-ḫu-ul
3) GIŠ.gu-za-lá ki-an-a-na-šú-a-aš na-ri-eri$_{11}$-gal-la
4) dingir-zi sag-èn-tar-é-kiš-nu-gál-la me-nun-na šu-du$_7$
5) lugal-mu-ra

1–5) For the god Ningišzida, champion, who *emits* a radiance and fearsome splendour, whose face ..., chair-bearer of the netherworld, counsellor of the underworld, reliable god, who looks after the Ekišnugal, who perfectly executes the princely *me*s, my lord,

6) ^{d}*ri-im*-^{d}EN.ZU
7) nita-kala-ga
8) sipa KA-sa$_6$-sa$_6$-ge-nibru.KI
9) me giš-ḫur-eridu.KI-ga kù-kù-ge
10) ú-a-úri.KI-ma

6–14) I, Rīm-Sîn, mighty man, shepherd who prays ardently for Nippur, who purifies the *me*s and rites of Eridu, provider of Ur, who looks after Girsu (and) the district of Lagaš, who renovated the temples of the gods, king of Larsa,

---

2.5 Copy: UD; text: di. 3.1, 7 -gal-⟨la⟩. 3.2 ki-an-na-a-KI-šú-a-aš. 3.5 omits line. 4.8 -gál-⟨la⟩. 9.5 kù-kù-ge$_4$.

11) sag-èn-tar-gír-su.KI ki-lagaš.KI-a
12) lú é-dingir-re-e-ne šu-gibil bí-in-ak
13) lugal-larsa.KI-ma
14) lugal-ki-en-gi-ki-uri-me-en

king of the land of Sumer and Akkad,

15) u$_4$ ugnim unu.KI
16) ì-si-in.KI KÁ.DINGIR.RA.KI
17) *ra-pi$_5$-qum*.KI *su-ti-um*.KI-ma
18) GIŠ.tukul mu-sìg-ga
19) mè-ba ÌR-ne-ne lugal-unu.KI-ga mu-dab$_5$-ba

15–19) when I smote with weapons the army of Uruk, Isin, Babylon, Rapiqum, and Sutium (and) seized ÌR-ne-ne, king of Uruk, in that battle,

20) inim-an lugal-dingir-re-e-ne-ta
21) du$_{11}$-ga-maḫ-^{d}en-líl lugal-gá-ta
22) ^{d}nin-líl nin-gá-ta
23) ^{d}nin-urta ur-sag-kala-ga á-zi-da du-gá-ta
24) ^{d}núska(PA.LU) sukkal-maḫ ad-da-é-gal-gá-ta

20–24) (when) by the word of the god An, king of the gods, by the supreme decree of the god Enlil, my lord, of the goddess Ninlil, my lady, of the god Ninurta, mighty champion who goes for me at the right hand of the god Nuska, supreme messenger, father of my palace,

25) géštu ^{d}en-ki-ke$_4$ ma-an-sum-ma-ta
26) ^{d}nin-ḫur-sag du$_{10}$ ki si-ig-ge$_4$-gá-ta
27) giskim-sa$_6$-ga-^{d}nanna-ta
28) nam-nir-gál-^{d}utu lugal-gá-ta
29) á-ág-gá-sa$_6$-ga ^{d}iškur-ta
30) usu-^{d}nergal dingir-sag-du-gá-ta

25–30) by the wisdom that the god Enki gave to me, by the goddess Ninḫursag who fills the earth with good things for me, by the favourable omen of the god Nanna, by the authority of the god Utu, my lord, by the splendid command of the god Iškur, by the might of the god Nergal, the god who created me,

31) ^{d}inanna nin-mè-gá-ta
32) ^{d}nin-in-si-na nin-á-gá-ta
33) ^{d}nin-šen-šen-na ma-UD-gá-ta

31–33) by the goddess Inanna, lady of my battle, by the goddess Ninisina, lady of my strength, by the god Ninšenšena who shines for me,

34) uru-didli-ma-da-unu.KI-ga mu-sì-sì-ga
35) nam-ra-ak nì-ga a-na-gál-la-bi
36) larsa.KI-šè
37) im-mi-ku$_4$-ra

34–37) the booty, as much as there was, of the various cities of the land of Uruk which I smote which I brought into Larsa:

38) u$_4$-ba ^{d}nin-giš-zi-da
39) lugal-mu-ra
40) KA-sa$_6$-sa$_6$-ge$_4$-da-mu-dè
41) é-nì-ge-na
42) ki-tuš-ki-ág-gá-ni
43) nam-ti-mu-šè mu-na-dù
44) sag-bi mu-ni-íl
45) ḫur-sag-gin$_7$ mu-na-mú

38–45) at that time, as I prayed ardently to my lord, the god Ningišzida, I built for him, for my own life, the Enigena ('House of righteousness'), his beloved residence. I raised its head (and) made it grow up like a mountain for him.

11

An inscription known from cones found at Ur and vicinity, as well as a tablet copy, deals with the construction of a storehouse for the god Nanna in the city of Ur.

15.5 ugnim(KA.LU.ÚB.GAR). **15**.5, 7 unu$_5$.KI. **16**.5, 7 KÁ.DINGIR.RA.⟨KI⟩. **17**.5, 7 *ra-pi-qum*.⟨KI⟩ *su-ti-um*.⟨KI⟩. **19**.3 ÌR-ne-⟨ne⟩. **19**.5 lugal-AB×ME.KI-ga. **19**.7 ⸢unu$_5$⸣.KI-ga. **21**.5 ^{d}en-líl-«ta». **23**.5 Copy: kala-LUGAL; text: kala-ga. **24**.1–2 nuska(PA.TÚG). **26**.2 si-ig-ge$_4$-⟨gá⟩-⸢ta⸣. **34**.5 ma-da-AB×U.KI-ga. **40**.5 KA-sa$_6$-sa$_6$-ge$_4$-ta-mu-ni. **42**.3 [ki-ág-gá]-⸢a-ni⸣. **42**.5 ⟨ki⟩-ág-gá-a-ni. **43**.5 mu-na-NI.

CATALOGUE

Ex.	Museum number	Excavation number	Photo number	Ur provenance	Object	Dimensions (cm)	Lines preserved	cpn
1	BM 116425 (1923-11-10,10)	U 781	U 88	From well no. 1	Cone head	11.5 dia.	1-33	c
2	BM 116425 (1923-11-10,10)	U 781	U 88	As ex. 1	Cone shaft	9.8	1-33	c
3	IM 791	U 1633(?)	–	Found by Arabs at Mfaisit	Cone head	–	1-33	n
4	IM 791	U 1633(?)	–	As ex. 3	Cone shaft	–	Beginnings of lines	n
5	IM –	U 17900M	–	From no. 1, Broad Street	Clay tablet	–	Traces, 21-33	n
6	BCM 60 '76	U –	–	–	Cone shaft	4.5	1-7, 31-33	c

COMMENTARY

The master text is ex. 1.

For the date of this inscription see the discussion in the introduction to Rīm-Sîn I.

Vars. for ex. 3 are added from the notes of Edzard, Sumer 13 p. 184. Ex. 6 was kindly collated by A. George.

BIBLIOGRAPHY

1923 Woolley, AJ 3 pl. XXIV 2 (c) (exs. 1-2, photo)
1928 Gadd, UET 1 no. 139 (exs. 1-2, composite copy, edition; ex. 3, var.)
1929 Barton, RISA pp. 384-85 Rim-Sin 2 (edition)
1957 Edzard, Sumer 13 pp. 178 and 184 (exs. 3-4, study)
1961 Hallo, BiOr 18 p. 10 Rim-Sin 11 (study)
1965 Sollberger, UET 8 p. 31 no. 29 (exs. 1-5, study)
1968 Kärki, SKFZ pp. 81-82 Rīmsîn 11 (edition)
1979 George, Iraq 41 p. 122 no. 38 (ex. 6, study)
1980 Kärki, SAKAZ 1 pp. 155-57 Rīmsîn 11 (edition)

TEXT

1) ^{d}nanna
2) en-gal me-lám-ma sag-íl
3) an-ki-a pa-è
4) su-lim-dagal še-er-zi-bi mú-mú
5) un-šár-ra-aš u$_4$ gá-gá
6) nun-u$_{18}$-ru me-ni a-re-eš kal
7) nì-nam-ma-ni kù-kù-ug
8) dumu-zi-le-kur-gal-^{d}en-líl-le
9) nun ki-ág-é-kur-ra
10) lugal-a-ni-ir
11) *ri-im*-^{d}EN.ZU
12) sipa-gú-un-kár-nibru.KI
13) ú-a-uri$_5$.KI-ma
14) sag-èn-tar-
15) gír-su.KI-ki-lagaš.KI-a
16) me giš-ḫur-eridu.KI-ga šu-du$_7$-du$_7$
17) é-babbar-da ní-te-⸢ge$_{26}$⸣
18) lugal-larsa.KI-ma
19) lugal-ki-en-gi-ki-uri
20) lú é-dingir-re-e-⸢ne⸣
21) šu-gibil bí-in-ak-⸢a⸣

1-10) For the god Nanna, great lord, who raises (his) head in an aura, who shines forth brightly in heaven and earth, the one with a broad awe-inspiring radiance which keeps renewing its brilliance, who establishes light for all the people, mighty prince, whose *me*s are worthy of praise, who makes everything he has shine, handsome son of the great mountain, the god Enlil, prince beloved of Ekur, for his lord,

11-25) Rīm-Sîn, shepherd who bears tribute for Nippur, provider of Ur, who looks after Girsu (and) the district of Lagaš, who perfectly executes the *me*s and rites of Eridu, who reverences the Ebabbar, king of Larsa, king of the land of Sumer and Akkad, who renovated the temples of the gods, who greatly perfects the rites and pure lustration ceremonies, who stands daily uttering supplications and entreaties,

---

4.1-2 Copy shows érin su-lim; collation reveals no érin sign.
7.1 Copy: PIRIG+RU; text: ug. **12.2** «^{d}»n[ibru.KI].

22) giš-ḫur šu-luḫ-kù-ga
23) šu-gal mu-du$_7$-a
24) nam-šita$_x$(REC 316) a-ra-zu di
25) u$_4$-šú-uš-e gub-ba
26) é-šútum-kù-^{d}nanna
27) ki-tuš-ní-dúb-bu-da-ni
28) nam-ti-la-ni-šè
29) mu-na-dù
30) diri-u$_4$-bi-ta-šè
31) é-šu-sì-ga-bi mu-dagal
32) sag-bi im-mi-in-íl
33) gal-le-eš im-mi-in-gùn

26–29) built for him, for his own life, the Ešutumkunanna ('House – shining storehouse of the god Nanna'), his residence of relaxation.

30–33) He enlarged its *ešusiga* more than it had been previously. He raised its head there and grandly decorated it with colours.

12

The taking of the city of Uruk recorded in the name of year 21 of Rīm-Sîn I was a notable achievement of the Larsa king. After this point the king always had his name written with the prefixed DINGIR sign in his royal inscriptions. The taking of Uruk is alluded to in two inscriptions of Rīm-Sîn I. The first deals with the construction of the temple of the god Ninšubur in Ur. This inscription is dedicated to Ninšubur in his male aspect.

CATALOGUE

Ex.	Museum number	Ur provenance	Object	Dimensions (cm)	Lines preserved	cpn
1	BM 90898	From the southern mound	Diorite tablet	11.0×6.3×1.9	1–24	c
2	BCM 287 '35E	–	Cone shaft	11.0	1–12, 17–24	c

COMMENTARY

The master text is ex. 1.

Ex. 1, a stone foundation tablet, has no registration no. but probably came from Taylor's excavations at Ur.

Ex. 2 has no excavation no. preserved on it, but presumably came from Woolley's excavations at Ur, since many of the Birmingham Museum pieces appear to have come from that source. It was collated by A. George.

BIBLIOGRAPHY

1861 1 R pl. 3 no. x (ex. 1, copy)
1872 G. Smith, TSBA 1 p. 53 (translation)
1874 Lenormant, Études accadiennes 2 p. 351
1875 Ménant, Babylone et la Chaldée p. 90 (translation)
1892 Winckler, KB 3/1 pp. 94–95 Kudur-mabuk and Rim-Sin 3 (edition)
1904 Price, Rim-Sin p. 9 no. IV (edition)
1905 Thureau-Dangin, ISA pp. 308–309 Rîm-sin c (edition)
1907 Thureau-Dangin, SAK pp. 218–19 Rîm-sin c (edition)
1910 King, Early History pl. XXIX facing p. 288 (ex. 1, photo [obv. only])
1929 Barton, RISA pp. 328–29 Rim-Sin 4 (edition)
1961 Hallo, BiOr 18 p. 10 Rim-Sin 7 (study)
1968 Kärki, SKFZ pp. 75–76 Rīmsîn 7 (edition)
1979 George, Iraq 41 p. 122 no. 37 (ex. 2, study)
1980 Kärki, SAKAZ 1 p. 149 Rīmsîn 7 (edition)

26.3 é-šutum(GI.NA.AB.DU$_7$). **27.3** ki-tuš-ní-dúb-⟨bu⟩-da-ni.
33.1 im-⟨mi⟩-in-gùn.

TEXT

1) ^{d}nin-šubur
2) en-gal me-kìlib-ba ág-e
3) šà-KA-sa$_6$-ge gal-zu
4) sukkal-maḫ šà-kúš-ù-an-gal-la
5) du$_{11}$-ga-ni igi-šè du
6) lugal-a-ni-ir

1–6) For the god Ninšubur, great lord, who measures out all the *mes*, who knows the essence of prayer, supreme messenger (and) adviser of great An, whose word goes at the fore, for his lord,

7) ^{d}*ri-im*-^{d}EN.ZU
8) sipa-gú-un-[k]ár-nibru.KI
9) me giš-ḫur-eridu.KI-ga šu-du$_7$-du$_7$
10) ú-a-uri$_5$.KI-ma
11) é-babbar-da ní-te-ge$_{26}$
12) lugal-larsa.KI-m[a]
13) [l]ugal-ki-en-gi-ki-uri-ke$_4$

7–13) (I), Rīm-Sîn, shepherd who [b]ears tribute for Nippur, who perfectly executes the *mes* and rites of Eridu, provider of Ur, who reverences Ebabbar, king of Larsa, king of the land of Sumer and Akkad,

14) u$_4$ an ^{d}en-líl
15) ^{d}en-ki
16) dingir-gal-gal-e-ne
17) unu.KI uru-ul
18) šu-mu-šè ma-ni-in-si-eš-a

14–18) when the gods An, Enlil, (and) Enki, the great gods, entrusted Uruk, the ancient city, into my hands,

19) ^{d}nin-šubur lugal-mu-úr
20) KA-sa$_6$-sa$_6$-ge-da-mu-ta
21) é-á-ág-gá-sum-mu
22) ki-tuš-ki-ág-gá-ni
23) nam-ti-mu-šè
24) mu-na-dù

19–24) for the god Ninšubur, my lord, as I said an ardent prayer, I built for him, for my own life, the Eaagasumu ('House which gives the commands'), his beloved residence.

13

A cone excavated by de Sarzec at Telloh, ancient Girsu, deals with the construction of the temple of the god Ninšubur in that city. The inscription alludes in a temporal clause to the gods' granting control over the city of Uruk to Rīm-Sîn I. The inscription is dedicated to Ninšubur in his male aspect.

CATALOGUE

Ex.	Museum number	Provenance	Object	Lines preserved	cpn
1	MNB 1510	Telloh, 60 cm below pavement opposite entrance MM' to palace of Tell A	Head	1–37	c
2	MNB 1510	As ex. 1	Shaft	27–29	c

COMMENTARY

The master text is ex. 1.

A photo of the cone was published in de Sarzec, Découvertes 1 pl. 41 no. 1. In the table of contents of this vol. p. 11, under Cônes, this piece is mentioned with a cross-reference to p. 47 of vol. 2. In vol. 2 p. 47 no. 2 there is a description of a cone but no details are given about the text inscribed on it. We have assumed that the cone described there is the Rīm-Sîn I cone and that the provenance described on p. 47 refers to this piece.

The god Lugal-gudua who appears in line 19 is probably a tutelary deity of a city in the vicinity of Larsa, and should not be taken to allude to control by the Larsa dynasty over the city of Kutha in the north. It could refer to the god Nergal of Uṣarpara(n), a city whose capture is commemorated in the name of year 18 of Rīm-Sîn I, or to the tutelary deity of Dūrum, whose capture is commemorated in the name of year 20. The epithet in line 20 alludes to control over Uruk.

BIBLIOGRAPHY

1884–1912 de Sarzec, Découvertes 1 pl. 41 no. 1 (ex. 1, photo); 2 p. 47 no. 2 (provenance, study)

1904 Price, Rim-Sin pp. 178–79 no. VIII and pls. XI–XIII (copy, edition)

1905 Thureau-Dangin, ISA pp. 306–307 Rîm-sin a (edition)

1907 Thureau-Dangin, SAK pp. 216–17 Rîm-sin a (edition)

1929 Barton, RISA pp. 324–27 Rim-Sin 1 (edition)

1961 Hallo, BiOr 18 p. 11 Rim-Sin 16 (edition)

1968 Kärki, SKFZ pp. 87–88 Rīmsîn 16 (edition)

1980 Kärki, SAKAZ 1 pp. 163–65 Rīmsîn 16 (edition)

TEXT

1) ^{d}nin-šubur
2) en-gal umuš galga zà-íl
3) inim-zi-du$_{11}$-ga-ni nu-kàm-me
4) sukkal-maḫ ù-luḫ-gi$_{4}$-rin šu-du$_{7}$
5) á-ág-gá an-ki-a si-sá-e
6) ba-an-gi$_{4}$ sum-mu dingir-gal-gal-e-ne-er
7) a-ra-zu-e giš-tuk
8) lugal-mu-ra

1–8) For the god Ninšubur, great lord, who bears instruction and counsel, whose reliable decree cannot be overturned, supreme messenger, who holds the shining staff in (his) hand, who puts in order the commands in heaven and earth, who gives answers to the great gods, who listens to entreaties, my lord,

9) ^{d}*ri-im*-^{d}EN.ZU nita-kala-ga
10) šul giš-tu[k]-kur-gal-la
11) sipa-gú-un-kár-nibru.KI
12) me giš-ḫur-šu-du$_{7}$-eridu.KI-ga
13) engar-zi ú-a-úri.KI-ma
14) é-babbar-da ní-te-ge$_{26}$
15) sag-èn-tar-gír-su.KI-ki-lagaš.KI
16) KA-sa$_{6}$-sa$_{6}$-ge-b[i] ⸢maḫ⸣-a
17) é-babbar gal-gal-la-e
18) [n]idb[a] nu-šilig-ge
19) ^{d}lugal-gú-du$_{8}$-a-šè
20) sá-du$_{11}$ laḫ$_{5}$ é-an-na-šè
21) lugal-larsa.KI-ma
22) lugal-ki-en-gi-ki-uri-me-en

9–22) I, Rīm-Sîn, mighty man, youth who listen[s] to the great mountain (Enlil), shepherd who bears tribute for Nippur, who perfectly executes the *me*s and rites of Eridu, reliable farmer, provider of Ur, who reverences the Ebabbar, who looks after Girsu (and) the district of Lagaš, whose ardent prayer is supreme, who makes the Ebabbar great, who (makes) unceasing offerings to the god Lugal-gudua, who brings regular offerings to Eanna, king of Larsa, king of the land of Sumer and Akkad,

23) u$_{4}$ an ^{d}en-líl ^{d}en-ki
24) ù dingir-gal-gal-e-ne
25) unu.KI uru-ul
26) šu-mu-šè bí-in-si-eš-a

23–26) when the gods An, Enlil, Enki and the great gods entrusted Uruk, the ancient city, into my hands,

27) nam-bi-šè
28) ^{d}nin-šubur lugal-mu-ra
29) nam-ga-me-èš-ak-da-mu-dè
30) é-me-kìlib-ba-sag-íl
31) ki-tuš nam-dingir-bi-šè túm-ma

27–37) on account of this, as I established a colleagueship with the god Ninšubur my lord, I built for my own life the Emekilibasagil ('House which raises its head in the totality of the *me*s'), a residence suitable for his divinity. I enlar[ged] its

32) nam-ti-mu-šè
33) mu-na-dù
34) [di]ri-u_4-bi-ta-šè
35) é-šu-sì-ga-b[i m]u-da[gal]
36) temen-mu-pà-da-n[am]-lugal-mu
37) u_4-ul-šè im-mi-gar

ešusiga gre[ater] than it had been previously. I put there, for the future, my foundation inscription proclaiming my r[o]yal name.

14

An inscription found on a cone fragment should be attributed to Rīm-Sîn I.

COMMENTARY

The fragment is BM 119049 (1927-10-3,44), excavation no. U 2552, from Diqdiqqah. It is a fragment of a cone shaft, 9.5 cm long. The inscription was collated.

The taking of a number of minor cities culminating with the capture of Uruk, events commemorated in the names of years 17–18 and 20–21 of Rīm-Sîn I, is alluded to in the second col. of the cone. This makes certain the attribution of the piece to Rīm-Sîn I, not Warad-Sîn as previously suggested. It also gives us a *terminus post quem* for the inscription, that is, after year 21. The deed commemorated by the inscription itself should have been narrated after the nam-bi-šè 'on account of this' in ii 12′. Unfortunately, the text breaks off precisely at this point.

The provenance of this cone, Diqdiqqah, gives a clue as to what may have been commemorated by the text. Jacobsen has pointed out (Iraq 22 [1960] p. 181) that a large number of inscriptions found at Diqdiqqah deal with the digging of canals. A canal is mentioned in i 11′: [...]-x-^{d}nanna i_7-hé-gál-túm 'the ... Nanna [canal], the canal which brings abundance'. This suggests that the text may have dealt with the digging of a canal. If the name in line 11′ is restored [ti-lim-da]^{d}nanna, then a correlation with the name of year 23 of Rīm-Sîn I is possible, but not certain in view of the broken nature of the text.

En-ane-du, the *en* priestess, appears in i 4′.

In ii 2, a clear PA sign appears which might be part of the city name Uṣarpara, but not enough of the name is preserved to make a positive identification.

BIBLIOGRAPHY

1965 Sollberger, UET 8 no. 82 (copy, study)
1966 Falkenstein, BiOr 23 pp. 167–68 (study)
1977 Michalowski, Mesopotamia 12 p. 87 (study)
1980 Kärki, SAKAZ 1 pp. 137–38 Waradsîn 37 (edition)

TEXT

Col. i
Lacuna
1′) [x x x x N]E SI
2′) [x x x x g]iš-šub-bi
3′) [x x a]l bí-in-du_{11}-ga!
4′) [en-an]-e-du_7
5′) [en-ki]-ág-^{d}nanna
6′) [x] x-e šà-kù-ge pà-da
7′) [dumu]-*ku-du-ur-ma-⟨bu⟩-uk*
8′) [géštu] ^{d}en-ki-ke_4
9′) [mu-na-an]-sum-ma
10′) [me é-kiš-n]u-gál-ta mu-un-ur_4-ur_4
11′) [x x x]-x-^{d}nanna i_7-ḫé-gál-túm

Lacuna
i 1′–12′) ..., ... their destiny, ... [re]quested, [En-an]e-du, [be]loved [*en* priestess] of the god Nanna, ... chosen by the pure heart, [daughter] of Kudur-ma(b)uk, the one [to whom] Enki gave [intelligence], gathered the [*me*s] from [Ekišn]ugal. [The canal ...]-Nanna, the canal which brings abundance, ...,
Lacuna

12′) [x x x] TE nu-x-x-x-[x]
Lacuna
Col. ii
Lacuna
1′) [x x] ⌜kur-gal⌝ [x x x x]
2′) ⌜URU⌝.[x] x ⌜pa⌝ x x [x]
3′) URU.É-šu-⌜d⌝E[N.ZU.KI]
4′) URU.im-gur-dBIL.[GI.KI]
5′) BÀD.[KI]
6′) ki-sur-ra.[KI]
7′) unu.KI [l]ugal-⌜ne⌝-[ne]
8′) ù ma-da-ma-da-n[e-ne]
9′) šu-né sá bí-in-d[u₁₁-ga]
10′) ugu-ne-a bí-i[n-x (x)]
11′) bàd-bi ⌜im⌝-m[i-in-sì]
12′) nam-bi-[šè ...]
13′) [x] x x [...]
Lacuna

Lacuna
ii 1′-13′) [(*when*) by the *decree* of] the great mountain [(Enlil)...] he conquered the city ..., the city Bīt-Šū-S[în], the city Imgur-Gibi[l], Dūr[um], Kisurra, (and) Uruk — the[ir k]ings and th[eir] lands — he [...] over them, (and) [tore down] their walls. On account of this ...
Lacuna

15

An inscription known from a tablet copy excavated by Woolley at Ur deals with the digging of a canal.

COMMENTARY

The tablet is IM 85684, excavation no. U 7748, excavated from a hoard of 42 tablets and fragments found in the burnt level over the upper floors of rooms 5-6, no. 7 Quiet Street. The tablet measures 11.6×5.5 cm and the inscription was collated.

The first line of the text, which probably originally mentioned the gods An, Enlil, Enki, and Ninmaḫ (it is restored from line 55), suggests a date for this inscription of year 22 of Rīm-Sîn I or later, since the great triad of gods An, Enlil, and Enki appears for the first time in the name of year 22.

The Mama-šarrat canal, which appears in the text, is found in an archival text from Uruk, W 20384 (reference courtesy of M. Boehmer), suggesting that this canal flowed not too far from Uruk.

In line 3 the ùr sign is unclear. For ki-ùr as a dwelling see H. Behrens, Enlil and Ninlil p. 145.

Although a number of verbs in the section lines 25-54 have -n- before the verbal root, which is normally indicative of a third person verb, the whole passage should be considered to be in the first person.

BIBLIOGRAPHY

1965 Sollberger, UET 8 no. 86 (copy, study)
1966 Falkenstein, BiOr 23 p. 168 (study)
1967 Pettinato, Orientalia NS 36 p. 457 (study)
1971 Renger, ZA 61 p. 43 (study)
1971 Sollberger and Kupper, IRSA IVB14d (translation)
1980 Kärki, SAKAZ 1 pp. 173-76 Rīmsîn 27 (edition)

ii 9′ Copy: TÚG-né; text: šu-né.

TEXT

1) [u$_4$ an ^{d}en-líl ^{d}en-k]i ^{d}nin-maḫ-[bi]
2) [igi-zi] mu-un-ši-bar-[re-eš-a]
3) [larsa.KI] ki-ùr(*)-ki-ág-g[á-ne-ne]
4) [nam-bi] mu-un-tar-re-[eš-a]
5) [inim-nu-k]úr-ru-ba-ne-[n]e-a ù-tu-bi bí-n[é-eš-a]

1–5) [When the gods An, Enlil, Enk]i, (and) Ninmaḫ [truly] looked at ..., determined [the destiny of Larsa ..., their] beloved abode, (and) by their [un]alterable [word] decr[eed] its creation,

6) [bala]-n[am-ḫ]é a nu-šilig-g[e]
7) [sa$_{12}$-e]-eš mu-u[n]-rig$_8$-ge(*)-eš
8) [a-da-r]í ḫa-la-kalam-ma-ka
9) [a] I$_7$.idigna I$_7$.buranun-na-bi-da
10) ⸢u$_4$⸣-ul-lí-a-ta mu-un-tùm-bé-eš-a
11) u$_4$-na-me-ka a-bi nu-šilig-ge
12) maš-bi I$_7$.^{d}*ma-mi-šar-ra-at* i$_7$-ḫé-⸢gál⸣-kalam-ma
13) a-bi I$_7$.idign[a] I$_7$.buranun-[na-bi]-da
14) ù-ba-e-ni-[i]n-kar
15) a-ab-ba-šè [ḫ]a-ba-an-dé

6–15) they [gra]nted [a reign] of ab[undance] with unceasing water. [Perpe]tual water, the allotment of the nation, [water] which the Tigris and Euphrates had brought from ancient times, and which had never ceased, the Mami-šarrat canal, the canal of abundance of the nation, whose water was (from) the Tigris and Euphrates rivers, took half of it and poured it into the sea.

16) en ^{d}nu-nam-nir-e d[u$_{11}$-ga-né] sag ba-an-du
17) sipa-šà-du$_{10}$-ga-n[a-k]a-šè mu-un-ši-i[n-gur]
18) gù-ḫúl ù-mu-un-d[é na]m-du$_{10}$ mu-ni-in-⸢tar⸣

16–18) Lord Nunamnir, [whose] w[ord] excels, [turned] to the shepherd who pleases h[im], spo[ke] to him joyously, and determined a good destiny (for him).

19) i$_7$ ba-al-e-dè [k]i-en-gi ki-uri
20) a-ḫé-gál-la [tù]m-ù-dè
21) a-gàr-gal-gal-bi še-[gu-n]u mú-mú-dè
22) pú GIŠ.kiri$_6$-bi x [...] x làl geštin du$_8$-ù-dè
23) ambar-b[i] k[u$_6$ mušen] ul-e-eš gar-[ga]r-e-⟨dè⟩
24) kur-[ga]l ^{d}en-líl-le ⸢á⸣-gal [m]u-da-⸢an⸣-[á]g

19–24) [Gr]eat mountain, the god Enlil, laid a great commission on me (namely) to dig the canal, to bring water of abundance (to) the [l]and of Sumer and Akkad, to make its great fields grow the late grain, to make it[s] groves and orchards [and ...] produce date syrup and wine, to make it[s] swamps richly provide fi[sh and fowl].

25) sipa ní-tuk á-[^{d}en]-líl lugal-a-ni-šè ì-d[u-a]-me-en
26) ^{d}*ri-im-*^{d}EN.ZU-me-e[n l]ú-kur-gal ^{d}en-líl-lá-me-[e]n
27) [ig]i-gál-tuk géšt[u-z]i šu-du$_7$
28) ⸢^{d}⸣*ri-im-*^{d}EN.ZU sipa-[zi]-sag-gi$_6$-ga-me-[e]n
29) [g]éštu-dagal ^{d}en-[ki-ke$_4$] ma-ni-in-⸢sum⸣-ma-⸢a⸣
30) ⸢ù⸣-mu-ni-in-s[a$_6$] i$_7$-da bal-e-d[è]
31) [š]à-mu ḫé-bí-in-[túm]

25–31) I, the reverent shepherd who go[es] at the side of the god [En]lil, his lord, I, Rīm-Sîn, the [m]an of the great mountain, the god Enlil, I, the one who possesses [int]elligence, perfect in [tr]ue wis[dom], I, Rīm-Sîn, [reliable] shepherd of the black-headed people, made good (use) of the broad [wi]sdom which the god En[ki] gave to me and decided t[o] dig the canal.

32) [...]-le šà ù-mu-ni-x-[(x)]
33) [i$_7$]-bi zà-I$_7$.⸢^{d}*ma*⸣*-mi-šar-ra-at* i$_7$-[ḫé-gál-kalam-ma-ka]
34) [... ḫu]-⸢mu-ba⸣-a[l]
35) [...]
36) [x] galam-bi giš-ḫur ḫa-ba-ak x x [...]
37) [u]n-šár-ra nam-sipa-bi ^{d}en-líl ma-[an-sum-ma]
38) [si]g-ta IGI.NIM-šè ù-mu-u[n-nigin]
39) us[u]-⸢kala⸣-ga-mu-ta ḫu-mu-u[n-ki]n

32–47) After (my) [he]art ... I ..., I du[g] that [canal] alongside the Mami-šarrat canal, the canal [of abundance of the land]. ... I cleverly did the rites ..., I [assembled] from the highlands and the lowlands the numerous [pe]ople, whose shepherding the god Enlil had [given] to me and, by my great migh[t] I had the work [do]ne. I constructed (the canal's) two dikes (high) [li]ke a mountain, and made them [full of] an aura. I established ab[und]ant water ⟨in⟩ its intake, and

---

3 ki-ùr; text: ki-MES×UN. 7 Text: rig$_8$(PA.ḪÚB)-re-eš.

40) e-min-a-bi ḫur-sag-[gi]n$_7$ ù-mu-un-dím me-lám ḫu-m[u-du$_8$-du$_8$]
41) ka-bi a-ḫ[é-g]ál-la ù-bí-⟨in⟩-ge-e[n]
42) kun-bi ḫ[u]-mu-un-sù-e
43) gú-gú-bé ú-ši[m] giri$_{17}$-zal-a ḫu-mè-šár-šár
44) i$_7$-bi I$_7$.*túq-ma-at-*^{d}*èr-ra*
45) mu-bi ḫ[é-b]í-ib-sa$_4$
46) a-da-rí-I$_7$.idigna-⌜I$_7$⌝.buranun-na-bi-da
47) ḫu-[m]u-ni-in-gi$_4$

filled its reservoir. Along their banks I made splendid plants grow luxuriantly. I called that canal Tuqmat-Erra. I restored the perpetual water of the Tigris and Euphrates.

48) ^{d}*ri-im-*^{d}EN.ZU lugal-larsa.KI-ma
49) lugal-k[i]-en-gi-ki-uri-me-en
50) kalam-dagal-la-mu šuḫuš-bi ḫu-mu-un-g[e-e]n
51) uru á-dam-bi ki-bi-šè ḫé-mi-i[n]-gi$_4$
52) un-šár-ra-mu-šè ú-kú(*) a-nag ḫé-bi-[i]n-gar
53) ki-en-gi ki-uri gù-téš ù-bí-sè-ke
54) šà-^{d}en-líl-lá ḫu-mu-un-du$_{10}$

48–54) I, Rīm-Sîn, king of Larsa, king of the la[nd] of Sumer and Akkad, made f[ir]m the foundation of my extensive nation. I restored the cities and villages. I established there, for my numerous people, food to eat (and) water to drink. I made the land of Sumer and Akkad peaceful and contented the god Enlil.

55) nam-bi-šè an ^{d}en-líl ^{d}en-ki ^{d}nin-maḫ-bi
56) nam-ti-u$_4$-sù-rá^{ra} gá-ra ḫa-ma-ni-in-sum
57) [ba]la-ḫé-gál-la GIŠ.gu-za-suḫuš-gi-na
58) [s]ag-e-eš ḫa-ma-ab-rig$_7$-e-ne
59) [t]e-me-en-mu-pà-da-nam-lugal-gá-a ár ù-bí-sar
60) ⌜u$_4$⌝-ul-lí-a-šè un-šár-ra-a ár mu-un-ak-ak-ne

55–60) In return for this *may* the gods An, Enlil, Enki, and Ninmaḫ grant me a long life-span. May they [g]rant me a [re]ign of abundance (and) a throne with a secure [fo]undation. I wrote (my) praise there on a foundation inscription which proclaims my royal name (in order that) the numerous people sing (my) praises forever.

16

The building of a temple for the goddess Ninegal by Simat-Eštar, wife of Rīm-Sîn I, is recorded in two inscriptions. The first is a 28-line version inscribed on stone and copper foundation tablets from Larsa.

CATALOGUE

Ex.	Museum number	Registration number	Object	Dimensions (cm)	Lines preserved	cpn
1	BM 90899	76-5-14,1	Stone tablet	–	1–6, 12–28	n/c
2	BM 116662	1924-7-26,1	Limestone tablet	12.9×7.3×1.8	1–28	n/c
3	BM 116663	1924-7-26,2	Copper tablet	12.1×7.8×0.6	1–28	n/c
4	NM Ant 2091	–	Stone tablet	12.4×6.6×2.2	9–28	p
5	–	–	Bronze tablet	–	1–28	p

COMMENTARY

The master text is ex. 2.

Despite the comments of Kärki, SAKAZ 1 p. 147, there is no evidence of any of these tablets coming from Ur. All the pieces were purchased, none scientifically excavated. The companion cone version of this text, however, can definitely be shown to have come from Larsa, so we may assume the same for the tablet version.

The writing of the king's name with the prefixed DINGIR sign indicates a dating of this inscription to year

41 ka-bi-⟨a⟩ a-ḫ[é-g]ál-la. **52** Text: kú-ú, read ú-kú.

21 or later. Hence, the inscription is edited at this point.

Exs. 1-3 were collated on the rev. side only, from a display in the British Museum. The text of the obv. is entered from the copies of Winckler and Gadd. Ex. 4 was collated from a photo kindly provided by B. Peterson of the National Museum, Stockholm. Ex. 5, formerly in the collection of M. Yondorf, purchased from M. Messayeh, was collated from photos OI 56542–56543 through the courtesy of J. Brinkman. The actual tablet is not in the Oriental Institute at this time. Notes kindly provided by W. Hallo indicate that a bronze tablet and limestone tablet with this inscription were once in the collection of E.S. David, but since the present location of these pieces cannot be determined, they have not been included in our edition of this inscription.

BIBLIOGRAPHY

1887 Winckler, MAOV 1 pp. 17–18 no. 3 (ex. 1, copy)
1892 Winckler, KB 3/1 pp. 96–97 Kudur-mabuk and Rim-Sin 5 (edition)
1892 Winckler and Böhden, ABK no. 58 (ex. 1, copy)
1904 Price, Rim-Sin p. 16 no. XI (edition)
1905 Thureau-Dangin, ISA pp. 310–11 Rîm-sin d (edition)
1907 Thureau-Dangin, SAK pp. 218–19 Rîm-sin d (edition)
1910 King, Early History pl. XXIX facing p. 288 (ex. 1, photo [rev. only])
1926 Gadd, JRAS pp. 679–872 (exs. 2–3, composite copy, edition)
1929 Barton, RISA pp. 328–31 Rim-Sin 5 (edition)
1953 Haldar, BiOr 10 p. 13 no. 2 (ex. 4, study)
1961 Hallo, BiOr 18 p. 10 Rim-Sin 6 (study)
1968 Kärki, SKFZ pp. 74–75 Rīmsîn 6 (edition)
1980 Kärki, SAKAZ 1 pp. 147–48 Rīmsîn 6 (edition)

TEXT

1) ^{d}nin-é-gal
2) nin-gal me-kìlib šu-na dab$_5$-bé
3) un-šár-ra-aš igi-bi gál
4) na-ri-maḫ šita$_5$-dù-sag-gi$_6$
5) a-rá-bi zà nu-di
6) nir-gál ukkin-na du$_{11}$-ga-ni igi-šè du
7) mu-ni a-re-eš gi$_7$
8) dingir-zi ki-a-a-ugu-ni-ta
9) ka-ba-ni še-ga
10) dumu-gal-^{d}EN.ZU-na
11) nin-a-ni-ir
12) *si-ma-at*-^{d}INANNA
13) dam-ki-ág-
14) ^{d}*ri-im*-^{d}EN.ZU
15) lugal-larsa.KI-ma
16) dumu-munus-IR$_{11}$-^{d}nanna-ke$_4$
17) u$_4$ ^{d}nin-é-gal nin-a-né
18) mu-sa$_6$-ga-ni in-sa$_4$-a
19) é-á-ág-gá-kìlib-ur$_4$-ur$_4$
20) ki-tuš nam-dingir-bi-šè túm-ma
21) nam-ti-^{d}*ri-im*-^{d}EN.ZU
22) u$_4$-da-rí-šè gál-le-dè
23) ù nam-ti-la-ni-šè
24) mu-na-dù
25) diri-u$_4$-bi-ta-šè
26) é-šu-sì-ga-bi mu-un-dagal
27) temen-mu-pà-da-nam-nin-a-ka-na
28) u$_4$-sù-rá-šè im-mi-in-gar

1–11) For the goddess Ninegal, great lady, who holds all the *me*s in her hand, who looks at the numerous people, supreme adviser who looks after the black-headed people, whose ways are not rivalled, aristocrat, whose word excels, in the assembly whose name is noble (enough) for praise, reliable goddess from (her) father who engendered her, whose utterance is favourable, great daughter of the god Sîn, his lady,

12–16) Simat-Eštar, beloved spouse of Rīm-Sîn, king of Larsa, daughter of Warad-Nanna,

17–18) when the goddess Ninegal, her lady, called her good name,

19–24) she built for her Eaagakiliburur ('House which gathers all the commands'), the residence suitable for her divinity, to establish the life of Rīm-Sîn forever and for her own life.

25–26) She enlarged its *ešusiga* more than it had been previously.

27–28) She placed there for the future her foundation inscription proclaiming her queenly name.

3.1 Copy: un-šár-ra-nu; other exs. have un-sár-ra-aš.

17

The building of the temple of the goddess Ninegal by Simat-Eštar is also recorded in a 46-line cone inscription.

CATALOGUE

Ex.	Museum number	Registration number	Excavation number	Provenance	Object	Dimensions (cm)	Lines preserved	cpn
1	Ash 1922,159	–	–	Excavated at Senkereh	Shaft	17.0	1–46	c
2	Ash 1922,159	–	–	As ex. 1	Head	15.5 dia.	1–21, 24–44	c
3	BM 116426	1923-11-10,11	U 369	Larsa	Head	10.9 dia.	9–18, 27–45	c
4	YBC 2308	–	–	Larsa	Head	–	24–46	c
5	YBC 9892	–	–	Larsa	Head	–	13–20, 34–41	c
6	LB 2123	–	–	Larsa	Head	18.1 dia.	1–46, 18–46	c
7	FMNH 156002	–	–	Larsa	Shaft	16.0	1–46	c
8	BM 118077	1926-11-13,26	–	Larsa	Head	–	1–18, 24–46	c
9	BM 118078	1926-11-13,27	–	Larsa	Head	10.7	1–13, 24–27	c
10	IM no number	–	L 8330	Larsa, from room 24 off the courtyard of Ebabbar	Head	17.3 dia.	2–21, 23–46	c

COMMENTARY

The master text is ex. 1.

All the exs. were purchased with the exception of ex. 10, which was recently excavated at Larsa. The Ur registry indicates that ex. 3 was given an Ur excavation no. when it was brought to Woolley at Ur from Senkereh. This U no. may have prompted Kärki to list the provenance of this exemplar as Ur, but we may assume that all the pieces came originally from Larsa. Exs. 4–5 could be pieces of the same cone, but because this is uncertain, they are edited separately here. Ex. 4 was kindly collated by G. Beckman. Ex. 7 was listed by Hallo, BiOr 18 p. 10 Rim-Sin 6: v, as a duplicate of the stone inscription, here E4.2.14.16, but the piece is in fact a cone, a duplicate of this inscription; it is edited here through the courtesy of the trustees of the Field Museum, Chicago. Exs. 8–9 are edited here for the first time through the courtesy of the trustees of the British Museum.

In line 13, šu-nigin is taken as a synonym of nigin = *taiiāru* 'compassion', see AHw sub *ta(j)jāru*. Such an understanding is supported by the evidence of E4.2.9.15 line 27: nun šà-gur-ru šu-nigin$_4$-bi du$_{10}$ 'prince whose mercy and compassion are good'.

BIBLIOGRAPHY

1923 Langdon, OECT 1 pp. 20–22 (exs. 1–2, edition) and pl. 17 (ex. 1, copy)
1923 Woolley, AJ 3 pl. XXXIV 2 (ex. 3, photo)
1926 Gadd, JRAS pp. 679–80 (ex. 3, study)
1928 Gadd, UET 1 no. 143 (ex. 3, copy, edition)
1929 Barton, RISA pp. 326–29 Rim-Sin 3 (edition)
1937 Stephens, YOS 9 no. 122 (ex. 4, study)
1957 van Dijk, TLB 2 no. 16 (ex. 6, copy)
1961 Hallo, BiOr 18 p. 11 Rim-Sin 13 (study) and Rim-Sin 6 (ex. 7, study)
1968 Kärki, SKFZ pp. 83–84 Rīmsîn 13 (edition)
1971 Sollberger and Kupper, IRSA IVB14f (translation)
1980 Kärki, SAKAZ 1 pp. 158–59 Rīmsîn 13 (edition)
1985 Arnaud, Akkadica 44 p. 18 (ex. 10, study)
1987 Arnaud in Huot, Larsa et 'Oueili 1983 pp. 213–15 (ex. 10, edition) and pp. 219–20 figs. 1–2 (photo, copy)

TEXT

1) ^{d}nin-é-gal
2) nin-gal kìlib-sag-gi$_6$-šár-ra-ba
3) an ^{d}en-líl ^{d}en-ki-bi
4) šu-ni-šè bí-in-si-eš-a

1–17) For the goddess Ninegal, great lady, in whose hands the gods An, Enlil, and Enki have entrusted all the numerous black-headed people, who makes just verdicts and decisions, who

5) di eš-bar-bi si-sá-sá-e
6) sá-gar-gar èn-tar-tar gal-zu
7) gú-dingir-gal-gal-e-ne-ka
8) inim-maḫ-du$_{11}$-ga-ni nu-kàm-me
9) ki igi-zalag-ga-ni an-dagal-la dag-ga
10) ki igi-zi-bar-ra-na
11) ^{d}lamma nir-gál
12) bí-íb-sum-mu-a
13) dingir-arḫuš-sù šu-nigin-bi du$_{10}$
14) šùd a-ra-zu-e giš-tuk
15) dumu-gal-^{d}EN.ZU-na
16) á-ág-gá an-ki-a ur$_{4}$-ur$_{4}$
17) nin-a-ni-ir
18) *si-ma-at*-^{d}INANNA
19) dam-ki-ág-
20) ^{d}*ri-im*-^{d}EN.ZU
21) šul giš-tuk-^{d}en-líl-lá
22) igi-du$_{8}$-a-an-na šà-kù-ge pà-da
23) lugal ki-ág-dingir-gal-gal-e-ne
24) šu-íl-la-ni še-ga
25) sipa-gú-un-kár-nibru.KI
26) me giš-ḫur-šu-du$_{7}$-eridu.KI-ga
27) engar-zi ú-a-úri.KI-ma
28) é-babbar-da ní-te-ge$_{26}$
29) lugal-larsa.KI-ma
30) lugal-ki-engi-ki-uri-ke$_{4}$
31) munus-sun$_{5}$-na
32) me-te lugal-šè túm-ma
33) KA-sa$_{6}$-sa$_{6}$-ge-bi maḫ-a
34) ^{d}nin-é-gal-ka-šè
35) u$_{4}$ ^{d}nin-é-gal nin-a-né
36) mu-sa$_{6}$-ga-né gù-zi bí-in-dé-a
37) é-á-ág-gá-kìlib-ur$_{4}$-ur$_{4}$
38) ki-tuš nam-dingir-bi-šè túm-ma
39) sag-bi ḫur-sag-gal-gin$_{7}$ im-mi-in-íl
40) nam-ti-^{d}*ri-im*-^{d}EN.ZU
41) u$_{4}$-da-rí-šè gál-le-dè
42) ù nam-ti-la-ni-šè
43) mu-na-dù
44) temen-mu-pà-da-
45) nam-nin-a-ka-na
46) u$_{4}$-sù-rá-šè im-mi-in-gar

knows how (both) to give counsel and to confer, whose supreme spoken word cannot be overturned among all the great gods, who gives a trustworthy protective genius to the one on whom her bright eye, as she roams in the vast heaven, looks steadfastly, goddess with patient mercy, whose compassion is good, who listens to prayers and entreaties, great daughter of the god Suen, who gathers the commands of heaven and earth, her lady,

18–19) Simat-Eštar, beloved spouse

20–30) of Rīm-Sîn, youth who listens to the god Enlil, and looks at the god An, chosen in the pure heart, king beloved of the great gods, whose *šu-ila* prayers find favour, shepherd who bears tribute for Nippur, who perfectly executes the *me*s and rites of Eridu, reliable farmer, provider of Ur, who reverences Ebabbar, king of Larsa, king of the land of Sumer and Akkad,

31–34) (Simat-Eštar), the humble woman, ornament befitting the king, whose ardent prayer is the best (directed) to the goddess Ninegal,

35–36) when the goddess Ninegal, her lady, truly called her good name,

37–46) she raised the head of Eaagakiliburur ('House which gathers all the commands'), the residence suitable for her divinity, like a mountain. She built it for her in order that it be there forever for the life of Rīm-Sîn, and for her own life. She put there for the future her foundation inscription proclaiming her queenly name.

7.6 dingir-gal-gal-⟨e⟩-ne-ka. **8.10** -kàm-ma. **14.1–2** Copy: dam a-ra-zu-e; text: šùd a-ra-zu-e. **16.1–2** Copy: á-ág-gá ki-a; text: á-ág-gá an-ki-a. **16.6** an-ki-a kin-kin. **21.1–2, 6** Copy: giš-tuk-^{d}EN.ZU; text: giš-tuk-^{d}en-líl-lá. **22.7** pà-⟨da⟩. **25.1–2** Copy suggests ki-nibru.KI; text: kár-nibru.KI. **27.1–3, 6, 10** uri$_{5}$.KI-ma. **28.8** ní-tuk. **29.1** lársa(UD.AB).KI-ma. **42.1** u$_{4}$ nam-ti-la-ni-šè (as copied).

18

The name of the 30th year of Rīm-Sîn I commemorates the king's taking of the city of Isin. This deed is indirectly alluded to in a cone inscription excavated at Ur that deals with the construction of the temple of the goddess Ninsiana for in this inscription Rīm-Sîn I appears as the king of Larsa, Uruk, and Isin.

CATALOGUE

Ex.	Museum number	Registration number	Excavation number	Ur provenance	Object	Dimensions (cm)	Lines preserved	cpn
1	BM 116427	1923-11-10,12	U 752	From well no. 1	Shaft	12.0	1–40	c
2	BM 116427	1923-11-10,12	U 752	As ex. 1	Head	9.4 dia.	1–13, 21–36	c

COMMENTARY

The master text is ex. 1.

The goddess Ninsianna, a form of the goddess of Eštar in her aspect as the planet Venus, is addressed in line 16 as lugal 'lord', a title normally applied only to male divinities.

For the ki-ti of line 13 as a kind of protective spirit see CAD 9 (L) p. 61: ki.ti.la = *la-m[a-súm]*. Lines 12–15 are translated based on the parallel with E4.2.14.2006 lines 6–7: lú ⸢ní-te⸣-ge$_{26}$-[n]a ^{d}lamma bí-ib-⸢sum-mu⸣-a 'who gives a protective genius to the one who reverences him'.

BIBLIOGRAPHY

1928 Gadd, UET 1 no. 140 (copy, edition)
1929 Barton, RISA pp. 384–87 Rim-Sin 3 (edition)
1961 Hallo, BiOr 18 p. 11 Rim-Sin 14 (study)
1968 Kärki, SKFZ pp. 84–86 Rīmsîn 14 (edition)
1980 Kärki, SAKAZ 1 pp. 160–62 Rīmsîn 14 (edition)

TEXT

1) ^{d}nin-si$_4$-an-na
2) dingir an-sikil-ta gišgal-bi im-zalag
3) giš-nu$_{11}$-bi pa-è
4) an-ta-gál unu$_7$-gal-e si-a
5) ka-ba-a-ni še-ga
6) nir-gál ukkin-ta ḫé-àm-bi dugud-da
7) igi-šè-du-dingir-gal-e-ne
8) mes-sag me-galam-ma šu-du$_7$
9) umuš galga šu-zi an-na gar
10) di-ku$_5$ na-ri-maḫ
11) nì-zi nì-lul-la šid-šid
12) dingir-arḫuš-sù lú ní-te-ge$_{26}$-na
13) ^{d}lamma-silim-ma ki-ti bar-kù
14) u$_4$-nam-ti-la maḫ-a
15) bí-íb-gar-re-⸢a⸣
16) lugal-mu-ú[r]
17) ^{d}⸢*ri*⸣-*im*-^{d}EN.⸢ZU⸣

1–16) For the goddess Ninsianna, goddess whose station shines from clear heaven, whose light shines forth, lofty one, who fills the great hall, whose utterance is favourable, aristocrat, whose fiat (carries) weight in the assembly, who goes at the fore of the great gods, foremost heroine, who perfectly executes the artful *me*s, who truly puts instruction and counsel in heaven, judge, supreme adviser, who distinguishes (between) truth and falsehood, god with patient mercy, who provides a protective genius of well-being, a ... guardian spirit, and a very great life-span for the one who is in awe of her, fo[r] my lord (sic!),

17–26) I, Rīm-Sîn, mighty man, whose offerings

18) nita-kala-ga
19) nidba-bi maḫ-a
20) èš-e nibru.KI-šè
21) me giš-ḫur-šu-du$_7$-eridu.KI-ga
22) ú-a-zi-uri$_5$.KI-ma
23) é-babbar-da ní-te-ge$_{26}$
24) lugal-larsa.KI-ma
25) unu.KI ì-si-in.KI
26) lugal-ki-en-gi-ki-uri-me-en
27) u$_4$ ^{d}nin-si$_4$-an-na
28) gú-érim-gál-la-mu
29) šu-mu-šè bí-in-si-a
30) nam-bi-šè
31) ^{d}nin-si$_4$-an-na lugal-mu-ú[r]
32) nam-ga-me-èš-ak-da-mu-⸢dè⸣
33) é-eš-bar-zi-da
34) nam-dingir-bi-šè túm-ma
35) ki-tuš-šà-du$_{10}$-ga-na
36) ki-sikil-la ḫu-mu-dù
37) giš-ká-n[a]
38) gan-du$_7$-é-e-ke$_4$
39) u$_4$-sù-rá-šè
40) mu-mu ḫé-em-mi-sar

are the greatest for shrine Nippur, who perfectly executes the *me*s and rites of Eridu, reliable provider of Ur, who reverences Ebabbar, king of Larsa, Uruk, (and) Isin, king of the land of Sumer and Akkad,

27–29) when the goddess Ninsianna delivered all my enemies into my hands,

30–40) on account of this, for the goddess Ninsianna my lord (sic!), as I established a colleagueship (with her), I built in a pure place the Eešbarzida ('House of reliable decisions'), suitable for her divinity, her residence which pleases her. I wrote my name there, on the linte[l] (and) door jamb of the temple, for the future.

19

This text, a tablet copy of a royal inscription of Rīm-Sîn dating to the time of the conquest of Isin, deals with the construction of a temple(?), probably in Larsa, for the goddess Amagula, wife of the god Nergal.

COMMENTARY

The inscription is on YBC 8770, a purchased tablet, probably from Larsa. It measures 10.2×5.7×3.3 cm and was collated. It is edited here for the first time through the courtesy of the trustees of the Yale Babylonian Collection. For the probable location of the temple of the god Nergal at Larsa see commentary to E4.2.6.2002.

TEXT

1) ^{d}ama-gu-[la]
2) nin-gal ki-šár-ra kala [x (x)]
3) me-lám-ma-ni u$_{18}$-[ru]
4) dingir-ir$_9$-ra ní-gal-ḫuš [ri]
5) ní-bi un-e dul-l[a]
6) dam-ur-sag-kala-ga
7) en-^{d}nergal-ke$_4$
8) ki-⸢mè(?)⸣-a nam-nin-ni ak-a
9) dingir-zi lú-nam-ga-me-èš-ak-a
10) nam-ti bí-íb-bu-u$_4$-a

1–11) For the goddess Ama-gu[la], the great lady, who is mighty everywhere, [...] whose aura is gre[at], angry goddess, who [sits in] furious splendour, whose splendour cover[s] the people, spouse of the mighty champion, the lord Nergal, who in the field of *battle* exercises her ladyship, faithful goddess (for) the one who makes a colleagueship (with her), but who (also) snatches away life, my lady,

11) nin-mu-ra
12) ^{d}*ri-im*-^{d}EN.ZU
13) nita-kala-ga
14) lugal-larsa.KI-ma
15) unu.KI ì-si-in.KI
16) lugal-ki-en-gi-ki-uri-ke$_4$
17) u$_4$ ì-si-in.KI
18) uru-nam-lugal-la
19) šu-mu-šè im-mi-in-si-a
20) nam-bi-šè
21) ^{d}ama-gu-la nin-m[u-ra]
22) [...] x x x da x x
23) [...] x kár
24) [ki-tuš ní-dúb]-bu-da-na
25) [...] x im-mi-dù
26) [ḫur-sag-í]l-⟨la⟩-gin$_7$ ⌜mu⌝-íl
27) x [...] x x x-e-ke$_4$
28) x [...] ⌜im⌝-mi-mú

12–16) (I) Rīm-Sîn, mighty man, king of Larsa, Uruk, (and) Isin, king of the land of Sumer (and) Akkad,

17–19) when she entrusted into my hands Isin, the city of kingship,

20–28) on account of this [for] the goddess Amagula m[y] lady ... I built ... her [abode of relax]ation and raised it like a [lof]ty [mountain]. I caused it to grow up there ...

20

A cone from Ur deals with construction work undertaken by the *en* priestess En-ane-du in the Gipar at Ur.

COMMENTARY

The cone is BM 130729 (1949-10-13,1), from Ur, presented to the British Museum, no excavation no. or provenance known. It is a fragment of a cone head 15.4 cm in dia., with the shaft broken away. The inscription was collated.

The dating of this inscription is not entirely certain. The phrase kur-gú-érim-gál-la-ni šu-ni-šè bí-in-si-iš-⟨eš⟩-[a] 'they filled his hands with the foreign land, all his enemies' occurs for the first time in a slightly varied form in E4.2.14.18 lines 28–29, and may possibly be connected with the great victory over the city of Isin. This suggests a date of this text sometime in or after year 30.

For the translation of line 4 see Steible, Rīm-Sîn p. 64.

For the reading and translation of utaḫ-ḫe in line 5 see Civil, Orientalia NS 52 (1983) pp. 238–40.

In line 22 the sign immediately after the šeš is a -mu sign that has been erased.

In line 23 the second sign is: .

Line 34 follows the translation of Jacobsen apud Weadcock, Iraq 37 (1975) p. 109. An alternative reading is given by Charpin, Le clergé d'Ur p. 200: u$_4$-ba ÚNU.SIS.BA.AN.DU kislaḫ-nam-tar-ra-en-en-e-ne-libir-ra-me-eš: 'En ce temps-là, le mur de soutenement du cimitière des pretresses d'antan'. Charpin takes ÚNU.SIS.BA.AN.DU as a diri compound for Akkadian *kisû*, an interpretation not adopted here.

Lines 23–25, which are nominalized, seem to denote indirect speech, the prayer of En-ane-du.

BIBLIOGRAPHY

1951 Gadd, Iraq 13 pp. 27–39 (photo, copy, edition)
1953 M. Lambert, Sumer 9 pp. 94–97 (study)
1961 Hallo, BiOr 18 p. 10 Rim-Sin 8 (study)
1964 Falkenstein, Bagh. Mitt. 3 p. 37 (study)
1968 Kärki, SKFZ pp. 76–78 Rīmsîn 8 (edition)
1971 Sollberger and Kupper, IRSA IVB14h (translation)
1980 Kärki, SAKAZ 1 pp. 150–52 Rīmsîn 8 (edition)
1986 Charpin, Le clergé d'Ur pp. 199–206 (edition)

TEXT

1) en-an-e-du$_7$
2) en-^{d}nanna
3) nam-gal-nam-en-na šà-kù-ta nam-gi$_7$-an-na
4) šà-ki-ág ^{d}nin-gal-e nì-UD-nam-en-na bar šu-ta gar
5) me-te-é-kiš-nu-gál zà-ša$_4$-utaḫ-ḫe-u$_9$-na
6) ḫé-du$_7$-É.NUN-na u$_4$-sa-sa-ḫa kalam-šè è
7) aga-nam-en-⟨na⟩-šè kù-ge-eš-e túm-ma
8) giš-ḫur-šu-luḫ-nam-dingir-šè zi-⌜dè⌝-eš pà-da
9) nun ní-tuk du$_8$-maḫ-é-lugal-la-na-šè šu-luḫ-luḫ-ḫa-ta al-gub-bu

1–9) I, En-ane-du, *en* priestess of the god Nanna, (predestined) from the holy womb (for) the great fate of the office of an *en* (and) the nobility of heaven, beloved of the heart, on whose body the goddess Ningal by (her own) hand has put the radiance of the office of *en*, ornament of Ekišnugal, who rivals high heaven, ornament of the *agrun*, *bright* light coming forth for the nation, holy suited for the tiara of the office of *en*, truly chosen for the rites and lustration ceremonies of divinity, reverent princess who stands for the lustration ceremonies at the lofty *laver* of the palace,

10) en-an-⌜e⌝-du$_7$
11) en igi-du$_8$-a-^{d}nanna ^{d}nin-gal-bi
12) uri$_5$.KI uru.KI-zà-è-ki-en-gi-ra
13) ki-šu-tag-za-⌜na⌝-ru en ^{d}aš-ím-babbar-e
14) lú gi$_6$-pàr nam-en-bi-šè ki-sikil-la dù-a gal-bi túm-ma-me-en

10–14) I, En-ane-du, *en* priestess who looks at the gods Nanna and Ningal, greatly befitting (the city) Ur, foremost city of Sumer, where lyres play (and) the lord Ašimbabbar, the one who built a *gipar* for the office of *en* in a pure place,

15) u$_4$ ^{d}nanna ^{d}nin-gal-bi
16) sag-ki-zalag-ga-ne-ne-a igi-bar-ra-bi nam-ti-la
17) igi-ḫúl-la-bi mu-un-ši-in-⌜sum⌝-eš-àm
18) èš é-kiš-nu-gál ki-tuš-⌜nam-dingir-ne-ne-a⌝
19) mu-mu mi-ni-in-maḫ-eš-a
20) ka-mu sikil-la na[m-š]ita$_x$(REC 316)-nam-ti-la mu-un-gar-re-eš-àm
21) šu-si-sá-mu u$_4$-nam-ti-⌜^{d}⌝*ri-im*-^{d}EN.ZU
22) šeš-(erasure)-tam-ma-«na»-mu
23) sù-su$_x$-u$_5$-dè mu-un-dè-ri-⌜eš⌝-a
24) kur-gú-érim-gál-la-ni
25) šu-ni-šè b[í]-⌜in⌝-si-iš-«eš»-[a]

15–25) when the gods Nanna and Ningal looked (at me) with their shining faces, gave to me life (and) a joyful expression, (and) made my name supreme in the shrine Ekišnugal, residence of their divinity, they placed a sup[plic]ation of life in my pure mouth: that they take my extended hand in order to prolong the life-span of Rīm-Sîn, my twin brother, (and) that they deliver into his hands the foreign land, all his enemies.

26) u$_4$-ba gi$_6$-pàr-kù-⌜ga⌝ ki-tuš-nam-en-na-mu
27) sig$_4$-bi úr-bi-⌜ta⌝ nu-ús-sa
28) en-an-e-du$_7$
29) en mu-maḫ zi-dè-eš [sa$_4$]-a
30) dumu-*ku-du-ur-ma-bu-uk*-me-en
31) gi$_6$-pàr-kù-ga úr-bi sun-a sig$_4$-zi-du ḫé-ni-ús
32) é-gar$_8$-bi šu-si-tag-ga im dùl ḫu-mu-ak
33) é-bi gibil-bé-eš ḫu-mu-tu

26–33) At that time the shining *gipar*, residence of my office of *en*, its bricks not fitting their base, I, En-ane-du, *en* priestess, truly [called] by a supreme name, daughter of Kudur-mabuk, laid tightly fitting bricks on the old base of the shining *gipar*. I plastered its walls aligned to a finger. I gave a new form to that house.

34) u$_4$-ba únu šeš ba-an-tùm ki-u$_4$-nam-tar-ra-
35) en-en-e-ne-libir-ra-me-eš
36) ki-bi bàd nu-dub$_x$(URUDU) gú-gìr-bi EDIN.BÚR-bi ḫé-⌜šub⌝
37) en-nu-un ba-ra-gar ki-bi ba-ra-sikil

34–37) At that time the place of the 'Hall-that-brings-bitterness', the place of those (who had gone to their) destiny, the former *en* priestesses, was not surrounded by a wall, its accesses and ... had collapsed, there were no guards (and) the place was not pure (any more).

38) gá-e géštu-gal-zu-mu-ta
39) nam-tar u$_4$-da egir-ra ki-bi bí-kin-kin
40) diri-ki-ná-en-en-e-ne-libir-ra-me-eš
41) ú-zu-ug-dagal-la ḫu-mu-gar
42) ki-bi šub-ba bàd-gal-e ḫu-mu-dub$_x$(URUDU)
43) en-nu-un-kala-ga bí-gar ki-bi ḫu-mu-sikil

38–43) I, by my great wisdom, sought, for the future, places (of those who would go to their) destiny. I established a broad sacred area surpassing the graveyard of the former *en* priestesses. I surrounded that ruined place with a wall, established a strong watch, and purified that place.

44) mu-pà-da-nam-en-na-mu pà-pà-dè-dè

44–48) To proclaim my name chosen for the

45) kin-bi ki-bi-šè ḫé-em-mi-gar
46) temen ár-nam-en-na-mu mu-sar
47) u_4 a-na-gál-⸢la⸣-ka-ta ḫé-em-mi-ú[s]
48) bàd-b[i] ní-te-ge$_{26}$-mu ḫ[é-e]m-i ⸢mu-bi ḫé⸣-e[m]-mi-s[a$_4$]

office of *en*, I restored this work. I inscribed my foundation inscription with the praise of my office of *en* (and) lai[d] it there for as long as it might be. I named tha[t] wall 'Praise be the one who reverences me'.

21

An axe-head in the Iraq Museum bears an inscription indicating that it was the property of Rīm-Sîn I.

COMMENTARY

The piece is IM 11494, said to have been found at Khafajah. It measures 20 cm long. The inscription was collated from the published photo.

BIBLIOGRAPHY

1952 Maxwell-Hyslop, Iraq 14 pp. 118–19 and pl. XXXI (photo, edition)

TEXT

1) é-gal ^{d}*ri-im*-^{d}EN.ZU

1) Palace of Rīm-Sîn.

22

An inscribed cylinder seal of a wife of Rīm-Sîn I is in Berlin.

COMMENTARY

The inscription is on VA 3589, a cylinder seal of haematite 2.8 cm long, 1.6 cm in dia. The piece was purchased. The inscription was collated.

BIBLIOGRAPHY

1926 Unger, RLV 4/2 pl. 159g (photo, edition)
1940 Moortgat, VAR no. 322 (photo, edition)
1961 Hallo, BiOr 18 p. 11 Rim-Sin 24 (study)
1968 Kärki, SKFZ p. 92 Rīmsîn 24 (edition)
1971 Sollberger and Kupper, IRSA IVB14g (translation)
1980 Kärki, SAKAZ 1 p. 169 Rīmsîn 24 (edition)

TEXT

1) *be-el-ta-ni*	1) Bēltāni,
2) dumu-munus *ḫa-ba-an-nu-um*	2) daughter of Ḫabannum,
3) dam-^{d}*ri-im*-^{d}EN.ZU	3) wife of Rīm-Sîn,
4) lugal-larsa.KI-ma	4) king of Larsa.

23

A number of votive inscriptions are known in which someone dedicates an object for the life of Rīm-Sîn I. These are known either from inscriptions found on the actual object itself or from tablet copies.

The first votive inscription edited here belongs to one of Rīm-Sîn I's wives, Rīm-Sîn-Šala-bāštašu. It records the setting up and dedication of a stone basin to hold water for annointing purposes at the gate of the great courtyard of Inanna's Emeurur temple in Larsa. The construction by Rīm-Sîn of the Emeurur temple itself is recorded in E4.2.14.2.

COMMENTARY

The piece is YBC 2247, a purchased piece presumably originally from Larsa. It is a fragment of a stone col. measuring 38 cm high, 17 cm in dia. The vessel holding the water, now broken away, must have once been affixed to the top of the col. The inscription was collated.

BIBLIOGRAPHY

1937 Stephens, YOS 9 no. 31 (copy, study)
1957 Edzard, Zwischenzeit p. 61 n. 282 (study)
1961 Hallo, BiOr 18 p. 11 Rim-Sin 18 (study)
1968 Kärki, SKFZ pp. 89–91 Rīmsîn 18 (edition)
1971 Sollberger and Kupper, IRSA IVB14e (translation)
1980 Kärki, SAKAZ 1 pp. 165–67 Rīmsîn 18 (edition)

TEXT

1) ^{d}inanna 2) dingir-íb-ba gú-en-na sag-íl 3) an-ta-gál kur-kur-ra dalla 4) mùš-me-bi i-ši si 5) dingir-zi šà-gur-ru-bi du$_{10}$-ga 6) arḫuš-su$_{13}$ la-ra-aḫ nì-gig-ga 7) šu-dab$_{5}$-bé gal-zu-a-aš 8) nin-mu-ra	1–8) For the goddess Inanna, angry goddess, proud one in the throne room, lofty one who shines brightly in the foreign lands, whose face is full of radiance, reliable god, whose compassion is good, (with) patient mercy, who knows how to take by the hand those in dire straits and the sick, my lady,
9) nam-ti- 10) ^{d}*ri-im*-^{d}EN.ZU 11) lugal-larsa.KI-ma-šè 12) ù *li-ri-iš-ga-am-lum* dumu-munus-a-ni	9–12) for the life of Rīm-Sîn, king of Larsa, and Lirīš-gamlum, his daughter,
13) ^{d}*ri-im*-^{d}EN.ZU-^{d}*ša-la-ba-aš-ta-šu* 14) dam-ki-ág-^{d}*ri-im*-^{d}EN.ZU 15) dumu-munus-^{d}EN.ZU-*ma-gir*-ke$_{4}$	13–17) I, Rīm-Sîn-Šala-bāštašu, beloved wife of Rīm-Sîn, daughter of Sîn-māgir, humble woman, ornament suitable for kingship,

16) munus-sun$_5$-na 17) me-te nam-lugal-šè túm-ma-me(*)-en 18) u$_4$ nin-mu mu-nam-sa$_6$-ga	18) when my lady truly called me with a gracious name,
19) gù zi-dè-eš ma-an-dé-⟨a⟩ 20) nam-bi-šè ᵈinanna-ra 21) KA-sa$_6$-sa$_6$-ge-da-mu-dè 22) dug-NA$_4$.ú-šù 23) a-sikil-la šu-tag-ga-šè túm-ma 24) nì u$_4$-bi-ta nin-igi-du-mu-ne 25) ba-ra-an-dím-ma-a 26) ù-mu-dím	19–26) on account of this, as I prayed ardently to the goddess Inanna, I fashioned for her a vessel of diorite stone, suitable for clean water and adornment, a thing that previously no queen who preceded me had fashioned,
27) ká-kù-kisal-maḫ-é-me-ur$_4$-ur$_4$ 28) ki-u$_6$-di-kalam-ma-ka 29) ul-šè mu-ni-gub	27–29) and set it up there as a beautiful (thing) at the shining gate of the main courtyard of the Emeurur temple, in the place of wonder of the nation.
30) šu lú-ḫul LÚ×KÁRA.ÉŠ-ta 31) *li-ri-iš-ga-am-lum* kar-re-dè 32) á(*)-zág-aš-búru kuš-a-na gál-la 33) ní-nu-zu-úr sum-mu-dè 34) ŠÀ.ḪAL igi-ni-a zi-zi-i-dè 35) zi-né ùru-ak-dè	30–35) In order to save Lirīš-gamlum from the hand of evil-doers or brigands, to hand over the *asakku* and *ašbur* diseases that are in her body to [a demon] who fears nothing, to expel the ... something that is in her eye, to protect her life,
36) nam-ti *li-ri-iš-ga-am-lum* dumu-munus-mu 37) ù nam-ti-mu-šè 38) géme-ní-tuk-ni-me-en 39) a mu-na-ru	36–39) I, the servant who respects her (the goddess Inanna), dedicated (this vessel) for the life of Lirīš-gamlum, my daughter, and for my own life.
40) u$_4$-me-da u$_4$-da-egir-bi-šè 41) lú kin-ak-a-mu íb-zi-ir-re-a 42) ki-gub-ba-bi íb-da-ab-kúr-ru-a 43) ki-kúr-ra bí-íb-gub-bu-a 44) mu-sar-ra-ba šu bí-ib-ùr-a 45) mu-ni bí-ib-sar-re-a 46) áš-bala-ba-ke$_4$-eš 47) lú-kúr šu ba-an-zi-zi-i-a	40–47) (As for) the one who any day in the future destroys my work, alters the place where it stands, sets it up in a different place, erases its inscription, (and) writes his own name there (or) because of this curse incites another to do so,
48) lú-ba ᵈinanna nin-kur-kur-ra-ke$_4$ 49) šà-íb-ba lipiš-bal-a-né 50) áš-gig-ga ḫé-en-e	48–50) upon that man, may the goddess Inanna, lady of the foreign lands, with her angry heart and wrathful mood utter a terrible curse.

2001

A flat dish was dedicated by Iltani to the goddess Inanna of Zabala for Rīm-Sîn I.

COMMENTARY

The dish is NBC 6029, a purchased piece. It is made of gray limestone 26.2 cm in dia. with a height of 4.3 cm. The inscription was collated.

---

17 Text: túm-ma-a-en. **32** Text: DA-zág.

BIBLIOGRAPHY

1930 de Genouillac, RHR 101 pp. 220–22 (?)
1937 Stephens, YOS 9 no. 38 (copy, study)
1954 Leemans, SLB 1/2 p. 2 (study)
1961 Hallo, BiOr 18 p. 11 Rim-Sin 19 (study)
1968 Kärki, SKFZ p. 91 Rīmsîn 19 (edition)
1971 Sollberger and Kupper, IRSA IVB14j (translation)
1980 Kärki, SAKAZ 1 pp. 167–68 Rīmsîn 19 (edition)

TEXT

1) ᵈinanna-zabala.KI
2) nin-a-ni-ir
3) nam-ti-
4) *ri-im*-ᵈEN.ZU
5) lugal-larsa.KI-ma-šè
6) *il-ta-ni*
7) dumu-⌜munus⌝-DINGIR-⌜*ba*⌝-*ni*
8) NA₄.díli
9) nam-ti-la-ni-šè
10) in-na-an-ba

1–2) To the goddess Inanna of Zabala, her lady,

3–5) for the life of Rīm-Sîn, king of Larsa,

6–10) (and) for her own life, Iltani, the daughter of Ilum-bāni, presented this dish.

2002

A bowl was dedicated by Šallūrum to the goddess Inanna of Zabala for Rīm-Sîn I.

COMMENTARY

The bowl is A 7462 (Chicago), a purchased piece, and is made of hornblende-diorite. The inscription was collated from a photo in Chicago. It is edited here for the first time through the courtesy of the trustees of the Oriental Institute.

BIBLIOGRAPHY

1961 Hallo, BiOr 18 p. 11 Rim-Sin 20 (study)

TEXT

1) ᵈinanna-zabala.KI
2) nin-a-ni-ir
3) nam-ti-
4) ᵈ*ri-im*-ᵈEN.ZU
5) lugal-larsa.KI-ma-šè
6) *ša-al-lu-ru-um*
7) dumu-lú-ᵈasal-lú-ḫi
8) bur NA₄ pirig-gùn x
9) ìr ní-tuk-ni
10) in-na-an-ba

1–2) To the goddess Inanna of Zabala, his lady,

3–5) for the life of Rīm-Sîn, king of Larsa,

6–10) Šallūrum, the son of Lu-Asalluḫi, her reverent servant, presented (this) bowl of ... stone to her.

2003

A cup was dedicated by Ṣālilum to the god Lisi for Rīm-Sîn I.

COMMENTARY

The piece is YBC 2302, a purchased piece, provenance unknown. It is a cup of grey alabaster, 7 cm high with a dia. at the rim of 7.5 cm. The inscription was collated.

BIBLIOGRAPHY

1937 Stephens, YOS 9 no. 33 (copy, study)
1961 Hallo, BiOr 18 p. 11 Rim-Sin 21 (study)
1968 Kärki, SKFZ p. 91 Rīmsîn 21 (edition)
1971 Sollberger and Kupper, IRSA IVB14i (translation)
1980 Kärki, SAKAZ 1 p. 168 Rīmsîn 21 (edition)

TEXT

1) ^{d}li$_9$-si$_4$
2) ^{d}nin-sikil-la
3) nam-ti-
4) ^{d}*ri-im*-^{d}EN.ZU
5) *ṣa-li-lum*
6) dumu-^{d}nanna-ma-an-sum
7) in-na-ba

1–2) To the god Lisi (and) the goddess Ninsikila,

3–4) for the life of Rīm-Sîn,

5–7) Ṣālilum, the son of Nanna-mansum, presented (this cup).

2004

A stone vessel, probably once used to hold unguent, was dedicated by Šēp-Sîn to the god Mardu for Rīm-Sîn I.

COMMENTARY

The piece, which was in the collection of the Comtesse de Béhague, was apparently offered for sale to the Oriental Institute by E.S. David in March 1935 but not purchased. In 1987 it was shown to C.B.F. Walker in the British Museum prior to its sale by Sotheby's. The piece was collated by Walker and from OI photo 25281 through the courtesy of J.A. Brinkman. The no. A 1803 referred to by W. Hallo (BiOr 18 p. 11, Rim-Sin 22) is an internal reference number of the Oriental Institute and is not the museum no. of the piece itself.

For ša-u$_{19}$(URU)-ša as a type of vessel, cf. Hh XI 386 (Landsberger, MSL 7 p. 144) URUDU.šà-u$_{18}$.ša$_4$ = *sappi*.

For (NA$_4$).zú-gi$_6$ of line 8 see Ur$_5$-ra = *ḫubullum* XVI 392 (MSL 10 p. 15). It is there equated with Akkadian *ṣurrum* 'obsidian'. The Rīm-Sîn I vessel is made of rock-crystal. It is 9 cm high.

The cup has a gold band around the top and a silver band around the base, exactly as the inscription indicates.

BIBLIOGRAPHY

1961 Hallo, BiOr 18 p. 11 Rim-Sin 22 (study)
1963 Hallo, BiOr 20 p. 141 n. 91 (study)
1987 Anon., Antiquités et Objets d'Art. Collection de Martine, Comtesse de Béhague provenant de la Succession du Marquis de Ganay. Sotheby's, Monaco (Dec. 5, 1987) pp. 42–43 lot 66 (photo, translation).

TEXT

1) ᵈmar-dú
2) lugal-a-ni-ir
3) nam-ti-
4) ᵈ*ri-im*-ᵈEN.ZU
5) lugal-larsa.KI-ma-šè
6) *še-ep*-ᵈEN.ZU
7) dumu-*ip-qú-ša* a-zu-gal-ke$_4$
8) NA$_4$.ša-u$_{19}$(URU)-ša zú-gi$_6$
9) tùn-bi kù-GI
10) KU-bi kù-babbar gar-ra
11) ìr ní-tuk-ni
12) a mu-na-ru

1–2) To the god Mardu, his lord,

3–5) for the life of Rīm-Sîn, king of Larsa,

6–12) Šēp-Sîn, son of Ipquša, the chief physician, the servant who reverences him, dedicated to him (this) vessel of rock-crystal, whose lip is inlaid with gold (and) whose base is inlaid with silver.

2005

Two cones excavated at Nippur deal with the construction of a brick structure for the god Nergal by Ninurta-gāmil, the 'resident' of Nippur, for the life of Rīm-Sîn I.

CATALOGUE

Ex.	Museum number	Excavation number	Provenance	Object	Dimensions (cm)	Lines preserved	cpn
1	Ni 9620	Hilprecht expedition	Nippur, west of the Shaṭṭ en-Nil, opposite 'Tablet Hill'	Cone shaft frgm.	–	1–17	n
2	IM 58724	3N–T804	Nippur, from TA 197 XI foundation	Cone shaft	5.7 long 4.7 dia.	1–18	c

COMMENTARY

The existence of ex. 2 was kindly communicated by M. Civil and it was edited through the courtesy of the trustees of the Oriental Institute.

The cones presumably were once inserted in the brick structure referred to in the text. The inscription must date to year 21 of Rīm-Sîn or later because the king's name is written with the divine determinative.

For the official lú-tuš-a-nibru.KI of line 13 see Lu I 134 (MSL 12 p. 97).

BIBLIOGRAPHY

1896 Hilprecht, BE 1/2 no. 128 (ex. 1, copy, study)
1904 Price, Rim-Sin p. 15 no. IX (ex. 1, edition)
1905 Thureau-Dangin, ISA pp. 308–309 Rîm-sin b (ex. 1, edition)
1907 Thureau-Dangin, SAK pp. 216–19 Rîm-sin b (ex. 1, edition)
1910 Hilprecht, Deluge Story p. 8 n. 3 (ex. 1, study)
1929 Barton, RISA pp. 326–27 Rim-Sin 2 (ex. 1, edition)
1961 Hallo, BiOr 18 p. 11 Rim-Sin 23 (ex. 1, study)
1968 Kärki, SKFZ pp. 91–92 Rīmsîn 23 (ex. 1, edition)
1980 Kärki, SAKAZ 1 pp. 168–69 Rīmsîn 23 (ex. 1, edition)

TEXT

1) ^{d}nergal
2) en-maḫ usu ní-gùr
3) šíta-ḫuš-a zà-kéšda
4) pirig šu-zi-ga ù-na gub-ba
5) érim-šè gug-sar-ak
6) lugal-a-ni-ir
7) nam-ti-
8) ^{d}*ri-im*-^{d}EN.ZU
9) nita-kala-ga
10) lugal-larsa.KI-ma
11) lugal-ki-en-gi-ki-uri-ka-šè
12) ^{d}nin-urta-*ga-mi-il*
13) lú-tuš-a-nibru.KI
14) dumu-*na-ar-bu-um-ma*-ke$_4$
15) u$_4$ I$_7$.gibil
16) mu-un-ba-al-la
17) á-diri sig$_4$-al-ùr-ra
18) mu-na-an-dù

1–6) For the god Nergal, supreme lord, bearing might and a fearsome splendour, who carries the angry *šita* mace, lion with raised paws, angrily rampant, who wields the *scimitar* at the enemy, his lord,

7–11) for the life of Rīm-Sîn, mighty man, king of Larsa, king of the land of Sumer and Akkad,

12–14) Ninurta-gāmil, 'resident' of Nippur, son of Narbumma,

15–16) when (Rīm-Sîn) dug the 'New Canal',

17–18) built an *additional wing* of baked bricks.

2006

A tablet at Yale has the copy of a votive inscription for the life of Rīm-Sîn I.

COMMENTARY

The text is inscribed on YBC 7232, a clay tablet probably from Larsa, which was collated. It is edited here for the first time through the courtesy of the trustees of the Yale Babylonian Collection.

Since this inscription is known only from a copy on a clay tablet, not the original object, we cannot determine the nature of the votive object of line 14.

Lines 15–18 are restored from E4.2.14.2007 lines 16′–18′.

The personal name in line 12 finds a parallel in UET 2 Supplement no. 25, obv. ii′ line 2: bar-še-sag-a-sag.

TEXT

1) ^{d}DINGIR.MAR.DÚ
2) en-gal ní-⌜ḫuš-ri⌝
3) me-sikil-la zà-kešda
4) dingir-zi dumu-⌜ki⌝-ág-^{d}en-líl-[lá]

1–8) For the god DINGIR-MARDU, great lord, who sits in a fearsome splendour, who carries the pure *me*s, reliable god, son beloved [of] the god Enlil, who listens to prayers and supplications, who

5) šùd a-ra-⌜zu⌝-e giš-tuk
6) lú ⌜ní-te⌝-ge$_{26}$-[n]a
7) ^{d}lamma bí-ib-⌜sum-mu⌝-a
8) dingir-ra-ni-ir
9) nam-ti-
10) ^{d}*ri-im*-^{d}EN.ZU
11) lugal-larsa.KI-ma-šè
12) bára-še-sag-⌜nì⌝-sa$_{6}$-ga-ni
13) dumu *ra-ši*-^{d}*en*-[...]
14) ša-u$_{18}$(GIŠGAL)-ša x [...]
15) me-te lu[gal-bi-šè túm-ma]
16) [ù-mu-dím]
17) [sá-du$_{11}$ nì-sa$_{6}$-ga-ni]
18) ki[n-kin]-dè
19) zi-[...]
20) a-ra-[zu-šè]
21) ir$_{11}$ n[í-tuk-ni]
22) a mu-[na-ru]

gives a protective genius to the one who reverences [h]im, his god,

9–11) for the life of Rīm-Sîn, king of Larsa.

12–13) Bara-še-sag-ni-saga-ni, son of Raši-En[...]

14–16) [fashioned] a ... *votive object*, an ornament [befitting its] lo[rd],

17–22) and in order to s[eek his regular offerings, good things, for] life ..., (and) *prayers*, his servant who re[verences him], dedic[ated] it [to him].

2007

A tablet in the Yale collections bears a copy of an inscription with the dedication of a chair to a god by a servant of Rīm-Sîn I.

COMMENTARY

The tablet is YBC 7239, a purchased piece, probably from Larsa. It is a clay tablet 12.6×8×3.4 cm and the inscription was collated. It is edited here for the first time through the courtesy of the trustees of the Yale Babylonian Collection.

TEXT

1′) [...] x [...]
2′) [x] ^{d}lamm[a ...] x [...]
3′) [n]a-ri-[ma]ḫ AN [...]
4′) šùd a-⌜ra-zu⌝-e giš-t[uk]
5′) lú ⌜ní⌝-te-ge$_{26}$-[na]
6′) mu-⌜sa$_{6}$⌝-ga-ni
7′) gù-zi-[d]é ug-gal UD-e
8′) dingir-r[a]-ni-ir
9′) nam-ti-
10′) ^{d}*ri-i*[*m*]-^{d}EN.ZU
11′) lugal-l[ar]sa.KI-ma
12′) lugal-ki-e[n-g]i-ki-uri-x-šè
13′) ⌜^{d}⌝EN.[x]-*še-me-i*
14′) dumu ^{d}⌜UTU⌝-*ra-bi*-ke$_{4}$
15′) GIŠ.gu-[za ...] x
16′) me-⌜te-nam-lugal⌝-bi-šè túm-ma
17′) ⌜ù⌝-m[u]-dím
18′) ⌜sá⌝-du$_{11}$ nì-sa$_{6}$-ga-ni

1′–8′) [For the god ...], a protective geni[us ..., who ... supre]me advice ..., who list[ens] to prayers and supplications, who truly calls the good name of the one who reverences him, great lion ..., his god,

9′–12′) for the life of Rī[m]-Sîn, king of L[ar]sa, king of the land of Su[m]er and Akkad,

13′–21′) *S*[*în*]-šēmei, son of Šamaš-rabi, fashioned a cha[ir ...] suitable for his lordship, to seek his regular offerings, good things, and his servant who reverences him dedicated it to him.

19′) ⌜kin-kin⌝-dè
20′) ⌜ìr⌝ ní-tuk-ni
21′) a m[u]-na-ru

2008

A number of seals of servants of Rīm-Sîn are known which could date to the time of either Rīm-Sîn I or II. They are all arbitrarily edited under the heading Rīm-Sîn I. The first is a seal of the archivist of the palace.

COMMENTARY

The seal was in the collection of W. Baker and is now in the Metropolitan Museum, New York, accession number 1972.118.20.

BIBLIOGRAPHY

1961 Bothmer, Ancient Art no. 26 (photo of impression, translation)
1984 Montebello, Ancient Near Eastern Art p. 54 no. 77 (photo of seal and impression)

TEXT

1) *nu-úr*-^{d}UTU	1) Nūr-Šamaš,
2) ŠA13.DUB.BA ŠÀ É.GAL	2) archivist of the palace,
3) ÌR ^{d}*ri-im*-^{d}EN.ZU	3) servant of Rīm-Sîn.

2009

A cylinder seal of a servant of Rīm-Sîn was in the Collection de Clerq.

COMMENTARY

The inscription was collated from the published photo.

BIBLIOGRAPHY

1883 Ménant, Glyptique 1 fig. 92 (copy)
1888 de Clercq, Collection 1 no. 187 (photo, edition)
1961 Hallo, BiOr 18 p. 11 Rim-Sin 25: iv (study)
1968 Kärki, SKFZ p. 92 Rīmsîn 25 (conflated edition)
1980 Kärki, SAKAZ 1 p. 169 Rīmsîn 25 (edition)

TEXT

1) *da-na-tum*
2) DUMU ^{d}EN.ZU-*ta-a-ar*
3) IR$_{11}$ ^{d}*ri-im*-^{d}EN.ZU

1) Dannatum,
2) son of Sîn-tayyār,
3) servant of Rīm-Sîn.

2010

A cylinder seal of a servant of Rīm-Sîn is in the Newell Collection of Babylonian Seals at Yale.

COMMENTARY

The piece, NCBS 661, is of black-green moss agate and measures 3.2×1.8 cm. The inscription was collated from the published photo.

BIBLIOGRAPHY

1934 von der Osten, Newell no. 661 (photo, edition)
1961 Hallo, BiOr 18 p. 11 Rim-Sin 25: ii (study)
1968 Kärki, SKFZ p. 92 Rīmsîn 25 (conflated edition)
1980 Kärki, SAKAZ 1 p. 170 Rīmsîn 25 (edition)
1981 Buchanan and Hallo, Early Near Eastern Seals no. 788 (study)

TEXT

1) *a-ḫu-wa-qar*
2) DUMU *nu-úr-ì-lí-šu*
3) IR$_{11}$ ^{d}*ri-im*-^{d}EN.ZU

1) Aḫu-waqar,
2) son of Nūr-ilīšu,
3) servant of Rīm-Sîn.

2011

A cylinder seal in the collection of Mrs A. Brett, now in the Metropolitan Museum in New York, has an inscription of a servant of Rīm-Sîn.

COMMENTARY

The seal is no. 78 in the Brett Collection. It is a cylinder seal of mottled red and brown jasper 31.1 cm long, 1.5 cm in dia. The inscription was collated from the published photo.

BIBLIOGRAPHY

1936 von der Osten, Brett no. 78 (photo, study)
1961 Hallo, BiOr 18 p. 11 Rim-Sin 25: vi (study)
1968 Kärki, SKFZ p. 92 Rīmsîn 25 (conflated edition)
1980 Kärki, SAKAZ 1 p. 170 Rīmsîn 25 (edition)

TEXT

1) lú-^{d}mar-dú
2) DUMU ^{d}EN.ZU-*ub-lam*
3) IR$_{11}$ ^{d}*ri-im*-^{d}EN.ZU

1) Lu-Mardu,
2) son of Sîn-ublam,
3) servant of Rīm-Sîn.

2012

A number of seal impressions of servants of Rīm-Sîn I are known. The first is found on a tablet in the Yale collections.

COMMENTARY

The impression is on YBC 5681, a clay tablet dating to year 23 of Rīm-Sîn I. It was not collated.

BIBLIOGRAPHY

1941 Faust, YOS 8 no. 41 (copy)
1961 Hallo, BiOr 18 p. 11 Rim-Sin 25: vii (study)
1968 Kärki, SKFZ p. 92 Rīmsîn 25 (conflated edition)
1980 Kärki, SAKAZ 1 p. 170 Rīmsîn 25 (edition)

TEXT

1) *ši-ir-bu-ni*
2) DUMU *i-gi$_{4}$-gi$_{4}$*
3) ÌR ^{d}*ri-im*-^{d}EN.ZU

1) Širbūni,
2) son of Igigi,
3) servant of Rīm-Sîn.

2013

A seal impression of a servant of Rīm-Sîn I is found on a tablet in the Yale collections.

COMMENTARY

The impression is on YBC 4396, a clay tablet dating to year 31 of Rīm-Sîn I. The impression measures 1.3×2.6 cm and was collated.

BIBLIOGRAPHY

1941 Faust, YOS 8 no. 122 (copy)
1961 Hallo, BiOr 18 p. 11 Rim-Sin 25: iii (study)
1968 Kärki, SKFZ p. 92 Rīmsîn 25 (conflated edition)
1980 Kärki, SAKAZ 1 p. 170 Rīmsîn 25 (edition)

TEXT

1) *a-na-*[d]EN.ZU*-ták-la-ku*
2) DUMU *ip-qú-*[d]*na-na-a*
3) IR$_{11}$ [d]*ri-im-*[d]EN.ZU

1) Ana-Sîn-taklāku,
2) son of Ipqu-Nanāia,
3) servant of Rīm-Sîn.

2014

An impression of seal of a servant of Rīm-Sîn I is found in the Yale collections.

COMMENTARY

The impression is on YBC 7707, a clay tablet dating to year 58 of Rīm-Sîn I. The impression measures 1.2×2.7 cm and was collated.

BIBLIOGRAPHY

1941 Faust, YOS 8 no. 166 (copy)
1961 Hallo, BiOr 18 p. 11 Rim-Sin 25: i (study)
1968 Kärki, SKFZ p. 92 Rīmsîn 25 (conflated edition)
1980 Kärki, SAKAZ 1 p. 170 Rīmsîn 25 (edition)

TEXT

1) [d]IŠKUR*-ri-im-ì-lí*
2) DUMU *ip-qú-*[d]IŠKUR
3) [I]R$_{11}$ [d]*ri-im-*[d]EN.ZU

1) Adad-rīm-ilī,
2) son of Ipqu-Adad,
3) [se]rvant of Rīm-Sîn.

2015

The impression of a servant of Rīm-Sîn I is found on a tablet excavated by Woolley at Ur.

COMMENTARY

The impression is on the clay tablet BM 131287 (1953-4-11,122), excavation no. U 7827x from no. 7 Quiet Street. The impression measures 1.1×2.8 cm and was collated.

BIBLIOGRAPHY

1953 Figulla and Martin, UET 5 no. 277 (copy)
1961 Hallo, BiOr 18 p. 11 Rim-Sin 25: v (study)
1968 Kärki, SKFZ p. 92 Rīmsîn 25 (conflated edition)
1980 Kärki, SAKAZ 1 p. 170 Rīmsîn 25 (edition)

TEXT

1) i-din-⌜^{d}EN⌝.ZU
2) DUMU na-aw-ru-um-ì-lí
3) ì[R] ^{d}ri-⌜im⌝-^{d}EN.ZU

1) Iddin-Sîn,
2) son of Nawrum-ilī,
3) ser[vant] of Rīm-Sîn.

2016

The impression of a seal of a servant of Rīm-Sîn I is found on a tablet in the Iraq Museum.

COMMENTARY

The impression is on IM 10135, a tablet which was acquired through confiscation. The tablet dates to year 52 of Rīm-Sîn I. The impression was not collated. The name in the seal impression is restored from the name found in line 10 in the tablet and envelope.

BIBLIOGRAPHY

1966 van Dijk, Heidelberger Studien p. 241 no. 42 (study)
1968 van Dijk, TIM 5 no. 68 (copy)
1980 Kärki, SAKAZ 1 p. 170 Rīmsîn 25 (edition)

TEXT

1) ^{d}E[N.ZU-APIN]
2) [DU]MU DINGIR-iš-[me-an-ni]
3) [ì]R [^{d}r]i-im-^{d}EN.ZU

1) S[în-ēriš],
2) [s]on of Ilum-iš[meʾanni],
3) [se]rvant of [R]īm-Sîn.

2017

The impression of a seal of a servant of Rīm-Sîn I is known from a copy provided by V. Scheil.

COMMENTARY

The present whereabouts of the tablet containing this impression is not known, so the impression could not be collated. Noteworthy is the Elamite name of the father of the seal owner.

BIBLIOGRAPHY

1916 Scheil, RA 13 p. 10 no. 2 (copy, transliteration, study)

TEXT

1) *ig-mi-il-*ᵈEN.ZU
2) DUMU *ku-uk-ši-ga-at*
3) ÌR ᵈ*ri-im-*ᵈEN.ZU

1) Igmil-Sîn,
2) son of Kuk-šigat,
3) servant of Rīm-Sîn.

2018

A clay bulla excavated at Larsa contains three seal impressions. One of these is of a servant of Rīm-Sîn I.

COMMENTARY

The impression is found on L 7672, IM no. unknown, a clay bulla from the 'socketed pit' in room 13 of the courtyard of the Ebabbar temple at Larsa. It was not collated. The Rīm-Sîn mentioned in this inscription could be either Rīm-Sîn I or Rīm-Sîn II.

BIBLIOGRAPHY

1980 Arnaud, Sumer 36 p. 130 §2.3.7 no. 3 (edition)

TEXT

1) [x]-x-*ba-ni*
2) [UGULA KÙ].DÍM.ME.EŠ
3) [DUMU *ì*]-*lí-ip-pa-al-*[*sà-am*]
4) [IR$_{11}$ ᵈ]*ri-im-*ᵈ[EN.ZU]

1) [...]-bāni,
2) [overseer of the gold]smiths,
3) [son of I]lī-ippal[sam],
4) [servant of] Rīm-[Sîn].

2019

An impression of a seal of a servant of Rīm-Sîn I is found on a tablet in the Louvre.

COMMENTARY

The impression is on AO 24185, a tablet dated to year 23 of Rīm-Sîn I. The tablet was purchased, but its provenance as Larsa can be determined on internal evidence. The impression was not collated.

BIBLIOGRAPHY

1981 Arnaud, Syria 58 p. 75 no. 5 (edition)
1983 Arnaud in Huot, Larsa et 'Oueili 1978–1981 p. 248 no. 5 (edition)

TEXT

1) ^{d}EN.ZU-[...]
2) dumu *hu-sa-pu-[um]*
3) ìr ^{d}*ri-im-*^{d}EN.ZU

1) Sîn-[...],
2) son of Ḫusapu[m],
3) servant of Rīm-Sîn.

2020

The impression of a seal of a servant of Rīm-Sîn I is found on a tablet envelope in the Yale collections.

COMMENTARY

The impression is on NBC 9039. It was collated from the published photo. The royal name in line 3 must refer to Rīm-Sîn I, because it is written without the prefixed DINGIR sign. Rīm-Sîn II's name, in documents known so far, is written with the prefixed divine determinative.

The names in lines 1 and 2 appear to be foreign.

BIBLIOGRAPHY

1981 Buchanan and Hallo, Early Near Eastern Seals no. 787 (photo, edition)

TEXT

1) *ša-ši-in*
2) DUMU *ni-ip-pi*
3) ÌR *ri-im-*^{d}EN.ZU

1) Šašin,
2) son of Nippi,
3) servant of Rīm-Sîn.

2021

A lump of clay with an impression of a cylinder seal of a servant of the *en* priestess En-ane-du was excavated by Woolley at Ur.

COMMENTARY

The impression is on U 4888, a fragment of clay, probably from the Dublamaḫ at Ur. Its present whereabouts is not known. It was collated from the published photo.

BIBLIOGRAPHY

1951 Legrain, UE 10 no. 459 (photo, transliteration)
1961 Hallo, BiOr 18 p. 11 En-anedu 1 (study)
1968 Kärki, SKFZ p. 92 Enanedu 1 (edition)
1980 Kärki, SAKAZ 1 p. 176 Enanedu 1 (edition)

TEXT

1) *i-bi-*^{d}*en-líl*	1) Ibbi-Enlil,
2) DUMU *iš-du-ki-in*	2) son of Išdu-kīn,
3) IR$_{11}$ en-an-e-du$_{7}$	3) servant of En-ane-du.

Rīm-Sîn II

E4.2.15

During the eighth year of Samsu-iluna a certain Rīm-Sîn revolted at Larsa, and by the end of the year became master of most of southern Babylonia. He reigned for just over a year and a half in the south and tablets were dated by his two year names in the cities under his control. However, at the beginning of year 10 of Samsu-iluna, Rīm-Sîn was defeated by the king of Babylon. Here we designate this short reigned ruler as Rīm-Sîn II. Although no inscriptions of Rīm-Sîn II are extant, we do have impressions of a few seals of his servants.

2001

A small archive from Ur studied by D. Ormsby contains, for the most part, small receipts for various commodities such as butter and oil, dating to years 6–8 of Samsu-iluna and years 1–2 of Rīm-Sîn II. These receipts were received by Sîn-ibbīšu, the son of Sîn-iqīšam, who had been the *šandabbakkum* and *gudapsûm* priest of the god Nanna. The impression of the seal of Sîn-ibbīšu in which he appears as a servant of Rīm-Sîn II is on two tablets from this archive.

COMMENTARY

The impressions are found on U 3579 and U 3592 from the Dublamaḫ at Ur. They were collated by D. Charpin. The tablets are at present in Philadelphia.

BIBLIOGRAPHY

1972 Ormsby, JCS 24 p. 99 seal 2 (exs. 1–2, composite copy)
1980 Kärki, SAKAZ 1 p. 170 Rīmsîn 25 (edition)
1986 Charpin, Le clergé d'Ur p. 129 (transliteration)

TEXT

1) ᵈEN.ZU-*i*-[*bi-šu*]	1) Sîn-ib[bīšu],
2) DUMU ᵈEN.ZU-*i-qí-ša-am*	2) son of Sîn-iqīšam,
3) ÌR ᵈ*ri-im*-ᵈEN.Z[U]	3) servant of Rīm-Sî[n].

2002

A tablet from Larsa dated to a year of Rīm-Sîn II has the impression of three servants of Rīm-Sîn II. The first impression belongs to Ibbi-Sîn.

COMMENTARY

The tablet was in the Relph collection; its present whereabouts is unknown. The inscription was not available for collation.

BIBLIOGRAPHY

1917 Pinches, PSBA 39 p. 69 seal A (edition) and pl. IX no. h (copy)
1976 Stol, Studies in Old Babylonian History p. 51 (transliteration, study)

TEXT

1) [*i*]-*bi*-dEN.ZU
2) DUMU dEN.ZU-*be-el*-⸢*ap*⸣-*l*[*im*]
3) ÌR d*ri-im*-dEN.[ZU]

1) [I]bbi-Sîn,
2) son of Sîn-bēl-apl[im],
3) servant of Rīm-[S]în.

2003

The seal impression of Sîn-muštāl, governor of Larsa during the reign of Rīm-Sîn II, and servant of Rīm-Sîn II, appears on two tablets.

CATALOGUE

Ex.	Museum number	cpn
1	–	n
2	YBC 4234	p

COMMENTARY

The impression is found on the tablet mentioned in the previous inscription (ex. 1) and YBC 4234 (ex. 2). Ex. 2 was collated from the published photo.

BIBLIOGRAPHY

1917 Pinches, PSBA 39 p. 69 seal B (ex. 1, edition) and pl. IX no. i (ex. 1, copy)
1941 Faust, YOS 8 no. 54 (ex. 2, copy)
1976 Stol, Studies in Old Babylonian History p. 51 (transliteration, study)
1981 Buchanan, Early Near Eastern Seals no. 802 (ex. 2, photo, edition)

TEXT

1) ^{d}EN.ZU-*mu-uš-ta-al*	1) Sîn-muštāl,
2) DUMU ^{d}EN.ZU-*ma-gir*	2) son of Sîn-māgir,
3) ÌR ^{d}*ri-im*-^{d}EN.ZU	3) servant of Rīm-Sîn.

2004

An impression of a third servant of Rīm-Sîn II is found on the tablet in the Relph collection.

COMMENTARY

The tablet is the same as described in E4.2.15.2002. The inscription was not available for collation.

BIBLIOGRAPHY

1917 Pinches, PSBA 39 p. 69 seal C (edition) and pl. IX no. j (copy)
1976 Stol, Studies in Old Babylonian History p. 51 (transliteration, study)

TEXT

1) *li-pí-it*-^{d}E[N-X]	1) Lipit-E[N...],
2) DUMU ^{d}UTU-DINGIR-X-[X]	2) son of Šamaš-DINGIR-X-[X],
3) ÌR ^{d}*ri-im*-[^{d}EN.ZU]	3) servant of Rīm-[Sîn].

Unidentified Fragments

E4.2.0

A handful of inscriptions from Ur are known which probably belong to kings of the Larsa dynasty, but whose exact attribution is uncertain because of their fragmentary nature. These inscriptions are edited here.

1

A fragment of a cone shaft from Ur is too fragmentary to determine which event it commemorates.

COMMENTARY

The inscription is on BM 119059 (1927-10-3,54) from Ur, excavation no. U ha, provenance not known. It was not collated.

BIBLIOGRAPHY

1965 Sollberger, UET 8 no. 90 (copy, study)

TEXT

Lacuna
1′) [...]
2′) [...] si
3′) [...] x x
4′) [...] NE
5′) [...]-bar-ra
6′) [...]-ta(?)
7′) [...]-x-x-gál-la
8′) [...]-gá
9′) [...]-šè
10′) [...]-en
11′) [...]-x
Lacuna

1′–11′) No translation warranted.

2

A fragment of a cone head from Ur, excavation no. U ia, is too fragmentary to determine which deed it commemorated.

BIBLIOGRAPHY

1965 Sollberger, UET 8 no. 92 (copy)

TEXT

Lacuna
1′) [...] x x [...]-x-t[i]
2′) [...] x-ra dub/kišib-lá x [...]
3′) [...] á ma KU r[i ...]
4′) [... N]I gál-ta
[...] x t[i ...]
5′) [...] l[i ...]
Lacuna

1′–5′) No translation warranted.

3

A cone shaft fragment in the Iraq Museum bears an inscription of a ruler whose name is broken away.

COMMENTARY

The inscription is found on IM 5553, probably the second col. of a cone inscription. It was not collated.

If line 1 of this piece refers to the Ebabbar temple, then a connection of this inscription with the Larsa dynasty is not unlikely. The text could refer, alternatively, to the Ebabbar temple in Sippar.

BIBLIOGRAPHY

1957 Edzard, Sumer 13 p. 189 and pl. 4 (copy, transliteration)

TEXT

Col. i
(missing)
Col. ii
1) [é-báb]bar ([U]D.UD)
2) [é]-⌜ki(?)⌝-ág-gá-[ni]
3) [... gi]ri$_{17}$-zal-la sa[g x]
4) [mu]-na-⌜dù⌝

ii 1–4) built for him the [Ebab]bar, [his] beloved [temple, ...] of magnificence.

5) ⸢é⸣-ki-gar UD x [x] ka-ni x
6) x AN [x]
7) [KA-s]a$_6$-sa$_6$-g[e]-da-ni-t[a]
8) [(x)] u$_4$ ḫé-en-na-[x]
9) [x]-la ⸢ḫur⸣-sa$_6$-[x]
10) [...] ḫé-[...]
11) [x]-aš UD N[E ...]

ii 5–11) No translation warranted.

BABYLON

E4.3

About the beginning of the reign of Sūmû-El of Larsa, the Amorite chief Sūmû-abum installed himself as ruler of Babylon, a hitherto inconsequential town on the Araḫtum canal north of Dilbat. He founded a dynasty which was to rule from Babylon for 300 years. During the reigns of Sîn-muballiṭ and Ḫammu-rāpi, there was a great expansion in the realms of Babylon, culminating with Ḫammu-rāpi's defeat of Rīm-Sîn of Larsa as commemorated in the name of his 31st year. Babylon's hegemony over Sumer and Akkad was short-lived, however, and by the time of the end of the reign of Ḫammu-rāpi's successor, Samsu-iluna, control over the south was lost. Babylon was then reduced to a rump state controlling cities in its general vicinity such as Sippar and Kiš. The dynasty was brought to an end by the raid of the Hittite king Muršili in 1595 BC.

Sūmû-abum

E4.3.1

The first Old Babylonian king for whom we have any year names is Sūmû-abum. He reigned 14 years.

2001

A cylinder seal of a servant of Sūmû-abum is in Philadelphia.

COMMENTARY

The seal is CBS 1111, a piece purchased in Baghdad, original provenance unknown. It is made of serpentine and measures 2.05 cm long, 1.1 cm in dia. The inscription was collated.

BIBLIOGRAPHY

1922 Legrain, MJ 13 p. 66
1925 Legrain, PBS 14 no. 326 (photo, edition)

TEXT

1) *da-ga-ni-ia*	1) Daganīia,
2) ÌR *su-mu-a-bu-um*	2) servant of Sūmû-abum.

Sūmû-la-Il

E4.3.2

Sūmû-la-Il, Sūmû-abum's successor, reigned 36 years. Only seals or seal impressions of servants of this king are known.

2001

The first inscription is found on the seal of Akšakia.

COMMENTARY

The seal is in the Bibliothèque Nationale, Paris (no. 138), given to that institution by the Duke of Luynes in 1862, original provenance unknown. It is a cylinder seal of haematite measuring 2.2 cm long, 1.1 cm in dia. The inscription was collated from the published photo, which provides a reading different from that previously given.

BIBLIOGRAPHY

1910 Delaporte, Bibliothèque Nationale no. 138 (photo, edition)

TEXT

1) *akšak*.KI-*ia*	1) Akšakia,
2) ÌR *su-mu-la-ìl*	2) servant of Sūmû-la-Il.

2002

A seal bears the inscription of a servant of Sūmû-la-Il.

COMMENTARY

The object is BM 102556 (1908-4-11,64). The deity mentioned in the seal, Uraš, suggests that the seal came from Dilbat. It is a cylinder seal of serpentine, 2.55 cm long, 1.2 cm in dia. The inscription was collated by E. Sollberger.

BIBLIOGRAPHY

1986 Collon, Cylinder Seals 3 no. 79 (photo, edition)

TEXT

1) *be-lí-i-pa-al-sà-am*	1) Bēlī-ippalsam,
2) DUMU *ib-ni*-^{d}uraš	2) son of Ibni-Uraš,
3) IR$_{11}$ ^{d}uraš	3) servant of the god Uraš,
4) ù *su-mu-la-ìl*	4) and Sūmû-la-Il.

2003

A tablet in the British Museum bears the seal impression of a servant of Sūmû-la-Il.

COMMENTARY

The tablet is BM 82424 (Bu 91-5-9,2469) and was excavated at Sippar. The impression was not collated.

BIBLIOGRAPHY

1968 Finkelstein, CT 48 no. 29 (transliteration)

TEXT

1) *na-ka-ru-um*	1) Nakarum,
2) DUMU ^{d}EN.ZU-*e-ri-ba-am*	2) son of Sîn-erībam,
3) ÌR *su-mu-la-ìl*	3) servant of Sūmû-la-Il.

Sābium

E4.3.3

Sūmû-la-Il's successor Sābium ruled 14 years. Only seals or seal impressions mentioning the king are extant.

1

A cylinder seal of Ibbi-Sîn, son of Sābium, is in Philadelphia.

COMMENTARY

The piece is CBS 8978, purchased in Shatra in 1891, original provenance unknown but probably Babylon. It is made of reddish limestone measuring 2 cm long, 1.6 cm in dia. The inscription was collated.

An attribution of the RN in line 2 to the king of Babylon is not absolutely certain in view of the variant spelling.

BIBLIOGRAPHY

1925 Legrain, PBS 14 no. 327 (photo, edition)

TEXT

1) *i-bí-*^{d}EN.ZU	1) Ibbi-Sîn,
2) DUMU *sà-bu-um* LUGAL	2) son of Sābium, the king.

2001

A seal impression on a tablet in Baghdad names a servant of Sābium.

COMMENTARY

The impression is on IM 49164, a tablet purchased from G. Ḫayyāṭ. It was not collated.

BIBLIOGRAPHY

1968 van Dijk, TIM 5 no. 6 (copy)

TEXT

1) *ì-lí-⌜a⌝-*[x]	1) Ilī-a[...],
2) DUMU *di-nam-ì-lí*	2) son of Dinam-ilī,
3) ÌR *sà-bi-um*	3) servant of Sābium.

2002

A tablet dating to year 22 of Sābium bears the seal impression of a servant of Sābium.

COMMENTARY

The impression is on Bu 91-5-9,2189A. This is a tablet envelope which was shattered to get the tablet out, and thus the impression could not be collated from the original. It was collated from the published photo.

BIBLIOGRAPHY

1912-13 Waterman, AJSL 29 p. 203 bottom (photo)
1916 Waterman, Bus. Doc. p. 136 bottom (photo)

TEXT

1) [...]-^{d}EN.ZU	1) [...]-Sîn,
2) DUMU *pá-ka-šar*	2) son of Pāka-šar,
3) ÌR *sà-bi-um*	3) servant of Sābium.

2003

A tablet envelope in the British Museum bears the impression of a seal of a servant of Sābium.

COMMENTARY

The envelope is BM 80128 (89-10-14,658b) excavated at Sippar. The impression was not collated.

BIBLIOGRAPHY

1968 Finkelstein, CT 48 no. 21 (transliteration)

TEXT

1)	*ni-di-in*-x	1) Nidin-...,
2)	DUB.⌜SAR⌝	2) scribe,
3)	DUMU gìr-ni-ì-sa_6	3) son of Girini-isa,
4)	ÌR *sà-bi-um*	4) servant of Sābium.

2004

The impression of a seal of a servant of Sābium is on a tablet envelope in the Louvre.

COMMENTARY

The impression, found on AO 10778, excavated at Kiš, measures 4.1×2.1 cm. It was collated from the published photo.

BIBLIOGRAPHY

1925 de Genouillac, Kich 2 p. 42 pl. 35 D 19 (study)
1957 Edzard, Zwischenzeit p. 151 n. 795 (edition)
1959 Kupper, RA 53 p. 32 (edition)
1988 Blocher, RA 82 pp. 34–35 (photo, edition)

TEXT

1)	[d]AMAR.UTU-AN.DÙL-[x]	1) Marduk-ṣulūl[...],
2)	DUB.S[AR]	2) scri[be],
3)	DUMU *be*-x-x-[x]	3) son of Be...,
4)	ÌR *sà-bi-u*[*m*]	4) servant of Sābiu[m].

Apil-Sîn

E4.3.4

Apil-Sîn, Sābium's successor, reigned 18 years. No inscriptions are extant for this king as yet.

Sîn-muballiṭ

E4.3.5

Sîn-muballiṭ, Apil-Sîn's successor, reigned 20 years. No inscriptions of this king are known.

Ḫammu-rāpi

E4.3.6

Ḫammu-rāpi, Sîn-muballiṭ's successor, reigned 43 years. A number of inscriptions are extant for this important ruler.

1

The name of the fourth year of Ḫammu-rāpi commemorates the construction of the wall of the cloister (in Sippar). This deed is commemorated in a Sumerian brick inscription.

CATALOGUE

Ex.	Museum number	Dimensions (cm)	Lines preserved	cpn
1	Ash 1922,183	22.0×6.0×8.0	1–21	c
2	EŞ 9044	22.0×7.8×8.8	15–35	c

COMMENTARY

The provenance of ex. 1 was not known when it was acquired by the Ashmolean Museum, but since the duplicate is known to have come from Sippar we may assume that it did as well. Ex. 2 probably comes from V. Scheil's excavations at Sippar, but is not mentioned in his publication of the finds.

W. Hallo, followed by I. Kärki, suggested that the Ashmolean text might be an inscription of Rīm-Sîn, but collation reveals that it belongs to Ḫammu-rāpi.

BIBLIOGRAPHY

1923 Langdon, OECT 1 p. 60 and pl. 30 (ex. 1, copy, study)
1968 Kärki, SKFZ p. 71 Rīmsîn 1 (ex. 1, edition)
1980 Kärki, SAKAZ 1 pp. 141–42 Rīmsîn 1 (ex. 1, edition)
1981 Walker, CBI p. 129 (ex. 1, study)
1984 Frayne, ARRIM 2 pp. 28–30 (ex. 1–2, copy, edition)

TEXT

1) ⌜*ḫa*⌝-[*am*]-⌜*mu*⌝-*ra*-⌜*pí*⌝
2) l[ugal-kala-ga]
3) lu[gal-KÁ.DINGIR.RA.KI]
4) u$_4$ ⌜^{d}⌝utu lugal-mu
5) x x x a
6) x x x x ni

1–12) I, Ḫa[m]mu-rāpi, [mighty] k[ing], ki[ng of Babylon], when the god Utu, my lord, ..., ..., I, being one who heeds the word which he has spoken, spoke to me joyously (and) laid a commission on me to widen ...

7) x UD(?) x x x
8) dagal-e-dè
9) ⌜inim⌝ in-⌜du$_{11}$-ga-a⌝
10) ⌜giš⌝ in-tuk-ni-me-en
11) gù-ḫúl ma-an-dé
12) ⌜á⌝-bi ḫu-mu-da-an-ág
13) u$_{4}$-ba
14) ⌜šà⌝-gál diri-dè
15) a-gàr a-gar-ra
16) e ḫu-mu-si-ga
17) úgu-ba
18) bàd-gá-gi$_{4}$-a
19) ḫu-mu-dù

13–19) At that time, in order to increase (the amount of) food, I piled up a dike in the flooded field (and) built the wall of the cloister upon it.

20) šà-ba
21) I$_{7}$.^{d}a-a-ḫé-gál
22) ḫu-mu-ba-al
23) a-nam-ḫé
24) ḫé-bí-dé

20–24) I dug there the canal Aia-ḫegal ('Aia is abundance') and poured abundant water in it.

25) nam-bi-šè
26) ^{d}a-a
27) nin-zimbir.KI
28) ḫé-⌜en⌝-ši-ḫúl-le
29) ki-^{d}utu
30) nìta-dam-ni-da
31) ti-⌜u$_{4}$-sù⌝-rá
32) ⌜bala⌝-[n]am-x [...]
33) ⌜suḫuš(?)⌝ ḫé(?)-x x
34) x [...] ḫé-en-⌜ši⌝-[...]
35) [...] sa$_{12}$-e-[éš]
36) [ḫa-ma-ab-rig$_{7}$-ge]

25–36) On account of this may the goddess Aia, lady of Sippar, rejoice (and) with the god Utu, her spouse, gr[ant to me] a long life-span, a reign of ..., (and) a ... foundation ...

2

The name of year 23 of Ḫammu-rāpi commemorates the laying of the base of the wall of Sippar; that of year 25 the construction of the wall itself. These deeds are described in an inscription found on cones from Sippar in both a Sumerian and Akkadian version.

CATALOGUE

Sumerian version

Ex.	Museum number	Registration number	Object	Dimensions (cm)	Lines preserved	cpn
1	Ash 1923,306	–	Head	17.5 dia.	1-58, 68-77	c
2	Ash 1923,306	–	Shaft	9.2	1-21	c
3	BM 80142	89-10-14,666	Shaft	18.4	1-80	c
4	BM 80142	89-10-14,666	Head	10.9 dia.	39-48, 71-74	c
5	BM 56614	82-7-14,995A	Shaft	10.7	1-35, 37-46, 64-67	c
6	BM 56614	82-7-14,995A	Head	9.1	35-39	c

16.1 Copy: ḫu; brick: ri. **17**.2 omits this line. **19**.1 Copy: ḫu; brick: ri. **21**.1 I$_{7}$.⟨^{d}⟩a-a-ḫé-gá[l].

Sumerian version

Ex.	Museum number	Registration number	Object	Dimensions (cm)	Lines preserved	cpn
7	BM 80141	89-10-14,665	Head	18.3	1–23, 28–52, 55–78	c
8	BM 80141	89-10-14,665	Shaft	11.2	1–8, 19–41	c
9	BM –	AH 82-7-14, –	Frgm.	–	26–31	n

Akkadian version

Ex.	Museum number	Object	Dimensions (cm)	Lines preserved	cpn
1	CBS 11	Shaft	–	1–81	c
2	CBS 11	Head	–	6–21, 32–45	c
3	A 24645	Head	18.7 dia.	1–81	c
4	A 24645	Shaft	–	28–40	c

COMMENTARY

The master text is ex. 3 for the Sumerian version and ex. 1 for the Akkadian version. The translation follows the Akkadian version.

One cone (exs. 1–2) of the Akkadian version was purchased from the J. Shemtob collection. The other (exs. 3–4) was presented to the Oriental Institute from the M. Yondorf collection.

BIBLIOGRAPHY

Sumerian version
1887 Winckler, ZA 2 p. 123 (ex. 9, partial copy, study)
1923 Langdon, OECT 1 pp. 23–24 and pl. 18 (ex. 1, copy, edition)
1970 Matthews, First Dynasty of Babylon pp. 109–19 (exs. 1, 5–6, edition)
1971 Sollberger and Kupper, IRSA ɪᴠC6f (ex. 1, study)
1983 Kärki, SAKAZ 2 pp. 8–10 (ex. 1, edition)
1985 Sollberger and Walker, Mélanges Birot pp. 263–64 (exs. 1–8, transliteration, study)

Akkadian version
1915 Ungnad, PBS 7 no. 133 (exs. 1–2, photo, copy, edition)
1948 Gelb, JNES 7 pp. 267–71 (exs. 3–4, photo, edition)
1970 Matthews, First Dynasty of Babylon pp. 109–19 (edition)
1971 Sollberger and Kupper, IRSA ɪᴠC6f (translation)
1983 Kärki, SAKAZ 2 pp. 6–10 (edition)

TEXT

Sumerian	Akkadian	
1) u$_4$ ^{d}utu	1) *ì-nu* ^{d}UTU	1–12) When the god Šamaš, great lord of heaven and earth, king of the gods, with his shining face, joyfully looked at me, Ḫammu-rāpi, the prince, his favourite, granted to me everlasting kingship (and) a reign of long days,
2) en-gal-an-ki-bi-da	2) *be-lum ra-bi-um*	
	3) *ša ša-ma-i ù er-ṣe-tim*	
3) lugal-dingir-re-e-ne-ke$_4$	4) LUGAL *ša* DINGIR.DINGIR	
4) *ḫa-am-mu-ra-pí*	5) *ḫa-am-mu-ra-pí*	
5) nun-še-ga-ni-me-en	6) *ru-ba-am mi-gir-šu ia-ti*	
6) igi-zalag-ga-na	7) *in pa-ni-šu nam-ru-tim*	
7) ḫúl-la-bi	8) *ḫa-di-iš*	
8) mu-un-bar-re-en	9) *ip-pa-al-sa$_6$-ni*	
9) nam-lugal-da-rí	10) *šar-ru-tam da-rí-tám*	
10) bala u$_4$-sù-rá	11) BALA *u$_4$-mi ar-ku-tim*	
11) ma-ni-in-rig$_7$	12) *iš-ru-kam*	
12) suḫuš-ma-da	13) SUḪUŠ KALAM	13–27) made firm for me the

Sumerian version: **3.1** lugal-dingir-re-ne-⟨ke$_4$⟩. **5.1** Copy: sipa še-ga; cone: nun še-ga. **9.1** Copy: da-na; cone: da-rí. **12.1** Copy: dumu-na; cone: suḫuš.

Akkadian version: **3.1** TA *ša-ma-i*. **6.1** *mi-*ḪA*-šu*. **7.1** *in pa-⟨ni⟩-šu*.

Sumerian	Akkadian	English
13) nam-en-bi ak-dè	14) *ša a-na be-li-im*	foundation of the land which he had given me to rule, spoke to me by his pure word which cannot be changed to settle the people of Sippar and Babylon in peaceful abodes, (and) laid a great commission on me to build the wall of Sippar (and) to raise its head,
14) ma-an-sum-ma	15) *i-din-na-am*	
15) ma-ni-in-ge$_4$-en	16) *ù-ki-in-nam*	
16) zimbir.KI	17) *ni-šî* ZIMBIR.KI	
17) KÁ.DINGIR.RA.KI un-bi	18) *ù* KÁ.DINGIR.RA.KI	
18) ki-tuš-ne-ḫa tuš-ù-da	19) *šu-ba-at ne-eḫ-ti-im*	
	20) *šu-šu-ba-am*	
19) inim-kù-nu-kúr-ru-da-na	21) *in pí-šu el-li-im*	
20) bí-in-du$_{11}$-ga-a	22) *ša la na-ka-ar iq-bi-ù*	
21) bàd-zimbir.KI	23) BÀD ZIMBIR.KI	
22) dù-ù-da	24) *e-pé-ša-am*	
23) sag-bi íl-i-da	25) *re-ši-šu ul-la-a-am*	
24) á-gal ḫu-mu-da-an-ág	26) *ra-bi-iš lu-wa-er-ra-an-ni*	
25) u$_4$-ba	28) *i-nu-u$_4$-mi-šu*	28–35) at that time, I, Ḫammu-rāpi, mighty king, king of Babylon, reverent one, who heeds the god Šamaš, beloved of the goddess Aia, who contents the god Marduk, his lord,
26) *ḫa-am-mu-ra-pí*	29) *ḫa-am-mu-ra-pí*	
27) lugal-kala-ga	30) LUGAL *da-núm*	
28) lugal-KÁ.DINGIR.RA.KI	31) LUGAL KÁ.DINGIR.RA.KI	
29) ní-tuk	32) *na-a*ᵓ*-du-um še-mu* ^{d}UTU	
30) ^{d}utu-da giš-tuk		
31) ki-ág ^{d}šè-ri$_5$-da	33) *na-ra-am* ^{d}*a-a*	
32) šà-du$_{10}$-ga-^{d}AMAR.UTU	34) *mu-ṭi-ib li-ib-bi*	
33) lugal-la-ni-me-en	35) ^{d}AMAR.UTU *be-li-šu a-na-ku*	
34) usu-maḫ ^{d}utu-ke$_4$	36) *in e-mu-qí-in ṣi-ra-tim*	36–45) by the supreme might which the god Šamaš gave to me, with the levy of the army of my land, I raised the top of the foundation of the wall of Sippar with earth (until it was) like a great mountain. I built (that) high wall.
35) ma-ni-in-sum	38) *ša* ^{d}UTU *id-din-na-am*	
36) ugnim-zi-ga	39) *in ti-bu-ut*	
37) ma-da-mu-ta	40) *um-ma-an ma-ti-ia*	
38) uru$_4$-bàd-zimbir.KI	41) *uš-ši* BÀD ZIMBIR.KI	
39) saḫar-ta ḫur-sag-gal-gin$_7$	42) *in e-pé-ri*	
	43) *ki-ma* SA.DÚ*-im ra-bi-im*	
40) sag-bi ḫé-em-mi-íl	44) *re-ši-sú-nu lu ú-ul-li*	
41) bàd-maḫ ḫu-mu-dù	45) BÀD MAḪ *lu e-pu-uš*	
42) u$_4$-ul-lí-a-ta	46) *ša iš-tu u$_4$-um ṣi-a-tim*	46–50) That which from the past no king among the kings had built, for the god Šamaš, my lord I grandly built.
43) lugal-lugal-a-ni-ir	47) *šar-ru in* LUGAL*-rí*	
44) lugal na-me	48) *ma-na-ma la i-pu-šu*	
45) ba-ra-an-dím-ma		
46) ^{d}utu lugal-gá	49) *a-na* ^{d}UTU *be-li-ia*	
47) gal-bi ḫu-mu-na-dù	50) *ra-bi-iš lu e-pu-ús-súm*	
48) bàd-bi	51) BÀD *šu-ú*	51–55) The name of that wall is 'By the decree of the god Šamaš, may Ḫammu-rāpi have no rival'.
49) du$_{11}$-ga-^{d}utu-ta	52) *in qí-bi-it* ^{d}UTU	
50) *ḫa-am-mu-ra-pí*	53) *ḫa-am-mu-ra-pí*	
51) gaba-ri na-an-tuk-tuk	54) *ma-ḫi-ri a ir-ši*	
52) mu-bi-im	55) *šum-šu*	
53) bala-sa$_6$-ga-gá	56) *in* BALA*-ia dam-qí-im*	56–61) In my gracious reign which the god Šamaš called, I cancelled corvée duty for the god Šamaš for the men of Sippar, the ancient city of the god Šamaš.
54) ^{d}utu-ke$_4$	57) *ša* ^{d}UTU *ib-bi-ù*	
55) mu-un-sa$_4$-a		
56) zimbir.KI	58) ZIMBIR.KI	
57) uru.KI-ul-la-	59) URU.KI *ṣi-a-tim ša* ^{d}UTU	
58) ^{d}utu-ke$_4$		

Sumerian version: **15**.1 Copy: ma-ni-in-ge-en; cone: ma-ni-in-ge$_4$-en. **19**.1 Copy: inim-kù-ge RU-da-na; cone: inim-kù-nu-kúr-ru-da-na. **26**.1 *ḫa-am-mu-⟨ra⟩-pí*. **29**.1 Copy: ní-⌜gál⌝; cone: ní-tuk. **31**.1 Copy unclear; cone: ki-ág-^{d}šè-ri$_5$-[d]a. **34**.1 Copy unclear at end; cone: ^{d}⌜utu⌝-ke$_4$. **35**.7 ma-ni-in-sum-ma-ta. **36**.1 Copy unclear; cone: ugn[i]m ⌜zi-ga⌝. **43**.1 lugal lugal-e-ne-er. **47**.1 Copy: mu-na-IR; cone: mu-na-dù.

Akkadian version: **16**.1 *ù-ki-in-na*(erased)*-nam*. **16**.2 *ù-ki-in-na-*⌜*am*⌝. **19**.1 *ne-eḫ-ti-⟨im⟩*. **27**.3 *lu u-wa-⟨er⟩-ra-an-ni*. **34**.1 *li-⟨ib⟩-bi*. **38**.1 DA*-din-na-am*. **38**.2 *id-din-⟨na⟩-am*. **44**.3 *re-ši-su-nu*. **46**.3 *u$_4$-mi*. **47**.3 *šar-⟨ru⟩*. **59**.1 *ša* ⟨^{d}UTU⟩.

59) érin-bi GIŠ.dusu-ta	60) ÉRIN-*šu in* GIŠ.DUSU	
60) ^{d}utu-ra ḫé-bí-zi	61) *a-na* ^{d}UTU *lu as-sú-úḫ*	
61) i$_{7}$-bi	62) I$_{7}$-*šu lu aḫ-ri*	62–69) I dug its canal (and) provided perpetual water for its land. I heaped up plenty and abundance. I established joy for the people of Sippar.
62) ḫu-mu-ba-al		
63) ki-in-gub-ba	63) *a-na er-ṣe-ti-šu*	
64) a-da-rí	64) *me-e da-ru-tim*	
65) ḫé-em-mi-gar	65) *lu aš-ku-un*	
66) ḫi-nun ḫé-gál-bi	66) *nu-uḫ-ša-am ù* ḪÉ.GÁL	
67) ḫé-ni-gar-gar	67) *lu ú-kam-me-er*	
68) un-zimbir.KI-šè	68) *a-na ni-šī* ZIMBIR.KI	
69) asila ḫé-bí-gar	69) *ri-iš-tam lu aš-ku-un*	
70) nam-ti-gá	70) *a-na ba-la-ṭì-ia*	70–81) They pray (Sumerian: they prayed) for my life. I did what was pleasing to the god Šamaš, my lord, and the goddess Aia, my lady. I put my good name in the mouths of the people (in order) that they proclaim it daily like (that of) a god and that it not be forgotten, forever.
71) šùd ḫé-em-mi-rá-aš	71) *lu i-ka-ar-ra-ba*	
72) su-^{d}utu lugal-gá	72) *ša a-na* SU ^{d}UTU *be-li-ia*	
73) ^{d}a-a nin-mu	73) *ù* ^{d}*a-a be-el-ti-ia*	
74) du$_{10}$-ga-ra ḫé-bí-ak	74) *ṭa-a-bu lu e-pu-uš*	
75) mu-sa$_{6}$-ga-mu	75) *šu-mi dam-qá-am*	
76) u$_{4}$-šú-uš	76) *u$_{4}$-mi-ša-am*	
77) dingir-gin$_{7}$ pà-dè-da	77) *ki-ma* DINGIR *za-ka-ra-am*	
78) du-rí-šè	78) *ša a-na da-ar*	
79) nu-ḫa-lam-e	79) *la im-ma-aš-šu-ú*	
80) ka un-ta ḫé-bí-gar	80) *in pí-i ni-šī*	
	81) *lu aš-ku-un*	

3

This inscription, known from a Neo-Babylonian copy, deals with the construction by Ḫammu-rāpi of a storehouse for the god Enlil in the city of Babylon.

COMMENTARY

The tablet bearing this inscription is BM 46543 (81-8-30,9), from Rassam's excavations in Babylonia. The evidence of the colophon indicates that it originally came from Borsippa.

The colophon of the tablet indicates that the scribe Rēmūt-Gula copied this text from an inscription which was in the Enamtila temple. This shrine is elsewhere known to be the temple of the god(s) Enlil (and Ninurta) in Babylon. This agrees with the text, which is concerned with the god Enlil. After he made the copy in Babylon Rēmūt-Gula deposited it in Ezida, the temple of the god Nabû in Borsippa.

Although the copy shows a number of late orthographies, the titulary of the king recorded in it seems to reflect a genuine Ḫammu-rāpi inscription. The titulary of the king found here shows striking similarities to that of E4.3.6.2 dating to year 25. The mention in the text of Enlil's granting to Ḫammu-rāpi of the exercise of rule over the land would appear to refer to Nippur's recognition of Ḫammu-rāpi's hegemony, an event which must date around year 29, when year names of the Babylonian king are used for the first time at Nippur. However, it lacks the epithet 'king who made the four quarters obedient', an epithet

---

Akkadian version: **71**.1 [*i*]-*ka*-⟨*ar*⟩-*ra*-[*ba*]. **72**.1 *a-na* SU (cone:*dí*).

which probably alludes to the great battle commemorated in the name of year 30. All these facts suggest that the OB original of this text dates to year 29. The building of a storehouse for the god Enlil in Babylon at this time may be connected with the coincidental recognition of the hegemony of Ḫammu-rāpi by Nippur.

BIBLIOGRAPHY

1892 Jensen, KB 3/1 pp. 120–23 Hammurabi f (edition)
1898–1900 King, LIH no. 59 (copy, edition)
1968 Hunger, Kolophone no. 140 (edition of colophon only)
1970 Matthews, First Dynasty of Babylon pp. 149–52 (edition)
1971 Sollberger and Kupper, IRSA ɪᴠC6g (translation)
1983 Kärki, SAKAZ 2 pp. 10–11 (edition)

TEXT

1) *a-na* ^{d}*en-líl*
2) *be-li* GAL-*i*
3) *šá* AN-*e u* KI-*tim*
4) LUGAL DINGIR.DINGIR
5) *be-li-ia*
6) *ḫa-am-mu-ra-pí*
7) *ru-bu-ú me-gir* ^{d}50
8) *re-ʾ-ú na-ram* ^{d}NIN.LÍL
9) *pal-ḫu še-mu-ú* ^{d}UTU
10) *mu-ṭib lìb-bi* ^{d}AMAR.UTU
11) LUGAL *dan-nu*
12) LUGAL TIN.TIR.KI
13) *áš-ru pal-ḫu*
14) [...] x ⌜*a*⌝-*na-k*[*u*]
15) [*ì-n*]*u* ^{d}*en-líl* UN.MEŠ KUR-*ú*
16) ⌜*a*⌝-*na be-lu-ti e-pe-ši*
17) *id-di-na ṣer-re-es-sa*
18) *a-na* ŠU-*ia*
19) *ú-ma-al-li*
20) *i-nu-šú* ⟨*i-na*⟩ TIN.TIR.KI
21) URU *na-ar-me-šu*
22) É-*šu-tùm-me*
23) *ḫu-ud lib-bi-šú e-pu-uš*

Colophon

24) *šá* UGU MU.SAR.E *šá é-nam-ti-la*
25) *šá ḫa-am-mu-ra-pí* LUGAL ^{m}*re-mut-*^{d}*gu-la*
26) A LÚ.SAG.ÉRIN LÚ.ŠÁMAN.LÁ NAB-TUR *iš-ṭur-ma*
27) *ana* TIN ZI.ME-*šú* DU$_{10}$-*ub lìb-bi-šú u* GIŠ.TUK *su-pe-e-šú*
28) *i-na é-zi-da* É *na-ram* ^{d}MUATI *ú-ki-in*

1–5) For the god Enlil, great lord of heaven and earth, king of the gods, my lord,

6–14) I, Ḫammu-rāpi, prince, favourite of the god Enlil, shepherd beloved of the goddess Ninlil, reverent one, who heeds the god Šamaš, who contents the god Marduk, mighty king, king of Babylon, humble, reverent one, ...

15–19) [wh]en the god Enlil gave to me to rule the people of the land, (and) entrusted their lead-rope into my hands,

20–23) at that time, I built a storehouse which pleases him ⟨in⟩ Babylon, his beloved city.

Colophon

24–28) (Text) upon an inscription of the Enamtila temple, of Ḫammu-rāpi, the king. Rēmūt-Gula, descendant of Ša-rēš-ṣābim, the apprentice, junior ... wrote it and put it in Ezida, the temple beloved of the god Nabû, for his life, happiness, and the hearing of his prayers.

4

An inscribed stone block mentions Ḫammu-rāpi's defeat of his enemies.

COMMENTARY

The inscription is found on Sb 17738, now in the Louvre, a piece excavated at Susa which was collated. It is a fragmentary block of granite 56 cm long, 29 cm across, and 32 cm thick.

Collation reveals that some pieces at the extreme right of the inscription have broken away since the copy of Jéquier was made. We give the text as found in Jéquier's copy. The copy suggests that there may have been a second col. now broken away.

The date of this inscription is not entirely certain. It lacks the title 'king of all the Amorite land' which according to M. Stol (Studies in Old Babylonian History p. 84 n. 54) was adopted around year 34. It does have the epithet 'king who makes the four quarters be at peace'. This epithet is found in inscriptions commemorating the events which figure in the names of years 33 and 36, but does not appear in E4.3.6.2 connected with the name of year 25. The epithet was probably adopted by Ḫammu-rāpi after some notable military victory. The first military success recorded in a year name after year 25 is the defeat of Elam in year 30. The second is the defeat of Rīm-Sîn of Larsa in year 31. It is noteworthy that the divine pair An and Enlil appear in this text along with 'the great gods'. This particular phraseology is found only in the name of year 31 of Ḫammu-rāpi. The evidence assembled here suggests a date for this inscription around year 31.

This stone block was presumably a victory stele erected to commemorate the victory over either Elam or Rīm-Sîn of Larsa.

BIBLIOGRAPHY

1900 Scheil, MDP 2 pp. 83–85 (copy, edition)
1957 Hallo, Royal Titles pp. 55 and 139 (study)
1970 Matthews, First Dynasty of Babylon pp. 165–67 (edition)
1971 Sollberger and Kupper, IRSA IVC6k (translation)
1983 Kärki, SAKAZ 2 pp. 15–16 (edition)

TEXT

Col. i

1) [*ḫa-am-m*]*u*-⸢*ra*⸣-*pí*
2) [ni]ta-kala-g[a]
3) [l]ugal ur-[sag]
4) lugal-an-ub-[da]-límm[u-ba]
5) gù-téš-[a]
6) bí-in-sì-g[a]
7) še-g[a]-an-na-[x]
8) SI A [...]
9) KA [...]
10) ^{d}e[n-líl]
11) dalla-[è]

i 1–11) [Ḫamm]u-rāpi, mighty [ma]n, vali[ant k]ing, king who makes the four quarters be at peace, favourite of the god An, who [makes] splendid the ... [of] the god E[nlil],

12) u$_4$ [an]
13) ^{d}en-[líl]
14) nam-a-[ni]
15) bí-íb-⸢bùlug⸣-g[e$_{26}$]-eš-a
16) dingir-gal-gal-e-ne
17) mu-ni-in-sa$_4$-e[š]

i 12–17) when the gods [An] (and) En[lil] magnified [his] destiny (and) the great gods called him (by name),

18) giš-rab-ni-ta
19) lú-kúr
20) šu ḫé-íb-ri-ri-ge
21) ugni[m]
22) gú-dù-a-n[i] GIŠ.tukul-a-[ni]
23) giš [x] ḫé-bí-in-r[a]
24) šen-šen-[na]

i 18–28) with his fetters he tied up the enemy, [his] weapon smote the arm[y] that was hostile to hi[m], [in] combat he slew the ev[il] land. [His] force ... the *disobe*[*dient*]

---

7 Beginning of -ga now missing. 11 End of dalla now missing. 13 en- missing. 14 -a missing. 15 bùlug partially preserved.

25) kur gú-NE.[RU]-gál-la-š[è]
26) ḫé-bí-i[n]-ḫúb
27) á-kala-ga-[ni]
28) nu-še-[ga]
Col. ii (missing)

ii) (missing)

5

The name of year 31 of Ḫammu-rāpi commemorates the defeat of the city of Larsa and that of year 32 the defeat of the army of Ešnunna, Subartu, and Gutium and the conquest of the land of Mankiṣum. Various historical sources studied by D. Charpin (Mélanges Birot pp. 56–57) indicate that in addition to Rīm-Sîn of Larsa, Ḫammu-rāpi defeated Ṣillī-Sîn of Ešnunna at this time. Events dating to this general time period are described in two fragments of historical texts of Old Babylonian date from Babylon that should be attributed to Ḫammu-rāpi and are included here as E4.3.6.5 and E4.3.6.6.

COMMENTARY

This first text, written in Sumerian, is inscribed on VAT 17399, a fragment of a clay tablet 2.5×6 cm, excavated by Koldewey at Babylon. It apparently deals with the defeat of Larsa by Ḫammu-rāpi.

BIBLIOGRAPHY

1987 van Dijk, VAS 24 no. 77 (copy)

TEXT

1) [...] *ṣi-lí*-^{d}EN.ZU lugal áš-nu[n-na.KI ...]
2) [...] x lugal-e larsa.KI-ma gú-giš-gá-gá bí-ni-[in-ak]
3) [...] ḫul-ḫul-ta mu-un-dím-ma gìr-sì-lugal-[la ...]
4) [...] á/id sizkur-ak-bi lugal-ra [...]
5) [...] x x [...]
Lacuna

1–5) [...] Ṣillī-Sîn, king of Ešnu[nna ...], (Ḫammu-rāpi) the king, defeated Larsa [...] the [...] which he fashioned ..., the *girsequ* [*of*] the king [...] their making offerings, to the king [...] ... [...]
Lacuna

6

Regarding this text see the introduction to E4.3.6.5.

25 š[è] at end of line not indicated in copy.

COMMENTARY

This second text, written in Akkadian, is inscribed on VAT 17172, a fragment of a clay tablet, 6×7×3.5 cm, excavated by Koldewey at Babylon. It probably deals with Hammu-rāpi's defeat of Ṣillī-Sîn near Mankiṣum on the Upper Tigris.

The obv. contains 10 lines which, apart from a mention of *su-bar-tim* in line 5′, are too broken to render a coherent translation.

BIBLIOGRAPHY

1987 van Dijk, VAS 24 no. 79 (copy)

TEXT

Reverse	Reverse
Lacuna	Lacuna
1′) [...] ⸢*qá*⸣-*ab-l*[*a-am* ...]	1′) [...] bat[tle ...]
2′) [...] ⸢*a*⸣-*ar up-pu-ti* [...]	2′) [...] ...
3′) [...] I$_{7}$.IDIGNA *i-n*[*a* ...]	3′) [...] the Tigris river in [...]
4′) [... *bi*]-*ri-it ma-an-ki-ṣúm*.KI x *i-*[*na* ...]	4′) [...] in between Mankiṣum ... in [...]
5′) [...] *ṣi-it ma-an-ki-ṣúm*.KI *ka-ra-as-su* x	5′) [...] ... Mankiṣum, his army
6′) [*ṣi-lí*]-^{d}EN.ZU LUGAL *áš-nun-na*.KI	6′) [Ṣillī]-Sîn, king of Ešnunna,
7′) [...] x-*ti šu-a-ti iš-mu-ú*	7′) [...] they heard those ...
8′) [...] *ti-pu-uš iš-ku-nam-ma*	8′) [...] he established ... and
9′) [...] x.MEŠ *iš-tu pa-ṭi gu-ti-um*.KI *a-di* x	9′) [...] the ... from the border of Gutium to
10′) [...] x *iš-te-en la i*-x [...]	10′) [...] not one ... [...]
11′) [...] x x x *a-tim* LUGAL É.[GAL-*la-tim* ...]	11′) [...] ..., the king of *E*[*kallātum* ...]
12′) [...] x [...]	12′) [...] ... [...]
Lacuna	Lacuna

7

The name of year 33 of Ḫammu-rāpi commemorates the digging of the canal 'Ḫammu-rāpi is the abundance of the people'. This deed is recorded in a stone foundation tablet.

COMMENTARY

The tablet is N III 3489, now in the Louvre, a purchased piece of unknown provenance brought to France in 1858. It is a limestone tablet 21.5×8.0 cm, and the inscription was collated.

In addition to narrating the digging of the canal, the inscription also records the construction along its banks of the fortress of 'Dūr-Sîn-muballiṭ'. The foundation tablet presumably came from this fortress.

The cities mentioned in the correlating year name 33 — Nippur, Eridu, Ur, Larsa, Uruk and Isin — make it clear that Ḫammu-rāpi is referring to the digging of the Euphrates river in this inscription. Dūr-Sîn-muballiṭ mentioned in the text may be connected with the town Dūr-Sîn-muballiṭ which appears fairly frequently in OB archival sources. Its wall was previously built by Sîn-muballiṭ, as recorded in the name of his 10th year. The town probably lay on the ancient Euphrates somewhere north of Nippur. The work on the wall of Dūr-Sîn-muballiṭ around year 33 of Ḫammu-rāpi may be alluded to in an OB letter (see M. Stol, AbB 9 no. 2 lines 14–18).

BIBLIOGRAPHY

1863 Ménant, Inscriptions de Hammourabi pp. 2–3, 13–66, and pls. 1–3 (copy, edition)
1880 Ménant, Manuel p. 306
1892 Winckler and Böhden, ABK no. 68 (copy)
1892 Jensen, KB 3/1 pp. 122–25 Hammurabi g (edition)
1898–1900 King, LIH no. 95 (copy, edition)
1970 Matthews, First Dynasty of Babylon pp. 136–39 (edition)
1971 Sollberger and Kupper, IRSA ɪvC6j (translation)
1983 Kärki, SAKAZ 2 pp. 13–15 (edition)

TEXT

1) *ḫa-am-mu-ra-pí*
2) LUGAL *da-núm*
3) LUGAL KÁ.DINGIR.RA.KI
4) LUGAL *mu-uš-te-eš-mi*
5) *ki-ib-ra-tim ar-ba-im*
6) *ka-ši-id ir-ni-ti*
7) ^{d}AMAR.UTU
8) SIPA *mu-ṭi-ib*
9) *li-ib-bi-šu a-na-ku*
10) *ì-nu* AN *ù* ^{d}*en-líl*
11) KALAM *šu-me-rí-im*
12) *ù ak-ka-di-im*
13) *a-na be-li-im id-di-nu-nim*
14) *ṣe-er-ra-sí-na*
15) *a-na qá-ti-ia*
16) *u-ma-al-lu-ú*
17) I$_{7}$.*ḫa-am-mu-ra-pí-nu-ḫu-uš-ni-ši*
18) *ba-bi-la-at me-e* ḪÉ.GÁL
19) *a-na* KALAM *šu-me-rí-im*
20) *ù ak-ka-di-im lu aḫ-ri*
21) *ki-ša-di-ša ki-la-le-en*
22) *a-na me-re-šim lu u-te-er*
23) *ka-re-e áš-na-an*
24) *lu aš-tap-pa-ak*
25) *me-e da-ru-tim*
26) *a-na* KALAM *šu-me-rí-im*
27) *ù ak-ka-di-im lu aš-ku-un*
28) KALAM *šu-me-rí-im*
29) *ù ak-ka-di-im*
30) *ni-ši-šu-nu sa*$_{6}$*-ap-ḫa-tim*
31) *lu u-pa-aḫ-ḫi-ir*
32) *mi-ri-tam ù ma-aš-qí-tam*
33) *lu aš-ku*(*)*-un-ši-na-ši-im*
34) *in nu-uḫ-šim ù* ḪÉ.GÁL
35) *lu e-ri-ši-na-ti*
36) *šu-ba-at ne-eḫ-tim*
37) *lu u-še-ši-ib-ši-na-ti*
38) *ì-nu-mi-šu*
39) *ḫa-am-mu-ra-pí*
40) LUGAL *da-núm*
41) *mi-gir* DINGIR.GAL.GAL *a-na-ku*
42) *in e-mu-qé-en ga-aš-ra-tim*

1–9) I, Ḫammu-rāpi, mighty king, king of Babylon, king who makes the four quarters be at peace, who achieves the victory of the god Marduk, shepherd who contents him,

10–16) when the gods Anum and Enlil gave to me the land of Sumer and Akkad to rule, (and) entrusted their nose-rope into my hands,

17–20) I dug the canal Ḫammu-rāpi-nuḫuš-nišī ('Ḫammu-rāpi is the abundance of the people'), which brings abundant water to the land of Sumer and Akkad.

21–37) I turned both its banks into cultivated areas. I kept heaping up piles of grain. I provided perpetual water for the land of Sumer and Akkad (and) gathered the scattered peoples of the land of Sumer and Akkad (and) provided for them pastures and watering places. In abundance and plenty I shepherded them. I settled them in peaceful abodes.

38–49) At that time, I, Ḫammu-rāpi, mighty king, favourite of the great gods, by the mighty strength which the god Marduk gave to me, raised high a tall fortress with great (heaps of) earth, whose tops were like a mountain. I built (it) at

---

33 Text: lu.

43) *ša* ^{d}AMAR.UTU *id-di-nam*
44) BÀD *ṣi-ra-am*
45) *in e-pe-ri ra-bu-tim*
46) *ša* ⌜*re*⌝*-ša-šu-nu*
47) *ki-ma* ⌜SA⌝.DÚ*-im e-li-a*
48) *in* KA I$_{7}$.⌜*ḫa-am-mu*⌝*-ra-pí-*⌜*nu-ḫu*⌝*-uš-ni-ši*
49) *lu* ⌜*e*⌝*-pu-uš*

the intake of the Ḫammu-rāpi-nuḫuš-nišī canal.

50) BÀD ⌜*šu*⌝*-a-ti*
51) BÀD ⌜^{d}EN.ZU*-mu*⌝*-ba-lí-it*.KI
52) ⌜*a-bi*⌝*-im wa-li-di-ia*
53) ⌜*a-na*⌝ *šu-mi-im lu ab-bi*
54) ⌜*zi-kir*⌝ ^{d}⌜EN.ZU⌝*-mu-ba-lí-iṭ*
55) *a-bi-im wa-li-di-ia*
56) *in ki-ib-ra-tim*
57) *lu u-*⌜*še-pi*⌝

50–57) I named that fortress Dūr-Sîn-muballiṭ-abim-wālidiia ('Fort Sîn-muballiṭ, father who engendered me'). (Thus) I made the name of Sîn-muballiṭ, the father who engendered me, pre-eminent (throughout) the (four) quarters.

8

The name of year 36 of Ḫammu-rāpi commemorates construction work carried out on the Emeteursag, temple of the god Zababa at Kiš. This work is also recorded in a Sumerian text known in two slightly variant versions (E4.3.6.8–9) on bricks from the area of the ziqqurrat at Kiš (Uḫaimir).

CATALOGUE

Ex.	Museum number	Excavation number	Uḫaimir provenance	Dimensions (cm)	Lines preserved	cpn
1	AO 10619	–	–	18×10×7.6	1–6	c
2	Istanbul, not located	–	–	–	12–13	n
3	Ash 1924,636	–	–	12.9×7.8×6	1–5	c
4	Ash 1924,637	–	–	11.8×18×9.3	3–6	c
5	Ash 1932,649	–	–	20×13.5×7	7–13	c
6	Ash 1961,261	–	HMR 55, from trial trench well outside east corner of platform	23.3×20.4×7.8	5–13	c
7	Ash 1966,1049	–	–	14×8.2	9–12	c
8	IM 2140	Oxford-Field Museum expedition 1429	Found in temple area in rubbish	34×21 (half brick)	–	n

COMMENTARY

Exs. 1–2 were found by de Genouillac's expedition of 1912 to Kiš, the remainder by the Oxford-Field Museum expedition.

BIBLIOGRAPHY

1923–24 Langdon, AJSL 40 pp. 227 and 230 Brick B 3 (ex. 6, copy)
1924 Langdon, Kish 1 p. 14 and pl. XXXIV 3 (composite copy, edition)
1924 de Genouillac, Kich 1 pl. 1 no. 0.1 (ex. 2, copy)
1925 de Genouillac, Kich 2 pl. 2 no. 0.6 (ex. 1, copy)
1958 Borger, Orientalia NS 27 pp. 407–408 (study)
1961 Hallo, BiOr 18 p. 4 nn. 2–3 (study)
1970 Matthews, First Dynasty of Babylon pp. 146–48 (edition)
1971 Sollberger and Kupper, IRSA IVC6i (translation)
1978 Moorey, Kish fiche 1 A11 (exs. 3–7, study)
1981 Walker, CBI no. 48 (exs. 3–7, study)

1981 Grégoire, MVN 10 nos. 46–50 (exs. 3–7, composite copy, study)

1983 Kärki, SAKAZ 2 pp. 12–13 (edition)

TEXT

1) *ḫa-am-mu-ra-pí*
2) lugal-kala-ga
3) lugal-KÁ.DINGIR.RA.KI
4) lugal-da-ga-an-kur-mar-dú
5) lugal-ki-en-gi-ki-uri-ke$_4$
6) é-me-te-ur-sag
7) é-^{d}za-ba$_4$-ba$_4$
8) kiš.KI-a
9) *su-mu-la-ìl*
10) ad-da-na-ke$_4$
11) mu-un-dù-a
12) mu-un-sumun-àm
13) mu-na-ni-gibil

1–5) Ḫammu-rāpi, mighty king, king of Babylon, king of all the Amorite land, king of the land of Sumer and Akkad,

6–13) renovated for him (the god Zababa) the Emeteursag ('House — befitting a champion'), the temple of the god Zababa in Kiš, which Sūmû-la-Il, his forefather, had built (and) which had become dilapidated.

9

A brick inscription dealing with the construction of the ziqqurrat at Kiš is a variant 15-line version.

CATALOGUE

Ex.	Museum number	Excavation number	Dimensions (cm)	Lines preserved	cpn
1	Istanbul no number	–	–	4–15	c
2	Ash 1924,638	–	9.9×7.4×4.4	7–11	c
3	Ash 1966,1048	HMR 248	22.0×14.5×7.0	5–15	c

COMMENTARY

Ex. 1 was found by de Genouillac's expedition of 1912 to Kiš, exs. 2–3 by the Oxford-Field Museum.

E4.3.6.9 differs from the previous inscription by the omission of the ke$_4$ sign at the end of line 5 and the addition of the phrase ub-ta límmu-ba gù-téš-a sì-ge after line 5.

BIBLIOGRAPHY

1923–24 Langdon, AJSL 40 pp. 226–27 and 230 Brick B 8 (ex. 3, copy, edition)
1924 Langdon, Kish 1 p. 14 and pl. XXXIV 3 (composite copy, edition)
1924 de Genouillac, Kich 1 pl. 1 no. 0.3 (ex. 1, copy)
1958 Borger, Orientalia NS 27 pp. 407–408 (study)
1961 Hallo, BiOr 18 p. 4 nn. 2–3 (study)
1970 Matthews, First Dynasty of Babylon pp. 146–48 (edition)
1971 Sollberger and Kupper, IRSA IVC6i (translation)
1978 Moorey, Kish fiche 1 A11 (exs. 2–3, study)
1981 Walker, CBI no. 48 (exs. 2–3, study)
1981 Grégoire, MVN 10 nos. 51–52 (exs. 2–3, composite copy, study)
1983 Kärki, SAKAZ 2 pp. 12–13 (edition)

TEXT

1) [*ḫa-am-mu-ra-pí*]
2) [lugal-kala-ga]
3) [lugal-KÁ.DINGIR.RA.KI]
4) [lugal-da-ga-an]-kur-mar-dú
5) [luga]l-ki-en-gi-ki-uri
6) ⌜ub⌝-ta límmu-ba
7) gù-téš-a sì-ge
8) é-me-te-ur-sag
9) é-^{d}za-ba$_4$-ba$_4$
10) kiš.KI-a
11) *su-mu-la-ìl*
12) ad-da-na-ke$_4$
13) mu-un-dù-a
14) mu-un-sumun-àm
15) mu-na-ni-gibil

1–7) [Ḫammu-rāpi, mighty king, king of Babylon, king of all] the Amorite land, [kin]g of the land of Sumer and Akkad, who makes the four quarters be at peace,

8–15) renovated for him (the god Zababa) the Emeteursag ('House — befitting a champion'), the temple of the god Zababa in Kiš, which Sūmû-la-Il, his forefather, had built (and) which had become dilapidated.

10

The beginning of a royal inscription of Ḫammu-rāpi is preserved in a tablet copy now in the British Museum.

COMMENTARY

The tablet is BM 64265 (82-9-18,4241), from Rassam's excavations in Babylonia. Sollberger, Essays Finkelstein p. 197, indicates the tablet comes from Sippar. The tablet measures 8.2×6.9 cm and the inscription was collated.

The exact date of this inscription is uncertain. The titulary of the king here includes the phrase 'king of all the Amorite land' which Stol has suggested was adopted around year 34 of Ḫammu-rāpi. Part of the titulary of this inscription is strikingly similar to that found in the name of year 36 and the text probably dates to this general time period. The translation is restored from the year name.

Lines 4–11 provide the Sumerian equivalent of a section of the prologue of the Ḫammu-rāpi lawcode, col. iv 65ff.

BIBLIOGRAPHY

1970 Matthews, First Dynasty of Babylon pp. 162–64 (edition)
1971 Sollberger and Kupper, IRSA IVC6l (translation)
1977 Sollberger, Essays Finkelstein pp. 197–98 (edition) and p. 200 no. 1 (copy)

TEXT

1) *ḫa-am-mu-ra-pí* dingir-kalam-[ma-na]
2) lú an-né me-lám-nam-lugal-la mu-u[n-dul$_5$-la]
3) ^{d}en-líl-le nam-a-ni gal-le-eš bí-i[n-tar-ra]
4) ní-tuk KA-sì-sì-ke-dingir-gal-gal-e-ne
5) [šà-ba]l-bal-*su-mu-la-ìl* ibila-kala-ga-^{d}EN.ZU-*mu-ba-*[*l*]*í-iṭ*
6) [num]un-da-ri-a-nam-lugal-la
7) [luga]l-kala-ga lugal-KÁ.DINGIR.RA.KI

1–6) [I], Ḫammu-rāpi, god of [his] nation, the one whom the god An [has covered] with the aura of kingship, for whom the god Enlil has grandly [determined] his fate, reverent one, who prays fervently to the great gods, [off]spring of Sūmû-la-Il, mighty heir of Sîn-muba[ll]iṭ, eternal [se]ed of kingship,

7–16) mighty [ki]ng, king of Babylon, [kin]g of

8) [lug]al-da-ga-an-kur-mar-dú-[me-en]
9) du$_{11}$-ga-gu-la-an ^{d}en-líl-bi-da-k[e$_4$]
10) giskim-ti-^{d}utu ^{d}iškur-bi-da-ke$_4$
11) [usu]-maḫ-^{d}AMAR.UTU-a-ta
12) [me-lám-^{d}z]a-ba$_4$-ba$_4$ ^{d}inanna-e-ne-bi-t[a]
13) [zà-zi-da] gin-na-mu
14) [...] NI x [...]
15) [...] UD(?) x [...]
16) [...] x [...]
Lacuna

all the Amorite land. By the great decree of the gods An and Enlil, by the help of the gods Utu and Iškur, by the supreme [might] of the god Marduk, [I made surpassing] the [aura of the god Z]ababa and the goddess Inanna, who go [at] my [right side] ...
Lacuna

11

The name of year 40 of Ḫammu-rāpi commemorates activities involving the Emeslam temple in Kutha. These are probably to be connected with a royal inscription of Ḫammu-rāpi known from a tablet copy in the British Museum.

COMMENTARY

The tablet is BM 96952 (1902-10-11,6), a purchased tablet of unknown provenance. The inscription was collated from a photo.

The titulary of the king in this text is very similar to that in the preceding inscription.

The colophon indicates that the copy dates to the 14th year of Samsu-iluna.

For line 30, cf. E4.3.7.3 line 36: du$_6$ *ka-ár-me*-šè ḫé-ni-ku$_4$ 'I turned (the cities) into rubble heaps and ruins'. For line 31, cf. E4.2.13.1002 iii 8′.

BIBLIOGRAPHY

1985 Sollberger and Walker, Mélanges Birot pp. 257-63 (copy, edition)

TEXT

1) [^{d}lugal]-⸢gú-du$_8$-a⸣.[KI ...] x kur-gal
2) [... gab]a-⸢ri⸣ nu-tuku
3) pirig-bàn-da na[m-ka]la-ga-ni rig$_7$
4) [ní] ⸢me⸣-[l]ám-ma-ni k[ur]-kur-ra dul-lá
5) [x x ga]l-gal-la nam-ti-la gub-bu-ù(*)
6) [x (x)]-túm-mu
7) ⸢lugal ḫu⸣-luḫ-ḫa érin-⸢sag-gá du⸣-e
8) kur-gú-dé-a sì-sì-[ge]
9) igi-ḫuš-íl-la-a-ni(*) un bí-i[n-x]-⸢e⸣
10) li-li sì-sì-ge uru-bi ⸢KU da-ta⸣
11) dingir ⸢šà⸣-AŠ.DU-šè á-zi-[d]a [x x]-ús
12) *ḫa-am-mu-ra-p*[*í* x x x] x
13) ^{d}⸢lugal⸣-gú-du$_8$-a.⸢KI⸣ x [x x x]
14) ⸢*ḫa-am-mu-ra-pí* lugal an⸣-[né]

1-11) [(For) the god Lugal]-gudua [...] ... the great mountain (the underworld) [...], who has no [ri]val, fierce lion whose str[eng]th ..., who stands (at) ... the great [...] in life, who looks after the [...], terrifying king who [goes] at the head of the troops, who annihilates the enemy lands, ... at the lifting of his angry eye the people ..., *clothed* in joy ..., perfect god who goes at the right side,

12-26) Ḫammu-rāp[i, whose ... was ...] by the god Lugal-gudua, Ḫammu-rāpi, king [whose name was call]ed by the god An, whose [destiny]

5 Text: ḫul. 9 Text: dù.

15) [mu-ni mu-un-s]a$_4$
16) [^{d}en-líl-le] na[m-a]-⸢ni⸣
17) [ga]l-eš bí-i[n-d]u$_{11}$-ga
18) ^{d}mes-lam-t[i-è-a ...] x x
19) mu-un-n[a-...]-⸢la⸣
20) ⸢ní⸣-tuk KA-[sì-sì-ke-dingir-gal-gal-e-n]e
21) šà-ab-bal-[bal-*su-mu-l*]*a*-⸢*ì*⸣
22) ibila-kala-⸢ga⸣-[^{d}]⸢EN⸣.ZU-*mu-ba-lí-iṭ*
23) numun-da-ri-nam-lugal-⸢la⸣
24) lugal-kala-ga lugal-KÁ.DINGIR.RA.KI
25) lugal-da-ga-⟨an⟩-kur-mar-dú
26) lugal-ki-en-gi-uri.KI

was [gra]ndly decreed by [the god Enlil], whose ... was ... by the god Meslamt[iea], reverent one who pr[ays fervently to the great go]ds, descend[ant of Sūmû-l]a-Il, mighty heir of Sîn-muballiṭ, eternal seed of kingship, mighty king, king of Babylon, king of all the Amorite land, king of Sumer and Akkad,

27) u$_4$ má-rí.KI ù a-dam-bi
28) in-dab$_5$-bé
29) bàd-⸢bi⸣ mu-un-gul-la
30) kalam-⸢ma⸣ d[u$_6$ ka-á]r-me-⟨šè⟩ i-ni-in-ku$_4$-re

27–30) when he captured Mari and its villages, destroyed its wall, and turned the land into ru[bble heaps (and) ru]ins,

31) ⸢balag⸣ li-⸢li⸣-[ì]s-zabar
32) ⸢šìr⸣-kù-⸢ga⸣ mu-ni-in-gub x šà-bi du$_{10}$-ga
33) [x x] x x ⸢ga⸣ èš-mes-lam-šè túm-ma
34) x [x] x ⸢é⸣ sá-du$_{11}$-⸢ga⸣-ni-šè

31–34) he set up a lyre (and) a bronze kettledrum, (for) holy songs, which please the heart, a ... befitting shrine Emeslam, a ... for his house of regular offerings.

35) [^{d}mes-la]m-ti-è-a ù dingir-gal-gal-⟨e⟩-ne
36) šu-⸢nir⸣ [m]u-⸢un⸣-na-an-dím
37) nam-ti-la-[ni-šè] a mu-na-ru

35–37) (For) [the god Mesla]mtiea and the great gods he fashioned a standard (and) dedicated it [for his] own life.

38) ⸢^{d}mes-lam-ti⸣-è-a kir$_4$-šu-⸢gál⸣
39) sum-mu-da [x]
40) *ḫa-am-mu-ra-pí* [x]
41) nu-NI-tuku [...]
42) ⸢da⸣-ri-šè giš ⸢ḫé⸣-bí-TU[K.TUK]
43) x [x] x ⸢ḫé-na⸣-ab-sum-[mu]
44) nì x [x x] ⸢ḫé-na⸣-[x x]
45) [lú-á-nì]-ḫu[l]-⸢dím-ma⸣

38–45) To give prayers (to) the god Meslamtiea, Ḫammu-rāpi, ... may he listen forever. May he give [*life*] to him, may he ... to him. ...

46) [íb-ši-ág-gá]-a
47) [nì-dím-ma]-x
48) [íb-zi-r]e-[a]
49) mu-sar-ra-ba ⸢šu bí⸣-[in-ùr-a]
50) ⸢mu⸣-ni bí-in-sar-r[a]
51) áš-⸢bal⸣-a-⟨ke$_4$⟩-eš lú-érim-D[U]
52) ⸢šu⸣ ba-an-zi-zi-[a]

46–52) [As for the man who gives orders to do ev]il [against it], has my [handiwork destro]yed or [erases] its inscription and writes his own name, or because of this curse incites an evil man to do so,

53) [x] x ^{d}mes-lam-ti-è-⸢a⸣ [x x]
54) [x x] x sag x x x x [x (x)]
55) [x x x] na x [x]
56) [x x x-t]a-an-x
57) [x x x] x ni-šè ⸢ḫé⸣-ni-íb-si-sá
58) x x x x ga mi-ni-íb-tag-ga
59) x KI x x AN AN ḫé-éb-DI
60) mu-bi ⸢im⸣-[ḫ]ul-ḫul
61) dim$_4$-dim$_4$ nu-x-x-ri-bal lam-ma-a-ni
62) ki-tuš-a-ni al m[u-x x x]-ku$_4$
63) kar-šár-ra UD x x [x x] x x
64) nam nu-me-a x a-ni nam-me-gal-x

53–64) ... may the god Meslamtiea ...

65) èn-tukum(*)-⟨bi⟩-šè nam-ma-ni-kin

65–70) If he does this, so may he break out in

---

65 Text: èn-ŠU.GAR.TUR.PA-šè.

66) a-še-er a-gin$_7$ ḫé-búr
67) u$_4$-aš-a u$_4$-ti-le-da-ni
68) ḫé-éb-bé
69) suḫuš-a-ni (erasure) ḫé-⸢bu-re⸣
70) ⸢numun-a-ni⸣ ḫé-éb-ri-ri
(15 lines blank)

sighs of woe. May (the god) pronounce the time he has to live (to be) only one day. May he rip out his foundation and destroy his seed.

Colophon
1′) šu ⸢ba-la-ṭú⸣
2′) [iti api]n-⸢du$_8$-a u$_4$ 22-kam⸣
3′) [mu *sa-am*]-*su-i*-⸢*lu*⸣-[*na* lugal]-e
4′) 〈lugal〉 ⸢im⸣-gi-⸢gú⸣-[bar-ra]

Colophon
1′–4′) Hand of Balāṭu, [month Api]ndua, day 24, [year 14: Sam]su-ilu[na, the king slew] the rebellious enemy (kings).

12

The name of year 43 of Ḫammu-rāpi commemorates work on the wall of Sippar. This work is described in an inscription found in both Sumerian and Akkadian versions on small headless cones excavated at Sippar.

CATALOGUE

Sumerian version

Ex.	Museum number	Registration number	Sippar provenance	Object	Dimensions (cm)	Lines preserved	cpn
1	BM 54539	82-5-22,856	–	Shaft	5.0	1-4, 19-20, 21-24, 38-39	c
2	BM 91069(12212)	82-7-14,1031	–	Shaft	9.8	1-39	c
3	BM 91070(12213)	82-3-23,190	–	Shaft	8.7	1-39	c
4	BM 91079(12222)	Bu 91-5-9,2550	–	Shaft	8.5	1-39	c
5	BM 91154	Bu 88-5-12,111	–	Shaft	8.8	1-39	c
6	BM 25000	98-2-16,54	–	Barrel	9.5	1-39	c
7	Istanbul, Si 11846	–	From a private house	Shaft	5.7 dia.	1-5, 15-22, 38-39	c

Akkadian version

Ex.	Museum number	Regisration number	Object	Dimensions (cm)	Lines preserved	cpn
1	BM 91073(12216)	82-7-14,1027	Shaft	4.3	1-46	c
2	BM 91072(12215)	AH 82-3-23,191	Shaft	8.7	1-46	c
3	BM 91071(12214)	82-7-14,1037	Shaft	–	–	n
4	BM 91077(12220)	Bu 91-5-9,2548	Shaft	9.5	1-46	c
5	BM 91078(12221)	Bu 91-5-9,2549	Shaft	9.4	1-46	c
6	BM 91080(12223)	Bu 91-5-9,2551	Shaft	8.8	1-46	c
7	BM 40631	81-4-28,176	Shaft	8	1-12, 25-33	c
8	UCLM 9-1780	–	Shaft	9.5	8-20, 32-44	c
9	UCLM 9-1781	–	Shaft	9	1-8, 10, 16-46	c
10	YBC 2150	–	Small cylinder	8.8 long, 6.8 dia.	1-46	c

COMMENTARY

For the Sumerian version, exs. 1–3 come from Rassam's excavations, ex. 7 from Scheil's excavations, ex. 4 was purchased by Budge, ex. 5 was purchased from J. Shemtob, and ex. 6 was purchased from Homsey and Co.

BIBLIOGRAPHY

Sumerian version
1887 Winckler, ZA 2 pp. 120–21 (exs. 1–2, edition)
1887 Strassmaier, ZA 2 pp. 175–76 (exs. 1–2, composite copy)
1892 Jensen, KB 3/1 pp. 116–21 Hammurabi e (exs. 1–2, edition)
1892 Winckler and Böhden, ABK no. 73 (exs. 1–2, composite copy)
1898–1900 King, LIH no. 58 (ex. 1, copy; exs. 1–4, edition)
1902 Scheil, Sippar p. 65 (ex. 7, study)
1924 Gadd, Reading-book pp. 46–49 (copy, edition)
1970 Matthews, First Dynasty of Babylon pp. 128–35 (edition)
1971 Sollberger and Kupper, IRSA IVC6e (study)
1983 Kärki, SAKAZ 2 pp. 5–6 (edition)

Akkadian version
1887 Winckler, ZA 2 pp. 118–19 (exs. 1–3, edition)
1887 Strassmaier, ZA 2 pp. 174–75 (exs. 1–3, composite copy)
1892 Jensen, KB 3/1 pp. 117–21 Hammurabi e (exs. 1–3, edition)
1892 Winckler and Böhden, ABK no. 72 (exs. 1–3, composite copy)
1898 King, First Steps pp. 5–7 (edition)
1898–1900 King, LIH no. 57 (exs. 1–6, edition; ex. 1 copy; exs. 2–6, vars.)
1904 Harper, Assyrian and Babylonian Literature p. 2 (translation)
1923 Jean, Le Milieu Biblique pp. 109–10 (translation)
1932 Poebel, AS 3 pp. 4–7 (study)
1963 Borger, BAL^{1} 2 p. 1 (transliteration, study)
1970 Matthews, First Dynasty of Babylon pp. 128–35 (edition)
1971 Sollberger and Kupper, IRSA IVC6e (translation)
1978 Foxvog, RA 72 p. 42 (exs. 8–9, study)
1979 Borger, BAL^{2} 1 p. 1 (transliteration, study; ex. 7, study)
1983 Kärki, SAKAZ 2 pp. 4–5 (edition)

TEXT

Sumerian	Akkadian	
1) *ḫa-am-mu-ra-pí*	1) *ḫa-am-mu-ra-pí*	1–10) I, Ḫammu-rāpi, mighty king, king of Babylon, king of the four quarters, who builds up the land, king whose deeds are pleasing to the gods Šamaš and Marduk,
2) lugal-kala-ga	2) LUGAL *da-núm*	
3) lugal-KÁ.DINGIR.RA.KI	3) LUGAL KÁ.DINGIR.RA.KI	
4) lugal-an-ub-da-límmu	4) LUGAL *ki-ib-ra-tim ar-ba-im*	
5) kalam dím-dím-me	6) *ba-ni ma-tim*	
6) lugal nì-ak-ak-bi	7) LUGAL *ša ep-ša-tu-šu*	
7) su-^{d}utu	8) *a-na ši-ir* ^{d}UTU	
8) ^{d}AMAR.UTU-ra	9) *ù* ^{d}AMAR.UTU *ṭa-ba*	
9) ba-du$_{10}$-ga-me-en	10) *a-na-ku*	
10) bàd-zimbir.KI	11) BÀD	11–24) raised the head of the wall of Sippar with earth like a great mountain. I encircled it with a swamp. I dug the Euphrates as far as Sippar (and) made it reach a prosperous quay.
	12) *ša* ZIMBIR.KI	
11) saḫar-ta	13) *in e-pe-ri*	
12) ḫur-sag-gal-gin$_{7}$	14) *ki-ma* SA.DÚ-*im*	
	15) *ra-bi-im*	
13) sag-bi	16) *re-ši-šu*	
14) ḫé-em-mi-íl	17) *lu ù-ul-li*	
15) ambar-ra ḫu-mu-ni-nígin	18) *ap-pa-ra-am*	
	19) *lu uš-ta-ás-ḫi-ir-šu*	
16) I$_{7}$.buranun	20) I$_{7}$.BURANUN	
17) zimbir.KI-šè	21) *a-na* ZIMBIR.KI	
18) ḫu-mu-ba-al	22) *lu aḫ-re-a-am-ma*	
19) kar-silim-ma-ke$_{4}$	23) *kar šu-ul-mi-im*	
20) ḫu-mu-ni-ús	24) *lu ù-um-mi-sú*	
21) *ḫa-am-mu-ra-pí*	25) *ḫa-am-mu-ra-pí*	25–30) I, Ḫammu-rāpi, who builds up the land, whose deeds are pleasing to the gods Šamaš and Marduk,
22) kalam dím-dím-me	26) *ba-ni ma-tim*	
23) lugal nì-ak-ak-bi	27) LUGAL *ša ep-ša-tu-šu*	
24) su-^{d}utu	28) *a-na ši-ir* ^{d}UTU	
25) ^{d}AMAR.UTU-ra	29) *ù* ^{d}AMAR.UTU *ṭa-ba*	
26) ba-du$_{10}$-ga-me-en	30) *a-na-ku*	

Sumerian version: **14**.2, 3 ḫé-⟨em⟩-mi-íl. **22**.3 dím-⌜dím⌝-⟨me⟩.
Akkadian version: **13**.8, 9 omit. **17**.8 ⌜*lu*⌝ *ú-ul-li*. **19**.3 *lu ú-uš-ta-ás-ḫi-ir-šu*. **22**.10 *lu aḫ-re-a-⟨am⟩-ma*. **24**.1, 4, 6 *lu ù-um-mi-sú*. **24**.3, 5, 9, 10 *lu ú-um-mi-sú*. **24**.2 *lu ú-um-mi-su*.

27) zimbir.KI
28) KÁ.DINGIR.RA.KI-bi-da-ke$_4$
29) ki-tuš-ne-ḫa
30) du-rí-šè
31) ḫé-em-mi-tuš
32) *ḫa-am-mu-ra-pí*
33) še-ga-^{d}utu
34) ki-ág-^{d}AMAR.UTU-me-en
35) u$_4$-ul-lí-a-ta
36) lugal-lugal-e-ne-er
37) ba-ra-an-dím-ma
38) ^{d}utu lugal-gá
39) gal-bi ḫu-mu-na-dù

31) ZIMBIR.KI
32) *ù* KÁ.DINGIR.RA.KI
33) *šu-ba-at ne-eḫ-tim*
34) *a-na da-rí-a-tim*
35) *lu ù-še-ši-ib*
36) *ḫa-am-mu-ra-pí*
37) *mi-gi$_4$-ir* ^{d}UTU
38) *na-ra-am* ^{d}AMAR.UTU
39) *a-na-ku*
40) *ša iš-tu u$_4$-um*
41) *ṣi-a-tim*
42) LUGAL *in* LUGAL-*rí*
43) *la ib-ni-ù*
44) *a-na* ^{d}UTU *be-lí-ia*
45) *ra-bi-iš*
46) *lu e-pu-ús-su-um*

31–35) caused Sippar and Babylon to dwell in peaceful abodes, forever.

36–39) I, Ḫammu-rāpi, favourite of the god Šamaš, beloved of the god Marduk,

40–46) what from the past no one among the kings had done, I did in a grand fashion for the god Šamaš, my lord.

13

After his defeat of Rīm-Sîn of Larsa, an event commemorated in the name of year 31, Ḫammu-rāpi incorporated the realms of the Larsa ruler into his own domains. The king of Babylon was then responsible for the upkeep of the temples in the south. Various inscriptions deal with work undertaken on these southern temples. None of this work was commemorated in year names of the king, so the exact date of these inscriptions is uncertain apart from the fact that they date after year 31.

The first text is a stamped brick inscription in Akkadian dealing with the building of the Ebabbar temple for the god Šamaš in Larsa.

CATALOGUE

Ex.	Museum number	Registration/Excavation number	Larsa provenance	Dimensions (cm)	Lines preserved	cpn
1	BM 90133	1979-12-20,62	From northern corner base of red mound at Senkereh	33.5×32.5×9.0	1–9	c
2	BM 90134	1979-12-20,63	As ex. 1	34.5×34.5	1–9	c
3	BM 90135	51-1-1,285	As ex. 1	Face 33.0×32.5×7.5	1–9	c
4	BM 90135	51-1-1,285	As ex. 1	Edge 33.0×32.5×7.5	1–9	c
5	–	L 67–	From surface of tell	–	–	n
6	–	L 7096b	–	–	–	n
7	–	L 69–	–	–	–	n
8	–	L 70–	From surface of superior tell of Ebabbar	–	–	n

Sumerian version: **30**.3 omits this line.
Akkadian version: **35**.1, 4, 6, 9, 10 *lu ù-še-ši-ib*. **35**.2, 5, 8 *lu ú-še-ši-ib*. **46**.1 *lu e-pu-ús-sú-um*. **46**.6 *lu e-pu-⟨ús⟩-sú-um*.

COMMENTARY

Exs. 1–4 come from Loftus's excavations at Larsa. Exs. 5–8 come from the recent French excavations at the same site.

BIBLIOGRAPHY

1857 Loftus, Travels p. 250 (exs. 1–4, provenance)
1861 1 R pl. 4 no. xv 2 (exs. 1–4, composite copy)
1863 Ménant, Inscriptions de Hammourabi pp. 68–74 and pl. 6 no. 3 (copy, edition)
1863 Oppert, EM 1 p. 267
1872 G. Smith, TSBA 1 pp. 60–61 (translation)
1874 Lenormant, Études accadiennes 2 pp. 355
1875 G. Smith, RP os 5 p. 75 (translation)
1875 Ménant, Babylone et la Chaldée p. 110 (translation)
1880 Ménant, Manuel p. 306
1892 Jensen, KB 3/1 pp. 110–11 Hammurabi c (edition)
1898–1900 King, LIH no. 63 (ex. 2, copy; exs. 1–4, edition)
1922 BM Guide p. 62 nos. 138–40 (exs. 1–4, study)
1968 Birot, Syria 45 p. 242 (ex. 5, study)
1970 Matthews, First Dynasty of Babylon pp. 126–27 (edition)
1971 Sollberger and Kupper, IRSA IVC6a (translation)
1971 Arnaud, Syria 48 p. 292 (exs. 5–7, study)
1981 Walker, CBI no. 47 (exs. 1–4, study)
1983 Kärki, SAKAZ 2 p. 1 (edition)

TEXT

1) *ḫa-am-mu-ra-pí*	1) Ḫammu-rāpi,
2) lugal-kala-ga	2) mighty king,
3) lugal-	3–4) king of Babylon,
4) KÁ.DINGIR.RA.KI	
5) lugal-an-ub-da-límmu-ba-ke_4	5) king of the four quarters,
6) ba-dím	6–7) builder of Ebabbar ('Shining-white house'),
7) é-babbar	
8) é-^{d}utu	8–9) temple of the god Utu in Larsa.
9) larsa.KI-ma-ta	

14

Construction work by Ḫammu-rāpi on the Ebabbar temple in Larsa is also recorded on limestone foundation tablets. The Sumerian version of this text is complete, the Akkadian version fragmentary.

COMMENTARY

The Sumerian version is found on BM 91076, from Larsa, a limestone tablet 16.2×7.9 cm. The rev. side on display was collated.

The Akkadian piece is LB 974, a purchased piece, presumably originally from Larsa. It is a fragment of a limestone tablet 5×8.5 cm. The inscription was collated.

BIBLIOGRAPHY

Sumerian version
1898–1900 King, LIH no. 62 (copy, edition)
1905 King, CT 21 pls. 45–46 (copy)
1923 Jean, Le Milieu Biblique p. 110 (translation)
1970 Matthews, First Dynasty of Babylon pp. 120–25 (edition)
1971 Sollberger and Kupper, IRSA IVC6b (translation)
1983 Kärki, SAKAZ 2 pp. 1–2 (edition)

Akkadian version
1933 Böhl, Leiden Coll. 2 pp. 10–12 (edition)
1957 van Dijk, TLB 2 no. 15 (copy)
1970 Matthews, First Dynasty of Babylon pp. 120–25 (edition)
1971 Sollberger and Kupper, IRSA IVC6b (translation)
1983 Kärki, SAKAZ 2 p. 2 (edition)

TEXT

Sumerian	Akkadian	
1) ^{d}utu		1–3) For the god Utu, lord of heaven and earth, his lord,
2) en-an-ki-bi-da		
3) lugal-a-ni-ir		
4) *ḫa-am-mu-ra-pí*		4–16) Ḫammu-rāpi, the one called by the god An, who listens to the god Enlil, favourite of the god Utu, shepherd beloved of the god Marduk, mighty king, king of Babylon, king of the land of Sumer and Akkad, king of the four quarters, king who renovated the shrines of the great gods,
5) gù-dé-a-an-na		
6) ^{d}en-líl-da giš-tuk		
7) še-ga-^{d}utu	Lacuna	
8) sipa ki-ág-	1′) [SI]PA *n[a-ra-am]*	
9) ^{d}AMAR.UTU-ke$_4$	2′) ⌜^{d}⌝A[MAR.UTU]	
10) lugal-kala-ga	3′) [LUG]AL *d[a-núm]*	
11) lugal-KÁ.DINGIR.RA.KI	4′) [LU]GAL K[Á.DINGIR.RA.KI]	
12) lugal-ki-en-gi-ki-uri	5′) [L]UGAL [KALAM] *šu-me-r[í-im]*	
	6′) ⌜*ù*⌝ *ak-ka-d[i-im]*	
13) lugal-an-ub-da-límmu-ba-ke$_4$	7′) [L]UGAL *ki-ib-r[a-tim]*	
	8′) *[a]r-ba-[im]*	
14) lugal bára-bára-	9′) [L]UGAL *mu-[ud]-di-[iš]*	
15) dingir-gal-gal-e-ne	10′) [B]ÁRA.BÁRA DINGIR.GA[L.GAL]	
16) šu-gibil bí-in-ak-a		
17) u$_4$ ^{d}utu	11′) ⌜*i*⌝-*nu* ^{d}[UTU]	17–23) when the god Utu gave to him the land of Sumer and Akkad to rule (and) entrusted their nose-rope in his hands,
18) ki-en-gi ki-uri	12′) [KALAM]	
	13′) *[šu]-me-rí-[im]*	
	14′) *[ù] ak-ka-d[i-im]*	
19) nam-en-bi ak-dè	15′) *[a-n]a be-l[i-im]*	
20) mu-na-an-sum-ma-ta	16′) *[id]-d[i-nu-šum]*	
21) éš-kìri-bi	Lacuna	
22) šu-ni-šè		
23) bí-in-si-a		
24) ^{d}utu		24–30) for the god Utu, the lord in whom he trusts, in Larsa, the city of his rule, he built for him Ebabbar ('Shining-white house'), his beloved temple.
25) en giskim-ti-la-ni-ir		
26) larsa.KI-ma		
27) uru-nam-en-na-ka-na		
28) é-babbar		
29) é-ki-ág-gá-ni		
30) mu-na-ni-in-dù		

15

A number of bricks stamped with an inscription dealing with Ḫammu-rāpi's construction of the temple for the goddess Inanna in Zabala were found at Ibzaiḫ.

CATALOGUE

Ex.	Museum number	Excavation number	Provenance	Dimensions (cm)	Lines preserved	cpn
1	IM 36809	–	Ibzaiḫ(?)	33.5×33.5×7.7	1–9	c
2	IM 36808	–	Ibzaiḫ(?)	33.0×33.0×7.5	–	n
3	IM 36810	–	Ibzaiḫ	34.0×31.0×7.5	–	n
4	IM 36811	–	Ibzaiḫ(?)	34.0×30.0×9.3	–	n
5	IM 56800	–	Ibzaiḫ(?)	–	–	n
6	IM 59377	–	Ibzaiḫ(?)	33.5×33.5×9.0	–	n
7	–	–	Ibzaiḫ	–	1–9	c
8	–	Warka Survey 169	Ibzaiḫ	–	1–9	p
9	A 1144	–	Adab	8.4×6.4×2.3	7–9	n

COMMENTARY

Ex. 1, which was collated from its display in the Iraq Museum, was part of a lot of four bricks which entered the museum in September 1937. Although none of exs. 2–4 has been collated it is assumed that they bear the same inscription.

In late 1953 the site of Ibzaiḫ was visited by T. Jacobsen as part of the Archaeological Survey of Historical Mounds and Ancient Canals, and another example of the brick was found. This is probably ex. 6, which entered the museum shortly after this.

Ex. 7 was copied by E. Sollberger during a visit to the site and a transliteration kindly communicated for this edition. Ex. 8 was found during the Warka Survey's visit to Ibzaiḫ and published by Nissen in Adams, Countryside p. 217. It is collated from a photo kindly provided by H. Nissen. Ex. 9 was purportedly found during Bank's expedition to Bismaya, ancient Adab.

BIBLIOGRAPHY

1930 Luckenbill, Adab no. 12 (ex. 9, copy)
1951 Goetze, Sumer 11 p. 127 (ex. 6, study)
1971 Sollberger and Kupper, IRSA ɪᴠC6c (ex. 7, translation)
1972 Nissen in Adams, Countryside p. 217 (ex. 8, copy)
1976 Basmachi, Treasures of the Iraq Museum (Baghdad) p. 206 no. 13 (ex. 1, study [incorrectly said to come from Larsa])
1983 Kärki, SAKAZ 2 pp. 2–3 (edition)

TEXT

1) *ḫa-am-mu-ra-pí*
2) lugal-kala-ga
3) lugal-
4) KÁ.DINGIR.RA.KI
5) lugal-an-ub-da-límmu-ba-ke₄
6) ba-dím-
7) é-zi-kalam-ma
8) é-^{d}inanna
9) zabala.KI-ta

1) Ḫammu-rāpi,
2) mighty king,
3–4) king of Babylon,
5) king of the four quarters,
6–7) builder of Ezikalama ('House – the life of the land'),
8–9) temple of the goddess Inanna in Zabala.

16

The building of Inanna's temple in Zabala is also recorded in a Sumerian text inscribed on two foundation tablets.

CATALOGUE

Ex.	Museum number	Lines preserved	cpn
1	BM 90939	1-35	rev. c
2	IM 36809	1-15, 20-35	c

COMMENTARY

Ex. 1 has no registration no.; it must have entered the British Museum before 1861. Its provenance was listed simply as Chaldea.

Ex. 2 was confiscated and accessioned by the Iraq Museum. It is edited here through the courtesy of Dr. B. Ismail Khalil.

BIBLIOGRAPHY

1861 1 R pl. 4 no. xv 1 (ex. 1, copy)
1863 Ménant, Inscriptions de Hammourabi pp. 72-80 and pls. 4-5 (ex. 1, copy, edition)
1863 Oppert, EM 1 p. 270
1872 G. Smith, TSBA 1 p. 60 (translation)
1875 Lenormant, Études accadiennes 2 p. 356
1875 Ménant, Babylone et la Chaldée (Paris) p. 109 (translation)
1882 Amiaud, JA 20 p. 236
1892 Jensen, KB 3/1 pp. 106-109 Hammurabi a (edition)
1898-1900 King, LIH no. 61 (ex. 1, copy, edition)
1905 King, CT 21 pls. 43-44 (ex. 1, copy)
1922 BM Guide p. 87 no. 94 (ex. 1, study) and pl. XXXII after p. 86 (ex. 1, photo [rev. only])
1970 Matthews, First Dynasty of Babylon pp. 143-45 (edition)
1971 Sollberger and Kupper, IRSA IVC6d (translation)
1983 Kärki, SAKAZ 2 pp. 3-4 (edition)

TEXT

1) ^{d}inanna-zabala.KI
2) nin me-lám-ma-ni
3) an-ki-a dul-lá
4) nin-a-ni-ir
5) *ḫa-am-mu-ra-pí*
6) gù-dé-a-an-na
7) ^{d}en-líl-da giš-tuk
8) še-ga-^{d}utu
9) sipa šà-du$_{10}$-du$_{10}$-
10) ^{d}AMAR.UTU-ke$_4$
11) nun šà-kí-ág-
12) ^{d}inanna-ke$_4$
13) lugal-kala-ga
14) lugal-KÁ.DINGIR.RA.KI
15) lugal-ki-en-gi-ki-uri
16) lugal-an-ub-da-límmu-ba-ke$_4$
17) lugal bára-bára-
18) dingir-gal-gal-e-ne

1-4) For the goddess Inanna of Zabala, lady whose aura covers heaven and earth, his lady,

5-20) Ḫammu-rāpi, the one called by the god An, who listens to the god Enlil, favourite of the god Utu, the shepherd who pleases the god Marduk, prince beloved of the heart of the goddess Inanna, mighty king, king of Babylon, king of the land of Sumer and Akkad, king of the four quarters, king who renovated the sanctuaries of the great gods,

19) šu-gibil
20) bí-in-ak-a

21) u$_4$ ^{d}inanna
22) giskim-sa$_6$-ga-ni
23) ki-en-gi ki-uri
24) nam-en-bi ak-dè
25) mu-na-an-sum-ma-ta
26) éš-kìri-bi
27) šu-ni-šè
28) bí-in-si-a

21–28) after the goddess Inanna gave him her favourable omen to rule the land of Sumer and Akkad (and) entrusted their nose-rope in his hands,

29) ^{d}inanna
30) ki-ág-gá-ni-ir
31) zabala.KI
32) uru-nam-nin-a-ka-na
33) é-zi-kalam-ma
34) é-ki-ág-gá-ni
35) mu-na-ni-in-dù

29–35) for the goddess Inanna, his beloved, in Zabala, the city of her lady-ship, he built for her the Ezikalama ('House — life of the land'), her beloved temple.

17

A stone foundation tablet in Paris is inscribed with an Akkadian text recording the construction of a sanctuary for the god Marduk in the city of Borsippa.

COMMENTARY

The piece is MNB 1847, now in the Louvre, a purchased piece of unknown provenance, acquired before 1880. It presumably came from Borsippa. It is a limestone tablet 8.9×20.5×2.6 cm and the inscription was collated.

The phraseology of this inscription is very similar to that of E4.3.6.13 and 15 and probably dates to a period late in the reign. Tutu, tutelary deity of Borsippa, was identified in OB times with Marduk.

BIBLIOGRAPHY

1880 Ménant, RT 2 pp. 76–85 (copy in typescript, edition)
1884 Delitzsch, Die Sprache der Kossäer (Leipzig) p. 73 (edition)
1892 Jensen, KB 3/1 pp. 124–27 Hammurabi h (edition)
1892 Winckler and Böhden, ABK nos. 69–70 (copy)
1898–1900 King, LIH no. 94 (copy, edition)
1912 Delitzsch, AL^5 pp. 131–32 (copy)
1947 Böhl, Chrestomathy no. 28 (copy)
1963 Borger, BAL^1 2 p. 1 (transliteration); BAL^1 3 pl. 1 (copy in Neo-Assyrian script)
1970 Matthews, First Dynasty of Babylon pp. 140–42 (edition)
1971 Sollberger and Kupper, IRSA IVC6h (translation)
1979 Borger, BAL^2 1 p. 1 (transliteration); BAL^2 2 p. 285 (copy in Neo-Assyrian script)
1983 Kärki, SAKAZ 2 pp. 11–12 (edition)

TEXT

1) *a-na* ^{d}AMAR.UTU
2) *be-li-im ra-bi-im*
3) *na-di-in ḫé-gál*
4) *a-na ì-lí*
5) *be-el é-sag-íl*

1–7) For the god Marduk, great lord, who gives abundance to the gods, lord of Esagil and Ezida, his lord,

6) *ù é-zi-da*
7) *be-lí-šu*

8) *ḫa-am-mu-ra-pí*
9) *na-bi-ù* AN-*nim*
10) [*še*]-*mu* ^{d}*en-líl*
11) [*mi*]-gi_4-*ir*
12) ^{d}UTU
13) SIPA *na-ra-am*
14) ^{d}AMAR.UTU
15) LUGAL *da-núm*
16) LUGAL KALAM *šu-me-ri-im*
17) *ù ak-ka-di-im*
18) LUGAL *ki-ib-ra-tim*
19) *ar-ba-im*

8–19) Ḫammu-rāpi, the one called by the god Anum, who [lis]tens to the god Enlil, [fa]vourite of the god Šamaš, shepherd beloved of the god Marduk, mighty king, king of the land of Sumer and Akkad, king of the four quarters,

20) *ì-nu* ^{d}*en-líl*
21) KALAM *ù ni-šì*
22) *a-na be-li-im*
23) *id-di-nu-šum*
24) *ṣe-er-ra-sí-na*
25) *a-na qá-ti-šu*
26) *ú-ma-al-li-ù*

20–26) when the god Enlil gave the land and people to him to rule and entrusted their nose-rope in his hands,

27) *a-na* ^{d}AMAR.UTU
28) DINGIR *ba-ni-šu*
29) *in bar-sí-pa*.KI
30) URU *na-ra-mi-šu*
31) *é-zi-da*
32) BÁRA-*šu el-lam*
33) *ib-ni-šum*

27–33) for the god Marduk, the god who created him, he built Ezida, his shining sanctuary, in Borsippa, his beloved city.

18

In 1850 A.H. Layard excavated briefly at Tell Muḫammad, a site now within the modern city of Baghdad. Two bronze knobs with Ḫammu-rāpi's name were found there.

CATALOGUE

Ex.	Museum number	Registration number	Dimensions (cm)	Lines preserved	cpn
1	BM 22455	51-10-9,146	Height 4.4, dia. 6.4	1–2	c
2	BM 22456	N 615	Height 4.4, dia. 6.0	1–2	c

BIBLIOGRAPHY

1853 Layard, Discoveries p. 477 (exs. 1–2, provenance; ex. 2, copy)
1861 1 R pl. 4 no. xv 3 (ex. 1, copy)
1863 Ménant, Inscriptions de Hammourabi pp. 67–68 and pl. 6 no. 4 (copy, edition)
1898–1900 King, LIH nos. 64–65 (exs. 1–2, copy, edition)
1970 Matthews, First Dynasty of Babylon p. 155 (edition)

TEXT

1) É.GAL *ḫa-am-mu-ra-pí*

1) Palace of Ḫammu-rāpi.

19

An inscription of Ḫammu-rāpi known from a Neo-Babylonian copy on a clay tablet is too fragmentarily preserved to determine the purport of the text.

COMMENTARY

The tablet is BM 36255, a clay tablet 5.4×4.7 cm. The inscription was not collated.

BIBLIOGRAPHY

1898–1900 King, LIH no. 96 (copy, edition)
1970 Matthews, First Dynasty of Babylon pp. 153–54 (edition)

TEXT

Obverse
Col. i
1) [...]
2) [...]
Lacuna
Col. ii
1) *ḫa-am-mu-ra-pí*
2) ⌜LUGAL⌝ *da-núm*
Lacuna

ii 1–2) Ḫammu-rāpi, mighty king ...

Reverse
Col. i
Lacuna
1′) [...]
2′) [...]-BI
3′) [...]-KU
4′) [...] x BI
5′) [...] KU
6′) [...] x
7′) [...]
8′) [...]
9′) [...]
Col. ii
Lacuna
1′)
2′) *ḫ*[*i-pí*]
3′)
4′)
5′)

rev. i 1′ – ii 9′) (Translation not warranted)

6′) *ḫi-p*[*í*]
7′)
8′) x *ḫi-pu-ú*
9′)

20

A number of stone fragments of Old Babylonian date are known which bear inscriptions in both Sumerian and Akkadian which appear to be pieces of monuments once set up by Ḫammu-rāpi.

Fragments of a basalt monument were found by Woolley in the Giparku at Ur, room C. 7. These were published as UET 1 no. 146. A tablet which duplicates part of this inscription was published by J.A. van Dijk as TLB 2 no. 3 and edited by A. Sjöberg in ZA 54 (1961) pp. 51–70. Another duplicate is VAS 24 no. 41. Stone fragments in the Yale Babylonian collection published as YOS 9 nos. 39–61 are probably pieces of this same monument as is A 3518 in Chicago (information courtesy of M. Stol) and U 116117 = 1927-5-27,24A (unpublished). As Stol, Studies in Old Babylonian History p. 41, points out, the mention of Turkriš in UET 1 no. 146 indicates a date for this inscription late in the reign of Ḫammu-rāpi.

In addition to the Ur monument, a number of inscribed basalt fragments were found at Kiš. The first was picked up by Porter in 1818 (see Porter, Travels 2 pl. 77 and King, LIH no. 67). Subsequently pieces were found by the Oxford-Field Museum expedition to Kiš and published by J.-P. Grégoire in P. Moorey, Kish fiche E03–E06.

Both the pieces of the Ur and Kiš monuments are bilingual and hymnic in phraseology. They are therefore best classified as royal hymns rather than royal inscriptions, and as a result are not edited in this volume.

1001

An Old Babylonian copy of an inscription of a king who ruled Sippar but whose name is broken away from the presently available text is found on a clay tablet in the British Museum. It may have been an inscription of Ḫammu-rāpi.

COMMENTARY

The tablet is BM 54705 (82-5-22,1031), from Rassam's excavation at Sippar. The edition offered here was prepared from a preliminary transliteration provided by P. Michalowski, and a preliminary transliteration and a copy by B. Alster with suggested readings by U. Jeyes. Alster will publish the copy in a text volume, CT 58, as well as an edition of this and other Sippar pieces in a joint article with Jeyes. The piece is edited here with the permission of the trustees of the British Museum. The Akkadian glosses on the tablet are not edited here but will be studied in Alster's forthcoming edition.

The text is fragmentarily preserved and its contents uncertain. It seems to record (obv. 6′) the fashioning of a copper du$_8$ for the god Utu. The fact that the text comes from Sippar makes its attribution to one of the kings of the First Babylon dynasty highly likely. The language of the text is good Sumerian, typical of the royal inscriptions of Ḫammu-rāpi and Samsu-iluna but not of the later OB kings Ammī-ditāna or Ammī-ṣaduqa. The name of year 13 of Ḫammu-rāpi records the construction of a KI.LUGAL.GUB.BA and a du$_{8}$-maḫ, and it is possible that this deed was commemorated in the present inscription.

TEXT

Obverse	
Lacuna	Lacuna
1′) [...] e N[E ...]	1′) [O god Utu] ...,
2′) [... za]-⸢e⸣-da nu-⟨me-a⟩ lugal nu-[...]	2′) [...] without you no king [*is raised to kingship*],
3′) [...] za-e-me-en ⸢á⸣-[...]	3′) [...] you are ...,
4′) [... n]í-tuku še-ga-zu nam-nir-[gál ...]	4′) [...] one who reverences (you), your favourite, ... author[ity],
5′) x x [...] nì-kal-la-zu gal-bi n[am-...]	5′) [...] your (great) worth, grandly ...,
6′) URUDU.du$_{8}$-⸢šen-na⸣ máš-anše gal-bi dím-dím-ma te-me-⸢en⸣ [...] nam-ti-la-ni u$_{4}$-bi sù-sù-dam NI ba-ra-ni-i[n-...] é-bar$_{6}$-bar$_{6}$ é-ki-ág-zu du-rí-šè š[a-...]	6′) A shining copper du$_{8}$, grandly fashioned (with depictions of) wild animals, a ... base, in order to prolong his life-span ..., Ebabbar, your beloved temple, forever ...
7′) ^{d}utu lugal-e ní-te-ge$_{26}$ gal-zu-me-en gal-bi AN x [...] šà-du$_{10}$-ga ur$_{5}$-sa$_{6}$-ge an-ta ḫé-bí-í[b(?)-...] an-⸢ki⸣-bi-ta ḫé-mu-x-[...]	7′) O god Utu, lord: I am one who knows how to reverence (you), grandly ..., (with) a happy heart (and) good spirits may ..., may ... from heaven and earth
8′) ^{d}a-a nìta-dam-[zu ...] nì-ḫúl-la [...] ki-b[a ...]	8′) The goddess Aia [your] spouse ... in joy, ... in that place ...
Lacuna	Lacuna
Reverse	Reverse
Lacuna	Lacuna
1′) [...] x x x [...]	1′) [...], ...,
2′) [...] ki-gub-ba mu-ni-i[b-...]	2′) [who alters] the place where it stands,
3′) [...] x-bi ki-dúr-bi-a mu-ni-i[b-...]	3′) [who ...] its [...] in the place where it sits,
4′) á-úr-x [...] mu-ni-ib-dúr-x [...]	4′) [who] sets it (in) a secret place ...,
5′) mu-ni-íb-GÌR × GÁNA-*tenû* é-a kin-kúr-šè mu-ni-ib-x [...]	5′) who having ... it, ... it into the temple for a different function,
6′) é-azag ki igi nu-bar-re-da-šè i-ni-ib-ku$_{4}$-k[u$_{4}$-...]	6′) who brings it into a forbidden place where it is unaccessible,
7′) mu-sar-ra-gá ⸢šu bí⸣-íb-ùr-ru-a mu-ni bí-íb-s[ar-re-a]	7′) who erases my inscription and writes his own inscription on it, or who on account of this curse incites another to do so
8′) áš-bal-ba-ke$_{4}$-eš lú-kúr šu ba-an-zi-z[i-...]	8′) (or) who on account of this curse incites another to do so
9′) ù-bí-íb-ku$_{5}$-e nì-ḫul alam-gá in-ga-[...]	9′) and having broken it, further [does] evil to my image:
10′) lú-bi lugal ḫé-a en ḫé-a énsi ḫé-a ù nam-lú-ù[lu ḫé-a]	10′) that man — whether he be king, or lord, or governor or (any) man —
11′) íb-ba-gu-la-^{d}utu-ke$_{4}$ ḫé x x x x x x x [...]	11′) may the great wrath of the god Utu ...,
12′) eš-bar ḫa-lam-a-ni é-bar$_{6}$-bar$_{6}$-ta ḫu-m[u-...]	12′) may (the god Utu) [decree] from the Ebabbar temple the verdict: his destruction.
13′) an lugal-dingir-e-ne-ke$_{4}$ bala-ni zà mu-ni-í[b-...] uru x dul ka-ár-šè NI A nam-ḫa-lam ma-da ⸢NI GAR⸣ [...] mu-ru-ub-dingir-re-e-ne-e-ra inim m[i-... kíd]	13′) An, the king of the gods, will bring his reign [to an end].
14′) [...] x an-ki-⸢bi⸣-ta x-ḫul x-bún du$_{8}$-du$_{8}$ x x [...]	14′) ... his city into ruins and rubble heaps ... destruction, his land ..., will [slander him] in the

15′) [... k]i-mè-[še]n-šen-na gàr-dar-bi-šè ḫé-gál éren-ni-šè [...] x x x x x ḫé-bí-íb-[...]
16′) [... t]i-la nir-da-gu-la-ni ba-ni-x [...]
17′) [...] a-nir še-ša$_4$ ḫé-ni-ib-til-e [...]
18′) [...] x x UŠ ni x [...]
19′) [...] x [...]
Lacuna

midst of the gods, ... from heaven and earth ... release ... winds ...
15′) May ... assign him in the place of battle and combat to his foe, may ... to his troops,
16′) ... life, his great sin ...,
17′) ... may it end in sighs and laments,
18′) ... his *offspring* ...
19′) ...
Lacuna

2001

A limestone slab, probably a fragment of a *lamassu* figure, was dedicated by Itur-ašdum to the goddess Ašratum, wife of the god Amurrum, for the life of Ḫammu-rāpi.

COMMENTARY

The piece is BM 22454 (82-7-14,993), from objects of Rassam's excavations in Babylonia. The slab measures 36.2 × 38.8 cm and the inscription has been collated.

There has existed some confusion about the provenance of this inscription. Clay, YOR 6 p. 97, reiterated that the slab was found at Diyarbakir, but this is certainly incorrect. Wiseman subsequently suggested that the piece came from Sippar. This is indicated by Walker, who points out that the registration date and a report by Birch confirm that the slab was from that city.

The restoration of line 15 follows a suggestion of M. Stol.

BIBLIOGRAPHY

1894 Winckler, AOF 1 pp. 145–46 (study) and p. 198 (copy)
1898–1900 King, LIH no. 66 (copy, edition)
1899 Ball, Light from the East (London) p. 65 (photo)
1902 Pinches, Old Testament frontispiece (photo)
1906 E. Meyer, Sumerier und Semiten p. 14 (study)
1922 BM Guide p. 62 no. 141 (study)
1928 Hall, Sculpture pp. 31–32 (study) and pl. IXa (photo)
1957 Wiseman in Kupper, Nomades p. 176 and n. 2 (study)
1958 Wiseman, Illustrations p. 26 (photo)
1960 Parrot, Sumer fig. 374 (photo)
1961 Kupper, Amurru p. 62
1962 Strommenger and Hirmer, Mesopotamien pl. 161 (photo)
1970 Matthews, First Dynasty of Babylon pp. 156–57 (edition)
1971 Sollberger and Kupper, IRSA IVC6o (translation)
1976 Stol, Studies in Old Babylonian History p. 83 (study)
1980 Walker and Collon in de Meyer (ed.), Tell ed-Dēr 3 pp. 101–102 no. 53 (study)

TEXT

1) [^{d}aš]-ra-tum
2) ⸢é⸣-[g]i$_4$-a(erasure)-an-na
3) nam-nin-a túm-ma
4) nin-ḫi-li ma-az-bi
5) ḫur-sag-gá
6) mí-z[i]-dè-eš du$_{11}$-ga
7) nin-šà-lá-sù
8) nita-dam-a-ni-ir
9) KA ní-tuk-bi sa$_6$-ga
10) nin-a-ni-ir

1–10) For [the goddess Aš]ratum, daughter-in-law of the god An, the one suitable for ladyship, lady of voluptuousness and happiness, tenderly cared for in the mountain, lady with patient mercy, who prays reverently for her spouse, his lady,

11) nam-[ti]
12) *ḫa-am-mu-r[a-pí]*
13) lugal-mar-[dú]
14) *i-túr-aš-d[u-um]*
15) *ra-bi-a-an* I$_7$.[*s*]*í-lá-ku*
16) dumu-*šu-ba*-AN.A[N-ke$_4$]
17) ^{d}lamma me-te nam-di[ngir-ra-na]
18) ki-tuš-ki-ág-g[á-na]
19) ìr ní-t[uk-ni]
20) u$_6$-di-dè b[í-in-gub]

11–13) for the li[fe] of Ḫammu-r[āpi], king of the Amo[rites],

14–20) Itūr-ašd[um], chief of the [S]ilakku canal (district), son of Šubā-il[ān], the servant who re[verences her, set up] as a wonder a protective genius befitting her d[ivi]nity, [in her] beloved residence.

2002

A figurine in the Louvre contains a dedicatory inscription to the god Mardu for the life of Ḫammu-rāpi.

COMMENTARY

The piece is AO 15704, a purchased piece, said to be from Larsa. It is a base with a copper figurine 19.2 cm high in all, figure 14.5 cm high, base 13 cm long. The inscription was collated.

For a similar use of -šè found in line 12 compare E4.2.13.2001 line 8.

BIBLIOGRAPHY

1933 Dussaud and Thureau-Dangin, MP 33 pp. 1–8 and pl. I (photo, copy, edition)
1935 Zervos, L'art de la Mésopotamie p. 242 (photo)
1954 Frankfort, Art and Architecture pl. 64 (photo)
1961 Kupper, Amurru p. 80
1962 Strommenger and Hirmer, Mesopotamien pl. XXX (photo)
1969 Sollberger, Iraq 31 p. 92 and pl. x*a* (photo, edition)
1969 Moortgat, The Art of Ancient Mesopotamia pl. 218 (photo)
1970 Matthews, First Dynasty of Babylon pp. 158–59 (edition)
1971 Sollberger and Kupper, IRSA IVC6n (translation)
1975 Orthmann (ed.), Der alte Orient p. 294 no. xi (study) and pl. xi (photo)
1982 André-Leicknam, Naissance de l'écriture pp. 20 and 228 no. 170 (photo, study)
1984 Braun-Holzinger, Figürliche Bronzen pp. 53–54 no. 192 (study) and pl. 39 (photo)

TEXT

1) ^{d}mar-dú
2) dingir-ra-ni-ir
3) nam-ti-
4) *ḫa-am-mu-ra-pí*
5) lugal-KÁ.DINGIR.RA.KI
6) lú-^{d}nanna [...]
7) dumu-^{d}EN.ZU-*le-i*
8) alam šà-ne-ša$_4$ urudu
9) mùš-me-[bi] kù-GI-[gar]-ra
10) ⌜nam-ti-la-ni-še⌝
11) mu-na-an-dím
12) ìr-da-ni-šè
13) a mu-na-ru

1–2) For the god Mardu, his god,

3–5) for the life of Ḫammu-rāpi, king of Babylon,

6–11) Lu-Nanna, [...], son of Sîn-leʾi, fashioned for him, for his life, a suppliant statue of copper, [its] face [plat]ed with gold.

12–13) He dedicated it to him as his servant.

2003

A curious sandstone stamp in the form of a vase has an inscription in mirror writing mentioning Ḫammu-rāpi.

COMMENTARY

The piece is CBS 1126, provenance unknown, listed in BE 1/1 p. 49 as coming from the neighbourhood of Babylon. It measures 13.3 cm high, 12.2 cm in dia., and the inscription was collated.

BIBLIOGRAPHY

1893 Hilprecht, BE 1/1 no. 27 (copy, study)
1970 Matthews, First Dynasty of Babylon p. 160 (edition)

TEXT

1) x [...]
2) x [...]
3) *ḫa-am-m*[*u-ra-pí*]
4) ᵈEN.ZU-*a-ḫa-a*[*m-i-din-nam*]
5) dumu ìr-*ì-lí*-[...]
6) nam-KA-sa₆-g[a-ni-šè]
7) mu-na-an-⌜dím(?)⌝

1–7) [For the god ..., for the life of] Ḫamm[u-*rāpi*], Sîn-aḫa[m-iddinam], son of Warad-ili[..., on account of his] prayer, *fashioned* (this object) for him.

2004

An eye-stone in the British Museum has a prayer inscribed on it to the god Utu for the life of Ḫammu-rāpi.

COMMENTARY

The piece is BM 130829 (1949-11-12,6) from the collection of the Dukes of Northumberland (see W.G. Lambert, Iraq 41 [1979] p. 1). It is an eye-stone of brown and milky agate and the inscription was collated. It is edited here in full for the first time through the courtesy of the trustees of the British Museum.

BIBLIOGRAPHY

1951 Gadd, BMQ 16 p. 44 (translation, study)
1970 Matthews, First Dynasty of Babylon p. 161 (edition)
1971 Sollberger and Kupper, IRSA IVC6m (translation)
1983 Kärki, SAKAZ 2 p. 17 (study)

TEXT

1) ^{d}utu	1) O god Utu,
2) en-gal-an-ki-ke$_4$	2) great lord of heaven (and) earth,
3) *ḫa-am-mu-ra-pí*	3) (as for) Ḫammu-rāpi,
4) nun še-ga-zu	4) your favourite prince,
5) ⸢ti⸣-la-ì	5) make him live!

2005

The impressions of a seal of Sîn-iqīšam, the *šandabakkum* official and *gudapsûm* priest at Ur, servant of Ḫammu-rāpi, are found on a number of tablets excavated at Ur.

CATALOGUE

Ex.	Excavation number	Ur provenance	cpn
1	U 7700	From rubbish in ruins of no. 2 Quiet Street	n
2	U 7784	From no. 2 Quiet Street, room 4	n
3	U 3570	From the Dub-lal-maḫ	n
4	U 3572	As ex. 3	n
5	U 3574	As ex. 3	n
6	U 3575	As ex. 3	n
7	U 3578	As ex. 3	n
8	U 3580	As ex. 3	n
9	U 3582	As ex. 3	n
10	U 3583	As ex. 3	n
11	U 3584	As ex. 3	n
12	U 3586	As ex. 3	n
13	U 3587	As ex. 3	n
14	U 3589	As ex. 3	n
15	U 3591	As ex. 3	n

COMMENTARY

The tablets date to years 6–8 of Samsu-iluna.

BIBLIOGRAPHY

1928 Gadd, UET 1 no. 304 (exs. 1–2, composite copy)
1972 Ormsby, JCS 24 p. 99 seal 1 (exs. 3–15, composite copy)
1986 Charpin, Le clergé d'Ur p. 121 (edition, study)

TEXT

1) ^{d}EN.ZU-*i-qí-ša-a*[*m*]	1) Sîn-iqīša[m],
2) PISAN.DUB.BA GÚDA.ABZU-^{d}[*nanna*]	2) archivist (and) *gudapsûm* priest of the god [Nanna],
3) DUMU *ìl-šu-i-bí-*[*šu*]	3) son of Ilšu-ibbī[šu],
4) ÌR *ḫa-am-mu-ra-*[*pí*]	4) servant of Ḫammu-rā[pi].

2006

The impression of a seal of a servant of Ḫammu-rāpi is found on a tablet excavated by Woolley at Ur.

COMMENTARY

The impression is on IM 67708, excavation no. U 6705, from either room C. 20 or C. 21 of the Gipar-ku at Ur. It was not collated.

BIBLIOGRAPHY

1928 Gadd, UET 1 no. 147 (copy, edition)
1976 Woolley and Mallowan, UE 7 p. 224 (provenance)

TEXT

1) AN-*pi*$_4$-^{d}[...]	1) Anum-pî-[...],
2) DUMU *la-la-*[...]	2) son of Lala[...],
3) ÌR *ḫa-am-mu-ra-p*[*í*]	3) servant of Ḫammu-rāp[i].

2007

The impression of a seal of a different servant of Ḫammu-rāpi is found on the same tablet mentioned in the previous inscription. It was not collated.

BIBLIOGRAPHY

1928 Gadd, UET 1 no. 148 (copy, edition)
1976 Woolley and Mallowan, UE 7 p. 224 (provenance)

TEXT

1) x [...] ^{d}[...]	1) ...,
2) DUMU *ḫa-li-qum*	2) son of Ḫaliqum,
3) ÌR *ḫa-am-mu-ra-p*[*í*]	3) servant of Ḫammu-rāp[i].

2008

The impression of a seal of a servant of Ḫammu-rāpi is found on a letter envelope excavated at Nippur.

COMMENTARY

The impression is on CBS 8040, a fragment of an envelope of a letter. It was collated.

BIBLIOGRAPHY

1925 Legrain, PBS 14 no. 328 (edition)

TEXT

1) [*ḫa*]-*am-mu-ra-pí-ì*-[*li*]
2) [DU]MU *i-ri-ba-am*-[d][...]
3) [ì]R *ḫa-am-mu-ra*-[*pí*]

1) [Ḫa]mmu-rāpi-i[lī],
2) [s]on of Irībam-[...],
3) [ser]vant of Ḫammu-rā[pi].

2009

The impression of a seal of a servant of Ḫammu-rāpi is found on a door sealing excavated at Mari.

COMMENTARY

The impression is on ME 193, an object previously identified as a jar stopper. It was collated by D. Charpin who provides a different reading than that previously given by Dossin.

BIBLIOGRAPHY

1959 Parrot, Documents pp. 197–98 and pl. XLIX ME 193 (photo, study); Dossin p. 256 Nûr(?)-Marduk (edition)
1985 Beyer, MARI 4 p. 380 (study)
1988 Charpin, MARI 5 p. 661 (edition)

TEXT

1) [d]AMAR.UTU-*mu-ša-lim*
2) DUB.SAR
3) DUMU *sí-ia-tum*
4) IR_{11} *ḫa-am-mu-ra-pí*

1) Marduk-mušallim,
2) scribe,
3) son of Siatum,
4) servant of Ḫammu-rāpi.

2010

A number of impressions of seals of servants of Ḫammu-rāpi are found on tablets in the Vorderasiatisches Museum in Berlin. The first of these is the impression of Nabium-nāṣirum.

COMMENTARY

The impression is on VAT 644B, a clay envelope dating to year 31 of Ḫammu-rāpi, and was collated.

The name in the seal is restored from line 12 in the same tablet.

BIBLIOGRAPHY

1909 Ungnad, VAS 9 no. 43 (copy)

TEXT

1)	[d]*na-bi-um-*[*na-ṣi-rum*]	1) Nabium-[nāṣirum],
2)	DUMU dEN.ZU-x [...]	2) son of Sîn-[...],
3)	IR11 *ḫa-am-mu-ra-pí*	3) servant of Ḫammu-rāpi.

2011

The impression of a seal of Sîn-māgir, servant of Ḫammu-rāpi, is found on a tablet in Berlin.

COMMENTARY

The impression is on VAT 644B, a tablet envelope dating to year 31 of Ḫammu-rāpi, and was collated.

BIBLIOGRAPHY

1909 Ungnad, VAS 9 no. 43 (copy)

TEXT

1)	dEN.ZU-*ma-*[*gir*]	1) Sîn-mā[gir],
2)	DUMU *ṣíl-lì-za-*[...]	2) son of Ṣillī-za[...],
3)	IR11 *ḫa-am-mu-ra-*[*pí*]	3) servant of Ḫammu-rā[pi].

2012

The impression of a seal of a servant of Ḫammu-rāpi whose name is not entirely preserved is found on a tablet in Berlin.

COMMENTARY

The impression is on VAT 888, a tablet dating to year 25 of Ḫammu-rāpi, and was collated.

BIBLIOGRAPHY

1909 Ungnad, VAS 9 no. 107 (copy)

TEXT

1) ɪʀ₁₁-ᵈ[...]	1) Warad-[...],
2) [ᴅᴜ]ᴍᴜ *èr-ra-na-d*[*a*]	2) [s]on of Erra-nād[a],
3) ɪʀ₁₁ *ḫa-am-am-mu-r*[*a-pí*]	3) servant of Ḫammu-r[āpi].

2013

A fragmentary impression of a seal of a servant of Ḫammu-rāpi is found on a tablet envelope in Berlin.

COMMENTARY

The impression is on VAT 1295 and was collated.

BIBLIOGRAPHY

1909 Ungnad, VAS 9 no. 194 (copy)

TEXT

1) [...]	1) [...]
2) [ᴅᴜᴍᴜ ...]-*ra-at*	2) [son of ...]rat,
3) ìʀ *ḫa-am-mu-ra-pí*	3) servant of Ḫammu-rāpi.

2014

A cylinder seal of a servant of Ḫammu-rāpi is in the Bibliothèque Nationale in Paris.

COMMENTARY

The piece is Bibliothèque Nationale no. 200, a cylinder seal of serpentine, 3.2 cm long, 1.6 cm in dia., acquired from Botta in 1846. The inscription was collated.

BIBLIOGRAPHY

1848 Chabouillet, Catalogue no. 801 (1848)
1910 Delaporte, Revue archéologique 1 p. 25 fig. 2 (copy)
1910 Delaporte, Bibliothèque Nationale no. 200 (photo, copy, study)

TEXT

1) x x [x] x
2) [x x] x
3) ìR *ḫ[a-a]m-m[u]-ra-pí*

1) ...,
2) [...] ...,
3) servant of Ḫ[a]mm[u]-rāpi.

2015–17

Impressions of seals of three servants of Ḫammu-rāpi are found in the collection of the IVe Section de L'École Pratique des Hautes Études in Paris.

2015

The first of these is the seal of Ilum-pî-Šamaš.

COMMENTARY

The impression is on HE no. 135, a tablet dating to year 38 of Ḫammu-rāpi.

The name of the owner of the seal, broken away in the seal impression, is restored from line 4 of the tablet.

BIBLIOGRAPHY

1982 Durand, Doc. Cun. 1 p. 75 no. 50 (transliteration)

TEXT

1)	[DINGIR]-*pí*$_4$-[^{d}UTU]	1) [Ilum]-pî-[Šamaš],
2)	[DUMU] ^{d}EN.ZU-[...]	2) [son] of Sîn-[...],
3)	[ÌR] *ḫa-am-mu-*[*ra-pí*]	3) [servant] of Ḫammu-[rāpi].

2016

The impression of a seal of Šēp-Sîn is in the same collection.

COMMENTARY

The impression is on HE no. 126, a tablet dating to year 37 of Ḫammu-rāpi.

BIBLIOGRAPHY

1928 Boyer, Contribution pl. x no. 126 (copy)
1982 Durand, Doc. Cun. 1 p. 75 no. 62 (transliteration)

TEXT

1)	*še*$_{20}$-*ep*-^{d}EN.ZU	1) Šēp-Sîn,
2)	DUMU ^{d}UTU-*mu-ba-lí*-[*iṭ*]	2) son of Šamaš-muballi[ṭ],
3)	IR$_{11}$ *ḫa-am-mu-ra*-[*pí*]	3) servant of Ḫammu-rā[pi].

2017

The impression of a seal of Šamaš-lamassašu is found in the same collection.

COMMENTARY

The impression is on HE no. 139.

BIBLIOGRAPHY

1928 Boyer, Contribution pl. XIV no. 139 (copy)
1982 Durand, Doc. Cun. 1 p. 76 no. 66 (transliteration)

TEXT

1) ^{d}UTU-*la-ma-sà-šu*	1) Šamaš-lamassašu,
2) DUMU *mu-ḫ[a]-ad-[du-um]*	2) son of Muḫad[dûm],
3) IR$_{11}$ *ḫa-am-m[u-ra-pí]*	3) servant of Ḫamm[u-rāpi].

2018

A seal impression of a servant of Ḫammu-rāpi is found on a tablet recently excavated at Larsa.

COMMENTARY

The impression is on L 78.223, IM no. not yet known. It is a clay tablet from room 15 of the courtyard of the Ebabbar temple, dating to year 3 of Samsu-iluna. The impression was not collated.

BIBLIOGRAPHY

1981 Arnaud, Syria 58 p. 55 no. 89 (edition)
1983 Arnaud in Huot, Larsa et 'Oueili 1978–1981 p. 237 no. 89 (edition)

TEXT

1) x x BI-^{d}[...]	1) ...BI-[...],
2) DUMU ^{d}UTU-*na*-[...]	2) son of Šamaš-na[...],
3) ÌR$_{11}$ *ḫa-am-[mu-ra-pí]*	3) servant of Ḫam[mu-rāpi].

2019

The impressions of a seal of Aqba-ḫammu, the diviner, in which he appears as servant of Ḫammu-rāpi are found on a number of tablets excavated at Tell al-Rimah.

CATALOGUE

Ex.	Excavation number	Tell al Rimah provenance	cpn
1	TR 4298	Palace room VI	n
2	TR 4296	As ex. 1	n
3	TR 4297	As ex. 1	n
4	TR 5743	As ex. 1	n

BIBLIOGRAPHY

1976 Hawkins in Dalley, OBTR pp. 253–54 no. 14ii and pl. 109 no. 14ii (composite copy, edition)

TEXT

1) *[a]q-ba-⌜ḫa⌝-m[u]*
2) MÁŠ.ŠU.GÍD.GÍD
3) [DU]MU *ḫi-im-di-sa-ma-áš*
4) [Ì]R *ša ḫa-am-mu-ra-⌜pí⌝*

1) [A]qba-ḫamm[u],
2) diviner,
3) [s]on of Ḫimdi-Samaš,
4) [ser]vant of Ḫammu-rāpi.

2020

The impression of a seal of a servant of Ḫammu-rāpi is found on a tablet in the British Museum.

COMMENTARY

The impression is on BM 80128 (89-10-14,658b), a tablet case from Sippar. It was not collated.

BIBLIOGRAPHY

1968 Finkelstein, CT 48 no. 21 (transliteration)

TEXT

1) [d]UTU-*ḫa-[zi-ir]*
2) dumu *i-*[...]
3) ÌR *ḫa-[am-mu-ra-pí]*

1) Šamaš-ḫā[zir],
2) son of I-[...],
3) servant of Ḫa[mmu-rāpi].

2021

The impression of another servant seal of Ḫammu-rāpi is found on a tablet in the British Museum.

COMMENTARY

The impression is on BM 82395a (Bu 91-5-9,2457), from Sippar. It was not collated.

BIBLIOGRAPHY

1968 Finkelstein, CT 48 no. 53 (transliteration)

TEXT

1) ⌜dUTU-*li-wi-ir*⌝	1) Šamaš-liwwir,
2) DUMU dUTU-GIŠ.RU-GI [(x)]	2) son of Šamaš-isqam-kīn,
3) UGULA NU.B[AR]	3) overseer of the *kulmaš*[*ītum*] priestesses,
4) ÌR *ḫa-am-mu-ra-*[*pí*]	4) servant of Ḫammu-rā[pi].

2022

The impression of a seal of a servant of Ḫammu-rāpi is found on an envelope fragment in the Yale collections.

COMMENTARY

The impression is on MLC 1220, an envelope dating to year 18 of Ḫammu-rāpi. It was collated from the published photo.

BIBLIOGRAPHY

1981 Buchanan, Early Near Eastern Seals no. 791 (photo, edition)

TEXT

1) ⌜*i-ku*⌝-*un-pi*$_4$-x	1) Ikūn-pî-...,
2) ⌜SANGA⌝ d*za-ba*$_4$-[*ba*$_4$]	2) *sanga* priest of the god Zaba[ba],
3) DUMU ⌜dEN.ZU⌝-*ma-gir*	3) son of Sîn-māgir,
4) ÌR ⌜*ḫa-am-mu*⌝-[*ra-pí*]	4) servant of Ḫammu-[rāpi].

Samsu-iluna

E4.3.7

Ḫammu-rāpi was succeeded by his son Samsu-iluna, who reigned 38 years. A number of royal inscriptions are extant for this ruler.

1

The names of years 9–14 of Samsu-iluna all deal with military campaigns of the king. Perhaps to be connected with one of these is a historical or epic text in Akkadian known from a fragmentary tablet copy.

COMMENTARY

The text is found on VAT 17286, a frgm. of the upper half of a one- or two-col. tablet, 5×5×3 cm, that was excavated by Koldewey at Babylon. The script of the copy is of late OB or MB date.

BIBLIOGRAPHY

1987 van Dijk, VAS 24 no. 80 (copy)

TEXT

Obverse	
Lacuna	Lacuna
1′) x [x] x x *ḫa-wi-ri* [...]	1′) ... Ḫawiri ...
2′) *um-ma-an gu-la*-x-x [...]	2′–4′) He [smote] with his weapon the army of Gula-..., which had come to his (enemy's) aid.
3′) *ša a-na ti-il-lu-ti-šu* [*illiku*]	
4′) *in* GIŠ.TUKUL-*šu*(?) x-x-*as*(?)-*su* [...]	
5′) *ṣa*-⸢*a*(?)⸣-*al-ta ú*-x-[x]-*ṣi* [...]	5′) Combat ...,
6′) *ki-iṣ-ra* NI x x *ri ki/di* [...]	6′) the troops ...,
7′) *dan-na-tu-šu-nu mu* x x x x	7′) their strongholds ...,
8′) *ša in pa*-x [...]	8′) which in ...,
9′) I_7.x [...]	9′) the ... canal
Lacuna	Lacuna
Reverse	Reverse
Lacuna	Lacuna
1′) x x [...]	1′) ...,
2′) *in* É-x [...]	2′) in Bīt-...,

3′) *in sa-pa-*[*ni-šu* ...]	3′) having wiped [it] out
4′) *ú-ul ša*(?)-*ki-i*[*n* ...]	4′) ... was not *placed* ...

5′) *ú-ul it-ta-al-*[*la-ak*]	5′) He did not go ...
6′) *ta-am-ḫa-ar* [...]	6′) battle ...
7′) LUGAL *in* GABA *ši-nu* [...]	7′–8′) the king stood face to face against ...
8′) *iz-zi-iz* x x [...]	
9′) *sa-am-su-i-l*[*u-na* ...]	9′) Samsu-il[una ...]
10′) x-*ma na-aw-ra-a*[*m*]	10′) ... Nawra[m]
11′) x x x *su*(?)-*nu*(?) x	11′) ...
Lacuna	Lacuna

2

An inscription found at Nippur deals with the construction of the wall of Nippur by Samsu-iluna.

COMMENTARY

The inscription is on HS 2003, a headless clay cone, 8.8 cm long and 5.5 cm wide at the top. It was found in debris near the eastern corner of the court of the ziqqurrat by the Hilprecht expedition to Nippur. The cone is offered here through the courtesy of the authorities of the Friedrich-Schiller-Universität, Jena.

BIBLIOGRAPHY

1903 Hilprecht, Explorations pp. 480–82 (translation, study)
1910 Hilprecht, Deluge Story p. 8 n. 2 (study)
1969 Oelsner, WZJ 18 p. 54 no. 31 (study)

TEXT

1) [*sa-a*]*m-su-i-lu-na*	1–4) [Sa]msu-iluna, migh[ty ki]ng, [ki]ng of Babylon, [k]ing of the fou[r] quarters,
2) [LUG]AL *da-nú*[*m*]	
3) [LU]GAL KÁ.DINGIR.⸢RA⸣.KI	
4) [L]UGAL *ki-ib-ra-tim ar-ba-i*[*m*]	
5) ⸢*i*⸣-*nu* ^{d}EN.LÍL	5–11) when the god Enlil gave to him the four quarters to rule, (and) entrusted their nose-rope in his hands,
6) *ki-ib-ra-at ar-ba-im*	
7) *a-na be-li-im*	
8) ⸢*id*⸣-*di-nu*-⸢*šum*⸣	
9) *ṣe-ra*-⸢*as-si-na*⸣	
10) *a-na qà-ti*-⸢*šu*⸣	
11) *ú-ma-al*-⸢*li*⸣-*ma*	
12) ⸢*i*⸣-*nu*-[*ú-mi-š*]*u*	12–31) at that time, [Sa]msu-iluna, [shepherd w]ho pleases [the hear]t of the god M[ard]uk, [by] the lofty power which the great gods gave to him, by the wisdom which the god Ea granted him, widened more than it had been previou[sly] and raised high as a grea[t] mountain the wall of Nippur, (the wall) of Sîn-muballiṭ, [h]is grandfather.
13) [*sa-a*]*m*-⸢*su-i-lu*⸣-*n*[*a*]	
14) [SIPA *m*]*u-ṭi-i*[*b*]	
15) [*lìb-b*]*i* ^{d}A[MAR.U]TU	
16) [*in*] ⸢*e*⸣-*mu-qí-in*	
17) [*ṣ*]*i-ra-tim*	
18) *ša* DINGIR.GAL.GAL	
19) *id-di-nu-šum*	

20) *in ne-me-qí-im*
21) [*š*]*a é-a*
22) [*ú*]*-ša-at-li-mu-šum*
23) [B]ÀD N[IBR]U.⸢KI⸣
24) [*ša* ^{d}EN.ZU]*-m*[*u*]*-*⸢*ba*⸣*-l*[*í-i*]*ṭ*
25) *a-*[*b*]*i a-bi-*[*š*]*u*
26) ⸢*e*⸣*-li ša pa-n*[*a*]
27) ⸢*šu*⸣*-ba-as-*[*su*]
28) ⸢*ú*⸣*-*[*r*]*a-ap-pí-iš*
29) BÀD*-šu ki-ma*
30) [S]A.⸢DÚ⸣*-im ra-bí-i*[*m*]
31) *ú-ul-l*[*i*]
32) *ap-pa-ra-a*[*m*]
33) *uš-ta-ás-ḫir-*[*šu*]
34) I$_{7}$.BURA[NUN]
35) *iḫ-ri-a-a*[*m-ma*]
36) GÚ I$_{7}$.BUR⸢ANUN⸣
37) *ú-um-mi-s*⸢*u*⸣
38) [B]ÀD *šu-a-t*[*i*]
39) ⸢*mar*⸣*-kas ma-ta-t*[*im*]
40) [*a-n*]*a* ⸢*šu-mi*⸣*-im ib-b*[*i*]

32–40) He surrounded [it] with a moa[t]. He dug the Euphr[ates] and made the wall reach the bank of the Euphrates. He call[ed] that wall 'Band of the lan[ds]'.

41) ⸢*ni-ši*⸣ KALAM *šu-me-ri-*⸢*im*⸣
42) *ù ak-ka-di-*⸢*im*⸣
43) *šu-ba-at ne-eḫ-ti*[*m*]
44) *ú-še-ši-ib*
45) *a-bur-*⸢*ri*⸣
46) *u-šar-bí-iṣ*

41–46) He caused the people of the land of Sumer and Akkad to dwell in peaceful abodes. He made (them) lie down in pastures.

47) *zi-*[*k*]*ir* ^{d}EN.Z[U]*-mu-ba-lí-iṭ*
48) *a-bi a-bi-šu*
49) ⸢*in ki*⸣*-ib-ra-tim*
50) ⸢*ú*⸣*-še-pí*

47–50) He made the name of Sîn-muballiṭ, his grandfather, eminent in the lands.

3

The name of year 16 of Samsu-iluna records the building of the wall of Sippar. The name of year 18 commemorates the raising high of the Ebabbar temple in that city. These two events are described in an inscription known in Sumerian and Akkadian versions from cones found at Sippar. The line count for the translation follows the Akkadian version.

CATALOGUE

Sumerian version

Ex.	Museum number	Registration number	Object	Dimensions (cm)	Lines preserved	cpn
1	NBC 6102	–	Head	19.0 dia.	1–98	c
2	NBC 6102	–	Shaft	19.0	1–98	c
3	CBS 13884	–	Clay tablet	–	5–24, 37–56, 64–85, 93–98	c
4	CBS 469	–	Cone	–	3–26, 39–46	c
5	Ash 1922,257	–	Head	18.5 dia.	3–24, 31–33, 54–67, 79–97	c
6	BM 50678	82-3-23,169	Head	12.6 dia.	1–5, 27–31, 52–57, 76–85	c
7	BM 56612	AH 82-7-14,994A	Shaft	8.8	1–26, 28–35	c

Sumerian version

Ex.	Museum number	Registration number	Object	Dimensions (cm)	Lines preserved	cpn
8	BM 56612	AH 82-7-14,994A	Head	13.1 dia.	79–98	c
9	BM 56622	AH 82-7-14,1003	Head	12 dia.	10–23, 39–50, 69–74	c
10	IM 56377	–	Shaft	17.6	1–43, 46–98	c
11	IM 56377	–	Head	13.0 dia.	5–25, 28–49, 56–57, 59–64	c
12	IM 42097(?)	–	Shaft	15.5	1–10, 21–46, 51–78, 84–98	c
13	IM 56286	–	Shaft	8.0	12–33, 47–58	c
14	IM 56286	–	Head	12.0 dia.	31–41, 50–67, 77–97	c
15	IM 42094	–	Head	14.0 dia.	20–25, 42–49, 68–76, 96–98	c
16	IM 42092	–	Head	13.0 dia.	1–9, 24–39, 53–66	c
17	IM 42091	–	Head	13.0 dia.	18–26, 45–51, 73–75	c
18	IM 42093	–	Shaft	6.4	24–29, 31–34	c
19	IM 42093	–	Head	15.0 dia.	59–73, 85–98	c
20	BM 50830	AH 82-3-23,1824	Head	16.5 dia.	10–25, 36–48, 70–75, 91–98	c
21	BM 50830	AH 82-3-23,1824	Shaft	7.0	11–13	c
22	Museo Monserrat no number	–	Head	–	30–35, 54–61	c
23	BM 71943	AH 82-9-18,11946	Shaft	–	1–5, 31–38	c

Akkadian version

Ex.	Museum number	Registration number	Object	Dimensions (cm)	Lines preserved	cpn
1	BM 102404	1906-7-17,1	Shaft	18.5	1–123	c
2	BM 102404	1906-7-17,1	Head	20.0 dia.	3–31, 34–61, 64–94, 102–123	c
3	BM 115039	Ki 1902-5-10,37	Shaft	13.3	1–50, 52–82	c
4	BM 115039	Ki 1902-5-10,37	Head	11.0 dia.	11–25, 41–55, 76–83	c
5	BM 50815	82-3-23,1808	Head	9.6 dia.	24–30, 55–61	c
6	BM 56620	AH 82-7-14,999	Shaft	9.3	42–123	c
7	BM 49197	82-3-23,188	Shaft	4.0	1–25, 29–41, 43–45, 69–79	c
8	BM 49198	82-3-23,189	Shaft	–	1–21 (traces), 22–32, 33–39 (traces), 40–61, 62–77 (traces), 78–123	c
9	BM 49198	82-3-23,189	Head	–	1–20, 22, 32–50, 62–75, 99	c
10	Ash 1922,195	–	Shaft	7.0	47–56, 83–123	c
11	IM 56378	–	Shaft	18.0	1–123	c
12	IM 42096	–	Shaft	11.0	1–31, 39–123	c
13	IM 42095	–	Shaft	7.5	30–41, 70–83	c

COMMENTARY

For the Sumerian version, the master text is ex. 1. The line count here treats indented lines within one frame as one line, hence the different line count from that found on Stephens's copy.

Ex. 17 could not be located. Information about it is entered from E. Sollberger's description. Ex. 22 is known from a copy of M. Civil.

For the Akkadian version, the master text is ex. 1. Ex. 11, written in Akkadian, shows an orthography influenced by Sumerian.

BIBLIOGRAPHY

Sumerian version
1914 Poebel, PBS 5 no. 101 (ex. 3, copy)
1915 Poebel, OLZ 18 106–11 (ex. 3, edition)
1922 Legrain, PBS 13 no. 57 (ex. 4, copy)
1923 Langdon, OECT 1 pl. 31 (ex. 5, copy)
1924 Langdon, RA 21 pp. 120–25 (edition)
1937 Stephens, YOS 9 nos. 36–37 (exs. 1–2, copy)
1942–44 Thureau-Dangin, RA 39 pp. 5–17 (edition)
1957 Edzard, Sumer 13 pp. 178 and 188 (exs. 10–19, study)
1967 Sollberger, RA 61 p. 44 (exs. 1–5, 7–9, study)
1969 Sollberger, RA 63 p. 43 (exs. 10–19, study)
1970 Matthews, First Dynasty of Babylon pp. 201–20 (edition)
1971 Sollberger and Kupper, IRSA IVC7c (study)
1983 Kärki, SAKAZ 2 pp. 28–32 (edition)

Akkadian version
1923 Langdon, OECT 1 pl. 30 (ex. 10, copy)
1923 S. Smith, CT 37 pls. 1–4 (exs. 1–4, copy)
1924 S. Smith, RA 21 pp. 75–78 (edition)
1924 Langdon, RA 21 pp. 119–25 (edition)
1925 Gadd, JRAS pp. 94–99 (transliteration, study)
1926 Ungnad, JSOR 10 pp. 88–92 (edition)
1942–44 Thureau-Dangin, RA 39 pp. 5–17 (edition)
1957 Edzard, Sumer 13 pp. 188–89 (exs. 11–13, study)
1967 Sollberger, RA 61 pp. 39–44 (edition)
1969 Sollberger, RA 63 pp. 42–43 (exs. 11–13, study)
1970 Matthews, First Dynasty of Babylon pp. 201–20 (edition)
1971 Sollberger and Kupper, IRSA IVC7c (translation)
1983 Kärki, SAKAZ 2 pp. 25–32 (edition)

TEXT

Sumerian	Akkadian	
1) u$_{4}$ ^{d}en-líl-le	1) *ì-nu ^{d}en-líl*	1-7) When the god Enlil, king of the gods, great lord of the foreign lands, looked at the god Šamaš with his gracious face,
2) lugal-dingir-re-e-ne	2) LUGAL *ša ì-lí*	
3) en-gal-kur-kur-ra-ke$_{4}$	3) *be-lum ra-bi-um*	
	4) *ša ma-tá-tim*	
4) ^{d}utu-ra igi-sa$_{6}$-ga-na	5) *a-na* ^{d}UTU *in bu-ni-šu*	
	6) *dam-qú-tim*	
5) mu-un-ši-in-bar-ra-àm	7) *ip-pa-al-sú-ma*	
6) zimbir.KI	8) ZIMBIR.KI	8-24) (and) decreed to him, by his utterance that cannot be altered, to build the wall of Sippar, the ancient city, his cult city, to restore Ebabbar, to raise high as heaven the top of the ziqqurrat, his lofty *gigunna* temple, and to bring the gods Šamaš and Aia into their shining dwelling amidst joy and rejoicing,
7) uru-ul ki-šu-peš-a-ni	9) URU *ṣi-a-tim ma-ḫa-sú*	
8) bàd-bi dù-ù-dè	10) BÀD-*šu e-pé-ša-am*	
9) é-babbar-ra	11) *é-babbar a-na aš-ri-šu*	
10) ki-bé gi$_{4}$-gi$_{4}$-dè	12) *tu-ur-ra-am*	
11) u$_{6}$-nir gi-gun$_{4}$-na-maḫ-a-ni	13) U$_{6}$.NIR *gi-gu-na-šu*	
	14) *ṣi-ra-am*	
12) sag-bi an-gin$_{7}$ íl-i-dè	15) *re-ši-ša ki-ma ša-me-e*	
	16) *ul-la-a-am*	
13) ^{d}utu ^{d}šè-ri$_{5}$-da-bi	17) ^{d}UTU *ù ^{d}a-a*	
14) ki-tuš-kù-ne-ne-a	18) *a-na šu-ub-ti-šu-nu*	
	19) *el-le-tim*	
15) asila nì-ḫúl-ḫúl-la-bi-šè ku$_{4}$-ku$_{4}$-dè	20) *in re-ša-tim*	
	21) *ù ḫi-di-a-tim e-re-ba*	
16) inim nì-nu-kúr-ru-da-na	22) *in pí-šu ša la*	
	23) *ut-ta-ak-ka-ru*	
17) bí-in-du$_{11}$-ga-a	24) *iq-bi-ù*	
18) u$_{4}$-bi-a	25) *ì-nu-šu*	25-32) at that time, there was established joyfully for champion, youth Šamaš, the great destinies which the god Enlil had determined for Sippar and Ebabbar.
19) ur-sag šul ^{d}utu	26) UR.SAG ŠUL ^{d}UTU	
20) nam-gal ^{d}en-líl-le	27) *a-na ši-ma-tim ra-bi-a-tim*	
	28) *ša ^{d}en-líl*	
21) zimbir.KI é-babbar-ra	29) *a-na* ZIMBIR.KI	
22) mu-ni-in-tar-ra-šè	30) *ù é-babbar i-ši-mu*	
23) ḫúl-la-gin$_{7}$	31) *ki-ma ḫi-du-tim*	
24) im-ma-na-ni-íb-gar	32) *it-ta-aš-ka-an-šum*	
25) *sa-am-su-i-lu-na*	33) *sa-am-su-i-lu-na*	33-38) He joyfully called me, Samsu-iluna, the king created by his hand, (and) gave to me that (afore-alluded) commission.
26) lugal šu-du$_{11}$-ga-ni-me-en	34) *šar-ra-am li-pí-it*	
	35) *qá-ti-šu ia-ti*	
27) gù-ḫúl ma-an-dé	36) *ḫa-di-iš is-si-a-ni-ma*	
28) á-bi mu-da-an-ág	37) *te-er-tam šu-a-ti*	
	38) *ú-wa-e-ra-an-ni*	
29) u$_{4}$-bi-a	39) *ì-nu-šu na-ap-ḫa-ar*	39-46) At that time I defeated with weapons, eight times in the course of one year, the totality of the land of Sumer and Akkad which had become hostile against me.
30) kìlib-ki-en-gi ki-uri	40) *ma-at šu-me-ri-im*	
	41) *ù ak-ka-di-im*	
31) lú gú mu-da-ab-dù-uš-a	42) *ša i-zé-ru-ni-in-ni*	
32) šà-mu-aš-a-ka	43) *in li-ib-bu*	
	44) *ša-at-tim iš-ti-a-at*	
33) a-rá-8-àm	45) *a-di 8-šu*	

Sumerian version: **7**.1–3 ki-šu-KAD$_{4}$. **10**.4 ki-bi-šè. **13**.4 ^{d}šè-ri$_{5}$-da-IR. **17**.9 -du$_{11}$-ga-àm. **21**.10 é-babbar-ra omitted. **22**.10 -tar-ra-⟨šè⟩. **24**.2 ⸢im⸣-[m]a-na-ni-⸢íb(?)⸣-gar. **24**.4 Copy: -ni-i[n-...]; cone: -ni-[...]. **24**.5 Copy: im-ma-ni-ib-gar; cone: im-ma-na-ni-íb-gar. **33**.2, 22 -8-am$_{6}$.
Akkadian version: **3**.7, 9 *ra-bu-um*. **3**.11 *ra-bu-ù*. **3**.12 [*ra-b*]*i-ù*. **11**.11 *é-babbar-ra*. **13**.11 *gi-gun$_{4}$-na-šu*. **15**.7 AN-*e*. **16**.4, 7, 9 *ul-la-⟨a⟩-am*. **21**.1–2 omit *ù ḫi-di-a-tim*. **28**.11 [^{d}*e*]*n-líl-le*. **30**.11 *é-babbar-ra*. **32**.11 -*aš*(over erasure)-*šu*. **32**.13 -*aš-ka-an-šu*. **38**.1 Copy: *ú-wa-⟨e⟩-ra-an-ni*; cone: *ú-wa-e-ra-an-ni*. **40**.3, 7 *šu*-PI-*ri*-. **40**.11 *šu-me-rí-im*. **44**.2 Copy: *iš-ti-⟨a⟩-at*; cone: *iš-ti-a-at*. **44**.11 *iš-te-a-at*.

Sumerian	Akkadian	English
34) GIŠ.tukul-ta ḫé-em-mi-sìg	46) *in* GIŠ.TUKUL *lu a-du-uk*	
35) uru-didli gú-bar-ra-mu-ne	47) URU.URU *za-i-ri-ia*	47–54) I turned the cities of my enemies into rubble heaps and ruins. I tore out the roots of the enemies and evil ones from the land. I made the entirety of the nation dwell according to my decree.
36) du$_{6}$ *ka-ár-me*-šè ḫé-ni-ku$_{4}$	48) *a-na* DUL.DUL *ù kar-mi*	
	49) *lu ú-te-er*	
37) lú-érim	50) SUḪUŠ *a-ia-bi ù le-em-nim*	
38) lú-ḫul-gál		
39) suḫuš-bi kalam-ta ḫé-em-mi-bu	51) *in* KALAM *lu as-su-úḫ*	
40) kur-gú-si-a	52) *na-ap-ḫa-ar* KALAM	
41) du$_{11}$-ga-gá ḫu-mu-ni-tuš	53) *a-na qí-bi-ti-ia*	
	54) *lu ú-še-ši-ib*	
42) nì-u$_{4}$-ul-lí-a-ta	55) *ša iš-tu* *u$_{4}$-um ṣi-a-tim*	55–62) (Now), from the time when the brickwork of Ebabbar was (first) constructed, (since), among the former kings, the god Šamaš favoured none of them (and consequently) no one built the wall of Sippar for him,
43) sig$_{4}$-é-babbar-ra	56) *iš-tu* SIG$_{4}$ *é-babbar*	
44) ba-dím-ma-ta	57) *ib-ba-ni-ù*	
45) lugal-IGI.DU-ne-ne-er	58) *in* LUGAL *maḫ-ra*	
46) lugal-na-me	59) LUGAL *ma-am-ma-an*	
47) ^{d}utu ba-ra-mu-un-ši-in-še-ga-àm	60) ^{d}UTU *la im-gu-ru-ma*	
48) bàd-zimbir.KI	61) BÀD ZIMBIR.KI	
49) nu-mu-na-ta-an-dù-àm	62) *la i-pu-šu-šum-ma*	
50) *sa-am-su-i-lu-na*	63) *sa-am-su-i-lu-na*	63–81) I, Samsu-iluna, beloved of the gods Šamaš and Aia, mighty king, king of Babylon, king of the four quarters, king whose word finds favour with the gods Šamaš and Aia, by the decree of the gods Šamaš and Marduk, by the levy of the army of my land, in the course of that (same) year formed its bricks (and) raised high the wall of Sippar there like a great mountain.
51) ki-ág-^{d}utu	64) *na-ra-am* ^{d}UTU *ù* ^{d}*a-a*	
52) ^{d}šè-ri$_{5}$-da-bi		
53) lugal-kala-ga	65) LUGAL *da-núm*	
54) lugal-KÁ.DINGIR.RA.KI	66) LUGAL KÁ.DINGIR.RA.KI	
55) lugal-an-ub-da-límmu	67) LUGAL *ki-ib-ra-at ar-ba-im*	
56) lugal du$_{11}$-ga-ni	69) LUGAL *ša qí-bí-sú*	
57) ki-^{d}utu	70) *it-ti* ^{d}UTU *ù* ^{d}*a-a*	
58) ^{d}šè-ri$_{5}$-da-ta še-ga-me-en	71) *ma-ag-ra-at a-na-ku*	
59) du$_{11}$-ga-du$_{11}$-ga-^{d}utu	72) *in qí-bi-it* ^{d}UTU	
60) ^{d}AMAR.UTU-bi-da-ka	73) *ù* ^{d}AMAR.UTU	
61) ugnim-zi-ga-	74) *in ti-bu-ut*	
62) ma-da-mu-ta	75) *um-ma-an ma-ti-ia-ma*	
63) šà-mu-ba-ka	76) *in li-ib-bu*	
	77) *ša-at-tim šu-a-ti*	
64) sig$_{4}$-bi mu-ni-du$_{8}$	78) SIG$_{4}$-*šu al-bi-in*	
65) bàd-zimbir.KI	79) BÀD ZIMBIR.KI	
66) ḫur-sag-gal-gin$_{7}$ mi-ni-íl	80) *ki-ma* SA.DÚ-*im ra-bi-im*	
	81) *ú-ul-li*	
67) é-babbar-ra šu-gibil im-mi-ak	82) *é-babbar ú-ud-di-iš*	82–92) I renovated Ebabbar, raised high as heaven the head of the ziqqurrat, their lofty *gigunnu* temple, (and) brought the gods Šamaš, Adad, and Aia into their shining dwelling amidst joy and rejoicing.
68) u$_{6}$-nir gi-gun$_{4}$-na-maḫ-ne-ne	83) U$_{6}$.NIR	
	84) *gi-gu-na-šu-⟨nu⟩*	
	85) *ṣi-ra-am*	
69) sag-bi an-gin$_{7}$ mi-ni-íl	86) *re-ši-ša ki-ma ša-me-e*	
	87) *ú-ul-li*	

Sumerian version: **35**.7 uru.KI-di[dli ...]. **36**.1–2 *ka-ár-⟨me⟩*-šè. **37–39**.10–11 suḫuš-lú-érim lú-ḫul-gál kalam-ta ḫé-em-mi-bu. **40**.1 gú-GIŠ-a. **45**.9 IGI.DU-ne-ne-er: collated. **47**.3 -še-ga-à[m]: collated. **49**.3 ḫu-mu-na-ta-.
Akkadian version: **47**.3, 8, 11–12 *za-e-*. **49**.12 *lu-ú ù-te-er*. **50**.1–2, 11–12 omit *ù*. **50**.11 *a-a-bi*. **50**.4, 11–12 *lem-nim*. **51**.4 *in ma-tim lu as-sú-uḫ*. **52**.4, 8 *ma-tim*. **53**.11 *qí-bi-it-ia*. **53**.12 *qí-bi-ia-ti*. **54**.12 *lu-ú ù-še-ši-ib*. **56**.11 *é-babbar-ra*. **57**.2, 8 *ib-ba-nu-ú*. **57**.12 *ib-ba-nu-ù*. **59**.11–12 *ma-am-ma-am*. **60**.1, 5 *im-gur-ru-ma*. **65**.11 LUGAL KALA.GA. **68**.12 *ar-ba-i-im*. **69**.1–2 *qí-bi-sú*. **69**.6, 11, 12 *qí-bí-sú*. **74–75**.1 omits. **75**.12 *um-ma-a-an*. **76**.1–2, 11 omit *li-ib-bu*. **76**.13 *in li-ib-bi*. **77**.2 *ša-⟨at⟩-tim*. **77**.6 [...] x *šu-a-ti*. **77**.11 *ša-at-tim-ma*. **80**.11 *⟨ra⟩-bi-im*. **80**.12 *ša-di-im*. **82**.11 *é-babbar-ra*. **84**.10 *gi-gu-un-na-šu*. **84**.11 *gi-gun$_{4}$-na-šu*. **86**.8 AN-*e*. **87**.12 *⟨ú⟩-ul-li*.

70) ^{d}utu ^{d}iškur
71) ^{d}šè-ri$_{5}$-da-bi
72) ki-tuš-kù-ne-ne-a

73) asila nì-ḫúl-ḫúl-la-bi-šè
74) mi-ni-ku$_{4}$
75) é-babbar-ra
76) ^{d}lamma-sa$_{6}$-ga-bi im-mi-gi$_{4}$
77) su-^{d}utu ^{d}iškur
78) ^{d}šè-ri$_{5}$-da-bi
79) du$_{10}$-ga-ra im-mi-ak
80) nì-du$_{11}$-ga-^{d}utu
81) ^{d}AMAR.UTU-bi-da-ke$_{4}$
82) ki-bi-šè im-mi-gar
83) bàd-ba ^{d}utu
84) *sa-am-su-i-lu-na*-ra

85) nam-nir nam-kala-ga
86) ù nam-ti-la-ke$_{4}$
87) sag-e-éš mu-ni-in-rig$_{7}$
88) mu-bi-im
89) ur$_{5}$-šè-àm ^{d}utu
90) sag-nam-bára-ga-ni
91) ša-mu-un-íl-la
92) nam-ti šà-du$_{10}$-ga gi$_{16}$-sa ak-a

93) nam-lugal zà-ša$_{4}$ nu-tuk-a

94) GIŠ.gidru nì-si-sá
95) kalam-ge-en-ge-en
96) GIŠ.tukul kala-ga GIŠ.gaz lú-kúr-e-ne
97) nam-en ub-da-límmu-ba

98) du-rí-šè ak-da nì-ba-ni-éš mu-na-an-sum

88) ^{d}UTU ^{d}IŠKUR *ù* ^{d}*a-a*

89) *a-na šu-ub-ti-šu-nu*
90) *el-le-tim*
91) *in re-ša-tim ù ḫi-da-tim*
92) *ú-še-ri-ib*
93) *a-na é-babbar* ^{d}LAMMA-*šu*
94) *da-mi-iq-tam*
95) *ú-te-er*
96) *ša e-li* ^{d}UTU
97) ^{d}IŠKUR *ù* ^{d}*a-a*
98) *ṭa-bu e-pu-uš*
99) *qí-bi-it* ^{d}UTU
100) *ù* ^{d}AMAR.UTU
101) *a-na aš-ri-im aš-ku-un*
102) BÀD *šu-ú* ^{d}UTU
103) *a-na sa-am-su-i-lu-na*
104) *iš-ru-uk-šum*
105) *me-te-lu-tam du-un-nam*
106) *ù ba-la-ṭam šum-šu*

107) *a-na šu-a-ti* ^{d}UTU
108) *mu-ul-li re-eš*
109) *šar-ru-ti-šu*
110) *ba-la-ṭam ṭú-ub*
111) *li-ib-bi-im*
112) *da-ra-a-am*
113) *šar-ru-tam ša ša-ni-nam*
114) *la i-šu-ú*
115) GIDRU *mi-ša-ri-im*
116) *mu-ki-in-na-at* KALAM
117) GIŠ.TUKUL *da-an-nam*
118) *ma-aš-ka-aš na-ki-ri*
119) *be-lu-ut ki-ib-ra-at*
120) *ar-ba-im*
121) *a-na da-ar e-pé-ša-am*
122) *a-na qí-iš-ti-šu*
123) *id-di-iš-šum*

93–95) I returned to Ebabbar its favourable protective genius.

96–101) I did that which was pleasing to the gods Šamaš, Adad, and Aia. I fulfilled the decree of the gods Šamaš and Marduk.

102–106) The name of that wall is 'The god Šamaš has given to Samsu-iluna dominion, might and life'.

107–123) On account of this the god Šamaš, who exalts his kingship, gave to him as a gift life, everlasting happiness, kingship that has no rival, a sceptre of justice that makes the land firm, a mighty weapon that wipes out the enemies, (and) the rule of the four quarters, forever.

Sumerian version: **80**.2 ⸢IGI(?)⸣-du$_{11}$-ga. **84**.1 *sa-am-⸢su⸣-i-⸢lu⸣-na*-⸢me-en⸣. **89**.2 Despite copy: ur$_{5}$-šè-àm. **89**.5 Copy: ur$_{5}$-ra-àm; cone: ur$_{5}$-šè-àm. **93**.3 [nu]-tuk-àm. **95**.1 kalam-ge-en-ge-RI. **98**.1 nì-ba-DÙ-éš.

Akkadian version: **91**.1–2, 8 omit *ù ḫi-da-tim*. **91**.10 *i-na*. **91**.11 *ḫa-di-⸢a⸣-tim*. **91**.12 *ḫi-di-a-tim*. **92**.10 Collation: *ú-še-ri-ib*. **92**.11 *e-re-ba-am*. **93**.11 *é-babbar-ra*. **101**.1, 12 *aš-ri-⟨im⟩*. **105**.1 *du-nam*. **105**.10 *du-un-na-am*. **106**.12 *ba-la-ṭá-am*. **108**.12 *mu-⟨ul⟩-li*. **110**.6 *ba-la-aṭ*. **111**.11 *li-bi-ib-im*. **112**.11 *da-rí-a-am*. **112**.12 *da-ri-a-am*. **113**.12 ⸢*ša-ni*⸣-*na-am*. **115**.6, 12 GIŠ.GIDRU. **116**.1–2, 6 *mu-ki-⟨in⟩-na-at*. **116**.10 *ma-tim*. **116**.12 *ma-⸢ti⸣-ia*. **117**.1–2, 8 *dan-nam*. **117**.12 *da-nam*. **120**.12 *ar-ba-i-im*.

4

A copy of a royal inscription on a clay tablet fragment deals with the construction of a city wall. Column i of this inscription, if restored correctly, appears to refer to the events of year 10 of Samsu-iluna, the revolt of Rīm-Sîn II of Larsa, and therefore an attribution of the inscription to Samsu-iluna is likely.

COMMENTARY

The inscription is on a tablet that was once in a private collection, but whose present whereabouts is unknown. It probably came from Sippar.

The inscription might possibly be connected with the name of year 16 of Samsu-iluna dealing with the construction of the wall of Sippar. It mentions a clay *narû*, a fact that suggests that this tablet might be a copy of a foundation tablet or cylinder.

BIBLIOGRAPHY

1970 Matthews, First Dynasty of Babylon pp. 277–78 (edition) and pl. I (copy)

TEXT

Col. i
Lacuna
1′) [mu ... nu ...]-sa$_9$
2′) [*ri-im*-^{d}EN].ZU
3′) [... KI.EN].GI.[SAG].6
4′) [...-d]a
5′) [...-d]a
6′) [...].KI-ke$_4$
7′) [...]-da-bi
8′) [...]-x-ke$_4$
9′) [...]-du$_8$-du$_8$
10′) [...]-x-bi
Lacuna

Lacuna
i 1′–10′) [The year was not] half over [when *he killed* Rīm-S]în, [*king*] of [E]mu[tb]ala ...
Lacuna

Col. ii
Lacuna
1′) x x x [...]
2′) níg nun ki da x [...]
3′) bàd-si-bi x x [...]
4′) ḫur-sag-gin$_7$ m[u-...]
5′) sag-bi ba-ni-x-[...]
6′) bàd-bi ù-x-[...]
7′) u$_4$-ba ^{d}x [...]
8′) ^{d}utu lugal-din[gir-re-e-ne]
9′) u$_4$-gin$_7$ igi in-[... bar-re-eš]
10′) IM.na-rú-a [...]
11′) sag mu-un-na-ab-[...]
Lacuna

Lacuna
ii 1′–11′) ... [...], he [*raised*] its parapet like a mountain. Its head [...], its wall ... At that time the god ... (and) the god Utu, king [of the] g[ods], loo[ked at it] brightly. He [...] a clay foundation inscription for him.
Lacuna

5

The name of year 17 of Samsu-iluna records the restoration of a number of fortresses that had fallen into disrepair. This year name is probably to be correlated to an inscription of Samsu-iluna dealing with the restoration of six fortresses which had been built earlier by his predecessor Sūmû-la-Il. The inscription is known in a Sumerian and Akkadian version.

CATALOGUE

Sumerian version

Ex.	Museum number	Registration number	Provenance	Object	Dimensions (cm)	Lines preserved	cpn
1	BM 91083	AH 82-7-14,629	Sippar	Limestone foundation tablet	18.4 × 9.2	1-83	c
2	BM 22507	AH 82-7-14,1022	Sippar	Clay statuette	19.1 long, 7.7 dia.	1-83	c

Akkadian version

Ex.	Museum number	Provenance	Object	Dimensions (cm)	Lines preserved	cpn
1	VA 2645	Unknown	Limestone foundation tablet	17.5 × 8.7	1-83	c
2	BM 38402	Unknown	Fragment of clay tablet	7.6 × 14.0	1-17, 19-24, 26-48, 50-83	c

COMMENTARY

The master text is ex. 1 for both versions. The translation follows the Akkadian version. For the reading of the toponym in line 47 of the Sumerian version see I.J. Gelb, MAD 2 p. 210.

BIBLIOGRAPHY

Sumerian version
1888 Strassmaier, ZA 3 pp. 140 and 153-57 no. 15 (ex. 2, copy, study)
1898-1900 King, LIH nos. 98-99 (exs. 1-2, copy, edition)
1905 King, CT 21 pls. 47-50 (ex. 1, copy)
1922 BM Guide p. 88 no. 108 (ex. 2, study)
1923 Jean, Le Milieu Biblique pp. 110-11 (translation)
1924 Gadd, Reading-book pp. 58-65 (composite copy, edition)
1970 Matthews, First Dynasty of Babylon pp. 187-200 (edition)
1971 Sollberger and Kupper, IRSA ɪvC7b (study)
1980 Walker and Collon in de Meyer (ed.), Tell ed-Dēr 3 p. 103 no. 68 (ex. 1, study) p. 106 no. 98 (ex. 2, study)
1983 Kärki, SAKAZ 2 pp. 22-25 (edition)

Akkadian version
1892 Winckler and Böhden, ABK no. 74 (ex. 1, copy)
1892 Winckler, KB 3/1 pp. 130-33 Samsu-iluna (ex. 1, edition)
1898-1900 King, LIH no. 97 (ex. 2, copy; exs. 1-2, edition)
1907 Ungnad, VAS 1 no. 33 (ex. 1, copy)
1923 Jean, Le Milieu Biblique pp. 110-11 (translation)
1957 Edzard, Zwischenzeit pp. 124-25 (study)
1963 Borger, BAL[1] 2 pp. 47-48 (copy in Neo-Assyrian script, transliteration, study)
1970 Matthews, First Dynasty of Babylon pp. 187-200 (edition)
1979 Borger, BAL[2] 1 pp. 51-52 (copy in Neo-Assyrian script, transliteration, study)
1983 Kärki, SAKAZ 2 pp. 19-25 (edition)

TEXT

Sumerian

1) u$_4$ an ^{d}en-líl
2) lugal-an-ki-bi-da-ke$_4$
3) ^{d}AMAR.UTU dumu-sag-
4) ^{d}en-ki-ka-ra
5) igi-ḫúl-la-ne-ne-a
6) in-ši-in-bar-re-eš-a
7) nam-en-ub-da-límmu-ba
8) mu-na-an-sum-mu-uš-a
9) ^{d}a-nun-na-ke$_4$-ne-er
10) mu-maḫ-a mi-ni-in-⌈sa⌉$_4$-eš-a
11) KÁ.DINGIR.RA.KI
12) suḫuš an-ki-gin$_7$
13) mu-na-an-ge-né-⌈eš⌉-a
14) u$_4$-ba ^{d}AMAR.UTU
15) ^{d}en-líl-kalam-ma-na
16) dingir nam-⌈kù⌉-zu
17) an-dím-⌈dím⌉-me-a
18) *sa-⌈am-su-i⌉-lu-na*
19) lugal ⌈la-la⌉-ni ì-me-en-na-ta
20) kur-kur kìlib-ba-bi
21) nam-sipa-bi ak-dè
22) ma-an-sum
23) kalam-ma-ni
24) ú-sal-la nú-dè
25) un-dagal-la-ni
26) silim-ma du-rí-šè túm-túm-mu-dè
27) á-gal ḫu-mu-da-an-ág
28) *sa-am-su-i-lu-na*
29) lugal-kala-ga
30) lugal-KÁ.DINGIR.RA.KI
31) lugal an-ub-da-límmu-ba
32) gù-téš-a bí-in-sì-ga-me-en
33) usu-ní-gá
34) igi-gál-gal-mu-ta
35) bàd-an-za-gàr-^{d}en-líl-lá.KI
36) ^{d}nin-ḫur-sag-gá
37) ama in-dím-en-na-⟨mu⟩-uš
38) bàd-*pà-da*.KI
39) ^{d}iškur á-daḫ-mu-ke$_4$
40) bàd-*la-ga-ba*.KI
41) ^{d}nanna
42) dingir-sag-du-mu-šè
43) bàd URU *ia-bu-šum*.KI
44) ^{d}lugal-GIŠ.ásal

Akkadian

1) *ì-nu* AN ^{d}*en-líl*
2) *šar-ru ša* AN ⌈*ù*⌉ KI
3) *a-na* ^{d}AMAR.UTU
4) [DU]MU *re-eš-ti-im ša é-a*
5) *ḫa-di-iš ip-pa-al-su-šum*
6) *be-lu-ut ki-ib-ra-at ar-ba-im*
7) *i-din-nu-šum*
8) *in* ^{d}*a-nun-na-ki*
9) *šu-ma-am ṣi-ra-am i-bí-ù-šu*
10) KÁ.DINGIR.RA.KI
11) SUḪUŠ-*šu ki-ma* [AN] *ù* KI
12) [*ú*]-*ki-in-nu-šum*
13) *ì-nu-šu* ^{d}AMAR.UTU
14) [^{d}]*en-líl ma-ti-šu*
15) DINGIR *ba-ni ne-me-qí-im*
16) *a-na sa-am-su-i-lu-na*
17) LUGAL *la-le-šu ia-a-ti*
18) [Š]U.NÍGIN *ma-ta-tim*
19) [*a*]-*na re-ie-em i-din-nam*
20) [K]ALAM-*su a-bur-ri šu-ur-bu-ṣa-am*
21) *ni-ši-š*[*u ra-a*]*p-ša-tim*
22) *in šu-ul-mi-im*
23) *a-na da-ar i-tar-ra-am*
24) *ra-bi-iš lu ú-wa-e-ra-an-ni*
25) *sa-am-su-i-lu-na*
26) LUGAL *da-núm*
27) LUGAL KÁ.DINGIR.RA.KI
28) LUGAL *mu-uš-te-eš-mi*
29) *ki-ib-ra-at*
30) *ar-ba-im a-na-ku*
31) *in e-mu-uq ra-ma-ni-ia*
32) *in* IGI.GÁL-*ia ra-bi-im*
33) BÀD AN.ZA.GÀR-^{d}*en-líl*.KI
34) *a-na* ^{d}NIN.MAḪ
35) AMA *ba-ni-ti-ia*
36) BÀD *pà-da*.KI
37) *a-na* ^{d}IŠKUR *re-ṣi-*⌈*ia*⌉
38) BÀD *la-ga-ba*.[KI]
39) *a-na* ^{d}EN.[ZU] DINGIR *ba-ni-i*[*a*]
40) BÀD URU *ia-bu-šu*[*m*.KI]
41) *a-na* ^{d}LUGAL.ÁS[AL]

Translation

1–5) When the gods Anum and Enlil, the kings of heaven and earth, joyously looked at the god Marduk, first-born son of the god Ea,

6–9) gave to him the rule of the four quarters, called (his) exalted name in (the assembly of) the *Anunnaku* gods,

10–12) (and) made the foundation of Babylon firm for him like (that of) heaven and earth,
13–15) at that time, the god Marduk, the Enlil of his land, the god who creates wisdom,

16–24) gave to me, Samsu-iluna, king of his pleasure, the totality of the lands to shepherd (and) laid a great commission on me to make his nation lie down in pastures and to lead his extensive people in well-being, forever.

25–30) I, Samsu-iluna, mighty king, king of Babylon, king who makes the four quarters be at peace,

31–35) by my own might and by my great intelligence (I built) the fort Dimat-Enlil for the goddess Ninmaḫ, the mother who created me,
36–37) the fort Pada, for the god Adad, my helper,
38–39) the fort Lagaba for the god Sîn, the god who created me,

40–42) the fort Iabušum for the god Šar-ṣarbatim, who magnifies

---

Sumerian version: **5**.2 [igi-ḫúl]-la-né-ne-a. **20**.2 [kìli]b-ba-a-bi. **24**.2 nú-ù-dè. **40**.2 bàd-⌈gal⌉.

Akkadian version: **18**.2 [NIGIN KALAM]. **33**.1 Copy in VAS 1: AN.A.GÀR; text: AN.ZA.GÀR.

45) mu-nam-lugal-la-mu-um 46) bí-íb-gu-ul-la-aš	42) *mu-šar-bí-ù* ⟨*šum*⟩ *šar-ru-ti-ia*	my royal name,
47) bàd uru *gu-la-ba*$_{8}$.KI 48) ù bàd *ú-ṣi-a-na-èr-ra*.KI 49) ^{d}nergal 50) tun(UD + ḪÚB)-lú-érim-mu-um 51) bí-in-ak-a-aš	43) BÀD URU *gu-la-ba*$_{8}$.KI 44) *ù* BÀD *ú-ṣi-a-na-èr-r*[*a*] 45) *a-na* ^{d}*nergal* 46) *ḫa-ti a-a-b*[*i*]*-ia*	43–46) the fort Gulaba and the fort Ūṣi-ana-Erra for the god Nergal, who smites my enemies.
52) 6 bàd-gal-gal-la-bi 53) *su-mu-la-ìl* 54) a-a-gu-la-mu 55) pa-bíl-ga-5-kam-ma-mu 56) mi-ni-in-dù-a 57) nam-sumun-ba ní-te-a-*ne-ne-a*	47) 6 BÀD.[MEŠ *ra-bu*]*-tim šu-nu-ti* 48) *ša su-mu-*[*l*]*a-ìl* 49) *a-bi r*[*a-bi*]*-um* 50) *a-bi a-*[*bi*]*-ia* 51) *ḫa-a*[*m*]*-šum* ⌜*e*⌝*-pu-šu* 52) *in* [*l*]*a-*[*b*]*i-ru-ti-šu-nu* 53) *in r*[*a*]*-ma-ni-šu-nu* 54) *up-ta-as-sí-sú-ma*	47–54) These six great forts which Sūmû-la-Il, my great forefather, my fifth (generation) ancestor, had built: in their old age they had fallen into ruin on their own accord.
58) ì-šub-šub-bu-uš-àm 59) šà-iti-min-kam-ma-ta 60) sig$_{4}$-bi mi-ni-du$_{8}$ 61) gal-bi im-mi-dù 62) sag-ne-ne ḫur-sag-gin$_{7}$ mi-ni-íl	55) *in li-ib-bu* ITI.2.KAM 56) SIG$_{4}$*-šu-nu al-bi-in* 57) *ra-bi-iš e-pu-uš* 58) *re-ši-šu-nu ki-ma* SA.DÚ*-im ú-ul-li*	55–58) In the course of two months I formed their bricks and in a grand fashion built them. I raised their heads like a mountain.
63) kìlib-kur-kur-ra-ke$_{4}$ 64) suḫuš-bi m[i]-ni-ge-en 65) KÁ.DINGIR.RA.KI 66) mu-bi ḫu-mu-ni-maḫ 67) an-ub-da-límmu-ba ḫé-bí-diri 68) ní-me-lám- 69) nam-lugal-la-mu 70) zà-an-ki-ke$_{4}$ ḫé-en-dul	59) ŠU.NÍGIN *ma-ta-tim* SUḪUŠ*-ši-na ú-ki-in* 60) KÁ.DINGIR.RA.KI šum-šu 61) *lu ú-ṣi-ir* 62) *in ki-ib-ra-at ar-ba-im* 63) *lu ú-ša-tir-šu* 64) *pu-luḫ-ti* ME.LÁM *šar-ru-ti-ia* 65) *pa-aṭ* AN *ù er-ṣi-tim* 66) *lu ik-tum*	59–66) I made the foundation of the totality of the lands firm. I made the name of Babylon supreme (and) made it surpassing in the four quarters. The fearsome splendour and aura of my kingship covered the borders of heaven and earth.
71) ur$_{5}$-šè-àm 72) dingir-gal-gal-e-ne 73) igi-zalag-ga-ne-ne-a 74) ḫu-mu-ši-in-bar-re-eš 75) nam-ti-la ^{d}nanna-gin$_{7}$ 76) iti-iti-da mú-mú-da 77) nam-sipa-ub-⌜da⌝-límmu-ba 78) silim-ma du-rí-šè ak-da 79) šà-kur-ku-da-mu 80) dingir-gin$_{7}$ sá-di-da 81) u$_{4}$-šú-šè sag-íl-la 82) asila šà-ḫúl-la-ta du-du-da	67) *a-na šu-a-ti* DINGIR.GAL.GAL 68) *in bu-ni-šu-nu na-aw-ru-tim* 69) [*lu i*]*p-pa-al-sú-nim* 70) [*ba-la-ṭ*]*am ša ki-ma* ^{d}EN.ZU 71) *wa-a*[*r-ḫi*]*-ša-am* 72) *ú-t*[*e-e*]*d-di-šu* 73) *re-iu-ta*[*m ša*] *ki-ib-ra-*[*at*] *ar-ba-im* 74) *in šu-ul-mi-im* 75) *a-na da-ar e-pé-ša-am* 76) *ni-iz-ma-at li-ib-bi-ia* 77) *ki-ma* DINGIR *ka-ša-dam* 78) *u*$_{4}$*-mi-ša-am in re-ši-in e-li-a-tim* 79) *in* ⌜*ri*⌝*-ša-a-tim* 80) *ù ḫ*[*u-u*]*d li-ib-bi-im* 81) *a-ta-al-lu-kam*	67–83) On account of this the great gods looked at me with their shining faces (and) granted to me as a gift: a life that, like the god Sîn, is renewed monthly; to exercise the shepherdship of the four quarters in well-being forever; to attain the desire of my heart like a god; (and) to walk daily with head held high in joy and happiness.

Sumerian version: **52**.2 -gal-gal-⟨la⟩-bi. **69**.2 nam-lugal-la-mu-um. **76**.2 mú-mú-dam. **77**.2 nam-sipa-an-ub-ta-límmu-ba. Akkadian version: **42**.2 *mu-šar-bí-*⟨*ù*⟩. **44**.2 omits *ù*. **47**.2 BÀD.GAL.[GAL]. **58**.2 RA.SI-*šu*-[*nu*]. **59**.2 NIGIN KALAM. **60**.1 É.DINGIR.RA.KI. **63**.2 omits *-šu*. **65**.2 *ša-me-e*. **78**.2 [*in* RA].SI-*in*.

83) sa_{12}-e-eš ḫu-mu-rig_7-eš

82) *a-na še-ri-ik-tim*
83) *[l]u iš-ru-ku-nim*

Colophon (from LIH no. 97)
1) [... *im-g*]*i-id-di ṣa-ar-pa*
2) [...] x *ina qaq-qa-di-šu*
3) [... I]N.SAR
4) [...]-*ri*
5) [...] x *a*

Colophon (from LIH no. 97)
1-5) [...] fired [lon]g-tablet [which ...] from its top [... wr]ote ...

6

The name of year 22 of Samsu-iluna records the renovation of the ziqqurrat of the gods Zababa and Inanna at Kiš. This work is described in a 15-line Sumerian text stamped on bricks found in the area of the ziqqurrat at Uḫaimir-Kiš.

CATALOGUE

Ex.	Museum number	Excavation number	Uḫaimir provenance	Dimensions (cm)	Lines preserved	cpn
1	Istanbul(?) unlocated	–	–	–	4-9	n
2	Istanbul no number	–	–	–	5-9	c
3	IM 1624	HMR 14	Lying against SE face of platform about 1 metre below surface	35.0×35.0×4.0	–	n
4	Ash 1930,40	HMR 124	Found in rubbish on SW side of ziqqurrat platform 50 cm below surface	35.0×34.6×8.2	1-15	c
5	Ash 1966,1041	HMR 246	Platform, SW side, 1.5 m below brickwork	Face 28.0×27.0×9.7	2-15	c
6	Ash 1966,1041	HMR 246	As ex. 5	Edge as ex. 5	5-15	c
7	IM 1708	HMR 352	At south end of SE platform just below surface of ground	35.0×22.0	–	n
8	Ash 1924,635	–	–	7.0×14.5×3.3	11-15	c
9	Ash 1932,650	–	–	Edge 24.8×20.5×8.5	4-15	c
10	FMNH 156012	–	–	34.7×35.0×8.0	1-15	c
11	UM 35-43-1	None	Kiš(?)	Face and edge 34.5×27.0×8.0	–	n

COMMENTARY

Exs. 1-2 were found during de Genouillac's excavations at Kiš in 1921. Exs. 3-10 were found by the Oxford-Field Museum expedition to Kiš.

BIBLIOGRAPHY

1923-24 Langdon, AJSL 40 pp. 226 and 299 Brick B 2 (ex. 9, photo, copy, edition)
1924 Langdon, Kish 1 p. 15 and pl. XXXIV no. 1 (ex. 9, copy, edition)
1924 de Genouillac, Kich 1 pl. 1 no. 0.2 (ex. 1, copy)
1925 de Genouillac, Kich 2 pl. 2 no. 0.7 (ex. 2, copy)
1958 Borger, Orientalia NS 27 p. 408 (edition)
1970 Matthews, First Dynasty of Babylon pp. 258-59 (edition)
1971 Sollberger and Kupper, IRSA IVC7a (translation)
1972 Gibson, The City and Area of Kish (Miami) p. 97 n. 62 (exs. 3-4, study)
1978 Moorey, Kish fiche 1 A11-A12 (exs. 4-6, 8-9, study)
1981 Walker, CBI no. 49 (exs. 4-6, 8-9, study)
1981 Grégoire, MVN 10 no. 53 (ex. 4, copy, study)
1983 Kärki, SAKAZ 2 p. 19 (edition)

TEXT

1) *sa-am-su-i-lu-na*	1) Samsu-iluna,
2) lugal-kala-ga	2) mighty king,
3) lugal-	3–4) king of Babylon,
4) KÁ.DINGIR.RA.KI	
5) lugal-	5–6) king of Kiš,
6) kiš.KI-a	
7) lugal-	7–8) king of the four quarters,
8) an-ub-da-límmu-ba-ke$_4$	
9) u$_6$-nir ki-tuš-maḫ-	9–13) renovated the ziqqurrat, the lofty residence of the god Zababa and goddess Inanna in Kiš.
10) ^{d}za-ba$_4$-ba$_4$	
11) ^{d}inanna-bi-da-ke$_4$	
12) kiš.KI-a	
13) šu-gibil bí-in-ak	
14) sag-bi an-gin$_7$	14–15) He raised its head high as heaven.
15) mi-ni-in-íl	

7

The name of year 24 of Samsu-iluna commemorates two events. The first is the construction of the wall of Kiš. This deed is commemorated in a text known in both Sumerian and Akkadian versions inscribed on clay cylinders from Kiš.

CATALOGUE

Sumerian version

Ex.	Museum number	Excavation number	Uḫaimir provenance	Dimensions (cm)	Lines preserved	cpn
1	Ash 1962,353	–	–	11.3 long, 10.0 max. dia.	1–18, 50–57	c
2	Ash 1929,137	V 232	Surface	–	29–37, 59–75, 104–122	c
3	Ash 1924,1545	HMR 170	Surface	9.0 dia.	21–33, 71–80	c

Akkadian version

Ex.	Museum number	Excavation number	Uḫaimir provenance	Dimensions (cm)	Lines preserved	cpn
1	YBC 2296	–	–	15.2 long, 9.0 dia.	1–138	c
2	MLC 1304	–	–	7.6 long, 8.0 dia.	22–40, 73–74, 76–87	c
3	Ash 1929,138 (+) 1929,138bis	V 232 (+) V 203	Surface		1–13, 15–31, 51–57, 68–84, 113–114, 116–120	c
4	Ash 1924,621	HMR 621	House ruins	9.0 max. dia.	4–13, 51–59	c

COMMENTARY

The master text for the Akkadian version is ex. 1. The lines of the Sumerian frgms. are numbered in the charts according to the corresponding Akkadian line numbers. The line count for the translation follows the Akkadian version.

BIBLIOGRAPHY

Sumerian version
1930 Langdon, Kish 3 pl. xii left (ex. 2, copy)
1969 Sollberger, RA 63 pp. 29–40 (exs. 1-2, copy, edition)
1970 Matthews, First Dynasty of Babylon pp. 221–40 (exs. 1-3, edition)
1971 Sollberger and Kupper, IRSA ivC7d (translation)
1977 Gurney, Essays Finkelstein pp. 93 and 96–97 (ex. 3, copy; exs. 1-3, study)
1983 Kärki, SAKAZ 2 pp. 35–39 (edition)

Akkadian version
1930 Langdon, Kish 3 pl. xii right (ex. 3, partial copy)
1937 Stephens, YOS 9 no. 35 (ex. 1, copy)
1942 Thureau-Dangin, MAIB 43 pp. 239–41 (ex. 1, edition of lines 89–154)
1963 Borger, BAL[1] 2 pp. 48–49 (transliteration); BAL[1] 3 pls. 32–33 (copy in Neo-Assyrian script)
1969 Sollberger, RA 63 pp. 29–40 (edition)
1970 Matthews, First Dynasty of Babylon pp. 221–40 (edition)
1971 Sollberger and Kupper, IRSA ivC7d (translation)
1977 Gurney, Essays Finkelstein pp. 93 and 96–97 (ex. 4, copy, study; ex. 3, provenance)
1983 Kärki, SAKAZ 2 pp. 32–39 (edition)

TEXT

Sumerian
1) ^{d}en-l[íl nam-lugal-la-ni]
2) dingir-e-n[e-er]
3) íb-g[u-la ...]
4) sipa nam [tar-re]
5) ^{d}za-ba$_4$-ba$_4$ ^{d}in[anna]
6) [nun-g]al-e-ne-er
7) [g]ù-mur in-ak-eš-a-aš
8) [igi-kù-g]a-na nam-mu-[u]n-ne-ši-du$_8$
9) [uru] kiš.ki
10) [ki-šu-p]eš-sag-gá
11) [ki-tuš]-maḫ-a-ne-ne
12) [bàd]-bi dù-ù-dè
13) [sag]-bi diri nì-u$_4$-bi-da-ka íl-i-da
14) [šà-ga]-ni zi-dè-eš [na]m-mu-un-túm
15) [^{d}en]-líl en-gal
16) [du$_{11}$-ga-n]i šu nu-bal-e-dam
17) [nam] íb-tar-re-d[a]
18) [nu-kúr-r]u-[da]
Lacuna
1′) [ù-ma-a-n]i-sá-
2′) [du$_{11}$-ga]-ar
3′) [^{d}inanna dumu-munus-à]m
4′) [... ki-ág-gá]-na
5′) [nin nam-dingir-ra]-na
6′) [nu-mu-un]-da-sá-e-a-aš
7′) [igi-ḫúl-la-na m]u-un-ne-ši-
8′) [i]n-bar(erasure?)-ma
9′) [inim-šà-du$_{11}$]-ga-ke$_4$
10′) [mu-u]n-da-ab-bé

Akkadian
1) *^{d}en-líl ša be-lu-sú*
2) *a-na ì-lí šu-úr-ba-at*
3) sipa *mu-ši-im ši-ma-tim*
4) *^{d}za-ba$_4$-ba$_4$ ù* ^{d}inanna
5) *qar-du-tim i-na i-gi-gi*
6) *in bu-ni-šu el-lu-tim*
7) *i-mu-ur-šu-nu-ti-ma*
8) uru *kiš*.ki *ma-ḫa-za-am re-eš-ti-a-am*
9) *šu-ba-at-sú-nu ṣi-ir-tam*
10) bàd-*šu e-pé-ša-am*
11) *re-ši-šu e-li ša pa-na*
12) *ul-la-a-am*
13) *li-ib-ba-šu ki-ni-iš ub-lam-ma*
14) *^{d}en-líl be-lum ra-bi-um*
15) *ša qí-bí-sú*
16) *la uš-te-pe-el-lu*
17) *ši-ma-at i-ši-im-mu*
18) *la ut-ta-ak-ka-ru*
19) *^{d}za-ba$_4$-ba$_4$ a-píl-šu*
20) *dan-nam*
21) *ka-ši-id ir-ni-ti-šu*
22) ^{d}inanna *ma-ar-tam*
23) *na-ra-am-ta-šu*
24) *be-el-tam ša i-lu-sà*
25) *la iš-ša-an-na-nu*
26) *in bu-ni-šu ša ḫe-du-tim*
27) *ip-pa-li-sú-nu-ti-ma*
28) *a-wa-at ṭú-ub li-ib-bi-im*
29) *it-ti-šu-nu i-ta-a-wu*

1–7) The god Enlil, whose lordship is surpassing among the gods, shepherd who determines the destinies, with his shining face looked at the god Zababa and the goddess Eštar, the champions (Sumerian: the ones who speak the loudest) among the Igigi gods.

8–13) His heart truly moved him to build the wall of Kiš, the foremost cult city, their lofty dwelling (and) to raise its head higher than it had been previously.

14–29) The god Enlil, great lord, whose utterance cannot be changed – the destiny that he determines cannot be altered – looked with his joyful face at the god Zababa, his mighty oldest son, the one who achieves his victory, (and) at the goddess Eštar, his beloved daughter, the lady whose divinity is not rivalled, (and) spoke with them happy words:

Akkadian version: **5**.3 *i-gi$_4$-gi$_4$*. **5**.4 *in i-gi$_4$-gi$_4$*. **9**.1 *šu-bat-sú*(text: ba)*-nu*. **9**.3 *ṣi-ir-tá*[*m*]. **9**.4 [*š*]*u-ba-as-su-nu*. **18**.3 [*ut-ta-a*]*k-ka-ra*. **22**.2 [^{d}in]ann[a *ma-ra-sú*]. **23**.2 *na-ra-am-t*[*ám*]. **28**.1 *li-ib-bi-*⟨*im*⟩.

11′) [*sa-am-su-i-l*]*u-na*
12′) [sukkal-kal]a-ga
13′) [nu-kúš]-ù-mu
14′) [šà-túm-ma]-mu
15′) [ki-bi-šè gar-ra in-zu]-a

16′) [giš-nu$_{11}$-zalag-ga-ni ḫé-me-en-zé-e]n

Lacuna

30) *sa-am-su-i-lu-na*
31) *na-aš-pa-ri dan-nam*
32) *la a-ni-ḫa-am*
33) *ša bi-bil li-ib-bi-ia*
34) *a-na aš-ri-im*
35) *ša-ka-nam mu-du-ú*
36) *lu nu-úr-šu na-aw-ru-um*
37) *at-ta-nu-ma*
38) *it-ta-ku-nu*
39) *da-mi-iq-tum*
40) *li-ib-ši-šum-ma*
41) *a-a-bi-šu na-e-ra*
42) *za-e-ri-šu a-na qá-ti-šu*
43) ⸢*mu-ul*⸣*-li-a-ma*
44) ⸢URU *kiš*.KI⸣ BÀD-*šu li-pu-uš*
45) *e-*⸢*li*⸣ *ša pa-na li-ša-te-er*
46) *in šu-ba-at ṭú-ub* [*l*]*i-ib-bi-im*
47) *li-*[*š*]*e-ši-ib-ku-nu-ti*

30–47) 'Samsu-iluna (is) my mighty (and) untiring envoy who knows how to carry out the desire of my heart. May you be his shining light. May your good omen occur for him. Kill his enemies (and) deliver into his hands his foes (in order) that he might build the wall of Kiš, make it greater than it had been previously (and) make you dwell in a happy abode.'

1″) [dingir-e-ne-er š]ili[g-ga-me-eš]
2″) inim a-a-bi ^{d}[en-líl]
3″) in-ne-ši-in-du$_{11}$-[ga-aš]
4″) šà-bi ḫi-li-su$_{13}$ in-[ḫúl]
5″) *sa-am-su-i-lu-*[*na*]
6″) lugal-kala-ga sipa u[r-sag]
7″) šu-du$_{11}$-ga-ne-ne-er
8″) sag-ki nam-ti-la-bi
9″) zalag-ge-eš nam-mu-un-ši-i[n]-zi-ge-eš
10″) inim-ul mu-un-da-ab-bal-bal-e-ne

48) ^{d}⸢*za*⸣*-ba$_{4}$-ba$_{4}$ ù* ^{d}INANNA
49) *be-lu* ⸢*gi*⸣*-it-ma-lu-tum*
50) *ša-ga-pu-ru-tum in ì-lí*
51) *a-na a-wa-at a-bu-šu-nu*
52) ^{d}*en-líl*
53) *iq-bu-šu-nu-ši-im*
54) *li-ib-ba-šu-n*[*u*]
55) *re-ši-iš iḫ-du-ma*
56) *a-na sa-am-su-i-lu-na*
57) LUGAL *da-an-nim*
58) SIPA *qar-ra-dim*
59) *li-pí-it qá-ti-šu-nu*
60) *bu-ni-šu-nu ša ba-*⸢*la*⸣*-ṭim*
61) *na-aw-ri-iš iš-šu-šum-m*[*a*]
62) *el-ṣí-iš it-ti-šu i-ta-wu-ú*

48–62) The god Zababa and goddess Eštar, the perfect and powerful lords among the gods — their hearts merrily rejoiced at the words that their father Enlil had spoken to them. They raised their faces of life brightly towards Samsu-iluna, the mighty king, the valiant shepherd, the creation of their hands, and joyfully spoke with him:

11″) *sa-am-su-i-lu-na*
12″) numun-da-rí-dingir-e-ne-ke$_{4}$
13″) ḫé-du$_{7}$-nam-lugal-la
14″) ^{d}en-líl-le
15″) nam-tar-ra-zu mi-ni-íb-gal
16″) udug-za silim-ma-ta aka-dè
17″) á ba-me-da-an-ág
18″) zà-zi-da-za ù-su$_{8}$-en-dè-en
19″) lú gú mu-e-da-ab-dù-uš-a
20″) sag-giš ba-ab-ra-ra-an-dè-en

63) *sa-am-su-i-lu-n*[*a*]
64) NUMUN *ì-lí da-rí-*[*u*]*m*
65) *wu-sum šar-ru-*[*t*]*im*
66) ^{d}*en-líl ši-ma-*[*t*]*i-ka*
67) *ú-*⸢*šar*⸣*-bí*
68) *a-na ra-bi-ṣú-ti-ka in šu-ul-mi-im*
69) *e-pé-ši-im*
70) *ú-wa-*ʾ*i-ra-an-ni-a-ti*
71) *in im-ni-ka*
72) *ni-il-la-ak*
73) *za-i-ri-ka ni-na-a-ar*

63–79) 'O Samsu-iluna, eternal seed of the gods, one befitting kingship — Enlil has made your destiny very great. He has laid a commission on us to act as your guardians for (your) well-being. We will go at your right side, kill your enemies, and deliver your foes into your hands. (As for) Kiš, our fear-inspiring cult city, build its wall, make it greater than it was previously.'

Akkadian version: **55.4** *iḫ-du-*⸢*u*⸣*-*[*ma*].

21″) lú érim-gál-la-zu-ne
22″) šu-za mi-ni-íb-si-g[e]-en-⌜dè⌝-e[n]
23″) uru kiš.KI ki-š[u-peš ...] x [...]
24″) bàd-bi ù-[dù ...]
25″) nì-šu-IGI.[DU-na-da] diri-[bí-ib]
26″) *sa-am-s[u-i-lu-na]*
Lacuna

1‴) [DINGIR-*n*]*i* lu[gal áš-nun-na.KI]
2‴) inim-ma-na giš-[túg nu-un-na]-an-gá[l-la]
3‴) šu im-m[i-in-du$_8$]
4‴) GIŠ.si-gar gú-[dù-a-ta]
5‴) nam-mi-in-[túm]
6‴) zi-ni gír-[ta] im-mi-i[n-gaz]
7‴) gù-nigin-ki-en-g[i$_4$ ki-uri]
8‴) téš-a im-[mi-in-sì]
9‴) an-ub-da-lí[mmu-ba]
10‴) du$_{11}$-ga-na m[i-ni-in-tuš]
11‴) u$_4$-ba *sa-am-*[*su-i-lu-na*] nita-ka[la-ga]
12‴) usu-u[gnim]-ni-[ta]
13‴) uru kiš.[KI mu-un-dù]

74) *a-a-bi-ka a-na qá-ti-ka*
75) *nu-ma-al-la*
76) URU *kiš*.KI *ma-ḫa-az-ni ra-aš-ba-am*
77) BÀD-*šu bi-ni*
78) *e-li ša pa-na*
79) *šu-te-er-šu*
80) *sa-am-su-i-lu-na*
81) LUGAL *le-iu-um*
82) *še-mu* DINGIR.GAL.GAL
83) *a-na a-wa-at* ^{d}*za-ba*$_4$*-ba*$_4$
84) *ù* ^{d}INANNA *iq-bu-šum*
85) *ra-bí-iš it-kal-ma*
86) GIŠ.TUKUL.GIŠ.TUKUL-*šu*
87) *a-na na-ar a-a-bi*
88) *uš-*[*t*]*e-še-er*
89) KASKAL-*a*[*m*] *a-na ša-ka-aš*
90) *za-i-ri-šu*
91) *ú-še-er-di*
92) *ša-at-tum la im-šu-lam*
93) *ri-im-*^{d}EN.ZU
94) *mu-uš-ba-al-ki-it*
95) KI.EN.GI.SAG.6
96) *ša a-na šar-ru-ut larsa*.KI
97) *in-na-ši-ù*
98) *i-na-ar-ma*
99) *in er-ṣe-et kiš*.KI
100) *dam-tam e-li-šu iš-pu-uk*
101) 26 LUGAL *ḫa-am-ma-i*
102) *za-i-ri-šu i-na-ar*
103) *gi-me-er-šu-nu iš-ki-iš*
104) DINGIR-*ni* LUGAL *iš-nun-na*.KI
105) *la* ⌜*še-mu*⌝ *a-wa-ti-šu*
106) *i-ik-mi*
107) [*i*]*n* GIŠ.SI.GAR
108) *ú-ra-aš-šu-ma*
109) [*n*]*a-pí-iš-ta-šu*
110) *ú-ša-ri-iḫ*
111) ŠU.NIGIN [K]ALAM *šu-me-ri-im ù ak-ka-di-im*
112) *uš-te-eš-mi*
113) *ki-ib-ra-at er-bé-tim*
114) *a-na qí-bí-ti-šu*
115) *ú-še-ši-ib*
116) *ì-nu-mi-šu*
117) *sa-am-su-i-lu-na da-núm*
118) *in e-mu-uq um-ma-ni-šu-ma*
119) URU *kiš*.KI *ib-ni*

80–91) Samsu-iluna, the capable king, the one who listens to the great gods, was greatly encouraged by the words which the god Zababa and the goddess Eštar spoke to him. He made ready his weapons in order to kill his enemies and set out on an expedition to slaughter his foes.

92–115) The year was not half over when he killed Rīm-Sîn (II), who had caused Emutbala to rebel, (and) who had been elevated to the kingship of Larsa. In the land of Kiš he heaped up a burial mound over him. Twenty-six rebel kings, his foes, he killed; he destroyed all of them. He defeated Iluni, the king of Ešnunna, one who had not heeded his decrees, led him off in a neck-stock, and had his throat cut. He made the totality of the land of Sumer and Akkad be at peace, made the four quarters abide by his decree.

116–127) At that time, Samsu-iluna, the mighty, by means of the force of his army built the city of Kiš. He dug its canal, surrounded it with a moat, (and)

Akkadian version: **118**.2 *i-na* [...]. **118**.3 *i-na*.

14‴) *ḫi-ri-t*[*um*-bi mu-un-ba-al]

15‴) [s]aḫar-g[al-ta suḫuš-bi]

Lacuna

120) *ḫi-ri-sú iḫ-ri*
121) AMBAR *uš-ta-ás-ḫi-ir-šu*
122) *in e-pé-ri ra-bi-ù-tim*
123) SUḪUŠ.SUḪUŠ-*šu ki-ma* SA.DÚ-*im ú-ki-in*
124) SIG$_4$-*šu ú-ša-al-bi-in*
125) BÀD-*šu i-pu-uš*
126) *in* ŠÀ MU.1.A.KAM *re-ši-šu*
127) *e-li ša pa-na ú-ul-li*
128) *a-na šu-a-ti*
129) ^{d}*za-ba$_4$-ba$_4$ ù* ^{d}INANNA
130) *a-na sa-am-su-i-lu-na*
131) *ru-bé-em ta-li-mi-*⸢*šu*⸣*-nu*
132) *šu-ul-ma-am ù ba-la-ṭam*
133) *ša ki-ma* ^{d}EN.ZU
134) *ù* ^{d}UTU *da-rí-um*
135) *a-*[*n*]*a qí-i*[*š*]*-tim*
136) *li-qí-šu-šum*
137) *a-na še-ri-ik-tim*
138) *li-iš-ru-ku-šum*

with a great deal of earth made its foundations firm as a mountain. He formed its bricks and built its wall. In the course of one year he made its head rise up more than it had been before.

128–138) On account of this may the god Zababa and goddess Eštar grant as a present well-being and life which like the gods Sîn and Šamaš is eternal, to Samsu-iluna, the prince, their favourite brother; may they present it to him as a gift.

8

The second part of the name of year 24 of Samsu-iluna commemorates the construction of 'Fort Samsu-iluna' on the banks of the Turul (Diyala) river. This deed is described in a text inscribed on clay cylinders from Khafajah in both a Sumerian and Akkadian version. The provenance of ex. 2 tells us that Mound B at Khafajah was the site of Dūr-Samsu-iluna.

CATALOGUE

Sumerian version

Ex.	Museum number	Excavation number	Provenance	Dimensions (cm)	Lines preserved	cpn
1	VA 5951	BE 46430	Babylon, found at Merkes, K 222–2.10 m.	13.1 long 7.4 dia.	1–94	c
2	IM 42465	–	Khafajah, mound B from the north corner of a gate room of a large Old Babylonian building	–	1–94	c

COMMENTARY

The translation and line count follow the Sumerian version, which is complete. The master text is ex. 1, found during Koldewey's excavations at Babylon. Ex. 2 was collated from a cast of the cylinder in Philadelphia.

The only ex. of the Akkadian version is the cylinder fragment A 22088 (Chicago), excavation no. Kh 35-7-86, from mound B at Khafajah. It measures 9×6.7×3.8 cm and was collated by M. Civil.

BIBLIOGRAPHY

Sumerian version
1933–34 Poebel, AfO 9 pp. 241–92 (ex. 1, copy, edition)
1938 Speiser, BASOR 70 pp. 5 and 8–10 (ex. 2, photo, study)
1938 Delougaz, ILN Dec. p. 1026 and fig. 3 (ex. 2, photo, provenance)
1942 Thureau-Dangin, MAIB 43 pp. 243–46 (ex. 1, edition [omits i 2–24])
1942 Iraq Museum Guide pl. XXVII (ex. 2, photo)
1952 Delougaz, Pottery p. 123 and n. 198 (ex. 2, provenance)
1969 Sollberger, RA 63 p. 41 (exs. 1–2, study)
1970 Matthews, First Dynasty of Babylon pp. 241–54 (edition)
1971 Sollberger and Kupper, IRSA IVC7e (study)
1983 Kärki, SAKAZ 2 pp. 39–43 (edition)
1984 Römer, TUAT 1/4 pp. 325–28 (translation)

Akkadian version
1935–36 Frankfort, AJSL 52 p. 210 (provenance)
1938 Speiser, BASOR 70 pp. 8–9 (study)
1969 Sollberger, RA 63 p. 42 (edition)
1970 Matthews, First Dynasty of Babylon pp. 241–54 (edition)
1971 Sollberger and Kupper, IRSA IVC7e (study)
1983 Kärki, SAKAZ 2 pp. 41–43 (edition)

TEXT

Sumerian	Akkadian	
1) *sa-am-su-i-lu-na*		1–6) Samsu-iluna, mighty king, king of Babylon, king of Kiš, king who makes the four quarters be at peace,
2) lugal-kala-ga		
3) lugal-KÁ.DINGIR.RA.KI		
4) lugal-kiš.KI-a		
5) lugal gù-an-ub-da-límmu-ba-ke$_4$		
6) téš-a bí-in-sì-ga		
7) lugal á-ág-gá-		7–19) king who at the order of the gods An and Enlil slew all those who engaged in hostility against him, shepherd to whom the goddess Inanna gave her favourable omen and help, who bound the hands of all those who were disloyal, who made all evil ones disappear in the land,
8) an-^{d}en-líl-ka-ta		
9) nigin lú-gú mu-da-ab-dù-uš-a		
10) giš-gaz-šè		
11) bí-in-ak-a		
12) sipa ^{d}inanna-ke$_4$		
13) giškim-sa$_6$-ga-ni		
14) nam-á-daḫ-a-ni		
15) in-ak-a-àm		
16) lú an-da-gur-eš-a zà-til-ba		
17) šu in-ne-en-dù-a		
18) lú-érim-gál-la-ne-ne-a		
19) kalam-ma ú-gu mi-ni-in-dé-a		
20) u$_4$-zalag-ga un-šár-ra-ba		20–24) who caused bright daylight to come forth for the numerous people, foremost first-born son of Ḫammu-rāpi, the lord who extended the land,
21) íb-ta-an-è-a		
22) ibila-sag-kala	Lacuna	
23) *ḫa-am-mu-ra-pí*	1′) [*ḫa-am-mu-ra-p*]*í*	
24) en kalam-ma in-dagal-la-ke$_4$	2′) [*be-li*]-*im mu-ra-ap-*[*pí*]-*iš ma-tim*	
25) lugal-e ma-da-	3′) [LUGAL] *ša ma-at*	25–41) king who subjugated the land of Idamaraz from the border of Gutium to the border of Elam with his mighty weapon, who conquered the numerous people
26) *i-da-ma-ra-az*-ke$_4$	4′) [*i-d*]*a-ma-ra-a*[*z*.KI]	
27) zà-*gu-ti-um*.KI-ta	5′) [*iš-t*]*u pa-aṭ* [*g*]*u-ti-um*.[K]I	
28) en-na-zà-NIM.KI-ka-šè	6′) [*a-d*]*i pa-aṭ* [NI]M.[K]I-*tim*	
29) GIŠ.tukul-kala-ga-ni-ta	7′) *in ka-ak-ki-šu da-nim*	

Sumerian version: **9.2** mu-un-da-. **14.2** á omitted. **24.1** in-dagal-la-a; -a inscribed over another sign. **28.2** -zà-kur-NIM.KI-.

Sumerian	Akkadian	English
30) gú giš bí-in-gar-gar-ra	8′) [*ú*]-*ka*-[*a*]*n-ni-š*[*u*]	of the land of Idamaraz, who demolished all the various fortresses of the land of Warûm who had resisted him, who achieved his victory and made his strength apparent.
31) un-dagal-la-ma-da	Lacuna	
32) *i-da-ma-ra-az*-ka		
33) šu-ni sá bí-in-du$_{11}$-ga		
34) nigin bàd-didli-		
35) ma-da-*wa-ru-um*-ma-ke$_4$		
36) gú an-da-an-bar-eš-a		
37) GIŠ.al-ta bí-in-ra-a		
38) ù-ma-na		
39) sá bí-in-du$_{11}$-ga		
40) nam-á-gál-la-na		
41) pa-è bí-in-ak-a		
42) iti-min-àm ba-zal-la-ta		42–49) After two months had passed, having set free and given life to the people of the land of Idamaraz whom he had taken captive, (and) the troops of Ešnunna, as many prisoners as he had taken,
43) un-ma-da-*i-da-ma-ra-az*-ka		
44) nam-ra-aš bí-in-ak-a		
45) ù érin-áš-nun-na.KI-me-eš-a		
46) LÚ×KÁR-a en-na bí-in-dab-ba-aš		
47) šu mi-ni-in-bar-ra		
48) šu-nam-ti-la-ke$_4$		
49) in-ne-ši-in-gar-ra		
50) bàd-didli-ma-da		50–56) he (re)built the various fortresses of the land of Warûm which he had destroyed (and) regathered and resettled its scattered people.
51) *wa-ru-um*-ma-ke$_4$		
52) mu-un-gul-gul-la		
53) bí-in-dù-dù-a		
54) un-sag-du$_{11}$-ga-bi	Lacuna	
55) gú-ba nam-mu-un-ne-en-gar-ra	1″) ⌜*ú*⌝-*pa-aḫ-ḫi-ru-m*[*a*]	
56) ki-bi-šè bí-in-gi$_4$-a	2″) *a-na aš-ri-ši-n*[*a*] 3″ *ú-te-er-ru*	
57) u$_4$-ba *sa-am-su-i-lu-na* nita-kala-ga-e	4″) *ì-nu-mi-šu* 5″) *sa-am-su-i-lu-na da-núm*	57–65) At that time, Samsu-iluna, mighty man: in order that the people who dwelled along the banks of the Turul and Ṭabān rivers might reside in peaceful abodes; that they might have no one who terrified them; (and) in order that all the land might sing the praise of his mighty valour;
58) un gú-i$_7$-*dur-ùl*-	6″) *ni-ši wa-ši-ba-at* 7″) GÚ Í[D *tú*]*r-ù*[*l*]	
59) gú-I$_7$.*ṭa-ba-an*-na-ka	8″) *ù* Í[D *ṭ*]*a-ba-an*	
60) ba-dúr-ru-ne-eš-a		
61) ki-tuš-ne-ḫa-a tuš-ù-dè	9″) *šu-ba-at ne*-[*eḫ-tim*] 10″) *a-na šu-šu-b*[*i-im*]	
62) lú-ḫu-luḫ-ḫa nu-tuk-tuk-dè	11″) *m*[*u-gal-li-tam*] 12″) [*ana lā šuršêm*]	
63) á-kala-ga	Lacuna	
64) nam-ur-sag-gá-na		
65) kur-gú-si-a ka-tar-šè si-il-le-dè		
66) šà-iti-min-kam-ma-ka-àm		66–76) in the course of two months, on the bank of the Turul river, he built Fort Samsu-iluna. He dug its (surrounding) moat, piled up its earth there, formed
67) gú-I$_7$.*dur-ùl*-ka-ta		
68) bàd-*sa-am-su-i-lu-na-a*		
69) bí-in-dù		
70) I$_7$.*ḫi-ri-tum*-bi		

Sumerian version: **34**.2 Second half of didli sign is -ḫal rather than -aš. **45**.2 iš-nun-. **46**.2 lú-a. **50**.2 didli omitted. **51**.2 *wa-ri-um*-. **64**.2 nam-ur-sag-gá-ka-na. **65**.2 si-il-si-le-dè. **68**.2 omits -a at end.

71) im-mi-in-ba-al
72) saḫar-bi im-mi-in-dub
73) sig$_4$-bi mi-ni-íb-du$_8$
74) bàd-bi bí-in-dù
75) sag-bi ḫur-sag-gin$_7$
76) mu-ni-in-íl

its bricks, (and) built its wall. He raised its head like a mountain.

77) nam-bi-šè
78) an ^{d}en-líl
79) ^{d}AMAR.UTU
80) ^{d}en-ki
81) ^{d}inanna-bi-da-ke$_4$
82) GIŠ.tukul-kala-ga
83) gaba-ri nu-un-tuk-a
84) nam-ti ^{d}nanna
85) ^{d}utu-bi-gin$_7$-nam
86) gi$_{16}$-sa-aš ak-a
87) nam-a-ni-šè
88) mu-ni-in-tar-re-eš
89) sa$_{12}$-e-éš mu-ni-in-rig$_7$-eš

77–89) On account of this the gods An, Enlil, Marduk, Enki, and goddess Inanna determined as his destiny (and) gave to him: a mighty weapon that has no rival (and) a life that like (that of) the gods Nanna and Utu is eternal.

90) bàd-ne-e
91) ^{d}en-líl-le
92) *sa-am-su-i-lu-na*-ra
93) kalam lú gú mu-un-da-ab-dù-uš-a
94) mu-na-an-GAM-GAM mu-bi-im

90–94) The name of that wall is 'The god Enlil has made the land of those who had become hostile to him bow down to Samsu-iluna'.

9

The name of year 31 of Samsu-iluna records the fashioning of a statue of Samsu-iluna made of alabaster stone. This is possibly the same statue described in a royal inscription known from a fragment of a tablet copy now in Berlin.

COMMENTARY

The tablet is VAT 1433, purchased from the Hornsy collection, original provenance unknown. It measures 6.7×5.9 cm and the inscription was collated.

Lines 2′–3′, which contain the end of the geneaology of Samsu-iluna, reveal names found in the Assyrian King List, as well as the tablet with the genealogy of the Ḫammu-rāpi dynasty published by Finkelstein (see bibliography).

If this inscription does deal with the statue of the king referred to in the name of year 31, then the same event is probably described in a hymn of the goddess Inanna known from two exs., CBS 4568 = Langdon, PBS 10/2 no. 11 and CBS 6051A + N 6622 (unpublished; see Farber-Flügge, Kramer Anniversary pp. 177–81). In this text the goddess Inanna blesses a statue of the king presented to her by Samsu-iluna and sings the praises of the king. This accords well with the evidence of the royal inscription, which tells us that the statue was set up in Eturkalama, Inanna's temple in Babylon.

Sumerian version: **75**.2 omits this line. **81**.2 ù ^{d}inanna-. **93**.2 omits -ab-.

BIBLIOGRAPHY

1917 Schroeder, VAS 16 no. 156 (copy)
1921 Meissner, OLZ 24 18–19 (edition)
1965 Kraus, Könige pp. 7–9 (study)
1966 Finkelstein, JCS 20 p. 98 (study)
1970 Matthews, First Dynasty of Babylon pp. 255–57 (edition)

TEXT

Lacuna
1′) [...] x x [...]
2′) [...] *a-bi a-bi-šu*
3′) [...]-*bi-ga ḫa-ar-ḫa-ar ma-da-ra*
4′) x [...] ^{d}EN.ZU
5′) *a-na-ku* ⸢*sa*⸣-[*am*]-*su-i-lu-na*
6′) *ša* ALAM.NA$_4$.GIŠ.NU$_{11}$.GAL
7′) [*š*]*a* 60 + 20 + 4 GÚ *ši-bi-ir-tam*
8′) *iš-ti-a-at šu-uk-lu-ul-tam*
9′) *i-na* É.TÙR.KALAM.MA
10′) *uš-zi-zu*
11′) LUGAL *ša ki-ma ia-a-ti*
12′) *ša* ALAM NA$_4$.GIŠ.NU$_{11}$.GAL
13′) ⸢*ša*⸣ 60 + ⸢20 + 4⸣ GÚ *ši-bi-ir-tam iš-ti-a-at*
14′) [*š*]*u*-[*u*]*k-lu-ul-tam*
15′) [*i-n*]*a* É.TÙR.KALAM.MA
16′) [*u*]*š-za-az-zu*
17′) [*š*]*u-mi ki-ma sa-am-su-i-lu-na*
18′) [...] x ⸢*li*-IK⸣-x [...]
19′) [...] x [...]
Lacuna

Lacuna
1′–10′) [...] ... [...], his forefather, [...]biga, Ḫarḫar, Madara, [...] Sîn. I, Sa[m]su-iluna, who set up a statue of alabaster stone [o]f 84 talents, a perfect block, in the Eturkalama.

11′–19′) (As for) the king who like me sets up a statue of alabaster of 84 talents, a p[e]rfect block, [i]n Eturkalama, may *they proclaim* his name like (that of) Samsu-iluna.
Lacuna

1001

A tablet excavated by the Hilprecht expedition to Nippur contains a copy of one or more dedicatory inscriptions of a king of the first dynasty of Babylon. It should be probably attributed to either Ḫammu-rāpi or Samsu-iluna. The text mentions Marduk, Zarpanītum, and the Esagila temple in Babylon. It deals with the construction of some cult object, probably a throne or dais on which the deity sat. The name of the cult object, which is in Akkadian, appears in i 9′–10′.

Although the fragmentary nature of the text makes its contents obscure, it may be connected with the fashioning of a pair of daises for Marduk and Zarpanītum which is commemorated in the name of year 19 of Samsu-iluna. Hence the inscription is edited at this point.

COMMENTARY

The tablet is Ni 9694, now in Istanbul. The inscription was not collated.

We have assumed that the deity who figures throughout col. i is Zarpanītum, who is alluded to in i 11′.

BIBLIOGRAPHY

1969 Kramer, Çıg, and Kızılyay, ISET 1 p. 109 pl. 51 Ni 9694 (copy)
1972 Civil, Orientalia NS 41 p. 86 sub 9694 (study)

TEXT

Col. i
Lacuna
1′) [...] x x x
2′) [...]-x bí-in-sa$_4$-a
3′) [...-b]i bí-íb-íl-la
4′) [x-dingir-re]-⸢e⸣-ne-ka mi-ni-íb-gu-ul-la
5′) [...]-gal ní-ḫuš-bi ri-ga(*) ezen-ezen-da mi-ni-in-da-tuš
6′) [...] x x nam-en-na-ka dúr gal-le-eš in-na-an-gar
7′) [...] x x x la nì-sa$_6$-ga-ni(*)
8′) [á-z]i-da-na mi-ni-in-gub
9′) [...] *zi-ik-ru-uk-ki*
10′) [...] AN *li-ib-lu-uṭ* mu-bi-im

Lacuna
i 1′–5′) ..., which he named, its ... which he elevated, ... which he made great [in the *midst of the gods*], great [...] seated in a fearsome splendour, she sat down beside ...,
i 6′) ... on a ... of *en*-ship she grandly sat down.
i 7′–8′) ..., her good thing, he set up on her right [side].
i 9′–10′) 'May he live ... at your command' is its name.

11′) [x x] x-a-an-na dam-ki-ág-^{d}AMAR.UTU
12′) [... b]í-in-dág-dág-ga
13′) [...] x x bí-in-gar-ra
14′) [...] x-⸢in⸣-[x]
Lacuna

i 11′–14′) [...] ... of An, beloved wife of the god Marduk, ... which he made clean, which he set ...
Lacuna

Col. ii
Lacuna
1′) x x x x mu x [...]
2′) mu-ru-ub-dingir-re-e-ne x [...]
3′) ^{d}*zar-pa-ni-tum* ama-ugu-mu-um-[...]
4′) giš-tuk-a inim-gar x x [...]
5′) inim-^{d}AMAR.UTU lugal-x-[...]
6′) é-sag-íl-la x [...]
7′) ḫé-en-na-ab-ku$_4$-[ku$_4$-re]
8′) nam-zà-tag-ga [...]
9′) i$_7$-uru-na-ka [...]
10′) a-šà-uru-na-ka [...]
11′) EZEN PA dingir-e-ne-ke$_4$ [...]
12′) giš-tag-ga mu-⸢pà⸣-da [...] zà [...]
13′) x [...]
Lacuna

Lacuna
ii 1′–2′) ... among the gods ...
ii 3′–4′) Zarpanītum, the mother who bore me, ..., the one who hears, ... reports
ii 5′) the word of Marduk, king ...
ii 6′–7′) May he bring [... it into] Esagil for him/her.
ii 8′) the overthrow ...
ii 9′) In the canal of his city ...
ii 10′) In the field of his city ...
ii 11′) ... of the gods ...
ii 12′–13′) offerings, one who proclaims [his] name, [...] ...
Lacuna

---

i 5′ Tablet: bi. i 7′ Tablet: DÙ.

1002

A fragment of a barrel cylinder with an inscription of Old Babylonian date was found at Kiš. Unfortunately, the name of the king responsible for this inscription does not appear in the extant portion of the text. The similarities of the text to E4.3.7.7 lines 86–91 suggest that it might be an inscription of Samsu-iluna.

COMMENTARY

The piece is Ash 1931,142, the left end of a barrel cylinder with a maximum dia. of 8 cm. It was found at Kiš, Inghara YW 0.50 m. Akkadian. The inscription was collated.

BIBLIOGRAPHY

1970 Matthews, First Dynasty of Babylon pp. 279–80 (edition)
1977 Gurney, Essays Finkelstein pp. 93–94 and 97 (copy, edition)

TEXT

Lacuna
1′) ⌜^{d}*en-líl*⌝ *er-*⌜*ṣe-tim*⌝ x [...]
2′) GIŠ.TUKUL.GIŠ.⌜TUKUL⌝-*šu u*[*š-te-še-er* KASKAL-*am*]
3′) *a-na ša-qá-áš za-i-ri ú-ša-a*[*r-di* ...]
4′) ^{d}*za-*ba_4-ba_4 *ù* ^{d}INANNA EN.MEŠ [...]
5′) [*a-n*]*a šu-um-qú-ut* ⌜*a*⌝-[*a-bi-šu* ...]
6′) [*a-n*]*a ka-ša-ad ir-ni-i*[*t-ti-šu* ...]
7′) [*il*]*-li-ku re-ṣu-u*[*s-su* ...]
8′) [...] x ⌜*šu-mi iš*⌝*-ku-un* NUN [...]
Lacuna

Lacuna
1′) Enlil of the lands ... [...]
2′–3′) he pr[epared] his weapons and le[d an expedition] to crush his enemies.

4′–7′) The god Zababa and goddess Eštar, lords [... c]ame as [his] help [... t]o fell [his] e[nemies ...] (and) [t]o achieve [his] victory.

8′) He established *my* name [...]
Lacuna

2001

The impression of the seal of Ilšu-ibbīšu, *šandabakkum* and *gudapsûm* priest of Nanna, is found on two tablets excavated at Ur.

CATALOGUE

Ex.	Museum number	Excavation number	Provenance	cpn
1	–	U 6360	Ur, from the Gipar-ku, room C. 26 (Old Babylonian), or room 63 (Kassite period)	n
2	IM 67695	U 6367	As ex. 1	n

BIBLIOGRAPHY

1928 Gadd, UET 1 no. 149 (exs. 1–2, copy, edition)
1932–33 Burrows, Orientalia NS 1 p. 248 no. 3 (transliteration, study)
1965 Woolley, UE 8 p. 42 (provenance)
1976 Woolley and Mallowan, UE 7 p. 58 n. 13 and p. 223 (provenance)
1986 Charpin, Le clergé d'Ur p. 122 (edition)

TEXT

1) DINGIR-*šu-i-bi-šu*	1) Ilšu-ibbīšu,
2) PISAN.DUB.BA GÚDA.ABZU-^{d}nanna	2) archivist (and) *gudapsûm* priest of Nanna,
3) DUMU ^{d}EN.ZU-*i-qí-ša-am*	3) son of Sîn-iqīšam,
4) IR$_{11}$ *sa-am-su-i-lu-na*	4) servant of Samsu-iluna.

2002

The impression of another *šandabakkum* official is found on the same pair of tablets as E4.3.7.2001.

BIBLIOGRAPHY

1928 Gadd, UET 1 no. 151 (exs. 1–2, copy, edition)
1965 Woolley, UE 8 p. 42 (provenance)
1976 Woolley and Mallowan, UE 7 p. 58 n. 13 and p. 233 (provenance)

TEXT

1) [...]-*úḫ-pu-*⌜*um*⌝	1) [...]uḫpum,
2) PISAN.DUB.BA-^{d}nanna	2) archivist of Nanna,
3) DUMU AN-*pi*$_{4}$-*šu* GÚDA.[ABZU]	3) son of Anum-pîšu, *gud*[*apsûm*] priest,
4) IR$_{11}$ *sa-am-su-i-lu-na*	4) servant of Samsu-iluna.

2003

The impression of Aḫūšunu, servant of Samsu-iluna, is also found on the same two tablets as E4.3.7.2001.

BIBLIOGRAPHY

1928 Gadd, UET 1 no. 150 (exs. 1–2, copy, edition)
1965 Woolley, UE 8 p. 42 (provenance)
1976 Woolley and Mallowan, UE 7 p. 58 n. 13 and p. 233 (provenance)

TEXT

1)	*a-ḫu-šu-nu*	1) Aḫūšunu,
2)	DUMU *im-ṭi-*^{d}*en-líl*	2) son of Imṭi-Enlil,
3)	IR$_{11}$ *sa-am-su-i-lu-na*	3) servant of Samsu-iluna.

2004

The impression of a seal of a servant of Samsu-iluna is found on a tablet envelope in Washington.

COMMENTARY

The impression is on Catholic University of America no. 57 and measures 2 cm high. It was not collated.

BIBLIOGRAPHY

1957 Buchanan, JCS 11 pl. 1 after p. 42 nos. 7–9 and p. 46 (photo, study)
1957 Goetze, JCS 11 pp. 106–107 (edition)

TEXT

1)	^{d}asar-lú-ḫi-lú-t[i(?) ...]	1) Asalluḫi-lu-t[i...],
2)	[DUB].SAR	2) [sc]ribe,
3)	DUMU ^{d}AMAR.UTU-*mu-ša-*[*lim*]	3) son of Marduk-muša[llim],
4)	IR$_{11}$ *sa-am-su-i-lu-na*	4) servant of Samsu-iluna.

2005

A small tablet at Yale bears the impression of a seal of a servant of Samsu-iluna.

COMMENTARY

The impression is on NBC 1240, an undated tablet. The impression measures 1.1 × 2.2 cm and was collated.

BIBLIOGRAPHY

1920 Keiser, BIN 2 no. 105 (copy)
1923 Ungnad, HG 6 no. 1528 (translation)
1952–53 Weidner, AfO 16 p. 24 (study)
1969 Finkelstein apud Lambert, ZA 59 p. 101–102 (study)

TEXT

1) ^{d}*nin-urta-a-b[i]*
2) DUMU ^{d}[EN].⌜ZU⌝-x [x]
3) IR$_{11}$ *sa-[a]m-su-i-lu-na*

1) Ninurta-ab[ī],
2) son of [S]în-[...],
3) servant of Samsu-iluna.

2006

A tablet from Sippar dating to the reign of Ammī-ṣaduqa has the impression of a seal of a servant of Samsu-iluna.

COMMENTARY

The impression is on BM 80160 (Bu 91-5-9,276). It was collated.

BIBLIOGRAPHY

1964 Pinches, CT 45 no. 60 (copy)

TEXT

1) *šu-ì-[lí-šu]*
2) DUMU *i-din-*[...]
3) IR$_{11}$ *sa-am-s[u-i-lu-na]*

1) Šū-i[līšu],
2) son of Iddin-[...],
3) servant of Sams[u-iluna].

2007

A cylinder seal has the inscription of Dakīia, servant of Samsu-iluna.

COMMENTARY

The seal is University of Illinois, Urbana no. O-M 129. The inscription was collated from a published photo. The seal was formerly in the Kalebjian collection when published by Scheil.

R.A. Martin, in discussing this piece, thought that the Damiq-ilīšu mentioned in the text was the name of the king of Isin. However, since this is a rather common personal name, we see no reason to connect the Damiq-ilīšu of this seal with the Isin king.

BIBLIOGRAPHY

1916 Scheil, RA 13 p. 13 no. 4 (transliteration) and pl. II no. 13 (photo)
1940 Martin, Ancient Seals of the Near East = Anthropology leaflet 34, Field Museum of Natural History p. 18 no. 7 (photo) and p. 19 (edition, study)
1969 Dodson, Archaeology 22 p. 102 (photo)

TEXT

1) *da-ki-ia*	1) Dakīa,
2) DUMU *da-mi-iq-ì-lí-šu*	2) son of Damiq-ilīšu,
3) IR$_{11}$ *sa-am-su-i-lu-na*	3) servant of Samsu-iluna.

2008

The impression of a seal of Adad-rabi, servant of Samsu-iluna, is found on two clay tablets in Cambridge.

CATALOGUE

Ex.	Museum number	cpn
1	FM 27	n
2	FM 38	n

COMMENTARY

The tablets are Fitzwilliam Museum nos. 27 and 38. Adad-rabi's name is restored from the tablet.

BIBLIOGRAPHY

1963 Szlechter, Manchester 1 pl. I FM 38 and pl. XIII FM 27 (exs. 1–2, copy); Manchester 2 p. 131 and 136 (exs. 1–2, transliteration)

TEXT

1) ^{d}IŠKUR-*ra-[bi]*	1) Adad-ra[bi],
2) DUMU *ḫa-zi-r[u-u]m*	2) son of Ḫazir[u]m,
3) ÌR *sa-am-su-i-lu-[na]*	3) servant of Samsu-ilu[na].

2009

The impression of a servant of Samsu-iluna is found on a tablet in Geneva.

COMMENTARY

The impression is on MAH 16194 dating to year 24 of Samsu-iluna. It was not collated. Muḫuški appears as a GAL MAR.DÚ on the tablet.

BIBLIOGRAPHY

1958 Szlechter, Geneva 1 pl. XXIX top left (copy); Geneva 2 p. 56 (transliteration)

TEXT

1) *mu-ḫu-uš-ki*	1) Muḫuški,
2) ÌR *sa-am-su-i-lu-na*	2) servant of Samsu-iluna.

2010–20

A number of impressions of seals of servants of Samsu-iluna are found on tablets in the Yale collections published by Feigin in YOS 12. These are edited here as E4.3.7.2010–20.

2010

This seal impression is on a tablet dating to year 4.

COMMENTARY

The impression is on YBC 6381, measuring 1.3 cm high. It was collated. Collation provides a reading slightly different from that given by Feigin.

BIBLIOGRAPHY

1979 Feigin, YOS 12 no. 116 (copy)

TEXT

1) ⸢d⸣[...] x x [...]	1) ...,
2) [D]UB.[SAR]	2) [s]cr[ibe],
3) [D]UMU *li-pí-i*[*t*-...]	3) [s]on of Lipi[t-...],
4) IR$_{11}$ ^{d}sa-am-su-[i-lu-na]	4) servant of Samsu-[iluna].

2011

The impression is found on YBC 5564 dating to year 2. The impression measures 1.1 × 2 cm and was collated. Bara-ule-gara, which appears in the personal name in line 2, was possibly the tutelary deity of the city of Ṣarbillum (cf. the name of year 2 of Rīm-Sîn, RLA 2 p. 161).

BIBLIOGRAPHY

1979 Feigin, YOS 12 no. 46 (copy)

TEXT

1)	É-*r*[*a-bi*]	1) Bītum-r[abi],
2)	DUMU [d]bára-ul-e-gar-ra-[x (x)]	2) son of Bara-ule-gara[...],
3)	IR_{11} *sa-am-su-i-lu-*[*na*]	3) servant of Samsu-ilu[na].

2012

The impression is found on YBC 7978 and YBC 5510 dating to years 1 and 11 of Samsu-iluna. It was collated.

BIBLIOGRAPHY

1979 Feigin, YOS 12 nos. 29 and 343 (exs. 1–2, copy)

TEXT

1)	*i-din-*[d]EN.ZU	1) Iddin-Sîn,
2)	DUMU *a-bu-um-wa-qar*	2) son of Abum-waqar,
3)	IR_{11} *sa-am-su-i-lu-na*	3) servant of Samsu-iluna.

2013

The impression is found on YBC 5652 dated to year 23 of Samsu-iluna. It measures 1.2×2.3 cm and was collated.

TEXT

1)	[d]AMAR.UTU-*na-ṣ*[*i-ir*]	1) Marduk-nāṣ[ir],
2)	AB.[AB.DU_7]	2) *ab*[*abdûm*] priest,
3)	DUMU *ì-lí-*[...]	3) son of Ilī-[...],
4)	IR_{11} *sa-am-su-*[*i-lu-na*]	4) servant of Samsu-[iluna].

2014

The impression is found on YBC 5652 dated to year 23 of Samsu-iluna. It measures 1.2×2.3 cm and was collated.

BIBLIOGRAPHY

1979 Feigin, YOS 12 no. 430 (copy)

TEXT

1) ᵈAMAR.UTU-*zu-uq-qí-i*[*p*]	1) Marduk-zuqqi[p],
2) DUMU *a-ḫu-um-wa-qar*	2) son of Aḫum-waqar,
3) IR₁₁ ᵈ*sa*-[*am-su-i-lu-na*]	3) servant of Sa[msu-iluna].

2015

The impression is found on YBC 6746 and YBC 5397 dating to years 4 and 6 of Samsu-iluna.

COMMENTARY

The impressions measure 1×2.2 cm. Ex. 1 was collated.

Sîn-muštāl is elsewhere known to have served as governor of Larsa. His seal as servant of Rīm-Sîn II is edited as E4.2.15.2003.

BIBLIOGRAPHY

1976 Stol, Studies in Old Babylonian History p. 51 (study of Sîn-mūstāl)
1979 Feigin, YOS 12 nos. 113 and 167 (exs. 1–2, copy)

TEXT

1) ᵈEN.ZU-*mu-uš-ta*-[*al*]	1) Sîn-muštā[l],
2) DUMU ᵈEN.ZU-*ma-g*[*ir*]	2) son of Sîn-māg[ir],
3) IR₁₁ *sa-am-su-i-lu-n*[*a*]	3) servant of Samsu-ilun[a].

2016

The impression is found on YBC 7739 dating to year 5 of Samsu-iluna. It measures 1.2 cm and was collated.

BIBLIOGRAPHY

1979 Feigin, YOS 12 no. 142 (copy)

TEXT

1) *ṭà-ab-wa-ša-ab-[šu]* 1) Ṭāb-wašāb[šu],
2) DUMU *lu-pa-ḫír-qí-bi-[su]* 2) son of Lupaḫḫir-qibī[ssu],
3) IR₁₁ *sa-am-su-i-lu-[na]* 3) servant of Samsu-ilu[na].

2017

The impression is found on YBC 7972 dating to year 4 of Samsu-iluna. It measures 1.2×2.4 cm and was collated.

BIBLIOGRAPHY

1979 Feigin, YOS 12 no. 123 (copy)

TEXT

1) [d]UTU-AN.DÙL 1) Šamaš-ṣulūlī,
2) [DUMU] *nu-úr-ì-lí-šu* 2) [son] of Nūr-ilīšu,
3) [IR₁₁] *sa-am-s[u-i-lu-na]* 3) [servant] of Sams[u-iluna].

2018

The impression is found on YBC 8726 dating to year 17 of Samsu-iluna.

COMMENTARY

The impression, measuring 1.1 cm high, is not well preserved; it is difficult to read because the tablet has cracked into two pieces. It was collated.

BIBLIOGRAPHY

1979 Feigin, YOS 12 no. 388 (copy)

TEXT

1) [d]⸢UTU⸣-*na-ṣi-ir* 1) Šamaš-nāṣir,
2) DUMU *a-pi[l-...]* 2) son of Api[l-...],
3) IR₁₁ *sa-a[m-su-i-lu-na]* 3) servant of Sa[msu-iluna].

2019

The impression is found on YBC 6100 dating to year 6 of Samsu-iluna. It measures 1.4 × 2.9 cm and was collated.

BIBLIOGRAPHY

1979 Feigin, YOS 12 no. 173 (copy)

TEXT

1) dUTU-*na-ṣi-[ir]*	1) Šamaš-nāṣi[r],
2) DUMU *ša-lim-sag-[il]*	2) son of Šalim-sag[il],
3) IR11 *sa-am-su-i-⌜lu⌝-[na]*	3) servant of Samsu-ilu[na].

2020

The impression is found on YBC 6022 dating to year 25 of Samsu-iluna. It measures 1 cm high and was collated.

BIBLIOGRAPHY

1979 Feigin, YOS 12 no. 461 (copy)

TEXT

1) [...]	1) [...],
2) DU[B.SAR]	2) sc[ribe],
3) [DUMU ...]	3) [son of ...],
4) IR11 *sa-am-su-i-lu-na* lu[gal]	4) servant of Samsu-iluna, the ki[ng].

Abī-ešuḫ

E4.3.8

Samsu-iluna was succeeded by his son Abī-ešuḫ, who reigned 28 years. Very few royal inscriptions survive from his reign.

1

A year formula of Abī-ešuḫ records construction work of the king at the city of Luḫaia. This work is also commemorated in a royal inscription of Abī-ešuḫ known from copies on two tablet fragments, one of them bilingual. Luḫaia lay to the north of Babylon on the Araḫtum canal, the canal which flowed through Babylon.

CATALOGUE

Ex.	Museum number	Excavation number	Registration number	Dimensions (cm)	cpn
1	BM 38446	From Rassam's excavations in Babylonia	80-11-12,329	7.8×6.4	c
2	BM 55472+40125	–	82-7-4,45	7.7×7.0	c

COMMENTARY

The Sumerian version is a conflation of exs. 1 and 2. The line count follows ex. 1 for lines 1′–3′ and ex. 2 for lines 4′–21′.

The join of BM 40125 as the rev. of BM 55472 is new since the publication of the latter by E. Sollberger. The preceding information was kindly communicated by C.B.F. Walker. The translation and line count follow the Sumerian version.

Ex. 2 was purchased by Spartoli in Babylonia.

BIBLIOGRAPHY

1894 Winckler, AOF 1/2 p. 200 (ex. 1, copy)

1898–1900 King, LIH no. 68 (ex. 1, copy, edition)

1970 Matthews, First Dynasty of Babylon pp. 260–63 (exs. 1–2, edition)

1971 Sollberger and Kupper, IRSA ivC8a (exs. 1–2, translation)

1977 Sollberger, Essays Finkelstein pp. 198–200 (ex. 2, copy, edition)

1983 Kärki, SAKAZ 2 pp. 43–44 (edition)

TEXT

Sumerian	Akkadian	
Lacuna		
1′) ⌜šà⌝-[bal-bal]-	Lacuna	1′–2′) [Abī-ešuḫ] ... de[scendant]
2′) *s*[*u*]-*mu-la-ì*[*l*-ke$_4$]	1′) ⌜*ša*⌝ [*s*]*u*-[*mu-la*]-*ì*[*l*]	of S[ū]mû-la-I[l],
3′) ibi[la]-nir-g[á]l-	2′) DUMU.NITA *e*-⌜*te*⌝-*el-lu*[*m*]	3′–10′) princely hei[r] of Samsu-
4′) [*s*]*a-am-su-i-lu-na*-ke$_4$	3′) *ša sa-am-su-i-lu-n*[*a*]	iluna, eternal seed of kingship,
5′) [numu]n-[d]a-rí-	4′) NUMUN *da-rí-um*	mighty king, king of Babylon,
6′) [na]m-lugal-la-ke$_4$	5′) *ša šar-ru-tim*	king of the land of Sumer and
7′) [lugal-ka]la-ga	6′) LUGAL *da-nú*[*m*]	Akkad,
8′) [lugal-KÁ].DINGIR.RA.KI-a	7′) LUGAL KÁ.DINGIR.RA.[KI]	
9′) [lugal-ki-e]n-gi-ki-uri-ke$_4$	8′) LUGAL KALAM *šu*-[*me-ri-im*]	
10′) (blank)	9′) *ù ak-k*[*a-di-im*]	
11′) [lugal an-ub]-da-límmu-ba-ke$_4$	10′) LUGAL *mu-u*[*š-te-eš-mi*]	11′–12′) [king who makes the] four [quar]ters be at [pea]ce,
12′) [gù-téš-a] íb-sì-ga	11′) *ki-ib-r*[*a-at ar-ba-im*]	
	12′) *in* ⌜GÚ I$_7$⌝-*a*-⌜*ra-aḫ*⌝-*t*[*im*]	
13′) [*lu-ḫa-i*]*a*.KI	13′) *lu-ḫa-i*[*a*.KI]	13′–15′) Luḫaia, an abode of joy,
14′) [ki-tuš-s]ù-ga-ke$_4$	14′) *šu-ba-at re-ša-a-tim*	on the bank of the Araḫtum
15′) gú I$_7$.*a-ra-aḫ-tum*-ka-[t]a	Lacuna	canal,
16′) *ḫa-am-mu-ra-pí*		16′–20′) which Ḫammu-rāpi, [h]is
17′) ad-da-[n]i		forefather, had built, (and) which
18′) [b]í-in-dù-⌜a⌝		as a result of its old age had
19′) [n]am-sumun-bi-[ta]		become dilapidated,
20′) [ba]-gul-[la]		
21′) [gib]i[l-bi] mu-n[i-in-dù]		21′) he [built] a[ne]w.
Lacuna		
1″) [...]-šè	1″) (blank)	1″–9″) No translation warranted.
2″) [...]-a	2″) (blank)	
3″) [...]-x-gal	3″) *zi-ik*-x-[...]	
4″) [...]-eš-a-ta	4″) *ba-nu*-[...]	
5″) [...] gu-ul-lu-[...] x-aš	5″) *du-rí*-[...]	
6″) [...]-li	6″) *li*-x-[...]	
7″) [...] ḫé-mú-mú	7″) ^{d}[x] *li*-[...]	
8″) [... g]i$_{16}$-sa ḫé-em-[...]-x	8″) *ša* [...] *lu*	
9″) [...] x [...] x	9″) *šu-ba*-[...]	

2

An eye-stone acquired by the Ashmolean Museum contains the remains of a dedication to the goddess Ningal by Abī-ešuḫ.

COMMENTARY

The piece is Ash 1922,293, purchased in Mosul. It is made of onyx and measures 2.1 × 1.4 cm and was collated. The original eye-stone was later trimmed to resemble two joined eye-stones, around the edges of which was added: *ana* ^{d}*nin-gal* x ^{m}*aš-šur-uballiṭ*(TI) IGI-*ma*.

BIBLIOGRAPHY

1923 Langdon, RA 20 pp. 9–11 (copy, edition)
1970 Matthews, First Dynasty of Babylon pp. 264–65 (edition)
1971 Sollberger and Kupper, IRSA ɪᴠC8b (translation)
1983 Kärki, SAKAZ 2 p. 44 (edition)

TEXT

1) ᵈ⌜nin⌝-gal	1) For the goddess Ningal,
2) [n]in-a-ani-ir	2) his [l]ady,
3) ⌜*a*⌝-*bi-e-šu-uḫ*	3) Abī-ešuḫ,
4) lugal-ᴋᴀ́.ᴅɪɴɢɪʀ.[ʀᴀ].ᴋɪ-ke₄	4) king of Babylon,
5) [a mu-na-ru]	5) [dedicated] (this eye-stone).

1001

A fragment of a clay cylinder excavated at Kiš bears a Sumerian inscription that probably belonged to one of the kings of the Old Babylonian dynasty. It may be an inscription of Abī-ešuḫ.

COMMENTARY

The cylinder fragment is Ash 1924,616, which probably originally contained six cols., of which parts of the last three are at present preserved. It has a dia. of 6.7 cm and a height of 5.5 cm. The piece was excavated at Kiš (Tell Uḫaimir), temple area, the great wall E–F beneath brickwork, excavation no. HMR 194.

The inscription mentions the Tigris river (i 4′), a gate built against the rebellious land (ii 4′), the fashioning of a weapon (ii 5′), and the digging of a canal (ii 2′). These deeds may be connected respectively with the damming of the Tigris river commemorated in the name of year 'o' of Abī-ešuḫ, the mention of the Tigris gate (ká-gal-ɪ₇.idigna) of the year 'm', the fashioning of the mace of the god Marduk of year 'g', and the digging of the Zubi canal of year 'i'. In view of the tentative nature of these correlations a definite attribution of the inscription to Abī-ešuḫ cannot be proved, although the OB king appears as the most likely candidate as author of the text.

BIBLIOGRAPHY

1977 Gurney, Essays Finkelstein pp. 93 and 97 (copy, transliteration)

TEXT

Col. i	
Lacuna	Lacuna
1′) [...]-⌜ra⌝	i 1′) ...
2′) [...g]ù-dé-a	i 2′) ... called
3′) ⌜lugal⌝-dalla	i 3′) resplendent king,
4′) [l]ugal ⌜ɪ₇⌝.ɪᴅɪɢɴᴀ	i 4′) king of the Tigris river,
5′) [l]ugal ne-⌜sag⌝	i 5′) king who ... first fruit offerings
6′) x ɴᴇ [x] x	i 6′) ...
7′) [x] me-kur-k[ur] x	i 7′) ... of the foreign lands ...

Col. ii
Lacuna
1′) šul ⌜ka⌝-tar-a-⌜ni(?)⌝
2′) i_7-dè nu-ba[l]-⌜a⌝
3′) lugal am-am-kur ra-ra
4′) ká-ki-bala dím
5′) GIŠ.tukul-ḫuš dím
6′) [kur] dúb-dúb
Col. iii
Lacuna
1′) x […]
2′) gá(?) […]
3′) lú […]

Lacuna
ii 1′) the hero *whose* fame …
ii 2′) the canal not having been dug,
ii 3′) the king who smites the wild bulls of the foreign lands,
ii 4′) who built the gate against the rebellious land,
ii 5′) who fashioned the angry weapon,
ii 6′) which causes the [foreign land] to quake

Lacuna
iii 1′–3′) (No translation warranted)

2001

A seal impression of a servant of Abī-ešuḫ is in the Yale collections.

COMMENTARY

The impression is on MLC 2239, a tablet dating to year 20 of Ammī-ditāna. It was not collated.

BIBLIOGRAPHY

1972 Finkelstein, YOS 13 p. 92 no. 476 (transliteration)

TEXT

1) *la-ma-nu-um*
2) DUMU *be-el-ku-ul-la*
3) ÌR *a-bi-e-šu-uḫ*

1) Lamānum,
2) son of Bēl-kulla,
3) servant of Abī-ešuḫ.

2002

The impression of a seal of a servant of Abī-ešuḫ is found on two tablets dating to years ‘m’ and ‘y’ of Abī-ešuḫ.

COMMENTARY

The impression is on YBC 8385 and YBC 5885. It was not collated.

BIBLIOGRAPHY

1972 Finkelstein, YOS 13 p. 92 no. 488 (ex. 1, transliteration) and no. 383 (ex. 2, copy)

TEXT

1) *lu-uš-ta-mar*-^{d}IŠKUR	1) Luštāmar-Adad,
2) DUMU DUMU-ZIMBIR.KI	2) son of Mār-Sipparim,
3) ÌR *a-bi-e-šu-uḫ* lugal	3) servant of Abī-ešuḫ, the king.

2003

A seal impression on a tablet in the Yale collections gives the name of a servant of Abī-ešuḫ.

COMMENTARY

The impression is on MLC 1539, a tablet measuring 1.5×2.4 cm. It was collated.

BIBLIOGRAPHY

1972 Finkelstein, YOS 13 p. 90 no. 331 (transliteration)

TEXT

1) ^{d}NÀ-an-[da-sá]	1) Nabiʾum-an[dasa],
2) DUMU DINGIR-*šu-ib-*[*ni-šu*]	2) son of Ilšu-ib[nīšu],
3) [I]R$_{11}$ *a-bi-e-*[*šu-uḫ*]	3) [ser]vant of Abī-e[šuḫ].

2004

An impression of a seal of a servant of Abī-ešuḫ is found on a tablet in the University Museum of Manchester, England.

COMMENTARY

The impression is on UMM 36. It was not collated.

BIBLIOGRAPHY

1963 Szlechter, Manchester 1 pl. xxv (copy); Manchester 2 p. 56 (transliteration)

TEXT

1)	[...]	1) [...],
2)	DUMU *a-wi-il-*[...]	2) son of Awīl-[...],
3)	ÌR *a-bi-e-šu-uḫ*	3) servant of Abī-ešu[ḫ].

2005

A cylinder seal of a servant of Abī-ešuḫ is in Berlin.

COMMENTARY

The seal is VA 3242, made of red chalcedony, 2.5 cm long, 1.6 cm in dia. The impression was collated from the published photo.

BIBLIOGRAPHY

1940 Moortgat, VAR no. 494 (photo, edition)

TEXT

1)	*ìl-šu-na-ṣi-ir*	1) Ilšu-nāṣir,
2)	MÁŠ.ŠU.GÍD.GÍD	2) diviner,
3)	DUMU [d]AMAR.UTU-*na-ṣi-ir*	3) son of Marduk-nāṣir,
4)	IR_{11} *a-bi-e-šu-uḫ*-ke_4	4) servant of Abī-ešuḫ.

2006

Although the seal edited here is clearly a forgery, it may have been copied from a genuine original.

COMMENTARY

The object is BM 89101 (88-5-12,773), a forged cylinder seal of haematite. It measures 3.2 cm long, 1.4 cm in dia., and the inscription was collated by C.B.F. Walker.

BIBLIOGRAPHY

1986 Collon, Cylinder Seals 3 no. 617 (photo, edition)

TEXT

1)	*i-din-*^{d}UTU	1) Iddin-Šamaš,
2)	SANGA ^{d}nin-in-si-na	2) *sanga* priest of the goddess Ninisina,
3)	DUMU kù-^{d}nin-in-si-na	3) son of Ku-Ninisina,
4)	ÌR *a-bi-e-šu-uḫ*-ke$_{4}$	4) servant of Abī-ešuḫ.

2007

A seal in the Lands of the Bible Archaeology Foundation has an inscription of a servant of Abī-ešuḫ.

COMMENTARY

The seal is made of carnelian and measures 3.0 × 1.4 cm. The impression was collated from the published photo. The seal has been patched with modern plastic and the patch inscribed with badly formed signs to complete the inscription.

BIBLIOGRAPHY

1981 Williams-Forte in O. Muscarella (ed.), Ladders to Heaven pp. 106–107 no. 66 (photo, edition)

TEXT

1)	^{d}EN.ZU-*i-din-na*[*m*]	1) Sîn-iddina[m],
2)	UGULA DAM.⸢GÀR⸣	2) overseer of the merchants,
3)	DUMU ^{d}*še-rum-ba-n*[*i*]	3) son of Šērum-bān[i],
4)	ÌR *a-bi-e-šu-*[*uḫ*-ke$_{4}$]	4) servant of Abī-ešu[ḫ].

Ammī-ditāna

E4.3.9

Abī-ešuḫ was succeeded by his son Ammī-ditāna, who reigned 37 years. Two building inscriptions of the king are known.

1

An inscription of Ammī-ditāna deals with the king's construction of the wall of Babylon.

COMMENTARY

Ex. 1, a Neo-Babylonian tablet, bears the museum number BM 38308 (80-11-12,185) and is from Rassam's excavations in Babylonia. The tablet measures 6.4×7 cm and the inscription was not collated. Ex. 2, whose present location is unknown, is from Babylon, excavation no. BE 36067, from Merkes, 0.20 025^{11}. It is a fragment of a clay cylinder with parts of columns 1 and 2 preserved. The inscription was collated from Babylon photo 1594.

BIBLIOGRAPHY

1891 Pinches, RP NS 5 p. 102 (ex. 1, translation)
1894 Winckler, AOF 1/2 p. [199] (ex. 1, copy)
1898–1900 King, LIH no. 100 (ex. 1, copy, edition)
1923–24 Langdon, AJSL 40 p. 227 n. 4 (ex. 1, study)
1926 Ebeling, ATAT^{2} p. 338 (ex. 1, translation)
1959 von Soden, WZKM 55 p. 57 n. 1 (ex. 1, study)
1971 Sollberger and Kupper, IRSA IVC9a (ex. 1, translation)
1972 Alster, Orientalia NS 41 p. 350 n. 4 (ex. 1, study of colophon)
1977 Frymer-Kensky, The Judicial Ordeal in th ncient Near East p. 566 (ex. 1, study)
1983 Kärki, SAKAZ 2 p. 45 (ex. 1, edition)

TEXT

Col. i
1) *am-mi-di-*[*ta-n*]*a*
2) lugal-kala-[g]a
3) lugal-KÁ.DINGIR.RA.K[I]-a
4) lugal-kiš.K[I]-a
5) lugal-ki-en-gi-ki-u[ri.KI-k]e$_{4}$
6) lugal-da-ga-a[n]-kur-mar-dú.KI-a-me-en
7) šà-bal-bal-
8) *su-mu-la-ìl-*⌜*a*⌝
9) [d]umu-ur-sag-gal-
10) *a-bi-e-šu-uḫ*-a-me-en
11) še-[ga]-^{d}en-líl-lá

i 1–12) I, Ammī-di[tān]a, mighty king, king of Babylon, king of Kiš, king of the land of Sumer and Ak[kad], king of all the Amorite land, I, descendant of Sūmû-la-Il, [s]on of the great champion Abī-ešuḫ, favour[ite] of the god Enlil, belo[ved of the goddess ...]
Lacuna

12) ki-á[g-^{d}...]
Lacuna
Col. ii
1) ⌜KÁ⌝.DINGIR.RA.KI-a
2) uru.KI
3) nam-lugal-la-gá-a
4) inim-⌜maḫ(?)⌝-ni an-ki-[a] íb-ta-s[a$_4$-a]

ii 1–4) In Babylon, the city of my kingship, he cal[led] his lofty decree [in] heaven and earth.

5) u$_4$-bi-[a]
6) nam-kù-zu-[a]
7) ^{d}en-[ki-ke$_4$]
8) šu-a ḫé(?)-[...]-an-[...-gar-ra-ta]
9) x [...]
10) x [...]
Lacuna

ii 5–10) At that time, by the wisdom that the god En[ki verily granted] to me,
Lacuna

1′) [x] bi [...]
2′) [...] ki-tuš asila^{lá}-[ka]
3′) [ḫé]-bí-ni-dúr-ru

ii 1′–3′) I made (Babylon) dwell in an abode of joy.

4′) bàd-bi
5′) ^{d}asar-lú-ḫi
6′) lú im-a bí-in-búr-ru-da-a
7′) im ki-a ḫa-ra-ab-gá-gá
8′) mu-bi-i[m]

ii 4′–8′) The name of that wall is 'May Asarluḫi turn into clay in the underworld the one who makes a breach in the clay (of the wall)'.

Colophon (ex. 1)
šá ^{md}EN-*ú-ša-al-li-im*
⌜A⌝ ^{m}*d*[*a-bi*]-*bi* LÚ *a-ši-pu*

Colophon (ex. 1)
(Property) of Bēl-ušallim, son of D[ābi]bi, the exorcist.

2

A bilingual building inscription of Ammī-ditāna is known from a tablet copy now in the Brockmon Collection in Haifa.

COMMENTARY

The tablet is BT (Brockmon Tablets) 5, an OB copy from Nippur, and measures 11.5 × 10.5 × 2.8 cm. The obv. and rev. contain two cols. each and about two-thirds of the bottom part of this broken tablet remains. The line count and translation follow the Akkadian version.

The identification of the ŠAR-BI-*it* canal of line 27′ is uncertain. Perhaps it is connected with the town Ṣarbatum, the construction of whose wall gave its name to year 1 of Sîn-muballiṭ (see Stol, Studies in Old Babylonian History p. 28 n. 9).

BIBLIOGRAPHY

1910 Hilprecht, Deluge Story p. 9 and n. 1 (study)
1989 Kutscher, Brockmon Tablets pp. 103–107, 116, and 124 (photo, copy, edition)

TEXT

Sumerian

Lacuna

1′) [...-à]m
2′) [...]-bi-x-eš-ta
3′) [nam-en-na-mu]-šè
4′) [mas-šù nu-x-x]-ìl-da
5′) [ka-kù-ga]-ne-ne-ta [b]í-in-e-eš-⌜a⌝-ta
6′) [^{d}utu ^{d}]AMAR.UTU-bi-da
7′) bala-⌜gá⌝ ki in-ši-in-á[g-gá]-eš-a
8′) nam-lugal-la-mu
9′) an-ub-da-límmu-ba-àm
10′) íb-ta-an-diri-ge-eš-àm
11′) un sag-gi$_6$-ga-ke$_4$
12′) nam-en-na-ne-ne-a-⌜ta⌝
13′) ma-ra-an-til-le-[eš-à]m
14′) ki-en-gi ki-uri-[ke$_4$] si íb-ta-an-[sá]
15′) un-dagal-la ki-tuš-ne-[ḫa]-ta
16′) in-né-ni-dúr-ru
17′) šà ma-da-gá-aš bí-du$_{10}$
18′) u$_4$-bi-ta
19′) nam-kù-zu-a
20′) ^{d}en-ki-ke$_4$
21′) ma-an-sum-ma-ta
22′) un kalam-ma-gá ì-dagal-le-eš-a
23′) un ú-kú ù a-nag nir-gál-la-ta
24′) nir-gál-bi in-ne-en-lu-⌜un⌝-na-aš
25′) ú-sal-la-aš in-ne-éb-ta-n[ú]-ù-dè
26′) BÀD *am-mi-di-ta-na*.KI-a
27′) gú I$_7$.ŠAR-BI-*it*-ka-ta
28′) ki ^{d}utu-è-a-ta
29′) [k]i ^{d}utu-šú-a-bi-da-ta
30′) [x]-ne-ni-dím
31′) [bàd-gal]-gal-la-ni bí-dù
32′) [ḫur-sa]g-gin$_7$
33′) [ki] bí-íb-ta-a-ús
34′) [mu-maḫ]-a-mu
35′) [u$_4$-ul$_4$-lí-a-šè p]a bí-è
36′) [...]-bi
37′) [...]-le

Lacuna

Akkadian

Lacuna

1′) [...]
2′) *re-ši-⌜ia⌝ ú-u[l-l]i-[im]*
3′) *an be-lu-ti-i[a]*
4′) *ma-an-su-am la na-[šêm]*
5′) *in pí-i-šu-nu el-lim iq-[bûnim]*
6′) ^{d}UTU *ù* ^{d}AMAR.UTU
7′) *ra-i-mu* BALA-*ia*
8′) *šar-ru-ti*
9′) *in kib-ra-a-tim*
10′) *ú-ša-te-ru-ma*
11′) UN *ṣa-al-ma-at qá-qá-di-⌜im⌝*
12′) *an be-lim*
13′) *ú-ga-am-ma-ru-nim*
14′) *ma-at šu-me-ri-im ù ak-[kadîm]*
15′) *uš-te-še-er*
16′) *ni-ši ra-ap-ša-a-[tim]*
17′) *⌜šu⌝-bat ne-eḫ-tim ú-[šēšibšunūti]*
18′) ⌜ŠÀ⌝-*bi ma-ti-im ⌜ú⌝-[ṭīb]*
19′) *in u$_4$-m[i-šú]*
20′) *in ne-me-qí-i[m]*
21′) *ša* ^{d}*é-a i-di-nam*
22′) *a-na ni-ši ma-ti-ia ra-ap-ša-[tim]*
23′) *in ri-tim ù ma-aš-qí-tim ta-[klātim(?)]*
24′) *e-te[l]-li-iš re-ie*(PI)*-em*
25′) *a-bur-re šú-ur-bu-ṣi-ši-n[a]*
26′) BÀD *am-mi-di-ta-na*.KI
27′) *in pu-ut* I$_7$.ŠAR-BI-*i[t]*
28′) *in ṣi-it* ^{d}UTU-*ši*
29′) *in e-reb* ^{d}UTU-*ši*
30′) *ab-ni*
31′) *du-ra-na-šú-nu ra-bí-ù-tim*
32′) *ki-ma ša-du-i-im*
33′) *e-pu-uš*
34′) *ú-šar-ši-id*
35′) *šu-mi ṣi-ra-am*
36′) *an ṣe-a-tim*
37′) *ú-šu-[pí]*
38′) BÀD X-[X]

Lacuna

Translation

Lacuna

1′–5′) [Ammī-ditāna] ... (the gods) decreed by their pure utterance that I lift (high) my head and that no leader rise against my rule.

6′–18′) The gods Šamaš and Marduk, who love my reign, made my kingship surpassing in the (Sumerian ‘four’) quarters and wholly entrusted me to rule the black-headed people. I provided justice for the land of Sumer and Akkad and settled the widespread people in peaceful abodes. I made the (Sumerian ‘my’) land content.

19′–25′) At that time, by the wisdom that the god Ea gave to me, in order to superbly shepherd the widespread people of my land by means of fine pastures and watering places and to make them lie down in (safe) pastures,

26′–34′) I built Fort Ammī-ditāna on the bank of the ŠAR-BI-it canal, to the east and the west. I built its (Sumerian ‘his’, Akkadian ‘their’) great walls. I made them firm as a mountain.

35′–37′) I made my august name famous forever.

38′) The wall ...

Lacuna

2001

Impressions of seals of a large number of servants of Ammī-ditāna are known. These are edited here.

The first is found on two tablets from Sippar.

COMMENTARY

Ex. 1 is AO 2502. Ex. 2 is HG 96.

BIBLIOGRAPHY

1910 Thureau-Dangin, TCL 1 no. 151 (ex. 1, copy)
1923 Delaporte, Louvre 2 A 562 (ex. 1, edition)
1988 Charpin, RA 82 pp. 28–30 seal E (ex. 2, copy, edition)

TEXT

1) *e-tel-pi*$_4$-^{d}*na*-[*bi-um*]	1) Etil-pî-Na[bium],
2) SANGA ^{d}*a*-[*a*]	2) *sanga* priest of the goddess A[ia],
3) DUMU ^{d}AMAR.UTU-*mu-š*[*a-lim*]	3) son of Marduk-muš[allim],
4) [Ì]R *am*-⸢*mi-di*⸣-*t*[*a-na*]	4) [ser]vant of Ammī-dit[āna].

2002–10

Impressions of seals of a number of judges, servants of Ammī-ditāna, are found on a tablet dealing with a legal case dating to year 24 of Ammī-ditāna. These are edited here as E4.3.9.2002–10. The impressions are on AO 4657. They were not collated.

BIBLIOGRAPHY

1910 Thureau-Dangin, TCL 1 no. 157 (copy)
1910 Thureau-Dangin, RA 7 pp. 121–27 (edition)
1923 Delaporte, Louvre 2 A 567 (photo, edition [E4.3.9.2002 and 2004])
1982 Wilcke, Kraus Festschrift p. 463 (transliteration)

2002

TEXT

1) ⸢^{d}⸣EN.ZU-*iš-me-a*-[*ni*]	1) Sîn-išmeʾa[nni],
2) [DU]MU *ib-ni*-^{d}[...]	2) [s]on of Ibni-[...],
3) [I]R$_{11}$ *am-mi-da-ta*-[*na*-ke$_4$]	3) [ser]vant of Ammī-ditā[na].

2003

TEXT

1) ^{d}*tu-tu-na-ṣi-ir*	1) Tutu-nāṣir,
2) DI.KU$_5$	2) judge,
3) DUMU *ib-ni-*^{d}AMAR.UT[U]	3) son of Ibni-Mard[uk],
4) ÌR *am-mi-di-t*[*a-na*-ke$_4$]	4) servant of Ammī-dit[āna].

2004

TEXT

1) *ib-ni-*^{d}[UTU]	1) Ibni-[Šamaš],
2) DUMU IR$_{11}$-^{d}E[N.ZU]	2) son of Warad-S[în],
3) IR$_{11}$ *am-mi-di-ta-*[*na*-ke$_4$]	3) servant of Ammī-ditā[na].

2005

TEXT

1) DINGIR-*bu-ul-*[*li-iṭ*]	1) Ilum-bul[liṭ],
2) DUMU *i-ba-al-*[*lu-uṭ*]	2) son of Ibal[luṭ],
3) I[R]$_{11}$ *am-mi-di-t*[*a-na*-ke$_4$]	3) [ser]vant of Ammī-dit[āna].

2006

TEXT

1) *i-bi-*^{d}*n*[*i*]*n-*⸢*šubur*⸣	1) Ibbi-N[i]nšubur,
2) DUMU ⸢IR$_{11}$-^{d}EN.ZU⸣	2) son of Warad-Sîn,
3) IR$_{11}$ *am-mi-di-ta-*⸢*na*⸣-ke$_4$	3) servant of Ammī-ditāna.

2007

TEXT

1) *a-wi-i*[*l*]-^{d}*na-bi-um*	1) Awī[l]-Nabium,
2) [D]UMU *i-ba-al-lu-uṭ*	2) [s]on of Ibbaluṭ,
3) ÌR *am-mi-di-ta-na*	3) servant of Ammī-ditāna.

2008

TEXT

1) *šu-^{d}na-bi-u[m]*
2) DI.⌜KU$_{5}$⌝
3) DUMU ^{d}*na-bi-um-ga-mil*
4) IR$_{11}$ *am-mi-di-ta-na*-ke$_{4}$

1) Šū-Nabiu[m],
2) judge,
3) son of Nabium-gāmil,
4) servant of Ammī-ditāna.

2009

TEXT

1) *im-gur-*^{d}⌜EN⌝.Z[U]
2) [D]UMU ir$_{11}$-^{d}E[N.ZU]
3) ⌜IR$_{11}$⌝ [*am-mi-di-ta-na*-ke$_{4}$]

1) Imgur-Sî[n],
2) [s]on of Warad-S[în],
3) servant [of Ammī-ditāna].

2010

TEXT

1) *ú-ṭul-eš$_{4}$-tár*
2) DUMU *e-tel-pi$_{4}$*-^{d}AMAR.UTU
3) ÌR *am-mi-di-ta-na*-ke$_{4}$

1) Uṭul-Eštar,
2) son of Etel-pî-Marduk,
3) servant of Ammī-ditāna.

2011

A tablet in the University Museum of Manchester dating to year 31 of Ammī-ditāna has a seal impression of a servant of the king. A duplicate of this seal impression is in the Morgan Library Collection.

COMMENTARY

Ex. 1 is found on UMM G 59. It was not collated. Ex. 2 is found on MLC 2656.

BIBLIOGRAPHY

1963 Szlechter, Manchester 1 pl. xxx G 59 (ex. 1, copy); Manchester 2 p. 63 (ex. 1, transliteration)

1982 Wilcke, Kraus Festschrift p. 432 C (ex. 2, transliteration)

TEXT

1) *ìl-šu-ba-ni*
2) UGULA NIN.DINGIR ^{d}za-b[a$_4$-ba$_4$]
3) DUMU *ìl-šu-ib-ni*
4) ÌR *am-mi-di-ta-na*-k[e$_4$]

1) Ilšu-bāni,
2) overseer of the NIN.DINGIR priestess of the god Zab[aba],
3) son of Ilšu-ibni,
4) servant of Ammī-ditāna.

2012

Another tablet in the University Museum of Manchester has the impression of a servant of Ammī-ditāna.

COMMENTARY

The impression is on UMM G 5 from Sippar, dating to year 25 of Ammī-ditāna. It was not collated.

BIBLIOGRAPHY

1963 Szlechter, Manchester 1 pl. xxi G 5 (copy); Manchester 2 p. 145 (transliteration)

TEXT

1) *ab*-[...]
2) [DU]MU *na-bi*-^{d}[...]
3) [Ì]R ⌜*am*⌝-*mi-di-ta*-[*na*]

1) Ab[...],
2) [s]on of Nabi-[...],
3) [ser]vant of Ammī-ditā[na].

2013

The impression of Ilšu-ibni, overseer of the merchant bankers, servant of Ammī-ditāna, is found on three tablets from Sippar.

CATALOGUE

Ex.	Museum number	Registration number	cpn
1	AO 1671	–	n
2	BM 80161	Bu 91-5-9,277	n
3	BM 80217	Bu 91-5-9,346	n

COMMENTARY

R. Harris (Ancient Sippar p. 71) points out that Ilšu-ibni was unusual in holding the position of overseer of the merchant bankers, an office normally held for one year only, for a full 22 years during the reign of Ammī-ditāna.

TEXT

1)	*ìl-šu-ib-ni*	1) Ilšu-ibni,
2)	UGULA DAM.GÀR	2) overseer of the merchant bankers,
3)	DUMU ^{d}*èr-ra*-[...]	3) son of Erra-[...],
4)	IR_{11} *am-mi-di-ta*-[*na*]	4) servant of Ammī-ditā[na].

2014

The impression of a seal of Ibni-Marduk, the diviner, servant of Ammī-ditāna is found on a tablet in the British Museum.

COMMENTARY

The impression is on BM 80223 (Bu 91-5-9,353) dating to year 24 of Ammī-ditāna. It was not collated.

BIBLIOGRAPHY

1964 Pinches, CT 45 no. 50 (copy)

TEXT

1)	*ib-ni*-^{d}AMAR.UTU	1) Ibni-Marduk,
2)	MAŠ.ŠU.GÍD.GÍD	2) diviner,
3)	DUMU *ib-ni*-^{d}EN.ZU	3) son of Ibni-Sîn,
4)	ÌR *am-mi-di-ta-na*-ke_4	4) servant of Ammī-ditāna.

2015

The fragmentary impression of a servant of Ammī-ditāna is found on another tablet in the British Museum.

COMMENTARY

The impression is on BM 80157 (Bu 91-5-9,271), probably from Sippar. It was not collated.

BIBLIOGRAPHY

1964 Pinches, CT 45 no. 54 (transliteration)

TEXT

Lacuna
1′) [ÌR *am*]-*mi-di-ta*-[*na*]

Lacuna
1′) [servant of Am]mī-ditā[na].

2016

A broken seal impression of a servant of Ammī-ditāna is found on a tablet in the British Museum.

COMMENTARY

The impression is on BM 81466 (Bu 91-5-9,1598). It was not collated.

BIBLIOGRAPHY

1968 Finkelstein, CT 48 no. 102 (translation)

TEXT

1) [...]
2) [...]
3) DUMU ^{d}[...]
4) ÌR *am-mi-di-ta*-⸢*na*⸣

1–4) [...] son of [...], servant of Ammī-ditāna.

2017

Another fragmentary seal impression of a servant of Ammī-ditāna is found on a tablet in the British Museum.

COMMENTARY

The impression is on BM 78296 (Bu 88-5-12,161). It was not collated.

BIBLIOGRAPHY

1968 Finkelstein, CT 48 no. 50 (transliteration)

TEXT

1) ^{d}EN.ZU-[...]	1) Sîn-[...],
2) x x ^{d}[...]	2) ... [...],
3) ÌR *am-mi-[di-ta-na]*	3) servant of Ammī-[ditāna].

2018

A number of tablets in the Morgan Library Collection now at Yale published by Finkelstein in YOS 13 bear seal impressions of servants of Ammī-ditāna. These are edited here as E4.3.9.2018–24.

COMMENTARY

The first impression is that on MLC 70 dating to year 11. It measures 1.2 cm high and was collated.

BIBLIOGRAPHY

1972 Finkelstein, YOS 13 p. 86 no. 16C (transliteration)

TEXT

1) *ni-di-[...]*	1) Nidi[...],
2) DUMU ^{d}[...]	2) son of [...],
3) ÌR x *am-[mi-di-ta-na]*	3) servant of Am[mī-ditāna].

2019

The seal impression is on MLC 1540. It measures 1.8 × 1.9 cm and was collated.

BIBLIOGRAPHY

1972 Finkelstein, YOS 13 p. 89 no. 274 (transliteration)

TEXT

1) [...][d][...]	1) [...],
2) DUB.SAR	2) scribe,
3) DUMU *na-bi-*[d][...]	3) son of Nabi-[...],
4) ÌR *am-mi-di-[ta-na]*	4) servant of Ammī-di[tāna].

2020

The seal impression is on MLC 1694, dating to year 31 of Ammī-ditāna. It was not collated.

BIBLIOGRAPHY

1972 Finkelstein, YOS 13 p. 90 no. 348 (transliteration)

TEXT

1) *iš-me-*[d][EN.ZU]	1) Išme-[Sîn],
2) DUB.SAR	2) scribe,
3) DUMU [d]EN.ZU-*i-ri-[ba-am]*	3) son of Sîn-irī[bam],
4) ÌR *am-mi-di-ta-[na]*	4) servant of Ammī-ditā[na].

2021

The seal impression is on MLC 657 dating to year 13 of Ammī-ditāna. It was not collated. Sîn-nādin-šumi appears as *sanga* priest of the goddess Inanna of Kiš in YOS 13 no. 348 line 21.

BIBLIOGRAPHY

1972 Finkelstein, YOS 13 no. 94B (copy)
1982 Wilcke, Kraus Festschrift p. 455 C (transliteration)

TEXT

1) ^{d}EN.ZU-*na-di-i*[*n-šu-mi*]	1) Sîn-nādi[n-šumi],
2) SANGA ^{d}*za-ba*$_4$-[*ba*$_4$]	2) *sanga* priest of the god Zaba[ba],
3) DUMU ^{d}*za-ba*$_4$-[*ba*$_4$]-x-[x x]	3) son of Zaba[ba-...],
4) ÌR *am*-[*mi-di-ta-na*]	4) servant of Am[mī-ditāna].

2022

The seal impression is on MLC 661. It was not collated.

BIBLIOGRAPHY

1972 Finkelstein, YOS 13 no. 203F (copy)
1982 Wilcke, Kraus Festschrift p. 470 F (transliteration)

TEXT

1) ⸢*lu*⸣-*uš-ta-mar*-^{d}*za-b*[*a*$_4$-*ba*$_4$]	1) Luštamar-Zab[aba],
2) [DU]MU ^{d}AMAR.UTU-*mu-ša*-[*lim*]	2) [s]on of Marduk-muša[llim],
3) [Ì]R *am-mi-di-ta-n*[*a*-ke$_4$]	3) [ser]vant of Ammī-ditān[a].

2023

The impression is on MLC 1690 dating to year 10 of Ammī-ditāna. It was not collated.

BIBLIOGRAPHY

1972 Finkelstein, YOS 13 no. 532E (copy)

TEXT

1) *gi-mil*-^{d}[AMAR.UTU]	1) Gimil-[Marduk],
2) DUMU *be-el-šu-n*[*u*]	2) son of Bēlšun[u],
3) ÌR *am-mi-di-ta*-[*na*]	3) servant of Ammī-ditā[na].

2024

The impression is on MLC 70 and measures 2.1×2.4 cm. It was collated.

BIBLIOGRAPHY

1972 Finkelstein, YOS 13 no. 16A (copy)

TEXT

1)	ᵈEN.ZU-*i*-[...]	1) Sîn-i[...],
2)	SANGA ᵈ[...]	2) *sanga* priest of the god [...],
3)	[DUMU] ᵈnin-x-[...]	3) [son] of Nin-[...],
4)	[Ì]R *am-mi-di-*⌜*ta*⌝-[*na*]	4) [ser]vant of Ammī-ditā[na].

2025

A cylinder seal in the British Museum has the inscription of a servant of Ammī-ditāna.

COMMENTARY

The object is BM 89149, a cylinder seal of chalcedony which was acquired before 1900. It measures 3.3×1.4 cm and the inscription was collated by C.B.F. Walker.

The personal name Lāgamāl suggests that this seal may have come from Dilbat.

BIBLIOGRAPHY

1986 Collon, Cylinder Seals 3 no. 627 (photo, edition)

TEXT

1)	*i-din-*ᵈ*la-ga-ma-al*	1) Iddin-Lāgamāl,
2)	DUMU *a-lí-ta-li-mi*	2) son of Ali-talīmī,
3)	ÌR *am-mi-di-ta-na-*ke$_4$	3) servant of Ammī-ditāna.

2026

A seal which was for sale in Paris in 1988 bears the inscription of a servant of Ammī-ditāna.

COMMENTARY

The seal was 2.8 cm long with a diameter of 2.5 + cm. The transliteration is given here through the courtesy of W.G. Lambert.

TEXT

1) *gi-mil*-^{d}AMAR.UTU	1) Gimil-Marduk,
2) DUMU ^{d}EN.ZU-ILLAT-*su*	2) son of Sîn-illassu,
3) ÌR *am-mi-di-ta-na*-ke$_4$	3) servant of Ammī-ditāna.

2027

The impression of a seal of a servant of Ammī-ditāna is found on a tablet from Sippar.

COMMENTARY

The tablet is HG 96.

BIBLIOGRAPHY

1988 Charpin, RA 82 pp. 28–30 seal G (copy, edition)

TEXT

1) [INANNA.MA.AN.SUM]	1) [Eštar-iddinam],
2) GA[LA.MAḪ]	2) [chief] can[tor]
3) *an-nu-ni-*[*tim*]	3) of the goddess Annunī[tum],
4) DUMU ^{d}UTU(?)-[...]	4) son of *Šamaš*-[...],
5) ÌR *am-mi-di-t*[*a-na*-ke$_4$]	5) [ser]vant of Ammī-dit[āna].

Ammī-ṣaduqa

E4.3.10

Ammī-ditāna was succeeded by his son Ammī-ṣaduqa, who reigned 21 years. Two inscriptions of this king survive.

1

What remains of a bilingual copy of an inscription of Ammī-ṣaduqa deals with the fashioning of a *lamassu* figure by the king for a goddess, probably Eštar.

COMMENTARY

The tablet is Ni 833 + Ni 10753, at present in Istanbul, and the inscription was collated. Ni 10753 is edited here for the first time. According to Peters Ni 833 came from the ridge opposite 'Tablet Hill', on the west side of the šaṭṭ en-Nīl.

Although control over Nippur by the Babylon dynasty was lost around year 29 of Samsu-iluna, the existence of a date list of Ammī-ṣaduqa from Nippur (HS 189, see I. Bernhardt, TMH NF 5 no. 77) suggests that Babylon may have regained control over the city during the reign of Ammī-ṣaduqa. This may account for the existence of a copy of the OB king's inscription being made at Nippur.

Kraus indicates that the tablet has a NB script. According to M. Civil the inscription may well be a MB copy.

The tablet is divided into three cols. Col. i, of which the line-beginnings are not preserved, has phonetic writings of some of the Sumerian; col. ii has the Sumerian text, and col. iii the Akkadian. The Sumerian glosses and Akkadian col. appear in MB script; the 'logographic' Sumerian text in col. ii, however, is rendered in OB sign forms. The rev. was also inscribed, but so little remains of it today that an edition of the traces is not attempted here.

The Sumerian text of this inscription is artificial and difficult, and is probably a translation from the Akkadian original. Many of the Sumerian words in the text are equivalents that one might find in late lexical texts and commentaries. A detailed study of the Sumerian is beyond the scope of the present volume. The translation given here follows the Akkadian version, except in line 30′.

Lines 24′–26′ may be compared with the name of year 29 of Ammī-ditāna known in both a Sumerian and Akkadian version:

mu *am-mi-di-ta-na* lugal-e ^{d}lamma-^{d}lamma bar-sù-ga-ke$_4$ nam-ti-la-ni-šè šu-àm mú-mú-àm kù-GI-ḫuš-a na$_4$-kal-la-bi-da-ke$_4$ šu-àm bí-in-da-ra-du$_7$-a bí-in-⌜dím⌝-dím-ma-a ^{d}inanna nin-gal kiš.KI-a sag lugal-⌜la-na⌝-ke$_4$ an-ši-in-íb-íl-la-áš in-ne-en-tu-ra

ša-at-tu ša am-mi-di-ta-na šar-rum ^{d}*la-ma-sà-at méš-re-e ša a-na ba-la-ṭi-šu i-kar-ra-bu i-na* KÙ.GI *ú-ši-im ù* NA$_4$ *a-qar-tim ib-ni-i-ma a-na* ^{d}INANNA NIN.GAL KIŠ.KI.A *mu-ul-li-a-at šar-ú-ti-šu ú-še-lu-ú*

(Translation follows the Akkadian)
'The year: Ammī-ditāna, the king, fashioned protective genii of prosperity which pray for his life, out of red gold and precious stones, and dedicated them to the goddess Eštar, great lady of Kiš, the one who elevated his kingship.'

BIBLIOGRAPHY

1896 Hilprecht, BE 1/2 no. 129 (copy)
1910 Hilprecht, Deluge Story p. 9 n. 2 (study)
1923 Poebel, Grammatik p. 5 (study)
1933 Landsberger, M. von Oppenheim Festschrift p. 177 (study)
1933 von Soden, ZA 41 p. 107 n. 5 (study)
1947 Kraus, JCS 1 p. 115 n. 74 (study)
1951 Landsberger, MSL 2 pp. 3, 89, and 108 (study)
1958 Kraus, Edikt p. 12 (study)
1970 Matthews, First Dynasty of Babylon pp. 270–74 (edition)

TEXT

	Sumerian	Akkadian	
	Lacuna	Lacuna	Lacuna
1′)	[...]	*le-at* [x x x]	1′–3′) [For the goddess Eštar] mighty one of ..., [his] lady,
2′)	[...] x	*mu-um-ma* N[E-X X]	
3′)	[...]	*be-el-ti-*[*šu*]	
4′)	[*am-mi-ṣa-du*]*-qá*	*am-mi-ṣa-du-q*[*a*]	4′–7′) Ammī-ṣaduqa, mighty king, king of Babylon, who adores the bright one,
5′)	[...-m]a(?)	LUGAL *dan-núm*	
6′)	[....K]I(?)	LUGAL KÁ.DINGIR.RA.KI	
7′)	[...]	*ka-ri-ib na-na-ar-*⌜x⌝	
8′)	[...]	DUMU *a-ša-re-d*[*u*]	8′–10′) first-born son of Ammī-ditān[a], *father* ...,
9′)	[*am-m*]*i-*[*di-ta-na*]	[*š*]*a am-mi-di-ta-n*[*a*]	
10′)	pa$_4$-sag-[x x x] x	⌜*a-bi* x x x x *e*⌝ [x]	
11′)	ug AN ŠITA SAG PAP X-e	*i-nu* ⌜^{d}⌝[x x x x x]	11′–12′) After the god ... multiplied defeat,
12′)	nam-gár-dan tuddaḫ(DU$_8$ × 4)-a-ta	*ta*(?)*-r*[*i* x x x x x]	
13′)	ki-ZUM-urbingu (UR × UR)-ta	*um-ma-*⌜*an*⌝-[x x x x]	13′–15′) had thrown down the army of [...] (on) the battle-field,
14′)	ḪI × GADA aš-BULUG-ga	*ís-ki-*[*pu*]	
15′)	bí-i[n-b]u-bu-a-ta	*a-šar tam-ḫa-*[*ri*]	
16′)	zabar-ba bí-in-ḫal-àm	*te-eb tu-ku-ul-*[*ti-šu*]	16′–19′) after the onrush of [his] *weapons,* had crushed the princes, had stood in might over the enemy,
17′)	X KA PA-PA-a in-ak-a	*iḫ-tu-ú mu-tál-*[*li*]	
18′)	níg-a-rá-ta sag rim-ma	*in le-t*[*i*]	
19′)	in-ne-da-lu-ga-ta	*e-lu a-a-bi iz-za-a*[*z-zu*]	
20′)	ug-ba	*i-nu-*[*šu*]	20′–23′) at [that] time Ammī-ṣaduqa, shepherd favourite of Telī[tum] (i.e. the goddess Eštar),
21′)	*am-mi-ṣa-du-qá*	*am-mi-ṣa-du-*[*qa*]	
22′)	kuš$_7$ še$_{21}$-ga	*re-iu-*[*ú*]	
23′)	DINGIR-zíb-ba-ke$_4$	*mi-gir te-li-*[*ti*]	
24′)	ki-ti gi-da-ri-a	^{d}LAMMA *méš-ri-i*	24′–26′) [fashioned] a ... protective genius of prosperity which blesses him beneficently,
25′)	du$_{10}$-ba	*ša i-kar-ra-*[*bu*]	
26′)	šu an-è-a	*šu-ul-ma-ni-*[*iš*]	
27′)	ŠA kala-ga šita$_4$-a	*ši-ta ma tum ga qar* x [x]	27′–28′) (and) a ... which adorns the dais,

Sumerian	Akkadian	Translation
28′) bára(*)-gi$_4$-a LIŠ x ugun-du$_{11}$-ga	*ṣa-⌜pu⌝-a-aṭ pa-rak-k*[*i*]	
29′) za-kal-la galam-dù-dù-a	*ab-nam a-qar-tam ṣú-ud-du-*[*rat*]	29′–31′) sparkling with precious stones, *regular offerings, bread,* (and) *beer* ...
30′) sá-du$_{11}$(*) ninda kaš íb-⌜ra⌝-x x	[x x x] x *da* [x]	
31′) BU NA(?) S[A$_6$ X x x]	[...]	
Lacuna	Lacuna	Lacuna

Glosses
10′) [...] x du ud x x
11′) [...] x x ši-ta
12′) [...] gàr-da-an
[...] tu-ud-da-ḫa-a-ta
13′) [...] x x x ri-ta
14′) [...] ši
15′) [...] im
16′) [...]
17′) [...]-du-um
[...] x ag-ga
18′) [...-t]a
22′) [...] še-ba
25′) [ze-e]b-ba
27′) [... kal]a-ga ši-ta-a
30′) [...] x na-ri-bi

2

This text is a copy of an inscription of Ammī-ṣaduqa that is too broken to determine what event was being commemorated.

COMMENTARY

The text is BM 97196 (1902-10-11,230) from a purchased collection, provenance unknown. It is a clay cylinder 9 cm long, 8.1 cm in dia. It is published here for the first time through the courtesy of the trustees of the British Museum.

The attribution of the text is based on the restoration of the king's name in i 1.

In ii 5, *an* is taken as a form of the preposition *ana*.

TEXT

Text	Translation
Col. i	
1) [*am-mi-ṣa-du*]*-qá*	i 1–9) [Ammī-ṣadu]qa, [migh]ty [king, king of Babylon], ...
2) [LUGAL *dan-n*]*úm*	
3) [LUGAL KÁ.DINGIR.RA].KI	Lacuna
4) [...]	
5) [...] x	
6) [...] x	
7) [...] x	

Sumerian version: **28′** Text: ad. **30′** Text: sag.

8) [... *i*]*m*
9) [...] x
Lacuna
1′) [...] x
2′) [...]-*ma*

i 1′–2′) ...

Col. ii
1) *ḫa-di-iš i-kar-ra-ba-nim*
2) *in* u_4*-mi-šu*(?)
3) *i-na me-re-ši-im*
4) *ša* ᵈ*é-a iš-ru-kam*
5) *an ni-ši-ia ra-ap-ša-a-tim*
6) *ša a-bur-ri ú-šar-bí-ṣ*[*ú*]
7) [x] x ⌜*li*⌝ x
Lacuna

ii 1–7) they joyfully invoke blessings for me. At that time, by the wisdom which the god Ea gave to me, for my broad numerous people, whom I settled in safe pastures, ...
Lacuna

1′) [x x x]-*ú*
2′) [x x x] UD
3′) [x x]-x-*ia*
4′) DINGIR ŠE.GA-*ia liš-pu-uk*
5′) *la um-su*

ii 1′–5′) ..., ..., ..., for the god who listens to me may he pour out, ...

Colophon:
1) *éš-gàr e-tel*-KA-ᵈUTU
2) ŠU *ib-ni*-ᵈAMAR.UTU

Colophon:
1–2) Text of Etel-pî-Šamaš, (from) the hand of Ibni-Marduk.

2001

A copy of an inscription on a tablet from Sippar deals with the dedication by judge Gimil-Marduk of a statue to the god Utu for the life of Ammī-ṣaduqa.

COMMENTARY

The tablet is BM 92515 (Bu 88-5-12,48), purchased by Budge in Baghdad. According to E. Sollberger this tablet is originally from Sippar. It measures 10.8 × 5.8 × 2.7 cm and the inscription was collated.

E. Sollberger suggests that this might be an early Kassite copy, probably from an original monument. Kutscher, Brockmon Tablets p. 104, argues for a late OB date.

BIBLIOGRAPHY

1898–1900 King, LIH no. 69 (copy, edition)
1969 Sollberger, Iraq 31 pp. 90–92 (edition)
1970 Matthews, First Dynasty of Babylon pp. 266–69 (edition)
1971 Sollberger and Kupper, IRSA IVC10a (translation)
1983 Kärki, SAKAZ 2 p. 46 (edition)

TEXT

1) ᵈutu
2) en-gal-
3) dingir-re-e-ne-er
4) lugal-é-di-ku_5-ta

1–4) For the god Utu, great lord of the gods, lord of the Edikuta,

5) nam-ti-la-

5–9) [for] the life of Ammī-ṣaduqa, mighty king,

6) *am-mi-ṣa-du-qá-a*
7) lugal-kala-ga
8) lugal-KÁ.DINGIR.RA.K[I]
9) lugal-a-ni-i[r]
10) *gi-mil-*^{d}AMAR.⸢UTU⸣ di-ku$_{5}$
11) dumu *ṣíl-lí-*^{d}UTU
12) u$_{4}$ ^{d}utu lugal-a-ni
13) inim in-na-an-du$_{11}$-ga-ni
14) an-da-gin-na-ta
15) ⸢šà⸣-lá in-(erasure)-ši-in-sù-àm
16) zi nam-ti-la
17) in-na-an-ba-a
18) URUDU.alam šà-ne-ša$_{4}$
19) du$_{10}$ bí-in-gam-ma
20) mùš-me-bi ⸢kù-babbar⸣ gar-ra
21) šùd ⸢in⸣-na-an-[né]-⸢a⸣-ni
22) in-⸢na⸣-n[i]-⸢in-dím⸣
23) URUDU.⸢alam⸣-ne-e
24) igi-^{d}utu
25) é-di-ku$_{5}$-da-ta
26) du$_{11}$-ga-ni
27) in-ši-in-še-[g]a
28) mu-ni-[gub]

king of Babylon, his lord,

10–11) Gimil-Marduk, the judge, son of Ṣillī-Šamaš,

12–17) after the god Utu, his lord, had agreed to the word that he had spoken to him, he showed him mercy, (and) granted him breath and life.

18–22) He fashioned for him a copper suppliant statue, with its knee bent, its face plated with silver, uttering his prayer to him.

23–28) He [set up] this statue before the god Utu of Edikudata, who had agreed to his words.

2002

A tablet from Sippar now housed in Philadelphia, CBS 9478, bears impressions of four servant seals of Ammī-ṣaduqa. These are edited here as E4.3.10.2002–2005. Duplicate impressions of these are found on Bu 91-5-9,272.

COMMENTARY

The impression is on CBS 9478 B and Bu 91-5-9,272 H.

BIBLIOGRAPHY

1906 Ranke, BE 6/1 pl. x no. 15 (ex. 1, photo)
1982 Wilcke, Kraus Festschrift pp. 467–68 no. 11 H and no. 12 B (exs. 1–2, transliteration)

TEXT

1) ^{d}IŠKUR-MA.A[N.SUM]
2) UGULA DAM.[GÀR]
3) DUMU ^{d}IŠKUR-*ša*[*r*-X X]
4) IR$_{11}$ *am-mi-ṣa-du-*[*qá*]

1) Adad-[iddin]am,
2) overseer of the merchant [bankers],
3) son of Adad-ša[r-...],
4) servant of Ammī-ṣadu[qa].

2003

The impression is found on CBS 9478 C and Bu 91-5-9,272 I.

BIBLIOGRAPHY

1906 Ranke, BE 6/1 pl. x no. 15 (ex. 1, photo)
1982 Wilcke, Kraus Festschrift pp. 467-68 no. 11 I and no. 12 C (exs. 1-2, transliteration)

TEXT

1) *a-wi-il-*[d]IŠ[KUR]
2) *ra-bi sí-ik-kà-*[*tim*]
3) [D]UMU *ip-qú-*[d]*ša-*[*la*]
4) IR$_{11}$ *am-mi-ṣa-du-q*[*á*]

1) Awīl-A[dad],
2) *rabi sikka*[*tim*],
3) [s]on of Ipqu-Šā[la],
4) servant of Ammī-ṣaduq[a].

2004

The impression is found on CBS 9478 D and Bu 91-5-9,272 K.

BIBLIOGRAPHY

1906 Ranke, BE 6/1 pl. x no. 15 (ex. 1, transliteration)
1982 Wilcke, Kraus Festschrift pp. 467-68 no. 11 K and no. 12 D (exs. 1-2, transliteration)

TEXT

1) *i-din-eš$_4$-t*[*ár*]
2) DUMU *ip-qú-an-nu-ni-t*[*um*]
3) IR$_{11}$ *am-mi-ṣa-du-qá-*[ke$_4$]

1) Iddin-Ešt[ar],
2) son of Ipqu-Annunīt[um],
3) servant of Ammī-ṣaduqa.

2005

The impression is found on CBS 9478 E and Bu 91-5-9,272 E.

BIBLIOGRAPHY

1906 Ranke, BE 6/1 pl. x no. 15 (ex. 1, photo)
1982 Wilcke, Kraus Festschrift pp. 467-68 no. 11 L and no. 12 E (exs. 1-2, transliteration)

TEXT

1) *a-wi-il-*^{d}[UTU]
2) DUMU *i-din-*^{d}*nin-*[...]
3) IR$_{11}$ *am-mi-ṣa-du-qá-*[(ke$_4$)]

1) Awīl-[Šamaš],
2) son of Iddin-Nin[...],
3) servant of Ammī-ṣaduqa.

2006–2008

Three servant seals found on Bu 91-5-9,272, not duplicated by the seals found on CBS 9478, are edited as E4.3.10.2006–2008.

2006

BIBLIOGRAPHY

1982 Wilcke, Kraus Festschrift p. 467 A (transliteration)

TEXT

1) *a-wi-il-*^{d}E[N.ZU]
2) DUMU ^{d}EN.ZU-*be-el-a*[*p-lim*]
3) ÌR *am-mi-ṣa-du-*[*qá*-ke$_4$]

1) Awīl-S[în],
2) son of Sîn-bēl-a[plim],
3) servant of Ammī-ṣadu[qa].

2007

BIBLIOGRAPHY

1982 Wilcke, Kraus Festschrift p. 467 J (transliteration)

TEXT

1) ⸢^{d}⸣EN.ZU-*i-din-*[*nam*]
2) [DUMU] ^{d}IŠKUR-MA.[AN.SUM]
3) [ì]R *am-mi-*[*ṣa-du-qá*-ke$_4$]

1) Sîn-iddin[am],
2) [son] of Adad-[iddin]am,
3) [se]rvant of Ammī-[ṣaduqa].

2008

The impression was collated by C. Wilcke.

BIBLIOGRAPHY

1982 Wilcke, Kraus Festschrift p. 467 M (transliteration)

TEXT

1) [dAMAR].UTU-*mu-ša-lim*
2) [DUMU *ip-q*]*ú-an-nu-ni-t*[*um*]
3) [ÌR *am-m*]*i-ṣa-du-qá*-ke$_4$

1) [Mar]duk-mušallim,
2) [son of Ipq]u-Annunīt[um],
3) [servant of Amm]ī-ṣaduqa.

2009

A seal impression of a servant of Ammī-ṣaduqa is found on a tablet in the Bodleian Museum in Oxford.

COMMENTARY

The impression is on Bodleian B 12, from either Sippar or Dilbat. It was collated from the published photo.

BIBLIOGRAPHY

1966 Buchanan and Gurney, Ashmolean 1 p. 228 no. 551 seal B (photo, edition)

TEXT

1) dUTU-*nu-úr*-[*ì-li*]
2) X-AB.A dX
3) DUMU *ìl-šu-ib-ni*
4) ÌR *am-mi-ṣa-du-qa*

1) Šamaš-nūr-[ilī],
2) ... priest of the god ...,
3) son of Ilšu-ibni,
4) servant of Ammī-ṣaduqa.

2010–16

Seal impressions of servants of Ammī-ṣaduqa are found on a number of tablets in the Morgan Library Collection now at Yale which were published by Finkelstein in YOS 13. These are edited here as E4.3.10.2010–16.

2010

The first seal impression is found on MLC 1196 dating to year 11 of Ammī-ṣaduqa (exemplar 1) and MLC 2656 dating to year 3 of Ammī-ṣaduqa (exemplar 2).

BIBLIOGRAPHY

1972 Finkelstein, YOS 13 p. 86 no. 31 (ex. 1, transliteration)
1982 Wilcke, Kraus Festschrift p. 432 B (ex. 2, transliteration)

TEXT

1) *ib-ni-*^{d}*za-ba*$_{4}$*-b*[*a*$_{4}$]	1) Ibni-Zabab[a],
2) SANGA ^{d}*za-ba*$_{4}$*-b*[*a*$_{4}$]	2) *sanga* priest of the god Zabab[a],
3) DUMU ^{d}EN.ZU-*na-di-in-š*[*u-mi*]	3) son of Sîn-nādin-š[umi],
4) [Ì]R *am-mi-ṣa-du-qá*-k[e$_{4}$]	4) [se]rvant of Ammī-ṣaduqa.

2011

The impression is found on MLC 422 and MLC 1634 dating to years 8 and 10 of Ammī-ṣaduqa. It was not collated.

BIBLIOGRAPHY

1972 Finkelstein, YOS 13 p. 87 no. 70A and no. 196 (exs. 1–2, transliteration)

TEXT

1) *ri-iš*-É.DUB	1) Rīš-Edub,
2) UGULA.[GAL]	2) [chief] overseer,
3) DUMU *i-na-pa-li-šu*	3) son of Ina-palîšu,
4) [ÌR] *am-mi-*[*ṣa-du-qá*]	4) [servant] of Ammī-[ṣaduqa].

2012

The impression is found on MLC 658 dating to year 5 of Samsu-ditāna. It was not collated.

BIBLIOGRAPHY

1972 Finkelstein, YOS 13 p. 87 no. 202A (transliteration)

TEXT

1) *na-bi-ì-*[*lí-šu*]	1) Nabi-i[līšu],
2) UGULA MUNUS.SUḪUR.LÁ.MEŠ	2) overseer of the *kezrētu* women,
3) DUMU *i-din-*[d]*na-*[*na-a*]	3) son of Iddin-Na[nāia],
4) ÌR *am-mi-ṣa-du-qá*	4) servant of Ammī-ṣaduqa.

2013

The impression is found on MLC 206 dating to year 1 of Samsu-ditāna. It was not collated.

COMMENTARY

The name in line 1 is restored from line 4 of the tablet.

BIBLIOGRAPHY

1972 Finkelstein, YOS 13 p. 88 no. 268 (transliteration)

TEXT

1) [d]NANNA-[ŠÀ.LÁ.SÙ]	1) Nanna-[rēmēni],
2) GALA.MAḪ	2) chief cantor,
3) [DUMU] ME.A.I[M.RI.A.MU]	3) [son] of Ali-i[lattī],
4) ÌR *am-mi-*[*ṣa-du-qá*]	4) servant of Ammī-[ṣaduqa].

2014

The impression is found on MLC 1357 dating to year 5 of Samsu-ditāna (exemplar 1) and MLC 1331 dating to year 2 of Samsu-ditāna (exemplar 2).

COMMENTARY

Although Finkelstein edited these impressions as different inscriptions, collation reveals that they are two exs. of the same inscription. Charpin suggests Nanāia-ēriš was one of the priesthood of Uruk exiled to Kiš in late OB times.

BIBLIOGRAPHY

1972 Finkelstein, YOS 13 p. 89 no. 297 (ex. 1, transliteration) and no. 262B (ex. 2, copy)
1986 Charpin, Le clergé d'Ur p. 406 (study)

TEXT

1) ᵈ*na-na-a-e-ri-*[*iš*]	1) Nanāia-ēri[š],
2) IŠIB AN ᵈINANNA	2) *išippu* priest of the gods Anum and Eštar,
3) DUMU UNUG.KI-*li-*[*ib-lu-uṭ*]	3) son of Uruk-li[bluṭ],
4) ÌR *am-mi-ṣa-du-*[*qá*]	4) servant of Ammī-ṣadu[qa].

2015

The impression is found on MLC 212 dating to year 17+b of Ammī-ṣaduqa. It was not collated. The tablet probably came from Dilbat.

BIBLIOGRAPHY

1972 Finkelstein, YOS 13 no. 32 (copy)

TEXT

1) *i-din-*ᵈ*la-*[*ga-ma-al*]	1) Iddin-Lā[gamāl],
2) DUMU ᵈ*uraš-n*[*a-ṣi-ir*]	2) son of Uraš-n[āṣir],
3) IR_{11} *am-mi-ṣa-*[*du-qá*]	3) servant of Ammī-ṣa[duqa].

2016

The impression is found on MLC 661, whose date is broken away. It was collated by C. Wilcke.

BIBLIOGRAPHY

1972 Finkelstein, YOS 13 no. 203D (copy)
1982 Wilcke, Kraus Festschrift p. 470 D (transliteration)

TEXT

1) ⌜*i*⌝-*n*[*a-é-sag-íl-*NUMUN]	1) In[a-Esagil-zēru]
2) [SA]NGA ᵈIN[ANNA]	2) [*sa*]*nga* priest of the goddess Eš[tar],
3) [DU]MU *ri-iš-*ᵈAM[AR.UTU]	3) [s]on of Rīš-Ma[rduk],
4) [Ì]R *am-mi-ṣa-du-q*[*á*-ke_4]	4) [se]rvant of Ammī-ṣaduq[a].

Samsu-ditāna

E4.3.11

Samsu-ditāna, the successor of Ammī-ṣaduqa, reigned 31 years.

2001

A plaster impression of a seal of a servant of Samsu-ditāna is known.

COMMENTARY

The impression is Walters Art Gallery C 20. The provenance of the original seal is unknown but it probably came from Kiš. The impression was collated from the published photo.

For a Gimil-Nanāia who may be the same person as the one who appears in this impression see D. Charpin, Le clergé d'Ur p. 407.

BIBLIOGRAPHY

1939 Gordon, Iraq 6 pp. 13–14 no. 26 (edition) and pl. IV no. 26 (photo)
1975 Boehmer in Orthmann (ed.), Der alte Orient no. 268i (photo, study)

TEXT

1) *qí-iš-ti-*ᵈAMAR.⌜UTU⌝
2) IŠIB AN ᵈIN[ANNA]
3) DUMU *gi-mil-*ᵈ*na-na-a*
4) ÌR *sa-am-su-di-ta-na*

1) Qīšti-Marduk,
2) *išippu* priest of the gods Anum and Eš[tar],
3) son of Gimil-Nanāia,
4) servant of Samsu-ditāna.

2002

Impressions of seals of servants of Samsu-ditāna are found on tablets in the Morgan Library Collection. The first is the impression of Rīš-Marduk.

COMMENTARY

The impression is on MCL 603 and was collated by C. Wilcke.

BIBLIOGRAPHY

1972 Finkelstein, YOS 13 p. 87 no. 90 (transliteration)
1982 Wilcke, Kraus Festschrift p. 437 B′ (transliteration)

TEXT

1) *ri-iš-*^{d}[AMAR.UTU]	1) Rīš-[Marduk],
2) GALA.MA[Ḫ ^{d}*za-ba*$_4$*-ba*$_4$]	2) chie[f] chanter [of the god Zababa],
3) DUMU *e-*[...]	3) son of E[...],
4) ÌR *sa-am-*[*su-di-ta-na*]	4) servant of Sam[su-ditāna].

2003

Another servant seal impression is found on MLC 603. It was collated by C. Wilcke.

BIBLIOGRAPHY

1972 Finkelstein, YOS 13 p. 87 no. 90D (transliteration)
1982 Wilcke, Kraus Festschrift p. 437 C′ (transliteration)

TEXT

1) *a-wi-il-*^{d}[*é-a*]	1) Awīl-[Ea],
2) LÚ.EGIR.R[A (KIŠ.KI)]	2) replacement troop [(of Kiš)],
3) [D]UMU ^{d}*é-a-n*[*a-ṣi-ir*]	3) [s]on of Ea-n[āṣir],
4) ÌR *sa-am-su-di-ta-*[*na*]	4) servant of Samsu-ditā[na].

2004

The impression of a seal of Ilī-iqīšam is found on MLC 658. It was not collated.

BIBLIOGRAPHY

1972 Finkelstein, YOS 13 p. 88 no. 202C (transliteration)

TEXT

1) *ì-lí-i-qí-ša-*[*am*]	1) Ilī-iqīša[m],
2) UGULA [MUNUS.SUḪUR.LÁ.MEŠ]	2) overseer of the [*kezrētu* women],
3) DUMU ^{d}*uraš-...*	3) son of Uraš-...,
4) ÌR *sa-am-su-di-*[*ta-na*]	4) servant of Samsu-di[tāna].

2005

The impression is found on MLC 644. It was not collated.

BIBLIOGRAPHY

1972 Finkelstein, YOS 13 p. 93 no. 521D (transliteration)
1982 Wilcke, Kraus Festschrift p. 473 B (transliteration)

TEXT

1) LÚ-[^{d}*é-a*]	1) Awīl-[Ea],
2) DUMU ^{d}*é-*[*a-na-ṣi-ir*]	2) son of E[a-nāṣir],
3) ÌR *sa-am-su-di-ta-n*[*a*-ke$_4$]	3) servant of Samsu-ditān[a].

URUK

E4.4

The city of Uruk played an important role in the complex politics of the Isin-Larsa period, having a very checkered history during this period. It would appear that Isin gained control over the city part way through the reign of Ibbi-Sîn of Ur. Year x+7 of Išbi-Erra commemorates the designation of the *en* of Inanna, which Renger has suggested refers to the priest of that goddess in Uruk. Allusions to Inanna and the city are found sporadically in year names and hymns of the early Isin kings. The last king of Isin who appears to have controlled the city was Lipit-Eštar, as is evidenced by his titulary and the finding of a brick fragment (see E4.1.5.1 ex. 11).

After the reign of Lipit-Eštar the status of the city is uncertain. It may have been controlled by Gungunum of Larsa for awhile, since bricks of that ruler were found at the small site of Umm al-Wawīya not far away. The first evidence of independent rule at the city is found in the name of year 5 of Sūmû-Il of Larsa which records the defeat of the army of Uruk. In this earliest period of Uruk independence should be placed the reigns of Ālila-ḫadum and Sūmû-kanasa, two shadowy figures, apparently of Amorite stock (see Kienast, Kisurra pp. 20–21). They are not known from texts from Uruk itself, but rather from year names found on tablets from Kisurra, which commemorate deeds connected with the goddess Inanna and the 'lady of Eanna'. From this it has been assumed that these figures were kings of Uruk who controlled Kisurra as well, but this is not entirely certain. Ikūn-pî-Eštar (see E4.0.16) may possibly belong to this early time period as well.

Subsequent to this time period falls the rule of Sîn-kāšid who styled himself as king of the Amnānum. Sîn-kāšid has left us a large number of building inscriptions. He was succeeded by a number of generally short-reigned rulers for whom we have a small number of royal inscriptions as well as dated archival texts. During the reign of ÌR-nene, one of the successors of Sîn-kāšid, the city of Uruk was attacked by Larsa, as commemorated in the name of year 14 of Rīm-Sîn. After this the city had a brief period of independence until it was finally conquered by Larsa as commemorated in the name of year 21 of Rīm-Sîn. With this the independent rule of Uruk ceased. The city subsequently passed from the control of Larsa to Babylon during the reign of Ḫammu-rāpi. It revolted during the early part of the reign of Samsu-iluna, but rebellion was quickly put down by the king of Babylon. The history of the city during the late Old Babylonian period is obscure. Rīm-Anum is known to have controlled the city during the time of Samsu-iluna.

Sîn-kāšid

E4.4.1

The relationship of Sîn-kāšid to the previous rulers of Uruk is uncertain. It is noteworthy that he never mentions his father in any of his inscriptions. He may have started a new dynasty.

No date list has appeared for the reign of Sîn-kāšid. While the length of his reign is unknown, the large number of different building inscriptions left us suggests that it was fairly lengthy.

The chronological arrangement of the Sîn-kāšid texts is uncertain. The construction of the Eanna temple was probably undertaken early in the reign because it is alluded to in so many of the other inscriptions. Work on the palace was probably begun early in the reign as well.

1

From the viewpoint of Sîn-kāšid's own inscriptions, his most laudable feat was the restoration of the Eanna temple in Uruk. The epithet ú-a-é-an-na 'provider of Eanna' and the temporal clause u_4 é-an-na mu-dù-a 'when he built Eanna' appear in a number of the king's inscriptions.

A number of bricks found at Uruk bear a five-line inscription dealing with the construction of the Eanna temple.

CATALOGUE

Ex.	Museum number	Excavation number	Warka photo number	Uruk provenance	Dimensions (cm)	Lines preserved	cpn
1	BM 90267 (51-1-1,291)	–	–	From top of Eanna ziqqurrat	33.0×12.0×8.0	1-5	c
2	–	W 70	35	From slope of ziqqurrat core	–	1-4	p
3	VA 14658	W 1120	808	Oexvi2, area of Eanna	–	1-5	p
4	VA 14658	W 1161	808/809	Paxvi3, area of Eanna	23.0×25.0	1-5	p
5	VA 14658	W 1635b	808	Odxvi3/4, area of Eanna, surface find	–	1-5	p
6	VA 14658	W 1641	807	Oexv5, rubble in Eanna area	–	1-5	p
7	VA 14658	W 1701b	807	Odxv4, area of Eanna	–	1-5	p
8	IM 6920	W 2919	808	Paxv5, rubbish on ziqqurrat	25.0×15.0	1-5	p
9	VA 14658	W 3200b	809	Ocxvi2, in room 2 as door pivot box	–	1-5	p

COMMENTARY

Ex. 1 comes from Loftus's excavations at Uruk. Apparently there were scant remains of a high temple of Sîn-kāšid on the very top of the Eanna ziqqurrat from which ex. 1 was taken. Loftus writes (Travels in Chaldea and Susiana, p. 168): 'The summit of the existing ruin is perfectly flat, and measures 68 feet from north to south. At one point are traces of a brick superstructure, with inscriptions of Sinshada [= Sîn-kāšid] who lived about 1500 BC, and the rubbish, mixed with bitumen, on the exterior, appears to have fallen from it.' Ex. 2, from the 1912-13 Jordan's excavation season, came from this rubbish on the slope of the ziqqurrat. Exs. 3-9 from Jordan's 1928-29 season come either from the slope of the ziqqurrat or from the general area of Eanna.

BIBLIOGRAPHY

1857 Loftus, Travels p. 168 (ex. 1, provenance)
1861 1 R pl. 3 no. VII 1 (ex. 1, copy)
1872 G. Smith, TSBA 1 p. 41 no. 20 (translation)
1874 Lenormant, Études accadiennes 2 p. 324
1875 Ménant, Babylone et la Chaldée (Paris) p. 69 (translation)
1876 Schrader, ZDMG 29 p. 40 (edition)
1892 Winckler, KB 3/1 pp. 82-83 Sin-gašid 1 (edition)
1905 Thureau-Dangin, ISA pp. 314-15 Sin-gâšid a (edition)
1905 King, CT 21 pl. 12 (ex. 1, copy)
1907 Thureau-Dangin, SAK pp. 220-21 Sin-gâšid a (edition)
1922 BM Guide p. 61 no. 131 (ex. 1, study)
1928 Jordan, Uruk-Warka p. 49 no. 3 and pl. 25 no. 7 c-d (ex. 2, photo, copy, study)
1929 Barton, RISA pp. 332-33 Singashid 1 (edition)
1929 Schott, Eanna pp. 51-52 no. 7 (exs. 2-9, study) and pl. 25d no. 7 (copy)
1961 Hallo, BiOr 18 p. 11 Sin-kašid 1 (study)
1968 Kärki, SKFZ p. 93 Sînkāšid 1 (edition)
1971 Sollberger and Kupper, IRSA IVD1b (translation)
1980 Kärki, SAKAZ 1 pp. 176-77 Sînkāšid 1 (edition)
1981 Walker, CBI no. 53 (ex. 1, study)

TEXT

1) ᵈEN.ZU-*kà-ši-id*
2) dumu-ᵈnin-sún
3) lugal-unu.KI-ga
4) ba-dím
5) é-an-na

1) Sîn-kāšid,
2) son of the goddess Ninsun,
3) king of Uruk,
4-5) builder of Eanna.

2

Several examples were found at Uruk of stamped bricks and small tablets of baked clay with a seven-line inscription dealing with the construction of Sîn-kāšid's palace.

CATALOGUE

Ex.	Museum number	Excavation number	Warka photo number	Uruk provenance	Dimensions (cm)	Lines preserved	cpn
Bricks							
1	BM 90268 (51-1-1,290)	–	–	Rebuilt into entrance jamb of Wuswas gateway	35.0×33.5	1-7	c
2	BM 90294 (1979-12-20,182)	–	–	–	35.0×17.0×8.0	1-7	c
3	Istanbul no number	W 20c	9	From 'West-bau' (= Sîn-kāšid palace?)	35.6×34.5×8.5	1-7	p
4	Istanbul no number	W –	–	–	35.0×32.0×9.0	1-7	p
5	Berlin no number	W 940	811	From area of city	–	1-7	p
6	–	W 1211	810	Ocxv3 area of Eanna	–	1-7	p
7	IM 6921A	W 1982Aa	810	Area of Eanna	15.0×7.5	1-7	p

Ex.	Museum number	Excavation number	Warka photo number	Uruk provenance	Dimensions (cm)	Lines preserved	cpn
8	IM 6921B	W 1982Ab	–	As ex. 7	–	–	n
9	IM 6921C	W 1982Ac	–	As ex. 7	–	–	n
10	Berlin no number	W 3663	811	On NE slope of ziqqurrat	–	1–7	p
11	–	W –	–	Room 102 of Sîn-kāšid palace	–	1–7	p
Tablets							
12	U 298 (Istanbul)	W 558	230–231a	Sîn-kāšid palace under reed matting between the courses of brickwork of the palace wall	–	1–7	p
13	U 321	W 558	230–231b	As ex. 12	–	1–7	p
14	U 332	W 558	230–231d	As ex. 12	–	1–7	p
15	–	W 558	230–231f	As ex. 12	–	1–7	p
16	U 329	W 558	230–231i	As ex. 12	–	1–7	p
17	U 327	W 558	230–231j	As ex. 12	–	1–7	p
18	U 333	W 558	230–231k	As ex. 12	–	1–7	p
19		W 558	224–225c	As ex. 12	–	–	p
20		W 558	224–225d	As ex. 12	–	–	p
21		W 558	224–225e	As ex. 12	–	–	p
22		W 558	224–225f	As ex. 12	–	–	p
23		W 558	224–225g	As ex. 12	–	–	p
24		W 558	224–225k	As ex. 12	–	–	p
25	VAT 8813	W 558	–	As ex. 12	4.5×5.6×1.5	1–7	c
26	VAT 8814	W 558	–	As ex. 12	4.9×5.5×1.8	1–7	c
27	VAT 8815	W 558	–	As ex. 12	4.5×6.4×1.4	1–7	c
28	VAT 8817	W 558	–	As ex. 12	4.2×5.0×1.5	1–7	c
29	(see bibliography)	–	–	–	–	1–7	n
30	(see bibliography)	–	–	–	–	1–7(?)	n
31	Toledo, Ohio Museum of Arts, no. 16.65	–	–	–	–	–	n
32	IB 207	–	–	–	4.8×5.7	1–7	n
33	MAH 16187	–	–	–	4.8×6.5×2.0	1–7	c
34	St. Paul Public Library, no. 26	–	–	–	7.8×5.0	–	n
35	University of Minnesota Library, no. 13	–	–	–	6.4×4.7	–	n
36	MWA1	–	–	–	6.7×5.2×1.7	1–7	p
37	UCLM 9-2257	–	–	–	–	1–7	c
38	UCLM 9-2867	–	–	–	–	1–7	c
39	Oakland Museum no. 28–227	–	–	–	–	1–7	c
40	McGill Ethnological Collections, no. 2.5	–	–	–	6.1×5.4×2.5	1–7	c
41	ROM 910×209.210	–	–	–	–	1–7	c
42	IES, Cambridge, no. 122	–	–	–	5.5×5.0	1–7	n
43	IES, Cambridge, no. 128	–	–	–	5.0×4.0	1–7	n
44	FM, Cambridge, E2	–	–	–	5.5×4.5	1–7	n
45	Collection of Arnold Spaer, Jerusalem	–	–	–	5.3×4.2×1.8	1–7	n
46	Crocker Art Gallery no. 7	–	–	–	–	1–7	n
47	Newbury District Museum	–	–	–	6.0×4.5×2.1	1–7	c
48	BCM A.439'1982	–	–	–	6.0×4.8×2.1	1–7	c
49	BCM A.440'1982	–	–	–	6.2×5.3×2.1	1–7	c
50	BCM A.441'1982	–	–	–	5.5×4.8×2.2	1–7	c
51	BCM A.442'1982	–	–	–	6.9×5.0×2.2	1–7	c
52	BCM A.443'1982	–	–	–	6.1×4.7×2.1	1–7	c
53	BCM A.444'1982	–	–	–	6.4×4.7×2.0	1–7	c
54	Ash 1960,1170	–	–	–	5.6×4.3×1.7	1–7	n
55	Ash 1923,436	–	–	–	–	1–7?	n
56	St. Louis Art Museum, no. 133:22	–	–	–	–	–	n
57	Piepkorn Collection PS 1	–	–	–	–	–	n
58	Piepkorn Collection PS 2	–	–	–	–	–	n
59	PS 3	–	–	–	–	–	n

Ex.	Museum number	Excavation number	Warka photo number	Uruk provenance	Dimensions (cm)	Lines preserved	cpn
60	PS 7	–	–	–	–	–	n
61	PS 8	–	–	–	–	–	n
62	Cherkasy 4, Brooklyn Museum	–	–	–	6.2×4.9×2.0	1–7	c

COMMENTARY

Bricks

Ex. 1 comes from Loftus's excavations at Uruk. It was not found in situ but had been rebuilt into the entrance jamb of the Bīt-Rēš temple (Wuswas). Ex. 2 was not given a registration no. in the British Museum but is probably also from Loftus's excavations. Exs. 3–4 come from Jordan's excavations of 1912–13, ex. 3 apparently from the area of Sîn-kāšid's palace, if this is what is meant by the expression 'Westbau'. Ex. 3 now in Istanbul has deteriorated somewhat from the photo published in Uruk-Warka pl. 101a. Exs. 5–10 come from Jordan's 1928–29 season, mainly from the area of Eanna. The palace of Sîn-kāšid, itself, after a brief sounding in 1912–13, was systematically excavated during the 17th to 22nd seasons of the Uruk excavations, but the numerous bricks found there with the palace inscription appear not to have been registered. One example, ex. 11, whose inscription is legible in a published photo, represents these excavated bricks.

Tablets

In Jordan's 1912–13 season at Uruk a probe was made into the north-west area of the mound where it had been determined that clay tablets and cones with Sîn-kāšid's palace inscription were coming. Here a few rooms of Sîn-kāšid's palace were uncovered. In the wall of the palace reed mat layers packed with inscribed cones and tablets were laid every fourth course of the mud bricks. The cones and tablets were inscribed with texts E4.4.1.2–4. All these tablets and cones were given the excavation no. W 558. They are now in Istanbul and Berlin. Curiously, while tablets were found with an inscription identical to the brick inscriptions, no cones bore this inscription. With respect to the Warka excavation photos the letters a, b, c, etc. denote the objects from left to right, from top to bottom in the photo.

For inscriptions 2–4 there are many more exs. in various collections. A complete listing is not possible here.

BIBLIOGRAPHY

Bricks

1857 Loftus, Travels p. 184 (ex. 1, provenance)
1861 1 R pl. 3 no. VIII 2 (ex. 1, copy)
1872 G. Smith, TSBA 1 p. 41 (translation)
1874 Lenormant, Études accadiennes 2 p. 325
1875 Ménant, Babylone et la Chaldée (Paris) p. 69 (translation)
1892 Winckler, KB 3/1 pp. 82–83 Sin-gašid 2 (edition)
1905 Thureau-Dangin, ISA pp. 314–15 Sin-gâšid b (edition)
1905 King, CT 21 pl. 12 (ex. 1, copy)
1907 Thureau-Dangin, SAK pp. 222–23 Sin-gâšid b (edition)
1915 King, History pl. XVIII facing p. 210 (ex. 1, photo)
1922 BM Guide p. 61 no. 130 (exs. 1–2, study)
1928 Jordan, Uruk-Warka p. 56 no. 1, pl. 101 a, and pl. 107 g (ex. 3, photo, copy, edition)
1929 Barton, RISA pp. 332–33 Singashid 2 (edition)
1961 Hallo, BiOr 18 p. 11 Sin-kašid 2: i (ex. 1, study)
1963 Lenzen, UVB 19 pl. 22 B (ex. 11, photo)
1968 Kärki, SKFZ p. 93 Sînkāšid 2 (edition)
1971 Sollberger and Kupper, IRSA IVD1c (translation)
1980 Kärki, SAKAZ 1 p. 177 Sînkāšid 2 (edition)
1981 Walker, CBI no. 54 (exs. 1–2, study)

Tablets

1914–15 Duncan, AJSL 31 p. 216 type A (ex. 30, edition)
1915 King, PSBA 37 p. 23 no. 2 (ex. 29, edition)
1917–18 Langdon, AJSL 34 p. 123 (ex. 21, study)
1927 Deimel, Orientalia os 26 p. 67 no. 194 (ex. 32, transliteration)
1928 Jordan, Uruk-Warka pl. 104 a–b, d, f, and i–k (exs. 12–18, photo)
1929 Barton, RISA pp. 332–33 Singashid 5 (edition)
1932 Lutz, UCP 10/2 p. 185 (ex. 37 or 38, copy)
1951 Sollberger, JCS 5 p. 18 (ex. 33, study)
1961 Jones and Synder, Econ. Texts nos. 334 and 338 (exs. 34–35, study)
1963 Szlechter, Manchester 1 pl. LXVII (exs. 42–44, copy); Manchester 2 p. 216 (exs. 42–44, transliteration)
1965 Levy and Artzi, ʿAtiqot 4 no. 89 (ex. 45, copy, study)
1970 Pettinato, OrAnt 9 pp. 103–104 A and pl. III (ex. 36, photo, edition)
1976 Freedman, JANES 8 p. 36 (ex. 46, transliteration)
1978 Foxvog, RA 72 p. 42 (exs. 37–39, study)
1975 Freedman, St. Louis p. 10 (exs. 56–61, study)
1979 Snell, MVN 9 p. 21 Cherkasy 4 (ex. 62, study)
1981 Grégoire, MVN 10 nos. 30–31 (exs. 54–55, copy, study)
1985 van de Mieroop and Longman, RA 79 p. 18 (ex. 31, study)

TEXT

1)	ᵈEN.ZU-*kà-ši-id*	1) Sîn-kāšid,
2)	nita-kala-ga	2) mighty man,
3)	lugal-unu.KI-ga	3) king of Uruk,
4)	lugal-*am-na-nu-um*	4) king of the Amnānum,
5)	é-gal-	5–7) built his royal palace.
6)	nam-lugal-la-ka-ni	
7)	mu-dù	

3

A variant to the palace inscription (E4.4.1.2) of Sîn-kāšid adds the epithet 'provider of Eanna' to the titles of Sîn-kāšid. This version of the inscription is found on numerous tablets and cones.

CATALOGUE

Ex.	Museum number	Registration/Excavation number	Warka photo number	Uruk provenance	Dimensions (cm)	Lines preserved	cpn
Tablets							
1	U 335 (Istanbul)	W 558	230–231c	From Sîn-kāšid palace, under reed matting between courses of brickwork in palace wall	–	1–8	p
2	U 330	W 558	230–231e	As ex. 1	–	1–8	p
3	U 299	W 558	230–231h	As ex. 1	–	1–8	p
4	U 328	W 558	230–231m	As ex. 1	–	1–8	p
5	–	W 558	224–225a	As ex. 1	–	1–8	p
6	–	W 558	224–225b	As ex. 1	–	1–8	p
7	VAT 8811	W 558	–	As ex. 1	7.8×5.2×1.9	1–8	c
8	VAT 8816	W 558	–	As ex. 1	6.8×9.3×2.2	1–8	c
9	Heidelberg	W 19818	8185–8186	Sîn-kāšid palace, in small mud bricks of outer wall	8.4×5.7×2.6	1–8	p
10	IM -	W 19826a	8185–8186	Dcxiv3 on diagonal near wall in palace rubble	8.3×6.2×2.5	1–8	p
11	IM -	W 19826b	8185–8186	As ex. 10	8.3×5.5×2.25	1–8	p
12	Heidelberg	W 19826c	8185–8186	As ex. 10	7.3×5.3×2.2	1–8	p
13	Heidelberg	W 19826d	8187–8188	As ex. 10	8.9×5.7	6–8	c
14	IM -	W 19826e	8187–8188	As ex. 10	8.7×5.9×2.1	1–8	p
15	IM -	W 19916,1	–	Ddxiv5, between 5th and 6th course of mud bricks at outer corner of outer wall	8.2×6.3×2.4	–	n
16	Heidelberg	W 19916,2	–	As ex. 15	8.2×5.6×2.5	1–8	c
17	Heidelberg	W 20327,8	–	–	5.3×5.7	1–4	c
18	IM 63625	W 20451,2	–	Found in course of campaign	7.5×5.5	1–8	c
19	Heidelberg	W 20451,4	–	As ex. 18	8.8×5.7×2.3	1–8	n
20	Heidelberg	W 20451,6	–	As ex. 18	9.1×5.4×2.2	1–8	n
21	Heidelberg	W -----,8	–	As ex. 18	9.6×7.5×2.3	1–8	n
22	Private collection in Helsinki	–	–	–	8.5×5.5	1–8	n
23	Wengler 37 – now Altorientalisches Seminar Freie Üniversität Berlin	–	–	–	–	1–8	p
24	Private possession, in Venice	–	–	–	–	1–8	p
25	(see bibliography)	–	–	–	–	–	n
26	Likhochev collection	–	–	–	8.2×6.3		
27	Mission Museum of Werl, MWA2	–	–	–	5.4×4.7×1.9	1–8	p
28	MWA3	–	–	–	6.3×5.3×2.2	1–8	p
29	BCM 305'68	–	–	–	–	–	n

Ex.	Museum number	Registration/Excavation number	Warka photo number	Uruk provenance	Dimensions (cm)	Lines preserved	cpn
30	BCM A.445'1982	–	–	–	7.3×5.4×2.8	–	n
31	BCM A.446'1982	–	–	–	5.3×4.9×2.0	–	n
32	BCM A.447'1982	–	–	–	8.8×5.4×2.2	–	n
33	Ash 1951,380	–	–	–	8.5×6.1×2.0	1-8	n
34	IM 3267A	–	–	–	8.0×6.0	1-8	c
35	YBC 2165	–	–	–	8.2×6.3×2.5	1-8	c
36	Smith College no. 516	–	–	–	–	1-8	n
37	McGill Ethnological Collections, no. 11	–	–	–	4.7×5.5×1.9	1-8	c
38	McGill Ethnological Collections, no. 1.9	–	–	–	8.2×6.4×1.8	1-8	c
39	Manitoba Museum of Man and Nature 436Ah	–	–	–	9.6×6.3×2.6	1-8	c
40	Bibliothèque Nationale et Universitaire de Strasbourg	–	–	–	–	1-8	n
41	IES 125	–	–	–	–	1-8	n
42	HS 2010	–	–	–	9.8×6.2×2.2	1-8	c
Cones							
43	VA 5997	W 558	232 = WVDOG 51, pl. 106a v	From mud brick foundation of Sîn-kāšid palace	6.9	1-8	c
44	VA 5998	W 558	–	As ex. 43	5.2	1-8	c
45	VA 5999	W 558	–	As ex. 43	5.6	1-8	c
46	VA 6000	W 558	–	As ex. 43	6.1	1-8	c
47	VA 6001	W 558	–	As ex. 43	5.1	1-8	c
48	–	W 558	232 = WVDOG 51, pl. 106a v	As ex. 43	–	–	p
49	–	W 558	224-225	As ex. 43	–	–	p
50	Heidelberg	W 20021	–	Eaxiv4, room 30, in robber's pit	5.8	1-8	c
51	Heidelberg	W 20036	–	Ddxiv2, room 7 from mud brick of foundation	5.2	–	n
52	Heidelberg	W 20075	–	Ebxiv4, between mud bricks	5.1	1-8	c
53	Heidelberg	W 20114	–	Eaxiv3, from mud bricks of court 23, SE foundation	5.8	1-8	c
54	IM 63617	W 20134	–	Dexiv5, between mud bricks of foundation of wall between rooms 14 and 15	7.4	1-8	c
55	IM 63616	W 20139	–	Dexiv5, in foundation of wall between rooms 13 and 14	7.0	1-8	c
56	Heidelberg	W 20144	–	Dexiv5, from seam of mud brick foundation of inner corridor wall	7.4	1-8	c
57	IM 63655	W 20145,1	–	From mud brick foundation of palace	6.2	1-8	c
58	IM 63615	W 20450,1	–	From mud brick foundation of palace, found in course of season	5.8	1-8	c
59	Heidelberg	W 20450,2	–	As ex. 58	6.8	1-8	c
60	IM 63644	W 20450,3	–	As ex. 58	5.9	1-8	c
61	Heidelberg	W 20450,5	–	As ex. 58	–	–	n
62	IM 63646	W 20450,6	–	As ex. 58	5.8	1-8	c
63	IM 63647	W 20450,7	–	As ex. 58	6.7	1-8	c
64	Heidelberg	W 20450,8	–	As ex. 58	5.1	1-8?	n
65	IM 63648	W 20450,9	–	As ex. 58	6.8	1-8	c
66	IM 63649	W 20450,10	–	As ex. 58	6.6	1-8	c
67	Heidelberg	W 20450,11	–	As ex. 58	5.0	1-8	c
68	Heidelberg	W 20450,12	–	As ex. 58	5.9	1-8	c
69	Heidelberg	W 20450,13	–	As ex. 58	6.4	1-8	c
70	IM 63650	W 20450,14	–	As ex. 58	6.7	1-8	c
71	Heidelberg	W 20450,15	–	As ex. 58	6.3	1-8	c
72	Heidelberg	W 20450,16	–	As ex. 58	5.0	1-8?	n
73	IM 63651	W 20450,17	–	As ex. 58	7.0	1-8	c
74	IM 63652	W 20450,18	–	As ex. 58	6.8	1-8	c
75	Heidelberg	W 20450,20	–	As ex. 58	5.9	1-8	c
76	Heidelberg	W 20450,21	–	As ex. 58	–	–	n
77	Heidelberg	W 20450,22	–	As ex. 58	5.8	1-8	c
78	IM 63653	W 20450,23	–	As ex. 58	4.8	1-8	c
79	(see bibliography)	–		–	–	–	n
80	Likhochev collection	–	–	–	–	1-8	p
81	Museum of the Buffalo Society of Natural Sciences	–	–	–	–	–	n

Ex.	Museum number	Registration/Excavation number	Warka photo number	Uruk provenance	Dimensions (cm)	Lines preserved	cpn
82	In collection of S. Mercer	–	–	–	–	1–8	n
83	IB 198	–	–	–	–	1–8	n
84	(see bibliography)	–	–	–	–	–	n
85	YBC 2326	–	–	–	6.9	1–8	c
86	NBC 6060	–	–	–	5.9	1–8	c
87	MAH 16451	–	–	–	4.5	1–8	c
88	Smith College no. 516	–	–	–	–	1–8	n
89	IM 2888	–	–	–	5.0	1–8	c
90	IM 3267D	–	–	–	6.2	1–8	c
91	IM 3267E	–	–	–	6.3	1–8	c
92	IM 23091/1	–	–	–	4.2	1–8	c
93	IM 44292	–	–	–	7.0	1–8	c
94	IM 49874A	–	–	–	6.2	4–8	c
95	IM 49874B	–	–	–	5.0	1–4, 6–8	c
96	IM 49874C	–	–	–	5.5	4–8	c
97	IM 49874D	–	–	–	5.7	1–8	c
98	AO 66126	–	–	–	7.3	1–8	c
99	Institute of Archaeology, Hebrew University Jerusalem 128/27	–	–	–	6.5	1–8	n
100	Museum Haaretz, Tel Aviv 113/24	–	–	–	5.0	1–8	n
101	(see bibliography)	–	–	–	–	–	n
102	Mission Museum of Werl, MWB1	–	–	–	5.9	–	n
103	MWB2	–	–	–	5.7	–	n
104	MWB4	–	–	–	6.1	–	n
105	Piepkorn Collection PS 10	–	–	–	–	–	n
106	Piepkorn Collection PS 11	–	–	–	–	–	n
107	Piepkorn Collection PS 12	–	–	–	–	–	n
108	Piepkorn Collection PS 13	–	–	–	–	–	n
109	Piepkorn Collection PS 14	–	–	–	–	–	n
110	Piepkorn Collection PS 17	–	–	–	–	–	n
111	Piepkorn Collection PS 18	–	–	–	–	–	n
112	Piepkorn Collection PS 19	–	–	–	–	–	n
113	Piepkorn Collection PS 20	–	–	–	–	–	n
114	Piepkorn Collection PS 23	–	–	–	–	–	n
115	Crocker Art Gallery, Sacramento	–	–	–	–	1–8	n
116	UCLM 9–142	–	–	–	5.5	1–8	c
117	UCLM 9–2258	–	–	–	5.5	1–8	c
118	Cherkasy 25	–	–	–	6.4	–	n
119	BCM 305'68	–	–	–	–	–	n
120	BCM A.427'1982	–	–	–	5.3	–	n
121	BCM A.428'1982	–	–	–	4.9	–	n
122	BCM A.429'1982	–	–	–	4.1	–	n
123	BCM A.430'1982	–	–	–	5.5	–	n
124	BCM A.431.1982	–	–	–	6.3	–	n
125	BCM A.432'1982	–	–	–	6.2	–	n
126	BCM A.433'1982	–	–	–	6.4	–	n
127	S-G 2	–	–	–	–	1–8	n
128	Ash 1924,642	–	–	–	–	–	n
129	Ash 1924,643	–	–	–	–	–	n
130	Ash 1924,646	–	–	–	–	–	n
131	Ash 1924,647	–	–	–	–	–	n
132	Ash 1924,648	–	–	–	–	–	n
133	Ash 1953,100	–	–	–	–	–	n
134	McGill Ethnological Collections, no. 2.1	–	–	–	–	–	c
135	Newbury District Museum, S 365b	–	–	–	5.1	1–8	c
136	VA 8798	–	–	–	6.5	1–8	c
137	BM 26338	98–5–14,156	–	–	7.0	1–8	c
138	BM 113206	1915–4–10,4	–	–	6.7	1–8	c
139	BM 114182	1919–10–11,272	–	–	5.3	1–8	c
140	BM 114183	1919–10–11,273	–	–	5.8	1–8	c
141	IAC no. 445, Claremont College, California	–	–	–	3.4	1–8	c

COMMENTARY

Tablets

Exs. 1-8 come from a probe in the Sîn-kāšid palace area and were found during Jordan's 1912-13 season. All bear the excavation no. W 558. Exs. 9-21 come from the excavations in the Sîn-kāšid palace in seasons 17-22. Exs. 22-43 are all purchased pieces.

Cones

Exs. 1-7, now in Istanbul or Berlin, were found in the 1912-13 season at Warka in the probe of the Sîn-kāšid palace. They all bear the excavation no. W 558. Exs. 8-36, now in Heidelberg or Baghdad, were found in the excavations of the Sîn-kāšid palace in the 17th to 22nd seasons. Exs. 37-86 were all purchased pieces. Exs. 47-55 in the Iraq Museum were either confiscated or donated pieces, none arising from scientific excavations. Ex. 85, in Berlin, was acquired from another museum, not from the 1912-13 season.

BIBLIOGRAPHY

Tablets

1914 Holma, ZATH no. 10 (ex. 22, copy, edition)
1914-15 Duncan, AJSL 31 p. 216 type B (ex. 25, edition)
1915 Shileiko, VN p. 19 no. IX and pl. I no. 2 (ex. 26, photo, edition)
1923 Deimel, Orientalia os 6 p. 58 no. 4 (ex. 23, transliteration)
1928 Jordan, Uruk-Warka pl. 104 c, e, h, and m (exs. 1-4, photo) and pl. 107 f (copy)
1937 Stephens, YOS 9 no. 123 (ex. 35, study)
1960 Castellino, RSO 35 pp. 29-30 and pl. 2 photo B (ex. 24, photo, edition)
1961 Hallo, BiOr 18 p. 12 Sin-kašid 3 (study)
1963 Szlechter, Manchester 1 pl. LXX (ex. 41, copy); Manchester 2 p. 216 (ex. 41, transliteration)
1968 Kärki, SKFZ pp. 93-94 Sînkāšid 3 (edition)
1969 Oelsner, WZJ 18 p. 54 no. 30 (ex. 42, study)
1970 Pettinato, OrAnt 9 p. 108 and pls. IV-V (exs. 27-28, photo, study)
1971 Sollberger and Kupper, IRSA IVD1c n. a (translation)
1979 George, Iraq 41 p. 122 no. 30 (ex. 29, study)
1980 Kärki, SAKAZ 1 p. 178 Sînkāšid 3 (edition)
1981 Grégoire, MVN 10 no. 37 (ex. 33, copy, study)
1981 Charpin and Durand, Documents Strasbourg no. 148 (ex. 40, copy)
1987 Mauer, Bagh. Mitt. 18 p. 136 no. 1 (ex. 21, copy, edition)

Cones

1914-15 Duncan, AJSL 31 p. 216 type B (ex. 79, edition)
1915 Shileiko, VN p. 19 no. IX and pl. I no. 3 (ex. 80, photo, edition)
1915 Hussey, Bulletin of the Buffalo Society of Natural Sciences 11/2 p. 160 and pl. 19 no. 21 (ex. 81, copy, translation)
1926 Mercer, JSOR 10 p. 285 no. 8 (ex. 82, copy, edition)
1927 Deimel, Orientalia os 26 p. 67 no. 193 (ex. 83, transliteration)
1928 Jordan, Uruk-Warka pl. 106 a nos. i and vi (ex. 48, photo)
1930 Knopf, USCS 2 pp. 1-11 (ex. 141, photo, edition)
1937 Stephens, YOS 9 nos. 125-26 (exs. 85-86, study)
1951 Sollberger, JCS 5 p. 18 1.5b (ex. 87, study)
1952 Gordon, Smith College no. 37 (copy)
1957 Edzard, Sumer 13 p. 178 (exs. 89-97, study)
1960 Aynard, RA 54 p. 18 (ex. 98, transliteration)
1965 Levy and Artzi, ʿAtiqot 4 nos. 87-88 (exs. 99-100, copy, study)
1965 Kienast, JCS 19 p. 41 no. 60 (ex. 101, study)
1970 Pettinato, OrAnt 9 pp. 108-109 nos. 3-22 (exs. 52-53, 56, 59, 64, 62-69, 71-72, 75, 77, study), p. 108 nos. 8-10 (exs. 102-104, study), and pls. VIb and VII (exs. 102-104, photo)
1975 Freedman, St. Louis pp. 10-11 (exs. 105-114, study)
1976 Freedman, JANES 8 p. 36 (ex. 115, transliteration)
1978 Foxvog, RA 72 p. 42 (exs. 115-16, study)
1979 Snell, MVN 9 p. 21 Cherkasy 25 (ex. 118, study)
1981 Grégoire, MVN 10 nos. 38-44 (ex. 127, copy; exs. 127-133, study)
1987 Meltzer, Carl S. Knopf and the I.A.C. Tablet Collection (Claremont) p. 27 (ex. 141, study)

TEXT

1) ^{d}EN.ZU-*kà-ši-id*	1) Sîn-kāšid,
2) nita-kala-ga	2) mighty man,
3) lugal-unu.KI-ga	3) king of Uruk,
4) lugal-*am-na-nu-um*	4) king of the Amnānum,
5) ú-a-é-an-na	5) provider of Eanna,
6) é-gal-	6-8) built his royal palace.
7) nam-lugal-la-ka-ni	
8) mu-dù	

4

A variant of the palace inscription of Sîn-kāšid (E4.4.1.2) adds the phrase 'when he built Eanna' to the epithet 'provider of Eanna'. This form of the inscription is found on tablets and cones.

CATALOGUE

Ex.	Museum number	Excavation number	Warka photo number	Uruk provenance	Dimensions (cm)	Lines preserved	cpn
Tablets							
1	–	W 558	230–231 = WVDOG 51, pl. 104g	From Sîn-kāšid palace under reed matting between courses of brickwork in palace wall	–	1–10	p
2	IM 63624	W 20451,5	–	From mud brick foundation of Sîn-kāšid palace found in course of campaign	5.8×7.8	1–10	c
3	(see bibliography) (Duncan)	–	–	–	–	–	n
4	(see bibliography) (King)	–	–	–	–	1–10	p
5	Mayo, Ireland (Gwyn)	–	–	–	7.5×5.2	1–10	n
6	Kyoto, Japan	–	–	–	–	1–10	p
7	In private possession in Venice	–	–	–	–	1–10	p
8	Minneapolis Institute of Arts, 27	–	–	–	8.3	–	n
9	IES, Cambridge, no. 123	–	–	–	7.0×5.5	1–10	n
10	In possession of Raanan Sivan Jerusalem 13/1297	–	–	–	6.5×5.5×1.7	1–10	n
11	Piepkorn Collection PS 4	–	–	–	–	–	n
12	PS 5	–	–	–	–	–	n
13	PS 6	–	–	–	–	–	n
14	Ash 1924,679	–	–	–	7.6×5.1×2.1	1–10	n
15	BCM A.448'1982	–	–	–	7.4×5.2×2.2	–	n
16	BCM A.449'1982	–	–	–	7.7×5.0×2.2	–	n
17	BCM A.449'1982	–	–	–	7.5×4.9×2.4	–	n
18	Newbury Districy Museum no. S 439	–	–	–	7.8×5.8×2.7	1–10	c
19	ROM 910×209.76	–	–	–	–	1–10	c
20	Le musée d'art de Joliette, Québec	–	–	–	6.6×4.9	1–10	p
21	In private collection in Pasadena, California	–	–	–	7.1×5.4	1–10	c
22	Manitoba Museum of Man and Nature, H3.5-41	–	–	–	7.5×5.5×2.5	1–10	c
23	Manitoba Museum of Man and Nature, H3.5-21	–	–	–	7.8×5.2×2.5	1–6	c
24	Emory University, Atlanta, Georgia no. 115	–	–	–	7.0×5.6	1–10	c
25	–	W 24499	–	Surface find	7.1×5.4	1–10	p
Cones							
26	–	W 558	232 (= WVDOG 51, pl. 106a iii, iv, vii, viii?)	From mud brick foundation of palace of Sîn-kāšid	–	–	p

Ex.	Museum number	Excavation number	Warka photo number	Uruk provenance	Dimensions (cm)	Lines preserved	cpn
27	Heidelberg	W 20450,19	–	From mud brick foundation of palace, found in course of season	6.8	1-10	c
28	IM 63654	W 20450,19	–	As ex. 27	6.2	1-10	c
29	(see bibliography)	–	–	–	–	–	n
30	Toledo, Ohio no. 16.66	–	–	–	5.7	1-10	n
31	Toledo, Ohio no. 22.185	–	–	–	7.2	1-10	n
32	Mount Holyoke	–	–	–	–	–	n
33	IM 21152	–	–	–	5.2	1-10	c
34	IM 23091/2	–	–	–	5.6	1-10	c
35	IM 23091/3	–	–	–	6.2	1-10 (omits 5)	c
36	IM 23091/4	–	–	–	5.5	1-10	c
37	IM 23091/5	–	–	–	6.0	Completely worn, may or may not be this text	c
38	IM 23091/6	–	–	–	4.9	1-6, 8-10	c
39	IM 23091/7	–	–	–	5.2	1-10	c
40	IM 23091/8	–	–	–	6.3	1-10	c
41	IM 29864	–	–	–	6.2	1-10	c
42	IM 42099	–	–	–	5.9	1-10	c
43	IM 54445B	–	–	–	4.8	1-10	c
44	St. Paul Science Museum, no. 1	–	–	–	5.0	–	n
45	University of Minnesota Library, no. 14	–	–	–	5.4	–	n
46	Registration no. 34/1346 Tel Aviv, possession Moshe Harari	–	–	–	5.5	1-10	n
47	Kenrick Theological Seminary, no. 10	–	–	–	–	–	n
48	Piepkorn Collection, PS 9	–	–	–	–	–	n
49	PS 15	–	–	–	–	–	n
50	PS 16	–	–	–	–	–	n
51	PS 21	–	–	–	–	–	n
52	PS 22	–	–	–	–	–	n
53	Ash 1924,481	–	–	–	–	–	n
54	Ash 1924,644	–	–	–	–	–	n
55	Ash 1924,649	–	–	–	–	–	n
56	Ash 1967,1500	–	–	–	–	–	n
57	BCM A.434'1982	–	–	–	6.9	–	n
58	BCM A.435'1982	–	–	–	5.5	–	n
59	BCM A.436'1982	–	–	–	6.2	–	n
60	BCM A.437'1982	–	–	–	6.8	–	n
61	BCM A.438'1982	–	–	–	6.4	–	n
62	ROM 910×209.76	–	–	–	–	1-10	c
63	Oklahoma Historical Society 1.1983.1 = Stovall Museum, no. 620	–	–	–	6.5	1-10	c
64	–	W 24548	–	Surface find	5.8	1-10	p

COMMENTARY

Tablets

Ex. 1 from the 1912–13 season at Uruk bears the excavation no. W 558. Ex. 2 comes from the 19th season of excavations. Exs. 3–24 are purchased pieces.

Cones

Ex. 26 comes from the 1912–13 season and exs. 27–29 from the 19th season. Exs. 30–63 were purchased.

Information on exs. 57–61 comes from A. George, on ex. 63 from D. Snell, and on ex. 64 from R. Böhmer.

BIBLIOGRAPHY

Tablets

1914–15 Duncan, AJSL 31 p. 216 type C (ex. 3, edition)
1915 King, PSBA 37 p. 23 no. 1 and pl. 1 (ex. 4, photo, edition)
1922 Gwynn, Hermathena 19 pp. 273ff. (ex. 5)
1928 Jordan, Uruk-Warka pl. 104 a and g (ex. 1, photo), pl. 107 e (ex. 1, copy), and p. 56 no. 3 (edition)
1928 Nakahara, Kyoto no. 54 (ex. 6, photo, copy, edition)
1929 Barton, RISA pp. 332–33 Singashid 4 (edition)
1960 Castellino, RSO 35 pp. 29–30 and pl. 1 photo A (ex. 7, photo, edition)
1961 Hallo, BiOr 18 p. 12 Sin-kašid 4 (study)
1961 Jones and Synder, Econ. Texts no. 337 (ex. 8, study)
1963 Szlechter, Manchester 1 pl. LXX IES 125 (ex. 9, copy); Manchester 2 p. 216 (ex. 9, edition)
1965 Levy and Artzi, ʿAtiqot 4 no. 85 (ex. 10, copy, study)
1968 Kärki, SKFZ p. 94 Sînkāšid 4 (edition)
1971 Sollberger and Kupper, IRSA IVD1d (translation)
1975 Freedman, St. Louis p. 11 (exs. 11–13, study)
1980 Kärki, SAKAZ 1 p. 179 Sînkāšid 4 (edition)
1981 Grégoire, MVN 10 no. 32 (ex. 14, copy, study)

Cones

1914–15 Duncan, AJSL 31 p. 216 type C (study)
1917–18 Langdon, AJSL 34 p. 123 no. 30 (ex. 29, edition)
1918 Hussey, Mount Holyoke Alumni Quarterly, pp. 211ff. (ex. 32)
1928 Jordan, Uruk-Warka pl. 106 a nos. iii, iv, vii, and viii? (ex. 26, photo)
1957 Edzard, Sumer 13 p. 178 (exs. 33–43, study)
1961 Jones and Synder, Econ. Texts nos. 336 and 339 (exs. 44–45, study)
1965 Levy and Artzi, ʿAtiqot 4 no. 86 (ex. 46, copy, study)
1968 Kärki, SKFZ p. 94 Sînkāšid 4 (edition)
1971 Sollberger and Kupper, IRSA IVD1d (translation)
1975 Freedman, St. Louis p. 11 (exs. 47–52, study)
1980 Kärki, SAKAZ 1 p. 179 Sînkāšid 4 (edition)
1981 Grégoire, MVN 10 nos. 33–36 (exs. 53–56, study)
1985 van de Mieroop and Longman, RA 79 p. 18 no. 30 (exs. 30–31, study)

TEXT

1) ^{d}EN.ZU-*kà-ši-id*	1) Sîn-kāšid,
2) nita-kala-ga	2) mighty man,
3) lugal-unu.KI-ga	3) king of Uruk,
4) lugal-*am-na-nu-um*	4) king of the Amnānum,
5) ú-a-é-an-na	5) provider of Eanna,
6) u_4 é-an-na	6–7) when he built Eanna,
7) mu-dù-a	
8) é-gal-	8–10) he built his royal palace.
9) nam-lugal-la-ka-ni	
10) mu-dù	

5

A variant version of Sîn-kāšid's palace inscription (E4.4.1.2) is known from two headless cones.

CATALOGUE

Ex.	Museum number	Excavation number	Warka photo number	Uruk provenance	Dimensions (cm)	Lines preserved	cpn
1	IM 22623a	W 15712A	3475	In rubble between Ur-Nammu casement wall and ziqqurrat, SW side	5.9	1–9 (omits line 2)	c/p
2	Archaeological Museum, Florence	–	–	–	6.5	1–10	n

COMMENTARY

Ex. 1 omits line 2.

BIBLIOGRAPHY

1957 Edzard, Sumer 13 p. 178 (ex. 1, study)
1960 Oberhuber, Florenz 2 p. 11 (ex. 2, edition)

TEXT

1) ^{d}EN.ZU-*kà-ši-id*	1) Sîn-kāšid,
2) nita-kala-ga	2) mighty man,
3) lugal-unu.KI-ga	3) king of Uruk,
4) lugal-*am-na-nu-um*	4) king of the Amnānum,
5) ú-a-é-an-na	5) provider of Eanna,
6) u$_4$ é-an-na	6–7) when he built Eanna,
7) mu-dù-a	
8) é-gal-gibil	8–10) built his new palace Ekituššaḫula ('House — abode of rejoicing').
9) é ki-tuš-šà-ḫúl-la-ka-ni	
10) mu-dù	

6

Sîn-kāšid's construction work on a temple of the goddess Nanāia is recorded in an inscription found on a small cone excavated at Uruk.

COMMENTARY

The cone, VA 10962, excavation no. W 4152, is from the Arab dump of building J, in Qcxv2, and was left by grave robbers. Warka photos 729–732 show this piece. It is a small headless cone 7.2 cm long and the inscription was collated.

Schott read line 8 as é-[ḫé]-gál-la-ka-na, but collation reveals é-[šà]-ḫúl-la-ka-na.

The inclusion of the title nita-kala-ga 'mighty male' (line 5), found only in this inscription and the palace inscription, may indicate an early date for this inscription. The title seems to have been dropped in subsequent inscriptions of Sîn-kāšid.

The exact meaning of ib in line 7 is unsure. At Lagaš the Ibgal of Inanna of Enannatum was an oval structure. The same might be true of the ib in this text, but this is not certain.

BIBLIOGRAPHY

1930 Schott, Eanna p. 52 and pl. 25 no. 8 (copy, edition)
1961 Hallo, BiOr 18 p. 12 Sin-kašid 9 (study)
1968 Kärki, SKFZ p. 97 Sînkāšid 9 (edition)
1980 Kärki, SAKAZ 1 p. 183 Sînkāšid 9 (edition)

TEXT

1) ^{d}na-na-a	1–3) For the goddess Nanāia, lady adorned with charm, his lady,
2) nin-ḫi-li-sù	
3) nin-a-ni-ir	
4) ^{d}EN.ZU-*kà-ši-id*	4–6) Sîn-kāšid, mighty man, king of Uruk,
5) nita-kala-ga	

E4.4.1.5 line 2.1 omits.

6) lugal-unu.KI-ga
7) ib
8) é-[šà]-ḫúl-la-ka-na
9) mu-na-dù

7–9) built for her an *oval* in her E[ša]ḫula ('House of rejoicing').

7

A number of headless cones excavated at Uruk deal with Sîn-kāšid's construction of a *papāḫum* cella for the gods An and Inanna.

CATALOGUE

Ex.	Museum number	Excavation number	Warka photo number	Uruk provenance	Dimensions (cm)	Lines preserved	cpn
1	IM 22619	W 15368a	3221	Between casement wall of Ur-Nammu and ziqqurrat, Paxvi3	2.4	1–7, 13	c
2	IM 22620	W 15388a	3221	Between casement wall of Ur-Nammu and ziqqurrat, +21	3.0	5–13	c
3	IM 22623a	W 15712a	3475	In rubble between casement wall of Ur-Nammu and ziqqurrat SE side	5.8	4–12	c
4	VA –	W 15712b	3475	As ex. 3	5.1	3–7+ (all that was visible on photo)	p (partial)
5	VA –	W 15722	3478	As ex. 3	5.3	1–13	p (partial)
6	IM 22622	W 15870	3478	As ex. 3	5.2	1–13	c
7	BM 135964 (1973-10-30,1)	–	–	–	5.7	1–13	c

COMMENTARY

The provenance of these cones suggests that this structure may have been adjacent to the courtyard of the Eanna ziqqurrat.

Exs. 4–5 are in Berlin but their VA numbers are not known. Ex. 4 was partially collated from an excavation photo. Ex. 5 is entered from the published copy.

BIBLIOGRAPHY

1957 Edzard, Sumer 13 pp. 187–88 (exs. 1–2, 6, edition) and pl. 4a (ex. 6, copy)
1961 Hallo, BiOr 18 p. 12 Sin-kašid 6 (study)
1963 Falkenstein, Bagh. Mitt. 2 pl. 7 no. 2 (ex. 5, copy)
1968 Kärki, SKFZ p. 95 Sînkāšid 6 (edition)
1971 Sollberger and Kupper, IRSA ivD1e (translation)
1978 Glaeseman in al Khalesi, Mari Palace p. 72 and n. 5 (study)
1980 Kärki, SAKAZ 1 p. 180 Sînkāšid 6 (edition)

TEXT

1) an lugal-dingir-re-ne-ke$_4$
2) ^{d}inanna nin-an-ki-bi-da
3) nin-a-ni-ir
4) ^{d}EN.ZU-*kà-ši-id*
5) lugal-unu.KI-ga
6) lugal-*am-na-nu-um*
7) ú-a-é-an-na
8) u$_4$ é-an-na

1–3) For the god An, king of the gods, (and) the goddess Inanna, lady of heaven and earth, his lady,

4–7) Sîn-kāšid, king of Uruk, king of the Amnānum, provider of Eanna,

8–9) when he built Eanna,

9) mu-dù-a
10) é-pa-paḫ
11) é ki-tuš-
12) šà-ḫúl-la-ka-ne-ne
13) ḫu-mu-ne-dù

10–13) built for them the Epapaḫ, their house, abode of rejoicing.

8

The construction of a temple for the god Lugalbanda and goddess Ninsun by Sîn-kāšid is recorded in an inscription known from cones from Uruk as well as from a Neo-Babylonian copy on a tablet.

CATALOGUE

Ex.	Museum number	Registration/Excavation number	Warka photo number	Provenance	Object	Dimensions (cm)	Lines preserved	cpn
1	BM 91151	51-1-1,168	–	Uruk, no provenance	Head	–	5–9	c
2	BM 91151	51-1-1,168	–	As ex. 1	Shaft	–	1–23	c
3	BM 30071+91150	51-1-1,167+ 56-9-3,1485	–	As ex. 1	Head	–	1–23	n
4	BM 30071+91150	51-1-1,167+ 56-9-3,1485	–	As ex. 1	Shaft	–	1–23	n
5	VA 6218	–	–	–	Shaft	9.2	1–23	c
6	VA 10957	W 4867	906–910	Uruk, building J, from room with a drain, 50 cm NE of door, 60 cm from drain, level with it	Shaft	–	1–23	c
7	VA 10957	W 4867	–	As ex. 6	Head	–	2–14, 19–23	c
8	IM 14174	W –	–	Uruk, provenance not known	Shaft	9.5	1–23	c
9	IM 22617	W 15416	3222–3223	Paxvi4–3, NB houses (near Eanna enclosure wall)	Shaft	8.0	1–23	c
10	IM 60449	W 18912	–	Mb/cxv4, in rubble over house	Shaft	6.4	4–22	c
11	Heidelberg	W 19162	–	Uruk	Shaft	5.5	1–23	c
12	IM 63621	W 20106	8817–8818	Ebxiv5, in rubble of room 42 of Sîn-kāšid palace	Shaft	8.5	1–23	c
13	Heidelberg	W 20168	–	Rubble dump Sîn-kāšid palace	Shaft	8.1	1–14	c
14	Heidelberg	W 21272,1	10569–10573	Uruk, in sump drain in room 75 of palace of Sîn-kāšid	Head	13.3 dia.	1–23	p
15	Heidelberg(?)	W 21272,1	10569–10573	As ex. 14	Shaft	13.0	1–23	p
16	IM –	W 21272,2	10570–10573	As ex. 14	Head	10.0 dia.	3–4, 6–13, 16–23	c
17	IM –	W 21272,2	10570–10573	As ex. 14	Shaft	13.0	1–23	c
18	IM –	W 21272,3	10574–10577	As ex. 14	Head	12.0 dia.	1–13, 15–23	c
19	IM –	W 21272,3	10574–10577	As ex. 14	Shaft	11.5	1–10, 19–23	c
20	–	W 21272,4	10575, 10577	As ex. 14	Shaft	–	12–21	n
21	Heidelberg	W 22071	–	Oexvii2, in NB rubble	Shaft	12.8	1–6, 11–23	c
22	–	W 24558	–	Uruk, surface find	Head	11.3 dia.	–	n
23	Ash 1924,641	–	–	Uruk, –	Shaft	8.1	1–23	n
24	YBC 2186	–	–	Uruk, –	Shaft	8.8	1–23	c
25	YBC 13512	–	–	Uruk, –	Shaft	7.8	1–23	c
26	BM 91081	82-5-22,356	–	From Rassam's excavations in Babylonia; colophon suggests tablet is from Borsippa	Clay tablet	–	1–23	n

COMMENTARY

Exs. 1–4 come from Loftus's excavations at Uruk, provenance unknown. Exs. 5–21 come from the German excavations at the site. Ex. 22, which is very fragmentary, could belong to either E4.4.1.8 or 10; it is arbitrarily edited here. Exs. 23–25 are purchased pieces in various collections.

Ex. 26 is a NB copy on a clay tablet. The colophon indicates that it was copied from a stone tablet which

was in the Ezida temple in Borsippa:
GABA.RI NA$_4$.RÚ.A *šá* NA$_4$.ESI
NÍG.GA *é-zi-da* ^{md}AG-TIN-*su-iq-bi*
A ^{m}*mi-ṣir-a-a iš-ṭur*
'Copy of a royal inscription on diorite stone. Property of Ezida. Nabû-balāssu-iqbi, son of Miṣirāia, wrote (it).'

Although a number of these cones were actually found in the Sîn-kāšid palace area, a few were found in the Eanna area. The latter location is where Falkenstein suggested the temple of Lugalbanda and Ninsun may have been.

BIBLIOGRAPHY

1872 G. Smith, TSBA 1 pp. 41-42 no. 20 (translation)
1874 Lenormant, Études accadiennes 2 pp. 325-26 (study)
1875 Lenormant, Choix no. 64 (copy)
1875 Ménant, Babylone et la Chaldée (Paris) p. 69 (translation)
1886-87 Pinches, BOR 1 pp. 8-11 (ex. 26, copy, edition) and p. 11 (exs. 1-4, study)
1891 4 R^2 pl. 35 no. 3 (ex. 2, copy; exs. 1-4, 26, vars.)
1892 Winckler, KB 3/1 pp. 84-85 Sin-gašid 3 (edition)
1899 Bezold, Cat. 5 p. 2241 (exs. 1-4, 26, study)
1905 Thureau-Dangin, ISA pp. 314-15 Sin-gâšid c (edition)
1905 King, CT 21 pls. 13-14 (ex. 26, copy) and pls. 15-17 (exs. 1-4, copy)
1907 Thureau-Dangin, SAK pp. 222-23 Sin-gâšid c (edition)
1910 King, Early History pl. XXIX facing p. 288 (ex. 26, photo [obv. only])
1929 Barton, RISA pp. 332-33 Singashid 3 (edition)
1930 Schott, Eanna p. 52 no. 9 (exs. 6-7, edition) and pl. 26 no. 9 (ex. 6, copy)
1937 Stephens, YOS 9 no. 124 (ex. 24, study)
1957 Edzard, Sumer 13 p. 178 (exs. 8-9, study)
1961 Hallo, BiOr 18 p. 12 Sin-kašid 8 (study)
1963 Falkenstein, Bagh. Mitt. 2 p. 30 n. 125 (exs. 12-13, provenance) and p. 32 n. 142 (study)
1966 Bottéro, UVB 22 p. 58 nos. 121-25 (exs. 14-20, study)
1968 Kärki, SKFZ pp. 96-97 Sînkāšid 8 (edition)
1970 Pettinato, OrAnt 9 p. 105 D (edition), p. 108 (ex. 13, study), and p. 111 (ex. 21, study)
1971 Sollberger and Kupper, IRSA IVD1g (translation)
1980 Kärki, SAKAZ 1 pp. 181-83 Sînkāšid 8 (edition)
1981 Grégoire, MVN 10 no. 45 (ex. 23, copy, study)

TEXT

1) ^{d}lugal-bàn-da
2) dingir-ra-ni-ir
3) ^{d}nin-sún
4) ama-a-ni-ir
5) ^{d}EN.ZU-*kà-ši-id*
6) lugal-unu.KI-ga
7) lugal-*am-na-nu-um*
8) ú-a-é-an-na
9) u$_4$ é-an-na
10) mu-dù-a
11) é-kankal
12) é ki-tuš-
13) šà-ḫúl-la-ka-ne-ne
14) mu-ne-en-dù
15) bala-nam-lugal-la-ka-né
16) 3 še gur-ta
17) 12 ma-na síg-ta
18) 10 ma-na urudu-ta
19) 3 bán ì-giš-ta
20) ganba-ma-da-na-ka
21) kù-babbar 1 gín-e
22) ḫé-éb-da-sa$_{10}$
23) mu-a-ni mu-ḫé-gál-la ḫé-a

1-4) For the god Lugalbanda, his personal god, (and) for the goddess Ninsun, his mother,

5-8) Sîn-kāšid, king of Uruk, king of the Amnānum, provider of Eanna,

9-10) when he built Eanna,

11-14) built for them the Ekankal, their house, abode of rejoicing.

15-22) In his period of kingship, according to the market value of his land, 3 *gur* of barley, 12 minas of wool, 10 minas of copper, 3 *ban* of vegetable oil cost one shekel of silver.

23) May his years be years of abundance.

4.12 omits. **7**.13 omits. **13**.25 -ne-⟨ne⟩. **15-23**.13 omits. **15**.23 -ka-⟨né⟩. **18**.23 urudu-⟨ta⟩. **21**.2 1 «kù»-gín-e. **21**.23 ⟨1⟩ gín-e.

9

A cone found at Uruk deals with Sîn-kāšid's construction of a *gipar* for his daughter, the *nin-dingir* priestess of the god Lugalbanda.

CATALOGUE

Ex.	Museum number	Excavation number	Warka photo number	Uruk provenance	Object	Dimensions (cm)	Lines preserved	cpn
1	VA –	W 16062	3630–31	From area of Eanna, NW of water trough in mud brick wall of older mantel	Shaft	9.8 long	1–14	p
2	VA –	W 16062	3630–31	As ex. 1	Head	8.2 dia.	1–14	p

COMMENTARY

Falkenstein has suggested that the *gipar* was probably located in the Eanna area not far from the temple of Lugalbanda and Ninsun. The provenance of this cone in Eanna is concordant with such a suggestion. Exs. 1–2 were in Berlin but their VA number could not be determined.

BIBLIOGRAPHY

1937 Falkenstein, UVB 8 p. 24 (exs. 1–2, edition)
1961 Hallo, BiOr 18 p. 12 Sin-kašid 5 (study)
1963 Falkenstein, Bagh. Mitt. 2 p. 33 (study) and pl. 8 (exs. 1–2, copy)
1968 Kärki, SKFZ pp. 94–95 Sînkāšid 5 (edition)
1971 Sollberger and Kupper, IRSA IVD1f (translation)
1980 Kärki, SAKAZ 1 p. 180 Sînkāšid 5 (edition)

TEXT

1) ^{d}EN.ZU-*kà-ši-id*
2) lugal-unu.KI-ga
3) lugal-*am-na-nu-um*
4) ú-a-é-an-na
5) u$_4$ é-an-na
6) mu-dù-a
7) *ni-ši-i-ni-šu*
8) nin-dingir-^{d}lugal-bàn-da
9) dumu-munus-ki-ág-gá-ni-i[r]
10) nam-ti-la-ni-šè
11) ba-ḫun-gá
12) gi$_6$-pàr-kù
13) é-nam-nin-dingir-ra-ka-ni
14) mu-na-dù

1–4) Sîn-kāšid, king of Uruk, king of the Amnānum, provider of Eanna,

5–6) when he built Eanna,

7–11) for Nīši-īnīšu, *nin-dingir* priestess of the god Lugalbanda, his beloved daughter, who was installed on behalf of his life,

12–14) he built for her the shining *gipar*, house of her office of *nin-dingir* priestess.

10

The construction by Sîn-kāšid of a 'seat' for the god Enki in Uruk is recorded in an inscription found on three cones from that city.

CATALOGUE

Ex.	Museum number	Excavation number	Warka photo number	Uruk provenance	Object	Dimensions (cm)	Lines preserved	cpn
1	VA 10964	W 4919	906–910	Building J, most easterly inner court in corner	Shaft	8.3	1–21	c
2	IM 22621	W 15672	3478	Oexvii2	Shaft	7.7	1–3, 5–21	c
3	AO 8866	–	–	–	Shaft	8.2	1–21	c

BIBLIOGRAPHY

1930 Schott, Eanna p. 53 and pl. 26 no. 11 (ex. 1, copy, edition)
1957 Edzard, Sumer 13 pp. 178 and 186 (ex. 2, study)
1960 Aynard, RA 54 p. 18 (ex. 3, study)
1961 Hallo, BiOr 18 p. 12 Sin-kašid 7 (study)
1968 Kärki, SKFZ pp. 95–96 Sînkāšid 7 (edition)
1980 Kärki, SAKAZ 1 p. 181 Sînkāšid 7 (edition)

TEXT

1) ^{d}en-ki
2) en dumu-sag-maḫ-an-na
3) lugal-a-ni-ir
4) ^{d}EN.ZU-*kà-ši-id*
5) lugal-unu.KI-ga
6) lugal-*am-na-nu-um*
7) ú-a-é-an-na
8) u$_4$ é-an-na mu-dù-a
9) géštu nì-maḫ-a
10) mu-na-ni-in-sum-ma
11) ki-tuš-kù-ki-ág-gá-ni
12) mu-na-dù
13) bala-nam-lugal-la-ka-ni
14) 3 še gur-ta
15) 12 ma-na síg-ta
16) 10 ma-na urudu-ta
17) 3 bán ì-giš-ta
18) ganba-ma-da-na-ka
19) kù-babbar 1 gín-e
20) ḫé-éb-da-sa$_{10}$
21) mu-a-ni mu-ḫé-gál-la ḫé-a

1–3) For the god Enki, lofty eldest son of the god An, his lord,

4–7) Sîn-kāšid, king of Uruk, king of the Amnānum, provider of Eanna,

8) when he built Eanna,
9–10) (and the god Enki) gave him intelligence, a supreme thing,
11–12) built for him his beloved shining abode.

13–20) In his period of his kingship, according to the market value of his land, 3 *gur* of barley, 12 minas of wool, 10 minas of copper, 3 *ban* of vegetable oil cost one shekel of silver.

21) May his years be years of abundance.

10.2 Collation reveals mu-na-ni-in-⸢sum⸣-ma. **11**.3 -ki-ág-⟨gá⟩-ni.

11

Sîn-kāšid's construction of the temple of the goddess Ninisina in Uruk is recorded in an inscription found on clay cones excavated at Uruk.

CATALOGUE

Ex.	Museum number	Excavation number	Warka photo number	Uruk provenance	Object	Dimensions (cm)	Lines preserved	cpn
1	VA 10958	W 3704	655–661	Qexɪv4 on surface of slope	Head	13.5 dia.	1-7, 10–24	c
2	VA 10958	W 3704	655–661	As ex. 1	Shaft	13.9	1-24	c
3	IM 25682	W 4868	906–910	Building J, in 'apsu' about 1.5 metres under surface	Shaft	8.2	1-24	c
4	Heidelberg	W 19874	8281-8284	Area of Eanna excavations, in a rubble heap	Shaft	5.6	1-24	c
5	IM –	W 21318	10735–10738	Pbxᴠɪɪ3, surface find	Shaft	12.3	–	n

BIBLIOGRAPHY

1928 Schott, Eanna p. 53 no. 10 (exs. 1-3, edition) and pl. 26 no. 10 (exs. 1-2, conflated copy)
1957 Edzard, Sumer 13 pp. 178, 186–87, and pl. 4b (ex. 3, copy, edition)
1961 Hallo, BiOr 18 p. 12 Sin-kašid 10 (study)
1966 Bottéro, UVB 22 p. 62 no. 155 (ex. 5, study)
1968 Kärki, SKFZ p. 97 Sînkāšid 10 (edition)
1980 Kärki, SAKAZ 1 p. 183 Sînkāšid 10 (edition)

TEXT

1) ^{d}nin-in-si-na
2) šim-mú-un-šár-ra-ba
3) a-zu-gal-sag-gi$_6$-ga
4) nin-a-ni-ir
5) ^{d}EN.ZU-*kà-ši-id*
6) lugal-unu.KI-ga
7) lugal-*am-na-nu-um*
8) engar-maḫ
9) gur$_7$-ra dub-bu
10) ú-a-é-an-na
11) é-gal-maḫ
12) é-nam-nin-a-ka-ni
13) mu-na-dù
14) u$_4$-ba bala-
15) nam-lugal-la-gá
16) 3 še gur-ta
17) 12 ma-na síg-ta
18) 10 ma-na urudu-ta
19) 3 bán ì-giš-ta
20) ganba-
21) ma-da-gá-ka
22) kù-babbar 1 gín-e

1–4) For the goddess Ninisina, incantation priestess of the the numerous people, chief physician of the black-headed (people), his lady,

5–10) Sîn-kāšid, king of Uruk, king of the Amnānum, supreme farmer, who heaps up (grain), provider of Eanna,

11–13) built for her the Egal-maḫ, house of her ladyship.

14–23) At that time in the period of my kingship, according to the market value of my land, 3 *gur* of barley, 12 minas of wool, 10 minas of copper, 3 *ban* of vegetable oil cost one shekel of silver.

1.1 Kärki: ⟨^{d}⟩nin-; collation: [^{d}]. **2.1** Kärki: šim-mú-kalam-ma; collation: sim-mú-un-šár-ra-ba. **9.3** gur$_7$-ra-dub-bu. **9.2** dub-b[é]. **9.4** ⌜gur$_7$⌝-x x [x]. **15.1** Copy indistinct; collation: nam-lugal-la-gá. **22.1** 1 gín-⟨e⟩.

23) ḫé-éb-da-sa$_{10}$
24) mu-mu mu-ḫé-gál-la ḫé-a

24) May my years be years of abundance.

12

An inscription known from two cones found at Uruk deals with Sîn-kāšid's construction of a temple for the god Iškur.

CATALOGUE

Ex.	Museum number	Excavation number	Warka photo number	Uruk provenance	Object	Dimensions (cm)	Lines preserved	cpn
1	Heidelberg(?)	W 18139	6059–6060, 6067–6069	Qbxɪv5 in rubble before NE casement wall on court side	Cone	–	–	n
2	IM –	W 20328	9436, 38, 9446, 47	Obxvɪ4 from surface rubble	Shaft	4.2	1–18	p

COMMENTARY

The edition follows the published copy of ex. 2, which was partially collated from photos. Ex. 2 was not located in the Iraq Museum. Ex. 1 was not collated and the vars. for it are listed from Falkenstein's edition of the inscription.

BIBLIOGRAPHY

1963 Falkenstein, Bagh. Mitt. 2 pp. 50–51 (exs. 1–2, edition) and pl. 6 no. 2 (ex. 2, copy)
1980 Kärki, SAKAZ 1 pp. 184–85 Sînkāšid 11 (edition)

TEXT

1) ⸢^{d}⸣iškur dumu-an-[na]
2) ⸢kù⸣-gál-an-ki-[ra]
3) lugal-a-ni-i[r]
4) ^{d}EN.ZU-*kà*-[*ši-id*]
5) [lu]gal-unu.KI-[ga]
6) [lu]gal-*am-na-nu*-[*um*]
7) ⸢é⸣ u$_{4}$-gal-gin$_{7}$ ki-ḫuš-[a dù-a]
8) ⸢é⸣-ki-ág-gá-[ni]
9) mu-na-[dù]
10) ⸢u$_{4}$⸣-ba bala-nam-lugal-l[a-ka-na]
11) ⸢3⸣ še gur-[ta]
12) [12] ma-⸢na⸣ [síg-ta]
13) [10] ma-⸢na⸣ [urudu-ta]
14) ⸢3⸣ bán ì-giš-[ta]
15) [gan]ba-⸢ma⸣-da-na-[ka]
16) [kù]-⸢babbar⸣ 1 ⸢gín⸣-[e]
17) [ḫé]-éb-da-[sa$_{10}$]

1–3) For the god Iškur, son of the god An, canal inspector of heaven and earth, his lord,

4–6) Sîn-kā[šid, ki]ng of Uruk, [ki]ng of the Amnān[um],

7–9) bu[ilt] for him Eugal-gin-kiḫuš[a-dua] ('House — like a great storm [set in] a wild place'), [his] beloved temple.

10–17) At that time, in the period of [his] kingship, according to the [mar]ket value of his land, 3 *gur* of barley, [12] minas of [wool, 10] minas of [copper], 3 *ban* of vegetable oil [cost] one shekel of [sil]ver.

2.1 -an-ki-r[a]. **10.1** -nam-lugal-la-g[á-ka]. **15.1** ma-da-gá-k[a].

18) [m]u-a-ni mu-ḫ[é-gál-la ḫé-a]

18) [May] his [ye]ars [be] years of ab[undance].

13

A year name found on a tablet from Uruk deals with (the construction) of the city of Dūrum by an unnamed king, probably Sîn-kāšid (see A. Falkenstein, Bagh. Mitt. 2 [1963] pp. 10 and 27). In the great oven on the north-west wall of the pillared hall 28 of the Sîn-kāšid palace a large number of clay cones were found with two inscriptions of Sîn-kāšid. The cones were to be sent to two temples that were under construction in Dūrum, a small city probably not far from Uruk. The cones never made it to their intended destination.

The first inscription deals with the construction of the temple of the god Lugal-Irra, tutelary deity of Dūrum.

CATALOGUE

Ex.	Museum number	Excavation number	Warka photo number	Object	Dimensions (cm)	Lines preserved	cpn
1	IM –	W 21415,1	11008	Head	11.6 dia.	1–20	p
2	IM –	W 21415,1	11009–11012	Shaft	12.2	1–20	p
3	IM –	W 21415,2	11008	Head	11.8	1–20	c
4	IM –	W 21415,2	11009–11012	Shaft	10.7	1–20	c
5	IM –	W 21415,4	–	Head	11.5 dia.	1–9, 11–18	c
6	IM –	W 21415,4	–	Shaft	13.0	1–20	c
7	IM –	W 21415,8	–	Head	–	1–20	n
8	IM –	W 21415,8	–	Shaft	–	1–20	n
9	IM –	W 21415,19	–	Head	12.0 dia.	1–20	c
10	IM –	W 21415,19	–	Shaft	9.0	1–20	c
11	Heidelberg	W 21415,21	–	Head	12.1 dia.	1–20	c
12	Heidelberg	W 21415,21	–	Shaft	10.2	1–20	c
13	Heidelberg	W 21415,22	–	Head	11.0 dia.	1–20	c
14	Heidelberg	W 21415,22	–	Shaft	12.5	1–20	c
15	Heidelberg	W 21415,23	–	Head	11.5 dia.	1–20	c
16	Heidelberg	W 21415,23	–	Shaft	12.6	1–20	c
17	Heidelberg	W 21415,25	–	Head	12.6	1–10, 15–20	c
18	Heidelberg	W 21415,25	–	Shaft	12.4	1–17, 20	c
19	Heidelberg	W 21415,26	–	Head	12.0 dia.	1–10, 12–20	c
20	Heidelberg	W 21415,26	–	Shaft	12.0	1–7	c
21	Heidelberg	W 21415,28	–	Head	11.5 dia.	1–20	c
22	Heidelberg	W 21415,28	–	Shaft	11.0	1–20 (omits 16–17)	c
23	Heidelberg	W 21415,33	–	Head	11.7 dia.	1–20	c
24	Heidelberg	W 21415,33	–	Shaft	11.3	1–20	c
25	Heidelberg	W 21415,37	–	Head	13.5 dia.	1–20	c
26	Heidelberg	W 21415,38	–	Head	11.8 dia.	1–20	c
27	Heidelberg	W 21415,38	–	Shaft	10.8	1–20	c
28	Heidelberg	W 21415,39	–	Head	11.9 dia.	1–20	c
29	Heidelberg	W 21415,39	–	Shaft	11.0	1–20	c
30	Heidelberg	W 21415,40	–	Head	11.5 dia.	1–20	c
31	Heidelberg	W 21415,40	–	Shaft	12.0	1–20	c
32	IM –	W 21415,41	–	Head	11.3 dia.	1–20	c
33	IM –	W 21415,41	–	Shaft	12.5	1–20	c
34	IM –	W 21415,xx	–	Head	10.5 dia.	2–9, 13–20	c
35	IM –	W 21415,xx	–	Shaft	10.2	1–20	c
36	Heidelberg	W 21415,xx	–	Head	12.2 dia.	1–20	c
37	Heidelberg	W 21415,xx	–	Shaft	12.9	1–20	c
38	IM –	W 21415,119	–	Shaft (small headless cone)	8.5	1–20	c

18.1 [mu]-mu mu-.

Ex.	Museum number	Excavation number	Warka photo number	Object	Dimensions (cm)	Lines preserved	cpn
39	–	W 21415,120	11024–11027	Shaft	–	–	n
40	In private possession in Freiburg	–	–	Shaft	10.2	1–20	n

COMMENTARY

The shaft of ex. 25 has text E4.4.1.14.

BIBLIOGRAPHY

1966 Falkenstein, UVB 22 p. 29 (exs. 7–8, edition); Nissen pl. 23bis a (ex. 7, copy) and pl. 23ter a (ex. 8, copy)

1970 Pettinato, OrAnt 9 pp. 105–106 E (edition) pp. 109–11 (exs. 11–24, 26–31, 36–37, study)

1975 Steible, ArOr 43 pp. 346–52 and pl. 2 (ex. 40, copy, edition)

1977 Michalowski, Mesopotamia 12 p. 86 (study)

1980 Kärki, SAKAZ 1 pp. 185–86 Sînkāšid 12 (edition)

TEXT

1) ^{d}lugal-ir$_9$-ra
2) lugal-BÀD.KI-ma
3) lugal-a-ni-ir
4) ^{d}EN.ZU-*kà-ši-id*
5) lugal-unu.KI-ga
6) lugal-*am-na-nu-um*
7) GÌR.NÍTA-BÀD.KI-ma
8) é-ní-ḫuš-íl
9) su-zi-íl-la-na
10) ḫu-mu-na-dù
11) u$_4$-ba bala-
12) nam-lugal-la-gá
13) 3 še gur-ta
14) 12 ma-na síg-ta
15) 10 ma-na urudu-ta
16) 3 bán ì-giš-ta
17) ganba-ma-da-gá-ka
18) kù-babbar 1 gín-e
19) ḫé-éb-da-sa$_{10}$
20) mu-mu mu-ḫé-gál-la ḫé-a

1–3) For the god Lugal-Irra, lord of Dūrum, his lord,

4–7) Sîn-kāšid, king of Uruk, king of the Amnānum, military governor of Dūrum,

8–10) built for him *his* Eniḫušil ('House that bears a fearsome splendour') bearing a frightful brightness.

11–19) At that time, in my period of kingship, according to the market value in my land, 3 *gur* of barley, 12 minas of wool, 10 minas of copper, 3 *ban* of vegetable oil cost one shekel of silver.

20) May my years be years of abundance.

14

The second inscription found in the oven at Uruk (see introduction to E4.4.1.13) deals with the construction of the temple of the god Meslamtaea, the second tutelary deity of Dūrum.

8.9 é-ní-ní-íl. **8–20**.8 omits. **9**.7–8 su-zi-íl-⟨la⟩-na. **9**.14 ⌜su⌝-zi-íl-⌜la-ni⌝. **9**.22 su-zi-íl-⌜la⌝-ni. **13**.14 3 še-gur-⟨ta⟩. **16**.22, 31 omits. **17**.14 ganba-ma-da-⟨gá⟩-ka. **17**.22 omits.

CATALOGUE

Ex.	Museum number	Excavation number	Object	Dimensions (cm)	Lines preserved	cpn
1	IM 69483	W 21415,9	Head	11.8 dia.	1–20	c
2	IM 69483	W 21415,9	Shaft	10.2	1–20	c
3	IM 64919	W 21415,xx	Head	–	1–20	c
4	IM 64916	W 21415,xx	Shaft	–	–	n
5	IM –	W 21415,xx	Head	–	1–20	c
6	IM –	W 21415,xx	Shaft	–	–	n
7	Heidelberg	W 21415,12	Head	13.0 dia.	1–20	c
8	Heidelberg	W 21415,12	Shaft	12.3	1–20	c
9	Heidelberg	W 21415,14	Head	12.7 dia.	1–20	c
10	Heidelberg	W 21415,14	Shaft	12.4	1–20	c
11	Heidelberg	W 21415,16	Head	12.8 dia.	1–20	c
12	Heidelberg	W 21415,16	Shaft	11.8	1–20	c
13	Heidelberg	W 21415,18	Head	13.3 dia.	1–20	c
14	Heidelberg	W 21415,18	Shaft	12.7	1–20	c
15	Heidelberg	W 21415,20	Head	12.2 dia.	1–20	c
16	Heidelberg	W 21415,20	Shaft	12.3	1–20	c
17	Heidelberg	W 21415,24	Head	11.6 dia.	1–16, 18–19	c
18	Heidelberg	W 21415,24	Shaft	12.0 dia.	1–20	c
19	Heidelberg	W 21415,27	Head	11.5 dia.	1–16	c
20	Heidelberg	W 21415,27	Shaft	14.0	1–13, 16–20	c
21	Heidelberg	W 21415,29	Head	11.4 dia.	1–20	c
22	Heidelberg	W 21415,29	Shaft	11.2	1–20	c
23	Heidelberg	W 21415,30	Head	11.5 dia.	1–20	c
24	Heidelberg	W 21415,30	Shaft	11.8	1–20 (omits 5–6, 16)	c
25	Heidelberg	W 21415,31	Head	11.8 dia.	1–20	c
26	Heidelberg	W 21415,31	Shaft	13.5	1–20	c
27	Heidelberg	W 21415,32	Head	12.9 dia.	1–20	c
28	Heidelberg	W 21415,32	Shaft	12.3	1–20	c
29	Heidelberg	W 21415,34	Head	12.0 dia.	1–20	c
30	Heidelberg	W 21415,34	Shaft	10.8	1–20 (omits 9)	c
31	Heidelberg	W 21415,36	Head	12.0 dia.	1–19	c
32	Heidelberg	W 21415,36	Shaft	11.8	1–20	c
33	Heidelberg	W 21415,37	Shaft	11.9	1–20	c
34	IM –	W 21415,42	Head	12.5 dia.	1–15	c
35	IM –	W 21415,42	Shaft	11.4	1–20	c
36	BM 118081 (1926-11-13,30)	–	Shaft	9.6	8–18	c
37	Smithsonian Institution	–	Head	11.0 dia.	1–20	n
38	Smithsonian Institution	–	Shaft	10.5	1–20	n

COMMENTARY

Exs. 3 and 5 were collated from cones on display in the Nasirīya Museum. Only the heads of these cones were visible. Neither the IM nor Warka number could be determined for ex. 5.

Ex. 36 was purchased from Gejou around 1926 and exs. 37–38 in Baghdad in 1941. The latter cone (exs. 37–38) is said to have come from Warka. The head of ex. 33 has text E4.4.1.13.

BIBLIOGRAPHY

1966 Falkenstein, UVB 22 p. 30 (exs. 9–10, edition); Nissen pl. 23bis b (ex. 9, copy) and pl. 23ter b (ex. 10, copy)

1970 Pettinato, OrAnt 9 pp. 106–107 F (edition) and pp. 109–11 (exs. 7–33, study)

1974 Owen, JCS 26 p. 63 (exs. 37–38, study) and p. 64 (ex. 37, copy)

1980 Kärki, SAKAZ 1 p. 186 Sînkāšid 13 (edition)

TEXT

1) ^{d}mes-lam-ta-è-a 2) lugal-BÀD.KI-ma 3) lugal-a-ni-ir	1–3) For the god Meslamtaea, lord of Dūrum, his lord,
4) ^{d}EN.ZU-*kà-ši-id* 5) lugal-unu.KI-ga 6) lugal-*am-na-nu-um* 7) GÌR.NÍTA-BÀD.KI-ma	4–7) Sîn-kāšid, king of Uruk, king of the Amnānum, military governor of Dūrum,
8) é-mes-lam 9) me-lám-gùr-na 10) ḫu-mu-na-dù	8–10) built for him his Emeslam, which bears an aura.
11) u_4-ba bala- 12) nam-lugal-la-gá 13) 3 še gur-ta 14) 12 ma-na síg-ta 15) 10 ma-na urudu-ta 16) 3 bán ì-giš-ta 17) ganba-ma-da-gá-ka 18) kù-babbar 1 gín-e 19) ḫé-éb-da-sa_{10}	11–19) At that time, in my period of kingship, according to the market value of my land, 3 *gur* of barley, 12 minas of wool, 10 minas of copper, 3 *ban* of vegetable oil cost one shekel of silver.
20) mu-mu mu-ḫé-gál-la ḫé-a	20) May my years be years of plenty.

15

A foundation tablet of baked clay in the British Museum deals with the construction of a temple by Sîn-kāšid.

COMMENTARY

Although catalogued as part of the Kuyunjik Collection, Walker suggests that K 7855 may have been found by Loftus at Uruk in 1851 or 1854. The tablet is of gray baked clay and measures 7.1 × 6.1 cm. The inscription was collated.

BIBLIOGRAPHY

1970 Walker, AfO 23 pp. 88–89 (copy, edition)
1980 Kärki, SAKAZ 1 pp. 186–87 Sînkāšid 14 (edition)

1.10, 27, 31, 32 ^{d}mes-lam-ta-è-⟨a⟩. **1**.12 ^{d}mes-lam-ta-⟨UD⟩. DU-a. **1**.20 ^{d}mes-lam-⟨ta⟩-è-a. **3**.26 -a- with two added horizontal wedges. **5**.24 omits. **5**.18, 22, 28 lugal-unu_5(AB).KI-ga. **6**.12 ⌜lugal⌝-*am-na*-⌜*nu*⌝-⟨*um*⟩. **6**.24 omits. **8**.12 omits. **9**.2 me-lám-gùr-ru-na. **9**.9, 30 omit. **9**.14 me-lám-gùr-ni. **12**.12 ⌜nam⌝-lugal-⟨la⟩-gá. **14**.9 ma-⟨na⟩. **14**.31 ⟨síg⟩-ta. **15**.9 urudu-⟨ta⟩. **16**.9, 14, 24 omit. **16**.37 3 bán «gur». **17**.9 omits. **17**.12 ⌜ganba⌝-ma-da-gá-⟨ka⟩. **17**.18 ganba-ma-da-KU-ka. **17**.32 ⌜ganba⌝-ma-da-⌜ta(?)⌝. **18**.9 kù-ba[bbar] ⌜1⌝ ma-na. **18**.12 1 gín-⟨e⟩. **19**.20 ḫé-eb-da-sa_{10}. **20**.9 mu-x-ḫé-[g]ál-⟨la⟩. **20**.18 ḫé-ME. **20**.35 ⟨ḫé-a⟩.

TEXT

1) [^{d}...]
2) [...] x [...]
3) ⸢lugal-a-ni⸣-[ir]
4) ^{d}EN.ZU-*kà-ši-i*[*d*]
5) sipa nì-nam-šár-ra-unu.K[I-ga]
6) engar-maḫ gur$_7$ dub-d[ub-bu]
7) dingir-dingir-re-[ne]
8) ú-a-é-an-[na]
9) GÌR.NÍTA-BÀD.K[I-ma]
10) lugal unu.KI-g[a]
11) lugal-*am-na-nu*-[*um*]
12) ⸢é⸣-[...]
13) [...] x x x am-d[u$_7$...]
14) [...]-e-ne am-gin$_7$ du$_7$-⸢ru⸣
15) [ḫu-m]u-na-dù
16) [u$_4$-ba bala]-nam-lugal-la-gá
17) [3] ⸢še⸣ gur-ta
18) [12] ma-na síg-ta
19) [10] ma-na urudu-ta
20) ⸢3 bán(?)⸣ ì-giš-ta
21) ⸢ganba-ma⸣-da-gá-ka
22) [kù-babbar] 1 gín-e
23) [ḫé-éb]-da-sa$_{10}$
24) [mu-mu mu-ḫ]é-gál-la ḫé-⸢a⸣

1-3) [For the god ...], ..., *his lord,*

4-11) Sîn-kāši[d], shepherd who makes everything abundant for Uruk, supreme farmer who hea[ps] up grain for the gods, provider of Ean[na], military governor of Dūrum, king of Uruk, king of the Amnānu[m],

12-15) built for him E[...], ... butting bull, ... butting like a bull.

16-23) [At that time] in my [period] of kingship, according to the market value of my land, [3] *gur* of barley, [12] minas of wool, [10] minas of copper, 3 *ban* of vegetable oil co[st] one shekel of [silver].

24) May [my years be years of a]bundance.

16

A seal impression found on three clay bullae from the palace of Sîn-kāšid bears an inscription of Šallurtum, the wife of Sîn-kāšid and daughter of Sūmû-la-Il, king of Babylon. This provides an example of a diplomatic marriage in Mesopotamia.

CATALOGUE

Ex.	Museum number	Excavation number	Warka photo number	Provenance	Dimensions (cm)	Lines preserved	cpn
1	Heidelberg	W 20212,1	8814	From palace of Sîn-kāšid, Ebxɪv3, in a corner where square mud bricks meet palace foundation	4.5×7.6	1-4	p
2	IM –	W 20212,2	8814	As ex. 1	4.4×4.3	1-4	p
3	Heidelberg	W 20212,3	8815	As ex. 1	2.5×3.4	1-4	p

BIBLIOGRAPHY

1963 Strommenger, UVB 19 p. 41 (exs. 1-3, edition) and pl. 19a (exs. 1-2, photo)
1963 Falkenstein, Bagh. Mitt. 2 pp. 6-7 (exs. 1-3, edition) and pl. 7 no. 1 (exs. 1-2, photo)
1971 Sollberger and Kupper, IRSA ɪvD1a (translation)
1980 Kärki, SAKAZ 1 pp. 187-88 Sînkāšid 15 (edition)

TEXT

1) *ša-lu-ur-tum*
2) DUMU.MUNUS *su-mu-la-ìl* LUGAL
3) DAM ^{d}EN.ZU-*kà-ši-id* LUGAL
4) KI.ÁG.A.NI

1) Šallurtum,
2) daughter of Sūmû-la-Il, the king,
3) wife of Sîn-kāšid, the king,
4) his beloved.

Sîn-irībam

E4.4.2

Sîn-kāšid was succeeded by Sîn-irībam. Although year names of this king have appeared on tablets, no inscriptions are at present extant for this ruler.

Sîn-gāmil

E4.4.3

Sîn-irībam was succeeded by his son Sîn-gāmil as ruler of Uruk. Three inscriptions are known which date to the reign of this ruler.

1

The first inscription deals with the construction of the Emeurur, temple of the goddess Nanāia in Uruk.

COMMENTARY

The inscription is found on IM 33476, excavation no. W 16934, a brick found in two pieces at Uruk 1/2 m down in sandy rubble on the underside of the Old Babylonian wall, east of the Bīt-Resh which was a continuation of the Seleucid wall. The brick measures 21×22×9.5 cm and the inscription was collated from Warka photos 4524–4525.

Collation of lines 12–18 from the photos suggests a slightly different reading from that of the previous editor.

Bearing in mind the close connections between the goddesses Inanna and Nanāia, this work on the Nanāia temple may be related to the renovation of the shrines of the gods An and Inanna recorded in a year name of Sîn-gāmil.

BIBLIOGRAPHY

1935 Falkenstein, UVB 6 p. 38 (study)
1937 Heinrich, UVB 9 p. 27 (provenance)
1957 Edzard, Zwischenzeit p. 155 n. 821 (study)
1963 Falkenstein, Bagh. Mitt. 2 pp. 51–52 and pl. 9 (copy, edition)
1971 Sollberger and Kupper, IRSA IVD3a (translation)
1980 Kärki, SAKAZ 1 pp. 188–89 Sîngāmil 3 (edition)

TEXT

1) ⸢d⸣na-na-a
2) [d]umu-ki-⸢ág⸣-[a]n-n[a]
3) [n]in-a-ni-ir
4) [dEN.Z]U-*ga-mi-il*
5) [n]ita-kal[a]-ga
6) [lu]gal-unu.KI-ga
7) [lu]gal-*am*-[*na*]-*nu-um*
8) [dumu dEN].ZU-*i-ri-ba-am*
9) [é]-me-ur₄-ur₄
10) [é]-la-la-ka-ni

1–3) For the goddess Nanāia, [d]aughter beloved of the god [A]n, his [l]ady,

4–8) [Sî]n-gāmil, mighty [m]an, [k]ing of Uruk, [k]ing of the Am[nā]num, [son of Sî]n-irībam,

9–11) [b]uilt the [E]meurur ('[House] which gathers the *me*s'), her [house] of delight.

11) [mu]-na-dù	
12) [x x-a]b-[d]a-tuš	12–18) He [*ins*]*talled* her. For ... he renovated it and, ...
13) [...] a-x-aš un-gibil	
14) [...] x x x x-a	
15) [...]-ra-ba	
16) [...]-⸢e⸣ x-⸢sù(?)⸣	
17) [...] x x x [g]ál	
18) [...]-a	

2001

An inscription on a limestone tablet in the British Museum deals with the construction of a temple for the god Nergal in the city of Uṣarpara(n) by Anam, the future king of Uruk, for the life of Sîn-gāmil, the contemporary ruler of Uruk.

COMMENTARY

The tablet is BM 91082 (82-7-14,181) from Rassam's excavations in Babylonia from a collection mainly from the city of Sippar. The tablet was collated.

Uṣarpara(n) was a small city probably not far from Uruk.

BIBLIOGRAPHY

1892 Winckler, KB 3/1 pp. 84–85 Sin-gâmil (edition)
1905 King, CT 21 pl. 17 (copy)
1907 Thureau-Dangin, SAK pp. 222–23 Sin-gâmil a (edition)
1910 King, Early History pl. XXIX facing p. 288 (photo [obv. only])
1929 Barton, RISA pp. 334–35 Singamil 1 (edition)
1961 Hallo, BiOr 18 p. 12 Sin-gamil 2 (study)
1968 Kärki, SKFZ p. 98 Sîngāmil 1 (edition)
1971 Sollberger and Kupper, IRSA IVD3b (translation)
1980 Kärki, SAKAZ 1 p. 188 Sîngāmil 1 (edition)

TEXT

1) ^{d}nergal	1–3) For the god Nergal, lord of Uṣarpara, his lord,
2) lugal-*ú-ṣar-pa-ra*.KI	
3) lugal-a-ni-ir	
4) nam-ti	4–6) for the life of Sîn-gāmil, king of Uruk,
5) ^{d}EN.ZU-*ga-mi-il*	
6) lugal-unu.KI-ga	
7) an-àm pisan-dub-ba	7–10) Anam, archivist, son of Ilān-šemeā, built his temple.
8) dumu-$^{\text{DINGIR}}_{\text{DINGIR}}$-*še-me-a*	
9) é-a-ni	
10) mu-un-dù	

2002

An inscription noted by Scheil deals with the construction of something, probably a temple, for the goddess Kanisura, by Anam, future king, for the life of Sîn-gāmil, king of Uruk.

COMMENTARY

Only a description of this text was given by Scheil. The present whereabouts of the piece is not known.

Scheil left two lines (5–6) untransliterated in his description of the piece. These have been restored according to parallels with E4.4.3.2001, following Kärki.

Kanisura was a deity belonging to the pantheon of Uruk. She appears with An-Inanna and Nanāia in a text cited by Charpin, Le clergé d'Ur pp. 411–12.

BIBLIOGRAPHY

1915 Scheil, RA 12 p. 193 (copy, edition)
1961 Hallo, BiOr 18 p. 12 Sin-gamil 1 (study)
1968 Kärki, SKFZ p. 98 Sîngāmil 1 (edition)
1980 Kärki, SAKAZ 1 p. 188 Sîngāmil 1 (edition)

TEXT

1) [d]kà-ni-sur-ra
2) nin-i_7-turun-gal
3) nin-a-ni-ir
4) an-àm pisan-dub-ba
5) [nam-ti-[d]EN.ZU-*ga-mi-il*]
6) [lugal-unu.KI-ga é-a-ni]
7) mu-na-dù

1–3) For the goddess Kanisura, lady of the Iturungal canal, his lady,

4–7) Anam, archivist, built for her [her temple, for the life of Sîn-gāmil, king of Uruk].

Ilum-gāmil

E4.4.4

Sîn-gāmil was succeeded by his brother Ilum-gāmil as king of Uruk. One inscription is known which mentions this ruler.

2001

A cone deals with the construction of a temple of the god Iškur by Ubār-Adad for the life of Ilum-gāmil.

COMMENTARY

The cone is in the possession of a private collector. It measures 14.5 cm long and the inscription was not collated.

BIBLIOGRAPHY

1964 Biggs, Studies Oppenheim pp. 1–5 (copy, edition)
1971 Sollberger and Kupper, IRSA IVD4a (translation)
1980 Kärki, SAKAZ 1 p. 189 Ilumgāmil 1 (edition)

TEXT

1) ^{d}iškur
2) en ní-gal-an-ki
3) dingir-ra-ni-ir
4) nam-ti-
5) DINGIR-*ga-mi-il*
6) lugal-unu.KI-ga
7) dumu-^{d}EN.ZU-*i-ri-ba-am*
8) *u-bar*-^{d}IŠKUR
9) ìr-da-ni
10) dumu-*a-pil-ku-bi*
11) é-sag-gi$_4$-a-ni-⸢du$_{10}$⸣
12) ki-tuš-nam-en-na-ni
13) mu-na-an-dù
14) ⸢ù⸣ nam-[ti]-la-ni-šè
15) zi-dè-eš
16) mu-na-túm-mu

1–3) For the god Iškur, lord, fearsome splendour of heaven and earth, his lord,

4–7) for the life of Ilum-gāmil, king of Uruk, son of Sîn-irībam,

8–16) Ubār-Adad, his servant, son of Apil-Kūbi, built the Esaggianidu, ('House – whose closing is good'), the residence of his office of *en*, and thereby made it truly befitting his own li[fe].

Etēia

E4.4.5

A king Etēia is mentioned in one economic text found at Uruk (see Falkenstein, Bagh. Mitt. 2 p. 35). Although the placement of this ruler in the Uruk dynasty is not certain, Falkenstein has suggested that he may have followed Ilum-gāmil. No inscriptions of the king are known.

Anam

E4.4.6

Four year names and seven royal inscriptions are known for Anam (or Dingiram), a successor of Ilum-gāmil.

1

We know most about Anam's concern for the renovation of the Eanna area in Uruk. Part of this work involved the restoration of the *gipar*, residence of the *en* priest(ess) for the goddess Inanna. A year name of the king mentions the gate of a *gipar*, presumably the one belonging to Inanna. Two inscriptions of Anam deal with this structure. The first is a foundation inscription recording the construction of the outer courtyard of the *gipar*.

CATALOGUE

Ex.	Museum number	Registration number	Provenance	Object	Dimensions (cm)	Lines preserved	cpn
1	BM 113207	1915-4-10,5	Uruk(?)	Stone tablet	8.2×5.9×1.6	1-12	c
2	YBC 2291	–	Uruk(?)	Limestone tablet	10.0×6.8×1.5	1-12	c

COMMENTARY

Both exs. are purchased pieces.

BIBLIOGRAPHY

1921 Gadd, CT 36 pl. 5 (ex. 1, copy)
1929 Barton, RISA pp. 334-35 Singamil 3 (edition)
1937 Stephens, YOS 9 no. 65 (ex. 2, copy)
1961 Hallo, BiOr 18 p. 12 An-am 3 (study)
1968 Kärki, SKFZ p. 99 Anam 3 (edition)
1971 Sollberger and Kupper, IRSA IVD6d (tanslation)
1980 Kärki, SAKAZ 1 pp. 190-91 Anam 3 (edition)

TEXT

1) ᵈinanna
2) nin-gal-é-an-na
3) nin-a-ni-ir
4) an-àm

1-3) For the goddess Inanna, great lady of Eanna, his lady,

4-8) Anam, true shepherd of Uruk, favourite of

5) sipa-zi-unu.KI-ga	the gods An and Inanna, beloved son of the goddess Inanna,
6) še-ga-an-^{d}inanna	
7) dumu-ki-ág-	
8) ^{d}inanna-ke$_4$	
9) kisal-bar-ra-	9–12) built for her the outer courtyard of the *gipar* of the *en* priest(ess), her abode of rejoicing.
10) é-gi$_6$-pàr-en-na	
11) ki-tuš-šà-ḫúl-la-na	
12) mu-na-dù	

2

A longer inscription at present in the Yale collections deals with the construction of a *gipar* of the goddess Inanna by Anam.

COMMENTARY

The text is YBC 2145, a purchased piece, presumably originally from Uruk. It is a limestone tablet, measuring 28×21.2×6 cm, and the inscription was collated.

BIBLIOGRAPHY

1915 Clay, YOS 1 no. 36 (copy, edition)
1922–23 Langdon, AJSL 39 pp. 139–40 (edition)
1929 Barton, RISA pp. 334–35 Singamil 5 (edition)
1961 Hallo, BiOr 18 p. 12 An-am 4 (study)
1963 Falkenstein, Bagh. Mitt. 2 pp. 53–54 (edition)
1968 Kärki, SKFZ pp. 99–100 Anam 4 (edition)
1971 Sollberger and Kupper, IRSA IVD6e (translation)
1980 Kärki, SAKAZ 1 p. 191 Anam 4 (edition)

TEXT

1) ^{d}inanna	1–3) For the goddess Inanna, great lady of Eanna, my lady,
2) nin-gal-é-an-na	
3) nin-mu-ra	
4) an-àm sipa-zi-	4–9) I Anam, true shepherd of Uruk, disciplined steward, favourite of the gods An and Inanna, beloved son of the goddess Inanna.
5) unu.KI-ga-ke$_4$	
6) agrig-šu-dim$_4$-ma	
7) še-ga-an-^{d}inanna	
8) dumu-ki-ág-	
9) ^{d}inanna-a-me-en	
10) u$_4$ é-an-^{d}inanna	10–15) When I renovated and restored the temple of the gods An (and) Inanna, the ancient work of divine Ur-Nammu and Šulgi,
11) nì-dím-dím-libir-ra	
12) ^{d}ur-^{d}nammu	
13) ^{d}šul-gi-ra-ke$_4$	
14) mu-un-gibil$_4$-a	
15) ki-bé bí-gi$_4$-a	
16) é-gi$_6$-pàr-en-na	16–19) I founded there the *gipar* of the *en* priest(ess), his/her abode of rejoicing, suitable for her delight.
17) ki-tuš-šà-ḫúl-la(*)-na	
18) la-la-bi-šè túm-ma	

---

17 Text: EN.

19) mu-un-ki-gar
20) é-gibil$_4$-gin$_7$
21) ḫu-mu-ù-tu

20–21) I created it as if it were a new temple.

22) GIŠ.ig-gal-gal-eren-a
23) GIŠ.*e-lam-ma-kum*
24) ḫur-sag(*)-ta DU-a
25) GIŠ.ig-ì-šéš
26) KUŠ-á(*)-si(*)-bi
27) alam-sa$_6$-ga
28) ul zabar-ḫuš šu-du$_7$
29) me-te-é-e-ke$_4$
30) ba-ab-du$_7$
31) é-bé ḫu-mu-si-si

22–31) I filled that temple with very large doors of cedar and *elamakkum* wood brought from the mountains, door(s) annointed with oil, with leather *straps*, beautiful statues, a *star* inlaid with awesome bronze ornaments of the temple that were suitable.

32) lú mu-sar-ra-ba
33) šu bí-íb-ùr-a
34) mu-ni
35) bí-íb-sar-re-a
36) an-gal
37) a-a-dingir-re-e-ne
38) ^{d}inanna nin-an-ki-ke$_4$
39) áš-ḫul-bi
40) ḫé-em-bal-eš

32–40) [As for] the man who erases this inscription and writes his own name, may great An, father of the gods, (and) the goddess Inanna, lady of heaven and earth, inflict on him a terrible curse.

3

An unplaced year name belonging to one of the successors of Sîn-kāšid deals with the restoration(?) of the old temple of the gods An and Inanna. The renovation of the old temple of An is recorded in a door socket of Anam found at Uruk, a fact which allows a probable attribution of the year name.

COMMENTARY

The door socket is in the Iraq Museum, IM no. as yet undetermined. The excavation no. is W 16906, found in OdXVI 1, +23.08 metres high. The piece was collated from Warka photo 4526.

BIBLIOGRAPHY

1938 Falkenstein, UVB 9 p. 15 and pl. 28a (copy, edition)
1961 Hallo, BiOr 18 p. 12 An-am 5 (study)
1968 Kärki, SKFZ p. 100 Anam 5 (edition)
1971 Sollberger and Kupper, IRSA IVD6b (translation)
1980 Kärki, SAKAZ 1 pp. 192–93 Anam 5 (edition)

24 Text: KA. **26** -á-si-; text: -DA-LAGAB-.

TEXT

1) an lugal-dingir-re-e-ne
2) lugal-a-ni-ir
3) ^{d}inanna nin-gal-é-an-na
4) nin-a-ni-ir
5) an-àm sipa-zi
6) unu.KI-ga
7) dumu-ki-ág-
8) ^{d}inanna-ke$_4$
9) u$_4$ é-a-ni-libir
10) mu-un-gibil
11) ki-bé bí-in-gi$_4$-a
12) GIŠ.ig-ì-šéš
13) al-gub-bu

1–4) For the god An, king of the gods, his lord, (and) the goddess Inanna, great lady of Eanna, his lady,

5–8) Anam, true shepherd of Uruk, beloved son of the goddess Inanna,

9–11) when he renovated her ancient temple and restored it

12–13) set up a door anointed with oil.

4

A short inscription found on stone tablets alludes to Anam's construction of the wall of Uruk.

CATALOGUE

Ex.	Museum number	Provenance	Object	Dimensions (cm)	Lines preserved	cpn
1	CBS 103	Said to come from neighbourhood of Babylon, presumably originally from Uruk	Soapstone tablet	4.8×4.0×0.8	1–8	c
2	In private possession in Jerusalem	Uruk(?)	Soapstone tablet frgm.	3.0×4.0×0.8	4–12	p
3	National Museum of Man, Ottawa, no. XXIV.H33c	Uruk(?)	Stone tablet	4.8×4.0×1.1	1–12	c

BIBLIOGRAPHY

1893 Hilprecht, BE 1/1 no. 26 (ex. 1, copy, study)
1893–95 Hommel, PSBA 16 pp. 13–15 (ex. 1, copy, edition)
1894 Hilprecht, Assyriaca pp. 101–106 (study)
1895 Winckler, AOF 1 pp. 274–75 (edition)
1896 Hilprecht, BE 1/2 p. 48 n. 3 (study)
1900 Jensen, KB 6/1 pp. 268–71 no. IIa (edition)
1900 Radau, EBH p. 227 (edition)
1905 Thureau-Dangin, ISA pp. 316–17 Sin-gâmil b (edition)
1907 Thureau-Dangin, SAK pp. 222–23 Sin-gâmil b (edition)
1929 Barton, RISA pp. 334–35 Singamil 2 (edition)
1961 Hallo, BiOr 18 p. 12 An-am 1 (study)
1968 Kärki, SKFZ p. 98 Anam 1 (edition)
1971 Sollberger and Kupper, IRSA IVD6a (translation)
1971 Tournay, Studies Albright pp. 453–57 (ex. 2, photo, partial edition)
1980 Kärki, SAKAZ 1 p. 190 Anam 1 (edition)
1983 Sweet, ARRIM 1 p. 23 (ex. 3, edition)

TEXT

1) an-àm
2) ab-ba-ugnim-
3) unu.KI-ga-ke$_4$
4) dumu-$^{\text{DINGIR}}_{\text{DINGIR}}$-*še-me-a*
5) bàd-unu.KI-ga
6) níg-dím-dím-libir-ra

1–4) Anam, chief of the army of Uruk, son of Ilān-šemeā,

5–8) who restored the wall of Uruk, the ancient work of divine Gilgameš,

7)	^{d}bìl-ga-meš-ke$_4$	
8)	ki-bé bí-in-gi$_4$-a	
9)	a nígin-na-ba	9–12) constructed it (the wall) for him (divine Gilgameš) in baked bricks in order that water might roar in its (the wall's) surrounding (moat).
10)	gu-nu-un-di-dàm	
11)	sig$_4$-al-ùr-ra-ta	
12)	mu-na-dù	

5

The fashioning of a gù-nun-di-dam also figures in an inscription of Anam in the Yale collections.

COMMENTARY

The inscription is found on YBC 2152, a purchased tablet, presumably originally from Uruk. It is a limestone tablet measuring 6.7×4.8×1.7 cm, and the inscription was collated.

BIBLIOGRAPHY

1913–14 Johns, AJSL 30 pp. 290–91 (edition)
1915 Clay, YOS 1 no. 35 (copy, edition)
1929 Barton, RISA pp. 334–35 Singamil 4 (edition)
1961 Hallo, BiOr 18 p. 12 An-am 2 (study)
1968 Kärki, SKFZ p. 99 Anam 2 (edition)
1971 Sollberger and Kupper, IRSA IVD6c (translation)
1980 Kärki, SAKAZ 1 p. 190 Anam 2 (edition)

TEXT

1)	^{d}inanna	1–2) For the goddess Inanna, his lady,
2)	nin-a-ni-ir	
3)	an-âm sipa-zi	3–6) Anam, true shepherd of Uruk, beloved son of the goddess Inanna,
4)	unu.KI-ga	
5)	dumu-ki-ág	
6)	^{d}inanna-ke$_4$	
7)	⌜u$_4$⌝ é-a-ni-libir	7–9) when he renovated her ancient temple and restored it
8)	mu-un-gibil	
9)	ki-bé bí-gi$_4$-a	
10)	a gù-nun-di-dam	10–11) built the (moat) 'Roaring water'.
11)	mu-un-dù	

6

A fragment of a badly preserved inscription of Anam excavated at Uruk deals with some goddess, possibly Inanna, whose name is broken away.

COMMENTARY

The piece is in the Iraq Museum, IM no. not known, excavation no. W 16591, found at Uruk, Paxvi5, 1.30 m under the Sargon casement wall. The inscription was not collated.

BIBLIOGRAPHY

1963 Falkenstein, Bagh. Mitt. 2 p. 54 and pl. 9 no. 2 (copy, edition)
1980 Kärki, SAKAZ 1 p. 193 Anam 6 (edition)

TEXT

1) ^{d}[inanna]
2) nin-a-n[i-ir]
3) an-àm [sipa-zi]-
4) u[nu.KI-ga]
Lacuna
1') en-n[a ...]
2') mu-u[n-...]

1–2) [For] the goddess [Inanna], hi[s] lady,

3–4) Anam, [true shepherd of] U[ruk],
Lacuna

1'–2') ...

2001

A cylinder seal in the Yale collections bears the name of a servant of Anam.

COMMENTARY

The piece is NBC 1199, a cylinder seal of carnelian, 2.5×1.4 cm, which was purchased and which probably originally came from Uruk. The inscription was collated from the published photo.

BIBLIOGRAPHY

1981 Buchanan and Hallo, Early Near Eastern Seals no. 769 (photo, edition)

TEXT

1) *ì-lí-i-dí-nam*
2) DUMU *ma-a-nu-um*
3) IR$_{11}$ an-àm

1) Ilī-iddinam,
2) son of Mānum,
3) servant of Anam.

2002

An impression of a servant of Anam is found on a tablet excavated at Uruk.

COMMENTARY

The tablet bearing the seal impression is W 20472,202 and the impression is 2.7 cm high. It was not collated.

BIBLIOGRAPHY

1988 Sanati-Müller, Bagh. Mitt. 19 p. 538 no. 43 seal d (copy, edition)

TEXT

1) ⌜*ì*⌝-*pí-iq-eš*$_4$-*tár*	1) Ipiq-Eštar,
2) DUMU *a-pu-ú-um*	2) son of Apûm,
3) ÌR an-àm	3) servant of Anam.

ÌR-ne-ne

E4.4.7

Four year names of ÌR-ne-ne, successor of Anam, are known from the Uruk tablets. This king's defeat is commemorated in the name of year 14 of Rīm-Sîn of Larsa. While no royal inscriptions of this ruler have appeared, impressions of seals of two of his servants are known.

2001

Impressions of the first servant seal are found on four tablets excavated at Uruk. The impressions were transliterated by H. Waetzoldt and are published here through the courtesy of M. Boehmer.

COMMENTARY

The tablets are W 20472,62, 20472,69, 20472,77 (tablet), and 20472,77 (envelope).

BIBLIOGRAPHY

1988 Sanati-Müller, Bagh. Mitt. 19 pp. 489–537 (exs. 1–4, copy, edition)

TEXT

1) *i-ni-é-*[x-x]
2) DUMU *pi-iq-qum*
3) ÌR ÌR-ne-ne

1) I-ni-é-[...],
2) son of Pīqqum,
3) servant of ÌR-ne-ne.

2002

The second servant seal is impressed on a tablet envelope excavated at Uruk.

COMMENTARY

The impression is found on W 20472,202a.

BIBLIOGRAPHY

1988 Sanati-Müller, Bagh. Mitt. 19 p. 538 no. 43 seal b (copy, edition)

TEXT

1) *i-din-*[d]*na-*[*na-a*]	1) Iddin-Na[nāia],
2) DUMU [d]EN.ZU-*i-ri-*[*ba-am*]	2) son of Sîn-irī[bam],
3) ÌR ÌR-ne-ne	3) servant of ÌR-ne-ne.

2003

An impression of a servant of ÌR-ne-ne is found on a tablet excavated at Uruk.

COMMENTARY

The impression is rolled on W 20472,19, which was not collated.

BIBLIOGRAPHY

1988 Sanati-Müller, Bagh. Mitt. 19 p. 489 (copy, edition)

TEXT

1) *na-bi-ì-lí-šu*	1) Nabi-ilīšu,
2) DUMU [d]EN.ZU-*kà-ši-id*	2) son of Sîn-kāšid,
3) ÌR ÌR-ne-ne	3) servant of ÌR-ne-ne.

Rīm-Anum

E4.4.8

A number of Old Babylonian tablets are known which belong to an archive dealing with distribution of flour for the *bīt asīrī* 'house of the prisoners', and which bear year names of the ruler Rīm-Anum. The city from which Rīm-Anum ruled is not known. A number of tablets bearing his year names were excavated at Uruk and the king's servant seals are conveniently edited at this point. M. Ellis (see bibliography) has demonstrated that Rīm-Anum was a contemporary of Samsu-iluna of Babylon.

BIBLIOGRAPHY

1963 Falkenstein, Bagh. Mitt. 2 pp. 39–40 (study)
1986 M. Ellis, RA 80 pp. 65–72 (study)

2001

The impression of the seal of Nabi-ilīšu, the archivist, servant of Rīm-Anum, is found on a number of tablets.

CATALOGUE

Ex.	Museum number	Registration number	cpn
1	VAT 3928	–	n
2	VAT 3965	–	n
3	VAT 3863	–	n
4	VAT 3878	–	n
5	BM 14030	96-4-2,130	n
6	BM 14070	96-4-2,172	n
7	BM 14074	96-4-2,176	n
8	BM 14075	96-4-2,177	n
9	BM 14077	96-4-2,179	n
10	BM 14079	96-4-2,181	n
11	BM 14080	96-4-2,182	n
12	BM 14082	96-4-2,184	n
13	BM 14084	96-4-2,186	n
14	BM 14087	96-4-2,189	n
15	BM 14092	96-4-2,194	n
16	BM 14154	96-4-2,256	n
17	BM 14175	96-4-2,276	n
18	BM 14188	96-4-2,289	n

BIBLIOGRAPHY

1914 Figulla, VAS 13 nos. 48–49, 53, and 55 (exs. 1–4, copy)
1978 Loretz, UF 10 pp. 122–36 nos. 5, 12, 15, 17–19, 21–22, 24–25, 27, 30, 32, 34, 36–37 (exs. 5–18, transliteration)
1986 M. Ellis, RA 80 p. 69 and n. 25 (study)

TEXT

1) *na-bí-ì-lí-šu*	1) Nabi-ilīšu,
2) PISAN.DUB.BA	2) archivist,
3) DUMU *la-ki-ta-re-me-ni*	3) son of Lakīta-rēmēni,
4) ÌR *ri-im-*^{d}*a-nu-um*	4) servant of Rīm-Anum.

2002

The impression of the seal of Apil-Amurrûm, servant of Rīm-Anum, is found on three tablets in the British Museum.

CATALOGUE

Ex.	Museum number	Registration number	cpn
1	BM 14030	96-4-2,130	n
2	BM 14061	96-4-2,162	n
3	BM 14065	96-4-2,166	n

BIBLIOGRAPHY

1978 Loretz, UF 10 pp. 124 and 126–27 nos. 5, 10, and 12 (exs. 1–3, transliteration)

TEXT

1) *a-pi-il-*^{d}MAR.DÚ	1) Apil-Amurrûm,
2) DUMU ^{d}šul-[gi-...]	2) son of Šul[gi- ...],
3) ÌR *ri-im-*^{d}*a-n*[*u-um*]	3) servant of Rīm-An[um].

2003

The impression of another servant of Rīm-Anum is found on two tablets in Berlin.

COMMENTARY

The impression is on VAT 3855 and VAT 3875, which were not collated.

BIBLIOGRAPHY

1914 Figulla, VAS 13 nos. 52, 54 (ex. 1–2, copy)

TEXT

1) ^{d}EN.ZU-*i*-[...]
2) [P]ISAN.DUB.[BA]
3) DUMU *i-din*-[...]
4) ÌR *ri-im*-^{d}[*a-nu-um*]

1) Sîn-i[...]
2) archivist,
3) son of Iddin-[...],
4) servant of Rīm-[Anum].

Nabi-ilīšu

E4.4.9

A year name found on a tablet from Uruk discussed by Falkenstein (Bagh. Mitt. 2 [1963] p. 12 no. 23) deals with the accession year of king Nabi-ilīšu. Falkenstein suggested that this might be the same Nabi-ilīšu who appears in the seal impression treated here as E4.4.8.2001. If so, Nabi-ilīšu probably followed Rīm-Anum as king. No servant seals of this ruler are at present known.

BIBLIOGRAPHY

1963 Falkenstein, Bagh. Mitt. 2 pp. 40–41 (study)
1987 Mauer, Bagh. Mitt. 18 p. 147 no. 22 (study)

EŠNUNNA

E4.5

Year 3 of Ibbi-Sîn marks the last year name of the Ur king used in Ešnunna (see R. Whiting, AfO 34 [1987] p. 33), after which the city was independent. The first attested independent ruler of the city, Šū-ilīia, adopted the title 'king', and used his own year names. His reign is contemporary with Ibbi-Sîn's and his inscriptions will be edited in RIME 3.

After the reign of Šū-ilīia, kingship of Ešnunna passed to the god Tišpak. While employing their own year names, succeeding rulers of the city down to the reign of Ipiq-Adad II served simply as governor (ÉNSI) under the god Tišpak. Beginning in the time of Ipiq-Adad II, the rulers of Ešnunna adopted the title lugal 'king' and sometimes used the prefixed divine determinative in the writing of their names.

Nūr-aḫum

E4.5.1

The first Isin period governor of Ešnunna was Nūr-aḫum, who was installed by Išbi-Erra of Isin. This ruler is mentioned in the literary letter of Puzur-Šulgi to Ibbi-Sîn (see F. Ali, Sumer 26 [1970] p. 162 line 37) and ruled at least seven years.

1

Bricks with the standard inscription of Nūr-aḫum were found at Ešnunna.

COMMENTARY

The only listed example of this inscription is As 31:T.50a, a brick from the Nūr-aḫum palace. The present location of the brick is not known and it was not available for collation.

BIBLIOGRAPHY

1940 Jacobsen, Gimilsin Temple p. 135 no. 2 (edition) and pl. 14 no. 2 (copy)

1961 Hallo, BiOr 18 p. 12 Ešnunna 1: i (study)

1971 Sollberger and Kupper, IRSA IVE1a (translation)

TEXT

1) *nu-úr-a-ḫu-um*
2) *na-ra-am* ^d^*tišpak*
3) ÉNSI
4) *áš-nun-na*.KI

1) Nūr-aḫum,
2) beloved of the god Tišpak,
3–4) governor of Ešnunna.

2

Diplomatic marriages are commonly attested in ancient Mesopotamian history. Nūr-aḫum married his daughter to a certain Ušašum, the son of an important Amorite chief, Abda-Il. An impression of a seal granted to Ušašum by his father-in-law Nūr-aḫum is found on a tablet excavated at Ešnunna.

COMMENTARY

The seal impression is found on As 30:T.757 =(?) As 30:450, found at N 31:1 in the Šū-ilīia–Nūr-aḫum palace. The impression was collated by R. Whiting.

Ušašum and his father Abda-Il appear on a tablet (BIN 9 no. 316 lines 13-14) dating to year x+10 of Išbi-Erra. This confirms that the reign of Nūr-aḫum was contemporary, at least in part, with the reign of Išbi-Erra.

BIBLIOGRAPHY

1940 Jacobsen, Gimilsin Temple p. 145 no. 10 (edition)
1961 Hallo, BiOr 18 p. 14 Ešnunna 21: ii (study)
1976 Stol, Studies in Old Babylonian History p. 87 (study)
1977 Franke in Gibson and Biggs, Seals p. 63 (study)
1987 Whiting, Letters p. 26 and pl. 27 (copy, edition)

TEXT

1) ⌜*nu*⌝-*ur-a-ḫu-um*
2) *na-ra-am* ^d^*tišpak*
3) [ÉNSI]
4) [*éš-nun-na*.KI]
5) [*a-na*]
6) *ú-ša-*⌜*šum*⌝
7) *e-mi-šu*
8) DUMU *ab-*⌜*da-il*⌝
9) [*ra-bí*]-*an*
10) [*a-mu-r*]*i-im*
11) [*i-q*]*i*$_4$-*iš*

1-4) Nūr-aḫum, beloved of the god Tišpak, [governor of Ešnunna],

5-11) [pres]ented (this seal) [to] Ušašum, his son-in-law, son of Abda-Il, [Amor]ite [chi]ef.

2001

The seal impression of Ūṣi-dannum, cupbearer (sagi) of Nūr-aḫum, is found on three clay tablets excavated at Ešnunna.

CATALOGUE

Ex.	Excavation number	Provenance	cpn
1	As 30:T.462	Ešnunna, M 31:1, from the Šū-ilīia–Nūr-aḫum palace	c
2	As 31:T.224	O 30:18, from the Itūrīia temple	c
3	As 31:T.244	As ex. 2	c

COMMENTARY

Jacobsen read the fourth line of the inscription ⌜*warad*(?)⌝ ŠU(?) GAB(?), but collation by Whiting reveals that it reads SÌLA.ŠU.DU$_8$ = SAGI.

Ex. 2 is actually a different seal impression of Ūṣi-dannum. Line 3 reads *ú-ṣi-*⌜*da-nu-um*⌝ and line 4 SAGI ⌜ÌR.ZU⌝.

BIBLIOGRAPHY

1940 Jacobsen, Gimilsin Temple p. 145 no. 11 (edition)
1961 Hallo, BiOr 18 p. 14 Ešnunna 21: ii (study)
1971 Sollberger and Kupper, IRSA ɪᴠE1b (translation)

TEXT

1) *nu-úr-a-ḫu-um*	1) Nūr-aḫum,
2) *na-ra-am* ^{d}*tišpak*	2) beloved of the god Tišpak –
3) *ú-ṣi-da-num*	3) Ūṣi-dannum,
4) SAGI	4) cupbearer,
5) [ÌR.ZU]	5) [your servant].

2002

The impression of a seal of Ur-Šara, another cupbearer of Nūr-aḫum, is found on two clay tablets excavated at Ešnunna.

CATALOGUE

Ex.	Excavation number	Provenance	cpn
1	As 31:207	Ešnunna	c
2	As 31:193	P 31:2, Bilalama palace	c

COMMENTARY

The tablet with ex. 2 contains the year name, mu NIM ì-im-zi 'the year he roused Elam', which consequently should be attributed to Nūr-aḫum. The seal impression, given here for the first time, is edited through the courtesy of the trustees of the Oriental Institute.

TEXT

1) *nu-úr-a-ḫu-um*	1) Nūr-aḫum,
2) ÉNSI	2–3) governor of Ešnunna –
3) *áš-nun*.KI	
4) ur-^{d}šára	4) Ur-Šara,
5) SAGI	5) cupbearer,
6) ÌR.ZU	6) your servant.

E4.5.1.2001 line 4.2 adds ⌜ÌR.ZU⌝.

2003

The seal impression of a scribe of Nūr-aḫum is found on a tablet excavated at Ešnunna.

COMMENTARY

The tablet is As 31:T.412 found under L 31:2, the Bilalama palace. The impression was collated by R. Whiting, who offers a reading slightly modified from Jacobsen's previous publication (cf. line 5).

BIBLIOGRAPHY

1940 Jacobsen, Gimilsin Temple p. 144 no. 9 (edition)
1961 Hallo, BiOr 18 p. 14 Ešnunna 21: ii (study)

TEXT

1) [*nu-úr-a*]-*ḫu-um*	1) [Nūr-a]ḫum,
2) [*na-ra-a*]*m* ^{d}*tišpak*	2) [belove]d of the god Tišpak –
3) [...]-*ša-bi*-⸢x⸣	3) [...]šabi[...],
4) [DUB].SAR	4) [scr]ibe,
5) [DUMU ...-*k*]*um*	5) [son of ...k]um,
6) ÌR.ZU	6) your servant.

2004

The seal impression of a servant of Nūr-aḫum is found on a tablet excavated at Ešnunna.

COMMENTARY

The impression is on As 31:T.266 from O 30:18, the Bilalama palace. The piece is edited here for the first time through the courtesy of the trustees of the Oriental Institute.

The tablet has a line, *a-a-ni-šu* ŠU BA.AN.TI, to be connected with the PN of line 3.

TEXT

1) *nu-úr-a-ḫu-um*	1) Nūr-aḫum,
2) *na-ra-am* ^{d}*tišpak*	2) beloved of the god Tišpak –
3) *a*-NI-NI-⸢*šu*⸣	3) A-NI-NI-šu,
4) ÌR.ZU	4) your servant.

Kirikiri

E4.5.2

Nūr-aḫum was succeeded by Kirikiri, who apparently was his brother. Two year names are known for this ruler. The combined rule of Nūr-aḫum and Kirikiri probably lasted about fifteen years.

1

No building inscriptions of Kirikiri have come to light. However, we do have a cylinder seal which the governor presented to his son Bilalama, the future governor of Ešnunna. We also have a clay sealing with an impression of this very seal.

Kirikiri is a non-Semitic name of a type common among the Elamites.

CATALOGUE

Ex.	Museum number	Excavation number	Provenance	Object	Dimensions (cm)	Lines preserved	cpn
1	A 7468	As 30:1000	Ešnunna, uncertain locus in the Bilalama palace	Cylinder seal of lapis lazuli	2.8 × 1.5 1.6 dia.	1–10	c
2	–	As 31:T.256	O 30:17, in a doorway between O 30:17 and 18 in the Itūrīia temple	Seal impression on clay tablet	–	–	n

COMMENTARY

Ex. 1 is the seal. Ex. 2 is an impression of that seal.

BIBLIOGRAPHY

1932 Jacobsen, OIC 13 pp. 42–44 (ex. 1, edition) and p. 19 fig. 14 (ex. 1, photo)

1940 Jacobsen, Gimilsin Temple p. 145 no. 12 (exs. 1–2, edition)

1955 Frankfort and Jacobsen, Cylinder Seals no. 709 (ex. 1, photo; exs. 1–2, edition)

1961 Hallo, BiOr 18 p. 14 Ešnunna 21: iii (study)

1971 Sollberger and Kupper, IRSA ivE2a (translation)

1987 Collon, First Impressions no. 500 (exs. 1–2, photo, study)

TEXT

1) ^{d}*tišpak*	1) O god Tišpak,
2) LUGAL *da-núm*	2) mighty king,
3) LUGAL *ma-at wa-ri-im*	3) king of the land of Warûm –
4) *ki-ri-ki-ri*	4) Kirikiri,
5) ÉNSI	5-6) governor of Ešnunna,
6) *áš-nun-na*.KI	
7) *a-na*	7-10) presented (this seal) to Bilalama, his son.
8) *bi-la-la-ma*	
9) DUMU.NI-*šu*	
10) *i-qi$_4$-iš*	

Bilalama

E4.5.3

Bilalama succeeded his father, Kirikiri, as governor of Ešnunna and reigned at least 20 years. His reign was contemporary, at least in part, with that of Šū-ilīšu of Isin. His year names mention clashes with the Amorites and building activities in Ešnunna. Bilalama's name occurs in the variant writing *bi/bíl-la-ma*.

1

The standard inscription of Bilalama is found on stamped bricks excavated from the palace at Ešnunna.

CATALOGUE

Ex.	Museum number	Excavation number	Provenance	Dimensions (cm)	Lines preserved	cpn
1	IM 23838	As 31:740	Ešnunna, from the Bilalama palace	31.5×31.5×8.0	–	n
2	A 9009	As 31:741	As ex. 1	32.0×32.0	1-5	c
3	A 9010	As 31:741a	As ex. 1	32.5×15.8	1-5	c
4	LB no number	–	Ešnunna	33.0×33.5×6.0	1-5	c
5	LB no number	–	Ešnunna	32.5×15.0×7.0	1-5	c

COMMENTARY

Exs. 1-3 were excavated at Ešnunna; exs. 4-5 were purchased. The Tell Asmar bricks were reassigned new numbers from those published by Jacobsen in the Gimilsin Temple. Here we cite the new numbers and refer the reader to Jacobsen's publication for the old numbers.

BIBLIOGRAPHY

1940 Jacobsen, Gimilsin Temple p. 135 no. 3 (edition) and pl. 14 no. 3 (copy)

1961 Hallo, BiOr 18 p. 12 Ešnunna 1: ii (study)

1971 Sollberger and Kupper, IRSA ɪvE3a (study)

TEXT

1) *bi-la-la-ma*	1) Bilalama,
2) *na-ra-am*	2) beloved of the god Tišpak,
3) ^{d}*tišpak*	3–4) governor of Ešnunna.
3) ÉNSI	
4) *áš-nun-na*.KI	

2

A year name of Bilalama deals with the construction of the Esikil, temple of Tišpak, city god of Ešnunna. An inscription recording this work is stamped on bricks found in the Bilalama palace in Ešnunna.

CATALOGUE

Ex.	Museum number	Excavation number	Provenance	Dimensions (cm)	Lines preserved	cpn
1	IM 23836	As 31:738	Ešnunna, from the Bilalama palace	36.0×18.0×8.0	–	n
2	A 8994	As 31:739	As ex. 1	36.0×17.5×7.8	1–10	c
3	A 8995	As 31:739a	As ex. 1	35.0×36.0×8.5	1–10	c
4	LB no number	–	Ešnunna	35.0×35.0×8.4	1–10	c

COMMENTARY

Ex. 3 is edited here for the first time.

BIBLIOGRAPHY

1932 Jacobsen, OIC 13 p. 45 (edition)
1932 ILN Oct. 1 p. 504 fig. 11 (photo)
1940 Jacobsen, Gimilsin Temple pp. 135–36 no. 4 (edition) and pl. 14 no. 4 (copy)
1961 Hallo, BiOr 18 p. 13 Ešnunna 8 (study)
1971 Sollberger and Kupper, IRSA IVE3b (translation)

TEXT

1) *a-na* ^{d}*tišpak*	1) For the god Tišpak,
2) *be-lí-šu*	2) his lord,
3) *bi-la-la-ma*	3) Bilalama,
4) *na-ra-am-šu*	4–5) his beloved and his envoy,
5) *ù na-áš-pár-šu*	
6) ÉNSI	6–7) governor of Ešnunna,
7) *áš-nun*.KI	
8) é-sikil-*am*	8–10) built the Esikil, which he loves.
9) *ša i-ra-a-mu*	
10) *ib-ni*	

9.4 *ša i-ra-am-mu*.

3

A cylinder seal in a private collection has an inscription which indicates that the seal was granted by Bilalama to his daughter, probably Mê-Kūbi.

COMMENTARY

The lapis lazuli cylinder seal was in the collection of Col. Norman Colville and was sold at Sotheby's or Christie's in the late 1970s. The transliteration offered here is given through the courtesy of C.B.F. Walker.

Walker's transliteration had *a-na* [x x]-*ga* for line 4. This has been emended to allow an attribution of the cylinder to Mê-Kūbi. A *ga* sign could be easily confused with a *bi* sign.

TEXT

1) *bi-la-ma*
2) ÉNSI
3) *áš-nun-na*.KI
4) *a-na* [*me-ku*]-*bi*
5) *ma-ar-ti-šu*
6) *i-qi*$_4$-*iš*

1) Bilalama,
2–3) governor of Ešnunna,

4–6) presented (this seal) to [Mê-Kū]bi, his daughter.

4

Mê-Kūbi, Bilalama's daughter, was married to Tan-ruḫuratir of Elam. As queen, she has left us bricks dealing with the construction of the temple of the goddess Inanna in Susa.

CATALOGUE

Ex.	Museum number	Excavation number	Dimensions (cm)	Lines preserved	cpn
1	Sb 14746	Susa 1741	25.4 × 16.3 × 8.5	1–8	c
2	Sb 14749	–	20.8 × 18.1 × 7.3	1–8	c
3	–	–	–	8–14	n
4	Sb 14747	Susa 6087	19.5 × 17.3 × 8	1–9	c
5	Sb 14748	Susa 1757	8.4 × 10.2 × 9.8	4–8	c

COMMENTARY

Ex. 3, known in copy only, was not located in the Louvre.

BIBLIOGRAPHY

1900 Scheil, MDP 2 p. 80 and pl. 15 no. 6 (ex. 1, photo, edition)
1905 Thureau-Dangin, ISA pp. 258–59 Dan-ruḫuratir (ex. 1, edition)
1907 Thureau-Dangin, SAK pp. 180–81 Dan-ruḫuratir (ex. 1, edition)
1913 Scheil, MDP 14 pp. 24–25 (exs. 2–3, copy, edition)
1929 Barton, RISA pp. 160–61 Dan-rukhuratir 1–2 (ex. 1–3, edition)
1932–33 Poebel, AJSL 49 p. 137 (edition)
1957 Edzard, Zwischenzeit p. 72 (study)
1957 Gelb, MAD 3 p. 167 (study)
1961 Hallo, BiOr 18 p. 13 Ešnunna 7 (study)
1971 Sollberger and Kupper, IRSA ɪᴠO2a (translation)

TEXT

1) ᵈinanna 2) nin-uru$_{17}$-an-na 3) nin-a-ni-ir	1–3) For the goddess Inanna, great lady of heaven, her lady,
4) *me-ku-bi* 5) dumu-munus-*bíl-la-ma* 6) énsi 7) *áš-nun*.ᴋɪ 8) dam-ki-á[g]-	4–8) Mê-Kūbi, daughter of Bilalama, governor of Ešnunna,
9) *tan-ᵈru-ḫu-ra-ti-ir* 10) énsi 11) ᴍùš.ᴇʀᴇɴ.ᴋɪ	9–11) belove[d] wife of Tan-ruḫuratir, governor of Susa,
12) nam-ti-la-ni-šè 13) é-ᵈinanna 14) mu-na-dù	12–14) built the temple of the goddess Inanna for her own life.

5

The name of a son of Bilalama appears on a duck weight in the Iraq Museum collections.

COMMENTARY

The piece is IM 49311, confiscated at Amarah. It is a duck weight made of black diorite, 21 × 13.5 × 11 cm, and the inscription was collated from its display in the Babylon Museum. It is edited here for the first time through the courtesy of Dr B. Khalil Ismail.

The personal name in line 3 appears to be Amorite.

TEXT

1) 10 ᴍᴀ.ɴᴀ 2) ɢɪ.ɴᴀ	1–2) 10 minas approved,
3) *ša-li-la-mi-il$_5$-ku-um*	3) Šālil-la-Milkum,
4) ᴅᴜᴍᴜ *bi-la-ma*	4) son of Bilalama.

2001

The impression of a seal of Wusum-bēlī, servant of Bilalama, is found on three clay tablets excavated at Ešnunna.

CATALOGUE

Ex.	Excavation number	Provenance	cpn
1	As 30:T.462	Ešnunna, M 31:1, from the Šū-iliia–Nūr-aḫum palace	n
2	As 31:T.224	O 30:18, from the Itūriia temple	c
3	As 31:T.244	O 30:18, from the Itūriia temple	n

BIBLIOGRAPHY

1940 Jacobsen, Gimilsin Temple p. 146 no. 16 (edition)

TEXT

1) *bi-la-la-ma*	1) Bilalama,
2) *na-ra-am* ^{d}*tišpak*	2) beloved of the god Tišpak,
3) ÉNSI	3–4) governor of Ešnunna –
4) *áš-nun-na*.KI	
5) *wu-súm-be-lí*	5) Wusum-bēlī,
6) DUMU LÚ-*ša-lim*	6) son of Awīl-šalim,
7) ÌR.ZU	7) your servant.

2002

An impression of a seal which indicates that it was granted by Bilalama to Wusum-bēlī, here designated as a chanter, was found on a tablet excavated at Ešnunna.

COMMENTARY

The tablet has an excavation no. As 31:T.266 and comes from O 30:18, the Bilalama palace. The tablet was collated by R. Whiting.

The restoration of lines 9–10 is based on parallels with other 'granting' seals. It does not appear in the seal impression itself.

BIBLIOGRAPHY

1940 Jacobsen, Gimilsin Temple p. 147 no. 17 (edition)

TEXT

1) [*b*]*i-la-la-ma*
2) [*na*]*-ra-am*
3) ^{d}*tišpak*
4) ÉNSI
5) [*áš-nun-na*.KI]
6) *a*-[*na*]
7) *wu-súm-be-lí*
8) NAR
9) [DUMU LÚ-*ša-lim*]
10) [*i-qi*$_4$*-iš*]

1–10) [B]ilalama, [be]loved of the god Tišpak, governor [of Ešnunna, granted] (this seal) t[o] Wusum-bēlī, the chanter, [son of Awīl-šalim].

2003

The impression of a seal of the scribe Puzur-Tišpak, servant of Bilalama, is found on clay tablets excavated at Ešnunna.

CATALOGUE

Ex.	Excavation number	Provenance	cpn
1	As 30:T.225	Ešnunna, K 31:1, from the Bilalama palace	n
2	As 30:T.413	From the Bilalama palace	n
3	As 30:T.457	K 31, from the Bilalama palace	n

BIBLIOGRAPHY

1940 Jacobsen, Gimilsin Temple p. 146 no. 15 (edition)
1961 Hallo, BiOr 18 p. 14 Ešnunna 21: iv (study)

TEXT

1) *bi-la-la-ma*
2) *na-ra-am* ^{d}*tišpak*
3) ÉNSI
4) [*áš*]*-nun*.KI
5) *puzur*$_4$-^{d}*tišpak*
6) DUB:SAR
7) DUMU *nu-úr*-^{d}EN.ZU
8) ÌR.ZU

1) Bilalama,
2) beloved of the god Tišpak,
3–4) governor of [Eš]nunna –

5) Puzur-Tišpak,
6) scribe,
7) son of Nūr-Sîn,
8) your servant.

2004

The seal impression of a seal of a servant of Bilalama is found on six clay tablets excavated at Ešnunna.

CATALOGUE

Ex.	Excavation number	Provenance	cpn
1	As 30:T.730	Ešnunna, room O 30:4, in the Bilalama palace; burned layer	c
2	As 30:T.732	As ex. 1	c
3	As 30:T.735	As ex. 1	c
4	As 30:T.736	–	c
5	As 30:T.738	As ex. 1; level 32, 50	c
6	As 30:T.745	As ex. 1; level 31, 30	c

BIBLIOGRAPHY

1940 Jacobsen, Gimilsin Temple p. 147 nos. 18 b–e (study)
1987 Whiting, AfO 34 p. 32 n. 15 (exs. 1–6, edition)

TEXT

1) *bi-la-la-ma*	1) Bilalama,
2) *na-ra-am* ^d^*tišpak*	2) beloved of the god Tišpak,
3) ÉNSI	3–4) governor of Ešnunna –
4) *áš-nun*.KI	
5) *ì l-šu-dan*	5) Ilšu-dān,
6) DUB.SAR	6) scribe,
7) DUMU ur-^d^nin-sún	7) son of Ur-Ninsun,
8) ÌR.ZU	8) your servant.

2005

The seal impression of a seal of a servant of Bilalama is found on two clay tablets excavated at Ešnunna.

CATALOGUE

Ex.	Excavation number	Provenance	cpn
1	As 30:T.742	Ešnunna, room O 30:4 of the Bilalama palace in the vertical shaft sunk into the niche of the temple, level 30 (or 30, 50)	c
2	As 30:T.752	As ex. 1; level 31, 30	c

BIBLIOGRAPHY

1987 Whiting, AfO 34 pp. 32–33 and n. 20 (exs. 1–2, edition)

TEXT

1) *bi-la-la-ma*	1) Bilalama,
2) *na-ra-am* ^{d}*tišpak*	2) beloved of the god Tišpak –
3) lugal-inim-du$_{10}$ DUB.SAR	3) Lugal-inim-du, scribe,
4) DUMU šeš-kal-[l]a ÌR.ZU	4) son of Šeš-kalla, your servant.

2006

The seal of a servant of Bilalama is found in a private American collection.

COMMENTARY

The inscription was collated from a photo of the seal kindly provided by R. Biggs.

TEXT

1) *i-šar-pá-dan*	1) Išar-padān,
2) NE-*za-um*	2) ... –
3) ÌR *bi-la-la-ma*	3) servant of Bilalama.

2007

The impression of a seal of a servant of Mê-Kūbi, queen of Tanruḫuratir, was excavated at Susa.

COMMENTARY

The impression is found on Sb 7390, a strip of clay perhaps used to seal a door, excavated at the Ville Royale by R. Ghirshman, level VI. It was collated from the published photo.

BIBLIOGRAPHY

1968 Ghirshman, Arts asiatiques 17 pp. 6 and 29 fig. 8
1972 Amiet, MDP 43/1 pp. 209–10 (study) and p. 216 no. 1676 (edition); MDP 43/2 pl. 34 no. 1676 (copy) and pl. 156 no. 1676 (photo)

TEXT

1) *me-ku-bi*	1) Mê-Kūbi,
2) NIN GU.LA	2) great queen –
3) a-a-bàn-da x	3) Aia-banda, ...,
4) DUB.SAR ÌR.ZU	4) scribe, your servant.

Išar-rāmāšu

E4.5.4

Bilalama appears to have been succeeded by Išar-rāmāšu as governor of Ešnunna. Only one inscription is known for this ruler.

1

The standard inscription of Išar-rāmāšu is found on bricks excavated in the Palace of the Three Rulers at Ešnunna.

CATALOGUE

Ex.	Museum number	Excavation number	Provenance	Dimensions (cm)	Lines preserved	cpn
1	IM 23842	As 31:742	Ešnunna, from the Palace of the Three Rulers	35.5×35.5×8.0	–	n
2	A 8992	As 31:743	As ex. 1	35.8×35.6×7.2	1–5	c
3	A 8993	As 31:743a	As ex. 1	34.3×17.1×8.2	1–5	c
4	(see bibliography)		Ešnunna		1–5	n

COMMENTARY

The present whereabouts of ex. 4 is not known.

BIBLIOGRAPHY

1892 Pognon, Le Muséon p. 253 no. 4 (ex. 4, copy, study)
1892–93 Pinches, BOR 6 p. 67 no. IV (ex. 4, copy, edition)
1905 Thureau-Dangin, ISA pp. 250–51 [ ]mašu (ex. 4, edition)
1907 Thureau-Dangin, SAK pp. 174–75 [ ]mašu (ex. 4, edition)
1929 Barton, RISA pp. 152–53 ...mashu 1 (ex. 4, edition)
1940 Jacobsen, Gimilsin Temple p. 136 no. 5 (exs. 1–3, edition) and pl. 14 no. 5 (copy)
1961 Hallo, BiOr 18 p. 13 Ešnunna 1: iii (study)
1971 Sollberger and Kupper, IRSA IVE4 (translation)

TEXT

1) *i-šar-ra-ma-šu*	1) Išar-rāmāšu,
2) *na-ra-am*	2–3) beloved of the god Tišpak,
3) ^{d}*tišpak*	
4) ÉNSI	4–5) governor of Ešnunna.
5) *áš-nun-na*.KI	

Uṣur-awassu

E4.5.5

Išar-rāmāšu was succeeded by Uṣur-awassu, a ruler known only from year names and seal impressions. A man by the same name appears in an Ešnunna tablet as 'the man of Dēr' and in another tablet as the ambassador of Ilum-muttabbil of Dēr (see E4.12.2). Frankfort and Jacobsen have suggested that Uṣur-awassu may have been installed as ruler of Ešnunna by Ilum-muttabbil of Dēr.

1

The first seal impression, found on clay tablets, is a nine-line text belonging to the governor himself, dedicated to the god Tišpak.

CATALOGUE

Ex.	Excavation number	Provenance	cpn
1	As 30:T.226	Ešnunna, from a dump	n
2	As 30:T.352	N 30:7, from the Bilalama palace	n
3	As 30:T.353	O 30:15, from the Bilalama palace	n

BIBLIOGRAPHY

1940 Jacobsen, Gimilsin Temple p. 147 no. 19 (exs. 1-3, edition)

1961 Hallo, BiOr 18 p. 13 Ešnunna 14 (study)

1971 Sollberger and Kupper, IRSA ɪᴠE5a (translation)

TEXT

1) ᵈ*tišpak*	1) The god Tišpak,
2) LUGAL *da-núm*	2) mighty king,
3) LUGAL *ma-at wa-ri-im*	3) king of the land of Warûm –
4) *ú-ṣur-a-wa-sú*	4) Uṣur-awassu,
5) *na-ra-am-šu*	5–6) his beloved and his envoy,
6) *ù na-áš-pár-šu*	
7) ÉNSI	7–8) governor of Ešnunna,
8) *áš-nun-na*.KI	
9) ÌR-*sú*	9) (is) his servant.

2001-2004

A number of legal documents, including sixty tablets dealing with real estate sales, were found in a vertical drain in a room of the palace by the Oriental Institute excavations at Tell Asmar.

On the tablets dealing with house sales the seal of the *kakikkum* official appears. On tablets dealing with the sale of fields, it is the *šassukkum* official whose seal is impressed (R. Whiting, personal communication). Thus, as a consequence of this archive, we know the names of these officials at Ešnunna from the time of Uṣur-awassu down to Warassa. Here we have edited the seal impressions of these officials, first among the servants of the Ešnunna governors, as E4.5.5.2001-2004.

2001

The seal impression of Ilānum, *kakikkum* official during the reign of Uṣur-awassu, is attested on three tablets found at Ešnunna.

CATALOGUE

Ex.	Museum number	Excavation number	Provenance	cpn
1	–	As 30:T.232	Ešnunna, from the vertical pottery drain in O 30:7	c
2	–	As 31:T.58	P 32:6, 40 cm above houses below Southern Building	c
3	A 22160	As 35:T.96	From 'House with Temple bricks in S. 41'	c

COMMENTARY

The name in line 4 appears to be Hurrian.

BIBLIOGRAPHY

1940 Jacobsen, Gimilsin Temple p. 148 no. 20 (ex. 1, edition)
1961 Hallo, BiOr 18 p. 14 Ešnunna 21: v (study)
1977 Whiting in Gibson and Biggs, Seals p. 71 (exs. 1-3, edition)

TEXT

1) [*ú-ṣur-a-wa*]*-sú*
2) *na-ra-am* ^{d}*tišpak*
3) *i-la-nu-um*
4) DUMU *tíš-é-la*
5) DUB.SAR
6) [ÌR.ZU]

1) [Uṣur-awa]ssu,
2) beloved of the god Tišpak –
3) Ilānum,
4) son of Tiš-ela,
5-6) scribe, [your servant].

2002

The seal of Ḫumzum, *šassukkum* official during the reign of Uṣur-awassu, is found on a tablet excavated at Ešnunna.

COMMENTARY

The tablet is As 30:T.519, from the vertical pottery drain in O 30:7. The impression was collated by R. Whiting.

BIBLIOGRAPHY

1977 Whiting in Gibson and Biggs, Seals p. 71 (edition)

TEXT

1) *ú-ṣur-a-wa-sú*	1) Uṣur-awassu,
2) *na-ra-am* ᵈ*tišpak*	2) beloved of the god Tišpak,
3) ÉNSI *áš-nun-na*.KI	3) governor of Ešnunna –
4) *ḫu-um-zum*	4) Ḫumzum,
5) DUB.SAR	5) scribe,
6) DUMU *a-bi-lu-lu*	6) son of Abī-lulu.

2003

The seal impression of Bēlī-kibrī, servant of Uṣur-awassu, is found on a tablet excavated at Ešnunna.

COMMENTARY

The seal impression is on As 31:616, found in a dump. It was not collated.

BIBLIOGRAPHY

1940 Jacobsen, Gimilsin Temple p. 148 no. 21 (edition) and p. 216 fig. 102 i (photo, copy)
1955 Frankfort and Jacobsen, Cylinder Seals no. 726 (photo, edition)
1961 Hallo, BiOr 18 p. 14 Ešnunna 21: v (study)
1971 Sollberger and Kupper, IRSA IVE5b (translation)

TEXT

1) *ú-ṣur-a-wa-s*[*ú*]	1) Uṣur-awass[u],
2) ÉNSI *áš-nun*.KI	2) governor of Ešnunna –
3) *be-lí-ki-ib-ri*	3) Bēlī-kibrī,
4) ÌR.ZU	4) your servant.

2004

The impression of what is probably a seal of a servant of Uṣur-awassu is found on a tablet excavated at Ešnunna.

COMMENTARY

The tablet is As 30:T.440, found in L 31:7 in the Bilalama palace. The impression was not collated.

BIBLIOGRAPHY

1940 Jacobsen, Gimilsin Temple p. 148 no. 21a (edition)
1961 Hallo, BiOr 18 p. 14 Ešnunna 21: v (study)

TEXT

1) [*ú*]-*ṣur-a-w*[*a-sú*]	1) [U]ṣur-aw[assu],
2) [É]NS[I] *áš-n*[*un*.KI]	2) [g]overn[or] of Ešn[unna] –
3) [...]-*e*-[...]	3) ...,
4) [...]-*a*-[...]	4) ...

Azūzum

E4.5.6

Uṣur-awassu was succeeded by Azūzum as governor of Ešnunna. He is known from one brick inscription and a few seal impressions of his servants.

1

The standard inscription of Azūzum is found on bricks excavated from the Palace of the Three Rulers at Ešnunna.

CATALOGUE

Ex.	Museum number	Excavation number	Provenance	Dimensions (cm)	Lines preserved	cpn
1	IM 23837	As 31:744	Ešnunna, from the Palace of the Three Rulers	33.0×32.0×8.0	–	n
2	A 9011	As 31:745	As ex. 1	32.0×31.5×7.4	1-5	c
3	A 9012	As 31:745a	As ex. 1	32.3×16.0	1-5	c

BIBLIOGRAPHY

1940 Jacobsen, Gimilsin Temple p. 136 no. 6 (edition) and pl. 15 no. 6 (copy)

1961 Hallo, BiOr 18 p. 13 Ešnunna 1: iv (study)

1971 Sollberger and Kupper, IRSA ɪᴠE6a (study)

TEXT

1) *a-zu-zum*
2) *na-ra-am*
3) ^{d}*tišpak*
4) ÉNSI
5) *áš-nun-na*.KI

1) Azūzum,
2–3) beloved of the god Tišpak,
4–5) governor of Ešnunna.

2

An impression of a seal of the governor Azūzum is found on a tablet excavated at Ešnunna.

COMMENTARY

The impression is on As 30:T.224 found in M 31:1, from the Bilalama palace. The inscription was not collated.

BIBLIOGRAPHY

1940 Jacobsen, Gimilsin Temple p. 148 no. 23 (edition)
1961 Hallo, BiOr 18 p. 13 Ešnunna 15 (study)
1971 Sollberger and Kupper, IRSA IVE6b (translation)

TEXT

1) ᵈ*tišpak*	1) O god Tišpak,
2) LUGAL *da-núm*	2) mighty king,
3) LUGAL *áš-nun*.KI	3) king of Ešnunna –
4) *a-zu-zum*	4) Azūzum,
5) *na-ra-*[*am*]	5–6) belov[ed] of the god Tišpak,
6) ᵈ*tišpak*	
7) ÉNSI	7–8) governor of Ešnunna,
8) *áš-nun-na*.KI	
9) ÌR.ZU	9) your servant.

3

An impression of a different seal of governor Azūzum is on a tablet excavated at Ešnunna.

COMMENTARY

The impression is found on As 30:T.355, from N 30:11, in the Ur-Ninmar palace. It was not collated.

BIBLIOGRAPHY

1940 Jacobsen, Gimilsin Temple p. 148 no. 22 (edition)
1961 Hallo, BiOr 18 p. 13 Ešnunna 16 (study)
1971 Sollberger and Kupper, IRSA IVE6c (translation)

TEXT

1) ᵈ*tišpak*	1) O god Tišpak,
2) LUGAL *da-núm*	2) mighty king,
3) LUGAL *ma-at wa-ri-im*	3) king of the land of Warûm –
4) *a-zu-zum*	4) Azūzum,
5) ÉNSI	5–6) governor of Ešnunna,
6) *áš-nun*.KI	
7) ÌR.ZU	7) your servant.

2001

The impression of a seal of Attā-ilī, *šassukkum* official during the reign of Azūzum, appears on a tablet excavated at Ešnunna.

COMMENTARY

The impression is found on As 30:T.559, from the vertical pottery drain in O 30:7. It was collated by R. Whiting, and is edited here through the courtesy of the trustees of the Oriental Institute.

BIBLIOGRAPHY

1977 Whiting in Gibson and Biggs, Seals p. 71 (transliteration)

TEXT

1) *a-zu-zum*	1) Azūzum,
2) ÉNSI	2–3) governor of Ešnunna –
3) *áš-nun-na*.KI	
4) *a-at-ta-ì-lí*	4) Attā-ilī,
5) DUB.SAR ÌR.ZU	5) scribe, your servant.

2002

The impression of a seal of Iddin-Sîn, *kakikkum* official during the reign of Azūzum, is found on three clay tablets excavated at Ešnunna.

CATALOGUE

Ex.	Excavation number	Provenance	cpn
1	As 30:T.511	Ešnunna, from the vertical pottery drain in O 30:7	c
2	As 30:T.544	As ex. 1	c
3	As 30:T.578	As ex. 1	c

BIBLIOGRAPHY

1977 Whiting in Gibson and Biggs, Seals p. 71 (transliteration)

TEXT

1) *a-zu-zum*	1) Azūzum,
2) *na-ra-am* ^{d}*tišpak*	2) beloved of the god Tišpak –
3) *i-din-*^{d}EN.ZU DUB.SAR	3) Iddin-Sîn, scribe,
4) DUMU *dan-*^{d}*tišpak*	4) son of Dān-Tišpak,
5) ÌR.ZU	5) your servant.

Ur-Ninmar

E4.5.7

Azūzum was succeeded by Ur-Ninmar as governor of Ešnunna. A few year names and inscriptions are known for this ruler. For the reading of the name Ninmar, see R. Whiting, ZA 75 (1985) pp. 1–3.

1

The standard inscription of Ur-Ninmar is found on bricks excavated from the Palace of the Three Rulers and the Ur-Ninmar palace.

CATALOGUE

Ex.	Museum number	Excavation number	Provenance	Dimensions (cm)	Lines preserved	cpn
1	IM -	As 31:746	Ešnunna, from the Palace of the Three Rulers or the Ur-Ninmar palace	–	–	n
2	IM -	As 31:747	As ex. 1	–	–	n
3	A 8990	As 31:747a	As ex. 1	31.5×31.5	1-5	c
4	ROM 910×209.573	–	Ešnunna	–	1-5	c
5	Collection of J. Mariaud de Serres, Paris	–	Ešnunna	34.0×16.0×6.5	–	n

BIBLIOGRAPHY

1940 Jacobsen, Gimilsin Temple p. 136 no. 7 (edition) and pl. 15 no. 7 (copy)

1961 Hallo, BiOr 18 p. 13 Ešnunna 1: v (study)

1971 Sollberger and Kupper, IRSA ɪvE7a (study)

1981 Grégoire, MVN 10 no. 29 (ex. 5, study)

TEXT

1) ur-^{d}nin-mar	1) Ur-Ninmar,
2) *na-ra-am*	2–3) beloved of the god Tišpak,
3) ^{d}*tišpak*	
4) ÉNSI	4–5) governor of Ešnunna.
5) *áš-nun-na*.KI	

2

The impression of a seal of governor Ur-Ninmar is found on a tablet excavated at Ešnunna.

COMMENTARY

The seal impression is on As 30:T.201, from O 30:1, top layer of the Ipiq-Adad I–Ibāl-pî-El I palace. It was not collated.

BIBLIOGRAPHY

1940 Jacobsen, Gimilsin Temple p. 151 no. 34 (edition)
1961 Hallo, BiOr 18 p. 13 Ešnunna 17 (study)
1971 Sollberger and Kupper, IRSA IVE7b (translation)

TEXT

1) ^{d}*tišpak*	1) O god Tišpak,
2) LUGAL *da-núm*	2) mighty king –
3) ur-^{d}nin-mar.KI	3) Ur-Ninmar,
4) ÉNSI	4–5) governor of Ešnunna,
5) *áš-nun-na*.KI	
6) ÌR.ZU	6) your servant.

3

A fragment of an impression of a seal of Ur-Ninmar dated to the time when his father was governor of Ešnunna was excavated at Ešnunna (Tell Asmar). Unfortunately, the name of the father, presumably Azūzum or Uṣur-awassu, is not preserved.

COMMENTARY

The impression is found on As 30:T.450 and was collated by R. Whiting.

BIBLIOGRAPHY

1987 Whiting, AfO 34 p. 35 (copy, edition)

TEXT

1) [...]	1) [...],
2) ÉN[SI *áš-nun*.KI]	2) gov[ernor of Ešnunna],
3) ur-^{d}nin-⌜mar⌝.[KI]	3) Ur-Ninmar,
4) DUMU.N[I]	4) h[is] son.

4

An impression of a seal of Ipiq-Adad, future governor of Ešnunna, dating to the time when his father Ur-Ninmar was governor of that city, is on a tablet excavated at Ešnunna (Tell Asmar).

COMMENTARY

The impression is found on As 30:T.118, from O 30:5, in the Ipiq-Adad I palace. It was not collated.

BIBLIOGRAPHY

1940 Jacobsen, Gimilsin Temple p. 151 no. 35 (edition)
1961 Hallo, BiOr 18 p. 14 Ešnunna 21: vi (study)

TEXT

1) ⌜ur⌝-^{d}nin.mar.KI	1) Ur-Ninmar,
2) *na-⌜ra-am⌝* ^{d}*⌜tišpak⌝*	2) beloved of the god Tišpak,
3) [*i-pí*]*-iq-*^{d}IŠKUR	3) [Ip]iq-Adad,
4) [DUMU].A.NA	4) his [son].

2001

The impression of a seal of Iddin-Sîn, *kakikkum* official under Ur-Ninmar, is found on a number of clay tablets excavated at Ešnunna. This is the same man who served as *kakikkum* during the reign of Azūzum.

CATALOGUE

Ex.	Excavation number	Provenance	cpn
1	As 30:T.356	From the vertical pottery drain in O 30:7	n
2	As 30:T.513	As ex. 1	n
3	As 30:T.535	As ex. 1	n
4	As 30:T.540	As ex. 1	n
5	As 30:T.573	As ex. 1	n

BIBLIOGRAPHY

1977 Whiting in Gibson and Biggs, Seals p. 71 (transliteration)

TEXT

1) ur-^{d}nin-mar.KI
2) *na-ra-am* ^{d}*tišpak*
3) *i-din*-^{d}EN.ZU DUB.SAR
4) DUMU *dan*-^{d}*tišpak* ÌR.ZU

1) Ur-Ninmar,
2) beloved of the god Tišpak —
3) Iddin-Sîn, scribe,
4) son of Dān-Tišpak, your servant.

2002

Iddin-Sîn was succeeded by his son Iddin-Amurrum in the post of *kakikkum* at Ešnunna during the reign of Ur-Ninmar. His seal impression is found on a tablet excavated at Ešnunna.

COMMENTARY

The impression is on As 30:T.565, from the vertical drain in O 30:7 at Ešnunna. It was collated by R. Whiting, and is edited here through the courtesy of the trustees of the Oriental Institute.

BIBLIOGRAPHY

1977 Whiting in Gibson and Biggs, Seals p. 72 (transliteration)

TEXT

1) ur-^{d}nin-mar.KI
2) ÉNSI *áš-nun-na*.KI
3) *i-din*-^{d}MAR.DÚ DUB.SAR
4) DUMU *i-din*-^{d}EN.ZU ÌR.ZU

1) Ur-Ninmar,
2) governor of Ešnunna —
3) Iddin-Amurrum, scribe,
4) son of Iddin-Sîn, your servant.

2003

Ḫumzum, *šassukkum* official during the reign of Uṣur-awassu, continued in that post during the reign of Ur-Ninmar, when a seal recognizing the new ruler was cut. The impression of that seal is found on a number of clay tablets excavated at Ešnunna.

CATALOGUE

Ex.	Excavation number	Provenance	cpn
1	As 30:T.491	Ešnunna, from the vertical pottery drain in O 30:7	n
2	As 30:T.521 + 522	As ex. 1	n
3	As 30:T.527	As ex. 1	n
4	As 30:T.563	As ex. 1	n
5	As 30:T.567(?)	As ex. 1	n
6	As 30:T.570	As ex. 1	n
7	As 30:T.579	As ex. 1	n

COMMENTARY

The meaning of DUR.ŠUB.BA in line 4 is unknown.

BIBLIOGRAPHY

1977 Whiting in Gibson and Biggs, Seals p. 71 (transliteration)

TEXT

1) ur-^{d}nin-mar.KI	1) Ur-Ninmar,
2) ÉNSI *áš-nun-na*.KI	2) governor of Ešnunna –
3) *ḫu-um-zum* DUB.SAR	3) Ḫumzum, scribe,
4) DUR.ŠUB.BA	4) ...,
5) DUMU *a-bi-lu-lu* ÌR.ZU	5) son of Abī-lulu, your servant.

2004

Ḫumzum was followed in the post of *šassukkum* at Ešnunna by his son Kuruza. The seal impression of Kuruza appears on a number of tablets excavated at Ešnunna.

CATALOGUE

Ex.	Excavation number	Provenance	cpn
1	As 30:T.493	Ešnunna, from the vertical pottery drain in O 30:7	n
2	As 30:T.554	As ex. 1	n
3	As 30:T.574	As ex. 1	n

COMMENTARY

According to T. Jacobsen, Gimilsin Temple p. 151, the RN of As 30:T.493 reads ur-^{d}nin-[...]. Jacobsen suggested a restoration ur-^{d}nin-[giš-zi-da], which was followed by Whiting in Gibson and Biggs, Seals p. 72. However, collation of other examples of this impression by Whiting (personal communication) reveals that it should be restored ur-^{d}nin-[mar.KI].

BIBLIOGRAPHY

1977 Whiting in Gibson and Biggs, Seals p. 72 (transliteration)

TEXT

1) ur-^{d}nin-mar.KI	1) Ur-Ninmar,
2) *na-ra-am* ^{d}*tišpak*	2) beloved of the god Tišpak,
3) ÉNSI *áš-nun-na*.KI	3) governor of Ešnunna –
4) *ku-ru-za* DUB.SAR	4) Kuruza, scribe,
5) DUMU *ḫu-um-zum* ÌR.ZU	5) son of Ḫumzum, your servant.

2005

Kuruza, in turn, was succeeded by his son Sîn-iddinam in the post of *šassukkum* at Ešnunna, probably late in the reign of Ur-Ninmar. The impression of the seal of Sîn-iddinam is found on two clay tablets excavated at Ešnunna.

CATALOGUE

Ex.	Excavation number	Provenance	cpn
1	As 30:T.552	Ešnunna, from the vertical pottery drain in O 30:7	n
2	As 30:T.524(?)	As ex. 1	n

COMMENTARY

The seal impression is edited here for the first time through the courtesy of the trustees of the Oriental Institute.

TEXT

1) ur-^{d}nin-mar.KI	1) Ur-Ninmar,
2) ÉNSI *áš-nun-na*.KI	2) governor of Ešnunna –
3) ^{d}EN.ZU-*i-din-nam*	3) Sîn-iddinam,
4) DUB.SAR DUR.ŠUB.BA	4) scribe, ...,
5) DUMU *ku-ru-za* ÌR.ZU	5) son of Kuruza, your servant.

Ur-Ningišzida

E4.5.8

Ur-Ninmar was succeeded by Ur-Ningišzida as governor of Ešnunna. A few year names, one brick inscription, and several seal impressions refer to this ruler.

1

The standard inscription of Ur-Ningišzida is known from stamped bricks from Ešnunna.

CATALOGUE

Ex.	Museum number	Excavation number	Provenance	Dimensions (cm)	Lines preserved	cpn
1	A 8991	As 31:748	Ešnunna, from the Ur-Ninmar palace O 29:3	32.5×16.0×7.6	1-5	c
2	A 8986	As 31:749	From the Ur-Ninmar palace	33.6×33.1×6.5	1-5	c
3	A 8987	As 31:749a	As ex. 2	33.5×33.0×7.0	1-5	c
4	IM 25603	As 31:763	P 33:8, level 33, 20	–	–	n
5	(see bibliography)	–	Ešnunna		1-5	n
6	EAH 110	–	Ešnunna(?) said to have come from Nippur	–	1-5	n
7	EAH 111	–	As ex. 6	–	1-5	n
8	Ash 1924,628	–	–	26.5×25.0×6.5	1-5	c
9	LB no number	–	–	32.5×32.5×7.2	1-5	c
10	UCLM 9-1765	–	–	33.0×33.0×7.0	1-5	c
11	Bristol Museum H 4361	–	–	16.0×6.0	–	n
12	Arch. Museum Florence 94051	–	–	34.0×35.5×7.5	1-5	p
13	Arch. Museum Florence 94067	–	–	10.5×8.0	2-5	p

COMMENTARY

Ex. 8 was incorrectly attributed to Ur-Ninmar by Grégoire, MVN 10 no. 28. Collation of the piece agrees with Langdon's and Walker's attribution of the piece to Ur-Ningišzida. Ex. 4 is trapezoidal in shape.

BIBLIOGRAPHY

1892 Pognon, Le Muséon pp. 250 and 253 (ex. 5, copy, translation)
1892–93 Pinches, BOR 6 p. 67 no. II (ex. 5, copy, edition)
1900 Radau, EBH pp. 433–34 (exs. 6-7, composite copy, edition)
1905 Thureau-Dangin, ISA pp. 248–49 Ur-nin-giš-zi-da (edition)
1907 Thureau-Dangin, SAK pp. 174–75 Ur-nin-giš-zi-da (edition)
1924 Langdon, Kish 1 p. 113 (ex. 8, edition)
1929 Barton, RISA pp. 152–53 Ur-Ningišzida 1 (edition)
1940 Jacobsen, Gimilsin Temple p. 136 no. 8 (exs. 1–3,

edition) and pl. 15 no. 8 (copy)
1961 Hallo, BiOr 18 p. 13 Ešnunna 1: vi (study)
1971 Sollberger and Kupper, IRSA ɪᴠE8a (study)
1978 Foxvog, RA 72 p. 42 (ex. 10, study)
1979 Snell, MVN 9 p. 21 (exs. 6–7, study)
1981 Grégoire, MVN 10 no. 28 (ex. 8, copy, study)
1981 Walker, CBI no. 51 (exs. 8, 11, study)

TEXT

1) ur-^{d}nin-giš-zi-da
2) *na-ra-am*
3) ^{d}*tišpak*
4) ÉNSI
5) *áš-nun-na*.KI

1) Ur-Ningišzida,
2–3) beloved of the god Tišpak,
4–5) governor of Ešnunna.

2

A number of statues were excavated at Susa which had been taken there as booty from Ešnunna by the Elamite king Šutruk-Naḫḫunte. On one of these, a standing stone statue, traces of an original inscription indicate that it had once been brought into the temple of the god Tišpak of Ešnunna by Ur-Ningišzida.

COMMENTARY

The statue is Sb 57, excavation no. Susa 6089. The inscription was collated by G. Frame.

Although W. Hallo, BiOr 18 (1961) p. 13, indicated that this statue was published in MDP 6 p. 12 and pl. 3, the statue found there is a different one without an Akkadian inscription.

A broken year name found on a tablet dating to about this time period refers to the fashioning of a seated stone statue. The tablet, As 30:T.493, has a seal impression of a servant of a ruler whose name is not fully preserved: ur-^{d}nin-[...]. A restoration Ur-Ninmar or Ur-Ningišzida is possible. Jacobsen suggested Ur-Ningišzida and suggested a connection with the statue edited here as E4.5.8.2. However, duplicates of this impression studied by R. Whiting (personal communication) indicate that the name should be read Ur-Ninmar, and hence the year name probably refers to a statue of Ur-Ninmar.

BIBLIOGRAPHY

1940 Jacobsen, Gimilsin Temple p. 185 (edition)
1961 Hallo, BiOr 18 p. 13 Ešnunna 9 (study)
1971 Sollberger and Kupper, IRSA ɪᴠE8c (translation)

TEXT

1) ⸢*a-na*⸣
2) [^{d}]*t*[*išpak*]
3) [*be*]-⸢*lí*⸣-[*šu*]
4) u[r-^{d}nin-giš-z]i-[da]
5) É[NSI]
6) *áš-nun*-⸢*na*.KI⸣
7) ⸢*a*⸣-*n*[*a*]
8) ⸢É ^{d}⸣[*tišpak*]
9) ⸢*a*⸣-[*na ba-l*]*a*-⸢*ṭi-šu*⸣
10) ⸢*ú-še*⸣-[*r*]*i*-⸢*ib*⸣

1–3) For [the god] T[išpak, his lo]rd,
4) U[r-Ningišz]i[da],
5–6) gov[ernor] of Ešnunna,
7–10) had (this statue) brought in[to] the temple of the god [Tišpak] f[or] his own [l]ife.

3

The seal of Erra-bāni, son of Ur-Ningišzida, is in Berlin.

COMMENTARY

The object is VA 3113, a piece purchased in 1901 with unknown provenance, probably originally from Ešnunna. It is a cylinder seal of lapis lazuli, 2.28 cm long, 1.5 cm in dia. The inscription was collated from the published photo.

Although Moortgat, VAR no. 254, assigned this seal to the Ur III period, the inscription dates it securely to Isin-Larsa times.

BIBLIOGRAPHY

1902 Scheil, RT 24 p. 25 (transliteration)
1909 Messerschmidt, Berliner Museen Amtliche Berichte 30 p. 128 fig. 82 (photo, study)
1909 Ungnad, OLZ 12 161–62 (edition)
1915 Prinz, Altorientalische Symbolik (Berlin) p. 58 no. 7 and pl. 12 no. 12 (photo, edition)
1940 Moortgat, VAR no. 254 (photo, edition)
1940 Jacobsen, Gimilsin Temple p. 113 and fig. 98 (photo, study)
1961 Hallo, BiOr 18 p. 14 Ešnunna 21: viii (study)
1971 Sollberger and Kupper, IRSA IVE8b (translation)
1987 Collon, First Impressions no. 459 (photo, study)

TEXT

1) ur-^{d}nin-giš-zi-da
2) ÉNSI *áš-nun*.KI
3) *èr-ra-ba-ni*
4) DUMU.NI
5) *i-qi$_{4}$-iš*

1) Ur-Ningišzida,
2) governor of Ešnunna,
3–5) presented (this seal) to Erra-bāni, his son.

2001

Iddin-Amurrum, who began his career as *šassukkum* official during the reign of Ur-Ninmar, continued in that position during the reign of Ur-Ningišzida. His seal impression dedicated to his new master is found on three clay tablets excavated at Ešnunna.

CATALOGUE

Ex.	Excavation number	Provenance	cpn
1	As 30:T.530	Ešnunna, from the vertical pottery drain in O 30:7	n
2	As 30:T.550	As ex. 1	n
3	As 30:T.560	As ex. 1	n

BIBLIOGRAPHY

1977 Whiting in Gibson and Biggs, Seals p. 72 (transliteration)

TEXT

1) ur-^{d}nin-giš-zi-da	1) Ur-Ningišzida,
2) ÉNSI *áš-nun-na*.KI	2) governor of Ešnunna –
3) *i-din*-^{d}MAR.DÚ	3) Iddin-Amurrum,
4) DUB.SAR DUR.ŠUB.BA	4) scribe, ...,
5) DUMU *i-din*-^{d}EN.ZU	5) son of Iddin-Sîn,
6) ÌR.ZU	6) your servant.

2002

Sîn-iddinam, the *šassukkum* official who began his tenure of office during the reign of Ur-Ninmar, continued in that post during the reign of Ur-Ningišzida. His seal impression as servant of Ur-Ningišzida is found on five clay tablets excavated at Ešnunna.

CATALOGUE

Ex.	Excavation number	Provenance	cpn
1	As 30:T.509	Ešnunna, from the vertical pottery drain in O 30:7	n
2	As 30:T.531	As ex. 1	n
3	As 30:T.533	As ex. 1	n
4	As 30:T.536	As ex. 1	n
5	As 30:T.551	As ex. 1	n

BIBLIOGRAPHY

1977 Whiting in Gibson and Biggs, Seals p. 72 (transliteration)

TEXT

1) ur-^{d}nin-giš-zi-da	1) Ur-Ningišzida,
2) ÉNSI *áš-nun-na*.KI	2) governor of Ešnunna –
3) ^{d}EN.ZU-*i-din-nam*	3) Sîn-iddinam,
4) DUB.SAR DUR.ŠUB.BA	4) scribe, ...,
5) DUMU *ku-ru-za* ÌR.ZU	5) son of Kuruza, your servant.

2003

Sîn-iddinam appears to have been followed in the office of *šassukkum* at Ešnunna by a certain Šū-Enlil, who was not his son. The latter's seal impression is found on two clay tablets excavated at Ešnunna.

CATALOGUE

Ex.	Excavation number	Provenance	Lines preserved	cpn
1	As 30:T.532	Ešnunna, from the vertical pottery drain in O 30:7	1–5	c
2	As 30:T.560	As ex. 1	1–5	c

COMMENTARY

The impressions actually come from two different seals, but have been edited together here since the difference in the inscription is merely in the division of the lines.

BIBLIOGRAPHY

1977 Whiting in Gibson and Biggs, Seals p. 72 (transliteration)

TEXT

1) ur-^{d}nin-giš-zi-da	1) Ur-Ningišzida,
2) ÉNSI *áš-nun-na*.KI	2) governor of Ešnunna –
3) *šu-^{d}en-líl*	3) Šū-Enlil,
4) DUB.SAR	4) scribe,
5) DUMU *ki-nam-iš-ti*	5) son of Kīnam-išti,
6) [ÌR.ZU]	6) [your servant].

2004

The seal impression of a servant of Ur-Ningišzida is found on a tablet excavated at Ešnunna.

2.2 writes ÉNSI *áš-nun-na*.KI in two lines.

COMMENTARY

The impression is on As 31:T.381, from O 30:8, the Bilalama palace. The impression was previously published by Jacobsen, Gimilsin temple p. 151 no. 36. Collation by R. Whiting yields a slightly modified reading.

BIBLIOGRAPHY

1940 Jacobsen, Gimilsin Temple p. 151 no. 36 (edition)
1961 Hallo, BiOr 18 p. 14 Ešnunna 21: vii (study)

TEXT

1) ur-^{d}nin-giš-[zi-da]	1) Ur-Ningiš[zida],
2) ÉNSI [*áš-nun-na*.KI]	2) governor [of Ešnunna] –
3) *en-num*-[...]	3) Ennum-[...],
4) DUMU *šu*-[...]	4) son of Šū-[...],
5) ÌR.ZU	5) your servant.

Ipiq-Adad I

E4.5.9

Ur-Ningišzida was succeeded by Ipiq-Adad, son of Ur-Ninmar, as governor of Ešnunna, the first of two governors to bear that name. Four or five year names may be attributed to this ruler. Whereas the later Ipiq-Adad adopted the title 'king of Ešnunna' along with the prefixed divine determinative in the writing of his name, Ipiq-Adad I used the title 'governor of Ešnunna' throughout his reign, and his name never has the divine determinative. The inscriptions edited here are generally assigned to the earlier ruler on the basis of their archaeological context.

1

The standard inscription of Ipiq-Adad I is found on stamped bricks excavated from the Ipiq-Adad I palace.

CATALOGUE

Ex.	Museum number	Excavation number	Provenance	Dimensions (cm)	Lines preserved	cpn
1	IM –	As 31:750	Ešnunna, from the Ipiq-Adad I palace	–	–	n
2	A 9007	As 31:751	As ex. 1	33.5×34.0×8.3	1-5	c
3	A 9008	As 31:751a	As ex. 1	32.0×15.5×8.3	1-5	c
4	LB no number	–	Ešnunna(?)	34.0×33.5×8.0	1-5	c
5	ROM 931×44.62	–	Ešnunna(?)	–	1-5	c

COMMENTARY

Exs. 1-3 were excavated at Ešnunna in an archaeological context which makes their attribution to Ipiq-Adad I certain. Exs. 4-5 were purchased, the latter by Meek in Iraq, and could date either to Ipiq-Adad I or to the earlier part of the reign of Ipiq-Adad II before he adopted the title 'king of Ešnunna'. They are arbitrarily included here.

BIBLIOGRAPHY

1940 Jacobsen, Gimilsin Temple p. 137 no. 9 (edition) and pl. 15 no. 9 (copy)

1961 Hallo, BiOr 18 p. 13 Ešnunna 1: vii (study)

1971 Sollberger and Kupper, IRSA IVE9a (study)

TEXT

1) *i-pí-iq*-^{d}IŠKUR
2) *na-ra-am*
3) ^{d}*tišpak*
4) ÉNSI
5) *áš-nun-na*.KI

1) Ipiq-Adad,
2–3) beloved of the god Tišpak,
4–5) governor of Ešnunna.

2

The impression of a seal of Ipiq-Adad I is found on a number of tablets excavated at Ešnunna. Their archaeological context makes their attribution to Ipiq-Adad I certain.

CATALOGUE

Ex.	Excavation number	Provenance	cpn
1	As 30:T.104	Ešnunna, P 29:6 top layer, Ipiq-Adad I–Ibāl-pî-el I palace	n
2	As 30:T.227	P 30:1, Ipiq-Adad I–Ibāl-pî-el I palace	n
3	As 30:T.293	Dump	n
4	As 30:T.421	O 30:5, top layer, Ipiq-Adad I–Ibāl-pî-el I palace	n
5	As 30:T.422	As ex. 4	n
6	As 30:T.423	As ex. 4	n
7	As 30:T.645	P 31:1, Ipiq-Adad I palace	n
8	As 30:T.669	As ex. 7	n
9	As 31:T.363	M 33, in street	n
10	As 31:T.673	M 32:6, –	n

BIBLIOGRAPHY

1940 Jacobsen, Gimilsin Temple p. 152 no. 40 (edition)
1961 Hallo, BiOr 18 p. 13 Ešnunna 18 (study)
1971 Sollberger and Kupper, IRSA IVE9b (translation)

TEXT

1) *i-pí-iq*-^{d}IŠKUR
2) *na-ra-am* ^{d}*tišpak*
3) ÉNSI *áš-nun-na*.KI
4) DUMU ur-^{d}nin-mar.KI

1) Ipiq-Adad,
2) beloved of the god Tišpak,
3) governor of Ešnunna,
4) son of Ur-Ninmar.

2001

Iddin-Amurrum, the *kakikkum* official who served under Ur-Ningišzida, continued in that post into the reign of Ipiq-Adad I, when a seal for his new master was cut. Impressions of that seal are found on two clay tablets excavated at Ešnunna.

CATALOGUE

Ex.	Excavation number	Provenance	cpn
1	As 30:T.549	Ešnunna, from the vertical pottery drain in O 30:7	n
2	As 30:T.781	As ex. 1	n

COMMENTARY

The inscription is edited here for the first time through the courtesy of the trustees of the Oriental Institute.

BIBLIOGRAPHY

1977 Whiting in Gibson and Biggs, Seals p. 72 (transliteration)

TEXT

1) *i-pí-iq-*[d]IŠKUR
2) ÉNSI *áš-nun-na*.KI
3) *i-din-*[d]MAR.DÚ DUB.SAR
4) DUMU *i-din-*[d]EN.ZU ÌR.ZU

1) Ipiq-Adad,
2) governor of Ešnunna —
3) Iddin-Amurrum, scribe,
4) son of Iddin-Sîn, your servant.

2002

A different seal of Iddin-Amurrum is found on three clay tablets excavated at Ešnunna.

CATALOGUE

Ex.	Excavation number	Provenance	cpn
1	As 30:T.512	Ešnunna, from the vertical drain in O 30:7	n
2	As 30:T.523	As ex. 1	n
3	As 30:T.553	As ex. 1	n

BIBLIOGRAPHY

1977 Whiting in Gibson and Biggs, Seals p. 72 (transliteration)

TEXT

1) *i-pí-iq-*^{d}IŠKUR	1) Ipiq-Adad,
2) ÉNSI *áš-nun-na*.KI	2) governor of Ešnunna –
3) *i-din-*^{d}MAR-DÚ	3) Iddin-Amurrum,
4) DUB.SAR DUR.ŠUB.BA	4) scribe, ...,
5) [DUMU *i-din-*^{d}EN.ZU ÌR.ZU]	5) [son of Iddin-Sîn, your servant].

2003

The seal impression of Erra-bāni, another *kakikkum* official who served under Ipiq-Adad I, is found on two clay tablets excavated at Ešnunna.

CATALOGUE

Ex.	Excavation number	Provenance	cpn
1	As 30:T.506	Ešnunna, from the vertical pottery drain in O 30:7	n
2	As 30:T.534	As ex. 1	n

BIBLIOGRAPHY

1977 Whiting in Gibson and Biggs, Seals pp. 72–73 (transliteration)

TEXT

1) *i-pí-iq-*^{d}IŠKUR	1) Ipiq-Adad,
2) *na-ra-am* ^{d}*tišpak*	2) beloved of the god Tišpak,
3) ÉNSI	3–4) governor of Ešnunna –
4) *áš-nun-na*.KI	
5) *èr-ra-ba-ni* DUB.SAR	5) Erra-bāni, scribe,
6) DUMU *šu-*^{d}*ṭa-ba-an*	6) son of Šū-Ṭabān,
7) ÌR.ZU	7) your servant.

2004

The impression of a seal of Šū-Enlil, who had served as *šassukkum* official during the reign of Ur-Ningišzida, acknowledges Ipiq-Adad I as lord. It is found on a number of clay tablets excavated at Ešnunna.

CATALOGUE

Ex.	Excavation number	Provenance	cpn
1	As 30:T.134	Ešnunna, M 31:6, Ipiq-Adad I–Ibāl-pî-el I palace	n
2	As 30:T.172	M 31:12, Ipiq-Adad I–Ibāl-pî-el I palace	n
3	As 30:T.180	As ex. 2	n
4	As 30:T.194	As ex. 2	n
5	As 30:T.195	As ex. 2	n
6	As 30:T.197	As ex. 2	n

BIBLIOGRAPHY

1940 Jacobsen, Gimilsin Temple p. 153 no. 42 (edition)
1961 Hallo, BiOr 18 p. 14 Ešnunna 21: ix (study)
1971 Sollberger and Kupper, IRSA IVE9c (translation)

TEXT

1) *i-pí-iq*-dIŠKUR
2) ÉNSI *áš-nun-na*.KI
3) *šu*-d*en-líl* DUB.SAR
4) DUMU *ki-nam-iš-ti*
5) [ÌR].ZU

1) Ipiq-Adad,
2) governor of Ešnunna —
3) Šū-Enlil, scribe,
4) son of Kīnam-išti,
5) your [servant].

2005

Sîn-iddinam, who served as *šassukkum* official during the reigns of Ur-Ninmar and Ur-Ningišzida, continued in that post during the reign of Ipiq-Adad I, as is evidenced by a seal impression.

COMMENTARY

The impression is found on As 30:T.625, from P 30:1 Ipiq-Adad I–Ibāl-pî-El I level. It was collated by R. Whiting (personal communication), who offers a slightly different reading from that previously given by Jacobsen (cf. line 3).

BIBLIOGRAPHY

1940 Jacobsen, Gimilsin Temple p. 153 no. 44 (edition)
1961 Hallo, BiOr 18 p. 14 Ešnunna 21: ix (study)

TEXT

1) [*i-pí-i*]*q*-dIŠKUR
2) [ÉNSI] *áš-nun-na*.KI
3) dEN.ZU-*i-din-nam* DUB.SAR
4) DUMU *ku-ru-za*
5) ÌR.ZU

1) [Ipi]q-Adad,
2) [governor] of Ešnunna —
3) Sîn-iddinam, scribe,
4) son of Kuruza,
5) your servant.

2006

The seal impression of Šumi-aḫīia, who served as *šassukkum* official during part of the reign of Ipiq-Adad I, is found on two clay tablets excavated at Ešnunna.

CATALOGUE

Ex.	Excavation number	Provenance	cpn
1	As 30:T.490+T.508	Ešnunna, from the vertical pottery drain in O 30:7	n
2	As 30:T.520	As ex. 1	n

BIBLIOGRAPHY

1977 Whiting in Gibson and Biggs, Seals p. 72 (transliteration)

TEXT

1) *i-pí-iq-*^{d}IŠKUR	1) Ipiq-Adad,
2) ÉNSI	2–3) governor of Ešnunna –
3) *áš-nun-na.*KI	
4) *šu-mi-a-ḫi-a*	4) Šumi-aḫīia,
5) DUB.SAR	5) scribe,
6) DUMU *a*-x x-*um*	6) son of A...um,
7) ÌR.ZU	7) your servant.

2007

The seal impression of Ikū(n)-pî-Eštar acknowledges Ipiq-Adad I as governor of Ešnunna.

COMMENTARY

The seal impression is found on As 31:T.268, collated by R. Whiting. It is edited here for the first time through the courtesy of the trustees of the Oriental Institute. The impression was wrongly attributed as one example of seal legend 40 by Jacobsen, Gimilsin Temple p. 152.

BIBLIOGRAPHY

1940 Jacobsen, Gimilsin Temple p. 152 no. 40 (As 31:T.268)

TEXT

1) *i-pí-iq-*[d]IŠKUR	1) Ipiq-Adad,
2) ÉNSI *áš-nun-na*.KI	2) governor of Ešnunna –
3) *i-ku-pí-eš₄-tár*	3) Ikū(n)-pî-Eštar,
4) DUMU *i-din-*[d]*ma-lik*	4) son of Iddin-Malik.

2008

A fragmentary seal impression of a servant of Ipiq-Adad I is found on a tablet excavated at Ešnunna.

COMMENTARY

The tablet is As 30:T.125, found at M 31:6, Ipiq-Adad I–Ibāl-pî-El I palace. The impression was not collated.

BIBLIOGRAPHY

1940 Jacobsen, Gimilsin Temple p. 153 no. 45 (edition)
1961 Hallo, BiOr 18 p. 14 Ešnunna 21: ix (study)

TEXT

1) [...]	1) [...],
2) [...]	2) [...],
3) ÌR *i-pí-iq-*[d][IŠKUR]	3) servant of Ipiq-[Adad].

2009

Another fragmentary seal impression mentioning Ipiq-Adad I appears on a tablet excavated at Ešnunna.

COMMENTARY

The impression is found on As 30:T.203, from M 31:1, Ipiq-Adad I–Ibāl-pî-El I palace. It was not collated.

BIBLIOGRAPHY

1940 Jacobsen, Gimilsin Temple p. 153 no. 46 (edition)
1961 Hallo, BiOr 18 p. 14 Ešnunna 21: ix (study)

TEXT

1) [...]-*ma-at-gi*(?)-*mi-i*[*l* ...]	1) [...]mat-gimi[l ...],
2) [... *i*]-*pí-iq*-^{d}IŠKUR	2) [... I]piq-Adad,
3) [...]-*a*(?)-*ni*(?) *wa-ru*-[...]	3) ...

Abdi-Eraḫ, Šiqlānum

E4.5.9a

A tablet recording the death of Šiqlānum was found on a tablet from a hoard in a pottery drain at Ešnunna. Jacobsen thought that this Šiqlānum was a ruler of Ešnunna. However, since a death of a ruler is never commemorated in the year name of a state of which he was head, Šiqlānum must have been a ruler of some city other than Ešnunna.

The assignment of Abdi-Eraḫ as ruler of Ešnunna, which was based on the occurrence of the name in a year name on a tablet from Tell Asmar, is unlikely (see R. Whiting, Letters p. 31). Thus it appears that neither Šiqlānum nor Abdi-Eraḫ was a ruler of Ešnunna.

BIBLIOGRAPHY

1932 Jacobsen, OIC 13 pp. 49–50 (study)
1940 Jacobsen, Gimilsin Temple pp. 120–21 (study)
1987 Whiting, Letters pp. 30–33 (study)

Šarrīia

E4.5.10

Ipiq-Adad I appears to have been succeeded by Šarrīia as ruler of Ešnunna.

1

Bricks stamped with the standard inscription of Šarrīia were found at Ešnunna.

COMMENTARY

The only ex. of this brick which was located is A 9002, As 31:762. It measures 33.5 × 33 cm and the inscription was collated. Jacobsen mentions two bricks, As 30:T.308 coming from N 30:3, not their original context. One of these could be our ex. 1. The other, probably in the Iraq Museum, has not been located.

BIBLIOGRAPHY

1940 Jacobsen, Gimilsin Temple p. 137 no. 10 (edition) and pl. 15 no. 10 (copy)
1961 Hallo, BiOr 18 p. 13 Ešnunna 1: viii (study)
1971 Sollberger and Kupper, IRSA IVE12 (study)

TEXT

1) *[ša]r-ri-ia*	1) [Ša]rrīia,
2) *na-ra-am*	2–3) beloved of the god Tišpak,
3) *[d]tišpak*	
4) ÉNSI	4–5) governor of Ešnunna.
5) *áš-nun-na*.KI	

Warassa

E4.5.11

Šarrīia was succeeded by Warassa as governor of Ešnunna. During his reign Tutub (Khafajah) and Išur were captured by Ešnunna.

While it was known that the reigns of Warassa and Bēlakum followed that of Šarrīia, the exact order of succession was not certain. The tablet As 30:T.575 mentions that Šarrīia was the father of Bēlakum. Based on this information, Jacobsen tentatively put Bēlakum as the successor of Šarrīia. The possibility existed, however, as Jacobsen pointed out, that Warassa and Bēlakum were brothers. In this case, either one of them could have succeeded Šarrīia. The evidence of E4.5.11.2001, a seal of an official who served under Ipiq-Adad I and Warassa but who is not attested among tablets dating to the reign of Bēlakum, indicates that Warassa preceded Bēlakum as governor of Ešnunna.

2001

This seal of Erra-bāni, *kakikkum* official of Ipiq-Adad I, indicates that he continued in that post during the reign of Warassa.

COMMENTARY

The seal is As 33:372 found in the dump formed during the 1930–31 seasons by material from the Old Palace.

The inscription was collated from the published photo.

BIBLIOGRAPHY

1940 Jacobsen, Gimilsin Temple p. 154 no. 47 (edition)
1955 Jacobsen, Cylinder Seals no. 724 (photo, edition)
1961 Hallo, BiOr 18 p. 14 Ešnunna 21: x (study)
1971 Sollberger and Kupper, IRSA IVE14a (translation)

TEXT

1) ÌR-[*sà*]
2) ÉNSI *áš-n*[*un-na*.KI]
3) *èr-ra-ba-ni* DU[B.SAR]
4) DUMU *šu*-^{d}*ṭa-b*[*a-an*]
5) ÌR.[ZU]

1) Waras[sa],
2) governor of Ešn[unna] –
3) Erra-bāni, sc[ribe],
4) son of Šū-Ṭab[ān],
5) [your] servant.

2002

The seal impression of Lu-ibgal, who served as *šassukkum* official under Warassa, is on a tablet excavated at Ešnunna.

COMMENTARY

The impression is found on As 30:T.523 + 561. It was not collated.

BIBLIOGRAPHY

1977 Whiting in Gibson and Biggs, Seals p. 73 (transliteration)

TEXT

1) ÌR-*sà*	1) Warassa,
2) ÉNSI	2–3) governor of Ešnunna –
3) *áš-nun-na*.KI	
4) lú-ib-gal	4) Lu-ibgal,
5) DUB.SAR	5) scribe,
6) ⌜DUMU⌝ x x x x	6) son of ...,
7) ÌR.ZU	7) your servant.

Bēlakum

E4.5.12

Warassa was succeeded by Bēlakum, apparently his brother, as governor of Ešnunna. About seven year names are known which may be attributed to this ruler. About this time Ešnunna gained control over Nērebtum.

1

Bricks stamped with the standard inscription of Bēlakum were excavated at Ešnunna.

CATALOGUE

Ex.	Museum number	Excavation number	Provenance	Dimensions (cm)	Lines preserved	cpn
1	–	As 30:T.304	Ešnunna, loose in soil of N 30:3	–	1–5	n
2	IM 23833	As 31:758	Q 32:6	33.0×33.0×6.5	–	n
3	A 8988	As 31:759	Q 33:8	32.0×32.7	1–5	c
4	A 8989	As 31:759a	N 31:6	30.4×25.7×6.0	1–5	c
5	(see bibliography)	–	Ešnunna(?)	–	1–5	n

BIBLIOGRAPHY

1892 Pognon, Le Muséon pp. 251 and 253 no. 3 (ex. 5, copy, translation)
1892–93 Pinches, BOR 6 p. 67 no. III (ex. 5, copy, edition)
1900 Radau, EBH p. 424 (ex. 5, transliteration)
1905 Thureau-Dangin, ISA pp. 250–51 Belaku (ex. 5, edition)
1907 Thureau-Dangin, SAK pp. 174–75 Belaku (ex. 5, edition)
1929 Barton, RISA pp. 152–53 Belaku 1 (ex. 5, edition)
1940 Jacobsen, Gimilsin Temple p. 137 no. 11 (ex. 1, edition), p. 91 (exs. 2–3, provenance), and pl. 15 no. 11 (ex. 1, copy)
1961 Hallo, BiOr 18 p. 13 Ešnunna 1: ix (study)
1971 Sollberger and Kupper, IRSA IVE13 (study)

TEXT

1) *be-la-kum*	1) Bēlakum,
2) *na-ra-am*	2–3) beloved of the god Tišpak,
3) ^{d}*tišpak*	
4) ÉNSI	4–5) governor of Ešnunna.
5) *áš-nun-na*.KI	

2001

A seal impression of Ennum-Sîn, *kakikkum* official at Ešnunna, appears on a tablet dated to year 1 of Bēlakum. The name of the governor of Ešnunna is broken away in this seal impression. It could have been Bēlakum, or possibly Warassa.

COMMENTARY

The impression is found on As 30:T.496 from the vertical drain in O 30: 7. It was collated by R. Whiting and edited here through the courtesy of the trustees of the Oriental Institute.

BIBLIOGRAPHY

1977 Whiting in Gibson and Biggs, Seals p. 73 (transliteration)

TEXT

1) [*be-la-kum*]	1) [Bēlakum],
2) *na-ra-am* ^{d}*tišpak*	2) beloved of the god Tišpak,
3) ÉNSI *áš-nun-na*.KI	3) governor of Ešnunna –
4) *en-num*-^{d}EN.ZU	4) Ennum-Sîn,
5) DUB.SAR DUR.ŠUB.BA	5) scribe, ...,
6) DUMU *i-din*-^{d}MAR.DÚ	6) son of Iddin-Amurrum,
7) ÌR.ZU	7) your servant.

2002

The seal impression of Lalûm, *kakikkum* official during the reign of Bēlakum, is found on two clay tablets excavated at Ešnunna.

CATALOGUE

Ex.	Excavation number	Provenance	cpn
1	As 30:T.542	Ešnunna, from the vertical pottery drain in O 30:7	n
2	As 30:T.782	As ex. 1	n

BIBLIOGRAPHY

1977 Whiting in Gibson and Biggs, Seals p. 73 (transliteration)

TEXT

1) *be-la-kum*	1) Bēlakum,
2) ÉNSI *áš-nun-na*.KI	2) governor of Ešnunna –
3) *la-lu-um* DUB.SAR	3) Lalûm, scribe,
4) DUMU *i-din-*^{d}MAR.DÚ	4) son of Iddin-Amurrum,
5) [ÌR.ZU]	5) [your servant].

2003

A seal impression of Lalûm appears on two clay tablets excavated at Ešnunna in which he functions as the *šassukkum* official.

CATALOGUE

Ex.	Excavation number	Provenance	cpn
1	As 30:T.507	Ešnunna, from the vertical pottery drain in O 30:7	n
2	As 30:T.548 + 703	As ex. 1	n

BIBLIOGRAPHY

1977 Whiting in Gibson and Biggs, Seals p. 73 (transliteration)

TEXT

1) *la-lu-um*	1) Lalûm,
2) DUB.SAR DUR.ŠUB.BA	2) scribe, ...,
3) DUMU *i-din-*^{d}MAR.DÚ	3) son of Iddin-Amurrum,
4) ⌜ÌR *be-la*⌝*-kum*	4) servant of Bēlakum.

2004

The seal impression of Attā-waqar, another *šassukkum* official who served during the reign of Bēlakum, is found on three clay tablets excavated at Ešnunna.

CATALOGUE

Ex.	Excavation number	Provenance	cpn
1	As 30:T.492	Ešnunna, from the vertical pottery drain in O 30:7	n
2	As 30:T.516	As ex. 1	n
3	As 30:T.569	As ex. 1	n

BIBLIOGRAPHY

1977 Whiting in Gibson and Biggs, Seals p. 73 (transliteration)

TEXT

1) *be-la-kum*	1) Bēlakum,
2) *na-ra-am* ^{d}*tišpak*	2) beloved of the god Tišpak,
3) ÉNSI	3–4) governor of Ešnunna –
4) *áš-nun-na*.KI	
5) *a-ta-wa-qar*	5) Attā-waqar,
6) DUB.SAR	6) scribe,
7) DUMU *iš-me*-^{d}EN.ZU	7) son of Išme-Sîn,
8) ÌR.ZU	8) your servant.

2005

The impression of Lalûm, a *šassukkum* official under Bēlakum, is found on a tablet excavated at Ešnunna. This is a different Lalûm from the one whose seal impression appears in E4.5.12.2002–2003.

COMMENTARY

The impression is on As 30:T.525 + 546, in the vertical pottery drain in O 30:7. It was not collated.

BIBLIOGRAPHY

1977 Whiting in Gibson and Biggs, Seals p. 73 (transliteration)

TEXT

1) *be-la-kum*	1) Bēlakum,
2) ÉNSI	2–3) governor of Ešnunna –
3) *áš-nun-na*.KI	
4) *la-lu-um*	4) Lalûm,
5) DUB.SAR	5) scribe,
6) DUMU *šu*-^{d}*ti*[*špak*]	6) son of Šū-Ti[špak],
7) [ÌR.ZU]	7) [your servant].

2006

The seal impression of Ibni-Tišpak, *šassukkum* official under Bēlakum, is found on a tablet excavated at Ešnunna.

COMMENTARY

The impression is impressed on As 30:T.504, from the vertical pottery drain in O 30:7. Collation by R. Whiting yields a different reading from that previously indicated by Jacobsen.

BIBLIOGRAPHY

1977 Whiting in Gibson and Biggs, Seals p. 73 (transliteration)

TEXT

1) *[be-la]-kum*	1) [Bēla]kum,
2) *na-ra-am* ᵈ*tišpak*	2) beloved of the god Tišpak –
3) *ib-ni-*ᵈ⌜*tišpak*⌝	3) Ibni-Tišpak,
4) DUB.[SAR]	4) scr[ibe],
5) DUMU ÌR-[...]	5) son of Warad-[...],
6) ÌR.[ZU]	6) [your] servant.

2007

The seal impression of Sîn-abūšu, servant of Bēlakum, is found on two clay tablets excavated at Ešnunna.

CATALOGUE

Ex.	Excavation number	Provenance	cpn
1	As 30:T.83	Ešnunna, O 30:3, higher than the Bilalama level	c
2	As 30:T.81	As ex. 1	c

COMMENTARY

The impression is published here for the first time through the courtesy of R. Whiting.

TEXT

1) ᵈEN.ZU-*a-bu-šu*	1) Sîn-abūšu,
2) DUB.SAR	2) scribe,
3) DUMU ur-ᵈEN.ZU	3) son of Ur-Sîn,
4) ⌜ÌR⌝ *be-*⌜*la-kum*⌝	4) servant of Bēlakum.

Ibāl-pî-El I

E4.5.13

Bēlakum was succeeded by Ibāl-pî-El, the first of two rulers of Ešnunna who bore that name. Ibāl-pî-El I can be distinguished in his building inscriptions from his later namesake because he served simply as 'governor' (énsi) of Ešnunna. Ibāl-pî-El II, in contrast, in the building inscriptions at present available, always appears as 'king' (lugal). Assignment of seals and seal impressions of servants of these two rulers is more difficult, because the titulary of the rulers does not normally appear in these inscriptions. These are attributed here according to their archaeological context.

1

A number of bricks stamped with the standard inscription of Ibāl-pî-El I were found at Ešnunna.

CATALOGUE

Ex.	Museum number	Excavation number	Provenance	Dimensions (cm)	Lines preserved	cpn
1	IM 25604	As 31:752	Ešnunna, from the Ibāl-pî-El I palace	–	–	n
2	A 8996	As 31:753	As ex. 1	35.0×35.0×8.2	1–4	c
3	IM 23834	As 31:794	P 27:9, under a wall at level 32, 30 in a private house	36.0×29.5×8.0	–	n
4	A 8998	As 31:795b	As ex. 3	Trapezoidal: 29.0 long, 23.0 high short end, 37.0 high long end, 7.1 thick	1–4	c
5	A 8999	As 31:795a	As ex. 3	Trapezoidal: 29.0 long, 24.0 high short end, 37.0 high long end, 7.7 thick	1–4	c
6	(see bibliography)	–	Ešnunna	–	1–4	n

COMMENTARY

Exs. 1–2 are rectangular bricks; exs. 3–5 are trapezoidal in shape, probably well-head bricks.

Jacobsen, Gimilsin Temple p. 138, expressed some uncertainty as to the dating of exs. 3–5. He provisionally assigned the bricks to Ibāl-pî-El I.

Hallo (BiOr 18 p. 13, Ešnunna 1 x.) mentions a brick of Ibāl-pî-El I in the Liagre Böhl collection. This could not be located in Leiden. There is a brick of Ibāl-pî-El II in that collection (see E4.5.20.1) that was not mentioned by Hallo and which might be this brick.

BIBLIOGRAPHY

1892 Pognon, Le Muséon pp. 250 and 253 no. 1 (ex. 6, copy, translation)

1892–93 Pinches, BOR 6 p. 67 no. I (ex. 6, copy, edition)

1900 Radau, EBH p. 434 (ex. 6, transliteration)

1905 Thureau-Dangin, ISA pp. 248–49 Ibalpel (ex. 6, edition)

1907 Thureau-Dangin, SAK pp. 174–75 Ibalpel (ex. 6, edition)

1929 Barton, RISA pp. 152–53 Ibalpel 1 (ex. 6, edition)

1940 Jacobsen, Gimilsin Temple p. 137 no. 12 (exs. 1–2, edition), pl. 16 no. 12 (exs. 1–2, copy), pp. 137–38 no. 12a (exs. 3–5, edition), and pl. 16 no. 12a (exs. 3–5, copy)

1961 Hallo, BiOr 18 p. 13 Ešnunna 1: x (study)

1971 Sollberger and Kupper, IRSA IVE15a (study)

TEXT

1) *i-ba-al-pi-el*
2) *na-ra-am*
3) ^{d}*tišpak*
4) ÉNSI
5) *áš-nun-na*.KI

1) Ibāl-pî-El,
2–3) beloved of the god Tišpak,
4–5) governor of Ešnunna.

2

The impression of a seal probably granted by Ibāl-pî-El I to his wife is found on a tablet excavated at Ešnunna.

COMMENTARY

The impression is on As 30:T.119, from P 29:1, from the surface of the mound. It was not collated.

We have restored line 5, following Jacobsen, as DAM-[*šu*].

BIBLIOGRAPHY

1940 Jacobsen, Gimilsin Temple p. 154 no. 47a (edition)

1971 Sollberger and Kupper, IRSA IVE15b (translation)

TEXT

1) ⸢*i*⸣-*ba*-[*al-pi-el*]
2) ÉNS[I]
3) *áš-nun*-[*na*.KI]
4) *a-na nir*(?)-[...]
5) DAM-[*šu*]
6) [*i-qi*$_4$-*iš*]

1–6) Ibā[l-pî-El], govern[or] of Ešnun[na, granted] (this seal) to *Nir*-[..., his] wife.

2001

The impression of the seal of Ašūb-li-El, servant of Ibāl-pî-El I, is found on four clay tablets excavated at Ešnunna.

CATALOGUE

Ex.	Excavation number	Provenance	cpn
1	As 30:T.216	Ešnunna, N 30:5,from the Ipiq-Adad I–Ibāl-pî-El I level	n
2	As 30:T.633	O 30:7, Bilalama palace level	n
3	As 30:T.634	N 31:1,Ipiq-Adad I–Ibāl-pî-El I palace	n
4	As 31:T.669	As ex. 3	n

BIBLIOGRAPHY

1940 Jacobsen, Gimilsin Temple p. 154 no. 48 (exs. 1–4, conflated edition)
1961 Hallo, BiOr 18 p. 14 Ešnunna 21: xi (study)

TEXT

1) *a-šu-ub-li-el*
2) ÌR *i-ba-al-pi-el*

1) Ašūb-li-El,
2) servant of Ibāl-pî-el.

2002

The impression of the seal of Tišpak-nāṣir, servant of Ibāl-pî-El I, appears on a tablet excavated at Ešnunna.

COMMENTARY

The impression is found on As 30:T.142, from M 31:1, from the Ipiq-Adad I–Ibāl-pî-El I palace. It was not collated.

BIBLIOGRAPHY

1940 Jacobsen, Gimilsin Temple p. 154 no. 49 (edition)
1961 Hallo, BiOr 18 p. 14 Ešnunna 21: xi (study)
1971 Sollberger and Kupper, IRSA IVE15c (translation)

TEXT

1) ᵈ*tišpak-na-ṣi-ir*	1) Tišpak-nāṣir,
2) DUB.SAR	2) scribe,
3) DUMU ur-ᵈnin-ì-si-na	3) son of Ur-Ninisina,
4) ÌR *i-ba-al-pi-el*	4) servant of Ibāl-pî-El.

2003

The impression of the seal of Warad-Adad, servant of Ibāl-pî-El I, is on a tablet excavated at Ešnunna.

COMMENTARY

The impression is found on As 30:T.54, from O 29:7, top layer (Ipiq-Adad I–Ibāl-pî-El I). It was not collated.

BIBLIOGRAPHY

1940 Jacobsen, Gimilsin Temple p. 154 no. 50 (edition)
1961 Hallo, BiOr 18 p. 14 Ešnunna 21: xi (study)

TEXT

1) ÌR-ᵈIŠKUR	1) Warad-Adad,
2) DUMU *a-bu-*[...]	2) son of Abu-[...],
3) ÌR *i-ba-al-pi-el*	3) servant of Ibāl-pî-El.

2004

A seal impression of a servant of Ibāl-pî-El I is found on a tablet from Ishchali.

COMMENTARY

The seal impression is found on UCLM 9-2395 from Ishchali.

The attribution of this impression to a servant of Ibāl-pî-El I rather than Ibāl-pî-El II is determined by the titulary found on the seal. While the year name dealing with the ivory throne of Tišpak on this tablet does appear as a year name of Ibāl-pî-El II (see Greengus, OBTI p. 31 no. 37), it also appears on a tablet from the pottery drain in O 30:7 which contained tablets dating to the time of Uṣur-awassu to Ibāl-pî-El I (see Jacobsen, OIP 43 p. 190 no. 111). Apparently it was a year name used by both Ibāl-pî-El I and II.

S. Greengus, Ishchali Documents p. 119, notes that the tablet bearing this seal impression is written in an archaic script. This supports an attribution of the seal inscription to Ibāl-pî-El I. Control over Kiti by Ešnunna seems to have been gained by Bēlakum, one of whose year names deals with the introduction of the statue of the goddess Inanna of Kiti into her temple, possibly in Kiti/Nērebtum. The evidence of this seal impression indicates that control over Kiti by Ešnunna continued into the time of Ibāl-pî-El I.

BIBLIOGRAPHY

1931 Lutz, UCP 10/1 p. 69 TN 36 (transliteration)
1986 Greengus, Ishchali Documents p. 118 (edition)

TEXT

1) *i-ba-al-pi-el*	1) Ibāl-pî-El,
2) *na-ra-am* ^{d}*tišpak*	2) beloved of the god Tišpak,
3) ÉNSI *áš-nun-na*.KI	3) governor of Ešnunna –
4) *na-bi*-^{d}EN.ZU	4) Nabi-Sîn,
5) ⌜KA⌝.KI	5) *kakikkum* official,
6) [DUM]U ur-é-ninnu	6) [so]n of Ur-Eninnu,
7) [ÌR.ZU]	7) [your servant].

Ipiq-Adad II

E4.5.14

Ibāl-pî-El I was succeeded by his son Ipiq-Adad, the second ruler of Ešnunna by that name. The evidence of the 'Assyrian Chronicle' texts published by Birot (see MARI 4 pp. 233–34) indicates that Ipiq-Adad II reigned a minimum of 37 years. During his reign he adopted the title 'king' (LUGAL), which had not been used at Ešnunna since the time of Šū-ilīia. Ipiq-Adad II greatly expanded Ešnunna's domains, prompting him to adopt the title 'enlarger of Ešnunna' (*murappiš ešnunna*).

1

At his accession Ipiq-Adad II appears to have taken the traditional title 'governor of Ešnunna' as evidenced by bricks found at the highest levels of the Ibāl-pî-El I palace at Ešnunna.

COMMENTARY

The only brick which bears this inscription is IM 23835, As 31:764, found at N 30:5, a pavement just below the surface directly above the building remains of Ibāl-pî-El I. It measures 32.5 × 32.5 × 8 cm and the inscription was not collated.

Doubts were expressed by Jacobsen, Gimilsin Temple pp. 138–39, about the attribution of this inscription. The stratigraphic evidence argued for an attribution to Ipiq-Adad II. The epigraphy of the text, however, suggested an earlier date. Weighing the various evidence, Jacobsen opted for an attribution to Ipiq-Adad II.

BIBLIOGRAPHY

1940 Jacobsen, Gimilsin Temple p. 138 no. 13a (edition), pp. 138–39 (study), pl. 16 no. 13a (copy), and p. 82 (provenance)

1961 Hallo, BiOr 18 p. 13 Ešnunna 1: xi (study)

1971 Sollberger and Kupper, IRSA IVE16a (translation)

TEXT

1) *i-pí-iq*-^{d}IŠKUR	1) Ipiq-Adad,
2) *na-ra-am*	2–3) beloved of the god Tišpak,
3) ^{d}*tišpak*	
4) ÉNSI	4–5) governor of Ešnunna.
5) *áš-nun-na*.KI	

2

Bricks stamped with an inscription of Ipiq-Adad II in which he appears as 'king' (LUGAL) were found in the paving of a street south of the palace.

CATALOGUE

Ex.	Museum number	Excavation number	Provenance	Dimensions (cm)	Lines preserved	cpn
1	IM –	As 31:756	Ešnunna, from street west of P 30	–	–	n
2	A 9003	As 31:757	As ex. 1	–	–	n
3	A 9004	As 31:757a	As ex. 1	–	–	n
4	LB no number	–	Ešnunna	41.0×41.0×7.4	1–8	c

COMMENTARY

The only ex. of this inscription which was located, ex. 4, is incomplete. The text given is that established by Jacobsen.

BIBLIOGRAPHY

1932 Jacobsen, OIC 13 p. 48 (ex. 1, edition)
1940 Jacobsen, Gimilsin Temple p. 138 no. 13 (edition), pl. 16 no. 13 (copy), pp. 83 and 117 (provenance)
1961 Hallo, BiOr 18 p. 13 Ešnunna 2 (study)
1971 Sollberger and Kupper, IRSA IVE16b (translation)

TEXT

1) [d]*i-pí-iq*-[d]IŠKUR	1) Ipiq-Adad,
2) LUGAL *da-núm*	2) mighty king,
3) LUGAL *mu-ra-pí-iš*	3–4) king who enlarges Ešnunna,
4) *èš-nun-na*.KI	
5) SIPA *ṣa-al-ma-at*	5–6) shepherd of the black-headed (people),
6) *qá-qá-di-im*	
7) *na-ra-am* [d]*tišpak*	7) beloved of the god Tišpak,
8) DUMU *i-ba-al-pi-el*	8) son of Ibāl-pî-El.

3

The capture of the city of Nērebtum is mentioned in the 'Assyrian Chronicle' texts published by Birot (see MARI 4 p. 229) in a section dealing with events dating to the reign of Ipiq-Adad II. This probably refers to Ipiq-Adad II's capture of the city. His control over Nērebtum had been known previously because of the find of tablets at Ishchali dated with his year names.

Probably in connection with the capture of the city of Nērebtum

Ipiq-Adad II undertook construction work on the Eštar-Kitītum temple, the chief shrine of Nērebtum. Bricks found in the temple describe the donation of the city as a whole by Ipiq-Adad II to the goddess Eštar.

COMMENTARY

No excavation nos. or museum nos. are known for the bricks with this inscription. They are known only from a note of Jacobsen. The transliteration offered here is a reconstruction based on this note; the inscription was not available for collation.

BIBLIOGRAPHY

1940 Jacobsen, Gimilsin Temple p. 116 (study)
1955 Harris, JCS 9 p. 33 n. 15 (study)
1979 Greengus, OBTI p. 1 n. 1 (study)

TEXT

1) *a-na* dINANNA *ki-ti-tum*	1) To the goddess Eštar-Kitītum,
2) d*i-pí-iq*-dIŠKUR	2) Ipiq-Adad,
3) LUGAL *da-núm*	3) mighty king,
4) LUGAL *mu-ra-pí-iš*	4–5) king who enlarges Ešnunna,
5) *èš-nun-na*.KI	
6) SIPA *ṣa-al-ma-at*	6–7) shepherd of the black-headed (people),
7) *qá-qá-di-im*	
8) *na-ra-am* d*tišpak*	8) beloved of the god Tišpak,
9) DUMU *i-ba-al-pi-el*	9) son of Ibāl-pî-El,
10) *ne-re-eb-tum*.KI *i-qí-si-im*	10) presented Nērebtum to her.

4

An eye-stone in Copenhagen bears an inscription of Ipiq-Adad II.

COMMENTARY

The inscription is in the Institute of Archaeology at the University of Copenhagen. It is said to have come from Luristan. It is an agate eye-stone 2.1 cm in dia. with a thickness of 0.6 cm. The inscription was collated from the published photo.

We note the title 'king of the world' applied to Ipiq-Adad in line 2. This makes an attribution of the piece to Ipiq-Adad II certain.

BIBLIOGRAPHY

1965–66 Laessøe, AcOr 29 pp. 243–45 and pl. 3 (photo, copy, edition)
1969 Lambert, RA 63 p. 69 (study)

TEXT

1) ^{d}*i-pí-iq*-^{d}IŠKUR	1) Ipiq-Adad,
2) LUGAL KIŠ-*im*	2) king of the world,
3) DUMU *i-ba-al-pi-el*	3) son of Ibāl-pî-El.

1001

The seal impression of a son of Ibāl-pî-El I is found on two clay tablets excavated at Ešnunna. Unfortunately, the name of this personage is not preserved on either of the tablets. The title 'beloved of Nin-[...]' in line 2′ suggests that this was the impression of a king's seal, not a seal belonging to a prince; thus an attribution of the inscription to Ipiq-Adad II seems reasonably certain.

CATALOGUE

Ex.	Excavation number	Provenance	cpn
1	As 30:T.179	Ešnunna, from the Ipiq-Adad I-Ibāl-pî-El I palace	n
2	As 30:T.183	As ex. 1	n

BIBLIOGRAPHY

1940 Jacobsen, Gimilsin Temple p. 155 no. 51 (exs. 1–2, edition)

TEXT

Lacuna	Lacuna
1′) KI.ÁG ^{d}*ni*[*n*-...]	1′) beloved of N[in-...],
2′) DUMU *i-ba-al-pi-el*	2′) son of Ibāl-pî-El.

2001

Part way through the reign of Ipiq-Adad II, as part of the expansion of Ešnunna's domains, the city of Šaduppûm came under the control of Ešnunna. This is evidenced by the find of tablets with year names of Ipiq-Adad II at Tell Ḫarmal.

At this time a certain engraver named Ammar-ilam dedicated a stone cylinder to Bēl-gašir, the tutelary deity of Šaduppûm at this time, for the life of Ipiq-Adad II.

COMMENTARY

The object is IM 51080, from Tell Ḥarmal, excavation no. HL 1–91. It is a small votive cylinder of agate with the inscription written in the positive. The inscription was not collated.

In this inscription Ipiq-Adad II appears as king and his name is written with the prefixed divine determinative.

For Bēl-gašir as lord of Šaduppûm see D. Charpin, NABU 4 (1987) p. 67.

BIBLIOGRAPHY

1946 Baqir, Sumer 2 p. 25 (transliteration)
1971 Sollberger and Kupper, IRSA IVE16c (translation)

TEXT

1) *a-na* ᵈ*be-el-ga-ši-ir*	1) To the god Bēl-gašir,
2) *be-lí-šu*	2) his lord,
3) *a-na ba-la-aṭ*	3–4) for the life of Ipiq-Adad,
4) ᵈ*i-pí-iq*-ᵈIŠKUR	
5) LUGAL *èš-nun-na*.KI	5) king of Ešnunna,
6) *a-ma-ar*-DINGIR BUR.GUL	6) Ammar-ilam, engraver,
7) DUMU *ḫa-du-um*	7) son of Ḫadûm,
8) *i-qí-iš*	8) presented (this cylinder).

2002

The expansion of Ešnunna under Ipiq-Adad II included the incorporation of the city of Dūr-Rīmuš into the realms of Ešnunna. At this time a citizen of Dūr-Rīmuš dedicated a small inscribed cylinder to the god Mīšar, tutelary deity of Dūr-Rīmuš, for the life of Ipiq-Adad II.

COMMENTARY

The piece is AO 21117, a purchased piece of unknown provenance. It is a votive cylinder of pale amethyst 2.7 cm long with a circumference of 5 cm with the inscription written in the positive. The inscription was collated from a photo by W.G. Lambert.

BIBLIOGRAPHY

1962 Nougayrol, Syria 39 pp. 189–90 (copy, edition)
1971 Sollberger and Kupper, IRSA IVE16d (translation)

TEXT

1) [*a*]-*na* ^{d}*mi-š*[*a*]*r*	1) [T]o the god Mīš[a]r
2) [*š*]*a* BÀD-*ri*-⸢*mu-uš*.KI⸣	2) [o]f Dūr-Rīmuš,
3) *a-na ba-la-aṭ*	3–4) for the life of Ipiq-A[dad],
4) ^{d}*i-pí-iq*-^{d}IŠ[KUR]	
5) LUGAL KIŠ	5) king of the world,
6) [D]UMU *i-ba-al-pi-el*	6) [s]on of Ibāl-pî-El,
7) [*b*]*e-lí-š*[*u*]	7) hi[s l]ord,
8) x x *ba/zu-ra-ma*	8) ...-ba/zu-rāma,
9) [DU]MU *ka-ab-zu-u*[*m*]	9) [s]on of Kabzu[m],
10) ⸢*i*⸣-*qí-i*[*š*]	10) present[ed] (this cylinder).

2003

A small cylinder in a private collection in Venice bears a dedicatory inscription for the life of Ipiq-Adad II.

COMMENTARY

The cylinder measures 5.5 cm long, 2.8 cm in dia. The transliteration is offered here through the courtesy of F.M. Fales.

TEXT

1) [*a-n*]*a* ^{d}[...]	1–2) [T]o the god [...], hi[s l]ord,
2) [*b*]*e-lí-š*[*u*]	
3) [*a*]-*na ba-la-a*[*ṭ*]	3–6) [f]or the lif[e of I]piq-[Adad, k]ing of the wo[rld, s]on of Ibāl-pî-E[l],
4) [*i*]-*pí-iq*-^{d}[IŠKUR]	
5) [LU]GAL K[IŠ]	
6) [DU]MU *i-ba-al-pi-e*[*l*]	
7) [x *t*]*u ta/ša ki/na* x	7–9) ..., [son] of Iṣi-sūmû-abu[m, p]resente[d] (this cylinder).
8) [DUMU] *i-ṣi-su-mu-a-bu-u*[*m*]	
9) [*i*]-*qí-i*[*š*]	

2004

A cylinder seal in Paris bears the inscription of a servant of Ipiq-Adad. Here the ruler's name is written without the prefixed divine determinative. It could have belonged to either Ipiq-Adad I or Ipiq-Adad II. We have arbitrarily assigned the seal to the latter ruler.

COMMENTARY

The object is Bibliothèque Nationale no. 198. It is a cylinder seal of haematite 2.1 cm long, 1.2 cm in dia. The inscription was collated from the published photograph.

BIBLIOGRAPHY

1848 Chabouillet, Catalogue no. 804
1910 Delaporte, Bibliothèque Nationale no. 198 (photo, edition)
1953 Weidner, JKF 2 pp. 135–36 (transliteration, study)

TEXT

1) *ab-ba-lu-u[m]*
2) IR₁₁ *i-pí-iq-*^{d}IŠKUR

1) Abbalu[m],
2) servant of Ipiq-Adad.

2005

A cylinder seal in London bears the inscription of a servant of Ipiq-Adad II.

COMMENTARY

The seal is BM 89298 (25-5-3,R159) from the Rich collection. The seal is made of haematite, and is 2.35 cm long, 1.3 cm in dia. The inscription was collated by E. Sollberger.

The writing of the ruler's name with the prefixed divine determinative ensures an attribution to Ipiq-Adad II.

BIBLIOGRAPHY

1842–43 Cullimore, Oriental Cylinders no. 29 (copy)
1986 Collon, Cylinder Seals III no. 345 (photo, edition)
1987 Collon, First Impressions no. 170 (photo, study)

TEXT

1) *ḫa-ab-de-e-*^{d}IŠKUR
2) DUMU *nu-úr-ku-bi*
3) ÌR ^{d}*i-pí-iq-*^{d}IŠKUR

1) Ḫabdê-Addu,
2) son of Nūr-Kūbi,
3) servant of Ipiq-Adad.

2006

The seal impression of a servant of Ipiq-Adad II is found on three tablets excavated at Ishchali.

CATALOGUE

Ex.	Museum number	Lines preserved	cpn
1	A 7792	1–3	n
2	A 7898	1–3	n
3	A 7913	1–3	n

COMMENTARY

The copy of ex. 1 indicates a writing of the king's name in line three without the prefixed divine determinative. The composite copy of exs. 1–3 shows the name with a prefixed DINGIR. Perhaps two different seals of the same servant are in question here, a new one being cut when the king adopted the divine determinative in the writing of his name.

BIBLIOGRAPHY

1979 Greengus, OBTI nos. 123 and 205–206 (composite copy at no. 205)
1986 Greengus, Ishchali Documents pp. 55 and 72 (transliteration)

TEXT

1) AN/DINGIR-*pi₄*-[...]
2) DUMU *a-mur-na-ar-bi-š*[*u*]
3) ÌR ᵈ*i-pí-iq*-ᵈ⌜IŠKUR⌝

1) Anum/Ilum-pî-[...],
2) son of Amur-narbīš[u],
3) servant of Ipiq-Adad.

2007

The impression of a seal of another servant of Ipiq-Adad II is found on a tablet from ancient Nērebtum.

COMMENTARY

The seal is impressed on A 7675, from Ishchali, exact provenance not known. The impression was not collated.

The seal impression, which is only partially preserved, is restored from Greengus, OBTI no. 265 lines 9–10.

BIBLIOGRAPHY

1979 Greengus, OBTI no. 232 (copy)

TEXT

1) ᵈ⌜EN⌝.ZU-*e*-⌜*ri-ba-am*⌝
2) D[UMU *na-ra-am*]-⌜*ì-li*⌝-*šu*
3) ⌜ÌR⌝ *i-pí*-⌜*iq*⌝-ᵈIŠKUR

1) Sîn-erībam,
2) s[on of Narām]-ilīšu,
3) servant of Ipiq-Adad.

2008

The impression of a servant of Ipiq-Adad II is found on a tablet excavated at Ishchali.

COMMENTARY

The impression is on A 22010, Ish 35:T.120 from 1 v 32. It was not collated.

BIBLIOGRAPHY

1979 Greengus, OBTI no. 246 (copy)

TEXT

1) ⌜DINGIR⌝-*ma-ì-*⌜*lí-šu*⌝	1) Iluma-ilīšu,
2) [DU]MU ⌜*i*⌝-*lí-é-*[*a*]	2) [so]n of Ili-E[a],
3) [Ì]R *i-pí-iq-*[d][IŠKUR]	3) [ser]vant of Ipiq-[Adad].

2009

The impression of a servant of Ipiq-Adad II is found on a tablet in the Yale collections.

COMMENTARY

The impression is on NBC 7309, a purchased tablet which was not collated.

The writing of the ruler's name with the prefixed divine determinative assures an attribution to Ipiq-Adad II.

BIBLIOGRAPHY

1960 Simmons, JCS 14 p. 49 (transliteration)
1981 Buchanan and Hallo, Early Near Eastern Seals no. 762 (photo, edition)

TEXT

1) *akšak*.KI-*še-mi*	1) Akšak-šemi,
2) DUMU ÌR-*sà*	2) son of Warassa,
3) ÌR [d]*i-pí-iq-*[d]IŠKUR	3) servant of Ipiq-Adad.

Narām-Sîn

E4.5.15

Ipiq-Adad II was succeeded by his son Narām-Sîn, who reigned at least nine years. Like his father, Narām-Sîn appears in his inscriptions as 'king of Ešnunna' and uses the prefixed divine determinative in the writing of his name. He also adopted the title 'king of the world' (LUGAL *kiššatim*) found in a few examples of his year names (see Simmons, JCS 13 [1959] p. 76), and used by his father in two inscriptions.

1

Bricks stamped with the standard inscription of Narām-Sîn were excavated at Ešnunna.

CATALOGUE

Ex.	Museum number	Excavation number	Provenance	Dimensions (cm)	Lines preserved	cpn
1	IM 23841	As 31:760	Ešnunna, from N 32:2, drain in street south of palace	33.0×24.0×7.0	–	n
2	A 9000	As 31:761	As ex. 1	33.7×25.0×7.0	1-5	c
3	A 9001	As 31:761a	As ex. 1	20.5×11.0×6.8	1-5	c

COMMENTARY

The two exs. of this text that were collated do not give a complete text. The text given is that provided by Jacobsen, a composite based on the evidence of several exs. In addition to the bricks listed here, some were found in the Narām-Sîn Audience Hall.

BIBLIOGRAPHY

1932 Jacobsen, OIC 13 p. 47 (edition)
1940 Jacobsen, Gimilsin Temple p. 139 no. 14 (edition), pl. 17 no. 14 (copy), and pp. 84-86 and 117 (provenance)
1961 Hallo, BiOr 18 p. 13 Ešnunna 3 (study)
1971 Sollberger and Kupper, IRSA IVE17a (translation)

TEXT

1) ^{d}*na-ra-am-*^{d}EN.ZU
2) LUGAL *da-an-nu-um*
3) LUGAL *èš-nun-na*.KI
4) *na-ra-am* ^{d}*tišpak*
5) DUMU *i-pí-iq-*^{d}IŠKUR

1) Narām-Sîn,
2) mighty king,
3) king of Ešnunna,
4) beloved of the god Tišpak,
5) son of Ipiq-Adad.

2

A small piece of hard white stone, perhaps an amulet, inscribed with a text of Narām-Sîn, was discovered in the 1850s on the island of Cythera in the Aegean Sea.

COMMENTARY

The piece was said to have come from a tomb near Kastri on Cythera. The whereabouts of the piece today is not known. It was therefore not available for collation. The only copy of it, made by a non-Assyriologist, is very poor and several signs cannot be read.

BIBLIOGRAPHY

1853 Leake, Transactions of the Royal Society of Literature of the United Kingdom, 2nd series no. 4 pp. 257–58 (copy, study)
1897 Köhler, SPAW pp. 262–65 (study)
1929 Unger, RLV 13 pl. 58A and p. 313 (study, edition)
1938 Thomas, JHS 58 p. 256 (copy, study)
1939 Weidner, JHS 59 pp. 137–38 (copy, transliteration, study)
1940 Jacobsen, Gimilsin Temple p. 139 no. 14 (transliteration, study)
1953 Weidner, JKF 2 pp. 131–32 (study)
1962 Nougayrol, Syria 39 p. 190 (study)
1971 Sollberger and Kupper, IRSA IVE17b (translation)
1973 Coldstream and Huxley (eds.), Kythera p. 33 (study)
1983 Butz in Potts (ed.), Dilmun p. 119 (edition)

TEXT

1) *a-na* ^{d}x x x
2) *ša* x x.KI
3) ^{md}*na-ra-am-*^{d}EN.ZU
4) DUMU ^{d}*i-pí-iq-*^{d}IŠKUR
5) *a-na ba-la-ṭì-šu*
6) [*i-qí-iš*]

1–2) To the god ... of ...,

3–6) Narām-Sîn, son of Ipiq-Adad, [presented] (this object) for his (own) life.

2001

A cylinder seal found in Cyprus once belonged to a servant of Narām-Sîn.

COMMENTARY

The seal was found among the temple treasure of Kurium, Cyprus. The seal is now in the Cesnola collection of the Metropolitan Museum of Art in New York. The inscription was collated from the published photo.

BIBLIOGRAPHY

1877 di Cesnola, Cyprus (London) pl. 31 after p. 392
1877 Sayce, TSBA 5 pp. 441–42 (copy, edition)
1897 Tomkims, Abraham and his Age p. xxviii and pl. x (photo, study)
1899 Ball, Light from the East (London) p. 53 (photo, translation)
1910 Ward, Seals no. 1158 (copy)
1910 King, Early History pp. 343–44 (study)
1911 Ungnad, OLZ 14 226 (study)
1914 Myres, Handbook of the Cesnola Collection pp. 429–31 (photo, translation)
1953 Weidner, JKF 2 pp. 128–29 and pl. 26 after p. 224 (photo, study)
1957–58 Nagel, AfO 18 p. 321 no. 35 (study)
1961 Hallo, BiOr 18 p. 14 Ešnunna 21: xiii (study)

TEXT

1) DUMU-^{d}*eš$_4$-tá*[*r*]
2) DUMU DINGIR-*ba-ni*
3) ÌR ^{d}*na-ra-am*-^{d}EN.Z[U]

1) Mār-Ešta[r],
2) son of Ilum-bāni,
3) servant of Narām-Sî[n].

2002

A seal now in Boston once belonged to a servant of Narām-Sîn.

COMMENTARY

The seal is in the Boston Museum of Fine Arts, no. 93.1483. It measures 2.7 cm long, 1.6 cm in dia. The inscription was collated by T. Kendall.

The third line was added after the seal and inscription were finished.

BIBLIOGRAPHY

1897 Scheil, RT 19 pp. 47–48 (copy in Neo-Assyrian script, translation)
1939 Frankfort, Cylinder Seals pl. XXVIIb (photo)
1953 Weidner, JKF 2 p. 130 (transliteration)

TEXT

1) *iš-gu-um-èr-ra*
2) DUMU ÌR-*ì-lí-šu*
3) ÌR *na-ra-am*-^{d}EN.ZU

1) Išgum-Erra,
2) son of Warad-ilīšu,
3) servant of Narām-Sîn.

2003

Before the reign of Ipiq-Adad II, it appears that the city of Mê-Turran on the upper Diyala river was independent, since we have a brick inscription of a ruler of that city (see E4.16.1.1). A year name of Ipiq-Adad II (see S. Greengus, OBTI p. 31 no. 40) refers to the capture of the city. The city apparently continued under the control of Ešnunna during the reign of Narām-Sîn, since a tablet with a seal impression of a servant of the king was recently excavated at Tell Ḥaddād, ancient Mê-Turran.

COMMENTARY

The impression is found on a tablet, IM no. as yet unknown, excavation no. Haddad 497. A transliteration of the impression is given here through the courtesy of A. Kamil.

TEXT

1) *puzur*$_4$*-ì1-a-ba*$_4$
2) DUMU *ì1-a-ba*$_4$*-na-ṣir*
3) ÌR [*na*]*-ra-am-*^{d}EN.ZU

1) Puzur-Ilaba,
2) son of Ilaba-nāṣir,
3) servant of [Na]rām-Sîn.

2004

A seal now in Los Angeles bears the inscription of a servant of Narām-Sîn.

COMMENTARY

The seal is in the Haermaneck collection of the Los Angeles County Museum of Art, no. M.76.174.380. The inscription was collated from the published photograph.

The glyptic of this seal may have been recut since the strong use of the drill suggests 'a fairly late date in the Old Babylonian period in or after the time of Samsu-iluna'.

BIBLIOGRAPHY

1981 Porada in Moorey et al., Ancient Bronzes p. 225 no. 1187 (photo, study); Renger p. 261 no. 1187 (edition)

TEXT

1) *še-le-bu-*[*um*]
2) [D]UMU [*li*]*-pí-it-eš*$_4$*-t*[*ár*]
3) ÌR ^{d}*na-ra-am-*^{d}EN.Z[U]

1) Šēlebu[m],
2) [s]on of [Li]pit-Ešt[ar],
3) servant of Narām-Sî[n].

Dannum-tāḫaz

E4.5.16

The exact place of this ruler in the Ešnunna dynasty has been uncertain. M. Ellis (JCS 37 [1985] pp. 61–85) and D. Charpin (Mélanges Birot p. 54) have argued that the reign of this ruler should be placed between Narām-Sîn and Dādușa. No building inscriptions of Dannum-tāḫaz have yet appeared. We have only the evidence of three servant seals of the king.

2001

The first servant seal impression is found on a tablet now at Yale.

COMMENTARY

The impression is on NBC 8548, a purchased tablet, perhaps from Tell Ḥarmal. It was not collated. For the reading of the divine name see E. Weidner, AfK 2 (1924–25) p. 13 line 14.

BIBLIOGRAPHY

1961 Simmons, JCS 15 p. 83 (transliteration)
1978 Simmons, YOS 14 pl. CXXII seal no. 114 (copy) and p. 3 with n. 8 (transliteration, study)
1985 M. Ellis, JCS 37 pp. 65–66 (study)
1985 Charpin, Mélanges Birot p. 54 n. 22 (transliteration)

TEXT

1) ^{d}EN.ZU-*im-ma-tim* DUB.SAR
2) DUMU *puzur$_4$-^{d}sakkud*
3) ÌR *da-an-nu-um-ta-ḫa-az*

1) Sîn-īn-mātim, scribe,
2) son of Puzur-Sakkud,
3) servant of Dannum-tāḫaz.

2002

The impression of a seal of a servant of Dannum-tāḫaz is found on a tablet now in the Iraq Museum.

COMMENTARY

The impression is on IM 10682, a purchased tablet. It was not collated.

BIBLIOGRAPHY

1968 van Dijk, TIM 5 no. 19 (copy)
1970 van Dijk, AfO 23 pp. 64–65 (transliteration, study)
1985 M. Ellis, JCS 37 p. 66 (study)
1985 Charpin, Mélanges Birot p. 54 n. 21 (transliteration)

TEXT

1) [*na-ra-am*]-*ì-lí-šu*	1) [Narām]-ilīšu,
2) DUMU DINGIR-*šu-i-bi-šu*	2) son of Ilšu-ibbīšu,
3) ÌR ⸢*da-an-nu-um*⸣-*ta-ḫ*[*a-az*]	3) servant of Dannum-tāḫ[az].

2003

The impression of a seal of a servant of Dannum-tāḫaz is found on a tablet envelope excavated at Ishchali.

COMMENTARY

The impression is on A 7634, excavation no. and provenance not known. It was not collated.

BIBLIOGRAPHY

1979 Greengus, OBTI pl. 18 no. 34 seal A (copy)

TEXT

1) *a-li-ia*	1) Alīia,
2) DUMU *iš-bi-èr-ra*	2) son of Išbi-Erra,
3) ÌR *da-nu-um-ta-ḫa-az*	3) servant of Dannum-tāḫaz.

Ibni-Erra

E4.5.17

A certain Ibni-Erra is known from the brick inscription of Iqīš-Tišpak, ruler of Ešnunna, to have been the father of the same. No royal inscriptions or servant seal impressions are known for this ruler; one year name is known (see S. Simmons, JCS 13 p. 118 no. 41 lines 19–20).

Iqīš-Tišpak

E4.5.18

The placement of the reign of Iqīš-Tišpak, known only from one brick inscription and a few year names, is uncertain. In the archive of Gidānum from Tell Ḫarmal year names of this ruler appear along with those of Ipiq-Adad II, Narām-Sîn, and Dannum-tāḫaz. This suggests that Iqīš-Tišpak reigned before Ibāl-pî-El II, not after him, as has sometimes been suggested. Since it is certain that Narām-Sîn succeeded Ipiq-Adad II and that Ibāl-pî-El II immediately followed Dādušа, the reign of Iqīš-Tišpak should be placed between those of Narām-Sîn and Dāduša. However, it is not certain whether the reign of Iqīš-Tišpak is to be placed before or after Dannum-tāḫaz.

A number of historical problems arise concerning the reign of Iqīš-Tišpak. First, we note the short duration of his reign. Secondly, while we know that Dāduša and Narām-Sîn were both sons of Ipiq-Adad II, Iqīš-Tišpak was not. Furthermore, while both Narām-Sîn and Dāduša styled themselves as kings of Ešnunna, Iqīš-Tišpak appears in his brick inscription simply as 'servant of Tišpak, governor of Ešnunna'. A year name of Dannum-tāḫaz, however, does refer to him as 'king'.

All these observations suggest that there may have been at this time a brief interregnum at Ešnunna. We note in this connection a temporal clause in a text dating to year 22 of Rīm-Sîn I: 'when the troops of Iamutbalum gathered in Maškan-šāpir for the expedition to (against) Ešnunna' (see M. Stol, Studies in Old Babylonian History pp. 64–65). It is to be noted that year 22 of Rīm-Sîn I falls roughly in the time period between the reigns of Narām-Sîn and Dāduša. If the expedition was successful and managed to install a puppet ruler in Ešnunna for a brief time as 'governor' (*iššiakum*), then this could account for the brief reign of Iqīš-Tišpak.

1

A brick inscription of Iqīš-Tišpak was found at Ešnunna.

COMMENTARY

The inscription is on As 33:T.10a, found in the filling used to raise the floor of the Audience Hall of Narām-Sîn. The brick has not been located.

BIBLIOGRAPHY

1940 Jacobsen, Gimilsin Temple p. 139 no. 16 (edition) and pl. 18 no. 16 (copy)
1961 Hallo, BiOr 18 p. 13 Ešnunna 6 (study)
1971 Sollberger and Kupper, IRSA IVE22a (translation)

TEXT

1) *i-⸢qí-iš⸣-*^{d}*tišpak*	1) Iqīš-Tišpak,
2) ÌR *ša* ^{d}*⸢tišpak⸣*	2) servant of the god Tišpak,
3) ÉNSI	3–4) governor of Ešnunna,
4) *eš-nun-na*.KI	
5) DUMU *ib-ni-èr-ra*	5) son of Ibni-Erra.

2001

The impression of a seal of a servant of Iqīš-Tišpak is found on a tablet excavated at Ešnunna.

COMMENTARY

The tablet is As 30:T.162 from M 31:11, the Ipiq-Adad I–Ibāl-pî-El I palace. The impression was not collated.

BIBLIOGRAPHY

1940 Jacobsen, Gimilsin Temple p. 155 no. 52 (edition)

TEXT

1) [...]	1) [...],
2) ÌR *i-qí-iš-*^{d}*t*[*išpak*]	2) servant of Iqīš-T[išpak].

Dādušа

E4.5.19

After the brief reigns of Dannum-tāḫaz and Iqīš-Tišpak, Dāduša, son of Ipiq-Adad II, held the throne of Ešnunna. He reigned at least nine years and adopted the title 'king of Ešnunna' like his father. At this time Ešnunna controlled a large number of cities in the Diyala region such as Šaduppûm, Nērebtum, and Mê-Turran, and it is from these sites that we have a number of impressions of servant seals of the king. Only one monumental text of the king is known from Ešnunna itself.

1

The name of the last year of Dāduša commemorates the defeat of the city of Qabarā. This conquest is narrated in a victory stele.

COMMENTARY

The stele is IM 95200 found in a field near Tell Asmar. It is 180×37×18.5 cm. This inscription will be edited by Dr B. Kh. Ismail.

BIBLIOGRAPHY

1986 Khalil Ismail, Oberhuber Festschrift pp. 105–108 (study)

2

The 'Assyrian Chronicle' texts edited by Birot (see MARI 4 pp. 219–42) document bellicose relations between the cities of Ešnunna and Aššur during the reign of Ipiq-Adad II. If Narām-Sîn of Ešnunna is the same as the Narām-Sîn who appears in the Assyrian King List, then it would appear that Ešnunna controlled Aššur for a time. Further evidence of this contact is provided by the finding at Aššur of a duck weight granted by Dāduša to his daughter.

COMMENTARY

The inscription is found on Ass 5925, from Aššur gravel rubble eC6I. The duck weight is pictured in Ass ph 708 from which it was collated.

Sollberger and Kupper, following Schroeder, restored two lines 'to Tišpak, his lord' at the beginning of the text, but neither the shape of the weight nor parallels with other donation inscriptions support such a restoration. If the inscription were in fact dedicated to Tišpak the line referring to Inibšina should read 'for the life of Inibšina', which is not found.

BIBLIOGRAPHY

1914 Schroeder, OLZ 17 246 (edition)
1918 Unger, Katalog 3 no. 179 pp. 26–27
1922 Schroeder, KAH 2 no. 3 (copy)
1940 Jacobsen, Gimilsin Temple p. 117 n. 5 (partial transliteration)
1944 Gelb, Hurrians p. 67 n. 151 (study)
1961 Hallo, BiOr 18 p. 13 Ešnunna 12 (study)
1971 Sollberger and Kupper, IRSA IVE18a (translation)

TEXT

1) ^{d}*da-d[u-ša]*	1) Dād[uša],
2) DUMU ^{d}*i-pí-iq*-^{d}IŠKUR	2) son of Ipiq-Adad,
3) LUGAL *èš-nun-na*.KI	3) king of Ešnunna,
4) *a-na i-ni-ib-ši-na*	4–5) grante[d] (this weight) to Inibšina, his daughter.
5) DUMU.MÍ.A.NI *iš-ru-u[k]*	

2001

The city of Šaduppûm which came under the control of Ešnunna during the reign of Ipiq-Adad II remained so during the reign of Dāduša. A seal impression of a servant of Dāduša is found on a tablet excavated at Šaduppûm (Tell Ḥarmal).

COMMENTARY

The impression is on IM 52922, which was collated.

BIBLIOGRAPHY

1958 Goetze, Sumer 14 p. 5 (study)

TEXT

1) *zi-im-ri*-BI-X	1) Zimrī-BI-...
2) DUMU *i*-ZI-X-X	2) son of I-ZI-...
3) ÌR *da-du-ša*	3) servant of Dāduša.

2002

The impression of a seal of a servant of Dāduša is found on three clay tablets excavated at Šaduppûm (Tell Ḫarmal).

CATALOGUE

Ex.	Museum number	Provenance	cpn
1	IM 51187	Tell Ḫarmal, room 133, level II	n
2	IM 51295	Room 136, level II	n
3	IM 51461	As ex. 1	n

BIBLIOGRAPHY

1972 M. Ellis, JCS 24 p. 69 no. 2 (exs. 1–3, composite copy)

TEXT

1) *ku-bu-lu-u*[*m*]
2) DUMU ᵈEN.ZU-*mu-ba-lí-i*[*t*]
3) ÌR *da-du-ša*

1) Kubullu[m],
2) son of Sîn-muballi[ṭ],
3) servant of Dāduša.

2003

The seal impression of a servant of Dāduša is found on three clay tablets excavated at Šaduppûm (Tell Ḫarmal).

CATALOGUE

Ex.	Museum number	Provenance	cpn
1	IM 51203	Tell Ḫarmal, room 143, level II	n
2	IM 51211	As ex. 1	n
3	IM 51598	Room 134, level II	n

BIBLIOGRAPHY

1972 M. Ellis, JCS 24 p. 69 no. 12 (exs. 1–3, composite copy)

TEXT

1) ^{d}EN.ZU-*e-ri-ba-am*	1) Sîn-erībam,
2) DUMU ^{d}EN.ZU-*mu-ba-li-iṭ*	2) son of Sîn-muballiṭ,
3) ÌR ^{d}*da-du-ša*	3) servant of Dāduša.

2004

The seal impressions of two servants of Dāduša are found on a tablet in the Yale collections which probably came from Šaduppûm (Tell Ḥarmal). The impressions are edited as E4.5.19.2004 and 2005.

COMMENTARY

The impression is on NBC 5304. It was not collated.

BIBLIOGRAPHY

1961 Simmons, JCS 15 p. 82 (transliteration)
1978 Simmons, YOS 14 pl. CXX seal no. 77 (copy)

TEXT

1) *a-píl-ku-*[*bi*]	1) Apil-Kū[bi],
2) DUMU *pu-ḫu-*[*um*]	2) son of Pūḫu[m],
3) ÌR *da-du-*[*ša*]	3) servant of Dādu[ša].

2005

See the introduction to E4.5.19.2004.

BIBLIOGRAPHY

1961 Simmons, JCS 15 p. 82 (transliteration)
1978 Simmons, YOS 14 pl. CXXIII seal no. 153 (copy)

TEXT

1) ^{d}*èr-ra-na-*[*da*]	1) Erra-nā[da],
2) DUMU ^{d}EN.ZU-*i-qí-*[*ša-am*]	2) son of Sîn-iqī[šam],
3) ÌR ⌜*da*⌝-*d*[*u-ša*]	3) servant of Dād[uša].

2006

The seal impression of a servant of Dāduša is found on a tablet in the Yale collections which internal evidence indicates comes from Šaduppûm (Tell Ḫarmal).

COMMENTARY

The impression is on YBC 11151. It was not collated.

BIBLIOGRAPHY

1960 Simmons, JCS 14 p. 30 (transliteration)
1978 Simmons, YOS 14 pl. CXVIII seal no. 10 (copy)

TEXT

1) *ib-ni-e-ra-*⌜*aḫ*⌝	1) Ibni-Eraḫ,
2) DUMU *su-mu-*[*e*]*-ra-aḫ*	2) son of Sūmû-[E]raḫ,
3) ÌR *da-du-ša*	3) servant of Dāduša.

2007

The seal impression of a servant of Dāduša is found on a tablet in the Yale collections which probably comes from Šaduppûm (Tell Ḫarmal).

COMMENTARY

The impression is on NBC 9206. It was not collated.

BIBLIOGRAPHY

1961 Simmons, JCS 15 p. 81 (transliteration)
1978 Simmons, YOS 14 pl. CXXIII seal no. 151 (copy)

TEXT

1) [*t*]*u-tu-ub.*KI*-še-mi*	1) [T]utub-šemi,
2) [DUMU] *ša-eš*$_4$*-tár*	2) [son] of Ša-Eštar,
3) [ÌR *d*]*a-du-ša*	3) [servant of D]āduša.

2008

The city of Nērebtum, which fell under the control of Ešnunna during the reign of Ipiq-Adad II, remained so during the reign of Dāduša. The seal impression of the *sanga* priest of the goddess Kitītum is found on two clay tablets excavated at Ishchali.

CATALOGUE

Ex.	Museum number	Provenance	cpn
1	A 7722	Ishcali, provenance not known	n
2	A 7796	As ex. 1	n

BIBLIOGRAPHY

1979 Greengus, OBTI nos. 132 and 231 (exs. 1-2, copy)

TEXT

1) [*i*]*n-bu-*[*ša*]	1) [I]nbu[ša],
2) [S]ANGA ^{d}*ki-ti-tu*[*m*]	2) [*s*]*anga* priest of the goddess Kitītu[m],
3) DUMU *ig-mil-*^{d}EN.Z[U]	3) son of Igmil-Sî[n],
4) [Ì]R *da-du-ša*	4) [se]rvant of Dāduša.

2009–12

The impressions of four seals of servants of Dāduša are found on a purchased tablet originally from Ishchali now at Berkeley (UCLM 9-2431). They are edited as E4.5.19.2009–12.

2009

BIBLIOGRAPHY

1931 Lutz, UCP 10/1 p. 73 TN 91 (transliteration)
1986 Greengus, Ishchali Documents p. 158 seal C (edition)

TEXT

1) *a-bu-wa-qar*	1) Abu-waqar,
2) DUMU ^{d}EN.ZU-*še-mi*	2) son of Sîn-šemi,
3) ÌR *da-du-ša*	3) servant of Dāduša.

2010

BIBLIOGRAPHY

1931 Lutz, UCP 10/1 p. 73 TN 91 (transliteration)
1986 Greengus, Ishchali Documents p. 158 seal B (edition)

TEXT

1) DINGIR/AN-*um-pí-ša*	1) Ilum/Anum-pîša,
2) DUMU ^{d}EN.ZU-*i-*⌜*qí*⌝*-ša-am*	2) son of Sîn-iqīšam,
3) ÌR *da-du-ša*	3) servant of Dāduša.

2011

BIBLIOGRAPHY

1931 Lutz, UCP 10/1 p. 73 TN 91 (transliteration)
1986 Greengus, Ishchali Documents p. 158 seal A (edition)

TEXT

1) ^{d}EN.ZU-*mu-ba-al-lí-iṭ*	1) Sîn-muballiṭ,
2) DUMU *ki-ir-ki-ru-um*	2) son of Kirkirum,
3) ÌR *da-du-ša*	3) servant of Dāduša.

2012

BIBLIOGRAPHY

1931 Lutz, UCP 10/1 p. 73 TN 91 (transliteration)
1986 Greengus, Ishchali Documents p. 158 seal D (edition)

TEXT

1) *za-ab-*[...]	1) Zab-[...],
2) DUMU *i-*X*-ru-*X	2) son of I...ru...,
3) ÌR *da-du-š*[*a*]	3) servant of Dāduš[a].

2013

The impression of a seal of a servant of Dāduša is found on a tablet from Ishchali.

COMMENTARY

The tablet is UCLM 9-2338.

BIBLIOGRAPHY

1931 Lutz, UCP 10/1 p. 75 TN 107 (partial transliteration)
1986 Greengus, Ishchali Documents p. 172 seal C (edition)

TEXT

1) [d]EN.ZU*-ga-mi-*X	1) Sîn-gāmil,
2) DUMU *a-ḫi-um-mi-šu*	2) son of Aḫi-ummīšu,
3) ÌR [*da*]*-du-ša*	3) servant of [Dā]duša.

2014–21

The city of Mê-Turran, which had fallen to Ipiq-Adad II, remained part of the domains of Ešnunna during the reign of Dāduša. The 'Assyrian Chronicle' texts published by Birot mention this city in connection with king Dāduša (see MARI 4 p. 231 E5). Eight seal impressions of servants of Dāduša are found on tablets excavated at Tell Ḥaddād, ancient Mê-Turran. They are edited here, as E4.5.19.2014–21, through the courtesy of A. Kamil.

2014

The first seal impression is found on Tell Ḥaddād 496. The name is restored from the tablet.

TEXT

1) [*ḫu-bi-ra-nu-um*]
2) DUMU KI-[*šu*]-*ša*
3) IR₁₁ *da-du-ša*

1) [Ḫabirānum],
2) son of KI[šu]ša,
3) servant of Dāduša.

2015

The impression is on Tell Ḥaddād no. 494.

TEXT

1) *i-lu-ni*
2) MÁŠ.ŠU.GÍD.GÍD
3) DUMU ᵈUTU-*ra-bi*
4) IR₁₁ *da-du-ša*

1) Iluni,
2) diviner,
3) son of Šamaš-rabi,
4) servant of Dāduša.

2016

The impression is found on Tell Ḥaddād no. 494.

TEXT

1) [*i*]-*lí*-[*ib*]-*ba*-[*ni*]
2) [DU]MU [*aq*]-*ba-ḫu-u*[*m*]
3) IR₁₁ *da-du*-[*ša*]

1) [I]lī-[ib]ba[ni],
2) [s]on of [Aq]ba-aḫu[m],
3) servant of Dādu[ša].

2017

The impression is on Tell Ḥaddād no. 503.

TEXT

1) *e-za*-[*tum*]
2) [DUMU ...]
3) IR₁₁ ⸢*da-du*⸣-*ša*

1) Eza[tum],
2) [son of ...],
3) servant of Dāduša.

2018

The impression is on Tell Ḥaddād no. 496.

TEXT

1) ᵈ*ši-bu-um-re-me-ni*	1) Šībum-rēmēnī,
2) DUMU *na-ra-am-*ᵈEN.ZU	2) son of Narām-Sîn,
3) IR_{11} *da-du-ša*	3) servant of Dāduša.

2019

The impression is found on Tell Ḥaddād no. 497.

TEXT

1) IR_{11}-ᵈ*tišpak*	1) Warad-Tišpak,
2) DUMU *im-gur-*ᵈEN.ZU	2) son of Imgur-Sîn,
3) IR_{11} *da-du-ša*	3) servant of Dāduša.

2020

The impression is on Tell Ḥaddād no. 497.

TEXT

1) *i-túr-aš-du-um*	1) Itūr-Ašdum,
2) DUMU *ak-ša-ia*	2) son of Akšāia,
3) IR_{11} *da-du-ša*	3) servant of Dāduša.

2021

The impression is on Tell Ḥaddād no. 501.

TEXT

1) *i-pí-iq*-AN-*tim*	1) Ipiq-Antim,
2) DUMU ⌜*ḫu*⌝-*du-šu-u*[*m*]	2) son of Ḫuddūšu[m],
3) IR$_{11}$ ⌜*da*⌝-[*du-ša*]	3) servant of Dā[duša].

2022

The impression of a seal of a servant of Dāduša is found on a tablet excavated at Mari.

COMMENTARY

The tablet was excavated from room 100 of the Old Babylonian palace at Mari. The inscription was collated by D. Charpin and J.-M. Durand.

BIBLIOGRAPHY

1957 Bottéro, ARMT 7 no. 292 (edition)
1983 Charpin and Durand, MARI 2 p. 99 no. 292 (transliteration) and p. 115 no. 292 (copy)

TEXT

1) ÌR-^{d}*tišpak*	1) Warad-Tišpak,
2) DUMU *i-din*-[...]	2) son of Iddin-[...],
3) ÌR *da-d*[*u-ša*]	3) servant of Dād[uša].

2023

A clay sealing excavated at Tell Leilan bears the inscription of a servant of a ruler whose name is fragmentarily preserved, but which seems to be Dāduša.

COMMENTARY

The impression is found on L 85-116. The legend measures 2.3 cm high and was collated by R. Whiting. It is offered through the courtesy of D.H. Weiss.

TEXT

1) [*n*]*a-ra-am-ì-lí*-[*šu*]	1) [N]arām-ilī[šu],
2) [DUMU] *ra-ba-ša-r*[*u-um*]	2) [son] of Raba-šarr[um],
3) [ÌR] ⌜*da-du*⌝-[*ša*]	3) [servant] of Dādu[ša].

Ibāl-pî-El II

E4.5.20

Dāduša was succeeded by his son Ibāl-pî-El, the second ruler of Ešnunna by that name. He ruled about 14 years. Ibāl-pî-El II adopted the title 'king' (lugal). This distinguishes him in his inscriptions from his earlier namesake who served merely as 'governor' (énsi). However, unlike Dāduša, Narām-Sîn, and Ipiq-Adad II, Ibāl-pî-El II never used the prefixed divine determinative in the writing of his name.

1

A number of bricks were found at Ešnunna stamped with the standard inscription of Ibāl-pî-El II.

CATALOGUE

Ex.	Museum number	Excavation number	Provenance	Dimensions (cm)	Lines preserved	cpn
1	Chicago, no number	As 31:754	Ešnunna, from N 32:2, a drain in street south of palace	33.0×32.7	1-5	c
2	A 9005	As 31:755	As ex. 1	31.0×31.0×8.0	1-5	c
3	A 9006	As 31:755a	As ex. 1	31.4×31.4×7.5	1-5	c
4	VA 3134	–	Ešnunna	12.0×10.0	2-5	c
5	BM 115038 (1979-12-20,387)	–	Said to have come from Samsâbâd near Bushire	39.5×39.5	1-5	n
6	Leiden, no number	–	Ešnunna(?)	31.5×32.0×7.5	1-5	c

BIBLIOGRAPHY

1907 Ungnad, VAS 1 no. 113 (ex. 4, copy)
1909 Ungnad, OLZ 12 161–62 (ex. 4, edition)
1914 Schroeder, OLZ 17 247 (ex. 4, transliteration [incorrectly attributed to Ipiq-Adad II])
1940 Jacobsen, Gimilsin Temple p. 139 no. 15 (exs. 1–3, edition), pl. 17 no. 15 (copy), and p. 139 (ex. 4, study)
1961 Hallo, BiOr 18 p. 13 Ešnunna 4 (study)
1971 Sollberger and Kupper, IRSA IVE19a (translation)
1981 Walker, CBI no. 50 (ex. 5, study)

TEXT

1) *i-ba-al-pi-el*
2) LUGAL *da-an-nu-um*
3) LUGAL *èš-nun-na*.KI
4) *na-ra-am* ᵈ*tišpak*
5) DUMU *da-du-ša*

1) Ibāl-pî-El,
2) mighty king,
3) king of Ešnunna,
4) beloved of the god Tišpak,
5) son of Dāduša.

2

A gold ring of unknown provenance mentions Ibāl-pî-El. It could have belonged to either of the Ešnunna rulers of that name and it is arbitrarily included here.

COMMENTARY

The ring was in the private possession of M. Feuardent; its present whereabouts is unknown. The inscription was collated by W.G. Lambert (in London). The diameter of the hoop is 2.4 cm.

BIBLIOGRAPHY

1930 Scheil, RA 27 p. 98 (edition)
1987 Anon., Antiquités et Objets d'Art. Collection de Martine, Comtesse de Béhague provenant de la Succession du Marquis de Ganay. Sotheby's, Monaco, Dec. 5, 1987, lot 3 (study)

TEXT

1) É.GAL *i-ba-al-pi-el*	1) Palace of Ibāl-pî-El.

3

Ešnunna's control over Šaduppûm continued during the reign of Ibāl-pî-El II. An impression of a royal seal was found on a tablet excavated at Šaduppûm (Tell Ḥarmal).

COMMENTARY

The seal impression is on IM 51251 from Tell Ḥarmal, which was collated.

BIBLIOGRAPHY

1958 Goetze, Sumer 14 pp. 5 and 23–24 (edition)

TEXT

1) [*i*]*-ba-al-pi-el*	1) [I]bāl-pî-El,
2) [LUGA]L KALA.G[A]	2) might[y kin]g,
3) [LUGA]L *èš-nun-na*.KI	3) [kin]g of Ešnunna,
4) [LUGA]L *pa-li-iḫ* AN/^{d}[x]	4) [kin]g who reveres An/the god ...,
5) [*na*]*-ra-am* ^{d}*tiš*[*pak*]	5) [be]loved of the god Tiš[pak],
6) [DUM]U *da-du-ša*	6) [so]n of Dāduša.

2001–2007

A number of impressions of seals of servants of Ibāl-pî-El II were excavated at Tell Ḥarmal. These are edited here as E4.5.20.2001-2007.

2001

This impression is found on IM 51278, from room 134, level II. It was not collated.

BIBLIOGRAPHY

1972 M. Ellis, JCS 24 p. 69 no. 1 (copy)

TEXT

1) *a-ad-uš-šu*	1) Aduššu,
2) DUMU *a*-PI-*du-um*	2) son of A-PI-dum,
3) ÌR *i-ba-al-pi-el*	3) servant of Ibāl-pî-El.

2002

The impression is on IM 51296, from room 133, level II. It was not collated.

BIBLIOGRAPHY

1972 M. Ellis, JCS 24 p. 69 no. 3 (copy)

TEXT

1) *iš-ḫi-li-il*	1) Išḫi-li-El,
2) DUMU *si*$_{20}$-*ma-nu-um*	2) son of Simānum,
3) ÌR *i-ba-al-pi-e*[*l*]	3) servant of Ibāl-pî-E[l].

2003

The seal impression is on IM 51403, from room 136, level II. It was not collated.

BIBLIOGRAPHY

1972 M. Ellis, JCS 24 p. 69 no. 5 (copy)

TEXT

1) *mu*-[...]	1) Mu...,
2) DUMU *a*-x x x x	2) son of A...,
3) ÌR *i-ba-al-pi-el*	3) servant of Ibāl-pî-El.

2004

The seal impression is on IM 51468, from court 110, level II. It was not collated.

BIBLIOGRAPHY

1972 M. Ellis, JCS 24 p. 69 no. 6 (copy)

TEXT

1) *še-le-bu-um*	1) Šēlebum,
2) DUMU *ú-pí*-DINGIR	2) son of Ūpi-El,
3) ÌR *i-ba-al-pi-el*	3) servant of Ibāl-pî-El.

2005

The seal impression is found on two tablets, IM 51185 and IM 51191, both from room 133, level II. The impressions were not collated.

BIBLIOGRAPHY

1972 M. Ellis, JCS 24 p. 69 no. 10 (exs. 1–2, composite copy)

TEXT

1) *im-gur-*[d]EN.ZU	1) Imgur-Sîn,
2) DUMU [d]EN.ZU-*e-ri-ba-am*	2) son of Sîn-erībam,
3) ÌR *i-ba-al-pi-el*	3) servant of Ibāl-pî-El.

2006

The seal impression is on IM 51190, from room 133, level II. It was not collated.

BIBLIOGRAPHY

1972 M. Ellis, JCS 24 p. 69 no. 13 (copy)

TEXT

1) *a-ma-ar-ì-lí*	1) Ammar-ilī,
2) DUMU *i-di-šum*	2) son of Idišum,
3) ÌR *i-ba-al-pi-el*	3) servant of Ibāl-pî-El.

2007

The seal impression of a servant of Ibāl-pî-El II is found on three tablets, one at Yale and the other two excavated at Šaduppûm (Tell Ḫarmal) and now in Baghdad.

COMMENTARY

The Yale tablet is NBC 8262. The others are IM 52156, from room 133, level II at Tell Ḫarmal and IM 51239 also from Tell Ḫarmal, provenance not recorded. None were collated.

BIBLIOGRAPHY

1959 Simmons, JCS 13 pp. 106–107 (ex. 1, transliteration; ex. 3, study)
1972 M. Ellis, JCS 24 p. 69 no. 14 (ex. 2, copy)
1978 Simmons, YOS 14 pl. CXVIII seal no. 1 (ex. 1, copy)

TEXT

1) *tu-tu-ub.*KI-*m*[*a-gir*]	1) Tutub-m[agir],
2) DUMU *im-gur-*[d]EN.ZU	2) son of Imgur-Sîn,
3) ÌR *i-ba-al-pi-el*	3) servant of Ibāl-pî-El.

2008

The seal impression of a servant of Ibāl-pî-El II is known from two tablets.

COMMENTARY

The impressions are found on NBC 5359 and IM 51548, the latter from Tell Ḥarmal.

BIBLIOGRAPHY

1943 Alexander, BIN 7 no. 85 case (ex. 1, copy)
1959 Simmons, JCS 13 p. 116 (ex. 1, transliteration; ex. 2, study)

TEXT

1) ^{d}nanna-ma-an-sum	1) Nanna-mansum,
2) DUMU *nu-úr-li-bi*	2) son of Nūr-libbi,
3) ÌR *i-ba-al-pi-el*	3) servant of Ibāl-pî-El.

2009

A tablet at Yale bears the seal impressions of two servants of Ibāl-pî-El II. The first is edited here.

COMMENTARY

The tablet is NBC 5304, which was not collated. The name is restored *ig-mi-*⟨*il*⟩*-ìl*, by a comparison with line 27 of the tablet which reads: *ig-mil-ìl*.

BIBLIOGRAPHY

1978 Simmons, YOS 14 pl. CXXIII seal no. 152 (copy)

TEXT

1) *i-di-ia-tum*	1) Idīiatum,
2) DUMU *ig-mi-*⟨*il*⟩-DINGIR	2) son of Igmi(l)-Il,
3) ÌR *i-ba-al-pi-el*	3) servant of Ibāl-pî-El.

2010

The second impression on NBC 5304 (cf. E4.5.20.2009) is edited here; it was not collated.

BIBLIOGRAPHY

1978 Simmons, YOS 14 pl. CXXIII seal no. 154 (copy)

TEXT

1) *a-ḫu-ni*	1) Aḫūni,
2) MÁŠ.ŠU.GÍD.GÍD	2) diviner,
3) DUMU *i-pí-iq-ši-na*	3) son of Ipiqšina,
4) ÌR ⸢*i*⸣-[*b*]*a-a*[*l-pi-el*]	4) servant of Ibā[l-pî-El].

2011

Ešnunna continued to control the city of Nērebtum during the reign of Ibāl-pî-El II. Inbuša, who had served as *sanga* priest of the goddess Eštar Kitītum during the reign of Dāduša, continued in that post during the reign of Ibāl-pî-El II. His seal impression dedicated to Ibāl-pî-El II is on a tablet excavated at Ishchali.

COMMENTARY

The impression is found on A 7640, exact provenance at Ishchali not known. It was not collated.

BIBLIOGRAPHY

1979 Greengus, OBTI no. 131 (copy)

TEXT

1) *in-*[*b*]*u-ša*	1) In[b]uša,
2) SANGA ^{d}*ki-ti-tum*	2) *sanga* priest of the goddess Kitītum,
3) DUMU *ig-mil-*^{d}EN.ZU	3) son of Igmil-Sîn,
4) [ÌR *i*]*-ba-a*[*l-pi-el*]	4) [servant of I]bā[l-pî-El].

2012

Inbuša was succeeded in the office of *sanga* priest of the goddess Eštar Kitītum by his brother Abisum. His seal impression dedicated to Ibāl-pî-El II is found on a number of tablets excavated at Ishchali. For the reading of the name as Abisum, see M. Ellis, JCS 37 (1985) p. 68 n. 30.

CATALOGUE

Ex.	Museum number	Excavation number	Provenance	Lines preserved	cpn
1	A 21917	Ish 34:T.74	Ishchali, 6 Q:30	2–4	n
2	A 7836	–	Ishchali, no provenance	–	n
3	A 7777	–	As ex. 2	–	n
4	A 7766	–	As ex. 2	1–4	n
5	A 7725	–	As ex. 2	1–2	n
6	IM 6940	–	Ishchali(?)	1–4	n

BIBLIOGRAPHY

1979 Greengus, OBTI nos. 114–17 (exs. 1–2, 4–5 copy) and p. 4 (study)
1965 van Dijk, TIM 2 no. 5 (ex. 6, copy)
1985 M. Ellis, JCS 37 p. 68 n. 30 (study)
1986 Greengus, Ishchali Documents pp. 52–53 (exs. 2, 3, 5; transliteration)

TEXT

1) *a-bi-sú-um*
2) SANGA ^{d}*ki-ti-tum*
3) DUMU *ig-mil-*^{d}EN.ZU
4) ÌR *i-ba-al-pi-el*

1) Abisum,
2) *sanga* priest of the goddess Kitītum,
3) son of Igmil-Sîn,
4) servant of Ibāl-pî-El.

2013

The seal impression of a servant of Ibāl-pî-El is found on two tablets from Ishchali.

CATALOGUE

Ex.	Museum number	Provenance	Lines preserved	cpn
1	UCLM 9-2338	Ishchali	1–3	c
2	IM 10865	Said to come from Abū Ḥabba	1–3	n

COMMENTARY

Ex. 1 is a purchased tablet from Ishchali. The seal impression on it was collated by D. Foxvog. Ex. 2, in the Iraq Museum, is supposed to have come from Abū Ḥabba, ancient Sippar, but the fact that it duplicates ex. 1 indicates that the tablet probably came from Ishchali as well.

BIBLIOGRAPHY

1931 Lutz, UCP 10/1 p. 69 TN 36 (ex. 1, transliteration)
1968 van Dijk, TIM 5 no. 21 (ex. 2, copy)

TEXT

1) *a-lí-ba-ni-šu*	1) Ali-bānīšu,
2) DUMU *šu-*^{d}EN.ZU	2) son of Šū-Sîn,
3) ÌR *i-ba-al-pi-el*	3) servant of Ibāl-pî-El.

2014

The fragmentary seal impression of a servant of Ibāl-pî-El II is found on a tablet excavated at Ishchali.

COMMENTARY

The tablet is A 7671, from Ishchali, excavation no. and provenance not known. The impression was not collated.

BIBLIOGRAPHY

1979 Greengus, OBTI no. 233 (copy)

TEXT

1) [...]-*ša*-[...]	1) [...]-ša-[...],
2) D[UMU] X-*ta*-⌜*ku*⌝-*ru*	2) s[on] of ...-takuru,
3) ÌR *i-ba-al*-⌜*pí*⌝-*e*[*l*]	3) servant of Ibāl-pî-E[l].

2015

The impression of a servant of Ibāl-pî-El II is found on a tablet excavated at Ishchali.

COMMENTARY

The impression is on A 21962, excavation no. Ish 35:T.25, from 2 S 29. It was not collated.

BIBLIOGRAPHY

1979 Greengus, OBTI no. 298 (copy)

TEXT

1) ⸢d⸣EN.ZU-*mu-b[a-lí-iṭ]*	1) Sîn-mub[alliṭ],
2) DUMU kù-dna[nna]	2) son of Ku-Na[nna],
3) ÌR *i-ba-al-pi-el*	3) servant of Ibāl-pî-El.

2016–22

Ešnunna continued to control Mê-Turran during the reign of Ibāl-pî-El II. Impressions of seals of servants of Ibāl-pî-El II were found on tablets excavated at Tell Ḥaddād and are edited as E4.5.20.2016–22.

2016

The impression is on Ḥaddād 424. The transliteration offered here is given through the courtesy of A. Kamil.

TEXT

1) *be-el-šu-nu*	1) Bēlšunu,
2) DUMU ÌR-dMAR.DÚ	2) son of Warad-Amurrum,
3) ÌR *i-ba-al-pi-el*	3) servant of Ibāl-pî-El.

2017

The impression is on Ḥaddād no. 525.

COMMENTARY

Kuzzi also appears as a servant of Ṣillī-Sîn (see E4.5.21.2002).

TEXT

1) *ku-*⸢*uz*⸣*-zi*	1) Kuzzi,
2) DUMU *nu-úr-ri*	2) son of Nurri,
3) ⸢ÌR *i-ba-al*⸣*-pi-el*	3) servant of Ibāl-pî-El.

2018

The impression is on Ḥaddād no. 524.

TEXT

1) *b[e]-el-šu-nu*	1) Bēlšunu,
2) DUMU ÌR-^{d}MAR-DÚ	2) son of Warad-Amurrum,
3) ÌR *i-ba-al-pi-el*	3) servant of Ibāl-pî-El.

2019

The impression is on Ḥaddād no. 496.

COMMENTARY

One notes the coincidence of the father's and son's names with the names of two kings of the Old Babylonian dynasty.

TEXT

1) *ḫa-am-mu-ra-[p]í*	1) Ḫammu-rā[p]i,
2) DUMU ^{d}EN.ZU-*mu-ba-lí-iṭ*	2) son of Sîn-muballiṭ,
3) [ÌR *i-ba*]-⸢*al-pi-el*⸣	3) [servant of Ib]āl-pî-El.

2020

The impression is on Ḥaddād no. 496.

TEXT

1) *i-pí-iq-[eš$_4$-tár]*	1) Ipiq-[Eštar],
2) DU[MU] *na-bi-ì-[lí]*	2) so[n] of Nabi-i[lī],
3) [Ì]R *i-ba-al-[pi-el]*	3) [se]rvant of Ibāl-[pî-El].

2021

The impression is on Ḥaddād no. 496.

TEXT

1) *ša-du-um-ra-bi*	1) Šadûm-rabi,
2) DUMU *na-bi-ì-lí*	2) son of Nabi-ilī,
3) ÌR *i-ba-al-pi-el*	3) servant of Ibāl-pî-El.

2022

The impression is found on Ḥaddād no. 496.

TEXT

1) ME-*ab-sú-um*	1) ME-apsûm,
2) DUMU *e-za-tum*	2) son of Ezatum,
3) ⸢ÌR *i-ba-al*⸣-[*pi-el*]	3) servant of Ibāl-[pî-El].

2023

The seal of a certain Ila-rāḫīia, servant of Ibāl-pî-El II, is impressed on a tablet excavated at Mari.

COMMENTARY

The tablet bearing this impression was excavated from room 108 of the Old Babylonian palace at Mari, and published as ARMT 8 no. 52. It is now in the Deir ez-Zor museum.

The tablet is dated by the eponymn Aḫīiaia, son of Takigi. Charpin (MARI 4 p. 250) suggests that this tablet may have been drawn up not at Mari, but rather at a city once under the domination of Ibāl-pî-El II which was subsequently conquered by the king of Mari.

BIBLIOGRAPHY

1957–58 Boyer, ARM(T) 8 no. 52 (copy, edition)
1960 Falkenstein, BiOr 17 p. 178 (study)

TEXT

1) *i-la-ra-ḫi-ia*	1) Ila-rāḫīia,
2) DUMU *bu-ṣi-ia*	2) son of Būṣīia,
3) ÌR *i-ba-al-pi-el*	3) servant of Ibāl-pî-El.

2024

A second seal impression on the previously mentioned tablet (E4.5.20.2023) is that of another servant of Ibāl-pî-El II.

COMMENTARY

This second impression was not copied by Boyer in ARM 8, but is available from the copy of Charpin.

BIBLIOGRAPHY

1983 Charpin, MARI 2 p. 65 no. 52 (transliteration) and p. 72 no. 52 (copy)

TEXT

1) *e-tel-pi*$_4$-^{d}UTU	1) Etel-pî-Šamaš,
2) DUMU *ḫa-ià-ma-lik*	2) son of Ḫaia-malik,
3) ÌR *i-ba-a*[*l*]-*p*[*i-el*]	3) servant of Ibā[l]-p[î-El].

2025

A seal of unknown provenance in Moscow bears the inscription of a servant of Ibāl-pî-El. We have arbitrarily included the inscription here under Ibāl-pî-El II.

COMMENTARY

The seal is in the Pushkin State Museum of Fine Art, Moscow, no. 51. The inscription was collated from the published photo.

BIBLIOGRAPHY

1957–58 Weidner, AfO 18 p. 123 Abb. 2 (photo, edition)

TEXT

1) *a-ḫi-ša-gi-iš*	1) Aḫī-šāgiš,
2) DUMU *ú-ku-un-pí-ia*	2) son of Ukūn-pîia,
3) ÌR *i-ba-al-pi-el*	3) servant of Ibāl-pî-El.

2026

A seal of unknown provenance in Los Angeles bears the inscription of a servant of Ibāl-pî-El. It is arbitrarily included here among the inscriptions of Ibāl-pî-El II.

COMMENTARY

The seal is in the Haermaneck collection of the Los Angeles County Museum of Art, M.76.174.379. It is 2.6 cm long and 1.5 cm in dia. The inscription was collated from the published photograph. The PN in line 2 is Elamite; see R. Zadok, The Elamite Onomasticon p. 8.

BIBLIOGRAPHY

1981 Porada in Moorey et al., Ancient Bronzes pp. 224–25 no. 1186 (photo, study); Renger p. 261 no. 1186 (edition)

TEXT

1) ᵈEN.ZU-*mu-ba-lí-iṭ*	1) Sîn-muballiṭ,
2) DUMU *a-ta-ú-ri*	2) son of Atta-uri,
3) ÌR *i-ba-al-pi-el*	3) servant of Ibāl-pî-El.

Ṣillī-Sîn

E4.5.21

Following the reign of Ibāl-pî-El II, Ešnunna may have been briefly under the control of Elam; in some tablets published in TIM 4, probably from Ešnunna, oaths by the god Tišpak and the *sukkalmaḫ*, and seal impressions of Kuduzuluš, king of Elam (see D. Charpin, Studies Birot p. 52), appear. After this Ešnunna was ruled by Ṣillī-Sîn. A number of year names of this ruler are now known from tablets excavated at Tell Ḥaddād (see R.R. Jāsim, Sumer 40 p. 100 [Arabic section]).

1

A brick bearing an inscription of Ṣillī-Sîn was excavated at Ešnunna.

COMMENTARY

The inscription is found on As 33:T.10b, a brick from the filling used to raise the floor of Narām-Sîn's Audience Hall. The brick was not available for collation.

The first sign in Ṣillī-Sîn's name, broken away in the brick, is restored here as *ṣíl*(MI) rather than the *ṣi-* proposed by Jacobsen. This is because this writing appears in the seal impressions edited here.

Ṣillī-Sîn appears in this brick inscription as 'governor' (énsi) of Ešnunna. However, a year name of the ruler refers to his accession as 'king' (lugal) (see S. Greengus, OBTI p. 34 no. 27).

BIBLIOGRAPHY

1940 Jacobsen, Gimilsin Temple p. 140 no. 17 (edition) and pl. 18 no. 17 (copy)

1961 Hallo, BiOr 18 p. 13 Ešnunna 5 (study)

1971 Sollberger and Kupper, IRSA IVE20a (translation)

TEXT

1) [*ṣíl*]-⸢*lí*⸣-^{d}⸢EN.ZU⸣
2) [ÌR *š*]*a* ^{d}*tišpak*
3) [ÉN]SI
4) [*èš-nun*]-*na*.KI
5) [DUMU ...]-^{d}⸢*še*⸣-*rum*

1) [Ṣil]lī-Sîn,
2) [servant o]f the god Tišpak,
3–4) [gov]ernor of [Ešnun]na,

5) [son of ...]-Šērum.

2001

A cylinder seal in the Yale collections has an inscription of a servant of Ṣillī-Sîn.

COMMENTARY

The piece is NBC 9118, made of haematite, 2.1 cm long, 1.0 cm in dia. It is a purchased piece of unknown provenance. The inscription was collated from the published photo.

BIBLIOGRAPHY

1981 Buchanan and Hallo, Early Near Eastern Seals no. 899 (photo, edition)

TEXT

1) *ig-mil*-[d]EN.ZU	1) Igmil-Sîn,
2) DUMU *ra-ma-nu*	2) son of Rammānu,
3) ÌR *ṣíl-lí*-[d]EN.ZU	3) servant of Ṣillī-Sîn.

2002

Ešnunna's control over Mê-Turran appears to have continued during the reign of Ṣillī-Sîn. A seal impression of a servant of the Ešnunna ruler is found on a tablet excavated at Tell Ḥaddād.

COMMENTARY

The impression is on Ḥaddād 492, seal d, IM number as yet unassigned. The transliteration is given through the courtesy of A. Kamil. Kuzzi appears as a servant of Ibāl-pî-El in E4.5.20.2017.

TEXT

1) *ku-uz-zi*	1) Kuzzi,
2) DUMU *nu-ri*	2) son of Nurri,
3) ÌR *ṣíl-lí*-[d]E[N.ZU]	3) servant of Ṣillī-S[în].

2003

A seal impression of a servant of Ṣillī-Sîn is on a tablet in the British Museum.

COMMENTARY

The impression is on BM 78403 (Bu 88-5-12,303) from Sippar. It was not collated.

BIBLIOGRAPHY

1976 Walker, CT 52 no. 29 (copy)
1977 Kraus, AbB 7 no. 29 (edition)

TEXT

1) ur-^{d}me-kal-kal	1) Ur-Mekalkal,
2) DUMU *bu-tum*	2) son of Butum,
3) ÌR *ṣíl-lí*-^{d}EN.ZU	3) servant of Ṣillī-Sîn.

Ibbi-Sîn

E4.5.22

Two tablets found at Ishchali bear the year name of a certain Ibbi-Sîn (see bibliography). Greengus has suggested that this refers to a ruler of Ešnunna who reigned after Ibāl-pî-El II. His relationship to Ṣillī-Sîn is uncertain. No inscriptions are known for Ibbi-Sîn.

BIBLIOGRAPHY

1979 Greengus, OBTI p. 32 no. 41 (study)
1986 Greengus, Ishchali Documents p. 182 (study)

Iluni

E4.5.23

Iluni, king of Ešnunna, figures in a royal inscription of Samsu-iluna; see E4.3.7.7. A year name of this king appears on a tablet from Ur now in Paris (see Charpin, Le clergé d'Ur pp. 174–75).

2001

An impression of a seal of a servant of Iluni appears on a tablet from Ur.

COMMENTARY

The impression is found on U 3581, a small tag. This object is one of a large group of tags, most of which are said to have come from the Dublamaḫ. Charpin points out that the tags published by Ormsby may originally have been from the archives of the Ganunmaḫ at Ur.

BIBLIOGRAPHY

1972 Ormsby, JCS 24 p. 99 seal 3 (copy)
1985 M. Ellis, JCS 37 p. 62 n. 3 (study)
1986 Charpin, Le clergé d'Ur p. 127 no. 11 (copy, edition)

TEXT

1) dEN.ZU-*i-bi-š*[*u*]
2) DUMU dEN.ZU-*i-qí-ša*-[*am*]
3) ÌR d*i-lu*-[*ni*]

1) Sîn-ibbīš[u],
2) son of Sîn-iqīša[m],
3) servant of Ilu[ni].

Aḫūšina

E4.5.24

A year name on an unpublished tablet in the British Museum (BM 79898) deals with Abī-ešuḫ's defeat of Aḫūšina, king of Ešnunna (C.B.F. Walker, personal communication). No inscriptions of this king survive.

BIBLIOGRAPHY

1985 M. Ellis, JCS 37 p. 62 n. 3 (study)

MARI

E4.6

Before the advent of the dynasty of Iaḫdun-Līm, Mari was ruled by a long series of viceroys (*šakkanakkū*). The relative dating of these figures has been uncertain for a long time. The recent discovery and publication by Durand of two lists of *šakkanakku*s (see MARI 4 pp. 152–59) has shed much light on this question.

Assuming the identity of the Puzur-Eštar who appears in one of the lists with a *šakkanakkum* by that name attested in various Ur III texts studied by Goetze, a relative chronology of the Mari rulers with the Ur III kings can be determined. The last of these Ur III period *šakkanakku*s, Ḫanun-Dagān, reigned during the last half of the reign of Ibbi-Sîn of Ur. Unfortunately, after this point, when the present volume commences, the evidence from the *šakkanakku* lists is full of lacunae. About 13 *šakkanakku*s should be placed in the gap between Ḫanun-Dagān and the beginning of Iaḫdun-Līm's reign. At present the names of six viceroys are known for this period. These are included here in the chronological order established by Durand.

Iṣi-Dagān

E4.6.1

2001

A text, attested on two seal impressions on a lump of clay excavated at Aššur, bears the name of a servant of Iṣi-Dagān.

COMMENTARY

The impressions are found on VA 7885, excavation no. S 21976h, from the forecourt of Ištar temple E at Aššur, a level generally dated to the Ur III period. It is a lump of unbaked clay, with the impression measuring 2.7 × 1.5 cm. The inscription was not collated.

The interpretation of this impression as a seal of a servant of Iṣi-Dagān, rather than of the governor himself, follows the reading suggested by Durand. The reading ŠABRA in line 4 as a title of Irmaš-Dagān is based on an interpretation of the signs in the field of the seal as part of the seal inscription.

While it is certain that the reign of Iṣi-Dagān followed that of Ḫanun-Dagān, the gap between the two *šakkanakku*s, if any, is not known. The stratigraphy argues for a date very early in the Isin–Larsa period.

BIBLIOGRAPHY

1914 Andrae, MDOG 54 p. 23 (transliteration, study)
1914 Ungnad, OLZ 17 434–44 (study)
1922 Andrae, AIT pp. 102–103 no. 147 (edition) and fig. 76b (copy)
1934 Thureau-Dangin, RA 31 p. 138 (study)
1957 Kupper, Nomades pp. 206–207 n. 4 (study)
1971 Kupper, RA 65 p. 116 (transliteration, study)
1971 Sollberger and Kupper, IRSA IVF1a (translation)
1985 Durand, MARI 4 pp. 149–50 (transliteration, study)

TEXT

1) *i-ṣí-*[d]*da-gan*	1) Iṣi-Dagān,
2) GÌR.NÍTA *ma-rí*	2) viceroy of Mari,
3) *ìr-maš-*[d]*da-ga*[*n*]	3) Irmaš-Dagā[n],
4) ŠABRA	4) the supervisor.

2002

A seal mentioning Iṣi-Dagān is in the British Museum.

COMMENTARY

The seal is BM 139951 (1985-7-15,1). It measures 2.6 × 1.3 cm and is made of a dark stone, probably chlorite.

BIBLIOGRAPHY

1987 Collon and Finkel, MARI 5 pp. 602–604 (photo, copy, edition)
1987 Collon, First Impressions no. 120 (photo, study)

TEXT

1) *i-ṣí-*[d]*da-gan*	1) Iṣi-Dagān,
2) GÌR.NÍT[A]	2) viceroy
3) *ma-rí*.K[I]	3) of Mari,
4) x x	4) ...
5) *zi*(?) *du*(?) x (x) [x]	5) ...

Ennin-Dagān

E4.6.2

1

A seal impression of Ennin-Dagān, military governor of Mari, is found on a clay lump excavated at Mari.

COMMENTARY

The impression is on ME 14, a clay door sealing. It was collated from the published photo. Previously this impression was attributed to Tūra-Dagān, but collation of the piece by J.-M. Durand gives the reading found here. The restoration of the name of Ennin-Dagān's father as Iṣi-Dagān is not supported by collation of the photo.

BIBLIOGRAPHY

1959 Parrot, Documents pp. 156–57 Cylindre I de Tûra-Dagan (study); Dossin p. 251 Cylindre I de Tûra-Dagan (edition) and pl. XLV ME 14 (photo)
1971 Kupper, RA 65 p. 113 (transliteration)
1971 Sollberger and Kupper, IRSA IVF2a (translation)
1981 Durand, RA 75 p. 180 (transliteration)
1985 Durand, MARI 4 p. 150 (transliteration) and p. 155 (study)
1985 Beyer, MARI 4 p. 377 (study)

TEXT

1) [*en*]-*nin*-[d][*d*]*a-gan*	1) [En]nin-[D]agān,
2) [G]ÌR.NÍTA	2–3) [v]iceroy of [Mar]i,
3) [*ma-r*]*í*.KI	
4) [...]-[d]*da-gan*	4) [son of ...]-Dagān,
5) [GÌR].NÍTA	5) [vice]roy.

Itūr-[...]

E4.6.3

1

A certain Itūr-[...] appears as viceroy and father of Tīr-Dagān, in a sealing of the latter (see E4.6.5.1). We thus know that Itūr-[...] ruled Mari before Tīr-Dagān. Tīr-Dagān appears as the next to last military governor of Mari in the *šakkanakku* list published by Durand. He probably reigned shortly before the accession of Iaḫdun-Līm. Since Iṣi-Dagān and Ennin-Dagān are thought to have reigned at the beginning of the Isin–Larsa period, and Itūr-[...] not too long before the accession of Iaḫdun-Līm, there may be a number of as yet unattested viceroys in the gap between these two figures. No inscriptions of Itūr-[...] are known.

Amer-Nūnu

E4.6.4

1

The impression of a seal of Amer-Nūnu, viceroy of Mari, is found on a lump of clay from Mari. Am[er-Nūnu] appears in the list of *šakkanakku* s published by Durand immediately preceding Tīr-Dagān.

COMMENTARY

The impression is found on ME 57, a clay lump, possibly a door sealing, excavated at Mari. The inscription was collated from the published photo.

The name of the viceroy was previously read as Mer-[...].

According to J.-M. Durand (MARI 4 p. 152 n. 36) Amer-Nūnu was probably the son of Itūr-[...] and brother of Tīr-Dagān.

BIBLIOGRAPHY

1959 Parrot, Documents p. 157 Cylindre de Mer (study); Dossin p. 251 Cylindre de Mer-... (edition) and pl. XLV ME 57 (photo)

1971 Kupper, RA 65 p. 113 (transliteration)

1981 Durand, RA 75 p. 180 (transliteration)

1985 Durand, MARI 4 p. 150 (transliteration) and p. 152 with n. 35 (study)

1985 Beyer, MARI 4 p. 377 (study)

TEXT

1) [*a*]-*me-er-*[d]*nu-nu*	1) [A]mer-Nūnu,
2) G[ÌR.NÍTA]	2–3) v[iceroy] of M[ari],
3) *m*[*a-rí*.KI]	
4) [DUMU *i-tur-*...]	4) [son of Itūr-...],
5) [GÌR.NÍTA]	5) [viceroy].

Tīr-Dagān

E4.6.5

1

The impression of a seal of Tīr-Dagān, viceroy of Mari, is found on two clay lumps excavated at Mari. Tīr-Dagān appears in the next to last position in a *šakkanakku* list published by J.-M. Durand.

CATALOGUE

Ex.	Excavation number	Provenance	Object	cpn
1	ME 196	Mari	Seal impression on clay door sealing	p
2	ME 64	Mari	Seal impression on clay lump, possibly door sealing	p

BIBLIOGRAPHY

1959 Parrot, Documents p. 159 Déesse et personnage virile (ex. 1, study); Dossin p. 252 (ex. 1, edition) and pl. XLV ME 196 (photo); Barrelet and Parrot pp. 157–58 Dieu au cercle et au bâton (ex. 2, study); Dossin p. 250 Cylindre du shakkanakkum X (edition) and pl. XLV ME 64 (photo)

1971 Kupper, RA 65 pp. 113–14 (exs. 1–2, transliteration, study)

1985 Durand, MARI 4 p. 150 (exs. 1–2, transliteration) and p. 152 n. 36 (study)

1985 Beyer, MARI 4 pp. 377–78 (exs. 1–2, study)

TEXT

1) *ti-ir-*[d]*d*[*a-gan*]
2) GÌR.NÍTA
3) *ma-rí.*[KI]
4) DUMU *i-túr-*d[...]
5) GÌR.[NÍTA]

1) Tīr-D[agān],
2–3) viceroy of Mari,
4) son of Itūr-[...],
5) vice[roy].

Dagān-[...]

E4.6.6

The last name in the list of viceroys published by J.-M. Durand reads Dagān-[...]. No inscriptions or seal impressions of this viceroy have yet come to light.

Iaggid-Līm

E4.6.7

After a long period of rule by viceroys at Mari there appears a sequence of rulers who styled themselves as 'king' (LUGAL). The first of these was Iaḫdun-Līm.

Iaḫdun-Līm's father, Iaggid-Līm, is mentioned in a letter from Mari that describes a confrontation between him and Ila-kabkabû, the father of Šamšī-Adad. Durand has suggested that Iaggid-Līm was not actually a ruler of Mari, but ruled instead at the nearby city of Ṣuprum. Perhaps as a result of a military defeat, Iaḫdun-Līm abandoned Ṣuprum and installed himself as king at Mari.

2001

No monumental texts of Iaggid-Līm have yet appeared. There is, however, a seal of a servant of the king. While Iaggid-Līm may not have actually reigned at Mari, this is a convenient place to edit this inscription.

COMMENTARY

The object is in the Kunst-historisches Museum, Vienna, Ägyptisches Semitisches Sammlung, no. 1198. It is a cylinder seal of purple-grey haematite, 3 cm long, 1.6 cm in dia. The inscription was collated from the published photo.

H. Hunger incorrectly read the name of the servant's father as *qi-iš-ti*-dA.É in line 2.

For the latest discussion of the career of Iaggid-Līm, see J.-M. Durand, MARI 4 pp. 166–70.

BIBLIOGRAPHY

1957–58 Weidner, AfO 18 pp. 122–23 and Abb. 1 (photo, edition, study)

1966 Unger, Siegelbildforschung pp. 41–42 no. 10 (study)

1981 Hunger in Bleibtreu (ed.), Rollsiegel aus dem Vorderen Orient (Wien) p. 56 no. 65 (photo, edition)

1987 Collon, First Impressions no. 171 (photo, study)

TEXT

1) *iš-me*-DINGIR DUB.SAR
2) DUMU *qí-iš-ti-ìl-a-ba*4
3) ÌR *ia-gi-id-li-i*[*m*]

1) Išme-Ilum, scribe,
2) son of Qīšti-Ilaba,
3) servant of Iaggid-Lī[m].

Iaḫdun-Līm

E4.6.8

Iaggid-Līm was succeeded by his son Iaḫdun-Līm, who reigned as king of Mari. Although we do not know the length of the rule of this important ruler, a number of his year names are extant. He was a contemporary of Šamšī-Adad of Aššur.

1

A cone inscription found in the Old Babylonian palace at Mari deals with the foundation of Dūr-Iaḫdun-Līm. This settlement is probably to be located on the right bank of the Euphrates near the confluence with the Ḫabur.

COMMENTARY

The text is inscribed on AO 18236, the fragmentary head of a large cone (39 cm in dia.). It was found in a corner of room 18 of the palace at Mari and has been collated.

BIBLIOGRAPHY

1936 Parrot, Syria 17 p. 23 and fig. 12 (photo, provenance)
1936 Thureau-Dangin, RA 33 pp. 49–54 (photo, edition)
1952 Oppenheim, JNES 11 p. 137 (study)
1953 Laessøe, JCS 7 p. 22 (study)
1954 Landsberger, JCS 8 p. 35 n. 26 (study)
1955 Dossin, Syria 32 pp. 27–28 (study)
1967 Lambert CRRA I 15 pp. 36–37 (study)
1971 Sollberger and Kupper, IRSA IVF6a (transliteration)
1976 Kupper, Kramer Anniversary pp. 301–303 (edition)
1984 Safren, RA 78 p. 123 (study)

TEXT

1) *ia-aḫ-du-un-li-im*
2) DUMU *ia-gi*(*)*-id-li-im*
3) LUGAL *ma-ri*.KI
4) *tu-ut-tu-ul*.KI
5) *ù ma-at ḫa-na*
6) LUGAL KALA.GA
7) *ga-me-er*
8) GÚ I_7.BURANUN.NA

1–8) Iaḫdun-Līm, son of Iaggid-Līm, king of Mari, Tuttul, and the land of Ḫana, mighty king, who controls the banks of the Euphrates —

---

2 Text: ZI.

9) ^{d}*da-gan*
10) *šar-ru-ti ib-bi*
11) GIŠ.TUKUL KALA.GA
12) *mu-ša-am-qí-it*
13) LUGAL.MEŠ *na-ki-ri-ia*
14) *id-di-nam-ma*

9–14) the god Dagān proclaimed my kingship (and) gave to me a mighty weapon that fells my royal enemies.

15) 7 LUGAL.MEŠ
16) *ab-bu-ú ḫa-na*
17) *ša uq-ta-ab-bi-lu-nim*
18) *ak-mi-šu-nu-ti*
19) *ma-at-sú-nu*
20) *a-na i-di-ia ú-te-er*

15–20) Seven kings, leaders of Ḫana who had fought against me, I defeated. I annexed their lands.

21) *ḫi-ip-pí*
22) *ša* GÚ I$_7$.BURANUN.NA
23) *as-sú-uḫ-ma*
24) *ma-ti šu-ub-tam*
25) *ne-eḫ-tam ú-še-ši-ib*
26) *na-ra-a-tim*
27) *ú-pé-et-ti*
28) *da-la-a-am*
29) *i-na ma-ti-ia*
30) *ú-ḫa-al-li-iq*
31) BÀD *ma-ri*.KI *e-pu-uš*
32) *ù ḫi-ri-sú aḫ-ri*
33) BÀD *ter-qá*.KI *e-pu-úš*
34) *ù ḫi-ri-sú aḫ-ri*

21–34) I removed the ... of the banks of the Euphrates and made my land dwell in peace. I opened canals and did away with the drawing of water in my land. I built the wall of Mari and dug its moat. I built the wall of Terqa and dug its moat.

35) *ù i-na sa-we-e*
36) *qá-qá-ar*
37) *na-aṣ-mi-im*
38) *ša iš-tu u$_4$-um ṣí-a-tim*
39) LUGAL *šum-šu*
40) *a-lam la i-pu-šu*
41) *a-na-ku la-la-am*
42) *ar-ši-i-ma*
43) *a-lam e-pu-úš*
44) *ḫi-ri-sú aḫ-ri*
45) BÀD-*ia-aḫ-du-li-im*
46) *šum-šu ab-bi*
47) *ù na-ra-am ep-te-šum-ma*
48) I$_7$-*i-ši-im-ia-aḫ-du-li-im*
49) *šum-šu ab-bi*

35–49) Now in a waste, a land of thirst, in which from days of old no king had built a city, I took pleasure in building a city. I dug its moat [and] called it Dūr-Iaḫdun-Līm ('Fort Iaḫdun-Līm'). I opened a canal for it and called it Išīm-Iaḫdun-Līm ('Iaḫdun-Līm has determined (its) destiny').

50) *ma-a-ti ú-ra-ap-pí-iš*
51) *iš$_6$-de ma-ri*.KI
52) *ù ma-ti-ia ú-ki-in-ma*
53) *a-na u$_4$-um ṣí-a-tim*
54) *šu-mi aš-ku-un*

50–54) I enlarged my land, established the foundations of Mari and my land, and established my fame until distant days.

55) *ša te-em-me-ni-ia*
56) *ú-na-ak-ka-ru-ma*
57) *te-em-me-ni-šu*
58) *i-ša-ak-ka-nu*

55–58) (As for) the man who removes my foundation deposits and puts his own foundation deposits (in their places),

59) *a-wi-lum šu-ú*
60) *lu* LUGAL *lu* ÉNSI
61) AN *ù* ^{d}*en-líl*
62) *er-re-tam le-mu-ut-tam*
63) *li-ru-ru-šu*

59–63) that man, whether he be a king or governor — may the gods Anum and Enlil inflict a terrible curse on him.

64) ^{d}UTU *ka-ak-ki-šu*
65) *ù ka-ak-ki*
66) *um-ma-ni-šu*
67) *li-iš-bi-ir*
68) ^{d}*ašnan ù* ^{d}*šákkan*
69) *ma-sú li-ik-ki-a*

64–69) May the god Šamaš smash his weapon and the weapon of his army. May the gods Ašnan and Šakkan impoverish his land.

70) *a-bu-ul ma-ti-šu*
71) *li-ki-la nu-ku-ra-tum*
72) *qá-ab-lum li-ib-ta-ri*
73) *i-na ma-ti-šu*
74) LUGAL-*sú a-di ba-al-ṭú*
75) u_4*-mi-ša-am ḫi-di-ir-tum*
76) *li-im-ta-aḫ-ḫa-ar*
77) AN *ù* ^{d}*en-líl lu ra-bi-iṣ le-mu-ti-šu*
78) *a-na da-ri-a-tim*

70–78) May hostilities close the gate of his land and may battle keep raging in his land. As long as he lives may bad news daily confront his rule. May the gods Anum and Enlil be the bailiffs of his misfortune forever.

2

Nine examples of large baked bricks inscribed with an account of the building of the temple of the god Šamaš in Mari by Iaḫdun-Līm were excavated from the foundations of that temple.

CATALOGUE

Ex.	Museum number	Registration number	Excavation number	Dimensions (cm)	cpn
1	Damascus	2169	M 2802	41.0×41.0	c
2	Aleppo	2173	M 2806	–	c
3	Aleppo	2174	M 2807	–	c
4	Damascus	2170	M 2803	–	c (partial)
5	Not located	(2175)	M 2808	–	n
6	AO 21815	2177	M 2928	40.0×40.0	c
7	Damascus	2171	M 2804	41.5×41.5	c
8	Damascus	2172	M 2805	–	c (partial)
9	Damascus	2176	M 2900	41.0×41.0	c

COMMENTARY

The text is arranged in versions of four or five cols., with varying line arrangements. The master text is ex. 1, which is followed except for lines 10, 18, 42, 56, 90, 105, and 120, where corrections have been made from other exs. The interested reader can check the scores.

BIBLIOGRAPHY

1954 Parrot, Syria 31 pp. 160–61 (ex. 9, photo; exs. 1–9, provenance)
1955 Dossin, Syria 32 pp. 1–28 and pls. 1–2 (ex. 1, photo, copy; exs. 1–9, edition)
1957 Kupper, Nomades pp. 50–51 (study)
1958 Dossin, RA 52 pp. 60–62 (study)
1958 Gelb, Lingua degli Amoriti p. 154 (study)
1960 Kraus, JNES 19 p. 129 n. 82 (study)
1962 Lancellotti, Grammatica della Lingua Accadica (Jerusalem) pp. 3*–10* (copy in Neo-Assyrian script)
1963 Borger, BiOr 20 p. 48 (study)
1965 von Soden, JSS 10 p. 123 (study)
1965 Malamat, Landsberger Festschrift pp. 367–70 (partial translation, study)
1967 Lambert, CRRA I 15 pp. 36–37 (study)
1969 Oppenheim, ANET^{3} pp. 556–57 (translation)

1971 Sollberger and Kupper, IRSA ivF6b (translation)
1982 André-Leicknam, Naissance de l'écriture pp. 95–97 no. 57 (ex. 6, photo, study)
1984 Borger, TUAT 1/4 p. 355 (partial translation)
1987 Durand, NABU p. 45 no. 85 (study)

TEXT

1) *a-na* ^{d}UTU LUGAL *ša-me-e*
2) *ù er-ṣe-ti-im*
3) *ša-pí-iṭ* DINGIR.MEŠ *ù a-wi-lu-tim*
4) *ša me-še-ru-um i-si-ik-šu-ma*
5) *ki-na-tum a-na še-ri-ik-ti-im*
6) *ša-ar-ka-šu-um*
7) *re-i ṣa-al-ma-at qa-qa-di-im*
8) DINGIR *šu-pí-im*
9) *da-ia-an ša-ki-in na-pí-iš-tim*
10) *ma-gi-ir te-ès-li-ti-im*
11) *še-mi ik-ri-bi*
12) *le-qí un-ne-ni-im*
13) *na-di-in ba-la-aṭ ṭú-ub li-bi-im*
14) *ša* u_4*-mi ar-ku-ti-im*
15) *a-na pa-li-ḫi-šu*
16) *ša ma-ri.*KI *be-li-šu*

1–16) To the god Šamaš, king of heaven and earth, judge of gods and mankind, whose concern is justice, to whom truth has been given as a gift, shepherd of the black-headed (people), resplendent god, judge of those endowed with life, who is favourably inclined to supplications, who heeds prayers, who accepts entreaties, who gives a long-lasting life of joy to him who reveres him, who is the lord of Mari:

17) ^{m}*ia-aḫ-du-un-li-im*
18) DUMU *ia-gi-id-li-im*
19) LUGAL *ma-ri.*KI *ù ma-at ḫa-na*
20) *pé-ti* I_7.DA.ḪI.A
21) *e-pí-iš du-ri*
22) *mu-re-ti na-re-e na-bi šu-mi*
23) *ša-ki-in nu-uḫ-ši-im*
24) *ù* ḪÉ.GÁL*-lim a-na ni-ši-šu*
25) *mu-ša-ab-ši mi-im-ma šum-šu*
26) *i-na ma-ti-šu*
27) LUGAL *dan-nu-um eṭ-lu-um šu-pu-um*

17–27) Iaḫdun-Līm, son of Iaggid-Līm, king of Mari and the land of Ḫana, opener of canals, builder of walls, erector of steles proclaiming (his) name, provider of abundance and plenty for his people, who makes whatever (is needed) appear in his land, mighty king, magnificent youth,

28) *i-nu-ma* ^{d}UTU *te-ès-li-sú*
29) *im-gu-ru-šu*
30) *ù qí-bi-sú iš-mu-ú*
31) ^{d}UTU *ia-aḫ-du-un-li-im*
32) *ù-da-ad-ma*
33) *i-na i-di-šu il-li-ik-ma*

28–33) when the god Šamaš agreed to his supplications and listened to his words, the god Šamaš quickly came and went at the side of Iaḫdun-Līm.

34) *ša iš-tu* u_4*-um ṣa-at*
35) *a-lam ma-ri.*KI DINGIR *ib-nu-ú*
36) LUGAL *ma-ma-an wa-ši-ib ma-ri.*KI
37) *ti-a-am-ta-am la ik-šu-du*
38) KUR GIŠ.ERIN *ù* GIŠ.TAŠKARIN
39) KUR*-i ra-bu-tim la ik-šu-du*
40) *ù i-ṣí-šu-nu la ik-ki-su*

34–40) From distant days when the god El built Mari, no king resident in Mari reached the sea, reached the mountains of cedar and boxwood, the great mountains, and cut down their trees,

41) ^{m}*ia-aḫ-du-un-li-im*

41–50) (but) Iaḫdun-Līm, son of Iaggid-Līm,

1.4–9 *ša-mi-e*. **2**.4–9 *er-ṣé-tim*. **3**.4–9 *i-li-im*. **3**.4–6 *a-wi-lu-ti-im*. **4**.4–9 *mi-še-ru-um*. **5**.2 *šu-ri-ik-ti-im*. **5**.4–9 *še-ri-ik-tim*. **6**.4–9 *ša-ar-ka-šum*. **10**.1, 3, 6, 9 *ma-zi-ir*. **10**.4, 6 *te-es-li-tim*. **10**.7–9 *te-ès-li-tim*. **12**.4–9 *ù-ne-ni-im*. **14**.4–9 *ar-ku-tim*. **16**.4–9 *ma-rí.*KI. **18**.1, 3, 6, 9 *ia-zi-id-li-im*. **19**.4–9 *ma-rí.*KI. **20**.8 *na-ti* instead of *pé-ti*. **20**.4–9 *na-ra-tim*. **24**.4–9 ḪÉ.GAL. **27**.4–9 *da-an-nu-um*. **33**.6 *íl-li-ik-ma*. **35**.4–9 *ma-rí.*KI. **35**.4–6 *i-lu-um*. **36**.4–9 *ma-rí.*KI. **37**.4–9 *ta-am-ta-am*. **38**.4–9 *ša-di e-ri-ni-im*. **38**.4–6 *ta-ás-ka-ri-nim*. **38**.7–9 *ta-ás-ka-ri-ni-im*. **39**.4–6 *ša-di-i*. **39**.7–9 *ša-di*. **39**.7–9 *ra-bu-ti*. **39**.7–9 *la* «*šu*» *ik-šu-du*.

42) DUMU *ia-gi-id-li-im*
43) LUGAL *gu-uš-ru-um ri-im šur-ri*
44) *i-na le-ù-tim*
45) *ù ga-mi-ru-tim*
46) *a-na ki-ša-ad ti-a-am-tim*
47) *il-li-ik-ma*
48) *a-na a-a-ab-ba ni-qí šar-ru-ti-šu*
49) *ra-bi-a-am iq-qí*
50) *ù ṣa-bu-šu i-na qé-re-eb a-a-ab-ba*

powerful king, wild bull of kings, by means of his strength and overpowering might went to the shore of the sea, and made a great offering (befitting) his kingship to the Sea. His troops bathed themselves in the Sea.

51) *me-e ir-mu-uk*
52) *a-na* KUR GIŠ.ERIN *ù* GIŠ.TAŠKARIN
53) KUR-*i ra-bu-tim i-ru-um-ma*
54) GIŠ.TAŠKARIN GIŠ.ERIN GIŠ.ŠU.ÚR.MAN
55) *ù* GIŠ *e-lam-ma-ka-am*
56) *i-ṣí an-nu-ti-in ik-ki-is*
57) *ḫa-mu-ṣa-am iḫ-mu-uṣ*(*)*-ma*
58) *šu-mi-šu iš-ta-ka-an*
59) *ù li-ù-sú ù-we-di*
60) *ma-ta-am ša-ti ša ki-ša-ad a-a-ab-ba*
61) *ù-ka-an-ni-iš*
62) *a-na pí-im ù-še-ši-ib-ši*
63) *wa-ar-ki-šu ù-ša-li-ik-ši*
64) *bi-il-ta-am ka-ia-an-ta-am*
65) *i-mi-sú-nu-ti-ma*
66) *ù bi-la-sú-nu na-šu-ni-iš-šum*

51–66) (Next) he entered into the cedar and boxwood mountains, the great mountains, and cut down these trees – box, cedar, cypress, and *elammakum*. He made a commemorative monument, established his fame, and proclaimed his might. He made that land on the shore of the Sea submit, made it subject to his decree, and made it follow him. Having imposed a permanent tribute on them, they now bring their tribute to him.

67) *i-na ša-at-tim-ma ša-a-ti*
68) ^{m}*la-ú-um* LUGAL *sa-ma-nim.*KI
69) *ù ma-at ub-ra-bi-im*
70) ^{m}*ba-aḫ-lu-ku-li-im* LUGAL *tu-tu-ul.*KI
71) *ù ma-at am-na-ni-im*
72) ^{m}*a-ia-lum* LUGAL *a-ba-at-tim.*KI
73) *ù ma-at ra-ab-bi-im*
74) LUGAL.MEŠ *an-nu-tu-un*
75) *i-ki-ru-šu-ma*
76) *a-na ti-lu-ti-šu-nu*
77) *ṣa-ab su-mu-e-pu-uḫ*
78) *ša ma-at ia-am-ḫa-ad.*KI
79) *il-li-ka-am-ma*
80) *i-na a-li-im sa-ma-nim.*KI
81) *um-ma-at tur-mi-im*
82) *iš-ti-ni-iš ip-ḫu-ru-šum-ma*
83) *i-na ka-ak-ki-im da-an-nim*
84) 3 LUGAL.MEŠ *an-nu-ti-in*
85) *ša tur-mi-im ik-mi*
86) *ṣa-ba-šu-nu ù ṣa-bi ti-la-ti-šu-nu i-du-uk*

67–91) In that same year, – Laʾum, king of Samānum and the land of the Ubrabium, Baḫlukullim, king of Tuttul and the land of the Amnānum, Aiālum, king of Abattum and the land of the Rabbum – these kings rebelled against him. The troops of Sūmû-Epuḫ of the land of Iamḫad came as auxiliary troops (to rescue him) and in the city of Samānum the tribes gathered together against him, but by means of (his) mighty weapon he defeated these three kings of ... He vanquished their troops and their auxiliaries and inflicted a defeat on them. He heaped up their dead bodies. He tore down their walls and made them into mounds of rubble.

42.1, 3, 6, 9 *ia-zi-id-li-im*. **45**.4–6 *ga-mi-ru-ti-im*. **46**.4–6 *ta-am-ti-im*. **46**.7–9 *ta-am-tim*. **48**.4–9 *a-ia-ba*. **48**.4–9 *ni-iq*. **49**.4–9 *ra-ba-am*. **49**.7–9 *i-qí*. **50**.4–9 *a-ia-ba*. **51**.4–9 *mi-e*. **52**.4–9 *ša-di*. **52**.4–6 *e-ri-nim*. **52**.7–9 *e-ri-ni-im*. **52**.4–9 *ta-ás-ka-ri-nim*. **53**.4–9 *ša-di-i*. **54**.4–9 GIŠ *ta-ás-ka-ri-na-am*. **54**.4–6 *e-ri-na-am*. **54**.7–9 *e-ri-nam*. **54**.4–9 GIŠ *šu-ur-mi-na-am*. **55**.4–9 omit GIŠ. **56**.2–3 *an-nu-ut-ti-in*. **56**.1 *i-ki-is*. **57**.1–3 *iḫ-mu-uṣ*(ŠE + RI)*-ma*. **57**.4–9 *iḫ-mu-uṣ$_4$-ma*. **60**.4–9 *a-ia-ba*. **61**.4–9 *ù-ka-ni-iš*. **62**.2 *ù-še-ši-«*DIŠ*»-ib-ši*. **64**.2 *bi-il-tá-am*. **64**.2 *ka-ia-an-tá-am*. **65** Copy: *su*; bricks: *sú*. **66**.4–9 *na-šu-ni-šum*. **67**.4–6 *ša-tim-ma ša-a-ti*. **67**.7–9 *ša-ti-ma ša-ti*. **68**.5 ^{m}*li-ú-um*. **68**.7–9 and possibly 5 *sa-ma-ni-im.*KI. **71**.7–9 *am-na-nim*. **72**.6 «DIŠ» LUGAL. **72**.4–9 *a-ba-tim.*KI. **73**.4–9 *ra-bi-im*. **74**.4–9 *šar-ru*. **79**.5–9 *il-li-kam-ma*. **80**.4–9 *sa-ma-ni-im.*KI. **82**.7–9 *-šum-šu*. **83**.4–9 *ka-ki-im*. **83**.4–6 *da-an-ni-im*. **84**.4–9 *šar-ri*. **86**.4–9 *ṣa-ab ti-la-ti-šu-nu*.

87) *da-aw-da-šu-nu im-ḫa-aṣ*
88) *gu-ru-un ša-al-ma-ti-šu-nu iš-ku-un*
89) *du-ra-ni-šu-nu iq-qú-ur-ma*
90) *a-na ti-li ù ka-ar-mi*
91) *iš-ku-un-šu-nu-ti*
92) *a-lam ḫa-ma-an*.KI *um-ma-at ḫa-na*
93) *ša a-bu-ú ḫa-na ka-lu-šu-nu i-pu-šu-šu*
94) *iq-qú-ur-šu-ma*
95) *a-na ti-li ù ka-ar-mi iš-ku-un-šu*
96) *ù šar-ra-šu ka-ṣú-ri-ḫa-la ik-mi*
97) *ma-sú-nu it-ba-al*
98) *ù ki-ša-ad pu-ra-tim ig-mu-ur-ma*

92–98) The city of Ḫaman, of the tribe of Ḫaneans, which all the leaders of Ḫana had built, he destroyed and made into mounds of rubble. Now, he defeated their king, Kaṣuri-Ḫāla. Having taken away their population he controlled the banks of the Euphrates.

99) *a-na ba-la-ṭì-šu* É ^{d}UTU *be-li-šu*
100) É *ša i-pí-iš-ta-am šu-uk-lu-lu-ma*
101) *um-me-nu-ta-am qú-ut-tu-ú*
102) *sí-ma-at i-lu-ti-šu i-pu-ús-su-um-ma*
103) *i-na šu-ba-at ra-bu-ti-šu*
104) *ù-še-ši-ib-šu šum* É *ša-tu*
105) *e-gi-ir-za-la-an-ki i-bi*
106) É *ta-ši-la-at ša-mé-e*
107) *ù er-ṣé-tim*

99–107) For his own life he built the temple of the god Šamaš, his lord, a temple whose construction was perfect with finished workmanship, befitting his divinity. He installed him in his majestic dwelling. He named that temple Egirzalanki ('House — rejoicing of heaven and earth').

108) ^{d}UTU *wa-ši-ib bi-tim ša-tu*
109) *a-na ia-aḫ-du-un-li-im ba-ni bi-ti-šu*
110) *šar-ri-im na-ra-am li-bi-šu*
111) *ka-ak-ka-am da-an-na-am*
112) *ka-ši-id a-ia-bi*
113) *pa-la-am ar-ka-am*
114) *ša ṭú-ub li-bi-im*
115) *ù ša-na-at* ḪÉ.GÁL-*li ri-ša-tim*
116) *a-na u*$_{4}$*-mi da-ru-tim*
117) *li-iš-ru-uk-šum*

108–117) May the god Šamaš, who lives in that temple, grant to Iaḫdun-Līm, the builder of his temple, the king beloved of his heart, a mighty weapon which overwhelms the enemies (and) a long reign of happiness and years of joyous abundance, forever.

118) *ša bi-ta-am ša-tu*
119) *ù-ša-al-pa-tu*
120) *a-na le-mu-tim*
121) *ù la da-mi-iq-tim i-ku-pu-šum*
122) *a-su-ra-šu la ù-da-na-nu*
123) *ma-aq-tu-sú la uš-za-zu*
124) *ù ni-in-da-ba-am*
125) *i-pa-ra-su-šu-um*
126) *šu-mi ša-aṭ-ra-am i-pa-ši-ṭú*
127) *ù ù-ša-ap-ša-ṭú*
128) *šum-šu la ša-aṭ-ra-am i-ša-ṭá-ru*
129) *ù ù-ša-áš-ṭá-ru*
130) *ù a-šu-um er-re-tim*
131) *ša-ni-a-am ù-ša-ḫa-zu*

118–131) (As for) the one who destroys that temple, who ... it to evil and no good, who does not strengthen its foundation, does not set up what has fallen down, and cuts its regular offerings off from it, who effaces my name or has it effaced and writes his own name previously not there, or has it written there, or because of (these) curses incites another to do so,

132) *a-wi-lum šu-ú lu šar-ru-um*
133) *lu ša-ka-na-ku-um*
134) *lu ra-bi-a-nu-um*

132–136) that man, whether he be king, viceroy, mayor, or common man,

---

90.1 *⟨ka⟩-ar-mi*. **91**.3 *iš-kur-un-⌜šu⌝-⟨nu⟩-ti*. **92**.2 *ḫa-me-an*.KI. **93**.3 *ka-lu-⟨šu-nu⟩*. **96**.7–9 ^{m}*ka-ṣú-ri-ḫa-la*. **98**.9 *ig-mu-«ru»-ur-ma*. **100**.4–9 *bi-ta-am*. **100**.8 inserts DIŠ after *bi-ta-am* and *i-pí-iš-ta-am*. **101**.4–9 *qú-tu-ú*. **102**.4–9 *i-pu-su-ma*. **104**.3 *ú-še-⌜ši-ib⌝-šu*. **104**.4–6 *bi-tim*. **104**.7–9 *bi-ti-im*. **105**.3, 6 *e-zi-ir-*. **105**.1 *e-z[i(?)-ir]-*. **105**.4–9 *ib-bi*. **106**.4–6 *bi-tum*. **106**.2, 5 *ša-me-e*. **107**.7–9 *er-ṣé-ti-im*. **111**.7 *dá-an-na-am*. **111**.7–9 *ka-ka-am*. **112**.9 *ka-ši-id-«id»*. **115**.4–6 ḪÉ.GAL-*li-im*. **115**.7–9 ḪÉ.GAL. **115**.7–9 *ri-ša-ti-im*. **116**.7–9 *da-ru-ti-im*. **120**.1 *le-mu-u[t]-tim*. **125**.4, 6 *i-pa-ra-su-šum*. **125**.5 *i-*PI*-ra-su-šum*. **130**.4, 5, 7–9 *aš-šum*. **130**.6 *aš-šu-um*. **131**.7–9 *ša-na-am*. **134**.4–9 *ra-ba-nu-um*.

135) *lu a-wi-lu-tum šum-ša*
136) *a-wi-lam ša-tu*
137) ^{d}*en-líl ša-pí-iṭ i-li*
138) *šar-ru-sú li-ma-ṭì*
139) *i-na ka-al šar-ri*
140) ^{d}EN.ZU *a-ḫu-um ra-bu-um*
141) *i-na i-li aḫ-ḫi-šu*
142) *er-re-ta-am ra-bi-ta-am*
143) *li-ru-ur-šu*
144) ^{d}*nè-eri*$_{11}$*-gal be-el ka-ak-ki-im*
145) *ka-ak-ka-šu li-iš-bi-ir-ma*
146) *mu-ti a-ii*(PI)*-im-ḫu-ur*
147) *é-a šar ši-im-tim*
148) *ši-im-ta-šu li-le-mi-in*
149) ^{d}*a-a ka-la-tum*
150) *be-el-tum ra-bi-tum*
151) *lu mu-le-mi-na-at a-wa-ti-šu*
152) *i-na ma-ḫa-ar* ^{d}UTU *a-na da-ri-a-tim*
153) ^{d}*bu-né-né šu-ka-al* ^{d}UTU *ra-bu-um*
154) *na-pí-iš-ta-šu li-ki-is*
155) *ze-ra-šu li-il-qú-ut-ma*
156) *pí-ri-iḫ-šu ù šum-šu*
157) *i-na ma-ḫa-ar* ^{d}UTU *a-ii*(PI)*-ta-la-ak*

137–157) may the god Enlil, judge of the gods, make his kingship smaller than that of any other king. May the god Sîn, the elder brother among the gods, his brothers, inflict on him a great curse. May the god Nergal, the lord of the weapon, smash his weapon in order that he not confront warriors. May the god Ea, king of destiny, assign him an evil destiny (and) may the goddess bride Aia, the great lady, put in a bad word about him before the god Šamaš forever. May the god Bunene, the great vizier of the god Šamaš, cut his throat; may he take away his progeny and may his offspring and descendants not walk before the god Šamaš.

3

The impression of a seal of Inibšina, daughter of Iaḫdun-Līm and *ugbabtum* priestess of the god Adad (see Batto, Women at Mari pp. 59–60 and 86), is found on a tablet excavated at Mari.

COMMENTARY

The impression is on ARMT 21 no. 104 from room 160 of the palace. The inscription was not collated.

BIBLIOGRAPHY

1983 Durand, ARMT 21 p. 569 seal 5 (transliteration)

TEXT

1) *i-ni-ib-[ši-na]*
2) [D]AM ^{d}[IŠKUR]
3) [DU]MU.MUNUS *ia-aḫ-du-[li-im]*

1) Inib[šina],
2) [w]ife of the god [Adad],
3) [dau]ghter of Iaḫdun-[Līm].

136.3 *a-wi-lum*. **138**.2, 4–9 *ša-ru-sú*. **144**.4–9 *ka-ki-im*. **145**.7–9 *ka-ka-šu*. **147**.4–6 *ši-im-ti-im*. **149**.7–9 *ka-la-tu*. **150**.7–9 *be-el-tu*. **150**.4–9 *ra-bi-tu*. **152**.7–9 *da-ri-tim*. **153**.9 *šu-ka-«lu»-al*. **154**.2 *na-pí-iš-tá-šu*. **155**.9 *li-il-qú-ut-⟨ma⟩*. **157**.2 *a-ii*(PI)*-i-ta-la-ak*.

4

A different seal of Inibšina is found on a tablet excavated at Mari.

COMMENTARY

The impression is on ARMT 11 no. 191, which is now in the Deir ez-Zor Museum. The piece came from room 111 of the palace and was not collated.

BIBLIOGRAPHY

1963 Burke, ARMT 11 no. 191 (transliteration)

TEXT

1) [*i-ni*]-*ib*-[*ši-na*]	1) [In]ib[šina],
2) DUMU.MUNUS *ia-aḫ-du*-[*li-im*]	2) daughter of Iaḫdun-[Līm],
3) GÉME [d][IŠKUR]	3) female servant of the god [Adad].

5

The seal impression of Iamama, daughter of Iaḫdun-Līm and wife of the diviner Asqudum, is known from a sealing from Mari.

COMMENTARY

The impression is found on the tablet TH 82.218 in the Deir ez-Zor Museum. It was found in Sounding A, room xv. The inscription was not collated.

BIBLIOGRAPHY

1985 Charpin, MARI 4 p. 456 (edition)
1988 Charpin in Young (ed.), Mari at 50 p. 62 (study)

TEXT

1) [f]*ia-ma-ma*	1) Iamama,
2) DUMU.MUNUS *ia-aḫ-du-li-⟨im⟩*	2) daughter of Iaḫdun-Līm,
3) DAM.A.NI *às-qú-di-im*	3) wife of Asqudum.

6

Impressions of a seal of Nagiḫa[...], daughter of Iaḫdun-Līm, are on two bullae found at Acem höyük in Turkey.

COMMENTARY

The impressions are on Ac (Acem höyük) i 1047 and i 1377, now in the Archaeological Museum in Ankara. They were collated through the courtesy of V. Donbaz.

BIBLIOGRAPHY

1980 Özgüç in Porada (ed.), Ancient Art in Seals (New Jersey) p. 65 (study), p. 81 fig. III–3a,b (study), and p. [89] fig. III–3a,b (photo)
1985 Veenhof, MARI 4 p. 194 n. 13 (study)
1986 Charpin and Durand, RA 80 p. 152 and n. 56 (edition, study)
1987 Collon, First Impressions no. 186 (photo, study)
1988 Charpin in Young (ed.), Mari at 50 p. 72 n. 65 (study)

TEXT

1) [*n*]*a-gi-ḫa-*[...]
2) DUMU.MUNUS *ia-aḫ-du-li-*[*im*]
3) LUGAL *ma-ri.*[KI]
4) *ù ma-at* DUMU *si-im-*[*a-al*]

1) [N]agiḫa[...]
2) daughter of Iaḫdun-Lī[m],
3–4) king of Mari and the land of the Simʾ[ālites].

2001

Impressions of a seal of Ḫamatil, servant of Iaḫdun-Līm, who served as chief steward during the reigns of Iaḫdun-Līm and Sūmû-Iamam are known from a sealing from Mari.

COMMENTARY

The impressions are found on M 11801 from room 108 of the palace. They were not collated.

We read the name here as Ḫamatil, following D. Charpin.

BIBLIOGRAPHY

1972 Sasson, RA 66 p. 179 (study)
1984 Charpin, MARI 3 p. 257 (copy, transliteration)

TEXT

1) [ḫ]a-ma-til DUB.SAR
2) [ì]R *ia-aḫ-du-li-im*

1) [Ḫ]amatil, scribe,
2) [se]rvant of Iaḫdun-Līm.

2002

The impression of a seal of Ilī-Epuḫ, servant of Iaḫdun-Līm, is found on a clay sealing from Mari.

COMMENTARY

The impression is on ME 199, a clay sealing 4.5 × 3.3 cm. The inscription was collated from the published photo.

BIBLIOGRAPHY

1959 Parrot, Documents p. 160 (study); Dossin p. 252 (edition) and pl. XLVII no. 199 (photo)

TEXT

1) *ì-lí-e-*⌊*pu-u*⌋*ḫ*
2) IR₁₁ *ia-a*[*ḫ-du-li-im*]

1) Ilī-E[p]uḫ,
2) servant of Ia[ḫdun-Līm].

2003

The impression of a seal of a servant of Iaḫdun-Līm whose name is not entirely preserved is found on a number of sealings from Mari.

COMMENTARY

The impression is on ME 4, 166, and 201. It was previously edited in MAM 2/3 as cylinder III of Zimrī-Līm. D. Charpin points out that collation of the published photo indicates that it is a seal of a servant of Iaḫdun-Līm.

BIBLIOGRAPHY

1959 Parrot, Documents p. 166 Cylindre III de Zimrilim (study); Dossin p. 253 Cylindre III de Zimrilim (edition) and pl. 46 nos. 201 and 166 (photo)
1985 Beyer, MARI 4 p. 378 (study)
1988 Charpin in Young (ed.), Mari at 50 p. 70 (transliteration, study)

TEXT

1) [...]-*ma*-DINGIR
2) [ì]R *ia-aḫ-du-un-l*[*i-im*]

1) [...]ma-Il,
2) [ser]vant of Iaḫdun-L[īm].

2004

Impressions of a seal of Baninum, servant of Iaḫdun-Līm, are found on a tablet envelope excavated at Mari.

COMMENTARY

The impressions are on M 13044 from room 160 of the palace. They were collated from the published photo.

The editors of this seal point out that the seal originally contained only lines 1–3. Lines 4–6 were added later. Mulḫân found in line 2 is attested as a geographical name and probably lay in the southern domains of Mari. Charpin and Durand suggest that Baninum may have been in charge of this city.

BIBLIOGRAPHY

1985 Charpin and Durand, MARI 4 pp. 323–24 (photo, copy, edition)

TEXT

1) [*b*]*a-ni-nu-um*
2) [...] *mu-ul-ḫa*-[*an*]
3) [ì]R *ia-aḫ-du-un-li*-[*im*]
4) *mu-te-er pi-ri-iḫ*
5) *ia-aḫ-du-un-li-im*
6) [*a-n*]*a iš-ri-te*$_9$-[*šu*]

1) [B]aninum,
2) [... of (the city of)] Mulhâ[n],
3) [se]rvant of Iaḫdun-Lī[m].
4–6) *restorer of the descendants* of Iaḫdun-Līm.

Sūmû-Iamam

E4.6.9

Iaḫdun-Līm was succeeded on the throne of Mari by Sūmû-Iamam, whose origins are obscure; he may have been a usurper. Only two year names are known for this ruler and none of his inscriptions are extant.

Šamšī-Adad

E4.6.10

Sometime during the last half of his reign, Šamšī-Adad, king of Ekallātum and Aššur, captured the city of Mari and ended the short rule of Sūmû-Iamam. A number of inscriptions of this ruler are known from copies found at Mari which have recently been edited by D. Charpin. All the Šamšī-Adad inscriptions are edited in RIMA 1.

Iasmaḫ-Addu

E4.6.11

Šamšī-Adad installed his son Iasmaḫ-Addu at Mari to control the area of Mari and lands to the north of it.

1

A statue found at Mari was dedicated to the god Šamaš by Iasmaḫ-Addu.

COMMENTARY

The statue is Aleppo Museum no. M 7917. It was found on the surface of the mound at Mari and taken to Aleppo by Lieutenant Cabane, hence the frequent designation of this piece as Statue Cabane. It is a headless statue of greyish limestone that was collated from the published photo. According to Moortgat-Correns the inscription was carved on a statue of an earlier ruler of Mari.

BIBLIOGRAPHY

1934 Thureau-Dangin, RA 31 p. 144 (photo, edition)

1939 Thureau-Dangin, Dussaud Festschrift pp. 157–59 (photo, edition)

1961 Borger, EAK 1 p. 18 and n. 1 (study)

1972 Grayson, ARI 1 §§159–62 (translation)

1986 Moortgat-Correns in M. Kelly-Buccellati (ed.), Studies Porada pp. 183–88 and pls. 36–37 (photo, study)

TEXT

1) *[ia-á]s-ma-aḫ-*^{d}IŠKUR	1–3) [Ia]smaḫ-Addu, ap[point]ee of the god Enlil, [so]n of Šamšī-Adad,
2) *š[a-k]i-in* ^{d}*en-líl*	
3) [DUM]U ^{d}UTU-*ši*-^{d}IŠKUR	
4) *a-na* ^{d}UTU	4–5) for the god Šamaš, his lord,
5) *be-lí-šu*	
6) [...]	6–10) ...
7) [...]	
8) *[m]u*(?)*-te-*[...]	
9) [...]	
10) [...] *ni* [...]	
11) *[i]-na q[é]-r[e-e]b*	11–15) [had] (this statue) fashioned in [the city of] M[ari, wh]ich he l[ov]es, and [de]dicated (it).
12) *[a-al] m[a-ri.*K]I	
13) *[š]a i-r[a-a]m-mu*	
14) *[ú-še]-p[í-i]š-ma*	

15) [*ú-š*]*e-li*
16) (blank)
17) *ša šu-mi*
18) *ša-aṭ-ra-am*
19) *ú-ša-sà-ku-ma*
20) *šum-šu ú-ša-á*[*š-ṭa*]*-ru*
21) [^{d}]UTU *be-lí*
22) [SU]ḪUŠ-[*š*]*u*
23) [*li*]*-sú-uḫ*
24) [*ù*] Š[E.NUMU]N-*šu*
25) [*l*]*i-il-qú-ut*

16) (blank)
17–20) He who removes my inscribed name and has his (own) name ins[cri]bed,

21–25) [may the god Šamaš], my lord, [r]ip out [h]is [fo]undation [and] destroy his progeny.

2

A clay tablet from Mari has a copy of an inscription of Iasmaḫ-Addu that deals with the votive offering of a pair of silver bags to the goddess Eštar, resident of the temple Ešabanna.

COMMENTARY

The inscription is found on M 8332, a clay tablet measuring 6.5×4.4×2.8 cm, from room 115 of Zimrī-Līm's palace. The tablet is not completely preserved, but since the inscription appears to have been written three times on the tablet, an almost complete text can be determined. The inscription was collated from the published photo.

A conflated text of the three copies is given here. The three separate copies are given in the scores.

BIBLIOGRAPHY

1984 Charpin, MARI 3 pp. 53–55 no. 5 (edition), p. 71 (photo), and p. 75 (copy)

TEXT

1) *a-na eš*$_{4}$*-tár be-le-et er-ṣ*[*é-tim*]
2) *wa-ši-ba-at é-šà-*[*b*]*a-an-na* X
3) *še-me-et ik-ri-bi be-*[*el-ti-šu*]
4) ^{m}*ia-ás-ma-aḫ-*^{d}[IŠKUR]
5) DUMU ^{d}UTU-*ši*-^{d}IŠKUR
6) *ik-ru-ub-ši-im*
7) 2 *na-da-tim* KÙ.B[ABBAR]
8) *ša i-na* DUMU.MEŠ *um-me-nu-tim*
9) *šu-uk-lu-*[*lu*]
10) *ik-ru-u*[*b*]

1–3) To the goddess Eštar, lady of the underw[orld], resident of Ešabanna, who listens to prayers, [his] la[dy],
4–6) Iasmaḫ-[Addu], son of Šamšī-Adad, made a vow to her.

7–10) He dedicat[ed] two si[lver] bags that were perfectly (fashioned) by the artisans.

3

The beginning of a copy of an inscription of Iasmaḫ-Addu dedicated to the god Mullil of Terqa is found on a tablet excavated at Mari.

COMMENTARY

The inscription is on M 11906, a clay tablet 5.1×4×2.1 cm from room 108 of Zimrī-Līm's palace. It was collated from the published photo.

The name Mullil, which appears in this text, is the Emesal form of Enlil, chief god of the Sumerian pantheon. Charpin indicates that in the 'Zimrī-Līm Epic' Dagān of Terqa is identified with Nunamnir, another name of Enlil. Hence, we should see in this text a reference to Mullil as a form of the god Dagān of Terqa.

BIBLIOGRAPHY

1982 Talon, AIPHOS 26 p. 115 (edition)
1984 Charpin, MARI 3 pp. 55–56 no. 6 (edition), p. 71 (photo), and p. 76 (copy)
1985 Charpin, RA 79 p. 91 (study)

TEXT

1) *a-na m*[*u-u*]*l-li-*[*il še-mi*]
2) *ik-ri-bi wa-ši-*[*i*]*b*
3) *tu-ut-tu-ul*.KI
4) ^{m}*ia-ás-ma-aḫ-*^{d}IŠKUR
5) [DU]MU ^{d}UTU-*ši*-^{d}IŠKUR
6) [*i-n*]*u-ma i-na a-aḫ* I$_{7}$.BURANUN.NA
7) [...] x x
8) [...]
9) [...]
10) [...]
Lacuna

1–3) To (the god) M[u]lli[l, the one who listens to] prayers, who dwells in Tuttul,

4–10) Iasmaḫ-Addu, [s]on of Šamšī-Adad, [wh]en on the banks of the Euphrates ...
Lacuna

4

A clay tablet from Mari has a copy of an inscription in which Izamu, female servant of Iasmaḫ-Addu, dedicates a statue to the goddess Eštar.

COMMENTARY

The copy of the inscription is found on A 2273 (Paris), a clay tablet 7.3×5×2.5 cm. It was collated from the published photo.

Izamu is known elsewhere to have been a secondary wife of Iasmaḫ-Addu.

BIBLIOGRAPHY

1984 Charpin, MARI 3 pp. 56–57 no. 7 (edition), p. 71 (photo), and p. 77 (copy)
1985 Durand, MARI 4 p. 412 no. 4 (study)

TEXT

Lacuna
1′) [...]-*et* [...]
2′) [*še*]-*me-et ik-r*[*i-bi*]
3′) *be-el-ti-š*[*a*]
4′) [^{f}]*i-za-mu* SUḪU[R.LÁ]
5′) [*m*]*u-da-am-m*[*i-qa-at*]
6′) [*n*]*i*-[*i*]*š* ŠU *be-li*-[*ša*]
7′) [^{m}]*ia-ás-ma-a*[*ḫ*-^{d}IŠKUR]
8′) [*i-nu-m*]*a* eš$_4$-*tár be-el*-[*ti*]
9′) [*i*]*k-r*[*i-bi*]-*ia*
10′) x x x [...]
11′) *ta-ás-l*[*i-ti*]
12′) [...]
13′) [A]LAM-*ša*
14′) [*ak*]-*ru-ub-š*[*i-i*]*m*
15′) [A]LAM *ša i-n*[*a*]
16′) [DUMU].MEŠ *um-me-nu-t*[*i*]*m*
17′) [*šu*]-*uk-lu-lu*
18′) [*ak*]-*ru-ub-ši-i*[*m* x]
Lacuna

Lacuna
1′–3′) [To the goddess Eštar], who ..., who [l]istens to pra[yers], he[r] lady,

4′–7′) Izamu, the *kez*[*ertum*] priestess, makes the prayer of her lord Iasma[ḫ-Addu] find favour,

8′–12′) [wh]en the goddess Eštar, [my] lady, [heard] my pra[ye]rs [and granted my] requ[est],

13′–14′) I [de]dicated her [s]tatue to h[e]r.

15′–18′) I [de]dicated to he[r a s]tatue that was [pe]rfectly (fashioned) by the crafts[men].
Lacuna

2001

A clay tablet from Mari has a copy of an inscription of a servant of Iasmaḫ-Addu, probably the governor of Terqa. Unfortunately neither the object dedicated on behalf of Iasmaḫ-Addu nor the deity to whom it was dedicated is preserved on the tablet.

COMMENTARY

The tablet is M 8455 from room 115 of the palace of Zimrī-Līm at Mari. It measures 5.8×6×3 cm. The inscription was collated from the published photo.

BIBLIOGRAPHY

1984 Charpin, MARI 3 pp. 58–60 no. 8 (edition), p. 71 (photo), and p. 77 (copy)

TEXT

Lacuna
1′) [*ša-ki-i*]*n te-er-q*[*a*.KI]
2′) [*a-al tu-u*]*k-la-t*[*i*]
3′) [*b*]*e-li-šu* [*i*]*a-ás-ma-aḫ-*^{d}IŠKUR
4′) DUMU ^{d}UTU-*ši*-^{d}IŠKUR
5′) LUGAL BÀD-*ia-ás-ma-aḫ*-^{d}IŠKUR
6′) ÉNSI ^{d}*da-gan ù eš*$_{4}$*-tár*
7′) *a-na ia-ás-ma-aḫ*-^{d}IŠKUR
8′) [*be-l*]*í-šu*
9′) [*i-na a-a*]*ḫ* I$_{7}$.BURANUN.[NA]
10′) [...]-*i a-mu-ri*-x-[...]
11′) [...] x *ma-ri*-[...]
Lacuna

Lacuna
1′–6′) ..., [govern]or of Terq[a, sec]ure [city] of his [l]ord [I]asmaḫ-Addu, son of Šamsī-Adad, lord of Dūr-Iasmaḫ-Addu, governor of the god Dagān and the goddess Eštar,

7′–11′) for Iasmaḫ-Addu, his [lo]rd, [on the ba]nks of the Euphrates ...
Lacuna

2002

A seal impression found on clay sealings from Mari bears the name of Sîn-muballiṭ, servant of Iasmaḫ-Addu.

COMMENTARY

The impression is on ME 218, and on no. 72-132, the latter from room 115 of the palace. They were not collated. Ex. 1 was previously assigned to Sîn-mūdû by G. Dossin.

BIBLIOGRAPHY

1959 Parrot, Documents p. 161 (study)
1984 Charpin, MARI 3 p. 59 n. 46 (study)
1985 Beyer, MARI 4 p. 378 (study)
1988 Charpin in Young (ed.), Mari at 50 p. 65 (edition)

TEXT

1) [*ia-ás*]*-ma-aḫ*-^{d}IŠKUR
2) [*da*]-*núm*
3) [*na*]-*ra-am eš*$_{4}$-*tár*
4) [^{d}]EN.ZU-*mu-ba-li*-[*iṭ*]
5) [ÌR].ZU

1) [Ias]maḫ-Addu,
2) [the mi]ghty,
3) [be]loved of (the goddess) Eštar,
4) Sîn-muballi[ṭ],
5) your [servant].

2003

An impression of a seal of Anāku-ilumma, servant of Iasmaḫ-Addu, is found on two clay sealings from Mari.

COMMENTARY

The impression is on M 6088 and M 7769 from room 115 of the palace. They were not collated.

BIBLIOGRAPHY

1984 Charpin, MARI 3 pp. 58–59 n. 46 (study)
1988 Charpin in Young (ed.), Mari at 50 p. 65 (edition)

TEXT

1) *[ia]-ás-ma-aḫ-*[ᵈIŠKUR]	1) [I]asmaḫ-[Addu],
2) *ša-ki-in* ᵈ*da-[gan]*	2) appointee of the god Da[gān],
3) *a-na-ku-*DINGIR-*ma* Ì[R.ZU]	3) Anāku-ilumma, [your] se[rvant].

2004

The seal impression of Ikšud-appašu, possibly the governor of Šubat-Šamaš, is found on a tablet envelope from Mari.

COMMENTARY

The impression is on ME 251, a tablet envelope found in room 108 of Zimrī-Līm's palace. The inscription was collated from the published photo.

BIBLIOGRAPHY

1958 Boyer, ARMT 8 pp. 4–7 Envelope du no. 1 (study)
1959 Parrot, Documents p. 234 fig. 120 (photo)
1982 Durand, MARI 1 p. 93 no. 1 sceau 3 (transliteration)
1983 Charpin, MARI 2 p. 61 (study) and p. 69 no. 1 sceau 3 (copy)
1984 Charpin, MARI 3 p. 58 (study)

TEXT

1) *ik-šu-ud-ap-pa-šu*	1) Ikšud-appašu,
2) *ša-kí-[i]n ma-tim*	2) governor of the land,
3) ÌR *ia-ás-[ma-a]ḫ-*ᵈIŠKUR	3) servant of Ias[ma]ḫ-Addu.

2005

The impression of a seal of Zakirum, servant of Iasmaḫ-Addu, is also found on the previously mentioned tablet envelope (E4.6.11.2004).

BIBLIOGRAPHY

1959 Parrot, Documents p. 234 fig. 120 (photo)
1982 Durand, MARI 1 p. 93 (transliteration)
1983 Charpin, MARI 2 p. 69 no. 1 sceau 2 (copy)

TEXT

1) *za-ki-rum*
2) [ì]R *ia-ás-ma-aḫ-*[d][IŠKUR]

1) Zakirum,
2) [se]rvant of Iasmaḫ-[Addu].

2006

The impression of a seal of Kirbāia, servant of Iasmaḫ-Addu, is found on a clay sealing excavated at Mari.

COMMENTARY

The sealing is on ME 231. Dossin gave a reading for the first line of this seal impression that differs from that which collation by Durand and Charpin provides.

BIBLIOGRAPHY

1959 Parrot, Documents p. 161 ME 231 (study) and pl. 47 ME 231 (photo); Dossin p. 252–53 (edition)
1985 Beyer, MARI 4 p. 378 (study)

TEXT

1) [*k*]*i-ir-ba-ia*
2) [ì]R *ia-ás-ma-aḫ-*[d][IŠKUR]

1) [K]irbāia,
2) [se]rvant of Iasmaḫ-[Addu].

2007

The impression of a seal of a servant of Iasmaḫ-Addu whose name is not fully preserved is found on two clay sealings from Mari.

COMMENTARY

The impression is on ME 55 and 179. They were not collated.

BIBLIOGRAPHY

1959 Parrot, Documents pp. 160–61 ME 55 and 179 (study) and pl. 47 ME 179 (photo); Dossin pp. 252–53 ME 55 and 179 (edition)
1985 Beyer, MARI 4 p. 378 (study)

TEXT

1) ^{d}*en-l*[*íl*-...]
2) ÌR *ia-ás*-[*ma-aḫ*-^{d}IŠKUR]

1) Enl[il-...],
2) servant of Ias[maḫ-Addu].

2008

The impressions of a seal of Iawi-Ilā, servant of Iasmaḫ-Addu, are known from a number of tablets excavated at Tell Leilan, ancient Šubat-Enlil.

COMMENTARY

The impressions are found on the tablets L 85-105, L 85-132, L 85-140, L 85-141, L 85-437, and L 85-438. They were collated by D. Parayre, and are published here through the courtesy of Dr H. Weiss.

Iawi-Ilā could be the same figure who appears in the Mari tablets as a high functionary resident in Upper Mesopotamia.

TEXT

1) *ia-wi*-[DINGIR]
2) DUMU *ma-nu-um-šu-uk*-[*lu-ul*]
3) ÌR *ia-ás-ma-aḫ*-^{d}[IŠKUR]

1) Iawi-[Ilā],
2) son of Mannum-šuk[lul],
3) servant of Iasmaḫ-[Addu].

2009

The impression of the seal of Bini-maraṣ, servant of Iasmaḫ-Addu, is known from a tablet excavated at Mari.

COMMENTARY

The impression is found on ARM 23 no. 290 = M 18400, from room 215 of the palace. The transliteration of this previously unpublished impression is offered through the courtesy of D. Charpin.

TEXT

1) *bi-ni-ma-ra*-[*aṣ*]
2) DUMU *bu-gu*-x-[...]
3) ÌR *ia-ás-ma-aḫ*-[^{d}IŠKUR]

1) Bini-mara[ṣ],
2) son of Bugu-[...],
3) servant of Iasmaḫ-[Addu].

Zimrī-Līm

E4.6.12

After a period of rule by Šamšī-Adad and his son Iasmaḫ-Addu at Mari, Zimrī-Līm, the son of Iaḫdun-Līm, gained control over the city of Mari and ruled there about fifteen years before being defeated by Ḫammu-rāpi of Babylon.

1

A tablet with a copy of a triumphal inscription first published by G. Dossin mentions Iasmaḫ-Addu, and was taken by the first editor to refer to a defeat of the same by Zimrī-Līm. A reinterpretation of the text by D. Charpin and J.-M. Durand suggested instead that it commemorates a victory of Iasmaḫ-Addu and his brother Išme-Dagān. A critique of this latter interpretation by M. Anbar favours the original attribution of the text to Zimrī-Līm, which is followed here. Since the defeat of Iasmaḫ-Addu must have been the event which allowed Zimrī-Līm to seize Mari, this text is edited here as the first inscription of Zimrī-Līm.

COMMENTARY

The inscription is found on tablet 485 from room 108 of Zimrī-Līm's palace at Mari. It is a clay tablet 18.5×7.7×2.2 cm. It was collated from the published photo.

BIBLIOGRAPHY

1971 Dossin, Syria 48 pp. 1–6 (copy, transliteration, study)
1972 Sasson, RA 66 p. 177 (study)
1985 Charpin and Durand, MARI 4 pp. 319–22 (photo, study)
1987 Anbar, BiOr 44 p. 182 (study)

TEXT

Lacuna
1′) [*d*]*a*-[*aw-da-a-am*]
2′) [*ša*] *iš-m*[*e*-^{d}*da-gan*]
3′) [LUG]AL É.[GAL-*la-tim*]
4′) [*i-na kur-d*]*a*.[KI *i-du-ku*]
5′) [...]
6′) [...] x [...]
7′) [... *kur*]-*da*.KI

Lacuna
1′–11′) [(Zimrī-Līm) d]e[feated] Išm[e-Dagān, kin]g of E[kallātum, at the city of Kurd]ā. [... *From* the city of Kur]dā [by the p]aths of Mount Saggar [with a f]orce of his own troops [and x] hundred Ḫaneans (Zimrī-Līm) wen[t, and de]feated ...

8′) *[i-na a]l-ka-⟨ka⟩-ti* KUR-*i* ^{d}*ságar*
9′) *[it-ti um]-ma-a-at* AGA.ÚS *ra-ma-ni-šu*
10′) *[ù* x] *me-tim ḫa-na il-li-i-i[k-ma]*
11′) *[da-a]w-da-a-am i-du-u[k]*
12′) *[ù b]u-ul-šu ú-te-ra-a[m]*
13′) [x *me]-tim da-aw-da-a-am [i-du-uk]*
14′) [x *l]i-mi* ÁB.ḪI.A 30 *li-[mi* UDU.ḪI.A]
15′) *[i-na* K]Á É.GAL-*la-tim*.KI-*[ma]*
16′) [LÚ.M]EŠ *su-ḫu-ú*.KI *ú-te-[lu-ú]*
17′) [x *l]i-im* 2 *me-tim* 1 *šu-ši*
18′) *[da]-⌜aw⌝-da-a-am*
19′) *[ša] ia-ás-maḫ*-^{d}IŠ[KUR]
20′) *[i-na] ti-iz-ra-aḫ*.KI *i-du-[uk]*
21′) [x *m]e-tim na-ak-rum ša* SA[G]
22′) [LUG]AL KÁ.DINGIR.RA.[KI]
23′) *[a-n]a* KÁ.DINGIR.RA.KI *i-[tu-úr]*
24′) *[i-na] ta-ia-ar-ti-[šu-nu]*
25′) *[a-di* ...].KI *iḫ-ši-[i-ma]*
26′) *[im-ḫ]u-ur-šu-nu-ti-[ma]*
27′) [x *me-tim] ṣa-ba-am i-d[u-uk]*
28′) [...] *ti-il-mu-u[n]*
Lacuna

12′–16′) He [also] brought back his [h]erds. [He defe]ated [x hun]dred (troops). The Suḫeans brou[ght x th]ousand cows and 30 thou[sand sheep even] to the [ga]te of Ekallātum.

17′–20′) [(Zimrī-Līm) d]efeate[d x th]ousand, two hundred sixty (troops and) Iasmaḫ-A[ddu at] Tizraḫ.

21′–27′) [x] hundred of the enemy, escor[ts of the ki]ng of Babylon, re[turned t]o Babylon. [On their] return, having followed them [to ...] in silence, he [con]fronted them [and] he defea[ted x hundred] troops.

28′) Tilmu[n ...]
Lacuna

2

Bricks found in Zimrī-Līm's palace at Mari bear a stamped inscription commemorating construction work of the king. One of the bricks was found in situ in a stairway.

COMMENTARY

The excavation numbers of the bricks are not known. The inscription was collated from the published photo.

BIBLIOGRAPHY

1936 Thureau-Dangin, RA 33 pp. 169–71 (photo, edition)
1938 Dossin, Syria 19 pl. XVI (photo)
1971 Sollberger and Kupper, IRSA IVF7a (translation)

TEXT

1) *zi-im-ri-li-im*
2) LUGAL KALA.GA
3) *mu-še-pí-iš*
4) *ši-ip-ri-im*
5) *ša i-lí*

1) Zimrī-Līm,
2) mighty king,
3–5) who has carried out the work for the gods.

3

The construction of an ice storage house in Terqa by Zimrī-Līm is commemorated in an inscription known from three clay tablet fragments from Terqa.

CATALOGUE

Ex.	Museum number	Excavation number	Provenance	Dimensions (cm)	Lines preserved	cpn
1	–	Found by Herzfeld	Terqa	6.3×6.5×3.2	1–6, 9–14	n
2	AO 20161	Purchased by M. Hamelin in Syria	Terqa	5.8×7.2×2.9	2–13	c
3	DeZ 1857	TQ4-T1 Level 4, Locus 9 in Islamic filling	Terqa, SG 10	–	3–7	c

BIBLIOGRAPHY

1914 Herzfeld, RA 11 pp. 134–37 no. 12 (ex. 1, photo, copy, edition)
1936 Thureau-Dangin, RA 33 pp. 53 and 169 (ex. 1, study)
1947 Nougayrol, CRAIB pp. 265–72 (ex. 2, copy, edition)
1971 Sollberger and Kupper, IRSA IVF7b (exs. 1–2, translation)
1978–79 Rouault, SMS 2/7 p. 2 no. 1 (ex. 3, copy, edition) and pl. I no. 1 (photo)

TEXT

1) ^{m}*zi-i*[*m-ri-li-im*]
2) DUMU *ia-aḫ-d*[*u-un-li-im*]
3) LUGAL *ma-ri.*[KI *tu-ut-tu-ul.*KI]
4) *ù ma-a-at* [*ḫa-na.*KI]
5) *e-pí-iš* É *šu-*[*ri-pí-im*]
6) *ša iš-tu pa-*⸢*na*⸣ L[UGAL]
7) *i-na a-aḫ* ⸢I$_7$⸣.[BURANUN.KI]
8) *ma-am-ma-an l*[*a*(*) *i-pu-šu*]
9) *šu-ri-pa-am ša* ⸢*ša*⸣ x x [...]
10) *úš-te-bi-ir* [...]
11) *i-na a-aḫ* I$_7$.BURANU[N.KI]
12) É *šu-ri-p*[*í-im*]
13) *i-na ter-q*[*a.*KI ...]
14) *na-ra-ma-at* ⸢^{d}⸣[*da-gan* ...]

1) Zi[mrī-Līm]
2) son of Iaḫd[un-Līm],
3) king of Mari, [Tuttul],
4) and the land [of Ḫana],
5–8) builder of an i[ce]-house, (something) which formerly n[o] k[ing had built] on the bank of the [Euphrates],

9–10) had ice of ... brought over

11–14) and [had] an ic[e]-house [built] on the bank of the Euphrat[es], in Terq[a, the *city*] beloved of the god [Dagān].

4

Impressions of three different royal seals of Zimrī-Līm are known. The longest of these has an eight-line inscription.

8.2 has *š*[*u*(?) ...], likely an error for *la*.

COMMENTARY

The impression is found on the following sealings: ME 3, 16a, 16b, 20–21, 27, 29, 31, 35–36, 40, and 48–49. The same impression was also found on Tell al Rimah 4332, probably fragments of an envelope of a letter of Zimrī-Līm sent to Ḫadnû-rāpi, ruler of Qaṭṭarā.

BIBLIOGRAPHY

1959 Parrot, Documents pp. 162–64 Cylindre I de Zimri-Lim (study) and pl. 46 ME 3, 16a (photo); Dossin p. 253 Cylindre I de Zimri-Lim (edition)

1971 Sollberger and Kupper, IRSA IVF7c (translation)

1976 Hawkins in Dalley, OBTR p. 250 and pl. 107 no. 5 (ex. 14, copy, edition); Dalley p. 1 (ex. 14, study)

1985 Beyer, MARI 4 p. 378 (exs. 1–13, study)

TEXT

1) *zi-im-ri-li-im*	1) Zimrī-Līm,
2) *ša-ki-in* ^{d}*da-gan*	2) appointee of the god Dagān,
3) *na-ra-am* ^{d}*en-líl*	3) beloved of the god Enlil,
4) *ga-mi-ir*	4–5) who controls the banks of the Euphrates,
5) *aḫ* I₇.BURANUN.KI	
6) LUGAL *ma-ri*.KI	6–7) king of Mari and the land of Ḫana,
7) *ù ma-a-at ḫa-na*	
8) DUMU *ia-aḫ-du-un-li-im*	8) son of Iaḫdun-Līm.

5

Impressions of a six-line royal seal of Zimrī-Līm are also known from clay sealings and tablets excavated at Mari.

COMMENTARY

The impressions are found on the following sealings: ME 53–54, 180, and 238; and the following tablets: ARM(T) 9 nos. 33, 36, 46, 186–187, 191, and 297 from room 5 of the palace; ARMT 21 nos. 93, 237 from room 160 of the palace; ARMT 23 no. 226 from room 108 of the palace; ARMT 24 nos. 6, 94, 109, 124, 131, 138, 154–155, 166, 268, 280, 299, and 306 from room Y or Z of the palace.

BIBLIOGRAPHY

1959 Parrot, Documents pp. 165–66 Cylindre II de Zimri-Lim (study) and pl. 46 ME 180 (photo); Dossin p. 253 Cylindre II de Zimri-Lim (edition)

1960 Birot, ARM(T) 9 nos. 33, 36, 46, 186–87, 191, and 297 (copy, edition)

1971 Sollberger and Kupper, IRSA IVF7d (translation)

1983 Durand, ARMT 21 p. 569 seal 16 (study)

1984 Joannès in Bardet, et al., ARMT 23 p. 200 no. 226 (study)

1985 Talon, ARMT 24 p. 209 seal 1 (study)

1985 Beyer, MARI 4 p. 378 (study)

TEXT

1)	*zi-im-ri-li-im*	1) Zimrī-Līm,
2)	*ša-ki-in* ^{d}*da-gan*	2) appointee of the god Dagān,
3)	*na-ra-am* ^{d}*en-líl*	3) beloved of the god Enlil,
4)	LUGAL *ma-ri*.KI	4–5) king of Mari and the land of Ḫana,
5)	*ù ma-at ḫa-na*	
6)	DUMU *ia-aḫ-du-un-li-im*	6) son of Iaḫdun-Līm.

6

A seal impression of a third cylinder of Zimrī-Līm is found on the envelope of a letter addressed by Zimrī-Līm to Tiš-Ulme, king of Mardaman.

COMMENTARY

The impression is on tablet no. 72–15 from room 115 of the palace. It was collated from the published photo.

BIBLIOGRAPHY

1985 Charpin and Durand, MARI 4 pp. 336–38 (photo, copy, edition)
1988 Charpin in Young (ed.), Mari at 50 p. 72 (edition)

TEXT

1)	*zi-im-ri-li-i*[*m*]	1) Zimrī-Lī[m],
2)	[*n*]*a-ra-am* ^{d}*da-gan*	2) [b]eloved of the god Dagān,
3)	[*š*]*a-ki-in* ^{d}[...]	3) [ap]pointee of the god [...]
4)	LUGAL *ma-ri*.[KI]	4–5) king of Mari and the land of Ḫ[ana],
5)	*ù ma-at ḫ*[*a-na*]	
6)	DUMU *ḫa-at-ni-*^{d}[IŠKUR]	6) son of Ḫadnī-[Addu].

7

The seal impression of Šibtu, the chief wife of Zimrī-Līm, daughter of Iarīm-Līm I, king of Iamḫad, is found on five sealings from Mari.

COMMENTARY

The impression is on ME 69, 181, 207, 216, and M 18025, the last from room 133 of the palace. ME 181 and 69 were collated from the published photos.

BIBLIOGRAPHY

1959 Parrot, Documents p. 168 (study) and p. 167 fig. 103 ME 181 (photo); Dossin p. 254 (edition) and pl. XLVI ME 69 (photo)

1985 Beyer, MARI 4 p. 378 (study)

1988 Charpin in Young (ed.), Mari at 50 p. 73 (edition)

TEXT

1) ^{f}*ši-ib-*[*tu*]	1) Šib[tu],
2) DUMU.MUNUS *ia-ri-im-li-im*	2) daughter of Iarīm-Līm,
3) DAM *zi-im-ri-li-im*	3) wife of Zimrī-Līm.

8

The impression of a seal of Iatarāia, a secondary wife of Zimrī-Līm, is found on a sealing from Mari.

COMMENTARY

The impression is on ME 170, which was previously incorrectly attributed to a female servant of Zimrī-Līm. It was collated by D. Charpin.

BIBLIOGRAPHY

1959 Parrot, Documents pl. XLVIII ME 170 (photo); Dossin p. 255 ME 170 (edition)

1974 Batto, Women at Mari pp. 21 and 23 (study)

1988 Charpin in Young (ed.), Mari at 50 p. 73 (edition)

TEXT

1) ^{f}*ia-ta-ra-i*[*a*]	1) Iatarāi[a],
2) GÉME *zi-im-ri-li-im*	2) female servant of Zimrī-Līm.

2001

Impressions of a large number of servants of Zimrī-Līm are known from the Mari documents. Here the seals in which the titulary of the king appears are edited first. Five seal legends give Zimrī-Līm the title 'mighty king'. The first of these is the seal of Abum-Il.

COMMENTARY

The impression is found on ME 272. It was collated from the published photos.

BIBLIOGRAPHY

1959 Parrot, Documents p. 242 Cylindre de Abu-um-il (study), p. 241 fig. 129 ME 272 (photo), and pl. LIV ME 272 (photo)
1988 Charpin in Young (ed.), Mari at 50 p. 65 (study)

TEXT

1) [z]*i-im-ri-l*[*i-im*]	1) [Z]imrī-L[īm],
2) LUGAL KALA.[GA]	2) might[y] king,
3) [*a-b*]*u-um*-DINGIR Ì[R.ZU]	3) [Ab]um-Il [your] se[rvant].

2002

Zimrī-Līm is called 'mighty king' in the seal of Sammētar. This personage was a high official at the palace of Mari, and later governor of the land of Suḫi.

COMMENTARY

The impression is found on A 3583 (Paris) from room 108 of the palace. It was not collated.

BIBLIOGRAPHY

1984 Joannès in Bardet, et al., ARMT 23 p. 201 no. 227 (transliteration)
1988 Charpin in Young (ed.), Mari at 50 p. 65 (study)

TEXT

1) *zi-im-ri-li-im*	1) Zimrī-Līm,
2) LUGAL KALA.GA	2) mighty king,
3) *sa-am-mé-tar*	3) Sammētar,
4) DUMU *la-i-im*	4) son of Laʾum.

2003

Zimrī-Līm appears as 'mighty king' in the impression of Šunuḫra-Ḫālu, personal secretary of the king.

COMMENTARY

The impression is found on ME 165 and 220. They were collated from the published photographs. This impression was previously edited as cylinder 4 of Zimrī-Līm, but collation of it by Durand indicates that it is in fact an impression of Šunuḫra-Ḫālu.

BIBLIOGRAPHY

1959 Parrot, Documents pp. 166–67 Cylindre IV de Zimri-Lim ME 165 and 220 (study), p. 167 fig. 103a ME 220 (photo), and pl. XLVI ME 165 and ME 220b (photo)
1985 Beyer, MARI 4 p. 378 (study)
1988 Charpin in Young (ed.), Mari at 50 p. 66 (edition)

TEXT

1) *zi-im-ri-li-im* — 1) Zimrī-Līm,
2) LUGAL KALA.GA — 2) mighty king,
3) *šu-nu-uḫ-ra-ḫa-lu* — 3) Šunuḫra-Ḫālu.

2004

A two-line version of the seal of Šunuḫra-Ḫālu is also known.

COMMENTARY

The impression is found on ME 18, which was collated from the published photo.

BIBLIOGRAPHY

1959 Parrot, Documents p. 194 Cylindre de Šunuḫ-raḫalu (study) and pl. XLIX ME 18 (photo); Dossin p. 256 Šunuḫ-raḫalu (edition)
1985 Beyer, MARI 4 p. 380 (study)
1988 Charpin in Young (ed.), Mari at 50 p. 66 (edition)

TEXT

1) [*šu-n*]*u-uḫ-ra-ḫa-*[*lu*] — 1) [Šun]uḫra-Ḫā[lu],
2) [ì]R *zi-im-ri-li-i*[*m*] — 2) [se]rvant of Zimrī-Lī[m].

2005

Zimrī-Līm appears as 'mighty king' in a seal impression of Šūbnalû, an official of the palace at Mari.

COMMENTARY

The impression is found on ARMT 21 no. 349 from room 134 of the palace, ARMT 24 no. 206 from room Y or Z of the palace, and M 13185 from room 79 of the palace.

BIBLIOGRAPHY

1983 Durand, ARMT 21 p. 569 seal 12 (transliteration)
1985 Talon, ARMT 24 p. 209 seal 5 (transliteration)
1988 Charpin in Young (ed.), Mari at 50 p. 66 (edition)

TEXT

1) *zi-im-ri-l*[*i-im*]	1) Zimrī-L[īm],
2) LUGAL *da*-[*núm*]	2) mi[ghty] king,
3) *šu-ub-na-lu-ú* [ÌR.ZU]	3) Šūbnalû, [your servant].

2006

A two-line version of the seal legend of Šūbnalû is also known.

COMMENTARY

The impression is found on ME 290 from Atelier 217 at Mari, which was collated from the published photo.

BIBLIOGRAPHY

1959 Parrot, Documents pp. 211–12 Cylindre d'un serviteur de Zimri-Lim (study) and p. 212 fig. 114 (photo); Dossin p. 257 ME 290 (edition)
1985 Beyer, MARI 4 p. 381 (study)
1988 Charpin in Young (ed.), Mari at 50 p. 66 (edition)

TEXT

1) [*šu*]-*ub-na-lu-ú*	1) [Š]ūbnalû,
2) [ÌR] *zi-im-ri-li-im*	2) [servant] of Zimrī-Līm.

2007

The title 'mighty king' also appears in a broken seal impression which probably is to be attributed to a servant of Zimrī-Līm.

COMMENTARY

The impression is found on ARMT 21 no. 181 from room 160 of the palace. It was not collated.

BIBLIOGRAPHY

1983 Durand, ARMT 21 p. 569 seal 19 (transliteration)

TEXT

1) [*zi-im-ri-li-im*]	1) [Zimrī-Līm]
2) [LUGAL] KALA.[GA]	2) might[y king],
3) [...] x ^{d}*nu-muš-*[*da*]	3) [...]-Numuš[da],
4) [DUMU ...]-*ri*-[...]	4) [son of ...]ri[...].

2008

In three seal legends Zimrī-Līm appears with the title 'beloved of the god Dagān'. The first of these is the seal of Puzur-Šamaš.

COMMENTARY

The impression is found on the tablet S 110, no. 259, from room 110 of the palace of Zimrī-Līm at Mari. It was not collated.

BIBLIOGRAPHY

1956–57 Bottéro, ARM(T) 7 no. 259 (copy, edition)
1960 Birot, ARMT 9 p. 251 n. 5 (study)
1983 Charpin and Durand, MARI 2 p. 96 no. 259 (transliteration) and p. 114 no. 259 (copy)
1988 Charpin in Young (ed.), Mari at 50 p. 66 (study)

TEXT

1) *zi-im-ri-li-*[*im*]	1) Zimrī-Lī[m],
2) *na-ra-am-*^{d}*da-*[*gan*]	2) beloved of the god Da[gān],
3) *puzur*$_4$-^{d}UT[U]	3) Puzur-Šam[aš],
4) [DUMU] x-*i-ia*-[x]	4) [son] of ...

2009

Zimrī-Līm appears with the title 'beloved of the god Dagān' in the seal legend of Ripʾi-Dagān, a high official.

COMMENTARY

The impression appears on the tablet 72.132 from room 115 of the palace. It was not collated.

BIBLIOGRAPHY

1988 Charpin in Young (ed.), Mari at 50 p. 66 (study)

TEXT

1) [*z*]*i-i*[*m-ri-li-im*]	1) [Z]i[mrī-Līm],
2) [*na*]*-ra-*[*am* ^{d}*dagan*]	2) [be]lov[ed of the god Dagān],
3) [*ri*]*-ip-i-*^{d}[*da-gan*]	3) [R]ipʾi-[Dagān],
4) [DU]MU *na-lu-*[...]	4) [s]on of Nalu-[...].

2010

Zimrī-Līm also appears with the title 'beloved of Dagān' in the seal legend of Iaḫad-maraṣ.

COMMENTARY

The impression appears on M 15180 from room 52 of the palace and M 18177 from room 143 of the palace.

The transliteration of this previously unpublished impression is given through the courtesy of D. Charpin.

BIBLIOGRAPHY

1988 Charpin in Young (ed.), Mari at 50 p. 66 (study)

TEXT

1) *zi-im-ri-li-im*	1) Zimrī-Līm,
2) *na-ra-am* ^{d}*da-gan*	2) beloved of the god Dagān,
3) *ia-ḫa-ad-ma-ra-aṣ*	3) Iaḫad-maraṣ
4) ÌR.[ZU]	4) [your] servant.

2011

Zimrī-Līm appears as the 'appointee of the god Dagān' in the seal of Asqudum, the diviner.

COMMENTARY

A tablet published by Dossin in 1950 bears the incomplete impression of a seal of Asqudum. The impression is also found on several tablets from the large house excavated in 'chantier A' at Mari. This house probably belonged to Asqudum. It also figures on a large number of administrative texts from rooms 108, 143, 160, and 215 (especially the last two) of the palace at Mari. In total a dossier of 137 tablets bear Asqudum's seal impression.

BIBLIOGRAPHY

1950 Dossin, Studia Mariana p. 42 (edition)
1983 Durand, ARMT 21 p. 569 seal 2 (transliteration)
1984 Lafont in Bardet, et al., ARM 23 nos. 60, 246–71, 274–333, and 496–503; pp. 231–33 (transliteration, study)
1985 Charpin, MARI 4 p. 456 (edition)
1988 Charpin in Young (ed.), Mari at 50 p. 61 (edition)

TEXT

1) *zi-im-ri-li-im*	1) Zimrī-Līm,
2) *ša-ki-in* ᵈ*da-gan*	2) appointee of the god Dagān,
3) *às-qú-du-um*	3) Asqudum,
4) MÁŠ.ŠU.GÍD.GÍD	4) the diviner.

2012

The impression of the seal of Kabi-Addu, the son of Asqudum, is found on a number of clay sealings from Mari.

COMMENTARY

The impressions are on M 7027 from room 115, 10455 from room 24, 13230 from room 79, 18523 = ARMT 23 no. 395 from room 215 of the palace, and TH 80.117 from Sounding A, room xv. They were not collated.

BIBLIOGRAPHY

1983 Beyer, MARI 2 pp. 50–51 and fig. 8 (copy, edition)
1984 Beyer, MARI 3 pp. 255–56 and fig. 1 (copy, study)
1984 Lafont in Bardet, et al., ARMT 23 p. 307 no. 395 (study)
1985 Charpin, MARI 4 p. 456 (edition)
1987 Collon, First Impressions no. 182 (copy, study)
1988 Charpin in Young (ed.), Mari at 50 p. 62 (edition)

TEXT

1) *ka-bi*-ᵈIŠKUR	1) Kabi-Adad,
2) DUMU *às-qú-di-im*	2) son of Asqudum,
3) ÌR *zi-im-ri-li-im*	3) servant of Zimrī-Līm.

2013

Zimrī-Līm appears with the title 'appointee of Adad' in the seal impression of Dabiʾum.

COMMENTARY

The impression is found on M 18358, from room 215 of the palace. It was not collated.

The reading of the PN in line 4 is determined by a variant *ia-wi-i-la*; see ARMT 16/1 p. 237.

BIBLIOGRAPHY

1984 Lafont in Bardet, et al., ARMT 23 p. 277 no. 345 (transliteration)
1988 Charpin in Young (ed.), Mari at 50 p. 66 (study)

TEXT

1) *zi-im-ri-li-im*
2) *ša-ki-in* dIŠKUR
3) *da-bi-um* [N]A(?).G[A]DA(?)
4) DUMU *ia-wi*-DINGIR ÌR.ZU

1) Zimrī-Līm,
2) appointee of the god Adad,
3) Dabiʾum, the *herdsman*,
4) son of Iawi-Ilā, your servant.

2014

Impressions of a seal of Ana-Sîn-taklāku, servant of Zimrī-Līm, are found on a large number of clay sealings from Mari. The seal which once belonged to Ana-Sîn-taklāku is also known.

COMMENTARY

The impressions are on ME 71–131, 198, 205–206, 221, and 234. The seal is AO 21988 purchased in Tehran. The inscription on the seal has been erased and a new one cut for a different owner, Adad-šarrum, son of Šamāiatum. The impression was collated from the published photos.

BIBLIOGRAPHY

1959 Parrot, Documents pp. 169–85 (study), p. 170 fig. 104 ME 71 and 72 (photo), p. 172 fig. 105 ME 75 (photo), and p. 173 fig. 106 ME 80 and 81a (photo); Dossin p. 254 Ana-Sin-taklâtku (edition) and pl. XLVIII ME 71a, 72, 73, 80, and 81a (photo)
1966 Parrot, Syria 43, pp. 333–35 (photo of impression, study)
1973 [Amiet], Bas-reliefs imaginaires de l'ancien Orient no. 352 (photo, study)
1985 Beyer, MARI 4 pp. 378–80 (study)
1987 Collon, First Impressions no. 191 (photo, study of seal)

TEXT

1) *a-na-*dEN.ZU-*ták-la-ku*
2) DUMU *da-ri-iš-li-bur*
3) ÌR *zi-im-ri-li-im*

1) Ana-Sîn-taklāku,
2) son of Dāriš-libūr,
3) servant of Zimrī-Līm.

2015

The seal impression of Iassi-Dagān, servant of Zimrī-Līm, is found on a tablet envelope excavated at Mari.

COMMENTARY

The impression is on ME 41 and was collated from the published photo. Iassi-Dagān is known from other sources to have been the commander of the troops.

BIBLIOGRAPHY

1959 Parrot, Documents p. 187 (study) and p. 186 fig. 107 (photo); Dossin p. 254 (edition)

TEXT

1) [*ia*]-*ás-si-*^{d}*da*-[*gan*]	1) [I]assi-Da[gān],
2) [DUMU] *la-i*-[*im*]	2) [son] of La'u[m],
3) [ÌR *z*]*i-im-ri-l*[*i-im*]	3) [servant of Z]imrī-L[īm].

2016

Impressions of a seal of Ilu-kānum, servant of Zimrī-Līm, are found on numerous sealings from Mari. Ilu-kānum was in charge of the kitchen supplies at Mari.

COMMENTARY

The impressions are on ME 32, ME 264 = ARMT 7 no. 155 from room 110 of the palace, ME 267, ARMT 9 no. 44 from room 5 of the palace; ARMT 11 nos. 12, 32, 36, 236 from room 111 of the palace; ARMT 12 nos. 106, 146, 695 from room 5 of the palace; and ARMT 21 no. 424 from room 160 of the palace. Bottéro indicated a var. writing of the name of his transliteration of ARMT 7 no. 155, but collation of this piece, ME 264 in Parrot, Documents pl. 53, shows that it is the same as the other impressions.

BIBLIOGRAPHY

1956–57 Bottéro, ARM(T) 7 no. 155 (copy, edition)

1959 Parrot, Documents pp. 188–89 Cylindre de Ilkanum ME 32 (study); Dossin p. 255 ME 32 (edition) and pl. LVI ME 32 (photo); Parrot and Barrelet p. 233 Cylindre au nom de Iluka-El ME 264 (study), pl. LIII ME 264 (photo), p. 239 Le cylindre de Iluka-El ME 267 (study), p. 239 fig. 126 ME 267 (photo), and pl. LIII ME 267 (photo)

1960 Birot, ARM(T) 9 no. 44 (copy, edition)

1963 Burke, ARMT 11 nos. 12, 32, 36, and 236 (transliteration)

1964 Birot, ARMT 12 nos. 106, 146, and 695 (study)

1983 Durand, ARMT 21 p. 569 seal 4 (transliteration)

1983 Charpin and Durand, MARI 2 p. 82 no. 155 (transliteration)

TEXT

1)	DINGIR-*ka-nu-um*	1) Ilu-kānum,
2)	ÌR *zi-im-ri-li-im*	2) servant of Zimrī-Līm.

2017

Seal impressions of Ummum-ṭābat, female servant of Šamšī-Adad, are known from Mari. Durand has suggested that she may have been a wife of Šamšī-Adad (see MARI 4 [1985] p. 408). Ummum-ṭābat continued to function at Mari under Zimrī-Līm. At that time a seal acknowledging her new master was cut, and impressions of this seal are found on a number of tablets from Mari.

COMMENTARY

The impressions are on ARMT 9 no. 58 from room 5 of the palace, ARMT 11 no. 93 from room 111 of the palace, ARMT 12 nos. 108 and 723 from room 5 of the palace. The impressions on these tablets, now in the Deir ez-Zor Museum, were not collated.

BIBLIOGRAPHY

1960 Birot, ARMT 9 no. 58 (study)
1963 Burke, ARMT 11 no. 93 (transliteration)
1964 Birot, ARMT 12 nos. 108 and 723 (edition)
1985 Durand, MARI 4 p. 408 (study)
1988 Charpin in Young (ed.), Mari at 50 p. 67 (edition)

TEXT

1)	AMA.DU$_{10}$.[GA]	1) Ummum-ṭāb[at],
2)	GÉME *š*[*a*]	2) female servant o[f]
3)	*zi-im-ri-li-im*	3) Zimrī-Līm.

2018

The impression of a seal of Mukannišum, servant of Zimrī-Līm, is found on a number of sealings from Mari. Mukannišum was in charge of the palace workshops at Mari.

COMMENTARY

The impressions are on ME 1 = ARMT 9 no. 27a from room 5; ARMT 7 nos. 90, 283 from room 110; ARMT 9 no. 127 from room 5; ARMT 21 nos. 145, 149 from room 160; ARMT 22 no. 335 from room 135; ARMT 23 no. 229 = A 3548 from room 108; ARMT 24 nos. 113, 123, and 125 from rooms Y and Z of the palace.

BIBLIOGRAPHY

1957 Bottéro, ARMT 7 nos. 90 and 283 (edition)
1959 Parrot, Documents pp. 189–90 Cylindre I de Mukannishum ME 1 (study); Dossin p. 255 Cylindre I de Mukannishum ME 1 (edition) and pls. XLI–XLII ME 1 (photo)
1960 Birot, ARM(T) 9 no. 127 (copy, edition)
1983 Durand, ARMT 21 p. 569 seal 8 (transliteration)
1983 Kupper, ARMT 22/2 pp. 538–39 no. 335 (edition)
1984 Joannès in Bardet, et al., ARMT 23 p. 203 no. 229 (transliteration)
1985 Talon, ARMT 24 p. 209 seal 3 (transliteration)

TEXT

1) *mu-ka-an-ni-šum*	1) Mukannišum,
2) DUMU *ḫa-ab-di-ba-aḫ-la-ti*	2) son of Ḫabdi-Baḫlati,
3) ÌR *zi-im-ri-li-im*	3) servant of Zimrī-Līm.

2019

A variant seal impression of Mukannišum is found on a clay sealing excavated at Mari.

COMMENTARY

The impression is on ME 43. It was collated from the published photo.

BIBLIOGRAPHY

1959 Parrot, Documents pp. 190–91 Cylindre II de Mukannishum (study); Dossin p. 255 Cylindre II de Mukannishum (edition) and pl. XLVIII ME 43 (photo)
1985 Beyer, MARI 4 p. 380 (study)

TEXT

1) *mu-ka-an-ni-šum*	1) Mukannišum,
2) ÌR *zi-im-ri-li-im*	2) servant of Zimrī-Līm.

2020

The seal impression of Iasīm-sūmû, archivist (*šandabakkum*) at Mari, is found on a number of sealings from Mari. Iasīm-sūmû was in charge of the personnel and records at Mari.

COMMENTARY

The impressions are on ME 30, 211–212, 240; ARMT 9 no. 276 from room 5; ARMT 22 no. 283 from room 135; ARMT 23 no. 391 = M 18519 from room 215; ARMT 24 nos. 121, 181, and 264–65 from rooms Y and Z of the palace.

BIBLIOGRAPHY

1959 Parrot, Documents pp. 192–93 Cylindre de Iasîm-Sumû (study) and p. 193 fig. 110 ME 30, 211, and 212 (photo); Dossin p. 256 Iasîm-Sumû (edition) and pl. XLVIII ME 212 (photo)
1960 Birot, ARM(T) 9 no. 276 (copy, edition)
1983 Kupper, ARMT 22/2 pp. 446–47 no. 283 (edition)
1984 Lafont in Bardet, et al., ARMT 23 p. 306 no. 391 (transliteration)
1985 Talon, ARMT 24 p. 209 seal 2 (transliteration)
1987 Collon, First Impressions no. 184 (drawing, study)

TEXT

1) *ia-si-im-su-mu-ú*
2) ŠÀ.DUB.BA
3) DUMU *a-bi-e-ra-aḫ*
4) ÌR *zi-im-ri-li-im*

1) Iasīm-sūmû,
2) archivist,
3) son of Abī-Eraḫ,
4) servant of Zimrī-Līm.

2021

The seal impression of Iluna-Kirišu, servant of Zimrī-Līm, is found on a number of sealings from Mari.

COMMENTARY

The impression is on ME 6–8, 12–13, 15, 17, 24, 228, and 244. It was collated from the published photos.

BIBLIOGRAPHY

1959 Parrot, Documents pp. 194–97 (study) and p. 194 fig. 11 ME 6, 8, and 12 (photo); Dossin p. 256 (edition) and pl. XLIX ME 12, 8, and 244 (photo)
1985 Beyer, MARI 4 p. 380 (study)

TEXT

1) *i-lu-na-ki-ri-[šu]*
2) [Ì]R *zi-im-ri-li-[im]*

1) Iluna-Kiri[šu],
2) [se]rvant of Zimrī-Lī[m].

2022

Impressions of three different seals of Dāriš-libūr, servant of Zimrī-Līm, are found on various tablets and sealings excavated at Mari. The actual text on the three different seals is identical; hence we edit the three seals together here.

COMMENTARY

The impressions are as follows: Impression 1: ME 5, 19, 25–26, 130–164, 187, 202–204, 214, 223, 226, 230, 237, and ARMT 24 no. 193; Impression 2 from rooms Y and Z of the palace: ME 185, 190, 195, and 215; Impression 3: ME 210. The impressions were collated from the published photo.

BIBLIOGRAPHY

1959 Parrot, Documents pp. 198–211 (study), p. 198 fig. 112 ME 5 (photo), and p. 200 fig. 113 ME 130–31 and 134 (photo); Dossin p. 256 Cylindres II–III Dâriš-Lîbur (edition) and pl. XLIX ME 131 (photo)

1985 Talon, ARMT 24 p. 209 seal 4 (transliteration)

1985 Beyer, MARI 4 pp. 380–81 (study)

TEXT

1) *da-ri-iš-li-bur*	1) Dāriš-libūr,
2) DUMU *li-bur-na-di-in-šu*	2) son of Libūr-nādinšu,
3) ÌR *zi-im-ri-li-im*	3) servant of Zimrī-Līm.

2023

The impression of a seal of Šarkassum-mātum, servant of Zimrī-Līm, is found on two sealings from Mari.

COMMENTARY

The impression is on ARMT 7 no. 122, now in the Deir ez-Zor Museum, from room 110 of the palace and ARMT 21 no. 141 from room 160 of the palace.

BIBLIOGRAPHY

1956–57 Bottéro, ARM(T) 7 no. 122 (copy, edition)

1983 Charpin and Durand, MARI 2 pp. 80 and 103 (copy, transliteration)

1983 Durand, ARMT 21 p. 569 seal 11 (transliteration)

1984 Durand, MARI 3 p. 130 (study)

TEXT

1) *šar-ka-sú-ma-[tum]*
2) IR₁₁ *zi-im-ri-l[i-im]*

1) Šarkassum-mā[tum],
2) servant of Zimrī-L[īm].

2024

The impression of a seal of Iarʾip-Dagān, servant of Zimrī-Līm, is found on tablets from Mari.

COMMENTARY

The impression is on ARMT 8 no. 90 from room 108 of the palace and ARMT 9 no. 5 from room 5 of the palace. Both pieces are now in the Deir ez-Zor Museum.

BIBLIOGRAPHY

1957–58 Boyer, ARM(T) 8 no. 90 (copy, edition)
1960 Birot, ARM(T) 9 no. 5 (copy, edition)
1983 Charpin, MARI 2 p. 67 no. 90 (transliteration) and p. 74 no. 90 (copy)

TEXT

1) *ia-ar-ip-*^{d}*d[a-gan]*
2) DUMU *puzur₄-*^{d}*m[a-ma]*
3) [Ì]R *zi-im-ri-[li-im]*

1) Iarʾip-D[agān],
2) son of Puzur-M[ama],
3) [se]rvant of Zimrī-[Līm].

2025

Impressions of a seal of Iantin-Eraḫ, servant of Zimrī-Līm, are found on a number of tablets from Mari. Iantin-Eraḫ was the commander of the Ḫanean troops, who appears in some documents as the *ša sikkatim* official.

COMMENTARY

The impressions are on ARMT 21 no. 148 from room 160 and ARMT 23 no. 390 = M 18518 and no. 617 = M 18712 from room 215 of the palace.

BIBLIOGRAPHY

1972 Marzal, Orientalia NS 41 pp. 374–76 (study of the functions of Iantin-Eraḫ)
1983 Durand, ARMT 21 p. 569 seal 14 (transliteration)
1984 Lafont in Bardet, et al., ARMT 23 p. 305 no. 390 (transliteration); Villard p. 577 no. 617 (transliteration)

TEXT

1) *ia-an-ti-in-e-ra-aḫ* 1) Iantin-Eraḫ,
2) DUMU *a-ḫu-a-tar* 2) son of Aḫu-atar,
3) ÌR *zi-im-ri-li-im* 3) servant of Zimrī-Līm.

2026

Impressions of Iabni-Il, servant of Zimrī-Līm, are found on a number of tablets from Mari.

COMMENTARY

The impressions are on ARMT 22 nos. 301 and 336 from room 135 and possibly on ME 34 and 232. These latter pieces are broken; only *ia-ab-ni* is preserved on them.

BIBLIOGRAPHY

1959 Parrot, Documents p. 192 Cylindre de Iabni ME 34 and 232 (study); Dossin p. 255 Cylindre de Iabni-... ME 34 and 232 (edition) and pl. XLIX ME 34 (photo)
1983 Kupper, ARMT 22/2 pp. 466–67 no. 301 and pp. 538–39 no. 336 (edition)
1985 Beyer, MARI 4 p. 380 (study)

TEXT

1) *ia-ab-ni*-DINGIR 1) Iabni-Il,
2) DUMU *ab-di-e-r*[*a-aḫ*] 2) son of Abdi-Er[aḫ],
3) ÌR *zi-im-ri-li-im* 3) servant of Zimrī-Līm.

2027

The impression of a seal of Aḫum, servant of Zimrī-Līm, is found on two tablets from Mari.

COMMENTARY

The impression is on ARMT 21 nos. 63 and 80, both from room 160 of the palace.

BIBLIOGRAPHY

1983 Durand, ARMT 21 p. 569 seal 1 (transliteration)

TEXT

1) *a-ḫu-*[*um*]	1) Aḫu[m],
2) DUMU *ki-nu-um-wa-*[*qar*]	2) servant of Kīnum-wa[qar],
3) ÌR *zi-im-ri-li-*[*im*]	3) servant of Zimrī-Lī[m].

2028

The impression of the seal of Dagān-šadûni, servant of Zimrī-Līm, is found on two tablets from Mari.

COMMENTARY

The impression is on ARMT 21 nos. 64 and 81 from room 160 of the palace.

BIBLIOGRAPHY

1983 Durand, ARMT 21 p. 569 seal 3 (transliteration)

TEXT

1) [d]*da-gan-*[KUR-*ni*]	1) Dagān-[šadûni],
2) ÌR *zi-im-ri-*[*li-im*]	2) servant of Zimrī-[Līm].

2029

The impression of a seal of Ṣidqi-Epuḫ, a high official in the palace at Mari, is found on a tablet from Mari.

COMMENTARY

The impression is on ARMT 21 no. 143 from room 160 of the palace.

BIBLIOGRAPHY

1983 Durand, ARMT 21 p. 569 seal 10 (transliteration)

TEXT

1) [*ṣ*]*í-id-qí-e-*[*pu-uḫ*]	1) [Ṣ]idqi-E[puḫ],
2) [ì]R *zi-im-ri-l*[*i-im*]	2) [se]rvant of Zimrī-L[īm].

2030

The impression of a seal of Etel-pî-šarrim, the administrator of the workshops at Mari, is found on a tablet from Mari.

COMMENTARY

The impression is on M 18450 = ARMT 23 no. 521 from room 215 of the palace.

BIBLIOGRAPHY

1984 Charpin in Bardet, et al., ARMT 23 p. 445 no. 521 (transliteration)

TEXT

1) *e-tel-pi*$_4$-[LUGAL]	1) Etel-pî-[šarrim],
2) DUMU *a*-X-*ri*-[...]	2) son of A-x-ri-[...],
3) ÌR *zi-im-ri*-[*li-im*]	3) servant of Zimrī-[Līm].

2031

The impression of a seal of Adad-muballiṭ, servant of Zimrī-Līm, is found on a tablet from Mari.

COMMENTARY

The impression is on M 12114 = ARMT 23 no. 551 from room 108 of the palace.

BIBLIOGRAPHY

1984 Villard in Bardet, et al., ARMT 23 p. 523 no. 551 (transliteration)

TEXT

1) ^{d}IŠKUR-*mu-ba-lí-iṭ*	1) Adad-muballiṭ,
2) DUMU ÌR-^{d}EN.[x]	2) son of Warad-EN[...],
3) ÌR *zi-im-ri-li-im*	3) servant of Zimrī-Līm.

2032

The impression of a seal of Šamaš-nāṣir, servant of Zimrī-Līm, is found on two tablets from Mari.

COMMENTARY

The impression is on A 3539 (Paris) = ARMT 23 no. 466 from room 108 of the palace and ARMT 24 no. 304 from room Y or Z of the palace.

BIBLIOGRAPHY

1984 Soubeyran in Bardet, et al., ARMT 23 p. 410 no. 466 (transliteration)
1985 Talon, ARMT 24 p. 210 seal 14 (transliteration)

TEXT

1) ^{d}UTU-*na-ṣi-ir*	1) Šamaš-nāṣir,
2) ÌR *zi-im-ri-li-im*	2) servant of Zimrī-Līm.

2033

The impression of a seal of Iašūb-Nār, servant of Zimrī-Līm, is found on a tablet from Mari.

COMMENTARY

The impression is on ARMT 23 no. 419 = A 18068 (Paris) from room 133 of the palace.

BIBLIOGRAPHY

1984 Lafont in Bardet, et al., ARMT 23 p. 316 no. 419 (transliteration)

TEXT

1) *ia-šu-ub-na-ar*	1) Iašūb-Nār,
2) DUMU *ṣíl-lí*-^{d}[...]	2) son of Ṣillī-[...],
3) ÌR *zi-im-ri-li-im*	3) servant of Zimrī-Līm.

2034

The impression of a seal of Bāli-Eraḫ, steward of the palace of Mari, is found on a tablet from Mari.

COMMENTARY

The impression is on ARMT 24 no. 285 from room Y or Z of the palace.

BIBLIOGRAPHY

1985 Talon, ARMT 24 p. 209 seal 7 (transliteration)

TEXT

1) [*b*]*a-li-e-*[*ra-aḫ*]
2) DUMU *me-sí-*[*ia-an*]
3) ÌR *zi-*[*i*]*m-r*[*i-li-im*]

1) [B]āli-E[raḫ],
2) son of Mesi[ān],
3) servant of Zimr[ī-Līm].

2035

The impression of a seal of a servant of Zimrī-Līm whose name is not preserved is found on a clay sealing excavated at Mari.

COMMENTARY

The impression is on ME 37. It was collated from the published photo.

BIBLIOGRAPHY

1959 Parrot, Documents p. 187 (study) and p. 187 fig. 108 (photo); Dossin p. 254 Cylindre de x, serviteur de Zimrilim (edition)
1985 Beyer, MARI 4 p. 380 (study)

TEXT

1) [...]
2) DUMU [...]
3) ÌR *z*[*i-im-ri-li-im*]

1) [...],
2) son of [...],
3) servant of Z[imrī-Līm].

2036

The impression of another servant of Zimrī-Līm whose name is not preserved is found on a clay sealing from Mari.

COMMENTARY

The impression is on ME 192 and was not collated.

BIBLIOGRAPHY

1959 Parrot, Documents pp. 187–88 Cylindre de x, serviteur de Zimri-Lim (photo, study); Dossin p. 254 (edition), p. 187 fig 108 (photo), and pl. XLIX ME 192 (photo)

TEXT

1) *ma-*⌜*lik*(?)⌝-[...]	1) Malik-[...],
2) [DUMU ...]	2) [son of ...],
3) ÌR *z*[*i-im*]-*r*[*i*]-*l*[*i-im*]	3) servant of Z[im]r[ī]-L[īm].

2037

The impression of a seal of a servant of Zimrī-Līm whose name is not fully preserved is found on a tablet from Mari.

COMMENTARY

The impression is on ARMT 24 no. 236 from room Y or Z of the palace. It was not collated.

BIBLIOGRAPHY

1985 Talon, ARMT 24 p. 210 seal 15 (transliteration)

TEXT

1) [...]-^{d}EN.ZU	1) [...]-Sîn,
2) [...] x x	2) [...] ...,
3) [ÌR] *zi-im-r*[*i-li-im*]	3) [servant] of Zimr[ī-Līm].

2038

The impression of a seal of a servant of Zimrī-Līm, whose name is almost entirely broken away, is found on a tablet from Mari.

COMMENTARY

The impression is on ARMT 8 no. 41, now in the Deir ez-Zor Museum, from room 108 of the palace. It was collated by D. Charpin.

BIBLIOGRAPHY

1958 Boyer, ARMT 8 p. 64 no. 41 (study)
1983 Charpin, MARI 2 p. 64 no. 41 (transliteration) and p. 72 no. 41–1 (copy)

TEXT

1) [x] x [x] x [...]
2) [Ì]R *zi-i*[*m-r*]*i-l*[*i-im*]

1) ...,
2) [se]rvant of Zi[mr]ī-L[īm].

2039

The impression of a seal of a servant of Zimrī-Līm whose name is largely broken away is found on two tablets from Mari.

COMMENTARY

The impressions are on ARMT 9 nos. 254 and 261 from room 5 of the palace. The tablets bearing these impressions are now in the Deir ez-Zor Museum.

BIBLIOGRAPHY

1960 Birot, ARM(T) 9 nos. 254 and 261 (copy, edition); ARMT 9 p. 250 (study)

TEXT

1) [x]-*šu*-[...]
2) [Ì]R *zi-im-ri-li*-[*im*]

1) [x]-šu-[...],
2) [ser]vant of Zimrī-Lī[m].

2040

The impression of a seal of a servant of Zimrī-Līm whose name is largely lost is found on a tablet from Mari.

COMMENTARY

The impression is on ARMT 12 no. 699 from room 5 of the palace. It was not collated. The PN in line 2 appears to be Hurrian.

BIBLIOGRAPHY

1964 Birot, ARMT 12 no. 699 (edition)

TEXT

1) *na-bi*-[...]	1) Nabi-[...],
2) DUMU *eḫ-li*-[...]	2) son of Eḫli-[...],
3) [Ì]R *zi*-[*im-ri-li-im*]	3) [ser]vant of Zi[mrī-Līm].

2041

A seal in the Hague bears the inscription of a servant of Zimrī-Līm.

COMMENTARY

The seal, ex. 1, is the Hague Collection no. 97. It is a purchased piece of unknown provenance acquired in 1823. The seal is made of haematite and measures 2.5 × 1.5 cm. The inscription was collated from the published photo.

A modern copy of this seal, ex. 2 made of lapis lazuli, 2.8 × 1.8 cm, is in the Pierpoint Morgan Library. A third modern copy, ex. 3, is in the Staatliche Museum in Berlin, Vorderasiatische Abteilung (see Porada, Corpus p. 162).

BIBLIOGRAPHY

1802 Denon, Voyage pl. 124 no. 9
1847 Lajard, Mithra pl. VII no. 1
1878 Ménant, Catalogue la Haye pp. 42–43 and pl. 5 no. 25 (ex. 1, edition)
1920 Ward, Morgan no. 104 (ex. 2, copy, study)
1948 Porada, Corpus no. 1151 (ex. 2, photo, study)
1951 Van Buren, JCS 5 p. 134 n. 5 (study)
1952 Zadoks-Josephus Jitta and Frankena, Catalogue sommaire no. 61 (ex. 1, photo, edition)
1952 Leemans, SLB 1/1 p. 10 n. 33 (study)
1953 Weidner, JKF 2 pp. 136–37 (ex. 2, transliteration, study)

TEXT

1) *nu-úr*-^{d}EN.ZU	1) Nūr-Sîn,
2) ÌR *zi-im-ri-li-im*	2) servant of Zimrī-Līm.

KISURRA

E4.7

The city of Kisurra (modern Abū Ḥaṭab), just north of ancient Šuruppak (Fara), had a checkered history in Old Babylonian times. The city was independent for a time and then fell under the control of such cities as Uruk, Marad, Isin, and the Mananā kings. It was finally conquered by Rīm-Sîn of Larsa, as commemorated in the name of the 20th year of the king. Inscriptions of one of its independent rulers, Itūr-Šamaš, are known.

Itūr-Šamaš

E4.7.1

A number of year names of Itūr-Šamaš are found on tablets excavated at Kisurra.

1

One inscription of this ruler is known.

COMMENTARY

The bricks are reported to have come from Abū Ḥaṭab but no exact provenance or excavation nos. are known. None of the Itūr-Šamaš bricks could be located in Istanbul or Berlin. The inscription was collated from Babylon photo 1145, which shows the brick which was published in MDOG 15 p. 13.

The last sign in line 3 was read as -ke$_4$ by Hommel, Stol, and Heltzer. Collation of the excavation photo reveals a clear *-ma*.

BIBLIOGRAPHY

1902 Koldewey, MDOG 15 p. 13 (copy); Messerschmidt pp. 13–14 (translation, study)

1904 Hommel, Grundriss der Geographie und Geschichte des alten Orients (Munich) pp. 352–53 (study)

1905 Thureau-Dangin, ISA pp. 214–15 Itûr-šamaš (edition)

1907 Thureau-Dangin, SAK pp. 152–53 Itûr-šamaš (edition)

1929 Barton, RISA pp. 150–51 Itur-Šamaš 1 (edition)

1957 Edzard, Zwischenzeit p. 136 n. 716 (study)

1971 Sollberger and Kupper, IRSA ɪᴠL1a (translation)

1976 Stol, Studies in Old Babylonian History p. 86 (transliteration, study)

1978 Kienast, Kisurra 1 p. 14 (edition)

1981 Heltzer, Suteans p. 105 (edition)

TEXT

1) *i-túr-*^{d}UTU	1) Itūr-Šamaš,
2) *ra-bí-an*	2–3) chief of the Rabbeans,
3) *ra-ba-bi-ma*	
4) DUMU *i-din-*DINGIR	4) son of Iddin-Ilum,
5) ÉNSI	5–6) governor of Kisurra,
6) *ki-sur-ra.*KI	
7) KI.ÁG ^{d}UTU	7–8) beloved of the god Šamaš and the goddess Annunītum.
8) *ù an-nu-ni-tum*	

2001

The impression of a servant seal of Itūr-Šamaš is found on a tablet in the British Museum.

COMMENTARY

The impression is on BM 14120 (96-4-2,222). The tablet dates to year 1 of Manna-balti-El of the Mananā dynasty. The inscription was not collated.

BIBLIOGRAPHY

1961 Figulla, Cat. 1 p. 170 sub 14120 (study)
1971 Sollberger and Kupper, IRSA ivL1a n. 1 (study)
1983 Sommerfeld, ZA 73 p. 212 (transliteration)

TEXT

1) *[a]-wi-lum*
2) DUB.[SAR]
3) ÌR *i-túr*-dUTU

1) [A]wīlum,
2) scr[ibe],
3) servant of Itūr-Šamaš.

KIŠ

E4.8

The once important city of Kiš had a very checkered history in Isin–Larsa/Old Babylonian times. With the accession of Išbi-Erra, the city became a dependency of Isin under the local governor Šū-Enlil (see F. Ali, Sumer 26 [1970] p. 162 line 38). Later the city gained its independence under a local ruler, Ašdūni-iarīm. Following this the city came under the control of the king of Marad, Sūmû-ditān. It regained its independence once again under Iawiʾum only to be dominated by the kings of the Mananā and Babylon dynasties.

BIBLIOGRAPHY

1957 Edzard, Zwischenzeit pp. 130–35 (study)

Ašdūni-iarīm

E4.8.1

An early independent ruler of Kiš was Ašdūni-iarīm, who is known from a cone inscription found in a long and short form.

1

The cone in the British Museum deals with Ašdūni-iarīm's defeat of his enemies, the construction of a wall, and the digging of canals.

COMMENTARY

The inscription is on BM 108854 (1914-4-7,20), a purchased small clay cone, and was collated. The cone may have originally come from the wall of Kiš.

The emendation of line 38 to *ed-ki*(*)-*ši-ma* suggested by von Soden, OLZ 55 (1960) 488, is not supported by collation. SÚ.A of line 17 is considered to be a logogram, a var. of im.a.sù = *ṭi-du* 'clay' (see MSL 7 p. 99 line 389).

BIBLIOGRAPHY

1921 Gadd, CT 36 pl. 4 (copy)
1929 Barton, RISA pp. 336-37 Ashduni-erim 2 (edition)
1957 Edzard, Zwischenzeit pp. 130-31 (study)
1960 von Soden, OLZ 55 488 (line 38, study)
1971 Sollberger and Kupper, IRSA ɪvK1a (translation)
1978 Moorey, Kish p. 174 (study)

TEXT

1) [*áš-d*]*u-ni-a-ri-im*
2) [NITA KAL]A.GA
3) [*na-ra-am*] ⸢d⸣INANNA
4) [*mi-gir*] ⸢d⸣*za-*ba_4*-*ba_4
5) [LUGAL K]IŠ.KI
6) [*i-n*]*u-mi*
7) [*ki-i*]*b-ra-tum*
8) [*er*]-*bi-im*
9) [*i*]-*ki-ra-ni-ni-ma*
10) [*sa*]-*ma-ni*
11) [*š*]*a-na-tim*
12) [*t*]*a-ḫa-za-am*
13) ⸢*e*⸣-*pu-uš-ma*

1–5) [Ašd]ūni-iarīm, [migh]ty [man, beloved] of the goddess Eštar, [favourite] of the god Zababa, [king of K]iš,

6–13) [wh]en the [f]our [qu]arters became hostile against me, I made [b]attle for [ei]ght [y]ears.

14) *i-na sa-mu-un-tim*
15) *ša-tim*
16) *ma-ḫi-ri*
17) *a-na* SÚ.A
18) [*l*]*u i-tu-úr*

14–18) In the eighth year my adversary was turned to clay.

19) *um-ma-ni*
20) *a-na ša-la-aš*
21) *me-at-*⸢*tim*⸣
22) *lu* ⸢*i*⸣*-tu-*⸢*úr*⸣

19–22) My army was reduced to three hundred (men).

23) *i-nu-mi*
24) ^{d}*za-ba*$_4$*-ba*$_4$ *be-lí*
25) *i-di-na-an-na*
26) *ù eš*$_4$*-tár be-el-ti*
27) [*t*]*a-pu-ti*
28) ⸢*i*⸣*-li-ku-na*

23–28) When the god Zababa, my lord, made a (favourable) judgement for me and the goddess Eštar, my lady, came to my [h]elp,

29) [*a-k*]*a-al* ⟨*pa-ta-ni-ia*⟩
30) [*é*]*l-qí-ma*
31) [*a*]*-na ḫa-ra-an*
32) ⸢*ú*⸣*-ma-ka-al*
33) *a-li-*[*ik-ma*]
34) *er-bi-e* ⸢*ú*⸣*-m*[*i*]
35) *ma-ta-am*
36) *na-ki-ir-ta-am*
37) *lu ú-ka-ni-iš*

29–37) I took some [f]ood ⟨to eat⟩ and we[nt] on an expedition of only a day. (But) for forty days I made the enemy land bow down (to me).

38) *ed-di-ši-ma*
39) BÀD *i-nu-úḫ-*⸢DINGIR⸣
40) *lu e-pu-uš*
41) *ù* I$_7$.*im-gur-eš*$_4$*-tár*
42) *lu aḫ-ri*

38–42) I built anew the wall Inūḫ-Ilum and dug the canal Imgur-Eštar.

43) *i-na e-bu-ri-šu-ma*
44) *ki-ib-ra-tum*
45) *er-bé-tim*
46) *i-ki-ra-ni-ni-ma*
47) BÀD BAR(*) KIŠ.K[I]
48) *lu e-pu-uš*
49) *ù* I$_7$.NUN.DI
50) *i-na ši-na ú-mi*
51) *lu es-ke-er*

43–51) That summer the four quarters became hostile against me and I built the outer wall of Kiš. In two days I dammed up the Nundi canal.

2

A second, shorter version of the Ašdūni-iarīm inscription is in the Louvre.

COMMENTARY

The text is inscribed on the shaft of AO 5645, which is a small cone, 11.5 cm long, 5 cm in dia. It was not collated.

---

47 BAR written over erasure.

BIBLIOGRAPHY

1911 Thureau-Dangin, RA 8 pp. 65–67 (copy, edition)
1929 Barton, RISA pp. 336–37 Ashduni-erim 1 (edition)
1957 Edzard, Zwischenzeit pp. 130–31 (study)
1960 von Soden, OLZ 55 488 (line 37, study)
1971 Sollberger and Kupper, IRSA ɪᴠK1a (study)

TEXT

1) *áš-du-ni-e-ri-im* 2) NITA KALA.GA 3) [L]UGAL KIŠ.KI	1–3) Ašdūni-iarīm, mighty man, [k]ing of Kiš,
4) ⌜*i*⌝*-nu-mi* 5) *ki-ib-ra-tum* 6) *er-bi-im* 7) *i-ki-ra-ni-ni-ma* 8) *sa-ma-ni* 9) *ša-na-tim* 10) *ta-ḫa-za-am* 11) ⌜*e*⌝*-pu-uš-ma*	4–11) when the four quarters became hostile against me, I made battle for eight years.
12) *i-na sa-mu-un-tim* 13) *ša-ti-im* 14) *ma-ḫi-ri* 15) *a-na* SÚ.A 16) *lu i-tu-úr*	12–16) In the eighth year my adversary was turned to clay.
17) ⌜*ú*⌝*-ma-ni* 18) *a-na ša-la-aš* 19) *me-at-tim* 20) *lu i-tu-úr*	17–20) My army was reduced to three hundred (men).
21) *i-nu-mi* 22) ^{d}*za-ba*$_{4}$*-ba*$_{4}$ *be-lí* 23) *i-di-na-an-na* 24) *ù eš*$_{4}$*-tár be-el-ti* 25) *ta-pu-ti* 26) *i-li-ku-na*	21–26) When the god Zababa, my lord, made a (favourable) judgement for me and the goddess Eštar, my lady, came to my help.
27) *a-ka-al* 28) *pa-ta-ni-ia* 29) *él-qí-ma* 30) *a-na ḫa-ra-an* 31) *ú-ma-ka-al* 32) *a-li-ik-ma*	27–32) I took some food to eat and went on an expedition of only a day;
33) 40 *u*$_{4}$*-mi* 34) *ma-ta-am* 35) *na-ki-ir-ta-am* 36) *lu ú-ka-ni-iš*	33–36) (but) for forty days I made the enemy land bow down (to me).
37) *ed-di-ši-ma* 38) BÀD GAL 39) *ša* KIŠ.KI 40) *lu e-pu-uš*	37–40) I built anew the great wall of Kiš.

Iawiʾum

E4.8.2

Kiš had a short period of independence under a certain Iawiʾum, who is known only from archival texts. No inscriptions are extant for this ruler.

BIBLIOGRAPHY

1957 Edzard, Zwischenzeit p. 131 (study)

MUTALÛ

E4.9

The ancient town of Mutalû was a small settlement located at modern Išān Dhaḥāk, 18 miles north-east of Kiš. Bricks with an inscription of its local ruler, GA/BI-NI/IR-ma-bi-de-e, were found there.

GA/BI-NI/IR-ma-bi-de-e

E4.9.1

1

The bricks are Ash 1924,624 and 1924,633 found by the Oxford-Field Museum expedition to Išān Dhaḥāk.

COMMENTARY

The bricks were stamped on the face and measure 33.5×33.0×6.0/5.0 cm. The stamp measures 7.3×5.9 cm.

Langdon recounts finding four exs. of this brick. Only two could be located in the Ashmolean Museum.

The reading of the PN in line 3 is uncertain. The occurrence of the term *ra-bi-an* 'chief' assures an OB date for this inscription (see M. Stol, Studies in Old Babylonian History p. 73).

BIBLIOGRAPHY

1924 Langdon, Kish 1 pp. 40–41 (edition)
1976 Stol, Studies in Old Babylonian History p. 80 (edition)
1981 Walker, CBI no. 52 (transliteration, study)

TEXT

1) GA/BI-NI/IR-*ma-bi-de-e*
2) DUMU *ma-*⌜*sa*(?)⌝*-lum*
3) *ra-bi-an*
4) *ba-ab-ti-šu*
5) *i-na e-mu-qì-šu*
6) BÀD *ša* ⌜*mu*⌝*-ta-lu*.KI
7) *i-pu-uš*

1) GA/BI-NI/IR-ma-bi-de-e,
2) son of Masalum,
3–4) chief of his quarter,

5–7) built the wall of Mutalû by his (own) means.

MANANĀ

E4.10

A number of rulers are known for a dynasty whose capital city has not yet been definitely determined but which may have been the city of Ilip. The most important of these rulers was Mananā, whose name is used here to designate the dynasty as a whole.

BIBLIOGRAPHY

1978 Charpin, RA 72 pp. 13–40 (study)
1989 Edzard, RLA 7/5–6 p. 332 (study)

Contemporary with the Mananā dynasty was the Marad–Kazallu kingdom, whose Amorite rulers controlled cities along the combined courses of the Araḫtum and Kazallu canals. In archival texts mentioning the rulers of this kingdom, oaths are sworn by either the god Lugal-marada, city god of Marad, apparently the southern capital of the kingdom, or the god Numušda, tutelary deity of Kazallu, the northern capital. While the names of several of its rulers — Ibni-šadûm, Sūmû-ditān, Iamsi-El, Alum-piʾû, and Sūmû-numḫim — are known, in contrast to the Mananā dynasty, no royal inscriptions, royal seals, or servant seals are known for the rulers of this dynasty.

BIBLIOGRAPHY

1957 Edzard, Zwischenzeit pp. 127–29 (study)
1980 Stol, AfO 27 p. 162 (study)

Ḫalium

E4.10.1

The first king of this dynasty for whom we have any year names is Ḫalium. No inscriptions of this ruler are known.

Abdi-Eraḫ

E4.10.2

The reign of Abdi-Eraḫ comes after that of Ḫalium. In addition to his capital city, Ilip, this king probably also controlled Kiš, as is evidenced by the title 'king of Kiš' found in his one known royal inscription. A letter found at Tell Asmar dated to the reign of Ipiq-Adad I of Ešnunna (see R. Whiting, Letters pp. 96–97 no. 40) refers to a certain Abdi-Eraḫ, probably the ruler of the Mananā dynasty.

1

A cone inscription of Abdi-Eraḫ deals with the construction of a city wall. The attribution of this text to Abdi-Eraḫ is based on a restoration of the name in line 1. The city wall in question is unknown. It might have been that of Ilip or Kiš.

CATALOGUE

Ex.	Museum number	Provenance	Object	Lines preserved	cpn
1	IM 10787	Acquired, provenance unknown	Clay cone head	1–5	c
2	IM 10788	As ex. 1	Clay cone head	1–8	c

BIBLIOGRAPHY

1957 Edzard, Sumer 13 p. 188 and pl. 2 (exs. 1–2, copy, edition)

TEXT

1) *ab-di-*[*e-ra-aḫ*]
2) DUMU *ḫu-zu-*[...]
3) LUGAL K[IŠ.KI]
4) *ša-am-š*[*i-*...]
5) BÀ[D ...]
6) *a-*[...]
7) x [...]
8) *i-*[*pu-uš*]

1) Abdi-[Eraḫ],
2) son of Ḫuzu[...],
3) king of K[iš],
4–8) ..., b[uilt] the wa[ll ...]

Mananā

E4.10.3

The reign of Mananā should be placed after that of Abdi-Eraḫ. Although numerous year names are known for this ruler, no royal inscriptions or servant seals are extant.

Nāqimum

E4.10.4

The exact place of Nāqimum in the Mananā dynasty is uncertain. No inscriptions are known for this ruler.

Aḫī-maraṣ

E4.10.5

This ruler is known only from one year name and no inscriptions are available for this king.

Sūmû-iamutbala

E4.10.6

2001

The reign of Sūmû-iamutbala should be placed after those of Nāqimum and Aḫī-maraṣ. While a number of year names are known for this ruler, only one seal of a servant of the king is known.

COMMENTARY

The seal is BM 134757 (1966-2-18,18) from the Spencer-Churchill Collection, provenance unknown. It is a lapis lazuli seal 2.48 cm long, 1.45 cm in dia., and was collated by E. Sollberger.

BIBLIOGRAPHY

1986 Collon, Cylinder Seals III no. 56 (photo, edition)
1987 Collon, First Impressions no. 535 (photo, study)

TEXT

1) dEN.ZU-*iš-me-a-ni*
2) DUMU dEN.ZU-*i-din-nam*
3) ÌR *su-mu-ia-mu-ut-ba-la*

1) Sîn-išmeʾanni,
2) son of Sîn-iddinam,
3) servant of Sūmû-iamutbala.

Manium

E4.10.7

A synchronism between year 32 of Sūmû-la-Il of Babylon and Manium indicates that this ruler reigned shortly after Sūmû-iamutbala.

2001

A seal of a servant of Manium is in the University Museum in Philadelphia.

COMMENTARY

The seal is CBS 14440, a haematite seal measuring 2.4 × 1.3 cm. It is a purchased piece from the Maxwell Sommerville Collection. The piece was collated from the published photo.

BIBLIOGRAPHY

1925 Legrain, PBS 14 no. 329 (photo, edition)
1962 Hallo, HUCA 33 p. 19 and n. 174 (study)

TEXT

1) ᵈEN.ZU-*e-ri-ba*-[*am*]	1) Sîn-erība[m],
2) DUMU ᵈEN.ZU-*en-nam*	2) son of Sîn-ennam,
3) ÌR *ma-ni-um*	3) servant of Manium.

MALGIUM

E4.11

The important city of Malgium, as yet unlocated, has provided inscriptions of two of its rulers for the Old Babylonian period, Ipiq-Eštar and Takil-ilissu.

The relative dating of the reigns of Ipiq-Eštar and Takil-ilissu is not certain. Edzard suggested that the Ipiq-Eštar inscription is to be dated after the Takil-ilissu inscription. C. Wilcke and R. Kutscher, however, have argued for a date before this, a scheme followed here.

BIBLIOGRAPHY

1988 Kutscher, RLA 7/3–4 pp. 300-304 (study)

Ipiq-Eštar

E4.11.1

1

A cone in Berlin deals with the destruction of the temple and orchard of the goddess Bēlet-Ilī in Malgium and its subsequent reconstruction and replanting by Ipiq-Eštar.

COMMENTARY

The clay cone is VA 3359, a purchased piece, provenance unknown, presumably originally from Malgium. The dia. of the head is 21.5 cm and the length of the shaft 12 cm. The cone was collated.

The reading of line 11 follows a suggestion of C. Wilcke and R. Kutscher, which is supported by collation.

According to a letter cited by D. Charpin (Archives Épistolaires 1/2 p. 154), Ipiq-Eštar was a contemporary of Ḫammu-rāpi of Babylon. Destructions of the city are noted in the names of years 10 and 35 of the Babylonian ruler.

BIBLIOGRAPHY

1905 Scheil, OLZ 8 512–13 no. 1 (study)
1907 Messerschmidt, VAS 1 no. 32 (copy)
1917-18 Schroeder, ZA 31 pp. 91–99 (edition)
1954 Landsberger, JCS 8 p. 38 (study)
1957 Edzard, Zwischenzeit pp. 159–60 (study)
1971 Sollberger and Kupper, IRSA ivM2a (translation)
1978 Kutscher and Wilcke, ZA 68 p. 100 n. 25 (study)
1985 Veenhof, RA 79 pp. 190–91 (study)
1988 Kutscher, RLA 7/3–4 p. 302 (study)

TEXT

1) ^{d}*i-pí-iq-eš$_4$-tár* LUGAL
2) *ši-ki*(*)-*in* ^{d}EN.KI ^{d}*dam-ki-na*
3) LUGAL *ma-al-gi-im*.KI
4) DUMU *a-píl-ì-lí-šu*
5) *i-nu* AN ^{d}*en-líl* DINGIR.MAḪ
6) *ù* ^{d}*é-a šar-ri*
7) *mi-li-ik ma-tim im-l*[*i*]-*ku*
8) *wa-ši-ib* LU-*im be-el pi-ri-iš-tim*
9) *ú-tá-di a-na ḫi-ir-ti-šu*
10) *el-le-tim* ^{d}*dam-ki-na*
11) *ar-ḫi-iš-mi mu-uḫ-ri ḫi-ṭa*
12) *šu-ti-qí ma-ru-uš-ta-am*
13) *a-na wa-ar-ki-a-tim*

1–4) Ipiq-Eštar, king *created* by the god Ea (and) the goddess Damkina, king of Malgium, son of Apil-ilīšu,

5–7) when the gods Anum, Enlil, Bēlet-Ilī, and Ea, my king, had taken counsel about the land,

8–17) the one who dwells in the *apsû*, the master of secrets (Ea), informed his wife, the goddess, pure Damkina, (saying): 'Quickly now, take away the offence! Ward off the evil! In the future, (as for) Malgium, your city, may its foundations be secure. May (its) kingship, the dynasty, last a long

---

2 Text: NA.

14) *lu ki-na iš-da-šu*
15) *ma-al-gu-um*.KI *a-al-ki*
16) *šar-ru-tum* BALA-*um* [*l*]*i*-⟨*ri*⟩-*ik*
17) *a ip-pa-ar-ku i-na* é-nam-ti-la
18) *i-nu-mi-šu ur-dam ma-a-tum*
19) *i na-ap-ḫa-ri ka-lu-šu*
20) *iš-ku-un ḫa-ba-ra-tam ra-bi-tam*
21) *ù ma-ru-uš-tam i*-⸢*pu*⸣-*u*[*š*]
22) *ú-ša-al-pí-it ki-iṣ-ṣa-a*[*m*]
23) *šu-ba-at* DINGIR.MAḪ *ra-bi-tim*
24) *ù mi-lam ra-aš-ba-am* GIŠ.KIRI$_6$-*ša i*-⸢*ki-is*⸣
25) ^{d}*i-pí-iq-eš*$_4$-*tár* LUGAL *na-ʾa-du*
26) *bi-ni-it qá-ti-šu*
27) *ša* ^{d}*é-a a-na-ku*
28) *i-na šu-ur-ri* ^{d}*é-a* ^{d}*dam-ki-na*
29) *a-na wa-ar-du*-⟨*ti*⟩-*šu-nu ir-šu-nin-ni*
30) ⸢*e*⸣-[*p*]*u-uš ab-ni bi-ta-am*
31) *a-na* DINGIR.MAḪ *um-mi-ia*
32) *áz-qú-up-ši-im* GIŠ.KIRI$_6$-*a-am el-lam*
33) *sí-ma-at i-lu-ti-ša*
34) *ú-ša-aš-ki-in* SÁ.DU$_{11}$ ⸢*in*⸣-*bi-im*
35) *a-na da-a-ar-i-tam maḫ-ri-ša*
36) *ab-bi šum* É *é-ki-tuš-geštu*$_x$(GIŠ.PI)
37) *ú-te-er-ši-im pa*(*)-*ra-ka*-⟨*am*⟩ *pa-ni-a-am*
38) *ù šu-ba-sà ar-mi*
39) *ša te-em-me-ni ú-da-ap-pa-ru*
40) DINGIR.MAḪ *er-re-tam ra-bi-tam*
41) *li*-⸢*ru*⸣-*ur-šu*

time; may it never cease in Enamtila.'

18–21) At that time all the land in its entirety came down, made a great clamour, and performed an evil deed.

22–24) It destroyed the sanctuar[y], the dwelling of the goddess, great Bēlet-ilī, and cut down its awe-inspiring height (of trees), her orchard.
25–38) I, Ipiq-Eštar, pious king, creation of the hand of the god Ea, as soon as the gods Ea and Damkina took me into their service, founded and built a temple for the goddess Bēlet-ilī, my mother. I planted for her a shining garden, befitting her divinity. I established forever regular offerings of fruit before her. I named it Ekitušgeštu ('House — abode of intelligence'). I returned to her her former shrine and founded her residence.

39–41) (As for) the one who removes my foundation inscription, may the goddess Bēlet-ilī inflict on him a great curse.

---

37 Text: NI.

Takil-ilissu

E4.11.2

1

Two inscriptions of Takil-ilissu are known. The first deals with the construction of a supporting wall around Enamtila, the temple of the god Ea in Malgium.

COMMENTARY

The inscription is on a brick in the Musées Royaux du Cinquantenaire in Brussels, no. O 265. It is said to have come from Ahymer, that is Kiš, and is a baked brick 36×9×13 cm, with the inscription running down the edge. The inscription was not collated.

BIBLIOGRAPHY

1912 Scheil, RT 34 pp. 104–105 (study)

1925 Speleers, Recueil pp. 115–16 no. 329 (copy, transliteration)

1937–39 Jacobsen, AfO 12 pp. 363–66 (copy, edition)

1971 Sollberger and Kupper, IRSA ɪᴠM1a (translation)

1978 Kutscher and Wilcke, ZA 68 pp. 127–28 (edition)

1988 Kutscher, RLA 7/3–4 p. 301 (study)

TEXT

1) ^{d}*ta-ki-il-ì-lí-su*
2) [L]UGAL *dan-nu-um*
3) [L]UGAL *ma-al-gi-im*
4) DUMU ^{d}*ištaran-a-su*
5) ⌜*i*⌝*-nu-ma* ^{d}*é-a*
6) ⌜^{d}⌝*dam-ki-na*
7) [*a-n*]*a re-ú-ut ma-al-gi-im*
8) [*š*]*u-mi ib-bu-ú*
9) ^{d}*é-a-ma be-li*
10) ⌜*i*⌝*-na* KA-*šu el-li-im*
11) [*i*]*q-bi-a-am-ma*
12) *i-nu-mi-šu é-nam-ti-*[*l*]*a*
13) *a-na li-wi-ti-šu*
14) [*k*]*i-sà-a-am ra-bi-a-am*
15) [*š*]*a* SIG$_4$.AL.ÙR.RA
16) [*š*]*a ki-ma ša-me-e*
17) [*i*]*š-da-šu ki-na*
18) [*a*]*l-wi-šu-ma*
19) [*š*]*u-ma-am da-ri-a-am*

1–4) Takil-ilissu, mighty [k]ing, [k]ing of Malgium, son of Ištaran-asu —

5–11) when the gods Ea (and) Damkina called my [n]ame [f]or the shepherdship of Malgium, (and when) the god Ea himself, my lord, [s]poke to me with his pure mouth,

12–21) at that time I [en]circled Enamtila in its circumference with a great supporting [w]all [o]f baked bricks, [wh]ose [fo]undation was as firm as heaven. I established the eternal [n]ame of my kingship.

20) *ša šar-ru-ti-ia*
21) *lu aš-ku-un*

22) *ša šu-mi ša-aṭ-ra-am*
23) *i-pa-aš-ši-ṭú-ma*
24) ⸢*šum*⸣-*šu i-ša-aṭ-ṭa-ru*
25) [*li-d*]*a-pí-ir li-di-da-ma*
26) [*šum-š*]*u ša-aṭ-ra-am*
27) [*a-na aš-r*]*i-šu la ú-ta-ar-ru*

22–27) (As for) the one who erases my inscribed name and writes his (own) name, may he quickly disappear and may his inscribed name not be [res]tored.

28) [LÚ] ⸢*šu*⸣-*ú lu* LUGAL *lu* EN *lu* ⸢GUDU$_4$⸣
29) [*lu ša*] ⸢*i*⸣-*na a-wi-lu-tim*
30) [*šu-m*]*a-am na-bu-ú*
31) [^{d}]⸢*é*⸣-*a* ^{d}*dam-ki-na*
32) [*i-š*]*i-sú li-sú-ḫu*
33) *ze-ra-*[*šu*] *li-il-qú-tu*

28–33) That [man], whether he be a king, a lord, or a *pašīšum* priest, or any member of the human race, may the gods Ea (and) Damkina rip out his [founda]tion and destroy [his] seed.

34) ^{d}ARA SUKKAL.MAḪ *ša* ^{d}*é-a*
35) *lu ra-bi-iṣ le-mu-ut-ti-*⸢*šu*⸣
36) *ša la na-ka-ri-im*
37) *a-na da-ri-a-tim*

34–37) May the god Ara, head vizier of the god Ea, forever be his evil spirit who cannot be countermanded.

2

Two bricks bear an inscription dealing with Takil-ilissu's construction of temples for the gods Anum, Ninšubur, and Ulmaššītum in Malgium.

CATALOGUE

Ex.	Museum number	Excavation number	Provenance	Object	Lines preserved	Dimensions (cm)	cpn
1	IM –	IB 1014	Isin, in rubble of a MB house, right frgm. 332.60N/17.80E, +8.51; left frgm. 345.70N/11.65E, +7.27	Inscribed brick-face	13–32, 45–65, 83–97	38.4×26.9×8.0	p
2	IM –	IB 1014	As ex. 1	Inscribed right and lower brick-edge	23–97	7.3 cm wide	p
3	YBC 2185	–	Not known, presumably originally from Malgium	Inscribed brick-face	36–97	24.5×33.5×8.5	p
4	YBC 2185	–	As ex. 3	Inscribed right and lower brick-edge	8–30, 64–77	8.3 cm wide	p

COMMENTARY

The inscription was collated from the published photos. Exs. 3 and 4 were purchased.

BIBLIOGRAPHY

1978 Kutscher and Wilcke, ZA 68 pp. 95–126 (exs. 1–2, photo, copy, edition)
1988 Kutscher, RLA 7/3–4 pp. 301–302 (exs. 1–4, study)

TEXT

1) [^{d}*ta-ki-il-ì-lí-su*]
2) [LUGAL *dan-nu-um*]
3) [LUGAL *ma-al-gi-im*]
4) [DUMU ^{d}*ištarān-a-su*]

1–4) [Takil-ilissu, mighty king, king of Malgium, son of Ištarān-asu],

5) [*i-nu-ma an-num*]
6) [*a-na re-ú-ut ma-al-gi-im*]
7) [*šu-mi ib-bu-ú*]

5–7) [when the god Anum called my name for the shepherdship of Malgium],

8) ⌜*a*⌝-*n*[*a an-nim ra-bi-i-im*]
9) *mu*-⌜*ki*⌝-*i*[*n* GIŠ.GU.ZA]
10) *šar-ru-ti*-[*ia* É-*sú*]
11) *ša i-na* MU.ŠÁ[R *i-na-ḫu*]
12) *a-ḫi-iṭ ú-ud-di*-[*iš-ma*]

8–12) fo[r the god, great Anum], who establish[es the throne of my] kingship, I examined and renew[ed his temple] which over many yea[r]s [had become dilapidated].

13) *na-ap-ta-an a*-[...] x
14) *a-ka-al-šu el-lam*
15) *me-šu na-aḫ-du-tim*
16) U4.SAKAR *ù* U4.15.KAM
17) *aš-ta-ak-ka-an-šum-ma*

13–17) I regularly set for him the ... meals, his clean food, his holy water on the days of the new moon and the full moon.

18) *ù a-na* ^{d}*nin-šubur*
19) *i-si-iq* SUKKAL.MAḪ-*ti-šu*
20) *i-na na-ap-ta-an*
21) *an-nim ra-i-mi-šu*
22) *la uš-pa-ar-ku-ú*
23) *lu ú-ša-aš-ki-in-šum*

18–23) I also established without end for the god Ninšubur the portion of his supreme office of vizier from the meals of the god Anum, who loves him.

24) *a-na* ^{d}*ul-maš-ši-tum*
25) *na-bi-a-at šu-mi-ia*
26) *é-maš šu-ba-at pu-sú-um-mi-ša*
27) KISAL *ra-bi-a-am*
28) *šu-ba-at ni-ši ma-da-tim*

24–28) For the goddess Ulmaššītum, the one who proclaims my name — Emaš, the dwelling of her veil, the great courtyard, place of the numerous people,

29) É *ri-ša-a-tim* KISAL(?) *ḫi-du-ti-šu*
30) *ša ši-i ù* ^{d}*nin-šubur*
31) ⌜*ḫi*⌝-*du-ut* ḪÉ.GÁL-*im*
32) *i-si-in ḫu-du li-ib-bi-im*
33) [*i-n*]*a*(?) *li-ib-bi-*[*i*]*m*
34) ⌜*i*⌝-*te-né-ep-p*[*u*(?)-*š*]*u*(?)

29–34) a temple of joy (and) courtyard of his pleasure within which she and the god Ninšubur celebrate constantly the delight of abundant (food) and the festival of pleasure —

35) *i-na tam-li-im ra*(?)-*bi-im*
36) ⌜*iš-di-šu*⌝ *i-na ma*(?)-x-*tim*
37) x [x] x [x]-*ma*

35–37) with a great terrace I *made firm* its foundations in ...

38) *ma-ḫa*(?)-*ra-tim ša* SIG4.AL.ÙR.RA
39) *ma*(?)-*ni*(?)-*ḫa* x [...] KISAL
40) *si-ma-at i-lu-ti-ša*
41) ⌜*ù*(?) *eṭ*(?)⌝-*lu-ti-ia e-pu-uš-ma*

38–41) I made a ... of baked bricks ... a courtyard befitting her divinity and my youth and

42) [^{d}*d*]*a-an*-É *ù* ^{d}*ra-šu-ub*-É
43) *ne-ši na-aš-pa-ri-ša*
44) *a-li-ku*-⟨*ut*⟩ *i-di*-«x»-*ša*
45) *a-šar ma-aq-qí-it šar-ri*
46) *ma-aṣ-ḫa-at ni-ši ma-da-tim*
47) *lu ú-še-ši-ib-šu-nu-ti*

42–47) installed [D]ān-Bītim and Rašub-Bītim, her escort lions, that go at her side at the place of the *maqqītum* offerings of the king (and) of the cereal offerings of the numerous people.

48) KÁ/É *a-ḫi-iṭ a-la-ak-ta-šu*
49) *uš-ta-as-sí-iq-ma*

48–57) I examined the temple/gate and put in order its routines there and in that temple. I

29.1, 2 *ri-ša-tim*. **43**.2 ⌜*na*⌝-[*aš*]-*pá-r*[*i*]-*ša*. **44**.3 *a-li-ku*-⟨*ut*⟩; other exs. broken at this point. **44**.2 *i-d*[*i*]-*ša*. **47**.1 *lu* ⌜*ú*⌝-x-*še-eb-šu-š*[*i*(?)]-*ib*-x-*šu-nu*-[*ti*].

50) *sà-ás-ka-a-am el-lam*
51) *ku-ul-ma-ša-am*
52) ⸢2⸣ ME.ZÉ *ti-gi-a-tim*
53) *ši-it-ra-am ra-bi-a-am*
54) *ḫu-bu-ra-am wa-ás-ma-am*
55) *ša a-na zi-mi i-lu-ti-ša*
56) *ra-bi-[tim(?)] šu-lu-ku*
57) *i-na* É *ša-a-ti lu ar-mi*

established pure *sasqûm* flour, a *kulmāšum*, two *manzû* drums for the lady drummers, a great curtain, an appropriate beer vat most suitable for the radiance of her great divinity.

58) *ša te-em-me-ni ú-uk-ka-šu*
59) *šu-mi ša-aṭ-ra-am*
60) *ú-da-ap-pa-ru-ma*
61) *šum-šu i-ša-aṭ-ta-ru*

58–61) (As for) the one who takes away my foundation inscriptions, and removes my inscribed name and writes his own name,

62) É(?) *li-ḫi-iṭ*
63) *ma-la-a-tim li-id-di-iš*
64) *ta-am-li-a-am li-ma-al-le-e*

62–64) may he examine the temple, renew its parts, and build up the terrace.

65) *šum* ^{d}*ta-ki-il-ì-lí-su* LUGAL
66) *a-na aš-ri-šu la ú-ta-ar-ru*
67) *a-wi-lum šu-ú lu* LUGAL
68) *lu* GÌR.NÍTA *lu* GUDU$_4$
69) *lu ša i-na a-wi-lu-tim*
70) *šu-ma-am na-bu-ú*

65–66) He who does not restore to its place the name of Takil-ilissu, the king,
67–70) that man — whether he be king, viceroy, *pašīšum* priest, or any member of the human race —

71) AN *šar-rum ša ì-lí ra-bu-tim*
72) *li-ik-ke-el-mi-ma šar-ru-*⸢*sú*⸣
73) *i-ši-it-ta-šu li-sú-úḫ*
74) *šar-ru-ut-sú i-na ta-ni-ḫi-im*
75) *li-iq-ta-at-ti*

71–73) may the god Anum, king of the great gods, look at him angrily and rip out the foundation of his kingship.
74–75) May his kingship end in sighs.

76) *an-nu-ni-tum*
77) *ra-i-ma-at pa-li-ia*
78) *li-bu-ús-sú-ma*
79) *ma-ru-uš-ta-am ra-bi-tam*
80) *li-iš-ku-un i-na zu-um-ri-šu*
81) *ar-nam ša la ib-šu-ú*
82) *i-na ni-ši ma-ti-ma*

76–82) May the goddess Annunītum, who loves my rule, destroy him and put a great pain in his body, a punishment which never has been among the people.

83) ^{d}*ul-maš-ši-tum*
84) *na-bi-a-at šu-mi-ia*
85) *mi-li-ik ḫa-la-qí-šu*
86) *pu-ru-sé la ba-la-ṭì-šu*
87) *a-na da-a-ar li-iq-bi*

83–87) May the goddess Ulamaššītum, who proclaims my name, announce the decree of his destruction and the decision of his eternal death.

88) ^{d}*nin-šubur* SUKKAL.AN.NA
89) *mu-*⸢*úḫ*⸣*-ḫa-šu*
90) *li-im-ḫa-aṣ-ma*
91) *ṭe$_4$-em-[š]u li-ša-an-ni*

88–91) May the god Ninšubur, vizier of the god Anum, smite [h]is forehead and disturb his reason.

92) ^{d}*da-an-*É ^{d}*ra-šu-ub-*É(?)
93) *it-ti* ⸢*an-nu*⸣*-ni-tum*
94) *ù* ^{d}*ul-maš-ši-tum*
95) *lu mu-le-em-mi-in*
96) *i-gi-ir-ri-i-šu-nu*
97) *a-na da-ri-a-tim*

92–97) May Dān-Bītim and Rašub-Bītim with the goddesses Anunītum and Ulmaššītum cause bad omens for him forever.

50.1 *sà-áš-*x-x*-am*. **50.3** *sà*(Brick: A)*-ás-ka-a-am*. **51.2** [*ku*]*-ul-ma-ša-*x*-am*. **57.1** *ša-ti*. **57.2** *ša-*x*-ti*. **58.1** *ú-ka-šu*. **58.2** ⸢*ú-ka*⸣-[*šu*]. **64.1** *ta-am-li-am*. **64.1** *li-ma-le-*⸢*e*⸣. **64.2** ⸢*li*⸣-[*m*]*a-l*[*e*]-[(x)]. **66.2** ⸢*a-na*⸣ *aš-ri-*x x. **69.3** *a-wi-*«LUM»*-lu-tim*. **72.2** [*l*]*i-*⸢*ki*⸣*-il-*⸢*mi*⸣*-ma*. **72.3** *li-ik-ke-el-mi-šu-ma* ⟨*šar-ru-sú*⟩. **74.2** *šar-ru-sú*. **84.1** [*n*]*a-bi-a*[*t*]. **84.2** [*n*]*a-bi-at*. **89.1** ⸢*mu*⸣-[*ḫ*]*a-šu*. **89.2** [*m*]*u-ḫa-šu*.

DĒR

E4.12

The important ancient city of Dēr, modern Tell al-ʿAqar near Badra, became independent following the Ur III period. Inscriptions of three of its rulers are known.

Nidnuša

E4.12.1

1

A fragmentary inscription of Nidnuša, viceroy of Dēr, is in the Yale collections.

COMMENTARY

The inscription is on YBC 2354, a purchased piece, provenance unknown, but presumably originally from Dēr. It is a piece of black limestone that was collated.

BIBLIOGRAPHY

1937 Stephens, YOS 9 no. 62 (copy, study)
1957 Edzard, Zwischenzeit pp. 68–69 (edition)
1971 Sollberger and Kupper, IRSA ivH1a (translation)

TEXT

1) ⸢^{d}⸣*ni-id-*⸢*nu-ša*⸣
2) NITA KALA.[G]A
3) *mi-gir* ^{d}*ištaran*
4) *na-ra-am* ^{d}INANNA
5) GÌR.NITA
6) BÀD.AN.KI
7) *da-ia-an ki-na-tim*
8) *la ḫa-bi-il*$_5$ *a-wi-lim*
9) *mu-uš-te*$_9$*-ši-ir ḫa-ab-lim*
10) *ù ḫa-bi-il*$_5$*-tim*
11) *ša-ki-in me-ša-ri-im*
12) *mu-ḫa-li-iq* ⸢*ra-gi-im*⸣
13) [x] x [...]
Lacuna

1–13) Nidnuša, mighty man, favourite of the god Ištarān, beloved of the goddess Eštar, viceroy of Dēr, just judge, who oppresses no one, who sets free the oppressed man and woman, who establishes justice, who destroys the evil man, ...
...
Lacuna

Ilum/Anum-muttabbil

E4.12.2

Two inscriptions are extant for Ilum-muttabbil (possibly to be read Anum-muttabbil), viceroy of Dēr. Ilum-muttabbil was a contemporary of Bilalama of Ešnunna and Šū-ilīšu of Isin (see R. Whiting, Letters p. 56 no. 13 line 5′).

1

A mace head in the British Museum bears an inscription of Ilum-muttabbil.

COMMENTARY

The object is BM 91084 (51-10-9,152), purchased from H.C. Rawlinson. It is an oval stone mace head that was not collated.

BIBLIOGRAPHY

1873 Lenormant, Choix no. 5 (copy)
1889 Winckler, Untersuchungen p. 156 no. 7 (copy)
1892 Winckler and Böhden, ABK no. 16 (copy)
1897 Thureau-Dangin, RA 4 p. 42 n. 4 (study)
1900 Radau, EBH pp. 255–56 n. 12 (edition)
1900 Scheil, MDP 2 pp. 75–76 (edition)
1905 King, CT 21 pl. 1 (copy)
1905 Thureau-Dangin, ISA pp. 250–51 Anu-mutabil (edition)
1907 Thureau-Dangin, SAK pp. 176–77 Anu-mutabil (edition)
1929 Barton, RISA pp. 166–67 Anu-mutabil 1 (edition)
1971 Sollberger and Kupper, IRSA IVH2a (translation)
1982 Steinkeller, ZA 72 p. 239 n. 4 (study)

TEXT

1) DINGIR-*mu-ta-bíl*
2) NITA KALA.GA
3) *mi-gir*
4) d*ištaran*
5) *na-ra-am*
6) dINANNA
7) GÌR.NITA
8) BÀD.AN.KI
9) *ma-ḫi-iṣ*
10) *qá-qá-ad*
11) *um-ma-an*
12) *an-ša-an*.KI

1–16) Ilum-muttabbil, mighty man, favourite of the god Ištarān, beloved of the goddess Eštar, viceroy of Dēr, who defeated completely the army of Anšan, Elam, (and) Simaški and aided Paraḫsum.

13) NIM-*tim*
14) *si-maš-ki-im*
15) *ù re-eṣ*
16) *pá-ra-aḫ-si-im*.KI

2

A fragmentary inscription known from a stone block, possibly a piece of a door socket, and a stamped brick fragment deals with Ilum-muttabbil's construction of something for Ištarān, the chief god of Dēr. The inscription may have dealt with the construction of the god's temple, but this is uncertain.

CATALOGUE

Ex.	Museum number	Provenance	Object	Dimensions (cm)	Lines preserved	cpn
1	Musée Royaux du Cinquantenaire, Brussels, no. O 239	Said to have come from Kermanshah	Frgm. of greyish granite, perhaps a piece of door socket	26.0 × 27.0	1–13, 24–37	n
2	IM 58333	From Tell al-ʿAqar or Tell Beiram near Badra	Frgm. of stamped brick	18.0 × 23.0 × 8.0	1–14, 16–24	n

BIBLIOGRAPHY

1925 Speleers, Recueil pl. 1 0.262 (ex. 1, copy)
1927–28 Jacobsen, AJSL 44 pp. 261–63 (ex. 1, edition)
1957 Edzard, Zwischenzeit p. 67 n. 322 (exs. 1–2, study)
1959 Edzard, Sumer 15 p. 26 and pl. 3 after p. 28 no. 12 (ex. 2, copy, study)
1971 Sollberger and Kupper, IRSA IVH2b (translation)
1982 Steinkeller, ZA 72 p. 239 n. 4 (study)

TEXT

1) *a-na*
2) ^{d}*i*[*š*]*taran*
3) *da-nim*
4) LUGAL BÀD.AN.KI
5) *ù* LUGAL
6) SA.DÚ-*im*
7) *be-lí-šu*

1–7) For the god I[š]tarān, the mighty, lord of Dēr, and lord of the mountain, his lord,

8) DINGIR-*mu-ta-bíl*
9) NITA KALA.GA
10) *mi-gi*[*r*]
11) ^{d}*ištaran*
12) *na-r*[*a-a*]*m*
13) ^{d}[INANNA]
14) GÌR.[NÍTA]

8–22) Ilum-muttabbil, mighty man, favouri[te] of the god Ištarān, belo[ve]d of the goddess [Eštar], vice[roy of Dēr] who def[eated] com[pletely] the ar[my] of Anša[n] (and) Simaš[ki] and ai[ded] Para[ḫsum].

3.1 ⌜*da-an*⌝-*nim*. 6.2 SA.DÚ-*i*.

15) [BÀD.AN.KI]
16) *ma-[ḫi-iṣ]*
17) *qá-[qá-ad]*
18) *um-m[a-an]*
19) *an-ša-[an]*
20) *si-maš-[ki-im]*
21) *ù r[e-eṣ]*
22) *pá-ra-[aḫ-si-im*.KI]
23) ⌜*í*⌝*-[nu-ma]*
24) *i-na ti-ir-ti*
25) [d]*ištaran*
26) *be-lí-šu*
27) *qá-qá-ad*
28) *um-ma-nim*
29) *[s]í-a-ti*
30) *im-ḫa-ṣu-na*
31) *ik-ru-ub-ma*
32) *ik-ri-bi-šu*
33) [d]*ištaran*
34) *iš-me-ma*

23–34) w[hen] by the command of the god Ištarān, his lord, he defeated completely [t]hat army, he prayed and the god Ištarān heard his prayer.

35) *a-na ba-la-ṭì-šu*
36) *[ù] ba-la-*⌜*aṭ*⌝
37) *[ma]-ti-*⌜*šu*⌝
Lacuna

35–37) He [...] for his own life [and] for the life of his [la]nd.
Lacuna

2001

A cylinder seal bears the inscription of a servant of Ilum-muttabbil.

COMMENTARY

The seal is in the Morgan Library, no. 68, a purchased piece. It is a cylinder of rock crystal, 3.1 cm long, 1.7 cm in dia. The seal legend measures 1.5 × 1.3 cm and the inscription was collated from the published photo.

BIBLIOGRAPHY

1916 Scheil, RA 13 pp. 134–35 (edition)
1920 Ward, Morgan no. 68
1948 Porada, Corpus no. 278 (photo, edition)
1961 Hallo, BiOr 18 p. 14 §v (study)

TEXT

1) DINGIR-*mu-ta-b[íl]*
2) GÌR.NÍTA
3) BÀD.AN.KI
4) *ba-zi-a*
5) SAG.DÙN ÌR.Z[U]

1) Ilum-muttabb[il],
2–3) viceroy of Dēr,
4) Bazīia,
5) cadastre official, you[r] servant.

[...]-ba

E4.12.3

1

A seal impression of a viceroy of Dēr, whose name is not fully preserved, is found on a tablet excavated at Ešnunna.

COMMENTARY

The tablet is As 30:T 255, from N 31:13 in, or slightly below, the Ipiq-Adad I–Ibāl-pî-El I palace. The inscription was collated by R. Whiting.

The provenance of this tablet indicates that this ruler of Dēr dates to a period later than Ilum-muttabbil.

BIBLIOGRAPHY

1940 Jacobsen, Gimilsin Temple pp. 155–56 (edition)
1957 Edzard, Zwischenzeit p. 67 n. 322 (study)
1987 Whiting, Letters p. 119 and pl. 27 Supplement 3 (copy, edition)

TEXT

1) ^{d}*ištaran*
2) *da-núm*
3) [LU]GAL BÀD.AN.KI
4) [...]-*ba*
5) [NITA KALA.GA]
6) *mi-gir* ^{d}*i*[*štaran*]
7) *na-ra-am* ^{d}[INANNA]
8) GÌR.[NITA]
9) [BÀD.AN.KI]
10) [ÌR.ZU]

1) Ištarān,
2) the mighty,
3) [lo]rd of Dēr –
4) [...]-ba,
5) [mighty man],
6) favourite of the god I[štarān],
7) beloved of [the goddess Eštar],
8–9) vice[roy of Dēr],
10) [your servant].

Iašūb-Iaḫad

E4.12.4

A ruler of Dēr by the name Iašūb-Iaḫad is mentioned in a letter published by G. Dossin. No inscriptions of this ruler are known.

BIBLIOGRAPHY

1956 Dossin, Syria 33 pp. 63–69 (study)
1985 Sasson, Mélanges Birot pp. 237–55 (study]

DINIKTUM

E4.13

The city of Diniktum was located somewhere in the Diyala region, possibly at or near Tell Muḥammad, in the south-east section of modern Baghdad. Inscriptions of two of its rulers are known.

Itūr-šarrum

E4.13.1

1

A seal impression on a tablet envelope excavated at Ešnunna bears the inscription of a ruler of Diniktum whose name is broken, but which should probably be restored as Itūr-šarrum.

COMMENTARY

The impression is rolled on As 30:T.133, a tablet envelope from M 31:6 found in association with sealings of servants of Ipiq-Adad I. This suggests a date for Itūr-šarrum before that of Sîn-gāmil.

BIBLIOGRAPHY

1987 Whiting, Letters p. 119 and pl. 27 Supplement 2 (copy, edition)

TEXT

1) ⌜*i*⌝-*túr-š*[*ar-ru-um*]	1) Itūr-š[arrum],
2) *ra-bí-an* MAR.DÚ	2–3) Amo[rite] chief of Dini[ktum],
3) *ša di-ni-i*[*k-tim*]	
4) [DUMU] ⌜*ì-lí*⌝-[...]	4) [son] of Ilī-[...].

Sîn-gāmil

E4.13.2

He figures in a letter published by Dossin (Syria 33 [1956] pp. 63–69) as king of Diniktum.

1

Sîn-gāmil was a contemporary of Iarīm-Līm I of Iamḫad, Zimrī-Līm of Mari, and Ḫammu-rāpi of Babylon. This text appears on bricks.

CATALOGUE

Ex.	Museum number	Excavation number	Provenance	Object	Dimensions (cm)	Lines preserved	cpn
1	IM 10794	None, presented by E. Musayyeh	Said to have come from Tell Abu Hurmah = (?) Tell Ḥarmal	Stamped brick	18.0 × 14.0	1–4	n
2	MB 2922	None	Brought into the Iraq Museum by a local resident in spring 1960	Stamped well or cistern brick	–	1–4	c

COMMENTARY

Although ex. 1 probably came from Tell Ḥarmal, this site cannot be Diniktum, because it is known to be ancient Šaduppûm.

Ex. 2, a well or cistern brick, was on display in the Iraq Museum (1985). It bears the Arabic notation MB 2922, the significance of which is unclear (Baghdad Museum ?). According to Adams, Baghdad p. 165, it is supposed to be from site 851 far off to the east of the Diyala. This is almost certainly a mistake based on a confusion of the records.

BIBLIOGRAPHY

1946 S. Smith, Sumer 12 pp. 19–21 (ex. 1, copy, edition)
1956 Dossin, Syria 33 p. 68 (edition)
1957 Kupper, Nomades pp. 192–93 (transliteration, study)
1957 Edzard, Zwischenzeit p. 37 n. 157 (study)
1961 J. Lewy, HUCA 32 p. 51 n. 115 (edition)
1965 Sollberger, UET 8 p. 12 n. to no. 65 (study)
1965 Adams, Baghdad p. 165 site no. 851 (ex. 2, edition, incorrect provenance)
1971 Sollberger and Kupper, IRSA IVJ1a (translation)
1976 Stol, Studies in Old Babylonian History p. 88 (transliteration, study)

TEXT

1) ᵈEN.ZU-*ga-mi-il*	1) Sîn-gāmil,
2) *ra-bí-an* MAR.DÚ	2–3) Amorite chief of Diniktum,
3) *ša di-ni-ik-tim*.KI	
4) DUMU ᵈEN.ZU-*še-mi*	4) son of Sîn-šemi.

2001

The impression of what may be the seal of a servant of Sîn-gāmil was found on a tablet excavated at Tell Leilan.

COMMENTARY

The impression is on L 85-495 excavated in the Lower Town. It was collated by D. Parayre and is edited here through the courtesy of H. Weiss.

TEXT

1) [x]-*lí-i-din-nam* x	1) [...]li-iddinam ...,
2) [ÌR] ᵈEN.ZU-*ga-mil*	2) [servant] of Sîn-gāmil.

DIYALA REGION

E4.14

An important dynasty which ruled a number of cities in the Diyala basin area appears in documents dating to the general time period of Sūmû-la-Il of Babylon. Unfortunately we do not yet know which city served as the home of this dynasty. We do, however, know the names of at least three of its rulers, Ammī-dušur, Sîn-abūšu, and Ikūn-pî-Sîn. Inscriptions and seal impressions belonging to these kings are edited here.

Ammī-dušur

E4.14.1

Ammī-dušur is known from a number of year names. Although no royal inscriptions of this king are known, we do have the text of a treaty between Ammī-dušur and Sūmû-numḫim, king of Šadlaš.

BIBLIOGRAPHY

1979 Greengus, OBTI pp. 74–77 no. 326 (edition of treaty)

Sîn-abūšu

E4.14.2

Sîn-abūšu is known from a large number of year names found in an archive edited by F. Rashid (see bibliography). He must have reigned about twenty years, and controlled many cities in the Diyala region including Šaduppûm, Nērebtum, Tutub, Dūr-Rimuš, Šulgi-Nanna, Dūr-Sîn-abūšu, and Aškuzum.

BIBLIOGRAPHY

1965 Rashid, Archiv Nūršamaš pp. 6–16

1001

A fragment of a clay cylinder was found at Ishchali. Although the name of the ruler responsible for it is not preserved, it should probably be attributed to Sîn-abūšu.

COMMENTARY

The cylinder comes from the foundations of the Inanna Kitītum temple at Ishchali. The excavation no. and present location of this cylinder are not known. The transliteration of this previously unpublished piece is from Th. Jacobsen and is edited through the courtesy of the trustees of the Oriental Institute.

The attribution of this piece is not certain; the inscription alludes to control over Tutub, and since it was found at Ishchali/Nērebtum we may assume that the king of this inscription controlled both these cities. Of the Diyala area kings who preceded Ipiq-Adad II, conqueror of Nērebtum for Ešnunna, Išme-Bali, Ammī-dušur, Sîn-abūšu, and Ikūn-pî-Sîn are all known to have controlled both Tutub and Nērebtum. The inscription refers to something of a huge size that Jacobsen has suggested (personal communication) must have been a canal. Sîn-abūšu had a canal dug which he had named after himself and commemorated in one of his year names. Although no certain attribution of this inscription can be made at this time, Sîn-abūšu seems to be the most likely candidate as the author of this inscription.

TEXT

Col. i (missing)	i) (missing)
Col. ii	
1) [...] *tu-tu-ub*.KI	ii 1–4) [When the god ...] looked [faithfully] at [...], Tutub [and] its land, its [cities] and villages,
2) [ù] ma-da-bi	
3) [uru] ⸢ù⸣ á-dam-bi-šè	
4) [igi-zi mu-ši-i]n-bar-ra-a	

5) [ki-b]i-šè
6) [im-ši-g]i$_{4}$-gi$_{4}$
7) [...-n]e-ne
8) [mu-u]n-gub
9) [...] mu
Lacuna

Col. iii (missing)

Col. iv
1) 5 d[anna gíd-bi-im]
2) 1 ½ nin[dan dagal-bi-im]
3) á-dah̬-⸢^{d}⸣[...]
4) usu-ušumgal-mu
5) á-dah̬-^{d}mar-[dú]
6) dingir-sag-du-m[u]
7) [ù] ^{d}inanna *ki-ti*.[KI-ta]

Lacuna

ii 5–6) he [rest]ored them

ii 7–9) (and) set up their ... .
Lacuna

iii) (missing)

iv 1–7) [I dug a canal whose length] was 5 [*danna*, whose width was] 1 ½ *nin*[*dan*] – with the help of the god [...], (with) my strength of a dragon, (with) the help of the god Mar[du], the god who created m[e, and with] (the help of) the goddesss Inanna of Kiti
Lacuna

2001

The impression of a seal of a servant of Sîn-abūšu is found on a tablet in the collection of the Lowie Museum of Anthropology, University of California, Berkeley.

COMMENTARY

The tablet numbered UCLM 9-2864 bears this inscription.

BIBLIOGRAPHY

1986 Greengus, Ishchali Documents p. 185 (transliteration)

TEXT

1) ÌR ^{d}NANNA
2) DUMU ^{d}EN.ZU-*ki-ma-ì-lí*-⸢*ia*⸣
3) ÌR ^{d}EN.ZU-*a-bu-šu*

1) Warad-Nanna,
2) son of Sîn-kīma-ilīia,
3) servant of Sîn-abūšu.

Ikūn-pî-Sîn

E4.14.3

Archival evidence indicates that Ikūn-pî-Sîn, who succeeded Sîn-abūšu, controlled both Nērebtum and Tutub. One year name of the king is known (see R. Harris, JCS 9 p. 47 no. 25).

1

An impression of a seal of Ikūn-pî-Sîn dedicated to the god Išar-kīdissu, probable spouse of Inanna Kitītum, is found on two tablets excavated at Ishchali.

Išar-kīdissu, apparently some form of the god Nergal, appears to have been an important deity at Ishchali. Leemans has discussed a possible connection of this god with the cult of Eštar (see Ishtar of Lagaba and Her Dress pp. 24–26). The evidence of Greengus OBTI 77 lines 12–13 suggests that Išar-kīdissu was the consort of the goddess Inanna Kitītum (see OBTI pp. 6–7). For the deity Išar-Kīdissu see W.G. Lambert, RLA 5 p. 173.

CATALOGUE

Ex.	Museum number	Excavation number	Provenance	Object	cpn
1	A 21957	Ish 35:T.14	Ishchali, 5 v 31	Seal impression on clay tablet	n
2	A 21966	Ish 35:T.32	Ishchali, 3 v 30	Seal impression on clay tablet	n

BIBLIOGRAPHY

1979 Greengus, OBTI no. 26 (exs. 1–2, composite copy) and p. 21 n. 103 (study)
1986 Greengus, Ishchali Documents p. 24 (ex. 1, edition)

TEXT

1) ^{d}*i*-⸢*šar*⸣-[*ki-di-su*]	1) [To] the god Išar-[kīdissu],
2) lugal-a-ni-[ir]	2) his lord,
3) *i-ku-un-pi*$_4$-^{d}EN.ZU	3) Ikūn-pî-Sîn
4) [in-na-an-ba]	4) [presented (this seal)].

2001

An impression of a servant seal of Ikūn-pî-Sîn is found on a jar cover excavated at Ishchali.

COMMENTARY

The impression is on Ish 34:T.72, found at 2–P.30, floor II. It is at present in the Iraq Museum. This information was communicated by S. Greengus, from the field notes of T. Jacobsen.

BIBLIOGRAPHY

1955 Harris, JCS 9 p. 55 (study)
1987 Whiting, Letters p. 32 n. 112 (study)

TEXT

1) [...] X-*šu*	1) [...]...šu,
2) [...] GAL	2) great [...],
3) [DUMU ...]-*re-me-ni*	3) [son of ...]-rēmēnī,
4) ÌR ⌜*i-ku*⌝-*un-pi*$_4$-^{d}EN.ZU	4) servant of Ikūn-pî-Sîn.

2002

Another seal impression on the previously mentioned jar cover names a servant of Ikūn-pî-Sîn.

COMMENTARY

This inscription results from a conflation of two partially preserved seal impressions.

BIBLIOGRAPHY

1986 Greengus, Ishchali Documents p. 24 (transliteration)

TEXT

1) *be-la-nu-um*	1) Bēlānum,
2) DUMU *e-te-el-lum*	2) son of Etellum,
3) ÌR ⌜*i-ku-un-pi*$_4$-^{d}EN.ZU⌝	3) servant of Ikūn-pî-Sîn.

Ibbīšu-Malik

E4.14.4

Impressions of seals of two other Diyala area rulers who may or may not have belonged to the Sîn-abūšu dynasty but who date to this general time period are edited here. The first of these is Ibbīšu-Malik.

2001

The impression of a seal of a servant of Ibbīšu-Malik is found on A 7829, a tablet from Ishchali, whose exact provenance is not known. It was collated by S. Greengus.

BIBLIOGRAPHY

1979 Greengus, OBTI no. 130 (copy)

TEXT

1) ᵈUTU-*mu-*⸢*uš-te-pi-iš*⸣	1) Šamaš-muštēpiš,
2) ÌR *i-bi-šu-*ᵈ*ma-lik*	2) servant of Ibbīšu-Malik.

Iadkur-Il

E4.14.5

The ruler Iadkur-Il is known from a year name on tablets excavated at Khafajah and Tell al-Ḍibāʿi, which commemorate his death (see T. Baqir, Sumer 5 p. 143 no. 5 and R. Harris, JCS 9 p. 47 no. 12).

2001

A seal impression of a servant of this ruler is known from Tell al-Ḍibāʿi.

COMMENTARY

The impression is found on IM 52774 from level v at Tell al-Ḍibāʿi. It was not collated.

BIBLIOGRAPHY

1949 Baqir, Sumer 5 p. 141 (transliteration)

TEXT

1) *ḫa-li-ṣum*	1) Ḫaliṣum,
2) DUMU *ta-an-ta-nu-um*	2) son of Tantanum,
3) ÌR *ia-ad-kur*-DINGIR	3) servant of Iadkur-Il.

ŠADLAŠ

E4.15

The city of Šadlaš, whose exact location is unknown, must have lain in the Diyala region. Inscriptions of two of its Old Babylonian rulers are known.

Sūmû-Amnānim

E4.15.1

Two inscriptions are known for Sūmû-Amnānim, king of Šadlaš.

1

An inscription of Sūmû-Amnānim dealing with the construction of temples for the goddess Eštar is known from Ishchali.

COMMENTARY

The inscription is found on two stamped brick fragments, one of which was found on the surface at Ishchali, the other in the uppermost stratum 6 R 35. According to notes of T. Jacobsen, the stamp of this inscription measures 16.5 × 12.25 cm. The inscription given here follows the transliteration offered in Greengus, OBTI p. 2 n. 6. None of the pieces could be located. According to Jacobsen, the inscription deals with the construction of the é-gibil$_4$ and é-maḫ for the goddess.

BIBLIOGRAPHY

1979 Greengus, OBTI p. 2 n. 6 (transliteration)

TEXT

1) *a-na* dINANNA
2) ⸢*su*⸣-*mu-am*$_7$-*na*-⸢*nim*⸣
3) LUGAL *ša-ad-la*-[*aš*.KI]
4) É ⸢X X⸣
5) *ù* [...]
Lacuna

1) For the goddess Eštar,
2) Sūmû-Amnānim,
3) king of Šadla[š],
4–5) [built] the temple ... and [the temple ...].
Lacuna

2

A basalt ex-voto excavated at Tell al-Ḍibāʿi contains a dedication to a goddess, probably Eštar, by Sūmû-Amnānim.

COMMENTARY

The object, apparently a chair or bench for offerings, was excavated in 1965 at Tell al-Ḍibāʿi. The reading of the text follows the copy of F. Rashid.

BIBLIOGRAPHY

1967 Rashid, Sumer 23 p. 178 [Arabic section] (copy, edition)
1979 Greengus, OBTI p. 2 n. 6 (transliteration)

TEXT

1) ᵈ[INANNA]	1) To the goddess [Eštar],
2) NIN *ša-ad-la-á*[*š*.KI]	2) lady of Šadla[š],
3) *ra-im-ti*	3) the one who loves (him),
4) *su-mu-am*$_7$-*na-ni*[*m*]	4) Sūmû-Amnāni[m],
5) *šar ša-ad-la*-[*áš*.KI]	5) king of Šadla[š],
6) *i-qí-iš*	6) presented (this object).

Sūmû-Samas

E4.15.2

Another ruler of Šadlaš, Sūmû-Samas, is known.

1

An impression of the seal of Sūmû-Samas appears on a tablet in the British Museum.

COMMENTARY

The impression is found on BM 80746 (Bu 91-5-9,884) probably from Sippar. It was not collated.

BIBLIOGRAPHY

1968 Finkelstein, CT 48 no. 83 (transliteration)
1976 Stol, Studies in Old Babylonian History p. 86 (transliteration, study)

TEXT

1) *su-mu-*dUTU	1) Sūmû-Samas,
2) DUMU *a-pil-*dEN.ZU	2) son of Apil-Sîn,
3) *ra-bi-a-an*	3–4) chief of Amnān (and) Šadlaš.
4) *am-na-an ša-ad-la-áš*	

Sūmû-numḫim

E4.15.3

A third king of Šadlaš is known, Sūmû-numḫim. He appears in a treaty between himself, ruler of Šadlaš, and Ammī-dušur, ruler of Nērebtum. No royal inscriptions of this ruler are known.

BIBLIOGRAPHY

1979 Greengus, OBTI pp. 74–77 (edition)

MÊ-TURRAN

E4.16

The important ancient city of Mê-Turran 'Waters of the Diyala' has been identified by Iraqi excavators at the modern sites of Tell Ḥaddād and Tell al-Sib, not far from modern Diyala north of the Jebel Ḥamrīn. A year formula of Ipiq-Adad II commemorates the capture of the city (see S. Greengus, OBTI p. 31 no. 40). The city appears to have stayed under the control of Ešnunna down to the time of Ṣillī-Sîn. An inscription of what may be a local Amorite ruler of the city dealing with the construction of the city walls was found by an Iraqi excavation team.

Arīm-Līm

E4.16.1

1

One inscription is known for Arīm-Līm, who ruled Mê-Turran.

COMMENTARY

The object is a stone foundation tablet reused as a door socket, excavated from Tell Ḥaddād, exact provenance and IM no. not determined. The text is offered here through the courtesy of F. Al-Rawi.

Arīm-Līm might possibly be the same figure as Iarīm-Līm, whose death is commemorated in the year name concluding the treaty between Šadlaš and Nērebtum (see Greengus, OBTI pp. 74–77). If so, he was a contemporary of Sūmû-la-Il of Babylon, and ruled Mê-Turran before the defeat of the city by Ipiq-Adad II of Ešnunna.

TEXT

1) *a-ri-im-li-im*	1) Arīm-Līm,
2) DUMU *i-ba-a-a*	2) son of Ibāia,
3) *ra-bí-an* MAR.D[Ú]	3) Amori[te] chief,
4) BÀD-*am*	4–6) built the wall of Mê-Turran
5) *ša me-tu-ra-an*.KI	
6) *i-pu-uš*	
7) *ù* GIŠ.IG-*tim*	7–8) and fixed (its) doors.
8) *ir-te*	
9) *i-na* KÁ.GAL-*tim*	9–11) In (its) gates he placed foundatio[n] inscriptions.
10) *tem-me-n*[*i*]	
11) *iš-ku-un*	

BATIR

E4.17

The city of Batir, which appears in Early Dynastic times in the form Badar or Madar, lay near or on the Diyala river near the junction with the Jebel Ḥamrīn.

Aiiabum

E4.17.1

1

A brick of an independent ruler of Old Babylonian date of the city of Batir was excavated at Tell al-Suleimah. Tell al-Suleimah may, therefore, mark the site of ancient Batir.

COMMENTARY

The inscription was collated from an excavation photo and is published here through the courtesy of Dr B.Kh. Ismail. No IM no. or exact provenance for the piece is known.

BIBLIOGRAPHY

1985 Rashid, Sumer 40 p. 56 (study)

TEXT

1) *a*-⌜*ia*⌝-*bu*-⌜*um*⌝	1) Aiiabum,
2) DUMU *a*-x x x x	2) son of ...,
3) *ra-bí-an* x x	3) ... chief
4) *ša ba*-⌜*ti*⌝-*ir*.[KI]	4) of Batir,
5) *a-na ba-la-ṭì-š*[*u*]	5–7) built the temple of the goddess Batirītum for hi[s] (own) life.
6) É ^{d}*ba-ti-ri*-⌜*tum*⌝	
7) *i-pu-uš*	

LULLUBUM

E4.18

The land of Lullubum lay in the mountainous area east of Mesopotamia, probably in the greater vicinity of modern Suleimānīyah. An inscription of one of its rulers, Anubanini, probably dates to the early Isin-Larsa period.

BIBLIOGRAPHY

1988 Klengel, RLA 7/3–4 pp. 164–68

Anubanini

E4.18.1

1

The inscription of Anubanini is found on a rock face near Sar-i-pūl-i-Zohāb.

COMMENTARY

The edition given here follows that of D. Edzard based on photos of the inscription taken by L. Trümpelmann.

The date of this inscription is not certain. In ii 4 the status constructus of *bēlum* appears as *be-el*. In inscriptions E4.1.1.2002 and 2004 dating to the reign of Išbi-Erra this word appears in the earlier form *be-al*. In inscription E4.1.4.9 dating to the time of Išme-Dagān *be-el* appears. This feature, in addition to others discussed by Edzard (AfO 24 [1973] pp. 74–75), suggests that the Anubanini inscription dates to the early Isin-Larsa period.

BIBLIOGRAPHY

1839 H. Rawlinson, JRGS 9 p. 37 (study)
1842 Flandin and Coste, Voyage en Perse 1 pl. 208 A (drawing)
1851 Flandin and Coste, Voyage en Perse. Relation du voyage p. 460 (study)
1865 G. Rawlinson, The Five Great Monarchies vol. 3 (London) p. 436 (drawing)
1893 de Morgan and Scheil, RT 14 pp. 100–105 (copy, edition)
1893 Hilprecht, BE 1/1 pp. 14–15 (study)
1896 de Morgan, MSP 4/1 pp. 160–70 pl. XI
1900 Scheil, MDP 2 pp. 67–68 (edition)
1905 Thureau-Dangin, ISA pp. 246–47 Anu-bânîni (edition)
1907 Thureau-Dangin, SAK pp. 172–73 Anu-bânîni (edition)
1910 Herzfeld, Iranisches Felsreliefs (Berlin) pp. 62 and 192 (study)
1915 Prinz, Altorientalische Symbolik (Berlin) pl. XIV, 1 (drawing)
1920 Herzfeld, Am Tor von Asien (Berlin) pp. 3–5 and fig. 1 (copy, study)
1928 Weissbach, RLA 1/2 p. 110 (study)
1929 Barton, RISA pp. 150–51 Anubanini 1 (edition)
1931 Contenau, Manuel 2 pp. 763–65 and fig. 541 (drawing, study)
1936 Cameron, Iran p. 41 (study)
1941 Herzfeld, Iran in the Ancient Near East (London) pp. 183–84 and fig. 297 (drawing, study)
1942 Debevoise, JNES 1 pp. 80–81 and fig. 2 (drawing, study)
1944 Diez, Iranisches Kunst pp. 114–15 and fig. 72 (drawing, study)
1956 von der Osten, Die Welt der Perser p. 25 (study)
1957 Hallo, Royal Titles pp. 97–98 (study)
1961 Moscati, Atti Lincei 8/10/2 p. 81 (study)
1962 Cameron, 25. Kongress 1 p. 242 (study)
1963 Hirsch, AfO 20 p. 32 (study)
1965 Porada, The Art of Ancient Iran (New York) pp. 40–41 and fig. 15 (drawing, study)
1966 Vanden Berghe, Archéologie de l'Iran ancien (Leiden) pp. 98–101 and pl. 123c (drawing, study)
1966 Brentjes, Das Altertum 12 p. 131 (study)
1967 Calmeyer, CRRA 15 p. 169 (study)
1969 Pritchard, ANEP[2] no. 524 (drawing, study)
1973 Boese, Studia Iranica 2 p. 46 n. 3 (study)
1973 Edzard, AfO 24 pp. 73–75 (edition)
1975 Seidl in Orthmann (ed.), Der alte Orient no. 183 (photo, study)
1976 Hrouda, Edzard and Trümpelmann, Iranische Denkmäler 2/7 pp. 7–11 and pl. 5–6 (photo, copy, drawing, edition)
1982 Börker-Klähn, Bildstelen pp. 138–39 no. 31 (photo, study)
1985 M. Walker, The Tigris Frontier pp. 163–67 (study)
1988 Klengel, RLA 7/3–4 p. 165 §4 (study)

TEXT

Col. i	
1) [AN]-*nu-ba-ni-ni*	i 1–3) [An]ubanini, mighty [k]ing, [k]ing of Lullubum,
2) [LU]GAL *da-núm*	
3) [L]UGAL *lu-lu-bí*.KI-*im*	
4) *ṣa-l*[*a-a*]*m-šu*	i 4–8) had an im[ag]e of himself and an image of the goddess Eštar set up on mount Batir.
5) *ù ṣa-lam* ^{d}INANNA	
6) *i-na ša-du-im*	
7) *ba-ti-ir*	
8) [*u*]*š-zi*(*)-*iz*	
9) *ša ṣa-al-mi-in*	i 9–12) He who removes these two images and inscription
10) *an-ni-in*	
11) *ù ṭup-pá-am*	
12) *ù-ša-sà-ku*	
13) [A]N-*nu-um*	i 13–21) may the gods [A]num and Antum, Enlil and Ninlil, Adad and Eštar, Sîn and Šamaš, ...
14) *ù an-tum*	
15) ^{d}*en-líl*	
16) *ù* ^{d}NIN.LÍL	
17) ^{d}IŠKUR	
18) *ù* ^{d}INANNA	
19) ^{d}EN.ZU	
20) *ù* ^{d}UTU	
21) [x (x)] x LUM	
22) [...]	i 22–23) [...]
23) [...]	
Col. ii	
1) ^{d}*nin*-x	ii 1–6) May the gods Nin... and [...], En[...] and the lord of [...] x [...], the [g]re[at] gods and ...
2) *ù* ^{d}[...]	
3) ^{d}*en*-[x]	
4) *be-el* [x x x] x [x (x)]	
5) *i-lu* [*r*]*a-b*[*í-ú-tum*]	
6) *ù ša*-x-[x (x)]	
7) *er-ra-tá*[*m*]	ii 7–11) inflict on him an evil curse. May they destroy his seed.
8) *le-mu-tám*	
9) *li-ru-ru-uš*	
10) *zé-ra-šu*	
11) *li-il-qú-tú*	
12) *ti-am-t*[*um*]	ii 12–22) The Upp[er] and Lo[wer] Se[a] ...
13) *e-li-t*[*um*]	
14) *ù ša-p*[*il-tum*]	
15) *ša* x x	
16) *a* x [...]	
17) *ù* [x] TI(?)	
18) [...]	
19) *a* [x (x)] *lu* x	
20) [...]	
21) *šu* x [x (x)]	
22) *ù* [x x] *šu*	
Col. iii	
1) *li*-x-*la*	iii 1) May ...
2) *a* x x x	iii 2–10) ...

i 8 Text: GI.

3) [...] x
4) [...] *š*[*u*]
5) [...] x
Lacuna (3 lines missing)
9) *ša* [...]
10) *lu*(?) x [...]
11) *a-i* IB-[...]
Lacuna (5 lines missing)
17) x [...]
Lacuna (c. 11 lines missing)

iii 11) May it not [...]
Lacuna

SIMURRUM

E4.19

The important city of Simurrum, which lay in the east Transtigridian region not too far from the Jebel Ḥamrīn, was frequently the object of campaigns by both the Old Akkadian and Ur III kings. With the collapse of the Ur III empire Simurrum appears to have become an independent state. In an archival document dating to year x + 19 of Išbi-Erra (BIN 9 no. 421), there is mentioned a diplomatic gift from Isin for the king of Simurrum, and an ambassador from Simurrum figures in the same tablet.

A handful of inscriptions are extant which mention king Iddi(n)-Sîn and his son Zabazuna, kings of Simurrum. The provenance of these inscriptions, four near the city of Rania in Iraq and one at Sar-i-pūl-Zohāb in western Iran, shows the wide area that was controlled by Simurrum at this time.

A certain Iddi(n)-Sîn, possibly a reference to the king of Simurrum, is mentioned in a letter found at Tell Asmar, which may have been sent to Nūr-aḫum of Ešnunna (see R. Whiting, Letters p. 37 no. 2 line 8). A seal impression of a servant of Zabazuna found at Ešnunna dates, according to Whiting, to the period after the end of the Ur III, but before the time of Bilalama. A certain *za-ba-zi-in-núm* who appears in a letter to Bilalama found at Tell Asmar (see Whiting, Letters p. 56 no. 13 line 10′) might possibly refer to Zabazuna of Simurrum. If so, it would indicate that Zabazuna was a contemporary of Bilalama of Ešnunna. These facts suggest that the reigns of Iddi(n)-Sîn and Zabazuna were contemporary with that of Išbi-Erra of Isin.

BIBLIOGRAPHY

1978 Hallo, RHA 36 pp. 71–81 (study of pre-OB Simurrum)

Iddi(n)-Sîn

E4.19.1

A number of inscriptions are known which date to the reign of Iddi(n)-Sîn, but which were commissioned by his son Zabazuna near the ancient city of Kulunnum. This city is probably to be located near Bardi Sanjian not far from modern Rania.

1

The first of these inscriptions deals with a table set up for the goddess Eštar following the defeat of the city of Kulunnum.

COMMENTARY

The piece is IM 81364, from Bardi Sanjian in Bītwāta. It was not found in situ. It is a rectangular block of stone; the inscription was collated from the published photo.

In line 62 there is a clear *ma* at the end. This is probably a mistake for *la*, which is found in E4.19.1.4 (unpublished) at the corresponding point. The translation assumes a reading *la* instead of *ma*.

BIBLIOGRAPHY

1978 al Fouadi, Sumer 34 pp. 122–26 text A (photo, conflated edition)

TEXT

1) ^{d}*i-dì-*^{d}EN.ZU	1–3) Iddi(n)-Sîn, mighty king, king of Simurrum,
2) LUGAL *da-núm*	
3) LUGAL *si-mu-ri-im*.KI	
4) ^{d}*za-ba-zu-na*	4–5) Zabazuna (is) his son –
5) DUMU-NI	
6) *ku-lu-un-nu-um*.KI	6–11) Kulunnum rebelled and waged war against Zabazuna.
7) *ik-ki-ir-ma*	
8) *a-na*	
9) ^{d}*za-ba-zu-na*	
10) *gi-ra-am*	
11) *i-ta-ba-al*	
12) *ša* ^{d}*za-ba-zu-na*	12–21) The gods Adad, Eštar, and Nišba heard the word of Zabazuna – he destroyed the city (of Kulunnum) and consecrated it to those gods.
13) *a-wa-sú*	
14) ^{d}IŠKUR	
15) ^{d}INANNA	

16) *ù* ^{d}*ni-iš-ba*
17) *iš-me-ú-ma*
18) *a-lam ú-ḫa-li-iq-ma*
19) *a-na i-li*
20) *šu-nu-ti*
21) *ú-qá-dì-ís-sú*
22) GIŠ.BANŠUR-*am*
23) *ša* ^{d}INANNA
24) *be-el-ti-šu*
25) *iš-ku-un*

22–25) He set up a table of the goddess Eštar, his lady.

26) *ša i-pi*$_5$*-iš-ti*
27) *ù-ša-sà-ku*
28) *ù ši-ṭì-ir-ti*
29) *ú-pá-sà-sú*
30) *a-na šu-mi*
31) *er-re-ti-šu*
32) *ša-ni-am*
33) *ú-ša-ḫa-zu*

26–33) He who removes my work, or erases my inscription or because of its curse incites another (to do so),

34) *a-wi-lam*
35) *šu-a-ti*
36) AN
37) ^{d}*en-líl*
38) ^{d}*nin-ḫur-sag*
39) ^{d}EN.KI
40) ^{d}EN.ZU
41) ^{d}IŠKUR
42) *be-el* GIŠ.TUKUL
43) ^{d}UTU
44) *be-el* DI.KU$_5$.DA
45) ^{d}INANNA
46) *be-la-at ta-ḫa-zi-im*
47) ^{d}*nin*-AN-*si*$_4$*-an-na*
48) *ì-lí*
49) ^{d}*ni-iš-ba*
50) *be-li*
51) *er-re-tám*
52) *le-mu-tám*
53) *li-ru-ru-uš*

34–53) that man – may the gods Anum, Enlil, Ninḫursag, Ea, Sîn, and Adad, lord of the weapon, Šamaš, lord of judgements, Eštar, lady of battle, Ninsianna, my god, (and) the god Nišba, my lord, inflict on him an evil curse.

54) NUMUN-*šu*
55) *li-il-qú-⟨tú⟩-ma*
56) SUḪUŠ-*su*
57) *li-su-ḫu*

54–57) May they destroy his seed and rip out his foundation.

58) IBILA *ù* MU
59) *a i-dì-nu-šum*
60) *ba-la-ṭum*
61) *lu ik-ki-ib-šu*
62) *ki-ma ša-la*(*)
63) *e-bu-ri-im*
64) *i-na ṣe-er*
65) *um-ma-ni-su*
66) *lu ma-ru-uṣ*

58–66) May they not grant him heir or offspring. May life be his taboo. As (when) there is *no* harvest may it be difficult for his people.

---

62 Text: *ma*.

2

A second stone block found in Bītwāta deals with the setting up of a table for the god Adad by Zabazuna.

COMMENTARY

The piece is IM 81365, from Bardi Sanjian in Bītwāta. It was not found in situ. It is a rectangular block of stone. The text, which is not complete, was collated from the published photo.

BIBLIOGRAPHY

1978 al Fouadi, Sumer 34 pp. 122–26 text B (photo, conflated edition)

TEXT

1) ^{d}*i-dì-*^{d}EN.ZU
2) LUGAL *da-núm*
3) LUGAL *si-mu-ri-im*.KI

1–3) Iddi(n)-Sîn, mighty king, king of Simurrum,

4) ^{d}*za-ba-zu-na*
5) DUMU-NI

4–5) Zabazuna (is) his son –

6) *ku-lu-un-nu-um*.KI
7) *ik-ki-ir-ma*
8) *a-na*
9) ^{d}*za-ba-zu-na*
10) *gi-ra-am*
11) *i-ta-ba-al*

6–11) Kulunnum rebelled and waged war against Zabazuna.

12) *ša* ^{d}*za-ba-zu-na*
13) *a-wa-sú*
14) ^{d}IŠKUR
15) ^{d}INANNA
16) *ù* ^{d}*ni-iš-ba*
17) *iš-me-ú-ma*
18) *a-lam ú-ḫa-li-iq-ma*
19) *a-na i-li*
20) *šu-nu-ti*
21) *ú-qá-dì-ís-sú*

12–21) The gods Adad, Eštar, and Nišba heard the word of Zabazuna – he destroyed the city of (Kulunnum) and consecrated it to those gods.

22) GIŠ.BANŠUR-*am*
23) *ša* ^{d}IŠKUR
24) *be-lí-šu*
25) *iš-ku-un*

22–25) He set up a table of the god Adad, his lord.

26) *ša i-*pi_{5}*-iš-ti*
27) *ú-[ša-sà]-ku*
28) *ù [ší-ṭì-ir]-ti*
29) *ú-[pa-sà]-sú*
30) ⸢*a*⸣*-[na šu]-mi*
31) *[er-re-ti]-su*
Lacuna

26–31) He who re[move]s my work and er[as]es my [inscript]ion, or because of its [curse]
Lacuna

3

An inscription on a third stone block found in Bītwāta deals with the setting up of a throne for the god Nišba by Zabazuna.

COMMENTARY

The inscription, a join of two pieces, IM 81366+81367, appears on a rectangular block of stone which was not found in situ. The inscription was collated from the published photo.

BIBLIOGRAPHY

1978 al Fouadi, Sumer 34 pp. 122–26 text C (photo, conflated edition)

TEXT

1) ^{d}*i-dì*-^{d}EN.ZU 2) LUGAL *da-núm* 3) LUGAL *si-mu-ri-im*.KI	1–3) Iddi(n)-Sîn, mighty king, king of Simurrum,
4) ^{d}*za-ba-zu-na* 5) DUMU.NI	4–5) Zabazuna (is) his son–
6) *ku-lu-un-nu-um*.KI 7) [*i*]*k-ki-ir-ma* 8) [*a*]*-na* 9) [^{d}*za-ba*]*-zu-*⸢*na*⸣ 10) [*gi*]-⸢*ra*⸣-[*am*] 11) [*i-t*]*a-ba-al*	6–11) Kulunnum became [h]ostile and [w]aged [w]a[r ag]ainst [Zaba]zuna.
12) [*š*]*a* ^{d}*za-ba-zu-na* 13) *a-wa-sú* 14) ^{d}IŠKUR 15) ^{d}INANNA 16) *ù* ^{d}*ni-iš-ba* 17) *iš-me-ú-ma* 18) *a-lam ú-ḫa-li-iq-ma* 19) *a-na i-li* 20) *šu-nu-tu* 21) *ú-qá-dì-íš-sú*	12–21) The gods Adad, Eštar, and Nišba heard the word [o]f Zabazuna – he destroyed the city (of Kulunnum) and consecrated it to those gods.
22) GIŠ.GU.ZA-*am* 23) *ša* ^{d}*ni-iš-ba* 24) *be-lí-šu* 25) *iš-ku-un*	22–25) He set up a throne of the god Nišba his lord.
26) *ša i-pi*$_{5}$*-iš-ti* 27) *ú-ša-sà-ku* 28) *ù ší-ṭì-ir-ti* 29) *ú-pá-sà-sú* 30) ⸢*a*⸣*-na šu-mi* 31) [*er-r*]*e-ti-šu* Lacuna	26–31) He who removes my work, erases my inscription, or because of its [cu]rse ... Lacuna

4

Three pieces of inscribed rock, probably from the same provenance as the previously edited inscriptions (E4.19.1-3), contain a triumphal inscription of Iddi(n)-Sîn. They are at present in the Israel Museum in Jerusalem.

COMMENTARY

The inscriptions on fragments A and C are to be published by A. Shaffer.

BIBLIOGRAPHY

1978 al Fouadi, Sumer 34 pp. 126-28 (photo, study)

1001

A rock relief in western Iran bears an inscription in three columns. The first column, which undoubtedly contained the name of the ruler for whom the inscription was carved, is almost completely broken away. The attribution of this piece is uncertain, but it probably belongs to Iddi(n)-Sîn or his son Zabazuna.

COMMENTARY

The relief is inscribed on a rock face north of the village of Sar-i-pūl-i-Zohāb. Our edition follows that of Edzard, prepared from photos of L. Trümpelmann. The inscription was collated from the published photos.

Edzard suggested that the inscription might belong to Anubanini, because traces in the first col. seemed to refer to this ruler. However, the orthograpy of this text differs from that of the Anubanini text found some 200 metres away, and the fact that the curse formula is virtually identical to that found in the Iddi(n)-Sîn texts makes an attribution to this ruler, or his son, most likely.

Lines 29-41 are restored from E4.19.1.1-3.

Line 39: The copy of Edzard suggests ^{d}*n*[*in*]. Collation of the photos supports a reading [*b*]*e-e*[*l*].

Line 43: Traces in the photos support a reading [*ta*]-*ḫa-zi-im*.

BIBLIOGRAPHY

1839 H. Rawlinson, JRGS 9 p. 37 (study)
1842 Flandin and Coste, Voyage en Perse 1 pp. 168 (study, drawing)
1851 Flandin and Coste, Voyage en Perse. Relation du voyage p. 461 (study)
1896 de Morgan, MSP 4/1 pp. 156, 160, and fig. 146 (photo, study)
1910 Herzfeld, Iranisches Felsreliefs (Berlin) p. 193 fig. 86 (photo, study)
1920 Herzfeld, Am Tor von Asien (Berlin) pp. 5-6 with fig. 2 and pls. III-IV (photo, drawing, study)
1921 Herzfeld, Der Islam 11 p. 126
1941 Herzfeld, Iran in the Ancient Near East (London) p. 184 (study)
1942 Debevoise, JNES 1 p. 80 (study)
1944 Diez, Iranisches Kunst p. 115 (study)

1956 von der Osten, Die Welt der Perser p. 25 and pl. 11 (photo, study)
1962 Cameron, 25. Kongress 1 pp. 242–43 (study)
1966 Vanden Berghe, Archéologie de l'Iran ancien (Leiden) p. 101 and pl. 125d (photo, study)
1973 Edzard, AfO 24 pp. 75–77 (edition)
1976 Hrouda, Edzard, and Trümpelmann, Iranische Denkmäler 2/7 pp. 4–6, pls. 1–4, and pl. 6 (photo, copy, edition)
1982 Börker-Klähn, Bildstelen p. 138 no. 30 (study)
1985 M. Walker, The Tigris Frontier pp. 179–83 (edition)

TEXT

Col. i
[...]
2) [...]
3) [...]
4) ⌜x⌝ *za-ba-*[*zu-na*]
5) [DU]MU-[*ni*]

i 1–5) [...] Zaba[zuna] is [his s]on.

Col. ii
1) [...]
2) *ú-*[...]
3) *di*(?) x [...]
4) x [...]
5) DIŠ GI NA [x (x)]
6) x-*a*(?)-PI-x-[*tim*] *ra-bí-a-tim*
7) A.MU.[R]U
8) x x x [x (x)]
9) *i* NE [x (x)]
10) x [x (x)]
11) *ú*-PI-x [x]
12) x x [...]
13) *kà-la-*[x (x)]
14) *ú-*[...]
15) AN [x] x [...]
16) *qar-*[...]
17) x T[I x (x)] x [...]
18) [x] x x x [x]
19) *ú-kà-ni-i*[*š*]-*sú-*[*n*]*u-ti*
20) AL[A]M
21) *i-na š*[*a*(?)-*du-im*]
22) [*b*]*a-*[*ti-i*]*r*.KI
23) [*u*]*š-*[*zi*]-*i*[*z*]
24) *ša* [ALAM]-*am*
25) *an-n*[*i-am*]
26) *ú-*[*ša-sà-ku*]
27) [*a-na šum-mi*]
28) [*er-re-ti-šu*]
29) [*ša-ni-am*]
30) [*ú-ša-ḫa-zu*]
31) [*a-wi-lam*]
32) [*šu-a-ti*]
33) A[N]
34) ^{d}[*en-líl*]
35) [^{d}*nin-ḫur-sag*]
36) [^{d}EN.KI]
37) [^{d}EN].ZU
38) [^{d}IŠKUR]
39) [*b*]*e-e*[*l* GIŠ.TUKUL]

ii 1–7) ... to the great ... he dedicated.

ii 8–18) No translation warranted.

ii 19) ... he made them bow down.

ii 20–23) He [s]et up an im[a]ge on M[ount B]a[ti]r.

ii 24–26) He who [removes] th[is image]

ii 27–30) [or on account of this curse incites another to do so]

ii 31–50) [that man] — may the gods A[num, Enlil, Ninḫursag, Ea, S]în, [Adad, l]or[d of the weapon, Šamaš], lor[d of judgements, E]štar, lady of [b]attle, Ninsianna, my gods, (and) N[i]šba, [my lord], inflict on him an evil cu[rse].

40) [^{d}UTU]
41) ⌜*be*⌝-*e*[*l* DI.KU$_{5}$.DA]
42) ^{d}[I]NANNA
43) *b*[*e*]-*la-at* [*ta*]-⌜*ḫa-zi-im*⌝
44) ^{d}*nin*-AN-*si*$_{4}$-*an-na*
45) *ì-lí*
46) ^{d}*n*[*i-i*]*š-ba*
47) [*be-lí*]
48) *er*-[*ra-tám*]
49) *le-mu-tám*
50) *li-ru-ru-uš*
51) NU[MUN-*š*]*u*
52) *li*-[*il-qú-tú-ma*]
53) S[UḪUŠ-*sú*]
54) [*l*]*i*-[*sú-ḫu*]
55) IBI[L]A
56) *ù* [MU]

Col. iii
1) *a i-d*[*ì-n*]*u-šum*
2) [*b*]*a-l*[*a*]*-tum*
3) [*l*]*u i*[*k-k*]*i-i*[*b-šu*]

ii 51–54) May [they destroy h]is s[eed] and r[ip out his] fo[undation].

ii 55 – iii 3) May they not gr[an]t him heir or [offspring. M]ay life be [his] taboo.

Zabazuna

E4.19.2

Iddi(n)-Sîn was succeeded by his son Zabazuna as king of Simurrum. Two inscriptions are known which mention him as king.

2001

The first inscription is carved on a cylinder seal in the British Museum.

COMMENTARY

The seal is BM 102055, a piece acquired from Géjou, whose original provenance is unknown. It is a cylinder seal of green facies 3.25 cm long, 1.5 cm in dia. The inscription was collated from the published photo.

The servant in this seal bears a Hurrian name.

BIBLIOGRAPHY

1980 Sollberger, AnSt 30 pp. 63–64 and pl. IV (photo, edition)
1982 Collon, Cylinder Seals II no. 451 (photo, edition)
1987 Collon, First Impressions no. 121 (photo, study)

TEXT

1) ^{d}*za-ba-zu-na*	1) Zabazuna,
2) LUGAL *da-núm*	2) mighty king,
3) *te-ḫe-eš-a-tal*	3) Teḫeš-atal,
4) DUB.SAR	4) scribe,
5) ÌR.ZU	5) your servant.

2002

A seal impression on a tablet found at Ešnunna has the inscription of a servant of Zabazuna.

COMMENTARY

The seal impression is on As 30:T.223. There is some discrepancy in the records as to the exact level at which this tablet was found. It seems to have been found at level 31,20 at O 30:10. This is beneath the burned layer of the Bilalama level, but above the floor of the Ituriia temple. Whiting writes (AfO 34 [1987] p. 30): 'it seems most probable that the sealing belongs after the end of the Ur III period (at Ešnunna) but before the time of Bilalama ...'

In line 3 ⌜*ib*⌝-*ri* is a rendering of the Hurrian word *ewri* 'lord'.

BIBLIOGRAPHY

1940 Jacobsen, Gimilsin Temple p. 146 no. 13 (edition)
1978 al Fouadi, Sumer 34 p. 129 n. 6 (study)
1980 Sollberger, AnSt 30 pp. 63–64 (study)
1987 Whiting, AfO 34 p. 30 (copy, edition)

TEXT

1) [^{d}*za*]-*ba-zu-na*
2) LUGAL *da-núm*
3) [*z*]*i-li*-⌜*ib*⌝-*ri*
4) [...] x x [...]
5) [...] x x [...] x

1–5) [Za]bazuna, mighty king, [Z]ili-ewri, ...

ḪURŠĪTUM

E4.20

References to the city and land of Ḫuršītum appear in a handful of Old Babylonian texts. A brick inscription of one of its rulers is known.

BIBLIOGRAPHY

1975 Röllig, RLA 4/6–7 p. 522 (study)

Pūḫīia

E4.20.1

1

Stamped bricks bearing an inscription of Pūḫīia, king of the land of Ḫuršītum, were found near Tūz Ḫurmatı where the Aq-su, a tributary of the Al-ʿadhaim, breaks through the Jebel Ḥamrīn. This gives us an idea of the general location of the land of Ḫuršītum.

CATALOGUE

Ex.	Museum number	Provenance	Dimensions (cm)	Lines preserved	cpn
1	–	Tūz-Ḫurmatı	–	1–4	n
2	–	–	–	1–4	n
3	VA 3308	–	34.0×32.2	1–4	n

COMMENTARY

Ex. 3 is now missing. Ex. 2 was purchased in Kirkuk, while ex. 3 was purchased from Gegou in Paris, 1904.

BIBLIOGRAPHY

1894 Scheil, RT 16 p. 186 (ex. 1, copy, translation)
1897 Scheil, RT 19 p. 64 (ex. 2, partial copy, translation)
1905 Thureau-Dangin, ISA pp. 246–47 Buḫia (edition)
1907 Messerschmidt, VAS 1 no. 115 (ex. 3, copy)
1907 Thureau-Dangin, SAK pp. 172–73 Puḫia (edition)
1929 Barton, RISA pp. 168–69 Pukhia (edition)
1971 Sollberger and Kupper, IRSA ivN1a (translation)

TEXT

1) É.GAL *pu-ḫi-ia*
2) DUMU *a-si-ri-im*
3) LUGAL *ma-a-at*
4) *ḫu-ur-ši-tim*

1) Palace of Pūḫīia,
2) son of Asīrum,
3–4) king of the land of Ḫuršītum.

QABARĀ

E4.21

The city of Qabarā, which lay somewhere in the land around Urbilum, was a very important city in Old Babylonian times when it was attacked by the armies of Šamšī-Adad of Ekallātum (see RIMA 1 A.0.39.1001) and Dāduša of Ešnunna (see E4.5.19.1). In the stele of Dāduša which describes this attack, the name of the king of Qabarā, Bunu-Eštar, is revealed.

Bunu-Eštar

E4.21.1

2001

A seal of a servant of Bunu-Eštar was found at Ešnunna.

COMMENTARY

The seal has the excavation no. As 33:385, from P 27:8, the Audience Hall of Narām-Sîn, surface. It was collated from the published photo.

The provenance of this piece suggests it might have been a piece of booty brought back from Dāduša's siege of the city of Qabarā.

Jacobsen read the ruler's name as *bu-kur-*^{d}*eš*$_4$*-tár*, but collation of the photo reveals *bu-nu-*^{d}*eš*$_4$*-tár*. The fact that the owner of the seal and his father bear Hurrian names accords well with attribution of this seal to a servant of the king of Qabarā, since Qabarā lay in a Hurrian-speaking area.

BIBLIOGRAPHY

1955 Jacobsen, Cylinder Seals no. 729 (photo, edition)

TEXT

1) *e-ki-*^{d}IŠKUR	1) Eki-Tešup,
2) DUMU *a-ta-ta-wi-ra*	2) son of Atatawira,
3) ÌR *bu-nu-*^{d}*eš*$_4$*-tár*	3) servant of Bunu-Eštar.

ITABALḪUM

E4.22

Itabalḫum appears to have been a state in the north-east Zagros region.

Pišenden

E4.22.1

Pišenden, one of the rulers of Itabalḫum, was probably a contemporary of king Dāduša of Ešnunna.

1

A seal known from impressions on three fragments of clay envelopes bears the inscription of Pišenden and gives us the name of his father and son.

COMMENTARY

The impressions are found on SH 890, SH 817b, and an unnumbered fragment excavated at Tell Šamšārah, ancient Šušarrā. They were collated by J. Eidem.

BIBLIOGRAPHY

1989 Eidem and Møller, MARI 6 [forthcoming] (edition)

TEXT

1) ^{m}*pi-še-e*[*n-de-en*]	1) Piše[nden],
2) DUMU ^{m}*tu-ba*(?)-*az*(?)-*ti*	2) son of *Tubazti*,
3) LUGAL *ma-*[*a*]*t i-ta-bá+al-ḫ*[*i*]	3) king of the la[n]d of Itabalḫ[um],
4) *wa-li-*[*i*]*d ta-bi-ti*	4) begett[e]r of Tabitu.

ḪANA

E4.23

After the destruction of Mari by Ḫammu-rāpi, the state of Ḫana on the Middle Euphrates, with its capital at ancient Terqa, modern Tell ᶜAsherah, emerged as an important power. A number of rulers of Ḫana are known, chiefly from their year names and seal impressions. Tablets recently excavated at Tell ᶜAsherah shed new light on the rulers of this kingdom, supplementing what was already known from earlier chance finds from that site.

BIBLIOGRAPHY

1988 Buccellati, BASOR 270 pp. 43–61 (study)

Iapaḫ-sūmû-abu

E4.23.1

A contract excavated at Terqa bears the name of a king that is not entirely preserved, but which should probably be restored Iapaḫ-sūm[û-abu] (see O. Rouault, TFR 1 no. 8 line 20). The Terqa tablet mentioning this ruler is typologically similar to the Mari tablets and probably post-dates the destruction of Mari by only a few years. This ruler may have been one of the first kings of Ḫana. A text from Alalaḫ (see Wiseman, Alalakh no. 56 line 47) mentions a man by this name as UGULA *ḫana* 'overseer of the Ḫaneans' and if this is a reference to king Iapaḫ-sūmû-abu, it would indicate that he was a contemporary of Abba-Il of Aleppo. No inscriptions or seal impressions of this king have come to light.

BIBLIOGRAPHY

1984 Rouault, TFR 1 p. 4 (study)
1988 Buccellati, BASOR 270 pp. 50–51 (study)

Iṣi-sūmû-abu

E4.23.2

A king by the name of Iṣi-sūmû-abu appears in a contract excavated at Terqa (see O. Rouault, TFR 1 no. 9 line 19). He probably reigned before Iadiḫ-abu but whether he reigned before or after Iapaḫ-sūmû-abu is not certain. No inscriptions or seal impressions of this king or his servants are yet attested.

BIBLIOGRAPHY

1984 Rouault, TFR 1 p. 4 (study)
1988 Buccellati, BASOR 270 pp. 50–51 (study)

Iadiḫ-abu

E4.23.3

The name of year 28 of Samsu-iluna commemorates a victory of the Babylonian king over Iadiḫ-abu and Muti-ḫuršana. The former name probably refers to a king of Ḫana who is attested in a number of tablets excavated at Terqa. No inscriptions of the king or seal impressions of his servants are known at present.

BIBLIOGRAPHY

1984 Rouault, TFR 1 p. 4 (study)
1988 Buccellati, BASOR 270 p. 53 (study)

Kaštiliašu

E4.23.4

The reign of Kaštiliašu of Ḫana probably followed that of Iadiḫ-abu but whether he was an immediate successor or not is not known. Kaštiliašu may have been a Babylonian installed by Samsu-iluna at Terqa after his defeat of Iadiḫ-abu and not a native Ḫanean ruler, for the onomastica from Terqa does not reveal the presence of Kassites in the population of the city.

2001

A seal impression of a servant of Kaštiliašu was excavated at Terqa.

COMMENTARY

The impressions are found on TQ5-T105, a bulla sealing a jar, and TQ5-T99, another bulla. Both were found in area C at Tell ʿAsherah, in structure D, room 3, the ceremonial area of the temple of Ninkarak.

This same servant appears in a tablet from Terqa published by Thureau-Dangin and Dhorme (Syria 5 [1924] pp. 272–73).

BIBLIOGRAPHY

1984 Rouault, TFR 1 pp. 4–5 (study)
1988 Buccellati, BASOR 270 p. 58 (edition)

TEXT

1) [*gi*]-*mil*-^{d}*nin-kar*-[*ra-ak*]
2) [DUMU] *ar-ši-a*-[*ḫu-um*]
3) [Ì]R *ìl-a*-[*ba*$_4$]
4) [*ù k*]*a-aš-ti-li-i*[*a-šu*]

1) [Gi]mil-Ninkar[ak],
2) [son] of Arši-a[ḫum],
3) [se]rvant of Ila[ba],
4) [and K]aštili[ašu].

Šunuḫrû-Ammu

E4.23.5

A document dated to the reign of Šunuḫrû-Ammu was found on the floor of level 2 of the Ninkarak temple at Terqa. This indicates that the reign of this ruler should be placed after Kaštiliašu, for whom dated documents were found on the floor of level 3 of the same temple. While a number of year names are attested for this king, no inscriptions or seal impressions of his servants are known at present.

BIBLIOGRAPHY

1957 Goetze, JCS 11 p. 64 (study)
1988 Buccellati, BASOR 270 p. 54 (study)

Ammī-madar

E4.23.6

A tablet from Deir ez-Zor bears a year name of a king of Ḫana, Ammī-madar. In the body of the text Ammī-madar appears as the son of Šunuḫrû-Ammu. We can be certain, therefore, that Ammī-madar followed Šunuḫrû-Ammu as king of Ḫana, probably as his immediate successor. No inscriptions or seal impressions are known for this ruler.

BIBLIOGRAPHY

1909 Ungnad, VAS 7 no. 204 (copy of tablet with year formula)
1988 Buccellati, BASOR 270 p. 54 (study)

Išar-Līm

E4.23.7

1

A tablet picked up at Terqa bears the seal impression of Išar-Līm, king of the land of Ḫana.

COMMENTARY

The impression is found on AO 2673, a clay tablet. It was not collated.

BIBLIOGRAPHY

1897 Thureau-Dangin, RA 4 p. 86 and pl. XXXII no. 85 (copy, translation)
1910 Delaporte, RA 7 p. 147 and pl. IV no. 1 a–c (photo, translation)
1910 Thureau-Dangin, TCL 1 no. 237 (copy)
1913 Schorr, Urkunden no. 219 (transliteration)
1923 Delaporte, Louvre 2 A 594 (copy, edition)
1926 Unger, RLV 4/2 pl. 160 (copy)
1937 Stephens, RA 34 p. 180 (study)
1937 Herzfeld, AMI 8 p. 105 fig. 1 (copy, study)
1947 Nougayrol, RA 41 p. 43 nn. 2–3 (study)
1957 Goetze, JCS 11 p. 63 (transliteration, study)
1957–58 Nagel, AfO 18 p. 257 n. 23 (study)
1971 Sollberger and Kupper, IRSA IVG1a (translation)
1981 Lambert, UF 13 p. 301 (edition)
1987 Collon, MARI 5 pp. 149–50 (photo, copy, edition)
1987 Collon, First Impressions no. 199 (copy, study)
1988 Buccellati, BASOR 270 p. 54 (study)

TEXT

1) *i-šar-li-i*[*m*]	1) Išar-Lī[m],
2) LUGAL KUR *ḫa-n*[*a*]	2) king of the land of Ḫan[a],
3) DUMU *i-din-*^{d}*ka-ak-k*[*a*]	3) son of Iddin-Kakk[a],
4) *na-ra-am ì-l*[*a*]-*b*[a_4]	4) beloved of the gods Il[a]b[a]
5) *ù* ^{d}*d*[*a*]-*gan*	5) and D[a]gān.

Iggid-Līm

E4.23.8

1

A contract excavated at Terqa (TPR 7 no. 4) mentions the name of king Iggid-Līm in an oath. There is a fragmentarily preserved seal impression, probably of a ruler of Ḫana, on the edge of a tablet. We would expect, based on parallels with other Terqa tablets, that this was an impression of the seal of Iggid-Līm; unfortunately, little of the impression remains. A second example of this seal impression on a tablet in the Rosen collection (RBC 779) does allow a more complete restoration of the seal inscription.

A variety of evidence assembled by A. Podany (Chronology pp. 56–59) suggests that Išar-Līm was the father of Iggid-Līm.

BIBLIOGRAPHY

1979 Rouault, TPR 7 no. 4 (copy, edition of tablet mentioning Iggid-Līm)

1988 Podany, Chronology pp. 55–57 (exs. 1–2, transliteration, study)

1988 Buccellati, BASOR 270 p. 54 (study)

TEXT

1) [*i-gi-id-li-im*]
2) [É]NSI ^{d}[*da-g*]*an*
3) [L]UGAL KUR *ḫa-*⌜*na*⌝
4) [DU]MU *i-šar-*[*l*]*i-im*
5) [Ì]R [*ìl-a-ba*$_{4}$ *ù* ^{d}]*da-*[*gan*]

1–5) [Iggid-Līm, g]overnor of the god [Dag]ān, [k]ing of the land of Ḫana, [s]on of Išar-[L]īm, [se]rvant [of the gods Ilaba and] Da[gan].

Isiḫ-Dagān

E4.23.9

1

The impression of a seal of Isiḫ-Dagān, son of Iggid-Līm and king of the land of Ḫana, is found on a tablet from Terqa.

COMMENTARY

The impression is on AO 20162, a tablet purchased by Mr. Hamelin from Terqa. The tablet measures 4.0×7.0 cm. The seal impression was collated by D. Collon and B. André-Leicknam. Collation of the seal impression by D. Collon gives the name of Isiḫ-Dagān's father as Iggid-L[īm] correcting the earlier reading *zi*(?)-*it*(?)-*r*[*i*(?)] suggested by Goetze.

BIBLIOGRAPHY

1947 Nougayrol, RA 41 pp. 42–46 (copy, edition)
1957 Goetze, JCS 11 p. 64 (transliteration, study)
1987 Collon, MARI 5 pp. 147–49 (photo, copy, edition)
1987 Collon, First Impressions no. 198 (copy, study)
1988 Buccellati, BASOR 270 p. 54 (study)

TEXT

1) *i-si-iḫ-*^{d}*da-gan*
2) ÉNSI ^{d}*da-gan*
3) [LUGAL KUR *ḫ*]*a-n*[*a*]
4) DUMU *i-gi-id-l*[*i-im*]
5) ÌR *ìl-a-*[*ba₄*]
6) *ù* ^{d}*da-g*[*an*]

1) Isiḫ-Dagān,
2) governor of the god Dagān,
3) [king of the land of Ḫ]an[a],
4) son of Iggid-L[īm],
5) servant of the gods Ila[ba]
6) and Dag[ān].

Ḫammu-rāpi

E4.23.10

The impression of a seal of Ḫammu-rāpi, king of the land of Ḫana, is found on two tablets.

1

A year name of Ḫammu-rāpi (BRM 4 no. 52) mentions a canal stretching from Dūr-Išar-Līm to Dūr-Iggid-Līm. These forts were probably named after the kings of Ḫana and indicate that the reign of Ḫammu-rāpi followed that of Iggid-Līm.

COMMENTARY

Ex. 1 is on YBC 6518, from Dura-Europus, field no. K 757, found imbedded in an unbaked mud brick which formed part of the wall of the temple of Atargatis between rooms 4 and 6 of square H2. It was collated by W. Hallo. Ex. 2 is found on MLC 613. It was collated by A. Podany.

BIBLIOGRAPHY

1907 Johns, PSBA 29 pp. 177–84 (copy of tablet of ex. 2, edition)
1923 Clay, BRM 4 no. 52 (ex. 2, copy)
1937 Stephens, RA 34 pp. 183–90 (ex. 1, copy, edition)
1957 Goetze, JCS 11 p. 64 (exs. 1–2, transliteration, study)
1972 Sollberger and Kupper, IRSA ɪᴠG2a (ex. 1, translation)
1976 Hallo and Porada, Ancient Mesopotamian Art and Selected Texts pp. 38–42 and pl. 14 (ex. 2, photo, study)
1981 Buchanan, Early Near Eastern Seals no. 1030 (ex. 1, study)
1981 Lambert, UF 13 pp. 300–301 (ex. 1, edition)
1987 Collon, MARI 5 pp. 149–51 (ex. 1, edition)
1988 Buccellati, BASOR 270 pp. 54–55 (study)

TEXT

1)	[*ḫ*]*a-am-mu-r*[*a-pí*]	1) [Ḫ]ammu-r[āpi],
2)	⌜ÉNSI⌝ ^{d}⌜*da-gan*⌝	2) governor of the gods Dagān,
3)	*ù ìl-a-ba*$_4$	3) and Il-aba,
4)	LUGAL KUR *ḫa-na*	4) king of the land of Ḫana,
5)	[DUMU (x)] *a-g*[*i*(?)-x-x-x]	5) [son of] Ag[i-...],
6)	ÌR *ìl-*[*a-ba*$_4$]	6) servant of the gods Il-[aba]
7)	*ù* ⌜^{d}⌝*d*[*a-gan*]	7) and D[agān].

2

A duck weight in the Louvre bears the inscription of Ammu-rāpi, king of the land of Ḫana.

COMMENTARY

The duck weight is AO 9047. It is made of agate and is 2.4 cm long. The inscription was not collated.

The reading of the divine name in line 3 is uncertain.

BIBLIOGRAPHY

1924 Thureau-Dangin, Syria 5 pp. 275–76 (copy, edition)
1954 Balkan, Kassit. Stud. p. 105 (study)
1971 Sollberger and Kupper, IRSA IVG2b (translation)

TEXT

1) ᵐ*am-mu-ra-pí*
2) LUGAL KUR *ḫa-na*.KI
3) *a-na* ᵈDU.ZA.BI
4) IN.NA.AN.BA

1) Ammu-rāpi,
2) king of the land of Ḫana,
3–4) presented this (duck weight) to the god DUZABI.

BUZURAN

E4.24

The city of Buzuran appears to have been situated a little downstream from Mari. What may be the copy of an inscription of the king of Buzuran appears on a cylinder seal in a private collection.

Ia᾽ūš-Addu

E4.24.1

1

The seal is in the Jonathan P. Rosen Collection in New York City. It measures 2.4 cm long and is made of obsidian. It was collated from the published photo. Ia᾽ūš-Addu appears in the Mari texts as a contemporary of Zimrī-Līm of Mari (see Birot, Kupper, and Rouault, ARMT 16/1 p. 236).

BIBLIOGRAPHY

1987 Collon, First Impressions no. 192 (photo, study)

TEXT

1) KIŠIB *ia-uš*-[d]IŠKUR	1) Seal of Ia᾽ūš-Addu,
2) LUGAL *bu-zu*(?)*-ra-an*	2) king of Buzuran.

QAṬṬARĀ/KARANĀ

E4.25

The British excavations at Tell al Rimah have shed considerable light on the political fortunes of an Old Babylonian city whose ancient name is not entirely certain. Arguments have been put forward for an identification of Tell al Rimah with Karanā, Qaṭṭarā, or Razamā. Here we have opted for the identification with Qaṭṭarā following D. Charpin and J.-M. Durand. Most recently Kh. Nashef has suggested an identification of ancient Karanā with modern Tell Ḫamīra, 16 kilometres east of Tell al Rimah.

The two cities at Qaṭṭarā and Karanā appear to have lain close to one another and to have served alternately as capitals of a small kingdom contemporary with that of Zimrī-Līm of Mari.

BIBLIOGRAPHY

1980 Groneberg, Rép. Géogr. 3 p. 190 (study)
1987 Charpin and Durand, RA 82 pp. 125–46 (study)
1988 Nashef, WO 19 pp. 35–39 (study)

BI/GA-ID/DA-ḫa-X

E4.25.1

2001

The seal impression of Ilī-Samaš, servant of a ruler, the reading of whose name is uncertain, is found on a number of tablets excavated at Tell al Rimah.

COMMENTARY

The impressions are on tablets found by the temple stairway; the exact date of these tablets is not known. Some of them are dated by eponyms which date to the time of Šamšī-Adad.

Here we list the excavation numbers of tablets bearing this seal impression and the number of the text as treated in Dalley, et al., OBTR: TR 4922 = 283, TR 4924 = 284, TR 4943 = 285, TR 4925 = 286, TR 4937 = 288, and TR 4952 = 317.

As Dalley points out, the name of the ruler (line 3) could be read *pí-it-ḫa-⸢na⸣*, but such an Anatolian name is unexpected.

BIBLIOGRAPHY

1976 Hawkins in Dalley, OBTR pp. 248–49 and pl. 107 no. 1 (copy, edition)

TEXT

1) *ì-lí-sa-ma-*[*áš*]
2) DUMU *iq-qa-at-*[d]⸢UTU/IŠKUR⸣
3) ÌR BI/GA-ID/DA-ḪA-X [...]

1) Ilī-Sama[š],
2) son of Iqqat-Šamaš/Adad,
3) servant of BI/GA-ID/DA-ḫa-X.

Samu-Addu

E4.25.2

Indirect evidence suggests that Samu-Addu served as ruler of Qaṭṭarā, probably as a vassal of Šamšī-Adad during the reign of the Assyrian king. No inscriptions of this ruler are extant. Impressions of a seal of his daughter Iltani are known. These are treated under E4.25.5 Aqba-Ḫammû.

BIBLIOGRAPHY

1976 Dalley, OBTR p. 33 (study)

Ḫadnû-rāpi

E4.25.3

A certain Ḫadnû-rāpi appears to have taken control over Qaṭṭarā when Zimrī-Līm took the throne of Mari from the Assyrians. He is referred to as ruler of Qaṭṭarā in a letter published by D. Charpin and J.-M. Durand (RA 81 [1987] p. 134). This ruler is attested in seal impressions of two of his servants.

2001

The broken name of a servant of Ḫadnû-rāpi is on a tablet excavated at Tell al Rimah.

COMMENTARY

The impression is found on TR 5695, from room 12 of the palace at Tell al Rimah. It was not collated.

BIBLIOGRAPHY

1976 Hawkins in Dalley, OBTR pp. 251–52 and pl. 108 no. 9 (copy, edition)

TEXT

1) ⌜*i*⌝-*ba-al*-[...]	1) Ibāl-[...],
2) ⌜DUMU⌝ *a-ḫu*-x-x-x	2) son of Aḫu-...,
3) ⌜ÌR *ḫa*⌝-*ad-nu*-⌜*ra-pi*⌝	3) servant of Ḫadnû-rāpi.

2002

The impression of another servant of Ḫadnû-rāpi is found on a number of clay sealings excavated at Tell al Rimah.

COMMENTARY

The impression is on TR 5678–80, 5683, and 5686, from the gap between the walls north of room 16 of the palace.

BIBLIOGRAPHY

1976 Hawkins in Dalley, OBTR p. 252 and pl. 108 no. 11 (copy, edition)

TEXT

1) *be-lí*-IGI.DU	1) Bēlī-ašarēd,
2) DUMU *zi-li-ba-an*	2) son of Ziliban,
3) ÌR *ḫa-ad-nu-ra-pí*	3) servant of Ḫadnû-rāpi.

Aškur-Addu

E4.25.4

Following the reign of Ḫadnû-rāpi, Aškur-Addu, who D. Charpin and J.-M. Durand suggest (see RA 81 [1987] p. 146) was ruler of the neighbouring city of Karanā, gained control over Qaṭṭarā (Tell al Rimah).

1

A seal impression of Aškur-Addu is on a clay sealing excavated at Tell al Rimah.

COMMENTARY

The impression is found on TR 5691, from room 12 of the palace. It was not collated.

BIBLIOGRAPHY

1970 D. Oates, Iraq 32 pp. 5–6 (study)
1972 D. Oates, Iraq 34 p. 86 (study)
1976 Hawkins in Dalley, OBTR p. 251 and pl. 108 no. 7 (copy, edition)

TEXT

1) [*aš*]-*kur*-^{d}[IŠKUR]	1) [Aš]kur-[Addu],
2) ⸢*pa*⸣-*li-iḫ* ⸢^{d}⸣[...]	2–3) who reveres the gods [...] (and) Lāgam[āl],
3) [^{d}]*la-ga-m*[*a-al*]	
4) [...] x [...]	4) ...

2

The impression of a certain Bini-šakin, son of Aškur-Addu, is known from a seal impression excavated at Tell al Rimah.

COMMENTARY

The impression is on two clay sealings, TR 5692 and TR 5693, probably parts of the same sealing found in room 12 of the palace.

Since this seal dates to Aškur-Addu's time and since there is no evidence that Bini-šakin ever ruled at Tell al Rimah, his seal is edited under the heading of his father.

BIBLIOGRAPHY

1970 D. Oates, Iraq 32 p. 5 (study)
1972 D. Oates, Iraq 34 p. 86 (study)
1976 Hawkins in Dalley, OBTR p. 251 and pl. 108 no. 8 (copy, edition)
1987 Collon, First Impressions no. 181 (copy, study)

TEXT

1) *bi-ni-ša-ki-in*	1) Bini-šakin,
2) DUMU SAG.KAL LUGAL	2) foremost son of the king,
3) ÌR *aš-kur-*ᵈIŠKUR	3) servant of Aškur-Addu.

Aqba-Ḫammû

E4.25.5

A certain Aqba-Ḫammû seems to have taken the throne of Karanā from Aškur-Addu. A seal of this man reveals that he had served as diviner before he became king. He appears to have served as an independent ruler of Karanā and then to have become a vassal of Ḫammu-rāpi of Babylon. Impressions of a seal of his wife and a number of seals of his servants are known.

1

The impression of a seal of Iltani, wife of Aqba-Ḫammû, daughter of Samu-Addu, is found on a number of tablets and envelope fragments excavated at Tell al Rimah. The queen seems to have been resident at Qaṭṭarā (Tell al Rimah).

COMMENTARY

The excavation and publication numbers of the impressions are: TR 4291 = 180, TR 4297 = 198, TR 4289 = 191, TR 4290 = 192, TR 4294 = 193, TR 4295 = 194, TR 4299 = 200, TR 4319 = seal 13, and TR 4320 = seal 13, all from room 6 of the palace.

BIBLIOGRAPHY

1968 Page, Iraq 30 p. 91 (study)
1976 Hawkins in Dalley, OBTR p. 253 and pl. 109 no. 13 (copy, edition)

TEXT

1) ^{f}*il-ta-ni*	1) Iltani,
2) DUMU.MUNUS *sa-mu-*^{d}IŠKUR	2) daughter of Samu-Addu,
3) DAM *aq-ba-ḫa-mu*	3) wife of Aqba-Ḫammû.

2001

The impression of a seal of Ḫadnû-tanūḫa, servant of Aqba-Ḫammû, was impressed on tablets found in the 'Wine Archive' excavated at Tell al Rimah.

COMMENTARY

The impressions are on tablets from the wine archive found in debris overlying the junction between the walls of rooms 16 and 21 of the palace. Their excavation and publication numbers are: TR 5718 = 254, TR 5717 = 257, TR 5727 = 258, TR 5716 = 259, and TR 5726 = 262.

BIBLIOGRAPHY

1976 Hawkins in Dalley, OBTR pp. 252–53 and pl. 108 no. 12 (copy, edition)

TEXT

1) ⌜*ḫa*⌝-*ad-nu-ta-nu-*[*ḫa*]	1) Ḫadnû-tanū[ḫa],
2) [DU]MU *ḫi-da-ti-*PA-x [...]	2) [so]n of Ḫidati-PA[..]
3) ⌜ÌR⌝ *aq-ba-ḫa-m*[*u*]	3) servant of Aqba-Ḫam[mû].

2002

The impression of a seal of Kiṣṣurum, servant of Aqba-Ḫammû, is on a tablet and envelope fragments excavated at Tell al Rimah.

COMMENTARY

The impression is found on TR 4288 = 195 and TR 4325, from room 6 of the palace.

BIBLIOGRAPHY

1968 Page, Iraq 30 p. 91 (study)
1976 Hawkins in Dalley, OBTR p. 254 and pl. 109 no. 15 (copy, edition)

TEXT

1) ⌜*ki*⌝-*iṣ-ṣú-*⌜*rum*⌝	1) Kiṣṣurum,
2) DUMU *ab-du-*x-[...]	2) son of Abdu-[...],
3) ÌR *aq-ba-ḫa-*⌜*mu*⌝	3) servant of Aqba-Ḫammû.

2003

Impressions of a seal of Inib-Šamaš, servant of Aqba-Ḫammû, are found on a tablet excavated at Tell al Rimah.

COMMENTARY

The impressions are on TR 4292 = 196, from room 6 of the palace.

BIBLIOGRAPHY

1968 Page, Iraq 30 p. 91 (study)
1976 Hawkins in Dalley, OBTR p. 254 and pl. 109 no. 16 (copy, edition)

TEXT

1) *i-ni-ib*-⌜dUTU⌝
2) DUMU *za-ak*-⌜*ku*⌝-[*ú*]
3) ÌR *aq-ba-ḫa*-⌜*mu*⌝

1) Inib-Šamaš,
2) son of Zakkû,
3) servant of Aqba-Ḫammû.

2004

A seal of a servant of Aqba-Ḫammû, presumably the ruler of Qaṭṭarā, was found by Woolley at Tell Atshana in Syria.

COMMENTARY

The seal is BM 126173, excavation number AT/38/119, from Tell Atshana, ancient Alalaḫ, from room 16 of the Level IV palace. It is a cylinder seal of haematite, 2.8 cm long, 1.35 cm in dia. The inscription was collated from the published photo.

The seal was reused and recut with Mitannian elements.

BIBLIOGRAPHY

1939 Woolley, AJ 19 pl. XIII (photo)
1955 Woolley, Alalakh p. 121 and pl. LXIV no. 75 (photo, provenance)
1959 Kupper, RA 53 p. 97 n. 2 (study)
1976 Dalley, OBTR p. 32 (study)
1979 Lambert, Iraq 41 p. 11 (study)
1982 Collon, The Alalakh Cylinder Seals pp. 47–49 and pl. 4 no. 15 (photo, copy, edition)
1987 Collon, First Impressions no. 185 (photo, study)

TEXT

1) *qar-ra-du-um*	1) Qarrādum,
2) DUMU *i-din-*[d]*de-ri-tum*	2) son of Iddin-Dērītum,
3) ÌR *aq-ba-ḫa-mu*	3) servant of Aqba-Ḫammû.

RAZAMĀ

E4.26

The city of Razamā, which lay not far from ancient Qaṭṭarā, was an important city in Old Babylonian times. It was the object of a siege by Ṣillī-Sîn of Ešnunna, who headed a coalition that included Ešnunna, Elam, Andariq, and probably Išme-Dagān of Assyria. The event was used to name one of Ṣillī-Sîn's years (see A.K. Muḥammad, Studies on the Unpublished Cuneiform Texts, Diyala Region, Ḥamrin Basin, Tell Ḥaddād, M.A. thesis, Baghdad [1985] pp. 81–83).

One inscription of Šarrum-kīma-kalima, ruler of Razamā, is known. He appears in the documents from Mari and Tell al Rimah in the shorter form Šarrāia. He probably was the ruler of Razamā when the city was attacked by Ṣillī-Sîn.

BIBLIOGRAPHY

1976 Dalley et al., OBTR pp. 7–11 (study)

Šarrum-kīma-kalima

E4.26.1

1

A text from Tell al Rimah records Šarrum-kīma-kalima's building of a palace in Razamā.

COMMENTARY

The inscription is found on TR 5708, excavated at Tell al Rimah from the palace area, site C, buried in a repaired section of a wall in building of level 5. It is a circular plaque of baked clay 12.5 cm in dia. and was collated from its display in the Iraq Museum.

BIBLIOGRAPHY

1970 Walker, Iraq 32 pp. 27–30 (copy, edition)
1976 Walker in Dalley, OBTR p. 193 no. 277 (edition); Dalley pp. 34–35 (study)

TEXT

1) LUGAL-*ki-ma-ka-li-ma*	1) Šarrum-kīma-kalima,
2) DUMU *a-ni-iš-ki-ba-al*	2) son of Aniškibal,
3) *ba-ni* É.GAL-*lim*	3) builder of the palace
4) *i-na qé-er-bu*	4–5) in Razamā,
5) *ra-za-ma-a*.KI	
6) *ra-bi-ti-šu*	6) his *capital city*.

ŠEḪNĀ

E4.27

Recent archaeological research at Tell Leilan coupled with new information from the Mari archives informs us that the ancient name of Tell Leilan was Šeḫnā, and that this city served as capital of the land of Apum. When Šamšī-Adad made the city his capital he re-named it Šubat-Enlil.

Seal impressions of five rulers who controlled Šeḫnā after the death of Šamšī-Adad have been found on tablets and sealings from Tell Leilan. These are edited here by kind permission of H. Weiss.

BIBLIOGRAPHY

1987 Charpin, MARI 5 pp. 129–40

Turum-natki

E4.27.1

The first of the post-Šamšī-Adad rulers at Šeḫnā was Turum-natki, who died in Zimrī-Līm year 3′ and was buried in Apum (see D. Charpin, MARI 4 p. 136).

2001

Impressions of a seal of a servant of Turum-natki were found on two tablets excavated at Tell Leilan.

COMMENTARY

The impressions are on L 82–74–75. They were collated by R. Whiting.

BIBLIOGRAPHY

1983 Weiss, AAAS 33 p. 60 no. 3 and p. 66 fig. 12 (copy, translation)
1985 Weiss, MARI 4 p. 282 fig. 10 and p. 283 no. 3 (copy, translation)

TEXT

1) *a-píl-ì-lí-šu*	1) Apil-ilīšu,
2) DUMU *a-lí-ba-ni-šu*	2) son of Ali-bānīšu,
3) IR₁₁ *tu-rum-na-at-*⌜*ki*⌝	3) servant of Turum-natki.

Ḫaia-abum

E4.27.2

Ḫaia-abum was installed as king in Apum in year 4′ of Zimrī-Līm following the death of Turum-natki (see D. Charpin, MARI 4 p. 136).

2001

Seal impressions of a servant of this ruler were excavated at Tell Leilan.

COMMENTARY

The impression was found on 277 sealings including L 82–76 from room 8 of the Building Level II temple at Tell Leilan.

BIBLIOGRAPHY

1983 Weiss, AAAS 33 p. 60 no. 4 and p. 67 fig. 13 (copy, translation)
1985 Weiss, MARI 4 p. 282 fig. 11 and p. 283 no. 4 (copy, translation)

TEXT

1) *be-lí-e-mu-qí*	1) Bēlī-emūqī,
2) IR$_{11}$ *ḫa-ia-a-bu-um*	2) servant of Ḫaia-abum,
3) IR$_{11}$ ^{d}IŠKUR	3) servant of Adad.

Tilabnû

E4.27.3

The Tell Leilan archives indicate that Mutīia was succeeded by his son Tilabnû as ruler of Šeḫnā.

1

A seal of Tilabnû is found on a tablet from Tell Leilan inscribed with a treaty between the king of Apum and the king of Kaḫat.

COMMENTARY

The impression is on L 87–1362+. It is offered through the courtesy of J. Eidem.

TEXT

1) *ti-la-ab-nu-ú*	1) Tilabnû,
2) DUMU *da-ri-e-pu-uḫ*	2) son of Dāri-Epuḫ,
3) LUGAL *ma-a-at a-pí*	3) king of the land of Apum.

2001

A seal impression of a servant of Tilabnû is found on sealings excavated in 1985 and 1987 in the Lower Town.

COMMENTARY

The impression is on L 85–435, 454, 492, and L 87–894, and was collated by D. Parayre, who kindly communicated this transliteration.

TEXT

1) *ba-a-*[*ia*]*-nu*	1) Bai[iā]nu,
2) DUMU *ḫa-*[*ka*]*-mu*	2) son of Ḫa[ka]mu,
3) ÌR *ti-l*[*a-a*]*b-nu-*⌜*ú*⌝	3) servant of Til[a]bnû.

2002

The fragmentary impression of a seal of a servant of Tilabnû was found on a sealing in the Lower Town.

COMMENTARY

The impression is on L 85-435. It was collated by R. Whiting.

TEXT

1) [...]	1) [...],
2) [DUMU ...]	2) [son of ...],
3) [ÌR] ⌜*ti-la*⌝*-ab-nu-*⌜*ú*⌝	3) [servant] of Tilabnû.

Mutīia

E4.27.4

Documents excavated in 1985 and 1987 from Tell Leilan indicate that a certain Mutīia served as ruler in Šeḫnā during the reign of Samsu-iluna of Babylon. Šeḫnā may have been under the control of Ḫammu-rāpi of Iamḫad at this time. Mutīia appears to be a hypocoristicon of the name Mutu-Abiḫ found in E4.27.4.2.

1

An impression of a seal of Mutīia is found on a treaty fragment excavated at Tell Leilan.

COMMENTARY

The seal impression is on L 87–617. It is offered through the courtesy of J. Eidem.

TEXT

1) *mu-ti-a*	1) Mutīia,
2) [DUMU] *ḫa-lu-e-bi-iḫ*	2) [son] of Ḫālu-Ebiḫ,
3) LUGAL *ma-a-at a-pí-im*.KI	3) king of the land of Apum.

2

Another seal probably belonging to Mutīia (written in the fuller form Mutu-Abiḫ) is on a number of sealings from Tell Leilan.

COMMENTARY

The impressions are found on the sealings L85-134, 135, L87-184, 243, 383, 384, 445, and 646, from the Lower Town. The text published here is from J. Eidem.

TEXT

1) *mu-tu-a-bi-[iḫ]*
2) DUMU *ḫa-lu-e-bi-[iḫ]*
3) *na-ra-am* ᵈIŠKUR
4) *ù* ᵈNIN-*a-pí-im*

1) Mutu-Abi[ḫ],
2) son of Ḫālu-Ebi[ḫ],
3) beloved of the god Adad
4) and the goddess Bēlet-Apim.

2001

The impression of a servant of Mutīia is on a number of sealings excavated in 1985.

COMMENTARY

The impressions are found on L 85-117 to L 85-122, excavated in the Lower Town. They were collated by D. Parayre, who kindly communicated this transliteration.

TEXT

1) *ḫa-ar-ra-ma-ni-šu*
2) ÌR *mu-ti-ia*

1) Ḫar-ramānīšu,
2) servant of Mutīia.

2002

Seal impressions of another servant of Mutīia are found on a number of tablets from Tell Leilan.

COMMENTARY

The impressions are on L 87-137, 183, 246, 250, 257, 398, 422, and 1286. The inscription is published here through the courtesy of J. Eidem. The PN in line 2 appears to be Elamite (see R. Zadok, The Elamite Onomasticon p. 47).

TEXT

1) *te-ki-*[...]
2) DUMU *lu-ul-lu-uz-zi*
3) ÌR *mu-ti-ia*

1) Teki-[...],
2) son of Lullu-uzzi,
3) servant of Mutīia.

Iakūn-ašar

E4.27.5

The name of year 23 of Samsu-iluna deals with the defeat of Šeḫnā and its king Iakūn-ašar. An administrative text from Tell Leilan refers to a certain Iakūn-ašar as the 'man of Ilanṣurā' (J. Eidem, personal communication). He may have usurped power at Šeḫnā, only to be defeated by Samsu-iluna.

1

Impressions of a seal of Iakūn-ašar, king of the land of Apum, were found on tablets and sealings from Tell Leilan.

COMMENTARY

The impressions were found on L 85-80-87 and 123-124 from the Lower Town at Tell Leilan. These previously unpublished impressions are given here through the courtesy of D. Parayre.

BIBLIOGRAPHY

1987 Charpin, MARI 5 p. 136 and n. 39 (study)
1987 Collon, First Impressions no. 183 (copy, study)

TEXT

1) *ia-ku-un-a-ša*[*r*]	1) Iakūn-aša[r],
2) DUMU *da-ri-e-pu-u*[*ḫ*]	2) son of Dāri-Epu[ḫ],
3) LUGAL *ma-a-at a-pí-im.*[KI]	3) king of the land of Apum.

2001

A number of sealings fron Tell Leilan bear impressions of servants of Iakūn-ašar. The name of the first is not preserved.

COMMENTARY

The impression is found on L 87-370 from the Lower Town. It was collated by J. Eidem, who communicated this transliteration.

TEXT

1) [...] x [...]
2) [DUMU *ḫa*(?)-*z*]*i-ip-te-*[*šu-ub*]
3) [ÌR *i*]*a-ku-un-a-*[*šar*]

1) [...] ... [...],
2) [son of Ḫaz]ip-Te[šup],
3) [servant of I]akūn-a[šar].

2002

A number of tablets from Tell Leilan bear impressions of the seal of Ummī-waqra[t].

COMMENTARY

The impressions are found on L 87-263, 267, 309, 375, and 379 from the Lower Town. The transliteration is from J. Eidem, who collated the impression.

TEXT

1) f*um-mi-wa-aq-ra-a*[*t*]
2) [G]ÉME *ia-k*[*u-un-a-šar*]

1) Ummī-waqra[t],
2) [fem]ale servant of Iak[ūn-ašar].

2003

Impressions of the seal of Sîn-idd[in] are on several tablets from Tell Leilan.

COMMENTARY

The impressions are found on L 87-296, 818, 822-23, 985, 987-88, 994-95, 1251-53, 1256-58, 1260, 1262, 1264, 1266, 1268-69, 1272, and 1386 from the Lower Town. The inscription was collated by J. Eidem.

TEXT

1) dEN.ZU-*i-di-*[*in*]
2) DUMU *ab-ba-n*[*i* ...]
3) ÌR *ia-k*[*u-un-a-šar*]

1) Sîn-idd[in],
2) son of Abban[i ...],
3) servant of Iak[ūn-ašar].

ANDARIQ

E4.28

The Mari documents reveal the existence of a number of kings of Andariq, an important city in northern Mesopotamia, as yet unlocated.

Qarni-Līm

E4.28.1

Qarni-Līm, king of Andariq, ruled during the early part of the reign of Zimrī-Līm of Mari. No inscriptions of this ruler have come to light.

Atamrum

E4.28.2

Qarni-Līm was succeeded by Atamrum as king of Andariq. No inscriptions of this ruler are known.

Ḫimdīia

E4.28.3

Ḫimdīia once served under Atamrum, but later became king of Andariq itself towards the end of the reign of Zimrī-Līm.

2001

A seal of a servant of this ruler is in the Louvre.

COMMENTARY

The seal is MN (Musées Nationaux) 101, provenance unknown. It is a cylinder seal of haematite, 2.3 cm long, 1.1 cm in dia. The inscription was collated from the published photo.

BIBLIOGRAPHY

1923 Delaporte, Louvre 2 p. 131 A 385 and pl. 81 fig. 14 (photo, edition)
1959 Kupper, RA 53 p. 98 (study)

TEXT

1) *ia-am-ṣí-ḫa-ad-nu-ú*	1) Iamṣi-Ḫadnû,
2) DUMU *ba-ri-ia*	2) son of Barīia,
3) ÌR *ḫi-im-di-ia*	3) servant of Ḫimdīia.

2002

An impression of a seal of a servant of Ḫimdīia is on sealings and tablets excavated at Tell Leilan.

COMMENTARY

The impression is found on L85-128 and L87-892, 912, 1275 from the Lower Town. It was collated by D. Parayre, who kindly communicated the transliteration. It is edited here through the courtesy of H. Weiss.

TEXT

1) ^dUTU-DINGIR-[KALA.GA]	1) Šamaš-ilum-[dannum],
2) ÌR *ḫi-im-di-[ia]*	2) servant of Ḫimdī[ia].

Ḫadnī-Addu

E4.28.4

Ḫadnī-Addu was a king of Upper Mesopotamia allied to king Atamrum of Andariq (see Kupper, RA 53 p. 99). Although not a king of Andariq, inscriptions referring to him are edited at this point.

2001

A seal of a servant of Ḫadnī-Addu is in the Louvre.

COMMENTARY

The seal is AO 1634, provenance unknown. It is a cylinder seal of haematite, 2.2 cm long, 1.0 cm in dia. It was collated from the published photo.

BIBLIOGRAPHY

1910 Ward, Seals no. 881 (copy)

1923 Delaporte, Louvre 2 p. 193 A 914 and pl. 96 fig. 12b (photo, edition)

1959 Kupper, RA 53 p. 99 (study)

TEXT

1) *ḫa-qa-t*[*a*]	1) Ḫaqat[a],
2) [D]UMU *pa-ta-al-l*[*a*]	2) [s]on of Patall[a],
3) [Ì]R *ḫa-ad-ni-a-d*[*u*]	3) [se]rvant of Ḫadnī-Add[u].

2002

The impression of a seal of Addu-dūri, a secondary wife of Ḫadnī-Addu, is on a few sealings from Mari.

COMMENTARY

The impressions are found on ME 227 (= ARMT 7 no. 193 = ex. 1), ME 273 (= ARMT 24 no. 128 = ex. 2), and M 13161 (= ex. 3). They were collated from the published photos.

BIBLIOGRAPHY

1957 Bottéro, ARMT 7 p. 90 no. 193 (ex. 1, edition)
1959 Parrot, Documents p. 191, Cylindre de Addu-dûri (ex. 1, study), p. 191 fig. 109 (ex. 1, photo), p. 242 Cylindre de Addu-dûri (ex. 2, study), and pl. 54 (ex. 2, photo); Dossin p. 255 (ex. 1, edition)
1983 Charpin and Durand, MARI 2 pp. 86 and 107 no. 193 (ex. 1, copy, transliteration)
1985 Talon, ARMT 24 p. 209 seal 13 (ex. 2, transliteration)
1988 Charpin in Young (ed.), Mari at 50 p. 73 (ex. 3, edition)

TEXT

1) ^{fd}IŠKUR-*du-ri*
2) GÉME *ḫa-ad-ni*-^{d}IŠ[KUR]

1) Addu-dūri,
2) female servant of Ḫadnī-Ad[du].

ILĀNṢURĀ

E4.29

The important city of Ilānṣurā was located in northern Mesopotamia somewhere in the Ḫabur triangle. Seals or seal impressions of servants of one of its rulers, Ḫaia-sūmû, are known.

Ḫaia-sūmû

E4.29.1

Ḫaia-sūmû was ruler of Ilānṣurā during the reign of Zimrī-Līm of Mari.

2001

A seal of a servant of Ḫaia-sūmû is in the Louvre.

COMMENTARY

The seal is AO 6257, a purchased piece of unknown provenance. It is a cylinder seal of serpentine, 1.8 × 1.0 cm. The inscription was collated from the published photo.

BIBLIOGRAPHY

1923 Delaporte, Louvre 2 p. 126 A 337 and pl. 79 fig. 21 (photo, edition)

1959 Kupper, RA 53 p. 98 (study)

1979 Birot, et al., ARMT 16/1 p. 106 (for the writing Ḫaia-sūmû)

TEXT

1) *ì-lí-ṣí-id-qí*	1) Ilī-ṣidqī,
2) ÌR *ḫa-ià-su-mu*	2) servant of Ḫaia-sūmû.

2002

A small tablet from Mari recording the disbursement of fish for Ḫaia-sūmû in Ilānṣurā bears the seal impression of a servant of Ḫaia-sūmû.

COMMENTARY

The seal impression is found on ARMT 21 no. 88.

BIBLIOGRAPHY

1983 Durand, ARMT 21 p. 569 seal 17 (transliteration)

TEXT

1) [*ṣí*]-*id-qí*-[...]
2) [DUMU] *ša-at-tum-k*[*i*-...]
3) [ÌR] *ḫa-ià-su-ú*-[*mu*]

1) [Ṣ]idqī-[...],
2) [son] of Šattum-k[i-...],
3) [servant] of Ḫaia-sū[mû].

2003

A seal of a servant of Ḫaia-sūmû is in a private American collection. The transliteration of this piece is offered through the courtesy of W.W. Hallo.

TEXT

1) ^{d}*da-gan-ṣí-nu-š*[*u*]
2) ÌR *ḫa-ià-sú-mu*-⸢*ú*⸣

1) Dagān-ṣīnuš[u],
2) servant of Ḫaia-sūmû.

AŠNAKKUM

E4.30

The important city of Ašnakkum was located somewhere in the Ḫabur basin.

Sammētar

E4.30.1

Sammētar, king of Ašnakkum, is mentioned in the Mari letters.

2001

An impression of a servant of Sammētar probably refers to this king.

COMMENTARY

The impression is found on ARMT 24 no. 85.

BIBLIOGRAPHY

1985 Talon, ARMT 24 p. 209 seal 6 (transliteration)

TEXT

1) *ia-mu-ut-ḫa-*[*ma-di*]	1) Iamūt-ḫa[madī],
2) ÌR *sa-am-mi-*[*e-tar*]	2) servant of Sammē[tar].

KAḪAT

E4.31

The ancient city of Kaḫat has been located at modern Tell Barri on the Jaghjagh River (see G. Dossin, AAS 11/12 pp. 197–206).

Iamsi-Ḫadnû

E4.31.1

1

A seal impression of Iamsi-Ḫadnû, king of Kaḫat, a contemporary of Tilabnû of Šeḫnā, is found on a treaty excavated at Tell Leilan.

COMMENTARY

The impression is on L87–1362+. It is offered here through the courtesy of J. Eidem.

TEXT

1) *ia-am-sí-ḫa-ad-nu-ú*	1) Iamsi-Ḫadnû,
2) DUMU *ás-di-ni-ḫi-im*	2) son of Asdī-niḫim,
3) LUGAL *ka-ḫa-at*	3) king of Kaḫat.

CARCHEMISH

E4.32

The names of three kings of ancient Carchemish, modern Jerablus on the Upper Euphrates, are found in the Mari archives. Seals or seal impressions mentioning one of these rulers are known.

Aplaḫanda

E4.32.1

Documents from Mari dating to the time of Iasmaḫ-Addu and Zimrī-Līm mention Aplaḫanda (variants Apliḫanda/Apliḫa(n)di), king of Carchemish. Seals or seal impressions of his daughter and his servants are known.

1

The first seal belonged to a daughter of the king, Matrunna.

COMMENTARY

The seal is in the Metropolitan Museum in New York, MMA L 55.49.139, formerly Moore no. 130. It was found at Ras al-Shamra before the start of the excavations there. It is a cylinder seal of haematite, 2.4 cm long and 1.2 cm in dia. The inscription was collated from the published photo. The goddess Kubaba who figures in line 3 was the tutelary deity of Carchemish.

BIBLIOGRAPHY

1929 Virolleaud, Syria 10 p. 308 (study)
1928–29 Albright, AfO 5 p. 229 (edition)
1929–30 Dussaud, Babyloniaca 11 pp. 166–68 and pl. 4 no. 1 (photo, transliteration, study)
1936 Virolleaud, Danel pp. 2–3 (study)
1938 Dossin, RA 35 p. 115 (photo, transliteration, study)
1940 Eisen, Moore no. 130 (photo, edition)
1953 Dussaud, Prélydiens, Hittites et Achéens p. 105 (translation)
1955 Moortgat-Correns, ZA 51 p. 98 (study)
1958 Nagel and Strommenger, JCS 12 p. 118 (study)
1962 Nougayrol, Syria 39 p. 188 n. 2 (study)
1976 Williams-Forte, Ancient Near Eastern Seals no. 11 (photo, edition)
1987 Collon, First Impressions no. 189 (photo, study)

TEXT

1) *ma-at-ru-un-na*
2) DUMU.MUNUS *ap-la-ḫa-an-da*
3) GÉME ^{d}*ku-ba-ba*

1) Matrunna,
2) daughter of Aplaḫanda,
3) female servant of the goddess Kubaba.

2001

A servant seal of Aplaḫanda is in the Louvre.

COMMENTARY

The seal is AO 21116, a purchased piece of unknown provenance. It is a cylinder seal of haematite, 1.8 × 1 cm. The inscription was collated from the published photo.

BIBLIOGRAPHY

1962 Nougayrol, Syria 39 p. 188 (edition), p. 190 (copy)
1962 [Hotel Drouot] Cachets et Cylindres Orientaux lot 56 (photo)
1973 [Amiet], Bas reliefs imaginaires de l'Ancien Orient d'après les cachets et les sceaux-cylindres (Paris) no. 350 (study)
1987 Collon, First Impressions no. 190 (photo, study)

TEXT

1) *ṭà-ab-be-li*
2) ÌR *ap-la-ḫa-an-d*[*a*]

1) Ṭāb-bēlī,
2) servant of Aplaḫand[a].

2002

A seal of a servant of Aplaḫanda is in the Marcopoli collection.

COMMENTARY

The seal is Teissier, Marcopoli 442. It is a cylinder seal of haematite, 2.2 × 1.3 cm. The inscription was collated from the published photo.

BIBLIOGRAPHY

1984 Teissier, Marcopoli no. 442 (photo, edition)
1987 Durand, NABU p. 28 no. 51 (copy, transliteration)
1987 Collon, First Impressions no. 541 (photo, study)

TEXT

1) *aḫ-zi-ib-kar*$_x$(TE)*-kà-mi*[*š*]
2) DUMU *na-ra-am-*[DINGIR]
3) ÌR *ap-li-ḫa-an-d*[*a*]

1) Aḫzib-Karkami[š],
2) son of Narām-[Ili],
3) servant of Aplaḫand[a].

2003

Impressions of a seal mentioning Aplaḫanda are found on two bullae excavated at Acem höyük in Turkey.

COMMENTARY

The impressions are on Ac i 1051 and Ac i 1053 now in the Archaeological Museum in Ankara. They were collated through the courtesy of V. Donbaz.

BIBLIOGRAPHY

1977 Özgüc, Belleten 41 pl. IV no. 11 (photo)
1980 Özgüc in Porada (ed.), Ancient Art in Seals (New Jersey) p. 67 (study), p. 82 sub fig. III–11 (study), and p. 91 fig. III–11a,b (photo)

TEXT

Lacuna
1′) [ÌR] *ap-li*-⌜*ḫa*⌝-[*du*]

Lacuna
1′) [servant] of Aplaḫan[da].

2004

An impression of another seal mentioning Aplaḫanda is found on a bulla from Acem höyük.

COMMENTARY

The impression is on Ac i 1052, a clay bulla now in the Archaeological Museum in Ankara. It was collated through the courtesy of V. Donbaz.

BIBLIOGRAPHY

1977 Özgüc, Belleten 41 pl. VI no. 17 (photo)
1980 Özgüc in Porada (ed.), Ancient Art in Seals (New Jersey) p. 69 (study), p. 82 sub fig. III–17 (study), and p. 92 fig. III–17 (photo)
1987 Collon, First Impressions no. 188 (photo, study)

TEXT

1) [...] X BI-[...]
2) [GÉME *a*]*p-li-ḫa-d*[*u*]
3) [D]AM LUG[AL]

1) [...]BI[...],
2) [female servant of A]plaḫand[a],
3) [w]ife of the ki[ng].

Iatar-amī

E4.32.2

Documents from Mari reveal that Aplaḫanda of Carchemish was succeeded by his son Iatar-amī, who was a contemporary of Zimrī-Līm of Mari. No inscriptions of this ruler have yet come to light.

Iaḫdun-Līm

E4.32.3

An economic document recently published by J.-M. Durand (NABU 1988 p. 2) refers to a certain *ia-aḫ-du-li-im* 'king of Carchemish'. According to B. Lafont (NABU 1988 pp. 2–3) Iaḫdun-Līm succeeded his brother Iatar-amī as king of Carchemish. No inscriptions of this ruler are extant.

IAMḪAD

E4.33

A large number of tablets excavated by Woolley at Tell Atshana on the bend of the Orontes in Syria, ancient Alalaḫ, date back to the 18th century BC. The information from these tablets coupled with that obtained from the Mari archives sheds much light on the rulers of the ancient kingdom of Iamḫad.

Sūmû-Epuḫ

E4.33.1

A seal impression from Mari recently published by D. Charpin (see bibliography), if restored correctly, indicates that Sūmû-Epuḫ was the father of Iarīm-Līm I, king of Iamḫad (see E4.33.2.1). The exact status of Sūmû-Epuḫ, whether king or not, is not known. He appears in an inscription of Iaḫdun-Līm (see E4.6.8.2 lines 77–78) in connection with the land of Iamḫad.

BIBLIOGRAPHY

1965 Klengel, Geschichte Syriens pp. 111–15 (study)
1988 Charpin in Young (ed.), Mari at 50 pp. 74–75 (study)

Iarīm-Līm I

E4.33.2

Mari documents dating to the time of Zimrī-Līm reveal the existence of Iarīm-Līm I, king of Aleppo and the land of Iamḫad. This man is designated here Iarīm-Līm I to distinguish him from his later name-sakes.

BIBLIOGRAPHY

1965 Klengel, Geschichte Syriens pp. 115–23 (study)

1

An impression of a seal of Iarīm-Līm I found on a tablet envelope from Mari was published by D. Charpin.

COMMENTARY

The impression is on Mari 8090, a small tablet envelope fragment, 2.5×2 cm. The envelope presumably once encased a letter from Iarīm-Līm I to the ruler of Mari.

BIBLIOGRAPHY

1988 Charpin in Young (ed.), Mari at 50 pp. 74–75 (edition)

TEXT

1) *ia-ri-im-*[*li-im*]	1) Iarīm-[Līm],
2) DUMU *su-mu-*⌜*e*⌝-[*pu-uḫ*]	2) son of Sūmû-E[puḫ],
3) [LU]GAL *ia-*[*am-ḫa-ad*]	3) [k]ing of Ia[mḫad],
4) [*n*]*a-ra-*[*am* ᵈIŠKUR]	4) [b]elove[d of the god Adad].

2

Šibtu, the daughter of Iarīm-Līm I of Iamḫad, was married to Zimrī-Līm, king of Mari. Her seal is edited in the Mari section dealing with Zimrī-Līm (see E4.6.12.7).

2001

A seal of a servant of Iarīm-Līm is in Paris. To which of the three kings of Iamḫad who bore this name this seal is to be attributed cannot be determined. It is arbitrarily included under Iarīm-Līm I.

COMMENTARY

The seal is in the Bibliothèque Nationale, no. 496, brought to France by Cousinéry in 1817 and acquired from the Collection Lajard in 1846. It is a haematite cylinder seal 2.7 cm long, 1.1 cm in dia. The inscription was collated from the published photo.

BIBLIOGRAPHY

1886 Ménant, Glyptique 2 p. 117 and fig. 110 (copy, study)
1910 Delaporte, Bibliothèque Nationale no. 496 (photo, edition)
1951 Van Buren, JCS 5 pp. 133–34 (photo, edition)
1953 Weidner, JKF 2 pp. 138–39 (transliteration, study)
1954 Landsberger, JCS 8 p. 60 n. 126 (study)
1987 Collon, First Impressions no. 215 (photo, study)

TEXT

1) *a-ia-a-ḫu-⌜i⌝*
2) ÌR *ia-ri-im-li-im*

1) Aia-aḫūʾī,
2) servant of Iarīm-Līm.

Ḫammu-rāpi I

E4.33.3

Iarīm-Līm I of Iamḫad was succeeded by his son Ḫammu-rāpi I.

BIBLIOGRAPHY

1965 Klengel, Geschichte Syriens pp. 123–27 (study)

2001

A cylinder seal of a servant of Ḫammu-rāpi, which probably refers to one of the two kings of Iamḫad who bore this name, was found in Turkey. It is arbitrarily included here.

COMMENTARY

The present location of the cylinder, found at Firakdin, has not been determined; it may be in Ankara. The inscription was collated from the published photo.

BIBLIOGRAPHY

1955 Özgüç, Belleten 19 pp. 304–305 and fig. 32 (photo, edition)

TEXT

1) *[qí-ī]š-ti-*^{d}IŠKUR	1) [Qī]štī-Addu,
2) [DUMU *ḫ*]*a-ad-nu-a-bi*	2) [son of Ḫ]adnû-abī,
3) [ÌR *ḫ*]*a-am-mu-ra-pí*	3) [servant of Ḫ]ammu-rāpi.

2002

The impression of a seal of a servant of Ḫammu-rāpi edited here shows a number of Syrian motifs that indicate that this Ḫammu-rāpi must have been one of the kings of the Iamḫad dynasty. It is arbitrarily included under Ḫammu-rāpi I.

COMMENTARY

The present whereabouts of this seal is not known. The impression measures 2.9 cm high and it was collated from the published photo.

BIBLIOGRAPHY

1987 Collon, First Impressions no. 544 (photo, study)

TEXT

1) *ši-ri-mu-a ša* GIŠ.ŠAR	1) Širimuʾa, gardener,
2) DUMU *ki-ḫu-uš-ti-ia-ri*	2) son of Kiḫuštiari,
3) ÌR *ḫa-am-mu-ra-pí*	3) servant of Ḫammu-rāpi.

Abba-Il

E4.33.4

Ḫammu-rāpi I of Iamḫad was succeeded by his son Abba-Il. The reading of the royal name is uncertain; it could be Abba-Il or Abban.

BIBLIOGRAPHY

1965 Klengel, Geschichte Syriens pp. 151–54 (study)

1

The impressions of a seal of Abba-Il are found on various tablet envelope fragments excavated at Tell Atshana.

CATALOGUE

Ex.	Museum number	Excavation number	Provenance	Dimensions (cm)	cpn
1	Antakya 7327	ATT/39/184	Tell Atshana, level VII palace, room 11	2.3 long, 3.2 long with caps, 1.5 dia.	n
2	Antakya 7876	ATT/39/156A	As ex. 1	As ex. 1	n
3	Antakya 7900+9140	ATT/39/184	As ex. 1	As ex. 1	n
4	Antakya 7960-1	ATT/39/153	As ex. 1	As ex. 1	n

BIBLIOGRAPHY

1953 Wiseman, Alalakh no. 444 seal b (copy, translation)
1955 Woolley, Alalakh p. 266 nos. 145–52 (study)
1974 Safadi, UF 6 p. 322 and pl. XIX no. 132 (copy, transliteration, study)
1975 Collon, AOAT 27 p. 6 no. 3 (photo, copy, transliteration, study)
1987 Collon, First Impressions no. 542 (copy, study)

TEXT

1) *ab-ba-ìl*
2) DUMU *ḫa-am-mu-ra-pí*
3) LUGAL *ia-am-ḫa-ad*
4) *na-ra-am* ᵈIŠKUR

1) Abba-Il,
2) son of Ḫammu-rāpi,
3) king of Iamḫad,
4) beloved of the god Adad.

2

Impressions of a different seal, the name of whose owner is broken away, but which should probably be restored as Abba-Il, are found on tablet envelopes excavated at Tell Atshana.

CATALOGUE

Ex.	Museum number	Excavation number	Provenance	cpn
1	Antakya 7322	ATT/39/184	Tell Atshana, level VII palace, room 11	n
2	Antakya 7761	ATT/39/183	As ex. 1	n
3	Antakya 7900	ATT/39/184	As ex. 1	n
4	Antakya 7960–1	ATT/39/153	As ex. 1	n

BIBLIOGRAPHY

1974 Safadi, UF 6 p. 322 no. 134 (study)
1975 Collon, AOAT 27 p. 7 no. 4 (photo, copy, transliteration, study)

TEXT

1) [*ab-ba-ìl*]	1) [Abba-Il],
2) [DUMU *ḫa-am*]*-mu-ra-*[*pí*]	2) [son of Ḫam]mu-rā[pi],
3) [LU]GAL *ia-am-ḫa-a*[*d*]	3) [k]ing of Iamḫa[d],
4) [*n*]*a-ra-am* ᵈIŠ[KUR]	4) [b]eloved of the god Ad[ad].

2001

The seal impression of a servant of a ruler whose name is probably to be restored Abba-Il is found on a tablet envelope excavated at Tell Atshana.

COMMENTARY

The impression is on Antakya 7900, excavation no. ATT/39/184, from the level VII palace, room 11.

BIBLIOGRAPHY

1975 Collon, AOAT 27 p. 94 no. 175 (copy, transliteration, study)

TEXT

1) *ku-li*-x-[...]
2) ìR *ab-b*[*a-il*]

1) Kuli-[...],
2) servant of Abb[a-Il].

Iarīm-Līm II

E4.33.5

Abba-Il was succeeded by his son Iarīm-Līm II as king of Iamḫad.

BIBLIOGRAPHY

1965 Klengel, Geschichte Syriens pp. 154–55 (study)

1

The impressions of a seal of Iarīm-Līm II are found on a number of tablet envelopes excavated at Tell Atshana.

CATALOGUE

Ex.	Museum number	Excavation number	Provenance	Dimensions (cm)	cpn
1	Antakya 7761	ATT/39/183	Tell Atshana, level VII palace	2.2 long, 2.95 long with caps, 1.3 dia.	n
2	Antakya 7960-1	ATT/39/153	As ex. 1	As ex. 1	n
3	Antakya 9140	ATT/39/184	As ex. 1	As ex. 1	n

BIBLIOGRAPHY

1953 Wiseman, Alalakh no. 444 seal a (copy, translation)
1975 Collon, AOAT 27 p. 8 no. 5 (photo, copy, transliteration, study)

TEXT

1) *ia-ri-im-li-im*	1) Iarīm-Līm,
2) DUMU *ab-ba-ìl*	2) son of Abba-Il,
3) LUGAL *ia-am-ḫa-ad*	3) king of Iamḫad,
4) *na-ra-am* ᵈIŠ[KUR]	4) beloved of the god Ad[ad].

2001

The impression of a servant of Iarīm-Līm, probably the second ruler of that name at Iamḫad, is found on a tablet envelope excavated at Tell Atshana.

COMMENTARY

The impression is on BM 131449A, excavation no. ATT/39/113b, from the level VII palace, room 11.

We note the appearance of the name of the goddess Kubaba, tutelary deity of Carchemish, in the name of the seal owner.

BIBLIOGRAPHY

1953 Wiseman, Alalakh no. 7 seal f (copy, edition)
1955 Woolley, Alalakh p. 262 and pl. 60 no. 12A (copy, study)
1974 Safadi, UF 6 p. 323 and pl. XXI no. 145 (copy, transliteration, study)
1975 Collon, AOAT 27 p. 19 no. 20 (copy, transliteration, study)

TEXT

1) *ì-ni-ku-bá-b*[*á*]	1) Ini-Kubab[a],
2) ÌR *ia-ri-im-li-im*	2) servant of Iarīm-Līm,
3) *na-ra-am* ᵈIŠ[KUR]	3) beloved of the god Ad[ad].

2002

The impression of a seal of a servant of Iarīm-Līm II, either the king of Iamḫad or the governor of Alalaḫ by that name, is found on a tablet envelope excavated at Tell Atshana. It is arbitrarily included as an inscription of the king of Iamḫad.

COMMENTARY

The impression is on BM 131449A, excavation no. ATT/39/113b, from the level VII palace, room 11.

BIBLIOGRAPHY

1948 Woolley, AJ 28 p. 14 and pl. 9
1953 Wiseman, Alalakh no. 7 seal c (copy, edition)
1955 Woolley, Alalakh p. 262 and pl. 60 no. 12B (photo, study)
1974 Safadi, UF 6 p. 316 and pl. II no. 4 (copy, study)
1975 Collon, AOAT 27 p. 77 no. 141 (copy, transliteration, study)

TEXT

1) *sa-am-šu-*^{d}IŠKUR
2) UGULA DAM.GÀR
3) DUMU *ir-pa-a-[du]*
4) ÌR *ia-ri-im-[li-im]*

1) Samšû-Addu,
2) overseer of the merchant bankers,
3) son of Irpaʾ-A[ddu],
4) servant of Iarīm-[Līm].

2003

The impression of a seal of a vizier of Iarīm-Līm II is found on a tablet envelope excavated at Tell Atshana.

COMMENTARY

The impression is on Antakya 7900, excavation no. ATT/39/184, from the level VII palace, room 11.

BIBLIOGRAPHY

1975 Collon, AOAT 27 p. 94 no. 174 (copy, transliteration, study)

TEXT

1) *we-ri-[ki-ba]*
2) SUKKAL *ia-[ri-im-li-im]*
3) [Ì]R [...]

1) Weri[kiba],
2) vizier of Ia[rīm-Līm],
3) [se]rvant of [...].

2004

The impression of the seal of another servant of Iarīm-Līm II is found on a tablet envelope excavated at Tell Atshana.

COMMENTARY

The impression is on Antakya 7322, excavation no. ATT/39/184, from the level VII palace, room 11. It was collated from the published photo. Line 5 does not appear to be in the original field cut for the seal legend (contra D. Collon).

BIBLIOGRAPHY

1975 Collon, AOAT 27 p. 78 no. 143 (photo, copy, transliteration, study)

TEXT

1) *ša* ^{d}IŠKUR x [...]
2) *sú-mi-a-*[*du*]
3) DUMU *ab-du-da-*[*gan*]
4) *ma*(?)-*ḫi-ir da-*x [...]
5) ÌR *ia-ri-i*[*m-li-im*]

1) Belonging to the god Adad [...] –
2) Sumī-A[ddu],
3) son of Abdu-Da[gān],
4) ...,
5) servant of Iarī[m-Līm].

Niqmī-Epuḫ

E4.33.6

Iarīm-Līm II was succeeded by his son Niqmī-Epuḫ as king of Iamḫad.

BIBLIOGRAPHY

1965 Klengel, Geschichte Syriens pp. 155–56 (study)

1

The impression of a seal of Niqmī-Epuḫ is found on a number of tablet envelopes excavated at Tell Atshana. It was collated from the published photo.

CATALOGUE

Ex.	Museum number	Excavation number	Provenance	Dimensions (cm)	cpn
1	Antakya 7318	ATT/39/184	Tell Atshana, level VII palace, room 11	2.75 long, 2.95 long with caps, 1.3 dia.	n
2	Antakya 7900	ATT/39/184	As ex. 1	As ex. 1	n
3	BM 131449A	ATT/39/1136	As ex. 1	As ex. 1	n

BIBLIOGRAPHY

1953 Wiseman, Alalakh no. 7 seal e (copy, edition)
1955 Woolley, Alalakh p. 262 and pl. 60 no. 12A (photo, study) and p. 266 and pl. 67 no. 145 (photo, study)
1974 Safadi, UF 6 p. 322 and pl. XX no. 141 (copy, transliteration, study)
1975 Collon, AOAT 27 p. 9 no. 6 (photo, copy, transliteration, study)
1987 Collon, First Impressions no. 214 (copy, study)

TEXT

1) *ni-iq-mi-e-p[u-uḫ]*
2) DUMU *ia-ri-im-li-i[m]*
3) LUGAL *ia-am-ḫa-a[d]*
4) *na-ra-am* ^{d}[IŠKUR]

1) Niqmī-Ep[uḫ],
2) son of Iarīm-Lī[m],
3) king of Iamḫa[d],
4) beloved of the god [Adad].

2001

The impression of a seal of the vizier of Niqmī-Epuḫ is found on tablet envelopes excavated at Tell Atshana.

CATALOGUE

Ex.	Museum number	Excavation number	Provenance	Dimensions (cm)	cpn
1	Antakya 7960-1 + 7900	ATT/39/153 + 184	Tell Atshana, level VII palace, room 11	2.2 long with caps	n
2	BM 131449A	ATT/39/113b	From the level VII palace, room 2	As ex. 1	n

BIBLIOGRAPHY

1953 Wiseman, Alalakh no. 7 seal b (copy, edition)
1974 Safadi, UF 6 p. 322 no. 142 (transliteration, study)
1975 Collon, AOAT 27 p. 18 no. 19 (copy, transliteration, study)

TEXT

1) *na-aḫ-mi-*ᵈ*da-gan*
2) SUKKAL *ni-iq-mi-e-pu-uḫ*
3) *na-ra-am* ᵈIŠKUR

1) Naḫmī-Dagān,
2) vizier of Niqmī-Epuḫ,
3) beloved of the god Adad.

Irkabtum

E4.33.7

Niqmī-Epuḫ seems to have had a number of sons, three of whom succeeded him on the throne of Iamḫad. The exact order of their succession is not certain. Here we follow the scheme suggested by D. Collon (see AOAT 27 pp. 143–45).

BIBLIOGRAPHY

1965 Klengel, Geschichte Syriens pp. 156–57 (study)

1

The seal impression of Irkabtum, son of Niqmī-Epuḫ, is on a tablet envelope excavated at Tell Atshana.

COMMENTARY

The impression is found on BM 131648, excavation no. ATT 39/30, from the level VII palace, room 2.

BIBLIOGRAPHY

1953 Wiseman, Alalakh no. 443 seal a (copy, transliteration)
1975 Collon, AOAT 27 p. 10 no. 8 (copy, transliteration, study)

TEXT

1) [*ir-k*]*ab*-[*tum*]	1) [Irk]ab[tum],
2) [DU]MU *ni-iq-mi-e-pu-u*[*ḫ*]	2) [s]on of Niqmī-Epu[ḫ],
3) LUGAL *ia-am-ḫa*-[*ad*]	3) king of Iamḫa[d],
4) *na-ra-am* [^{d}IŠKUR]	4) beloved of [the god Adad].

Iarīm-Līm III

E4.33.8

Irkabtum seems to have been succeeded by his brother Iarīm-Līm III as king of Iamḫad.

BIBLIOGRAPHY

1965 Klengel, Geschichte Syriens pp. 157–61 (study)

1

The impression of a seal of Iarīm-Līm III is on a tablet envelope excavated at Tell Atshana.

COMMENTARY

The impression is found on Antakya 8880. It was collated from the published photo.

BIBLIOGRAPHY

1975 Collon, AOAT 27 p. 11 no. 10 (photo, copy, transliteration, study)

TEXT

1) *[ia]-ri-im-[li-im]*	1) [Ia]rīm-[Līm],
2) [DUMU] *ni-i[q-mi-e-pu-uḫ]*	2) [son] of Ni[qmī-Epuḫ],
3) LUGAL *i[a-am-ḫa-ad]*	3) king of I[amḫad],
4) *na-ra-a[m* ^{d}IŠKUR]	4) belov[ed of the god Adad].

2001

Impressions of a seal of a servant of Iarīm-Līm III are found on a tablet envelope excavated at Tell Atshana.

CATALOGUE

Ex.	Museum number	Excavation number	Provenance	Dimensions (cm)	cpn
1	Antakya 3206	ATT/39/153	Tell Atshana, level VII palace, room 11	About 1.1 dia.	p
2	Antakya 7327	ATT/39/184	As ex. 1	As ex. 1	p
3	Antakya 7960–1	ATT/39/153	As ex. 1	As ex. 1	p

BIBLIOGRAPHY

1975 Collon, AOAT 27 p. 76 no. 140 (copy, transliteration, study)

TEXT

1) [*i*]*a*(?)-*bi*-[...]
2) [DUM]U *id-na*-[...]
3) [ÌR] *ia-ri-im-l*[*i-im*]

1) [I]abi-[...],
2) [so]n of Idna-[...],
3) [servant] of Iarīm-L[īm].

Ḫammu-rāpi II

E4.33.9

Iarīm-Līm III was succeeded by Ḫammu-rāpi II as king of Iamḫad. No inscriptions of this ruler are known at present.

BIBLIOGRAPHY

1965 Klengel, Geschichte Syriens pp. 161–62 (study)

ALALAḪ

E4.34

In addition to information about the rulers of the kingdom of Iamḫad, the Alalaḫ tablets give us the names of various governors of Alalaḫ during late Old Babylonian times. Their inscriptions are edited at this point.

Iarīm-Līm

E4.34.1

Abba-Il, king of Iamḫad, installed his brother Iarīm-Līm as ruler in Alalaḫ.

1

A historical text known from a copy on a tablet deals with the installation of Iarīm-Līm by Abba-Il and the dedication of a statue(?) of Iarīm-Līm to the temple of the goddess Eštar.

COMMENTARY

The text is inscribed on BM 131446, excavation no. ATT/39/83, from the level VII palace, room 11, at Alalaḫ. It is a clay tablet 11 × 6.4 cm.

A diorite head found in the level VII temple at Alalaḫ (see L. Woolley, Alalakh pl. 47), as Woolley suggests (pp. 235–37), may belong to a statue of Iarīm-Līm, possibly the same one which may be mentioned in this inscription.

BIBLIOGRAPHY

1953 Wiseman, Alalakh no. 1 (copy, edition)
1957 Albright, BASOR 146 pp. 27–28 (study)
1957 S. Smith, RSO 32 p. 177–78 (translation, study)
1965 Klengel, Geschichte Syriens pp. 136–37 (partial edition)
1980 Naʾaman, JNES 39 pp. 209–14 (edition)
1985 Dietrich and Loretz, TUAT 1/5 pp. 497–98 (translation)

TEXT

1) *i-nu-ma aḫ-ḫu-šu* ^{m}*ab-ba-ìl be-el-šu-nu ib-ba-al-ki-tu*
2) ^{m}*ab-ba-ìl* LUGAL-*r*[*u i-n*]*a* ⸢*tu-ku*⸣*-u*[*l-ti*] ^{d}IŠKUR
3) ^{d}*ḫé-pát ù* GIŠ.ŠUKUR [... *ša* ^{d}*eš*$_{4}$*-tár*] *a-na* URU *ir-ri-de*.KI *il-lik-ma*
4) URU *ir-ri-de*.KI *iṣ-*⸢*ba-at*⸣ [*ù ṣ*]*a-ab-šu ik-šu-ud*

1–4) When his allies rebelled against Abba-Il, their lord, Abba-Il, the ki[ng], with the help of the gods Adad, Ḫepat, and the spear [of Eštar], went to Irride, captured Irride, and defeated its troops.

5) *i-na* ⸢*u*$_{4}$⸣*-mi-šu* ^{m}[*ab*]*-ba-ì*[*l*] *a-na pu-ḫa-at*
6) URU *ir-ri-de*.⸢KI⸣ [*š*]*a a-b*[*i-š*]*u* ⸢*id*⸣*-di-na-am*
7) *i-na na-ra-*[*am*] *li-ib-bi-šu* URU *a-la-la-aḫ*.KI
8) ⸢*i*⸣-[*i*]*d-di-in*$_{4}$ ⸢*ù*⸣ [*i*]*-na u*$_{4}$*-mi-šu* ^{m}*ia-ri-*⸢*im*⸣*-li-im*
9) DU[MU ^{m}*ḫa-am-mu*]*-ra-pí* ÌR ^{m}*ab-ba-ìl* [ALAM-*šu*]

5–10) At that time Abba-Il, in exchange for Irride which his father granted, gave Alalaḫ of his own free will. And at that time, Iarīm-Līm, s[on of Ḫammu]-rāpi, servant of Abba-Il, dedicated [a statue of himself to the temple] of the goddess Eštar.

10) [*a-na* É] ⸢^{d}⸣*eš*$_4$*-tár ú-še-li*
11) [... ^{m}*ab*]*-ba-ìl ša ia-ri-im-li-im*
12) x [...] ⸢*a*⸣-[*l*]*a-am pu-ḫa-at a-li-im*
13) ⸢*id-di-na-aš*⸣*-šu ša a-wa-at ab-ba-ìl i-pu-šu*
14) *ú-na-ak-ka-ru a-na ia-ri-im-li-im*
15) *ù pí-ir-ḫi-šu ú-la-am-ma-nu*
16) ^{d}IŠKUR *i-na* GIŠ.TUKUL *ša qa-ti-šu li-iḫ-bu-us-su*
17) ^{d}*ḫé-pát* ^{d}*eš*$_4$*-tár* GIŠ.SUKUR*-šu li-iš-bi-ir*
18) ^{d}*eš*$_4$*-tár a-na qa-ti mu-ka-aš-ši-di-šu li-ma-al-li-šu*
19) ^{d}*eš*$_4$*-tár* SAG.UR.SAG *pa-ra-ú-ra-am*
20) *i-na bi-ir-ki-šu li-te-eb-bi*

11–15) [... Ab]ba-Il who Iarīm-Līm ... gave him a city in exchange for a city. Whoever changes the affair which Abba-Il has done and injures Iarīm-Līm and his posterity:

16–20) may the god Adad crush him with the weapon which is in his hand; may the goddesses Ḫepat and Eštar shatter his spear; may the goddess Eštar deliver him into the hand of his pursuers; and may the goddess Eštar (as with) a eunuch cause *potency* to leave his private parts.

Ammī-taqūmma

E4.34.2

Ammī-taqūmma, ruler of Alalaḫ, was the son of a certain Iarīm-Līm. We cannot determine at present whether this Iarīm-Līm was the king of Iamḫad or the governor of Alalaḫ of that name.

1

Impressions of a seal of Ammī-taqūmma are found on a number of tablet envelopes excavated at Tell Atshana.

CATALOGUE

Ex.	Museum number	Excavation number	Provenance	Dimensions (cm)	cpn
1	Antakya 3206	ATT/39/153	Tell Atshana, level VII palace, room 11	2.0 long, 0.9 dia.	n
2	Antakya 7322	ATT/39/184	As ex. 1	As ex. 1	n
3	Antakya 7327	ATT/39/184	As ex. 1	As ex. 1	n
4	BM 131648	ATT/39/30	Level VII palace, room 2	As ex. 1	n

BIBLIOGRAPHY

1953 Wiseman, Alalakh no. 443 seal b (copy, translation)
1974 Safadi, UF 6 p. 322 and pl. XX no. 144 (copy, transliteration, study)
1975 Collon, AOAT 27 p. 15 no. 14 (copy, transliteration, study)

TEXT

1) *[a]m-mi-ta-qum-m[a]*
2) [DUMU *i*]*a-ri-im-li-i*[*m*]
3) *šar a-la-la-a*[*ḫ*]
4) [*na*]-*ra-am* ᵈ[IŠKUR]

1) [A]mmī-taqūmm[a],
2) [son of I]arīm-Lī[m],
3) king of Alala[ḫ],
4) [be]loved of the god [Adad].

Ḫammu-rāpi

E4.34.3

A certain Ḫammu-rāpi, son of Ammī-taqūmma, probably succeeded his father as governor of Alalaḫ. No inscriptions of this ruler have yet come to light.

BIBLIOGRAPHY

1953 Wiseman, Alalakh pp. 33–34 no. 6 (study)

TUBA

E4.35

Tuba was a minor city which at some times was part of the kingdom of Alalaḫ. The names of three of its kings are known.

Sumī-rapa

E4.35.1

1

The plaster impression of a seal of Sumī-rapa, king of Tuba, is in the Louvre.

COMMENTARY

The impression measures 3.7 cm high and was collated from the published photo.

BIBLIOGRAPHY

1962 Nougayrol and Amiet, RA 56 pp. 169–74 (photo, edition)
1987 Collon, First Impressions no. 543 (photo, study)

TEXT

1) ^{d}IŠKUR *na-bi šu-mi-ia*	1) (For) the god Adad who proclaims my name,
2) [^{d}EN].ZU *ra-im pá-li-ia*	2) [(and) the god S]în, who loves my rule,
3) *su-[m]i-ra-pa*	3) Su[m]ī-rapa,
4) DUMU ⸢*ia-ri*⸣*-im-li-im*	4) son of Iarīm-Līm,
5) LUGAL URU *tu-ba*.KI	5) king of the city of Tuba,
6) *na-ra-*⸢*am*⸣-^{d}*eš*$_{4}$*-tár*	6) beloved of the goddess Eštar,
7) NA$_{4}$.KIŠIB ⸢KIŠIB⸣.ḪI.A	7) seal of seals.

Ammu-sama

E4.35.2

1

A tablet excavated at Tell Atshana (see D. Wiseman, Alalakh no. 11 lines 18 and 31) mentions a certain Ammu-sama, 'ruler' of Tuba. A seal impression found on the envelope of this tablet names Ammu-sama with the title of king, presumably of Tuba.

COMMENTARY

The impression is on Antakya 7960–1, excavation no. ATT/39/153, joining Antakya 7900 (ATT/39/184), from the level VII palace, room 11.

BIBLIOGRAPHY

1975 Collon, AOAT 27 p. 20 no. 23 (copy, transliteration, study)

TEXT

1) *am-mu-*[*sa-ma*]	1) Ammu-[sama],
2) [DU]MU *ni-iq-*[*mi*]-⸢*e*⸣-[*pu-uḫ*]	2) [s]on of Niq[mī]-E[puḫ],
3) [LU]GAL [*tu-ba*.KI]	3) [ki]ng of [Tuba].

Irkabtum

E4.35.3

Irkabtum, king of Tuba, is mentioned in D. Wiseman, Alalakh no. 367 lines 13–14. No seal impressions of this king or his servants are known at present.

EBLA

E4.36

The status of the city of Ebla in Isin–Larsa/Old Babylonian times is uncertain. The finding of a monument of a certain Ibbiṭ-Līm, probably dating to late Ur III times (on the date see D. Owen and R. Veenker in L. Cagni [ed.], Ebla 1975–1985 pp. 269–73), suggests that the city gained its independence at the collapse of the Ur III empire. A seal impression of a son of a certain Indilimgur who ruled Ebla around 1725 BC is known. Later, a year name of Ammī-taqūmma of Alalaḫ records the marriage of a son of Ammī-taqūmma to the daughter of the *en* of Ebla (see Wiseman, Alalakh p. 43 no. 35), a fact suggesting that the city was a vassal of Alalaḫ at that time.

Indilimgur

E4.36.1

1

A number of fragments of jar shoulders excavated at Tell Mardiḫ bear the seal impression of a son of Indilimgur. Indilimgur appears in a year name on a tablet excavated at Tell Mardiḫ (see P. Matthiae, Académie des Inscriptions et Belles-Lettres, Comptes Rendus 1980 pp. 116–17), so we may assume that he was an independent ruler who controlled Ebla. Whether his son Marat-ewari[...] succeeded his father is not known. P. Matthiae dates the seal impression to about 1725 BC.

CATALOGUE

Ex.	Museum number	Excavation number	Tell Mardikh Provenance	Dimensions (cm)	Lines preserved	cpn
1	National Museum, Damascus	TM 65.B.264a + b + c	Sector B, Western Palace	7.9 × 2.5	1–2	p
2	Archaeological Museum, Aleppo	TM 66.B.207	As ex. 1	As ex. 1	1–2	p
3	–	TM –	As ex. 1	As ex. 1	1–2	n

BIBLIOGRAPHY

1966 Liverani, MAIS 1965 pp. 51–55 no. 9 and pl. LXXIX 3–4 (ex. 1, photo, study)

1967 Liverani, MAIS 1966 p. 56 no. 1 and pl. LIX 1 (ex. 2, photo, study)

1969 Matthiae, Syria 46 pp. 1–43 and pls. I–II (exs. 1–2, photo, study)

1980 Matthiae, Ebla An Empire Rediscovered p. 138 fig. 32 (drawing), pl. 3b following p. 224 (ex. 2, photo)

1980 Kühne, Das Rollsiegel in Syrien no. 35 (exs. 1–2 study; ex. 2, photo, composite drawing)

1982 Homes-Fredericq, et al., Sceaux-Cylindres de Syrie no. 35 (exs. 1–2, study, drawing)

1984 Matthiae, Biblical Archaeologist 47 p. 22 (ex. 3, photo)

1985 Matthiae, I tesori di Ebla (Rome) pl. 87 (exs. 1–2, photo, study)

1987 Collon, First Impressions no. 545 (composite copy, study)

TEXT

1) ^{m}*ma-rat-e-wa-ri-*[...]
2) DUMU *in-di-lim-gur*

1) Marat-ewari[...],
2) son of Indilimgur.

UNIDENTIFIED CITIES

E4.0

A number of seals or seal impressions of Old Babylonian date are known in which the owner of the seal appears as the 'servant' (ìR) of another man. Using the principle put forward by E. Weidner in JKF 2 (1953) pp. 127–28, we may assume that the name following the designation 'servant' is that of a ruler. The importance of this ruler, however, could vary from that of a petty local ruler to that of the king of Babylon. We have edited in this volume servant seals under the appropriate sections when the rulers were known from other sources. However, a number of servant seals remain whose rulers are otherwise unknown. These seal inscriptions and other miscellaneous inscriptions of unidentified rulers are edited in this section.

Ammī-ištamar

E4.0.1

1

A vase bears a votive inscription of a certain Ammī-ištamar, who probably bore the title 'Amorite chief'. Unfortunately, we do not know where this ruler was based.

COMMENTARY

The inscription is found on an onyx vase donated by the Baron Edmond de Rothschild to the Cabinet de Médailles. It is said to have come from Nippur. The vase has an external dia. of 8 cm and a height of 15 cm. The inscription was collated from the published photo.

The restoration of line 6 is not entirely certain. M. Stol suggested a reading [*ra-bi*]-⌜*a*⌝-*an* MAR.TU, but the traces before the *-an* sign in the photo favour a reading [*b*]*i-* rather than ⌜*a*⌝. The title 'Amorite chief' agrees with the name of the dedicator of the vase, which is clearly Amorite.

The divine name in lines 1–2 [d]NIN-*šuk-nir* is probably a var. of the name which appears as d*be-la-at-šuḫ-nir* in Ur III sources.

BIBLIOGRAPHY

1911 Fossey, Babyloniaca 4 pp. 248–49 and pl. va (photo, edition)

1976 Stol, Studies in Old Babylonian History p. 87 (transliteration, study)

1981 Heltzer, Suteans p. 5 n. 33 (edition)

TEXT

1) [*a*]-*na* 2) [d]NIN-*šuk-nir* 3) [*be*]-*el-ti-šu*	1–3) [T]o [the goddess] Bēlet-Šuknir, his [l]ady,
4) [*am-m*]*i-iš-ta-mar* 5) [x *d*]*i-da-ni-um* 6) [*ra-b*]*í-an* MAR.DÚ	4–6) [Amm]ī-ištamar, [... of the D]idānum, Amorite [chi]ef,
7) [*a-n*]*a ba-la-ṭì-šu* 8) *i-qí-iš*	7–8) presented (this vase) [fo]r his own life.

Unknown Ruler

E4.0.2

1

A cone fragment in the British Museum bears the inscription of a ruler whose name is not preserved.

COMMENTARY

The fragment bears the registration no. 1931-10-10,364. Although this registration group includes pieces excavated by Woolley at Ur there is no information about the provenance of this particular piece. The fragment measures 4.7×6 cm. About one-third of the circumference is preserved. The inscription was collated by R.F.G. Sweet and is published here through the courtesy of C.B.F. Walker.

The occurrence of the lam sign at the end of line 8′ suggests a possible connection with é-mes-lam, the temple of the god Nergal.

TEXT

1′) [....K]I
2′) [...].KI
3′) [...]-da-
4′) [... n]i-šè
5′) [... n]a-a
6′) [... š]e-ga-⌜ni⌝
7′) [...] dím(?)
8′) [...] lam
9′) [...] x x

1′–9′) No translation warranted.

Šū-Kakka

E4.0.3

1

A fragmentary seal impression on a tablet from Ešnunna has the inscription of king Šū-Kakka, whose city is unknown.

COMMENTARY

The impression is on As 31:T.661, found in the dump of the Bilalama excavations. Although the tablet bearing the impression lacks an archaeological context, a man called Šū-Kakka, probably the ruler of the same name, does appear in a tablet from Ešnunna dating to the reign of Bilalama. The transliteration of this seal inscription is offered through the courtesy of R. Whiting.

In view of the connection of the god Kakka with the city of Maškan-šarrum, king Šū-Kakka may have been the ruler of that city on the middle Tigris.

BIBLIOGRAPHY

1987 Whiting, AfO 34 pp. 34–35 (copy, edition)

TEXT

1) ⸢^{d}⸣*šu-kak-kà*	1) Šū-Kakka,
2) [LUGAL] KALA.GA	2) mighty [king],
3) [^{d}UTU M]A.DA.NA	3) [sun/king] of his [la]nd,
4) [...]-⸢*um*⸣	4) to [...]um
Lacuna	Lacuna
1′) [*i-q*]*i*$_4$(?)-[*iš*]	1′) [he gr]an[ted] (this seal).

Ambuna-aḫi

E4.0.4

1

The seal of the chief Ambuna-aḫi is in Paris.

COMMENTARY

The seal is in the collection of Mme Vendryès. It was collated from the published photo.

BIBLIOGRAPHY

1985 Parayre, Mélanges Birot, pp. 233–34 (photo, copy, translation, study)
1985 Charpin, RA 79 p. 191 (transliteration, study)

TEXT

1) *am-bu-na-a-ḫi*	1) Ambuna-aḫi,
2) DUMU *i-ša-nu-um*	2) son of Išānûm,
3) *ra-bí-a-nu-um*	3) chief.

Abī-maraṣ

E4.0.5

2001

The seal of a servant of Abī-maraṣ is in the British Museum.

COMMENTARY

The seal is BM 89011 (43-11-17,2), from the Sir Keith Jackson collection, found at Hillah, near Babylon, in 1829. It is a cylinder seal of haematite, 2.7 cm long, 1.6 cm in dia.

BIBLIOGRAPHY

1847 Lajard, Mithra pl. LXIVA no. 5
1898 Jastrow, Bildermappe no. 142
1910 Ward, Seals no. 445 (copy)
1939 Frankfort, Cylinder Seals pl. XXVIIIa (photo [wrongly numbered 11068])
1941 Balkan, Sumerolojı Araştırmaları (Istanbul) p. 899 (photo)
1966 Unger, Siegelbildforschung p. 60 (study)
1986 Collon, Cylinder Seals III no. 420 (photo, edition)

TEXT

1) *ḫa-a-lí-lu-ú*
2) DUMU *ḫu-nu-bi-im*
3) ÌR *a-bi-ma-ra-aṣ*

1) Ḫalilû,
2) son of Ḫunnubum,
3) servant of Abī-maraṣ.

Abī-nu-x

E4.0.6

2001

BIBLIOGRAPHY

1899 Ball, Light From the East (London) p. 20 (photo)

TEXT

1) [d]nanna-ki-ág
2) DUMU *ma-nu-um-ša-ni-in-š*[*u*]
3) ÌR *a-bi-nu*-X

1) Nanna-kiag,
2) son of Mannum-šāninš[u],
3) servant of Abī-nu-x.

Adad-ilušu

E4.0.7

2001

An impression of a seal of a servant of Adad-ilušu appears on a tablet dated to year 13 of Sūmû-El of Larsa.

COMMENTARY

The impression is found on NBC 5410 and measures 2.2 cm high. It was collated from the published photo.

BIBLIOGRAPHY

1943 Alexander, BIN 7 no. 108 (copy)
1970 Walters, Water p. 113 text 83 (for restoration of the seal)
1981 Buchanan and Hallo, Early Near Eastern Seals no. 752 (photo, edition)

TEXT

1) [...]
2) ÌR [d]IŠKUR DINGIR-*šu*

1) [...],
2) servant of Adad-ilušu.

Addu-mālik

E4.0.8

2001

The seal of a servant of Addu-mālik is in the Jonathan P. Rosen Collection in New York.

COMMENTARY

A transliteration of this seal is provided through the courtesy of W. Hallo.

TEXT

1) *ab-di-an-na*	1) Abdi-Anna,
2) DUMU *ḫi-ni-*ᵈ*da-gan*	2) son of Ḫinnī-Dagān,
3) ÌR ᵈIŠKUR-*ma-lik*	3) servant of Addu-mālik.

Adad-qarrād

E4.0.9

2001

The seal of a servant of Adad-qarrād is in the British Museum.

COMMENTARY

The seal is BM 102524 (1908-4-11,32). The original provenance of the piece is unknown. It is a cylinder seal of quartz, variety chalcedony (red jasper), and measures 2.65 cm long, 1.7 cm in dia.

BIBLIOGRAPHY

1986 Collon, Cylinder Seals III no. 42 (photo, edition)

TEXT

1) *ú-qá-eš$_4$-tár*
2) DUMU *šar-ru-um-*^{d}IŠKUR
3) ÌR ^{d}IŠKUR-UR.SAG

1) Uqqâ-Eštar,
2) son of Šarrum-Adad,
3) servant of Adad-qarrād.

Awīl-Ili

E4.0.10

2001

The seal of a servant of Awīl-Ili is in the Morgan Library Collection.

COMMENTARY

The seal is no. 553 in E. Porada's catalogue of the collection. It was collated from the published photo.

A city named URU *a-wi-il*$_5$*-ì-lí* occurs in an economic tablet from Larsa which probably dates to the time of Rīm-Sîn (see VAS no. 104 ii 19).

BIBLIOGRAPHY

1948 Porada, Corpus no. 553 (photo, edition)
1962 Hallo, HUCA 33 p. 20 (study)

TEXT

1) *ab-di-e-ra-aḫ*
2) DUMU *la-i-um*
3) ÌR *a-wi-il*-DINGIR

1) Abdi-Eraḫ,
2) son of Laʾium,
3) servant of Awīl-Ili.

Iakūn-Dīri

E4.0.11

2001

Iakūn-Dīri was a king of Upper Mesopotamia allied to Zimrī-Līm. The seal of a servant of this king is in the Louvre.

COMMENTARY

The seal is KL (Cabinet Langpérier) q 51, provenance unknown. It is a cylinder seal of haematite, 2.5 cm long, 1.3 cm in dia. The inscription was collated from the published photo.

BIBLIOGRAPHY

1923 Delaporte, Louvre 2 A 418 and pl. 82 fig. 13 (photo, edition)

1959 Kupper, RA 53 pp. 98–99 (study)

TEXT

1) *ia-mu-ut-ku-lu-uḫ*	1) Iamūt-Kuluḫ,
2) DUMU *ḫa-ab-du-e-ra-aḫ*	2) son of Ḫabdu-Eraḫ,
3) ÌR *ia-ku-un-di-r*[*i*]	3) servant of Iakūn-Dīr[i].

Ilānī

E4.0.12

2001

The seal of a servant of Ilānī is in New York.

COMMENTARY

The seal is Metropolitan Museum of Art no. 43.102.35, from the Rogers Fund, 1943. The impression measures 2.4 cm high and was collated from the published photo.

BIBLIOGRAPHY

1966 Metropolitan Museum of Art, Ancient Near Eastern Art p. 16 fig. 26 (photo)

TEXT

1) dUTU-TAR-DI	1) Šamaš-pāris-dīnim,
2) ÌR *i-la-ni*	2) servant of Ilānī.

Ilum-mutnen

E4.0.13

2001

A late Old Babylonian seal bears the inscription of a servant of Ilum-mutnen.

COMMENTARY

The seal is in the Danish National Museum, no. 10031, a piece purchased in Syria. It was collated from the published photo. In line 2 Šuqab is a Kassite deity, a fact that suggests a late OB date for this seal.

BIBLIOGRAPHY

1960 Ravn, Catalogue no. 88 (photo, edition)

TEXT

1) *i-bur-eš₄-tár*	1) Ibūr-Eštar,
2) DUMU *ri-iš-ᵈšu-qa-ab*	2) son of Rīš-Šuqab,
3) ÌR DINGIR-*mu-ut-nen*	3) servant of Ilum-mutnen.

Mutuša

E4.0.14

2001

A seal impression bears the inscription of a servant of Mutuša, a ruler otherwise unknown.

COMMENTARY

The impression was shown to C.B.F. Walker, who kindly communicated a transliteration of the text.

TEXT

1) *iš-me-èr-ra*	1) Išme-Erra,
2) DUMU *ì-lí-ba-ni*	2) son of Ilī-bāni,
3) ÌR *mu-tu-ša*	3) servant of Mutuša.

Nūr-Surutar

E4.0.15

2001

A seal of a servant of Nūr-Surutar is in the Ashmolean Museum.

COMMENTARY

The object is Ash 1921,948, a cylinder seal of dark green serpentine, 2.1 × 1.1 cm. It comes from the John's collection, and may be from the Diyala region. The inscription was collated from the published photo.

BIBLIOGRAPHY

1966 Buchanan and Gurney, Ashmolean 1 no. 531 (photo, edition)

TEXT

1) *im-ṣí-é-a*	1) Imṣi-Ea,
2) ÌR *nu-úr-*^{d}*su-ru-tar*	2) servant of Nūr-Surutar.

Pî-Eštar

E4.0.16

2001

A seal of a servant of Pî-Eštar is in the British Museum.

COMMENTARY

The seal is BM 121209 (1930-3-9,1), presented by C. Smith. It is made of haematite and measures 2.25 × 1.1 cm. It was collated from the published photo.

The name Pî-Eštar may possibly be an abbreviated form of the name Ikūn-pî-Eštar, a year name of whom appears on an economic text excavated at Nippur (see M. Sigrist, Sattukku p. 43). The name also appears in a fragment of the Sumerian King List (see T. Jacobsen, SKL p. 8). In the King List fragment Ikūn-pî-Eštar is followed immediately by Sūmû-abum (of Babylon). The Nippur archive studied by Sigrist otherwise starts with Lipit-Enlil of Isin, and it is likely that Ikūn-pî-Eštar preceded that king in control of Nippur. Jacobsen suggests that Ikūn-pî-Eštar may have been a ruler of Uruk. That Uruk was an independent power at this time is confirmed by the name of year 5 of Sūmû-El of Larsa, probably a contemporary of Ikūn-pî-Eštar, which commemorates the defeat of the army of Uruk.

BIBLIOGRAPHY

1986 Collon, Cylinder Seals III no. 171 (photo, edition)

TEXT

1) [x] x x [x] x	1) ...
2) [x] x x x	2) ...
3) IR$_{11}$ *pi-i-eš$_4$-tár*	3) servant of Pî-Eštar.

Pulsuna-Addu

E4.0.17

2001

The seal of a servant of Pulsuna-Addu is in the Yale collections.

COMMENTARY

The object is NBC 8915, a cylinder seal of haematite, 1.7 × 0.9 cm. The inscription was collated from the published photo.

BIBLIOGRAPHY

1981 Buchanan and Hallo, Early Near Eastern Seals no. 1136 (photo, edition)

TEXT

1) *da-di-e-ba-al*	1) Dādī-Ebal,
2) IR$_{11}$ *pu-ul-sú-na-*^{d}IŠKUR	2) servant of Pulsuna-Addu.

Šamḫum

E4.0.18

2001

A seal of a servant of Šamḫum is in the British Museum.

COMMENTARY

The object is BM 114401 (1920-5-14,1), presented to the museum, provenance unknown. It is a cylinder seal of haematite 2.35 cm long, 1.35 cm in dia.

A place-name Dūr-Šamḫum appears in a tablet from Ishchali (Greengus, OBTI no. 305 lines 26 and 30). A certain Šamḫum appears in the expression DUMU.ME *ša-am-ḫi-im* 'sons of Šamḫum' in a letter to Ipiq-Adad I of Ešnunna (see R. Whiting, Letters pp. 98-99 no. 42 line 9'). If this is the same person who appears as ruler in the seal, then the evidence of the letter would indicate that he was a contemporary of Ipiq-Adad I, and that he probably ruled in the Diyala region.

BIBLIOGRAPHY

1986 Collon, Cylinder Seals III no. 543 (photo, edition)

TEXT

1) ÌR-[d]IŠKUR	1) Warad-Adad,
2) DUMU *ṣa-li-lum*	2) son of Ṣālilum,
3) ÌR *ša-am-ḫu-um*	3) servant of Šamḫum.

Šaram

E4.0.19

2001

The seal of a servant of Šaram is found in the University Museum in Philadelphia.

COMMENTARY

The piece is CBS 5046, purchased in Baghdad in 1890, provenance unknown. It is a concave cylinder seal of haematite, 2.0×0.9 cm. The inscription was collated from the published photo.

BIBLIOGRAPHY

1925 Legrain, PBS 14 no. 360 (photo, edition)
1962 Hallo, HUCA 33 p. 20 and n. 180 (study)

TEXT

1) *ka-lu-um*
2) DUMU *a-lí-a-ḫu-ia*
3) ÌR *ša-ra-am*

1) Kalum,
2) son of Ali-aḫūia,
3) servant of Šaram.

Ūṣi-nawir

E4.0.20

2001

The seal of a servant of Ūṣi-nawir is in the University Museum in Philadelphia.

COMMENTARY

The piece is CBS 14434 from the Maxwell Sommerville Collection. It is a concave cylinder seal of haematite, 2.4×1.1 cm. The inscription was collated from the published photo.

BIBLIOGRAPHY

1925 Legrain, PBS 14 no. 366 (photo, edition)
1962 Hallo, HUCA 33 p. 20 and n. 181 (study)

TEXT

1) *nu-úr-be-lí*
2) DUMU *ur-na-mi-iš*
3) IR$_{11}$ *ú-ṣí-na-wi-ir*

1) Nūr-bēlī,
2) son of Urnamiš,
3) servant of Ūṣi-nawir.

Index of Museum Numbers

Ashmolean

Birmingham

British Museum

Chicago

Free Library, Philadelphia

Hatay Museum, Antakya

Iraq Museum

Istanbul

Louvre

Lowie Museum

Vorderasiatisches Museum

Yale

MISCELLANEOUS

Archaeological Museum, Ankara

Archaeological Museum, Florence

Australian Institute of Archaeology, Melbourne

Bibliothèque Nationale, Paris

Bodleian Museum, Oxford

Bristol Museum

Brockmon Collection, Haifa

Brooklyn Museum

Catholic University of America

Medelhavsmuseet, Stockholm

No.	E4.
MM 1974:26	1.3.1

Metropolitan Museum of Art

No.	E4.	No.	E4.
MMA 43.102.35	0.12.2001	MMA L 55.49.139	32.1.1
MMA 59.41.84	1.7.1.4		

Minneapolis Institute of Arts

No.	E4.
27	4.1.4.8

Mission Museum of Werl

No.	E4.	No.	E4.
MWA1	4.1.2.36	MWB1	4.1.3.102
MWA2	4.1.3.27	MWB2	4.1.3.103
MWA3	4.1.3.28	MWB4	4.1.3.104

Morgan Library

No.	E4.
68	12.2.2001
553	0.10.2001

Musée d'Art et d'Histoire, Geneva

No.	E4.
MAH 16194	3.7.2009
MAH 16451	4.1.3.87

Musée de Rouen

No.	E4.
HG 96	3.9.2001.2
HG 96	3.9.2027

Musées Royaux du Cinquantenaire, Brussels

No.	E4.
O 239	12.2.2.1
O 265	11.2.1

Museum of Arts, Toledo

No.	E4.	No.	E4.
16.65	4.1.2.31	22.185	4.1.4.31
16.66	4.1.4.30		

Museum of Civilization, Ottawa

No.	E4.
XXIV.H33c	4.6.4.3

Museum of Fine Arts, Boston

No.	E4.	No.	E4.
MFAB 37.1151	2.13.12.2	MFAB 93.1483	5.15.2002
MFAB 41.814	2.13.22.8		

Museum Haaretz, Tel Aviv

No.	E4.
113/24	4.1.3.100

National Museum, Stockholm

No.	E4.
NM Ant 2091	2.14.16.4

Newbury District Museum

No.	E4.
S 365b	4.1.3.135
S 439	4.1.4.18

Oakland Museum

No.	E4.
28-227	4.1.2.39

Oklahoma Historical Society

No.	E4.
1.1983.1	4.1.4.63

Pontificium Institutum Biblicum, Rome

No.	E4.
IB 198	4.1.3.83
IB 207	4.1.2.32

Pushkin State Museum of Fine Arts, Moscow

No.	E4.
51	5.20.2025

Royal Ontario Museum

No.	E4.	No.	E4.
ROM 910 × 209.76	4.1.4.19	ROM 910 × 209.573	5.7.1.4
ROM 910 × 209.76	4.1.4.62	ROM 931 × 44.62	5.9.1.5
ROM 910 × 209.210	4.1.2.41		

Smith College

No.	E4.
516	4.1.3.36
516	4.1.3.88

Index of Excavation Numbers

Tell Atshana

No.	E4.	No.	E4.	No.	E4.	No.	E4.
AT/38/119	25.5.2004	ATT/39/153	33.4.1.4	ATT/39/156A	33.4.1.2	ATT/39/184	33.5.1.3
ATT/39/30	33.7.1	ATT/39/153	33.4.2.4	ATT/39/183	33.4.2.2	ATT/39/184	33.5.2003–2004
ATT/39/30	34.2.1.4	ATT/39/153	33.5.1.2	ATT/39/183	33.5.1.1		
ATT/39/83	34.1.1	ATT/39/153	33.8.2001.1	ATT/39/184	33.4.1.1	ATT/39/184	33.6.1.1–2
ATT/39/113b	33.5.2001–2002	ATT/39/153	33.8.2001.3	ATT/39/184	33.4.1.3	ATT/39/184	33.8.2001.2
ATT/39/113b	33.6.1.3	ATT/39/153	34.2.1.1	ATT/39/184	33.4.2.1	ATT/39/184	34.2.1.2–3
ATT/39/113b	33.6.2001.2	ATT/39/153 +	33.6.2001.1	ATT/39/184	33.4.2.3	ATT/39/184 +	33.6.2001.1
ATT/39/113b	33.8.2001	ATT/39/153 +	34.2.1	ATT/39/184	33.4.2001	ATT/39/184 +	34.2.1

Isin

No.	E4.	No.	E4.	No.	E4.	No.	E4.
IB 192	1.5.3.1	IB 335	1.4.5.2	IB 939	1.14.3.2	IB 1392(*)	1.13.3
IB 198	4.1.3.83	IB 336	1.5.3.3	IB 953	1.10.10.2	IB 1411	1.13.3
IB 207	4.1.2.32	IB 340	1.5.4.6	IB 1014	11.2.2.1–2	IB 1481	1.15.3
IB 282A	1.5.1.12	IB 341	1.5.4.7	IB 1016	1.5.3.4	IB 1537	1.4.9
IB 282B	1.5.1.13	IB 380	1.11.1.3–4	IB 1084	1.4.5.5	IB 1607a	1.4.5.6
IB 282C	1.5.1.14	IB 422	1.14.3.3	IB 1090	1.15.1.5	IB 1607b	1.4.5.7
IB 311	1.4.5.1	IB 594	1.10.1.4	IB 1153	1.11.1.5–6	IB 1608	1.4.5.8
IB 322	1.5.4.1	IB 688	1.10.2.1	IB 1217	1.10.2.3	IB 1609	1.4.5.9
IB 323	1.5.4.2	IB 774	1.4.5.3–4	IB 1289	1.5.3.5	IB 1610	1.14.1.1
IB 324	1.5.4.3	IB 855	1.10.2.2	IB 1291	1.15.2.3	IB 1639	1.4.5.10
IB 325	1.5.4.4	IB 932	1.10.7.2–3	IB 1337	1.13.2	IB 1640	1.4.5.11
IB 333	1.5.3.2	IB 937	1.6.1.40	IB 1384	1.5.3.6	IB 1641	1.4.5.12
IB 334	1.5.4.5	IB 938	1.14.3.1	IB 1387	1.2.3.1–2		

Larsa

No.	E4.	No.	E4.	No.	E4.	No.	E4.
L [33]4	2.8.7.2	L 67–	3.6.13.5	L 7096	2.4.1.3	L 74–	2.5.3.7
L [33]7	2.9.2.3	L 6911	2.9.3.3	L 7096b	3.6.13.6	L 74101	2.8.1.4
L [33]25	2.8.7.3	L 69–	2.5.3.6	L 7098	2.6.2.2	L 74817	2.8.1.5
L [33]57A	2.6.2002	L 69–	2.9.3.4	L 7099	2.9.3.6	L 7672	2.14.2018
L [33]82	2.9.8	L 69–	3.6.13.7	L 70101	2.9.3.7	L 78.223	3.6.2018
L [33]298	2.8.7.4	L 7039	2.9.3.5	L 70–	2.4.1.4	L 78250	2.13.8
L [33]307	2.9.4.1	L 7081	2.5.3.3	L 70–	2.4.1.5	L 78300	2.9.6.1
L 67–	2.4.1.1	L 7082	2.8.1.2	L 70–	2.5.3.4	L 8330	2.14.17.10
L 67–	2.6.2.1	L 7091	2.4.1.2	L 70–	2.5.3.5		
L 67–	2.8.1.1	L 7092	2.8.1.3	L 70–	2.9.3.8		
L 67–	2.9.3.2	L 7095	2.9.4.2	L 70–	3.6.13.8		

Tell Leilan

No.	E4.	No.	E4.	No.	E4.	No.	E4.
L82-74-76	27.1.2001	L85-437	6.11.2008	L87-267	27.5.2002	L87-818	27.5.2003
L85-80-87	27.5.1	L85-438	6.11.2008	L87-296	27.5.2003	L87-822-23	27.5.2003
L85-105	6.11.2008	L85-454	27.3.2001	L87-309	27.5.2002	L87-892	28.3.2002
L85-116	5.19.2023	L85-492	27.3.2001	L87-370	27.5.2001	L87-894	27.3.2001
L85-117-122	27.4.2001	L85-495	13.2.2001	L87-375	27.5.2002	L87-912	28.3.2002
L85-123-124	27.5.1	L87-137	27.4.2002	L87-379	27.5.2002	L87-985	27.5.2003
L85-128	28.3.2002	L87-183	27.4.2002	L87-383	27.4.2	L87-987-88	27.5.2003
L85-132	6.11.2008	L87-184	27.4.2	L87-384	27.4.2	L87-994-95	27.5.2003
L85-134	27.4.2	L87-243	27.4.2	L87-398	27.4.2002	L87-1251-53	27.5.2003
L85-135	27.4.2	L87-246	27.4.2002	L87-422	27.4.2002	L87-1256-58	27.5.2003
L85-140	6.11.2008	L87-250	27.4.2002	L87-445	27.4.2	L87-1260	27.5.2003
L85-141	6.11.2008	L87-257	27.4.2002	L87-617	27.4.1	L87-1262	27.5.2003
L85-435	27.3.2001–2002	L87-263	27.5.2002	L87-646	27.4.2	L87-1266	27.5.2003

Mari

Nippur

Tell al Rimah

Ur

Warka

MISCELLANEOUS

Tell Abū Duwari

Ashur

Babylon

Dura-Europus

Eridu

Tell Ḥaddād

Tell Ḥarmal

Concordances of Selected Publications

Hallo, BiOr 18

No.	E4.
Išbi-Irra 1: i	1.1.2010
Išbi-Irra 1: ii	1.1.2009
Išbi-Irra 1: iii	1.1.2007
Išbi-Irra 1: iv	1.1.2002
Išbi-Irra 1: v	1.1.2005
Išbi-Irra 1: vi	1.1.2001
Išbi-Irra 2	1.1.1
Šu-ilišu 1	1.2.1
Iddin-Dagan 2	1.3.2
Išme-Dagan 1	1.4.1
Išme-Dagan 2	1.4.2
Išme-Dagan 3	1.4.7
Išme-Dagan 4	1.4.3
Išme-Dagan 5	1.4.4
Išme-Dagan 6	1.4.11
Išme-Dagan 7	1.4.5
Išme-Dagan 8	1.4.13
Išme-Dagan 9	1.4.12
Išme-Dagan 10	1.4.2001
Išme-Dagan 12	1.4.6
Lipit-Ištar 1	1.5.1
Lipit-Ištar 2	1.5.4
Lipit-Ištar 3	1.5.5
Lipit-Ištar 4	1.5.6
Lipit-Ištar 5	1.5.3
Lipit-Ištar 6	1.5.9
Lipit-Ištar 7	1.5.8
Lipit-Ištar 8	1.5.2001
Lipit-Ištar 9	1.5.2002
Lipit-Ištar 10	1.5.2003
Ur-Ninurta 1	1.6.1
Ur-Ninurta 2	1.6.2
Bur-Sin 1	1.7.1
Bur-Sin 2	1.7.2
Bur-Sin 3	1.7.3
Bur-Sin 4	1.7.2006
Bur-Sin 5	1.7.2005
Enlil-bani 1	1.10.1
Enlil-bani 2	1.10.2-3
Enlil-bani 3: ii	1.10.5
Enlil-bani 4	1.10.6
Zambia 1	1.11.1
Ur-dukuga 1	1.13.1
Sin-magir 1	1.14.1
Sin-magir 2	1.14.2
Sin-magir 3	1.14.2001
Sin-magir 4	1.14.2002
Damiq-ilišu 1	1.15.1
Damiq-ilišu 2	1.15.2
Gungunum 1	2.5.3
Gungunum 2	2.5.1
Gungunum 3	2.5.2
Abisare 1	2.6.2001
Abisare 2	2.6.2002
Abisare 3	2.6.2003
Sumu-il 1	2.7.1
Sumu-il 2	2.7.2
Sumu-il 3	2.7.2002
Sumu-il 4	2.7.2001
Sumu-il 5	2.7.2004
Sumu-il 6	2.7.2007
Nur-Adad 1	2.8.5
Nur-Adad 2	2.8.2
Nur-Adad 3	2.8.3
Nur-Adad 4	2.8.4
Nur-Adad 6: i	2.8.2007
Nur-Adad 6: ii	2.8.2001
Nur-Adad 6: iii	2.8.2009
Nur-Adad 6: iv	2.8.2006
Nur-Adad 6: v	2.8.2005
Nur-Adad 6: vi	2.8.2004
Nur-Adad 6: vii	2.8.2010
Nur-Adad 6: viii	2.8.2003
Nur-Adad 6: ix	2.8.2008
Nur-Adad 6: x	2.8.2011
Nur-Adad 6: xi	2.8.2002
Sin-iddinam 1	2.9.13
Sin-iddinam 2	2.9.10
Sin-iddinam 3	2.9.11
Sin-iddinam 4	2.9.12
Sin-iddinam 5	2.9.5
Sin-iddinam 6	2.9.2
Sin-iddinam 7	2.9.14
Sin-iddinam 8	2.9.9
Sin-iddinam 9	2.9.7
Sin-eribam 1	2.10.1
Sin-eribam 2	2.10.2001
Sin-eribam 3	2.10.2002
Ṣilli-Adad 1	2.12.1
Warad-Sin 1	2.13.18
Warad-Sin 2	2.13.25
Warad-Sin 3	2.13.9
Warad-Sin 4	2.13.19
Warad-Sin 5	2.13.11
Warad-Sin 6	2.13.12
Warad-Sin 7	2.13.22
Warad-Sin 8	2.13.27
Warad-Sin 9	2.13.6
Warad-Sin 10	2.13.16
Warad-Sin 11	2.13.10
Warad-Sin 12	2.13.23
Warad-Sin 13	2.13.3
Warad-Sin 14	2.13.1
Warad-Sin 15	2.13.24
Warad-Sin 16	2.13.4
Warad-Sin 17	2.13.26
Warad-Sin 18	2.13.20
Warad-Sin 19	2.13.15
Warad-Sin 20	2.13.30
Warad-Sin 21	2.13.31
Warad-Sin 22	2.13.32
Warad-Sin 24	2.13.32
Warad-Sin 25: i	2.13.2004
Warad-Sin 25: ii	2.13.2005
Warad-Sin 25: iii	2.13.2002
Warad-Sin 26	2.13.7
Warad-Sin 27	2.13.14
Warad-Sin 28	2.13.13
Kudur-mabuk 1	2.13a.2
Rim-Sin 2	2.14.1
Rim-Sin 3	2.14.6
Rim-Sin 4	2.14.2
Rim-Sin 5	2.14.3
Rim-Sin 6	2.14.16
Rim-Sin 7	2.14.12
Rim-Sin 8	2.14.20
Rim-Sin 9	2.14.4
Rim-Sin 9	2.14.9
Rim-Sin 11	2.14.11
Rim-Sin 12	2.14.5
Rim-Sin 13	2.14.17
Rim-Sin 14	2.14.18
Rim-Sin 15	2.14.8
Rim-Sin 16	2.14.13
Rim-Sin 17	2.14.7
Rim-Sin 18	2.14.23
Rim-Sin 19	2.14.2001
Rim-Sin 20	2.14.2002
Rim-Sin 21	2.14.2003
Rim-Sin 22	2.14.2004
Rim-Sin 23	2.14.2005
Rim-Sin 24	2.14.22
Rim-Sin 25: i	2.14.2014
Rim-Sin 25: ii	2.14.2010
Rim-Sin 25: iii	2.14.2013
Rim-Sin 25: iv	2.14.2009
Rim-Sin 25: v	2.14.2015
Rim-Sin 25: vi	2.14.2011
Rim-Sin 25: vii	2.14.2012
En-anedu 1	2.14.2021
Sin-kašid 1	4.1.1
Sin-kašid 2: i	4.1.2
Sin-kašid 3	4.1.3
Sin-kašid 4	4.1.4
Sin-kašid 5	4.1.9
Sin-kašid 6	4.1.7
Sin-kašid 7	4.1.10
Sin-kašid 8	4.1.8
Sin-kašid 9	4.1.6
Sin-kašid 10	4.1.11
Sin-gamil 1	4.3.2002
Sin-gamil 2	4.3.2001
An-am 1	4.6.4
An-am 2	4.6.5
An-am 3	4.6.1
An-am 4	4.6.2
An-am 5	4.6.3
Ešnunna 1: i	5.1.1
Ešnunna 1: ii	5.3.1
Ešnunna 1: iii	5.4.1
Ešnunna 1: iv	5.6.1
Ešnunna 1: v	5.7.1
Ešnunna 1: vi	5.8.1
Ešnunna 1: vii	5.9.1
Ešnunna 1: viii	5.10.1
Ešnunna 1: ix	5.12.1
Ešnunna 1: x	5.13.1
Ešnunna 1: xi	5.14.1
Ešnunna 2	5.14.2
Ešnunna 3	5.15.1
Ešnunna 4	5.20.1
Ešnunna 5	5.21.1
Ešnunna 6	5.18.1
Ešnunna 7	5.3.4
Ešnunna 8	5.3.2
Ešnunna 9	5.8.2
Ešnunna 12	5.19.2
Ešnunna 14	5.5.1
Ešnunna 15	5.6.2
Ešnunna 16	5.6.3
Ešnunna 17	5.7.2
Ešnunna 18	5.9.2
Ešnunna 21: ii	5.1.2, 2001, 2003
Ešnunna 21: iii	5.2.1
Ešnunna 21: iv	5.3.2003

No.	E4.
Ešnunna 21: v	5.5.2001, 2003-2004
Ešnunna 21: vi	5.7.4
Ešnunna 21: vii	5.8.2004
Ešnunna 21: viii	5.8.3
Ešnunna 21: ix	5.9.2004-2005, 2008-2009
Ešnunna 21: x	5.11.2001
Ešnunna 21: xi	5.13.2001-2003
Ešnunna 21: xiii	5.15.2001
§V	12.2.2001

Kärki, SAKAZ 1

No.	E4.
Išbierra 1	1.1.2001, 2002, 2005, 2007, 2009-2010
Išbierra 2	1.1.1
Šuilīšu 1	1.2.1
Šuilīšu 2	1.2.2
Iddindagān 1	1.3.2001
Iddindagān 2	1.3.2
Iddindagān 3	1.3.3
Išmedagān 1	1.4.1
Išmedagān 2	1.4.2
Išmedagān 3	1.4.7
Išmedagān 4	1.4.3
Išmedagān 5	1.4.4
Išmedagān 6	1.4.11
Išmedagān 7	1.4.5
Išmedagān 8	1.4.13
Išmedagān 9	1.4.12
Išmedagān 10	1.4.2001
Išmedagān 11	1.4.10
Išmedagān 12	1.4.6
Lipiteštar 1	1.5.1
Lipiteštar 2	1.5.4
Lipiteštar 3	1.5.5
Lipiteštar 4	1.5.6
Lipiteštar 5	1.5.3
Lipiteštar 6	1.5.9
Lipiteštar 7	1.5.8
Lipiteštar 8	1.5.2001
Lipiteštar 9	1.5.2002
Lipiteštar 10	1.5.2003
Urninurta 1	1.6.1
Urninurta 2	1.6.2
Būrsîn 1	1.7.1
Būrsîn 2	1.7.2
Būrsîn 3	1.7.3
Būrsîn 4	1.7.2006
Būrsîn 5	1.7.2005
Būrsîn 6	1.7.2003
Būrsîn 7	1.7.2004
Enlilbāni 1	1.10.1
Enlilbāni 2	1.10.2
Enlilbāni 3	1.10.5
Enlilbāni 4	1.10.6
Enlilbāni 5	1.10.9
Enlilbāni 6	1.10.8
Enlilbāni 7	1.10.11
Enlilbāni 8	1.10.4
Enlilbāni 9	1.10.7
Zambīja 1	1.11.1
Urdukuga 1	1.13.1
Sînmāgir 1	1.14.1
Sînmāgir 2	1.14.2
Sînmāgir 3	1.14.2001
Sînmāgir 4	1.14.2002
Damiqilīšu 1	1.15.1
Damiqilīšu 2	1.15.2
Damiqilīšu 3	1.2.4
Zabāja 1	2.4.1
Gungunum 1	2.5.3
Gungunum 2	2.5.1
Gungunum 3	2.5.2
Abīsarē 1	2.6.2001
Abīsarē 2	2.6.2002
Abīsarē 3	2.6.2003
Abīsarē 4	2.6.1
Abīsarē 5	2.6.2
Sumuel 1	2.7.1
Sumuel 2	2.7.2
Sumuel 3	2.7.2002
Sumuel 4	2.7.2001
Sumuel 5	2.7.2004
Sumuel 6	2.7.2007
Nūradad 1	2.8.5
Nūradad 2	2.8.2
Nūradad 3	2.8.3
Nūradad 4	2.8.4
Nūradad 6	2.8.2001, 2003-12
Nūradad 7	2.8.1
Sîniddinam 1	2.9.13
Sîniddinam 2	2.9.10
Sîniddinam 3	2.9.11
Sîniddinam 4	2.9.12
Sîniddinam 5	2.9.5
Sîniddinam 6	2.9.2
Sîniddinam 7	2.9.14
Sîniddinam 8	2.9.9
Sîniddinam 9	2.9.7
Sîniddinam 10	2.9.2001-2013
Sîniddinam 13	2.9.1
Sîniddinam 14	2.9.6
Sîniddinam 15	2.9.3
Sîniddinam 16	2.9.4
Sînirībam 1	2.10.1
Sînirībam 2	2.10.2001
Sînirībam 3	2.10.2002
Sîniqīšam 1	2.11.2
Sîniqīšam 2	2.11.2001
Ṣillīadad 1	2.12.1
Waradsîn 1	2.13.18
Waradsîn 2	2.13.25
Waradsîn 3	2.13.9
Waradsîn 4	2.13.19
Waradsîn 5	2.13.11
Waradsîn 6	2.13.12
Waradsîn 7	2.13.22
Waradsîn 8	2.13.27
Waradsîn 9	2.13.6
Waradsîn 10	2.13.16
Waradsîn 11	2.13.10
Waradsîn 12	2.13.23
Waradsîn 13	2.13.3
Waradsîn 14	2.13.1
Waradsîn 15	2.13.24
Waradsîn 16	2.13.4
Waradsîn 17	2.13.26
Waradsîn 18	2.13.20.4
Waradsîn 19	2.13.15
Waradsîn 20	2.13.30
Waradsîn 21	2.13.31
Waradsîn 22	2.13.32
Waradsîn 23	2.13.33
Waradsîn 24	2.13.32
Waradsîn 25	2.13.2002, 2004-2005
Waradsîn 26	2.13.7
Waradsîn 27	2.13.14
Waradsîn 28	2.13.13
Waradsîn 29	2.13.21
Waradsîn 30	2.13.2
Waradsîn 31	2.13.2001
Waradsîn 32	2.13.20.5
Waradsîn 33	2.13.28
Waradsîn 34	2.12.2
Waradsîn 35	2.13.1002
Waradsîn 36	2.13.20.6-7
Waradsîn 37	2.14.14
Waradsîn 38	2.13.1001
Waradsîn 39	2.13.17
Kudurmabuk 1	2.13a.2
Kudurmabuk 2	2.13a.1
Rīmsîn 1	3.6.1
Rīmsîn 2	2.14.1
Rīmsîn 3	2.14.6
Rīmsîn 4	2.14.2
Rīmsîn 5	2.14.3
Rīmsîn 6	2.14.16
Rīmsîn 7	2.14.12
Rīmsîn 8	2.14.20
Rīmsîn 9	2.14.4
Rīmsîn 10	2.14.9
Rīmsîn 11	2.14.11
Rīmsîn 12	2.14.5
Rīmsîn 13	2.14.17
Rīmsîn 14	2.14.18
Rīmsîn 15	2.14.8
Rīmsîn 16	2.14.13
Rīmsîn 17	2.14.7
Rīmsîn 18	2.14.23
Rīmsîn 19	2.14.2001
Rīmsîn 21	2.14.2003
Rīmsîn 23	2.14.2005
Rīmsîn 24	2.14.22
Rīmsîn 25	2.14.2009-2016
Rīmsîn 25	2.15.2001
Rīmsîn 26	2.14.10
Rīmsîn 27	2.14.15
Enanedu 1	2.14.2021
Sînkāšid 1	4.1.1
Sînkāšid 2	4.1.2
Sînkāšid 3	4.1.3
Sînkāšid 4	4.1.4
Sînkāšid 5	4.1.9
Sînkāšid 6	4.1.7
Sînkāšid 7	4.1.10
Sînkāšid 8	4.1.8
Sînkāšid 9	4.1.6
Sînkāšid 10	4.1.11
Sînkāšid 11	4.1.12
Sînkāšid 12	4.1.13
Sînkāšid 13	4.1.14
Sînkāšid 14	4.1.15
Sînkāšid 15	4.1.16
Sîngāmil 1	4.3.2001
Sîngāmil 1	4.3.2002
Sîngāmil 3	4.3.1
Ilumgāmil 1	4.4.2001
Anam 1	4.6.4
Anam 2	4.6.5
Anam 3	4.6.1
Anam 4	4.6.2
Anam 5	4.6.3
Anam 6	4.6.6

Sollberger and Kupper, IRSA

No.	E4.
ivA1a	1.1.2009
ivA1b	1.1.2005
ivA2a	1.2.1
ivA2b	1.2.2
ivA3a	1.3.2
ivA3a	1.13.1
ivA4a	1.4.7
ivA4b	1.4.11
ivA4b	1.14.2001
ivA4c	1.4.5
ivA4c	1.14.2002
ivA4d	1.4.12
ivA4e	1.4.13
ivA5a	1.5.5
ivA5a	1.15.1
ivA5b	1.5.3
ivA5c	1.5.4
ivA5d	1.5.8
ivA5e	1.5.2001
ivA5f	1.5.2002
ivA6a	1.6.1
ivA6a	2.6.1
ivA7a	1.7.1
ivA7b	1.7.2
ivA7c	1.7.3
ivA7d	1.7.2005
ivA10a	1.10.2-3
ivA10b	1.10.6
ivA10c	1.10.5
ivA11a	1.11.1
ivA14a	1.14.2
ivA15b	1.15.2
ivB4a	2.4.1
ivB5a	2.5.3
ivB5b	2.5.1
ivB6b	2.6.2001
ivB6c	2.6.2002
ivB6d	2.6.2003
ivB7a	2.7.1
ivB7b	2.7.2
ivB7c	2.7.2001
ivB7d	2.7.2004
ivB8a	2.8.5
ivB8b	2.8.3
ivB8c	2.8.4
ivB8d	2.8.2005
ivB9a	2.9.10
ivB9b	2.9.6
ivB9c	2.9.2
ivB10a	2.10.1
ivB11a	2.11.2
ivB12a	2.12.1
ivB13a	2.13.21
ivB13b	2.13.19
ivB13c	2.13.25
ivB13d	2.13.11
ivB13e	2.13.26
ivB13g	2.13.9
ivB13i	2.13.3
ivB13j	2.13a.2
ivB14a	2.14.3
ivB14b	2.14.6
ivB14c	2.14.10
ivB14d	2.14.15
ivB14e	2.14.23
ivB14f	2.14.17
ivB14g	2.14.22
ivB14h	2.14.20
ivB14i	2.14.2003
ivB14j	2.14.2001
ivB15a	2.13.33
ivC6a	3.6.13
ivC6b	3.6.14
ivC6c	3.6.15
ivC6d	3.6.16
ivC6e	3.6.12
ivC6f	3.6.2
ivC6g	3.6.3
ivC6h	3.6.17
ivC6i	3.6.8-9
ivC6j	3.6.7
ivC6k	3.6.4
ivC6l	3.6.10
ivC6m	3.6.2004
ivC6n	3.6.2002
ivC6o	3.6.2001
ivC7a	3.7.6
ivC7b	3.7.5
ivC7c	3.7.3
ivC7d	3.7.7
ivC7e	3.7.8
ivC8a	3.8.1
ivC8b	3.8.2
ivC9a	3.9.1
ivC10a	3.10.2001
ivD1a	4.1.16
ivD1b	4.1.1
ivD1c	4.1.2
ivD1d	4.1.4
ivD1e	4.1.7
ivD1f	4.1.9
ivD1g	4.1.8
ivD3a	4.3.1
ivD3b	4.3.2001
ivD4a	4.4.2001
ivD6a	4.6.4
ivD6b	4.6.3
ivD6c	4.6.5
ivD6d	4.6.1
ivD6e	4.6.2
ivE1a	5.1.1
ivE1b	5.1.2001
ivE2a	5.2.1
ivE3a	5.3.1
ivE3b	5.3.2
ivE4	5.4.1
ivE5a	5.5.1
ivE5b	5.5.2003
ivE6a	5.6.1
ivE6b	5.6.2
ivE6c	5.6.3
ivE7a	5.7.1
ivE7b	5.7.2
ivE8a	5.8.1
ivE8b	5.8.3
ivE8c	5.8.2
ivE9a	5.9.1
ivE9b	5.9.2
ivE9c	5.9.2004
ivE12	5.10.1
ivE13	5.12.1
ivE14a	5.11.2001
ivE15a	5.13.1
ivE15b	5.13.2
ivE15c	5.13.2002
ivE16a	5.14.1
ivE16b	5.14.2
ivE16c	5.14.2001
ivE16d	5.14.2002
ivE17a	5.15.1
ivE17b	5.15.2
ivE18a	5.19.2
ivE19a	5.20.1
ivE20a	5.21.1
ivE22a	5.18.1
ivF1a	6.1.2001
ivF2a	6.2.1
ivF6a	6.8.1
ivF6b	6.8.2
ivF7a	6.12.2
ivF7b	6.12.3
ivF7c	6.12.4
ivF7d	6.12.5
ivG1a	23.7.1
ivG2a	23.10.1
ivG2b	23.10.2
ivH1a	12.1.1
ivH2a	12.2.1
ivH2b	12.2.2
ivJ1a	13.2.1
ivK1a	8.1.1-2
ivL1a	7.1.1
ivM1a	11.2.1
ivM2a	11.1.1
ivN1a	20.1.1
ivO2a	5.3.4

Thureau-Dangin, SAK

No.	E4.
Itûr-šamaš	7.1.1
Puḫia	20.1.1
Anu-bânîni	18.1.1
Ur-nin-giš-zi-da	5.8.1
Ibalpel	5.13.1
Belaku	5.12.1
[ ]mašu	5.4.1
Anu-mutabil	12.2.1
Dan-ruḫuratir	5.3.4
Ur-nin-IB	1.6.1
Pûr-sin a	1.7.1
Pûr-sin b	1.7.2005
Lipit-ištar	1.5.6
Sin-mâgir	1.14.1
Išme-dagan	1.4.2
Gungunu a	2.5.3
Gungunu b	2.5.2
Aus der Zeit Gungunus	1.4.4
Sumu-ilu	2.7.2001
Nûr-immer	2.8.2
Sin-idinnam a	2.9.14
Sin-idinnam b	2.9.9
Sin-idinnam c	2.9.7
Sin-idinnam d	2.9.11
Arad-sin a	2.13.9
Arad-sin b	2.13.18
Arad-sin c	2.13.16
Arad-sin d	2.13.22
Arad-sin e	2.13.11
Arad-sin f	2.13.12
Rîm-sin a	2.14.13
Rîm-sin b	2.14.2005
Rîm-sin c	2.14.12
Rîm-sin d	2.14.16
Rîm-sin e	2.14.2
Rîm-sin f	2.14.3
Sin-gâšid a	4.1.1
Sin-gâšid b	4.1.2
Sin-gâšid c	4.1.8
Sin-gâmil a	4.3.2001
Sin-gâmil b	4.6.4

v.ingramcontent.com/pod-product-compliance
Source LLC
80826
00046B/1279